Note to the Student:

This text was created to provide you with a high-quality educational resource. As a publisher specializing in college texts for business and economics, our goal is to provide you with learning materials that will serve you well in your college studies and throughout your career.

The educational process involves learning, retention, and the application of concepts and principles. You can accelerate your learning efforts by utilizing the supplements accompanying this text:

The **STUDY GUIDE**, prepared by the author is designed to help you better your performance in your Cost Accounting course. The guide includes objectives, definitions, and true/false, fill-in-the-blank, and matching questions. Answers to all questions are included in the Study Guide, providing verification of responses as well as explanation as to why the statement is true or false.

Ramblewood Manufacturing, by Leland Mansuetti and Keith Weidkamp, both of Sierra College, is a computerized simulation that can be used with your Cost Accounting course.

These learning aids are designed to improve your performance in the course by highlighting key points in the text and providing you with assistance in mastering basic concepts. Check your local bookstore or ask the manager to place an order for you today.

We at Irwin sincerely hope that this text package will assist you in reaching your goals both now and in the future.

Cost Accounting: Using a Cost Management Approach

THE IRWIN SERIES IN UNDERGRADUATE ACCOUNTING

Bernstein
**Financial Statement Analysis:
Theory, Application and
Interpretation**
Fifth Edition

Bernstein and Maksy
**Cases in Financial Statement
Reporting and Analysis**
Second Edition

Boatsman, Griffin, Vickrey and
Williams
Advanced Accounting
Seventh Edition

Boockholdt
Accounting Information Systems
Fourth Edition

Booker, Caldwell, Gallbreath, and
Rand
   Ready Slides
   Ready Shows
   Ready Notes
**Power Point Classroom
Presentation Products**

Carse and Slater
Payroll Accounting
1996 Edition

Danos and Imhoff
**Introduction to Financial
Accounting**
Second Edition

Dyckman, Dukes and Davis
Intermediate Accounting
Third Edition

Edwards, Hermanson and Maher
**Principles of Financial and
Managerial Accounting**
Revised Edition

Engler, Bernstein and Lambert
Advanced Accounting
Third Edition

Engstrom and Hay
**Essentials of Accounting for
Governmental and Not-for-Profit
Organizations**
Fourth Edition

Engstrom and Hay
**Essentials of Governmental
Accounting for Public
Administrators**

Epstein and Spalding
**The Accountant's Guide to Legal
Liability and Ethics**

Ferris
**Financial Accounting and
Corporate Reporting: A Casebook**
Fourth Edition

Garrison and Noreen
Managerial Accounting
Seventh Edition

Hay and Wilson
**Accounting for Governmental
and Nonprofit Entities**
Tenth Edition

Hermanson and Edwards
**Financial Accounting: A Business
Perspective**
Sixth Edition

Hermanson, Edwards and Maher
**Accounting: A Business
Perspective**
Sixth Edition

Hermanson and Walker
**Computerized Accounting with
Peachtree Complete© Accounting,
Version 8.0**

Hoyle
Advanced Accounting
Fourth Edition

Koerber
College Accounting
Revised Edition

Larson and Miller
Financial Accounting
Sixth Edition

Larson
**Fundamental Accounting
Principles**
Fourteenth Edition

Larson, Spoede and Miller
**Fundamentals of Financial and
Managerial Accounting**

Libby, Libby and Short
Financial Accounting

Maher and Deakin
Cost Accounting
Fourth Edition

Mansuetti and Weidkamp
**Introductory/Intermediate
Practice Set Series**
Fourth Edition

Marshall and McManus
**Accounting: What the Numbers
Mean**
Third Edition

Miller, Redding and Bahnson
**The FASB: The People, the
Process and the Politics**
Third Edition

Morris
Short Audit Case
Seventh Edition

Mueller, Gernon and Meek
**Accounting: An International
Perspective**
Third Edition

Pasewark and Louwers
**Real World Accounting Series
   Athletronics, Inc.
   Shoe Business, Inc.
   Understanding Corporate
   Annual Reports**

Pany and Whittington
Auditing

Peters and Peters
College Accounting
Second Edition

Pratt and Kulsrud
**Corporate, Partnership, Estate
and Gift Taxation, 1996 Edition**

Pratt and Kulsrud
Federal Taxation, 1996 Edition

Pratt and Kulsrud
Individual Taxation, 1996 Edition

Rayburn
**Cost Accounting: Using a Cost
Management Approach**
Sixth Edition

Robertson
Auditing
Eighth Edition

Schrader
**College Accounting: A Small
Business Approach**
Second Edition

Van Breda and Hendriksen
Accounting Theory
Sixth Edition

Whittington and Pany
Principles of Auditing
Eleventh Edition

Yacht
**Computer Accounting with
Peachtree® for Microsoft®
Windows® Release 3.0**

Yacht and Terry
**Computer Accounting for
Microsoft® Windows®**

Sixth Edition

Cost Accounting: Using a Cost Management Approach

Letricia Gayle Rayburn

Professor of Accountancy
Southeast Missouri State University

IRWIN

Chicago • Bogotá • Boston • Buenos Aires • Caracas
London • Madrid • Mexico City • Sydney • Toronto

Times Mirror
Higher Education Group

Irwin Book Team
Sponsoring editor: Mark Pfaltzgraff
Associate marketing manager: Heather L. Woods
Editorial assistant: Ted Brown
Project editor   Jean Lou Hess
Production supervisor: Kim Meriwether/Bob Lange
Designer: Laurie J. Entringer
Compositor: Douglas & Gayle, Ltd.
Typeface: 10/12 Times Roman
Printer: Von Hoffman Press, Inc.

Library of Congress Cataloging-in-Publication Data

Rayburn, Letricia Gayle.
    Cost accounting : using a cost management approach / Letricia
Gayle Rayburn.
        p.   cm.—(The Irwin series in undergraduate accounting)
    Includes index.
    ISBN 0-256-17480-6   ISBN 0-256-20689-9 (International Student Edition)
    1. Cost accounting.   2. Managerial accounting.   I. Title.
II. Series.
HF5686.C8R3638   1996
657' .042—dc20   95–23347

Printed in the United States of America
1 2 3 4 5 6 7 8 9 0 VH 2 1 0 9 8 7 6 5

Preface

Organization of Book

New developments in the cost/management accounting field bring opportunities as well as threats. Failure to incorporate new ideas and techniques in an organization's operations can lead to failure if its competitor implements these innovations first. Because the information that cost accounting provides is so powerful, it shapes the future of companies as well as nations. Efficient cost management systems provide superior information for improved decision making. Managers are then able to more efficiently allocate resources and measure and control operations. With a superior cost management system, a company can dominate global commerce, becoming more profitable.

This book considers the needs of its customers—the students, the teachers, and employers. It is designed to develop critical thinking and communication skills by encouraging professors to teach students how to think. Its emphasis on the cost management approach recognizes that product costing for inventory valuation and income determination is only one of cost accounting's many purposes—certainly not its primary purpose. It further emphasizes that methods of determining product cost must reflect the current manufacturing and service environment. This book's discussion and illustrations of activity-based management and costing emphasize continuous improvement.

Because the text is adaptable, it can be used by instructors with different teaching objectives and instructional methods. The book's organization allows instructors much flexibility in selecting chapters to meet their course objectives. Instructors can skip chapters or rearrange the sequence of chapters because each chapter is self-contained. End-of-the chapter materials covering topics from more than one chapter are clearly labeled to allow flexibility.

Adopters of previous editions report using this book after a first course in accounting principles or financial accounting. An orientation to accounting terminology and the financial reporting systems is a helpful prerequisite. However, it is not necessary for students to have completed a course in managerial or cost accounting before using this book.

This book identifies concepts and principles of cost accounting in a clear, concise, and straightforward manner. Discussions are supported by extensive examples. The first chapters discuss cost accounting concepts concerned with cost collection—

factors that influence such managerial decisions as sales price determination. The last part of the book emphasizes the application of cost concepts in cost management analysis and quantitative tools for decision making.

To aid the student, each chapter begins with measurable learning objectives that focus on important areas of coverage. Each chapter also includes a list of important terms and concepts.

The mix of assignment material includes questions that review concepts and procedures, exercises that review the direct applications of the basic concepts, problems of varying difficulty that enhance the learning process and cover the concepts in greater depth, and relevant cases that illustrate the practical problems associated with concept implementation. The cases are thought-provoking and designed to stimulate class discussion and develop written and oral communication skills.

This book contains such a variety of problems and cases that there is sufficient material to challenge students who have had previous courses in management accounting or a varied background in accounting and related fields. The sixth edition contains extensive material concerned with activity-based management and costing for both manufacturing and marketing activities. Its discussion on service industry costing recognizes the need to accurately determine the cost of providing services in an expanding service-oriented environment.

The chapter sequence does not undermine the mix and match possibilities for selecting course content. Chapters in the book are grouped into six major topic modules which include the following features.

*Part I
Cost/Management
Accounting
Concepts*

Chapter 1—Cost Accounting in a Contemporary Environment discusses the impact of automation on cost accounting and the growth of Activity-Based Management, Life-cycle Costing, and Target Costing. The danger of integrating cost data with the financial accounting system is presented. A clear distinction is made between cost accounting as needed for financial reporting and cost accounting for supporting decision making and performance evaluation.

Chapter 2—Cost Concepts and Cost Flows presents the basic cost concepts, emphasizing the flow of costs through inventory accounts until they are disposed of as expenses on the income statement. The discussion uses volume-related cost drivers to apply overhead. Cost of goods manufacturing statements using actual and applied overhead trace the manufacturing inventory flow. The chapter further discusses the impact of computer-integrated manufacturing on cost mix, labor-based application rates, and quality control.

Chapter 3—Cost Behavior and Cost Estimation discusses the relationship of fixed and variable behavior patterns, unit and total costs and relevant range. Students are encouraged to learn to apply regression analysis technology and understand the criteria for its analysis rather than memorizing its mathematical foundations. The regression analysis discussion includes criteria for regression analysis, effect of outlier observations, relevant range and linearity, and cost functions and linearity.

Chapter 4—Volume-Based Cost Assignments first compares various capacity levels since many students have trouble understanding how capacity relates to application rates for overhead. Illustrations of the direct, step, and linear algebra methods of overhead assignment allow students to compare the benefits of each approach. The chapter presents the criteria for selecting a single versus plantwide application rate. Analyzing the over- or underapplied overhead balance in spending and volume variances encourage identification of nonvalued activities and wasted costs.

Chapter 5—Activity-Based Cost Systems and Strategic Cost Analysis emphasizes the use of benchmarking when determining which activities are value-added or nonvalue-added. The chapter presents the focus of strategic cost analysis on the positioning and potential penetration of products and services in the marketplace. The impact of product diversity and volume diversity illustrates the importance of activity-based management. Illustrations apply materials acquisition and handling costs on nonvolume-related cost drivers. The chapter discusses the role of product life-cycle costing and the theory of constraints in achieving continuous improvement.

Part II
Product Cost
Allocation and
Accumulation
Procedures

Chapter 6—Job Order Costing illustrates job order costing and compares it to process costing and operation costing. Internal control surrounding basic documents such as material requisitions and job order sheets prevent miscosting. The chapter explains that because direct material is often insignificant for service organizations and service labor-related costs are usually larger than other costs, service organizations's costing systems differ from manufacturers. The result is that a service organization's predetermined overhead rate is frequently based on labor.

Chapter 7—Process Costing—Weighted-Average and FIFO Costing introduces process costing in a unique way as students are encouraged to think of a snowball gathering snow (cost) as it travels from one department to another. This analogy communicates the essence of how costs accumulate in a process system. Process costing is placed in this chapter sequence because it is difficult to cover this topic before the student has seen how product costing works. A discussion of the impact of flexible manufacturing and just-in-time on process costing questions the future use of equivalent units. An appendix illustrates completed and not transferred inventory.

Chapter 8—Process Costing—Addition of Materials and Lost Units presents additional complexities encountered in process costing systems when concentrated mixtures are diluted and units lost. The chapter presents the impact of timing of inspections, quality control, and zero defect programs on cost efficiency.

Chapter 9—Joint Product and By-Product Costing discusses the necessity of allocating joint costs for financial reporting and illustrates the physical or market bases of assigning joint costs. The chapter explains why managers need a differential cost analysis, not joint cost allocations, when deciding whether to process further.

Part III
Cost Data for
Performance
Evaluation

Chapter 10—Strategic Planning and Budgeting shows that strategic planning provides the compass for a companies' activities in its quest to determine and meet customer needs. Comparisons of fixed (static) and flexible (variable) budgets encourage recognition of the influence of volume achieved on cost behavior. Discussions emphasize determining the cost of acquired resources not utilized. The information flow outlines the interrelationships between production-related budgets.

Chapter 11—Nonmanufacturing Budgets, Forecasted Statements, and Behavioral Issues discusses the role of cash budgets in cash management and the importance of marketing budgets. The chapter exposes students to the use of budgets for performance evaluation and the resulting behavioral implications.

Chapter 12—Target Costing, Kaizen Costing, and Standard Cost for Material and Labor and **Chapter 13—Standard Costs for Factory Overhead Variance** first present the calculations for material, labor, and overhead variances and then emphasize finding the responsible factor for the variance and taking corrective action. These chapters represent target costs as market-driven standards. Kaizen costing is presented as a means of ensuring continuous improvement by supporting the cost reduction process in the manufacturing phase. These chapters emphasize the relationship of variances and the importance of managers monitoring efficiency and volume variances to prevent excess inventory. By placing standard costing later in the textbook, students have prior exposure to product costing and can understand that standard costs can be used for both job order and process systems.

Part IV
Cost Planning and
Control

Chapter 14—Cost-Volume-Profit Analysis discusses the contribution margin concept and breakeven analysis with emphasis on the manipulation of the cost-volume profit formula. This helps the student understand the usefulness of differentiating between fixed and variable costs. If instructors prefer to introduce cost-volume-profit analysis earlier, they can present Chapter 14 before or immediately after Chapter 3.

 Chapter 15—Product Quality and Inventory Management in a JIT Environment discusses the impact of JIT, decreased setup times, and shorter lead times on the validity of EOQ. The chapter presents various methods of recording material waste and the importance of selecting inventory controls that match the value of inventory. An appendix illustrates inventory costing for students with an inadequate foundation in these concepts.

 Chapter 16—Payroll Accounting and Incentive Plans demonstrates the basic entries for labor distribution, payroll tax, and indirect or fringe benefits. The chapter illustrates incentive compensation plans and the impact of JIT on these plans. Students understand the role of learning curve theory in establishing incentive plans and labor standards.

Part V
Cost Accounting/
Cost Management
for Decision
Making

Chapter 17—Decision Models and Cost Analysis under Uncertainty presents decision models, including differential analysis and cost studies under uncertainty. Payoff tables are introduced using probabilities in deciding whether to investigate variances from standards or budgets. The expected value of investigating variances in a two-state environment are compared to the present value of the extra costs of not investigating.

 Chapter 18—Performance Evaluation and Segment Analysis illustrates ROI, residual income, and other short-run measures of evaluating performance. The chapter illustrates the dangers of evaluating only short-term results and encourages the use of multiple performance measures, including nonfinancial evaluations.

 Chapter 19—Transfer Pricing in Multidivisional Companies presents the objective of alternative transfer pricing models. The chapter discusses the related behavioral implications of a selected transfer pricing method (i.e., internal competition, suboptimization, and other dysfunctional behavior).

 Chapter 20—Capital Budgeting outlines discounted cash flow methods as well as the payback and unadjusted return on investment alternative models. The chapter illustrates how to calculate the cost of capital.

 Chapter 21—Capital Budgeting—Additional Topics illustrates sensitivity analysis in cash flow and economic life estimates and inflation in the capital budgeting process. The impact of automation on traditional capital budgeting models and the improvements needed in these models is discussed. Aftertax analysis of equipment replacement is demonstrated through use of the total-cost and differential-cost approaches.

Chapter 22—Activity-Based Management for Marketing and Pricing Decisions uniquely presents setting marketing standards on activity-based costing drivers. The chapter outlines the steps to implementing ABC for marketing activities. This chapter demonstrates the diversity of contexts in which cost accounting concepts and decision making techniques apply by illustrating the influence of cost on product pricing.

Part VI
Analysis of Costs
and Profits

Chapter 23—Variable Costing illustrates the advantage of using variable (direct) costing for internal use. The chapter presents the weaknesses of an absorption costing system relying on phantom profits and how variable costing overcomes misconceptions of full costing. The chapter also includes the dangers of using variable costing with a numerical example of how variable (direct) costing can lead to poor pricing practices.

Chapter 24—Revenue Variances, Material Mix and Yield Variances, and Labor Mix and Yield Variances presents price, volume, quantity, and mix variances for revenue and production. The chapter illustrates market size and market share variances as a breakdown of the sales quantity variance.

Chapter 25—Gantt Charts, PERT, and Decision Tree Analysis explains quantitative concepts in a straightforward manner with relevant examples. Pert-cost analysis is illustrated in choosing when to crash. Variance analysis and PERT-cost are demonstrated. The roll-back concept is used in decision tree analysis.

Chapter 26—Linear Programming and the Cost Accountant defines the role of the cost accountant in applying linear programming with emphasis on understanding the effect of constraints and developing the objective function.

Strengths of Fifth Edition Retained

The chapter sequence continues to allow instructors flexibility in the chapter material; however, chapters do not exist in isolation. The topics flow evenly through the chapters. Using different costs for different purposes remains a strong emphasis. This focus helps students understand the importance of professional judgment in choosing the most appropriate cost concept for specific situations.

Cost concepts and cost accumulation topics are covered first. This is most appropriate since robotics and automated manufacturing cause a change in cost mix and behavior. The idea that accounting exists to provide useful information is reinforced and is an integral part of each chapter. Not only do readers learn how information is produced in cost accounting systems, but they are encouraged to examine how it can be used by management.

Unlike many other cost accounting texts which virtually ignore marketing and distribution costs, this book contends that evaluating segment performance only on production costs provides inaccurate estimates of relative profitability. The sixth edition expands the chapter on distribution and marketing costs, which has been included since the textbook's first edition. This chapter now demonstrates the role of activity-based cost drivers in pricing decisions and evaluating marketing performance.

Deficiencies of traditional capital budgeting models and performance measures continue to be emphasized. Such quantitative tools as PERT and linear programming continue to be integrated into the text rather than included in supplements or appendices. This helps students understand quantitative applications more easily and see how they can use them effectively.

A detailed outline in Chapter 13 shows the relationships between the two-, three-, and four-variance method for overhead variances so that students quickly realize that they are not learning completely different variance sets. This understanding of relationships allows students to evaluate which method they prefer and to better understand why the four-variance method is generally preferred.

The book includes many well-written exercises, problems, and cases designed to improve the students' writing and critical thinking skills. The book's numerous decision making cases encourage students to understand the interrelationship of other disciplines with cost accounting. The textbook is also designed to increase students' thinking power by including capstone cases at the conclusion of each part. These cases test the students' understanding and knowledge of cost accounting systems. Several of these do this by asking students to evaluate a present system, some of which managers have failed to update when they automated their factories. The author wrote all problems and tested them in class so she could see first hand which areas were not clear enough in their first draft form and then revised the text as needed.

The end-of-chapter material continues to be representative of the text coverage and gives sufficient practice in applications. There are no distractions in the problem material that undermine successful completion in this student-oriented text. The cases are very interesting and provide an opportunity for the professor to discuss some of the ideas presented in the cases in more detail and from a different perspective.

Changes in Content and Pedagogy of Sixth Edition

Many changes have been made to the content of the sixth edition to reflect the changing nature of cost accounting and the impact of customer focus, automation, JIT, quality control, and other new manufacturing techniques on the needs for cost management information.

Major changes to the content of the sixth edition are:

1. A new chapter discusses activity-based cost systems and strategic cost analysis. Discussions on the use of strategic cost analysis, product life cycle costing, and theory of constraints to distinguish between value-added and nonvalue-added activities are included. Illustration of activity-based costing encourages students to use non-volume based cost drivers when product and volume diversity exists.

2. The inclusion of current cost management practices exposes students to real-world examples. These examples reinforce the text material.

3. The text includes more end-of-chapter material that encourages students to use critical thinking in making decisions. Some of these exercises have missing data which requires students to work backwards and not memorize a rote approach to problem solving.

4. The capstone cases presented at the end of each section are effective for team projects. The cases include written and/or oral communications assignments.

5. While the clear, concise writing structure has been retained, most of the materials has been rewritten to a more active writing style to reflect the exciting, changing nature of cost accounting. By removing some of the nice but unnecessary prose, the readability is enhanced without losing content.

6. To assume even greater importance of cost accounting in a company's value chain, the book encourages recognition of the availability of alternative measures of performance evaluation. Importance of nonfinancial measures of performance and multiple measures of performance are given increased coverage.

7. Coverage of the text has been broadened to include more of the conceptual framework and decision making analysis underlying the treatment of cost accounting procedures.

8. The more liberal use of graphics and flowcharts is useful in helping students step from a procedural level of thinking to higher levels of thought in developing more refined abstract reasoning skills.

Supplements to the Sixth Edition

Supplements for Students

Student Guide by Rayburn that is keyed to each chapter of the book. This workbook provides a detailed outline of each chapter, a review of the important new terms and concepts, matching questions containing true-false questions, completion questions, and exercises. Answers to all questions are included in the Study Guide, which provides verification of responses as well as explanation as to why the statement is true or false. Since the student workbook is prepared by the textbook author, there is a strong carryover to the textbook material.

List of Key Figures prepared by the textbook author provides check figures for each exercise, problem, and case; these lists are provided in quantity to instructors for distribution.

Video—The Richard D. Irwin Managerial/Cost Accounting video series contains fifteen 10–15-minute segments covering such topics as capital budgeting, the design of a cost accounting system, process and job order costing, and service and activity-based costing. Prepared by Pacific Lutheran University in Seattle, Washington, the videos are free upon adoption. This video series is designed to strengthen classroom presentations and enhance student interest in the subject matter.

Spreadsheet Applications Template Software (SPATS)—Many additional exercises, problems, and cases can be solved using SPATS. It contains innovatively designed templates based on Lotus® 1-2-3® and includes an effective tutorial on Lotus® 1-2-3®. Available in both DOS and Windows® versions. SPATS can be ordered with the text or as a separate item.

Supplements for Instructors

Solutions Manual by Rayburn. Detailed solutions to all questions, exercises, problems, and cases in the textbook. Comments on alternative teaching approaches and solutions are included. The solution manual includes hints on how to improve critical thinking and communication skills.

Solution Transparencies—Overhead transparencies of solutions are designed for easy viewing in the classroom and are available for every exercise and problem in the text.

ComputTest 4—This improved microcomputer version of the testbank allows editing of questions; provides up to 99 versions of each test; and allows question selection based on type of question or level of difficulty. Available in Windows®, DOS, or Macintosh version. The author wrote the testbank.

ACKNOWLEDGMENTS

First, I acknowledge the support of my husband, Mike, and children, Douglass and Beverly, to writing this book and its accompanying materials. Also, I acknowledge the encouragement given by my parents, Harold and Myrtle Douglass.

Many students have worked the problems to ensure that they are as error-free as possible, and they have contributed ideas for more effectively presenting the concepts.

Appreciation also goes to the American Institute of Certified Public Accountants, the Institute of Certified Management Accountants, and the Institute of Internal Auditors, Inc., for their permission to use questions and/or unofficial answers from their past professional examinations. Problems from the Uniform CPA Examination are designated (AICPA), from the Certified Management Accountants Examination (CMA), and from the Certified Internal Auditing Examination (CIA).

More than any other objective, I want this textbook to motive students to learn and develop problem solving techniques; further, I want them to view cost/management accounting as exciting and valuable. To achieve this, my goal is to make this textbook the best possible teaching tool for cost accounting professors. Further, I want to make it easier for professors to develop in their students critical thinking skills and an inextinguishable thirst for knowledge. Suggestions and comments regarding the textbook and related materials are encouraged and welcome.

Letricia Gayle Rayburn

Brief Contents

Contents

Part II

Product Cost Allocation and Accumulation Procedures

6   Job Order Costing   159

Part III

Cost Data for Performance Evaluation

Part V

Cost Accounting/Cost Management for Decision Making

17   Decision Models and Cost Analysis under Uncertainty   545

18   Performance Evaluation and Segment Analysis   578

Part VI

Analysis of Costs and Profits

23   Variable Costing   743

24   Revenue Variances, Material Mix and Yield Variances, and Labor Mix and Yield Variances   774

25   Gantt Charts, PERT, and Decision Tree Analysis   802

26   Linear Programming and the Cost Accountant   839

PART I

Cost Management Accounting Concepts

Cost Accounting in a Contemporary Environment

Chapter Objectives

After studying this chapter, you should be able to:

1. Contrast cost accounting and financial accounting.
2. Discuss the role of cost accountants and their interaction with various players in the automated environment of manufacturing.
3. Explain the changes cost management concepts are making to traditional accounting systems.
4. Identify the professional certifications available for cost accountants.

Introduction

As you study cost accounting, you will find many ways to use cost analysis in personal decision making. For example, assume you earn $15,000 annually, and you question whether to further your formal education. If you decide to return to school, you must give up your job and its $15,000 salary, which is an opportunity cost. This sacrifice of the lost salary, in addition to costs of tuition and books, must be matched against the future benefits of having increased your education.

After joining the business world, you will use cost data to help your company respond quickly to changing market conditions by tailoring products to different consumer tastes and demands. Adapting cost accounting systems to better meet management's needs is crucial to an organization's survival when competing in global markets. Rather than spending much of your time tracking incurred costs—referred to as cost control—your objective will be to improve operations by determining which activities add value. Adopting a goal of continuous improvement forces the systematic and continuous elimination of waste whether it involves people's time, materials, or capital not spent on activities adding value to products or services required by customers.

Your responsibility as a cost accountant is to add value by providing strategic information that focuses management's attention wherever change will be most beneficial. Note the direct link between cost accounting practices and corporate goals. In today's automated environment, cost accountants use their management control systems to support and reinforce manufacturing strategies. Thus, you will discover that as a cost accountant you play more of an influencing role than an informing role.

What Is Cost Accounting?

You are entering the study of cost accounting, but what is this subject all about? **Cost accounting** identifies, defines, measures, reports, and analyzes the various elements of direct and indirect costs associated with producing and marketing goods and services. Cost accounting also measures performance, product quality, and productivity. Cost accounting is broad and extends beyond calculating product costs for inventory valuation, which external reporting requirements largely dictate. In fact, cost accounting's focus is shifting from inventory valuation for financial reporting to costing for decision making.

The main objective of cost accounting is communicating both financial and nonfinancial information to management for planning, controlling, and evaluating resources. Cost accounting supplies information that enables management to make more informed decisions. Thus, modern cost accounting often is called **management accounting** because managers use accounting data to guide their decisions.

Cost Management Systems

Managers distribute resources to meet organizational goals. Because of limited resources, managers should rely on cost data in deciding which actions provide optimal returns to the company. In arriving at these decisions, they can use cost management information to direct day-to-day operations and supply feedback to evaluate and control performance.

Comparison of Cost Accounting with Financial Accounting

Financial accountants prepare information for external parties on the status of assets, liabilities, and equity. Financial accounting also reports results of operations, changes in owners' equity, and cash flow for an accounting period. Creditors, present owners, potential owners, employees, and the public at large use financial accounting reports in decision making. Both external financial accounting and internal management analysis require cost information. Accountants develop cost data for inventory valuation and income determination; both are concerns of financial accounting.

Usually, cost information used for external reporting is irrelevant for actual management decision making. When results from reported production activity require more than one day to reach manufacturing managers, corrective action is not likely to occur and effectiveness is lost. It is usually better to provide incomplete, perhaps less precise, data to managers quickly than to provide complete information too late to affect any of their decisions or actions. Thus, an organization needs two different accounting systems with different degrees of completeness and timeliness.

Cost Defined

Cost measures the economic sacrifice made to achieve an organization's goal. For a product, cost represents the monetary measurement of resources used, such as material, labor, and overhead. For a service, cost is the monetary sacrifice made to provide the service. Accountants generally use cost with other descriptive terms, such as *historical, product, prime, labor,* or *material.* Each of these terms defines some characteristic of the cost measurement process or an aspect of the object being measured.

Different Costs for Different Purposes.   Cost systems are designed to collect, summarize, and report costs for the purpose of product costing, inventory valuation, or operational control/performance measurement. These various purposes influence the collecting, summarizing, and reporting process. Thus, accountants use different costs for different purposes as the type, purpose, and nature of a cost define its usage. Cost accountants use professional judgment in choosing the most appropriate cost concept for specific situations.

Roles of Controller and Cost Accountant

A common title given to the chief accounting officer and manager of the accounting department in a company is **controller.** Controllers play a significant role in planning and controlling activities by helping managers in the decision-making process. A controller designs systems to prepare internal reports for management and external reports for the public and government. The controller's functions also include analyzing profitability and establishing budgets. In addition, the controller may prepare special managerial revenue and cost analyses. For example, controllers compare the cost of making parts with their purchase cost.

As a member of the controller's department, a **cost accountant** is responsible for collecting product costs and preparing accurate and timely reports to evaluate and control company operations. Cost accountants assemble, classify, and summarize financial and economic data on the production and pricing of goods or services. Cost accountants have greater responsibilities in a manufacturing company than in a retail firm that purchases ready-for-sale merchandise.

Current Cost Management Practice

Kmart, the nation's No. 2 retailer has gone back to a strategy it put on hold in 1992. In January 1994, Kmart's chief executive announced an end to a self-imposed, year-old freeze on plans to refurbish, expand, or relocate Kmart's aging core stores. This retailer continues to experiment with new Super Kmart centers, megaretail stores selling both groceries and Kmart's traditional discount wares under the same roof.

Changing directions is a habit at Kmart; in the past it bought a chain of warehouse stores, regional cafeterias, drugstores, and a chain of off-price apparel stores. The current strategy is to focus on specialty retailing. The chief executive admits they are still in an experimental stage.

James B. Treece, "KMART: Slick Moves—Or Running in Place?" *BusinessWeek,* January 17, 1994, p. 28.

A controller's duties differ significantly from those of a treasurer. A **treasurer** primarily manages cash. A treasurer's duties include arranging short-term financing, maintaining banking and investor relationships, temporarily investing excess funds, and supervising customer credit and collection activities.

Planning and Control Activities

Cost accountants play an important role in coordinating external and internal data so managers can formulate better plans and control activities. In the planning phases, cost accounting helps management by providing budgets reflecting cost estimates of material, labor, technology, and robotics. A company uses cost accounting data in selecting the best methods of attaining goals when reviewing alternative courses of action.

While planning activities are future oriented, control activities involve monitoring present production processes and reporting variations from budgets and plans. Cost accountants issue progress reports that summarize the costs of activities to show the efficiency of divisions. By comparing actual results with the budget amounts, they identify areas of deviation where problems may be developing. Cost accounting, then, provides **feedback,** or information about current performance designed to encourage needed changes.

Cost Analysis.   Cost accountants obtain cost information from a variety of sources. Some of this information, such as vendor invoices, becomes the basis for journal entries. Similarly, they use engineering time and motion studies, timekeepers' records, and planning schedules from production supervisors in cost analysis. Cost analysis techniques include breakeven analysis, comparative cost analysis, capital expenditure analysis, and budgeting techniques. After determining what is actually happening, accountants should identify available alternatives. Then they use professional judgment to apply and interpret the results of each costing technique. For example, although breakeven analysis indicates the capacity at which operations become profitable, it assumes a static condition in which sales prices and expenses are constant. However, such factors do not remain constant in the real world. For instance, inflation, supply, and demand cause sales prices and expenses to vary.

Cost-Benefit Approach.   In accounting there is a direct relationship between the amount of time and funds management is willing to spend on cost analysis and the degree of reliability desired. If a company wants detailed records with a high degree of accuracy, managers should provide additional time and money for compiling and maintaining cost information. However, managers should use cost analysis and control techniques only when the anticipated benefits in helping achieve management goals exceed the cost. This is the primary criterion for choosing among alternative accounting approaches and is the **cost-benefit approach.**

Cross-Functional Structures

Traditional organizational structure groups machines by functions and individuals by skills. Parts travel great distances in traditional factories because all grinding machines and drilling machines are in one location. Separating responsibility fails to recognize the interdependencies between decisions made by one company division on the performance of another division. A **cross-functional structure** encourages cooperation and partnership among employees, customers, suppliers, and labor unions rather than viewing these parties as adversaries. In addition, companies must be able to respond quickly to these parties' needs and requests. However, traditional organizational structures lack this flexibility to respond rapidly to the multiple simultaneous changes these demands require.

Instead, a **networking form of organization** crosses functional and organizational boundaries to better meet customers' demands. A cross-functional team is a small group of individuals that crosses departmental boundaries and levels of hierarchy. In **computer-integrated manufacturing (CIM),** digital control links the entire factory together—from design to production. CIM removes the barrier between accounting, engineering, and manufacturing. Rather than separating these functions, cross-functional structures bring them together to promote team-based management. Team members with varying skills are more successful in improving operations, identifying and solving problems, and conducting research.

Improved factory layout eliminates wasted space by bringing together operators who sequentially process a product, allowing greater cross-functional decision making and coordination. This networking system encourages accounting, manufacturing, engineering, design, testing, quality control, and marketing to work closely together throughout the product development stage. Workers perform tasks in parallel, not in sequence. The traditional cycle is to design a product first and to perform cost accounting, manufacturing, and quality control functions second. Such tools as **computer-aided design (CAD)** and **computer-aided manufacturing (CAM)** apply computer technology to any or all aspects of the production process from design to fabrication. These tools facilitate closer interaction between personnel. Integrated manufacturing systems better prepare companies to compete in global markets.

What Cost Accountants Do

Within this network, cost accountants work closely with many people in other departments. In meeting the information needs of other departments, cost accountants gather, report, and analyze cost data. They also collect all costs of making goods or providing services. They use such cost data for income measurement and inventory valuation. These data also help management plan and make operating decisions. As part of their jobs, cost accountants interpret results, report them to management, and provide analyses that assist decision making in the following departments:

1. *Marketing.* The marketing department develops sales forecasts to facilitate preparing a product's manufacturing schedule. Cost estimates, competition, supply, demand, environmental influences, and the state of technology determine the sales price.

2. *Engineering.* Cost accountants and engineers translate specifications for new products into estimated costs. Accountants work closely with marketing and engineering in the **target costing** process which involves deciding what to sell, determining the price that competition will allow, and then managing costs to allow a desired profit margin. If cost estimates do not fit the target cost, engineers make design changes.

3. *Manufacturing.* Cost accountants work closely with production personnel to measure and report manufacturing costs. By evaluating the efficiency of the production departments in scheduling and transforming material into finished units, they can improve methods.

4. *Systems design.* Cost accountants are becoming more involved in designing CIM systems and databases corresponding to cost accounting needs. The ideal is for cost accountants, engineers, and systems designers to develop a flexible production process that responds to changing market needs.

5. *Treasurer.* The treasurer uses budgets and related accounting reports developed by cost accountants to forecast cash and working capital requirements. Detailed cash reports indicate when there will be excess funds to invest.

6. *Financial accounting.* Cost accountants work closely with financial accountants who use cost information in valuing inventory for external reporting and income determination. In many companies, cost accountants may also perform financial accounting activities.

7. *Personnel.* Personnel administers the wage rates and pay methods used in calculating each employee's pay. This department maintains adequate labor records for legal and cost analysis purposes.

Ethics in Business

Cost accountants have responsibilities to their employers, to others in their organizations, and to themselves. While their positions involve collecting, analyzing, and reporting operating information, their conduct must be ethical. Their ethics require that they exercise initiative and good judgment in providing management with information having a potentially adverse economic impact, such as reports about poor product quality, cost overruns, and abuses of company policy. They should communicate to management not only their professional judgments or opinions but also favorable and unfavorable data. They should protect proprietary information and follow the chain of command.

Controllers are responsible for internal control and for ensuring that employees follow company policies and enforce controls necessary to achieve the firm's objectives. Before proceeding with any questionable actions, controllers should determine whether they are violating professional standards, personal principles, or the company's code of ethics.

A code of ethics provides formal guidance as cost accountants face ethical dilemmas in the business world. In Exhibit 1–1, the standards of ethical conduct are from the Institute of Management Accountants' (formerly National Association of Accountants) *Statement on Management Accounting*, 1983; they discuss how to resolve ethical conflicts.

EXHIBIT 1–1   Standards of Ethical Conduct for Management Accountants

---

Management accountants have an obligation to the organizations they serve, their profession, the public, and themselves to maintain the highest standards of ethical conduct. In recognition of this obligation, the Institute of Certified Management Accountants and the National Association of Accountants have promulgated the following standards of ethical conduct for management accountants. Adherence to these standards is integral to achieving the Objective of Management Accounting. Management accountants shall not commit acts contrary to these standards nor shall they condone the commission of such acts by others within their organizations.

Competence

Management accountants have a responsibility to:

* Maintain an appropriate level of professional competence by ongoing development of their knowledge and skills.
* Perform their professional duties in accordance with relevant laws, regulations, and technical standards.
* Prepare complete and clear reports and recommendations after appropriate analysis of relevant and reliable information.

Confidentiality

Management accountants have a responsibility to:

* Refrain from disclosing confidential information acquired in the course of their work except when authorized, unless legally obligated to do so.
* Inform subordinates as appropriate regarding the confidentiality of information acquired in the course of their work and monitor their activities to assure the maintenance of that confidentiality.
* Refrain from using or appearing to use confidential information acquired in the course of their work for unethical or illegal advantage either personally or through third parties.

Integrity

Management accountants have a responsibility to:

* Avoid actual or apparent conflicts of interest and advise all appropriate parties of any potential conflict.
* Refrain from engaging in any activity that would prejudice their ability to carry out their duties ethically.
* Refuse any gift, favor, or hospitality that would influence or would appear to influence their actions.
* Refrain from either actively or passively subverting the attainment of the organization's legitimate and ethical objectives.
* Recognize and communicate professional limitations or other constraints that would preclude responsible judgment or successful performance of an activity.
* Communicate unfavorable as well as favorable information and professional judgments or opinions.
* Refrain from engaging in or supporting any activity that would discredit the profession.

Objectivity

Management accountants have a responsibility to:

* Communicate information fairly and objectively.
* Disclose fully all relevant information that could reasonably be expected to influence an intended user's understanding of the reports, comments, and recommendations presented.

Resolution of Ethical Conflict

In applying the standards of ethical conduct, management accountants may encounter problems in identifying unethical behavior or in resolving an ethical conflict. When faced with significant ethical issues, management accountants should follow the established policies of the organization bearing on the resolution of such conflict. If these policies do not resolve the ethical conflict, management accountants should consider the following courses of action:

* Discuss such problems with the immediate superior except when it appears that the superior is involved, in which case the problem should be presented initially to the next higher managerial level. If a satisfactory resolution cannot be achieved when the problem is initially presented, submit the issues to the next higher managerial level. If the immediate superior is the chief executive officer, or equivalent, the acceptable reviewing authority may be a group such as the audit committee, executive committee, board of directors, board of trustees, or owners. Contact with levels above the immediate superior should be initiated only with the superior's knowledge, assuming the superior is not involved.
* Clarify relevant concepts by confidential discussion with an objective advisor to obtain an understanding of possible courses of action.
* If the ethical conflict still exists after exhausting all levels of internal review, the management accountant may have no other recourse on significant matters than to resign from the organization and to submit an informative memorandum to an appropriate representative of the organization.

Except where legally prescribed, communication of such problems to authorities or individuals not employed or engaged by the organization is not considered appropriate.

Productivity

Current Cost Management Practice

After experiencing a drop in earnings of 70 percent, Compaq Computer Corporation asked its customers what was wrong. Customers indicated they could not find the salespersons. After conducting a study, Compaq found there was not a shortage of salespersons, but rather too many were organizing their time badly. Compaq decided to automate rather than populate and cut its sales force by a third, saving $10 million annually in salary and rent. A toll-free number was set up to answer routine inquiries, freeing the salespersons to focus on developing new business and servicing accounts. Computer and communications technologies in home offices boosted the surviving salespeople's productivity. Salespersons have more freedom to set their work hours while providing their customers with a higher quality service.

R. Lee Sullivan, "The Office That Never Closes," *Forbes*, May 23, 1994, pp. 212–13.

Automation and Cost Management Concepts

Mass production of a mature product with known characteristics and a stable technology was the basis of traditional cost accounting models. With automation, the labor content in manufacturing processes diminishes while other costs increase. Automated manufacturing usually requires large investments in engineering design and in new processes.

The traditional cost accounting model assumes each company mass produces few standardized items. Mass production was a primary means of cost savings; however, automation reduces the cost of changing manufacturing from one product line to another. Thus, automation permits companies to manufacture many small batches of various products in a short time. Such changes create a need for new types of cost accounting systems.

The **cost management concept** recognizes this shift in cost structure when providing product cost information. Estimated product costs influence new product introduction decisions, product design, and the marketing efforts given a product line. Product costs also play an important role in setting prices. Instead of focusing attention on what occurred, cost management emphasizes the future impact of economic conditions. Next we summarize some of the major changes cost accounting systems must undergo as manufacturers move toward the factory of the future.

Flexible Manufacturing Systems

Flexible manufacturing systems use computer-controlled production processes, including CAD/CAM, programmable machine tools, and robots. Because flexible manufacturing reduces setup or changeover times, companies can efficiently manufacture a wide variety of products in small batches. A **product life cycle** is the time between designing and introducing a new product and removing it from the market because of insufficient demand. Product life cycles are getting shorter and the rate of engineering change is increasing; it appears that this rate will continue to increase. Manufacturing one product and then another requires the frequent moving of equipment. Machine tools that are self-contained and shock-resistant offer advantages because today machine mobility is increasingly important.

Flexible manufacturing systems shift the emphasis from large-scale manufacturing of standard products to highly automated job shop environments. Job shops manufacture items in small batches for specific customers. Thus, a company is better equipped to alter product lines as product life cycles become shorter. When properly organized and arranged, computer-controlled machine tools also improve product quality and reliability. Combining these tools with computer scheduling and reporting leads to shorter production runs, lower inventory levels, and lower overall costs.

Total Quality Management

In addition to purchasing flexible machines easily adaptable to changing markets, firms use **total quality management (TQM),** a process of continuous improvement to achieve full customer satisfaction. Quality is providing customers with products and services that consistently meet their needs and expectations. Rather than waiting to inspect items at the end of the production line or striving to stay within acceptable tolerance limits, TQM's goal is eliminating all waste. Waste is anything other than the minimum amount of labor, machines, materials, and facilities. Cost accountants are adopting the **zero defects** concept, whose performance standard is to *do it right the first time.* Operators, not the inspector, become responsible for zero defects. Operators stop the manufacturing process to take immediate corrective action on discovery of an error or defect.

Value-Added Activities

A companywide operating philosophy to remove waste identifies and eliminates nonvalued activities. **Nonvalue-added time** represents the time a part is delayed, moved, or inspected. It is *wasted time* because no value is created for a customer when the product is not being processed. Inefficiencies in production cause nonvalue-added activities. **Throughput time** is value-added time plus nonvalue-added time. Throughput time represents the interval between starting a part in manufacturing and shipping that finished part to a customer. To increase profits, cost accountants must look for ways to reduce throughput time.

Just-in-Time Concept

The **Just-In-Time (JIT) management philosophy** minimizes throughput time by emphasizing continuous improvements. JIT reduces inventories by achieving a continuous production process. In a JIT setting, employees keep on hand only the inventory needed in production until the next order arrives. Having fewer goods on hand not only requires less warehouse space and storage equipment but also reduces inventory holding cost, while realizing gains in productivity.

Pull Rather Than Push System

The essence of JIT is a **pull system,** rather than a **push system.** Using a pull system, managers realize that it is better to not produce than to manufacture unnecessary parts resulting in excessive inventories. The factory production line operates on a demand-pull basis. The demand created by downstream workstations initiates activity at each workstation. Producing goods only for stock is in sharp contrast with the demands of CIM and JIT pull production and delivery systems. Under JIT, when marketing receives a sales order, manufacturing pulls a sales order through its process. Sales, not production, generate funds for the company. A pull system operates most efficiently where schedules are sufficiently level so a manufacturing process can react to the pull signals.

Service

Current Cost Management Practice

Hewlett-Packard, one of the computer giants, faced with competition from smaller rivals, is beating the odds by continuing to grow fast. Corporate planning is mainly bottom up as each business unit sends projections based on trends and market potential up the hierarchy. H-P executives have an enviable degree of freedom so they can reinvest the capital their businesses generate or attack markets in their own ways. They also are experimenting with ways to extend autonomy to the rank and file by allowing employees to answer phones and respond to customers' questions. The CEO at H-P recognizes that his job is to encourage people to work together, but he can't order them to do it. One approach is to allow teams to pick their own supervisors; this gives employees a strong interest in seeing their managers succeed. H-P learned that while its managers resent being told what to do, they are not too proud to copycat good ideas. The company also encourages their managers to ask other managers for help. Their philosophy is that it is hard for an employee to say no if another employee asks for help, but employees would resent a company telling them they have to do things a certain way.

Alan Deutschman, "How H-P Continues to Grow and Grow," *Fortune* 129, no. 9 (May 2, 1994), pp. 90–100.

Activity-Based Management

Today, cost accountants recognize that manufacturing and providing services are related activities. Thus, they direct attention to the cost of these activities. The **activity-based management** system links resource consumption to the activities a company performs and costs the activities to products or customers. Activity-based management uses **activity-based costing** (also called **transaction-based costing**) to measure and control these relationships. Activity-based costing (ABC) results from the belief that products consume activities; product design determines which activities the products consume. An **activity** is a process or procedure causing work. Examples include moving parts, performing engineering change orders, and establishing vendor relations. ABC is a cost planning system emphasizing an ongoing process of improvement. ABC encourages an identification of value- and nonvalue-added activities to eliminate nonvalue-added activities.

Life-Cycle Costing

Combining activity-based management and life-cycle costing illustrates the impact of alternative product designs on product costs. **Life-cycle costing** tracks and collects the costs attributable to each product or service from its initial research and development to final marketing to customers—thus, the term *cradle to grave* costing. Life-cycle costing recognizes that the design stage holds great promise for supporting low-cost production. By the time new products enter the production stage, opportunities to economize are limited. In addition to production costs, life-cycle costing studies preproduction and postproduction costs. For example, accountants estimate the cost of furnishing spare parts and services for the product involved.

Spending more effort in estimating costs in the preproduction stages reduces the number of parts and promotes the use of standard parts across the production lines, also lowering costs. Using standard parts lowers material costs because it creates possibilities for more aggressive volume buying. Also, when manufacturers use rigidly specified equipment designed to make only one product, this product is expensive because the specialized equipment often becomes worthless at the end of the life cycle.

Global

Current Cost Management Practice

Will Fujitsu be spared the layoff trauma that IBM went through? In its favor Fujitsu is more than a computer company as it began in telecommunications. Also, it claims to be at the forefront of asynchronous transfer mode switch technology; this is the key device that will make possible an electronic superhighway. Fujitsu is wisely trying to protect its greatest asset, its mainframe client list. It plans to show its clients how to downsize their computers.

Kathleen Morris, "What IBM Could Have Done," *Financial World*, March 15, 1994, pp. 32–39.

Target Costing

Life-cycle costing encourages **target costing,** an approach that determines what a product or service should cost, based on its sales price less a target profit. Rather than using the traditional approach of marking up costs, this is a market-driven way of examining the relationship of price and costs. Target costing uses market research to estimate what consumers will pay for a specific product. After subtracting an acceptable profit from the estimated sales price, managers compare the target cost with the expected cost. If expected costs exceed target costs, a company can (1) change the product design or manufacturing and marketing operations to cut costs, (2) accept a lower profit margin, or (3) not introduce the product or service because it cannot earn the profit margin desired.

Change in Performance Evaluation

The adoption of JIT, life-cycle costing, and other innovative management techniques requires an analysis of current performance evaluation systems. Often traditional labor productivity measures become irrelevant. The use of a single short-term profit measure, such as net income, may not reflect the ability of managers, especially those receiving bonuses for rapid profit improvement. Short-term profits are not reliable indicators of good management because profits can increase solely due to acquiring another company, deferring maintenance, or cutting out research and other discretionary expenses. Thus, manufacturers that successfully compete in the global market use multiple methods for measuring performance and improving productivity, quality, and cost visibility as discussed in Chapter 18.

Goal Congruence.   These performance measures should encourage managers to achieve overall organizational goals. To do this, a company breaks down its goals into subgoals for individual managers. These subgoals should be consistent with the company's overall goals. Such **goal congruence** is an ideal that is difficult to achieve, for individuals bring their own aspirations into the company and try to fulfill their own goals as much as possible. Individual employees adopt management's goals as long as the resulting benefits outweigh the required sacrifices. For example, an important personal goal of individual employees is to earn enough money to meet their families' physical and social needs. This may conflict with the goals of the company, because higher employee salaries mean lower company profits. In addition, managers often increase their functional responsibilities and the number of employees reporting to them to obtain power and prestige. The result is an inefficient organizational structure.

Rather than having only one dominant goal, an organization is more likely to have many operating subgoals that yield overall goals. Because multiple goals exist, accountants may have difficulty determining the enterprise's true overall goals. Top managers may hand down what each inaccurately considers are the company's goals. Thus, the accountant may not know if an action is congruent with overall goals or not. To help overcome these communication problems while also recognizing that goal congruence is difficult to achieve, managers should agree on company goals. After they carefully explain these goals, employees can better understand their responsibility in goal achievement. Managers should try to set company goals that also satisfy employee goals.

Professional Organizations

Several organizations in the private sector have professional certifying examinations for cost accountants. This book includes problems from these examinations. Other organizations influencing cost accounting development, such as the Cost Accounting Standards Board and the Internal Revenue Service, are agencies of the federal government.

Professional Certifications

Institute of Management Accountants (IMA). The IMA established the **Certified Management Accountant (CMA)** examination. Candidates must pass a series of uniform national examinations that include four parts: economics, finance, and management; financial accounting and reporting; management reporting, analysis, and behavioral issues; and decision analysis and information systems. The CMA exam tests cost accounting knowledge extensively. Candidates must meet specific experience and education requirements. Test dates are in June and December.

American Institute of Certified Public Accountants (AICPA). The AICPA prepares, administers, and grades the **Certified Public Accountant (CPA)** examination consisting of four parts: auditing; business law and professional responsibility; accounting and reporting (taxation, managerial-cost, and governmental and not-for-profit organizations); and financial accounting and reporting. The CPA exam has specific experience and education requirements. Test dates are in May and November.

The Institute of Internal Auditors (IIA). The IIA develops the **Certified Internal Auditing (CIA)** exam that consists of the following four parts: internal audit process, internal audit skills, management control information technology, and the audit environment. This certification program also has experience and education requirements.

Society of Cost Estimating and Analysis. Enhancing the efficiency and effectiveness of cost and pricing activities in proprietary industry, not-for-profit organizations, and governments is a goal of the Society of Cost Estimating and Analysis.

The **Certified Cost Estimator/Analyst** designation is a certification by the society that an individual possesses high estimating or analysis accomplishment and capability. To receive this designation, an applicant must meet education and/or job experience criteria and pass a written examination.

Summary

This chapter defines cost accounting and explains the functions of cost accountants and their relationships with other departments in an organization. Cost accountants are important members of the management team because their role extends far beyond accumulating product costs for inventory valuation. They have flexibility in preparing cost accounting analyses and reports in a manner that best meets the company's planning and control needs. Thus, modern cost accounting systems better reflect the manufacturing processes that actually occur on the factory floor. Also, market-driven accounting practices enable companies to more effectively meet global competition.

Modern methods for costing products, such as activity-based management, trace the costs of resources by the activities needed to produce individual products. In a transaction-related ABC system, units that originate the activities are charged for their costs. ABC identifies activities that add value and encourages the use of designs that reduce the demand for high-cost activities. Identification and elimination of waste emphasize continuous improvement, thus lowering product cost.

Important Terms and Concepts

Cost accounting   4
Management accounting   4
Cost   5
Controller   5
Cost accountant   5
Treasurer   6
Feedback   6
Cost-benefit approach   7
Cross-functional structure   7
Networking form of organization   7
Computer-integrated manufacturing (CIM)   7
Computer-aided design (CAD)   7
Computer-aided manufacturing (CAM)   7
Target costing   8
Cost management concept   10
Flexible manufacturing systems   10
Product life cycle   10
Total quality management   11

Zero defects   11
Nonvalue-added time   11
Throughput time   11
Just-in-time (JIT) management philosophy   11
Pull system   12
Push system   12
Activity-based management/costing (transaction-based costing)   12
Activity   12
Life-cycle costing   12
Target costing   13
Goal congruence   13
Certified Management Accountant (CMA)   14
Certified Public Accountant (CPA)   14
Certified Internal Auditor (CIA)   14
Certified Cost Estimator/Analyst   15

Ethical Dilemma

Jan Brown can remember discussing the Standards of Ethical Conduct for Management Accountants in detail as a student. From these discussions, Brown remembers professors stating that many events in their professional careers were going to be maybe situations depending on the circumstances rather than straight yes or no decisions. Brown especially remembers these past discussions after reviewing the president's latest expense report.

Brown has never seen Division President Ron Smith's employment contract, but each time Brown questions Smith about a lavish expense, such as entertainment or contributions, Smith repeatedly tells Brown that the lavish entertainment reimbursements are part of an approved compensation package. Smith also justifies some of the entertainment as a cost incurred in interviewing potential employees. Moreover, at frequent intervals Smith expresses the strong opinion that all companies owe their presidents some leeway in documenting expenditures if these presidents have made significant contributions in the past in building their organizations to profitable market positions.

Following the president's directions, Brown approved the disbursements in the past. However, recently these expenses are increasing at an even higher rate. Now, instead of true entertainment vouchers, Brown is beginning to see invoices for luggage, expensive clothing, household furnishings, and other nonbusiness, personal items. Occasionally, Brown questions the appropriateness of the expense. The president insists that the corporate officers only look at the divisional profits, and they agree that such items are fringe benefits. Thus, Smith tells Brown to pay for such expenses. Fortunately, demand for the company's product is high and the division is profitable despite the large travel and entertainment expenditures.

Required:

How much padding of expenses is acceptable, if any? How can accountants protect themselves in this regard? Does using the firm's telephone for personal calls or the company's copying machine for personal duplication make a person a thief? What about taking pencils and stationery home for personal use?

Problem for Self-Study

Information Needed

There will always be a trade-off in data gathering between the cost of acquiring additional data and the benefit of these data. A system becomes too expensive when it produces more reports than management can or will use. This also has a detrimental effect on the morale of the employees who have prepared the reports. They cannot feel pride in their work when they see that it is not fulfilling a purpose. Accountants should strive to strike an optimum balance between the cost of the information and the benefits of this information.

Required:

Discuss the types of information needed for controlling a company.

Solution to Problem for Self-Study

The following classification summarizes the various types of information needed in controlling companies:

1. Progress reports indicating how efficiently various divisions are performing. The feedback loop in the company's accounting system helps answer questions relating to the level of efficiency.

2. Information that directs attention to areas where problems are developing.

3. Information that helps evaluate which one of several alternatives to decisions or ways of performing jobs is best. Problem-solving questions that fall into this classification can be related to the response function or the area in which action variables are linked with environmental variables.

Review Questions

1. Support or disclaim this statement: "Cost accounting fills a need generated by the financial reporting process for inventory valuation."
2. Define cost accounting. How does it differ from financial accounting?
3. Support your agreement or disagreement with the statement: "Different costs should be used for different purposes."
4. Explain why the accounting system that is most valuable to management is one that raises questions, not answers questions.
5. Compare and contrast the duties of the controller, treasurer, and cost accountant.
6. Who should be involved in designing a cost accounting system so that it meets management's needs?
7. Define the term *feedback*. What role does cost accounting play in providing feedback to management?
8. Discuss the relationship of the cost accountant and other departments within the company.
9. Explain why cost accounting professionals should support and encourage senior executives to approach problems by asking, "What can we do about it?" rather than "What happened?" What impact does this approach to problem analysis have on developing cost data that are meaningful?

Exercises

E1–1 Applying Control Function
After much investigation, the Crews Company decided to use its own employees in adding another floor to their present building. A $400,000 budget was approved. Managers estimated that the project would take two years for completion. They transferred some employees from production of ZERXO, which was experiencing depressed sales. Because no employees belonged to a union, the company had this flexibility.

Sales of ZERXO became even more depressed after construction began. Market research, however, indicated that this was only a temporary decline and that production should not be halted on this line. After consultation, management decided to offer additional ZERXO workers the chance to transfer to building construction.

Periodically, top management inspected the building site so they had a general idea of the stage of completion. The assistant plant manager assumed the position of building supervisor and furnished top management with a review of operations only on request.

Because of these additional workers, construction was completed in one and one-half years, but at a cost of $440,000. The construction passed all building codes and also met all the company's specifications.

Required:

Do you believe the control function was effectively applied? It not, what control techniques should have been used?

E1–2 Evaluating Cost Accounting Responsibility System

Recently you were hired as a cost accountant for the Elliott Manufacturing Company. On your first day at work, the controller gave you a schedule for preparing cost reports; it appears rather tight. The controller stresses that the cost statements and analyses must be on the president's desk by 9 A.M. on the specified day.

After the accounting period ends, you must work overtime to be certain that the statements are prepared on time. A fellow accountant tells you not to spend too much time on the reports, since there is never any feedback. He also comments, "Don't get any bright ideas and suggest to the controller that we start investigating any deviations from planned results, since our workload is heavy enough now."

Required:

List the strong points and weak points of the present cost accounting reporting system.

E1–3 Problems with Organizational Structure

You have accepted a job as budget director for the Ace Manufacturing Company. As part of your orientation program, you receive the following organization chart:

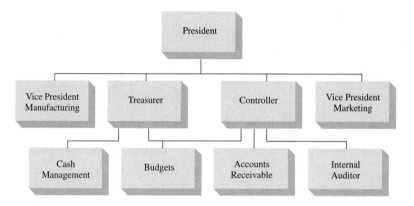

The treasurer calls you into his office for a confidential discussion. He informs you of rumors that he will be selected to succeed the retiring president. You decide not to tell the treasurer that no one else has informed you of such rumors.

Later, you visit the president. He stresses how important he believes budgets are to the company and has decided that you should report directly to him. When you ask the president for a copy of the budget procedures, he explains that such manuals are not necessary. Instead he is confident that you can initiate and handle all budgeting matters with your staff authority.

Required:

What problems with the organizational structure does the company face? What potential problems do you see in your new job as budget director? What solution to these problems would you suggest?

E1–4 Compliance with Procedure Manual

Before the purchasing department of the Scott Company accepts a requisition, they require a series of signatures. Normally, the requisition moves through intracompany mail to each person whose signature is required, and then to the purchasing department, where purchasing employees place a written order with an outside vendor.

When supervisors need an item in a hurry, they expedite the procedure by carrying the requisition to each person whose signature is required. If they cannot reach a person whose authorizing approval is required, they obtain alternative signatures. In some cases, secretaries provide the signature, either using a signature stamp or signing a superior's name to the requisition.

After accumulating all the necessary authorizations, supervisors may personally take their requisitions to the purchasing department and plead for rapid handling of the orders. If they are successful in convincing the purchasing agent of the urgency of the order, the purchasing agent places a verbal purchase order with the vendor, saving additional time.

The policy manual states that all requisitions must have supporting documents. If it is convenient for supervisors to attach these data, they do so. Otherwise, they either attach no supporting documents or some miscellaneous documents which contain little useful information. Employees readily agree that often the authorized signer may approve the requisition after only superficial examination of the supporting documents.

Required:

a. Do the documents resulting from the short-cut procedure provide adequate evidence of compliance with the procedure manual? What changes would you make to handle rush orders?
b. Assume you are the accounts payable clerk at the Scott Company and have received a copy of the policy manual which states that purchase requisitions in good form must support all purchase invoices. What would you do if you continually receive purchase requisitions that do not have supporting documents or have supervisors' names signed by their secretaries?

E1–5 Controlling Excess Inventory

Henderson County Hospital is a 700-bed hospital employing 18 pharmacists. Most of the drugs they dispense are prepacked; however, they do compound and prepare baby formula and intravenous solutions. In the preparation of these products, they use the drug *lactose,* purchased in one-pound containers.

The hospital's purchasing agent places an order for lactose when the supply on hand reaches the established reorder point. The chief pharmacist then places a weekly requisition for the lactose he estimates will be needed.

One year ago, the hospital experienced a critical shortage of lactose due to Federal Drug Administration restrictions on the manufacturers. During this time the hospital was unable to obtain enough lactose to compound and mix the required baby formula and intravenous solution. They had to purchase the baby formula and intravenous solution already mixed at a significantly increased cost. For the last six months the chief pharmacist has directly ordered from the supplier an extra supply of lactose to ensure against another shortage. This supply is stored in the pharmacy department.

The controller was unaware of this situation until the external auditors asked management if the large supply of lactose was necessary.

Required:

Suggest controls that would prevent the carrying of excess inventory.

E1–6 Meaning of the Term "Cost"

You are a partner in the consulting firm of Ernest, Inc. One of your clients has asked your assistance in explaining the term *cost* as used in accounting. The client relates the following incidents using the term *cost:*

Critical Thought

1. A sales supervisor in a large automobile dealership encourages a prospective customer to buy a new car by agreeing to sell at the dealership's *cost.* When the customer again asked what the price would be, the sales supervisor assured the customer of only paying *cost* by signing the agreement. Further, the dealership would not be making any profit from the sale.

2. The owner of Jones Furniture Store explained to the company's banker why company income was down by stating, "My *costs* this year increased 25 percent. Because revenues did not increase this much, income is lower."
3. In viewing an income statement, the client notices that *cost* of goods sold is deducted from sales to give gross margin.

Required:

Determine whether cost is correctly used in these incidents and what connotation it has in each.

Writing

E1–7 Traditional Concepts of Control

Traditionally, accountants used control techniques to meet the goals established by a few people at the top of the organization. Usually top management's principal objective was profit maximization. Further, these managers assumed that employees had the capacity to act in only limited ways and were not adaptive to specific situations. They believed employees were motivated primarily by economic forces. In turn, managers assumed the needs which the workers wanted to satisfy were those at the bottom of the hierarchy of needs. Self-esteem and self-actualization were not included. According to this traditional view, work was an unpleasant task that employees avoided whenever possible. A company needed tight controls to achieve any level of productivity. Thus, according to classical theories of control, the primary function of accounting is to achieve profit maximization. The accounting system serves as a control device reflecting unfavorable performance through unfavorable variances in comparing actual results to standards. The accounting system is designed to be objective and neutral in its evaluation since managers compare performance against overall organizational goals. Managers view this comparison with a high degree of certainty and rationality because they assume that accountants have only one correct way to report financial data.

Required:

Write a memo to an associate with limited business background contrasting traditional and modern concepts of cost control; include discussions of employee behavior, the organization's objectives, and accounting's role.

Cases

Critical Thought

C1–8 Cost Information Needed

Having had experience in metal handling, John Douglass decided to invest a part of his savings, form his own company, and be his own boss. He realizes that his company will have to be small, especially at first. However, Douglass believes that his savings will be large enough to provide an initial down payment for equipment and supplies. He has talked with a local banker and received the bank's backing to borrow limited funds for working capital.

Douglass' analysis of the market reveals that the concern for energy conservation will encourage consumers to install woodburning fireplaces. He has designed self-contained units with enough flue pipe to reach an 8-foot ceiling. Some models include a reducer and a grate along with brass ornaments; lower-priced models do not include these items. The more expensive models include glass paneled doors. Prices of the fireplaces range from $500 to $800, depending on the model. Douglass will employ two people who can install the fireplaces. Customers can have the fireplaces delivered or pick them up at the factory.

After investigating the vacant buildings available, Douglass secured a lease on a building. The building is adequate for initial production. Douglass plans to start operations with five employees and gradually hire another five. At the end of the first year, 10 employees will work one shift. His long-range plans include adding enough employees for a second shift in two to three years.

Douglass and an engineer have drawn up plans for two standard styles of fireplace-heaters. They expect to complete three more plans before operations begin next month. Douglass has not yet hired a full-time engineer. The part-time engineer will prepare plans for custom-made fireplace-heaters for an additional fee.

Douglass does not know how much advertising to use; however, he realizes he will have to compete with several fireplace firms in his city. He plans to advertise custom work in designing and installing fireplace-heaters for new homes. Also, Douglass plans to emphasize the standard models for older homes that already have flues. He has talked with several local residential building contractors and is considering giving them a discount to get customers.

John Douglass realizes the importance of maintaining adequate accounting records, but he is reluctant to spend much of his time in detailed cost analysis. He believes he can more profitably spend his time in production activities. He questions if checkbook stubs and a few other records will be sufficient for tax return and management purposes.

Required:

List the types of records Douglass needs for internal and for external purposes and explain why each is necessary.

Writing

C1–9 Cost Accounting Requirements for a Service Agency

Even though the volume of revenues has been steadily rising at the Treadwell Advertising Agency, its costs have been increasing at a faster rate. Thus, the ratio of profit to net revenue has decreased. Treadwell's principal source of revenue is commissions earned for placing advertisements in various communication media, such as television, magazines, and newspapers. Publishers and other communications companies bill Treadwell at a scheduled rate less a 12 percent commission. Treadwell in turn bills its clients at the full scheduled rate in addition to any special artwork or research requested by the client. To make a profit, Treadwell's costs must be less than the 12 percent commission.

At present there are three departments: copy, art, and production. Each department has its own facilities with production having more equipment because it is responsible for conducting the mechanical aspects of the jobs, such as obtaining engravings, plates, printing, and photographs. Its staff salaries include those for the administrator, account executive, copywriters, artists, and production personnel. The account executive is the principal contact person between the agency and the client. Periodically, it must make outside purchases of mechanical and artwork items such as engravings and photographs for its clients.

Treadwell is now having problems with several clients who expect special artwork and research without an additional charge. Service charges are made based on the staff hours required to develop pamphlets, folders, or booklets. Treadwell adds a flat 5 percent for an estimate of the cost of any supplies required to this hourly charge. However, because one of its large clients complained so bitterly last month over its service charge, Treadwell dropped part of the fee. Treadwell management made the charge elimination because it recognizes that a large part of its costs are for creative skills. These skills are difficult to quantify, as all artists and writers have dry spells in which productivity is less than normal.

The company tries to accumulate the direct costs involved on jobs for which service charges are made. However, Treadwell readily admits that these records lack accuracy. Also, there has never been any continuous costing of its services. Treadwell only has a general idea of which client services are more profitable than others.

Required:

Describe the accounting information the company needs. How should top and middle managers each use this information?

Critical Thought

C1–10 Potential Organizational Problem

Two engineers, an accountant, and an attorney organized the Hammond Company. The principal business activity is the manufacture and assembly of factory machinery. In addition, the company performs contract work for governmental units. Not only does the company have a healthy domestic market, but sales to European countries have also continued to grow.

In the early stages of organization, Hammond's external auditor performed most of the accounting work, organized the books and set up bookkeeping procedures. Hammond still uses very informal budgets employing approximations of factory overhead, marketing, and administrative expenses. Since cash is a critical issue, the main responsibility of the vice president of finance is preparing detailed cash flow projections. A secretary keeps the cost records. Hammond uses accounting information only to a limited extent; however, the firm keeps fairly adequate cost records on the government contract work since government auditors require it.

The president assists the vice president of finance in closely checking the cash position and receivables. Quarterly income statements are prepared by the external auditors, these statements are examined closely since the company is strongly profit motivated. Project engineers also play an important role in cost control because each development program is budgeted or funded for a specific amount of money. Each project engineer has the responsibility for developing the product within the specified budget. If the engineers meet their budgets, they are rewarded with bonuses; otherwise, they are penalized even to the extent of termination.

The project engineer's tasks is difficult because of not only many complex design problems but also time and budget constraints. Many of the company's engineers have erred in designing technically perfect products so expensive to produce that sales prices were prohibitive. It is not surprising, then, that the average project engineer believes cost accounting data are a nuisance that impedes efforts to arrive at a superior design.

When the number of employees and sales increase, management believes it will become necessary to substantially refine accounting and cost-control procedures. A controller will be hired to establish a simple budgeting system and introduce a rudimentary standard cost system for production work. Management plans to employ an outside engineering firm to establish material, labor, and overhead standards that will be scientific goals or yardsticks to measure the efficiency of factory employees.

Required:

a. Problems among the accounting, production, marketing, and engineering staffs are anticipated as the company grows; mention five potential problems.
b. Give several factors in support of management's philosophy of using small organizational units.

C1–11 Behavioral Impact of Nonverbal Communications

Writing

Accountants communicate through a variety of channels; written messages and verbal exchanges appear as the most obvious. However, they also exhibit communication by their facial expressions, tone of voice, manner of dress, use of office space and decor, personal appearance, and other nonverbal signals. When nonverbal signals accompany a verbal message, they may reinforce it or contradict the verbal message.

Sometimes the physical or nonverbal communication better reflects an individual's true feelings than either written or oral communication. This is probably true because most written or oral communication is a conscious effort by the individual; nonverbal is more of an unconscious response. The following accountants present barriers to effective communication by their nonverbal signals:

In meeting the recently hired staff lawyer, Accountant A says, "I am so glad to meet you. If you play tennis or golf, let's get together very soon." Due to the busy work schedule, Accountant A remained seated behind a stack of reports on his desk and did not make eye contact with the lawyer.

As controller of the company, Accountant B has many subordinate staff accountants. However, she is a recent graduate of a master's program that introduced her to the merits of participative management. She prides herself on applying this concept throughout the accounting department. In her office operations, the following occurs:

1. Accountant B often keeps subordinates waiting for conferences simply to prove her status.

2. Accountant B considers herself very intelligent and in conversation often helps subordinates and peers complete their sentences.

3. Recognizing that her time is very important, Accountant B accepts phone calls and outside interruptions when in discussion with others.

Accountant C's most common body position when listening to a speaker is to sit with arms folded and legs crossed.

Accountant D addresses subordinates over a large, uncluttered desk, even though there are other chairs and tables available within the office.

Accountant E uses Accountant F's office as an exit since this is a closer route to the elevator than through the hall.

Required:

a. Describe the behavioral message given by each of these five accountants.
b. Discuss the impact of these behavioral messages on the organization's future and the receivers of these messages.
c. Suggest how each of these accountants can improve his or her communication process.

Cost Concepts and Cost Flows

Chapter Objectives

After studying this chapter, you should be able to:

1. Contrast the different uses of cost accounting for retail, service, and manufacturing organizations.
2. Identify the components of production, marketing, and administration costs.
3. Demonstrate the flow of manufacturing costs through the materials, work in process, and finished goods inventory accounts as reflected in the cost of goods manufactured and sold statements.
4. Explain the effect of automation on volume-based overhead application rates.

Introduction

A market-driven philosophy demands rapid cost information beginning from the product conception to its final distribution, service, and follow-up. Managers use product cost information for a variety of strategic decisions, including pricing, accepting or rejecting sales orders, and selecting which products to make. If accounting systems generate inaccurate cost data, companies may sell their products for less than cost. Without accurate costs, product designers may select designs that fail to add value. This chapter describes the procedure for tracking cost flows that leads to effective decision making and introduces the cost of goods manufactured statement that shows an overview of cost flows.

Cost Accounting for Retailing, Service, and Manufacturing Organizations

Accurate cost information is important whether a company engages in retailing, manufacturing, or service operations. Each of these industries has the same basic financial statements; these normally consist of the balance sheet (also called the statement of financial position) and related statements of income, retained earnings, and cash flow.

- *Retailers* and other merchandising companies sell goods in substantially the same physical form in which they purchased them. A retailer generally has only one inventory account, called *Merchandise Inventory;* it shows finished goods available for sale.
- *Manufacturing companies* convert materials into finished goods and generally have four inventory accounts: Direct Materials Inventory, Factory Supplies Inventory, Work in Process Inventory, and Finished Goods Inventory. Direct Materials shows the cost of materials available for processing; Work in Process, the cost of uncompleted goods; and Finished Goods, the cost of completed goods.
- *Service organizations* have little or no inventory and their output is often intangible, such as health services, and difficult to define. Public accounting and consulting firms are service organizations that have tangible outputs, such as audit reports. Service companies usually employ significant amounts of labor; they can be for-profit or not-for-profit organizations. Their inventory accounts are usually a supplies inventory for material items used in rendering services. Service companies may have Work in Process accounts, but usually they do not have finished goods inventory accounts. Their workers convert inputs, including their own efforts, into finished services and these inputs require costing. Corresponding to a manufacturer's work in process, professional service organizations may have unbilled work consisting of costs incurred for clients. Service organizations do not have finished goods inventories.

Exhibit 2–1 illustrates the current asset section of a balance sheet for a retailer. Exhibit 2–2 shows a manufacturer's typical current assets. The four manufacturing inventory accounts often appear under one inventory caption on a balance sheet. However, Exhibit 2–2 details them for illustrative purposes.

EXHIBIT 2–1

WALTHER RETAIL COMPANY	
Balance Sheet	
As of December 31, 19X1	
Assets	
Current assets:	
Cash	$ 20,000
Accounts receivable	75,000
Merchandise inventory	183,000
Total Current assets	$278,000

EXHIBIT 2–2

WELLS MANUFACTURING COMPANY		
Balance Sheet		
As of December 31, 19X1		
Assets		
Current assets:		
Cash.		$ 20,000
Accounts receivable.		75,000
Direct materials inventory	$ 32,000	
Factory supplies inventory	6,000	
Work in process inventory	31,000	
Finished goods inventory	114,000	183,000
Total current assets.		$278,000

A retail company buys a finished product, places a price tag on it, and displays it for sale. The retailer has an invoice from the supplier as evidence of what the product costs. In contrast, production accounting is more involved because the manufacturer accumulates the costs of materials, labor, and overhead to determine product costs. Through the application of labor, machinery, equipment, and other productive elements, manufacturers convert raw materials into finished products.

Manufacturing Inventory Accounts

Direct Materials Inventory or Materials Inventory, an asset account shown in Exhibit 2–2, reports raw material on hand that will become a part of the finished product. **Factory Supplies Inventory** represents supplies to be used in factory maintenance, repair, and cleaning.

A **Work in Process Inventory** account collects costs incurred in manufacturing a finished product. At any balance sheet date, usually some units are only partially completed. At the end of a period, the Work in Process Inventory account shows the production costs of these semifinished units. Goods in Process Inventory is another name for this account. A **Finished Goods Inventory** account accumulates the cost of finished products until sold. At their sale, their cost is transferred to a Cost of Goods Sold account. A finished product is sold (1) to another manufacturer that further refines it or uses it as a component of a product, (2) to a wholesaler or retailer for resale, or (3) directly to the final consumer.

Current Cost Management Practice

Service

The main thrust of Sears, Roebuck & Company's ambitious restructuring and repositioning program is to sell low-priced but fashionable apparel. The realization that they are a mall-based, moderate-price retailer puts them head-to-head with JC Penney. To emphasize its distinction of being a full-line department store, Sears is advertising itself as a "whole store." Sears does not intend to drop its hard lines and auto business to focus on apparel as Penney did. Sears's critics are happy with the change because profit margins are higher in apparel. This change also shows that Sears has focused on its most likely customers, the women shoppers who dominate in regional malls.

Robert Stowe England, "Penny-Wise?" *Financial World,* April 26, 1994, pp. 36–39.

Production, Marketing, and Administrative Costs

All costs fall into one of three general classifications: production, marketing, and administrative. **Production costs** include the direct material, direct labor, and factory overhead incurred to produce a good or service. Product engineering and design costs occurring before manufacturing are also production costs. **Marketing costs** result from selling and delivering products and include the costs of promoting sales and retaining customers, as well as transportation, warehousing, and other distribution costs. **Administrative costs** result from directing and controlling the company and for general activities such as personnel and legal functions. They include management and financial accounting salaries, clerical costs, telephone costs, and rental fees. Both production and marketing functions incur administrative costs.

Even though production costs are generally treated as **product costs** and included in either work in process or finished goods inventories, marketing and administrative costs are generally treated as **period costs.** Period costs are charged against revenue in each accounting period. Product costs do not become the *cost of sales* charged against revenue until the sales of the product on which costs were incurred.

Direct Material

Direct material is any raw material that becomes an identifiable part of the finished product. For example, in manufacturing men's shirts, the fabric is direct material. Accountants separately record and trace all direct material required in manufacturing to specific products. Companies buy direct materials in various forms. They buy some direct material in a finished state and assemble the component parts into their final product. In the manufacture of television sets, companies often purchase electronic components, cabinets, and TV tubes. Workers assemble these components in finished appliances. Other companies purchase direct material in a raw state and apply labor, machinery, and equipment to change it into another form. Sugar processors, for instance, cut and cook raw sugar cane before it becomes a finished product. In either case, receipt of direct material costing $55,000 requires the following entry using a perpetual inventory system:

Direct Materials Inventory	55,000	
Cash or a liability account		55,000

This entry records the actual use of direct material costing $39,000 in production:

| Work in Process Inventory . . . . | 39,000 | |
| Direct Materials Inventory . . . . | | 39,000 |

Direct Labor

Direct labor costs are the wages earned by workers who transform the material from its raw state to a finished product. For example, the wages paid to shirt factory workers who cut fabric and sew the pieces are direct labor costs. Only the wages earned by those workers involved in the physical manufacture of the product are direct labor costs. This entry records direct labor wages of $10,000:

| Work in Process Inventory . . . . | 10,000 | |
| Payroll Payable . . . . | | 10,000 |

Factory Overhead

Factory overhead is sometimes called *manufacturing overhead* or *factory burden*. Even though the term *indirect manufacturing overhead* better describes this cost element, this book uses the briefer term *factory overhead*. Factory overhead includes all production costs other than direct material and direct labor. The emphasis here is on the term *production costs*; factory overhead excludes marketing and administrative expenses. For example, a salesperson's salary is a marketing expense; salaries earned by top management, the controller, and the financial accountant are usually administrative expenses. However, an inventory control clerk or timekeeper's wage is factory overhead.

Examples of Factory Overhead.   Factory overhead includes **indirect materials,** which are the operating, repair, and janitorial supplies used in the factory. Indirect materials also may include small, insignificant items of material costs whose cost is relatively small in relation to the cost of all other raw materials, such as thread used in sewing shirts.

Plant superintendents and other skilled and unskilled workers, such as janitors, repairers, and supervisors, do not actually work on the product, so their earnings are not charged as direct labor costs. Also, the results of their efforts are not as easily traceable to the finished product. Thus, their earnings are usually a part of the **indirect labor** costs and charged to factory overhead.

In addition to indirect material and indirect labor, factory overhead includes such costs as rent, taxes, insurance, and depreciation on manufacturing facilities. Factory overhead also includes other occupancy costs such as light, heat, and power used in manufacturing facilities. In addition, the wage and salary payments called direct labor costs may not include employee benefits. Employers pay not only the gross wages an employee earns but also employee benefits, such as Social Security, unemployment compensation, vacation and holiday pay, sick pay, and life and health insurance. Even though employee benefit costs that relate to direct labor workers are direct labor costs, many companies find it easier to treat all employee benefit costs as indirect costs that are later costed to all products.

Prime and Conversion Costs

Direct material and direct labor comprise the **prime cost** of a product. Usually accountants can easily and accurately measure these two cost elements. Managers maintain accurate records showing the cost of material used in manufacturing a specific

---

Global

Current Cost Management Practice

While Motorola continues to enjoy an enviable reputation, the issue now is whether Motorola can keep getting better as it keeps getting bigger. Pioneering advances in self-directed work teams, training, and business process reengineering helped it earn this reputation. Motorola, the country's top practitioner of total quality management, has no labor unions. The question is whether Motorola will fall victim to the bureaucracy and complacency that have afflicted other large American businesses. Motorola now faces a new set of challenges—most of them brought on by its own explosive growth. As it expands internationally, Motorola must tailor its approaches of empowerment and decentralization to cultures unfamiliar with these concepts. Also, Motorola must keep its workers motivated and energized—even in the face of record-breaking success.

Ronald Henkoff, "Keeping Motorola on a Roll," *Fortune*, April 18, 1994, pp. 67–78.

---

product or service. Clock cards or other time records report the time that each worker spends on a job. Multiplying the worker's basic wage rate by the time indicated determines the direct labor cost. Direct labor and factory overhead costs are called **conversion costs** or *processing costs*. Operations converting raw material into a finished product incur both direct labor and factory overhead costs.

Application of Factory Overhead

On completion of a product, clerks transfer the accumulated costs in Work in Process to the Finished Goods Inventory account. The amount transferred is the sum of the three factory cost elements: direct material, direct labor, and factory overhead. They obtain actual direct material and direct labor costs by adding the direct material and the labor costs charged as shown earlier in the entries debiting Work in Process. Determination of factory overhead costs is more complicated because cost accountants cannot calculate total actual factory overhead costs for an accounting period until it ends.

In addition, actual factory overhead costs may vary considerably from month to month; so, the value assigned to inventory can fluctuate considerably when using *actual* costs. For example, a New England desk manufacturer incurs fuel expense to heat the factory in January, but not in June. However, it is unreasonable to sell a desk manufactured in June at a different price from a similar one made in January. The company assigns estimated overhead to units manufactured so desks produced in January bear the same dollar amount of overhead as those manufactured in June.

To provide timely product costing data and to decrease fluctuations in overhead costs assigned to inventory, a company estimates its overhead costs for an attainable volume to arrive at a factory overhead application rate. Then accountants use this rate to assign factory overhead to different departments and jobs. Detailed budgets support each estimated factory overhead item. If managers budget $75,000 in factory overhead costs for the year and estimate that total machine-hours will be 1,500, the factory overhead application rate is as follows:

$$\frac{\$75,000 \text{ estimated factory overhead}}{1,500 \text{ estimated machine-hours}} = \$50 \text{ per machine-hour}$$

For every machine-hour used to finish a product, the factory overhead cost is applied at $50 per machine-hour. Accountants do not enter the $75,000 budgeted factory overhead in the journal or ledger as it is used for determining the application rate. Note that $75,000 is entirely too small to represent realistic factory overhead; we use very few digits in our illustrations to keep them simple.

In a highly automated factory, machine-hours may be the most accurate overhead application basis because many factory overhead costs, such as repairs and maintenance, depreciation, insurance, and property taxes, relate to machine utilization. Machine-hours is one basis for applying factory overhead; other commonly used bases include work cells, machine setups, direct labor-hours, and units of production. A **work cell** is a product-oriented work center that includes the machines and tools necessary to efficiently produce a family of parts. As you learn later, the appropriateness of the basis depends on whether the environment is labor-paced or machine-paced and whether it reflects the factor that causes the cost to occur. Each department may have its own specific factory overhead application rate, or accountants may use a plantwide rate.

Accountants must apply indirect costs included in factory overhead to the product at various stages of production to reflect the full cost of production. A journal entry can be made for each overhead application. For example, when finishing a product on the fifth day of the month, a journal entry applying $50 for every machine-hour charged to the product or job is appropriate. However, this practice involves much time and effort and is not practical. A simpler approach is to separately record the amount of **factory overhead applied** for each job on its cost sheet (as illustrated in Chapter 6). Then accountants prepare a summary entry at the end of the accounting period for the total factory overhead applied to each job finished during the period. At the end of each accounting period, accountants also must apply factory overhead to the partially finished units remaining in Work in Process Inventory. All production during the period, whether or not completed at the end of each accounting period, must receive an overhead application for the period.

Entry to Apply Overhead

The entry to record applied overhead involves a debit to Work in Process Inventory and a credit to Factory Overhead Control. Assume that 1,440 machine-hours were incurred on all jobs and the factory overhead application rate is $50 per machine-hour. The following journal entry records this:

Work in Process Inventory.	72,000	
Factory Overhead Control (1,440 hours × $50		
factory overhead application rate = $72,000). .		72,000

Control Account.   The Factory Overhead Control account is the same as any control account, such as the Accounts Receivable Control account used in financial accounting. In addition, Factory Overhead Control is a suspense or clearing account designed to accumulate actual and applied overhead. Accountants charge actual factory overhead costs to Factory Overhead Control as costs accrue throughout the accounting period. Factory Overhead Control is a general ledger account supported by a subsidiary ledger that details various factory overhead costs. The subsidiary ledger listing the separate cost items is necessary for management planning and control purposes. Management would not be able to analyze the details of factory overhead cost without in-depth accounting for each cost.

Assume that actual annual manufacturing overhead is $72,500 consisting of such cost items as supplies, indirect labor, depreciation, and rent. In this example, the production accounts involved would appear as follows at the end of the accounting period after posting the entry to apply overhead:

Work in Process Inventory

Actual direct material	39,000
Actual direct labor	10,000
Applied manufacturing overhead	72,000

Factory Overhead Control

Actual—factory supplies	5,000	*Applied*	72,000
indirect labor	33,000	($50 × 1,440 actual machine-hours)	
depreciation	28,000		
other factory overhead	6,500		
Total actual overhead	72,500		

Factory Overhead Applied Account.   An acceptable practice some companies use is to accumulate applied overhead in a separate Factory Overhead Applied account. They debit Factory Overhead Control for actual costs and credit Factory Overhead Applied for the estimated applied overhead when debiting Work in Process Inventory. When using a separate Factory Overhead Applied account, the transaction flow would appear as follows (Work in Process Inventory is not affected):

Suspense **Factory Overhead Control**		*Suspense* **Factory Overhead Applied**	
Actual 72,500			*Applied* 72,000

Overhead was applied to job or work orders for a total of $72,000 using the applied overhead rate of $50 per machine-hour. Even though the Factory Overhead Control account shows only one credit entry for $72,000, overhead is applied to each product and the $72,000 is a total for the year. Chapter 6 illustrates subsidiary records detailing the overhead application.

Disposition of Under- or Overapplied Overhead

The debit balance of $500 in the Factory Overhead Control account indicates that the actual overhead costs incurred exceeded the amount of overhead applied to production for the period. Overhead is underapplied or underabsorbed when this occurs. If the overhead applied to production is greater than total actual factory overhead costs incurred, the credit balance in a Factory Overhead Control account indicates that factory overhead has been overapplied or overabsorbed. Cost accountants periodically analyze actual factory overhead costs to determine the reasons for the over- or underabsorption.

Accountants close Factory Overhead Control accounts at year-end. If the amount necessary to close the Factory Overhead Control account is not significant, they close the over- or underapplied amount into the Cost of Goods Sold account. When the amount is significant, either in relation to the total cost of goods sold, total operating income, or some other test of materiality, accountants distribute the over- or underapplied overhead between work in process, finished goods, and cost of sales based on the relative proportion of units sold and units remaining in the inventories. For practical reasons, accountants prorate the over- or underapplied balance only when the amount materially affects inventory valuations.

Manufacturing Inventory Flows

Exhibit 2–3 illustrates the flow of costs through the four inventory accounts, Factory Supplies, Direct Materials, Work in Process, and Finished Goods. Exhibits 2–4 and 2–7 illustrate the cost of goods manufactured statement using the dollar amounts assumed for these T accounts. Accountants charge Work in Process for direct materials issued from the storeroom to a production department.

Accountants charge Factory Overhead Control for supplies and insignificant materials as indirect material. The Factory Overhead Control account is a general ledger cost control account. Actual factory costs such as indirect material, indirect labor, insurance, and depreciation are charged as debits to this account. This account collects only factory-related costs. Depreciation, insurance, and rent on the office building and office equipment are not part of factory overhead. Instead, an Administrative Expense Control account accumulates these costs.

Cost of Goods Manufactured Statement Using Applied Overhead

Cost accountants are primarily responsible for preparing the **cost of goods manufactured statement,** illustrated in Exhibit 2–4. The *statement of manufacturing costs* or, more briefly, the *manufacturing statement* is another name for this statement. The purpose of the cost of goods manufactured statement is to support the statement of income by summarizing all production costs for an accounting period.

EXHIBIT 2–3   Inventory Account

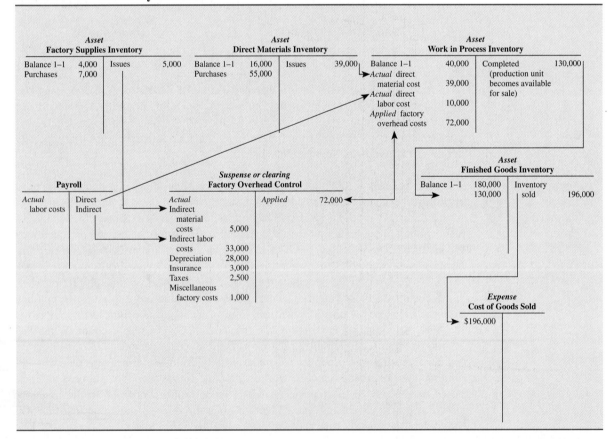

EXHIBIT 2–4   Cost of Goods Manufactured Statement Using Applied Overhead

WELLS MANUFACTURING COMPANY
Cost of Goods Manufactured Statement
For the Year Ended December 31, 19X1

Direct materials inventory, January 1, 19X1	$16,000	
Add: Net material purchases	55,000	
Direct materials available for use	$71,000	
Less: Direct materials inventory, December 31, 19X1	32,000	
Direct materials used		$ 39,000
Direct labor		10,000
Factory overhead costs applied		72,000
Total manufacturing costs for the period		$121,000
Add: Work in process inventory, January 1, 19X1		40,000
Manufacturing costs to account for		$161,000
Less: Work in process inventory, December 31, 19X1		31,000
Costs of goods manufactured		$130,000

These production costs consist primarily of the three elements discussed previously—direct material, direct labor, and factory overhead.

The cost of goods statement in Exhibit 2–4 shows operations used $39,000 direct material and $10,000 direct labor. As illustrated earlier, overhead was applied at the rate of $50 per machine-hour throughout the period, giving a total of $72,000 absorbed. Because the statement in Exhibit 2–4 shows applied factory overhead totaling $72,000, it does not also show actual overhead. When the cost of goods manufactured statement shows applied overhead, rather than actual overhead, it is usually advisable to verify and tie in actual costs as well. In Exhibit 2–5, cost of goods sold receives the $500 underapplied overhead reconciling amount. Accountants prorate significant over- or underapplied amounts between inventories and cost of sales.

Adding the beginning balance of Work in Process to the total manufacturing cost for the period gives the amount of costs put in production during the period. The resulting manufacturing costs to account for represents costs associated with either goods manufactured or goods remaining unfinished. The ending balance in Work in Process Inventory represents the cost of incomplete units at the end of the accounting period.

Manufacturer's Statement of Income

Exhibit 2–5 illustrates a manufacturer's income statement that picks up the cost of goods manufactured shown in Exhibit 2–4. Accountants add underapplied overhead and deduct overapplied overhead from Cost of Goods Sold as illustrated for the $500 underapplied factory overhead in Exhibit 2–5. A manufacturer's statement of income and cost of goods manufactured can be combined into one statement, but accountants often report only the cost of goods sold on the statement of income.

Retailer's Statement of Income

One difference between a manufacturer's income statement and the retailer's income statement appearing in Exhibit 2–6 lies in the terminology used. Because retailers buy only finished goods, *Merchandise Inventory* is their inventory account. *Purchases* are the goods retailers buy. Regardless of the number of inventory accounts used or their titles, the essential factor is understanding that costs flow through inventory accounts until their final disposition as income statement expenses.

EXHIBIT 2–5

WELLS MANUFACTURING COMPANY
Statement of Income
For the Year Ended December 31, 19X1

Net sales		$299,500
Less: Cost of goods sold:		
Finished goods inventory, January 1	$180,000	
Add: Cost of goods manufactured	130,000	
Cost of goods available for sale.	$310,000	
Less: Finished goods inventory, December 31	114,000	
Cost of goods sold	196,000	
Add: Underapplied factory overhead	500	196,500
Gross margin		103,000
Marketing and administrative expense:		
Less: Marketing expenses.	$ 38,000	
Administrative expenses	35,000	
Total.		73,000
Income before taxes		$ 30,000
Less: Income taxes		10,000
Net income.		$ 20,000

EXHIBIT 2–6

WALTHER RETAIL COMPANY
Statement of Income
For the Year Ended December 31, 19X1

Net sales		$299,500
Less: Cost of goods sold:		
Merchandise inventory, January 1	$240,000	
Add: Net purchases	139,500	
Cost of goods available for sale.	$379,500	
Less: Merchandise inventory, December 31	183,000	
Cost of goods sold		196,500
Gross margin		$103,000
Marketing and administrative expense:		
Less: Marketing expenses.	$ 38,000	
Administrative expenses	35,000	
Total.		73,000
Income before taxes		$ 30,000
Less: Income taxes		10,000
Net income.		$ 20,000

Cost of Goods Manufactured Statement Using Actual Overhead

Alternatively, Exhibit 2–7 illustrates using actual overhead instead of applied overhead on the cost of goods manufactured statement. For illustrative purposes, Exhibit 2–7 lists only a few items of actual factory overhead. Analysis of inventory flow for factory supplies reveals that $5,000 of indirect materials (factory supplies)

EXHIBIT 2–7   Cost of Goods Manufactured Statement Using Actual Overhead

WELLS MANUFACTURING COMPANY
Cost of Goods Manufactured Statement
For the Year Ended December 31, 19X1

Direct materials inventory, January 1, 19X1	$16,000	
Add: Net material purchases	55,000	
Direct materials available for use	$71,000	
Less: Direct materials inventory, December 31, 19X1	32,000	
Direct materials used		$ 39,000
Direct labor		10,000
Factory overhead costs:		
Factory supplies, January 1, 19X1	$ 4,000	
Add: Purchases	7,000	
Supplies available for use	11,000	
Less: Factory supplies, December 31, 19X1	6,000	
Indirect materials used	5,000	
Indirect labor	33,000	
Depreciation	28,000	
Insurance	3,000	
Taxes	2,500	
Miscellaneous	1,000	
Total factory overhead costs		72,500
Total manufacturing costs for the period		$121,500
Add: Work in process inventory, January 1, 19X1		40,000
Manufacturing costs to account for		$161,500
Less: Work in process inventory, December 31, 19X1 . . .		31,000
Cost of goods manufactured		$130,500

were actually used and charged to overhead. Actual factory overhead costs total $72,500. There is no adjustment to cost of goods sold for over- or underapplied overhead on the income statement when using only actual factory overhead.

Statement Equations.   The following equations will help you understand the cost flow on the cost of goods manufactured statement and the statement of income. These equations correspond to lines on the cost of goods manufactured statement and statement of income. (Note if you are using a perpetual inventory system, direct material used, cost of goods manufactured, and cost of goods sold would equal credits to their respective inventory accounts.)

On Cost of Goods Manufactured Statement.

Direct materials inventory, beginning balance $+$ Net material purchases $=$ Direct materials available for use

Direct materials available for use $-$ Direct materials inventory, ending balance $=$ Direct materials used

Direct materials used $+$ Direct labor $+$ Factory overhead $=$ Total manufacturing costs for the period

Total manufacturing costs for the period $+$ Work in process inventory, beginning balance $=$ Manufacturing costs to account for

Manufacturing costs to account for $-$ Work in process inventory, ending balance $=$ Cost of goods manufactured

Strategic Planning

Current Cost Management Practice

The board of Delta Air Lines approved a $2 billion cost-cutting plan and announced that everything else is open for negotiation. An all-out war on costs sums up Delta's grand turn-around plan. The board plans to eliminate 15,000 jobs or 20 percent of their work force in three years. Competitors are skeptical, suggesting Delta's plan may not go far enough as every airline is scrambling to cut costs. The benchmark for what defines a low-cost carrier is heading constantly lower. Delta does have a big advantage because only its pilots and dispatchers are unionized, which allows management to easily make some work rule changes.

David Greising, "A Destination, but No Flight Plan—Delta Plots a New Course," *BusinessWeek*, May 16, 1994, pp. 74–75.

On Statement of Income.

$$\begin{matrix} \text{Beginning finished} \\ \text{goods inventory} \end{matrix} + \begin{matrix} \text{Cost of goods} \\ \text{manufactured} \end{matrix} = \begin{matrix} \text{Cost of goods} \\ \text{available for sale} \end{matrix}$$

Cost of goods available for sale $-$ Ending finished goods inventory $=$ Cost of goods sold

Net sales $-$ Cost of goods sold $=$ Gross margin

Gross margin $-$ Operating expenses $=$ Net income

Inventory Physical Flow

Note the similarity between the flow of costs through a retailer's merchandise inventory and a manufacturer's inventory accounts. Exhibit 2–8 illustrates the similarity in all inventory accounts. A retailer buys finished goods and makes them available for sale. A manufacturer buys direct materials and adds labor and overhead to produce finished goods for sale. In summary, net purchases, as presented in the cost of goods sold section of a retailer's income statement, is equivalent to the cost of goods manufactured as presented on a manufacturer's income statement. As a reminder, finished goods is usually the only inventory sold. Because the raw material (including direct materials and factory supplies) in a manufacturing company is not generally ready for sale, the total of beginning materials inventory and net purchases represents the materials available for use. Manufacturers usually do not buy partially completed products for the work in process inventory or items for the finished goods inventory from an outside supplier. Instead, they produce this inventory using direct materials, direct labor, and overhead.

Volume-Related Cost Drivers

Although we expressed activity volume in machine-hours when estimating the $50 factory overhead application rate, this may not be the **cost driver** or factor that causes the activity to occur. For example, if many factory overhead costs relate to labor, the most accurate application basis is either direct labor-hours or direct labor-dollars. Accountants ensure they properly apply costs by analyzing the components of factory overhead. It is helpful for managers to visualize the route of a product as it travels through different factory processes. Then they can consider the causes or cost of the benefits received in each process the product goes through.

The overriding principle is to apply overhead costs to products and other objects based on the causes of costs or the benefits received rather than some arbitrary basis. Increasingly, accountants expect **nonvolume-related** (also known as **nonunit-related**)

EXHIBIT 2–8

	Retail Accounting			*Manufacturing Accounting*
Merchandise inventory:			Raw material inventory:	
	Beginning inventory			Beginning inventory
Plus:	Net purchases		Plus:	Net material purchases
Equals:	Available for sale		Equals:	Available for use
Minus:	Ending inventory		Minus:	Ending inventory
Equals:	Cost of goods sold		Equals:	Raw material used
	Manufacturing Accounting			*Manufacturing Accounting*
Work in process inventory:			Finished goods inventory:	
	Beginning inventory			Beginning inventory
Plus:	Cost of direct material, direct labor, and overhead		Plus:	Cost of goods manufactured
Equals:	Manufacturing costs to account for		Equals:	Available for sale
Minus:	Ending inventory		Minus:	Ending inventory
Equals:	Costs of goods manufactured		Equals:	Cost of goods sold

EXHIBIT 2–9   Determination of Factory Overhead Rates

Estimated total factory overhead	$75,000
Estimated machine-hours for period	1,500 hours
Estimated material costs for period	$60,000
Estimated units to be produced in the period	500
Estimated direct labor costs for period @ $15 per hour	$18,750
Estimated direct labor-hours for period	1,250 hours

activities such as numbers of inspections, setups, or scheduling transactions to be the factors that drive overhead cost. However, in introducing overhead application methods, it is easier to use **volume-related (unit-related) application bases** for illustration. Thus, we express activity in these five terms based on the data in Exhibit 2–9 and compare the different rates: (1) machine-hours, (2) direct materials cost, (3) units of production, (4) direct labor costs or dollars, or (5) direct labor-hours. (Chapter 5 illustrates activity-based management using both volume-related and nonvolume-related application bases.)

Machine-Hours

As illustrated earlier, the calculation using machine-hours as a base for applying factory overhead is as follows, given the data from Exhibit 2–9:

$$\frac{\$75,000 \text{ estimated factory overhead}}{1,500 \text{ estimated machine-hours}} = \$50 \text{ per machine-hour}$$

Some companies have a fixed relationship between direct labor and machine-hours; for instance, one direct labor worker is stationed at each machine. If this is true, the company can use either direct labor-hours or direct labor costs (if all workers in the department receive approximately the same wage per hour) rather than machine-hours as the application base. This may be easier because wage and labor-hour data are already computed.

Direct Materials Cost

Direct materials cost is an appropriate base if there is a logical relationship between direct materials usage and overhead costs. This occurs if each product involves about the same material costs or if the same amount of material is applied per hour. Also, if many of the overhead costs result from materials handling, direct materials is a valid basis. The formula for computing the overhead application rate with direct materials cost as the base, using the data from Exhibit 2-9 is as follows:

$$\frac{\$75,000 \text{ estimated factory overhead}}{\$60,000 \text{ estimated materials costs}} = 125 \text{ percent of materials cost}$$

Units of Production

Companies that manufacture only one product or have a simple production process use the unit of production base. Firms manufacturing more than one product, however, find another base is more appropriate because units produced rarely receive equal manufacturing effort. Rather than relying strictly on the unit of production basis, a company may assign points to the units produced to obtain a better apportionment of overhead. Also, nonmanufacturing organizations use variations; for example, a health care institution uses the number of beds. A marketing company may use the number of sales calls or miles traveled by salespersons; colleges and universities may use the number of students enrolled in different programs. The formula for determining the factory overhead rate, using the units of production data in Exhibit 2–9, is as follows:

$$\frac{\$75,000 \text{ estimated factory overhead}}{500 \text{ estimated units}} = \$150 \text{ per unit}$$

Direct Labor Cost

When using direct labor cost as a base for applying factory overhead, we assume that higher-paid workers are incurring a larger share of factory overhead than are lower-paid workers. Such a condition exists if the more highly paid, better-trained workers operate the more expensive and more sophisticated machinery and plant facilities. Direct labor cost is appropriate if overhead costs include many employee benefits based on a percentage of employees' base pay. The rate using direct labor costs as the application base is as follows:

$$\frac{\$75,000 \text{ estimated factory overhead}}{\$18,750 \text{ estimated direct labor costs}} = 400 \text{ percent of direct labor costs}$$

Weaknesses of Labor Cost Base.   Such a high relationship of overhead to labor is typical in an automated factory. Under these circumstances, labor-based application rates give the false impression that a causal relationship exists between the incurrence of direct labor and overhead costs. Another basis, such as machine-hours or work cells, would be more appropriate in this situation.

Using direct labor costs as an application base has additional weaknesses when factory overhead represents resources consumed over time, such as heat, light, power, insurance, rent, and taxes. Because all direct labor workers do not earn the same rate per hour, cost centers using higher-paid workers receive more applied factory overhead. However, much of their factory overhead results from use of the facilities. For example, assume that actual wages paid amounted to $15.30 per hour and that actual hours were 1,250 as budgeted. Total factory overhead applied would be

$15.30 × 1,250 hours = $19,125 × 400 percent = $76,500 factory overhead applied. If, instead, actual wages paid equaled the $15 budgeted, factory overhead applied is $15 × 1,250 hours = $18,750 × 400 percent = $75,000. Thus, the cost center applies more dollars of overhead by paying a higher labor rate than planned. In turn, a comparison of this larger amount of $76,500 applied factory overhead to $75,000 actual factory overhead results in overapplied factory overhead if actual factory overhead followed the expected behavior pattern.

Departmental rates based on direct labor dollars do overcome part of this weakness as long as workers within each department receive an hourly rate that is in the same range. Also, rather than use actual direct labor dollars, Chapter 13 introduces the use of standard or budgeted direct labor rates. Another weakness in applying factory overhead on the basis of actual direct labor dollars is that an inefficient use of direct labor causes an excessive amount of applied factory overhead.

Direct Labor-Hours   If many factory overhead costs relate to the use of labor-hours, as in labor-paced manufacturing settings, direct labor-hours is an appropriate base. However, the use of direct labor-hours may require additional computations, because someone must compute these hours for each job using information on labor time tickets. Using the data from Exhibit 2–9, we compute the application rate using direct labor-hours as the base as follows:

$$\frac{\$75,000 \text{ estimated factory overhead}}{1,250 \text{ estimated direct labor-hours}} = \$60 \text{ per direct labor-hour}$$

Using actual direct labor-hours as an application base has inherent weaknesses. Assume workers took three hours to produce each unit when two and one-half hours of direct labor were budgeted to finish each product unit. The standard of two and one-half direct labor-hours would be a better basis for applying factory overhead than would applying overhead on the additional inefficient one-half hour of labor per unit.

Impact of Computer-Integrated Manufacturing

Computer-integrated manufacturing (CIM) reduces direct labor costs. CIM promotes cross-training in which employees set up production runs, inspect production, operate, repair and maintain machinery, and enter accounting data. In turn, this places more emphasis on monitoring overhead.

Cost Mix   The traditional overhead cost mix averaged 50 to 60 percent of direct labor cost. However, in today's automated factories, overhead is usually 400 to 500 percent of direct labor costs. Although the proportion of these elements can vary significantly from industry to industry, typically material is 40 to 50 percent of total production cost, labor is 10 to 30 percent, and overhead is 30 to 40 percent.

The composition of overhead also is changing as factories automate. New overhead cost categories are emerging. For example, indirect labor includes manufacturing technicians, equipment maintenance labor, and machine operators who all were formerly direct laborers. Existing overhead categories, such as equipment main-

Productivity

Current Cost Management Practice

ITT Automotive, a large automotive component supplier, reviewed its accounts payable function from a total quality management perspective. ITT began by investigating software to automate the matching process for productive inventory items at all operations and support the consolidation of the accounts payable function. The firm found productive inventory invoices accounted for 70 percent of the dollar value of purchased goods, but represented only 35 percent of the volume of invoices processed. Thus, simply automating productive inventory invoice processing would have a limited impact on the activities of accounts payable personnel.

ITT's next step was analyzing how the operating unit acquired and paid for such noninventory goods as shop, maintenance, and office supplies. The company found the accounts payable personnel spent considerable time on such nonvalue-adding activities as printing checks, stuffing envelopes, and filing paperwork. After much study, ITT Automotive adopted a fully operational pilot program that reengineered the process by using procurement cards. A procurement or corporate purchasing card is a credit card allowing an employee to charge a purchase for which full payment must be made by the company in 30–45 days. Using these cards allowed ITT to reduce mailroom and postage costs, accounts payable personnel, and much paperwork. By receiving and paying its bill electronically, the arrangement almost becomes a paperless system.

Richard J. Palmer, "Reengineering Payables at ITT Automotive," *Management Accounting,* July 1994, pp. 38–42.

tenance, utilities, and manufacturing supplies, are becoming increasingly significant. The extensive use of capital equipment in automated factories causes depreciation to increase regardless of production volumes.

Eliminate Direct Labor Category.   Highly automated work cells using activity-based costing often do not divide workers into direct and indirect laborers because operations use the resources of all employees. Many companies also view labor as fixed because they do not hire and fire by the job. Thus, companies may combine direct labor costs with overhead when it is a very low percentage of product cost. Such systems record labor costs in overhead accounts, and apply overhead costs on a new base, such as machine-time or process-time.

Labor-Based Application Rate

Direct labor has been an acceptable basis for overhead application in the past because manufacturing processes were highly labor intensive. Some managers continue to support direct labor as an application basis because they believe that reducing direct labor is essential for ongoing cost improvements. Applying overhead on direct labor creates strong proautomation incentives. However, more managers believe direct labor-hours and direct labor costs are not good predictors of the value added to a product because of changes in cost mix. A basic flaw is that a direct labor application base does not correctly represent the amount of resources consumed by the product during the routing process in many computer-aided manufacturing systems. Thus, in today's automated environment, applying overhead on direct labor often distorts true manufacturing cost performance and distracts management attention from increasing overhead, staff, and other indirect costs. A direct labor application base may encourage managers to monitor the absorption of overhead, rather than to eliminate waste. For example, if the overhead rate is 600 percent of direct labor, the costing system implies to product designers that direct labor is very expensive. Thus, a design change reducing direct labor cost by $1 for a product results in an apparent savings of $6 in overhead. However, in reality, a design change reducing labor usually results in increased overhead because of engineering change activities.

Quality Control

More companies are realizing that to be competitive they must change from the conventional produce-and-rework-if-defective routine to a zero defects concept. Material costs also change dramatically as a result of the new emphasis on quality throughout the manufacturing process. With emphasis on reducing scrap and rework costs, material utilization increases, with yields approaching 100 percent. However, the implementation of total quality control involves a companywide commitment from top management down to factory employees. Elimination of defects involves coordinated group efforts.

Summary

Direct labor was an acceptable basis for overhead application in the past when production included highly labor-intensive processes. However, today's automated companies report their composition of manufacturing costs is changing with overhead comprising a large portion of the product costs while the labor cost percentage decreases. New labor categories are evolving because machine fabrication and assembly workers are now manufacturing and engineering technicians, process control specialists, and equipment maintenance technicians. To avoid misleading product cost data, costing systems must reflect this shift in cost structure. Activity-based costing using different cost drivers may better show this new cost mix.

Important Terms and Concepts

Ethical Dilemma

*Ethics of Charging
Exempt Employees'
Labor Cost*

Many companies sell products and services using cost reimbursement contracts, primarily for federal government agencies. These companies also bid for other contracts and use cost data extensively in this competitive bidding. They find it critical to have meaningful and complete information about effort expended on a project or activity. These companies normally use professional labor in a direct or billable capacity; for example, their attorneys work on various liability suits and their marketing professionals work on advertising campaigns and product development.

The Fair Labor Standards Act, passed in 1938, requires employers to pay all nonexempt employees an hourly rate of one and one-half times their standard hourly rate for work performed in excess of 40 hours per week. The act expressly exempts management and professional employees. Management employees are defined as those responsible for a broad range of activities, who direct the activities of other employees and are concerned with the policies and overall direction of the enterprise. Professional employees are defined as those whose duties require broad and in-depth knowledge acquired through education, training, and experience. This category includes lawyers, accountants, engineers, consultants, teachers, and physicians.

The following illustrates one method of allocating the labor cost of a research engineer earning $1,100 weekly. The engineer consistently works 52 hours each week. Assume the engineer equally divides time between an internal project with a fixed price contract and a cost-plus contract whose fee is 20 percent of total cost. Since the engineer is under pressure to complete the cost-plus contract, he works on the cost-plus contract first each day. Assume indirect labor costs for vacation, health insurance, and pensions average 80 percent of direct labor. Since the research engineer is overrunning the cost estimate of the internal project, the accountant fears her company will not show a profit on this contract because of these cost overruns. Thus, the accountant suggests costing the project as follows:

	Cost-Plus	Internal Project
Direct labor-hours	26 (½ × 52 hours)	14 (40–26 hours assigned to cost plus contract)
Direct labor amount	$ 715*	$385†
Indirect cost at 80% of direct labor	572	308
Total costs	$1,287	$693
Fee at 20%	257	—
Total	$1,544	$693

*$1,100/40 hours = $27.50 per hour; $27.50 × 26 hours = $715.
†$27.50 × 14 hours = $385.

Required:

a. If you think this costing procedure is unethical, explain why.
b. If you see aspects of this costing procedure that you consider unethical, suggest an alternative costing procedure that is more ethical.
c. List some advantages and disadvantages of the costing procedure the accountant proposed and the costing procedure you propose.
d. What behavioral issues do you see for the costing procedure proposed by the accountant and the costing procedure you propose?
e. What costing procedure do you consider most appropriate?

Problem for Self-Study

Cost of Goods Manufactured Statement and Income Statement

Data from the records of Brian Company show the following:

Accounts receivable	$ 7,600
Administrative expense control	10,500
Cash	100
Depreciation on factory building	3,000
Direct labor	4,000
Direct materials inventory, December 31, 19X1	2,500
Direct materials inventory, January 1, 19X1	5,000
Factory miscellaneous expense	350
Factory insurance	500
Indirect labor	390
Indirect materials used	250
Marketing expense control	9,000
Purchase discounts on direct materials	100
Purchases of direct materials	7,500
Sales	38,500
Work in process, December 31, 19X1	5,060
Work in process, January 1, 19X1	2,800

There were 650 units completed and transferred to the finished goods storeroom during the year. Finished goods inventory on January 1 contained 50 units at a cost of $1,500. Sales during the year totaled 600 units. Inventory is costed out on a FIFO basis.

Required:

From the data given, prepare a cost of goods manufactured statement and an income statement for Brian Company for the year 19X1. Round all unit costs to two decimal places.

Solution to Problem for Self-Study

BRIAN COMPANY
Cost of Goods Manufactured
For the Year Ended December 31, 19X1

Direct materials inventory, January 1, 19X1		$ 5,000	
Purchases	$7,500		
Less: Purchase discounts	100	7,400	
Direct materials available for use		$12,400	
Less: Direct materials inventory, December 31, 19X1		2,500	
Direct materials used			$ 9,900
Direct labor			4,000
Factory overhead:			
Depreciation		$ 3,000	
Insurance		500	
Indirect materials		250	
Indirect labor		390	
Miscellaneous		350	4,490
Total current manufacturing costs			$18,390
Add: Work in process January 1, 19X1			2,800
Total costs to account for			$21,190
Less: Work in process, December 31, 19X1			5,060
Cost of goods manufactured			$16,130

BRIAN COMPANY
Income Statement
For the Year Ended December 31, 19X1

Sales..		$38,500
Beginning finished goods, 50 units	$ 1,500	
Cost of goods manufactured	16,130	
Cost of goods available for sale.......................	$17,630	
Less: Ending finished goods (100 × $24.82*).............	2,482	
Cost of goods sold		15,148
Gross margin.....................................		$23,352
Administrative expense..............................	$10,500	
Marketing expense.................................	9,000	19,500
Income before income taxes		$ 3,852

*$16,130/650 units = $24.82 unit cost.

Review Questions

1. How do the inventory accounts of service organizations, merchandisers, and manufacturers differ? What type of costs do typical production inventory accounts contain?

2. Why do many companies use applied rates for factory overhead as opposed to actual factory overhead rates?

3. Explain the difference between direct and indirect material and direct and indirect labor in terms that a nonaccountant could understand. Is it feasible to trace down every item of material that goes into a finished product?

4. Outline the basic component parts of an inventory cost flow. (Hint: You may find a model helpful.)

5. What cost component do prime costs and conversion costs share? What cost components differ between the two?

6. Indicate whether the following costs are production, marketing, or administrative costs.
    a. Advertising.
    b. Factory rent.
    c. Insurance on factory machinery.
    d. Warehousing and handling costs.
    e. Property taxes on factory building.
    f. Depreciation on the sales executive's office.
    g. Wages of production workers.
    h. Materials used to make finished units.
    i. Production superintendent's wages.
    j. Financial accounting salaries.

7. Under which conditions would it be appropriate to use direct material costs as an application base?

8. Which of the following are examples of period rather than product costs for a manufacturing company?
    a. Advertising campaign.
    b. Insurance on factory machines.
    c. Depreciation of factory building.
    d. Wages of salespersons.
    e. Factory machinery repairs.
    f. Wages of machine operators.

9. When would it be most appropriate to use the direct labor cost basis for applying factory overhead?

10. Define the primary production cost elements.

Exercises

Writing

E2–1 Criteria of Cost Drivers
Write a memo to the production manager that discusses the criteria that an activity measure should meet, whether it is units of production, direct labor costs, direct labor-hours, machine-hours, or materials costs.

E2–2 Determining Costs Put into Process, Goods Manufactured and Sold
The following account balances were on the books of Clayton Company on May 1 and May 31:

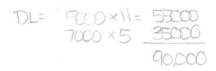

	May 1	May 31
Direct materials inventory	$20,000	$11,000
Work in process inventory	61,000	58,000
Finished goods inventory	50,000	43,000

Direct materials of $31,000 were purchased during the month while 5,000 hours of direct labor were incurred in the Mixing Department and 7,000 direct labor-hours were incurred in the Finishing Department. The labor rate for the Mixing Department was $11.00 and $5.00 for the Finishing Department. Factory overhead is applied at $6 per direct labor-hour in the Mixing Department and 200 percent of the direct labor costs in the Finishing Department.

Required:
Without preparing a formal statement of income, determine:
   a. Total manufacturing costs for the period.
   b. Cost of goods manufactured.
   c. Cost of goods sold.

E2–3 Significant Underapplied Overhead
Assume that a company has a large underapplied factory overhead balance and top management encourages the accountant to treat the balance as a period cost. Write a memo to the president explaining the effect on the financial statements if this policy is followed.

Writing

E2–4 Cost of Goods Manufactured and Income Statements
Butcher Company provides the following data for its year ended July 31, 19X2:

Administrative expenses	$ 195,000
Direct labor cost (53,000 hours)	424,000
Gross margin	1,500,000
Marketing expenses	600,000
Sales	3,500,000

Factory overhead is applied at the rate of 40 percent of direct labor dollars. Selected inventory accounts have these beginning and ending balances:

	August 1, 19X1	July 31, 19X2
Work in process	$192,000	$150,000
Finished goods	655,000	590,000

Required:

Prepare a cost of goods manufactured statement and an income statement.

E2–5 Determining Factory Overhead Rates Using Various Bases

Fourth Company provides you with the following estimated data for the next period for preparing factory overhead application rates:

Estimated total factory overhead	$525,000
Estimated machine-hours for period	375,000 hours
Estimated material costs for period	$700,000
Estimated number of units to be produced in the period	140,000
Estimated direct labor costs for period	$500,000
Estimated direct labor-hours for period	125,000 hours

Required:

Because the company is undecided about which basis to use, management asks that you prepare the overhead rate based on the following:
  a. Machine-hours.
  b. Direct materials cost.
  c. Units of production.
  d. Direct labor costs or dollars.
  e. Direct labor-hours.

Problems

Critical Thought

P2–6 Compensating for Others' Perceived Errors

The top management team of Uddin Company has recently become aware of a tactic that has become widespread throughout its organization. They describe this tactic as "Don't trust anyone—I must make sure that I compensate for the lack of ability and integrity of other employees with whom I deal." The extra steps that departments take in carefully checking over any products received from internal departments demonstrates these tactics. Many production supervisors keep a separate set of records that report flaws and inefficiencies detected in other department's performance. Some even keep tabs on the time employees of other departments spend on coffee breaks just in case this documentation ever becomes necessary to support their views about the inefficiencies of others.

This concerns top management deeply because they take pride in the employees they recruited. They believe most employees are sincere and dedicated and want the operation to be a success.

Required:

Does top management have a legitimate concern or is this just normal for employees to engage in such tactics? Should management take any steps to alleviate the current situation?

Critical Thought

P2–7 Cost of Goods Manufactured Statement with Unknowns

A review of Liberty Company's cost of goods manufactured statement for the fiscal year ended July 31, 19X2, discloses the following information and relationships concerning its single product.

1. Beginning work in process totaling $60,008 represents 52 percent of the ending work in process.
2. Factory overhead was applied to work in process at 40 percent of direct labor dollars.
3. Of the total manufacturing cost, applied factory overhead represents 20 percent.
4. Total costs to account for are $700,008.

Required:

a. Prepare the cost of goods manufactured statement for the year ended July 31, 19X2, in good form. Show supporting computations.
b. To test your understanding of the relationship of one cost component to another, recast the cost of goods manufactured statement using the following information and relationships:
   (1) Beginning work in process totaled $60,008 and ending work in process inventory is 52 percent of the beginning work in process inventory.
   (2) Direct labor is 40 percent of factory overhead.
   (3) Of the total manufacturing cost, applied factory overhead represents 20 percent.
   (4) Total costs to account for are $700,008.
c. If your statements in Requirements *a* and *b* differ, explain why.

SPATS

P2–8 Cost of Goods Manufactured Statement and Income Statement

Data from the records of Douglass Company show the following:

Direct material inventory, January 1, 19X1	$10,000
Purchase discount on direct material.	200
Accounts receivable	15,000
Direct labor	8,000
Administrative expense control	21,000
Indirect material used	500
Work in process, January 1, 19X1	5,600
Sales	77,000
Direct material inventory, December 31, 19X1	5,500
Indirect labor	780
Purchases of direct material.	15,500
Cash	200
Factory insurance	1,000
Depreciation on factory building	6,000
Factory miscellaneous expense.	700
Work in process, December 31, 19X1.	10,120
Marketing expense control.	18,000

There were 1,300 units completed and transferred to the finished goods storeroom during the year. Finished goods inventory on January 1 contained 100 units at a value of $3,000. Sales during the year totaled 1,200 units. Inventory is costed out on a first-in, first-out basis.

Required:

From these data, prepare a cost of goods manufactured statement and an income statement for Douglass Company for the year 19X1. Round all unit cost to two decimal places.

SPATS

P2–9 Combined Manufacturing and Income Statement

These data are from Rasher Manufacturing Company's books on October 31, 19X2:

	In Thousands	
	Debits	Credits
Direct labor.	$22,000	
Direct materials inventory, November 1, 19X1	7,000	
Finished goods inventory, November 1, 19X1	6,600	
Work in process inventory, November 1, 19X1	8,400	
Factory overhead, actual.	8,900	
Purchases of direct materials	15,000	
Purchase discounts.		$ 800
Sales		80,000
Sales discounts	900	
Other data:		
Direct materials inventory, October 31, 19X2	5,600	
Finished goods inventory, October 31, 19X2.	4,800	
Work in process inventory, October 31, 19X2	9,200	

Required:

Prepare a combined statement of cost of goods manufactured and income statement through the calculation of gross margin.

P2–10 Manufacturing and Income Statement

The following data are from the records of the AYO Company:

Direct material used	$ 34,250
Gross margin	69,600
Direct labor	60,380
Sales.	221,400
Work in process, January 1, 19X1	8,060
Work in process, December 31, 19X1.	12,070
Administrative expenses	23,700
Finished goods inventory, December 31, 19X1	31,500
Marketing expenses	18,050
Finished goods inventory, January 1, 19X1	16,700

Required:

Prepare a cost of goods manufactured statement and an income statement for the AYO Company. (HINT: You must work backwards to find the missing factory overhead costs. The key to the problem involves first finding cost of goods sold. You may find it easier to prepare the cost of goods manufactured format and fill in the information supplied before determining the missing information.)

P2–11 Cost of Goods Manufactured and Factory Overhead Application Rate

Sallie Company applies factory overhead on the basis of a rate per direct labor-hour. The company provides you with the following data for the month of May 19X1. Selected inventories have the following balances:

	May 1	May 31
Work in process	$78,000	$85,000
Finished goods	81,000	60,000

Prime costs for the month were:

Direct material used	48,000
Direct labor (45,000 actual labor-hours)	294,000

Sales have increased 20 percent over April's net sales of $500,000; as a result, gross margin for May is $190,000. Actual factory overhead for May is $58,100.

Required:

    a. Prepare a cost of goods manufactured statement showing only applied factory overhead. Also prepare a formal income statement.

    b. Determine the factory overhead application rate.

    c. Determine the amount of over- or underapplied overhead.

Critical Thought

SPATS

P2–12 Budgeted Cost of Goods Manufactured Statement and Income Statement Using FIFO, LIFO, and Weighted-Average Inventory Costing

Management of Boston Company expects to sell 60,000 units of the only product that it manufactures. The firm forecasts the sales price to be $150 per unit. There are 8,500 units remaining in finished goods inventory on May 31, 19X1, at a cost of $493,000. The company expects work in process inventory to remain unchanged and desires to have 12,500 units in finished goods inventory at the end of May 19X2.

Each unit of finished product requires three gallons of material costing $4 per gallon. Each unit takes four hours of direct labor; the cost of direct labor is $8 per hour. Factory overhead is applied on the basis of $5 per direct labor-hour. Marketing costs at this budgeted level are $1,500,000; estimated administrative costs are $1,000,000.

Required (Chapter 15 Appendix reviews inventory costing.):

    a. Prepare a budgeted cost of goods manufactured statement and statement of income using FIFO costing.

    b. Assume instead that the company uses LIFO costing; determine the ending finished goods inventory.

    c. Assume instead that the company uses weighted-average costing; determine the ending finished goods inventory. Round to two decimal points.

    d. Which inventory method is preferred for tax purposes? Explain why.

    e. Is Boston Company using a Just-in-Time management philosophy? Explain your answer.

P2–13 Factory Overhead Application Rate for Use in Cost of Goods Manufactured Statement

Cleopatra Company manufactures special motors for industrial use. A computerized costing system accumulates production costs. At the beginning of June, assembly line operations have been changed due to the installation of a processing machine that took over some of the work previously performed by direct labor workers. The following data are available at the beginning of June:

Direct materials inventory, June 1		$15,000
Work in process inventory, June 1		
Direct materials	$1,500	
Direct labor (300 hours)	1,800	
Factory overhead applied.	750	
Total	$4,050	

During the month of June the following activities occurred:

1. Direct labor totaled 4,500 hours at $6 per hour.
2. Direct materials costing $18,900 were purchased.

At the end of June, inventories consisted of the following:

Direct materials inventory, June 30		$16,500
Work in process inventory, June 30		
Direct materials	$ 5,500	
Direct labor (600 hours)	3,600	
Factory overhead applied.	2,460	
Total	$11,560	

Required:

Prepare a detailed cost of goods manufactured statement for June.

P2–14 Budgeted Cost of Goods Manufactured Statement and Income Statement Using FIFO, LIFO, and Weighted-Average Inventory Costing

Peasant Company produces and sells only one product. For the next year ending May 31, 19X2, management expects to sell 96,000 units at an $80 sales price per unit. There are 7,000 units remaining in finished goods inventory at the end of the current year at a cost of $315,000. Management wants to have 10,000 units in finished goods inventory at the end of the period. The company wishes to maintain the end of period level of partially completed units.

Each unit requires eight gallons of direct material. Only one direct material is used; it costs $2 per gallon. Two hours of direct labor are required before completion of each unit; the cost of direct labor is $10 per hour. Factory overhead is applied on the basis of $6 per direct labor-hour. Budgeted marketing costs at this level are $1,200,000; administrative costs are expected to be $600,000.

Required (Chapter 15 Appendix reviews inventory costing.):

a. Prepare a budgeted cost of goods manufactured statement and statement of income using FIFO costing.
b. Assume that the company uses LIFO costing instead; determine the ending finished goods inventory.
c. Assume that the company uses weighted-average costing instead; determine the ending finished good inventory. Round to two decimal points.

P2–15 Journal Entry Preparation Using Factory Overhead Subsidiary Ledger

Amy Wells Company, Inc., gives you the following information concerning their August monthly operations. Before the year began, management decided to apply factory overhead on machine-hours. Estimated yearly factory overhead was $220,500 for the budgeted direct labor-hours of 9,000. On August 1, 19X3, the balance in Finished Goods Inventory was $16,160, in Work in Process, $3,100; in Direct Materials Inventory, $2,850; and in Factory Supplies Inventory, $1,600. The company has a subsidiary ledger to record the details of its factory overhead.

1. Direct materials of $21,700 were purchased on account.
2. Direct materials of $15,600 were issued out of the storeroom for use in production.
3. Direct materials of $1,200 were issued out of the storeroom to be used as maintenance supplies.
4. Analysis of the payroll records revealed the following (ignore payroll deductions):

	Hours	Payroll Costs
Direct laborers	2,000	$60,000
Superintendents	350	4,000
Factory repairers.	250	1,500
Factory janitorial staff.	800	4,500
Marketing staff.	500	9,000
Administrative staff	700	10,000
		$89,000

5. Apply factory overhead; machine-hours were 760.

6. Miscellaneous factory expense of $700 was paid for in cash.

7. Analysis of the monthly depreciation schedules revealed the following:

	Amount
Factory building.	$2,650
Factory machinery	3,010
Office building (one-third of the building is occupied by the marketing staff)	900
Office equipment (one-fourth of this is used by the marketing staff).	400
	$6,960

8. Analysis of the insurance register revealed that the following prepaid insurance has expired this month:

Coverage:	Factory building.	$350
	Factory equipment	295
	Office building.	150
	Office equipment	80
		$875

9. A physical count was made of the inventory on hand at August 31, 19X3. The balances were as follows:

Direct materials.	$ 7,750
Factory supplies	400
Work in process	2,945
Finished goods	17,180

The differences reflect the costs transferred. The difference in finished goods inventory reflects goods that were sold on account at a markup on cost of 35 percent. (This markup was calculated before over- or underapplied overhead is closed.)

10. Record the closing of all revenue and expense accounts.

Required:

Prepare the general journal entries to record the monthly operations using a factory overhead subsidiary ledger.

Case

C2–16 Informal Organizations

When Ann Watts returned to the business environment as a cost accountant after taking off five years to raise her family, she vowed that she would not listen to office gossip. Her philosophy was that what she did not know cannot hurt her. For a while she stayed true to this vow and refused to talk about the personal lives of co-workers when she had lunch with other employees.

However, she began to wonder if she was making a mistake trying to isolate herself from the office grapevine. She noticed that she seemed to have more trouble getting along with her co-workers and supervisors. Watts did not have the benefit of the behind-the-scene information about these people's personal lives. For instance, last week when she delivered last month's cost of goods manufactured statement to the controller, he was rude to her and began asking for explanations why direct material and direct labor costs had increased so drastically during the last quarter. When she was unable to give a concise answer, he immediately told her to have a detailed report on his desk by 8:00 the next morning.

By the time she arrived back at her office from this meeting, she was seriously considering resigning. Her secretary, noting the distraught look on her face, asked what was the matter. After Watts told her what had happened, the secretary remarked, "Oh, don't you know? His 16-year-old son wrecked the family car last night. While no one was badly hurt, he completely destroyed his new sports car."

This started Watts thinking that maybe she should become more a part of the group. Yet, she dreaded the thoughts of trying to separate herself from some of the obsessive gossipers she had seen around the company. However, Watts also remembered several other events that had left her with egg on her face.

Once, for example, when the vice president asked her at an office party how she liked the change in office dress code, she had quickly remarked, "I think it is completely old-fashioned not to allow the company's female professional staff to wear pant suits to their jobs. Further, I believe this is discrimination." Later, she learned that it was this vice president who had pressed so hard for the change in dress code to prohibit pant suits. His argument had been that the company paid these ladies high enough salaries to require that they dress accordingly. Most of the women employees had resented the change to a more formal dress code, but they had limited their verbal outbursts to discussions among themselves.

In view of these recent events, Watts questions her approach to the working environment and wonders if she should change her tactics regarding the informal communication system.

Required:

    a. Compare the sources of power and authority for an informal organization with those of the formal organization.

    b. Explain the factors that cause the development of informal organizations within the formal organization structure of companies.

    c. Discuss ways an informal communication system can be beneficial to the management process in achieving the organization's goals.

    d. Describe the ways formal and informal communication systems differ as to accuracy and speed of communication. What is the impact that communication has on employees?

    e. Discuss (1) what employees can learn from office talk and (2) what its dangers are.

    f. Explain why Ann Watts has or has not made an error in her approach to the informal work group.

Cost Behavior and Cost Estimation

Chapter Objectives

After studying this chapter, you should be able to:

1. Understand cost behavior patterns and the impact of automated manufacturing on these patterns.

2. Identify the important role of cost accountants in advising management about predicted cost behavior.

3. Use cost estimation methods, including regression analysis, to separate costs into their fixed and variable components.

4. Prepare cost estimating functions for determining budgeted costs to compare with actual costs.

Introduction

Cost behavior concerns how *total* and *unit* costs vary with changes in activity or volume. To better estimate and control cost, understanding its behavior is essential. Because of the large investment in equipment, the importance of cost behavior analysis increases as factories become more automated. Activity-based costing (ABC) questions the traditional model using a fixed and variable costs dichotomy. ABC reports the rate at which activities consume resources as well as why they use the resources. Rather than assuming a single mix of cost behavior, the cost management approach examines how to improve profits by managing cost interrelationships.

Cost Behavior Patterns

Fixed and Variable Costs

Analyzing cost behavior patterns is an important function of cost accountants. Total **variable costs** vary in direct proportion to changes in the cost driver. Total **fixed costs** remain the same despite changes in the cost driver; depreciation, insurance premiums, and rent payments are examples. **Semivariable (mixed) costs** behave as partly variable and partly fixed; that is, they vary, but less than proportionately. Costs of indirect material, indirect labor, and utilities may be semivariable. For instance, there is a fixed monthly electricity cost plus a per kilowatt-hour charge.

Finding a strictly fixed or strictly variable cost in practice is difficult; many costs fall into a semivariable group that displays both fixed and variable characteristics. There is usually little difficulty in determining whether a direct material or direct labor cost in a labor-paced environment is fixed or variable; generally, these costs are variable. Direct labor in a machine-paced, automated factory tends to be a fixed cost. However, overhead cost behavior is harder to determine because some overhead costs vary erratically with production. Before semivariable costs can be used in cost estimates such as budgets, accountants segregate them into their fixed and variable components. This chapter discusses methods for making this distinction.

Fixed costs can be either committed costs or discretionary costs. **Committed costs** are the result of previous managerial actions. Depreciation and property taxes on the manufacturing facilities are committed costs. After acquiring an asset, committed costs are not changed unless economic circumstances indicate a change in the depreciation method or useful life, or the asset is sold.

Other costs, such as factory supervision, are **discretionary costs** because management uses its professional judgment each period in deciding the amount of such costs. These costs also are called programmed or managed costs. Many marketing and administrative costs are discretionary costs. Changes in economic conditions and technology as well as plant layout and facilities location affect management's decision about the level of discretionary costs. For example, if a competitor's product is more technologically advanced, management may find it urgent to change the product design. This design change may involve an employee training program. Such costs arise from periodic appropriation decisions reflecting top management decisions. If unfavorable conditions develop for the company, managers may drastically reduce these costs for a given year. Even though there is often no clear line between committed and discretionary costs, the distinction is useful for planning and control decisions.

Strategic Planning

Current Cost Management Practice

As companies streamline operations, managers are dismantling bureaucracies and questioning the benefits of vertical integration. One alternative is a strategy that focuses internal operations on a small set of critical core activities. Nonessential services are then outsourced to external vendors who can offer advantages, such as flexibility, cost, and access to the latest technology. Sun Microsystems, a maker of computer workstations, has been referred to as an intellectual holding company because it concentrates on hardware and software design and outsources almost everything else in its value chain. Cost accountants can help decide which activities should be performed within the firm and which should be bought externally. Understanding a firm's value chain and the relationship among its service activities is the beginning step in preparing an outsourcing study.

Ralph E. Drtina, "The Outsourcing Decision," *Management Accounting,* March 1994, pp. 56–62.

We must distinguish between short- and long-run periods in relation to fixed and variable costs. In the long run, there are no committed costs. Should management decide not to operate their plant facilities, usually they can cancel the lease agreement and avoid the rent payment. In the short run, however, management cannot inform the lessor that operations have ceased and they wish to terminate the lease immediately. When a cost is fixed, it is fixed for a certain short period—a month or a year. People, machines, and other resources come in lumpy amounts; not all costs are variable in the long run.

Relevant Range

The **relevant range** is the specific period and designated range of production volume or activity for defining fixed and variable costs. If fixed costs are $100,000 for a year, we assume they remain the same for a certain volume range; for example, 1,000 to 3,000 units. When management finds an expansion of production facilities is necessary, it may either move to a larger plant or use the present facilities with additional shifts. In either case, this change in the production facilities or the number of work shifts can cause a change in the relevant range. This change in the relevant range can affect *total* fixed costs. Although some fixed costs, such as depreciation, do not change unless a company acquires new equipment or a larger plant, other fixed costs may increase. For example, a company may hire more plant supervisors.

Total fixed costs are time-related rather than activity- or volume-related when compared to variable costs. Price changes experienced in a different accounting period affect fixed costs. For example, even if the same number of shifts work next year, or the plant size remains the same, the salary level paid to the plant supervisors or rent on present plant facilities may increase. This increase may affect total fixed costs. Thus, total fixed costs remain the same only if we assume the relevant range does not change and prices remain constant.

The top illustration in Exhibit 3–1 shows the fixed costs for activities on either side of the relevant range when companies make major salary adjustments or changes in plant facilities. The fixed cost function depicted often is called a *step function.* Because in practice fixed costs are usually not graphed according to this conceptual analysis, the lower illustration shows the practical analysis of fixed costs. The probability of a company's activity being outside the relevant range is usually small so $100,000 becomes the fixed-costs level.

EXHIBIT 3–1   Conceptual Analysis and Practical Analysis of Fixed Costs

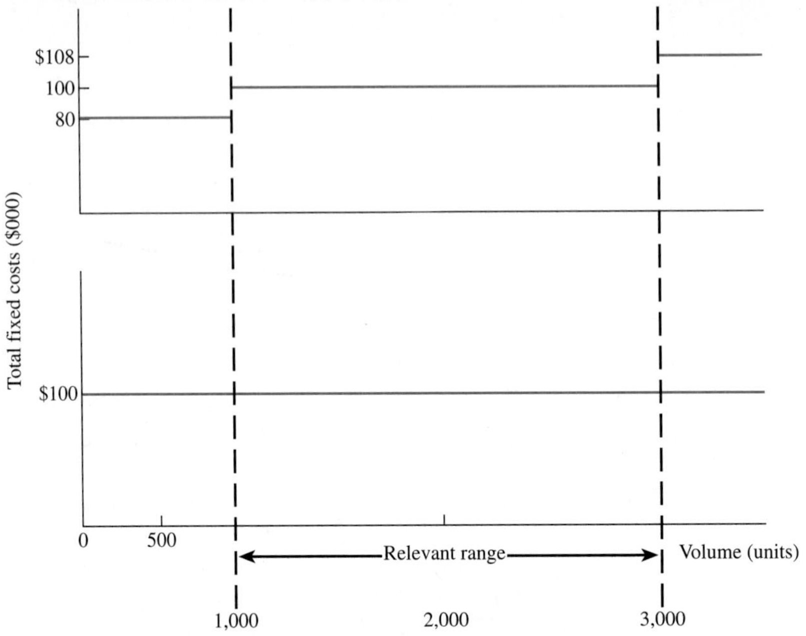

Nonlinear Relationships

The basic assumption of relevant range applies to variable costs as shown in Exhibit 3–2. Accountants assume variable costs are constant (represented graphically by a straight line) while economists often assume a curve more accurately represents the underlying variable cost relationship as compared to volume. Economists argue quite convincingly that at higher levels of activity, there might be overcrowding, fatigue, or breakdowns in communications causing variable costs to increase per activity level rather than maintain the constant (linear) relationship that accountants usually assume exists for cost analysis and control purposes. Also, while learning their jobs, workers may waste more raw material or labor-hours at lower activity levels.

Outside the relevant range, raw material, labor, utilities used, and other variable costs may not behave directly with changes in volume. Economists plot variable costs as in the top graph of Exhibit 3–2, showing variable costs are not strictly affected in direct proportion to volume outside the relevant range. Exhibit 3–2 shows costs increase at a decreasing rate for volumes up to 1,000 units; production costs increase faster than the assumed linear rate beyond 3,000 units. However, between 1,000 and 3,000 units, each unit appears to contain the same amount of cost. This range provides linear cost behavior; in practice, we draw total variable costs as shown in the bottom graph in Exhibit 3–2. Economies and diseconomies of scale can cause nonlinear cost behavior. For example, quantity discounts could cause cost per unit to decrease up to 1,000 units in Exhibit 3–2. However, as long as we limit decision making to the relevant range, misleading interpretation does not result.

Unit versus Total Costs

Unit Fixed versus Total Fixed Costs.   Accountants express fixed and variable costs either as unit costs or in total. Exhibit 3-3 illustrates these concepts but omits the relevant range; total fixed cost for rent is $100. We divide lump-sum fixed cost by volume to give unit fixed cost. For example, if the company produces one shirt, the unit fixed cost is $100; if it produces two shirts, the unit fixed cost is $50 ($100 total fixed cost ÷ 2 units); if it produces 10 shirts, the unit fixed cost is $10 ($100 total fixed cost ÷ 10 units); and so forth.

Unit Variable versus Total Variable Costs.   Exhibit 3–3 also graphs total variable costs and unit variable costs. The relationship between total variable cost and volume is direct; *total variable* costs increase in proportion to volume increases. However, *unit variable* cost remains constant. Assume that a worker uses three yards of material to make each shirt and that total material cost is $20 per shirt. Exhibit 3–3 shows the total variable costs are $20 for one shirt. Total variable costs are $200 when producing 10 shirts; the unit variable cost remains $20 per shirt.

Total Cost per Unit versus Total Cost.   We plot total cost by adding the fixed and variable cost curves. Total cost increases with output because of variable costs. We compute total cost per unit, sometimes called *average cost,* by dividing total cost by the units produced. For example, the total cost to produce two shirts is $140 ($100 fixed cost + $40 variable cost) or $70 total cost per shirt ($140/2 units). Average unit cost decreases with output because we spread the $100 fixed cost over more shirts.

EXHIBIT 3–2   **Conceptual Analysis and Practical Analysis of Variable Costs**

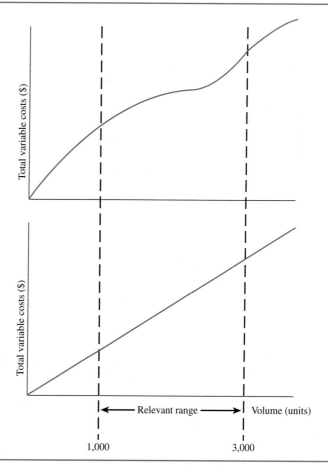

EXHIBIT 3–3   Cost Behavior Patterns Summarized

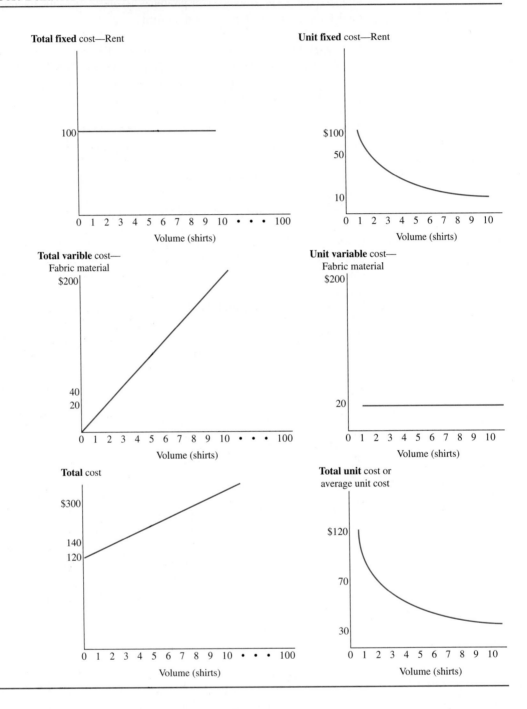

Semivariable (Mixed) Costs

Semivariable or mixed costs vary with volume changes, but the proportional relationship found in variable costs is missing. Part of semivariable costs are costs that a company incurs regardless of the level of work performed, such as supervision, inspection, or wages of standby repairers. The total cost increases as companies attain

EXHIBIT 3–4   **Total Semivariable Costs—Step-Type**

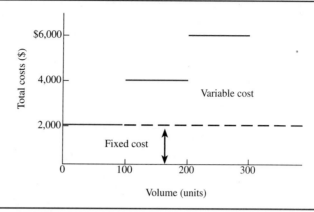

higher activity levels because more supervisors, inspectors, and repairers are needed to support a higher production level. In reality, therefore, the costs of processing, monitoring, and expediting are often step functions (e.g., fixed over a certain range of activities). Semivariable costs also are called *semifixed costs.*

Step-Type Semivariable Costs.   Exhibit 3–4 shows a **step cost,** one of the many forms that semivariable costs can take. Assume that a person inspects 100 units per month and earns $2,000 monthly. The company hires a second inspector when volume increases beyond 100 units, and total inspection costs become $4,000. The company hires a third inspector when volume reaches 300 units, and so forth. The $2,000 earned by the first inspector represents the fixed portion of the semivariable cost, reflecting the minimum cost of supplying inspection service. The difference between $2,000 and the amount paid is the variable portion related to usage.

Maintenance and repair of factory machinery and equipment may follow the semivariable pattern shown in Exhibit 3–5. Management may decide a good preventive maintenance policy is to keep one repairer at the plant and pay the person $1,800 per month. As volume increases, the company needs more repairers and additional repair supplies. The $1,800 salary of the first repairer is the fixed component. The remainder of the semivariable costs is the variable portion that may increase at a constant or increasing rate. The variable cost portion in Exhibit 3–5 increases at a constant rate.

In practice, cost behavior patterns vary and many cost structures are not linear. For instance, a semivariable cost such as electricity increases either at a decreasing or increasing rate. Utility companies charge a fixed monthly fee for service—a base charge that is constant for the period—and a demand charge that varies with consumption. With increasing amounts of energy consumed, unit variable cost may decrease. On the other hand, a penalty for greater consumption may increase the variable costs at an increasing rate.

Importance of Cost Behavior to Service Organizations

Even though our discussion of fixed and variable costs is based on manufacturing companies, analysis of cost behavior is important to all organizations, including not-for-profit and service industries. Effectively managing universities, hospitals, and for-profit service organizations requires an understanding of these concepts. Many of these organizations have a unique cost mix. For example, fixed costs account for 60 to 80 percent of total hospital costs. However, unlike many organizations of

Exhibit 3–5   Total Semivariable Factory Overhead—Increasing at a Constant Rate

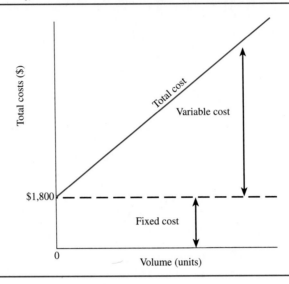

this type, labor costs largely comprise hospitals' fixed costs. Labor costs, unlike depreciation, require a cash flow out. This is a characteristic of labor-intensive organizations. Also, hospitals usually allocate 10 to 15 percent of their space for standby emergency events giving them built-in idle capacity. This prevents hospitals from enjoying the advantages of higher profits that a capital-intensive organization realizes at higher volumes beyond the breakeven volume. Thus, the cost structure of health care institutions presents challenges to accountants because of their labor-intensive and capital-intensive characteristics.

Impact of Automated Manufacturing

Exhibit 3-3 shows unit fixed costs decrease as volume increases. If the plant produces only one unit, the *unit* fixed cost is $100. The cost impact of idle capacity concerns managers because at this low volume total product costs may not be recoverable at competitive prices. As companies produce more units, unit fixed costs decrease. Thus, today's managers have gained experience under a strict discipline based on economies of scale.

Economies of Scale and Scope

Economies of scale assume that because changeover costs are high, companies should avoid changing from manufacturing one product line to another. Thus, longer production runs of standard products lower unit cost. In a traditional production setting, frequent setups and changeovers result in more machine downtime and spoilage, more indirect labor-hours, and less efficient use of direct labor. Because these developments reflect poorly on a supervisor's performance, supervisors learn to run only large batches regardless of the need for the goods being processed or the priority of the batch. Long runs result in a better ratio of direct to indirect labor. This reasoning argues for big batches and long production runs—bigger is better in virtually any circumstance.

Current Cost Management Practice

Service

Hard-nosed businesspersons are using embarrassingly romantic terms to describe the new order of supplier-customer relationships. They report, it is like a marriage—committing to one relationship. They talk this way because close customer-supplier relationships help trim costs, improve quality by disseminating quality-enhancing management techniques across company boundaries and by enlisting each supplier's technological expertise in designing and making parts. Bailey, a unit of Elsap Bailey Process Automation, treats some suppliers almost like departments of its own company. Bailey stocks only enough inventory for a few days of operation, rather than two to three months, like it used to carry. One of its major suppliers, Montreal-based Future Electronics is hooked on with an electronic data interchange system so when a bin of parts falls below a designated level, a Bailey employee passes a laser scanner over the bin's bar code, instantly alerting Future to send the parts at once. With more companies forming a network of related companies, they are learning to cooperate to meet competition.

Myron Magnet, "The New Golden Rule of Business," *Fortune,* February 21, 1994, pp. 60–64.

Plant managers reason that when a troublesome operation is running well, they should produce many parts so there is no need to run the line again for a long time. For example, producing 50,000 units of the same product is easier than producing five 10,000-piece batches of different models or products—even though the same physical volume of products is manufactured. Producing five different batches requires more scheduling and setups, more placing, receiving, inspecting, and storing of product orders, and more shipping of orders. Even more critical, the assumptions of economies of scale have guided the development of technology, encouraging profitable rigidity and discouraging expensive change.

With computer-integrated manufacturing (CIM) systems becoming more widespread, however, cost accountants are questioning the assumption that increased production volume always leads to increases in profits. More and more managers are realizing that it is better not to produce than to manufacture an unnecessary part to be stored in inventory. Large inventories stored for future use may become obsolete before their sale. Thus, companies are recognizing that sales, not production, generate profits; producing for inventory is not necessarily a value-added activity. Cost accountants are considering market demand when applying variable-fixed cost relationships.

Using **economies-of-scope logic,** companies vary rather than standardize products. Now they manufacture many custom products that reflect consumer demands. An operating system reflecting economies-of-scope logic is responsive to consumer demands. The economies-of-scope concept assumes that flexibility and variety create profits rather than expenses as under economies-of-scale logic. Shorter product life cycles, shorter setup times, more flexibility in multipurpose automated manufacturing equipment, and emphasis on quality partly explain less emphasis on economies of scale thinking and recognition of economies of scope. Manufacturing facilities using an economies-of-scope philosophy are flexible to quickly capture changing customer demands.

In selecting plant size, it may be more economical to acquire a plant capacity greater than the requirements of most months. Thus, current production can satisfy peak demands. Stockpiling inventories to meet peak demand would be necessary if plant capacity were lower. When a company acquires manufacturing facilities to handle its expected needs, management may lease excess space to outside parties until it needs more space. It also may be profitable to operate an additional shift rather than expand plant facilities because the increased usage reduces the building's idle capacity. Actually, the decision to increase the number of shifts depends on many other factors. Even with a pay differential, the company may not be able to hire enough employees for a midnight shift. In addition, it may be necessary to have the plant idle for certain periods for cleaning and maintenance.

Cost Behavior

Direct material and direct labor are usually variable costs in a labor-paced environment. For example, if production of a unit requires one pound of plastic costing $40 and two direct labor-hours costing $10 per hour, we assume these per unit figures do not change when production changes. By contrast, the per unit factory overhead cost includes both fixed and variable costs. Production of another unit does not increase total fixed costs such as rent and insurance. However, variable factory costs such as indirect material may increase directly with volume changes. Semivariable factory overhead costs such as inspection, repairs, and maintenance vary, but not in direct proportion to volume changes.

Currently, automation is having an impact on the traditional view of cost behavior. In the new automated factory, direct labor has essentially become a fixed cost, not a variable cost. The labor cost that remains in a CIM system represents wages for the initial machine and material loading, but only for a single shift during a three-shift operation. Process engineers and industrial engineers are assembling equipment, setting up runs, and monitoring the processes. Some factory workers operate sophisticated equipment, while other workers monitor quality at various stations throughout the plant.

These trained factory workers are likely paid on a fixed salary basis, rather than on an hourly basis. Thus, materials, operating supplies, and energy are often the only significant components of variable manufacturing costs in the new environment. Accountants are adapting traditional cost accounting techniques to fit management's needs in environments where direct labor is a fixed cost and overhead is neither traceable to nor associated with labor.

Variable Costs in the Short Run.   Even though accountants usually consider direct material and direct labor as variable costs, their behavior is often semivariable. However, direct material is variable more often than direct labor. Managers can acquire materials when needed or place materials in inventory until their use. A company does not use direct material if management decides not to produce on a particular day. However, direct labor is variable with capacity only if labor hours can be accurately and rapidly adjusted to the activity level. As a result, most labor costs—even direct labor, which is generally considered a variable cost—behave in some semivariable fashion in practice. Usually, though, in a labor-paced environment, the fixed portion of direct labor is so small in relation to total labor costs that accountants call the total a variable cost. By ignoring these complexities, we assume we can stop direct labor costs quickly and easily in the short run if management decides not to produce. As a result, direct labor costs tend to be variable when measured over a longer period, say, a month or year, and within a relevant range. The high rate of unemployment during recessionary times is additional support for classifying direct labor as largely a variable cost. The fixed cost inherent in supervisory wages, however, may be significant enough that accountants separate the fixed and variable elements. Also, the trend toward automation significantly affects the behavior pattern of labor cost.

Fixed Costs in the Short Run.   Management cannot eliminate fixed costs easily in the short run. If company managers plan to manufacture, for example, they have to buy or rent a building and incur either depreciation or rent expense on the building. The company also incurs such fixed costs as insurance on plant facilities and wages for a plant superintendent. Then, even if management decides to stop production, the plant superintendent must receive due notice and probably termination pay. Also, the company must sublease or sell the plant, machinery, and equipment. Therefore, it takes some time before management eliminates all fixed costs.

Cost Estimation

In estimating cost behavior, **cost estimation studies** attempt to predict relationships based on an activity level or **cost driver** affecting costs. In practice, managers frequently encounter such cost drivers as machine-hours, transactions, units of sales, work cells, order size, direct labor hours, value of materials, and quality requirements. The **cost estimating function** is:

$$y = a + bx$$

where *y* represents total cost, *a* equals the fixed component that does not change with activity levels, *b* refers to variable costs, and *x* represents the activity volume. The costs predicted (the dependent variable) is *y* in the preceding formula; *x* in the formula represents the independent variable. We call the independent variable the *explanatory variable,* or cost driver. It is usually a measure of activity controllable by a decision maker. In cost estimation, we identify some independent variable (the activity) and the functional relationships that permit computation of the corresponding value of the dependent variable (the costs). Cost behavior models are correlational rather than causal; in a **causal model,** *x* results in *y,* while in a **correlational model,** occurrences or movement in *y* are associated with occurrences or movements in *x.*

Cost Functions and Linearity

Accountants frequently use linear cost functions to estimate the relationships of total costs to a specific range of output or input. When relating total costs to output, several assumptions provide adequate conditions for linearity to exist. One of these assumptions is that the cost of securing each input must be a linear function of the quantity acquired. For example, there are no quantity discounts on the direct material purchased—the unit cost is identical regardless of the quantity bought. As shown in Exhibit 3–2, even if the cost is not linear over the entire range of volume, there may be a range that permits a linearity assumption within specified output limits. Another assumption is that each finished product contains the same amount of direct labor or direct material.

We also assume that all input acquired is fully utilized. In estimating cost behavior, we further assume that variations in a single variable, such as machine hours, can explain variations in the total cost level. After making these assumptions, we find the underlying cost behavior pattern of each cost, more frequently called a **cost function.** Then we can estimate costs based on projections of the behavior of the independent variable.

Cost Estimation Methods

Accountants use several methods to measure the variability of costs when volume changes. Some methods rely on historical data in determining the fixed and variable elements. Some approaches emphasize statistical analysis, while others stress engineering studies. Each of the methods also differs in cost; thus, cost-benefit analysis often dictates which methods are applied. Because each method has its advantages and disadvantages, managers should never use one method to the exclusion of others.

We commonly use the following five cost estimation methods in practice to separate mixed costs into their variable and fixed components:

1. Industrial engineering estimates.
2. Account analysis.
3. Scattergraph (visual fit).
4. High-low method.
5. Regression analysis.

Many companies combine several of these methods to estimate the relation between cost behavior and cost drivers or activity levels simultaneously so they can compare results. In fact, accountants may have to go through the cycle several times using different independent variables (cost drivers) before finally finding an acceptable cost function.

Industrial Engineering Approach

With an industrial engineering approach, the focus is on what the cost should be to produce a finished product using the company's production facilities most efficiently. The engineering approach uses time-and-motion studies and production specifications in determining which cost components are needed. Companies with standard cost systems widely use the engineering approach. **Cost standards** are scientifically predetermined costs of production used as a basis for measurement and comparison.

An engineering approach analyzes the relationships between inputs and outputs by carefully studying each phase of the manufacturing process together with the kinds of work performed and the costs involved. Completion times for each manufacturing step are added and serve as a basis for estimating direct labor costs. Cost estimates for material are obtained from engineering drawings and specification sheets.

Engineering estimates often help reveal areas where slack and inefficiencies exist. A benefit to the engineering approach is that it details each step required in operations to compare with similar operations in other settings. However, the engineering method is costly and fails to plan and control some overhead costs.

Account Analysis

Using account analysis, accountants examine and classify each ledger account as variable, fixed, or mixed. They break down mixed accounts into their variable and fixed components. They base these classifications on experience, on inspection of cost behavior for several past periods, or on managers' intuitive feelings. Assume, for instance, that management has estimated $1,090 variable costs and $1,430 fixed costs to make 100 units using 500 machine-hours. Since machine-hours drive variable costs in our example, they are stated as $1,090/500 machine-hours = $2.18. Using our cost equation, we have:

Factory overhead costs = $1,430 + $2.18 per machine-hour

And for 550 machine-hours, we have

Factory overhead = $1,430 + $2.18 (550) = $1,430 + $1,199 = $2,629

The degree to which accountants analyze ledger accounts to obtain historical cost data varies from a superficial inspection of the cost accounts to a detailed analysis of cost behavior over time. In any case, this analysis should determine whether any factors other than output are influencing costs. Such factors might include seasonal changes, the introduction of robots, new products or manufacturing processes, and other conditions that make historical cost data inappropriate for predicting cost activity relationships. For example, assume a company establishes an austerity program during a recession. In this situation, managers control costs so tightly that cost behavior differs considerably from what it would be under more relaxed conditions.

A danger in this approach is that many managers may assume a cost's behavior without further analysis. For example, managers may classify direct labor as variable because traditionally in a labor-paced environment this has been true. In an automated factory, however, any remaining direct labor cost is likely to be fixed.

Scattergraph

The **scattergraph** (also known as a **scattergram**) is a simple analysis method employing only two variables, such as cost and machine-hours. Exhibit 3–6 shows the data for 12 observations of electricity, a semivariable cost. After gathering such data, the first step is to plot the costs on the vertical, or *Y*, axis of a graph. The second step is to plot the variable measuring activity level, perhaps machine-hours or work cells, on the horizontal, or *X*, axis. Exhibit 3–7 illustrates the statistical scattergraph for these figures. Each point on the graph represents 1 of the 12 cost observations. For example, we plot the data for June on the horizontal axis (30,000 machine-hours) and on the vertical axis ($61,300 cost). The activity base used for applying electricity cost is machine-hours because usually there is a correlation between electricity costs and machine-hours. However, some other basis may be more appropriate.

EXHIBIT 3–6   Observations of Semivariable Costs

	Volume (Machine-Hours)	Electricity Costs
January	35,000	$ 65,000
February	28,000	59,800
March	34,000	64,100
April.	42,000	67,800
May	37,000	70,000
June	30,000	61,300
July.	25,000	57,800
August	22,000	55,600
September	20,000	54,200
October.	37,000	71,000
November	45,000	72,000
December	41,000	65,000
	396,000	$763,600

EXHIBIT 3–7   Statistical Scattergraph

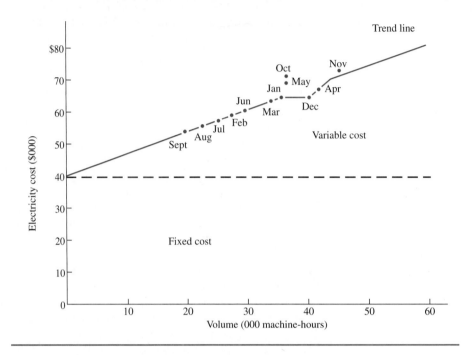

Number of Observations.   For simplicity, we are using cost data for only 12 months; this may be adequate if production activity levels (machine-hours in our case) and costs are highly stable. A rule of thumb is to use monthly data for three years if the production process has not changed significantly. If, however, a flexible manufacturing system using robots and other computer-controlled production processes has replaced a labor-oriented production process, we would use cost data representing only the automated systems in cost estimating methods.

Trend Line.   We may fit the **trend line (line of best fit)** mathematically or visually; it was plotted by visual inspection in Exhibit 3–7. It should be fitted so there is an equal distance between the plotted points above and below the trend line. The fixed component of $40,000 in Exhibit 3–7 is determined where the trend line intersects the vertical axis. From these figures, a quick estimate of variable costs per hour can be made for the electricity cost in Exhibit 3–6 assuming fixed costs of $40,000 per month:

	$763,600	total annual costs
Less	480,000	total annual fixed costs ($40,000 monthly fixed costs $\times$ 12)
	$283,600	total annual variable costs

$$\frac{\$283,600 \text{ total annual variable costs}}{396,000 \text{ machine-hours}} = \$0.7161 \text{ variable cost per machine-hour}$$

Merely plotting points on a graph and visually fitting a trend line may not be adequate to give a clear indication of cost behavior. For example, distortion may result due to the scale of axes. Although the scattergraph is simple to apply and understand, it is not objective. Two accountants might easily fit two very differ-ent lines to the same set of data, each believing he or she has the better fit. In addition, there may, in fact, be no correlation between the variables. This should be apparent when the points are plotted on the scattergraph. Sometimes when we fit the trend line by visual inspection (thus the name *visual fit*), personal bias may distort the true picture. Because misleading generalizations about cost behavior can result, we should use a more accurate study of cost behavior than the scatter-graph.

High-Low Method   If we can describe the cost-activity relationship by a straight line, we may use any two points on a scattergraph in the estimating procedures. Usually, we select the lowest and the highest activity levels; thus, the name, **high-low method.** The **two-point method** is another name for the high-low method. However, these levels should be within the relevant range because we define fixed and vari-able costs in relation to a specific period of time and a designated range of volume or activity. The costs chosen should represent the normal cost incurred at these levels; all excessive costs resulting from abnormal conditions should be removed.

Exhibit 3–8 shows how the high-low technique separates the fixed and variable elements of electricity cost using the data from Exhibit 3–6. We calculate the vari-able rate by dividing the change in costs by the change in activity base, which is machine-hours for electricity.

Cost Estimating Function.   After determining whether costs are fixed or vari-able, accountants enter them into the cost estimating function for predicting future costs. The function for electricity is $39,960 per month, plus $0.712 per machine-hour. We divide the change in the semivariable cost of $17,800 by the change of 25,000 hours to give a variable cost rate of $0.712 per machine-hour. The increase in costs when the volume changed from 20,000 to 45,000 machine-hours results from variable costs only. The variable cost per hour remains the same while the total variable cost increases. Total fixed costs remain the same at the high and low capacity levels.

EXHIBIT 3–8   High-Low Method of Separating Fixed and Variable Costs

	Machine-Hours	Cost of Electricity
High capacity—November	45,000	$72,000
Low capacity—September	20,000	54,200
Change in hours and semivariable costs	25,000	$17,800

$$\text{Variable rate} = \frac{\text{Change in semivariable costs}}{\text{Change in machine-hours}} = \frac{\$17,800}{25,000} = \$0.712 \text{ per machine-hour}$$

	Low	High
Total costs	$54,200	$72,000
Variable costs—$0.712 per machine-hour	14,240	32,040
Fixed costs	$39,960	$39,960

EXHIBIT 3–9   Diagram of High-Low Cost Estimates

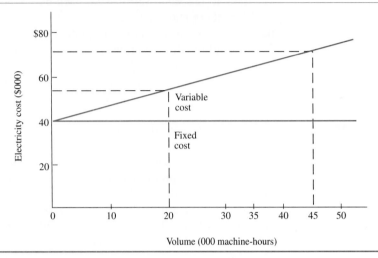

Volume (000 machine-hours)

Diagram of High-Low Estimates.   Exhibit 3–9 shows the construction of the high-low line. We plot the high and low points of 20,000 and 45,000 machine-hours with their respective total costs. The fixed element is the intersection of the cost line with the vertical axis. The high-low technique assumes that the costs for all volumes between these two points fall along a straight line. Thus, we can draw a cost line between these two activity levels. For example, electricity costs at 35,000 machine-hours total nearly $65,000 of which $39,960 is fixed and the remainder, variable. The high-low method uses less information about cost behavior than does the scattergraph because we plot only two data points. We plotted 12 points in our scattergraph in Exhibit 3–7, recognizing then that we were simplifying our illustration by using only 12 points.

Regression Analysis   The use of statistical techniques to analyze cost behavior provides a more scientific analysis. Some of the statistical methods for separating fixed and variable cost elements are beyond the scope of this book. However, the least squares method, sometimes called *simple regression analysis,* is a relatively simple, effective approach. We use **regression analysis** to measure the average amount of change in a dependent variable, such as electricity, that is associated with unit increases in the amounts of one or more independent variables, such as machine-hours. A major advantage of regression analysis over the high-low technique is inclusion of all data points, rather than just the high and the low, in specifying the relation.

Least Squares Method.   The **least squares method** is the most widely used regression analysis. It is based on the straight-line equation ($y = a + bx$) with y representing the costs; a, the fixed component; b, the variable element; and x, the volume. This method is most appropriate when data have a uniform variance of deviations along the trend line. If the cost is fixed, the slope coefficient b is zero; if the cost is variable, the intercept a equals zero in the cost function. For semivariable or mixed costs, both a and b have positive values.

Exhibit 3–10 shows the manual computations for the least squares method using the cost data from Exhibit 3–6. We divide the total of 396,000 for Column 1, representing machine-hours for each observation, by the 12 observations to give an

EXHIBIT 3–10   Manual Calculation of Least Squares Method

Month	(1) Machine-Hours (x)	(2) Difference from Average of 33,000 hours (X)	(3) Total Electricity Costs (y) (00s)	(4) Difference from Average of $636.33 (Y) (0s)	(5) Column (2) Squared (X²)	(6) Column (2) × Column (4) (XY) (00s)
January	35,000	2,000	$ 650	13.67	4,000,000	$ 27,340
February . . .	28,000	− 5,000	598	− 38.33	25,000,000	191,650
March	34,000	1,000	641	4.67	1,000,000	4,670
April	42,000	9,000	678	41.67	81,000,000	375,030
May	37,000	4,000	700	63.66	16,000,000	254,640
June	30,000	− 3,000	613	− 23.33	9,000,000	69,990
July	25,000	− 8,000	578	− 58.33	64,000,000	466,640
August	22,000	− 11,000	556	− 80.33	121,000,000	883,630
September . .	20,000	− 13,000	542	− 94.33	169,000,000	1,226,290
October	37,000	4,000	710	73.66	16,000,000	294,640
November . .	45,000	12,000	720	83.66	144,000,000	1,003,920
December . .	41,000	8,000	650	13.66	64,000,000	109,280
Total	396,000	−0−	$ 7,636	−0−	714,000,000	$4,907,720
Average	33,000		$636.33			

a = Fixed component
b = Variable component
x = Volume
X = Deviations from average of x
y = Costs
Y = Deviations from average of y

Using the straight-line equation, the computation is

$$y = a + bx$$

$$\text{where } b = \frac{\Sigma XY}{\Sigma X^2} = \frac{\$490,772,000}{714,000,000} = \$0.687$$

$$y = a + bx$$
$$\$63,633 = a + (0.687 \times 33,000)$$
$$\$63,633 = a + \$22,671$$
$$\$63,633 - \$22,671 = a$$
$$a = \$40,962 \text{ (the fixed cost)}$$

Cost estimating function: $40,962 + $0.687 per machine-hour

average of 33,000 hours. We divide the annual total cost of $763,600 in Column 3 by 12 observations to give an average of $63,633. We enter the differences from the average in Columns 2 and 4. The differences in Column 2 are squared, and the square is entered in Column 5 and totaled. Column 6 represents the extension of the data in Columns 2 and 4 with the results added.

Exhibit 3–10 shows cost behavior as dependent on a single measure of machine-hours. However, more than one factor may cause a cost to vary. This book illustrates only simple regression analysis that considers one independent variable. Multiple regression analysis is a further expansion of the least squares method allowing the consideration of more than one independent variable. We can expand the straight-line equation ($y = a + bx$) used in simple regression to include more than one independent variable. By including two independent variables, the equation becomes $y = a + bx + cz$ with c the rate of cost variability for z, an additional independent variable. Although multiple regression is beyond the scope of this book, computer applications make the estimation quite simple.

Exhibit 3–11   The Least Squares Method Using a Computer Application

	Regression Statistics			
R square.	0.86			
Standard error.	2375.57			
Number of observations.	12			

	Coefficients	*Standard Error*	*T-statistic*	*P-Value*
Intercept	40,949.30	3,012.89	13.59	3.20E–08
Volume	0.69	0.09	7.73	9.02E–06

Cost estimating function: $40,949.30 + $0.69 per machine-hour

Using a Computer for Regression. The least squares method is time-consuming to apply manually, especially when we consider more than one independent variable; a computer can make the computations quickly. The regression capabilities in a computer spreadsheet program can estimate the linear cost function shown in Exhibit 3–11. The typical output from a computer regression package includes the estimated intercept and slope coefficient, their respective standard errors, and t-statistics. The t-statistic provides a test for the hypothesis that the estimated coefficient is different from zero. In this case, both our fixed costs and variable unit costs are significantly greater than zero (at a probability level less than 0.01).

Even though this chapter gives the mathematical details of the manual process, you may be as well served by devoting your time and effort only to the preprogrammed microcomputer applications that have been written for this book. Accountants' primary concerns are knowing what data to seek, the criteria the data must meet, and interpretation of the results.

Establishing Correlation. The scattergraph in Exhibit 3–7 was verified visually with a reasonable degree of correlation. If perfect correlation existed, all plotted points would fall on the regression line. We can use several statistics to measure the relation between x (machine-hours) and y (electricity cost). The **correlation coefficient** (r) is the most commonly used statistic, as the square of this coefficient expresses the extent to which the changes in x explain the variation in y. The closer the r value is to either $+1$ or -1, the stronger the statistical relation between the two variables. As r approaches -1, a negative, or inverse, relation is implied, meaning the dependent variable (y) decreases as the independent variable (x) increases. On the other hand, as r approaches $+1$, a positive relation is implied, meaning the dependent variable (y) increases as the independent variable (x) increases.

We find the **coefficient of determination** (r^2) by squaring the correlation coefficient. Exhibit 3–12 uses the data in Exhibit 3–6 to provide the figures needed in the manual computation of the correlation analysis formula.

In column 3, each independent variable (x) is multiplied by its corresponding dependent variable (y). Each x value and each y value are squared and entered in Columns 4 and 5, respectively. After totaling all columns, we enter the figures in the following formula. We designate the number of observations (the 12 months in Exhibit 3–12) as n and also use it. (Note that we omitted the computation and show the formula and result.)

EXHIBIT 3–12   Correlation Analysis Data

Month	(1) Machine-Hours (x)	(2) Electricity Cost (y) (00s)	(3) xy (00s)	(4) x² (00s)	(5) y² (00s)
January	35,000	$ 650	22,750,000	1,225,000,000	422,500
February	28,000	598	16,744,000	784,000,000	357,604
March	34,000	641	21,794,000	1,156,000,000	410,881
April.	42,000	678	28,476,000	1,764,000,000	459,684
May	37,000	700	25,900,000	1,369,000,000	490,000
June	30,000	613	18,390,000	900,000,000	375,769
July	25,000	578	14,450,000	625,000,000	334,084
August	22,000	556	12,232,000	484,000,000	309,136
September	20,000	542	10,840,000	400,000,000	293,764
October.	37,000	710	26,270,000	1,369,000,000	504,100
November	45,000	720	32,400,000	2,025,000,000	518,400
December	41,000	650	26,650,000	1,681,000,000	422,500
Total	396,000	$7,636	256,896,000	13,782,000,000	4,898,422

$$r = \frac{n\Sigma xy - (\Sigma x)(\Sigma y)}{\sqrt{[n\Sigma x^2 - (\Sigma x)^2]\,[n\Sigma y^2 - (\Sigma y)^2]}}$$

$$= \frac{(12)(256,896,000) - (396,000)(7,636)}{\sqrt{[(12)(13,782,000,000) - (396,000)(396,000)]\,[(12)(4,898,422) - (7,636)(7,636)]}}$$

$$r = +0.92558$$

$$r^2 = 0.8567$$

Application of the correlation analysis technique to these data reveals a coefficient of determination of 0.8567. If instead, we used a computer application, Exhibit 3–11 indicates that the coefficient of determination for these cost data is 0.86. From this we interpret that more than 85 percent of the change in electricity cost can be explained by the change in machine-hours. Accountants can use this relationship to calculate the electricity overhead rate. However, we are not saying that machine-hours is the best measure of activity as there may be a better measure that we have not considered. We need caution in interpreting this relation. Coefficients of correlation and determination are most meaningful in a model comparison context and high coefficients are often unacceptable while, on other data sets, even relatively low coefficients are all that can be hoped for.

Criteria for Regression Analysis

The results computed using the least squares method differ slightly from those determined by the scattergraph. The least squares method is more objective because personal bias does not enter into fitting the trend line. However, to be of benefit, regression analysis must meet certain criteria:

1. Reasonableness of relationship—A reasonable degree of correlation must exist that meets economic and professional judgment. For example, a high correlation between hemlines and stock prices may indicate only that these

two variables move together. This is a **spurious correlation,** a high correlation between two variables that do not seem related at all. We need knowledge of cost behavior and the production function to give plausibility to a relationship. The independent variables under consideration should have some reasonable economic relationship. It is advisable to plot the data first on a scattergraph to be certain there is a reasonable degree of correlation.

2. Examination of r^2 or other tests of goodness of fit help in interpreting the extent to which the independent variable accounts for the variability in the dependent variable. In arriving at the best fit for a pair of variables, regression fits a line to a set of data points such that the sum of the squares of the vertical deviations of the data points is minimized. In selecting the variable with the best fit, we should choose the variable having the smaller sum of square deviations. The coefficient of determination, r^2, embodies this same information, and most computer programs generate this ratio.

3. The following conditions must hold for appropriate regression analysis:
   a. Representative observations.
   b. Linearity in the relevant range.
   c. Constant variance.
   d. Independence.
   e. Normality.
   f. Absence of multicolinearity, which applies only to multiple regression.

Representative Observations.   In applying regression analysis, we assume that observations come from a uniform population. For example, the least squares method in Exhibits 3–10 and 3–11 used machine-hours and electricity costs for the same current period as shown in Exhibit 3–6. The scattergraph in Exhibit 3–13 indicates that one unusual observation can have a pronounced effect on the regression line. An accountant might decide to throw out the unusual observation called the **outlier.** Using cheaper skills of labor or grades of material than are normally available could cause this unusual event with its low cost in relation to volume. Expense adjustments that are clearly abnormal also cause outliers. We can justify omitting observations that are not representative of normal operating conditions from the regression analysis.

Linearity in the Relevant Range.   Linearity must exist between x and y using the equation $(y = a + bx)$. We can check the presence of linearity by plotting the data on a scattergram if there is one independent variable. The role of the relevant range is very important in interpreting the scattergraph. As discussed earlier in this chapter and illustrated in Exhibit 3–2, the linearity assumption must hold for the relevant range that is under consideration. It is dangerous to extrapolate beyond the relevant range.

Constant Variance.   In applying regression analysis, the spread of observations around the regression line must be constant throughout the entire range of observations. Exhibit 3–14 indicates constant variance or **homoscedasticity,** while Exhibit 3–15 indicates that nonconstant variance or **heteroscedasticity** exists, and the constant variance criteria is not met. We often find heteroscedasticity in cost data because it is reasonable to expect a higher degree of variability of costs at high levels of volume than at low levels.

EXHIBIT 3–13   Effect of Outlier Observation

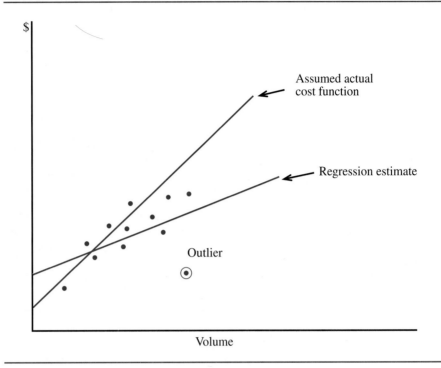

EXHIBIT 3–14   Observations Having Constant Variance

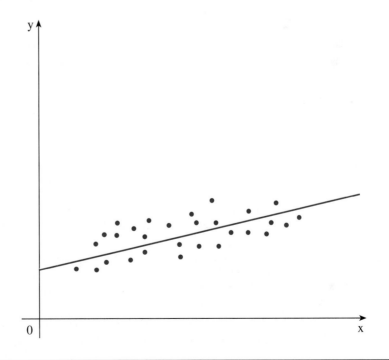

EXHIBIT 3–15   Observations Lacking Constant Variance

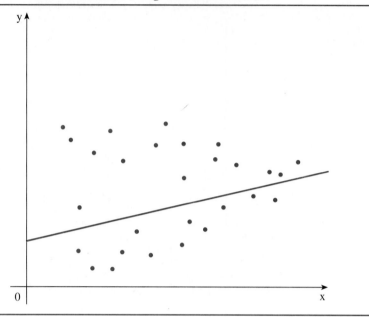

EXHIBIT 3–16   Autocorrelation

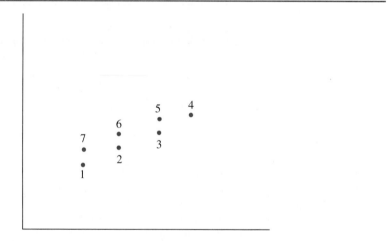

Independence.   According to the independence condition, the sequence of observations makes no difference in the level of costs. For example, costs follow one pattern when volume increases, but a different pattern when volume decreases. We frequently see this "stickiness of costs" with direct labor costs because companies hire workers when production volume increases, but do not lay off these same workers as quickly when volume decreases. **Autocorrelation** exists when this assumption of observations is not met. We use statistical tests, such as the Durbin–Watson, to detect autocorrelation. Plotting and numbering the points as shown in Exhibit 3–16 also can detect autocorrelation. An autocorrelation problem exists if there is a pattern in the plotted residuals.

Productivity

Current Cost Management Practice

Managers at Alvery, Inc., a St. Louis maker of conveyors, wonder if production can keep up with demand. Fadal Engineering Co., a machine-tool maker, also finds machine-tool orders are the best in five years. Despite disastrous economies in Europe and Japan, U.S. makers of factory machinery can compete because they have become the low-cost producers. U.S. labor is cheaper. Managers report they have done much work in getting their cost base in line. They report enthusiastic discussions with suppliers on improving efficiency and chopping prices. Not surprising, business looks strongest for producers whose machines promise lower costs and higher quality. Another sign is that those producers who recognize the importance of the customer will report increased earnings.

Zachary Schiller, "No Rust on This Market," *BusinessWeek,* January 10, 1994, p. 73.

Normality.   We use normality criteria—that the points around the regression line are normally distributed—to make probability statements using the **standard error of the estimate.** This is a measure of how far the actual cost figures deviate from an estimate of cost. We know that the level of cost at each activity level cannot be perfectly estimated. Yet, the standard error of the estimate gives a means for estimating the amount of error that reasonably can be expected around the best estimate of the dependent variable.

Absence of Multicolinearity.   The absence of **multicolinearity** is applicable only to multiple regression with two or more independent variables. Multicolinearity exists when the independent variables are highly correlated with each other.

The results of cost behavior studies like those discussed earlier may differ significantly from prestudy predictions. Cost accountants, therefore, should not presume to estimate the relationship of cost changes to volume variations without conducting such studies of cost behavior patterns.

Budgeted Allowances Using Cost Estimating Function

Accountants separate costs into their fixed and variable components using one of the cost estimating methods presented earlier, such as high-low or least squares. This allows them to better budget costs. Following is a simple illustration of using the cost estimating function in budgeting. (Chapter 10 gives an extensive description of this budgeting approach.) Assume we estimate factory supplies as strictly variable at $6.14 per machine-hour and monthly factory rent, a fixed cost, at $25,000. Exhibit 3–11 separates electricity, a semivariable cost, into $40,949 fixed and $0.69 variable per machine-hour using the least squares method. Adding the variable costs ($6.14 + $0.69 = $6.83) and the fixed costs ($25,000 + $40,949 = $65,949) of factory supplies, electricity, and rent, the cost estimating function for total overhead is $6.83 + $65,949. If monthly capacity is budgeted at 30,000 hours, this yields an applied overhead rate of $3.50 as shown in Exhibit 3–17. Assume further that the company works 28,000 machine-hours during the

EXHIBIT 3–17

Factory Overhead Budget at 30,000 Budgeted Hours

	Variable		*Fixed*	*Total*
Factory supplies......	$18,420	($6.14 × 30,000)		$ 18,420
Electricity	20,700	($0.69 × 30,000)	$40,949	61,649
Rent			25,000	25,000
	$39,120		$65,949	$105,069
Application rate	$3.50	($105,069 ÷ 30,000 hours)		

Factory Overhead Budget at 28,000 Actual Hours

	Variable		*Fixed*	*Total*	*Actual*	*Variance*	
Factory supplies......	$17,192	($6.14 × 28,000)		$ 17,192	$ 18,300	$1,108	Unfavorable
Electricity	19,320	($0.69 × 28,000)	$40,949	60,269	58,800	1,469	Favorable
Rent			25,000	25,000	25,500	500	Unfavorable
	$36,512		$65,949	$102,461	$102,600	$ 139	Unfavorable
Factory overhead applied ($3.50 × 28,000)					98,000		
Underapplied overhead					$ 4,600		

month, resulting in $3.50 × 28,000 = $98,000 applied factory overhead. At the end of the month, we determine budgeted amounts for the actual capacity worked using the cost estimating function as shown in Exhibit 3–17. Monthly variances result assuming actual costs of $18,300 for supplies, $58,800 for electricity, and $25,500 for rent. A comparison of $102,600 total actual overhead with $98,000 applied yields $4,600 underapplied overhead.

Summary

With CIM facilitating flexible manufacturing systems, cost accountants are now rethinking the assumption of economies of scale and further studying the behavior of costs when volume changes. In practice, few costs are strictly variable or strictly fixed because countless factors affect cost behavior. Direct labor is truly a variable cost only if the company pays workers on a piecework basis and maintains a tight control over labor costs. Indirect labor costs often fall into the semivariable category because companies need some indirect labor employees for standby services. Companies acquire direct material as needed, thus making materials a variable cost.

While we have demonstrated several techniques such as the high-low, scattergraph, and least squares methods to segregate costs into fixed and variable components, the task in practice is more involved. Costs may vary due to several factors besides volume changes. The methods available to cost accountants may sometimes be inadequate to obtain more than a hint of the causal factors. With some data sets, even relatively low coefficients are all that can be obtained. However, this is much better than carelessly lumping costs into variable and fixed categories without any analysis.

Important Terms and Concepts

Ethical Dilemma

Ethics of Cost Accountants

Webber, Inc., recently developed a new glass casserole dish. Webber promotes the dish as being not only highly attractive but also able to withstand intense oven heat for extended periods. In advertising the new product, marketing personnel have stressed the reason that its price is higher than competitors' is because it is more durable and easier to clean.

Inspection occurs at different stages of the manufacturing operation. Webber can rework dishes rejected during testing at the firing stage if the cracks are not large and only appear in the top surface. Webber then sells these dishes as first-quality products.

Mary Brown, the cost accountant, has become close friends with Jane Stone, one of the marketing managers. Recently, Stone mentioned that they were spending much time answering customer complaints concerning excessive breakage of these casserole dishes. That prompted Brown to ask the quality control engineer to check into the matter. After many tests, the engineer ascertained that reworking does not bring the product up to standard. In fact, test results reveal that 1 in 12 of the reworked dishes will break within three years' usage.

At Brown's request, the engineer investigated other types of reworking techniques but found that their costs outweighed any benefit. Further, after using the current reworking procedure, there is no test to determine which dish is likely to be the one that breaks.

Brown has followed the long-standing policy of highlighting to the board of directors any cost data that has potential adverse effects. Thus, she believes it is her responsibility to include the rework problem in a report she prepared for the next monthly board meeting.

However, when the plant supervisor and other production personnel previewed the report, they immediately called Brown's supervisor, the controller, and demanded that the information given to the board not mention the rework problem. Instead, they convinced the controller to mention the problem only briefly in the oral presentation rather than highlight it in a written report. They rationalize that consumers expect all glass cooking utensils to break eventually anyway. Brown felt strongly that the data are important and believed the quality engineer would agree with her. However, his only remark was "Well, Mary, you just have to go with the flow and hide the problem."

Required:

 a. What ethical considerations do the following individuals have in this matter?
   (1) Mary Brown, cost accountant.
   (2) Quality control engineer.
   (3) Controller.
   (4) Plant supervisor.
 b. Explain what Mary Brown should do in this situation.

Problem for Self-Study

High-Low Method

Skelly, Inc., has provided the following actual cost data for your use in determining variable factory overhead costs and fixed factory overhead costs for budgeting purposes:

	Three Quarters Ago	*Two Quarters Ago*	*One Quarter Ago*
Machine-hours	70,000	80,000	100,000
Direct material	$147,000	$168,000	$ 210,000
Direct labor	350,000	400,000	500,000
Factory insurance	8,000	9,000	11,000
Indirect labor	14,200	15,800	19,000
Factory inspection costs.	10,300	11,200	13,000
Indirect material	4,000	5,100	5,500
Factory utilities.	10,000	11,800	14,200
Salespersons' salaries	190,000	210,500	250,000
Advertising.	56,000	64,000	80,000
Executive salaries	90,000	90,000	90,000
Total.	$879,500	$985,400	$1,192,700

Required:

Determine an overall variable factory overhead rate per machine-hour and total fixed factory overhead using the high-low method, assuming management believes no other major factors affect cost behavior.

Solution to Problem for Self-Study

Skelly, Inc.

Factory overhead costs for:

	(70,000 hrs.) *Lowest Activity*	*(100,000 hrs.)* *Highest Activty*
Factory insurance	$ 8,000	$11,000
Indirect labor	14,200	19,000
Factory inspection costs	10,300	13,000
Indirect material	4,000	5,500
Factory utilities	10,000	14,200
	$46,500	$62,700

$$\frac{\$16,200 \text{ difference in total overhead}}{30,000 \text{ hours difference in volume for}} = \$0.54 \text{ variable overhead rate}$$
highest and lowest activity

$62,700	Total overhead for 100,000 hours
54,000	Variable overhead for 100,000 hours (100,000 hours × $0.54)
$ 8,700	Budgeted fixed overhead

Review Questions

1. Discuss how the calculation of overhead rates is used in cost control evaluation.

2. Determine the budgeted fixed overhead and the variable overhead rate for indirect labor if the two budgets are: 1,000 units—$4,000; 3,000 units—$8,000. Can you compute the fixed overhead application rate for this company?

3. A company wants to realize a profit of $150,000. Its salespeople plan to sell 100,000 units of a product for $15 each; fixed costs are $250,000. To realize this desired profit, what would variable costs be?

4. Understanding cost behavior is vital to all organizations, but it is crucial to hospitals because their patterns of cost differ from most manufacturing firms. Discuss why you think the cost structure of health care institutions presents additional challenges and indicate whether you think a hospital is a capital intensive organization.

5. Is depreciation cost a fixed or variable cost? Indicate the factor determining whether the cost is fixed or variable.

6. In analyzing cost behavior, why must the accountant guard against feeding large amounts of data to the computer and letting a regression program find a relationship among the variables?

7. What factors cause costs to vary?

8. If total costs for Ban Company are $280,000 for 600,000 machine-hours and $310,000 for 700,000 machine-hours, what are the budgeted fixed costs for the year?

9. State why you agree or disagree with this statement: The basic concept in cost estimation is to estimate the relation between costs and the variables affecting costs. What is likely to be determined by a cost-estimation study?

10. Briefly explain three assumptions of regression analysis.

Exercises

Critical Thought

E3–1 Unit Cost under Seasonal Conditions

Fairleigh, Inc., makes children's toys. The company uses a chain of merchandisers for retail distribution. Even though sales and production increase dramatically near the end of the year, management maintains enough manufacturing activity to keep its labor force employed year round. Data for the first quarter's production when 60,000 toys were sold at $5 each is:

Direct material	$120,000
Commissions on sales	3,000
Wages and salaries	38,000
Administrative expenses	25,000
Distribution expenses	24,000

Required:

    a. Give the total cost per unit sold.

    b. Assume that direct material and commissions vary in relation to sales volume while other costs remain fixed; what profit would the company make the last quarter if it sells 100,000 toys?

    c. Determine the total cost per unit sold in the last quarter.

    d. List additional problems companies operating like Fairleigh would encounter.

E3–2 High-Low Method

Bartell, Inc., wishes to determine the fixed portion of its semivariable expense, electricity, as measured against direct labor-hours, for the first three months of the year. Information for this period is as follows:

	Direct Labor-Hours	*Electricity Expense*
January	3,000	$600
February	3,400	635
March	3,200	618

Required:

What is the company's variable and fixed portion of electricity expense? (Carry the unit variable cost to four decimal places but round fixed costs to the nearest dollar.)

E3–3 Data Observation

You have plotted the data points below and are now ready to begin a regression analysis.

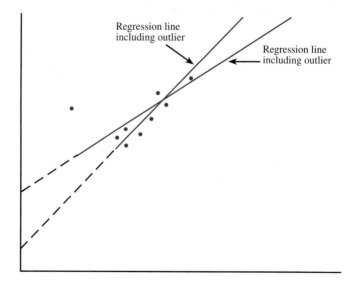

Required:

    a. Do you see anything that should be done before running the regression?

    b. What could have caused any unusual observations that you detect in the preceding graph?

Critical Thought

E3–4 Cost Behavior Patterns

Stallings Company provides you with a summary of its total budgeted production costs at three production levels:

	Volume in Units		
	1,000	*2,000*	*3,000*
Cost A.	$5,000	$5,000	$5,000
Cost B.	1,400	1,800	2,200
Cost C.	3,000	6,000	9,000
Cost D.	2,000	2,000	2,500

Required:

   a. Indicate the cost behavior for Costs A through D.
   b. What would the total budgeted cost be for Costs A and C if the company produces 2,500 units?
   c. Give an example of a production cost that could have the same type of behavior as each of Costs A through D.

E3–5 Regression Diagram

The controller for Stern, Inc., prepared this regression diagram drawing a line of best fit (trend line) for factory overhead and wages. The line of best fit in this diagram is described by the formula $y = a + bx$.

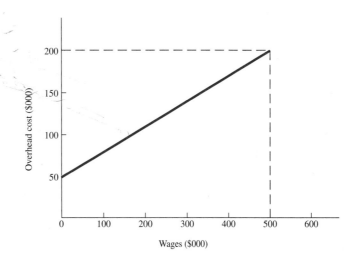

Required:

   a. Determine the slope of the line of best fit in numerical terms.
   b. Give the estimated overhead if wages amount to $750,000.

E3–6 High-Low Approach

The total monthly overhead budget for Deb Corporation is given for two volume levels:

8,000 machine-hours	$5,000,000
12,000 machine-hours (budgeted capacity)	6,800,000

Required:

a. Management asks you for an approximate fundamental measure of fixed and variable cost behavior using the high-low method as follows:
   (1) Prepare the mathematical analysis.
   (2) Diagram the high-low estimates.
b. After the month ends, you find that 11,200 hours were actually worked and total overhead costs incurred amounted to $6,774,000. Prepare a simple budget using the cost estimating formula and indicate whether the total overhead variance is favorable or unfavorable.

Problems

P3–7 Cost-Volume Relationships Illustrated in Graphs: Total Cost

In the graphs shown, assume that *total* costs for the Greer Company are measured on the vertical axis while the horizontal axis measures the volume or activity level.

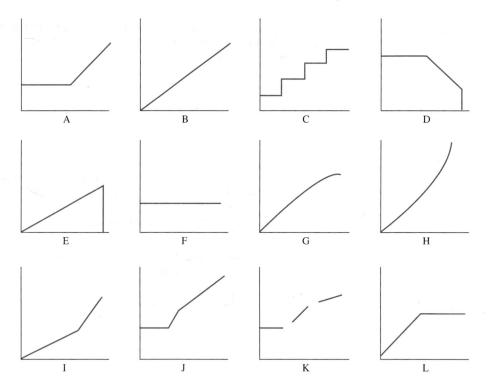

Required:

Indicate the graph that best describes the cost-volume relationship in the following situations (a graph may be used more than once). (Hint: The emphasis is placed on total cost, not unit cost.)

a. The purchasing department is unable to obtain a discount on the direct material used until production increases enough to buy in large quantities.
b. Depreciation on the building is calculated using a straight-line method.
c. The company has an agreement with an outside repair organization that will provide a certain number of hours of repair work for a fixed fee. Greer has agreed to pay a fee per hour of repair work when more hours are required.

d. Depreciation on the factory equipment is calculated on a machine-hour basis.

e. The salaries of manufacturing supervisors when the span of control of each supervisor is overseeing the production of 1,000 units.

f. The company has agreed to pay a certain fee for each mold used in making Product A. After they manufacture and sell a specified quantity of Product A, the company will not be required to pay the fee at that volume and any past fees paid will be refunded. The supplier paying for the use of the mold believes that if enough Product A is introduced into the market, it will stimulate other customers.

g. A supplier of a direct material item has agreed to furnish the material at $1.10 per pound. However, since this supplier has limited capacity, another supplier, whose price is $1.50 per pound, must be used when demand exceeds the first supplier's ability to furnish materials.

h. The electricity bill is determined as follows:

> 0—500 kilowatt-hours. . . . . . . $1.00 per kilowatt-hour used
> 501—600 kilowatt-hours. . . . . . .   1.15 per kilowatt-hour used
> 601—700 kilowatt-hours. . . . . . .   1.30 per kilowatt-hour used
> 701—800 kilowatt-hours. . . . . . .   1.45 per kilowatt-hour used
> And so forth

i. In its effort to attract industry, the Chamber of Commerce furnished the organization with a building on which there is a rent of $500,000 less $1 for each direct labor-hour worked in excess of 100,000 hours. The agreement also specifies that after the organization works 300,000 hours, there will be no rent.

j. The lease agreement on the equipment is as follows:

> Minimum $600 per month (this covers up to 500 machine-hours)
> Next 200 machine-hours . . . . $3 per hour
> Next 200 machine-hours . . . .   2 per hour
> Above 900 machine-hours . . . .   1 per hour

k. An agreement with an advertising agency specifies that $0.15 per unit sold will be charged with a maximum payment of $10,000 for their work in developing an advertising campaign.

l. The cost of material and direct labor used in production.

P3–8 Statistical Scattergraph and Least Squares Method

The data for six bimonthly cost observations of the Steve Douglass Company follow:

	Direct Labor-Hours	Costs
January–February	100,000	$14,000
March–April.	75,000	8,000
May–June.	130,000	17,000
July–August	25,000	6,250
September–October	60,000	11,000
November–December	90,000	15,750

Required:

a. Plot a statistical scattergraph from the data to obtain the fixed and variable cost elements.

b. Use the least squares method to determine the fixed and variable cost elements.

P3–9 Cost-Volume Relationships Illustrated in Graphs: Unit Cost

In the graphs shown, assume that unit costs for Butcher Company are measured on the vertical axis while the horizontal axis measures production volume.

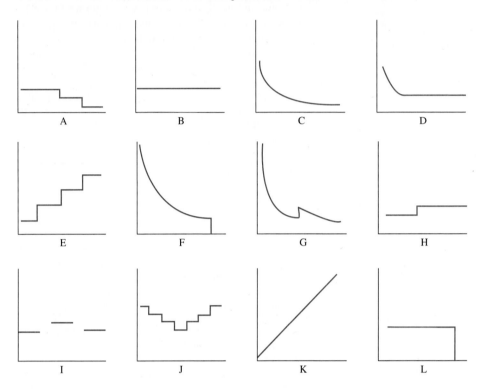

Required:

Indicate the graph that best describes the cost-volume relationship in the following situations (a graph may be used more than once). (Hint: The emphasis is placed on unit cost, not total cost.)

- *a.* Depreciation is calculated on a units-of-production basis.
- *b.* For a fixed fee, a service maintenance company provides a specific number of hours of repair work. When more hours of repair work are needed, Butcher has agreed to pay a stated fee per hour.
- *c.* One component of each finished unit requires two hours of direct labor costing $10 per hour.
- *d.* Depreciation is calculated on a straight-line basis.
- *e.* Salaries of inspection personnel: each earning $1,000 per period and having a span of control of 100 units.
- *f.* Discounts are not available on material purchased unless the company purchases 1,000 gallons or more per period; increasing discounts are available for each additional 500 gallons purchased.
- *g.* Butcher has a limited number of Department B workers so that when production exceeds a specified number of units per period, these laborers must work in excess of 40 hours per week and be paid time and one-half.

h. In its effort to stimulate employment in the region, the Chamber of Commerce has leased the building to Butcher Company under the following conditions: a $12,000 minimum rent covering production up to 2,000 labor-hours; if production exceeds that level per period, there is no rent charge.

i. The present supplier of disposable molds has a limited capacity. When production capacity exceeds a specified number of units, a more expensive mold supplier must be used.

j. Butcher has agreed to pay a certain fee for each plastic container used for each finished product. After a specified number of products are manufactured each period, there will be no charge for any container used since the supplier believes that advertising for the containers will be sufficient to warrant this arrangement.

k. Containers in which the product is packaged can be purchased according to the following price schedule:

Packages	Per Unit Cost
1—100.	$3.00
101—200.	2.75
201—300.	2.50
301—400.	2.25
401—500.	2.50
501—600.	2.75
601—700.	3.00

SPATS

P3–10 High-Low Method

Smile, Inc., has provided the following actual cost data for your use in determining variable factory overhead costs and fixed factory overhead costs for budgeting purposes:

	Quarters		
	Spring	*Summer*	*Fall*
Machine hours	70,000	80,000	90,000
Direct material	$147,000	$168,000	$ 189,000
Direct labor	350,000	400,000	450,000
Factory overhead.	50,400	56,700	63,000
Salespersons' salaries	182,000	208,000	234,000
Warehousing.	56,000	64,000	72,000
Executive salaries	90,000	90,000	90,000
	$875,400	$986,700	$1,098,000

Required:

a. Determine an overall variable factory overhead rate per machine-hour and total fixed factory overhead using the high-low method, assuming management believes no other major factors affect cost behavior.

b. Determine the cost estimating function for factory overhead.

c. Give the budgeted amount in each of the six accounts if the m   ⸳nt of Smile, Inc., budgets 83,600 machine-hours for the winter quarter.

SPATS

P3–11 Least Squares

During your examination of the financial statements of Imperial Company, you wish to analyze selected aspects of the company's operations. Machine-hours and maintenance costs for the first four months of 19X1, which you believe are representative for the year, were as follows:

Month	Machine-Hours	Total Maintenance Costs
January	2,800	$ 3,200
February	3,200	3,600
March	4,400	4,400
April	3,600	3,852
	14,000	$15,052

Required:

Use the least squares method to determine the fixed and variable cost elements.

P3–12 Cost Estimating Formula and Budget Preparation

Phoenix, Inc., plans to produce 10,000 motors each month. Time and motion studies reveal it takes five machine-hours per motor. The established monthly manufacturing overhead budget is:

Maintenance and repairs	$130,000
Utilities	157,500
Factory supplies	67,500
Rent	30,000
Insurance	18,000
	$403,000

Maintenance and repairs, utilities, and factory supplies vary directly with production. Assume a rental contract with a specified monthly payment and monthly insurance payments. At the end of the month, the accountant determined that workers made 9,120 motors in 45,600 actual machine-hours. Actual manufacturing costs were:

Maintenance and repairs	$118,000
Utilities	144,100
Factory supplies	63,400
Rent	32,000
Insurance	16,500
	$374,000

Required:

a. What is the cost estimating formula for each fixed and variable cost? Express the total cost estimating formula on the basis of machine-hours.
b. Prepare a budget for the actual production level and determine variances from budget for each detailed expense.
c. List some factors that could cause the variances you determined in Requirement *b*.

SPATS

P3–13 Least Squares and Scattergraph

Sand, Inc., has experienced difficulty in estimating its costs at various levels of occupancy for its hotel. Management believes that this difficulty is part of the reason that they are not maintaining the profitability of past years. In an attempt to predict its cost-behavior patterns, managers spent much time analyzing past data and future trends.

Except for housekeeping services, managers have separated all department costs into variable and fixed costs. Costs in this area do not seem to demonstrate a strictly fixed or strictly variable pattern. The following are housekeeping costs over the past several months, along with the number of rooms occupied:

Month	Rooms Occupied (000)	Housekeeping Costs
January	3	$15,100
February	4	16,900
March	8	22,100
April	5	16,300
May	10	22,696
June	6	16,800
July	7	17,200
August	6	17,000
September	5	16,500

You are to determine whether these costs contain a mixture of variable and fixed cost elements.

Required:

a. Use the least squares method to determine the variable and fixed cost elements in total housekeeping costs. (You may compute the variable rate in thousands of rooms occupied or divide by 1,000 and express the variable rate per room occupied since the data are in thousands of rooms.)

b. Express the data determined in Requirement *a* for housekeeping in a cost estimating formula.

c. Prepare a scattergraph using the preceding data. Place cost on the vertical axis and rooms occupied (the activity) on the horizontal axis. Fit a regression line to the plotted points by simple visual inspection.

d. Do housekeeping costs contain both variable and fixed cost elements? If so, what is the approximate total fixed cost and the approximate variable cost per room occupied based on the scattergraph?

Writing

P3–14 Concepts and Considerations in Using Regression (CIA)

A Canadian bank has many branch offices. To help prepare budgets for its branch offices, the bank hired the services of a consulting firm. The consulting firm studied the past behavior of different types of costs at several of the branches and, using regression analysis, developed mathematical models to predict costs at the branch offices. One of the regression models developed was:

$$CPC = 200 + 5H + 0.01P$$

where

CPC = Check processing cost per month
H = Labor-hours per month in the check processing department
P = Number of checks processed per month

The consulting company reported that the coefficient of determination (R^2) of the regression equation was 0.96. The standard error of the regression was reported to be $50. In the report, they explained that a standard error of $50 implied that, with the probability of 0.95, the actual check processing cost would lie within ± $98 of that estimated by the model. The report also included the following information about the 35 branch banks from which the data were gathered to develop the model:

	Labor-Hours per Month	Checks Processed per Month
Minimum value	120	50,000
Maximum value	600	300,000

Required:

a. Interpret the terms $5H$ and $0.01P$ in the regression model.
b. During a particular month, one of the branch offices used 250 labor-hours to process 120,000 checks and incurred a check processing cost of $2,870. Explain clearly how to use the regression model to determine whether the operations of the check processing department at this branch office should be examined in more detail. (*Please note.* You are not asked to evaluate this branch's operations but only to explain how the regression model and associated analysis could be used in determining the need for further examination.)
c. The bank is planning to open a new branch office. Management estimates that the labor-hours per month will average 1,200 and that the checks processed per month will average 650,000. Management plans to use the preceding model for estimating the check processing cost at this new branch. Identify relevant considerations in using the model developed for the 35 branch banks to estimate the costs for the new branch.

P3–15 Regression Analysis Theory (CMA)
The controller of the Connecticut Electronics Company believes that identification of the variable and fixed components of the firm's costs will enable the firm to make better planning and control decisions. Among the costs the controller is concerned about is the behavior of indirect supplies expense. He believes there is some correlation between the machine-hours worked and the amount of indirect supplies used.

A member of the controller's staff has suggested that a simple linear regression model be used to determine the cost behavior of the indirect supplies. The following regression equation was developed from 40 pairs of observations using the least squares method of regression. The regression equation and related measures are as follows:

$$S = \$200 = \$4H$$

where

$$S = \text{Total monthly costs of indirect supplies}$$
$$H = \text{Machine-hours per month}$$

Standard error of estimate: $S_e = 100$
Coefficient of correlation: $r = .87$

Required:

a. When a simple linear regression model is used to make inferences about a population relationship from sample data, what assumptions must be made before the inferences can be accepted as valid?

b. Assume the assumptions identified in Requirement *a* are satisfied for the indirect supplies expense of Connecticut Electronics Company.
  (1) Explain the meaning of 200 and 4 in the regression equation $S = \$200 + \$4H$.
  (2) Calculate the estimated cost of indirect supplies if 900 machine-hours are to be used during a month.
c. Explain briefly what the
  (1) Coefficient of correlation measures.
  (2) Value of the coefficient of correlation ($r = .87$) indicates if Connecticut Electronics Company wishes to predict the total cost of indirect supplies on the basis of estimated machine-hours.

Case

C3–16 Determining Information Needed from an Accounting System

Plywood Plastics Manufacturing Company was formed as a partnership 25 years ago by Buell Edmonds and Harold Douglass after Edmonds, a successful business executive in the floor-covering business, acquired a plastics franchise. His new product was to be bonded with plywood and used for sink tops, paneling, and tabletops. Edmonds and Douglass were long-time friends, and Edmonds thought Douglass had the technical expertise to successfully produce a product. For years, Douglass had been an industrial arts teacher in a large metropolitan school district.

Each partner invested $5,000 in the business, and the partnership leased space behind a garage. Edmonds worked for the business in an administrative capacity, while Douglass worked part-time, mainly at night and on Saturdays. After approximately two years, since the business was prospering, the company moved to a larger location at which time each partner invested additional money.

Originally, the company's business consisted of custom-made products for new and remodeled homes; however, it gradually expanded operations so that emphasis shifted from single custom orders to larger commercial orders. Eventually, the bulk of its business came from several large national motel chains and one large, national mail-order house. Operations expanded to the extent that Plywood Plastics was producing custom countertops for mail-order catalog sales for the entire United States and Canada. In addition, it was shipping vanity tops and bathroom sink tops all over the world for the motel chains. After the purchase of new, modern equipment, Plywood Plastics began producing rough-slab products for sale to several large makers of kitchen tables; these firms further processed the products.

By this time, Douglass had resigned from his teaching position and was working full time with the company. Eventually, Plywood Plastics became a corporation with each partner receiving 50 percent of the stock and Douglass was named the general manager. Ten years ago, when Edmonds retired, Douglass purchased his holdings and became the sole owner. Five years later, Douglass sold all his holdings to a group of six investors; however, he remained a member of the board of directors since the investors owed him a portion of the sale price that was secured by collateral in the company.

Immediately after the sale, the assistant manager, who was one of the six investors, became president and general manager. Within one year a very profitable business began to lose money, at which time the board fired the manager and rehired Douglass on a daily consulting-fee basis. Within six months, Plywood Plastics was once again experiencing sizable profits; however, since Douglass did not want to remain active, the board hired another full-time manager and president. Profits have decreased to the point where the company was breaking even.

At present, the company has a work force of 40 employees, a reduction from the 100 workers employed during peak production. Although the production work force has been cut, the administrative staff remains the same—a general manager, two bookkeepers, and two salespersons. The company remains approximately one month behind in filling orders, presenting some problems since its competitors are able to fill orders much more quickly. Often the company is unable to begin processing an order after it is received because the material necessary must be ordered first. The only finished goods inventory produced for stock are vanity tops processed for the mail-order company; all other items are manufactured only after an order is received.

Plywood and plastic constitute the two main raw material inputs. The manufacturing process operates on an assembly line with the following four main steps involved:

1. A section where the plywood and plastic are glued together.
2. A section where any necessary bending takes place.
3. A section where the slab is cut to specifications.
4. The final section where any molding or other refinements take place.

When Douglass was general manager, he would call the three factory supervisors into his office and give them their work orders for the day. When the regular assembly line employees reported each day, material necessary for production had already been obtained from the storeroom. Because of his long experience, Douglass correctly estimated the labor-hours needed for each batch of products; this allowed the manager to forecast profits per square feet of production with a high degree of accuracy. During each workday, Douglass would check with the supervisors on the progress of each job.

The company does not have a cost accounting system nor does it maintain a perpetual inventory system. Even though the company is closing its books each month, a physical inventory is taken only once per quarter; management estimates inventory values for other months. The firm determines earnings only for months in which management has estimated the inventory values. It values finished goods at 80 percent of sales price, and work in process at 70 percent of sales price. A local CPA firm prepares the year-end statements and tax returns.

Required:

What recommendations would you make for improving the company's profitability? Include in your recommendations the type of information the company needs from its accounting system.

CHAPTER 4

Volume-Based Cost Assignments

Chapter Objectives

After studying this chapter, you should be able to:

1. Apply criteria in selecting appropriate plant capacity and cost drivers.
2. Explain the concepts of traceability that distinguish direct costs from indirect costs.
3. Allocate service department overhead to producing departments to determine overhead application rates.
4. Prepare overhead variances for a normal costing system, recognizing they represent over- or underapplied overhead.

Introduction

There is no one true cost of a good or service unless a company manufactures only one product or provides only one service. In that case, this one good or service receives all costs. Otherwise, accountants must allocate costs incurred for all products or services among the products and services. Methods of allocating costs from departments and activities to products are known as **cost allocations, cost assignments, cost distributions,** or **cost apportionments.** For example, in manufacturing, accountants must allocate the cost of service departments such as factory office, maintenance, and materials storeroom to production departments. Production departments then apply total factory overhead costs to units they manufacture. Similarly, for cost reimbursement purposes, hospitals allocate personnel and equipment costs to patient care centers, while colleges and universities allocate administrative costs to graduate and undergraduate programs to determine a cost per enrolled student.

Plant Capacity Concepts

Chapter 2 illustrated overhead application rates calculated on various volume-related or unit-related bases. However, we postponed the question of which capacity to use in estimating factory overhead rates until this chapter. Accountants budget costs in relation to one specific sales or production volume used for estimating the predetermined factory overhead application rate. Because of the impact of volume changes on fixed and variable costs, the capacity level chosen affects the factory overhead costs applied to the product. In determining factory overhead application rates, accountants distinguish between idle capacity and excess capacity. **Idle capacity** is the temporary nonuse of facilities resulting from a decrease in demand for the company's products or services. **Excess capacity** refers to facilities that are simply not necessary.

The capacity selected depends on whether management uses a short-range or long-range viewpoint and how much allowance management wants to make for possible volume interruptions. Also, experience with the respective industry or company within the industry provides information in selecting the activity level. Next, we discuss these four capacity approaches: theoretical, practical, normal, and expected actual capacity.

Theoretical capacity.   **Theoretical capacity** (also called the **maximum or ideal capacity**) assumes all personnel and equipment operate at peak efficiency using 100 percent of plant capacity. Theoretical capacity is unrealistic; it fails to include normal interruptions for machine breakdowns or maintenance. Thus, accountants usually do not consider theoretical capacity a feasible basis for determining cost allocation rates. However, managers use theoretical capacity to help measure efficiency of operations by providing ideal figures for comparison.

Practical capacity.   **Practical capacity** does not consider idle time due to inadequate sales demand. This production volume occurs when demand for the company's products causes the plant to operate continuously. Practical capacity represents the maximum output at which departments or divisions can operate efficiently; thus, unused capacity costs are not assigned to products. Although this level varies

---

Global

Current Cost Management Practice

BMW took swifter cost reduction measures than its competitors; this strategy helped it weather the European recession. Its wage bill accounts for 20 percent of revenues, compared to 25–27 percent for its rivals. The company also has beaten its rivals in materials management, cutting down inventories, and in just-in-time production. BMW's cost reduction strategy proved rewarding: BMW was the only German car maker to make money in 1993, and it became number one among European car exporters for the first time.

Nick Gilbert, "BMW Goes a-Rovin," *Financial World,* May 24, 1994, pp. 24-28.

---

from company to company, managers usually consider practical capacity as approximately 80 to 90 percent of theoretical capacity. Practical capacity is more realistic than theoretical capacity. It allows for unavoidable delays due to holidays, vacations, time off for weekends, and machine breakdowns.

Normal capacity.   **Normal capacity** includes consideration of both idle time due to limited sales orders and human and equipment inefficiencies. It represents an average sales demand expected to exist over a long enough period that includes seasonal and cyclical fluctuations. Managers should review sales figures for a sufficient number of years to observe cyclical changes. Because normal capacity evens out the cyclical changes, it is a more appropriate basis for applying overhead under most circumstances.

Expected Actual Capacity.   **Expected actual capacity** is the production volume necessary to meet sales demand for the next year. This short-range concept does not attempt to even out the cyclical changes in sales demand. If product costs strongly influence the pricing policies or if a company uses cost-plus contracts extensively—as in government contracting—there is a danger using the expected actual activity level in a seasonal or cyclical business. Fixed unit costs would decrease in peak production periods when using the expected actual activity level as the basis for applying factory overhead. Under these conditions, the sales price for these units would be lower in a cost-plus contract than when manufacturing the units in a slack period.

Comparison of Capacity Levels

After a company decides on a specific capacity level, it estimates its variable and fixed costs for the period. For simplicity, Chapter 2 did not divide the overhead application rate into its fixed and variable components as is necessary. In Exhibit 4–1 several activity levels illustrate the effect of the capacity level on the estimated fixed factory overhead rate. One level, called the **denominator capacity,** is chosen for recording purposes. Exhibit 4–1 uses a volume-related basis (machine-hours), but the effect on fixed unit cost would be the same if we used a nonvolume-related basis, such as number of setup hours or other transactions. (You will learn more about volume- and nonvolume-related bases in the next chapter.)

Effect on Unit Fixed Costs.   In Exhibit 4–1, total fixed costs remain at $87,750 within the relevant range of the various capacity volumes listed. When using higher capacity levels, the fixed factory overhead rate is lower than when using the normal or

EXHIBIT 4–1   Capacity Level Effect on Estimated Fixed Factory Overhead

Actual	Theoretical	Capacity Practical	Normal	Expected
Capacity level	100%	85%	75%	60%
Machine-hours.	6,000	5,100	4,500	3,600
Estimated factory overhead:				
Variable overhead @ $16.50				
per machine-hour	$ 99,000	$ 84,150	$ 74,250	$ 59,400
Fixed overhead	87,750	87,750	87,750	87,750
Total overhead	$186,750	$171,900	$162,000	$147,150
Factory overhead rate per machine-hour:				
Variable overhead.	$16.50	$16.50	$16.50	$16.50
Fixed overhead	14.63	17.20	19.50	24.38
Total overhead	$31.13	$33.70	$36.00	$40.88

expected actual capacity. This results because we spread fixed overhead over a greater number of machine-hours. For example, if we use 3,600 machine-hours, the fixed factory overhead rate is $24.38 per machine-hour ($87,750/3,600 hours). If we use 6,000 machine-hours, the rate is $14.63 per machine-hour ($87,750/6,000 hours). The variable factory overhead rate remains a constant $16.50 per machine-hour at all capacity levels. Although we illustrate overhead rates for different activity levels in Exhibit 4-1, accountants must select one activity level to use for product costing.

Allocating Service Department Costs to Production (Operating) Departments

After choosing whether to use theoretical, practical, normal, or expected actual capacity, accountants accumulate costs for production and service departments. **Production** or **operating departments,** such as Fabricating, Assembly, and Finishing, directly process materials into finished goods or produce service revenue. **Service departments** provide support to other manufacturing departments and perform no production work. Service departments, such as Materials Handling and Repairs, do not actively engage in manufacturing the company's products. They help other departments' operations and contribute to their efficiency. Companies allocate service department costs to production departments so goods and services produced reflect the total full cost of production. Also, the allocation of service department costs makes user department managers aware of the cost of services they are using.

Service organizations.   While this discussion has centered around manufacturing activities, the production and service department concept is also applicable to nonmanufacturing service organizations, such as hospitals. For instance, the units that provide direct patient care, such as surgery, are a hospital's production departments. Service or ancillary departments are the administrative support departments, such as patient accounting and materials management.

Direct and Indirect Costs

When calculating overhead application rates, accountants must distinguish between direct and indirect costs. This distinction depends on the *attachability* or *traceability* of the cost element. Accountants do not allocate **direct costs** to the costing

EXHIBIT 4–2 Allocating Service Department Costs to Production (Operating) Departments

Service Department—Materials Handling
$43,500

Production Department—Assembly	44%	56%	Production Department—Treating	
Direct costs	$ 34,654		Direct costs	$ 25,846
Indirect costs	77,600		Indirect costs	78,900
Allocated service department costs. . .	19,140 ◄—	—► Allocated service department costs. . .	24,360
Total costs.	$131,394		Total costs.	$129,106
Divided by units produced	10,000		Units produced	4,300
Unit cost	$13.14		Unit cost	$30

center because they arise within the department or job and are clearly traced to this cost center. (Chapter 2 contrasts direct materials and direct labor costs to indirect materials and indirect labor costs, respectively.) **Indirect costs** (also called **common costs**) serve two or more costing centers. For example, rent and depreciation specifically used within the Assembly Department and wages paid to that department's workers are direct costs of the Assembly Department and require no allocations. However, rent and depreciation on the overall plant building is an indirect cost of the Assembly Department. Accountants must allocate indirect cost on some basis, such as square footage, before determining the total cost of that department. Electric power and other utilities are also indirect costs if each department is not individually metered. The term *indirect costs* thus refers to cost elements that accountants cannot trace to one costing center.

Because traceability is the key distinction between direct and indirect costs, we must define the object of costing (such as a product line, a department, or unit of inventory) before we can say whether a cost is direct or indirect. For example, the plant superintendent's salary and depreciation on the factory building are indirect costs for all service and production departments because we cannot trace these costs to only one department. However, when the object of costing is the overall company, the plant superintendent's salary and building depreciation are direct costs of production.

Exhibit 4–2 diagrams the flow of cost from one service department to two producing departments, Assembly and Treating, that manufacture the company's two products. We trace $34,654 direct costs, but allocate $77,600 indirect costs to the Assembly Department. In distributing indirect costs to production and service departments, we allocate utilities on square footage. Of the $43,500 direct and indirect service department cost, we allocate 44 percent or $19,140 to Assembly and 56 percent or $24,360, to Treating. These allocations represent another indirect cost. Dividing Assembly's $131,394 total costs by the 10,000 units produced yields approximately $13.14 per unit cost. Adding Treating's direct, indirect, and allocated service department costs and dividing by the 4,300 units produced yields an approximate $30 unit cost for inventory valuation and cost of goods sold.

Although no allocations are necessary for direct costs, indirect costs require a basis for allocations. A plant survey provides the information on which to allocate the indirect costs. We use the information in Exhibit 4–3 to allocate indirect costs and service department costs to production departments and then to determine overhead rates for production departments.

EXHIBIT 4–3   Collins Company Plant Survey *Step 1 of Stepn method*

	KWH	Employees	Estimated Cost of Materials Requested	Estimated Labor Hours of Repair Service Used	Square Footage	Direct Labor	Machine-Hours
Materials Handling	65,550	5			15,140		
Repairs and Maintenance	70,730	3	$ 30,000		9,460		
Building and Grounds	73,620	2	25,500	5,000			
Producing departments:							
Assembly	427,300	10	33,000	1,100	40,000	$157,500	2,140
Treating	362,800	15	42,000	2,300	30,000	22,500	4,500
Totals	1,000,000	35	$130,500	8,400	94,600	$180,000	6,640

Cost Allocation Basis.   The basis for allocating indirect costs must bear a relationship to the kind of services a department gives. For example, the number of purchase orders processed or costs of materials used by each department is an appropriate base for allocating purchasing department costs. An appropriate allocation base for a personnel department is the number of employees or labor-hours in each department. Similarly, the number of requisitions is appropriate for allocating materials handling costs. Service hours rendered is a typical allocation base for repairs and maintenance costs. We often allocate building occupancy costs on occupied floor space, although this allocation base is somewhat controversial. Using plant square footage presents some conflict because this assumes all space is equally desirable, regardless of the number of windows or location of space.

Cost accountants recognize that sometimes they must resort to an arbitrary basis because there is no clear cause-and-effect relationship between the basis and the cost. However, there is a danger in relying on a basis such as sales dollars, gross margin, or some other ability-to-bear basis. In such cases, an inaccurate cost allocation is likely to result. Instead, the cost accountant determines the basis that most accurately reflects services or benefits received. Accountants may use this data later for allocating service department costs to the other service departments and/or production departments.

Allocating Indirect Costs to Service and Producing Departments.   For simplicity, Exhibits 4–4 and 4–5 illustrate few direct and indirect costs; for example, they include only two indirect costs: electricity of $134,800 and superintendence of $70,000. The plant survey data in Exhibit 4–3 supplies the bases for allocating indirect costs. For instance, we allocate the indirect cost of electricity to both service and producing departments based on the kilowatt-hours (KWH) used within each department. The Materials Handling Department receives:

$$\frac{65,550 \text{ KWH}}{1,000,000 \text{ total KWH}} \times \$134,800 \text{ electricity cost} = \$8,840 \text{ (rounded)}$$

Likewise, the Materials Handling Department receives $10,000 superintendence cost:

$$\frac{5 \text{ Materials Handling employees}}{35 \text{ total employees}} \times \$70{,}000 \text{ total superintendence cost} = \$10{,}000$$

Allocating Indirect Costs versus Allocating Service Department Costs

Even though service departments, such as Janitorial Service and Materials Storeroom, support rather than directly manufacture products, production departments receive their costs before distribution to units of goods or services. There are several methods for allocating these costs:

1. **Direct method.** We allocate service department costs to production departments only.
2. **Step, sequential, or step-down method.** We allocate service department costs to some other service departments and to production departments that have received their services.
3. **Linear algebra.** (also called reciprocal, or matrix method.) The linear algebra method uses simultaneous equations to recognize that service departments render reciprocal services.

Whatever method of service department cost allocation we use, we begin the procedure by estimating the overhead costs for the entire plant.

Because producing departments, such as Assembly and Treating, are the only departments that physically work on the product, we assign all factory overhead costs to products through rates developed only for production departments. This means that we must allocate the costs of service departments, such as Repairs and Personnel, to producing departments before establishing a factory overhead application rate for the production departments. However, we allocate to production departments only the portion of service department costs that relates to the production/operating departments. For example, Personnel is a service department that serves both administration and production. We allocate administration's prorata share of the cost to administrative centers and treat this portion as a period cost. We allocate production's prorata share of Personnel cost to manufacturing centers and treat it as overhead (product) cost.

Before allocating service department costs to producing departments, however, we must estimate a service department's direct costs as well as its share of indirect costs. Accountants allocate indirect costs, such as superintendent's salary, to both producing and service departments on some logical basis. Allocated service department costs are indirect for the production department.

Note that tracing each department's direct costs and allocating indirect costs to each department are independent of the method of allocating service department costs. We illustrate the direct, step, and linear algebra methods next. For example, in Exhibits 4–4, 4–5 and 4–6, each service and production department has the same direct and indirect costs (e.g., Materials Handling has a total cost of $43,500). The exhibits, however, differ in the method of allocating each service department's direct and indirect costs.

Direct Method

Exhibit 4–4 illustrates the direct method in which production departments directly receive service department costs. It shows the allocation of the Materials Handling Department (service department) to Assembly and Treating (production departments). The Materials Handling Department's budgeted costs are $43,500 as shown in the second column in Exhibit 4–4. We allocate the Materials Handling Department costs based on the estimated cost of materials requisitioned, which is $33,000 for the Assembly Department and $42,000 for the Treating Department, totaling $75,000, as shown in Exhibit 4–3.

EXHIBIT 4–4   Direct Method of Allocating Budgeted Service Department Costs

COLLINS COMPANY
Allocation of Service Department Costs to Production Departments—Direct Method
For Year 19X1

	V or F	Service Departments			Production Departments		
		Materials Handling	*Repairs and Maintenance*	*Building and Grounds*	*Assembly*	*Treating*	*Total*
Direct costs:							
Indirect labor	V	$ 8,400	$ 6,780	$ 3,810	$ 10,064	$ 1,746	$ 30,800
Depreciation of equipment	F	16,260	13,935	17,615	24,590	24,100	96,500
Total departmental direct costs		24,660	20,715	21,425	34,654	25,846	127,300
Indirect costs and allocation base:							
Electricity (KWH)	V	8,840	9,535	9,925	57,600	48,900	134,800
Superintendence (no. of employees) .	F	10,000	6,000	4,000	20,000	30,000	70,000
Total departmental indirect costs		18,840	15,535	13,925	77,600	78,900	204,800
Total departmental overhead costs		$43,500	$36,250	$35,350	$112,254	$104,746	$332,100
Total variable departmental costs		$17,240	$16,315	$13,735	$ 67,664	$ 50,646	$165,600
Total fixed departmental costs		26,260	19,935	21,615	44,590	54,100	166,500
Total departmental factory overhead before distribution of service departments		43,500	36,250	35,350	112,254	104,746	332,100
Distribution of service department costs:							
Materials handling (estimated cost of materials requisitioned: Assembly, $33,000; Treating, $42,000)		(43,500)			19,140	24,360	
Repairs and maintenance (estimated labor-hours of service used: Assembly, 1,100; Treating, 2,300)			(36,250)		11,728	24,522	
Building and grounds (square footage: Assembly, 40,000; Treating, 30,000)				(35,350)	20,200	15,150	
Total factory overhead					$163,322	$168,778	$332,100
Allocation bases to apply to production:							
Direct labor cost					$157,500		
Machine-hours						4,500	
Total factory overhead rates					104% of direct labor cost	$37.50 per machine-hour	

Handwritten annotations:

assign direct costs
② Direct costs

③ allocate indirect cost to Service & production departments

④ Distribution of service department costs
33÷75×43500
42÷75×43500

⑤

⑥

EXHIBIT 4–5   Step Method of Allocating Budgeted Service Department Costs

COLLINS COMPANY
Allocation of Service Department Costs to Production Departments—Step Method
For Year 19X1

	V or F	Service Departments			Production Departments		
		Materials Handling	Repairs and Maintenance	Building and Grounds	Assembly	Treating	Total
Direct costs:							
Indirect labor	V	$ 8,400	$ 6,780	$ 3,810	$ 10,064	$ 1,746	$ 30,800
Depreciation of equipment	F	16,260	13,935	17,615	24,590	24,100	96,500
Total departmental direct costs		24,660	20,715	21,425	34,654	25,846	127,300
Indirect costs and allocation base:							
Electricity (KWH)	V	8,840	9,535	9,925	57,600	48,900	134,800
Superintendence (no. of employees) .	F	10,000	6,000	4,000	20,000	30,000	70,000
Total departmental indirect costs		18,840	15,535	13,925	77,600	78,900	204,800
Total departmental overhead costs		$43,500	$36,250	$35,350	$112,254	$104,746	$332,100
Total variable departmental costs		$17,240	$16,315	$13,735	$ 67,664	$ 50,646	$165,600
Total fixed departmental costs		26,260	19,935	21,615	44,590	54,100	166,500
Total departmental factory overhead before distribution of service departments		43,500	36,250	35,350	112,254	104,746	332,100
Distribution of service department costs:							
Materials handling (estimated cost of materials requisitioned: Repairs $30,000; Building, $25,500; Assembly, $33,000; Treating, $42,000)		(43,500)	10,000	8,500	11,001	13,999	
Total Repairs and Maintenance			46,250				
Repairs and maintenance (estimated labor-hours of service used: Building, 5,000, Assembly, 1,100; Treating, 2,300)			(46,250)	27,530	6,056	12,664	
Total Building and Grounds				71,380			
Building and Grounds (square footage: Assembly, 40,000; Treating, 30,000)				(71,380)	40,789	30,591	
Total variable and fixed overhead					$170,100	$162,000	$332,100
Allocation bases to apply to production:							
Direct labor cost					$157,500		
Machine-hours						4,500	
Total factory overhead rate					108% of direct labor cost	$36.00 per machine-hour	

This calculation allocates the Materials Handling Department's $43,500 costs to the Assembly Department:

$$\frac{\$33,000}{\$75,000} \times \$43,500 = \$19,140$$

And, this calculation allocates the Materials Handling Department's $43,500 costs to the Treating Department:

$$\frac{\$42,000}{\$75,000} \times \$43,500 = \$24,360$$

We allocate the other service department costs to Assembly and Treating in the same fashion. This method ignores allocating the costs of any Materials Handling services provided to other service departments. Thus, we add only Assembly's $33,000 materials to Treating's $42,000 materials for a total of $75,000 materials requisitions. The direct method is simple because the order of allocating each service department's costs does not matter.

Regardless of the allocation method used (direct, step, or linear algebra), after distributing all service department costs to production departments, we calculate the overhead rates for each production department. Exhibit 4–4 uses direct labor costs as the allocation base for the Assembly Department and machine-hours for the Treating Department. In deciding whether to use different bases for different departments, accountants study the cause-and-effect relationship between the cost and the cost allocation basis. After determining the departmental rate, accountants use the estimated overhead rate to apply overhead to the units produced.

Step Method

When using the step method of service cost allocation, accountants follow a sequence in distributing the costs of all service departments to other departments. Generally, they allocate the costs of the service department that serves the most other departments first, the department servicing the next greatest number second, and so forth. The last service department allocated is normally the one serving the fewest other departments. The step method illustrated in Exhibit 4–5 allocates Materials Handling Department costs to all other service and producing departments; Repairs and Maintenance receives $10,000 ($30,000/$130,500 × $43,500) costs. Then we allocate Repairs and Maintenance Department costs, including its share of the Materials Handling cost allocation, to all other departments. We do not allocate any of the $46,250 cost to the Materials Handling Department nor to the Repairs and Maintenance Department because these two departments are closed or are being closed out.

We determine the Building and Grounds' portion of the $46,250 as follows: 5,000/8,400 × $46,250 = $27,530. The distribution base is 5,000 + 1,100 + 2,300 = 8,400 service hours, as shown in Exhibit 4–3. Finally, we distribute the Building and Grounds costs that include the department's share of the Materials Handling and the Repairs and Maintenance cost allocations.

Normally, the step method is preferable to the direct method because it considers the benefits given by one service department to other service departments. However, the step method fails to recognize that, for example, the Building and Grounds Department may have given some reciprocal service to the Materials Handling and the Repairs and Maintenance departments. Since we previously allocated the costs of these departments, we allocate no Building and Grounds costs to these departments. Accountants prefer the linear algebra method because it takes into account these reciprocal services.

Linear Algebra or Reciprocal Method

Exhibit 4–6 illustrates the reciprocal method using linear algebra or simultaneous equations. This method achieves greater exactness than the step method because it recognizes reciprocity between service departments. However, we achieve this greater exactness only if the estimated level of service that departments give to each other is valid. For complex decisions about product pricing, or making or buying products, accountants use the linear algebra method to obtain a more precise allocation of costs.

Computer software packages now make it easy to apply the linear algebra method. However, we introduce this allocation procedure manually even though the figures become detailed. Because Exhibit 4–6 illustrates three service departments, three simultaneous equations are necessary. Additional service departments may require more simultaneous equations. In this case, accountants use matrix algebra to handle the series of equations.

We base the amount of service department cost assigned on the percentage of usage for each department. For example, Exhibit 4–6 indicates that the Treating Department uses 32 percent of the Materials Handling services. To determine this, we compare the Treating Department's $42,000 estimated materials requested to the $130,500 total, as shown in Exhibit 4–3 ($42,000/$130,500 = 32%). Assembly Department's share is $33,000/$130,500, or 25 percent. We compute the other departments' shares of Materials Handling in a similar manner. (Note we use some rounding of percents to keep the digits to two places and still equal 100 percent distribution of service department cost.) Likewise, we calculate Building and Grounds' 60 percent usage of Repairs and Maintenance as 5,000/8,400 labor hours, or 60 percent. Assembly receives 42 percent of Building and Grounds' total cost because its 40,000 square footage is 42 percent of the 94,600 total square footage.

After inserting these usage percentages in the simultaneous equations, we obtain the estimated total cost for each service department as shown in Exhibit 4–6. After solving all simultaneous equations, we distribute total estimated cost based on the usage percentages. For example, Assembly receives 25% × $56,468 total Materials Handling costs = $14,117, 13% × $57,343 Repairs and Maintenance = $7,455, and 42% × $81,049 Building and Grounds = $34,040. After distributing all service department cost to the producing departments, we divide the total estimated overhead by the allocation base to arrive at the application rate. Thus, $167,866 Assembly cost/$157,500 direct labor equals a rate of 107 percent.

Comparison of Direct, Step, and Linear Algebra Methods.   The overhead rates determined in Exhibit 4–4 using the direct method, in Exhibit 4–5 using the step method, and in Exhibit 4–6 using the linear algebra method vary slightly. For the Assembly Department, the basis is 104 percent of direct labor costs using the direct method, 108 percent using the step method, and 107 percent using the linear algebra method. For the Treating Department, the basis is $37.50 per machine-hour using the direct method, $36.00 using the step method, and $36.50 using the linear algebra method. Even though these results are close, do not conclude that the allocation method chosen makes little difference in other situations. We purposely kept the three exhibits simple, using few departments with small expenses. As stated earlier, the linear algebra method is the preferred method because it considers reciprocal services between departments.

EXHIBIT 4–6 **Linear Algebra Method of Allocating Budgeted Service Department Costs**

COLLINS COMPANY
Allocation of Service Department Costs to Production Departments—Linear Algebra Method
For Year 19X1

| | Service Departments | | | Production Departments | | |
	Materials Handling	Repairs and Maintenance	Building and Grounds	Assembly	Treating	Total
Department rendering service:						
Materials Handling	—	23%	20%	25%	32%	100%
Repairs and Maintenance	—	—	60	13	27	100
Building and Grounds	16%	10	—	42	32	100
Departmental costs before allocation						
of service department costs	$43,500	$36,250	$35,350	$112,254	$104,746	$332,100
Materials Handling Department allocation ...	(56,468)	12,988	11,293	14,117	18,070	
Repairs and Maintenance						
Department allocation	—	(57,343)	34,406	7,455	15,482	
Building and Grounds Department allocation	12,968	8,105	(81,049)	34,040	25,936	
Total overhead	-0-	-0-	-0-	$167,866	$164,234	$332,100
Allocation bases to apply overhead						
to production:						
Direct labor cost				$157,500		
Machine-hours					4,500	
Total factory overhead rate				107% of direct labor cost	$36.50 per machine-hour	

The three simultaneous equations to solve for the three unknowns are

Let M = Total costs of Materials Handling Department
R = Total costs of Repairs and Maintenance Department
B = Total costs of Building and Grounds Department

(1) $M = \$43,500 + .16B$
(2) $R = \$36,250 + .23M + .10B$
(3) $B = \$35,350 + .20M + .60R$

Substituting in (1)

$M = \$43,500 + .16 (\$35,350 + 20M + .60R)$
$M = \$43,500 + \$5,656 + .032M + .096R$
$.968M = \$49,156 + .096R$
$M = \$50,780.99 + .0991736R$

Substituting in (2)

$R = \$36,250 + .23(\$50,780.99 + .0991736R) + .10 [\$35,350 + .20(\$50,780.99 + .0991736R) + .60R]$
$R = \$36,250 + \$11,679.63 + .02281R + .10(\$35,350 + \$10,156.20 + .019835R + .60R)$
$R = \$36,250 + \$11,679.63 + .02281R + .10(\$45,506.20 + .619835R)$
$R = \$36,250 + \$11,679.63 + .02281R + \$4,550.62 + .0619835R$
$R = \$52,480.25 + .0847935R$
$.9152065R = \$52,480.25$
$R = \$57,342.52$ or rounded to $57,343

Substituting in (3)

$B = \$35,350 + .20[\$50,780.99 + .0991736(\$57,342.52)] + .60(\$57,342.52)$
$B = \$35,350 + .20(\$50,780.99 + \$5,686.86) + \$34,405.51$
$B = \$35,350 + .20(\$56,467.85) + \$34,405.51$
$B = \$35,350 + \$11,293.57 + \$34,405.51$
$B = \$81,049$

Substituting in (1)

$M = \$43,500 + .16(\$81,049)$
$M = \$43,500 + \$12,968$
$M = \$56,468$

Behavioral Aspects of Allocating Service Department Cost

By knowing service department rates in advance and allocating the cost of one department to others, department heads are more likely to question whether they really need the service before requesting it. When department managers realize they are not charged for services requested, they may request an excessive amount of service because they have little incentive to control costs.

Conversely, allocating service department costs may cause cost center managers to refrain from using needed services. For example, assume department managers realize that they are charged when they ask systems designers to evaluate and improve their information flows. By avoiding this expense, these managers may retain outdated and inefficient systems. When management wants to encourage producing departments to use specific services, accountants do not allocate these service department costs to users.

Another problem is that managers of service departments sometimes forget what their purpose really is—to provide support. They develop unrealistic charge rates to show a favorable financial picture for their service departments. When superiors monitor charge rates of both production and service departments, they can develop fairer rates for services.

Multiple Rates versus a Single, Plantwide Rate

The exhibits thus far have calculated departmental overhead rates. The procedure for applying factory overhead is the same whether using a single plantwide rate or multiple departmental rates. A consideration in selecting a plantwide rate or departmental rate is whether all departments use similar operating processes, direct labor, and machines. A single plantwide rate may be appropriate in a small plant with production moving through all departments. However, it is difficult to find such a manufacturing situation in the real world.

Accountants consider multiple overhead rates desirable when plants manufacture various products that do not go through the same departments or use the same technology. Under these manufacturing circumstances, products are subject to different cost drivers, such as worker-hours, machine-hours, throughput, order size, value of materials, or quality requirements.

Avoid Plantwide Rate.   A dangerous assumption made in using a single, plantwide rate is that a single factor causes costs to change. Since this is unlikely for most manufacturing processes, miscosting and mispricing of products often result. For example, if managers select direct labor as the single cost driver, a product line using more labor hours receives higher overhead. Because labor-hours have very little impact on how a technological environment drives overhead costs, this product line may be inaccurately applied overhead.

Exhibit 4–7 uses the departmental cost data from the step method illustrated in Exhibit 4–5, but bases departmental rates on machine-hours for both Assembly and Treating. The plant survey in Exhibit 4–3 gives the machine-hours. If an order receives more services from one department than from another, the use of a plantwide rate results in an inaccurate allocation of costs to the jobs. Order No. 1 in Exhibit 4–7 required eight hours of machine work from the Assembly Department, whose overhead application rate is larger, while it was a light user of the Treating Department machines. Use of the departmental rates results in $708 applied overhead. If, instead, Collins Company uses the plantwide rate, applied overhead is $500. Use of the departmental rates reflects the difference in time spent in each department. As illustrated in Exhibit 4–7, companies usually need department rates so different jobs bear their share of factory overhead. Otherwise, the application of overhead using a plantwide rate may not reflect actual uses of resources.

EXHIBIT 4–7

COLLINS COMPANY
Departmental Overhead Rates Contrasted to a Single Plantwide Overhead Rate
For Year 19X1

| | Departmental Rates | | Plantwide |
	Assembly	Treating	Rate
Budgeted overhead	$170,100	$162,000	$332,100
Machine-hours	2,140	4,500	6,640
Rate per machine-hour	$79.50	$36.00	$50
Overhead application to Order No. 1 using machine-hours:			
Assembly (8 machine-hours @ $79.50)			$ 636
Treating (2 machine-hours @ $36.00)			72
Total overhead applied using departmental rates			$708
Plantwide (10 hours @ $50)			$500

Productivity

Current Cost Management Practice

Motorola's defect-reduction program has helped earn it one of the finest reputations for quality in corporate America; this, in turn, is reflected in its high-earnings performance. Motorola's leaders fear that within a few years, rivals will have caught up and quality will have changed from a goal to a given. They plan to use responsiveness, adaptability, and creativity as their weapons against competition. To develop these attributes they are building a new campaign around lifelong learning. Motorola is dramatically increasing training for all employees for the purpose of having a workforce that is disciplined, yet free thinking. It dares to make such a large commitment in dollars for this initiative because its training to date has paid off.

Kevin Kelly, "Motorola: Training for the Millennium," *BusinessWeek,* March 28, 1994, pp. 158-63

Applied and Actual Factory Overhead

After a company decides whether it is using departmental or plantwide overhead application rates determined by either the direct (Exhibit 4–4), step (Exhibit 4–5), or linear algebra (Exhibit 4–6) method, it applies overhead to units produced. A **normal costing system** applies overhead on actual cost drivers. For example, for every machine-hour used in the Treating Department to finish a product, accountants apply factory overhead costs at $36.00 per machine-hour if using the step method. To have proper matching of actual overhead with applied overhead, we must apply factory overhead to all jobs (both complete and incomplete) worked on during the period. Note we do not enter budgeted factory overhead for a producing department (i.e., $162,000 for the Treating Department using the step method) in the journal or ledger because we use it for determining the application rate. A predetermined overhead rate usually stays the same throughout the year. During the time we apply overhead using estimated rates, we debit actual overhead to each service and producing department's Factory Overhead Control account.

Allocating Actual Service Department Variable and Fixed Costs

Dividing the budgeted variable service department costs by the budgeted units of service actually required yields the budgeted variable service department rate. For example, Materials Handling's budgeted variable cost is $17,240 (from Exhibit 4–4 or 4–5) and its budgeted cost driver is $130,500 materials requested (from Exhibit 4–3). The resulting variable cost rate is 13 percent per dollar of materials requested. Variable service department costs should be allocated based on the number of units of service provided. Since it is the responsibility of Materials Handling to control their costs, user departments' allocated actual variable costs are calculated as 13 percent multiplied by each department's actual dollars of materials requested. If Materials Handling's actual variable rate differs from the 13 percent budgeted rate, they must absorb it. By using a budgeted rate instead of the actual rate of variable service department costs, we do not distribute service department inefficiencies to other departments that cannot control them.

Actual fixed service department costs are not allocated to user departments. Instead, accountants allocate budgeted fixed costs on a predetermined, lump-sum basis. The basis used should reflect the long-run needs of the cost centers serviced, since such needs were given consideration when the company organized the service department and selected its capacity. A company should use the percentages of capacity provided for each department served as the basis for allocation. User departments should have to pay only for the budgeted fixed costs agreed to when developing the predetermined overhead rate. For example, in Exhibit 4–4 and 4–5, Materials Handling's budgeted fixed overhead is $26,260. If their actual fixed overhead at year-end totals $27,000, only $26,260 is distributed to user departments. The $740 difference between Materials Handling's actual fixed overhead and budgeted fixed overhead should remain with Materials Handling as part of their spending variance.

Spending and Volume Variances

Two variances—spending and volume—represent over- or underapplied overhead. Exhibit 4–8 contains the computation of the spending and volume variances for the Treating Department. The total of the spending variance and the volume variance equals the over- or underapplied overhead. We use the **cost estimating formula** introduced in Chapter 3 to determine a budget adjusted to actual capacity.

A **spending variance** (also called a **budget variance**) is due to incurring higher or lower costs on overhead items than originally estimated. Any time actual overhead exceeds budgeted overhead adjusted to actual capacity, the spending variance is unfavorable. Conversely, a favorable spending variance results when the actual overhead is less than the budgeted overhead for the actual capacity attained.

A **volume variance** (also called the **idle capacity variance**) is due to activity or volume factors. If actual production-hours exceed the planned or budgeted hours, the volume variance is favorable. On the other hand, idle capacity hours indicate the company used less volume than planned, and the volume variance is unfavorable. After computing the variances, accountants should determine the cause of any significant variance.

For simplicity, Exhibits 4–4 through 4–6 did not calculate a variable and fixed overhead rate. Calculating spending and volume variances requires computing variable and fixed overhead application rates using the same approach as presented for total overhead. Exhibit 4–8 illustrates the computation of these variances, assuming the Treating Department incurred 4,400 actual machine-hours and $164,149 actual factory overhead (which includes its share of service departments).

EXHIBIT 4–8   Spending and Volume Variances

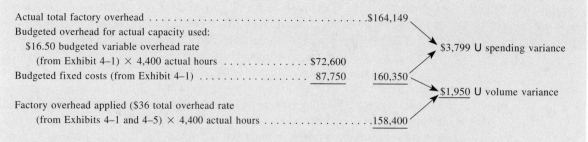

Actual total factory overhead $164,149

Budgeted overhead for actual capacity used:

$16.50 budgeted variable overhead rate

(from Exhibit 4–1) × 4,400 actual hours .... $72,600 $3,799 U spending variance

Budgeted fixed costs (from Exhibit 4–1) 87,750   160,350

$1,950 U volume variance

Factory overhead applied ($36 total overhead rate

(from Exhibits 4–1 and 4–5) × 4,400 actual hours 158,400

Total variance which is the difference between $164,149 actual and $158,400 applied overhead $5,749

The volume variance can also be computed by comparing budgeted capacity to actual capacity and multiplying by the budgeted fixed overhead rate: [4,500 budgeted hours (from Exhibits 4–1 and 4–5) − 4,400 actual hours] × $19.50 budgeted fixed overhead rate = $1,950 unfavorable volume variance

---

Spending and volume variances may be set up in ledger accounts as follows:

Total Overhead Spending Variance	3,799	
Overhead Volume Variance	1,950	
Factory Overhead Control—Treating Department .		5,749

An alternative treatment is to not establish ledger accounts for the variances and still receive the same benefit from the analysis as to their cause. This analysis is the important factor—not whether accountants journalize variances. We must close out the Factory Overhead Control account balance at the end of the accounting period.

Disposition of Over- or Underapplied Overhead

Accountants may have transferred any over- or underapplied overhead amount into spending and volume variances (in a journal entry similar to the preceding one). The variances are then (1) treated as a period cost and charged to Cost of Goods Sold or directly to Income Summary or (2) prorated to Work in Process Inventory, Finished Goods Inventory, and Cost of Goods Sold. Chapter 13 illustrates the proration.

If spending and volume variances recorded in ledger accounts are not material, accountants record the following entry using the data previously illustrated:

Cost of Goods Sold.........................	5,749	
Total Overhead Spending Variance		3,799
Overhead Volume Variance................		1,950

If, instead, the variances are not recorded in separate accounts, the entry becomes:

Cost of Goods Sold.........................	5,749	
Factory Overhead Control—Treating Department .		5,749

This entry closes out the Factory Overhead Control-Treating Department ledger account.

Summary

Before calculating factory overhead application rates, management decides which capacity level to adopt by weighing the practicability of the approach against setting a high level so that the fixed overhead per product unit is reduced. Because the product unit is routed only through production departments, accountants often establish estimated factory overhead rates only for production departments. They allocate the overhead costs of service departments in which no direct production work is performed to production departments.

After allocating all estimated factory costs to production departments, accountants determine the factory overhead application rate which they use throughout the period. At the end of the period, the difference between actual factory overhead and applied factory overhead reflects the over- or underapplied amount that can be further analyzed as spending and volume variances. Variance analysis provides a springboard for discovering the cause of differences between budgeted and actual costs and for achieving better control of factory overhead costs.

Important Terms and Concepts

Cost allocations, assignments, distributions, and apportionments   92
Idle capacity   92
Excess capacity   92
Theoretical (maximum or ideal) capacity   92
Practical capacity   92
Normal capacity   93
Expected actual capacity   93
Denominator capacity   93
Production (operating) departments   94
Service departments   94

Direct costs   94
Indirect or common costs   95
Direct method of allocation   97
Step (sequential, or step-down) method of allocation   97
Linear algebra (reciprocal) allocation method   97
Normal costing system   104
Cost estimating formula   105
Spending (budget) variance   105
Volume (idle capacity) variance   105

Problem for Self-Study

Developing Application Rates Using Linear Algebra (Reciprocal) Method
Direct and indirect departmental overhead budgets for the production and service departments of John Company are as follows:

Building Repairs	$ 87,000
Personnel Administration	99,000
Tooling	333,000
Fabricating	392,000
	$911,000

The following factory statistics are necessary to determine the percentage of service received from each service department. Number of repair-hours is used to allocate the building repairs department cost while number of employees is used for allocating Personnel Administration.

Departments	Repair Hours	Number of Employees	Machine-Hours
Building Repairs	12	6,640	—
Personnel Administration	96	1,115	—
Tooling.	264	10,624	27,925
Fabricating	240	15,936	19,685
	612	34,315	47,610

Required:

Using linear algebra, determine the overhead application rate per machine-hour. Round the application rate to the nearest dollar.

Solution to Problem for Self-Study

JOHN COMPANY

The departments receive the following percentages of service:

Department Rendering Service	Building Repair	Personnel Administration	Tooling	Fabricating
Maintenance	—	16% $\frac{96}{600}$	44% $\frac{264}{600}$	40% $\frac{240}{600}$
Administration	20% $\frac{6,640}{33,200}$	—	32% $\frac{10,624}{33,200}$	48% $\frac{15,936}{33,200}$

Let BR = Total costs of Building Repairs Department
P = Total costs of Personnel Administration Department
$BR = \$87,000 + .20P$
$P = \$99,000 + .16BR$
Substituting $BR = \$87,000 + .20(\$99,000 + .16BR)$
$BR = \$87,000 + \$19,800 + .032BR$
$.968BR = \$106,800$
$BR = \$110,331$
Substituting $P = \$99,000 + .16(\$110,331)$
$P = \$99,000 + \$17,653$
$P = \$116,653$

	Service		**Production**		
	Building Repairs	Personnel Administration	Tooling	Fabricating	Total
Department overhead	$87,000	$99,000	$333,000	$392,000	$911,000
Building Repair	(110,331)	17,653	48,546	44,132	
			(16% × $110,331)	(44% × $110,331)	(40% × $110,331)
Personnel Administration	23,331	(116,653)	37,329	55,993	
	(20% × $116,653)		(32% × $116,653)	(48% × $116,653)	
Estimated Production Department Overhead			$418,875	$492,125	$911,000
Base: Machine-hour			27,925	19,685	
Rate per machine-hour			$15	$25	

Review Questions

1. Distinguish between production and service departments and give examples of each type.
2. Contrast idle capacity and excess capacity.
3. Distinguish between direct and indirect costs and give examples of each.
4. *a.* What is the normal criteria for selecting the fair basis of cost allocation?
   b. If the criteria or relationship you indicated cannot be identified, how should cost elements be allocated?
5. If a company uses cost-plus contracts extensively in a business that is seasonal or cyclical, what capacity level would be most appropriate? Why is it necessary to specify the activity level at which managers budget operations?
6. What factors would you consider in determining whether to adopt department rates for applying factory overhead rather than using a single plantwide rate?
7. In interviewing several manufacturing firms operating in the same industry, you find that Company A's factory overhead application rate is $2 per direct labor-hour while Company B's rate is $2.50 per direct labor-hour. Can you conclude that Company A is more efficient? Why or why not?
8. Distinguish between spending and volume variances. How is each computed?
9. What factors could cause a company to have both unfavorable spending and volume variances?
10. During interviews you determine that Company C has a favorable volume variance, while Company D, which is of like size and operations, has an unfavorable volume variance. In stating the cause of the idle capacity variance, can you conclude that Company C is more efficient? Explain why or why not.

Exercises

E4–1 Volume and Spending Variances
A cost accountant estimates that next year's normal capacity for the Susan Douglass Company will be 40,000 machine-hours. At this level, managers estimate fixed costs at $140,000 with variable costs of $90,000. There were 41,000 actual machine-hours for the year ended February 28, 19X1, and total costs were $232,500.

Required:
   a. What is the fixed overhead rate at normal capacity?
   b. What is the total overhead rate used to apply factory overhead during the year?
   c. What is the amount of over- or underapplied factory overhead?
   d. Compute the volume variance and the spending variance for the year. Are they favorable or unfavorable? Prove your answer.

E4–2 Allocation of Indirect Cost
The details pertaining to the Utilities Department of Sun, Inc., are as follows:

Schedule of Kilowatt Hours

	Service Departments		Producing Departments		
	Repair	*Personnel*	*Mixing*	*Finishing*	*Total*
Needed at capacity production ...	19,800	25,200	18,000	27,000	90,000
Used during May	20,240	22,000	17,600	28,160	88,000

During the month of May the expense of operating the Utilities Department amounted to $17,400; of this amount $6,000 was considered to be fixed costs.

Required:

    a. What dollar amounts of the Utilities Department expense should be allocated to each producing and service department if fixed costs are allocated according to volume at capacity production and the variable costs according to actual usage?

    b. What are the reasons for allocating the costs of one service department to other service departments as well as to producing departments?

Writing

E4–3 Service Department Cost Allocation and Overhead Application Theory
Regarding the allocation of overhead,

    a. Discuss the theoretical merit of three different methods of allocating service department costs to production departments.

    b. Distinguish between direct and indirect costs and their relationship in determining overhead application rates for production departments.

    c. Discuss three different capacity approaches to use in estimating factory overhead and when (if ever) each would be appropriate.

    d. Give three different bases that are appropriate for use with a predetermined annual factory overhead rate and the objectives and criteria a company should use in selecting each of these bases.

E4–4 Spending and Volume Variances
Brown Company's budget formula is $93,000 fixed overhead plus a variable rate of $5 per machine-hour, yielding a total application rate of $8. Actual machine-hours for the period were 31,800; actual factory overhead of $254,800 was reported.

Required:

Determine the spending and volume variances.

E4–5 Developing Application Rates Using Linear Algebra (Reciprocal) Method
Overhead budgets for the production and service departments of Lynn Company are as follows:

Maintenance	$ 75,000
General Factory Administration	92,000
Tooling	325,000
Processing	380,000
	$872,000

Accountants use the following factory statistics in determining the percentage of service received from each service department. The company uses the number of repair-hours to allocate the Maintenance Department cost and the number of employees for allocating General Factory Administration.

Departments	Repair Hours	Employees	Machine-Hours
Maintenance	10	6,480	
General Factory Administration	75	1,000	
Tooling	225	24,840	20,640
Processing	200	22,680	19,965
	510	55,000	40,605

Required:

Determine the overhead application rate per machine-hour using the linear algebra method.

E4–6 High-Low, Application Rates, and Variances

Jasper, Inc., uses machine-hours to apply factory overhead with an operating range between 1,000 and 6,000 hours per month. A normal capacity of 4,000 hours will be used for applying factory overhead. Fixed costs per month amount to $24,000 while the strictly variable factory overhead costs total $3 per hour. In addition, semivariable factory overhead cost for 6,000 machine-hours total $32,000, while those for 1,000 hours are budgeted to be $20,000.

Required:

a. Separate the semivariable costs into their fixed and variable components using the high-low method.
b. Compute the fixed and variable factory overhead application rates.
c. Determine spending and volume variances for a month in which 5,000 hours were worked and actual factory overhead totaled $70,400. Prove your answer.
d. Calculate a bid price for a customer who approached you during the month when machine-hour capacity was 5,000. How much should be allowed for factory overhead if this special order requires 250 machine-hours?

E4–7 Writing Assignment Concerning Overhead

Writing

Because you are a CPA with an excellent reputation in the city, Hammermill Company asks your advice concerning the assignment of overhead in its production process. The company manufactures a line of bathroom fixtures that includes pedestal sinks and drop-in sinks of vitreous china. Hammermill also produces solid brass bath fixtures. Business operations are subject to wide cyclical fluctuations because the sales volume follows new housing construction. Production personnel normally complete about 50 percent of their manufacturing in the last quarter of the calendar year to be ready to meet the heavy spring construction demand.

In addition to those fluctuations, material costs vary widely as a percentage of total factory cost because the company uses various combinations of brass, marble powder, and polyester resin. For example, the material cost of a specific item ranges from 20 to 65 percent of total inventoriable cost.

Hammermill's labor-intensive processing uses five departments. Even though all products use each of the departments, they are not used proportionately. Each department uses different labor skills. The plant wage rate ranges from $6 to $10.50 an hour. However, within each of the five individual departments, the spread between the high and low wage rate is less than 4 percent. Factory overhead ranges from 35 to 80 percent of conversion cost within each department.

Management specifically asks that you study the cost system with reference to these issues concerning overhead:

1. Using department overhead rate or plantwide rate.
2. Basing overhead rates on normal capacity or expected actual capacity.
3. Distributing factory overhead on direct labor-hour, direct labor cost, or material cost.

Required:

Write a memorandum to top management of Hammermill Company stating your position regarding the three different issues in question. Include reasons supporting your recommendations.

E4–8 Departmental and Plantwide Overhead Rates

Satterfield Manufacturing Company is undecided whether to adopt departmental factory overhead application rates for its Sewing and Treating departments or whether a plantwide rate would be adequate. You advise them to give you budgeted overhead for each department and data for one job so both approaches can be evaluated. They extract the following data from their records:

	Departments	
	Sewing	*Treating*
Supplies.	$ 600	$ 400
Superintendent's salaries	1,000	1,500
Indirect labor	1,500	4,900
Depreciation.	800	5,000
Repairs	4,100	3,000
Insurance	700	800
	$8,700	$15,600
Total direct labor-hours	400	520
Direct labor-hours on Job No. 414 .	10	2

Required:

a. Prepare departmental and a plantwide overhead rates. Then apply overhead to Job No. 414 using both approaches.

b. Evaluate the approaches indicating which you prefer.

Problems

P4–9 Effect of Capacity on Application Rate

Stal Company prepared the following information for 19X1 representing two different volumes:

	Percent of Capacity	
	70 Percent	*85 Percent*
Machine-hours	28,000	34,000
Variable factory overhead	$110,600	$134,300
Fixed factory overhead	$119,000	$119,000
Total factory overhead rate per machine-hour.	$ 8.20	$ 7.45

Factory overhead was applied based on the 85 percent capacity level; however, 28,000 machine-hours were used for the period.

Required:

a. Account for the difference in factory overhead rates between the two capacity levels.

b. If actual factory overhead were equal to the budgeted amount for the attained capacity, what is the total overhead variance for the year and what kind of variance is it?

P4–10 Cost Estimating Formula, Application Rates, Variances

Burton Company presents you with the following monthly factory overhead budgets that were prepared at the beginning of the year.

	Machine-Hours	
	50,000	*60,000*
Supplies.	$120,000	$144,000
Indirect labor	67,500	81,000
Utilities	162,500	195,000
Supervision salaries	10,000	10,000
Depreciation.	9,000	9,000
Insurance	8,000	8,000
Property taxes.	15,000	15,000
Total	$392,000	$462,000

At the end of the month, analysis of the cost records reveal that the following factory overhead was incurred in operating at 58,000 machine-hours:

Supplies	$136,000
Indirect labor	80,000
Utilities	190,000
Supervision salaries	10,200
Depreciation	8,880
Insurance	7,600
Property taxes	14,700
Total	$447,380

Required:

   a. Compute the cost estimating formula.

   b. Determine the factory overhead application rate using an estimated capacity of 60,000 hours.

   c. Determine variances for each of the factory overhead items, indicating whether they are favorable or unfavorable.

P4–11 Journal Entries to Record Spending and Volume Variances

Danden Manufacturing Company provides the following data concerning its operations for the year ended December 31, 19X1:

Estimated variable overhead rate per machine-hour	$2.50
Estimated total overhead rate per machine-hour	$6.00
Budgeted capacity	15,000 machine-hours
Actual capacity during year	15,200 machine-hours
Actual factory overhead costs	$96,000

Required:

   a. Compute the amount of overhead applied during the year and prepare the summary journal entry required to record this on the books.

   b. Determine the amount of the over- or underapplied overhead.

   c. Compute the factory overhead spending and volume variances.

   d. Prepare the journal entries required to journalize the variances and to close the Factory Overhead Control account; close variance to the Cost of Goods Sold account.

SPATS

P4–12 Step Method Use in Service Industry

Memorial Hospital consists of several revenue and nonrevenue centers. In determining the cost of each revenue center, accountants use the step method to allocate the direct cost of nonrevenue centers. The following information is available for a month:

	Direct Costs	Number of Employees	Square Footage	Pounds of Laundry	Order of Allocation
Nonrevenue cost centers:					
Personnel	$ 12,000	6	800	0	1
Housekeeping	50,875	40	900	1,210	2
Laundry	370,000	18	200	140	3
Revenue cost centers:					
Radiology	$1,400,000	20	1,000	1,350	
Pharmacy	1,000,000	10	400	50	
Physical Therapy	800,000	17	1,250	1,000	
Surgical unit	200,000	45	2,400	3,450	

Distribute nonrevenue cost centers in this order for these bases: Personnel's cost is allocated on the number of employees; Housekeeping, on square footage; and Laundry, on pounds of laundry.

Required:

Use the step method to allocate the costs of the nonrevenue cost centers to the revenue cost centers. Then arrive at application rates based on the following: Radiology—29,961 estimated patients served; Pharmacy—112,012 prescriptions filled; Physical Therapy—58,536 estimated patients served; and Surgical unit—22,422 patient days. Round to whole dollars in arriving at producing department's application rates.

SPATS

P4–13 Step and Direct Methods for Developing Overhead Rates

The producing departments at Lisa Lewis Company are Parts Fabrication and Assembly. The three service departments are Building, Administration, and Engineering. Building maintains the plant facilities and the grounds. Administration is responsible for the scheduling, control, and accounting functions, while engineering plans and designs parts and procedures. Following are the annual budgets of direct charges and the budgeted operating data for all the departments.

	Building	Administration	Engineering	Parts Fabrication	Assembly	Total
Direct cost:						
Indirect labor	$400	$600	$280	$1,000	$ 800	$3,080
Indirect materials	60	130	100	400	250	940
Indirect cost:						
Insurance	70	40	20	200	125	455
Depreciation	250	85	50	140	100	625
Total departmental costs	$780	$855	$450	$1,740	$1,275	$5,100
Floor space (sq. ft.)	150	200	100	600	400	1,450
Number of employees	15	25	10	200	115	365
Engineering-hours	15	10	5	100	80	210

Required:

    a. Allocate the costs of the service departments using the step method. First, allocate Building based on floor space; next, Administration based on number of employees; and finally, Engineering based on engineering-hours. Calculate factory overhead allocation rates using 800 estimated machine-hours for Parts Fabrication and 600 estimated machine-hours for Assembly.

    b. Compute an overhead allocation rate per service unit using the direct method which charges no service department for services provided by other service departments. Calculate factory overhead allocation rates using the same machine-hours as in Requirement *a.*

P4–14 Developing Application Rates Using the Linear Algebra (Reciprocal) Method

Princeton Company has prepared overhead budgets for the production and service departments (before allocation) as follows:

Employee Fitness	$ 20,000
Repair	60,000
Mixing	241,733
Finishing	220,892
	$542,625

Accountants use the following data to determine the percentage of service received from each service department. The company uses the number of employees for allocating Employee Fitness Department costs and square footage for the Repair Department.

Departments	Employees	Square Footage	Direct Labor Dollars
Employee Fitness	18	5,000	
Repair	175	2,000	
Mixing	280	15,000	$ 824,000
Finishing	245	30,000	600,500
	718	52,000	$1,424,500

Required:

(Round to whole dollars.)

    Using linear algebra, determine the overhead application rates for the production departments per direct labor dollar.

P 4–15 Plant Capacity Concepts

Writing

Olive Branch Manufacturing Company produces a ball valve used in water systems. The company has selected normal capacity for estimating costs and for establishing the factory overhead application rate. For the December 31, 19X3, year just ended, the plant operated at only 90 percent of normal capacity. As a result, there is underapplied overhead for the year.

    Olive Branch typically sells its valves for $160 each. However, at the beginning of 19X4, the firm received a one-time order for 1,000 units conditional on a unit sales price of $120. The controller is advocating that management accept the order. He mentions two factors influencing his recommendation: First, the total unit manufacturing cost of $130 is composed of $100 variable costs and $30 fixed costs. Second, the additional units can be manufactured within the company's normal capacity.

Required:

   a. Discuss the following capacity concepts:
     (1) Theoretical capacity.
     (2) Practical capacity.
     (3) Normal capacity.
     (4) Expected actual capacity.
   b. Discuss the financial aspects that should be analyzed before deciding whether or not to accept the order.
   c. Discuss the reason that the Factory Overhead Control account will probably reflect overapplied overhead for 19X4 if the order is accepted. Explain the disposition of any overapplied overhead.

Critical Thought

P 4–16 Explanation of Underabsorption of Overhead

The Brian Wilson Company is engaged in production of machinery; its accountant has applied factory overhead to its product on the basis of an average rate of 80 percent of direct labor cost. At the time it was established, this rate was based on the following information as to expected operations:

Direct labor-hours		150,000
Direct labor cost		$1,800,000
Average labor rate per hour		$ 12
Fixed overhead	$540,000	
Variable overhead	900,000	
Total overhead		$1,440,000

At the end of the first accounting period, the records disclosed the following information:

Direct labor-hours		148,000
Direct labor cost		$1,805,600
Average labor rate per hour		$ 12.20
Fixed overhead	$585,000	
Variable overhead	930,000	
Total actual overhead		$1,515,000
Underabsorbed overhead		$ 70,520

Management is concerned that the company failed to absorb overhead of $70,520 in the year's operations.

Required:

   a. Prepare an explanation for management showing why the $70,520 underabsorption existed. You are to compute and show the effect of variation in direct labor rates and direct labor-hours on the absorption of overhead.
   b. Evaluate the system currently being used to absorb overhead.

P 4–17 Developing Application Rates Using the Direct Method, Step Method, and Linear Algebra

Billy Long Company has departmentalized its operations into two service departments, General Factory Office and Employee Relations, and three production departments, Mixing, Fabricating, and Finishing. For the year ending December 31, the firm budgeted the following direct costs:

	General Factory Office	Employee Relations	Mixing	Fabricating	Finishing
Salaries and wages	$40,000	$70,000	$180,000	$210,000	$250,000
Depreciation	2,000	4,000	35,000	40,000	50,000
Supplies expense	1,000	5,000	18,000	16,000	20,000
	$43,000	$79,000	$233,000	$266,000	$320,000

→ *total indirect costs:* $9,900 $9,350 $43,100 $31,256 $36,900

The company estimates that indirect costs will be insurance expense, $32,200; rent, $49,000; and heating and lighting expense, $48,600. It will use the following bases to allocate indirect expenses:

1. Insurance expenses on the basis of equipment book values. The book value of the equipment in the departments is General Factory Office, $20,000; Employee Relations, $25,000; Mixing $130,000; Fabricating, $175,000; and Finishing, $110,000.

2. Rent expense on the basis of the amount and value of space occupied. The General Factory Office and the Mixing Department occupy space that is not as valuable because the rooms have no windows. Management believes that $20,000 of the rent expense should be allocated to these two departments in proportion to the space occupied and the balance to the remaining departments in proportion to the space occupied. The following amounts of space are occupied by the five departments; General Factory Office, 1,000 square feet; Employee Relations, 800 square feet; Mixing, 4,000 square feet; Fabricating, 2,000 square feet; and Finishing, 3,000 square feet.

3. Heating and lighting expense on the basis of floor space occupied.

General Factory Office is allocated first on the basis of labor-hours, and Employee Relations is allocated second on the basis of number of employees. The company provides the following estimated data for use in this allocation:

	General Factory Office	Employee Relations	Mixing	Fabricating	Finishing
Labor-hours	10,000	12,000	23,200	25,600	19,200
Number of employees	60	30	144	228	168
Machine-hours			63,540	105,800	85,725

Required:

a. Using the direct method, prepare departmental overhead expense allocations. Develop overhead rates per machine-hour.

b. Using the step method, prepare the same analysis as in Requirement *a*.

c. Using linear algebra, determine the application rate per machine-hour.

P 4–18 Calculating Volume Variances Using Practical, Normal, and Expected Actual Basis

The president of Oliphant Company has approached you for assistance in developing factory overhead application rates. Oliphant Company has been distributing actual factory overhead at the end of each month on the basis of direct labor-hours.

As a result, the hourly rate varies considerably and is of limited use in estimating prices for bidding purposes. Management believes that it is especially important to change methods before introducing a new product line.

Management and the cost accountant cannot agree on what capacity should be selected for applying factory overhead. However, they do all agree that machine-hours would be a better basis than direct labor-hours since 10 new machines have been purchased recently to highly automate the factory. Each machine costs $40,000 and is expected to produce 12 completed units per hour. Because of rapid technology in the field, the machines have an expected life of eight years at which time their salvage value is forecasted to equal the dismantling cost. Depreciation will be computed using the straight-line method. Based on engineering studies, practical capacity for each machine for each year is 2,200 hours.

The marketing department does not believe that it can sell enough the first year to allow each machine to operate at 2,200 hours. They believe that only 216,000 units can be sold the first year, with an average of 252,000 units in later years. The cost accountant believes that this average of 252,000 units should be used as normal capacity; however, the marketing manager disagrees, believing expected actual capacity of 216,000 units should be used instead. On the other hand, the president believes practical capacity should be the basis.

Estimated factory overhead is: variable costs—$5 per machine-hour; fixed costs excluding depreciation—$ 64,300 per year.

Required:

    a. Calculate fixed and variable factory overhead rates per machine-hour on a practical, normal, and expected actual basis. Round to two decimal places.

    b. Assuming that 216,000 units are produced next year and each machine produces 12 units per hour, determine the factory overhead applied and the volume variance under each of the three bases used in Requirement *a.*

    c. Based on your findings, which basis would you advise the company to use? Explain your answer by discussing the advantages and disadvantages of the methods available.

CHAPTER 5

Activity-Based Cost Systems and Strategic Cost Analysis

Chapter Objectives

After studying this chapter, you should be able to:

1. Determine when it is more appropriate to use nonvolume-based cost drivers than volume-based cost drivers.
2. Assign costs using activity-based costing with volume- and nonvolume-related cost drivers.
3. Apply materials acquisition and handling costs.
4. Use strategic cost analysis, product life-cycle costing, and theory of constraints to distinguish between value-added and nonvalue-added activities.

Service

Current Cost Management Practice

With the breakup of AT&T into smaller, more focused business units and the advent of price-cap regulation instead of the predefined return on investment regulation, its focus changed from allocating costs to managing. Since the company's business units compete in an open market, managers need accurate cost and profit information by service. Business managers are held accountable for profit, market share, and customer satisfaction within a smaller, more focused market. Previously, allocation of cost occurred most frequently on convenient, high-level volume drivers. Costs were not allocated according to service, customer segment, or actual activity being performed. Even though a new accounting system was developed, they still did not have a process that provided business unit managers with the ability to manage the cost of cost centers that allocated significant expenses to their income statements. A fact-based process identifying activities, activity cost drivers, and value added was missing. The process did not analyze the value of the activities that drove the cost. To remedy this problem, AT&T introduced ABC using a multi-stage cost driver analysis identifying drivers as activity, process, or resource related. Process modeling traced costs to outputs. After implementing ABC, benchmarking has ensured continued improvements.

Terrence Hobdy, Jeff Thomson, and Paul Sharman, "Activity-Based Management at AT&T," *Management Accounting*, April 1994, pp. 35-39.

Introduction

Developments in manufacturing and marketing, such as just-in-time manufacturing and increased emphasis on customer satisfaction, are exposing the deficiencies of conventional accounting performance measures. Traditionally, accountants considered volume-related cost drivers, such as machine-hours and units sold, as the only factors that caused activities and costs to occur. They used volume-related cost drivers to apply overhead from cost pools to products.

In addition to these changes in production operations, managers are questioning the appropriateness of cost behavior models using fixed and variable costs. These events lead to the introduction of **activity-based costing** (ABC). ABC (also called **transaction-based costing)** attempts to improve the accuracy of product and service costs by recognizing that some costs are more appropriately assigned on nonvolume bases. Instead of focusing on cost objects as does conventional costing, ABC recognizes the great diversity in activities performed. ABC reflects costs consumption by identifying drivers that can occur at multiple levels within an organization.

Activity-Based Costing

Rather than apply factory overhead costs to products based on departmental overhead rates as illustrated in Exhibits 4–4 through 4–6 in Chapter 4, ABC recognizes that performance of activities triggers the consumption of resources that accountants record as costs. ABC reports the rate at which activities consume resources as well as why an organization uses resources.

As defined in Chapter 1, an *activity* is a process or procedure that causes work. Examples are moving parts, performing engineering change orders, setting up machines for a production run, and establishing vendor relations through contacting vendors and setting requirements for purchases. Also included are receiving, disbursing, reorganizing the production flow, redesigning a product, and taking a customer order. ABC traces costs to the activities identified.

Activities/ Transactions as Cost Drivers

The assumption that costs vary only with changes in production volume is correct for such unit-related activities as production supplies and parts. However, many costs in plants do not vary with the volume of production but with transactions. Every time companies perform activities, they generate **transactions.** Every movement of materials from inventory to the shop floor requires a materials requisition (a transaction). Transactions generate overhead costs in such activities as inspection, setup, or scheduling. For example, purchasing department cost is driven by the number of purchase orders processed. The information systems department cost is driven by the amount of bills, parts, and materials to track and handle; engineering department cost by the number of engineering change orders; and setup cost by the number of setups and hours required. Rather than use the actual duration of the activity such as setup machine hours, using the number of transactions generated by an activity is more effective.

Volume-Related and Nonvolume-Related Cost Drivers

Traditionally, accountants considered volume-related cost drivers as the only factors that caused activities and costs to occur. They used volume-related cost drivers to apply overhead from cost pools to products. **Volume-based** or **unit-based drivers** are allocation measures based on product attributes, such as labor-hours, machine-hours, and materials cost. For example, assume a product generates a demand for machine-hours. In this situation, machine-hours is the cost driver that causes a certain pool of costs to increase. Machine-hours then are appropriate to use in allocating the costs in that pool.

However, some allocations require nonunit-related bases because volume does not drive all overhead costs. Instead, the complexity and diversity of the manufacturing process is the driver. Accountants should use bases that reflect cost drivers when allocating cost pools to products. **Cost drivers** are the factors that cause activities to occur; they capture the demand placed on an activity by a product or service.

When some product-related activities are unrelated to the number of units manufactured, using only volume-based (unit-based) allocations distorts product costs. For example, applying overhead on labor-hours incorrectly implies that a reduction in direct labor results in corresponding reductions in receiving, production control, and purchasing. Automating a process or shortening a production run does not reduce the number of purchase orders placed, shipments received, or batches scheduled.

Nonunit-level activities, such as setting up the machines, ordering parts, transporting parts to and from the machines, machining the parts, and controlling the part numbers are unrelated to the size of a production run. For example, doubling the size of the batch may not require doubling the number of setups. Thus, a unit-level cost driver, such as direct labor costs or machine-hours illustrated in Exhibits 4–4 to 4–6 in Chapter 4, fails to capture the complexity of the relationships between volume, batch size, and order size.

Traditionally in labor-paced environments, the error from using only volume-related allocation bases in reported product costs was not significant. Accountants could ignore this problem because the percentage of nonvolume-related costs was much smaller than it is today in high-technology environments. However, in manufacturing processes with high percentages of nonvolume-related costs, cost systems using only volume-related allocation bases produce inaccurate product costs as this chapter illustrates when discussing product and volume diversity. Also, the error in reported product costs increases significantly if companies manufacture products in highly varied lot sizes.

Levels of Cost Drivers

ABC classifies costs as they vary according to unit, batch, product, technology, customer, and facility activities: **unit-level activities** occur every time workers produce a unit; **batch-level activities** occur every time workers produce a batch; **product-sustaining activities** enable the manufacture and sale of a product, **technology-sustaining activities** enable a technology to produce a product, such as machine maintenance; **customer-sustaining activities** service customers and prospects, such as delivering a product; and **facility-sustaining activities** enable production or servicing to occur, such as paying rent. Then ABC assigns costs of activities to products using both volume- and nonvolume-based drivers.

ABC recognizes that different activities cause costs to vary with the diversity and complexity of products. Some activity costs do not vary with the number of units produced. For example, if total work cell costs add value to the product, accountants should accumulate these costs at the work cell level. Chapter 2 defines a **work cell** as a product-oriented work center that includes the machines and tools necessary to efficiently produce a family of parts. Accountants distribute the costs of the cell to products according to the cell time a product takes within each cell. How fast the inventory moves through the cell is called **inventory velocity.** Accountants use inventory velocity as the basis for assigning overhead to products in this situation.

Drivers for Unit- and Batch-Level Activities.   Surfaces machined, number of insertions, and direct labor-hours are typical cost drivers for unit-level activities. An example of a batch-level activity is the manufacture of circuit boards for which customers have specified the number and sizes of holes in the boards. Engineers make specifications for a tooling machine to process the correct number and sizes of holes. Personnel do not perform this activity for each product unit; instead, the setup activity benefits the entire batch. Setup hours, number of setups, number of purchase orders, materials-handling hours, and number of times handled are additional examples of ABC drivers at the batch level.

Drivers for Product-Level Activities.   Correcting a defect in product design is an example of a product-level activity. Workers do not perform this engineering change activity on each unit; instead, the activity benefits the entire product line. Another example of a product-level activity is advertising a specific product line. Marketing personnel do not perform this activity for each product unit. Instead, the marketing activity benefits the entire product line. The number of components or dies, ordering hours, number of times ordered, and number of part numbers maintained are additional examples of drivers for product-level activities.

Value-Added versus Nonvalue-Added Activities

By specifying each activity, managers determine the cost drivers regulating each value activity. Managers compare the skills and resources the company uses to perform each activity. ABC helps focus on high-cost activities by identifying resources being consumed by each activity. This helps link the costs and the activities that cause those costs. Customers determine the value of these activities by the price they are willing to pay for the product or service. This process encourages managers to identify **value-added activities** and eliminate **nonvalue-added activities.**

Nonvalue-added costs, such as those incurred while workers wait until materials are brought to the floor or until machines are operating properly, represents the difference between the lowest possible life-cycle cost and actual costs incurred. The goal of continuous improvement requires the systematic and continuous elimination of waste. Waste includes people's time, materials, and capital not spent on activities that add value to the products or services required by the customer.

For example, accountants can prepare cost analyses illustrating that companies further enhance efficiency of operations by having a more versatile, flexible work force capable of moving to where the work is and/or completing setup and preventive maintenance assignments. If direct labor workers are capable of performing minor maintenance and setup jobs, higher-paid engineers can analyze product design, improve efficiency, or perform other more challenging duties. Workers should perform educational, setup, and preventive maintenance activities during slack times. Calculating the time workers wait each day and costing this time may lead to better production scheduling and a stimulus to increasing sales. Assigning managers the cost of their employees waiting for materials and machines to be ready for production may also encourage the transfer of workers between different production departments and product lines.

Benchmarking

Accountants often use benchmarking when determining which activities are value-added or nonvalue-added. **Benchmarking** is a process of comparing activities to world-class best practices. Managers compare activities to similar ones in another company or in a different department of their company. The objective is to identify the strengths and weaknesses of these products, processes, or services considered the best in the class. Then managers can imitate those ideas that are transferable. Benchmarking is a tool for continuous improvement because after identifying a best-practices activity, it becomes a target to beat. Merely copying practices from other companies, however, is insufficient unless the factor that resulted in success is first identified, whether it is effective training programs or empowering workers with relevant information.

Comparing ABC and Traditional Costing

Ignoring levels of cost drivers is serious if there is product diversity or volume diversity. **Product diversity** occurs when products consume activities and inputs in different proportions. As an example, product lines place different size, complexity, or material component demands on a firm's resources. Complex products may consume more nonunit-level inputs, such as machine setups, but not necessarily more machine hours or other unit-level inputs than less complex products. **Volume diversity** or **batch-size diversity** occurs when there is a difference in the number of units manufactured by product lines (i.e., companies manufacture products in different-size batches). Products having materials that take longer to machine may consume a disproportionate share of unit-level inputs; this is called **material diversity.**

Product Diversity   ABC does not include Materials Handling costs as a part of factory overhead and allocate it to producing departments, as illustrated in Exhibits 4–4 through 4–6. Instead, ABC arrives at an application rate per material move or some other transaction basis. The following illustration compares the conventional costing approach with the ABC method. Miscosting results if products are as diverse in their characteristics as are Products A and B.

	Product A	Product B
Units produced	10	10
Material moves per product line	3	7
Direct labor-hours per unit	435	435
Budgeted Materials Handling costs—$43,500		

Conventional costing yields the following application rate:

$$\frac{\$43,500 \text{ budgeted materials handling costs}}{(435 \times 10 \text{ Product A units}) + (435 \times 10 \text{ Product B units}) = 8,700 \text{ budgeted direct labor-hours}} =$$

$$\frac{\$43,500}{8,700} = \$5 \text{ application rate per direct labor-hour}$$

As shown in the following table, each unit of Product A and B absorbs the same amount of material handling costs even though Product B is a heavier user of this activity. Conventional costing fails to trace the large number of material moves for Product B.

	Product A	Product B
Total Material Handling costs applied to each product line	$21,750	$21,750
	($5 × 4,350 hrs.)	($5 × 4,350 hrs.)
Materials Handling costs per product unit	$2,175	$2,175
	($21,750 ÷ 10 units)	($21,750 ÷ 10 units)

Instead, ABC more accurately traces the cost drivers:

$$\frac{\$43,500 \text{ budgeted materials handling costs}}{10 \text{ budgeted material moves}} = \$4,350 \text{ application rate per material move}$$

	Product A	Product B
Total Materials Handling costs applied to each product line	$13,050	$30,450
	($4,350 × 3 moves)	($4,350 × 7 moves)
Materials Handling costs per product unit	$1,305	$3,045
	($13,050 ÷ 10 units)	($30,450 ÷ 10 units)

Product B requires more material moves and correctly receives more materials handling costs.

Product Diversity Further Illustrated.   Product diversity also is illustrated for Product C and Product D. Product C is a new undeveloped product with production and quality problems requiring many engineering changes. Product D is a more mature product and does not require as much engineering attention, which is a product-level activity.

	Product C	Product D
Units produced	400	400
Engineering change notices per product line	10	3
Unit cost per engineering change notice	$500	$500
Machine-hours per unit	2	3

A volume-based allocation yields the following application rate:

$$\frac{13 \text{ total change notices} \times \$500 \text{ unit cost} = \$6{,}500 \text{ budgeted engineering change costs}}{(2 \times 400 \text{ Product C units}) + (3 \times 400 \text{ Product D units}) = 2{,}000 \text{ budgeted machine-hours}} =$$

$$\frac{\$6{,}500}{2{,}000} = \$3.25 \text{ application rate per machine-hour}$$

	Product C	Product D
Total engineering change cost applied to each product line	$2,600	$3,900
	($3.25 × 800 hrs.)	($3.25 × 1,200 hrs.)
Engineering change cost per product unit	$6.50	$9.75
	($2,600 ÷ 400 units)	($3,900 ÷ 400 units)

Conventional costing indicates that Product C has a much lower cost per unit even though it consumes more than three times as much engineering change activity as Product D. A volume-based cost assignment fails to trace the high number of engineering changes for Product C. Because Product D accounts for more of the machine-hours, this product incorrectly absorbs more of the engineering costs. The result is a **cross-subsidy** in which one product absorbs costs that correctly belong to another product. Product C appears to cost less because this volume-based allocation averaged indirect costs.

If accountants use ABC, they trace the following costs according to engineering change notices that drive engineering costs:

	Product C	Product D
Total engineering change costs applied to each product line	$5,000	$1,500
	($500 × 10 eng. changes)	($500 × 3 eng. changes)
Engineering change costs per product unit	$12.50	$3.75
	($5,000 ÷ 400 units)	($1,500 ÷ 400 units)

Volume Diversity   The complexity of the product line and the special handling required for special low-volume products cause large amounts of overhead in modern multiproduct factories. Often the high-volume products, such as Product E, are subsidizing the low-volume specialty products, such as Product F.

	Product E	Product F
Units produced	1,000	100
Machine setup hours per product line	5	5
Machine hours per unit	2	2
Total budgeted machine setup-related cost—$8,800		

A traditional costing system uses the following application rate to allocate the machine setup-related cost to Products E and F:

$$\frac{\$8,800 \text{ budgeted machine setup cost}}{(2 \times 1,000 \text{ Product E units}) + (2 \times 100 \text{ Product F units}) = 2,200 \text{ budgeted machine-hours}} =$$

$$\frac{\$8,800}{2,200} = \$4 \text{ application rate per machine-hour}$$

	Product E	Product F
Total machine setup-related cost applied to each product line	$8,000	$800
	($4 × 2,000 hrs.)	($4 × 200 hrs.)
Machine setup-related cost per unit	$8	$8
	($8,000 ÷ 1,000 units)	($800 ÷ 100 units)

As a high-volume product, Product E consumes 10 times the machine-hours and subsequently receives 10 times the machine setup-related cost, even though it requires only five machine setups, as does Product F. Conventional costing overcosts Product E, the high-volume product, and undercosts Product F, the low-volume product. This results because the traditional cost system averages out product costs rather than reflecting volume-based differentials.

Specialty products, such as Product F, appear as high-profit items, even though they often are large losers. When allocating overhead across all products, inaccurate product costs result, hindering cost reduction and pricing strategies because management receives the wrong signals. For example, marketing managers may believe product proliferation is inexpensive and that low-volume, nonstandard products are no more costly than high-volume, standard products. Further, product engineers may believe that product design component proliferation is free. Engineers may incorrectly assume there is no cost penalty for using a variety of nonstandard parts and that standard and nonstandard parts cost the same.

When ABC is used, the cost driver is the number of setups:

$$\frac{\$8,800 \text{ budgeted machine setup cost}}{10 \text{ budgeted machine setup hours}} = \$880 \text{ application rate per machine setup-hour}$$

	Product E	Product F
Total machine setup-related cost applied to each product line	$4,400	$4,400
Machine setup-related cost per unit	$4.40	$44
	($4,400 ÷ 1,000 units)	($4,400 ÷ 100 units)

Each product line receives $4,400 machine setup-related cost because each line requires the same amount of engineering attention. However, more units of Product E share this total cost. Using ABC, accountants report the increased overhead that specialty products regularly incur rather than distort the cost picture through the traditional averaging effect.

Two-Stage Allocation Process

Both traditional and activity-based costing use a two-stage allocation process. We express the volume for the capacity level selected (i.e., theoretical, practical, normal, or expected actual capacity) in either volume-related (i.e., machine-hours, direct labor costs) or nonvolume-related cost drivers (i.e., setups or work cells). In the first stage, we assign costs to cost centers either through direct charges or some appropriate allocation basis such as floor space for rent. In the second stage of the following traditional volume-based system, we allocate costs to products using machine-hours or other bases that vary directly with the volume of products manufactured. In the second stage of an ABC system, we trace costs from activities to products based on the product's demand for these activities. This simplified example assumes only one production department with 84,000 budgeted machine-hours with these budgeted overhead costs and resulting application rate.

Machine depreciation and maintenance	$ 840,000
Receiving costs	418,600
Engineering costs	360,000
Machine setup costs	37,400
Inspection costs	192,000
	$1,848,000

Assume further that the company manufactures and sells three products with the following attributes:

	Product X	Product Y	Product Z	Total
Units produced and sold	28,000	18,000	6,000	
Unit direct material cost	$20	$15	$13	
Unit direct labor cost	$12	$14	$10	
Machine-hours required per unit	1.5	2	1	84,000
Number per product line:				
Receiving orders	16	40	200	256
Production orders	14	12	19	45
Production runs	4	8	22	34
Inspections	8	4	20	32

Know this →

EXHIBIT 5–1   Activity-Based Costing

The unit costs for the three products using ABC are

	Product X	Product Y	Product Z
Unit direct materials cost	$20.00	$15.00	$13.00
Unit direct labor cost	12.00	14.00	10.00
Machine-related overhead[a]	15.00	20.00	10.00
Receiving costs[b]	0.93	3.63	54.50
Engineering costs[c]	4.00	5.33	25.33
Machine setup costs[d]	0.16	0.49	4.03
Inspection costs[e]	1.71	1.33	20.00
Total	$53.80	$59.78	$136.86

a $$\frac{\$840,000 \text{ machine depreciation and maintenance}}{84,000 \text{ machine-hours}} = \$10 \text{ rate per machine-hour}$$

b $$\frac{\$418,600 \text{ receiving cost}}{256 \text{ number of receiving orders}} = \$1,635 \text{ rate per receiving order}$$

Product X: ($1,635 × 16) ÷ 28,000 units = $0.93
Product Y: ($1,635 × 40) ÷ 18,000 units = $3.63
Product Z: ($1,635 × 200) ÷ 6,000 units = $54.50

c $$\frac{\$360,000 \text{ engineering cost}}{45 \text{ number of production orders}} = \$8,000 \text{ rate per production order}$$

Product X: ($8,000 × 14) ÷ 28,000 units = $4.00
Product Y: ($8,000 × 12) ÷ 18,000 units = $5.33
Product Z: ($8,000 × 19) ÷ 6,000 units = $25.33

d $$\frac{\$37,400 \text{ machine setup cost}}{34 \text{ number of production runs}} = \$1,100 \text{ rate per production run}$$

Product X: ($1,100 × 4) ÷ 28,000 units = $0.16
Product Y: ($1,100 × 8) ÷ 18,000 units = $0.49
Product Z: ($1,100 × 22) ÷ 6,000 units = $4.03

e $$\frac{\$192,000 \text{ inspection cost}}{32 \text{ inspections}} = \$6,000 \text{ rate per inspection}$$

Product X: ($6,000 × 8) ÷ 28,000 units = $1.71
Product Y: ($6,000 × 4) ÷ 18,000 units = $1.33
Product Z: ($6,000 × 20) ÷ 6,000 units = $20.00

★ Using traditional costing:

Pohr = $$\frac{\$1,848,000 \text{ budgeted overhead cost}}{84,000 \text{ budgeted machine-hours}} = \$22 \text{ application rate per machine-hour}$$

	Material	Labor	Overhead

Product X costs: $20 + $12 + (1.5 hrs. × $22 = $33) = $65
Product Y costs: $15 + $14 + (2 hrs. × $22 = $44) = $73
Product Z costs: $13 + $10 + (1 hr. × $22 = $22) = $45

Productivity

Current Cost Management Practice

Previously Pennsylvania Blue Shield supported its complex decisions by making lengthy studies to gather extensive costs data. It followed the prescribed methods of financial recording and reporting as recommended by the Blue Cross Blue Shield Association. While this allocation methodology was adequate for product pricing, it failed to provide the level of information necessary for management decisions. In adopting ABC to provide this data, managers followed these steps:

1. Planning—identify company's critical issues, management's difficult decisions, corporate culture, and current approach to financial management.
2. Resolving issues—convince managers in this conservative culture that ABC is a win/win situation.
3. Training—show workers how ABC methodology differs from the traditional cost allocation system.
4. Procedural documentation—identify activities in various types of departments.
5. Expense analysis—distribute expenses to activity centers.
6. Collect first-stage drivers—align indirect expenses from the activity centers to activity pools using first-stage drivers.
7. Collect second-stage drivers—use specific measures such as volumes of claims or inquiries to assign activity cost to a product.
8. Automate the process.
9. Management training—educate management as to the many uses of the ABC data and how to play an interactive role in the process.

Angela Norkiewicz, "Nine Steps to Implementing ABC," *Management Accounting,* April 1994, pp. 28-33.

If, instead, we use activity-based costing, we allocate $840,000 equipment depreciation and maintenance on machine-hours, a volume-related cost driver, because these costs are volume driven. Costs of the other activities are transaction driven. We assign them on the nonvolume-related cost drivers indicated in Exhibit 5–1.

The following summary shows product costs for X, Y, and Z according to the two methods. It illustrates the distorted product costs that result under conventional costing by overcosting Products X and Y and undercosting Product Z, the low-volume product. This results because Product Z creates more transactions per unit of output than Products X and Y. This further illustrates that conventional costing systems are simplistic because they only consider volume- or unit-based allocations.

	Product X	*Product Y*	*Product Z*
Conventional approach	$65.00	$73.00	$ 45.00
Activity-based costing	53.80	59.78	136.86
Difference	$11.20	$13.22	$ 91.86

ABC for Materials Acquisition and Handling

Exhibits 4–4 through 4–6 in Chapter 4 included materials handling costs in overhead. However, accountants can use activity-based costing to assign any extra materials handling costs incurred because of the nature of an order. This approach can represent a phased strategy for introducing ABC into the cost accounting system. A strong argument exists for **applying materials acquisition and handling costs** to direct materials cost or increasing the factory overhead application rate on orders requiring extra handling. For instance, if a company estimates Purchasing Department costs at $70,000 and the dollar value of direct materials purchased at $1,000,000 for the next accounting period, the application rate is 7 percent, computed as follows. (Alternatively, accountants can use the number of purchase orders as the cost driver.)

$$\frac{\$70,000 \text{ estimated purchasing department cost}}{\$1,000,000 \text{ estimated purchases}} = 7 \text{ percent}$$

Assume estimated Receiving Department cost is $45,000 and managers expect receipt of goods costing $900,000. Using these estimates, they develop a 5 percent application rate for applying receiving costs. (An alternative cost driver is the estimated items to be received.)

$$\frac{\$45,000 \text{ estimated receiving department cost}}{\$900,000 \text{ estimated dollar value received}} = 5 \text{ percent}$$

If the company estimates Warehousing Department costs at $150,000 and the square footage to be 100,000, a $1.50 rate per square foot results. Number of items, dollar value of items warehoused, or warehousing days represent alternative cost drivers.

$$\frac{\$150,000 \text{ estimated warehousing costs}}{100,000 \text{ square feet estimated per period}} = \$1.50 \text{ per square foot}$$

The company could use the same approach for freight-in with the following estimate:

$$\frac{\$90,000 \text{ estimated freight-in}}{\$1,000,000 \text{ estimated material purchases}} = 9 \text{ percent}$$

Application of Materials Acquisition and Handling Costs Illustrated.

Assume that during the accounting period, the company purchased direct materials costing $60,000, received $58,000 of these materials ($2,000 are in transit), and used an area of 3,000 square feet. The following journal entries record the application of materials acquisition costs:

Direct Materials Inventory	17,000	
Purchasing Department Expense Control ($60,000 × 7%)		4,200
Receiving Department Expense Control ($58,000 × 5%)		2,900
Materials—Warehousing Department Expense Control		
(3,000 square feet × $1.50)		4,500
Freight-in ($60,000 × 9%)		5,400

We debit actual costs in the applicable expense control account. The applied amount is a credit. For example, if actual Purchasing Department costs total $4,500, there is a $300 underapplied balance in the Purchasing Department Expense Control account as follows:

Purchasing Department Expense Control

Actual expenses	4,500	*Applied* expense based on rate per purchase dollar	4,200

We close the balance of the over- or underapplied materials acquisition expenses either to Cost of Goods Sold or directly to the temporary ledger account used for closing revenues and expenses, the Income Summary. Note the similarity between the treatment for applying materials acquisition costs and that for applying factory overhead to units being manufactured. In both cases, actual costs are debits while the applied costs are credits to the ledger account.

Activity-Based Management

Activity-based costing yields much information about activities and the resources required to perform these activities. Thus, ABC is much more than a cost assignment process. ABC supplies the information and **activity-based management (ABM)** uses this information in various analyses designed to result in ongoing improvement. ABC contributes to cost reduction in marketing and administrative activities as well as improves product costing. The concepts underlying ABC—that activities consume resources and products require activities—apply as readily in service organizations as they do in manufacturing organizations.

Evaluating ABC

The traditional allocation of overhead on a labor-hours basis implies reducing direct labor results in a corresponding decrease in such costs as engineering, receiving, and purchasing. However, automating a production process does not reduce the number of engineering change notices, shipments received, or number of purchase orders placed. Allocating overhead on volume-paced drivers results in reliable product cost information only if the cost being allocated is triggered by units of output or varies in proportion to units of output. Thus, some allocations require nonunit-related bases because volume does not drive all costs. Instead, the complexity and diversity of the process is the driver.

Strengths of ABC

Traditional cost systems fail to recognize that nonvolume-related costs vary with such transactions as the number of inspections performed, the number of setups, and the quantity of scheduling. ABC does overcome distortions inherent in traditional cost information based on step down allocations using only volume-driven drivers. ABC further recognizes the causal relationship of cost drivers to activities. By focusing on the cost drivers of activities within business processes, managers can understand and act on the causes of costs, not their symptoms.

Companies with high overhead costs, a diversity of products, and wide variations in the batch size of production runs are most likely to benefit from ABC. ABC systems yield much information about activities and the resources required to perform these activities. By providing this information, ABC offers assistance in improving work processes by providing better information to help identify which activities require much work. Thus, managers have improved data that reveal what products and services really cost.

ABC information further encourages companies to evaluate activities to see which are nonvalued and can be eliminated. In a typical operation, workers spend much nonvalued time before they can perform productive work. However, direct labor workers cannot be expected to have responsibility over machine maintenance and setups unless they are adequately trained. Also, merely identifying nonvalued activities does not lower costs; managers must reduce excess resources or direct them into more productive areas.

As with traditional means of allocating overhead on volume-based cost drivers, an ABC system provides relevant data only if the costs in every activity are homogeneous and strictly proportional to their cost driver. The two assumptions underlying ABC are that (1) costs in each cost pool are driven by homogeneous activities and (2) costs in each cost pool are strictly proportional to the activity. The homogeneity assumption is violated if costs are driven by two or more not highly correlated activities and only one of the activities is used to assign all costs in the cost pool to products. The result is arbitrary allocations. The presence of nonlinear costs violate the proportionality assumption. For example, if a cost pool includes both variable and fixed costs and they are assigned to products as if they were both strictly variable. Also, ABC requires much operating data; current computer technology and the use of bar codes ease this information gathering.

Weaknesses of ABC   Critics argue that ABC fails to encourage managers to think about changing work processes to make business more competitive. Further, they question if ABC explicitly and systematically links activity with satisfaction of customer wants. This chapter earlier demonstrated product and volume diversity. Using ABC information, managers may assume abandoning the low-volume, newer products in favor of expanding the more mature products having higher margins improves their company's profitability. However, this short-term cost-cutting or margin-enhancing strategy may be counter to customers' wants. Managers may need to spend more of their time and budgets in the short run developing and improving the quality of their newer products.

ABC also may render misconceptions about lowering sales order handling costs by eliminating small orders that generate lower margins. While this strategy reduces the number of sales orders (the driver), customers may want frequent delivery of small lots at infrequent intervals. If there are competing companies willing to meet their needs, long-run profits may suffer by eliminating small orders. Instead, if customers prefer to order in small lot sizes, managers should then study the activities involved to see if any are nonvalued.

ABC also does not specifically conform to generally accepted accounting principles. ABC encourages the allocation of such nonproduct costs as research and development to products while committed product costs such as factory depreciation are not allocated to products. Therefore, most companies have used ABC for internal analysis and continued using their traditional cost system for external reporting.

Emphasizing ABC information also may cause managers to constantly encourage cost reduction. Critics argue that ABC does not encourage the identification and removal of constraints creating delay and excess. An overemphasis on cost reduction without regard to the constraints does not create an environment for learning about problems. A successful long-range global marketing strategy requires finding ways to reduce the costs of manufacturing or servicing the customers' wants in the form customers demand. This may mean more varied product lines or smaller-size products that initially cost more. Managers must be open to changing their work processes by eliminating delays and variation from processes.

Further, if a company's goal is to compete as the low-cost producer of goods or services, it has defined a very narrow niche for itself since there can be only one low-cost producer. Instead, a better approach is to create a differentiation from competition. In addition, a cost reduction program often rejects all decisions to improve quality without considering the cost of customer complaints.

Rather than focus on eliminating all costly processes without considering their impact on customers, managers should instead use ABC data to eliminate the nonvalued activities and waste in these processes. Calculating activity-based driver costs should help companies improve their operations by identifying waste.

Strategic Planning

To obtain optimum use from ABM, managers should prepare **strategic plans** establishing the organization's long-range objectives and the means to achieve them. Companies lacking a sustainable competitive edge will not survive for a long time as they must find a market niche. If they are not identifiably better or demonstrably cheaper, their markets will erode over time. Before operations begin, managers must decide what products or services to provide to what markets. They also must address the marketing and financing of these operations. In addition, strategic planning includes **strategic cost analysis** that concerns the positioning and potential penetration of products and services in the marketplace.

Strategic Cost Analysis

Managers having a good understanding of their company's cost structure have a significant advantage in competing. Strategic cost analysis uses cost data in developing superior strategies by looking at the likely positioning of a new product in the marketplace and its potential penetration. A company should try to select an effective **positioning** theme that makes target customers believe it is distinctive from its rivals. Managers may establish superior quality or service, or satisfy shifting customer requirements faster than competitors, or create a bonding or loyalty in their customer relationships. Alternatively, its positioning theme may include all of these characteristics.

By developing market segmentation, managers can decide whether a new product's position will attract customers from other market segments. This allows managers to access whether a new product will directly attack its mainstream business. Strategic cost analysis involves these three themes: value chain analysis, cost driver analysis, and competitive advantage analysis.

Value Chain Analysis

Each company's value chain reflects its market position, strategic choices, history, and the competitive forces in the market it serves. A **value chain** is the linked set of value-creating activities leading from raw material sources to the ultimate end use of the products or services produced. The activities in a value chain include manufacturing operations, marketing, service, and technology development. Managers use the value chain as a way of breaking down a company's strategic activities to understand cost behavior. Value chain analysis is a long-run approach which extends beyond the company's boundaries; the company is only one part of the overall chain of value-creating activities.

Cost Driver Analysis

The purpose of value chain analysis is to determine where managers can lower costs from design to distribution in the company's segment of the chain. Managers do this by analyzing changes in the costs of each value activity through **cost driver analysis** as discussed earlier in this chapter.

Service

Current Cost Management Practice

Olson Metal Products in Seguin, Texas, found the real potential of ABC is its ability to generate the data necessary to support the theory of constraints management process. The company found the activity analysis required to implement ABC also can reveal the capacity of individual resources. Since companies have many different resources and products, the interaction of capacity requirements and contribution margins can determine the appropriate product mix. This company found the throughput-oriented management philosophy advocated by the theory of constraints could exploit their available opportunities. Using resource requirement flowcharts, activity analysis helped Olson identify its key production constraint. Then it followed the theory of constraints philosophy and recognized the constraint as its profitability driver. By focusing on this profitability driver and selecting the best product mix, Olson's income increased.

Charlene Spoede, Emerson O Henke, and Mike Umble, "Using Activity Analysis to Locate Profitability Drivers," *Management Accounting*, May 1994, pp. 43–48.

Competitive Advantage Analysis

A company obtains competitive advantage if its product or distribution has different characteristics than its competitors'. For this competitive advantage to be relevant for strategic planning, customers must attribute a consistent difference in the product or distribution characteristics. For example, customers must believe that a company's product is of higher quality than competing brands. Competitive advantages also result from having a reputation based on prior actions or due to holding patents or licenses. For such competitive advantages to be effective, existing or potential competitors either cannot or will not take the actions required to eliminate these advantages. Manufacturing-related decisions affecting **competitive advantage analysis** include product design, process design, research and development, and relationship with suppliers.

In its strategic planning, a company may develop a sustainable competitive advantage either through controlling cost drivers or rearranging its value chain. Thus, managers decide either to compete on cost leadership or differentiation. Companies achieve cost leadership through economies of scale in manufacturing, tight cost control, learning curve effects, and cost minimization. If a company's goal is to compete as the low-cost producer of goods or service, it may have defined a very narrow niche for itself since there can be only one low-cost producer. A better approach may be to create a differentiation from competition. Differentiation occurs when customers believe a company's products or services are unique either because of superior customer service, dealer network, or product design.

Theory of Constraints

Since one of the criticisms of ABC is its failure to identify and remove constraints, managers should find adopting the theory of constraints concept beneficial. Eliyahu Goldratt's theory of constraints provides a precise focus on the goals of the organization and on the constraints that limit the accomplishments of those goals.[1] **Constraints,**

---

[1]Eliyahu M. Goldratt, *Theory of Constraints: What Is This Thing and How Should It be Implemented?,* (Croton-on-Hudson, NY: North River Press, 1990).

EXHIBIT 5–2   Identifying Constraints

	TVs	Computers	Total Minutes Needed	Percentage Available
Cutting machine	120	160	280	70% (280/400)
Tooling machine	200	280	480	120% (480/400)
Finishing machine	210	110	320	80% (320/400)

also known as the weakest links, are anything that limits performance. Constraints restrict an organization or individual from obtaining continuously higher levels of performance in reaching goals. They may be internal (such as policies or resources within the firm) or external and governed by outside forces that are beyond the control of management (such as laws of nature, government regulations, and market characteristics.) Constraints also can be both physical and policy-related. A resource constraint exists when demand for a resource exceeds its physical capacity. If market demand exceeds the resource capacity, a bottleneck exists and management should search for production mix alternatives to assure the most profitable use of limited resources.

Identifying and Exploiting Constraints

To illustrate how to identify and exploit constraints, assume Wells Company produces televisions and computers using three different machines. Assume each machine has 400 minutes available for processing each day. The market demand is 50 televisions and 28 computers each day. If the manufacture of televisions and computers requires the following usage of each of the machines, the tooling machine becomes the constraint as Exhibit 5–2 shows.

Throughput

Exhibit 5–3 illustrates the sales price, raw material cost and constraint time per television and computer. We are deducting only raw material costs to yield throughput; we could modify throughput by deducting all variable costs from selling price to yield contribution margin. **Throughput** is the rate at which the system generates money through sales. Production is not throughput if the product is not sold. By adopting throughput as a performance measure, managers try to reduce inventories and increase the throughput rate by attacking the causes of high inventory levels.

Because large inventories make it difficult to identify and solve quality problems and to respond to changing customer needs, companies should adopt performance measures that penalize inventory buildups. Throughput is a nontraditional performance measure that recognizes inventory profits are not real profits. **Throughput speeds,** defined as how long it takes the product to get through the manufacturing process, are shrinking as product life cycles decrease.

Optimum Product Mix.   Assume simply that Wells Company's only way to exploit the tooling machine constraint is to determine the optimum product mix. Exhibit 5-3 indicates that the throughput for each television is higher than for each computer. According to the theory of constraints approach, the tooling machine should produce 50 televisions each day with any remaining time used to make computers. Manufacturing 50 televisions requires 200 minutes of tooling machine time, leaving 200 minutes unused of the 400 total available. The product mix then is: 50 televisions and 20 computers (200 minutes extra/10 minutes per computer = 20).

EXHIBIT 5–3   Exploiting Constraints

Theory of Constraint Approach

	Televisions	Computers
Unit sales price	$1,200	$1,840
Raw material unit cost	500	1,000
Throughput	$ 700	$ 840
Constraint time (tooling machine minutes per product)	4	10
Throughput per constraint minute	$ 175	$ 84

Theory of constraints approach indicates televisions are preferred.

Traditional Approach

	Televisions	Computers
Unit sales price	$1,200	$1,840
Raw material unit cost	500	1,000
Throughput	$ 700	$ 840
Direct labor minutes per product	100	100
Dollars per labor minute	$ 7.00	$ 8.40

Traditional approach indicates computers are preferred.

If, instead Wells Company uses the traditional approach, Exhibit 5–3 shows computers are the priority because of the higher throughput per direct labor minute. Any excess time should be devoted to television manufacturing according to the traditional approach. The product mix then is: 28 computers and 30 televisions (120 minutes extra/4 minutes per television = 30).

Exhibit 5–4 compares income from the product mix determined using the theory of constraints (TOC) approach and the mix using the traditional approach. Assuming $10,000 operating expense, Exhibit 5–4 shows the product mix determined using the TOC approach yields a higher income. Rather than using the traditional focus on direct labor workers, exploiting the tooling machine constraint results in higher income. However, as the following five steps indicate, management should break the constraint of the tooling machine by adding more tooling machines, reducing the time televisions and computers spend in tooling operations, or other ways to reduce the limiting impact of the constraint.

EXHIBIT 5–4   Income Comparison Using TOC and Traditional Approach

	Theory of Constraint Approach			*Traditional Approach*		
Sales of Televisions	(50 × $1,200)		$60,000	(30 × $1,200)		$36,000
Sales of Computers	(20 × $1,840)		36,800	(28 × $1,840)		51,520
			$96,800			$87,520
Television material costs	(50 × $500)	$25,000		(30 × $500)	$15,000	
Computer material costs	(20 × $1,000)	20,000	45,000	(28 × $1,000)	28,000	43,000
Throughput			$51,800			$44,520
Operating expense			10,000			10,000
Income			$41,800			$34,520

The Five Steps of
Focusing

Goldratt's approach seeks continuous improvement by systematically breaking the constraints. He emphasizes that the approach to ongoing improvement of global operations is a sequence of tasks. Goldratt describes the following sequence of tasks identified as the five steps of focusing.

1. Identify the system's constraints.

2. Decide how to exploit the system's constraints. This may involve providing buffers to ensure that the constraint always has what it needs to work on and that workers can convert constraint output into system throughput without delay. Managers should take immediate steps to ensure the system constraint reaches and maintains its maximum rate of output. This usually requires detailed scheduling of the constraint and continuous monitoring of this schedule. When necessary, expediting is done to ensure that the constraint is never idle due to lack of material or operators. Managers make certain that the system makes the best use of every minute of constraint time which may involve manning the constraint through breaks and lunch hours to ensure that it never falls idle. The objective is to squeeze every drop of capacity out of the current resources without changing the system.

3. Subordinate everything else to the preceding decision. Workers manage all ancillary activities to support the production schedule for the constraint. They use every possible resource to assist the constraint to accomplish the mission.

4. Evaluate the system's constraints by providing for increased levels of a company's constraint capacity. The company may require new procedures, new equipment, new policies, new designs, and long lead times. In the meantime, exploitation and subordination in steps 2 and 3 sustain the highest obtainable level of throughput. Management begins to examine ways to break the constraint only at this point. However, it is tempting in an environment of abundant resources to go directly from constraint identification to evaluation process. However, many constraints can be broken without spending money by changing policies.

5. If, in the previous steps a constraint has been broken, go back to step 1.

100 Percent Use of All Resources.   According to the theory of constraints, companies should avoid 100 percent resource utilization as only maximum utilization of a constraint resource is desirable. If a resource is not a constraint, a company should desire no higher level of utilization than is necessary to keep its constraints fully utilized. For example, nonconstraining machines should not produce more than the constraining machines can handle, as this results in excess inventory. Instead, managers should productively use time saved on the nonconstraining machines elsewhere.

Averaging Utilization.   Like 100 percent utilization, transferring workers to achieve an average plantwide utilization on all resources is not an optimal solution. The capacity of the constraining resource should set the pace for the entire operation; there is no value in planning output beyond the capability of the constraining machines. If a company increases the capacity of its nonconstraining machine, whose output feeds the constraint operations, the opportunity for unwanted buildup of work in process and idle time increases.

The company should solve current problems in the constraining operations before attempting to raise capacity. A company should not increase capacity until it has exploited its constraint and subordinated the rest of its system. After examining causes of the present backlog, managers may find capacity is not the problem. The objective is getting the constraining machines working at 100 percent of their present capacity before attempting to add capacity to it. Adding resources to the constraint is expensive and offers no assurance of improvements. Instead, the biggest returns for the investment involved often arise from the exploiting and subordinating stages.

Performance Measures as Policy Constraints

Policy constraints may be rules to solve problems that no longer exist, such as rules designed to optimize local performance measures. A typical policy constraint that many companies suffer from is the end-of-reporting period hockey stick phenomena. This occurs when their plants issue shipments at a steady rate for a period, then shipments rise sharply, and drop even more rapidly to the original rate. They repeat this pattern at regular, predictable intervals with widely varying systems, processes, technology, and quality requirements. The hockey stick phenomena occurs because as the end of the reporting period approaches, corporate management is no longer interested in local performance; instead, its focus is the overall performance of the company. Corporate managers want to know how much product they will ship and how much money the company will make.

To maximize performance as a period is ending, shop managers use expensive overtime, frequent setups, and expediting to meet their quotas. They push shipments aggressively, emphasizing productivity over efficiency. Output increases, but at a significant cost. These shop managers resist stopping production on any machine because they know large lot sizes and infrequent schedule changes maximize efficiency and direct labor utilization. Since companies often do not punish shop managers for large in-process inventories or hold them responsible for scheduling or coordinating waves of material, these issues are of little concern for shop managers. Instead, managers uses additional inventory and indirect labor to solve their scheduling problems.

These performance measures create a management mindset that focuses on shipping targets and not cost control or constraint utilization. Corporate managers believe the company ships more product and makes more money than it would have by following other practices that focus on constraints. Unfortunately, companywide measures of quality, customer service, and productivity suffer.

Product Life-Cycle Costing

Admittedly, ABC does not solve all product costing problems or shortcomings in manufacturing. For example, it does not directly address life-cycle costing or performance measurements even though ABC supports these functions with valuable information. **Product life-cycle costing** refers to accumulating costs for activities that occur over the entire life cycle of a product. Following are the four stages of the product life cycle that managers generally accept:

1. **Introduction**—a low sales volume and high product introduction costs result in a loss situation; the company frequently has a near monopoly and uses intensive marketing activity to generate awareness of its product.

2. **Growth**—sales increase, costs per unit decline, and profits increase; cost per unit is the lowest as a result of large sales increases and production and distribution economies. Profits reach their highest level during the growth stage.

3. **Maturity**—costs increase as a result of product modifications, larger marketing mix expenditures, and other efforts to maintain market position; profits decline which causes weak companies to withdraw from the market; price competition intensifies as the factors responsible for the monopoly disappear. Gradually, identical products become available from many sources; marketing conditions become highly competitive and the rate of sales growth declines.

4. **Decline**—market for the product contracts causing sales and profits to decline and usually companies leave the market.

Expanded Life Cycle

Product life cycles are being compressed and new products introduced at a faster pace. With technology costs increasing as a percentage of total product costs, the life-cycle cost of a new product is 80 to 90 percent committed and locked in at the design phase. Thus, cost accountants need more involvement in the initial stages of the product life cycle because often planning and product design are ignored when considering the product life cycle. Traditionally, the focus has been only on the maturity and decline stages. Instead, the product life cycle should be expanded to include the following steps which are described next: planning, design, and production preparation. Exhibit 5–5 shows that 85 percent of the cost of a new product is committed after the design stage and that manufacturing can influence only about 10 to 15 percent of the cost.

- **Planning**—determining a product's concept, objective, and primary specifications for performance and design; schedule of product's design, production and marketing activities; establishing target costs, sales price, and volume. **Target cost** is the value to the end customer less margins along the value chain. If the price of raw materials increases, this does not add value to the end product. Under target costing, managers try to find ways to cut costs elsewhere by reworking the product's design. Using target costing, managers go to the end of the value chain—the customers—to find their acceptable price and then work back through all the stages of a product.

- **Design**—classifying the functional areas of a new product by use and value and assigning the target cost to the functional area of the new product; designing the basic product concept under the target cost; using rough cost estimates to determine whether the basic product concept is designed to fit the target cost; making design changes if the cost of general drawings is not within the target cost.

- **Production preparation**—designing the production process under target cost; preparing detailed cost estimates to determine whether production preparations are accomplished within the target cost.

Accountants have traditionally written off the costs of developing new products as overhead and there has been no attempt to match development costs to the actual products subsequently manufactured. Thus, new products do not bear any of the costs incurred prior to introduction. This causes managers to be penalized in the current period for developing products that might produce long-term benefits. Those managers who invest little effort in new-product development appear to have more efficient performance in the short-run.

EXHIBIT 5–5   Product Life-Cycle Costs

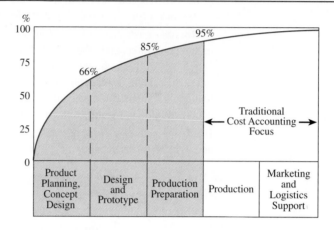

Instead, cost management should reduce costs by improving design and production techniques while still at the design stage because as Exhibit 5–5 shows, this is where companies incur the bulk of their product cost. The focus is on activities that occur prior to production to ensure the lowest total life-cycle cost. Front-end planning allows for detection of opportunities for eliminating waste; the tightest controls are placed on the design phases. Also, managers are recognizing that at the maturity and decline stage, they must decide if other products will contribute more per dollar of expenditure. Product life-cycle costing encourages management to determine what percentage of the company's sales, profits, and investment in assets falls into each stage of the product life cycle.

Summary

Conventional costing systems often hide the true causes of nonvolume-related activities. ABC improves cost allocations by measuring the cost and performance of process-related activities and assigns their cost based on both volume and nonvolume related drivers. Also, the use of value chain analysis to evaluate all of a company's activities from providers of raw materials to its customers encourages managers to identify and eliminate nonvalued activities.

Successful applications of ABC and strategic cost analysis generate data useful to operations personnel. This requires involving operational people in revamping the company's cost practices and cost system so it reflects their needs. This approach encourages operational people to buy in and sustain its use. ABC can result in a change in performance only if management takes the initiative. A costing system by itself cannot cause the change. Smart accounting personnel stay in the background and provide assistance; otherwise, operations personnel do not accept system changes.

Important Terms and Concepts

Problem for Self-Study
ABC and Traditional Cost Allocations for Hospitals

Midtown Hospital administrators know that the seriousness of patients' illnesses determines the skill and amount of nursing services the hospital requires. For example, their study of activities reveal that patients in Cardiac Care need eight times as much nursing care as new mothers in Maternity. Traditionally, the hospital has allocated its total nursing costs on the number of patient beds occupied. Some of the administrators do not believe ABC is warranted because so many of their costs, such as occupancy and dietary, are the same for all patients. Other administrators disagree and provide you with the following information relating to acuteness or seriousness levels of the Maternity patients. Total monthly nursing services costs—$450,000; 1,000 total days occupied by all departments monthly. For simplicity, only two departments are detailed out; data for the other departments are totaled. Assume the average acuteness level is 4 for these other departments.

	Monthly Patient Beds Occupied	*Acuteness Level*
Cardiac Care Department	100 days	8
Maternity Department	300 days	1
Other departments	600 days	4

Required:

Compare the hospital's current approach with an ABC approach using activity drivers of costs per day for each acuteness level. Discuss which approach more accurately reflects the actual service received.

Solution to Problem for Self-Study

Midtown Hospital

Using traditional costing to distribute nursing services:

Cardiac Care Department receives: 100/1,000 days × $450,000 = $45,000
Maternity Department receives: 300/1,000 days × $450,000 = $135,000

Using ABC costing:

Cardiac Care Department: 100 days × 8 =	800
Maternity Department: 300 days × 1 =	300
Other departments: 600 days × 4 =	2,400
	3,500

Cardiac Care Department receives: 800/3,500 acuteness days × $450,000 = $102,857
Maternity Department receives: 300/3,500 acuteness days × $450,000 = $38,571

Using activity drivers of cost per day for each acuteness level better reflects how much nursing care each patient receives; this will provide a better basis for charging patients. Some costs, such as dietary and occupancy costs, and maintenance, should continue to be allocated on a volume basis (number of patient beds occupied) with adjustment for level of acuteness.

Review Questions

1. Name six cost drivers typically used in ABC systems.

2. List benefits expected from ABC systems.

3. Explain how traditional cost systems frequently overcost high-volume products and undercost low-volume specialty products.

4. Do you think simple cost systems with limited cost pools provide enough information for companies to compete internationally? Provide support for your answer.

5. Why do ABC advocates argue that allocating overhead across all products hinders cost reduction and pricing strategies because management receives the wrong signals?

6. Discuss the two assumptions underlying ABC. Do these differ from the assumptions of a traditional costing system?

7. Suppose another manager suggests that the company engineer assist you, the cost accountant, in preparing a questionnaire that surveys what workers really do and for what product lines. Indicate whether you think this activity has value and what types of information you expect to find that could be of benefit.

8. *a.* What is the theoretical justification for applied rates for material acquisition and warehousing costs?
   b. Why aren't material acquisition and warehousing costs commonly applied in practice?

9. Assume a company uses benchmarking to find the best way to manufacture its products. After identifying these best world-class practices, it copies them and incorporates them into its own process. What dangers are there in this imitating approach?

Exercises

Writing

E5–1 Support of Multiple Cost Pools

The controller of your company is comfortable using a traditional cost system that is familiar. The argument presented for not detailing cost pools more is that there is always a trade-off in dividing cost pools into smaller units. Further, smaller cost pools inherently require more allocations of common costs. Opponents of changing to an ABC cost system argue that not only can it not be used for external reporting but also some of these additional allocations required become arbitrary merely because there is no strong cause-and-effect relationship.

Required:

Write a memo to the controller of your company discussing why you think simple cost systems with single cost pools are inadequate in today's competitive environment.

E5–2 Comparison of Allocations Using Traditional and ABC Costing Methods

Attaway Company provides the following information concerning its two product lines:

	Product A	Product B
Number of units produced	500	100
Machine setup hours per product line	30	30
Direct labor-hours per unit	2	2
Total budgeted machine setup-related cost—$36,000		

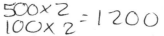

Required:

a. How much machine setup-related cost is allocated to each product line if Attaway Company uses a traditional cost allocation system based on direct labor-hours? What is the cost per unit for Product A and Product B?

b. If instead, Attaway Company uses activity-based costing, how much machine setup-related cost is allocated to Product A and B lines? What is the cost per unit for Product A and Product B?

c. Is overhead allocation to Product A and B lines evidence of product diversity or volume diversity?

Writing

E5–3 Written Communication Concerning Constraints

Write a memo to the Cheng Company president supporting your request for top managers to examine company policies to determine if they place constraints on operations that the managers can eliminate by changing the current policy. As a starting point, explain why you suggest the board examine the policies surrounding inventory and their requirement that managers must show evidence that they have tried to obtain the lowest price. Suggest other areas that typically present constraints to more profitable operations.

E5–4 Application Rates for Material Acquisition Costs

Turner Company applies material acquisition costs because many of their orders for materials require extra care and inspection. The bookkeeper provided the following estimates:

Annual estimated warehousing department costs	$ 112,000
Annual estimated purchasing department costs	120,000
Annual estimated freight-in	140,000
Annual estimated direct materials purchased	2,800,000
Annual estimated number of purchase orders	15,000

Actual data for the month are

Direct materials purchased	$ 300,000
Warehousing Department costs	12,350
Purchasing Department costs	11,800
Freight-in costs incurred	14,300
Number of purchase orders	1,500

Required:

a. Determine application rates, applying freight-in cost and Warehousing Department costs on the basis of materials cost purchased and Purchasing Department costs on the basis of purchase orders.

b. Prepare the journal entries to record both the actual costs incurred and the application of materials acquisition costs. Close the balance of the material acquisition ledger accounts to Cost of Goods Sold.

E5–5 Comparison of Allocations Using Traditional and ABC Costing Methods

Cappettini Company provides the following information concerning its two product lines:

	Product A	Product B
Units produced	10	20
Machine-hours per unit	3	4
Inspections per product line	5	1
Total budgeted inspection cost—$3,300		

Required:

a. Assume Cappettini Company uses activity-based costing; calculate how much inspection cost is allocated to each line. What is the cost per unit for Products A and B?

b. Determine how much inspection cost is allocated to each line if Cappettini Company uses a traditional cost allocation system based on machine-hours. What is the cost per unit for Products A and B?

c. Decide if overhead allocation to Product lines A and B is evidence of product diversity or volume diversity and explain why.

E5–6 ABC and Traditional Product-Level Cost Allocations

Holt, Inc., recently introduced a new motor designed for refrigerators. Because this was a new product design, engineers had to make 100 engineering changes, but only 300 changes for its other more mature product lines. Holt, Inc. allocated its engineering change costs of $100,000 along with other overhead in a single cost pool on the basis of machine-hours. An ABC study showed that engineering changes drive engineering change costs. Manufacturing the new motors accounted for 500 machine-hours of the 5,000 total machine-hours.

Required:

Concerning only the engineering change product-level costs, how much did the traditional cost system distort product-level costs for the new motor?

E5–7 Relating Service Costs to Levels

KLIZ, Inc. is a highly automated delivery service. Its operations are divided into three product lines: heavy-weight loads; light-weight loads; and highly perishable, rapid deliveries. The following are a sample of the costs it typically incurs each day:

1. Refrigeration for milk-related products.
2. Wages of office workers.

Critical Thought

3. Special wrapping paper for lighter loads.
4. Invoice forms for each delivery.
5. Salaries of three divisional managers.
6. Dry ice for floral deliveries.
7. Property taxes.
8. Maintenance of administrative offices.
9. Tires for heavy-duty trucks used for heavy-weight deliveries.
10. Central Office billing clerk's wages.
11. Depreciation on president's car owned by KLIZ.
12. Delivery request forms prepared by sender.

Required:

For each of these costs, indicate whether it is related to the unit level (U), the batch level (B), the product/process level (P), or the facility level or organization level (F). Also identify a logical cost driver for each cost and be able to support your choice of driver.

E5–8 Value-Added and Nonvalue-Added Activities

A sample from the value chart of the activities conducted by Bramwell, Inc., workers reveals the following tasks performed:

Critical Thought

1. An operator is manually counting parts because the counter on her machine no longer works.
2. Reworking products.
3. Pricing product.
4. Product sourcing.
5. Filing obsolete policies and procedures manuals in office cabinets.
6. A finishing operator is performing polishing rework rather than sending the parts back to the polishing department.
7. Inspecting.
8. Applying inappropriate performance measurements.
9. Grinding up scrap materials and sending them back through the process as raw materials.
10. Enforcing quality control standards.
11. Setting up a machine.
12. Polishing a precision optic because customers want outstanding optical performance.
13. Preparing financial statements.
14. Expediting products.
15. Processing a payment twice.
16. Moving a product.
17. Purchasing parts.
18. Receiving materials.
19. Disbursing parts.
20. Redesigning a product.
21. Mixing and pouring materials.

Required:

a. Indicate which of these activities are value-added.
b. Suggest a solution to avoid performing two of the activities that you indicated were nonvalued.
c. Defend your answer to whether Activity 13, Preparing financial statements, has value.

Problems

P5–9 Transaction Costing
Madeo Company budgets factory overhead for next year as:

Engineering	$ 64,000
Quality control inspections	280,000
Machine setups	66,000
Total budgeted costs	$410,000

Overhead has been applied on the basis of direct labor-hours; 16,400 direct labor-hours are budgeted for next year.

Madeo Company wonders whether an activity-based or transaction-based cost system which allocates overhead costs based on nonvolume-based cost drivers would result in improved costing. The activity-based cost drivers for next year's budgeted overhead costs are:

Engineering	1,600 engineering change notices
Quality control inspections	20,000 number of inspections
Machine setup hours	6,000 setup hours

Madeo provides the following data concerning producing 500 computers:

Machine-hours	1,000
Direct labor-hours	3,000
Number of engineering moves	200
Number of quality control inspections	40
Machine setups hours	30

Required:

a. What are the factory overhead costs per computer under a volume-based cost allocation system that applies overhead on direct labor-hours?

b. If an activity-based costing (transaction-based costing system) is implemented, what are the factory overhead costs per computer?

c. Assuming the direct materials and direct labor cost per unit is $400, what is the selling price of computers under both methods if the Madeo Company's gross margin is 40 percent of product costs? Management estimates this gross margin percent to cover other costs such as administrative expenses, marketing expenses, financial expenses, and research and development expenses, and yield a profit.

SPATS

P5–10 Journal Entries Recording Applied and Actual Material Costs
Bird Company uses the following estimates for applying materials acquisition costs:

Annual estimated Purchasing Department costs	$ 55,863,000
Annual estimated Inspection Department costs	$ 31,035,000
Annual estimated Receiving Department costs	$ 1,727,000
Annual estimated direct materials purchases	$620,700,000
Estimated items to be received	550,000

Required:

a. Develop application rates for the materials handling costs by applying Purchasing and Inspection Department costs on the basis of the dollar value of materials purchased and Receiving Department costs on the basis of items received. Freight on incoming material is available for each invoice.

b. Prepare the journal entries to record the actual cost of a purchase including the application of materials acquisition costs if 900 items are bought on account at a cost of $85,250 with freight cost of $1,430.

c. Using the following actual recorded data for the period, prepare journal entries to close the balances of the materials acquisition ledger accounts to Cost of Goods Sold.

Direct materials purchased (includes $85,250 purchased in Requirement *b*) . . . $625,000,000

Purchasing Department cost . . . . $ 56,274,000

Inspection Department cost . . . . $ 31,236,000

Receiving Department cost . . . . $ 1,640,000

Items received 545,500

SPATS

P5–11 Reconciling ABC and Traditional Costing

Merlin Company recently introduced a new product, which managers refer to as Special, to complement their other product, Regular. Accountants accumulate all overhead in a single cost pool and allocate it based on machine-hours. With the recent addition of an expanded computer system, Merlin decided to begin implementing ABC. A study reveals much overhead cost relates to machine setups and engineering changes. They select the number of setups and the number of engineering changes as the activity drivers for the two new cost pools. They will continue to use machine-hours as the base for allocating all remaining overhead. Accountants provide the following information about Merlin Company's most recent year of operations:

	Regular	*Special*	*Total*
Units produced	49,800	200	50,000
Direct material cost:			
Per unit	$ 20	$ 120	
Direct labor cost	$2,200,000	$300,000	$2,500,000
Machine hours	11,000	960	11,960
Machine setups	20	40	60
Engineering changes	400	600	1,000
Overhead:			
Machine setup-related			$ 240,000
Engineering-related			836,400
Other			1,913,600
Total overhead			$2,990,000

Required:

a. Using the current costing system, determine the total and unit cost for each product line.

b. Using the ABC costing system, determine the total and unit cost for each product line.

c. Reconcile the total and unit costs reported for Special by the two costing systems.

d. What percentage of Merlin's total overhead did the two costing systems treat differently? By what percentage did the cost of Special change as a result of the change in the system? Calculate each answer to the nearest whole percent.

P5–12 Just-In-Time and Profitability of Special Orders

Barc Inc. experiences intense price competition in manufacturing a special model of calculator. Barc Inc. has produced an average of 600,000 calculators per year over the past three years. They pride themselves on the product's high quality and find the introduction of new technology is the most promising marketing strategy. Management realizes their marketing program is very important since they presently operate at 75 percent of plant capacity. The product is sold at $300 in the market.

Estimated production costs of one calculator are as follows:

Direct material	$ 50
Direct labor	30
Variable overhead	55
Allocated overhead	47
Total production costs	$182

In an attempt to improve their product costing, management is considering adopting an activity-based costing (ABC) system and introducing just-in-time into the production system. Barc's accountants recognize that many indirect common product costs using a traditional accounting system are changed to direct traceable product costs using an ABC system that incorporates the JIT philosophy.

Barc recently received a special order from one of its dealers for 150,000 calculators at a unit bid sales price of $180. Because Barc has idle capacity, no increase in fixed costs would occur to meet the special order. To better compare their conventional costing system with an ABC system, they determined the following production costs using a JIT system and the allocation of production overhead based on an ABC system:

Direct materials	$ 50
Direct labor	35
Variable overhead	60
Fixed overhead	30
Total production costs	$175

Rather than use the traditional departmental overhead rates, an ABC system applies factory overhead costs to products based on cost drivers. Production personnel recognize that this may require a change in layout of factory equipment and the development of decentralized work cells. A JIT production system requires a zero-defect program in which no scrap or waste is allowed. Barc management plans to adopt the philosophy of total quality control. Management plans to maintain minimum inventory levels because JIT is a demand-pull approach.

Because workers in each cell are trained to perform various tasks within the cell, idle time is not permissible. This arrangement facilitates the traceability of costs to the final product. Direct labor costs are usually considered variable costs under traditional accounting systems. However, direct labor costs become fixed costs using an ABC system because workers perform a variety of tasks within a specific work cell.

Required:

a. Prepare computations using a traditional accounting system that indicates whether the special order should be accepted or rejected.
b. Prepare computations using ABC and JIT accounting systems to indicate whether the special order should be accepted or rejected.
c. Determine if the cost activities described in the case will result in different cost estimates and different contribution margins. Determine which cost accounting system is preferable for pricing this special order.

P5–13 Converting to ABC System

Oberle Company's Northern Territory manufactures a variety of products that are currently at different stages in their life cycles. As a result, some products are selling at a high volume while others are being introduced and have low volume. Northern Territory provides the following data for its most recent year of operations:

Factory overhead cost:		
Materials related:		
Materials handling	$ 218,000	
Materials receipts and processing	272,000	
Freight-in	120,000	$ 610,000

Machine related:

Machine operating cost	$ 504,000	
Machine setup cost	160,200	664,200
Other overhead		1,800,000
Total overhead		$3,074,200

Direct materials cost	$1,017,000
Direct labor-hours	400,000
Pounds of materials	150,000
Setup hours	420
Number of receipts	8,000
Machine-hours	36,000

Northern Territory uses volume-based cost drivers and allocates all materials-related overhead based on direct materials cost, all machine-related overhead based on machine-hours, and all remaining overhead based on direct labor-hours. However, consultants recently found that materials handling costs and machine setup costs are primarily related to the setup hours; materials receipts and processing costs primarily relate to the number of receipts; and freight-in primarily relates to pounds of materials received. The consultants' study makes no further recommendations.

Required:

a. Determine the three overhead rates currently used by Northern Territory that reflect volume-based cost drivers.
b. Make only the changes suggested by the consultants and establish an ABC system for Northern Territory. List the cost driver that you use to allocate each cost pool to products.
c. Determine the overhead rates that the ABC system should use for the most recent year based on the new cost drivers.

Cases

Writing

C5–14 Bottlenecks

Swang Company has a more than adequate supply of labor, but only one machine to finish the products after direct labor workers complete their tasks. There is sufficient market demand for their product so that the finishing machine is fully utilized. However, this capacity level uses only 80 percent of direct labor capacity, thus representing a nonbottleneck operation whose capacity exceeds market demand.

One of Swang's cost accountants argues that direct labor workers should be laid off so there is no excess capacity. She stresses that employing direct labor workers at the current 100 percent level results in excess labor costs and a lower profit for the company. Further, she argues that by fully implementing the labor resource, throughput is not improved because the finishing machine prevents the increase of sales.

Another cost accountant believes that the company has an obligation to keep all direct labor workers employed and offers another solution. He believes enough raw material should be purchased to keep all workers busy, thus fully utilizing labor.

A third accountant then asks if any consideration is being given to inventory profits or phantom profits in either of the solutions offered. At this point, the production and marketing managers remark that they are totally confused and want an explanation.

Required:

a. Explain why all plants should include at least one bottleneck operation whose capacity is less than or equal to market demand.

b. Explain if the labor resource should be fully implemented.

c. Explain if a company should have excess capacity everywhere to prevent bottlenecks.

d. Explain why you would or would not advise Swang Company to have only exact capacity everywhere.

e. Explain why you agree or disagree with the cost accountant's suggestion to purchase enough raw materials to keep workers fully utilized.

f. Define inventory profits and explain how are they achieved.

Writing

C5–15 Impact of Automation on Strategic Planning

Annual sales for automobiles produced by Meador, Inc., are in the range of $40–$50 million; annual sales increases for the past four years have averaged 6 percent. More than 800 persons are employed including national account salespersons and traveling sales representatives. The home office and production plant are located in Grand Rapids, Michigan, and all products are distributed in the western United States.

Marketing personnel pride themselves on their ability to convince management that additional varieties and features on their automobiles should be made available to the public. Thus, consumers now have an extensive range of options available.

Management contacted consultants to evaluate the plant to determine if newer technology would be cost effective. The consultants found a snake-type production process that fails to follow straight-line flows. They also pointed out several areas where robotics would be appropriate; however, management believes that it should approach this environment very slowly and has tentatively decided to install robotics to do a simple welding process, rather than utilize robots in the more complex painting and testing areas.

The consultants also were amazed at the vast amount of inventory Meador carries. In fact, the consultants summarized their feelings to top management in the following remark: "Inventory is evidence of all management's problems." The consultants suggested management adopt a just-in-time (JIT) inventory system. However, Meador's conservative management ignores this suggestion on the basis that their suppliers are entirely too unreliable and they don't want to miss a sale.

Meador uses a plantwide overhead rate applied on the basis of direct labor. Overhead is allocated to cost centers and then production departments assign product costs to products.

Required:

a. What major topics should be addressed in the company's strategic planning sessions ignoring whether the new technology is installed?

b. Why did you select the topics indicated in Requirement a?

c. What initial specific procedure will be followed each year in developing the master budget? Indicate the factors that will impact on this beginning budgeting step.

d. What is the impact on budget procedures of having so many options available for consumers?

e. What will be the effect on the following if the expensive new technology is correctly installed and implemented?
   (1) Labor and factory overhead budgets.
   (2) Product quality.

f. What is the meaning of the consultant's statement regarding inventory being evidence of management's problems?

g. What is your reaction to management's decision regarding JIT? What do you see as a solution to their real problem?

Critical Thought

C5–16 Theory of Constraints in Production

Whist Jewelers produces both expensive and inexpensive costume jewelry. Workers cut, polish, and then insert diamonds, emeralds, and fake stones in mountings in the finishing operations. Market demand for Whist jewelry averages 150 units weekly. Despite increased competition, Whist is unable to fully meet its market demand.

Writing

Whist uses cutting, polishing, and finishing machines in its operations. Production statistics reveal the cutting machines typically operate at 70 percent capacity, the polishing machines at 60 percent capacity, and the finishing machines at 80 percent capacity or 96 units per week. Maximum output for the cutting machines is 200 units during a 40-hour week, 180 units for the polishing machines, and 120 for the finishing machines. Despite this difference in utilization, typically there is a backlog of inventory awaiting finishing operations.

Whist's top managers agree that the company should use simple measures of performance that are easy to apply and effective. They recognize problems with their present production operations and performance measurement system. However, their board of directors is placing pressure to reduce both their financial and personnel resources. All Whist managers recognize the danger of adopting a business as usual approach. They admit that dramatically changing global relations, increased competition for scarce resources, and technological revolutions threaten the survival of slow responding companies. Yet, they lack agreement as to what their focus should be.

Bob, a Whist manager, suggests they establish self-managed work teams allowing each team to make and implement as many required decisions as possible. Bob also encourages the adoption of the total quality management philosophy and the related concept of Pareto analysis. The idea behind Pareto analysis is to prioritize opportunities for improvement by recognizing that approximately 20 percent of problems (or causes) are usually responsible for 80 percent of the impact (or symptoms). Before adopting this concept, managers agree they should identify what Whist's problems really are.

Mary, another manager, supports the idea of 100 percent use of all resources. Since the cutting and polishing machines are presently at 70 percent and 60 percent utilization respectively, which is below the finishing machines' utilization ratios, she suggests adding resources to these two operations to improve their labor efficiency. At the minimum, she believes Whist should average the utilization of all machines by transferring finishing operators to cutting and polishing operations so plantwide utilization on all machines is approximately 70 percent.

In opposition to Mary's suggestion, Sue, another Whist manager, argues that they should transfer some of the cutting and polishing machine operators to a second shift on the finishing machine. Sue believes the capacity of the finishing machines should set the pace for the entire operation. She emphasizes there is no value in planning output beyond the finishing operation's capability. Sue believes operations with additional capacity should work only to the rate of the finishing machines, the constraining factor. Sue argues that running the cutting and polishing operations beyond the rate set by the finishing machines is wasteful. Sue also questions the financial impact of hiring more cutting and polishing workers.

Bill, another manager, asks if somehow they could use the additional cutting and polishing capacity to off-load work from finishing operations. He also asks if there is a market for Whist to sell cut, polished, and unfinished stones without a mounting.

Gale, a Whist manager who recently joined the organization, suggests that instead of increasing the capacity of the finishing operations, Whist should investigate the cause of the finishing backlog. Rather than buy more finishing machines or hire more finishing workers, Gale believes Whist should take certain steps first. Since Whist is a complex web of processes, Gale questions whether changing one individual operation will impact other operations.

Whist's president reminds the group that their board of directors has an unwritten policy concerning utilization. As they have done in the past, the president expects the board to begin their own investigation of plant operations whenever any department's operations fall below 60 percent utilization. Thus, the president questions whether they should drop utilization on any machine below 60 percent. Instead, should they keep utilization at least 60 percent, and either work around the 60 percent utilization policy to prevent adverse reactions or let the chips fall where they may which has the potential of resulting in adverse reactions. The president agrees that they may be able to persuade the board to recognize the results sacrificed if the company strictly follows the 60 percent utilization policy. Managers believe if the board fails to remove this policy, the board must accept the financial trade-off of the results.

Additionally, the president reminds the managers of the general company policy limiting each work center to only 40 hours per week. Also, the president questions if the company should take any precautions to ensure that certain machine operations keep running. He questions the impact of disruptions in the supply of material to any one machine.

Also, all managers remember that at the beginning of each quarter, Whist rewards or punishes shop managers based on local measurements of efficiency or labor utilization. Thus, shop managers schedule large batch sizes and batches with minimum setups at each quarter's beginning. As the quarter approaches its end, shop managers receive increased pressure to accomplish the production quota. Managers use expensive overtime, frequent setups, and expediting to meet their quotas. Thus, output increases, but at a significant cost. These shop managers resist stopping production on any machine because they know large lot sizes and infrequent schedule changes maximize efficiency and direct labor utilization. Since the company does not punish shop managers for large in process inventories or hold them responsible for scheduling or coordinating waves of material, shop managers do not concern themselves with this. Instead, Whist uses additional inventory and indirect labor to solve these scheduling problems. Managers remember that such large inventories make it difficult to identify and solve quality problems and to respond to changing customer needs. While these steps improve departmental efficiency, companywide measures of quality, customer service, and productivity suffer.

As a starting point, the managers agree they need a list of the undesirable effects associated with the present production scheduling, their core problem, and what desirable effect or goal they wish to achieve. This leads the group in a heated discussion as to what Whist's primary goal really is. Some managers believe it is to be a good corporate citizen; others believe it is to increase market share or to provide jobs. This discussion encourages the managers to ask themselves if instead they should express the company's goal as making money now and in the future—whether this will facilitate other goals. Managers agree to conducting individual investigations and meeting later.

One week later at their agreed-on meeting, the managers reported the following from their initial investigation.

1. A finishing operator is manually counting parts because the counter on his machine no longer works.
2. Another finishing operator is performing polishing rework under the assumption that it is less expensive for her to correct the stones' polished surface rather than send them back to the polishing department.
3. Finishing operators perform at different levels of productivity, each using different work methods.

Required:

a. Define a constraint and list some typical constraints companies encounter in operations.
b. (1) What is Whist's constraint now? (2) What should Whist managers do first about this constraint? (3) If market demand was 100 units weekly, would it represent an initial constraint for Whist at present?
c. Indicate why you agree or disagree that a company should strive for 100 percent utilization of all resources.
d. What do you believe will be the result if Whist adopts Mary's suggestion of averaging utilization to 70 percent for all machines.
e. Evaluate Sue's suggestion.
f. Evaluate the suggestions of Bill and Gale.
g. What should the managers do based on their findings after a week's investigation?
h. Do you see any advantages of contradicting the board of directors' policy on utilization?
i. If each machine quits operating for five hours, indicate the units each machine would lose and the number produced assuming (1) present utilization and (2) 100 percent utilization.
j. At present, how many hours could the cutting and polishing machines each lose before they affect the finishing output quantity?

k. Suggest which machines should have the most protection to ensure there are no disruptions in operations. List what form this protection should take and support your answer with quantitative data.

l. What are the behavioral implications of managers who receive bonuses or punishment at the beginning of each quarter for production efficiency and labor utilization? How do these performance measures affect attempts to weaken Whist's constraints?

C5–17 Applying Theory of Constraint to Personal Decisions

Relate what you have learned from Whist operations in C5-16 about recognizing the weakest link by applying this theory to personal characteristics. Assume the goal of the following fictitious individuals is to obtain or keep a good-paying, rewarding job that offers them challenges.

Individual A is from a poor economic background and is working his way through college. His parents are very proud of his high grade point average, especially since they were never able to attend college. Even though they are giving him all their love and support, A recognizes that he lacks the social class of many of his fellow students. For instance, at a recent school dinner, he was at lost as to which fork to use for his salad; also he kept quiet during a discussion concerning the recent travels of some of his classmates. He did not want to admit that his travels were limited to a radius of 400 miles of his hometown.

Individual B is a well-rounded accounting major, having an outgoing personality along with a high grade point average and graduate admission testing scores. B's work this summer as an intern with a national public accounting firm is convincing him that university teaching/research should be his goal. B recognizes that he needs a Ph.D. to achieve this. After completing a normal course load in the fall semester, B will have enough hours to complete a masters degree. However, B is unsure if some of his transfer work from another university will meet all the course requirements. B cannot decide whether he should try to continue working during the upcoming fall and spring semester at the public accounting firm and take a reduced course load. B fears the academically recognized Ph.D. programs which he wants to enter will prohibit new admissions in the spring semester. He questions if they accept new enrollees only in the fall. Also, B is unsure if the national public accounting firm will provide employment next summer, especially if they learn of his plans to enter a Ph.D. program. Money is not a constraint as B's parents indicate they will support him financially whatever his decision.

Individual C is an international student studying accounting in the United States. C speaks English fairly well but has trouble understanding some of the slang and informal language that the English-speaking students use in her dorm. Even though she has found these students to be very friendly, C refuses to accept their invitations to go out to dinner or a movie. Instead, C prefers to associate only with students from her native land. As a result, C rarely participates in classroom discussions for fear she will speak incorrectly. However, C plans to stay in the United States after graduation even though the thought of interviewing causes a great terror.

Individual D is admittedly very shy, rarely expressing his opinion in groups. Even though D has a high grade point average, D has limited work experience and on-campus involvement. The thought of job interviewing also terrorizes D.

Individual E is an unemployed 40 year old, slightly overweight, parent of two children. E's spouse has a steady job and has no desire to change locations. E's undergraduate degree is in liberal arts. After investigating the master's curriculum in liberal arts and one in accounting-computer science at a nearby university, E discovers she could complete the liberal arts masters in two less years.

Individual F has been employed for 23 years in a fairly rewarding job that pays a comfortable salary. F earned a masters degree 20 years ago. After all these years, F knows all the job requirements and does not find the job very demanding. As a result, F has adequate off-job time to spend in family-related and leisure activities. However, recent rumors that F's company is considering closing appear to dampen her seemingly perfect world.

Required:

a. Identify the constraint or limiting factor that you think will prevent each of these individuals from achieving this goal. Suggest ways to overcome these constraints.

b. Relate Individual E's situation to what some critics argue is a current criticism of traditional cost accounting.

c. Assuming that international student C becomes very fluent in English, understanding both formal and informal conversations, what should C do then?

d. Thought-provoking questions which should *not* be written and turned in: What do you view is your constraint to prevent obtaining a top paying, challenging job assuming you are not a perfect individual? What immediate actions can you take about exploiting this constraint? Assume you eliminate this constraint, what should you do then?

Critical Thought

C5–18 Impact of Robots on Overhead Application (CMA)

Rose Bach has recently been hired as controller of Empco Inc., a sheet metal manufacturer. Empco has been in the sheet metal business for many years and is currently investigating ways to modernize its manufacturing process. At the first staff meeting Bach attended, Bob Kelley, chief engineer, presented a proposal for automating the Drilling Department. Kelley recommended that Empco purchase two robots that would have the capability of replacing the eight direct labor workers in the department. The cost savings outlined in Kelley's proposal included the elimination of direct labor cost in the Drilling Department plus a reduction of manufacturing overhead cost in the department to zero because Empco charges manufacturing overhead on the basis of direct labor dollars using a plantwide rate.

The president of Empco was puzzled by Kelley's explanation of cost savings, believing it made no sense. Bach agreed, explaining that as firms become more automated, they should rethink their manufacturing overhead systems. The president then asked Bach to look into the matter and prepare a report for the next staff meeting.

To refresh her knowledge, Bach reviewed articles on manufacturing overhead allocation for an automated factory and discussed the matter with some of her peers. Bach also gathered the following historical data on the manufacturing overhead rates experienced by Empco over the years. Bach wanted to have some departmental data to present at the meeting and, using Empco's accounting records, was able to estimate the annual averages for each manufacturing department in the 1980s.

	Historical Data		
Date	*Average Annual Direct Labor Cost*	*Average Annual Manufacturing Overhead Cost*	*Average Manufacturing Overhead Application Rate*
1940s	$1,000,000	$ 1,000,000	100%
1950s	1,200,000	3,000,000	250
1960s	2,000,000	7,000,000	350
1970s	3,000,000	12,000,000	400
1980s	4,000,000	20,000,000	500

	Annual Averages		
	Cutting Department	*Grinding Department*	*Drilling Department*
Direct labor	$ 2,000,000	$1,750,000	$ 250,000
Manufacturing labor	11,000,000	7,000,000	2,000,000

Required:

a. Disregarding the proposed use of robots in the Drilling Department, describe the short-comings of the system for applying overhead that is currently used by Empco Inc.

b. Explain the misconceptions underlying Bob Kelley's statement that the manufacturing overhead cost in the Drilling Department would be reduced to zero if the automation proposal was implemented.

c. Recommend ways to improve Empco Inc.'s method for applying overhead by describing how it should revise its overhead accounting system:

(1) In the Cutting and Grinding Departments.

(2) To accommodate the automation of the Drilling Department.

Capstone Case

Complete Cycle of Developing Rates, Applying Overhead, and Calculating Spending and Volume Variances

The following indirect factory overhead costs were budgeted for the Ethel Elizabeth Company for the year ended December 31, 19X1. The F or V notation indicates whether each cost is fixed or variable. The allocation bases also are given.

Indirect Costs	Amount	Fixed or Variable	Allocation Base
Depreciation of factory building	$10,000	F	Floor space
Factory superintendent's salary	20,000	F	Number of employees
Insurance on machinery	1,600	F	Investment in machinery
Power costs	40,000	V	Kilowatt-hours

In addition to these indirect costs, direct costs were budgeted for the three service departments (Factory Office, Maintenance, and Materials Storeroom) and the three production departments (Mixing, Assembly, and Finishing) as shown in the following exhibit:

Direct Costs	Factory Office	Maintenance	Materials Storeroom	Mixing	Assembly	Finishing	Total	F/V
Fuel, heat, and lights	$ 645	$1,763	$1,000	$ 480	$ 690	$ 570	$ 5,148	V
Water	140	220	175	285	475	705	2,000	V
Indirect material	215	180	190	1,200	1,600	1,115	4,500	V
Indirect materials	195	40	125	200	350	415	1,325	F
Indirect labor	500	600	800	200	600	1,000	3,700	V
Indirect labor	175	80	340	320	540	545	2,000	F
Total direct costs...........	$1,870	$2,883	$2,630	$2,685	$4,255	$4,350	$18,673	
Total variable costs	$1,500	$2,763	$2,165	$2,165	$3,365	$3,390	$15,348	V
Total fixed direct costs	370	120	465	520	890	960	3,325	F
Total direct costs	$1,870	$2,883	$2,630	$2,685	$4,255	$4,350	$18,673	

Managers took a plant survey and estimated the budgeted data:

Department	Square Feet	No. of Employees	Investment in Machinery	Kilowatt-Hours	Cost of Materials Used
Factory office	1,600	100	$ 500	800	$ 600
Maintenance	2,500	150	1,000	600	100
Materials storeroom ...	7,000	300	700	500	—
Mixing	10,000	550	15,000	47,000	5,000
Assembly	15,000	400	10,000	20,050	3,000
Finishing	13,900	500	12,800	11,050	2,000
Total	50,000	2,000	$40,000	80,000	$10,700

Required:

a. Using the step method, calculate the predetermined variable and fixed factory overhead rates for the three producing departments. The estimated allocation bases are Mixing, 81,778 direct labor-hours; Assembly, $134,275 direct labor dollars; and Finishing, 90,116 machine-hours. Allocate service departments in this order: Factory Office (on basis of employees), Maintenance (on basis of square feet), and Materials Storeroom (on basis of materials cost). Round to nearest dollar in allocating costs. (In allocating the indirect and service department costs, it will be helpful to distinguish between fixed and variable costs.)

b. Apply overhead to the three production departments using the factory overhead allocation rates you determined in Requirement a. Actual direct labor-hours in Mixing were 82,000 and direct labor dollars were $136,000 in Assembly; actual Finishing machine-hours were 85,000 hours. After distributing service department costs, total actual costs for the production departments were $43,618—Mixing; $30,051—Assembly; $25,748—Finishing. Calculate the over- or underapplied factory overhead for each department. (It is not necessary to distinguish between fixed and variable costs.)

c. Calculate spending and volume variances for each of the production departments.

PART II

Product Cost Allocation and Accumulation Procedures

CHAPTER
6

Job Order Costing

Chapter Objectives

After studying this chapter, you should be able to:

1. Identify the manufacturing characteristics that help determine whether a job order, process, or operation costing assignment is most appropriate.

2. Explain the source documents for the job cost sheet that accountants use to determine product costs.

3. Journalize basic entries associated with job order cost accounting systems.

4. Adapt job order costing to meet the specific needs of service organizations.

Introduction

Determining the cost of products and services is an important cost accounting function because it affects the success of contract bidding and product pricing. With increasing national and global competition, small costing disparities can have a large impact on whether a company survives. Also, rapid technological changes have increased the need for accurate cost information. These changes encourage managers to adopt strategies and product designs that improve the production process. Armed with accurate product costs, managers can assess each job's profitability. Product-costing data not only guide continuous improvement but are also required for external reporting.

Job Order, Process, and Operation Costing

After accumulating costs by departments or responsibility centers as presented in Chapter 4, accountants assign them to products or orders through either job order costing, process costing, or operation costing. Job order and process costing are the two polar extremes while operation costing represents a hybrid costing system. The nature of manufacturing activities determines which cost application system to use. Service organizations use costing systems similar to manufacturers except that usually they have no inventories. In providing services, they incur labor and overhead like manufacturing operations. Activity-based management, presented in Chapter 5, may be combined with either job order or process costing or a combination of these product costing systems.

Job Order Costing

With a **job order cost** system, costs are assigned to each job. A job may be an order, a contract, a unit of production, or a batch performed to meet customers' specifications. For example, job order costing is appropriate for printing or publishing companies, laundries, marketing firms preparing advertising campaigns, accounting firms performing audits or preparing tax returns, and any organization producing a tailor-made good or service according to customers' specific requirements. For example, a printing company uses job order costing because printers usually produce each printing order to one customer's specifications. A mechanic also uses job order costing to accumulate the costs of an automobile repair job. The mechanic collects the cost of repair parts and the direct labor-hours spent in repairing the car. Overhead costs are applied using an overhead rate. Accountants also use job order costing in the construction of commercial and residential buildings, ships, and machines. In addition, job order costing is appropriate for companies making different components for inventory.

Process Costing

Using a **process costing** system, accountants accumulate costs for each department for a time period and allocate costs among all the products manufactured during that period. Companies that mass produce homogeneous goods such as chemicals, petroleum, bakery goods, and canned food in a continuous production process use process costing. Direct material, direct labor, and applied factory overhead are accumulated for each department for a period, usually a month. At the end of the period, departmental cost is divided by the number of units produced to obtain a cost per unit. Process costing is discussed in detail in Chapters 7 and 8.

Strategic Planning

Current Cost Management Practice

Coleman's new CEO recognizes that its brand name is bigger than the company. As a result, they are trying to spread Coleman's name beyond the campground into hardware. The CEO believes his firm's reputation for rugged, reliable products will click with tradespeople and backyard handypersons, even if they have not pitched a tent in years. The company also is redesigning its approach to foreign markets, where its presence is still largely limited to camping goods. They had a major problem in Europe because Europeans preferred butane gas appliances, rather than Coleman's propane appliances. To remedy this situation, purchases of British and Italian camping equipment makers allowed Coleman to use its name on butane products. Coleman plans to squeeze even more value out of its brand name.

John Labate, "Coleman: Growing to Match Its Brand Name," *Fortune,* June 13, 1994, p. 114.

Operation (Hybrid) Costing

Each company develops its own product costing system that meets its specific needs. Many companies employ an **operation costing** system or **hybrid costing system** to manufacture goods having different direct materials but similar processing. An operation is a routine production method, technique, or step that is repetitively performed. Operating costing is appropriate for clothing, furniture, and food manufacturers. For example, a manufacturer of men's suits makes distinctions between batches of product, such as Style A men's suits and Style B suits. Various styles of men's suits require different fabrics (such as wool, cotton, or silk) and hand sewing operations, but similar machine sewing.

As in job order costing, accountants specifically allocate direct materials to the batches using operation costing. However, direct labor and overhead are absorbed in the same manner as under process costing. They apply conversion costs to all physical units passing through the operation by using a single average unit conversion cost for that operation. Operation costing best meets the needs of a batch manufacturer whose products have variations of a single design and require a varying sequence of standardized operations. Because job order and process costing represent the two ends of a continuum, companies adapt features from each to have a system that best reflects their actual processing.

Accounting for Materials in Job Order Systems

After a company receives materials, clerks classify them as direct materials if they become a part of the finished product, or indirect materials if they are used in the manufacturing process. A material requisition records the material flow. The **material (stores) requisition** form is a basic source document informing the cost accounting department that material has been issued. No material should be issued from the storeroom unless a material requisition is processed. This is a basic internal control procedure.

Material Requisitions and Issues

Exhibit 6–1 illustrates a typical manufacturing material requisition form indicating that Job No. 101 needs five pounds of thread and 15,000 yards of cloth in the Sewing Department. The material requisition not only fixes responsibility for the requisi-

EXHIBIT 6–1

MATERIAL REQUISITION

Requisition no: __911__

Department to be charged __Sewing Department__   Job No.: __101__   Date: __1/12/19X1__

Deliver to ___Sewing Department___   Date wanted ___1/15/19X1___

Quantity	Unit of measure	Description of item	Unit price	Extension
5	Pound	Cotton-polyester thread	$2/lb.	$10
15,000	Yard	72" 14 oz. cloth	$0.43/yd.	$6,450

___Bill Cox___	___Mary Miller___
Requested by	Issued by

---

tion of goods but also provides information for future reference. Requests for unusual material not normally carried in stock go to the Purchasing Department.

Issuance of Direct Material.   Material requisitions facilitate assigning material cost to a job or department. Companies use *issue slips* that serve the same purpose. Because the material requisition indicates the department requesting the material, it becomes the source document for recording the transfer of costs from Direct Materials Inventory to Work in Process Inventory or Factory Overhead. Accountants charge materials purchased for a specific contract directly to that contract.

Most companies accumulate material requisitions for a week or month and make one entry to record the raw material used; otherwise, a company would have many entries per month. However, for illustrative purposes, the following journal entry charges Job No. 101 for direct materials listed on the material requisition shown in Exhibit 6–1. Note that Job No. 101 is a subsidiary work in process account to the general ledger account.

Work in Process Inventory—Job No. 101	6,460	
Direct Materials Inventory		6,460

Issues of Indirect Material.   When the material requisition requests $1,000 of factory supplies, which are indirect materials, accountants charge Factory Overhead Control. And, they debit the indirect materials subsidiary ledger for Factory Overhead Control as follows:

Factory Overhead Control—Indirect Materials	1,000	
Factory Supplies Inventory		1,000

Material Credit Slips.   Clerks issue **material credit slips** when a department returns material to the storeroom. They also use these slips to correct errors in material issuance. The credit slip transfers the material accountability from the production department back to the storekeeper. Material credit slips transfer only reusable material. Changed or damaged materials become scrap. Material credit slips are the source document used by the accounting department to give credit to the department returning the material. In effect, they offset material requisitions. Normally an entry is made recording a batch of material credit slips. However, for illustrative purposes, the following entry records the issuance of a material credit slip:

Direct Materials Inventory	XXX	
Work in Process Inventory—Job No. 101		XXX

Labor Accounting

Accurate, understandable methods for calculating payroll are necessary. Probably no other area in accounting has more impact on the morale of employees than do employee wage and benefit policies. If only a few employees are unsure about how their gross and net wages are calculated or believe errors are involved, they can create discontent in their peer group. For this reason, companies should carefully explain the wage payment and employee benefit plans to all employees.

Variety of Labor Systems.   **Wages** designate hourly or piece-rate payment which represents a variable cost. **Salaries** describe a fixed periodic payment, such as a weekly or monthly payment. Even though a variety of payroll methods exists, understanding the basic labor accounting concepts presented in this chapter will allow you to readily adapt them to a company's particular payroll system.

Various laws require employers to withhold from the pay of employees certain taxes and to remit these amounts periodically to the proper authorities. These tax withholdings include federal, state, and city income taxes and Social Security taxes (FICA). Assume that payroll deductions are $103 for FICA taxes, $263 for federal income taxes, and $104 for state income taxes. The following journal entry charges both the general ledger account (Work in Process Inventory) and its subsidiary ledger account (Job No. 101) for $1,300 direct labor incurred in the Sewing Department:

Work in Process Inventory—Job No. 101	1,300	
FICA Taxes Witheld or Payable		103
Federal Income Tax Withheld		263
State Income Tax Withheld		104
Payroll Payable		830

Payroll Taxes.   Payroll taxes also are levied directly on the employer for the benefit of employees. The primary payroll taxes include Social Security (FICA), unemployment taxes, and state workers' compensation insurance. In addition to the FICA taxes withheld from employees' payroll checks, employers also pay FICA tax. Unemployment taxes and workers' compensation are not withholdings from employees; along with the employer's share of FICA, they are additional labor costs to the employer. The following entry records $103 FICA, $35 state unemployment, and $10 federal unemployment payroll tax on direct labor as an indirect cost by charging them to Factory Overhead Control. Chapter 16 illustrates an alternative method of recording payroll taxes by recording them as a direct cost to Work in Process Inventory.

Factory Overhead Control	148	
FICA Taxes Payable		103
State Unemployment Taxes Payable		35
Federal Unemployment Taxes Payable.		10

Labor-Related Costs.   Labor costs include more than the basic earnings computed for each employee on an hourly or piecework basis, and thus represent a significant amount of money. There are many labor-related costs, such as payroll taxes, as just illustrated. Bonuses, holiday and vacation pay, free uniforms, medical insurance, and retirement pensions are other labor-related costs. Studies have shown that employee benefits add at least 35 percent to the basic labor cost of the average employee. Costs of fringes vary considerably by industry and somewhat by the size of the company and the geographical region.

To account for these labor costs, payroll and cost accountants must work closely together. To effectively control labor costs, cost accountants maintain accurate, timely records of labor costs by job or department. Cost accountants prepare performance reports for each department reflecting the level of workers' efficiency. Payroll accountants are concerned that payroll records conform with government regulations and also provide the supporting data necessary to calculate each employee's gross pay, withholdings, and net pay.

Timekeeping Records

Well-documented time records are necessary to protect against overpayments. For hourly employees, some form of timecard ensures that each employee was on the job for the specified hours. In addition, hourly employees receive premiums when working night shifts, working overtime (usually work over 8 hours a day or 40 hours a week is paid at one and one-half times the normal earnings), and working on holidays (usually paid at twice the normal rate). Because of these premiums, timekeeping systems record the time of day, the particular days worked, and total hours per day and week. In addition, vacation days, sick days, and other absences must be reported and recorded for correct calculation of pay.

Timecard.   A **clock card** or **timecard** provides evidence of employees being on the work site. Employees fill out clock or timecards manually or use a clock punch. Each employee's timecard or sheet shows the dates worked as well as arrival and departure times.

Job Time Tickets.   Because employees' timecard only indicates the total time worked, companies need a **job time ticket** to show the time each employee spent on individual jobs during the day. Exhibit 6–2 illustrates an individual job time ticket reflecting where the employee worked during the day, the name of the employee working on a particular job, the time the employee started and stopped, and the rate of pay. Employees can prepare their own forms if the forms are readily available and if a minimum of time is required to complete them. In other instances, supervisors or dispatch clerks complete the forms when employees report to them for a new assignment.

EXHIBIT 6–2   Individual Job Time Ticket

Date _____   Employee name (or no.) _____

Time started _____   Job No. _____

Time stopped _____   Department_____

Hours worked_____   Pieces completed _____

Rate_____   Amount _____

Approved _____

EXHIBIT 6–3   Daily Job Time Ticket

Date _____   Employee name (or no.)_____

Started	Stopped	Hours	Job No.	Department

Job No.	Hours	Other work	Hours	Total Hours

Regular   Overtime

Daily Time Ticket.   Instead of having an employee prepare a new ticket for each job worked during the day, a **daily job time ticket** summarizes all jobs the worker performed. The daily job time ticket, as illustrated in Exhibit 6–3, eliminates having more than one ticket per employee each day. The ticket has a space for the starting and stopping time for each job worked on. A tabulation at the bottom of the daily time ticket allows for the accumulation of hours worked on each assignment before the hours are posted to a job cost sheet. Exhibit 6–3 also shows total regular and overtime hours. Supervisors review and approve timecards and job tickets.

Each day, the timekeeper collects the previous day's job time tickets and time-cards. After comparing the time reported on these, any differences are investigated. If the difference is small, it is idle time and charged to Factory Overhead. This often represents the time required for the worker to transfer from one job to another. When the job time ticket shows more hours than the timecard, the time-keeper determines the cause by consulting the employee and supervisor. After receiving completed timecards and job time tickets, the payroll department uses them in calculating employees' pay.

Factory Overhead Application

Factory overhead is an important concern of cost center managers, whatever their responsibilities. Factory overhead costs are all factory costs, except direct material and direct labor, and include many different costs from a variety of sources.

Accountants record different factory overhead costs in various ways. For example, certain costs such as electricity, fuel, and water are paid for each month, while other manufacturing costs, such as insurance, vacations, and holidays, are accrued and arise from adjusting journal entries made at the end of the relevant period. The source documents for some factory overhead costs, such as indirect material (material requisitions) and indirect labor (job time tickets), originate internally. Other overhead costs arise from source documents prepared outside the company. The source documents for fire insurance, property taxes, and utility expenses are vendor invoices. The coding of the source documents to the proper factory overhead account and cost center is vital to the success of the budgetary system.

As discussed in Chapter 2, distributing actual factory overhead usually is not practical so we use estimated factory overhead application rates. Wells Manufacturing Company's $50 estimated factory overhead rate is applied to the 300 machine-hours incurred in the Sewing Department and to the 220 machine-hours incurred in the Treating Department to arrive at the charge to Work in Process. We debit both the general ledger account and Job No. 101, the subsidiary work in process ledger account. The entry to record the overhead applied to Job No. 101 is

Work in Process Inventory—Job No. 101	26,000	
Factory Overhead Control		26,000

As the entry shows, we apply overhead before transferring a job to finished goods inventory. However, a job does not have to be finished for overhead to be applied. Factory overhead must be applied (1) when a job is completed and (2) at the end of the period to all unfinished jobs. Thus, to have proper matching of actual factory overhead and absorbed or applied overhead, factory overhead must be applied to both complete and incomplete jobs worked on during the period.

Job Cost Sheet

A **job cost sheet** is the basic document in job order costing that accumulates costs for each job. Since costs are accumulated for each batch or lot in a job order accounting system, job cost sheets indicate the direct material and direct labor incurred on a job, as well as the amount of overhead applied. The file of incomplete job cost sheets can serve as the subsidiary ledger for Work in Process Inventory. There are different forms of job cost sheets. For example, a patient's medical record listing the cost of all medical services rendered for that patient is a hospital's job cost sheet.

In Exhibit 6–4, the heading on the job cost sheet contains such information as the job order, customer, and date required. Accountants enter the material costs of $6,460 used in the Sewing Department and $1,540 used in the Treating Department on the job sheet. After computing job charges from the job time ticket, accountants also enter the labor cost on the job cost sheet. In addition, they enter the overhead applied on the job cost sheet so the total cost of the job is known when the job is completed.

EXHIBIT 6-4

JOB ORDER COST SHEET
WELLS MANUFACTURING COMPANY

Customer   Job No.___101___
   Douglass Warehouse, Inc.   Product___144″ #8 cloth (144 rolls)___
   309 North 12th Street   Date required___1/23/19X1___
   Murray, Kentucky 42071   Date Started___11/16/19X0___
   For stock_____   Date completed___1/20/19X1___

SEWING DEPARTMENT

Direct Materials			Direct Labor		Factory Overhead		
Date	**Requisition Number**	**Amount**	**Date**	**Amount**	**Date**	**Basis**	**Amount**
1/16/19X1	911	$6,460	1/18/19X1	$1,300	1/20/19X1	machine-hours	$15,000

TREATING DEPARTMENT

Direct Materials			Direct Labor		Factory Overhead		
Date	**Requisition Number**	**Amount**	**Date**	**Amount**	**Date**	**Basis**	**Amount**
1/18/19X1	914	$1,540	1/19/19X1	$ 700	1/20/19X1	machine-hours	$11,000

SUMMARY

	Sewing Department	Treating Department	Total
Selling price			$100,000
Incurred in prior period . . .	$20,000	$20,000	$40,000
Direct materials costs	6,460	1,540	8,000
Direct labor costs	1,300	700	2,000
Factory overhead applied .	15,000	11,000	26,000 → 76,000
Gross margin		76,000	$24,000 *Profit*

After the company finishes and sells Job No. 101, the accountant completes the summary at the bottom of the job cost sheet. The entry records the transfer of Job No. 101 to Finished Goods Inventory:

Finished Goods Inventory	76,000	
Work in Process—Job No. 101		76,000

Basic Journal Entries in Job Order Costing Summarized

The following journal entries summarize the basic transactions in a job order cost system used by the Wells Manufacturing Company, including the entries for Job No. 101 previously illustrated. In practice, special journals are normally used (i.e., sales entries are recorded in a sales journal, and cash payments in a cash disbursements journal); here we illustrate only a general journal.

The journal entries illustrated omit the subsidiary ledger account titles to emphasize the general ledger accounts. Also to simplify the illustrations, Wells Company is working on only three jobs, including Job No. 101 whose costs were journalized earlier. Exhibit 6–5 illustrates the posting of the following journal entries.

Direct and Indirect Materials Purchased.   The following entry records the purchase of direct or indirect raw material on account:

a.

Direct Materials Inventory	55,000	
Accounts Payable		55,000
Factory Supplies Inventory	7,000	
Accounts Payable		7,000

Direct and Indirect Materials Issued.   Assume the issuance of $8,000 direct materials for Job No. 101, $12,000 for Job No. 102, and $19,000 for Job No. 103. Work in Process Inventory receives $39,000 total direct materials issued. The job subsidiary ledger records the detailed costs of each job. The following entry also illustrates the issuance of $5,000 of factory supplies charged to Factory Overhead Control and the indirect materials subsidiary ledger account.

b.

Work in Process Inventory	39,000	
Job No. 101—8,000		
Job No. 102—12,000		
Job No. 103—19,000		
Factory Overhead Control—Indirect Materials	5,000	
Direct Materials Inventory		39,000
Factory Supplies Inventory		5,000

Factory Labor Incurred.   The following entry to Work in Process Inventory records the direct labor cost for the three jobs. Assume Job No. 101 incurred direct labor costs of $2,000; Job No. 102, $3,000; and Job No. 103, $5,000. Each amount is posted to the respective account in the subsidiary job ledger. The following entry also records $33,000 indirect labor in the Factory Overhead Control account and the factory overhead subsidiary ledger. The credit of $43,000 to Payroll Payable represents the gross amount of wages payable. Additional entries record taxes and other amounts withheld from the employees' wages and the employer's payroll taxes, which are ignored in this illustration for simplicity.

c.

Work in Process Inventory	10,000	
Job No. 101—2,000		
Job No. 102—3,000		
Job No. 103—5,000		
Factory Overhead Control—Indirect Labor	33,000	
Payroll Payable		43,000

Marketing and Administrative Salaries.   The following entry records the marketing and administrative salaries of $6,000 and $5,000. Although this entry can be combined with entry *c,* we separated it here to emphasize that only factory payroll is charged to Work in Process Inventory and Factory Overhead Control. Subsidiary ledgers detail both the Marketing Expense Control and the Administrative Expense Control, but Exhibit 6–5 does not show these.

d.

Marketing Expense Control	6,000	
Administrative Expense Control	5,000	
Payroll Payable		11,000

Factory Depreciation.   Assume that depreciation for the period is $15,000 on the factory building and $13,000 on the factory machinery and equipment. We charge the Factory Overhead Control account in the general ledger and the depreciation account in the factory overhead control subsidiary ledger for this period's depreciation. The credits are entered in the accumulated depreciation contra asset accounts.

e.

Factory Overhead Control—Depreciation Expense	28,000	
Accumulated Depreciation—Building		15,000
Accumulated Depreciation—		
Machinery and Equipment		13,000

Marketing and Administrative Depreciation.   A separate entry records depreciation on the office equipment used by sales and administrative personnel. Alternatively, we could make this entry at the time we record factory depreciation. We charge all other marketing and administrative costs to these control accounts and illustrate only payroll and depreciation.

f.

Marketing Expense Control	2,000	
Administrative Expense Control	5,000	
Accumulated Depreciation—		
Machinery and Equipment		7,000

Factory Insurance.   The following entry records the expiration of $3,000 of prepaid insurance on the factory building and equipment. Previously, accountants debited the Prepaid Insurance asset account at payment of the policy premium. An entry to the Factory Overhead Control account in the general ledger and to insurance expense in the factory overhead subsidiary ledger records this cost.

g.

Factory Overhead Control—Insurance Expense	3,000	
Prepaid Insurance		3,000

Property and Payroll Taxes.   Estimates for both the tax rate and tax base may be needed for factory property taxes even though the exact amount to be paid may not be known. Normally an accrual for the tax liability occurs when using an estimate based on the rates and bases applicable in the preceding period adjusted for possible changes in the tax rates or assessed values. To record estimated property taxes on the factory, we debit Factory Overhead Control and credit Taxes Payable. A similar entry records the employer's payroll tax as illustrated earlier for Job No. 101. An additional entry debits the taxes account in the factory overhead subsidiary ledger.

h.

Factory Overhead Control—Tax Expense	2,500	
Taxes Payable		2,500

When the taxes are paid, we debit Taxes Payable for the amount accrued and debit Prepaid Taxes for the amount applicable to future periods; cash is credited. To simplify the illustration, no adjustment for over- or underaccrual of taxes occurs at payment.

Factory Miscellaneous Costs. A debit to Factory Overhead Control in the general ledger and to the Miscellaneous Factory Cost account in the factory overhead subsidiary ledger records a $1,000 cash payment for miscellaneous factory costs. We credit the cash account in the general ledger. This exhibit omits all other individual entries to the Cash account. Other cash receipts totaled $191,000 and other cash disbursements totaled $185,000, including $73,000 for marketing and administrative expense and $30,000 for mortgage payments. The following entry records the payment for miscellaneous factory costs:

i.

Factory Overhead Control—Miscellaneous Factory Costs .	1,000	
Cash.		1,000

Factory Overhead Applied. Using the $50 per machine-hour application rate for Wells Manufacturing Company from Chapter 2, each job receives the following applied overhead based on the machine-hours incurred:

Job No. 101	$26,000 ($50 x 520 machine-hours)
Job No. 102	39,000 ($50 x 780 machine-hours)
Job No. 103	7,000 ($50 x 140 machine-hours)

This entry is a summary entry recording the total overhead applied for this period. It transfers $72,000 total overhead applied to Work in Process Inventory. The Factory Overhead Control account is credited as follows:

j.

Work in Process Inventory.	72,000	
Job No. 101—26,000		
Job No. 102—39,000		
Job No. 103—7,000		
Factory Overhead Control		72,000

Transfer to Finished Goods. Assume that during the period, Wells Company employees complete Job No. 101 and Job No. 102 and transfer them to Finished Goods Inventory. Job No. 101 had a beginning balance of $40,000; additions this period were direct material of $8,000, direct labor of $2,000, and factory overhead of $26,000. We transfer the $76,000, total cost of Job No. 101, from both the job ledger and Work in Process Inventory by credits to these accounts. Workers started and finished Job No. 102 this period; the total cost is $54,000. Job No. 103, with costs of $31,000, remains unfinished in Work in Process Inventory at the end of the period.

k.

Finished Goods Inventory	130,000	
Work in Process Inventory		130,000
Job No. 101—76,000		
Job No. 102—54,000		

Sale Is Made. To record the sale on account of Job No. 101 for $100,000, we debit Accounts Receivable and credit Sales. We charge Cost of Goods Sold for the $76,000 cost of Job No. 101. The credit of $76,000 to Finished Goods Inventory removes the cost of Job No. 101 from this asset account.

l.

Accounts Receivable.	100,000	
Sales		100,000
Cost of Goods Sold.	76,000	
Finished Goods Inventory		76,000

This journal entry does not illustrate additional sales on account totaling $199,500. A debit to Cost of Goods Sold and a credit to Finished Goods Inventory records the $120,000 cost of these sales. Assume $314,500 is received on account and credited to the accounts receivable ledger.

Underapplied Factory Overhead.   The balance in the Factory Overhead Control account at the end of the period arises because actual factory overhead amounted to $72,500, while the overhead applied was only $72,000. The difference of $500 represents an underapplication of overhead. Because this balance reflects inefficiencies of the current month, it is closed as a debit to Cost of Goods Sold. The credit of $500 closes Factory Overhead Control.

m.

Cost of Goods Sold.	500	
Factory Overhead Control		500

Subsidiary Factory Ledgers

Exhibit 6–5 illustrates the use of the Factory Overhead Control account in the general ledger and the need for using subsidiary ledger accounts to detail actual factory overhead costs. For most companies, the number of factory overhead costs is too great to set up individual accounts in the general ledger, so accountants establish individual overhead accounts in a subsidiary ledger. The total balance of all accounts in the factory overhead subsidiary ledger should equal the balance in the Factory Overhead Control account in the general ledger. The association between the Factory Overhead Control account and its subsidiary ledger is similar to that for accounts receivable and accounts payable general ledger accounts and their respective subsidiary ledgers. Accountants set up individual subsidiary ledger accounts for each expense by department or by cost center. Codes in the chart of accounts facilitate the distribution of actual factory overhead to specific expense accounts and also to departments and other cost centers. For example, Account No. 5141 can indicate that indirect material (code 514) is charged to Cost Center No. 1. Instead of using account code numbers, detail for departments can be calculated in other ways. For example, accountants prepare analysis sheets for each department to accumulate the actual factory overhead items incurred. Chapter 4 emphasizes the need for detailing actual factory overhead by department to develop departmental factory overhead applied rates.

Exhibit 6–5 also shows a job order subsidiary ledger. Normally, subsidiary ledgers for direct material inventory and finished goods inventory also are used, but Exhibit 6–5 does not illustrate these ledgers. The total of the three jobs in the work in process subsidiary ledger equal the balance of the Work in Process general ledger account: $76,000 (Job No. 101) + $54,000 (Job No. 102) + $31,000 (Job No. 103) = $161,000. Because subsidiary ledgers for work in process inventory and factory overhead control are usually more difficult to understand, Exhibit 6–5 illustrates these subsidiary ledgers.

For the resulting cost of goods manufactured statement and statement of income for Wells Manufacturing Company for the year ended December 31, 19X1, see Exhibits 2–4, 2–5, and 2–7 in Chapter 2.

EXHIBIT 6–5

Cash

Beginning balance	15,000	*(i)* Miscellaneous factory costs	1,000
Receipts	191,000	Disbursements	185,000
	206,000		186,000
Balance 20,000			

Accounts Receivable

Beginning balance	90,000	Received on account	314,500
(l) Sales	100,000		
Other sales	199,500		
	389,500		
Balance 75,000			

Direct Materials Inventory

Beginning balance	16,000	*(b)* Issues	39,000
(a) Purchases	55,000		
	71,000		
Balance 32,000			

Factory Supplies Inventory

Beginning balance	4,000	*(b)* Issues	5,000
(a) Purchases	7,000		
	11,000		
Balance 6,000			

Work in Process Inventory

Beginning balance	40,000	*(k)* Transfer to finished goods	130,000
(b) Direct material	39,000		
(c) Direct labor	10,000		
(j) Applied overhead	72,000		
	161,000		
Balance 31,000			

Finished Goods Inventory

Beginning balance	180,000	*(l)* Transfers to cost of	
(k) Transfers from		goods sold	76,000
work in process	130,000	Transferred to cost of goods	
	310,000	sold for other jobs sold	120,000
Balance 114,000			

Prepaid Insurance

Beginning balance	5,000	*(g)* Expired insurance	3,000
Balance 2,000			

Accumulated Depreciation—Building

		Beginning balance	40,000
		(e) Depreciation expense	15,000
		Balance	55,000

Accumulated Depreciation—Machinery and Equipment

		Beginning balance	15,000
		(e) Depreciation expense	13,000
		(f) Depreciation expense	7,000
		Balance	35,000

EXHIBIT 6–5   (continued)

Sales

(l) Sale on account	100,000
Other sales	199,500
	299,500

Cost of Goods Sold

(l) Sale	76,000
Other sales	120,000
(m) Underapplied overhead	500
Balance	196,500

Factory Overhead Control

(b) Indirect material	5,000	*(j)* Applied	72,000
(c) Indirect labor	33,000	*(m)* To close underapplied	500
(e) Depreciation	28,000		72,500
(g) Insurance	3,000		
(h) Taxes	2,500		
(i) Miscellaneous	1,000		
	72,500		

Marketing Expense Control

(d) Payroll	6,000
(f) Depreciation	2,000
Cash disbursements for other expenses	30,000
Balance	38,000

Administrative Expense Control

(d) Payroll	5,000
(f) Depreciation	5,000
Cash Disbursements for other expenses	25,000
Balance	35,000

Work in Process Subsidiary Ledger Accounts
Job No. 101

Beginning balance	40,000	*(k)* Transferred to finished goods	76,000
(b) Direct material	8,000		
(c) Direct labor	2,000		
(j) Applied overhead	26,000		
	76,000		

Job No. 102

(b) Direct material	12,000	*(k)* Transferred to finished goods	54,000
(c) Direct labor	3,000		
(j) Applied overhead	39,000		
	54,000		

Job No. 103

(b) Direct material	19,000
(c) Direct labor	5,000
(j) Applied overhead	7,000
	31,000

EXHIBIT 6–5   (concluded)

Factory Overhead Subsidiary Ledger
Indirect Material

(b)	5,000	

Indirect Labor

(c)	33,000	

Depreciation

(e)	28,000	

Insurance

(g)	3,000	

Taxes

(h)	2,500	

Miscellaneous Factory Costs

(i)	1,000	

Job Order Costing for Service Organizations

Although manufacturers use a job order sheet similar to that shown in Exhibit 6–4, service organizations perform jobs that differ from each other and use a variety of job order costing. Service organizations include print shops, repair shops, tailors, lawn service companies, and professional services such as medical, legal, veterinary, accounting, and consulting.

Two major differences in job order costing for manufacturers and service organizations are (1) because direct material is often insignificant for service organizations, it may be included in overhead rather than accounted for separately; and (2) service labor and labor-related costs are usually larger than other costs. As a result, a service organization's predetermined overhead rate is more frequently based on labor. For some service organizations, labor is often the only directly traceable cost. However, for legal and consulting services, long-distance telephone charges, photocopying, travel, and entertainment are directly traceable to the client or job.

Exhibit 6–6 shows a job cost sheet for optical service. Looking at this sheet, you can see that the ICD–9 code is the diagnosis and the CPT code is the type of professional service rendered. (All insurance carriers require forms to include a ICD–9 code and a CPT code.) The type of glasses sold is indicated in the optical service category. An optometrist who receives assignments agrees to accept what insurance pays even if this is less than the total charges. Accumulating the costs of each patient's tests, X-rays, and direct labor time spent allows professionals such as the

EXHIBIT 6–6

Bill Jones O.D., Family Optometry

			294 ¦ 00			294 ¦ 00		0	Jane Smith
DATE	FAMILY MEMBER	DESCRIPTION	CHARGES	PAYMENT ¦ ADJ. CREDITS		CURRENT BALANCE	PREVIOUS BALANCE		NAME

Medicare # _____

ICD-9 CODE: DIAGNOSIS
- 366.9 ☐ Cataract OD, OS, OU
- 372.14 ☐ Conjunctivitis Allergic
- 372.3 ☐ Conjunctivitis
- 918.1 ☐ Corneal Abrasion
- 371.50 ☐ Corneal Distrophy
- 370.00 ☐ Corneal Ulcer
- 362.53 ☐ Cystoid Macular Edema
- 250.0 ☐ Diabetes Mellitus
- 250.5 ☐ Diabetes Per History
- 375.15 ☐ Dry Eye Syndrome
- 379.91 ☒ Eye Pain
- 365.9 ☐ Glaucoma
- 784.0 ☒ Headache
- 370.9 ☐ Keratitis
- 377.30 ☐ Optic Neuritis
- 361.0 ☐ Retinal Tear
- 379.24 ☐ Vitreous Floaters
- ☐ _____

CPT CODE: PROFESSIONAL SERVICE   FEE
NEW   ESTAB   REFRACTION ☐YES☐NO
- 92020 ☐ Gonioscopy _____
- 92083 ☒ Visual Field Extended $120
- 92082 ☐ Visual Field, Quantitative _____
- 92283 ☐ Color Vision _____
- 92285 ☐ External Ocular Photography _____
- 92070 ☐ Therapeutic Treatment _____
- 92060 ☐ Sensorimotor Examination _____
- 99050 ☐ After Hours Service _____
- 99058 ☐ Emergency Service _____
- 99070 ☐ Supplies/Materials _____
- 99080 ☐ Special Reports _____
- 90605 ☐ Intermediate Consultation _____
- 65222 ☐ Corneal Foreign Body Removal _____
- 65435 ☐ Corneal Rust Ring _____
- 68800 ☐ Tear Duct Dilation _____
- 68840 ☐ Lacrimal Canaliculi _____
- ☐ _____

OPTICAL SERVICE

A		RX 1	RX 2
Frame		$100	___
Lenses		___	___
Oversize		___	___
Tint		___	___
Scratch Resist		___	___
Prism		___	___
Safety/Sports		___	___
Repair		___	___
A: Sub-Total	$ ___		

B: CONTACT	☐ Fitting		☐ Replacement
	⊙D	OS	OU
Soft ✗	65	___	___
Gas P. ___	___	___	___
Ext. W. ___	___	___	___
Hard ___	___	___	___
B: Sub-Total	$ 65		

Accept Assignment ☑ Yes ☐ No

Bill Jones   O.D.
Doctor's Signature

21830

PROFESSIONAL CHARGES $ 120
I hereby authorize the undersigned Physician to release any information acquired in the course of my examination or treatment.

Jane Smith   *1-10-19X5*
Signed (Patient, or Parent, if Minor)   Date

A & B Optical Total $	165
Sales Tax $	9
Professional Charges $	120

WHITE COPY/OFFICE   YELLOW COPY/PATIENT   PINK COPY/INSURANCE

TOTAL CHARGES $ 294

optometrist to estimate a profit margin on service performed for each patient or client. Job order sheets also can contain categories for the different labor skills showing the hours each charge.

Summary

Companies use either job order, process costing, or operation costing systems to assign costs to products. Activity-based management may be combined with these product costing systems. A batch, a contract, or an order receives costs using a job order system. Direct material and direct labor associated with each job are identified and accumulated on a job cost sheet. Because factory overhead resources usually cannot be traced to specific jobs, overhead is applied on a causal basis. This chapter illustrates the source documents and journal entries used in job order systems.

Process costing accumulates costs by departments for a time period and allocates costs among the products processed during the period. Process costing requires less record-keeping; however, the benefits of knowing the cost of each job may outweigh the added costs of a job costing system. A company may find that a hybrid of the process costing and job order costing systems best meets its needs; such systems are operation costing systems. Both service and manufacturing organizations should select the systems that best meet their individual needs.

Important Terms and Concepts

Job order costing   160
Process costing   160
Operation costing   161
Hybrid costing   161
Material (stores) requisition   161
Material credit slips   162

Wages   163
Salaries   163
Clock card (timecard)   164
Job time ticket   164
Daily job time ticket   165
Job cost sheet   166

Problem for Self-Study

Forecasted Income Statement Based on Projections Given

The following information regarding one unit of product has been abstracted from the records for the year ending March 31, 19X2, of Kohn Manufacturing Company:

	Per Unit	
Sales price	$100	
Direct materials	22	
Direct labor	15	
Variable factory overhead	10	
Fixed factory overhead	18	
Marketing expense	6	(35% is variable)
Administrative expense	4	(10% is variable)

Management is formulating a strategy to increase company sales; they want to sell more than the 4,200 units sold last year. The alternative being considered is a sales price reduction to stimulate sales. A 10 percent reduction in unit sales price will result in a 20 percent increase in the units sold. The existing plant facilities are adequate for producing the increased volume. Because the company will be able to take advantage of quantity discounts, direct materials cost will decrease by $2.00 per unit. There will be, however, an 8 percent increase in the labor cost per unit. No other changes are projected. Provide for no change in the level of inventories maintained.

Required:

a. Prepare a pro forma statement of income for the next year using the projections presented. No cost of goods manufactured statement is required; instead, detail the cost of sales on the statement of income.

b. Prepare a statement of income for the year ending March 31,19X2. Compare the income before taxes on this statement to that on the pro forma and advise management regarding the proposed price reduction and sales increase. Support your conclusions.

Solution to Problem
for Self-Study

a.

KOHN MANUFACTURING COMPANY
Pro Forma Statement of Income
For the Year Ending March 31, 19X3

Sales (4,200 units × 120%) × $90		$453,600
Cost of goods sold:		
Direct materials (5,040 units × $20)	$100,800	
Direct labor [5,040 units × ($15 × 108%)]	81,648	
Factory overhead—variable (5,040 units × $10)	50,400	
Factory overhead—fixed (4,200 units × $18)	75,600	
Total cost of goods sold		308,448
Gross margin		$145,152
Less: Marketing expense—variable [5,040 × (35% × $6)]	10,584	
Marketing expense—fixed [4,200 × (65% × $6)]	16,380	
Administrative expense—variable [5,040 × (10% × $4)]	2,016	
Administrative expense—fixed [4,200 × (90% × $4)]	15,120	44,100
Income before taxes		$101,052

b.

KOHN MANUFACTURING COMPANY
Statement of Income
For the Year Ending March 31, 19X2

Sales (4,200 units × $100)		$420,000
Cost of goods sold:		
Direct materials (4,200 units × $22)	$92,400	
Direct labor (4,200 units × $15)	63,000	
Variable factory overhead (4,200 units × $10)	42,000	
Fixed factory overhead (4,200 units × $18)	75,600	
Total cost of goods sold		273,000
Gross margin		$147,000
Less: Marketing expense—variable [4,200 × (35% × $6)]	$ 8,820	
Marketing expense—fixed [4,200 × (65% × $6)]	16,380	
Administrative expense—variable [4,200 × (10% × $4)]	1,680	
Administrative expense—fixed [4,200 × (90% × $4)]	15,120	42,000
Income before taxes		$105,000

Note: Management should not initiate the price reduction even though the number of units sold will increase. Income before taxes for 19X2 is higher than that projected for 19X3. Sales price and production should remain at the current levels.

Review Questions

1. Explain if all variable costs are direct costs and if all direct costs are variable.

2. Explain how you could use job order costing in a nonmanufacturing firm or industry.

3. Contrast job order and process costing systems. What factors dictate whether a job order or process cost system is more appropriate?

4. How does a dentist or veterinarian use the job cost sheets that you personally see?

5. What could cause a difference between the time reported on a time card and that shown on a job time ticket? How should this difference be reported?

6. If the total material cost of 100 units is $200 and a 10 percent increase in material cost is expected at the same time that an increase of 50 percent in volume of production is planned, what is next year's total budgeted cost of materials?

7. What is the source document for the distribution of direct labor costs to Work in Process Inventory and indirect labor costs to Factory Overhead Control?

8. What methods and documents are used to control materials inventories?

9. What form does the subsidiary ledger for a Work in Process Control account in a job order costing system take?

Exercises

E6–1 Journal Entries for Cost Transations

Pineapple Corporation has asked you to record the following data relating to factory labor and overhead for one period during the year. Before operations began, management estimated direct labor costs for the year at $120,000 and factory overhead costs at $72,000.

1. An analysis of store requisitions showed indirect material amounted to $15,000.

2. The labor time tickets showed that actual labor cost was $72,000 including indirect labor of $9,000. Ignore salary deductions.

3. Cash of $2,100 was paid for miscellaneous factory overhead expenses.

4. Depreciation was $3,000 for the building and $1,000 for machinery and equipment.

5. Insurance of $500 on the building and machinery and equipment expired.

6. Accrued taxes on the factory building and factory machinery and equipment were estimated to be $5,600.

7. Apply factory overhead and close the under- or overapplied amount to Cost of Goods Sold.

Required:

Prepare journal entries for the transactions.

E6–2 Manufacturing Statement; Factory Overhead Schedule

Lee Company records provide the following data:

Janitorial supplies, January 1, 19X1	$ 2,000
Janitorial supplies, December 31, 19X1	1,600
Janitorial supplies purchased	14,000
Direct labor (25,000 hours)	115,000
Depreciation	8,500
Property taxes	1,700
Direct materials, January 1, 19X1	65,000
Direct materials, December 31, 19X1	70,000
Direct materials purchased	80,000
Indirect labor	42,000
Work in process, January 1, 19X1	105,700
Work in process, December 31, 19X1	95,800
Utilities	30,000
Finished goods inventory, January 1, 19X1	120,600
Finished goods inventory, December 31, 19X1	115,000
Rent	22,000

Factory overhead is applied at 105 percent of direct labor cost.

Required:

Prepare a cost of goods manufactured and sold statement for the year ended December 31, 19X1, using actual factory overhead. Also prepare a separate schedule for factory overhead showing a calculation of over- or underapplied factory overhead.

Critical Thought

E6–3 Balances in Inventory Accounts, Over- or Underapplied Overhead

For Box, Inc.'s first month of operations, materials and labor costs charged to three jobs worked on in May were:

	Job No.		
	101	*102*	*103*
Direct materials	$3,000	$4,500	$1,800
Direct labor at $8 per hour	3,200	2,400	2,000

Overhead is applied at the rate of $6 per direct labor-hour. Jobs No. 101 and 102 were completed, Job No. 101 was sold; Job No. 103 remained incomplete at the end of the month.

Box, Inc., incurred these costs during the month:

Direct materials purchases	$25,000
Direct and indirect factory labor costs	8,500
Factory overhead excluding indirect labor	5,000

Required:

a. Determine the May 31 balances in each of the three inventory accounts.
b. Compute the amount of over- or underapplied overhead.
c. Prepare the entry to dispose of the over- or underapplied overhead, treating the entire amount as a period cost.

E6–4 Applying Overhead to Job

In 19X1, Jett Company began work on Job No. 218, incurring a direct materials cost of $1,200 and a direct labor cost of $4,209 representing an actual labor rate of $6.10. The factory overhead application rate was $4.75 per direct labor-hour for 19X1. After evaluating 19X1 variances and undertaking further study, management revised the factory overhead application rate in 19X2 to $4.90 per direct labor-hour. After additional material costing $500 and 100 hours of direct labor at a $6.15 labor rate were incurred in January 19X2, Job No. 218 was finished and sold to a customer for $14,000 on account.

Required:

a. Compute the balance in Job No. 218 subsidiary ledger account on December 31, 19X1, when the year ends.
b. Give all journal entries relating to Job No. 218 for 19X2.

E6–5 Determination of Job Cost

Cavitt Company uses a job order system for its two departments. Budgeted production costs for the year are as follows:

	Department A	Department B
Budgeted costs for year:		
Direct materials	$ 60,000	$ 80,000
Direct labor	150,000	200,000
Factory overhead	450,000	80,000
Actual cost charged to Job No. 86 during year:		
Direct materials	1,000	800
Direct labor	3,000	2,200

Cavitt applies manufacturing overhead to production orders on the basis of direct labor cost using departmental rates determined at the beginning of the year based on the annual budget.

Required:

Determine the total manufacturing cost associated with Job No. 86 for the year.

E6–6 Job Order Costing

Ink, Inc., began work on four jobs during the current month of operation. Two of the jobs, Job No. 12 and No. 31, were completed during the month. Their cost sheets indicate that all costs applicable to them have been recorded on these sheets but not journalized. The remaining two jobs, Job No. 21 and No. 42, are still in process at the end of the month; all appli-cable costs except factory overhead have been recorded on the related cost sheets for these two unfinished jobs; also these costs have not been journalized. A total of $583.30 of indirect materials and $1,404 of indirect labor were used during the month in addition to the materials and labor charged directly to the jobs.

Job No. 12		Job No. 21	
Direct materials	7,717.50	Direct materials	14,250.00
Direct labor	5,700.00	Direct labor	19,200.00
Factory overhead	2,679.00	Factory overhead	
Total	16,096.50		

Job No. 31		Job No. 42	
Direct materials	6,120.00	Direct materials	2,625.00
Direct labor	10,950.00	Direct labor	3,540.00
Factory overhead	5,146.50	Factory overhead	
Total	22,216.50		

Required:

Prepare an entry, in general journal form, to record each of the following operations for the month (one entry for each operation):

a. Direct and indirect materials used.

b. Direct and indirect labor used.

c. Application of factory overhead on the basis of direct labor cost using a single overhead rate to all four jobs.

d. Completion and transfer to the finished warehouse of Jobs No. 12 and No. 31.

Problems

P6–7 Journal Entries and Cost of Goods Manufactured Statement

Constance Company completed these selected transactions during May 19X1:

1. Purchased $50,000 direct materials and $5,000 factory supplies on account.
2. Issued direct materials costing $40,000 into production and $3,000 factory supplies.
3. Cash was paid for miscellaneous manufacturing expense costing $4,000.
4. The following adjusting entries were made on May 31:

Depreciation on factory machinery and equipment	$11,400
Insurance expired on factory machinery and equipment	$2,500

5. The factory payroll was accrued and distributed as follows:

Indirect labor	$13,000
Direct labor (9,000 hours)	$45,000

6. Factory overhead is applied at $4.00 per direct labor-hour.
7. The balance in Work in Process Inventory on May 1, 19X1, was $12,000; the balance on May 31, 19X1, was $16,000. Transfer the costs of goods completed to the finished goods storeroom.
8. The May 1, 19X1, balance in Finished Goods Inventory was $26,000 while the May 31, 19X1, balance was $20,000. Record the entry for the goods sold on account that were priced at 120 percent of cost.
9. Close the Factory Overhead Control and transfer any over- or underapplied overhead to cost of goods sold.

Required:

a. Prepare journal entries for these transactions using a factory overhead subsidiary ledger.
b. Prepare a cost of goods manufactured statement for the month using actual factory overhead.

P6–8 Forecasted Income Statement

The controller of Wren, Inc., presented the following summarized income statement for the year ended June 30, 19X1, to the board of directors:

Sales (1,600 units)		$360,000
Less: Cost of goods sold:		
Direct materials	$176,000	
Direct labor	32,000	
Factory overhead ($50,000 fixed)	130,000	
Cost of goods sold		338,000
Gross margin		$ 22,000
Less: Marketing and administrative expenses:		
Marketing expenses ($18,000 variable*)	$ 28,000	
Administrative expenses (fixed)	30,000	58,000
Operating loss		($36,000)

*Variable with sales dollars.

Since management is disappointed with operating results, plans are made to change the marketing strategy. With this change, an increase in sales volume of 25 percent is expected. The following increases in unit costs and expenses are also expected: direct materials, 10 percent; direct labor, 2 percent; variable factory overhead, 4 percent. Variable marketing expense will remain the same percentage of sales dollars while all fixed costs remain the same.

Required:

a. Prepare a forecasted income statement for the next year incorporating all expected changes.

b. Account for any change in the cost per unit sold; use a breakdown for production, marketing, and administrative unit costs.

SPATS

P6–9 Preparing Journal Entries, a Cost of Goods Manufactured Statement, and an Income Statement

A partial list of the account balances on November 1, 19X1, for the Don Manufacturing Company were Direct Materials, $65,000; Indirect Materials, $8,000; Work in Process, $70,000; and Finished Goods, $88,000. Transactions for the month include the following:

1. Purchased direct materials costing $30,000 and indirect materials costing $10,000 on account.

2. Paid cash for the factory rent, $1,500.

3. Issued material costing $28,160 to three jobs for the processing of units.

4. Janitorial supplies costing $1,080 and repair supplies costing $5,780 were issued from the storeroom.

5. Analysis of the payroll records revealed that direct labor of $43,000, indirect labor of $26,000, marketing salaries of $5,000, and administrative salaries of $6,000 were to be recorded. Ignore payroll deductions.

6. Depreciation on the factory machinery amounted to $2,770, and on the factory building to $2,850.

7. Insurance of $500 expired on the factory building and machinery.

8. The cost accountant has budgeted factory overhead for the year to be $450,000 and machine-hours to be 90,000. Machine-hours for November were 8,000. Record the application of overhead.

9. Paid cash for miscellaneous factory overhead of $330.

10. There were 3,000 finished units costing $150,000 transferred into the warehouse.

11. During the month, 4,000 units costing $200,000 were sold on account for $300,000.

12. It was determined that the reason for the difference in actual and applied factory overhead was inefficiencies in the operating conditions. Close the Factory Overhead account.

13. Other marketing expenses of $3,000 and administrative expenses of $4,600 were paid.

Required

a. Prepare journal entries to record the transactions for the month, using subsidiary ledger accounts for factory overhead.

b. Prepare a cost of goods manufactured statement using applied factory overhead costs and also prepare a statement of income for the month.

SPATS

P6–10 Journal Entries Using Determination of Factory Overhead Application Rate

Tabby Catfood, Inc., budgets to sell 11,000 cartons of cat food each period. For the next period, management wants to have an ending inventory of 2,000 cartons; beginning inventory for the period is 3,000 cartons. Fixed costs of operations each period are budgeted to be $125,000; 50,000 hours of direct labor will be required for planned production next period. Variable overhead per carton is estimated to be $2. A summary of operations for the period follows:

1. Direct materials costing $31,000 and indirect materials of $7,600 were purchased on account.

2. Materials requisitioned and factory labor used:

	Materials	Factory Labor	Direct Labor-Hours
Job No. 1	$ 1,500	$ 62,300	7,570
Job No. 2	21,800	21,600	5,500
Job No. 3	2,500	40,200	8,040
Job No. 4	11,060	81,700	16,200
Job No. 5	31,960	100,780	12,500
For general factory use	810	900	

3. Factory overhead costs incurred on account, $63,000.

4. Factory machinery and equipment depreciation totaled $80,000.

5. Jobs finished: Nos. 1, 2, and 4. Jobs 3 and 5: 60 percent complete; apply factory overhead.

6. Transferred into finished goods storeroom: Nos. 1, 2, and 4.

7. Job Nos. 2 and 4 were shipped and customers were billed for $75,000 and $180,000 respectively.

8. Close over- or underapplied factory overhead.

Required:

a. Prepare entries in general journal form to record the summarized operations.

b. Open T accounts for Work in Process Inventory and Finished Goods Inventory and post the appropriate entries using the identifying numbers as dates. Insert memorandum account balances as of the end of the month.

c. Support the balance in the Work in Process account with a schedule of unfinished jobs.

d. Support the balance in the Finished Goods account with a schedule of completed jobs on hand.

P6–11 Forecasted Income Statement Based on Projections Given
The following information regarding one unit of product has been abstracted from the records for the year ending March 31, 19X2, of Donnell Manufacturing Company:

	Per Unit
Sales price	$120
Direct materials	30
Direct labor	20
Variable factory overhead	15
Fixed factory overhead	20
Marketing expense	8 (35% is variable)
Administrative expense	6 (10% is variable)

Management is formulating a strategy to increase company sales over the 5,000 units sold last year. The alternative that is presently being considered is a sales price reduction to stimulate sales. It has been determined that a 10 percent reduction in unit sales price will result in a 20 percent increase in the number of units sold. The existing plant facilities are adequate for producing the increased volume. Because the company will be able to take advantage of quantity discounts, direct materials cost will decrease by $1.50 per unit. There will be, however, a 5 percent increase in the labor cost per unit. No other changes are projected. Provide for no change in the level of inventories maintained.

Required:

a. Prepare a pro forma statement of income for the next year using the projections presented. No cost of goods manufactured statement is required; instead, detail the cost of sales on the statement of income.

b. Prepare a statement of income for 19X2. Compare the income before taxes on this statement to that on the pro forma and advise management regarding the proposed price reduction and sales increase. Support your conclusions.

P6–12 Impact on Gross Margin with Volume and Cost Changes

One product line is manufactured by Bond Company with sales of this product line for 19X1 expected to be $300,000. The following data indicate the cost of goods sold:

Direct materials used	$ 60,000
Direct labor	80,000
Fixed factory overhead	28,000
Variable factory overhead	72,000
	$240,000

Company management expects costs to rise and at year-end predicts the following will occur in 19X2 unless the product is redesigned.

Not Redesigning Product

1. Material prices will average 6 percent higher while direct labor rates will average 12 percent higher. Variable factory overhead will vary in proportion to direct labor costs.
2. There will be an 8 percent decrease in the number of units sold in 19X2 if the sales price is increased to produce the same rate of gross margin as the 19X1 rate; gross margin is expressed as a percentage of sales.

Redesigning Product

If instead the product is redesigned according to the suggestions of the marketing department, a 15 percent increase can be obtained in the number of units sold with a 12 percent increase in the unit sales price. By changing the product, costs will be impacted as follows:

1. A lower grade of material will be used that has averaged 8 percent below the price of the material now being used, but 5 percent more of it would be required for each unit. The 8 percent difference in price is expected to continue for the year 19X2.
2. The company can use less-skilled workers whose average pay rate for 19X2 would be 5 percent below the average for 19X1 due to the change in processing methods planned. However, 10 percent more labor per unit would be required than was needed in 19X1.
3. Variable overhead is incurred directly in relation to production, and it is expected to increase 7 percent because of price changes and to increase an additional amount in proportion to the change in labor hours.

Required:

a. Rounding to whole dollars, determine prospective gross margin if:
   (1) The same product is continued for 19X2 and sold at a price to earn the same gross margin percentage.
   (2) The product is redesigned for 19X2.
b. Advise management as to whether the product should be redesigned.

P6–13 Projected Cost of Goods Manufactured and Income Statements

Management of Peru, Inc., desires to have 1,800 units in ending inventory of finished goods at the end of 19X3; production is assumed to occur evenly throughout the year. Direct materials and work in process inventories are so small that they can be ignored in the next year's forecasts. Marketing personnel predict that 19X3 sales will be 29,700 units at $15 per unit which represents a significant sales increase from the previous two years. Materials X and Y are mixed to form the finished product. A change in the production process is being made in 19X3 so that the quantity of Material X used in a unit of product will be decreased 4 percent while the quantity of Material Y used in a unit of product will be increased 5 percent. The price of Material X is expected to continue the percentage trend of the past two periods while the price of Material Y is expected to be $1.10 in 19X3. A wage increase of 5 percent was given in the middle of 19X1 and 19X2, and a similar increase is expected in the middle of 19X3. The amount of fixed factory overhead was $12,000 during 19X1 and 19X2 without any change expected for 19X3. Also, the variable unit factory overhead is expected to remain the same in 19X3 as in former years. FIFO costing is used. Production and sales data for 19X1 and 19X2 are as follows:

Units

	19X1	19X2
Beginning inventory	1,000	3,000
Production	10,000	12,000
	11,000	15,000
Sales	8,000	13,500
Ending inventory	3,000	1,500

Sales and Cost	19X1			19X2	
	Amount	Per Unit		Amount	Per Unit
Sales	$98,000			$195,750	
Cost of sales:					
Direct materials					
X $25,000			$36,000		
Y 10,000	$35,000	$3.50	12,000	$ 48,000	$4.00
Direct labor	20,000	2.00		25,200	2.10
Factory overhead ..	20,000	2.00		21,600	$1.80
Inventory variation	−15,000			+10,650	
Cost of sales	$60,000	$7.50		$105,450	$7.90
Gross margin	$38,000			$ 90,300	

Required:

a. Show how the inventory variation for 19X1 and 19X2 was computed.

b. Determine production requirements for 19X3.

c. Prepare projected 19X3 cost of goods manufactured statement supported by computations for costs of materials, labor, fixed and variable overhead. Carry per unit cost to three decimal places.

d. Prepare projected 19X3 income statement through gross margin showing inventory variation (increase or decrease).

SPATS

P6–14 Budgeted Income Statement and Cost of Goods Manufactured under Certain Assumptions

Barton Company's cost of goods manufactured and income statement for the year ended December 31, 19X1, follow. Beside the cost figures is an indication of whether they are variable (V) or/and fixed (F). The company produced 50,000 units in 19X1. Assume that finished goods inventory is carried at the average unit cost of production and material prices have been stable during 19X1.

BARTON COMPANY
Cost of Goods Manufactured
For the Year Ended December 31, 19X1

Direct materials:

Inventory, January 1, 19X1		-0-	
Purchases of direct material		$ 50,250	
Direct materials available		$ 50,250	
Inventory, December 31, 19X1		250	
Direct materials used		$ 50,000	V
Direct labor		35,000	V
Factory overhead:			
Utilities	$ 2,500	V	
Supervision	19,000	($5,000 V, $14,000 F)	
Miscellaneous overhead	$44,000	($ 4,000 V, $40,000 F)	65,500
Cost of goods manufactured			$150,500

BARTON COMPANY
Income Statement
For the Year Ended, December 31, 19X1

Sales			$409,500
Less: Cost of goods sold:			
Finished goods, January 1, 19X1	-0-		
Cost of goods manufactured	$150,500		
Cost of goods available	$150,500		
Finished goods, December 31, 19X1	13,545		
Cost of goods sold			136,955
Gross margin			$272,545
Less marketing and administrative expenses:			
Marketing expenses	$ 25,000	($16,380 V* $8,620 F)	
Administration expenses	25,000	F	50,000
Income before income taxes			$222,545

---

*Variable with sales dollars.

Required:

Show and *label* all calculations and supporting computations. Using the preceding information, prepare a budgeted income statement, including a schedule of cost of goods manufactured, for Barton Company for 19X2 under the following assumptions:

a. Unit sales prices will remain the same.
b. Variable cost per unit will remain the same.
c. Fixed costs will remain the same.
d. Sales will increase to 63,000 units.
e. Ending finished goods inventory, December 31, 19X2, will be 3,000 units and is to be carried at the average unit cost of production for 19X2.

P6–15 Preparing Journal Entries and Using a Subsidiary Ledger for Work in Process
Before operations begin for the year 19X2, the management of the Cent Company predicts factory overhead will be $51,200 while estimated machine-hours will be 6,400.

At the beginning of 19X2, the Work in Process account and the job order ledger appear as follows:

Work in Process Inventory		**Job No. 1**	
Balance	8,050	Direct material	2,200
		Direct labor	1,500
		Applied factory	
		overhead	1,050
		Balance	4,750

Job No. 2		**Job No. 3**	
Direct material	360	Direct material	570
Direct labor	475	Direct labor	280
Applied factory		Applied factory	
overhead	1,015	overhead	600
Balance	1,850	Balance	1,450

Required:

a. Record the following journal entries using general ledger accounts; in addition, use subsidiary ledger accounts for work in process assuming the company employs a perpetual inventory system.

Jan. 2   Purchased direct material of $3,000, repair supplies of $1,800, and factory supplies of $200 for cash.

4   Issued materials as follows:

Job No. 1	$ 200
Job No. 2	300
Job No. 3	1,000
Repair supplies	1,500

10   Job No. 1 was finished and transferred to the storeroom. It was determined that during the month of January, direct labor cost on this job was $450 while machine-hours totaled 230.

16   The following factory items were paid for in cash:

Rent	$700
Insurance	500
Miscellaneous expense	200

19   Additional material was issued from the materials storeroom:

To Job No. 2	$307
To Job No. 3	116
Factory supplies	80

20   Job No. 1 was sold for $7,500 on account.

24   Job No. 2 was finished and transferred to the storeroom. It was determined that during the month of January, direct labor cost on this job was $345 while machine-hours totaled 202.

31   Analysis of the time sheets showed the following unrecorded factory labor: Job No. 3, $225; factory supervision $150; and maintenance employees, $100.

31   Overhead was applied to the remaining jobs in process. Machine-hours on Job No. 3 during January amounted to 70 hours.

31   Depreciation of $775 on the factory building was recorded.

31   Close the over- or underapplied overhead to Cost of Goods Sold.

b. Prove your balance in Work in Process Inventory.

P6–16 Journal Entries and Cost of Goods Manufactured Statement
McElroy Company completed the following selected transactions during May 19X1:

Required:

a. Prepare journal entries for these transactions using a factory overhead subsidiary ledger.
   (1) Purchased $57,000 direct materials and $8,000 factory supplies on account.
   (2) Issued direct materials costing $36,000 into production and $5,000 factory supplies.
   (3) Cash was paid for miscellaneous manufacturing expense costing $4,000 and $6,000 for factory rent.
   (4) The following adjusting entries were made on May 31:

Depreciation on factory machinery and equipment	$1,400
Insurance expired on factory machinery and equipment	$2,500

   (5) The factory payroll was accrued and distributed as follows:

Indirect labor	$13,000
Direct labor (9,000 hours)	$45,000

   (6) Factory overhead is applied at $3.50 per direct labor-hour.
   (7) The balance in Work in Process inventory on May 1, 19X1, was $16,000; the balance on May 31, 19X1, was $13,000. Transfer the costs of goods completed to the finished goods storeroom.
   (8) The May 1, 19X1, balance in Finished Goods Inventory was $22,000 while the May 31, 19X1, balance was $26,000. Record the entry for the goods sold on account that were priced at 130 percent of cost.
   (9) Close the Factory Overhead Control and transfer any over- or underapplied overhead to cost of goods sold.
b. Prepare a cost of goods manufactured statement for the month showing only applied factory overhead.

P6–17 Using T-Account Analysis for Cost Flow Determination

Critical Thought

A mudslide destroyed many of the records of California Company on November 11, 19X7. For insurance reimbursement purposes, you have been asked to determine the cost of inventory destroyed. The company used a job order costing system. You have verified the following information:

1. At the beginning of the fiscal year on July 1, 19X7, the balances in these accounts were Direct Materials Inventory, $10,000; Factory Supplies Inventory, $4,000; Work in Process Inventory, $8,000; and Finished Goods Inventory, $14,000. The balance sheet also showed a $3,000 balance reflecting the liability for accrued payroll.
2. Direct materials costing $18,000 were purchased on account between July 1 and November 11.
3. A total of $17,000 direct materials and $2,000 factory supplies were issued to the factory.
4. A total of $35,000 was paid in factory wages between July 1 and November 11. Ignore all payroll deductions. On November 11 there were $2,000 accrued factory wages payable.
5. Of the factory wages, direct labor totaled $30,000.
6. The debits to the Factory Overhead account during the period before the mudslide totaled $20,000 excluding the indirect materials and indirect labor.
7. Overhead is applied using a rate of 85 percent of direct labor costs.
8. Goods costing $50,000 were finished and transferred to Finished Goods Inventory between July and November.

9. Goods costing $55,000 were sold this period.

10. The company follows the policy that if the balance in Factory Overhead is small, it is distributed to Cost of Goods Sold; otherwise it is apportioned among Work in Process, Finished Goods, and Cost of Goods Sold based on their balances before the apportionment.

Required:

Use T-account analysis in determining the November 11 balance of Direct Materials, Factory Supplies Inventory, Work in Process Inventory, and Finished Goods Inventory.

CHAPTER
7

Process Costing—Weighted-Average and FIFO

Chapter Objectives

After studying this chapter, you should be able to:

1. Contrast the difference between process, job order, and operation costing in assigning costs to products.
2. Discuss what characteristics of manufacturing procedures make process costing appropriate.
3. Prepare departmental cost of production reports using weighted-average and FIFO costing.
4. Explain the change an automated manufacturing environment has on process costing and equivalent unit calculations.

Introduction

Organizations assign costs to products through either job order costing, process costing, or operation costing. As you learned in Chapter 6, job order and process costing are the two polar extremes while operation costing represents a hybrid-costing system. The nature of manufacturing activities (i.e., whether they are automated or manual, whether they make customized products or standard products) determines which of the cost application systems is most appropriate.

Contrast between Job Order, Process, and Operation Costing

Process costing is an effective costing system for firms that employ assembly-line production to create a continuous flow of goods. After completing manufacturing, workers transfer units to the finished goods warehouse because these goods were not produced for a specific customer. All units in the specific product line are identical. In contrast, **job order** manufacturing normally begins only when a customer places an order. Each job receives varying amounts of skill and attention depending on the customer's specifications; thus, the unit cost per order differs. Managers determine total cost at the time each job order is finished. Exhibit 7–1 illustrates this, using the three jobs presented in Chapter 6. With process costing, accountants accumulate costs by operating centers for a given period. They determine total cost at the end of the costing period.

An **operation costing** system represents a hybrid method, having some of the characteristics of both process and job order costing. For example, in operation costing, accountants allocate direct materials specifically to the batches similar to job order costing. Like process costing, they apply direct labor and overhead to all physical units passing through the operation by using a single average unit conversion cost for the operation.

Companies use operation costing when manufacturing goods that have some common characteristics plus some individual characteristics. Operation costing meets the needs of a batch manufacturer whose products have variations of a single design and require a varying sequence of standardized operations. Job costing continues to be the best alternative for accumulating the cost of contracts and customized manufacturing. However, the trend is toward process costing systems and cost systems that are custom designed, such as operation costing.

Departmentalization of Work in Process Inventory

Process costing assumes a sequential flow from one department to other departments as units travel through the production process. The costs of processing increase the unit's cost as it moves from department to department while each performs its specific task. An easy way to visualize this flow is to think of a snowball gathering snow (costs) as it travels from one department to another. Process costing usually assumes that units do not skip departments. That is, all units leave the first department and take their costs with them to the second department, and so on to all departments. For example, Exhibit 7–1 illustrates the movement of units and costs through Departments A, B, and C. If this pattern

Global

Current Cost Management Practice

Matsushita is finding that its overseas network of factories is not only its most valued asset but one of its toughest management challenges. By having overseas plants, the company can tailor its home appliances and electronic devices to the idiosyncrasies of consumers in different countries. However, its success abroad is causing many overseas plants to compete with the company's factories in Japan. This puts pressure on Matsushita's managers and engineers to devise other, more advanced products to keep its Japanese employees gainfully busy. The company president believes their success in manufacturing abroad helps them more than it hurts because it provides a greater incentive to develop new products and technologies in Japan.

Brenton R. Schlender, "Matsushita Shows How to Go Global," *Fortune,* April 18, 1994, pp. 159–66.

varies, a flowchart outlining the movement of units is helpful. Individual departments maintain a Work in Process Inventory subsidiary ledger and costs are summarized by departments. In job order costing, a Work in Process Inventory subsidiary ledger is maintained for individual job orders, such as for Job Nos. 101, 102, and 103 as Exhibit 7–1 illustrates.

Equivalent Units

In a typical manufacturing operation, accountants assign some costs to unfinished units at the end of the period. Thus, a department's total cost is distributed to both the units finished in a period and the partially completed units in ending work in process inventory. Because partially completed units have used fewer resources than complete units, however, division of a department's total costs by physical units is inappropriate. Instead, accountants convert units in work in process inventory into **equivalent finished units** (also called **equivalent production** or **equivalent full units**) and distribute costs on that basis. For example, 320 equivalent units equal 800 units that are 40 percent complete in Exhibit 7–2's beginning inventory. Thus, 40 percent of the processing on these 800 units was done last period. The 60 percent processing to complete these 800 units will be done this period. Likewise, the costs incurred to process the 200 units in ending inventory to a 20 percent stage is expressed as the cost to complete 40 units. If unit cost is $4, we distribute $160 costs to these 200 units.

As illustrated for Exhibit 7–2, the stage of completion for each batch of work in process determines the equivalent units. The ease of calculating the percentage of completion varies among industries and depends on the availability of data about the amount of material and hours of labor required to finish a product. To better illustrate the costing procedure, the stages of completion in the exhibits and problems in Chapters 7 and 8 are more exact than is usually practical in actual manufacturing operations.

Before moving a unit to the next department, a unit must have completed the entire operating cycle of the department. After finishing in that department, the unit may still not be in a finished state ready for shipping to a customer. Only when it is leaving the company's final department is the product ready for a user.

EXHIBIT 7–1   Process and Job Order Costing Compared

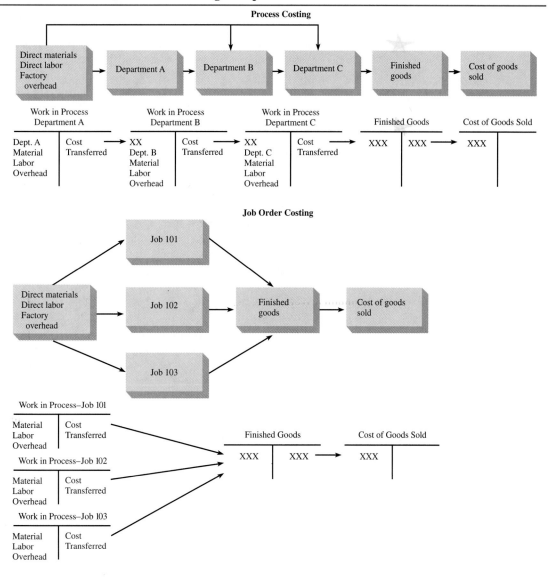

EXHIBIT 7–2   Flow of Units

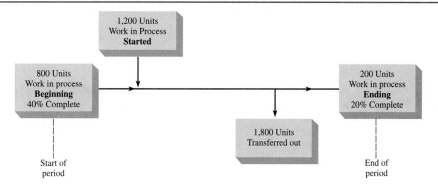

Weighted-Average and FIFO Costing

Two methods account for the beginning inventory costs in process costing:

 1. **Weighted-average costing:** We average the previous period costs of completing the beginning inventory to a semifinished state with the current period's costs to arrive at a unit cost. Units in beginning inventory receive the same unit cost as the units started and finished during the period; thus, all units transferred have an identical unit cost.

 2. **First-in, first-out (FIFO) costing:** The FIFO method separates the cost of the units finished from beginning inventory from the cost of the units started and finished during the period. We assume the beginning inventory cost flows out of work in process first. The cost of the goods transferred contains the cost of the goods finished that were in beginning inventory and the cost of the goods started and finished during the current period. We value ending work in process inventory at the unit cost of current production for the period. Dividing equivalent units into the production costs incurred in the current period only determines the unit cost of current production.

Difference in Equivalent Units.   FIFO equivalent units differ from units based on weighted-average costing because of the difference in the assumption concerning the cost flow of beginning inventory. Units are lost through spoilage, evaporation, and shrinkage during processing. The following weighted-average and FIFO equivalent units (EU) formulas exclude lost units that we introduce in Chapter 8:

EU, weighted-average costing	=	Units completed and transferred × 100%	+	Partially completed ending inventory × stage of completion		
EU, FIFO costing	=	Units completed and transferred × 100%	+	Partially completed ending inventory × stage of completion	−	Beginning inventory × stage of completion

To illustrate the calculation of EU, assume the following data for a department:

Units in beginning inventory (40% complete for all cost elements, $1,556 costs incurred to date)	800	
Units started in process during the current period	1,200	2,000
Units completed and transferred out	1,800	
Units in ending inventory (20% complete for all cost elements)	200	2,000

Using weighted average, EU are as follows:

EU, weighted average = 1,800 units transferred + 40 ending inventory = 1,840
(200 units × 20%)

EU calculated using FIFO costing differ as follows:

EU, FIFO = 1,800 units transferred + 40 ending inventory − 320 beginning inventory = 1,520
(200 units × 20%)   (800 units × 40%)

The next illustration shows the difference in distributing the beginning inventory costs under weighted average and FIFO, assuming $1,556 beginning inventory costs and $6,080 current costs.

Weighted-Average Costing

$$\frac{\$1,556 \text{ cost of beginning inventory} + \$6,080 \text{ current costs}}{1,840 \text{ weighted-average EU}} = \frac{\$7,636}{1,840} = \$4.15 \text{ average unit cost}$$

FIFO Costing

$$\frac{\$6,080 \text{ current costs}}{1,520 \text{ FIFO EU}} = \$4 \text{ current unit cost}$$

Sources of Units Transferred

Whether a firm uses FIFO or average costing, the total units transferred to the next department come from these two sources:

1. Beginning inventory.
2. Current production, also called **units started and finished** during the period. Note that units started and finished are not the same as units started in process or units transferred. **Units started in process** merely indicate that units were introduced into the production process; they may not have been finished at the end of the period. **Units transferred** come from both current production of units started and finished and from beginning inventory. The classification of *unit transferred* does not indicate the unit's source but merely that the unit left the department.

We always assume that a company finishes beginning inventory before starting units during the period. In weighted-average costing, the source of the units transferred does not matter because we cost out all units transferred during the period at an average. Using FIFO, we keep the costs of the units from these two sources separate. In the earlier example illustrating equivalent unit computations of the 1,800 units transferred, 800 come from beginning inventory and 1,000 from current production.

Cost of Production Report

In process costing, a **cost of production report** summarizes total and unit costs. Either each cost center or department makes such a report, or accountants combine individual reports of several departments. Regardless of the format chosen from the many available, an orderly approach to preparing the cost of production report is important. The following four steps provide a uniform approach; note these steps in parentheses in the chapter's exhibits.

Step 1. Prepare quantity schedule.
Step 2. Calculate equivalent units and unit costs.
Step 3. Determine the costs to account for.
Step 4. Distribute all costs and account for all costs.

Steps Illustrated Using Weighted-Average Costing

Exhibit 7–3 illustrates a cost of production report using the weighted-average method with only one department, simply called Department 1. Next we discuss each section of the cost of production report.

EXHIBIT 7–3

CASPARI COMPANY
Cost of Production Report—Weighted Average
For Month Ending January 31, 19X1

Department 1

Quantity schedule (Step 1):

Beginning inventory (all material, 2/3 labor and overhead)	600
Units started in process	7,600
Units transferred out	7,200
Ending inventory (all material, 1/5 labor and overhead)	1,000

(handwritten: 8,200 in / 8,200 out)

	Total Costs	Unit Costs

Costs to account for (Step 3): *(handwritten: input)*

Work in process—beginning inventory:

Material	$ 2,720	
Labor and overhead	5,000	
Total beginning inventory	$ 7,720	

Current costs in department:

Material	$13,680	$ 2.00
Labor and overhead	30,520	4.80
Total costs to account for	$51,920	$ 6.80

Costs accounted for as follows (Step 4): *(handwritten: output)*

Costs transferred out (7,200 × $6.80)		$48,960
Work in process—ending inventory:		
Material (1,000 × $2.00)	$ 2,000	
Labor and overhead (1,000 × 1/5 × $4.80)	960	2,960
Total costs accounted for		$51,920

Additional computations (Step 2):

	Transferred		Ending Inventory		
EU, Department 1, material	7,200	+	1,000	=	8,200
			(1,000 × 100%)		

$$\frac{\$2,720 + \$13,680}{8,200} = \frac{\$16,400}{8,200} = \$2.00$$

	Transferred		Ending Inventory		
EU, Department 1, labor and overhead	7,200	+	200	=	7,400
			(1,000 × 1/5)		

$$\frac{\$5,000 + \$30,520}{7,400} = \frac{\$35,520}{7,400} = \$4.80$$

(handwritten left margin: ★ labor + OH = conversion cost   ★ labor + mat'l = prime cost)

Step 1—Department 1's Quantity Schedule. A quantity schedule lists the units for which the department is responsible. This schedule accounts for all units started in the department. A quantity schedule shows the disposition of these units—whether transferred to finished goods or to the next department, lost, or remaining in ending inventory. This part of the cost of production report often is called the physical flow section; it concerns only whole units, regardless of their stage of completion.

The quantity schedule expresses units of the department's finished products in any appropriate measurement, such as feet, gallons, or pounds. We express all units in the same measure. Assume, for example, that a department produces shirts and each shirt requires two yards of fabric. If the department begins cutting and sewing 2,000 yards of fabric, the quantity schedule shows the starting of 1,000 units (2,000 yards/2 yards per shirt) in process because the units transferred out are expressed in finished shirts.

The quantity section shows that Department 1 placed 7,600 units into the production process. It had 600 units in beginning inventory, having all their material and two-thirds of their labor and overhead, with a total cost of $7,720. For ease in computing the equivalent units in Step 2, the quantity schedule shows the stage of completion next to the units.

At this introductory stage, you may wonder if the quantity schedule is worth your time and effort. In more complicated process costing operations, where units are added or lost, preparation of the quantity schedule assures accounting for all units.

Step 2—Department 1's Equivalent Units and Unit Costs.   The bottom of the cost of production report shows the computations for equivalent units and unit costs. Cost of production reports distributed to nonaccountants often omit the additional computation section. This explains why the steps are not shown in sequence in the body of the cost of production report. Regardless of whether units transferred came from beginning inventory or from current production, we add them to the equivalent units in ending inventory to determine total equivalent units of production. Since Department 1 introduces material at the beginning of the operations, we multiply the units in ending inventory by 100 percent in computing equivalent units for materials. They have all the material they need for completion. Because Department 1 adds labor and overhead evenly throughout the process, they are combined. Often the cost of production report labels labor and overhead costs as conversion costs. In computing the equivalent units for labor and factory overhead, we multiply the ending inventory by its one-fifth stage of completion. Before Department 1 transfers these units out, it must add an additional four-fifths in subsequent periods. To determine the labor and overhead unit costs, we convert these 1,000 partially completed units into 200 equivalent finished units. This is computed strictly for unit costing purposes; of course, there are still 1,000 unfinished units.

To determine the unit cost for materials, labor, and factory overhead, we consider equivalent units rather than total physical units. While the exhibits and problems in Chapters 7 and 8 carry unit cost out to four or five decimal places, accountants usually round total cost to whole dollars.

Weighted-average costing adds the individual cost in the beginning inventory to the current cost. Dividing the equivalent units into this total cost gives the unit cost. For example, units receive all their Department 1 material when they enter the production process. Even though the units in ending inventory are not complete, they have all their Department 1 material. Adding the $2,720 material cost of the semi-finished goods in beginning inventory to the $13,680 current material costs gives a total of $16,400 material cost; dividing that total by 8,200 equivalent units gives $2 unit cost. Department 1 labor and factory overhead require similar computations, which gives a $4.80 unit cost.

We insert each unit cost in the costs to account for section of the cost of production report to arrive at a total departmental unit cost of $6.80 (the total of the calculated equivalent unit costs). The total cost to account for, $51,920, cannot be divided by any one equivalent unit figure to arrive at the unit cost of $6.80 because material and conversion costs involve a different stage of completion.

Step 3—Department 1's Costs to Account for.   The costs that a department is responsible for may come from several sources. Costs of material, labor, and factory overhead assigned to partially completed units in last period's ending inventory become the cost of the current period's beginning inventory and are accounted for. Also, if a department is not the first processing center, units received into operations from previous departments have costs attached. In addition, each department incurs materials and/or labor and factory overhead in its own processing. For example, Department 1 incurred a direct material cost of $13,680 and direct labor cost and factory overhead totaling $30,520 during January. Adding the $7,720 beginning inventory to these current costs, we have to account for $51,920 total costs.

Conversion Costs.   Determining only the total costs for each processing department is inadequate for control purposes. Instead, the cost of production report summarizes by department three cost components—direct material, direct labor, and factory overhead. The report also determines unit costs for each of the three elements. When factory overhead is applied on the basis of direct labor or if direct labor is such a small percent of the total production cost as may be found in automated factories, the cost of production report may combine factory overhead and labor. These costs are simply itemized as conversion costs. The cost of production report can detail each item of factory overhead and calculate a unit cost for individual cost elements. For brevity, the cost of production reports in this book do not calculate unit costs for each item of factory overhead; instead, they show unit costs for total material, labor, and factory overhead or for total material and conversion costs.

Step 4—Distributing Department 1's Costs and Accounting for All Costs.   Companies distribute costs to cost centers that receive units transferred out of a department. Units remaining in the department and any lost units receive the remaining costs. Chapter 8 discusses the assignment of lost unit costs.

By multiplying the 7,200 units transferred out by the $6.80 unit cost, we get a total cost of $48,960 transferred. There is no need to itemize transferred costs by the three components of material, labor, and factory overhead; we use only the total unit cost of $6.80. Because the 1,000 units in ending inventory have all their material and are 100 percent complete, we multiply all units by the $2 unit cost. The ending inventory is only partially completed for labor and overhead; therefore, the units are multiplied by their one-fifth stage of completion (which is their equivalent units of 200) before being multiplied by the $4.80 labor and overhead unit cost. The $2,960 value of the ending inventory becomes the beginning inventory for the next period in Department 1.

Two parts comprise the cost section of the cost of production report. One part determines the total costs that we must account for, while the other section shows the disposition of these costs. There must be agreement between these two sections; otherwise, there is an error. Determining that the total costs accounted for of $51,920 equal the total costs that the department is responsible for completes the cost of production report.

FIFO Costing Illustrated

To demonstrate the difference between FIFO and weighted-average costing, Exhibit 7–4 uses the cost data from Exhibit 7–3 with the assumption that Caspari Company uses FIFO costing. The quantity schedules are identical. Using FIFO costing, accountants need not detail the cost of each component in beginning inventory, since they only use total inventory valuation. In comparing Exhibit 7–3 with Exhibit 7–4, note we use $7,720 total beginning inventory cost rather than itemized material and conversion costs. As you recall, weighted-average costing requires this detail to average the beginning inventory costs with current costs.

The difference between FIFO and weighted-average costing becomes clearer with the calculation of equivalent units in Exhibit 7–4. Calculated under FIFO, these represent current production only. Because we include the units completed and transferred from beginning inventory at 100 percent with the units started and finished to give total units transferred, the stage of completion of the beginning inventory is deducted in computing FIFO equivalent units.

EXHIBIT 7–4

CASPARI COMPANY
Cost of Production Report—FIFO
For Month Ending January 31, 19X1

		Department 1

Quantity schedule (Step 1):

Beginning inventory (all material, 2/3 labor and overhead)	600	
Units started in process	7,600	8,200
Units transferred out	7,200	
Ending inventory (all material, 1/5 labor and overhead)	1,000	8,200

	Total Costs	Unit Costs

Costs to account for (Step 3):

Work in process—beginning inventory:		
Material	$ 2,720	
Labor and overhead	5,000	
Total beginning inventory	$ 7,720	
Current costs in department:		
Material	$13,680	$ 1.80
Labor and overhead	30,520	4.36
Total costs to account for	$51,920	$ 6.16

Costs accounted for as follows (Step 4):

1.) Costs transferred out M,L,OH		
From beginning inventory:		
Value of beginning inventory	$ 7,720	
Labor and overhead added		
(600 × 1/3 × $4.36)	872	$8,592
2) From current production		
(6,600 × $6.16)		40,656
Total cost transferred out		49,248
Work in process—ending inventory:		
Material (1,000 × $1.80)	$ 1,800	
Labor and overhead (1,000 × 1/5 × $4.36)	872	2,672
Total costs accounted for		$51,920

Additional computations (Step 2):

	Transferred		Ending Inventory		Beginning Inventory		
EU, Department 1, material	7,200	+	1,000	−	600	=	7,600
$\frac{\$13,689}{7,600} = \$1.80$			(1,000 × 100%)		(600 × 100%)		
EU, Department 1, labor and overhead	7,200	+	200	−	400	=	7,000
$\frac{\$30,520}{7,000} = \$4.36$			(1,000 × 1/5)		(600 × 2/3)		

Different Formula for EU, FIFO.   The following formula for computing FIFO equivalent units differs slightly from that in Exhibit 7–4:

EU, FIFO	=	Units started and finished × 100%	+	Ending inventory × stage of completion	+	Beginning inventory × stage of completion to be added

Using this formula, the computation for labor and overhead in Department 1 in Exhibit 7–4 is as follows:

$$EU, FIFO = 6,600 \text{ started and finished}$$
$$+ \; 200 \text{ ending inventory} + 200 \text{ beginning inventory} = 7,000$$
$$(1,000 \times 1/5) \qquad\qquad (600 \times 1/3)$$

Units Started and Finished.   As illustrated in the formula, there is a difference between units transferred and units started and finished. The total units transferred come from the units started and finished in current production as well as from beginning inventory. For example, workers started 7,600 units in process but because 1,000 units remained in ending inventory, only 6,600 of the units were finished. This is an important point to remember in choosing the formula that appears easier. The correct use of either formula gives the same results.

Additional differences between FIFO and weighted average appear in determining the cost of the units transferred. Department 1 has 600 units in beginning inventory that need additional labor and overhead. The 600 units that reached a two-third stage of conversion cost completion last period receive an additional one-third equivalent units of conversion cost before being transferred out. For this reason, the 600 units are multiplied by one-third before being finally multiplied by $4.36 unit conversion cost. A transfer of 7,200 total units occurs; 600 of these units come from beginning inventory. This leaves 6,600 units started and finished in current production (7,200 total transferred − 600 transferred from beginning inventory = 6,600 transferred from current production). Do not calculate the units transferred from current production using this approach: 7,600 started in process − 1,000 units in ending inventory = 6,600 even though the same answer results. If this illustration contained the spoilage and dilution effects the next chapter presents, you would not have obtained the same answer. We assign $6.16 total departmental unit cost to each unit from current production. The ending inventory in Department 1 is multiplied by its stage of completion and the unit costs.

Subsequent Month and Department Using Weighted Average

January's ending work in process inventory valuation for Caspari Company becomes the beginning inventory for February. Exhibit 7–5 illustrates weighted-average costing for February using the ending inventory valuation for Department 1 from Exhibit 7–3. For example, to process Department 1's 1,000 units in beginning inventory into a semifinished state required costs of $2,960. Exhibit 7–5 adds data for a subsequent department to illustrate the transfer of costs. Department 2's quantity schedule indicates that 200 units were in beginning inventory when operations began. (Note that Department 2's January cost of production report was not illustrated.) Department 1 transferred 8,500 units during February to Department 2 for further processing. Unless stated otherwise, assume that units from the preceding department are introduced in subsequent departments at the beginning of operations. Department 2 adds

EXHIBIT 7–5

caspari company
Cost of Production Report—Weighted Average
For Month Ending February 28, 19X1

	Department 1		Department 2	

Quantity schedule (Step 1):

Beginning inventory (all material, $1/5$ labor and overhead)	1,000		($1/10$ M, $2/5$ L and OH) 200	
Units started in process	9,000	10,000	8,500	8,700
Units transferred to next department	8,500		8,100	
Ending inventory (all material, $1/3$ labor and overhead	1,500	10,000	($1/6$ M, $1/4$ L and OH) 600	8,700

	Total Costs	Unit Costs	Total Costs	Unit Costs
Costs to account for (Step 3):				
• Work in process—beginning inventory:				
Costs from preceding department	–0–		$ 1,300	
Material	$2,000		10	
Labor and overhead	960		875	
Total beginning inventory	$2,960		$ 2,185	
• Costs received from preceding department . .			56,100	$ 6.5977
• Current costs in department:				
Material	19,000	$ 2.10	3,680	0.4500
Labor and overhead	39,540	4.50	74,200	9.1000
Total costs to account for	$61,500	$ 6.60	$136,165	$16.1477
Costs accounted for as follows (Step 4):				
Costs transferred to next department (8,500 × $6.60)		$56,100	(8,100 × $16.1477) $130,796	
Work in process—ending inventory:				
Costs from preceding department			(600 × $6.5977) $ 3,959	
Material (1,500 × $2.10)	$3,150		(600 × $1/6$ × $0.45) 45	
Labor and overhead (1,500 × $1/3$ × $4.50)	2,250	5,400	(600 × $1/4$ × $9.10) 1,365	5,369
Total costs accounted for		$61,500		$136,165

Additional computations (Step 2):

	Transferred		Ending inventory		
EU, Department 1, material	8,500	+	1,500	=	10,000
$\dfrac{\$2,000 + \$19,000}{10,000} = \dfrac{\$21,000}{10,000} = \$2.10$			(1,500 × 100%)		
EU, Department 1, labor and overhead	8,500	+	500	=	9,000
$\dfrac{\$960 + \$39,540}{9,000} = \dfrac{\$40,500}{9,000} = \$4.50$			(1,500 × $1/3$)		
EU, Department 2, preceding department costs .	8,100	+	600	=	8,700
$\dfrac{\$1,300 + \$56,100}{8,700} = \dfrac{\$57,400}{8,700} = \$6.5977$			(600 × 100%)		
EU, Department 2, material	8,100	+	100	=	8,200
$\dfrac{\$10 + \$3,680}{8,200} = \dfrac{\$3,690}{8,200} = \$0.45$			(600 × $1/6$)		
EU, Department 2, labor and overhead	8,100	+	150	=	8,250
$\dfrac{\$875 + \$74,200}{8,250} = \dfrac{\$75,075}{8,250} = \$9.10$			(600 × $1/4$)		

material, labor, and factory overhead before the units become finished products ready for sale to a consumer. Of these 8,500 units, workers finished 8,100 units and transferred them to finished goods. Because Department 2 treats material differently, the ending inventory has only one-sixth of its materials needed for completion.

Department 2's Costs to Account for.   Adding currently incurred costs of material, labor, and factory overhead to beginning inventory costs yields the total costs to account for. Department 2 received 8,500 units from Department 1 and must account for the preceding department costs of these units, totaling $56,100. These costs from the preceding department include material, labor, and overhead. The arrows in Exhibit 7–5 denote both the transfer of units and the transfer of costs.

Because Department 2 adds material uniformly, neither the beginning nor ending inventory has all its material. Assume in February that Department 1 incurred $9,540 labor and $30,000 overhead, and Department 2 incurred $14,200 labor and $60,000 overhead. Because we add labor and factory overhead at the same pace, they are combined.

EU and Unit Costs.   We calculate equivalent units for the preceding department costs for departments subsequent to the first because units take on costs as they transfer from one department to another. (Think of the snowball gathering snow or costs, as it travels through the production process.) Units in Department 2 are 100 percent complete for prior department costs. This is the reason for including 8,100 units transferred and 600 units in ending inventory in their entirety rather than multiplying them by some fraction to determine equivalent units for the preceding department cost.

Using the weighted-average method, we average the costs assigned last month for beginning inventory to reach a semifinished stage with current costs. Breaking down the beginning inventory by individual cost elements, we add the cost of material, labor, and overhead to current costs *element by element*. For example in Exhibit 7–5, we average the $1,300 preceding department cost that the 200 units in Department 2's beginning inventory incurred in a prior period with the current cost of $56,100 transferred from Department 1. The resulting $6.5977 unit cost differs from the $6.60 Department 1 cost in Exhibit 7–5 because we average costs from a prior period with current costs. Avoid the temptation to carry the previous departmental unit cost, which is $6.60 in Exhibit 7–5, over to the next department; usually, the unit cost differs. (Note that if we were using more realistic numbers, the difference would likely be much more.)

Unit costs come out even to two decimal places in Department 1 but not in Department 2. As a result, we express unit costs in four decimal places in Department 2; this numerical precision helps to account for all costs. The cost of production report does not always balance if we round unit costs to two decimal places.

Disposition of Department 2's Costs.   After determining the unit costs for Department 2 for material, labor, and overhead, we add them to the previous department costs to arrive at a total unit cost of $16.1477. Each of the 8,100 units leaving Department 2 carries a cost of $16.1477, giving a total of $130,796 transferred to finished goods. Because all of the 600 units in ending inventory have been through a previous department, they each receive the averaged preceding department cost of $6.5977. Current costs assigned to ending inventory reflect the stage of completion. The final step is proving that the $136,165 cost is accounted for.

Current Cost Management Practice

Strategic Planning

Eli Lilly & Co. planned to spin off its medical device and diagnostics businesses and focus exclusively on its core pharmaceutical operations. This disvesture rid the company of products whose manufacture and marketing shared little with drugs, the company's main money-maker. Lilly has refocused on such key questions as: What do we have, what do we need, and who do we have that we don't need? The overall answer is that Lilly plans to emphasize its customer service and turn that message into results.

David Greising, "Randall Tobias Takes a Pruning Hook to Lilly," *BusinessWeek,* January 31, 1994, p. 32.

Subsequent Month and Department Using FIFO

Exhibit 7–6 illustrates FIFO costing for February using the Department 1 ending inventory valuation from Exhibit 7–4. The total costs of $55,799 transferred from Department 1 to Department 2 represent two batches—1,000 units finished during the period and 7,500 units started and finished in current production. Even though $55,799 transferred-in costs represent two batches, the cost is averaged after Department 2 receives the batches. In Exhibit 7–6, dividing the $55,799 total cost received by 8,500 equivalent units gives a single averaged preceding departmental cost of $6.5646, which differs slightly from the $6.6043 computed in Department 1.

Averaging within FIFO.   Accountants often call the FIFO method the modified or departmental FIFO method. FIFO costing is strictly applied within each department, but when transferring costs out, we use an averaging technique in the next department. Thus, all units received from a preceding department bear the same average unit cost. Accountants justify this slight modification because of the clerical cost involved in keeping costs strictly attached to each batch. Otherwise, the FIFO method would not be feasible in process costing because of the burdensome task of accounting for the mass of figures. If preferred, a company can use strict FIFO when the goods are transferred out of the last department into finished goods.

Materials Issued at Various Stages

When preparing cost of production reports, it becomes clear that because production processes differ, material enters the process at various stages. Rather than assume the introduction stage for material, you should obtain accurate information regarding the material issue point in the processing operation. For example, a shirt manufacturing process introduces fabric at the beginning of operations so cutting and sewing operations may begin. In other operations, such as the chemical industry, workers may add material in a continuous flow or at specific points in the manufacturing process. Other companies add some of the direct material at the end of a process in a department.

Journal Entries Using Process Costing

Similar to job order costing, entries accumulate direct material, direct labor, and factory overhead in process costing. However, instead of tracing costs to specific jobs or batches, we accumulate costs for departments or cost centers. Next, we explain journal entries for each cost component using data from Exhibit 7–6.

EXHIBIT 7-6

caspari company
Cost of Production Report—FIFO
For Month Ending February 28, 19X1

	Department 1			Department 2	
Quantity schedule (Step 1):					
Beginning inventory (all material,					
$^1/_5$ labor and overhead)	1,000		($^1/_{10}$ M, $^2/_5$ L & OH)	200	
Units started in process	9,000	10,000		8,500	8,700
Units transferred to next					
department	8,500			8,100	
Ending inventory (all material,					
$^1/_3$ labor and overhead	1,500	10,000	($^1/_6$ M, $^1/_4$ L & OH)	600	8,700

	Total Costs	Unit Costs		Total Costs	Unit Costs
Costs to account for (Step 3):					
Work in process—beginning inventory:					
Costs from preceding department	–0–			$ 1,300	
Material.	$1,800			10	
Labor and overhead	872			875	
Total beginning inventory	$2,672			$ 2,185	
Costs received from preceding department . .				55,799	$ 6.5646
Current costs in department:					
Material.	19,000	$2.1111		3,680	0.4499
Labor and overhead	39,540	4.4932		74,200	9.0820
Total costs to account for	$61,212	$6.6043		$135,864	$16.0965
Costs accounted for as follows (Step 4):					
Costs transferred to next department:					
From beginning inventory:					
Value of beginning inventory	$ 2,672			$ 2,185	
Material added	–0–		(200 × $^9/_{10}$ × $0.4499)	81	
Labor and overhead added					
(1,000 × $^4/_5$ × $4.4932)	3,595	$ 6,267	(200 × $^3/_5$ × $9.082)	1,090	$ 3,356
From current production					
(7,500 × $6.6043)		49,532	(7,900 × $16.0965)		127,162
Total cost transferred		$55,799			$130,518
Work in process—ending inventory:					
Costs from preceding department	–0–		(600 × $6.5646)	$ 3,939	
Material (1,500 × $2.1111)	$ 3,167		(600 × $^1/_6$ × $0.4499)	45	
Labor and overhead					
(1,500 × $^1/_3$ × $4.4932)	2,246	5,413	(600 × $^1/_4$ × $9.0820)	1,362	5,346
Total costs accounted for		$61,212			$135,864

Additional computations (Step 2):	Transferred		Ending Inventory		Beginning Inventory		
EU, Department 1, material	8,500	+	1,500	–	1,000	=	9,000
$\frac{\$19,000}{9,000} = \$2.1111$			(1,500 × 100%)		(1,000 × 100%)		
EU, Department 1, labor and overhead . . .	8,500	+	500	–	200	=	8,800
$\frac{\$39,540}{8,800} = \$4.4932$			(1,500 × $^1/_3$)		(1,000 × $^1/_5$)		
EU, Department 2, preceding department costs	8,100	+	600	–	200	=	8,500
$\frac{\$55,799}{8,500} = \$6.5646$			(600 × 100%)		(200 × 100%)		
EU, Department 2, material	8,100	+	100	–	20	=	8,180
$\frac{\$3,680}{8,180} = \$0.4499$			(600 × $^1/_6$)		(200 × $^1/_{10}$)		
EU, Department 2, labor and overhead . . .	8,100	+	150	–	80	=	8,170
$\frac{\$74,200}{8,170} = \$9.0820$			(600 × $^1/_4$)		(200 × $^2/_5$)		

Material Journal Entries Using Process Costing.   Chapter 6 describes material requisitions used in job order costing. In process costing, the material requisition indicates the department charged rather than the job order number. The entry charging Departments 1 and 2 for the material used during February is

Work in Process—Department 1—Direct Material	19,000	
Work in Process—Department 2—Direct Material	3,680	
Direct Materials Inventory		22,680

Labor Journal Entries Using Process Costing.   Process costing eliminates the detailed work of accumulating labor by jobs on job time tickets. Instead, daily or weekly time tickets or clock cards become the basis of distributing payroll charges. The following entry uses only a payroll summary account to distribute the payroll and ignores payroll deductions. A typical entry to allocate the direct labor charges for Exhibit 7–5 or 7–6 is as follows. (Remember that during February Department 1 incurred $9,540 labor and $30,000 overhead and Department 2 incurred $14,200 labor and $60,000 overhead; they are combined as conversion costs on Exhibits 7–5 and 7–6.)

Work in Process—Department 1—Direct Labor	9,540	
Work in Process—Department 2—Direct Labor	14,200	
Payroll		23,740

Factory Overhead Using Process Costing.   In a job order costing system, factory overhead application rates ease the costing of products. Rather than wait until the end of operations to distribute actual factory overhead, accountants use estimated factory overhead rates in job order costing. In certain process cost systems, on the other hand, accountants use actual factory overhead rather than applied factory overhead costs because they do not accumulate costs until the end of operations. If production is stable from one period to another and total fixed cost does not vary considerably, estimated factory overhead rates are unnecessary. Instead, the fixed cost per unit charged to the product represents that calculated under normal conditions. There is support for using only the actual cost if the processing department's fixed costs are a small percentage of the total departmental costs.

However, accountants use applied factory overhead rates if production is not stable and if the actual fixed costs per unit fluctuate considerably. For example, for seasonal work, production varies so much between peak and slack periods that costs would fluctuate considerably without the use of estimated factory overhead rates. The procedure for determining the factory overhead application rate is similar to that for job order costing. Accountants estimate total variable and fixed overhead for the period and select a base, such as estimated direct labor-hours or machine-hours, to compute the factory overhead application rate. Even though accountants may eventually charge actual factory overhead to the departments, they first accumulate actual costs in the Factory Overhead Control account. Subsidiary ledger accounts detail factory overhead. The following is a typical entry for Departments 1 and 2 assuming actual overhead totaled $90,000:

Factory Overhead Control	90,000	
Prepaid Insurance		XX
Accounts Payable		XX
Factory Supplies Inventory		XX
Accumulated Depreciation		XX
And so forth.		

Total of 90,000

Even if accountants use applied factory overhead rates to cost products, they also allocate actual factory overhead costs to departments. This allows a comparison of actual and applied factory overhead and determination of spending and volume variances as illustrated in Chapter 4. When accountants do not use estimated factory overhead application rates, they allocate actual factory overhead to calculate overhead cost for each product.

To allocate overhead to departments, we use factory overhead subsidiary ledger accounts or a separate departmental expense analysis to summarize actual costs by departments. If we use actual factory overhead rather than an estimated overhead rate to cost the products, we make the following entry to distribute actual factory overhead:

Work in Process—Department 1—Factory Overhead . .	30,000	
Work in Process—Department 2—Factory Overhead . .	60,000	
Factory Overhead Control		90,000

This becomes the source for the overhead charged to the departments, as shown on the cost of production report.

When using estimated factory overhead rates, we debit departmental Work in Process accounts and credit Factory Overhead Control for applied overhead based on estimated rates. The difference between actual and applied overhead remains in the Factory Overhead Control account.

Transfer of Costs between Departments.   In addition to assigning factory overhead, the process costing accountant records the transfer of costs between departments. When transmitting units from Department 1 to Department 2, the following journal entry records the transfer:

Work in Process—Department 2	55,799	
Work in Process—Department 1		55,799

The following entry transfers the finished units from Department 2 to the Finished Goods Inventory.

Finished Goods Inventory	130,518	
Work in Process—Department 2		130,518

Comparison of Weighted-Average and FIFO Costing.   As the chapter's exhibits illustrate, the difference using weighted-average and FIFO costing may be insignificant. This occurs if the raw material price does not fluctuate considerably between periods. In addition, because the production and inventory levels of most industries using process costing usually do not fluctuate, labor and overhead costs per unit stay approximately the same. While FIFO is strictly applied within each department, we average the costs received from previous departments when the units enter a new department. Although we recognize that FIFO would be burdensome if we did not use this averaging procedure, it does cause the FIFO method to lose some of its value because we average the costs assigned to the different batches. However, FIFO does provide better information about cost control in each department since we know current departmental costs for this period to compare with budgets.

Impact of Flexible Manufacturing and JIT on Process Costing

Traditional manufacturing environments use job orders as their primary scheduling and cost tracking tool. However, in a flexible manufacturing environment, the transfer of workers and even materials among job orders to ensure a smooth flow of process is frequent. Transfers of this type among jobs disrupt the accounting department's attempt to trace the costs of material, labor, and overhead to different job orders.

Also, job orders become less useful in an automated setting because companies are less likely to produce inventory for stock. Using flexible manufacturing, in which manufacturing of products begins only with the receipt of a sales order, lot sizes become too small to have a unique job order attached to each lot. Increasingly, accountants base their reports on periods rather than the closing of work orders.

Less Costing of Inventory Flow

Using traditional cost accounting, each inventory center separately records the movement of all inventory items from one center to another. However, the prevalence of JIT inventory policies has reduced the need for a detailed tracking of work in process inventory. Work in process inventory does not stay in one place long enough for the maintenance of accurate records as it flows through a manufacturing operation. Detailed inventory tracking is unnecessary in a JIT environment with a kanban pull system in which production is closely tied with sales. In companies using JIT, this inventory detail often creates vast amounts of paperwork and many reporting errors.

After implementing JIT, companies find they do not need to accumulate costs by individual job or workstation. Lot sizes become too small to have a unique job order attached to each lot. Also, data accumulation points are no longer at a department level because JIT does not departmentalize production.

Ignore EU Calculations in JIT

Accountants in automated manufacturing environments no longer calculate the equivalent units used in process costing to arrive at a unit cost. Companies that manufacture products only after receiving sales orders have insignificant inventory levels. In a successful JIT setting, the composition of inventory changes. There is little or no work in process inventory as a result of reduced lead time. Reduction of finished goods inventory levels occurs because the system is more responsive to customer needs. Elimination of obsolete and slow-moving categories results. Companies keep little raw material because of their ability to plan and coordinate vendor deliveries.

The insignificant inventory levels make the total units transferred and the units in current production (units started and finished) almost identical using JIT. As a result, accountants can forgo the calculation of equivalent units entirely and assign all current costs to the units transferred and none to unfinished inventory. As the levels of work in process and finished goods diminish, the need to separately allocate costs to ending inventories decreases because failing to assign costs to the small amounts of inventory may not be material. This saves much time and cost in the areas of data collection, analysis, and reporting. Ignoring equivalent units calculations does not materially affect reporting accuracy in a successful JIT operation.

Summary

In deciding whether to adopt process, job order, or operation costing, accountants must study the nature of the company's manufacturing operations. Process costing accumulates costs for a given period in each department. This approach differs from job order costing in which the job becomes the focal point for assigning costs. Process costing is adaptable for a company with assembly-line operations, where there is a continuous flow of products. Operation costing is more appropriate if direct materials can be specifically allocated to the batches and conversion costs can be applied to all physical units passing through the operation.

The weighted-average and FIFO methods are two approaches for handling beginning inventory cost in process costing. FIFO costing keeps the costs of the units in beginning inventory separate from the costs assigned to the units started and finished during the period. The computation of equivalent units differs with these two methods because of the treatment of beginning inventory.

Using JIT manufacturing, accountants can forgo the calculation of equivalent units entirely because there is little or no work in process as a result of reduced lead time. With a substantial reduction in the levels of work in process and finished goods inventories, the need to separately allocate costs to ending inventories decreases. JIT systems charge direct labor and factory overhead costs to cost of goods sold directly rather than to work in process and finished goods. The substantial reduction in accounting costs overrides the marginal decrease in the accuracy of product costs for these companies.

Job order costing may become less useful in an automated setting because lot sizes become too small to have a unique job order attached to each lot. Also, companies are less likely to be mass producing inventory for stock. Job and lot costing systems give way to process and operation costing approaches in flexible manufacturing.

Important Terms and Concepts

Appendix 7–A Completed and Not Transferred Inventory

In practice, transfer of all products finished during a period to the next department may not occur by the time accountants complete costing for that period. Thus, accountants add completed and not transferred units in the following equivalent unit formulas:

EU, Weighted-Average Costing	=	Units completed and transferred × 100%	+	Units completed and not transferred × 100%	+	Partially completed ending inventory × stage of completion

| EU, FIFO Costing | = | Units completed and transferred × 100% | + | Units completed and not transferred × 100% | + | Partially completed ending inventory × stage of completion | − | Beginning inventory × stage of completion |

EXHIBIT 7A–1

MARK MANUFACTURING COMPANY
Cost of Production Report—Weighted Average
For Month Ending December 31, 19X1

Mixing Department

Quantity schedule (Step 1):

Completed and on hand	500	
Semifinished inventory ($^1/_3$ material, $^1/_4$ conversion costs)	2,400	
Units started in process	10,000	12,900
Units transferred to next department	11,000	
Ending inventory (all material, $^2/_5$ conversion costs)	1,900	12,900

	Total Costs	Unit Costs
Costs to account for (Step 3):		
Work in process—completed inventory:		
Material	$ 1,000	
Conversion costs	5,750	
	$ 6,750	
Work in process—semifinished inventory:		
Material	1,600	
Conversion costs	6,300	
Total semifinished inventory	$ 7,900	
Current costs in department:		
Material	23,845	$ 2.05
Conversion costs	128,482	11.95
Total costs to account for	$166,977	$ 14.00

Costs accounted for as follows (Step 4):

Costs transferred to next department (11,000 × $14)		$154,000
Work in process—ending inventory:		
Material (1,900 × $2.05)	$ 3,895	
Conversion costs (1,900 × $^2/_5$ × $11.95)	9,082	12,977
Total costs accounted for		$166,977

Additional computations (Step 2):

	Transferred	+	Ending Inventory		
EU, Mixing Department, material	11,000	+	1,900	=	12,900
$\dfrac{\$1,000 + \$1,600 + \$23,845 = \$26,445}{12,900} = \$2.05$			(1,900 × 100%)		
EU, Mixing Department, conversion costs ..	11,000	+	760	=	11,760
$\dfrac{\$5,750 + \$6,300 + \$128,482 = \$140,532}{11,760} = \$11.95$			(1,900 × $^2/_5$)		

EXHIBIT 7A–2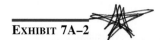

MARK MANUFACTURING COMPANY
Cost of Production Report—FIFO
For Month Ending December 31, 19X1

Mixing Department

Quantity schedule (Step 1):

Completed and on hand	500	
Semifinished inventory ($1/3$ material, $1/4$ conversion costs)	2,400	
Units started in process	10,000	12,900
Units transferred to next department	11,000	
Ending inventory (all material, $2/5$ conversion costs)	1,900	12,900

	Total Costs	Unit Costs
Costs to account for (Step 3):		
Work in process—completed inventory:		
Material	\$ 1,000	
Conversion costs	5,750	
	\$ 6,750	
Work in process—semifinished inventory:		
Material	\$1,600	
Conversion costs	6,300	
Total semifinished inventory	\$7,900	
Current cost in department:		
Material	23,845	\$ 2.0556
Conversion costs	128,482	12.0527
Total costs to account for	\$166,977	\$14.1083

Costs accounted for as follows (Step 4):		
Costs transferred to next department:		
From completed inventory		\$ 6,750
From semifinished inventory:		
Value of semifinished inventory	\$ 7,900	
Material added (2,400 $\times$ $2/3$ $\times$ \$2.0556)	3,289	
Conversion costs added (2,400 $\times$ $3/4$ $\times$ \$12.0527)	21,695	32,884
From current production (8,100 $\times$ \$14.1083)		114,277
Total cost transferred		\$153,911
Work in process—ending inventory:		
Material (1,900 $\times$ 100% $\times$ \$2.0556)	\$ 3,906	
Conversion costs (1,900 $\times$ $2/5$ $\times$ \$12.0527)	9,160	13,066
Total costs accounted for		\$166,977

Additional computations (Step 2):

	Transferred	+	Ending Inventory	–	Completed Inventory	–	Semifinished Inventory	=	
EU, Mixing Department, material	11,000	+	1,900	–	500	–	800	=	11,600
			(1,900 $\times$ 100%)		(500 $\times$ 100%)		(2,400 $\times$ $1/3$)		

$$\frac{\$23,845}{11,600} = \$2.0556$$

	Transferred	+	Ending Inventory	–	Completed Inventory	–	Semifinished Inventory	=	
EU, Mixing Department, conversion costs	11,000	+	760	–	500	–	600	=	10,660
			(1,900 $\times$ $2/5$)		(500 $\times$ 100%)		(2,400 $\times$ $1/4$)		

$$\frac{\$128,482}{10,660} = \$12.0527$$

Using Weighted-Average Costing.   Exhibit 7A–1 illustrates the weighted-average process costing approach when a department completes units in inventory but does not transfer them to the next department during the period in which they were finished. The Mixing Department in Exhibit 7A–1 has 500 completed units and 2,400 semifinished units in beginning inventory. Assume the Mixing Department completed the units on the last day of the previous month and did not have time to transfer them to the next department. The ending inventory for the previous month of November includes the completed units.

In this case, we include the cost allocated to both the completed and semifinished units with the current cost to arrive at the unit cost. In computing the Mixing Department material unit cost, we add the $1,000 material assigned to the completed units to the $1,600 assigned to the 2,400 units to reach a one-third stage of material processing along with the $23,845 current material cost. We divide $26,445 total material cost by the 12,900 material equivalent units to arrive at a $2.05 unit material cost in the Mixing Department. A similar computation for conversion costs arrives at $11.95 unit cost. We assign a total unit cost of $14 to all 11,000 units transferred (500 completed and not transferred last month + 2,400 semifinished units in beginning inventory finished this period + 8,100 units started and completed this period).

Using FIFO Costing.   Exhibit 7A–2 illustrates the procedure if Mark Manufacturing Company uses FIFO costing. In arriving at the unit cost, we divide only current cost by the equivalent units. We treat completed units as a separate batch of inventory that is transferred to the next department. The cost transferred comes from three sources: completed units on hand in beginning inventory, semifinished units from beginning inventory that are finished during the month, and units that are started and finished during the month.

Review Questions

1. Discuss the characteristics of the production process which determine whether to use job order costing or process costing.

2. Define equivalent units. Why is it necessary to compute equivalent units and how are they used?

3. Why is it suggested that the product unit under process costing may be visualized as a snowball as it travels from one department to another?

4. On the quantity schedule for a department, 1,000 units are indicated as finished and transferred; does this necessarily mean that the unit is in a finished stage ready for sale to a customer?

5. When would you advise using estimated factory overhead application rates in a process costing system?

6. Contrast how the costs of beginning inventory are treated in the weighted-average and FIFO costing approaches used in process costing.

7. What information about beginning inventory is needed for FIFO costing that is not needed to compute the unit costs under weighted-average costing?

8. Why is the FIFO method of accounting for beginning inventory costs sometimes referred to as the modified or departmental FIFO method? Why not use strict FIFO costing?

9. Why should the accountant be concerned about determining when material is issued into the production process?

10. What changes in job order and process costing systems do you expect will become more prevalent because of increased usage of flexible manufacturing and automation?

Exercises

E7–1 Calculating EU
Analysis of the records of the Burnett Company revealed the following:

Beginning inventory	3,000 units
1/5 of inventory is 1/3 complete	
4/5 of inventory is 1/4 complete	
Transferred	30,000 units
Started	32,000 units

Ending inventory
    1/5 of inventory is 1/10 complete
    4/5 of inventory is 3/4 complete

Required:

a. Calculate equivalent units for FIFO costing.
b. Calculate equivalent units for weighted-average costing.

Critical Thought

E7–2 FIFO Costing; Determining Costs
You are able to obtain only limited data from Steele Company before having to prepare cost sections of the production report. The ending balance in Work in Process for the previous month shows 500 units having three-fifths of their material at a cost of $324 and one-fifth of their conversion costs, which cost $68. After calculating material equivalent units of 3,800, management is glad to find that current material unit cost has decreased $0.02. But management is not pleased with the $0.05 increase in current unit conversion cost with conversion cost equivalent units of 3,200. A total of 3,100 units were transferred to the next department.

Required:

Prepare the costs to account for and the costs accounted for sections of a production report using FIFO costing.

E7–3 FIFO Process Costing: Costs Accounted for Section
Hastings Company places material in production at the beginning of operations. In September, material costs totaled $6,240; direct labor, $10,500; and factory overhead, $5,724. On September 1, there were 600 units in process, one-third completed as to direct labor and one-fourth completed as to factory overhead; these had a total cost of $1,310. There were 4,600 units completed and transferred during the month. Ending inventory consisted of 800 units, three-fourths completed as to direct labor and two-fifths completed as to factory overhead. The company uses the FIFO method of costing.

Required:

a. Determine the costs to be assigned to the units in ending inventory.
b. Determine the costs to be assigned to the units transferred.

E7–4 EU Calculations Using Weighted-Average and FIFO Costing
Determine finished equivalents for the following process of Watch Company:

	Mixing Department
Units in process—beginning	2,400
stage of completion except material	80%
Units received from prior department	30,000
Units transferred	28,000
Units in process—ending	4,400
stage of completion except material	60%

Workers issued materials at the beginning of the process in this second department of operations.

Required:

a. Determine the equivalent units using weighted-average costing for:
   (1) Preceding departmental cost.
   (2) Materials.
   (3) Conversion costs.
b. Repeat Requirement *a* using FIFO costing.

E7–5 FIFO Process Costing

Courtney Company places material in production at the beginning of operations. In April, material costs totaled $16,660; direct labor, $20,560; and factory overhead, $7,139. On April 1, there were 750 units in process, one-fifth completed as to direct labor and one-third completed as to factory overhead; these had a total cost of $2,788. There were 6,200 units completed and transferred during the month. Ending inventory consisted of 500 units, three-fourths completed as to direct labor and one-fifth completed as to factory overhead. The company uses the FIFO method of costing.

Required:

a. Calculate the cost to be assigned to the units transferred.
b. Calculate the cost to be assigned to the units in ending inventory.

Writing

E7–6 Theory of Process Costing

The following computations are for Creite's, Inc.'s cost of production report. The 200 units in beginning inventory have a total cost of $500.

EU, preceding department cost $= 1,000 + 100 - 200 = 900$

$$\frac{\$450}{900} = \$0.50$$

EU, materials $= 1,000 + 100 - 200 = 900$

$$\frac{\$990}{900} = \$1.10$$

EU, conversion costs $= 1,000 \quad + 25 \quad - \quad 80 \quad = 945$
$$\qquad\qquad\qquad\qquad (100 \times 25\%) \ (200 \times 40\%)$$

$$\frac{\$1,890}{945} = \$2$$

Required:

a. Explain why you know that this is not the first processing department.
b. (1) Identify the costing method (FIFO or weighted average) being used.
   (2) Give two reasons why you know this costing method is being used.

c. Why were 200 units deducted in computing the equivalent units for the preceding department cost?

d. Explain before what stage of operations material enters this department.

e. Explain why you could not work this problem on the data given using average costing.

E7–7 FIFO Costing; Calculating Current Cost

Department One of Bacon, Inc., provides the following limited data for May:

Beginning inventory (1,500 units):
Materials (10% stage of completion)	$ 450
Conversion cost (80% stage of completion)	$1,800
Units transferred	9,000

The ending inventory contains 600 units having 30 percent of material and 40 percent conversion cost. Due to a change in suppliers, material unit cost decreased $0.20 but the cheaper grade of material caused unit conversion cost to increase $0.40 from April.

Required:

Prepare a cost of production report for May using FlFO costing.

E7–8 FIFO Process Costing: Determining Current Cost

Because you are such an industrious cost accountant, you decide to return to the office tonight and finish the cost of production report you started during regular working hours. However, to your dismay, you find that the safe is locked up and you forgot to bring your keys. After extracting the work sheet from your drawer, you are delighted to find the following figures already recorded on it:

Bowden Company

Value of beginning inventory (880 units):
Material (1/4 stage of completion)	$242
Conversion costs (2/5 stage of completion)	$704
Units transferred	4,000
Units in ending inventory (having 1/3 material and	
1/5 conversion costs)	750

You remember that management was quite concerned that material cost had increased $0.05 per unit and conversion costs had an increase of $0.10 per unit from last period.

Required:

Prepare a cost of production report using FIFO costing.

Problems

Critical Thought

P7–9 Error in OH Application Rate for Process Costing System

You have been asked to review the cost records of Saber, Inc., and to make any changes needed to correct errors in the financial statements of March 31, 19X1. Saber, Inc., started operations on March 1,19X1, with no beginning inventories. Factory overhead costs are applied at 95 percent of direct labor cost. The determination was:

$$\frac{\$1,472,500 \text{ factory overhead costs budgeted}}{\$1,550,000 \text{ direct labor cost budgeted}} = 95 \text{ percent}$$

Work in process inventory of March 31 was fully complete for materials and one-third complete for conversion costs. Costs recorded for March were:

Direct material	$84,000
Direct labor	93,500

In the departmental budgets prepared for the year 19X1, the following are administrative expenses:

Factory accountants' salaries	$ 72,500
Payroll taxes applicable to factory	135,000
Depreciation on building and equipment	300,000

Factory operations utilize 60 percent of the building and its equipment. Financial statements prepared on March 31 showed the following:

Work in process inventory, March 31 (15,000 units)	$ 45,450
Finished goods inventory, March 31 (7,500 units)	44,175
Cost of sales for March (30,000 units)	176,700

Required:

a. Determine the corrected balances on March 31 for:
   (1) Work in process inventory.
   (2) Finished goods inventory.
   (3) Cost of goods sold.
b. Explain the impact on the financial statements of using the incorrect factory overhead application rate.

P7–10 Calculating Equivalent Units (CIA adapted)

The Brown Company manufactures hair spray in a three-department process. The Molding Department produces the plastic bottles and caps. The Mixing Department combines the raw materials for the hair spray and puts the mixture into bottles. The Packaging Department boxes the product and seals it in cellophane. A description of the departmental activities as well as the units associated with the work in process at the beginning of March were as follows:

Critical Thought

SPATS

Molding Department.   In the Molding Department, the plastic is added at the beginning of the process, overhead is uniformly incurred, and the only direct labor occurs at the end of the process. A worker trims the bottle and cap and places them on a conveyer for transport to the Mixing Department. The work in process at March 1 was 1,000 units estimated to be 50 percent complete.

Mixing Department.   All the materials for the hair spray are combined in a large vat, thoroughly mixed, and pumped into the plastic bottles conveyed from the Molding Department. The overhead costs for the Mixing Department are uniformly incurred during the mixing process. Materials and direct labor are added at the beginning of the process. At the beginning of March, no work in process existed in the Mixing Department.

Packaging Department.   The capped bottles are conveyed to the Packaging Department where they are automatically boxed. At the end of the process, the boxes are sealed in cellophane and a worker packs them in cases of 24 bottles each. The individual box is added at the beginning of the process and the cellophane, direct labor, and casing are added at the end of the process. Overhead is incurred uniformly; 960 units were considered to be 40 percent complete on March 1.

Plastic for 100,000 bottles and caps was added into production in March in the Molding Department. The work in process inventories at the end of March included: 2,000 units, 80 percent complete in the Molding Department; 1,000 units, 50 percent complete in the Mixing Department; and 640 units, 25 percent complete in the Packaging Department.

The Molding and Mixing Departments use weighted-average process costing, while the Packaging Department uses first-in, first-out process costing.

Required:

Complete the equivalent unit schedule for March for the three departments. Assume that Brown Company calculates equivalent units for each identifiable input in each department, and that no spoilage occurs in any of the processes.

P7–11 Weighted-Average Cost of Production Report

Jewel Company uses the weighted-average method of costing. The following data were accumulated in Department B for December. There were no lost units in December.

Beginning inventory:

Cost from Department A (preceding department)	$330
Department B material	150
Department B labor	250
Department B overhead	240

300 units (stage of completion: 1/4 material, 1/6 labor, 1/5 overhead)

Current costs:

Costs received from preceding department (600 units)	$ 733.80
Material	1,638.58
Labor	3,456.92
Overhead	2,811.75

Ending inventory (200 units, 1/5 material, 1/8 labor, 1/4 overhead)

Required:

Prepare a cost of production report for Department B for December.

P7–12 Average Costing, FIFO: Two Months

Amy Wells Production Company employs a process cost system in the manufacture of industrial chemicals. Three departments are involved in the process: Blending, Fabricating, and Finishing. No units are lost in the Fabricating Department. Data for January and February operations in the Fabricating Department are as follows:

	January	February
Beginning inventory	1,200	?
Stage of completion	3/5 material, 1/3 conversion costs	?
Received from preceding department	3,000	2,500
Ending inventory	800	900
Stage of completion	1/2 material, 1/4 conversion costs	1/3 material, 1/6 conversion costs
Value of beginning inventory:		
Costs from preceding department	$4,110	?
Material	1,350	?
Conversion costs	720	?
Costs received from preceding department	2,820	$3,225
Current material cost	4,928	3,910
Current conversion costs	864	1,128

Required:

a. Prepare a cost of production report using FIFO costing.
b. Prepare a cost of production report using weighted-average costing.

P7–13 Process Costing: FIFO and Weighted-Average Costing, Second Department
The following information is for Department 2 of the Tenn Company, for June 19X1. The company uses a process cost system.

Beginning inventory	600	units (1/3 material, 1/6 conversion costs)
Prior department costs	$ 925	
Material	$ 280	
Conversion costs	$ 270	
Received from previous department	5,000	units
Current costs:		
Material	$ 7,245	
Conversion costs	$13,832	
Costs received from prior department	$ 7,750	
Transferred	5,300	units
Ending inventory	300	units (1/4 material, 2/5 conversion costs)

Required:

a. Prepare a production cost report using FIFO.
b. Prepare a production cost report using the weighted-average method.

P7–14 FIFO and Average Process Costing: Third Department
Data for Department 3 of Key, Inc., for May follows; they use a process cost system.

Started in process	5,000	units
Current material cost	$ 4,675	
Current conversion costs	$16,926	
Costs from prior departments	$35,000	
Transferred	4,500	units
Beginning inventory	900	units
		(2/3 material,
		5/6 conversion costs)
Value of beginning inventory:		
Costs from prior departments	$ 6,100	
Material	$ 600	
Conversion costs	$ 3,075	
Ending inventory	1,400	units
		(1/4 material,
		1/5 conversion costs)

Required:

a. Prepare a production cost report using the FIFO method.
b. Prepare a production cost report using the weighted-average method.

SPATS

P7–15 Weighted-Average and FIFO Production Reports
Dawee Company uses a process costing system in the manufacture of industrial chemicals. According to the following data for Departments One and Two, there were several batches of units on hand when operations began for January:

	Department One	Department Two
Started in process	2,900 units	?
Beginning inventory	100 units	500 units
Value of beginning inventory and stage of completion:		
Costs from preceding department		$5,640
Material	$ 40 (1/4)	300 (1/5)
Labor	327 (3/5)	60 (1/10)
Overhead	75 (1/5)	100 (1/5)
Current costs:		
Material	$ 4,429	$7,095
Labor	$14,933	$3,025
Overhead	$ 9,804	$1,978
Ending inventory	500 units	800 units
Stage of completion	1/5 material	3/5 material
	3/5 labor	3/4 labor
	1/5 overhead	1/4 overhead

No completed units were on hand at the end of the month.

Required:

a. Prepare a cost of production report using weighted-average costing.
b. Prepare a cost of production report using FIFO costing.

P7–16 Process Costing: Completed and Semifinished Units in Beginning Inventory (Weighted-Average and FIFO Costing)

Reeves Company uses a process costing system in the Grinding Department and the Assembly Department. Several batches of finished units were on hand when operations began for February. Data from the records are as follows:

	Grinding Department	Assembly Department
Started in process	3,900 units	?
Completed and on hand	200 units	500 units
Value of completed units:		
Costs from preceding department . . .		$ 2,365
Material	$ 460	$ 400
Labor	$ 240	$ 825
Overhead	$ 100	$ 1,650
Semifinished units on hand	1,800 units	600 units
Value of semifinished units and stage of completion:		
Costs from preceding department . . .		$ 2,300
Material	$ 1,125 (1/6)	450 (1/3)
Labor	531 (1/4)	192 (1/5)
Overhead	336 (1/3)	495 (1/4)
Current costs:		
Material	$10,588	$ 2,975
Labor	$ 5,695	$ 7,728
Overhead	$ 2,420	$15,119
Ending Inventory	900 units	1,200 units
Stage of completion	(1/5 M, 1/3 L, 1/9 OH)	(1/6 M, 1/3 L, 1/4 OH)

There were no units completed and on hand at the end of the month.

Required:

a. Prepare a cost of production report using weighted-average costing.
b. Prepare a cost of production report using FIFO costing.

P7–17 Average Costing, FIFO for Two Months

Rosser Production Company employs a process cost system in the manufacture of industrial chemicals. Three departments are involved in the process: Mixing, Refining, and Finishing. No units are lost in the Refining Department. Data for January and February operations in the Refining Department are as follows:

	January	February
Beginning inventory	600	?
Stage of completion	3/4 material	?
	2/5 conversion costs	?
Received from preceding department . . .	1,500	2,000
Ending inventory	330	500
Stage of completion	2/3 material	4/5 material
	1/6 conversion costs	1/10 conversion costs
Value of beginning inventory:		
Costs from preceding department . . .	$1,170	?
Material cost	308	?
Conversion cost	132	?
Costs received from preceding department	3,000	$3,900
Current material cost	3,234	4,422
Current conversion costs	951	1,168

Required:

a. Prepare a cost of production report using FIFO costing.
b. Prepare a cost of production report using weighted-average costing.

SPATS

P7–18 Process Costing, Two Departments: Weighted-Average Costing and FIFO

William Manufacturing Company utilizes a process cost system for its two factory departments. After leaving the Fabricating Department, one-third of the goods finished are transferred to finished goods and sold immediately. The remainder is transferred to the Finishing Department.

The following data is from their records for the month ending January 31, 19X1:

	Fabricating Department	Finishing Department
Beginning inventory	100 units	500 units
Stage of completion	1/4 material	1/5 material
	3/5 conversion cost	1/10 conversion cost
Started in process	7,560 units	?
Ending inventory	700	1,140
Stage of completion	1/5 material	3/5 material
	2/7 conversion cost	3/4 conversion cost
Value of beginning inventory:		
Costs from preceding department		$4,157
Material	$ 65	30
Conversion costs	330	43
Current material cost	14,135	2,312
Current conversion cost	41,198	2,870

Required:

a. Prepare a cost of production report using weighted-average costing.
b. Prepare a cost of production report using FIFO costing. Assume the 100 units in beginning inventory are included in the units transferred to the Finishing Department.

P7–19 Two Departments, Two Batches in Inventory, FIFO and Weighted-Average Costing

C. Renshaw Manufacturing Company produces units in two departments, Mixing and Finishing. The company introduces material in both departments. It placed a total of 2,000 units in process in the Mixing Department during the month. There were two batches of beginning inventory in the Finishing Department. Data for the month of May follow:

	Mixing Department	Finishing Department	
	Batch Number 1	Batch Number 1	Batch Number 2
Units	100	400	250
Stage of completion	1/5	1/8 material	1/5 material
		3/5 labor	1/10 labor
		1/4 overhead	3/5 overhead
Costs of preceding department:		$1,200	$750
Material	$ 6	55	74
Labor	37	700	80
Overhead	55	260	380
Current costs:			
Material	2,350	$3,680	
Labor	1,692	5,369	
Overhead	1,598	5,450	

Each department had one batch of ending inventory. A total of 300 units were one-third complete as to all cost elements; they were in the Mixing Department ending inventory. The 200 units in the Finishing Department's ending inventory were three-fourths complete as to material; two-fifths, labor; and nine-tenths, overhead.

Required:

a. Prepare a cost of production report using FIFO costing.
b. Prepare a cost of production report using weighted-average costing.

Process Costing—Addition of Materials and Lost Units

Chapter Objectives

After studying this chapter, you should be able to:

1. Show the effect on product costs of additional materials.
2. Illustrate the costing procedure when the addition of material results in an increase in units to account for.
3. Prepare cost of production reports using FIFO and weighted-average costing when normal and abnormal losses occur.
4. Explain the impact of quality control concepts and zero defects programs on abnormal and normal losses.

Introduction

The preceding chapter introduces both the FIFO and weighted-average methods of process costing. However, Chapter 7 does not discuss many of the complexities that accountants encounter in process costing. For example, the computation of product costs becomes more difficult if the material added to production increases the units to account for or if the manufacturing operations lose units. This chapter illustrates the costing procedures for these complexities.

Addition of Material

The addition of material may either **increase the unit cost** of the product or **increase the number of units** for which managers must account. For example, shirt manufacturers issue fabric at the beginning of production operations. They later add material in the Finishing Department when workers sew on buttons. This added material—buttons—does not increase the number of shirts. The only effect is an increase in the unit cost. A similar situation occurs when workers add parts during the assembly of microwave ovens. There is no increase in the units to account for because workers are only changing the nature or character of the product. Chapter 7 introduces the costing procedure used when workers in departments subsequent to the first add materials that do not increase the number of units of product. Chapter 8 addresses the situation where materials that are added in departments subsequent to the first do increase the number of product units.

Effect of Addition of Materials on Total Units to Account for Using Weighted Average

Exhibit 8–1 illustrates the weighted-average costing procedure when the introduction of material increases the number of units. Department 2 adds 1,000 gallons of oil to dilute the 6,500-gallon paint mixture received from Department 1. This increases the units to account for to 7,500 gallons plus 500 gallons in beginning inventory. Because workers combine the oil and paint mixture so neither can be distinguished, we spread the preceding department cost over the entire 7,500 gallons.

Department 1 is purposely simple so we can emphasize Department 2. In addition, Exhibit 8–1 combines labor and factory overhead costs in the one category of conversion costs. Department 1 workers introduce material throughout the process; the only effect is that each product completed must absorb a $2 unit material cost. Because there is no beginning inventory in Department 1, all 6,500 units transferred to the next department come from current production. Each of the 6,500 units carries with it a $5 cost from the preceding department when transferred to Department 2. The ending inventory in Department 1 has received only one-fifth of its material and two-sevenths of its conversion costs. We multiply the units in ending inventory by their stage of completion and finally by the unit cost to arrive at a valuation.

Effect of Addition of Materials on Unit Costs Using Weighted Average

Immediately on arrival, Department 2 workers mix oils costing $6,380 with the 6,500 gallons of paint mixture. This results in an additional 1,000 units to account for. Accountants spread the cost from the preceding department over the combined oil and paint mixture using the following weighted-average equivalent unit computation that Chapter 7 introduced:

EU, preceding department costs = 7,400 transferred + 600 ending inventory = 8,000
(600 × 100%)

Strategic Planning

Current Cost Management Practice

The cola battle is raging anew, this time around the world. Pepsi is moving into foreign countries where Coca-Cola is sheltered from stiff competition, sells its drinks at high prices, earns large profits, and derives four-fifths of its total earnings. Pepsi's strategy involves these steps: (1) Set a winner's growth goals; if you act like No. 2, you always will be No. 2. (2) Hire people who love change and thrive on risk-taking. (3) Practice competitive techniques that upset the rules of the marketplace to throw a rival off balance. (4) Always anticipate the response you may provoke. What if the competitor comes back hitting harder? (5) Control distribution so you serve customers directly. Execution of a plan often drives success more than marketing.

Patricia Sellers, "Pepsi Opens a Second Front," *Fortune,* August 8, 1994, pp. 70-76.

$$\frac{\$2{,}000 \text{ Beg. Inv. Preced. Dept.} + \$32{,}500 \text{ Current Preced. Dept.}}{8{,}000 \text{ units}} = \frac{\$34{,}500}{8{,}000 \text{ units}} = \$4.313$$

The 7,400 units transferred come from a mixture of the units in beginning inventory, the units received from the preceding department, and the units added in Department 2.

Change in per Unit Cost.   The additional units added in Department 2 cause a decrease in cost per unit. We average the $2,000 cost from preceding department in beginning inventory with the $32,500 current costs received to arrive at a unit cost of $4.313. This is in contrast to the $5 per unit cost from Department 1. This difference partially arises because we spread the costs received from the preceding department over 1,000 additional units. For instance, if Department 2 workers did not dilute the paint mixture with 1,000 gallons of oil, unit cost would be $4.928 instead of $4.313, as follows:

$$\frac{\$2{,}000 \text{ Beg. Inv. Preced. Dept.} + \$32{,}500 \text{ Current Preced. Dept.}}{7{,}000 \text{ units}} = \frac{\$34{,}500}{7{,}000 \text{ units}} = \$4.928$$

This lower cost per unit illustrates unit cost changes from one department to another.

In addition, the 500 units in beginning inventory have a preceding department unit cost of $4 ($2,000 costs from the preceding department ÷ 500 units) which reduces the averaged preceding department per unit cost. (Remember these 500 units went through Department 2's diluting process last month.) Other factors can cause the per unit preceding department cost to differ from the cost calculated in the previous department. This chapter discusses normal loss of units and averaging with FIFO, which also can account for the change in unit cost for a department when units enter the subsequent department. Exhibit 8–4 illustrates these two factors.

We must arrive at a unit cost for each of the following: preceding department costs, Department 2 material, and Department 2 conversion costs. We should not average the $6,380 material cost with the $2,000 and $32,500 preceding department

EXHIBIT 8–1

WELLS MANUFACTURING COMPANY
Cost of Production Report—Weighted-Average Costing—Addition of Material
For the Month Ending January 31, 19X1

	Department 1		Department 2	
Quantity schedule (Step 1):				
Beginning inventory	–0–		($1/5$ M, $1/10$ CC) 500	
Received from preceding department	–0–		6,500 ✓	
Additional units put in process	–0–		1,000 ✓	
Started in process	7,200			
Total units to account for		7,200		8,000
Transferred to next department	6,500		7,400	
Ending inventory				
($1/5$ material, $2/7$ conversion costs)	700		($1/3$ M, $3/4$ CC) 600	
Total units accounted for		7,200		8,000

	Total Costs	Unit Costs	Total Costs	Unit Costs
Costs to account for (Step 3):				
Work in process—beginning inventory:				
Costs from preceding department			$ 2,000	
Material			80	
Conversion costs			43	
Total value of beginning inventory. . . .			$ 2,123	
Cost from preceding department			32,500 ✓	$ 4.313
Current costs:				
Material.	$13,280	$ 2.00	6,380 ✓	0.850
Conversion costs	20,100	3.00	6,865 ✓	0.880
Total costs to account for	$33,380	$ 5.00	$47,868	$ 6.043

Costs accounted for as follows (Step 4):				
Costs transferred to next				
department (6,500 × $5)	$32,500	(7,400 × $6.043)		$44,714*
Work in process—ending inventory:				
Costs from preceding department		(600 × $4.313)	$ 2,588	
Material (700 × $1/5$ × $2)	$ 280	(600 × $1/3$ × $0.85)	170	
Conversion costs (700 × $2/7$ × $3)	600	880	(600 × $3/4$ × $0.88)	396	3,154
Total costs accounted for		$33,380		$47,868

Additional computations (Step 2):

	Transferred	+	Ending inventory		
EU, Department 1, material	6,500	+	140	=	6,640
$\dfrac{\$13,280}{6,640} = \$2$			(700 × $1/5$)		
EU, Department 1, conversion costs	6,500	+	200	=	6,700
$\dfrac{\$20,100}{6,700} = \$3$			(700 × $2/7$)		
EU, Department 2, preceding department costs .	7,400	+	600	=	8,000
$\dfrac{\$2,000 + \$32,500}{8,000} = \dfrac{\$34,500}{8,000} = \$4.313$			(600 × 100%)		
EU, Department 2, material	7,400	+	200	=	7,600
$\dfrac{\$80 + \$6,380}{7,600} = \dfrac{\$6,460}{7,600} = \$0.850$			(600 × $1/3$)		
EU, Department 2, conversion costs	7,400	+	450	=	7,850
$\dfrac{\$43 + \$6,865}{7,850} = \dfrac{\$6,908}{7,850} = \$0.880$			(600 × $3/4$)		

*7,400 units × $6.043 = $44,718.20. To avoid decimal descrepancy, the cost transferred is computed as follows: $47,868 − $3,154 = $44,714.

costs, even though this material did result in 1,000 more units to account for. Instead, we compute a separate unit cost for material. In this example, Department 2 workers add material throughout the process, causing the material equivalent units to differ from the equivalent units for the preceding department.

The bottom of Exhibit 8–1 illustrates the computation for material and conversion costs. No difference exists between these computations and the ones presented for weighted-average costing in Chapter 7. Because the 600 units in ending inventory have been through the preceding department, we assign the adjusted unit cost of $4.313 to all 600 units. We determine a $3,154 inventory valuation by multiplying the units in ending inventory by their stage of completion and the cost per unit. A decimal discrepancy results because we carry the unit costs out to only three decimal places and use only whole dollars. When we multiply the 7,400 units transferred by the $6.043 unit cost in Department 2, the result is $44,718.20. However, if we add this figure to the $3,154 ending inventory valuation, the total does not equal the costs to account for. Because the difference is so small and we know it is caused by the use of whole dollars and three-digit unit costs, we transfer the costs out at a total of $44,714 ($47,868 costs to account for minus $3,154 ending inventory).

Effect of Addition of Materials on Total Units to Account for Using FIFO

Exhibit 8–2 uses Exhibit 8–1 data to illustrate the FIFO costing procedure for handling the increase in units. The basic costing procedures under weighted-average costing and FIFO remain the same as presented in the previous chapter. However, the increase in units from the diluting effect require additional accounting. Because there is no beginning inventory in Department 1, the equivalent units and unit costs are identical to those shown for the first department in Exhibit 8–1. However, differences arise in Department 2 because of the 500 units in beginning inventory. Using FIFO costing, we subtract the 500 units in beginning inventory in the equivalent units calculation for preceding department costs. We divide only the $32,500 cost transferred from Department 1 by the FIFO equivalent units to arrive at the following unit cost:

$$\frac{\$32,500 \text{ Current Preceding Department Cost}}{7,500 \text{ units}} = \$4.333$$

As in the weighted-average method illustrated in Exhibit 8–1, the preceding department unit cost has decreased because the base unit count has increased by 1,000 units. Since the increase in units comes from workers adding 1,000 gallons of oil before Department 2 processes the paint mixture, in Exhibit 8–2 we assume that the larger base unit count relates only to new production. However, if the increase in units develops because workers add materials continuously throughout the production process, the larger base unit count would relate to both new production and beginning inventory.

Effect of Addition of Materials on Unit Costs Using FIFO

Because we are using FIFO costing, we subtract the equivalent units in beginning inventory from units transferred and ending inventory to arrive at the unit material and conversion costs for Department 2. Rather than averaging the $2,123 value of beginning inventory in with current cost, we divide equivalent units into current costs only, as shown here:

$$\frac{\$6,380 \text{ current material}}{7,500 \text{ units}} = \$0.851 \qquad \frac{\$6,865 \text{ current conversion cost}}{7,800 \text{ units}} = \$0.880$$

EXHIBIT 8–2

WELLS MANUFACTURING COMPANY
Cost of Production Report—FIFO—Addition of Material
For the Month Ending January 31, 19X1

	Department 1		Department 2	
Quantity schedule (Step 1):				
Beginning inventory	–0–		($^1/_5$ M, $^1/_{10}$ CC)	500
Received from preceding department	–0–			6,500
Additional units put in process	–0–			1,000
Started in process	7,200			
Total units to account for		7,200		8,000
Transferred to next department	6,500			7,400
Ending inventory				
($^1/_5$ material, $^2/_7$ conversion costs)	700		($^1/_3$ M, $^3/_4$ CC)	600
Total units accounted for		7,200		8,000

	Total Costs	Unit Costs	Total Costs	Unit Costs
Costs to account for (Step 3):				
Work in process—beginning inventory:				
Costs from preceding department			$ 2,000	
Material.			80	
Conversion costs			43	
Total value of beginning inventory. . . .			$ 2,123	
Costs from preceding department.			32,500	$ 4.333
Current costs in department:				
Material.	$13,280	$ 2.00	6,380	0.851
Conversion costs	20,100	3.00	6,865	0.880
Total costs to account for	$33,380	$ 5.00	$47,868	$ 6.064
Costs accounted for as follows (Step 4):				
Costs transferred to next department:				
From beginning inventory:				
Value of beginning inventory			$ 2,123	
Material added			(500 × $^4/_5$ × $0.851) 341*	
Conversion costs added			(500 × $^9/_{10}$ × $0.880) 396	$ 2,860
From current production				
(6,500 × $5)		$32,500	(6,900 × $6.064)	41,842
Total cost transferred		$32,500		$44,702
Work in process—ending inventory:				
Costs from preceding department			(600 × $4.333) $ 2,600	
Material (700 × $^1/_5$ × $2)	$ 280		(600 × $^1/_3$ × $0.851) 170	
Conversion costs (700 × $^2/_7$ × $3) . . .	600	880	(600 × $^3/_4$ × $0.880) 396	3,166*
Total costs accounted for		$33,380		$47,868

Additional computations (Step 2):

*Rounded up $1 due to decimal discrepancy.

	Transferred	+	Ending Inventory	–	Beginning Inventory	=	
EU, Department 1, material	6,500	+	140 (700 × $^1/_5$)			=	6,640
$\frac{\$13,280}{6,640}$ = $2							
EU, Department 1, conversion costs	6,500	+	200 (700 × $^2/_7$)			=	6,700
$\frac{\$20,100}{6,700}$ = $3							
EU, Department 2, preceding department costs	7,400	+	600 (600 × .100%)	–	500 (500 × 100%)	=	7,500
$\frac{\$32,500}{7,500}$ = $4.333							
EU, Department 2, material	7,400	+	200 (600 × $^1/_3$)	–	100 (500 × $^1/_5$)	=	7,500
$\frac{\$6,380}{7,500}$ = $0.851							
EU, Department 2, conversion costs	7,400	+	450 (600 × $^3/_4$)	–	50 (500 × $^1/_{10}$)	=	7,800
$\frac{\$6,865}{7,800}$ = $0.880							

We apply material cost of $341 and conversion costs of $396 to the 500 units in beginning inventory before transferring them out of Department 2. Of the 7,400 total units transferred, workers started and finished 6,900 units during January. The $44,702 cost transferred represents two batches of production—500 units from beginning inventory and 6,900 units from current production. The 600 units in ending inventory each receive the adjusted preceding department unit cost of $4.333. We then compute the cost of completing ending inventory to a one-third material stage and three-fourths conversion costs stage. We complete the cost of production report by accounting for costs of $47,868.

Loss of Units

Manufacturing processes sometimes lose, as well as add, units. Units are lost because of spoilage, evaporation, and shrinkage. Even though the company wishes to avoid all possible losses, management may have to accept some spoilage and/or evaporation as an inherent part of the production process. For example, workers may spill or burn some ingredients used in candy manufacturing. In making furniture, workers may ruin lumber to the point that it cannot be sold as scrap, defective units, or spoiled goods. **Scrap** materials cannot be reused in the manufacturing process without additional refining. Scrap may or may not have market value. **Defective units** require extra work before they can be sold as first-quality products. On the other hand, **spoiled goods** contain such significant imperfections that no amount of additional material, labor, and overhead could turn them into perfect finished products.

Normal versus Abnormal Loss

Even though some industries recognize the loss of units is an unavoidable aspect of their specific manufacturing operations, each company should set normal tolerance limits for such losses. A loss within these limits is a **normal loss.** Loss of units outside these limits is an **abnormal** or **avoidable loss.** Managers usually set limits so they can estimate the number of units that will be lost. The nature of the loss and the point in the processing operations at which the loss takes place also help determine whether management classifies it as normal or abnormal. For example, during the cooking stage two vats containing semiprocessed ketchup suffer evaporation, a normal loss. However, an abnormal loss occurs if an errant forklift truck operator punctures one of the vats.

Normal Tolerance Limits

To help them distinguish between normal and abnormal loss of units, accountants assist production and engineering personnel in establishing tolerance limits. They can express **tolerance limits for normal loss** as a percentage of the good units that pass the inspection point of the operations. For example, if past inspections made at the end of processing yielded an average of 48 bad units for 1,000 units introduced into operations, the normal loss percentage would be 48/952 or 5 percent of good production. Managers would accept this percentage as the limit if their analysis verified that this loss was uncontrollable and an inherent part of operations. Suppose these managers discover that operations of a given period lose 100 units through spoilage. Assume further that workers complete 1,500 units, which passed inspection at the end of the operations. The normal loss associated with the good units finished would be 75 (5 percent $\times$ 1,500 good units). The remaining 25 units would be classified as abnormal loss.

Current Cost Management Practice

Global

According to the CEO of GTE Corporation, the time to improve your company is when you see the marketplace and technologies changing. GTE plans to replace 17,000 workers with computerized equipment. Despite expanding U.S. economic growth, some of America's biggest and best corporations are continuing to restructure by announcing significant layoffs and financial changes. Executives are nervous as they hear increasing demands for greater value from customers and feel the relentless pressure of global competition and fundamental shifts in technology.

Tim Smart, "Let the Good Times Roll—And a Few More Heads," *BusinessWeek,* January 31, 1994, pp. 28-29.

Accountants alternately express normal loss as a percent of total units processed. In this situation the normal loss is 48/100 or 4.8 percent of total units processed. Using either of these approaches, accountants then determine the cost of the normal and abnormal loss separately. This enables management to more easily recognize the investment lost through unavoidable and avoidable circumstances.

Quality Control Concepts and Zero Defects Programs

As more companies successfully adopt quality control concepts and zero defects programs, accounting for normal and abnormal losses may change. The **zero defects** performance standard emphasizes doing work right the first time. The zero defects philosophy is not limited to production efforts. Both service and manufacturing companies can realize a reduction in waste by eliminating poor practices and lackadaisical employee attitudes.

Produce-and-Rework-if-Defective Program

Traditionally, managers established an acceptable level of defects because they assumed that errors are inevitable. Such a policy encourages employees to operate at an established tolerance level. For example, if management allows a 2 percent defect level, most employees are satisfied if they attain this level. Employees typically do not strive to make further improvements—they operate to the tolerance level of authority. On the other hand, when managers set the defect level at zero, employees work harder to eliminate all defects.

On-the-Spot Correction

When a company adopts a quality control philosophy, employees pledge to make a constant conscious effort to do their jobs correctly the first time. Also, each worker takes personal responsibility for eliminating mistakes. Employees recognize that their individual contributions are a vital part of the organizationwide effort.

A zero defects program controls quality in the early manufacturing stages. Laborers inspect their work at each process to prevent defective parts from reaching the final process. When a mistake does occur, employees try to determine what caused the error. Then they consider what might be done to prevent similar mistakes in the future. Management relies on workers' self-inspection to reduce the number of full-time inspectors.

Regardless of how many inspectors are in a plant, errors are still likely to occur under conventional inspection systems. Traditionally, each inspector depends on the others to find the error. Sometimes, inspection workers may fail to note defects because they are confident the other inspectors will not see errors. Thus, they do not wish to discredit their colleagues.

Changing from the conventional produce-and-rework-if-defective routine to a zero defects concept involves a total commitment from top management down to factory employees. Companies need to retrain their employees before largely reducing spoilage and defective rates. And, managers must seriously encourage defect prevention.

Doing it right the first time sounds effective. But how can employees make products right the first time when the incoming material is off-color or their machines are not in good working condition? Managers must coordinate group efforts toward eliminating defects. For example, close association of an organization with its suppliers helps ensure the consistent quality of incoming materials.

Future Spoilage Minimized

Under the traditional produce-and-rework-if-defective routine, employees study any defect detected at the end of the line. They then use this information as feedback. However, the preferred approach is on-the-spot correction because it sharply reduces the time lag between the detection and correction of the defect. On-the-spot correction generally produces fewer defective units because of the immediate feedback workers receive.

Successful practice of quality control concepts emphasizes controlling and reducing all spoilage. Also, quality control recognizes that some waste can be minimized but never completely avoided. Examples include evaporation during processing, adherence of substances to containers during transfers of materials from one container to another, and cutting irregular shapes from a sheet of material.

Timing of Inspections

Whether a company operates under a traditional or modern inspection approach incurring abnormal or normal spoilage, a loss of units may occur at the beginning, midpoint, or end of operations within a department. Employees discover lost units at inspection. Traditionally, companies assumed losses occurred at the end of the department's process because they usually inspected operations then and recognized the loss. However, frequent on-the-spot inspection and correction often is less costly than applying cost to a unit that has already been spoiled. A trade-off usually occurs between the expense of additional inspections and the risk of unknowingly incurring material and conversion costs for a unit that has become spoiled.

Inspection at End of Operations

Exhibit 8–3 illustrates a cost of production report for a department that inspects units at the end of operations. Because inspection occurs at the end of processing, units in ending inventory are not inspected. Thus, because none of the units lost come from the current ending work in process inventory, the cost of lost units is charged only to the completed units. With these inspection arrangements, spoiled units complete the department's processing and receive the full departmental cost.

The department in Exhibit 8–3 loses 1,000 units to abnormal conditions and 2,500 units through normal causes. Because inspection occurs at the end of

EXHIBIT 8–3

REXFORD MANUFACTURING COMPANY—ASSEMBLY DEPARTMENT
Cost of Production Report
Weighted-Average Costing, Lost Units
Inspection at End of Processing
For the Month Ending June 19X5

Quantity schedule (Step 1):

Beginning inventory ($1/4$ M, $1/2$ CC)	500	
Started in production	7,200	7,700
Transferred	2,400	
Abnormal loss	1,000	
Normal Loss	2,500	
Ending inventory ($2/5$ M, $2/3$ CC)	1,800	7,700

	Total Costs	Unit Costs
Costs to account for (Step 3):		
Beginning inventory:		
Material	$ 750	
Conversion costs	2,880	
Costs of beginning inventory	$ 3,630	
Current costs:		
Material	$24,270	$ 3.7795
Conversion costs	52,920	7.8591
Total costs to account for	$80,820	$11.6386

Costs accounted for as follows (Step 4):

Costs transferred before normal loss (2,400 × $11.6386) ...... Joined w/	$27,933	
Costs of normal loss (2,500 × $11.6386) .... good units	29,096	
Total costs transferred		$57,029
Ending inventory:		
Materials (1,800 × $2/5$ × $3.7795)	$ 2,721	
Conversion costs (1,800 × $2/3$ × $7.8591)	9,431	
Total costs of ending inventory		12,152
Costs of abnormal loss (1,000 × $11.6386)		11,639
Total costs accounted for		$80,820

Additional computations (Step 2):

	Transferred	+	Ending Inventory	+	Abnormal Spoilage	+	Normal Spoilage	=	
EU, material =	2,400	+	720	+	1,000	+	2,500	=	6,620
$\dfrac{\$750 + \$24,270}{6,620} = \$3.7795$			(1,800 × $2/5$)						
EU, conversion costs =	2,400	+	1,200	+	1,000	+	2,500	=	7,100
$\dfrac{\$2,880 + \$52,920}{7,100} = \$7.8591$			(1,800 × $2/3$)						

processing, all spoiled units have been through the Assembly Department's entire operations. For this reason, the lost units are added in the following equivalent unit (EU) computations. Unit cost calculations also are given:

$$\begin{array}{c} \text{EU,} \\ \text{material} \end{array} = \begin{array}{c} 2,400 \\ \text{transferred} \end{array} + \begin{array}{c} 720 \text{ ending} \\ \text{inventory} \\ (1,800 \times 2/5) \end{array} + \begin{array}{c} 1,000 \text{ abnormal} \\ \text{loss} \end{array} + \begin{array}{c} 2,500 \text{ normal} \\ \text{loss} \end{array} = 6,620$$

$$\frac{\$750 \text{ beginning inventory materials} + \$24,270 \text{ current materials}}{6,620} = \frac{\$25,020}{6,620} = \$3.7795$$

$$\begin{array}{c} \text{EU,} \\ \text{conversion} \\ \text{cost} \end{array} = \begin{array}{c} 2,400 \\ \text{transferred} \end{array} + \begin{array}{c} 1,200 \text{ ending} \\ \text{inventory} \\ (1,800 \times 2/3) \end{array} + \begin{array}{c} 1,000 \text{ abnormal} \\ \text{loss} \end{array} + \begin{array}{c} 2,500 \text{ normal} \\ \text{loss} \end{array} = 7,100$$

$$\frac{\$2,880 \text{ beginning inventory conversion costs} + \$52,920 \text{ current conversion costs}}{7,100} = \frac{\$55,800}{7,100} = \$7.8591$$

Note that this is the same EU formula introduced in Chapter 7 except we added lost units at the stage of completion when they were discovered lost.

Cost of Abnormal and Normal Loss.   After calculating equivalent units for material and conversion costs, we assign the $11.6386 total unit cost to the 2,400 units transferred out of the department to arrive at a total of $27,933 (2,400 units × $11.6386). We also use the $11.6386 unit cost to arrive at the cost of the normal loss and the abnormal loss. The cost of the normal loss of units is 2,500 units × $11.6386 = $29,096. The cost of the abnormal loss of units is 1,000 units × $11.6386 = $11,639.

We then add the $29,096 cost charged to the units lost due to normal conditions to the $27,933 cost of the good units completed and transferred to arrive at a total cost transferred of $57,029. Thus, good units must absorb the cost of any normal loss. The 2,400 units leave with a total cost of $57,029 or at a higher unit cost than $11.6386. Note that the effect of the units lost through normal causes has been an increase in the cost of the good units. This higher cost reduces income when the company sells these units. Exhibit 8-3 illustrates only one department, and we assume the next department is Finished Goods. A separate journal entry is not needed to record the normal loss of units; the $29,096 cost is added to the $27,933 cost of the good units to transfer finished units out of the Assembly Department:

Finished Goods Inventory	57,029	
Work in Process—Assembly Department		57,029

This journal entry assumes that the 2,500 units lost because of normal conditions have no sales value. This is obviously the case if the normal loss was due to evaporation. If instead, scrap occurs on a regular basis and we assume that the company can sell the units spoiled because of normal conditions as irregulars or scrap material for $100, we assign net sales value to the spoilage. Spoilage is set up in an inventory account at this amount. We credit the Work in Process—Assembly Department account for the sales value of the spoilage. The good units completed now bear only a $28,996 cost ($29,096 cost of normal loss − $100 sales value of normal loss) due to the normal loss of units. The journal entry recording the spoilage and transfer to finished goods is

Spoiled Goods or Scrap Material Inventory	100	
Work in Process—Assembly Department		100
Finished Goods Inventory ($27,933 + $29,096 − $100).	56,929	
Work in Process—Assembly Department		56,929

This is the approach Chapter 15 suggests for accounting for scrap and spoiled goods. When the units lost through normal conditions are sold, the entry is as follows:

Cash or Accounts Receivable..................	100	
Spoiled Goods or Scrap Material Inventory		100

Journal Entry to Record Abnormal Loss. A separate entry records the abnormal loss of units. We treat normal loss as a product cost by assigning the loss to the good units completed. We treat abnormal loss as a period expense. For example, if we assume that the units lost through abnormal conditions have no salable value, the entry for the Assembly Department in Exhibit 8–3 is

Cost of Lost Units........................	11,639	
Work in Process—Assembly Department.......		11,639

Now assume that the company can sell the 1,000 spoiled units for $1 each. This entry sets up the inventory value of the units and removes the cost of the abnormal loss from the department:

Spoiled Goods or Scrap Materials Inventory	1,000	
Cost of Lost Units........................	10,639	
Work in Process—Assembly Department.......		11,639

The same type of entry as illustrated earlier records the sale of these spoiled goods or scrap material:

Cash or Accounts Receivable..................	1,000	
Spoiled Goods or Scrap Materials Inventory		1,000

Inspection at the Intermediate Point of Operations

Exhibit 8–4 illustrates FIFO costing where the Mixing Department inspects at the 40 percent stage of operations and the Finishing Department at the 75 percent stage of processing. However, note that inspections can occur, for example, at a 30 percent or a 50 percent stage of operation. We arbitrarily chose these points of inspection for illustration. There is no rule to inspect at the midpoint, at the beginning, or at the end of operations. Exhibit 8–4 rounds costs to whole dollars in both departments. Because workers add material at the beginning of operations in both departments, we include lost units in the equivalent unit calculation for material in both departments as follows:

EU, mixing material	5,500 = transferred	800 + ending inventory	500 + normal loss	200 + abnormal loss	600 − beginning inventory	= 6,400
EU, finishing material	4,500 = transferred	1,000 + ending inventory	400 + normal loss	100 + abnormal loss	500 − beginning inventory	= 5,500

Next, we must calculate the stage of completion of lost units at inspection. Since the Mixing Department detects the units lost at the 40 percent stage of operations, we assume they receive only 40 percent of their labor and overhead in this department. For example, we compute the equivalent units for labor in the Mixing Department as follows:

EU,	5,500	160	200	80	90	
Mixing =	transferred +	ending	+ normal	+ abnormal	− beginning	= 5,850
labor		inventory	loss	loss	inventory	
		(800 × 20%)	(500 × 40%)	(200 × 40%)	(600 × 15%)	

To determine the cost of abnormal and normal loss, we multiply all units by the unit material cost. The lost units receive only 40 percent of the mixing and 75 percent of the finishing conversion costs. The cost applied to the lost units in the Finishing Department represents work performed in the Mixing Department as well as in the Finishing Department. For example, to determine the cost of normal loss in the Finishing Department, Exhibit 8–4 shows the following computations on the cost of production report. The computation considers that the 400 units lost because of normal causes have all been through the Mixing Department and have received an adjusted cost of $10.418.

Costs of normal loss:
Cost from preceding department (400 × $10.418)	$4,167
Materials (400 × $0.582)	232
Labor (400 × 75% × $4.20)	1,260
Overhead (400 × 75% × $2.80)	840
Total cost of normal loss	$6,499

Assigning Current Costs to Units Spoiled.   An issue with FIFO costing is whether accountants should cost lost units at the current period's cost (as shown in all examples in this book) or at costs partly influenced by the cost of beginning work in process. Conceptually, if the units in beginning work in process have not passed the inspection stage, some will likely be lost in processing. However, for beginning work in process costs to influence the cost assigned to lost units, we must estimate the number of units spoiled from beginning inventory and the number of units started in the period and spoiled. Thus, the expedient procedure is to assume all losses are from current production and assign current costs to lost units as illustrated.

Change in per Unit Cost.   Units lost under normal conditions affect the unit cost of all units transferred. Note that the current unit cost in the Mixing Department shown in Exhibit 8–4 is $9.90. However, the cost increases to $10.418 in the Finishing Department because of the 500 lost units and averaging with FIFO. Averaging with FIFO occurs when the various batches of units transferred are received in the next department. In Exhibit 8–4, the Mixing Department transfers a 600-unit batch and a 4,900-unit batch to the Finishing Department. Combining the cost of the two batches affects the per unit cost in the subsequent department. The ending inventory and the lost units of the Finishing Department receive this higher $10.418 preceding department cost.

EXHIBIT 8-4

CRAWFORD PRODUCTION COMPANY
Cost of Production Report, FIFO—Inspection at Various Processing Points
For Month Ending January 31, 19X1

(handwritten: 40%) Mixing Department   *(handwritten: 75%)* Finishing Department

	Mixing Department		Finishing Department	
Quantity schedule (Step 1):				
Beginning inventory (all material, 15% labor, 10% overhead)	600		(all M, 30% L, 65% OH) 500	
Units started in process	6,400	7,000	5,500	6,000
Units transferred to next department	5,500		4,500	
Ending inventory (all material, 20% labor, 25% overhead	800		(all M, 40% L, 70% OH) 1,000	
Normal loss of units	500		400	
Abnormal loss of units	200	7,000	100	6,000

	Total Costs	Unit Costs		Total Costs	Unit Costs
Costs to account for (Step 3):					
Work in process—beginning inventory:					
Costs from preceding department	–0–			$ 5,200	
Material	$ 1,800			290	
Labor	260			600	
Overhead	230			910	
Total value of beginning inventory	$ 2,290			$ 7,000	
Costs received from preceding department				57,298	$ 10.418
Current cost in department:					
Material	$19,840	$ 3.10		3,201	0.582
Labor	16,380	2.80		21,525	4.200
Overhead	23,680	4.00		14,700	2.800
Total costs to account for	$62,190	$ 9.90		$103,724	$ 18.000

(handwritten note near Finishing beginning inventory: "Reflects 1051 units")

Costs accounted for as follows (Step 4):					
Costs transferred to next department:					
From beginning inventory:					
Value of beginning inventory	$ 2,290			$ 7,000	
Labor added (600 × 85% × $2.80)	1,428		(500 × 70% × $4.20)	1,470	
Overhead added (600 × 90% × $4)	2,160	$ 5,878	(500 × 35% × $2.80)	490	$ 8,960
From current production (4,900 × $9.90)		48,510	(4,000 × $18)		72,000
Total cost transferred before spoilage		$54,388			$ 80,960
Cost of normal loss:					
Costs from preceding department			(400 × $10.418)	$ 4,167	
Material (500 × $3.10)	$ 1,550		(400 × $0.582)	232	
Labor (500 × 40% × $2.80)	560		(400 × 75% × $4.20)	1,260	
Overhead (500 × 40% × $4)	800	2,910	(400 × 75% × $2.80)	840	6,499
Total cost transferred		$57,298			$ 87,459
Work in process—ending inventory:					
Costs from preceding department			(1,000 × $10.418)	$10,418	
Material (800 × $3.10)	$ 2,480		(1,000 × $0.582)	582	
Labor (800 × 20% × $2.80)	448		(1,000 × 40% × $4.20)	1,680	
Overhead (800 × 25% × $4)	800	3,728	(1,000 × 70% × $2.80)	1,960	14,640
Cost of abnormal loss:					
Cost from preceding department			(100 × $10.418)	$ 1,042	
Material (200 × $3.10)	$ 620		(100 × $0.582)	58	
Labor (200 × 40% × $2.80)	224		(100 × 75% × $4.20)	315	
Overhead (200 × 40% × $4)	320	1,164	(100 × 75% × $2.80)	210	1,625
Total costs accounted for		$62,190			$103,724

(continued)

EXHIBIT 8-4   *(concluded)*

Additional computations (Step 2):	Transferred +	Ending Inventory +	Normal Loss +	Abnormal Loss −	Beginning Inventory		
EU, Mixing, material $\dfrac{\$19,840}{6,400} = \$3.10$	5,500 +	800 +	500 +	200 −	600	=	6,400
EU, Mixing, labor $\dfrac{\$16,380}{5,850} = \$2.80$	5,500 +	160 (800 × 20%) +	200 (500 × 40%) +	80 (200 × 40%) −	90 (600 × 15%)	=	5,850
EU, Mixing, overhead $\dfrac{\$23,680}{5,920} = \$4.00$	5,500 +	200 (800 × 25%) +	200 (500 × 40%) +	80 (200 × 40%) −	60 (600 × 10%)	=	5,920
EU, Finishing, preceding department costs $\dfrac{\$57,298}{5,500} = \$10.418$	4,500 +	1,000 +	400 +	100 −	500	=	5,500
EU, Finishing, material $\dfrac{\$3,201}{5,500} = \$0.582$	4,500 +	1,000 +	400 +	100 −	500	=	5,500
EU, Finishing, labor $\dfrac{\$21,525}{5,125} = \$4.20$	4,500 +	400 (1,000 × 40%) +	300 (400 × 75%) +	75 (100 × 75%) −	150 (500 × 30%)	=	5,125
EU, Finishing, overhead $\dfrac{\$14,700}{5,250} = \$2.80$	4,500 +	700 (1,000 × 70%) +	300 (400 × 75%) +	75 (100 × 75%) −	325 (500 × 65%)	=	5,250

Assuming that none of the units lost has any salable value, the following journal entries are necessary to recognize the abnormal loss and to transfer the units from one department to another:

Cost of Lost Units (1,164 + 1,625)	2,789	
Work in Process—Mixing Department		1,164
Work in Process—Finishing Department		1,625
Work in Process—Finishing Department	57,298	
Work in Process—Mixing Department		57,298
Finished Goods Inventory	87,459	
Work in Process—Finishing Department		87,459

Allocation of Normal Loss

In Exhibit 8–4 we do not show **allocation of normal loss.** We do not allocate the cost of the normal loss of units to the units in ending inventory because they have not yet reached the inspection point in the production cycle. Instead, we assign the loss only to the units that have passed inspection. If, however, the ending inventory was more than 40 percent complete in the mixing operations or more than 75 percent complete in the finishing processing, we would assign the normal loss cost to both completed units and ending inventory. *Note we compare the stage in operations at*

*which inspection occurs to the stage of completion of the ending inventory in decid-
ing whether to assign normal loss cost to the units on hand that are partially complete
at the end of the period.*

Exhibit 8–5 illustrates the allocation of normal loss cost to units completed
and still in process using the same data as in Exhibit 8–3. However, instead of
inspection being at the end of operations, assume inspection is at the three-tenths
stage of completion. Thus, the 1,800 units in ending inventory have passed
inspection. We add the $43,200 costs before loss allocation of the 2,400 units
transferred to the $18,720 cost of the 1,800 semifinished units in ending inven-
tory, yielding a total of $61,920. Exhibit 8–5 shows the allocation of normal loss
cost:

$$\frac{\$43,200}{\$61,920} \times \$13,500 \text{ normal loss } = \$9,419 \text{ to the cost of the units transferred}$$

$$\frac{\$18,720}{\$61,920} \times \$13,500 \text{ normal loss } = \$4,081 \text{ to the ending inventory}$$

We add $9,419 to the cost of the good units transferred to give transferred costs total-
ing $52,619. Also, we add $4,081 to the ending inventory to yield a total valuation
of $22,801. Rather than spread normal loss costs over the units completed and still
in process on the basis of costs incurred, equivalent units (or less preferably, physical units) can be used as a basis. Problem for Self-Study 8–1 illustrates FIFO costing allocating normal loss costs on the basis of physical units.

We assign a total cost of $5,400 to the 1,000 units lost through inefficiencies
and other abnormalities and show this cost separately on the cost of production report.
The remaining steps in completing the cost of production report illustrated in Exhibit
8–5 are identical to those for other reports prepared using the weighted-average
approach.

Summary

As goods pass through manufacturing operations, accountants compute product unit costs to
determine inventory valuations. Different variables complicate the determination of product
cost in this process. The addition of material, for example, can cause an increase in unit cost
or in units to account for. It is much simpler if the material added does not increase the units
involved as Chapter 7 illustrated. The increase in the units to be accounted for resulting from
the addition of material requires that we calculate the preceding department unit cost again
to spread the cost over the increased units.

Companies lose units in processing because of uncontrollable factors, for example, shrinkage or evaporation. Management should determine normal tolerance limits for the loss expected.
Any loss exceeding these limits is an abnormal loss of units. Equivalent unit calculations
include lost units so the units lost receive a cost. The cost of abnormal loss of units is a
period cost. The point at which inspection occurs and lost units are detected determines whether
both ending inventory and units transferred or only units transferred receive the cost of the
normal loss of units. This method of indicating the cost of lost units provides an incentive
for management to become more conscious of ways to prevent losses. Increased use of the
zero defect concept also reduces losses.

EXHIBIT 8-5

3/30/10

REXFORD MANUFACTURING COMPANY—ASSEMBLY DEPARTMENT
Cost of Production Report—Weighted-Average Costing
Inspection at 30% Stage of Processing
For the Month Ending June 19X5

Quantity schedule (Step 1):

Beginning inventory ($\frac{1}{4}$ M, $\frac{1}{2}$ CC)	500	
Started in production	7,200	7,700
Transferred	2,400	
Abnormal loss	1,000	
Normal loss	2,500	
Ending inventory ($\frac{2}{5}$ M, $\frac{2}{3}$ CC)	1,800	7,700

	Total Costs	Unit Costs

Costs to account for (Step 3):

	Total Costs	Unit Costs
Beginning inventory:		
Material	$ 750	
Conversion costs	2,880	
Costs of beginning inventory	$ 3,630	
Current costs:		
Material	$24,270	$ 6.00
Conversion costs	52,920	12.00
Total costs to account for	$80,820	$ 18.00

Costs accounted for as follows (Step 4):

	Total Costs	Unit Costs
<u>Costs transferred</u> before loss		
allocation (2,400 × $18) ... *transferred*	$43,200	
Loss allocation ($43,200/$61,920) × $13,500	9,419	
Total costs transferred		$52,619
Ending inventory:		
Materials (1,800 × $\frac{2}{5}$ × $6)	$ 4,320	
Conversion costs (1,800 × $\frac{2}{3}$ × $12)	14,400	
<u>Costs of ending</u> inventory before		
loss allocation	$18,720 ✓	
Loss allocation ($18,720/$61,920) × $13,500	4,081	
Total cost of ending inventory		✓ 22,801
<u>Abnormal loss:</u>		
Material (1,000 × $\frac{3}{10}$ × $6)	$ 1,800	
Conversion costs (1,000 × $\frac{3}{10}$ × $12)	3,600	
Total costs of abnormal loss		5,400
Total costs accounted for		$80,820

61,920

Loss allocation:

	Total Costs	Unit Costs
Costs of normal loss:		
Material (2,500 × $\frac{3}{10}$ × $6)	$ 4,500	
Conversion costs (2,500 × $\frac{3}{10}$ × $12)	9,000	
Total cost of normal loss (2,500 × $\frac{3}{10}$)	$13,500	

DO FIRST

Additional computations (Step 2):

	Transferred	+	Ending Inventory	+	Abnormal Spoilage	+	Normal Spoilage		
EU, material =	2,400	+	720	+	300	+	750	=	4,170
$\frac{\$750 + \$24,270}{4,170} = \$6$			(1,800 × $\frac{2}{5}$)		(1,000 × $\frac{3}{10}$)		(2,500 × $\frac{3}{10}$)		
EU, conversion costs =	2,400	+	1,200	+	300	+	750	=	4,650
$\frac{\$2,880 + \$52,920}{4,650} = \$12$			(1,800 × $\frac{2}{3}$)						

if % completion of end. inv. ≥ % of inspection use % @ inspection for normal loss

Important Terms and Concepts

Addition of material that increases unit
 cost   222
Addition of material that yields a larger
 base unit count   222
Scrap   227
Defective units   227

Spoiled goods   227
Normal loss   227
Abnormal (or avoidable) loss   227
Tolerance limits for normal loss   227
Zero defects   228
Allocation of normal loss   235

Problem for Self-Study 8–1

FIFO, Normal Loss Allocated on Physical Units

Joseph Martin, Inc., uses process costing to account for its product. Operations take place in the Mixing Department. Since loss is inherent in the production process, management allocates this to its finished goods transferred and ending inventory. Inspection is made when the units are one-third complete in the department. Assume that at the inspection point, material and conversion costs are at the same stage of completion. A summary of the costs incurred is as follows:

Work in process beginning inventory, 400 units:
    Material ($1/4$ complete) . . . . $ 85
    Conversion costs ($2/5$ complete) . . . . 315 $ 400

Current period cost:
    Material 11,360
    Conversion costs 29,064

There were 15,000 units started in production in the Mixing Department, while 12,500 units were transferred to the Finishing Department: 2,000 units were incomplete at the end of the month having three-fourths of their material and three-fifths conversion costs.

Required:

Prepare a cost of production report using FIFO costing and allocate normal loss costs on physical units.

Solution to Problem for Self-Study 8–1

JOSEPH MARTIN, INC.
Cost of Production Report—FIFO
For Period Ending 19X1

Quantity schedule (Step 1):

Beginning inventory	400	($1/4$ M, $2/5$ L & OH)
Started in production	15,000	15,400
Transferred	12,500	
Still in process	2,000	($3/4$ M, $3/5$ L & OH)
Lost in process	900	15,400

Costs to account for (Step 3):	**Total Costs**	**Unit Costs**
Work in process—beginning	$ 400	
Current costs:		
Material	11,360	$ .80
Conversion costs	29,064	2.10
Total costs to account for	$40,824	$ 2.90

Solution to Problem
for Self-Study 8–1
(concluded)

Costs accounted for as follows (Step 4):

Transferred from beginning inventory:

Value of beginning inventory	$ 400	
Material added (400 × 3/4 × $.80)	240	
Conversion costs added (400 × 3/5 × $2.10)	504	
Total value of beginning inventory finished before loss allocation	$ 1,144	
Transferred from current production (12,100 × $2.90) .	35,090	
Costs transferred before loss allocation		$36,234
Loss allocation (12,500/14,500 × $870*)		750
Total costs transferred			$36,984

Work in process—ending:

Material (2,000 × 3/4 × $.80)	$ 1,200		
Conversion costs (2,000 × 3/5 × $2.10)	2,520		
Value of ending inventory before loss allocation		$ 3,720	
Loss allocation (2,000/14,500 × $870*)		120	3,840
Total costs accounted for			$40,824

Additional computations (Step 2):

EU, material = 12,500 + 1,500 + 300 − 100 = 14,200 $\dfrac{\$11,360}{14,200}$ = $ .80

EU, conversion costs = 12,500 + 1,200 + 300 − 160 = 13,840 $\dfrac{\$29,064}{13,840}$ = $ 2.10

*Loss allocation:
Loss = 900 × 1/3 × $2.90 = $870.

Problem for Self-Study 8–2

Addition of Material Increasing Base Unit Count; Unit Loss

Swann, Inc., manufactures a product known as CXI. For March 19X1, they have incurred the following cost:

	Department A		Department B	
Current costs:				
Materials	$35,451.00		$15,620.00	
Labor	25,680.00		30,091.28	
Overhead	21,838.00		12,744.00	
Beginning inventory:				
Prior department costs			$1,170.00	
Materials	$3,600.00		198.00	
Labor	810.00		72.00	
Overhead	540.00	4,950.00	55.00	1,495.00

The material introduced in Department B increases the number of units produced. The beginning inventory in Department A was composed of 1,200 units having one-third labor and one-fourth overhead. There were 11,700 units started in process in Department A. There were 12,000 units transferred; 600 units were in ending inventory involving one-sixth of their labor and one-third of their overhead. Of the remaining units, one-sixth were lost because a new worker failed to close a valve at the end of the process in Department A; the others represent a loss inherent in the production process. Inspection is made at the end of the process in Department A.

In Department B, 2,200 units of water were added to dilute the mixture received at the beginning of processing from Department A. There were 180 units in beginning inventory that were one-fifth complete for labor and one-third for overhead. There were 14,000 units transferred; 200 units were in ending inventory at a one-fourth stage of completion for labor and one-fifth for overhead. Of the remaining units, one-third were lost due to abnormal conditions, and two-thirds were lost due to normal production conditions.

Required:

a. Prepare a cost of production report using the FIFO method.

b. Prepare a cost of production report using the weighted-average costing method.

Solution to Problem for Self-Study 8–2   a. FIFO

·SWANN, INC.
Cost of Production Report—FIFO
For Month Ending March 30, 19X1

	Department A			Department B		
Quantity schedule (Step 1):						
Beginning inventory	1,200	(all M, ⅓ L, ¼ OH)		180	(all M, ⅕ L, ⅓ OH)	
Started into process	11,700					
Received from Department A ...				12,000		
Increase in units				2,200		
Total units to account for ..		12,900				14,380
Transferred	12,000			14,000		
Ending inventory	600	(all M, ⅙ L, ⅓ OH)		200	(all M, ¼ L, ⅕ OH)	
Normal loss of units	250			120		
Abnormal loss of units	50			60		
Total units to account for		12,900				14,380

	Total Costs	Unit Costs			Total Costs	Unit Costs
Costs to account for (Step 3):						
Beginning inventory	$ 4,950.00				$ 1,495.00	
Transferred in during month					85,181.00	$ 6.00
Added by department:						
Material	35,451.00	$ 3.03			15,620.00	1.10
Labor	25,680.00	2.14			30,091.28	2.12
Factory overhead	21,838.00	1.79			12,744.00	0.90
Total cost to be accounted for ...	$87,919.00	$ 6.96			$145,131.28	$ 10.12
Costs accounted for as follows (Step 4):						
Transferred:						
From beginning inventory	$ 4,950.00				$ 1,495.00	
Labor added (⅔ × 1,200 × $2.14)	1,712.00		(⁴⁄₅ × 180 × $2.12)		305.28	
Overhead added (¾ × 1,200 × $1.79)	1,611.00		(⅔ × 180 × $0.90)		108.00	
Transferred from beginning inventory .	$ 8,273.00				$ 1,908.28	
Transferred from current production						
(10,800 × $6.96)	75,168.00		(13,820 × $10.12)		139,858.40	
Total costs transferred before loss .	$83,441.00				$141,766.68	
Normal loss (250 × $6.96)	1,740.00		(120 × $10.12)		1,214.40	
Total costs transferred		$85,181.00				$142,981.08
Abnormal loss (50 × $6.96)		348.00				588.20*
Work in process—ending:						
Cost in Department A			(200 × $6.00)		$ 1,200.00	
Material (600 × $3.03)	$1,818.00		(200 × $1.10)		220.00	
Labor (100 × $2.14)	214.00		(50 × $2.12)		106.00	
Factory overhead (200 × $1.79)	358.00	2,390.00	(40 × $.90)		36.00	1,562.00
Total cost accounted for		$87,919.00				$145,131.28

Additional Computations (Step 2):
Department A

$$\text{EU, material} = 12,000 + 600 + 250 + 50 - 1,200 = 11,700; \frac{\$35,451}{11,700} = \$3.03$$

$$\text{EU, labor} = 12,000 + 100 + 250 + 50 - 400 = 12,000; \frac{\$25,680}{12,000} = \$2.14$$

$$\text{EU, OH} = 12,000 + 200 + 250 + 50 - 300 = 12,200; \frac{\$21,838}{12,200} = \$1.79$$

(continued)

*To avoid decimal discrepancy, abnormal loss is computed as follows: $145,131.28 − ($142,981.08 + $1,562.00) = $588.20.

Department B:
Prior Department Costs:

Units Transferred in .... 12,000 $\dfrac{\$85,181}{14,200}$ = $6.00 adjusted unit cost for prior department
Additional units put into process 2,200
                                          14,200

or EU, Department B, prior department costs = 14,000 + 200 + 120 + 60 − 180 = 14,200

EU, material = 14,000 + 200 + 120 + 60 − 180 = 14,200; $\dfrac{\$15,620}{14,200}$ = $1.10

EU, labor = 14,000 + 50 + 120 + 60 − 36 = 14,194; $\dfrac{\$30,091.28}{14,194}$ = $2.12

EU, OH = 14,000 + 40 + 120 + 60 − 60 = 14,160; $\dfrac{\$12,744.00}{14,160}$ = $0.90

b. Weighted average

SWANN, INC.
Cost of Production Report—Weighted Average For Month Ending March 30, 19X1

Quantity schedule (Step 1):		Department A	Department B	
Beginning inventory	1,200	(all M, 1/3 L, 1/4 OH)	180 (all M, 1/5 L, 1/3 OH)	
Started into process	11,700			
Received from Department A			12,000	
Increase in units			2,200	
Total units to account for		12,900		14,380
Transferred	12,000		14,000	
Ending inventory	600	(all M, 1/6 L & 1/3 OH)	200 (all M, 1/4 L, 1/5 OH)	
Normal loss of units	250		120	
Abnormal loss of units	50		60	
Total units to account for		12,900		14,380

	Total Costs	Unit Costs	Total Costs	Unit Costs
Costs to account for (Step 3):				
Beginning inventory:				
Prior department cost			$ 1,170.00	
Material	$ 3,600.00		198.00	
Labor	810.00		72.00	
Overhead	540.00		55.00	
Value of beginning inventory	$ 4,950.00		$ 1,495.00	
Costs received from preceding department:				
Transferred in during month			85,183.00	$ 6.00507
Added by department:				
Materials	35,451.00	$ 3.02721	15,620.00	1.10000
Labor	25,680.00	2.13629	30,091.28	2.11970
Factory overhead	21,838.00	1.79024	12,744.00	0.90007
Total costs to be accounted for ..	$87,919.00	$ 6.95374	$145,133.28	$ 10.12484
Costs accounted for as follows (Step 4):				
Transferred before loss (12,000 × $6.95374)		$83,445.00	(14,000 × $10.12484)	$141,747.76
Normal loss (250 × $6.95374)		1,738.00	(120 × $10.12484)	1,214.98
Total costs transferred		$85,183.00		$142,962.74
Abnormal loss (50 × $6.95374) ...		348.00		607.55*
Work in process:				
Prior department costs			(200 × $6.00507) $ 1,201.01	
Material (600 × $3.02721)	$ 1,816.00		(200 × $1.10) 220.00	
Labor (100 × $2.13629)	214.00		(50 × $2.1197) 105.98	
Factory overhead (200 × $1.79024)	358.00	2,388.00	(40 × $0.90007) 36.00	1,562.99
Total costs accounted for		$87,919.00		$145,133.28

*To avoid decimal discrepancy, abnormal loss is computed as follows: $145,133.28 − ($142,962.74 + $1,562.99) = $607.55.
Note: Costs accounted for in Department A are rounded to whole dollars while the costs in Department B are not. This is illustrated to show variations in practice employed by companies.

(continued)

*Solution to Problem
for Self-Study 8–2
(concluded)*

Additional computations (Step 2):

Department A

EU, material $= 12,000 + 600 + 250 + 50 = 12,900;$ $\dfrac{\$35,451 + \$3,600}{12,900} = \$3.02721$

EU, labor $= 12,000 + 100 + 250 + 50 = 12,400;$ $\dfrac{\$25,680 + \$810}{12,400} = \$2.13629$

EU, OH $= 12,000 + 200 + 250 + 50 = 12,500;$ $\dfrac{\$21,838 + \$540}{12,500} = \$1.79024$

Department B

EU, prior department costs $= 14,000 + 200 + 120 + 60 = 14,380;$ $\dfrac{\$1,170.00 + \$85,183.00}{14,380} = \$6.00507$

EU, material $= 14,000 + 200 + 120 + 60 = 14,380;$ $\dfrac{\$15,620.00 + \$198.00}{14,380} = \$1.10000$

EU, labor $= 14,000 + 50 + 120 + 60 = 14,230;$ $\dfrac{\$30,091.28 + \$72.00}{14,230} = \$2.11970$

EU, OH $= 14,000 + 40 + 120 + 60 = 14,220;$ $\dfrac{\$12,744.00 + \$55.00}{14,220} = \$0.90007$

Review Questions

1. Assume inspection is made at the beginning of operations in processing departments except the first department. *a.* What cost is assigned to the lost units? *b.* How would you allocate the cost of normal loss of units?

2. Why are the units lost through either normal or abnormal causes included in computing equivalent units?

3. *a.* Contrast the treatment for normal and abnormal loss in a process costing system.
   b. When would you allocate abnormal loss to cost of units produced under a process costing system?

4. Under an actual cost system, indicate reasons why the total unit cost determined in the first department under process costing could differ from the preceding department unit cost computed in the second department.

5. What is the FIFO equivalent unit calculation for material, labor, and overhead if material is added in processing at the beginning of operations and 12,800 units were started in production? Beginning inventory consisted of 2,600 units, one-fourth complete for labor and overhead, and ending inventory consisted of 1,500 units, three-fourths complete for labor and overhead. Inspection is at the two-thirds stage of production, and 600 units were found to be lost.

6. What factors would you consider in deciding at what points in the manufacturing operations to make inspections? Why is there a trade-off in selecting more frequent inspection points?

7. *a.* Assuming the company has units in beginning and ending inventory, indicate the equivalent unit computation for the preceding department cost when the units received from the preceding department are diluted with additional material creating an increase in units to account for using (1) weighted-average costing, and (2) FIFO costing.
   b. What effect on preceding department unit cost does this condition have?

8. Assume a process introduces one-half of the material needed at the beginning of operations with the remaining one-half material entering at the 60 percent stage of operation. If inspection is at the 30 percent stage of operations and 100 units are discovered to be defective at the inspection stage and are removed from operations, how many equivalent units of material should be included for the lost units?

9. Assume inspection is made at the midpoint of operations in a department subsequent to the first department and material is introduced at the beginning of operations. What cost is assigned to any lost units?

10. What are the equivalent units for material, labor, and overhead using the weighted-average method of product costing if: 1,200 units were started in process, 200 units were lost, and ending inventory consisted of 500 units, having one-fifth material, three-fifths labor, and four-fifths overhead. Inspection is at the end of the process.

11. What is the weakness in a system in which workers are continually compensating for others' perceived errors?

Exercises ✶hmwk

E8–1 Quantity Schedule and Equivalent Units under FIFO and Weighted Average

Blackmon Company introduces material at the beginning of operations in its process while adding conversion costs evenly throughout production. The following data is available for one period:

Received from preceding department	9,000 units
Units transferred to next department	7,500 units
Beginning inventory (20% processed)	660 units
Ending inventory (40% processed)	700 units
Current material cost	$18,132
Current conversion costs	$12,567
Material cost in beginning inventory	$ 1,188
Conversion costs in beginning inventory	$ 183

A total of 30 percent of the lost units were due to abnormal conditions. Inspection is at the 50 percent stage of operation.

Required:

a. Quantity schedule reflecting units lost.
b. Equivalent units and unit cost for material using:
   (1) FIFO costing.
   (2) Weighted-average costing.
c. Equivalent units and unit cost for conversion costs using:
   (1) FIFO costing.
   (2) Weighted-average costing.

E8–2 Equivalent Units for Addition of Material and Loss of Units

Immediately after the third department of Bennett, Inc., receives an 8,000 gallon batch of liquid from the second department, the mixture is diluted. At the end of operations in the third department, each finished gallon is packaged in containers, which is a material cost in the third department. Inspection occurs at the three-fifth stage of processing in Department 3.

   In the current month a total of 7,800 gallons were transferred while 600 gallons remained in ending inventory at a four-fifths stage of operations. Of those entering inspection this month, 70 percent pass inspection. One-fourth of the lost units are due to abnormal causes while the remaining are due to conditions experienced in a typical month. There was no beginning inventory in the third department.

Required:

a. Prepare a quantity schedule.
b. Determine equivalent units for preceding department cost, container material cost, and conversion costs.

E8–3 Equivalent Units for Lost Units

In the fourth department of David, Inc., inspection occurs at the 25 percent stage of processing. Material X is introduced at the beginning of operations while Material Y is added at the end of processing within the fourth department. During the current month, of the 600 units lost, two-thirds were due to normal causes.

Required:

Determine the equivalent units for the lost units for each of the following cost components. Break down into units due to normal and abnormal causes.
a. Prior department cost.
b. Conversion cost.
c. Material Y.
d. Material X.

E8–4 Equivalent Units and Unit Cost—Loss of Units

Judi Company experiences loss in the manufacture of its product. Inspection is at the 60 percent stage of production. Labor and overhead costs are added evenly up to the inspection point. Material is added at the beginning of operations. Beginning inventory consisted of 5,000 gallons, complete for 30 percent processing. Ending inventory consisted of 4,500 gallons, 80 percent complete for processing; 800 gallons were found to be lost. There were 20,000 gallons of materials started in the department.

Required:

a. Prepare a quantity schedule.
b. Determine equivalent units for material, labor, and overhead using FIFO costing.
c. Determine equivalent units for material, labor, and overhead using weighted-average costing.
d. Assume current costs were as follows:

Material, $40,000
Labor and overhead, $17,824
Beginning inventory was comprised of $10,250 material, and $2,389 labor and overhead.

(1) What is the unit cost using FIFO costing for material and labor and overhead?
(2) What is the unit cost using weighted-average costing for labor and overhead?

E8–5 Equivalent Unit Calculations

The Fabricating Department of Noland Company had 630 gallons of chemicals that were two-thirds complete in beginning inventory. When the 7,100 gallons received from the preceding department entered into fabricating operations, 3,600 gallons of another chemical were added to thin the solution. At the end of operations, 250 gallons of mixture were in ending inventory, four-fifths complete.

Required:

a. Indicate the equivalent unit calculation for the preceding department cost using
   (1) Weighted-average costing.
   (2) FIFO costing.
b. Indicate the equivalent unit calculation for the Fabricating department material and conversion costs using
   (1) Weighted-average costing.
   (2) FIFO costing.

E8–6 Costs Resulting from Losses

Mark, Inc., uses a weighted-average process cost system in manufacturing its single product. For each unit of finished product, four pounds of Material X are introduced at the start of the process, and two pounds of Material Y are added when the process is 50 percent complete. Labor and overhead costs are incurred uniformly throughout the process.

At the 40 percent stage of completion, inspection occurs and any spoiled units are scrapped with no recovery. Normal loss at that stage is expected to be 5 percent of the units processed up to that point. Normal loss costs are added to the cost of the good units completed, and abnormal loss costs are treated as an expense of the period. The following information applies to operations for October:

Work in process, October 1	6,000 units, 75% complete
Work in process, October 31	2,000 units, 25% complete
Total units lost including through	
abnormal factors	1,200 units
Good units transferred	24,600 units
Unit costs incurred:	
Material X, per pound	$6.00
Material Y, per pound	4.00
Conversion costs per equivalent unit	8.00

Required:

a. Determine the number of pounds of Material X and of Material Y that were put into production in October.
b. How much should be charged to October expense for abnormal loss costs?
c. Compute the total cost of the good units completed during October that will be transferred out.
d. Management has become aware of a material which, if added at the 60 percent state of completion, would extend the life of the product. If this material had been added during October's production run, what would be the direct effect on (1) costs due to lost units for the month (2) work in process at October 1, and (3) work in process at October 31 for your analysis? Show supporting calculations.

E8–7 Weighted Average and FIFO When Units Are Lost

Data relating to operations of Department Two of the McPatton Company are as follows:

Beginning work in process, 40% completed	600 units
Received from preceding department	3,200 units
Good units transferred out	2,500 units
Ending work in process, 20% completed	100 units
Cost in beginning inventory:	
Preceding department cost	$ 694
Conversion cost	354
	$1,048
Current cost:	
Preceding department cost	3,296
Material	5,000
Conversion cost	2,400

Thirty percent of the lost units were due to abnormal conditions. Inspection is at the 60 percent point of operations. Material in Department Two is added at the end of operations.

Required:

a. Units lost due to normal conditions.
b. Determine equivalent units and unit cost for:
   (1) Preceding departmental cost under weighted-average costing.

    (2) Conversion costs under weighted-average costing.

    (3) Material cost under weighted-average costing.

    (4) Preceding department cost under FIFO.

    (5) Conversion costs under FIFO.

    (6) Material cost under FIFO.

  c. Using weighted-average costing, determine:

    (1) Total costs transferred out to the next department.

    (2) Total costs of ending inventory.

    (3) Total costs of abnormal spoilage.

  d. Repeat Requirement *c* using FIFO costing.

E8–8 Allocation of Normal Loss

Analysis of Ronald, Inc.'s records reveals the following limited data. The equivalent units for material are 7,600 with a unit cost of $6.20, while conversion costs' equivalent units are 7,300 with a unit cost of $2.40. Workers transferred 5,800 units, 800 equivalent units of material remained in ending inventory, and 1,000 units were lost due to normal causes. There are 500 equivalent units of labor in ending inventory. Normal loss cost is allocated on costs incurred to date.

Required:

Prepare the cost to account for and costs accounted for sections of a production report.

Problems

P8–9 Cost of Production Report—FIFO, Lost Units

Tiff Company records the following data for March. Consider any units that are not accounted for to be lost through the normal process. Inspection occurs at the end of the process.

	Department 1
Beginning inventory—units	8,000 (100% material, 40% labor and overhead)
Units entered into process this month	34,000
Units transferred	32,000
Ending inventory—units	9,000 (100% material, 30% labor and overhead)
Beginning inventory cost:	
Prior department cost	–0–
Material	$ 4,000
Labor and overhead	7,000
Current costs:	
Material	21,200
Labor and overhead	67,970

Required:

Prepare a production cost report using the FIFO method.

SPATS

P8–10 Weighted-Average Costing, Normal Loss of Units

BAX Company has the following data for May. Consider any units that are not accounted for to be lost through the normal process. Inspection occurs at the end of the process.

	Department 1	
Beginning inventory—units	600	(80% material, 20% labor and overhead)
Units entered into process this month	9,600	
Units transferred	9,100	
Ending inventory—units	900	(100% material, 70% labor and overhead)
Beginning inventory cost:		
Prior department cost	–0–	
Material	$ 400	
Labor and overhead	120	
Current costs:		
Material	8,270	
Labor and overhead	10,803	

Required:

Prepare a production cost report using the weighted-average method.

Writing

P8–11 FlFO—Normal Loss Allocated

Texas, Inc., uses the FlFO method to account for its product. Operations take place in the preparation department. Since loss is inherent in the production process, management allocates the loss to its finished goods transferred and ending inventory on the basis of costs before the loss is allocated.

Inspection is at the point where the units reach a stage of one-fifth completion of operations in the department. Assume that material and conversion costs are at the same stage of completion at the inspection point.

A summary of the costs incurred for the month ending December 31, 19X1, is as follows:

Work in process beginning inventory (330 units—$1/5$ material, $1/3$ conversion costs stages of completion)	$ 118.00
Material	5,455.38
Conversion costs	8,779.68

There were 12,100 units started in production in the Preparation Department. There were 6,800 units transferred to the Finishing Department; 3,130 units were incomplete at the end of the month—these had one-half material and two-fifths conversion costs.

Required:

a. Prepare a cost of production report using FIFO costing. Allocate normal loss cost on costs incurred to date.
b. Explain if, with the data given in the problem, you could prepare a cost of production report for this department using weighted-average costing.

P8–12 Quantity Schedule Using FIFO Costing

Drake, Inc., uses two departments, A and B, for processing a chemical compound. Workers mix one pound of Chemical X with one pound of Chemical Y for the finished chemical compound. In Department A, they process and transfer one pound of Chemical X to Department B for further processing. Department B employees add one pound of Chemical Y when the process is 80 percent completed. After processing in Department B, the chemical compound is transferred to finished goods.

Spoilage occurs in Department A as 2 percent of Chemical X is lost within the first few seconds of processing. However, no spoilage occurs in Department B. Conversion costs are incurred uniformly throughout both departments. Drake uses FlFO costing. The following data are available for July:

	Department A	Department B
Work in process, July 1	10,000 pounds	12,000 pounds
Stage of completion for conversion		
costs (one batch per department)	25%	75%
Started or transferred in	55,000 pounds	?
Transferred out	50,000 good pounds	?
Work in process, July 31	?	?
Stage of completion for conversion		
costs (one batch per department)	20%	40%
Total equivalent pounds of		
material added in Department B	—	48,000 pounds

Required:

a. Prepare quantity schedules for each department.

b. Indicate the pounds started and completed for each department.

hmwk

P8–13 FIFO, Addition of Material That Increases Base Unit Count, and Journal Entries
Fatchett, Inc., produces a secret mixture called LEM in Departments 1 and 2. Fatchett uses the FIFO method of process costing.

In Department 1, the beginning inventory consisted of 250 units having one-fifth material and one-tenth labor and overhead added; the costs incurred are $60. There were 12,600 units started in process, while workers transferred 12,180 units to Department 2. There was no loss in either department. Ending inventory had two-fifths material and one-fifth labor and one-fifth overhead added.

Department 2 added a total of 5,000 units of purchased material to the units in process at the beginning of operations in the department. This material added in Department 2 increases the number of units manufactured.

There were 300 units in beginning inventory having one-third of their labor and one-third overhead. The total value of beginning inventory is $670. There were 364 units in ending inventory having one-fourth of their labor and one-fourth overhead. Department 2 adds all material at the beginning of operations.

Costs incurred in each department for June 19X1 are as follows:

	Department 1	Department 2
Material	$5,703.08	$11,338.80
Labor	3,809.59	13,856.67
Factory overhead	4,792.71	3,592.47

Required:

a. Prepare a cost of production report using the FlFO method.

b. Record all the journal entries required for Department 1 for the month.

SPATS

P8–14 Inspection at Midpoint of Operations and FIFO

Higg Company manufactures Products B in two departments, Mixing and Finishing. Inspection is at the midpoint of operations in both departments; if a spoiled unit is discovered, it is removed from the production process at that time. Both departments introduce all material at the beginning of the operation. Assume that at the inspection point conversion costs are at the same stage of completion.

The following information for January is from the company's books and production reports:

Production Data in Units	Mixing Department	Finishing Department
Opening inventory	1,000 units	600 units
Stage of completion	$3/5$ labor, $3/4$ overhead	$1/3$ labor, $1/4$ overhead
Started in process	7,000	(?)
Normal loss of units	350	300
Abnormal loss of units	150	100
Ending inventory	1,500	1,200
Stage of completion	$1/5$ labor, $1/3$ overhead	$1/4$ labor, $1/3$ overhead
Cost Data		
Work in process—beginning:		
Preceding department costs	—	$ 2,810
Material	$ 1,200	750
Labor	1,140	330
Overhead	1,800	346
Current costs:		
Material	10,500	7,800
Labor	11,900	10,915
Factory overhead	18,000	9,945

Required:

Prepare a cost of production report for January using the FIFO method of accounting for opening work in process inventories.

P8–15 Addition of Material—Weighted Average and FIFO

Dillard, Inc., is a successful manufacturer of paints. The minerals and paint pigments are mixed in the first department. For the month of October this beginning inventory consisted of 500 gallons of liquid that contained three-fifths of its material and one-fourth of its labor and overhead. At the end of October the mixture that remained was one-third complete with regard to ingredients and carried two-fifths of the conversion costs.

After the mixture leaves the Mixing Department, it is transferred to the next department where essential oils and water are added to the liquid. In October the Mixing Department started 3,000 gallons into production and transferred 3,200 gallons to the next department. The Finishing Department already had 400 gallons of this mixture in beginning inventory to which they had added one-fifth of their materials and three-fourths of the conversion costs. When the liquid was processed in the second department, 600 gallons of oils and water were added to it. At the end of October, 3,000 gallons had been transferred to finished goods and the ending inventory had two-thirds of its materials and one-fourth of its conversion costs. No units were lost in either department. Cost data is as follows:

	Mixing	Finishing
Work in process:		
Costs from preceding department		$1,202
Material	$ 295	192
Conversion costs	260	100
Current costs:		
Material	3,170	2,848
Conversion costs	6,380	1,022

Required:

a. Prepare a cost of production report using the weighted-average method.

b. Prepare a cost of production report using FIFO costing.

P8–16 Specific FIFO and Weighted-Average Cost Questions

Walker Company has three processing departments, A, B, C. Department B reveals the following information:

Work in process, January 1: 800 pounds	
Department A cost (100%)	$ 3,400
Department B material (80%)	2,500
Department B conversion costs (70%)	900
	$ 6,800
During January, 2,400 pounds from Department A plus	
1,000 pounds in Department B were put into process:	
Department A cost added in January	$10,200
Department B material cost added in January	7,800
Department B conversion costs added in January	3,000
Total costs to account for	$27,800

Completed in January and transferred to Department C: 3,000 pounds. Lost in January (150 pounds is considered a normal loss): 200 pounds. Work in process, January 31: 1,000 pounds.

Department A cost (100%)
Department B material (60%)
Department B conversion cost (40%)

Losses are discovered when the process reaches the 80 percent stage of completion for Department B material and Department B conversion costs. Department B finished and transferred all goods that reached the 80 percent stage this period.

Required:

a. Assume that Walker Company uses the first-in, first-out method of determining cost. Calculate each of the following:

(1) The total cost of the 3,000 good pounds completed and transferred to Department C.

(2) The total cost of the 50 pounds of abnormal loss.

(3) The total cost of the 1,000 pounds in the ending inventory.

b. Assume Walker Company uses the weighted-average method of determining cost. Calculate the following:

(1) The total cost of the 3,000 good pounds completed and transferred to Department C.

(2) The total cost of the 50 pounds of abnormal loss.

(3) The total cost of the 1,000 pounds in the ending inventory.

SPATS

P8–17 Addition of Material Using Weighted-Average and FIFO Costing

In refining chemicals David Johnson, Inc., uses two departments, No. 83 and No. 84. Management presently uses the weighted-average method of process costing but wants to investigate the impact of using FIFO costing. The following information is available for use in comparing the two costing approaches:

Chemicals originate in Department No. 83 where materials are added evenly throughout the process. Products leaving Department No. 83 are transferred to Department No. 84 where materials are added only at the 25 percent stage of operation. One gallon of diluting material is added to two gallons of concentrated materials from Department No. 83 at the 25 percent stage of the conversion process in Department No. 84. After mixing the materials and further refinement in Department No. 84, they are transferred to the next department. No gallons are lost in or between the departments due to tight controls. On November 1, Department No. 83 had a beginning inventory of 600 gallons, 40 percent complete as to the material and 10 percent as to conversion costs and 9,400 gallons were started in process. The ending inventory was 70 percent complete as to the materials and 25 percent as to conversion costs; 9,500 gallons were transferred to Department No. 84.

Department No. 84 entered into production its beginning inventory of 100 gallons which were 15 percent complete as to conversion costs, along with all the gallons received from the previous department. The 800 gallons in ending inventory were 80 percent complete as to conversion costs. Cost data are as follows:

	Department No. 83	Department No. 84
Work in process, November 1		
Cost from preceding department		$ 104
Material .... $ 90		–0–
Conversion costs	67	23
Current costs:		
Material	3,850	28,800
Conversion costs	10,713	21,337

Required:

a. Prepare a production report for November using the weighted-average method.

b. Using FIFO costing, prepare a cost of production report. Carry unit costs to six decimal places.

P8–18 Weighted-Average Costing, Normal Loss Allocated on Physical Units

Using the Joseph Martin Company data given in Problem for Self-Study 8–1, assume the company is using the weighted-average method and allocate normal loss costs on physical units.

P8–19 Combining Products from Different Departments Using Process Costing

Don Putnam produces an expensive line of small tools; its specialty is a line of axes. The company operates its own Handle Department and Foundry Department to produce the ax blades. The outputs from these two departments are then sent to the Assembly Department for finishing.

Equal parts, by weight, of pig iron, coke, and special alloy materials are introduced into the Foundry Department's furnace where the materials are reduced to molten metal that is poured into molds. A day in the Foundry Department involves these four steps:

1. Removing and cleaning the blades cast on the previous day. This step requires one-third of the labor cost of the Foundry Department.

2. Setting the molds for the current day's melt.

3. Loading and burning the melt for the day.

4. Pouring the metal into the molds.

The ax blades are finished in the Assembly Department and the wooden handles inserted. In the insertion process, handles are frequently broken; finally, the finished axes are transferred to the finished goods storeroom. An ax blade weighs one pound.

On May 1 there was no inventory in the Foundry Department. During May a total of 5,200 blades were completed and transferred to the Assembly Department. At the end of the month, 1,000 good, cleaned blades were on hand in the foundry, and 600 blades had been poured on the last day. A total of four tons of pig iron, coke, and alloy materials costing $9,600 were placed in production. Direct labor costs for the month totaled $42,550; factory overhead is applied at 40 percent of direct labor cost. Normally, some blades are not perfect and are lost before they are cleaned the next day.

On May 1 there were no handles on hand, but there were 500 ax blades in the Assembly Department on which no work had been done; their cost was $4,440. During May, 5,400 handles costing $11,340 were received in this department. All of the handles were used in completing 5,000 finished axes, but 700 blades on which no assembly work was performed remained in ending inventory. No assembly labor and overhead is assigned to the handles that are lost. Labor cost amounted to $15,000, and factory overhead is applied at 50 percent of direct labor cost.

Required:

Prepare cost of production reports for May for both departments using weighted-average cost. Normal loss cost is not allocated.

P8–20 FIFO Costing; Abnormal and Normal Loss

Inspection at the Cunningham Company occurs at the midpoint of processing. The company uses the FIFO method of processing. Both departments introduce material at the beginning of operations. Assume that at the inspection point, conversion costs are one-half complete. The following data from company records are for January 19X1:

	Department A	Department B
Beginning inventory	500 units	600 units
Stage of completion	3/4 labor	2/3 labor
	1/5 overhead	3/4 overhead
Units started in process	9,100	8,200
Normal loss of units	300	260
Abnormal loss of units	200	50
Ending inventory	900	350
Stage of completion	1/3 labor,	1/7 labor,
	1/6 overhead	2/5 overhead
Value of work in process, January 1, 19X1:		
Costs from preceding department	-0-	$3,240
Material	$ 645	660
Labor	1,035	470
Overhead	120	360
Current costs in department:		
Material	12,103	9,430
Labor	24,290	9,534
Overhead	10,030	6,444

Required:

Prepare a cost of production report for both departments.

P8–21 Normal and Abnormal Units (CMA)

APCO Company manufactures various lines of bicycles. Because of the high volume of each type of product, the company employs a process cost system using the weighted-average method to determine unit costs. Bicycle parts are manufactured in the Molding Department. The parts are consolidated into a single bike unit in the Molding Department and transferred to the Assembly Department where they are partially assembled. After assembly, the bicycle is sent to the Packing Department.

Accountants have completed cost per unit data for the 20-inch dirt bike through the Molding Department. Annual cost and production figures for the Assembly Department are presented in the following schedules:

Assembly Department Cost Data:

	Transferred in from Molding Department	Assembly Material	Assembly Conversion Costs	Total Cost of Dirt Bikes through Assembly
Prior period costs	$ 82,200	$ 6,660	$ 11,930	$ 100,790
Current period costs	1,237,800	96,840	236,590	1,571,230
Total costs	$1,320,000	$103,500	$248,520	$1,672,020

Assembly Department Production Data:

		Percent Complete		
	Bicycles	Transferred in	Assembly Material	Assembly Conversion
Beginning inventory	3,000	100%	100%	80%
Transferred in from				
Molding during year	45,000	100	—	—
Transferred out to				
Packing during year	40,000	100	100	100
Ending inventory	4,000	100	50	20

Inspectors identify defective bicycles at an inspection point when the assembly labor process is 70 percent complete; all assembly material has been added at this point of the process. The normal rejection percentage for defective bicycles is 5 percent of the bicycles reaching the inspection point. Any defective bicycles over and above the 5 percent quota are considered as abnormal. All defective bikes are removed from the production process and destroyed.

Required:

a. Compute the number of defective bikes that are considered to be
   (1) A normal amount of defective bikes.
   (2) An abnormal amount of defective bikes.
b. Compute the equivalent units of production for the year for
   (1) Bicycles transferred in from the Molding Department.
   (2) Bicycles produced with regard to Assembly material.
   (3) Bicycles produced with regard to Assembly conversion.

c. Compute the cost per equivalent unit for the fully assembled dirt bike.
d. Compute the amount of the total production cost of $ 1,672,020 that will be associated with
    (1) Normal defective units.
    (2) Abnormal defective units.
    (3) Good units completed in the Assembly Department.
    (4) Ending work in process inventory in the Assembly Department.
e. Describe how the applicable dollar amounts for the following items would be presented in the financial statements:
    (1) Normal defective units.
    (2) Abnormal defective units.
    (3) Completed units transferred into the Packing Department.
    (4) Ending work in process inventory in the Assembly Department.

Joint Product and By-Product Costing

Chapter Objectives

After studying this chapter, you should be able to:

1. Distinguish between joint products, by-products, and scrap.
2. Determine what value, if any, companies should assign to by-products before selling them.
3. Identify the reasons for allocating joint costs.
4. Choose the most appropriate method for distributing joint costs to by-products and joint products for inventory valuation.
5. Recognize the limitation of joint cost allocations for future planning and control.
6. Apply differential analysis in deciding whether to further process products.

Introduction

In many manufacturing operations, management has no choice but to produce several products simultaneously. Even though companies manufacture products in different proportions or quantities, they cannot produce one product without the other. For example, in the petroleum industry, the production of gasoline leads to the concurrent production of methane, ethane, raw kerosene, lube distillate, and waxes . A refinery cannot process only gasoline! Likewise, coal distillation gives us gas, coke, and other products; cotton ginning yields cotton fiber and cotton seed; and sugar refining results in sugar, molasses, and bagasse or plant residue.

Whether we call such products joint products or by-products depends on their relative importance. For example, gasoline, kerosene, lube distillate, and important gases are joint products, while such a relatively insignificant product as wax is a by-product. Many other processing operations, such as those handling raw milk, chemicals, and lumber, produce by-products and joint products.

Joint Products, By-Products, and Scrap

Joint products, also called **main products,** result from those manufacturing operations in which companies simultaneously produce two or more products of significant sales value. **By-products** are merely incidental products resulting from the processing of another product. The distinction between joint products and by-products depends largely on the market value of the products. Companies produce joint products in larger quantities. Joint products have larger market values and make a more meaningful contribution to revenue than by-products. Thus, by-products are a minor result of processing. Although a single by-product may make only a small contribution to revenue, a company's total by-products may make a significant contribution.

Because the dividing line between joint products and by-products is not rigid and is subject to change, managers need professional judgment to make the distinction. Management should be constantly alert for developments that could change a by-product into a more profitable product. For example, a product previously classified as a by-product may suddenly command a higher sales price and become a joint product. Likewise, the market for a joint product may diminish to the point that managers more accurately classify the product as a by-product.

As with by-products and joint products, often the distinction between by-products and scrap is not clear. **Scrap** is salable material resulting from the manufacturing process and having limited dollar value. In manufacturing shirts, for example, when employees lay and cut the pattern, any excess fabric between the pattern pieces is scrap. The excess fabric may have a minimal market value or workers may throw it in the waste bin. Because scrap occurs while producing shirts, manufacturers could classify it as a joint product or a by-product. However, it has so little value that it is questionable whether manufacturers should refer to this scrap as a product at all. The various methods illustrated in Chapter 15 for the treatment of scrap do not differ significantly from the accounting methods shown in this chapter for by-products. The correct way to treat both the market value of scrap and by-products is as a deduction from the cost of the main products.

Current Cost Management Practice

Global

With a new era of mobile communications dawning, a newcomer from Finland called Nokia is in a prime position to exploit it. This small, flexible company may be better suited to the new market than large companies with heavy bureaucracies. Rather than size being important, speed will be the key. Nokia is No. 1 in cellular phones in Europe and second only to Motorola in the United States. Because Nordic countries have vast stretches of relatively unpopulated land in their northern regions, mobile phones caught on fast. With such a small domestic market, Nokia had to export to survive.

It went global with a vengeance and avoided getting trapped into producing low value-added commodity products such as TVs. By focusing on fast-moving niche products where it had a natural advantage in its home market, Nokia remained flexible about its marketing strategy.

William Echikson, "Nokia—How to Win Markets Fast," *Forbes,* May 30, 1994, p. 114.

Joint Costs and Common Costs

To analyze production costs for joint products and by-products, we distinguish between joint costs and common costs. While the objective of assigning production costs to a costing center is the same for common costs and joint costs, this text does not use these terms interchangeably. The term **joint costs** is more restrictive; we limit it to those costs incurred to simultaneously process two or more products of significant market value. On the other hand, we associate **common costs** with the sharing of facilities by two or more users.

Common costs differ from joint costs because we can obtain common costs separately. Joint costs are the production costs incurred up to the point where products are separately identified. Joint costs are indivisible and must be assigned to products. Common costs include such service department costs as building repair and maintenance, cafeteria, and utilities. While each production department can have its own service department, companies usually incur common costs to effect cost savings. It is normally less expensive for production departments to share such facilities.

Accountants allocate service departments' costs on the basis of usage; for example, they allocate building occupancy costs on a square footage basis. As you recall, Chapter 4 discusses some of the problems of allocating common costs to departments. The theoretical and practical problems encountered in the treatment of common and joint costs are similar. However, most accountants (and this book) confine joint costs to the narrower meaning of the costs of manufacturing joint products before these products are separately identified.

Why Allocate Joint Costs?

Accountants allocate joint production costs to properly cost products and by-products. Each product's share of material, labor, and overhead costs is inseparable from that of every other product. When produced simultaneously, joint products and by-products do not have traceable, individual costs. Therefore, the allocation of joint production costs to products is necessary. This chapter later discusses various methods of joint cost allocation.

The reasons for allocating joint costs to arrive at product costs include the following:

1. To value inventories and compute cost of goods sold for both external financial and tax reporting. If we fail to assign joint costs to individual products, cost of goods sold includes all joint costs, and the joint products in ending inventories have zero joint cost.

2. To value inventory for insurance purposes. If a casualty loss occurs, the insured and the insurance company must agree on the value of the goods lost. One consideration in the settlement is the cost of goods lost. If joint products are destroyed, accountants must divide production costs between the products lost and those not lost.

3. To value inventory and compute a cost of goods sold for internal financial reporting. Many companies calculate executive compensation, at least partly, on the basis of each executive's segment or division earnings. If two or more segments sell a joint product, we must allocate the cost of material and processing to the products involved.

4. To determine cost reimbursement under contracts where a company sells only a portion of the jointly manufactured products or services or delivers to a single customer.

Split-Off Point and Separable Costs

To make reasonable cost allocations for joint products and by-products, accountants first determine the **split-off point.** At this point, they can identify joint products separately from by-products. Because it can occur at different stages in operations, the split-off point, also called the **point of separation,** may not be the same for all products. Second, accountants accumulate the costs incurred for the entire batch of products up to the split-off point and then distribute these costs among the units produced.

After the split-off point where products can be identified, production costs are more easily traceable. **Separable production costs** are material, labor, and overhead used in the later processing of the distinguishable products. Therefore, the cost of each joint product is its allocation of joint cost, plus the separable production costs necessary to put it in a salable condition.

Accounting for By-Products

All of the numerous approaches to costing by-products are variations of the following two methods:

1. *Assign an estimated cost to by-products equal to their net market value, or net realizable value.* We deduct this amount from the main or joint products' total production costs. Thus, we separate by-products from main products by transferring the amount of the by-products' net market value from Work in Process Inventory to By-Products Inventory. We compute **net market (realizable) value** as the market value of the by-products produced less the separable *(a)* production costs, *(b)* marketing costs, and *(c)* administrative costs. The only transaction when we sell by-products is an increase in Cash or Accounts Receivable and a decrease in By-Products Inventory.

2. *Do not assign an inventory value to by-products at their production.* Instead, any amount that can be attributable to by-products remains with the main products. We make a memo entry to record only the physical

amount of by-products manufactured. When we sell by-products, we record their entire net market value as other income by increasing Cash or Accounts Receivable and Other Income.

Net Market Value Assigned to By-Products Inventory.   The distinction between the two methods is the assignment or nonassignment of an estimated cost to by-products at their production. If the value of by-products is large enough to affect inventory or profits, assigning net market value to the by-products inventory when it is produced is preferable. Assigning net market value to by-products resembles the method employed in costing joint products. Also, this method identifies by-products at their production rather than waiting until their sale. Another advantage is that it provides a mechanism for management to make a desired percentage profit on by-products. To do this, we reduce the net market value by the amount of the desired profit, and main products bear more of the production costs.

Net Market Value of By-Products as Other Income.   If their value is so small that it does not affect inventory or profits, recording the net market value as other income is appropriate. The justification for this short-cut method is that the firm's intention is to produce main products, not by-products. Therefore, no part of the joint production costs is attributable to by-products. However, we must trace any separable costs to the by-products using the same approach as when we assign inventory value to by-products manufactured. When we sell the by-products, we deduct traceable by-product expenses from the sales proceeds.

Costing By-Products Illustrated   Exhibits 9–1 and 9–2 use the following data to illustrate the two basic methods of accounting for by-products:

	Joint (or Main) Products (Pounds)	By-Products (Pounds)
Production	50,000	20,000
Sales	48,000	19,000
Ending finished goods inventory	2,000	1,000
Sales value	$10 per pound	$1.10 per pound
No beginning finished goods inventory		

	Per Pound
Separable costs of by-products:	
Materials	$0.03
Labor	0.02
Factory overhead applied	0.01
Marketing costs applied	0.015
Administrative costs applied	0.025
	$0.10
Joint production costs for joint (main) products and by-products:	
Material	$ 50,000
Labor	150,000
Factory overhead	100,000
	$300,000

(continued)

$20,000 Marketing + $20,000 administrative costs of joint (main) products = $40,000

Income from by-products: 19,000 pounds sold × $1.00* = $19,000

Net market value, by-products: 20,000 pounds produced × $1.00* = $20,000

*($1.10 sales value − $0.10 separable cost of by-products)

Value of ending inventory of joint (main) product:

Method 1: Net market value of by-products produced assigned to inventory:

$$\frac{2{,}000 \text{ pounds}}{50{,}000 \text{ pounds}} \times \$280{,}000^\dagger = \$11{,}200$$

†($300,000 production cost − $20,000 by-products' net market value)

Method 2: Net market value of by-products as other income:

$$\frac{2{,}000 \text{ pounds}}{50{,}000 \text{ pounds}} \times \$300{,}000 = \$12{,}000$$

For aid in understanding the cost assignment, see diagram in Exhibit 9–1.

The Income Statement on the left in Exhibit 9–2 illustrates the assignment of net market value to by-product inventory. We deduct the $0.10 per pound of separable cost from $1.10 by-product sales value to give a net market value of $1.00 for the by-products. We then subtract the $20,000 total net market value for the by-products from the $300,000 total production cost yielding a net production cost for the joint product of $280,000. We assign the 2,000 pounds of joint product left in ending inventory a value equal to their net production cost (2,000 pounds/50,000 pounds × $280,000 = $11,200).

Exhibit 9–2 also illustrates the second basic method of accounting for by-products. We assign no value to the 20,000 pounds of by-products at the time of production. Instead, we report the $1.00 net market value per pound ($1.10 sales value less $0.10 cost of further processing and marketing and administrative costs) for the 19,000 pounds of by-products as other income. Because we do not reduce the main product's Finished Goods Inventory for the net market value of by-products, the ending inventory value is 2,000 pounds/50,000 pounds × $300,000 = $12,000.

Difference between Actual and Estimated Values.   If we deduct the net market (realizable) value of the by-products from the cost of production (method one illustrated in Exhibit 9–2), we assign the value credited to the cost of production to the By-Products Inventory account. Because we estimated the $1 net market value in Exhibit 9–2, a difference between the actual and estimated value of the by-products can arise. If the market value of the by-products is fairly stable, this difference should be small. It does not warrant restating the By-Products Inventory account and/or adjusting income from prior periods. We can show the difference as income or loss from by-product sales. If the difference is material, we may more properly classify the product involved as a joint or main product, not a by-product.

EXHIBIT 9–1

257 Jointproducts v. com.
256 Joint v. by prod.
258 Seperable costs

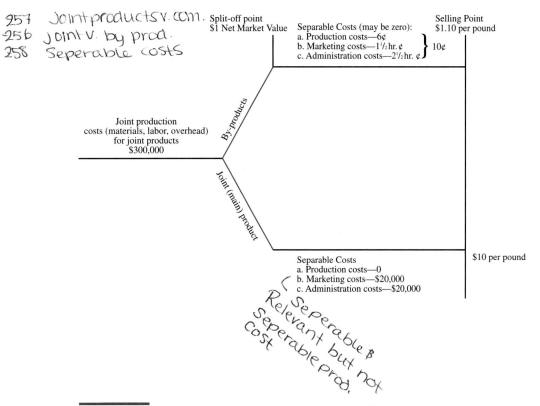

Split-off point
$1 Net Market Value

Separable Costs (may be zero):
a. Production costs—6¢
b. Marketing costs—1½ hr. ¢ } 10¢
c. Administration costs—2½ hr. ¢

Selling Point
$1.10 per pound

Joint production
costs (materials, labor, overhead)
for joint products
$300,000

By-products

Joint (main) product

Separable Costs
a. Production costs—0
b. Marketing costs—$20,000
c. Administration costs—$20,000

$10 per pound

(Seperable β
Relevant but not
seperable prod,
cost

EXHIBIT 9–2 Two Basic Methods of Accounting for By-Products

Income Statement		
	Method 1 *Net Market Value assigned* *to By-Products Inventory*	*Method 2* *No Value Assigned to* *By-Products Inventory;* *Net Market Value Treated* *as Other Income*
Sales, main (joint) products	$480,000	$480,000
Cost of sales:		
Joint production costs	$300,000	$300,000
Less net market value of all		
by-products produced	20,000	
Net production costs	$280,000	$300,000
Ending Inventory	11,200	12,000
Cost of sales	$268,800	$288,000
Gross Margin	$211,200	$192,000
Marketing		
and administrative expense	40,000	40,000
Operating income	$171,200	$152,000
Other income:		
Revenue from by-products sold		19,000
Income before taxes	$171,200	$171,000

Journal Entries for By-Products

Using the data given in Exhibit 9–2, the following journal entries record transactions using the first method in which we assign the net market value to By-Products Inventory. We charge the estimated net market value of $1 per pound to the account as follows:

By-Products Inventory........................	20,000	
Work in Process Inventory		20,000

As additional processing is completed, we charge separable production costs to the By-Products Inventory account:

By-Products Inventory (20,000 pounds × $0.06).....	1,200	
Materials		600
Payroll		400
Factory Overhead Costs..................		200

The application of marketing and administrative costs is:

By-Products Inventory (20,000 pounds × $0.04).....	800	
Marketing Expense Control		300
Administrative Expense Control		500

For simplicity, this assumes we apply all administrative and marketing costs to the 20,000 pounds produced, even though 1,000 pounds remain unsold. Assuming the 19,000 pounds of by-products are sold for cash at $1.10 per pound, the entry is as follows:

Cash (19,000 pounds × $1.10)	20,900	
By-Products Inventory....................		20,900

If the By-Products are sold for $1.25 instead of the $1.10 used for product costing, the entry would be as follows:

Cash (19,000 pounds × $1.25)	23,750	
By-Products Inventory....................		20,900
Gain on Sale of By-Products Inventory		
(19,000 pounds × $0.15)...............		2,850

The By-Products Inventory account appears as follows:

By-Products Inventory

20,000	20,900
1,200	
800	
22,000	
Balance 1,100	

We show the $1,100 balance in the By-Products Inventory ledger account as an asset on the balance sheet, along with the other inventory accounts.

Selecting a Method of Accounting for By-Products.   Practical as well as theoretical factors help determine which method of accounting for by-products is most appropriate. The importance of the by-products involved is an influencing factor. Deducting the net market value of the by-products manufactured from production costs has theoretical merit. However, this approach may not be practical. A company may have no assurance that it can sell the by-products or that the market value for selling will remain stable. The stability of the market and the reliability of the market value for the by-products help determine whether we assign a value before making the sale. The practical response to market instability is to recognize the sale of by-products only as income and assign no value to the by-products inventory. Even though this approach fails to properly match cost with revenue, the by-product's value may not merit assigning a value to the ending inventory of by-products and setting them up in a separate ledger account. If a company produces approximately the same amount of by-products every period, there is no material difference between the methods chosen. In addition, since by-products by definition have a small market value, the choice of the method may not significantly affect operating results.

Assignment of Costs to Joint Products

After selecting the method of by-product costing, we can allocate production costs to the joint (main) products. The physical measure and the market or sales value methods are the two basic costing procedures for doing this. We discuss the following variations of these two methods:

1. Physical measures: Quantity method. Average unit cost. Weighted factor.
2. Market or sales value: Gross market value. Net market (realizable) value (also known as relative sales value at the split-off).

Because physical measures require no estimates of a product's sales value, we may assign costs in a manner not proportionate to revenue producing capacity. Thus, we may allocate more cost to a product than the revenue it generates. Consequently, we may use market-based allocations so the assignment of costs results in a better matching of revenue and expense. Regardless of the method chosen to distribute joint costs, we may make arbitrary decisions merely because no alternatives appear preferable. For this reason, this chapter emphasizes that accountants use these methods for inventory valuation only and that the allocation method may have limited usefulness for control and planning.

Diagram Processing Operations.   Exhibit 9–3 portrays the manufacturing operations that we use to illustrate various joint cost allocations. The importance of diagramming the production process will become clearer later when we discuss multiple split-off points. Assume that the net market value of by-products a company manufactures is $10,000. We deduct the $10,000 from the joint cost of $150,000 to arrive at $140,000 net production cost that we assign to joint (main) products. This is the by-product costing approach illustrated in the left column in Exhibit 9–2. Assume also that each joint product has separable costs as indicated in Exhibit 9–3.

EXHIBIT 9–3   **Diagram of Manufacturing Operations**

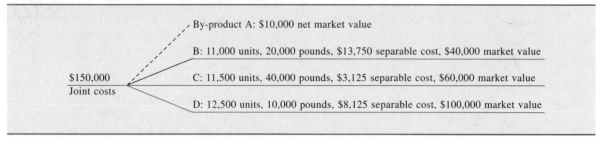

By-product A: $10,000 net market value

B: 11,000 units, 20,000 pounds, $13,750 separable cost, $40,000 market value

$150,000
Joint costs

C: 11,500 units, 40,000 pounds, $3,125 separable cost, $60,000 market value

D: 12,500 units, 10,000 pounds, $8,125 separable cost, $100,000 market value

Physical Measures

Exhibits 9–4 through 9–6 illustrate the **physical measures of allocating joint costs.**

Quantity Method.   Proponents of the **quantity method of joint cost allocations** argue that since all the joint products come from the original joint material, labor, and factory overhead, all products should receive a share of the joint costs based on a physical measure. This requires that all products be converted to the same physical measure, whether that is tons, gallons, or pounds. Exhibit 9–4 illustrates the assignment of net production cost to the three joint products on the basis of pounds. For example, since there were 20,000 pounds of Product B manufactured out of a total of 70,000 pounds of joint products for this batch, Joint Product B receives $40,000 of the joint costs (20,000/70,000 × $140,000 = $40,000). This procedure simply assumes it costs the same ($2 per pound in Exhibit 9–4) to produce a pound of output regardless of whether it is B, C, or D. For example, if this were a meat-packing operation, each pound of steak would be assumed to cost as much to process as a pound of hamburger. This method ignores the market value of the products involved.

After allocating the net costs of production to the joint products under the quantity method, we add the actual costs incurred after the split-off point (separable costs) to arrive at the inventory valuation. We show this at the bottom of Exhibit 9–4.

Average Unit Cost Approach.   Exhibit 9–5 illustrates the **average unit cost method of joint cost allocations.** It is a variation of the physical measure approach to joint product costing that assigns production costs on the basis of units, ignoring the weight or sales value of the products involved. We divide the total units into the net production costs to arrive at a joint cost per unit. As long as the units do not differ greatly, the weaknesses of this simple method are not too severe.

Weighted Factors.   Rather than use the number of units, pounds, or other physical measure processed as the basis for allocation, accountants may assign factors to each product. These weighted factors can reflect the varying amounts of time required to process the units, the difficulty of the processing procedures, the amount of material or labor used, and other factors that management considers significant. Exhibit 9–6 illustrates the **weighted factor method of joint cost allocation,** with the following assignment of points to joint products: Joint Product B, 10 points; C, 5 points; and D, 9 points.

historical

Physical measure

EXHIBIT 9–4   Use of Quantity Method in Allocating Joint Cost

Joint Products	Pounds	Distribution of Net Cost of Production
B	20,000	$\frac{20,000}{70,000} \times \$140,000 = \$\ 40,000$
C	40,000	$\frac{40,000}{70,000} \times \$140,000 = \ 80,000$
D	10,000	$\frac{10,000}{70,000} \times \$140,000 = \ 20,000$
	70,000	$140,000

A slightly different approach is to first obtain the net cost of production per pound. This cost is multiplied by the number of pounds in each joint product to obtain this cost distribution:

$$\frac{\$140,000 \text{ net production cost}}{70,000 \text{ pounds}} = \$2 \text{ net production cost per pound}$$

Joint Products	Distribution of Net Cost of Production
B	20,000 pounds × $2 = $ 40,000
C	40,000 pounds × $2 = 80,000
D	10,000 pounds × $2 = 20,000
	$140,000

After assigning the net costs of production, the inventory valuations are as follows:

Joint Products	Net Cost of Production	Separable Cost	Inventory Valuation
B	$ 40,000	$13,750	$ 53,750
C	80,000	3,125	83,125
D	20,000	8,125	28,125
	$140,000	$25,000	$165,000

EXHIBIT 9–5   Use of Average Unit Cost Method in Allocating Joint Costs

Joint Products	Units	Distribution of Net Cost of Production
B	11,000	$\frac{11,000}{35,000} \times \$140,000 = \$\ 44,000$
C	11,500	$\frac{11,500}{35,000} \times \$140,000 = \ 46,000$
D	12,500	$\frac{12,500}{35,000} \times \$140,000 = \ 50,000$
	35,000	$140,000

EXHIBIT 9–6   Use of Weighted Factor Method in Allocating Joint Costs

Joint products	Units	Points per Unit	Weighted Unit	Distribution of Net Cost of Production		
B	11,000	10	110,000	$\dfrac{110,000}{280,000}$ × $140,000	=	$ 55,000
C	11,500	5	57,500	$\dfrac{57,500}{280,000}$ × $140,000	=	28,750
D	12,500	9	112,500	$\dfrac{112,500}{280,000}$ × $140,000	=	56,250
	35,000		280,000			$140,000

Market or Sales Value

There are several variations of the **market or sales value method of joint product costing** in which accountants use the joint products' sales prices as the basis for allocation. Accountants base the market value approximation on the belief that if a product has a higher sales price, then it costs more to produce. Therefore, we prorate joint costs on the basis of the market value of the products manufactured. We use a weighted market value to reflect the various quantities of each product manufactured.

Gross Market Value.   Exhibit 9–7 illustrates the use of the **gross market value method of joint cost.** Gross market value is appropriate <u>only</u> if a company can sell its joint products at the split-off point without further processing. As there are no separable costs, the inventory valuation of the joint products is the joint costs assigned.

   The gross margin percentages (gross margin/sales) are identical for all three products because there are no costs after the split-off point. This identical gross margin demonstrates an important concept of the gross market value method—that revenue dollars from each joint product are assumed to make the same percentage contribution at the split-off point as the revenue dollars from every other joint product. Input costs are matched with revenues generated by each output.

EXHIBIT 9–7   Gross Market Value Method

Joint Products	Number of Units Produced	Market Value per Unit	Total Gross Market Value	Distribution of Net Cost of Production		
B	40,000	$1	$ 40,000	$\dfrac{\$40,000}{\$200,000}$ × $140,000	=	$ 28,000
C	30,000	$2	60,000	$\dfrac{\$60,000}{\$200,000}$ × $140,000	=	42,000
D	25,000	$4	100,000	$\dfrac{\$100,000}{\$200,000}$ × $140,000	=	70,000
			$200,000			$140,000

Assuming the sales prices shown in Exhibit 9–7 and no further processing cost, the gross margin of Joint Product B is $12,000 ($40,000 gross market value − $28,000 joint cost assigned). This results in a 30 percent gross margin for Product B: $12,000/ $40,000 = 30%.

An identical gross margin percentage is calculated for Product C of

$$\frac{\$60,000 - \$42,000}{\$60,000} = \frac{\$18,000}{\$60,000} = 30\%$$

And for Product D

$$\frac{\$100,000 - \$70,000}{\$100,000} = \frac{\$30,000}{\$100,000} = 30\%$$

The market value approach levels income; this smoothing and its simplicity is what makes the gross market approach attractive. However, allocations based on the market value approach have limited usefulness for control and planning.

Net Market (Realizable) Value or Relative Sales Value at the Split-Off.   Many products cannot be sold at the split-off point; instead, they must be processed further. Because no market value is available for these products at the split-off point, accountants use the **net market (realizable) method of joint cost allocation.** They estimate the market value by subtracting separable costs from the products' sales value after further processing. For example, each cut of meat requires varying amounts of processing before sale. If these separable costs are significant or vary considerably among products, we should consider these costs in allocating joint costs to the products.

For products with no market value at split-off, we use the **relative sales value at split-off method of joint cost allocations.** We determine an approximate market value at split-off by deducting the separable costs from the market value at the first possible point of sale. Exhibit 9–8 illustrates the procedures involved. Accountants presume the first sales point after split-off gives the best approximation of sales value at split-off even though several possible sales points are available. If the separable costs for each product vary, and separable costs are not proportional to gross sales value, as in Exhibit 9–8, the joint products are not equally profitable. After allocating the cost of production, we add the separable costs to arrive at the inventory valuation. We illustrate this at the bottom of Exhibit 9–8.

Multiple Split-Offs   The production process that illustrates the joint cost allocation methods in Exhibits 9–4 through 9–8 involves only one split-off point to simplify the discussion. However, many manufacturing operations contain multiple split-off points with separable costs for each stage. For example, suppose a company manufactures three joint products— E, F, and G—having sales prices per pound of $9, $12, and $11 respectively. Department 1 processes 100,000 pounds of raw material at a total cost of $250,000. Department 1 transfers 65 percent of the units to Department 2, where the material is further processed at a total additional cost of $80,000. Department 3 processes the other 35 percent of the units leaving Department 1 at a total additional cost of $11,000. Since evaporation occurs in Department 3, only 21,000 pounds emerge as Product G.

Prospective

EXHIBIT 9–8   Net Market (Realizable) Method of Allocating Net Costs of Production

Joint Products	Total Gross Market Value	Separable Cost	Net Market Value		Distribution of Net Cost to Production	
B......	$ 40,000	$13,750	$ 26,250	$\frac{\$26,250}{\$175,000}$ × $140,000 =	$ 21,000
C......	60,000	3,125	56,875	$\frac{\$56,875}{\$175,000}$ × $140,000 =	45,500
D......	100,000	8,125	91,875	$\frac{\$91,875}{\$175,000}$ × $140,000 =	73,500
	$200,000	$25,000	$175,000			$140,000

A different approach is to obtain the percentage of cost to market value. We multiply this percentage by each joint product's market value as follows:

$$\frac{\$140,000 \text{ net cost of production}}{\$175,000 \text{ net market value}} = 80\%$$

Joint Products	Net Market Value		Distribution of Net Cost of Production	
B...............	$ 26,250	80% ×	$26,250 =	$ 21,000
C...............	56,875	80% ×	$56,875 =	45,500
D...............	91,875	80% ×	$91,875 =	73,500
	$175,000			$140,000

Based on the net market method of allocating the net cost of production, the following inventory valuations result:

Joint Products	Net Cost of Production	Separable Cost	Inventory Valuation
B..................	$ 21,000	$13,750	$ 34,750
C..................	45,500	3,125	48,625
D..................	73,500	8,125	81,625
	$140,000	$25,000	$165,000

We transfer 80 percent of the units processed in Department 2 to Department 4. The units emerge as Product E after further processing costing $201,500. Department 5 processes the other 20 percent leaving Department 2 at a cost of $12,500. They emerge as Product F. Exhibit 9–9 illustrates the joint cost allocation for this multiple split-off example.

Inventories at Sales Price

Because it is difficult to find a joint costing approach that satisfies all needs, some companies avoid the joint costing issue completely by assigning sales value or sales value net of separable costs to products resulting from joint production. They ignore joint costs completely because they assign only the realizable value or net market value to inventory. However, carrying inventories at sales value or sales value net of separable cost recognizes profits before sales are made. Either approach is contrary to generally accepted inventory costing methods as variations in inventory can affect profit. For example, an increase in inventory can cause an increase in a company's income because less cost is assigned to the goods sold.

EXHIBIT 9–9   Multiple Split-Off Points

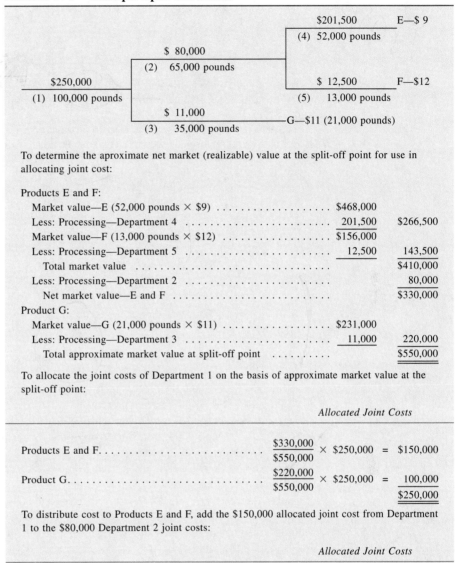

To determine the aproximate net market (realizable) value at the split-off point for use in allocating joint cost:

Products E and F:

Market value—E (52,000 pounds × $9)	$468,000	
Less: Processing—Department 4	201,500	$266,500
Market value—F (13,000 pounds × $12)	$156,000	
Less: Processing—Department 5	12,500	143,500
Total market value		$410,000
Less: Processing—Department 2		80,000
Net market value—E and F		$330,000

Product G:

Market value—G (21,000 pounds × $11)	$231,000	
Less: Processing—Department 3	11,000	220,000
Total approximate market value at split-off point		$550,000

To allocate the joint costs of Department 1 on the basis of approximate market value at the split-off point:

	Allocated Joint Costs

Products E and F. . . . . $\dfrac{\$330,000}{\$550,000}$ × $250,000 = $150,000

Product G. . . . . $\dfrac{\$220,000}{\$550,000}$ × $250,000 =   100,000

$250,000

To distribute cost to Products E and F, add the $150,000 allocated joint cost from Department 1 to the $80,000 Department 2 joint costs:

	Allocated Joint Costs

Product E. . . . . $\dfrac{\$266,500}{\$410,000}$ × $230,000 = $149,500

Product F. . . . . $\dfrac{\$143,500}{\$410,000}$ × $230,000 =   80,500

$230,000

To find the inventory valuation:

Products	Allocated Joint Costs +	Separable Costs =	Inventory Valuation
E.	$149,500	$201,500	$351,000
F.	80,500	12,500	93,000
G.	100,000	11,000	111,000
			$555,000

Current Cost Management Practice

The $200 billion drug industry is in seismic upheaval as giant multinational producers search for new products and wider distribution. Such moves as Roche Holding Ltd. agreeing to buy Syntex Corp. and SmithKline Beecham PLC's pact to buy Diversified Pharmaceutical Services, Inc., reflect a fundamental struggle for financial control in the health care business. Additionally, Pfizer Inc. agreed to venture with Value Health Inc., operator of the Value Rx drug middlemen. In just a few years, the balance of power has shifted dramatically. Hospitals have won clout by merging or forming purchasing alliances; they and other big drug buyers have contracted with benefit-management companies to negotiate lower prices on their behalf. To combat soft prices, the big producers are scrambling to build market share by selling more products. To fight the growing might of distributors, they are buying the distributors. For example, when Merck and SmithKline purchased Medco and Diversified, they essentially swallowed up the middlemen that have forced their margins down. In drugs, big has suddenly become much better.

Joseph Weber, Joan O'C. Hamilton, Gail Edmondson, and Paula Dwyer, "Drug-Merger Mania," *BusinessWeek,* May 16, 1994, pp. 30–31.

If, on the other hand, the joint costs are for perishable items with a rapid turnover, the use of sales prices as a basis for inventory valuation is less subject to criticism. In addition, if the normal profit percentage is small so there is little difference between cost and selling price, the approach is more defensible. Perhaps, the most sensible variation of this method is to deduct a normal profit percentage from the sales price net of separable cost. This procedure avoids the criticism that accountants recognize a profit before making a sale.

To summarize, in certain cases, cost accountants can employ arbitrary allocations without obvious harm. Although we may not be able to defend precisely the allocation method used, allocations are preferred to the extreme alternatives of assigning no value to ending inventory of joint products or assigning them market value. Valuing inventory at market value recognizes a profit for the products in inventory and overstates income.

Process Further Decision Making

Even though inventory valuation requires joint cost allocations, they are irrelevant for decision making. Managers frequently must decide what is the most profitable stage at which to sell products. In these situations, joint costs are sunk costs. As with all decision making, we should consider only future costs and revenues.

Irrelevance of Joint Costs

Chapter 17 discusses in detail that a sell or process further decision should rest on a differential revenue/cost analysis. We briefly mention it here to emphasize the limitation of joint product cost allocation procedures in decision making.

Differential costs, not joint product costs, are the only relevant costs we should consider in selecting the most profitable stage at which to sell a product. **Differential cost** is the extra cost incurred for different alternatives. When a company is considering further processing, incremental or differential cost is the additional cost for extending operations. **Differential revenue** is the additional revenue. We reserve this classification solely for those costs or revenues that change depending on the decision made. We compare differential revenue and differential cost to arrive at the extra earnings or differential earnings that result.

The following example briefly explains the analysis necessary to determine differential earnings. We assumed in Exhibit 9–8 that Product B has no market value at the split-off point but after incurring costs of $13,750 in processing, we can sell Product B for $40,000. Gross differential revenue is $40,000; differential cost is $13,750; and the **net differential revenue** is $26,250. In effect, the company loses $26,250 if it fails to further process Product B and merely disposes of the waste in an environmentally safe manner.

Erroneous Results Using Joint Costs

Erroneous decisions about when to sell a product can result if we use joint costs. For example, suppose an opportunity arises for the company to further process Product B at an additional cost of $15,000 to become Super Product B. Assume we can sell Super Product B for $52,000. If managers base their decision on joint cost allocations using either the net market value or quantity methods, the resulting margins would be those shown in Exhibit 9–10.

EXHIBIT 9–10   Incorrect Use of Joint Cost Allocation for Decision Making

	By Net Market (Realizable) Method		By Quantity Method	
Sales of Super Product B		$52,000		$52,000
Joint cost (from Exhibit 9–8) $21,000			(from Exhibit 9–4) $40,000	
Added cost 28,750		49,750	28,750	68,750
Margin		$ 2,250		$(16,750)

Product B now has separable costs totaling $28,750 ($13,750 to become Product B and $15,000 to become Super B). Because we normally determine the net market (realizable) value by the first sales possible after split-off, further processing to become Super B does not change the joint cost allocation as determined in Exhibit 9–8. The possibility of further processing Product B also does not change the $40,000 joint cost allocation under the quantity method presented in Exhibit 9–4. We simply add the separable cost to the joint cost allocation determined under each of the methods. The use of the net market value method indicates that further processing Product B would be profitable. Further processing is profitable even though it results in a margin smaller than the $5,250 [$40,000 sales − ($21,000 joint cost allocation + $13,750 separable cost)] determined without the additional processing. However, the quantity method indicates a loss of $16,750.

Exhibit 9–10 shows these approaches result in inconsistent margins. In addition, neither method is relevant to the decision. In deciding whether the additional processing would be profitable, the company should instead compare the additional separable cost with the additional revenue they would generate:

Additional revenue ($52,000 Super B − $40,000 Product B) $12,000
Additional separable cost 15,000
Net differential cost . . . . $ 3,000

If we consider no factors other than costs, the decision to sell the product as B rather than to process it further is appropriate.

Summary

Accountants face two important issues involving by-products and joint products: (1) the difficulty of allocating joint costs for inventory valuation or product costing purposes and (2) the use of differential analysis in identifying the most profitable point in the manufacturing cycle at which to sell products. We prefer basing further processing decisions on differential revenue/cost analysis, not allocated joint costs. Joint cost allocations have limited use in internal decision making because many managers think of only full costs. Thus, they are reluctant to continue manufacturing products that report book losses.

The chapter presents two basic methods of accounting for by-products. Accountants can assign a value to the by-products at their production or they can wait until their sale and record the income at that time. Accountants use two basic procedures to assign production costs to joint products—the physical measure and the market or sales value method. We can use gross market value as the basis for allocating joint cost, but it is appropriate only if we can sell the joint products in their state at the split-off point without further processing. If a joint product requires additional processing before its sale, we should subtract the separable costs incurred from the market value. We then use this as a basis for joint cost allocations. There is difficulty in deciding which is the most appropriate method of assigning joint cost because each of the allocation methods presented depends on different conditions and assumptions.

Important Terms and Concepts

Joint products   256
Main products   256
By-products   256
Scrap   256
Joint costs.   257
Common costs   257
Split-off point or point of separation   258
Separable production costs   258
Net market (realizable) value of by-products produced   258
Physical measures of joint cost allocations   264
Quantity method of joint cost allocations   264

Average unit cost method of joint cost allocations   264
Weighted factor method of joint cost allocations   264
Market or sales value methods of joint cost allocations   266
Gross market method of joint cost allocations   266
Net market (realizable) method of joint cost allocations   267
Relative sales value at the split-off method of joint cost allocations   267
Differential cost and revenue   271
Net differential revenue   271

Ethical Dilemma

Ethics of Obtaining Information about Competitors (CMA)

Mywrite Corporation designs and builds sophisticated machinery for manufacturers of micro-circuitry. The rapidity of technological advancement in this industry creates a continuing demand for highly complex, well-developed production equipment. Competition has grown in intensity in the struggle to meet market demands. Mywrite has managed to attract many bright engineers and always seems to be looking for talented people for all of its departments.

Ted Raull, cost accounting manager, has been with Mywrite for six months. He had been with a competitor previously but that company had failed to receive sufficient contracts to stay in business. He considered himself fortunate that Mywrite happened to be looking for cost accountants and applied for the job a few months before his old company was dissolved. Raull's initial impression of Mywrite's costing procedures was that they were not as good as those used by his former employer. Thus, he thought he could contribute toward improving the costing system.

Mark Philips, human resource manager, has asked Raull to interview a job applicant for a position in Mywrite's finance area. Philips indicated that the employee who usually conducts such interviews is attending an out-of-town convention. "This applicant is an excellent prospect. You're in a better position to evaluate the candidate anyway, Ted. Who knows, you may get some good information that will help us out. He's currently employed by Vestron, our biggest competitor," said Philips.

Raull was flattered that he was asked to conduct the interview, until he realized there was no opening in the finance area. Raull asked a friend in the Human Resource Department why Mywrite had advertised for a position that did not exist. His friend said, "We do it all the time. The ads attract people from our competitors, and in the course of the employment interview, they spill all kinds of useful information trying to impress us with their capabilities. We just listen and encourage them. Sometimes we even hire one. It sure keeps us informed and keeps us abreast of the competition. Vestron apparently has a financing arrangement that we'd like to know about."

Raull's reaction was that perhaps he and others at his old company had been used. In fact, he thinks that Mywrite's actions are unethical.

Required:

a. Explain why Mywrite Corporation's practice of obtaining information while interviewing people for nonexistent positions is unethical.

b. Ted Raull is trying to decide what action he should take with regard to the request of Mark Philips to conduct the interview of the Vestron employee.

 (1) Identify the appropriate alternatives for Raull to take in this situation.

 (2) Recommend the alternative identified in Requirement *b.1.* that Raull should take and explain why.

c. Discuss the responsibility, if any, that Ted Raull has to eliminate the practice of Mywrite's Human Resource Management Department of interviewing people for nonexistent positions.

Problem for Self-Study

Treating a Product as a Joint Product or a By-Product

The following gallons were jointly produced in a batch at the Montee Chemical Company: AXY—1,160; BXY—2,300; CXY—2,000; Waste—500. The market price per gallon of the chemicals is $40, $22, and $9.50, respectively. Joint costs of producing the batch consisted of $50,000 direct materials and $25,000 conversion costs.

Required:

Determine the cost per gallon for each product assuming:

a. Montee classifies chemicals AXY, BXY, and CXY as joint products, and uses the gross market value method to allocate joint costs. Round to the nearest dollar.

b. Treat chemical CXY as a by-product and deduct the net market value of the by-product processed from the production cost. Separable cost per gallon of chemical CXY is $2.

Solution to Problem for Self-Study

MONTEE CHEMICAL COMPANY

a.

Joint Products	Gallons Produced	Market Value per Gallon	Market Value	Distribution of Production Costs	
AXY	1,160	$40.00	$ 46,400	$30,000	$\dfrac{\$\ 46,400}{\$116,000} \times \$75,000*$
BXY	2,300	22.00	50,600	32,716	$\left(\dfrac{\$\ 50,600}{\$116,000} \times \$75,000\right)$
CXY	2,000	9.50	19,000	12,284	$\left(\dfrac{\$\ 19,000}{\$116,000} \times \$75,000\right)$
			$116,000	$75,000	

*$50,000 direct material + $25,000 conversion cost

Joint Products	Cost per Gallon
AXY	$\left(\$25.862\ \dfrac{\$30,000}{1,160}\ \text{gallons}\right)$
BXY	$\left(\$14.224\ \dfrac{\$32,716}{2,300}\ \text{gallons}\right)$
CXY	$\left(\$6.142\ \dfrac{\$12,284}{2,000}\ \text{gallons}\right)$

b.

Production cost			$75,000
Less by-product chemical CXY:			
Gross market value		$19,000	
Less separable cost (2,000 × $2)		4,000	15,000
Costs to allocate to joint products			$60,000

Joint Product	Distribution of Production Costs	
AXY	$28,701	$\left(\dfrac{\$46,400}{\$97,000} \times \$60,000\right)$
BXY	31,299	$\left(\dfrac{\$50,600}{\$97,000} \times \$60,000\right)$
	$60,000	

Product	Joint Cost per Gallon	Separable Costs	Inventory Value per Gallon
AXY	$24.742 ($28,701/1,160 gallons)		$24.742
BXY	13.608 ($31,299/2,300 gallons)		13.608
CXY	7.50 ($15,000/2,000 gallons)	$2.00	9.500

Review Questions

1. Why should managers be alert for market developments affecting their by-products and joint products?

2. *(a)* Contrast scrap, by-products, and joint products. *(b)* Under which conditions should a product be treated as a by-product rather than as a joint product?

3. Discuss the basic difference between the methods of accounting for by-products and for joint products.

4. When would it be appropriate to allocate all producing costs to the joint products and treat the recovery value of by-products as other income?

5. Which of the two major approaches to accounting for by-products usually results in a lower valuation of joint (main) product inventories?

6. Discuss the methods available for accounting for joint products and describe the advantages and weaknesses of each method.

7. *(a)* Why do the joint cost allocation methods illustrated in the chapter have limited usefulness in cost control and planning? *(b)* What type of cost analysis would yield results that management can use in deciding on the most profitable stage at which the joint products can be sold?

8. Define the relationship between the split-off point and separable costs.

9. Compare common costs with joint costs.

10. Since the choice of which joint allocation method to use often is arbitrary, why are these approximations necessary?

Exercises

Writing

E9–1 Cause-and-Effect Criterion

Sugar Farmers grows sugar beets; these large beets have a high natural sugar content that the company refines to produce commercial sugar. The sugar processing factory accepts only topped beets, whose leaves, stems, and crowns (called tops) are removed. Thus, the topping process is necessary for the marketability of all products. The first process when harvesting beets is to cut off the tops while the beets are still in the ground. Tractors pull machines over the beets; these machines cut off the tops, grind them and convey them into trucks that are driven along side. On delivery to the cattle feed processor, tops are weighted by the truck-load. Despite their small market value in relation to the beets, tops do have a significant value. After processing, tops are fed to cattle.

Tractors pull other machines over the topped beets to dig them from the ground and deposit them into a hopper. Later trucks transport these hoppers to the sugar refinery.

Accountants with the sugar grower question whether the cause-and-effect criterion should impact their treatment of the joint cost allocation. Managers often use the cause-and-effect criterion in cost allocations when they can identify the variable causing a cost to occur. A cause-and-effect relationship exists if a cost pool can be related directly to cost objectives. They question if sequential, rather than simultaneous, production processing of products should affect their decision.

Required:

Write a memo to these accountants explaining the following:

a. Whether tops are by-products or joint products.

b. Whether they should assign the cost of cutting tops solely to the beet tops or consider the cost of this process a joint cost.

c. Whether their decision to assign the cost of cutting tops solely to the beet tops or to treat this as a joint cost should be affected by the fact that the tops are identifiable from the sugar beets and can be weighed.

d. The role, if any, of the cause-and-effect criterion in joint cost allocations.

E9–2 Joint Product versus By-Product Costing

Oury Company's Chemicals X12 and YR8 are joint products; 20,000 gallons of X12 and 40,000 gallons of YR8 were produced. Their cost for April up to the point of separation was $350,000. No costs were incurred beyond that point. The selling price was $8 for X12 and $6 for YR8.

Required:

a. Determine the allocation of costs between joint products using the net market (realizable) method.

b. If, instead, the sales price for X12 is $2.50 per gallon and X12 is treated as a by-product and the sales price for YR8 remains at $6, determine the allocation of costs between the two products. The company follows the approach of deducting the market value of the by-products produced from production costs. Would you advise management to continue production using these market conditions?

E9–3 Net Market (Realizable) Value Method of Allocation

Cinnamon Refining Company produces three different chemicals. A batch costing $23,750 produces the following:

Chemicals	Gallons Produced and Sold	Unit Sales Price	Additional Cost beyond Split-Off
W	12,500	$4.00	$10,000
Y	5,000	8.00	5,000
Z	10,000	3.50	15,000

Required:

a. Using the net market (realizable) value method for allocating joint costs, determine the joint cost to be assigned to each product and the gross margin for each chemical.

b. The company is considering selling Chemical Y directly at the split-off point for $36,000. In the plant space used for the further processing of Chemical Y, Chemical Z can be processed even further to become Super Chemical Z which can be sold for $75,000. Additional costs of $38,000 would be incurred. What would you advise management to do? Support your answer with computations.

E9–4 Joint Cost Allocation and Sell or Process Further Decision

Texco Company manufactures three products, R, S, and T, from a particular joint process. Each product may be sold at split-off or may be processed further. Joint production costs for the period were $412,500. All costs of additional processing are of a variable nature and are directly traceable to the products involved. The following data are from company records:

Critical Thought

Joint Product	Units Produced	Total Sales Value at Split-off	Separable Costs	Sales Value after Further Processing
R	25,000	$550,000	$67,500	$590,000
S	15,000	300,000	24,000	340,000
T	10,000	150,000	32,000	210,000

Required:

a. Using the gross market value method, distribute joint cost to the joint products.

b. Using the quantity method, determine the joint costs to allocate to each group of joint products.

c. If management instead assigns weights of 3:1:2 to products R, S, and T respectively based on the engineering skills required, what is the joint cost allocation and the cost per actual unit produced?

d. What is the unit cost for each product group that is most relevant to a sell or process further decision?

e. Recommend which product(s) should be additionally processed to maximize net contribution to profits. Support your recommendation with a cost analysis.

E 9–5 Physical and Net Market Realizable Value Allocation Methods

Freedman Corporation uses a joint process to manufacture Products A, B, and C. Each product may be sold at its split-off point or processed further. Additional processing costs are entirely variable and traceable to the respective products manufactured. Joint production costs for 19X1 were $580,000. The following data are available:

Product	Units Produced	Sales Value after Additional Processing	Separable Costs
A	28,000	$200,000	$24,500
B	32,000	$250,000	$20,500
C	40,000	$280,000	$10,000

Required:

a. Determine the joint cost allocation and inventory value for each product, assuming all products are processed beyond the split-off point:
   (1) Using the physical method of allocation.
   (2) Using the net market (realizable) value method of allocation.

b. Assume Product A can be sold at the split-off point for $185,000. What would you advise management to do?

c. Assume Product C can be sold at split-off point for $265,000. What would you advise management to do?

E 9–6 Joint Products and By-Products

Allen Manufacturing Company produces one by-product, Cy-O, and three joint products—Di-O, Ey-O, and Fe-O. Joint costs of production totaled $508,000 for May. Because the skills needed to process each product vary, the engineering staff has provided points per pound. Data for each product follows:

	Pounds Produced	Points per Pound	Gross Total Market Value of Production	Separable Costs
Cy-O	500	—	$ 7,250	$ 1,050
Di-O	2,000	2	415,000	60,000
Ey-O	4,000	4	289,000	15,000
Fe-O	6,000	3	188,000	45,000

The company uses the approach of deducting the net market value of the by-products manufactured from production costs.

Required:

a. Using the weighted factor method in allocating joint costs, determine the distribution of production costs, total inventory valuation of each of the four products, and their unit costs. Would this method be acceptable for this set of circumstances?

b. Using the net market method in allocating joint costs, determine the distribution of production costs and total inventory valuation of each of the four products.

E 9–7 Classification of Products

At the Mitchell Company, chemicals are mixed in 4,000-gallon batches. The yield of one batch of raw material and the market prices are:

Chemical	Market Price per Gallon	Yield per Batch (Percent)
A	$50	20%
B	30	30
C	20	35
Waste	0	15

Direct material costs $21,600 per batch; conversion cost per batch is $20,000 at normal capacity.

Required:

Determine the cost per gallon for each product assuming:

a. Chemicals A, B, and C are classified as joint products, and the gross market value method is used to allocate joint costs.

b. Chemical C is a by-product and deduct the net market value of the by-product processed from the production cost. Separable cost per gallon of Chemical C is $11.

E9–8 Physical Basis and Net Market (Realizable) Value

Murray Company produces three main products: A, B, and C. It also has a residue Product DD that requires additional material and processing before it can be sold. The company assigns joint production costs to its Product DD equal to its market value less additional costs incurred after the split-off point. The products are manufactured in batches, costing $2,175. A batch produces the following:

Product	Volume (Gallons)	Market Value	Separable Cost
A	25	$ 770	$ 20
B	50	500	100
C	100	2,000	150
DD	30	100	25

Required:

a. Using the physical basis, determine the amount of production costs that should be allocated to all four products. Also indicate the inventory value for each product.
b. Using the net market (realizable) value, determine the amount of production costs that should be allocated to all four products. Also indicate the inventory value for each product.
c. Indicate the ending inventory valuation using the physical basis and the net market value method if 10 gallons of Product A, 18 gallons of B, 15 gallons of C, and 6 gallons of DD are on hand at the end of the period.

E9–9 Further Processing of Products
G. Porter Corporation uses a joint process in manufacturing product L, UL, SUL. Each product may be sold at its split-off point or processed further. None of the separable costs are fixed, and all are traceable to the respective product manufactured. Joint production costs total $45,000 and are allocated on the basis of the sales value at split-off point.

Sales Value and Separable Cost if Processed Further

Product	Sales Value at Split-Off	Separable Costs	Sales Value
L	$ 375,000	$23,750	$400,000
UL	325,000	22,250	340,000
SUL	300,000	24,000	324,000
	$1,000,000		

Required:

a. Determine the joint cost allocated to each product and the inventory valuation assuming the products are further processed.
b. For the company to maximize profits, what is your suggestion on each product?

Problems

P9–10 By-Product Costing
The following data are from the records of the Patterson Meat Packing Company:

	Joint Products	By-Products
Sales	120,000 pounds	15,000 pounds
Production	130,000 pounds	20,000 pounds
Estimated market value	$1.50 per pound	$0.39 per pound
Costs of further processing:		
Materials		0.08 per pound
Conversion cost		0.02 per pound
Marketing and administrative costs applied ...		0.06 per pound
Total production costs	$145,000	
Total marketing and administrative costs	22,000	

Required:

Using the two basic methods of accounting for by-products illustrated in the text, prepare income statements.

P9–11 Journal Entries (AICPA adapted)

Lares Confectioners, Inc., makes a candy bar called Rey, that sells for $0.50 per pound. The manufacturing process also yields a product known as Nagu. Without further processing, Nagu sells for $0.10 per pound. With further processing, Nagu sells for $0.30 per pound. During the month of April, total joint manufacturing costs up to the split-off point consisted of the following charges to work in process:

Raw materials	$150,000
Direct labor	120,000
Factory overhead	30,000

Production for the month was 394,000 pounds of Rey and 30,000 pounds of Nagu. To complete Nagu during the month of April and obtain a selling price of $0.30 per pound, further processing during April would entail the following additional costs:

Raw materials	$2,000
Direct labor	1,500
Factory overhead	500

Required:

Prepare the April journal entries for Nagu, if Nagu is

a. Transferred as a by-product at sales value to the warehouse without further processing, with a corresponding reduction of Rey's manufacturing costs.

b. Further processed as a by-product and transferred to the warehouse at net realizable value, with a corresponding reduction of Rey's manufacturing costs.

c. Further processed and transferred to finished goods, with joint costs being allocated to Rey and Nagu based on relative sales value at the split-off point.

P9–12 Multiple Split-Off; Inventory Valuation

SPATS

Forman, Inc., processes salmon meat and eggs into Products A, B, C, and D. Products A, B, and C are joint products; Product D is a by-product. The production processes for a given accounting period are as follows:

    In the Cleaning Department, 3,000,000 pounds of raw fish are processed at a cost of $600,000. After processing in the Cleaning Department, 2 percent of the fish processed is fish eggs that are transferred to the Egg Packing Department (Product A). An additional cost of $100,000 is incurred, and Product A is sold for $25 per pound.

Ninety-six percent of the processed fish is transferred to the Fish Processing Department. The remainder (2 percent) is considered a by-product (Product D) and is sold at $0.50 per pound as animal food with no additional processing. Selling expense to dispose of Product D is $5,000. The company accounts for this by crediting the net market value of by-products produced to the production costs of the main products.

In the Fish Processing Department, the meat is processed further at a cost of $800,000. In this department, the fish that is to become Product B is canned, and the fish that is to become Product C is bagged.

Seventy-five percent of the fish (Product B) is transferred to the Cooking Department at an additional cost of $700,000. After processing, B is sold at $2 per pound. The remaining fish (Product C) is transferred to the Freezing Department where additional costs of $300,000 are incurred. Product C is sold for $3 per pound.

Required:

a. Diagram the production process indicating the appropriate data associated with each product (i.e., quantities, separable cost, and gross market values).
b. Using the net market valuation method of allocating joint costs, determine the distribution of production costs and the total inventory valuations for each of the four products. Round to the nearest dollar.

P9–13 Joint Cost Allocation (CIA)

A company uses a single process to produce three joint products, E, M, and H. Raw materials in the amount of 100,000 gallons are processed in each batch to yield 40,000 gallons of E, 30,000 gallons of M, and 20,000 gallons of H. The joint costs of processing a batch of raw materials are

Materials (100,000 gallons)	$60,000
Conversion costs	75,000

After split-off, Product E can be sold for $1.50 per gallon. Product M and H must be processed further before they can be sold. The separate processing costs are $1.50 per gallon for Product M and $2.00 per gallon for Product H. Product M then can be sold for $3 per gallon and Product H for $4.25 per gallon.

During March, the company processed 100,000 gallons of raw materials. There were no inventories of finished product on hand on March 1. March sales were 30,000 gallons of E, 28,000 gallons of M, and 16,000 gallons of H. The company uses the net realizable value method for allocating joint costs.

Required:

a. Prepare a schedule showing the allocation of the $135,000 joint cost between Products E, M, and H. Clearly label your answer.
b. Prepare a statement of gross margin for Products E, M, and H for March.
c. Suppose Product E can be processed further into Product Super E by additional processing which costs $14,000; 35,000 gallons of Super E can be produced per batch of 100,000 gallons of raw materials. Super E can be sold for $2 per gallon. Will the company be better off by producing and selling Super E rather than Product E? Show computations to support your answer.

SPATS

Critical Thought

P9–14 Unit Cost Determination

Winter Fertilizer Company operates three departments. As a result of the unique process in each department, the company markets a variety of products.

All products originate in Department A. Raw materials are converted at this phase into three products: Z1, Z2, and Z3. Z1 is sold at this stage, but Z2 must be processed further before it can be marketed. Z3 could be sold at this stage, but Winter has chosen to subject it to additional processing.

Z2 is transferred to Department B. Here it is converted into Z2B and is sold at this stage.

Z3 is transferred to Department C. Here another raw material is added and Z3 is converted into Z3C, which is sold at this stage. In processing Z3 into Z3C, an incidental product, Z4, results. Winter has a customer for all the Z4 it produces; there are no additional processing costs beyond this point, neither are there any marketing or administrative costs allocable to Z4.

Because inventory costs are determined on a FIFO basis, the unit cost of the most recently produced items must be determined. Winter accounts for the by-product Z4 by deducting its net market value from the cost of production. An inspection of company records reveals the following information for March:

Department A:
Raw materials	$ 4,500
Conversion costs	45,000

Department B:
Conversion costs	6,120

Department C:
Raw materials	1,260
Conversion costs	30,000

Inventories:

	Pounds Produced	Ending Inventory February 28	Ending Inventory March 31	Sales Price per Pound
Z1	4,000			$4.32
Z2	3,200	320	120	
Z3	6,000	400	580	4.80
Z2B	3,060			6.00
Z3C	7,000			9.00
Z4	2,000			1.00

Required:

a. Compute Department A's cost per pound of Z1, Z2, and Z3 produced using the average unit cost method based on physical units for March.

b. Compute the costs as in Requirement *a* using the gross market value method.

c. Compute the cost per pound of Z3C produced in March. Assume for this computation that the cost per pound of Z3 produced is $3.90 in February and $4 in March.

P9–15 Determining Inventory Values

Wells Manufacturing Company produces petroleum products from crude oil. Bexene can be sold for $150 per gallon; however, Triane can only be sold for two-thirds of the Bexene sales price, while Rilane is sold at only one-fifth of the Bexene sales price. During August the factory's costs and output were as follows:

Production:	
Bexene	500 gallons
Triane	225 gallons
Rilane	50 gallons

Costs:	
Material	$35,480.00
Labor	21,001.00
Factory overhead	15,100.28
Packing and labeling, Bexene	575.00
Packing and labeling, Triane	63.00
Scrap recovery	340.64

The company deducts the net market value of the by-products produced from production costs.

Required:

a. Using the net market (realizable) method, compute the amount of joint cost that is to be allocated to each petroleum product. Treat the Rilane as a by-product and the other two as joint products.

b. What unit costs should be assigned as inventory value for each of the three petroleum products?

c. A chemical consulting firm offers to come into the factory and rework the Triane so that it can be sold as Bexene. The cost of doing this for the 225 gallons, which represent a month's average quantity, is as follows:

Material	$ 5,700
Labor	6,000
Variable factory overhead	1,800
	$13,500

What advice can you give management in regard to hiring these chemists?

P9–16 Allocating Joint Cost with Multiple Split-Off Points

Foster, Inc., manufactures three products, W, Y, and Z, in a joint process. Product Z is manufactured in two phases; in the first phase, raw materials are processed to produce two intermediates in fixed proportions. One of these intermediates is processed to yield a product called W. The other intermediate is converted into Product Z in a separate finishing operation that yields both finished Product Z and another product, Y. Product Y must be further processed before yielding a salable product. Product quantity, market price per gallon, and sales volume are as follows for a normal period:

	Gallons	*Market Price per Gallon*
Product W	70,000	$6
Product Y	50,000	3
Product Z	80,000	5

Processing cost is as follows:

	Product Processing			
	Basic Process	*W*	*Y–Z*	*Y*
Material	$ 54,000	$ 92,160	$ 40,000	$ 4,000
Direct labor	12,000	25,000	28,000	11,000
Variable factory overhead ...	18,000	12,000	12,000	8,000
Fixed factory overhead	16,000	17,000	41,840	27,000
Total	$100,000	$146,160	$121,840	$50,000

SPATS

Required:

Using the net market (realizable) method in allocating joint costs, determine the distribution of production costs and the inventoriable cost per gallon for each product.

P9–17 By-Product and Joint Costing under a Process Costing System

Ann Wilson Company produces two principal products known as AX and BX. Incidental to the production of these products, it manufactures a by-product known as Bypo. The company has three producing departments, which it identifies as Departments 1, 2, and 3. Raw materials are started in process in Department 1. On completion of processing in that department, 20 percent of the material is by-product and is transferred directly to stock. Twenty-five percent of the remaining output of Department 1 goes to Department 2 where it is made into AX, and the other 75 percent goes to Department 3 where it becomes BX. The processing of AX in Department 2 results in a gain in weight of material transferred into the department of 25 percent due to the addition of water at the start of the processing. There is no gain or loss of weight in the other processes.

The company considers the income from Bypo, after allowing $0.10 per pound for estimated marketing delivery costs, to be a reduction of the cost of the two principal products. The company assigns Department 1 costs to the two principal products in proportion to their net sales value at point of separation computed by deducting costs to be incurred in subsequent processes from the sales value of the products. Sales price and additional costs for each product are as follows:

Per Pound
AX—$24 sales price; $4 subsequent processing cost
BX—$18 sales price; $6 subsequent processing cost
Bypo—$.60 sales price; $0.10 marketing cost

The following information concerns the operations during May:

	Inventories		
	April 30 Quantity (Pounds)	*Value*	*May 31 Quantity (Pounds)*
Department 1	None		None
Department 2	400	$3,360	600
Department 3	200	1,560	800
Finished goods—AX	450	4,500	500
Finished goods—BX	1,000		600
Finished goods—Bypo	None		None

Inventories in process are estimated to be one-half complete in Departments 2 and 3, both at the first and last of the month.

	Costs	
	Material Used	*Labor and OH*
Department 1	$44,180	$52,000
Department 2	–0–	20,600
Department 3	–0–	73,800

The material used in Department 1 weighed 21,000 pounds. Prices as of May 31 are unchanged from those in effect during the month.

Required:

a. Prepare a statement showing costs and production by departments for May. The company uses the first-in, first-out method to cost production.
b. Prepare a schedule of inventory values for finished goods as of April 30.

P9–18 Inventory Values for Joint Products and By-Products

Young Corporation processes, cans, and sells two main orange products—orange sections and orange juice. Orange skin is treated as a by-product and sold to a candy-making company for further processing as candied orange peel. Young's production process begins in the Cutting Department where oranges are processed. The oranges are sterilized and the outside skin is cut away. The two main products and the by-product (orange skin for candy peel) are recognizable after processing in the Cutting Department. Each product is then transferred to a separate department for final processing.

Some of the peeled oranges are forwarded to the Sectioning Department where the oranges are sectioned and canned. Any juice generated during the sectioning operation is packed in the cans with the orange sections.

The remaining peeled oranges are forwarded to the Juicing Department where they are pulverized into a liquid. There is an evaporation loss equal to 10 percent of the weight of the good output which occurs as the juices are heated. The outside skin is cut and frozen in the Candy Peel Department.

Young Corporation uses the net market value method to assign costs of the joint process to its main products. The by-product is inventoried at its net market value.

The Cutting Department received a total of 50,000 pounds during September. The costs incurred in each department, the proportion by weight transferred to the two final processing departments, and the selling price of each end product follow:

Processing Data and Costs
September 19X1

	Costs Incurred	Product by Weight Transferred to Department (Percent)	Selling Price per Pound of the Final Product
Cutting	$14,000	—	—
Sectioning	3,500	50%	$1.00
Juicing	2,000	40	.50
Skin for candy peel	500	10	.20
	$20,000	100%	

Required:

Using the net market value method to determine inventory values for its main products and by-products, calculate:

a. (1) The pounds of oranges that result as output for orange sections, orange juice, and candy peel.
   (2) The net market value at the split-off point of the two main products.
   (3) The amount of the cost of the Cutting Department assigned to each main product and to the by-product.
   (4) The gross margins for each of the two main products.
b. (1) Why would management need to know gross margin information by main product?
   (2) Would this information be helpful in deciding whether to process the main products further?

P9–19 Methods of Accounting for By-Products

Cates Chemical Company provides the following data regarding its processing operations:

	By-Products	Joint Products
Sales	35,000 gallons	80,000 gallons
Production	40,000 gallons	100,000 gallons
Estimated market value	$7.50 per gallon	$50 per gallon
Costs of the further processing:		
Materials	1.25 per gallon	
Labor	0.40 per gallon	
Factory overhead applied	0.35 per gallon	
Marketing costs applied	0.30 per gallon	
Administrative costs applied	0.20 per gallon	
Total production costs		$1,500,000
Total marketing and administrative costs		120,000

Required:

a. Prepare income statements using the two basic methods of accounting for by-products.

b. Using the net market value method, prepare the journal entries to record the costs assigned to the by-products.

c. Assume that the market improves for the by-products and the 35,000 gallons are sold for cash at $8 per gallon. Record the entry.

P9–20 Numerous Split-Offs of Joint Products

Crawford Corporation produces two joint products: DX and EX. Additionally, FX is a by-product of DX. No joint cost is to be allocated to the by-product. The production processes for a given year are as follows:

The first department—Cutting— processes 117,000 pounds of direct material at a total cost of $150,000. After processing in the Cutting Department, workers transfer 62,000 pounds to the Mixing Department and 55,000 pounds (now EX) to the Fabricating Department.

The Mixing Department further processes the material at a total additional cost of $18,000. Of the pounds available, 50,000 pounds (now DX) go to the Finishing Department, and the remaining pounds emerge as FX, the by-product, to be sold at $2 per pound. Marketing expenses related to disposing of FX are $4,000.

The Finishing Department processes DX at a total additional cost of $8,400. After this processing, DX is ready for sale at $5 per pound.

The Fabricating Department processes EX at a total additional cost of $123,600. In this department, a normal loss of units of EX occurs which equals 10 percent of the good output of EX. The remaining good output of EX is then sold for $6 per pound.

Required:

a. Draw a diagram depicting the flow of pounds through the production cycle.

b. Prepare a schedule showing the allocation of the $150,000 joint cost between DX and EX using the net market value approach. The net market value of FX should be treated as an addition to the sales value of DX.

c. Disregard your answer to Requirement *b* and assume that $100,000 of total joint costs were appropriately allocated to DX. Assume also that there were 52,000 pounds of DX and 11,000 pounds of FX available to sell. Prepare a statement of gross margin for DX using the following facts:

(1) During the year, sales of DX were 70 percent of the pounds available for sale. There was no beginning inventory.

(2) The net market value of FX available for sale is to be deducted from the cost of producing DX. The ending inventory of DX is to be based on the net cost of production.

(3) Data relating to marketing cost are identical to those presented earlier.

Cases ·

Critical Thought

C9–21 Comparing Profitability of Subsequent Processing

Vickry, Inc., manufactures a product called FIN in the following four departments: Department 1, mixing; Department 2, cooking; Department 3, cooling; and Department 4, packing.

The first department weighs and mixes materials A and B. Department 2 cooks the mixture; 20 percent of the mixture is lost in evaporation at the end of the departmental process. The remaining 80 percent of the mixture is then sent to Department 3, where it is cooled. At the end of the cooling process, the top 90 percent of the mixture is transferred to Department 4, where it is bottled for shipment. The remaining 10 percent of the mixture represents sediments from the cooling process and is sold in bulk as a product called PRO for $3 a pound.

However, variations occur in the cooling process because of temperature changes, so that the percentage of PRO can be increased to as high as 30 percent of the Department 3 mixture. At a minimum, PRO will always be 10 percent of the Department 3 mixture. FIN sells for $10 a bottle.

A prospective use for PRO has been found, but it would require the establishment of a fifth department. This new product, NEW-PRO, would sell for $6 a pound. Producing this product requires adding two pounds of a new material to each pound of sediment obtained from Department 3. The additional processing would require 30 percent shrinkage of the resulting mixture. The following additional costs would result from processing NEW-PRO:

Materials	$ 0.60 per pound
Variable processing costs	$ 1.00 per pound of input
Fixed processing costs	$4,000 per month

Required:

a. Outline briefly the processing flow by departments describing the steps involved with their specific characteristics as to percentage lost and transferred.

b. Prepare statements based on the following cost data and production figures for a month. Show total production cost and gross profit for each of the following three situations assuming that all production is sold:

Material issues to Department 1:	Material A—6,000 @ $1.50 per pound
	Material B—4,000 @ $1.10 per pound

Conversion costs:

Department 1—$0.50 per pound of departmental output
Department 2—$0.40 per pound of departmental output
Department 3—$0.90 per pound of departmental output
Department 4—$0.20 per pound of departmental output (all is considered variable)

---

(1) PRO is produced at a rate of 10 percent of the Department 3 mixture with Department 3 cost allocated to both products on a per-pound basis.

(2) NEW-PRO is produced at 10 percent of Department 3 mixture.

(3) PRO is produced at 30 percent of the Department 3 mixture and NEW-PRO then is manufactured.

c. Explain which of the three alternatives you would advise adopting and list factors to consider in making this decision.

Capstone Case

Bases for Allocating

Sellar Cheese Company manufactures a high-quality cheddar cheese using fresh, sweet milk that it pasteurizes. The milk flows from the pasteurizer into stainless steel vats that hold 10,000 pounds of milk each. Sellar Company has found it takes about 11 pounds of milk to make 1 pound of cheddar cheese.

In making cheese, the curd, or solid parts, of milk must be separated from the whey, or liquid part. Sellar adds a starter culture of lactic acid bacteria to each vat to accomplish this separation. When the bacteria are distributed throughout the vat, the milk begins to ripen or ferment. Rennet extract, a substance from the lining of a calf's fourth stomach, is added to make the milk curdle. The milk then coagulates into a curd, or soft, semisolid mass.

Using paddles, workers stir the curd and whey before the mixture is heated to about 102°F to remove any remaining whey and to develop the proper firmness and acidity. Cheese workers drain the whey from the vat and push the curd to the sides.

Curd processing.   After the whey is drained off, workers place the curd in a machine that cuts it into pieces about 10 cm long and 13 ml thick. They salt the cut curd and press it into molds. The molds are stacked in a press and kept under great pressure overnight. The next morning, the cheese is removed and placed in a curing room where it remains for 90 days.

Whey processing.   Whey is drained off into vats where a preservative agent is added, which allows a two-month storage. After a short mixing and cooking process, the whey is refrigerated for sale to cattle-feed producers. Within the last few years, a new process has been developed in which soybeans are mixed with whey for livestock food. If whey is not further processed, it has no value and is poured down the drain.

Because Seller's cheddar cheese has such a fine reputation, the cheese is easy to sell at $4 per pound and is shipped as fast as it is cured. More effort is required to sell the whey, even though both are sold to the same food-producing companies by the same marketing force. Often, when the accumulation of whey becomes especially heavy and the date of spoilage is coming close, buyers are required to purchase some amount of whey to be able to buy the cheddar cheese. Sellar Company justifies this by arguing that they want to stimulate the use of whey in livestock food processing.

This is the reason Sellar's marketing manager was excited when Beyer Foods, Inc., offered to buy 100,000 pounds of whey for $0.50 per pound. However, Sellar's production manager argued that the $0.50 per pound offer should not be accepted because the cost of production is at least $0.80 per pound and probably more. The marketing manager points out that the production manager's insistence on $0.80 has led to a heavy accumulation of whey in refrigeration.

The production manager counters this argument by saying, "Your salespeople are so incompetent and so lacking in incentive that they would pour out the whey unless we had inventory controls."

Cost data.   Both managers realize they need assistance from the cost accountant and request the preparation of financial data for their use. After analysis of past results, the cost accountant indicates that Sellar Company processes 50,000 pounds of milk into cheese in the one eight-hour shift that operates daily.

Out of 10,000 pounds of milk processed, 1,400 pounds of output are saved—910 pounds of cheese and 490 pounds of whey that can be preserved. Raw milk costs $1,000 per 10,000 pounds, while lactic acid bacteria and rennet extract together average $150 per 10,000 pounds of milk. Labor and overhead costs average $800 per 10,000 pounds of milk processed through the stage where whey is drained off. Labor and overhead in curd processing average $500 per 910 pounds of cheese; salt averages $29 for a 910-pound batch.

In whey processing, the preservatives average $16 for a 490-pound batch. Labor and overhead per 490-pound batch average $25. Selling costs average $0.10 per finished pound each for the cheese and the whey.

Sellar Cheese Company *(concluded)*

Production manager's basis.   After studying the cost data, the production manager presents the following support for refusing the offer of $0.50 sales price per pound of whey:

$$\frac{\$1,000 \text{ milk} + \$150 \text{ bacteria and rennet extract}}{1,400 \text{ pounds of output}} = \$0.82$$

The production manager emphasizes that an $0.80 price per pound does not even cover the materials much less the labor and overhead.

Marketing manager's basis.   The marketing manager contends that the production manager's basis has no merit because it assumes that the company would just as soon make whey as cheese, and everyone knows that is a fallacy. Instead, the marketing manager presents the argument that the material for the cheese initially is worth more per pound than the material for the whey. Based on this contention, he presents the following analysis:

	Output of 10,000 Pounds of Milk	Market Price per Pound	Total Market Value	Percent of Total	Costs Applicable to Each	Cost per Pound
Cheese	910	$4.00	$3,640	93.7%	$1,827*	$2.00
Whey	490	.50	245	6.3	123	.25
			$3,885	100.0%	$1,950	

* 93.7% × ($1,000 + $150 + $800).

The production manager disagrees with the approach, arguing that the cost allocation should not be a function of their relative market prices. The marketing manager then asks, "Why not treat the whey as a by-product, because you'll agree that we prefer to process cheese all the time rather than whey if we could." Under this approach, the market value of the whey ($0.50) is deducted from the cost of operations and all income or loss is carried by the cheese.

The production manager does not completely agree with this approach because the cost allocated is still a function of the market value of the whey. The belief that an accurate cost is needed to establish sales policy is still strong.

Because of their inability to solve the issue, they consulted the controller and president to determine whether a $0.50 per pound sales offer for the whey should be accepted.

Required:

a. Evaluate the following bases proposed:
   (1) The production manager's allocation of material resulting in an $0.82 cost per pound of total output.
   (2) The marketing manager's allocation resulting in a $0.25 cost per pound of whey.
   (3) The marketing manager's by-product allocation.
b. Suggest other appropriate bases and determine the cost per pound of cheese and whey using these bases.
c. Determine if the offer of $0.50 per pound of whey should be accepted.

PART III

Cost Data for Performance Evaluation

CHAPTER 10

Strategic Planning and Budgeting

Chapter Objectives

After studying this chapter, you should be able to:

1. Discuss how top managers implement their important roles in strategic planning by providing the frameworks for effective budgeting.
2. Explain the advantages of budgets as a management tool for performance evaluation.
3. Distinguish between variances obtained using fixed budgets and variances obtained using flexible budgets.
4. Prepare budgets in the master budget plan.

Introduction

Budgeting is a means of coordinating the combined intelligence of an entire organization into a plan of action. This plan is based on past performance and governed by rational judgments about factors influencing the course of business in the future. Without the coordination provided by budgeting, department heads may follow courses beneficial for their own departments, but not for the overall company. Budgeting control is a companywide operation with a complete plan of execution—a program that encompasses much more than monetary aspects. Many behavioral factors are inherent in the budgeting process. For example, employees are more willing to accept departmental budgets if managers make honest attempts to explain the budgeting procedure and to involve them in the process.

Master budgets include both operating and financing budgets. This chapter discusses **operating budgets,** whose focus is the acquisition and use of scarce resources. As discussed in the next chapter, **financial budgets,** such as cash budgets, direct attention to acquiring funds to obtain resources. Chapters 20 and 21 discuss capital budgeting and provide definite procedures and methods for evaluating each proposed project's merit.

Accountants prepare effective operating budgets using a flexible budgeting approach. Flexible budgets are useful for determining the efficiency of operations because their use involves comparing the actual costs at an output level to a budget adjusted to that actual activity level. A flexible budgeting approach eliminates distortions due to volume variations.

Role of Strategic Planning

Through strategic planning top-level managers develop and implement long-term organizational goals and policies. **Strategic planning** provides the compass for a company's activities in its quest to determine and meet customer wants. Managers evaluate their organizations' strengths and weaknesses to emphasize external opportunities and internal strengths. Their strategic plans then provide direction in selecting what products or services to sell and what consumer markets to target. Also, these plans outline how to promote and distribute such products and services; budgets reflect these plans.

Managers prepare budgets in numerous ways depending on the strategic plans and desired complexity. Even simple budgets offer many external and internal advantages. Budgets make the decision-making process more effective by helping managers meet uncertainties. The objective of budgeting is to substitute deliberate, well-conceived business judgment for accidental success in enterprise management. Budgets should not be expressions of wishful thinking but rather descriptions of attainable objectives. Certainly, budgets reflect plans—managers must plan before preparing budgets.

Communication, Coordination, and Performance Evaluation

The general operating budget or annual profit plan is not only an important operating tool but also represents a formal communication channel within a company. In the initial phase of the budgetary process, managers are forced to communicate with each other. This process encourages necessary coordination among segment activities as managers consider the organization structure and interrelationship among

Strategic Planning

Current Cost Management Practice

Colgate's chief executive, Reuben Mark, expected to lift the firm's gross margin from 39 percent in 1984 to nearly 48 percent in 1993. The fatter gross margins are, the more a company can spend on advertising; advertising and promotion are investments in the value of any consumer franchise. Mark contended that 1994's sharp slippage in toothpaste and soap volume was brought on primarily by inventory adjustments by retailers when Colgate shifted its emphasis to an everyday low pricing policy. This policy uses price to encourage retailers to buy just enough for their immediate needs rather than stocking up several times a year when special promotional prices are offered. When Colgate introduced this policy, retailers had to run down their sizable inventories before placing new orders. The chief executive also is whittling away at costs, spending 60 percent of the company's $415 million 1994 capital spending budget on investments in cost reduction. The hurdle rate for such investment is a 20 percent aftertax return, suggesting that Mark plans to cut $50 million annually out of costs. Another part of Mark's strategy is to keep coming up with new high-margin products.

Howard Rudnitsky, "Making His Mark," *Forbes,* September 26, 1994, pp. 47–48.

segments. Because budgets force managers to plan, they exchange views about where they want the company to be in the next 5 or 10 years. In this process, different views of future company objectives usually arise; the budgeting process helps managers to compromise. When this compromise is not made, each company segment could follow a course of action that benefits only itself, not the entire company. If the budgeting process does not facilitate long-range planning, management is likely to be concerned with meeting only daily operational goals. Coordination is best achieved using a participative budgeting approach in which all managers provide input into the goal setting process.

Budgets represent management's formal commitment to take positive actions to make actual events correspond to the strategic plan. Profit plans also contain explicit statements concerning implementation of management objectives for a period of time; managers communicate these to all parties with control responsibility. Comparison of actual results with the profit plan forms the basis for management control, motivation, and performance evaluation.

Cost accounting provides the total and detailed costs of the products manufactured or the services provided by a company. To measure their efficiency, costs must be compared with a yardstick that was prepared in advance of production and that reflects a good level of performance. The most common method of evaluating actual performance is through budget analysis. Combining a standard cost system with budgets also leads to better performance of assigned tasks and goals.

Budgets and Standards

As discussed in Chapters 12 and 13, standard costs serve as building blocks when constructing budgets. Budgets are statements of expected costs and forecasts of production requirements. Budgets attempt to set up a predetermined standard of operations for a period or project taken as a whole, while standards are concerned with cost per unit. Thus, when using standard costs, the budget is largely a summary of standards for all items of revenue and expense.

The following list summarizes a few of the advantages a formalized system of budgeting or profit planning offers:

1. It obligates management to specify objectives for the short and long run.
2. It forces management to analyze future problems so they recognize alternative plans.
3. It directs effort and funds toward the most profitable of possible alternatives.
4. It emphasizes the need for coordination of all elements of a company since budgeting reveals a lack of control in an organization.
5. It serves as a means of communication.
6. It provides performance standards that serve as incentives to perform more effectively.
7. It indicates those areas lacking control by providing data used to analyze variances between actual and budgeted operations. These variances should provide the springboard for study of the source of the problem.

Principles of Budgeting

General principles apply to the budgeting process. Top management's support is crucial to the success of the budgetary program. Top management's philosophy toward budgeting soon filters down in the company even though executives may not realize their importance in the process. When managers view the budget as some mechanical process to complete as quickly as possible, their employees are less likely to give budget preparation much attention. The budgeting process also fails if management views budgets as a scapegoat on which to blame company problems. On the other hand, if management considers the budget an excellent means of planning and takes an active role in the budgeting process, a company is more likely to gain many benefits.

Relation to Organizational Structure and Environment

Accountants should design budgetary control systems around each organization's formal structure because of the necessary differentiation and integration between areas of the organization. Integration is especially important when the output of one area is the input of another area. **Decentralization** or **differentiation** is the degree to which managers have freedom to use their own management techniques and make their own decisions. Generally, the larger the organizational size and more complex the technology, the greater the degree of decentralization. The compilation of a comprehensive budget requires integration among segments.

The size and technology of an organization also determine the degree of individual participation in the budgeting process. In a small firm, many employees can participate, while participation in a large firm may be limited to managers. In high-technology firms, changes often occur so rapidly there is no time available for full participation. In low-technology firms, there can be a more definite period for preparation, allowing the additional time that participation requires.

Budgetary control systems cannot function properly in isolation from the operational context of the organization—the separation from reality makes them ineffective. The efficiency of a department depends on factors internal to a cost center, external to a cost center, and external to the company. The internal factors are more important for a production department. External factors are vital for a research and development department, and both external and exogenous factors play an essential role for a marketing department. To increase effectiveness, managers should consider the turbulence of the environment in selecting control mechanisms.

Budget Revisions

Changes in conditions both inside and outside the company may justify revising budgets, rather than using unattainable budgets. When companies fail to adjust budgets for external unforeseen situations, frustration can result. For example, additional competitors may enter the market and make meeting budgeted market share and sales unlikely, despite increased promotional expenditures. However, companies should not revise budgets every time they fail to meet budgeted goals because this type of revising defeats the control functions of budgets. Top managers usually approve or make budget revisions.

Budget Committee

Line management has the responsibility for the preparation of individual budgets. To do this, they need technical, unbiased assistance. The president or chief executive officer normally establishes budgeting principles. The budget committee generally directs and executes all budget procedures. The budget committee serves as a consulting body to the budget officer; members include the budget director and top executives representing all company financial segments.

Because the budget committee's functions include coordination of all planning, the committee should review and evaluate all reports prepared at the initiation of the budgetary system. A company can more easily eliminate duplication if the budget committee prepares a list of the reports to supply the information needed. The budget committee then asks other managers within the company whether these reports are sufficient. Otherwise, given the normal resistance to change, most managers would continue to request reports, even if they are redundant. After preparing budgets, the budget committee continues in an advisory capacity, periodically reviewing the budget and approving budget changes as conditions warrant.

Budget Manual.   The budget committee's functions also include reviewing and approving budget estimates and suggesting revisions. It should review segment budgets to determine whether they are excessively optimistic, conservative, or make provision for slack. The committee also has the responsibility of recommending action to improve efficiency where necessary. In addition, it is helpful for the budget committee to prepare a policy manual as a reference for implementation of a budget program. This manual has long-range usefulness because it documents procedures.

Budget Director.   The budget director, who serves in a staff capacity, is usually the controller or someone reporting to the controller. The budget director requests estimates of the cost of running each cost center from department heads and supervisors. Similarly, sales executives submit sales estimates. The budget director also should supply executives with information about past operations to guide them in the preparation of new budgets. Many accountants fail as budget directors, not because they lack accounting knowledge, but because they cannot recognize the administrative problems inherent in the budgeting process. The success of budget directors in generating goodwill toward themselves and the budget department is crucial to the success of the budget program.

Length of Budget Period

Generally, a company's budget corresponds to the fiscal period used in the accounting system. Budgets can be short or long range. While the long-range budget lacks the detail supplied by a short-range operational budget, it does provide broad guidelines. For example, a long-range budget covering as many as 5 or 10 years anticipates long-term needs and opportunities that may require the company to take definite steps in the short run. Because long-range budgets are subject to many changes, they may not be circulated among middle and lower management. Short-term budgets have the advantage of being more accurate since they reflect shorter periods.

Some companies prepare detailed **rolling,** also known as **continuous, budgets.** Using a rolling budget means that at the end of May of each year, the company adds a budget for May of the next year. As each month ends, companies add a new 12th month. With this method, companies always have a detailed 12-month budget in advance. Rolling budgets incorporate changing economic conditions into the plans each time companies add a new month. Budgeting thus becomes a continual process rather than a once-a-year task.

Other companies prepare their annual budgets in two phases. They detail the first half of the year and summarize the remaining six months by quarters in less detail. They prepare a new, short-range, detailed budget every six months, partly on the basis of earlier summarized data and partly on the results of the previous six months.

Bottom-Up Budgeting Approach

Budgets should follow the lines of responsibility and authority of organization charts. Clear lines of authority and responsibility can remove any questions about which individual to hold accountable for each expenditure. An organization chart should identify employees whose operations justify a budget.

There is little purpose to setting goals if the individuals who must meet these goals are unaware of their existence. Holding a person responsible for a level of achievement that he or she does not know about is an unfair management practice. Failure to communicate results to involved parties also is unfair. The more rapidly a company communicates results, the greater the chance that employees will make needed corrections and achieve more efficient performance.

The development of an annual profit plan employing a bottom-up approach uses the following steps. A **bottom-up approach** combines budgets at successively higher levels of management. This approach also indicates the level of management involved and the nature and direction of the communication process.

1. Identification of planning guidelines by top management. All levels of management are involved and communication is downward.
2. Preparation of the general operating budget or profit plan beginning with a sales budget. Lower levels of management receive sales targets providing a basis for the preparation of production budgets and other components. Consultation with a higher (middle) management level may be needed to arrive at certain aspects of the specific manager's budget. The communication process is primarily lateral with some upward communication possible.

3. Negotiation may be necessary to arrive at final plans; communication is upward.

4. Coordination and review of the profit plan; top-level management makes recommendations and returns the various plans to middle-level management. After middle management makes these changes, the plan is resubmitted for approval. Communication is generally downward; however, there may be some lateral communication during the adjustment phase.

5. Final approval and distribution of the formal plan; top management gives final approval and communicates its decision downward.

If the company is of any size, accomplishing these steps in implementing a budget takes time. Employees may resent the time and effort devoted to budgeting especially if managers present budgets as abstract listings of numerical data. Rather, managers should translate the quantitative data into individual human endeavor. This translation shows how the company's objectives will be reached and what equipment, material, and personnel are required. By involving employees, budgets are more likely to reflect changing conditions. Most companies experience drastically changeable market conditions and few completely predictable situations.

Fixed (Static) and Flexible (Variable) Budgeting

To reflect the changing environment and obtain the full advantages of budgeting, companies should use a flexible, not a fixed, budget. A **fixed** or **static budget** approach estimates costs for a single activity volume and does not adjust the budget when actual volume differs. Actual results are compared later with this one budget. Fixed budgeting is appropriate only if a company can estimate its operating volume within close limits and if the costs are behaving predictably. Few companies are fortunate enough to fall into this group. As a result of these factors, a fixed budget is generally not adequate.

A flexible budget is an alternative to the fixed budget. A **flexible,** or **variable, budget** adjusts revenues, costs, and expenses to the actual volume experienced, and compares these amounts to actual results. Flexible budgets incorporate changes in volume to provide a valid basis of comparison with actual costs.

Fixed and Flexible Budget Variances Compared

Exhibits 10–1 through 10–3 illustrate the problems that can arise from using a fixed or static budget and why flexible budgets are more appropriate. Flexible budgets also include revenue as well as variable and fixed marketing and administrative expenses. To simplify the example, the budgets illustrated in Exhibits 10–1 through 10–3 include only production costs.

Exhibit 10–1 shows the fixed budget for one cost center for January. Managers expected Cost Center A to produce 1,000 units, each requiring two hours of machine time, and they estimated costs at that level. However, monthly production was only 900 units. Exhibit 10–1 compares the costs incurred to produce 900 units with the fixed budget for 1,000 units. In this case, management may believe incorrectly that costs are under control because all variable costs have favorable variances. However, the variable costs to produce 900 units should be less than those to produce 1,000 units. Even though fixed costs are generally easier to estimate in the short run, actual fixed costs may vary from budgeted fixed costs. As shown in Exhibit 10–1, the two fixed costs vary from their budgeted amounts.

EXHIBIT 10–1 Performance Report Using Fixed Budget

	Budget	Actual	Variance	
COST CENTER A				
Performance Report Using a Fixed Budget				
For the Month Beginning January, 19X1				
Units	1,000	900	100	units
Machine-hours	2,000	1,800	200	hours
Variable costs:				
Direct material.....................	$ 1,000	$ 980	$ 20	favorable
Direct labor........................	4,000	3,820	180	favorable
Factory overhead:				
Indirect material	3,000	2,600	400	favorable
Indirect labor......................	8,500	8,400	100	favorable
Factory utilities....................	2,000	1,800	200	favorable
Total variable costs.................	$18,500	$17,600	$900	favorable
Fixed costs:				
Factory overhead:				
Depreciation—production equipment.......	$ 900	$ 960	$ 60	unfavorable
Rent—manufacturing building............	600	570	30	favorable
Total fixed costs....................	$ 1,500	$ 1,530	$ 30	unfavorable
Total costs	$20,000	$19,130	$870	favorable

Cost of Acquired Resources Not Utilized

Fixed budget variances mislead managers regarding the impact of not using all acquired resources. Fixed cost must now be shared by only 1,800 machine-hours rather than the estimated 2,000 hours. Cost Center A incurred idle capacity costs because it did not fully use its budgeted capacity. Managers cannot ignore market demand; if the consumer demand is only 900 units, a cost center should not produce 1,000 units. Instead, management needs to expand into other product lines or reduce its resource spending for capacity. Exhibits 10–2 and 10–3 depict a flexible (variable) budget, which more accurately describes the cost situation.

With flexible budgets, costs can be different in each month or in selected months according to seasonal variation and the activity of the cost center. Accountants, on the other hand, do not adjust fixed budgets to the actual volume attained. Instead, they base the fixed budget on certain definite assumed conditions and compare actual results with this point fixed in advance. A fixed budget is satisfactory only when a company can estimate its activities within close limits.

Exhibit 10–2 gives the **flexible budget formula** for fixed and variable cost behavior used to compute budgeted costs at any capacity level. In Chapter 3 we refer to this formula as the **cost estimating function** used to estimate cost behavior. The flexible budget formula for *production cost* is $18.50 per unit and $1,500 per month.

Expressing factory overhead on an hourly basis is often more appropriate than on a unit basis. Thus, we generally restate output in the quantity of labor or machine-hours it takes to produce budgeted units. In this case, factory overhead is $6.75 per machine-hour ($3,000 + $8,500 + $2,000 = $13,500/2,000 budgeted hours = $6.75) and $1,500 per month. Should Cost Center A select 1,600 machine-hours, rather than 2,000 machine-hours, as normal capacity, the budgeted production cost is $10.1875 per machine-hour ($16,300/1,600 budgeted hours = $10.1875).

EXHIBIT 10–2 Flexible Budgets Illustrated for Various Volume Levels

COST CENTER A
Flexible Budgets for Various Projected Activity Levels
January 19X1

	Various Levels of Activity (Budgeted)			Budget Formula
Units	800	1,000	1,400	
Machine-hours	1,600	2,000	2,800	
Variable costs:				
Direct materials	$ 800	$ 1,000	$ 1,400	$ 1.00 per unit
Direct labor	3,200	4,000	5,600	4.00 per unit
Indirect materials	2,400	3,000	4,200	3.00 per unit
Indirect labor	6,800	8,500	11,900	8.50 per unit
Factory utilities	1,600	2,000	2,800	2.00 per unit
Total variable costs	$14,800	$18,500	$25,900	$18.50 per unit
Fixed costs:				
Depreciation—production equipment	$ 900	$ 900	$ 900	$ 900 per month
Rent—manufacturing building	600	600	600	600 per month
Total fixed overhead	$ 1,500	$ 1,500	$ 1,500	$1,500 per month
Total costs	$16,300	$20,000	$27,400	$18.50 per unit and $1,500 per month
Cost per unit	$20.375	$ 20.00	$19.572	

Choice of Activity Level.   For simplicity, we expressed the flexible budget formula on a single basis, machine-hours. As Chapter 5 discusses, the type of activity determines which volume-related or nonvolume-related cost driver is most appropriate. For example, if accountants establish flexible budgets on direct labor-hours in a machine-paced environment, misleading conclusions may arise from the variances computed. Many variable overhead costs in an automated manufacturing setting do not vary with direct labor as assumed by a flexible budget formula expressed on a direct labor basis. Instead, variable overhead in an automated manufacturing setting varies with other measures of activity such as machine-hours, kilowatt-hours, setups, and materials.

Also, the use of only one activity measure reduces the ability of the cost system to predict the variation in cost with changes in the volume and mix of actual production. Instead, use of multiple bases for different cost centers better reflects cost behavior. By breaking their factories down into various production centers, companies can use different overhead rates on the basis of the level of technology, types of machines, and services in each center.

Exhibit 10–2 shows a series of three possible volumes—800, 1,000, and 1,400 units, all within the relevant range of this cost center. Accountants prepare these different flexible budgets for various levels of projected volume before operations begin on January 1, 19X1. Just because Exhibit 10–2 illustrates more than one budget, do not assume that accountants must prepare many budgets under a flexible budgeting approach. This is not correct. As shown in Exhibits 10–1 and 10–2, Cost Center A's preestablished budgets did not reflect in advance the actual volume obtained of 900 units or 1,800 machine-hours. Indeed, the chances are very small of preparing a budget in advance with a volume that coincides exactly with actual volume. A flexible budgeting approach only requires a forecast of total costs at the estimated volume level. If actual volume differs from expected volume, we adjust the budget to actual volume at the end of the period. By having a flexible budget formula, a budget adjusted to or allowed for actual volume is easy to compute at the end of the accounting period.

Using the data in Exhibit 10–1, an actual performance report using a flexible budget yields the variances for actual production shown in Exhibit 10–3. For example, we compare $8,400 actual indirect labor costs to $7,650 ($8.50 × 900 units = $7,650) budgeted costs, yielding a $750 unfavorable variance. Instead of a $900 favorable net variance for variable costs shown in a fixed budget in Exhibit 10–1, the variance is $950 unfavorable. Comparing the costs of operations for 900 units against a budget prepared for the same volume judges the efficiency of the cost center more accurately.

EXHIBIT 10–3 Performance Report Using Flexible Budget

COST CENTER A
Performance Report Using a Flexible Budget
Assuming 900 Units Produced
For the Month Beginning January, 19X1

	Budget Adjusted to Actual Volume	Actual	Variance
Units	900	900	–0–
Machine-hours	1,800	1,800	
Variable costs:			
Direct material	$ 900	$ 980	$ 80 unfavorable
Direct labor	3,600	3,820	220 unfavorable
Factory overhead:			
Indirect material	2,700	2,600	100 favorable
Indirect labor	7,650	8,400	750 unfavorable
Factory utilities	1,800	1,800	–0–
Total variable costs	$16,650	$17,600	$950 unfavorable
Fixed costs:			
Factory overhead:			
Depreciation—production equipment	$ 900	$ 960	$ 60 unfavorable
Rent—manufacturing building	600	570	30 favorable
Total fixed costs	$ 1,500	$ 1,530	$ 30 unfavorable
Total costs	$18,150	$19,130	$980 favorable

Master Budget

The master budget for a manufacturing company covers various types of budgets; additional budget schedules support many of these. This book illustrates the following types of budgets:

1. Sales budget broken down by

       a. Territory and product.

       b. Territory, product, and customer grouping.

  2. Production budget in units.

  3. Direct materials purchases budget.

  4. Direct labor budget.*

  5. Factory overhead budget.*

  6. Cost of goods sold budget.

  7. Marketing and administrative budgets. *(Chapter 11)*

  8. Research and development budget. *(Chapter 11)*

  9. Budgeted income statement. *(Chapter 11)*

10. Budgeted statement of cash receipts and disbursements. *(Chapter 11)*

11. Capital expenditure budget. *(Chapters 20 and 21)*

12. Budgeted balance sheet. *(Chapter 11)*

*Can be combined with direct material in a manufacturing budget estimate.

Master Budget Interrelationships	The budget preparation process flows from strategic plans through the sales budget supported by sales forecasts to the projected financial statements as shown in Exhibit 10–4. The resulting budgeted income statement and balance sheet incorporate elements from all budgets and schedules prepared. The budgeting process begins with management's plans and objectives for the next period. These plans result in various policy decisions concerning selling price, distribution network, advertising expenditures, and environmental influences. Managers prepare sales forecasts for the period (in units by product or product line) from this information. Multiplying units by selling price gives the sales budget in dollars.

Volume and inventory policies influence the preparation of the direct materials purchases budget and the production budget. Accountants base the cost of goods sold budget on expected production, sales volume, and inventory policy. They make detailed budgets for each major type of manufacturing, marketing, and administrative expense on both a cost center (responsibility) basis and in the aggregate. Accountants prepare a budgeted balance sheet using information contained in the budgeted income statement. Policy decisions about dividends, inventory, credit, capital expenditures, and financial plans also influence balance sheets.

Sales Forecasts

Before preparing the master budget, companies prepare a forecast of sales for the budget period. Sales forecasts usually determine the activity level on which a company establishes all budgets. However, if a company can sell more than it can produce, it must first consider its production constraint. For example, if a company can sell 1,000 units but its manufacturing facilities can produce only 750 units, it bases all budgets on a 750-units activity level unless it acquires additional production facilities.

Internal factors, such as the historical sales pattern, desired profit, product characteristics (whether it is a new product or a seasonal one), and sales force estimates also influence a sales forecast. Among other things, managers analyze previous period sales and other information for possible fluctuations caused by seasonal variations, economic cycles, and labor strikes. However, historical sales may not

EXHIBIT 10–4   Interrelationships among Strategic Plans and Budgets

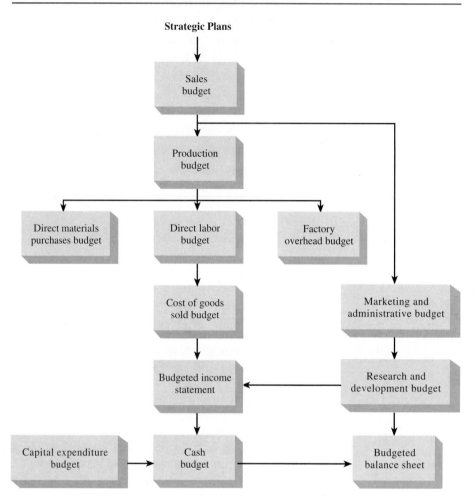

fully reflect previous period demand because most companies have no record of unfilled orders. A figure closer to past demand is unfilled orders added to past sales; unfortunately this figure usually is unavailable.

Many external economic and social conditions—such as government monetary and fiscal policies for taxation and international trade—and the technological, social, and legal environment affect future sales. Industry prospects, purchasing power of the population, population shifts, and changes in buying habits are important considerations. If managers can establish a causal relationship, more accurate sales estimates result. For example, historical data may reveal a relationship between a company's sales and personal discretionary income or gross national product. A company also may study the relationships of its products with each other. A company should make allowances for varying conditions that affect products, territories, or the strength of competitors. For example, changes in the company's sales promotion or that of its competitors affect sales.

Productivity

Current Cost Management Practice

While Pepsi-Cola North American may admit it got the wrong one, baby, wrong taste, wrong name, and wrong packaging and advertising on Crystal Pepsi, it is not ready to call it quits on this product. Crystal Pepsi represents the company's year-old stab at creating a clear cola. They plan to change the name to just Crystal and remove hints of cinnamon, ginger, and pepper, but keep it clear. Also, Crystal will be reincarnated as a citrus cola. Crystal Pepsi won only half of the U.S. soft-drink market projected for it the first year. Pepsi recognizes it was not able to satisfy people's taste. For the past three years, Pepsi has been at the forefront with an ambitious multibrand strategy that has led it into everything from fruit juices to iced tea to sports drinks. Pepsi's iced tea has made some inroads. However, industry consultants worry that the flurry of new products in its multibrand strategy has diverted Pepsi's attention from the mother brands of Pepsi and Diet Pepsi. They believe people are still loading up on fat, sugar, and caffeine—emphasizing that Pepsi's best assets may be those old-fashioned colas.

Laura Zinn, "Does Pepsi Have Too Many Products?" *BusinessWeek*, February 14, 1994, pp. 64–66.

*Employees'
Experienced
Judgment*

The methods of estimating future sales vary widely depending on the products sold and channels of distribution used. A company's sales force can supply supervisors with sales estimates for their territories. Not only is information gained from a first-hand source but this also can stimulate the salespersons' interest in the budgeting process. District marketing managers should review each of these individual estimates because often they are biased.

Executives also can refine sales estimates determined through other sources, as in the bottom-up approach. Executive experience provides subjective estimates of factors that are difficult to quantify, such as general economic and industry conditions, competition, and the quality of the sales force. At other times, companies begin their sales forecasting process with estimates from key executives.

*Trend and
Correlation
Analysis*

Past experience alone is not sufficient to forecast sales; therefore, most companies use a marketing research department or outside market research firm, that centrally develops and analyzes the sales forecast data. Using correlation analysis, cycle projection, and trend analysis, market researchers arrive at projected sales. The market research department also may use motivation research to measure the factors influencing consumers' decisions. They study the subconscious motives of buyers using word association, in-depth interviews, and other behavioral science techniques. Such techniques may be of more use in making industry forecasts than in a sales forecast for a single company. Statistical forecasting techniques are most effective for products having stable market patterns. For products with markets that fluctuate considerably and require extensive sales promotion, subjective estimates are appropriate.

Market researchers may study actual sales for several years in the past as well as for the corresponding period in the previous year to project a **trend.** Using only historical sales data in forecasting has some weaknesses because some of the company's policies may have changed, which, in turn, affects future sales. For example, improved quality may have created a higher demand for the product. The company may have adopted more liberal credit terms. Managers should give the most recent historical data more significance than older data when using moving averages of past sales data, rather than an average of all available data for specific past periods. Plotting sales for previous periods on a moving-average basis may forecast secular or long-term trends.

Correlation analysis attempts to establish the relationship between the values of two attributes—that is, the relationship between an economic indicator (independent variable) and sales (dependent variable). Companies frequently use an economic indicator such as the Gross National Product (GNP) or a forecast of personal income. To use this method, the indicator must be predictable. A relationship also must exist between the indicator and the product for which sales are being forecasted. For example, in predicting sales for baby bottles, the projected birthrate is the independent variable. This relationship can predict sales for the entire industry or for one firm.

To illustrate this sales forecasting method, assume a relationship between personal computers and per capita income. Managers can use regression analysis, introduced in Chapter 3, to estimate the linear relation between computers and income. Assume that regression analysis indicates that the line crosses the vertical axis at 150,000 personal computers and that the slope of the line is 12 personal computers per dollar of per capita income. Exhibit 10–5 plots this equation, $Y = 150,000 + 12x$. If managers predict a $20,000 per capita income, a sales forecast of 390,000 personal computers results.

EXHIBIT 10–5   Using Regression Analysis in Predicting Sales

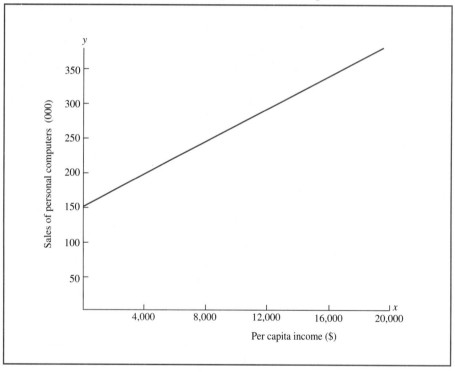

Documentation. Forecasters should document their underlying assumptions for each forecast, major sources of information, and the techniques used to arrive at the final forecast. Documentation of the data provides a good source for reviewing the accuracy of the forecast and for refining assumptions. If a sales forecast is unrealistic, all budgets, in turn, become poor planning tools.

EXHIBIT 10–6 Sales Budget

HART COMPANY
Sales Budget
For Year Ending December 31, 19X2

	Men's Pants		Suits		Dresses		
	Quantity	Sales	Quantity	Sales	Quantity	Sales	Total
January ...	100	$10,000	1,150	$138,000	800	$144,000	$292,000
February ..	120	$12,000	980	$117,600	770	$138,600	$268,200
March	110	$11,000	1,000	$120,000	650	$117,000	$248,000
April	115	$11,500	1,080	$129,600	600	$108,000	$249,100
May	140	$14,000	1,200	$144,000	680	$122,400	$280,400
June	150	$15,000	1,250	$150,000	725	$130,500	$295,500
July	145	$14,500	1,375	$165,000	780	$140,400	$319,900
August ...	155	$15,500	1,400	$168,000	820	$147,600	$331,100
September .	160	$16,000	1,500	$180,000	850	$153,000	$349,000
October ...	150	$15,000	1,600	$192,000	900	$162,000	$369,000
November .	145	$14,500	1,770	$212,400	925	$166,500	$393,400
December .	130	$13,000	1,800	$216,000	975	$175,500	$404,500
Total ...	1,620	$162,000	16,105	$1,932,600	9,475	$1,705,500	$3,800,100

Territorial Sales Budget

The sales budget in Exhibit 10–6 classifies product sales by months. A sales budget also can indicate whether purchasers are wholesalers, retailers, government agencies, or foreign buyers. With this customer breakdown, management can better determine the percentage of sales generated by each group. To simplify, the budgets illustrated in Exhibits 10–6 through 10–13 do not indicate customer groups or individual territories. They use only combined data.

Production-Related Budgets

After completing the sales budget, managers prepare a production budget stating the physical units to manufacture. The production budget is the sales budget adjusted for any changes in inventory, as follows:

Units to produce = Budgeted sales
　　　　　　　+ Desired ending finished goods inventory
　　　　　　　+ Desired equivalent units in ending work in process inventory
　　　　　　　− Beginning finished goods inventory
　　　　　　　− Equivalent units in beginning work in process inventory

　　　　Note that we can apply the budgeting formula, Sources = Uses, for many budgeting decisions. For example, Beginning inventory (a source) + Units to produce (a source) = Desired ending inventory (a use) + Budgeted withdrawals for sales (a use). Solving for units to produce, accountants mathematically derive the production budget from its necessary antecedent, the sales budget.

　　　　Although their sales may be of a seasonal nature, many companies tend to stabilize their production through inventory. That is, inventory is the buffer absorbing extra production when demand is slack and from which they draw units during heavy demand periods. If work in process inventory does not constitute a significant portion of the inventory, managers can ignore partially completed goods. They also can ignore them if a company does not extend the production cycle as in pull systems using a just-in-time approach. Assume Hart Company's records provide the following inventory data and their stage of completion. Management supplies desired ending inventory information.

	Work in Process Inventory				Finished Goods Inventory	
Product	*Beginning Units*	*Percent Processed*	*Ending Units*	*Percent Processed*	*Beginning Units*	*Ending Units*
Men's pants	50	10%	100	20%	65	80
Suits	200	40	300	50	395	350
Dresses	100	30	400	80	495	130

Production Budget

Exhibit 10–7 illustrates a production budget using work in process and finished goods inventory. The production budget in Exhibit 10–8 reflects production each quarter for one product. (Note we cannot add horizontally the equivalent units in inventory to yield the total for 19X2. Instead, we use 70 beginning and 100 ending equivalent units for the year.)

The two production budgets in Exhibits 10–7 and 10–8 are readily adaptable for a company manufacturing a standard product. However, for a company that manufactures only after receipt of a customer order, plans have to be less detailed. Preferably, a company uses standardized direct material parts in production, thus allowing it to budget in a similar manner. The important factor in job order costing, performing manufacturing to customer specification, is to avoid delays and costly overtime by properly routing and scheduling work through the factory.

To provide as smooth a flow of production as possible, management should coordinate the marketing and production budgets. Often marketing personnel are not fully aware of the plant capacity available. They may fail to consider what the company's manufacturing facilities can produce. They may have to shift marketing efforts

EXHIBIT 10–7   Total Production Budget

HART COMPANY
Total Production Budget
For Year Ending December 31, 19X2

	Men's Pants	*Suits*	*Dresses*
Units required for sales (from Exhibit 10–6)	1,620	16,105	9,475
Add ending inventory of finished units	80	350	130
Total finished units required	1,700	16,455	9,605
Less beginning inventory of finished units	65	395	495
Units to be transferred to finished goods	1,635	16,060	9,110
Add ending work in process inventory (in equivalent units)	20	150	320
	1,655	16,210	9,430
Less beginning work in process inventory (in equivalent units)	5	80	30
Equivalent units to be produced	1,650	16,130	9,400

EXHIBIT 10–8 Production Budget for One Product

HART COMPANY
Men's Pants Production Budget
By Quarter for Year Ending December 31, 19X2

	First	Second	Third	Fourth	Total
Planned pant sales	330	405	460	425	1,620
Desired ending equivalent units					
in inventory	60	65	85	100	100
Total units to provide for	390	470	545	525	1,720
Less beginning equivalent units					
in inventory	70	60	65	85	70
Pants to be produced	320	410	480	440	1,650

to avoid idle capacity and to fully utilize production facilities. Because the production budget determines the volume of manufacturing operations, it becomes the basis for the direct materials purchases budget, labor budget, and factory overhead budget.

Direct Materials Purchases Budget

After determining the number of units of each product they plan to manufacture, managers calculate the materials each operation requires. They then combine these requirements in a direct materials purchases budget, as shown in Exhibit 10–9. Managers prepare the budget in the unit of measure (pounds, yards, etc.) used for

EXHIBIT 10–9 Direct Materials Purchases Budget

HART COMPANY
Direct Material Purchases Budget
For Year Ending December 31, 19X2

	Fabric	Buttons	Total
Units needed for production (from below)	88,270	48,260	
Desired ending direct materials inventory	4,500	2,500	
Total material units to provide for	92,770	50,760	
Less: Beginning direct materials inventory	5,000	1,900	
Units to be purchased	87,770	48,860	
Unit purchase price	$ 2.50	$ 1.10	
Total purchase cost	$219,425	$53,746	$273,171

**Direct Material Usage
Production**

Finished Units	Men's Pants (1,650 Units)	Suits (16,130 Units)	Dresses (9,400 Units)	Total Direct Material Usage	Material Unit Cost	Cost of Material Used
Fabric (3 yards for pants,						
4 for suits, 2 for dresses) . .	4,950	64,520	18,800	88,270	$2.50	$220,675
Buttons (4 buttons for pants,						
2 for suits, 1 for dresses) . .	6,600	32,260	9,400	48,260	$1.10	53,086
						$273,761

the material. Exhibit 10–9 shows only two different material items to keep the illustration simple. Managers indicate the desired level of ending direct materials inventory they wish to maintain. If they use a **just-in-time system,** inventory represents only the amount needed in production until the next order arrives. They do not need to stockpile inventory. For the just-in-time system to operate efficiently, suppliers must be reliable and provide parts of high quality. Inventory records show the beginning direct materials inventory balance.

Exhibit 10–9 summarizes the annual direct material needs, with data obtained from the monthly budgets for each direct material. Exhibit 10–10 illustrates the production and inventory requirements for fabric material broken down on a quarterly basis. We can prepare a similar budget for each item of direct material, especially for the significant material items. Exhibits 10–9 and 10–10 show only direct material, since the factory overhead budget usually shows indirect material and supplies.

EXHIBIT 10–10   Purchases Budget for One Material

HART COMPANY
Fabric Material Purchase Budget
By Quarter for Year Ending December 31, 19X2

	First	Second	Third	Fourth	Total
Yards needed for production	17,955	19,370	23,385	27,560	88,270
Desired ending direct materials inventory	3,000	4,200	4,600	4,500	4,500
Total material units to provide for	20,955	23,570	27,985	32,060	92,770
Less: beginning direct materials inventory	5,000	3,000	4,200	4,600	5,000
Units to be purchased	15,955	20,570	23,785	27,460	87,770
Unit purchase price.	$ 2.50	$ 2.50	$ 2.50	$ 2.50	$ 2.50
Total purchase cost	$39,887	$51,425	$59,463	$68,650	$219,425

Note again that in determining units to purchase, we apply the formula, Sources = Uses, as follows: Beginning inventory (a source) + Purchases (a source) = Desired ending inventory (a use) + Units needed for production (a use). By solving for Purchases, we derive mathematically the direct materials purchases budget from its necessary antecedent, the production budget.

Direct Labor Budget

The direct labor budget reflects the number of units to be produced according to the production budget. Generally, this budget includes only direct labor as indirect labor is part of the factory overhead budget. The information provided in the direct labor budget guides a Personnel Department in filling positions so the required employee skills are available. By referring to the annual direct labor budget, the Personnel Department has time to make arrangements to either hire or lay off workers. After determining the number of direct labor-hours needed per period, accountants translate the hours into dollars by applying appropriate labor rates. Exhibit 10–11 illustrates a summarized annual direct labor budget assuming Hart Company pays only one wage rate. Each department should have detailed monthly budgets.

EXHIBIT 10–11   Direct Labor Budget

HART COMPANY
Direct Labor Budget
For the Year Ending December 31, 19X2

	Units Produced	Direct Labor-Hours per Unit	Total Hours	Total Budget @ $20 per Hour
Men's Pants..............	1,650	1	1,650	$ 33,000
Suits.................	16,130	.6	9,678	193,560
Dresses	9,400	1	9,400	188,000
			20,728	$414,560

Factory Overhead Budget

Even though we can group factory overhead expenses in several ways, such as by function, cost behavior, or department, usually we use the natural expense classification. However, the natural expense classification, which involves such categories as utilities, indirect labor, and indirect material, has limited usefulness for budgeting purposes. Instead, we should prepare factory overhead budgets for each cost center so the cost centers' supervisors are held accountable and responsible for the costs incurred. Budget should distinguish between controllable and noncontrollable costs so supervisors are held accountable for only those expenses over which they have control. An annual factory overhead budget similar to the one in Exhibit 10–12 summarizes each departmental factory overhead budget. Exhibit 10–12 shows a limited number of costs for the 37,900 machine-hours required for production. Assume men's pants require 1.8 machine hours, 1 hour for suits, and 2 hours for dresses [(1.8 machine-hours $\times$ 1,650 men's pants manufactured) + (1 machine-hour $\times$ 16,130 suits manufactured) + (2 machine-hours $\times$ 9,400 dresses manufactured) = 37,900 total machine-hours].

EXHIBIT 10–12

HART COMPANY
Factory Overhead Budget
For the Year Ending December 31, 19X2
(at budgeted capacity of 37,900 machine-hours)

Indirect material	$375,500	
Indirect labor	300,000	
Depreciation—variable portion...................	100,000	
Total variable overhead		$ 775,500
Insurance	$300,000	
Depreciation—fixed portion	878,000	
Supervision.................................	320,500	
Total fixed overhead		1,498,500
Total factory overhead		$2,274,000

($2,274,000 ÷ 37,900 machine-hours = $60 per machine-hour)
Relevant range is 37,000 to 38,000 machine-hours.

Cost of Goods Sold Budget

After determining the budgets for direct material, direct labor, and factory overhead, a cost of goods sold budget summarizes the data, as Exhibit 10–13 illustrates. The unit cost for each of the three products shown places a valuation on the ending balance of finished goods inventory. The accounting records provide the beginning balance of finished goods inventory.

EXHIBIT 10–13   Cost of Goods Sold Budget

HART COMPANY
Cost of Goods Sold Budget
For the Year Ending December 31, 19X2

Direct materials used (from Exhibit 10–9)	$ 273,761
Direct labor (from Exhibit 10–11)	414,560
Factory overhead (from Exhibit 10-12)	2,274,000
Total current manufacturing costs	$2,962,321
Add: Work in process January 1, 19X2 (per accounting records)	2,563
Total costs to account for	$2,964,884
Less: Work in process, December 31, 19X2 (see below)	62,180
Cost of goods manufactured	$2,902,704
Add: Finished goods January 1, 19X2 (per accounting records)	40,984
Cost of goods available for sale	$2,943,688
Less: Finished goods, December 31, 19X2 (see below)	59,655
Cost of goods sold	$2,884,033

	Unit Cost	Men's Pants Units	Men's Pants Amount	Suits Units	Suits Amount	Dresses Units	Dresses Amount
Fabric material	$ 2.50	3	$ 7.50	4	$10.00	2	$ 5.00
Buttons	1.10	4	4.40	2	2.20	1	1.10
Direct labor	20.00	1	20.00	0.6	12.00	1	20.00
Factory overhead	60.00	1.8	108.00	1	60.00	2	120.00
			$139.90		$84.20		$146.10

	Unit Cost	Work in Process Equivalent Units	Work in Process Total Amount	Finished Goods Units	Finished Goods Total Amount
Ending balance:					
Men's Pants	$ 139.90	20	$ 2,798	80	$11,192
Suits	84.20	150	12,630	350	29,470
Dresses	146.10	320	46,752	130	18,993
			$62,180		$59,655

Summary

Budgets can serve as excellent planning and control tools when managers devote attention to properly establishing them. Companies should conduct a careful study of the behavior of costs before preparing flexible budgets. Flexible budgeting evaluates the efficiency of operations by comparing actual costs incurred at an output level against a budget adjusted to that actual activity level. The flexible budget formula, also known as the cost estimating function, is prepared in advance of operations for each department or cost center, indicating both fixed costs and the variable cost rates per unit. Using flexible budgets, volume variations do not impact performance evaluation.

To be effective, those individuals responsible for the operations that the budget is measuring should participate in the budget setting process. They should know the criteria used in evaluation so they have a guide when incurring expenditures. The budgeting process allows for thorough review of operations. However, there is little value in merely determining that a difference between actual and budgeted performance exists. Instead, the true value of a budgetary program comes from identifying the causes of the variances. When used properly, budgets pave the way to higher morale and a better working relationship among employees and management.

Important Terms and Concepts

Problem for Self-Study

Flexible Budget Formula and Variances

Gula Company provides the following monthly budgets that were prepared at the beginning of the year. Budgeted capacity was set at 20,000 units:

	20,000	25,000
Units produced and sold		
Direct material	$ 30,000	$ 37,500
Direct labor	22,000	27,500
Factory utilities	60,000	75,000
Production supervision salaries	12,000	12,000
Sales promotion	10,000	12,500
Marketing manager's salary	8,000	8,000
Administrative salaries	32,000	32,000
	$174,000	$204,500

At the end of the month, analysis of the cost records reveals that Gula incurred the following costs and expenses in producing and selling 21,600 units:

Direct material	$33,000
Direct labor	25,100
Factory utilities	64,900
Production supervision salaries	12,500
Sales promotion	11,300
Marketing manager's salary	7,800
Administrative salaries	32,700
	$187,300

Required:

a. Determine the flexible budget formula for all costs/expenses, expressing variable costs on a per unit basis.
b. Compute the factory overhead application rate.
c. Determine variances for each line item using a flexible budget, indicating whether the variances are favorable or unfavorable.

Solution to Problem for Self-Study

Gula Company

a. Fixed costs:

Production supervision salaries	$ 12,000
Marketing manager's salary	8,000
Administrative salaries	32,000
	$ 52,000

Variable costs:

Direct material	1.50	($30,000/20,000)
Direct labor	1.10	($22,000/20,000)
Factory utilities	3.00	($60,000/20,000)
Sales promotion	0.50	($10,000/20,000)
	$ 6.10	

$6.10 per unit + $52,000 = flexible budget formula

b. $12,000/20,000 units = $0.60 fixed rate + $3.00 variable rate = $3.60 factory overhead application rate.

c.

	ActualCost	Budget for 21,600 units		Variance	
Direct material	$ 33,000	$32,400	($1.50 × 21,600)	$ 600	U
Direct labor	25,100	23,760	($1.10 × 21,600)	1,340	U
Factory utilities	64,900	64,800	($3.00 × 21,600)	100	U
Production supervision salaries	12,500	12,000		500	U
Sales promotion	11,300	10,800	($0.50 × 21,600)	500	U
Marketing manager's salary	7,800	8,000		200	F
Administrative salaries	32,700	32,000		700	U
	$187,300	$183,760		$3,540	U

F = Favorable; U = Unfavorable

Review Questions

1. Assume that to gain better insight into budgeting methods used in practice, you interview a number of business executives. You ask if they have a flexible budgeting approach and are surprised to find that they all reply, "Yes." What is amazing is that you know an accountant from one of the firms, and the accountant has told you that the company uses fixed budgeting. Why do you think they all gave you a positive answer?

2. Why is it important to have available the budget formula for a company's fixed and variable cost behavior?

3. What abilities does a budget director need to perform effectively?

4. Discuss the budgets a company should prepare as part of a master budget plan; discuss their interrelationships to each other.

5. Discuss several advantages and limitations of budgets, both for internal and external purposes.

6. How are predetermined overhead rates useful in the development of budgets?

7. What factors should be evaluated in deciding to purchase enough materials to maintain a large ending inventory?

8. If a company's policy is that each month's units of ending inventory should be equal to 130 percent of the next month's units of sale, what may this suggest?

9. As a newly hired cost accountant for a manufacturing firm, you find that a fixed budgeting system is being used. You immediately suggest a flexible budgeting approach. Your supervisor's reply is, "You haven't been here long enough to know how many hours it takes to set up only one budget! How can we ever have the time to prepare four or five detailed budgets on a series of volumes?" What is your reply to your supervisor?

10. What factors should be evaluated in deciding to purchase enough materials to maintain a large ending inventory?

Exercises

E10–1 Performance Report Using Flexible Budget

Assume Cost Center A produces 1,000 units in January 19X1, incurring the following actual costs:

Direct material	$ 1,100
Direct labor	4,270
Indirect material	2,920
Indirect labor	9,000
Factory utilities	1,910
Depreciation—production equipment	960
Rent—manufacturing building	570
Total costs	$20,730

Required:

a. Using the flexible budget formula given in Exhibit 10–2, determine variances for each line expense.

b. Explain if a flexible budget can incorporate revenue and nonmanufacturing costs as well as manufacturing costs.

E10–2 Factory Labor Budget

Elder Company manufactures Products A, B, and C in the Mixing, Fabricating, Finishing, and Wrapping Departments. Accountants developed standard costs for each product as follows for the budget year 19X1:

Product	19X1 Budgeted Unit Production	Mixing	Fabricating	Finishing	Wrapping	Total Standard Direct Labor-Hours per Unit
		Standard Hours per Unit				
A	200,000	0.6	1.0	0.4	0.2	2.2
B	400,000	1.0	——	2.8	0.6	4.4
C	300,000	1.6	3.0	——	0.4	5.0
Hourly labor rate		$6.00	$5.50	$7.50	$6.50	
Annual capacity in direct labor-hours		900,000	1,200,000	1,250,000	350,000	

Elder bases annual capacity on a normal two-shift operation; any hours required in excess of budgeted capacity are provided by overtime labor at 150 percent of normal hourly rates.

Required:

Prepare a direct labor-hour requirements schedule for 19X1 and related direct labor cost budget.

E10–3 Budgets Using Estimated Costs

Scott, Inc., mixes and bakes party-size birthday cakes. The standard cost of each unit in one of these cakes is

Flour	$ 8
Sugar and spices	12
Direct labor-mixing and cooking	45
Factory overhead	18
	$83

The estimated cost of flour is $1.60 per pound and $2 for sugar and spices. Scott pays direct labor workers $15 per hour.

Management expects to sell 10,000 birthday cakes in 19X1. Beginning inventory consists of finished goods (cakes)—800 units, flour—1,800 pounds, and sugar and spices—2,500 pounds. Desired ending inventory is finished goods—1,600 units; flour—2,200 pounds, and sugar and spices—3,600 pounds.

Required:

a. Prepare a production budget.
b. Prepare a direct materials purchases budget.
c. Prepare a direct labor budget.

E10–4 Production and Sales Budgets

Democrat, Inc., a producer of fine linen tablecloths, provides the following production records for the past four years. Tablecloths are provided in three different dimensions.

	Unit sales in 000s			
Product Line	Year 1	Year 2	Year 3	Year 4
36 × 48 inches	50	75	100	125
72 × 48 inches	200	220	242	266
105 × 72 inches	500	450	405	365

The trends over the past four years are expected to extend to Year 5. Inventory estimates for Year 5 are

Inventory in 000s

Product Line	Beginning	Ending
36 × 48 inches	10	20
72 × 48 inches	15	12
105 × 72 inches	25	25

Required:

Prepare sales and production forecasts for Year 5 in units by each product line. Round up to the next whole unit.

E10–5 Flexible Budget Formula and Preparation of Flexible Budget

Next year's monthly forecast for the Long Company indicates that the company will sell 10,000 units at a $25 per unit sales price. No change in inventory level is planned. Each unit will require three hours of machine time. Based on this volume, the monthly manufacturing overhead budget is

Variable overhead:	
Supplies.............	$ 94,500
Inspection	82,500
Repairs	33,000
Fixed overhead:	
Supervision	12,000
Depreciation.........	32,000
Insurance	8,000
	$262,000

At the end of the month it was determined that 28,500 machine-hours were used to produce 9,500 units. Actual manufacturing overhead costs were

Variable overhead:	
Supplies.............	$ 90,000
Inspection	78,100
Repairs	32,000
Fixed overhead:	
Supervision	12,100
Depreciation.........	31,800
Insurance	8,300
	$252,300

Required:

a. What is the flexible budget formula? Express the formula in machine-hours.
b. Prepare a flexible budget for actual volume and determine the variances by detailed expense. Indicate whether the variances are favorable or unfavorable.
c. If, instead, a fixed budget were used to determine variances, what would be the variances for supplies and repairs under these conditions?

E10–6 Production Requirements

Budgeted data for the Puryear Company indicates that 40,000 pounds of sugar are needed to remain in the ending inventory for processing its cola drink. Beginning sugar inventory is expected to contain 25,000 pounds. The expected cost per pound of sugar is 50 cents. The expected total cost of sugar purchases is $400,000.

Required:

From the information, compute the production requirements in pounds of sugar.

E10–7 Production Budget

Salabor Company produces three types of soft drinks. Following is the tentative sales budget for the winter season of the company year:

Soft Drink	Units
Cola	500,000
Grape soda	250,000
Ginger ale	425,000

These are the inventory levels:

| | **Work in Process Inventory** | | | | **Finished Goods Inventory** | |
| | **Beginning** | | **Ending** | | | |
	Units	*Percent processed*	*Units*	*Percent Processed*	*Beginning Units*	*Ending Units*
Cola.	3,000	45%	3,500	50%	15,000	16,500
Grape soda	5,000	33	4,215	40	13,000	11,350
Ginger ale	4,175	40	4,050	22	12,175	16,775

Required:

Prepare a production budget by product lines.

Problems

Writing

P10–8 Purposes of Budgets

Managers use budgets for planning and establishing goals for the future. Budgets also help managers evaluate past performance.

Required:

a. What areas of conflict are there between these two purposes of budgets?
b. How does allowing employees to participate in the budgeting process help solve these areas of conflict?

SPATS

P10–9 Material Purchases Budget

Parker Co. manufactures chairs, studio couches, and stools. Each piece of furniture requires varying quantities of material. Planned unit production of each product in 19X1 is 40,000 chairs, 20,000 couches, and 10,000 stools. The following summarizes direct material requirements for one unit of each product:

| | *Unit Material Requirements* | | | |
Product/Material	*Fabric*	*Oak Wood*	*Pine Wood*	*Metal*
Chair	2	3	—	1
Studio couch	3	—	2	—
Stool.	0.5	4	1	0.5

Beginning and desired ending inventory as well as unit costs are as follows for each direct material:

	Fabric	*Oak Wood*	*Pine Wood*	*Metal*
Inventory in units:				
January 1, 19X1	15,000	7,000	2,000	3,000
December 31, 19X1	6,000	2,000	4,000	5,000
19X1 unit cost	$2	$5	$4	$3

Direct material unit prices as budgeted are the delivered unit cost experienced.

Required:

Prepare a direct materials purchases budget for 19X1.

P10–10 Flexible Budget Preparation with Price Increases
Each unit produced by Paige, Inc., requires 0.4 hours of direct labor. Last year, when the company operated at 80 percent of capacity, 120,000 units were produced. The following percentages indicate the makeup of fixed and variable costs:

Fixed Costs	Percent	Variable Costs	Percent
Depreciation	35%	Factory supplies	20%
Rent	20	Utilities	40
Factory supervisor's salary	15	Indirect material	30
Insurance	30	Indirect labor	8
	100	Miscellaneous	2
			100

Management expects to increase next year's volume to 95 percent of capacity. Total factory overhead is expected to be $360,000 at this level, using a ratio of variable cost to fixed cost of 2:1, with variable costs based on direct labor-hours. Not included in the $360,000 is a recent notice of a 20 percent price increase from the utility company. This utilities price rise is expected regardless of any capacity changes. (Note that 2:1 variable to fixed cost ratio will not be in effect after the utilities price increase.)

Required:

a. Prepare a flexible budget for next year using 80, 95, 100, and 120 percent capacity levels; for each capacity level, determine the factory overhead rate per hour of production. Round to whole dollars for total costs, but carry variable cost per hour to five decimal places. Determine the budget formula for each line expense item.

b. Explain why the total factory overhead rate per hour has an inverse relationship to capacity.

P10–11 Budget Formula and Flexible Budget Preparation
Catree, Inc., plans to produce 2,000 tables next accounting period. Time and motion studies reveal it takes 10 machine-hours to manufacture each table. The established monthly factory overhead budget is as follows:

Fuel	$30,000
Repairs	15,000
Supplies	17,000
Depreciation	10,000
Rent	6,000
	$78,000

Assume depreciation is calculated on a straight-line basis and rent is paid monthly. At the end of the month, it is determined that 18,000 actual machine-hours were incurred to make 1,800 tables, and actual factory costs were as follows:

Fuel	$24,000
Repairs	12,000
Supplies	15,600
Depreciation	10,100
Rent	6,200
	$67,900

Required:

a. Prepare a fixed budget and determine variances from budget for each detailed expense.
b. What is the flexible budget formula for the fixed and variable cost behavior per direct labor-hour? (Express formula in machine-hours.)
c. Prepare a flexible budget for a production level of 18,000 machine-hours and determine variances from budget for each detailed expense.

P10–12 Monthly Sales Budgets; Sales Price and Volume Increase

Based on an average unit selling price of $100, monthly sales during 19X1 were as follows for the Lark Company:

January	$ 50,000
February	45,000
March	40,000
April	35,000
May	30,000
June	25,000
July	25,000
August	30,000
September	32,500
October	37,500
November	42,500
December	47,500
	$440,000

Since the company is faced with increasing labor cost, management plans to increase the sales price by 10 percent in 19X2. However, demand for this product is so high that sales volume is expected to increase by 40 percent even with this price increase. The seasonal sales pattern experienced in 19X1 is expected to continue throughout the next year.

Required:

a. Prepare a 19X2 sales budget by months.
b. If the average sales price is increased 20 percent in 19X2 with a projected sales volume increase of 15 percent, what will total 19X2 sales be?

P10–13 Static and Flexible Budgets

Rosmond Company presents you with the following monthly factory overhead budgets that were prepared at the beginning of the year. Budgeted capacity was set at 40,000 hours.

Direct labor-hours	*35,000*	*40,000*
Repair materials	$ 98,000	$112,000
Indirect labor	54,250	62,000
Utilities	108,500	124,000
Supervision salaries	12,000	12,000
Depreciation	11,000	11,000
Insurance	9,000	9,000
Rent	20,000	20,000
Total	$312,750	$350,000

At the end of the month, analysis of the cost records reveals that the following factory overhead was incurred in operating at 40,500 direct labor-hours:

Repair materials	$116,000
Indirect labor	62,600
Utilities	126,100
Supervision salaries	11,800
Depreciation	10,700
Insurance	9,110
Rent	21,500
Total	$357,810

Required:

a. Compute the flexible budget formula.
b. Determine the factory overhead application rate.
c. Determine variances for each of the factory overhead items, indicating whether they are favorable or unfavorable using a: (1) flexible budget; (2) static budget.
d. Compare your answers in Requirement *c* and indicate on which variance you would put more reliance.

SPATS

P10–14 Using Market Shares for Budget Preparation

Georgia, Inc., manufactures baby bottles and uses marketing research to estimate future sales. Research has shown that an average of 20 bottles is purchased per birth and that generally all 20 are bought within the same quarter of birth. The forecasted births for the Georgia, Inc., marketing area by quarter for 19X2 are first quarter—1,000; second quarter—1,200; third quarter—1,600; and fourth quarter—900.

Market research studies reveal that of the total market Georgia, Inc., expects its share to be 25 percent for the first quarter; 28 percent for the second quarter, 35 percent for the third quarter, and 40 percent for the fourth quarter. A $3 unit sales price is projected for Georgia's baby bottles.

Management would like to end each quarter with 15 percent of next quarter's sales in Finished Goods Inventory and 20 percent of next quarter's material requirements in Material Inventory. For year 19X3, quarter sales are expected to be 10 percent above this year's quarter sales. At the beginning of the first quarter of 19X2, there were 600 units in Finished Goods Inventory and 1,000 pounds of direct material. Each bottle requires 3/4 pounds of direct material which has an average cost of $0.60 a pound and 0.01 hours of direct labor. Direct labor workers are paid an average $15 per hour.

Required:

a. Using the market study, prepare a sales budget for the company.
b. Determine required quarterly production.
c. Determine production requirements for direct material and direct labor expressed in pounds and hours respectively. Round to the nearest whole pound or hour.
d. Prepare a material purchases budget for the material needed.
e. Determine the budgeted materials and labor costs by quarters.

P10–15 Preparation of Five Production Budgets

Grady Company manufactures and sells only one product, chemical B8. The finished goods inventory on May 1 costs $861,800 and contains 13,900 units. The finished goods inventory on May 31 is expected to contain 15,600 units. The company will sell its finished products for $80 per unit, and 85,000 units of finished goods are expected to be sold during the month. Only one kind of direct materials is used to produce each finished good. Six gallons of direct material are needed to produce each unit of finished goods.

Beginning direct material inventory on May 1 is expected to be 115,000 gallons, while ending direct material inventory is expected to be 113,800 gallons, and direct material is expected to continue costing $2.20 per gallon. FIFO inventory costing is used.

Two hours of direct labor are needed to produce each unit. Direct labor workers are paid $12 per hour.

Variable factory overhead at the budgeted level of operations is expected to amount to $1,184,840, while fixed factory overhead is expected to be $1 million. Factory overhead is applied to work in process on the basis of direct labor dollars.

Required:

Prepare the following:
a. Sales budget.
b. Production budget.
c. Direct materials purchases budget.
d. Direct labor budget.
e. Cost of goods sold budget.

P10–16 Flexible Budget Preparation at Various Volumes

Newsome Company asks that you assist them in analyzing the output of their flexible budgeting system. They give you the following data for May 19X1 in which 50,000 units were produced and sold. The company plans to maintain the present level of inventories.

Direct material	$ 59,800
Direct labor	117,000
Factory overhead	120,000
Marketing expenses	17,500
Administrative expenses	30,000

After studying the above data, you find that the industry experienced a shortage of material in May; as a result, prices were 15 percent higher than normal. The monthly labor costs were 10 percent lower than normal. Total factory overhead was 20 percent lower than what is considered normal; 35 percent of the factory overhead for a normal month is fixed. Salespersons are paid a commission equal to $0.25 per unit; the remainder of the marketing expense is fixed. Of the administrative expense, 75 percent represents fixed costs. Of the fixed costs, salaries account for $8,200. Administrative personnel earning a fixed salary received an 8 percent raise effective June 1.

Required:

a. Prepare flexible budgets at volumes of 40,000, 45,000 and 55,000 units for June operations. Determine the cost per unit for each volume level for both fixed and variable costs.
b. If 41,140 units were actually processed during June, which of the three budgets prepared in Requirement *a* would you use?

SPATS

P10–17 Territorial Sales and Production Budgets

Wise Company plans expansion into the northern territory after experiencing success in the southern territory. The company forecasts these northern territory sales based on southern territory forecasted sales data:

Forecasted sales data for the southern territory
for the quarter ending March 31, 19X2

	Beef Stew		**Soup**		**Chili**	
	Quantity	Unit sales price	Quantity	Unit sales price	Quantity	Unit sales price
January	90	$55	1,140	$10	790	$7.00
February	110	56	970	9	760	6.00
March	100	52	990	9	640	6.50

Management plans to introduce only beef stew and soup in the northern territory. Forecasts of sales quantities are based on a percentage of the southern market for each product, as shown:

	Beef Stew		**Soup**	
	Percentage of Southern Market	Unit Sales Price	Percentage of Southern Market	Unit Sales Price
January	60%	$55	10%	$7
February	50	57	15	7
March	50	57	18	8

On January 1, 19X2, an inventory count of beef stew revealed 32 finished units; 475 units of soup; and 130 units of chili. Management desires an ending inventory on January 31, 19X2, of 40 units of beef stew; 315 units of soup; and 150 units of chili. Material and labor requirements for each of the products are as follows:

	Beef Stew	Soup	Chili
Meat	2 pounds	4 pounds	6 pounds
Vegetables	3 gallons	2 gallons	4 gallons
Direct labor	2 hours	4 hours	3 hours

Meat costs $1.75 per pound, while vegetables are expected to cost $2.10 per gallon. Direct labor workers are under a union contract specifying that they receive $8 per hour. On January 1, 19X2, an inventory count showed that there were 1,000 pounds of meat and 1,575 gallons of vegetables. Management desires an ending inventory of each of these materials, which represents 25 percent of the material needed for the next monthly sales.

Required:

a. Prepare monthly sales budgets for the first quarter for each territory broken down for each of the three products. Round to the nearest dollar.

b. Prepare a production budget for January for both territories combined.

c. Prepare a direct materials purchases budget for January for both territories including any needed direct material usage budgets. Round to the nearest dollar.

d. Prepare a direct labor budget for January for both territories combined.

P10–18 Variances Using a Fixed and a Flexible Budgeting Approach
The 1,000-bed ARD Hospital is in a large metropolitan area. Because the hospital has a number of highly specialized physicians, it draws patients from a 300-mile radius. The hospital experiences greater capacity in the winter months, up to 95 percent occupancy; in the summer months capacity often declines to 75 percent occupancy. The administrator believes that 85 percent occupancy represents normal capacity, and this is the basis used for budgeting.

The January 19X3 budget for the laundry department is as follows:

1,000-BED ARD HOSPITAL—LAUNDRY DEPARTMENT
Fixed Budget
For the Month Beginning January 19X3

	Budget 850 Beds 85 Percent Capacity
Variable costs:	
Linen replacement	$ 12,801
Detergent and other cleaning supplies	6,290
Utilities	6,000
Total variable costs	$ 25,091
Fixed costs:	
Laundry supervisors' salaries	$ 10,180
Laundry washers' salaries	26,260
Laundry flatwork ironers	61,170
Laundry travel expense	190
Total fixed costs	$ 97,800
Total costs	$122,891

Due to an emphasis in the community on obtaining flu shots, the hospital had only an 80 percent occupancy in January. At the end of January, the controller determines that the hospital incurred the following actual costs:

Variable costs:	
Linen replacement	$ 12,640
Detergent and other cleaning supplies	6,000
Utilities	5,800
Total variable costs	$ 24,440
Fixed costs:	
Laundry supervisors' salaries	$ 11,010
Laundry washers' salaries	25,900
Laundry flatwork ironers	62,000
Laundry travel expense	200
Total fixed costs	$ 99,110
Total costs	$123,550

Required:

a. Compute the variances by line items for the laundry department for the month of January using the fixed budget given. Indicate if they are favorable (F) or unfavorable (U).

b. Comment on the budgeting approach used.

c. Assuming you convince the hospital administrators that they should adopt a flexible budgeting approach, construct a budget for 80 percent (800-bed), 85 percent (850-bed), and 90 percent (900-bed) occupancy and give the budget formula by line item.

d. Using the information you computed in Requirement c, perform variance analyses for each expense item using the appropriate flexible budget. Indicate if variances are favorable (F) or unfavorable (U).

Cases

Critical Thought

C10–19 Kanban Squares

In a recent move to adopt newer manufacturing techniques, Kreiger Company marked off kanban squares the size of one unit with yellow tape in the factory. An assembler at one table places a completed unit on the square within easy reach of the next assembler at the next table. No more units can be completed until the next assembler removes the unit from the kanban square.

This company also uses kanban squares to serve another purpose. Lights and a problem display board next to each workstation permit capture of problem causes. When assemblers do not have units in their kanban squares, they wait ten seconds for a unit to arrive. After ten seconds, they turn on a yellow light signaling a problem. The light tells subsequent assemblers that they also are going to be slowed down. The yellow light alerts the attention of the supervisor to find the real causes.

Kreiger management believes this is a better approach than the one often used by conventional manufacturing in which no one records the real causes. They argue that Kreiger workers have little reason to get embarrassed and go on the defensive. Rather than giving each assembler the uncomfortable feeling of being blamed for most of the shutdowns, high costs, poor housekeeping, and bad quality products, assemblers have the opportunity to state the factor beyond their control that causes the slow down. Assemblers explain the cause of the problem when the slowdown occurs, rather than trying to remember what the problem factor was several days later.

Kreiger also uses red lights throughout the production floor to signal major problems. With the adoption of the JIT concept, Kreiger's president reminded company management that job titles mean little and responsibilities blur when problems have to be fixed quickly. When a red light goes on, everyone must help to solve the problem before it becomes a disaster. As a result, engineers, plant managers, schedulers, and other salaried support production people are spending much less time in their offices. In fact, some of them are now suggesting that their offices, the computer, and computer staff should be moved closer to production operations. One advocate of the move made this observation: "We need to get the support people into the vacated space fast; otherwise, someone will revert to our old way and fill the space with inventory again when no one is looking."

Required:

a. Explain why the company has a policy that no units can be completed until the next kanban square on the assembly line is empty.
b. Do you think the kanban light system asks the question, "Why can't you keep up?" so that workers become defensive and argue that they have too much work to do? Or, do you view the light system as a way to give workers a chance to air their problems?
c. Give one advantage and one disadvantage you can see in moving:
    (1) Salaried support people's desks on the factory floor, intermingled with workstations.
    (2) The computer which supports manufacturing and its computer staff on the floor.

Writing

C10–20 Evaluating Budget Cuts

Thelma Ezell, Inc., is a small, dynamic, and very successful electronics company. In its first year of operations, management decided the accounting system must keep pace with the rapid changes taking place in the firm. Thus, the system has become complex. The original purpose of accounting was to provide profitability data for use by top management, since the major concerns of the company were survival and preparation for the future. If the company proved successful, the original members of the management team would receive sizable rewards in promotions and increases in stock ownership. As the company began to grow, however, the reporting system changed since there were fewer and fewer direct personal benefits from increases in corporate profits.

In the last few years, the focus has been on greater accomplishment. As a result, the accounting system has developed another set of reports that emphasize budget aspects rather than departmental profitability. These reports include the standard, or goal, to be used as a measuring stick of performance and the actual results of operation. Management has found that standards are more acceptable when operating personnel participate in their establishment; therefore, the division manager being evaluated is allowed sufficient voice in setting the standards. Budgets are determined at the division manager level and are discussed and revised until each division manager is satisfied with the budget for his or her division. Then each division manager subdivides this budget among the various departments.

Division managers are concerned primarily with their overall performance because they are judged on whether they meet the aggregate goals. Determining how these goals are achieved is the division manager's job. Generally, division managers believe that it is as bad to be under target as to be over target. If the division is under target, either the manager was too optimistic in the projection or the projection had slack in it; if over target, the projection was either incorrect or new, unplanned costs have appeared.

An insight into this budgeting process can be gained by examining a specific division. Jay Hugg's report at midyear shows his departments' goals and expenditures have been:

Department	Goal	Expenditures	Variance
A	$100,000	$110,000	$10,000 unfavorable
B	100,000	90,000	10,000 favorable
C	100,000	100,000	—
	$300,000	$300,000	$—

The original division budget was $600,000, equally divided among three departments. Hugg is concerned that Department A has exceeded its goal, but Department B has offset this variance, and the division as a whole is on target. Hugg is considering taking $10,000 out of B's budget and transferring it to A's.

Required:

a. Give your reactions to this budgeting system.

b. Explain if you would advise the division manager to make this trade-off of $10,000 between departments.

c. Assume that at midyear the entire division's budget must be cut.

   (1) How would you advise Hugg to pass the cut along to subordinate departments?

   (2) To what extent should human factors be considered in this decision?

   (3) Discuss the order in which specific budget items should be cut.

   (4) What do you think of a deep-cut approach that dictates an arbitrary cut of X percent across the board?

CHAPTER 11

Nonmanufacturing Budgets, Forecasted Statements, and Behavioral Issues

Chapter Objectives

After studying this chapter, you should be able to:

1. Prepare budgets for marketing, administrative, and research activities.
2. Estimate cash collections from credit sales and cash disbursements needed in preparing a cash budget.
3. Prepare a budgeted statement of income and balance sheet, including a gross profit analysis.
4. Compare appropriation, incremental, and zero-base budgeting.
5. Explain the inherent behavioral implications of budgeting and how the misuse of budgets prevents continuous improvement.

Current Cost Management Practice

Global

Nynex Corp. announced its need to slash its operating budget by up to 40 percent to remain competitive. The downsizing would eliminate 15,000 to 25,000 people from its payroll. Nynex plans to remake itself, reduce costs, improve customer service, and prepare for more aggressive competition in the years ahead. The players involved include a dynamic steely executive leading the effort, an outside consultant whose firm is billing the company $1 million a month to help with the downsizing, and employees who will become either survivors or resentful victims. The company hopes to avoid forced layoffs by enticing employees to accept buyout offers. Some critics believe massive downsizing has become a fad, a bone to throw Wall Street when investors began baying for cost cuts. Other critics maintain that large-scale staff reductions, even at profitable companies, are necessary to maintain competitiveness in a fast-changing global marketplace. However, the cost and trauma of large-scale layoffs is immeasurable.

John A. Byrne, "The Pain of Downsizing," *BusinessWeek,* May 9, 1994, pp. 60–69.

Introduction

As introduced in Chapter 10, budgets are important in internal control. If properly developed and followed, the budgetary process can be a springboard for many control techniques. Companies implement control by measuring and comparing actual results with budgeted plans at designated intervals. This chapter discusses marketing and administrative budgets, cash budgets, and forecasted statements. Also, this chapter emphasizes the importance of companywide participation and recognition of the human factors involved in the budgeting process.

Today many companies sell their products through a multitude of channels. To prevent excessive inventories, accurate forecasts from marketing personnel are essential. When budgets are unreliable, company resources are unavailable to produce needed goods or services. Thus, budgets provide a means for communications among accounting, production, and marketing personnel.

Marketing and Administrative Budgets

It is usually more difficult to control and budget marketing and administrative expenses than production costs because marketing and administrative functions lack standardization. However, companies can justify the extra effort required to set budgets for these functions because of the large expense involved. Exhibit 11–1 illustrates an annual marketing and administrative expense budget classified as to fixed and variable expenses. Accountants break down the annual budget on a monthly basis and then by individual expense budgets for each marketing function. This encourages managers to consider the factors affecting expenses. For example, the promotional budget should reflect the projects and dollars involved and the timing of the projects.

EXHIBIT 11-1   **Marketing and Administrative Expense Budget**

HART COMPANY
Marketing and Administrative Expense Budget
For Year Ending December 31, 19X2

Variable marketing expense:		
Salaries and wages..............................	$ 19,800	
Sales commissions...............................	20,000	
Advertising.....................................	20,000	
Traveling......................................	28,000	
Total variable marketing expenses.................		$ 87,800
Fixed marketing expenses:		
Warehousing....................................	$ 60,000	
Advertising....................................	30,000	
Marketing manager's salary......................	66,000	
Total fixed marketing expenses...................		156,000
Total marketing expenses.......................		$243,800
Variable administrative expense:		
Clerical wages.................................	$ 40,000	
Supplies......................................	20,213	
Total variable administrative expenses.............		$ 60,213
Fixed administrative expenses:		
Depreciation..................................	$ 90,000	
Salaries......................................	100,000	
Total fixed administrative expenses...............		190,000
Total administrative expenses....................		$250,213
Total marketing and administrative expenses..............		$494,013

Promotional Budgets

Promotional budgets are difficult to establish because so many factors influence the success of promotional campaigns. Promotional activities include advertising, personal selling, publicity, sales promotion, and public relations. Availability of money or credit, the salesperson's technique, and economic conditions are influences. The time lag between advertising expenditures and sales also increases the difficulty of setting the promotional budget. Often companies use one of the following bases for establishing the promotional budget: a percentage of sales, an amount per unit of product in budgeted sales, competitors' actions, an all we can afford amount, market research, or the task method.

Fixed Percentage of Sales.   Even though setting the promotional budget as a fixed percentage of sales is a popular approach because it makes additional funds available for following a favorable market, this method lacks flexibility. Also, we assume sales result from promotional activities rather than vice versa. It is more logical to use this approach to correlate advertising appropriations with forecasted sales.

Amount per Unit.   Instead of setting the promotional budget as a percentage of sales, managers may base the promotional budget on a unit cost per product grouping, per customer, or other segment. This approach is easily adapted with flexible budgeting using standard costs. For example, managers may set the promotional budget based on the cost per promotion item mailed, cost per newspaper inch, or cost per minute of radio or television time.

Competitors' Actions.   Companies may gauge their promotional expenditures by competitors' actions to avoid spending more than competitors. However, merely reacting to competitors causes a company to ignore its own competitive strengths. Instead, many factors, including demographics, should affect the specific type and kind of media used for advertising in each territory.

All We Can Afford.   Because advertising is a **discretionary cost** arising from periodic appropriation decisions that reflect top management policies, the size of the advertising budget may merely be the amount of funds available. If there are excess funds, companies increase their advertising budgets. The all we can afford method disregards the relationship between promotional costs and promotional effects; it funds promotional activities only after budgeting all other expenses.

Market Research.   Market research can determine the probable relationship between demographic characteristics and the promotional medium chosen. In determining promotional expenditures, marketing managers should consider the density of the population, whether the area is urban or rural, types of industry found in the market territory, the characteristics of the target market, and climate. To observe the returns from incremental increases in these costs, management can vary the amount spent on promotional activities in limited market areas.

Task Method or Sales Objective.   The task method establishes a definite promotional objective for each product, such as a desired level of customer awareness. The promotional budget is the total amount of money considered necessary to meet each product's objective.

Research and Development Budgets

A budget is the most useful tool for both planning and controlling research and development expenses. In the short run, a company must direct research and development efforts toward projects expected to earn a satisfactory rate of return on the funds invested. The long-run objective is assurance that research programs are in line with forecasted future market trends.

Budgets for research and development activities should be broken down by projects. Each project should then be broken down into departments or phases, and the completion date for each phase forecasted. Exhibit 11–2 illustrates a detailed budget for the development of the new product Zerxx, broken down by expense items for the three phases of the project. Overhead is applied on the basis of $30 per machine-hour to complete the different phases.

Status Reports.   Periodically, companies prepare a status report, as illustrated in Exhibit 11–3, for all phases or departments involved in each project. The expenditures incurred to date and the commitments made represent the **encumbered amount.** Accountants match encumbrances against the budget to determine the unexpended amount. If the unexpended amount is insufficient to complete the phase, a company should take corrective action and/or make budget revisions.

Exhibit 11–4 reviews three research projects in process. The cost summary shows costs incurred in previous periods and the current year's expenses. Adding future costs to these two expenses gives the expected total cost of the project. The inclusion of annual forecasted income assists in evaluating the project's success.

Time budget analysis.   Exhibit 11–5 compares actual hours spent on a project with the hours budgeted. Managers need this evaluation in addition to analyzing expenses. Product Zerxx used 27 more hours in development than forecasted.

EXHIBIT 11–2 New Product Budget

BUDGET FOR NEW PRODUCT ZERXX
Project director: Harold Douglas
Project number: 2118

	Department or Phase			
Expenses	Planning	Production	Promotion	Total Budget
Direct materials.	$ 4,000	$26,300	$ 2,700	$ 33,000
Labor costs.	1,000	29,000	6,000	36,000
Consulting fees	10,000	3,000	5,000	18,000
Indirect labor.	1,500	2,800	300	4,600
Supplies and other				
indirect material.	1,500	6,800	2,900	11,200
Equipment	–0–	40,000	–0–	40,000
Overhead allocation.	1,500	9,000	3,000	13,500
	$19,500	$116,900	$19,900	$156,300
Estimated machine-hours . . .	50	300	100	450
Completion date	May 31, 19X1	January 31, 19X2	April 30, 19X2	

EXHIBIT 11–3 Status Report for New Product

STATUS REPORT FOR NEW PRODUCT ZERXX—PROJECT NUMBER 2118
Production Department
December 31, 19X1

Expense	Budget	Expenditures to Date	Commitments	Encumbered	Unexpended
Direct materials.	$ 26,300	$ 25,100	$ 100	$ 25,200	$ 1,100
Labor cost.	29,000	20,000	1,000	21,000	8,000
Consulting fees	3,000	2,700	200	2,900	100
Indirect labor	2,800	2,300	700	3,000	(200)
Supplies and other					
indirect material. . . .	6,800	4,200	1,800	6,000	800
Equipment	40,000	40,000	–0–	40,000	–0–
Overhead allocation. . .	9,000	6,800	1,800	8,600	400
	$116,900	$101,100	$5,600	$106,700	$10,200

EXHIBIT 11–4 Research and Development Cost Summary

RESEARCH AND DEVELOPMENT COST SUMMARY
December 31, 19X1

Project	Project Description	Costs to January 1, 19X1	Year 19X1 Costs	Future Costs	Expected Total Costs	Annual Forecasted Income
2118	Product ZERXX	–0–	$101,100	$5,600	$106,700	$16,000
2119	Product YERXX	$5,000	4,000	3,000	12,000	4,000
2120	Improve Product AAX	1,000	15,000	2,000	18,000	5,000

EXHIBIT 11–5   Time Budget Analysis

TIME BUDGET ANALYSIS-PRODUCT ZERXX
MAY 31,19X2

Phase	Hour Budgeted	Actual Hours	Variance
Planning			
Product specification	20	24	4 unfavorable
Personnel involved	5	3	2 favorable
Research	6	8	2 unfavorable
Market analysis	10	7	3 favorable
Finance	9	14	5 unfavorable
	50	56	6 unfavorable
Production			
Personnel training	25	26	1 unfavorable
Purchasing	15	20	5 unfavorable
Control functions	10	8	2 favorable
Test runs	200	225	25 unfavorable
Product revisions	50	40	10 favorable
	300	319	19 unfavorable
Promotion			
Field testing	15	20	5 unfavorable
Advertising	85	82	3 favorable
	100	102	2 unfavorable
Total hours	450	477	27 unfavorable

Often the competition for market share makes time more important than dollars. Managers should compare the differential or extra revenue gained by introducing a product several months early and beating competition to market with the differential or extra cost of increasing production and market tests. They then should compare this differential income with the income estimated by following the original time schedule. These efforts to complete the project ahead of schedule are called **crashing** and are part of **Program Evaluation and Review Technique (PERT)** analysis. Chapter 25 discusses PERT-time and PERT-cost analyses involving networks that show paths to completion. A detailed timetable is essential to any new product introduction, whether it involves a simple method of preparing calendars or a more sophisticated computerized PERT network.

Cash Management

Effective management of cash plays an essential role in capital budgets and in the survival of a company. Failure to provide cash resources to meet liabilities as they come due is one of the most common causes of business failure. Collecting accounts receivable and making cash disbursements have always been functions of cash management. Today cash utilization also involves evaluating the cost of money or its ability to earn a return. Improvements in communication and transportation have facilitated the movement and clearing of funds. The expansion of business firms with subsidiaries in foreign countries has increased the problems of controlling and funding corporate operations.

Productivity

Current Cost Management Practice

American Standard's strategy for reducing working capital, especially inventories, is a model for mature industries. Its CEO plans for the worst by setting out to reduce its working capital. U.S. companies on average, use more than 15 cents in working capital from each $1 of sales. To get to zero, a company must push inventories so low they can be financed without borrowing. The idea is to deliver goods, and to bill customers more rapidly, then use the customer's money to pay for minimal stocks, without speeding up payments to suppliers. American Standard also introduced a lean manufacturing system called demand flow technology which involves plants manufacturing products as customers order them. Suppliers deliver straight to the assembly line, reducing stocks of parts, and plants ship the products as soon as they are completed, thus cutting finished goods inventory.

Shawn Tully, "The Prophet of Zero Working Capital," *Fortune,* June 13, 1994, pp. 113–14.

Many companies have reserves of cash and near-cash securities totaling more than immediate or expected future requirements because they make no analysis of how much cash they need to support expected activity levels. Companies generally have three objectives in managing their cash; in descending order they are security of principal, liquidity of principal, and yield. Often companies are willing to accept low **yields,** or rates or return, to achieve security and liquidity of principal. **Liquidity,** or the ability to meet debts as they come due, is also of concern. **Security of principal** refers to the protection, or assurance, that the obligation will be paid. Companies can justify a conservative policy if the cash balance is low and necessary to meet operating needs and emergencies. However, when these cash funds have grown to the point where they exceed projected or probable expected uses, this policy has less importance.

Centralization of Cash

High interest rates cause companies to reduce their cash balances and examine the age of their receivables. Rather than a piecemeal analysis by individual departments, a multidepartmental review of cash functions is critical to better cash management. Generally, there are advantages to having cash-handling functions centralized. With consolidated management of cash, receipts are deposited in centrally controlled bank accounts and branch disbursements are made from imprest funds or payroll accounts. Usually companies limit decentralized functions to the payment of local operating expenses and receipt of payment from local customers. Authority over major capital expenditures and functions, such as capital stock sales and income tax and dividend payments, are centralized. Centralization of cash also prevents the unauthorized payment of funds and helps control all bank borrowing. In addition, it is often more economical to have accounting and other paperwork related to cash centralized at a single location.

Earlier Availability of Receipts.   Cash management also requires improving cash collections. A review of credit, billing, discount, and collection procedures discloses opportunities to obtain prompt payments from customers. A review of credit policies determines whether the granting of credit is too strict and is cutting down the inflow of cash by rejecting sound sales. Conversely, the credit terms may be too liberal, increasing the number of slow-paying customers and bad-debt losses. Any delay in billing obviously results in delayed receipt of cash. Errors in bills mailed to customers also slow down cash receipts.

Cash Budgets

Forecasts of future cash receipts and disbursements, as shown in Exhibit 11–6, may reveal a company is holding unnecessary cash in bank accounts. Management needs both short- and long-range forecasts of cash positions. Long-range cash projections do not detail estimates of revenues and expenses because their purpose is to show long-term trends indicating whether working capital growth will generate funds when needed.

A budget showing expected cash receipts and disbursements indicates the months having cash shortages and excesses so managers can take corrective action in advance. Accountants usually prepare cash budgets for a year in the future, broken down by months, to ease the comparison of actual cash receipts and disbursements with budgeted amounts. For simplicity, Exhibit 11–6 illustrates a cash budget for only January, February, and December. The procedure used for Exhibit 11–6 is to estimate each expected source and disbursement of cash for the given period. Budgeted 19X2 sales come from Exhibit 10–6, the sales budget. The only source of cash assumed in Exhibit 11–6 is from charge sales, with 97 percent of the charge sales collected. Exhibit 11–6 assumes the following collection pattern and sales:

40% in the month of sale
30% in the month following sale
27% in the second month following sale
 3% uncollectible
100%
Actual charge sales:
   November, 19X1 . . . . $250,000
   December, 19X1 270,000

Exhibit 11–6 assumes the average markup on cost is 60 percent and management wishes to have 10 percent of next month's sales in ending inventory. Because cost is the basis of this markup, it represents 100 percent and sales represent 160 percent.

December 19X1 Cost of Goods Sold ($270,000 December 19X1 sales ÷ 160%)	$168,750
+ Desired ending inventory ($292,000 January 19X2 sales ÷ 160% = $182,500	
January Cost of Goods Sold; $182,500 × 10%)	18,250
	$187,000
− Beginning inventory (10% × $168,750 December cost of goods sold)	16,875
December 19X1 purchases if gross margin is expressed on *cost*	$170,125
January 19X2 Cost of Goods Sold ($292,000 January 19X2 sales ÷ 160%)	$182,500
+ Desired ending inventory ($268,200 February 19X2 sales ÷ 160% = $167,625	
February Cost of Goods Sold; $167,625 × 10%)	16,763
	$199,263
− Beginning inventory (10% × $182,500 January cost of goods sold)	18,250
January 19X2 purchases if gross margin is expressed on *cost*	$181,013

(continued)

EXHIBIT 11-6   Budgeted Cash Receipts and Disbursements

HART COMPANY
Budgeted Statement of Cash Receipts and Disbursements
For Year Ending December 31, 19X2

	January	February	December	Total
Cash sales	$100,000	$103,000	$110,000	
Cash receipts from charge sales:				
From November 19X1 sales:				
27% × $250,000	67,500			
From December 19X1 sales:				
30% × $270,000	81,000			
27% × $270,000		72,900		
From January 19X2 sales:				
40% × $292,000	116,800			
30% × $292,000		87,600		
From February 19X2 sales:				
40% × $268,200		107,280		
From October 19X2 sales:				
27% × $369,000			99,630	
From November 19X2 sales:				
30% × $393,400			118,020	
From December 19X2 sales:				
40% × $404,500			161,800	
Total receipts	$365,300	$370,780	$489,450	$4,720,000
Disbursements:				
Purchases:				
From December 19X1 purchases:				
80% × $170,125 × 98%	$133,378			
20% × $170,125	34,025			
From January 19X2 purchases:				
80% × $181,013 × 98%		$141,914		
20% × $181,013		36,202		
From November 19X2 purchases:				
80% × $246,568 × 98%			193,309	
20% × $246,568			49,314	
Fixed costs	120,000	120,000	125,000	
Variable costs:				
January sales:				
25% × $292,000 = $73,000				
30% × $73,000	21,900			
70% × $73,000		51,100		
February sales:				
25% × $268,200 = $67,050				
30% × $67,050		20,115		
November sales:				
25% × $393,400 = $98,350				
70% × $98,350			68,845	
December sales:				
25% × $404,500 = $101,125				
30% × $101,125			30,338	
Property taxes		1,532		
Dividends			1,897	
Equipment purchases	42,277			
Total disbursements	$351,580	$370,863	$468,703	$4,687,983
Excess of receipts over disbursements ..	$ 13,720	$ (83)	$ 20,747	$ 32,017
Beginning cash balance	20,100	33,820	31,370	20,100
Ending cash balance	$ 33,820	$ 33,737	$ 52,117	$ 52,117

November 19X2 Cost of Goods Sold ($393,400 November 19X2 sales ÷ 160%)	$245,875
+ Desired ending inventory ($404,500 December 19X2 sales ÷160% = $252,813	
December Cost of Goods Sold; $252,813 × 10%)	25,281
	$271,156
− Beginning inventory (10% × $245,875 November cost of goods sold)	24,588
November 19X2 purchases if gross margin is expressed on *cost*	$246,568

Assume instead management had expressed the gross margin markup on sales rather than *cost.* Then gross margin would be 60 percent of *sales,* cost of goods sold would be 40 percent of sales, and $157,804 November 19X2 purchases result as follows. (Purchases for the other months would be calculated similarly.)

November 19X2 Cost of Goods Sold ($393,400 November 19X2 sales × 40%)	$157,360
+ Desired ending inventory $404,500 December 19X2.sales × 40% × 10%	16,180
	$173,540
− Beginning inventory ($157,360 November cost of goods sold × 10%)	15,736
November 19X2 purchases if gross margin is expressed on *sales*	$157,804

Hart Company pays for 80 percent of each month's purchase by the 10th of the following month to take advantage of the 2 percent purchase discount. They pay gross for the remaining 20 percent in the month following purchase. Hart Company expects cash disbursements for fixed costs to be $120,000 per month for January and February, and $125,000 for the remainder of 19X2. (Remember that such fixed expenses as depreciation and amortization do not require a cash disbursement.) They expect cash disbursements for variable costs to be 25 percent of monthly sales; they pay for 30 percent of their variable costs in the month incurred and 70 percent in the following month.

Hart Company plans to pay $1,532 for property taxes in February and $1,897 in dividends in December. The cash balance on January 1 is $20,100 and $31,370 on December 1. They expect to pay equipment purchases totaling $42,277 in January. The total budget column in Exhibit 11–6 shows only total receipts and disbursements since the cash budget omits nine months for simplicity.

Determining Collections Based on Accounts Receivable Balances

Instead of estimating the collections of accounts receivable as in Exhibit 11–6, a company may forecast collections on the balances in its accounts receivable account identified by specific periods. For example, assume Clevenger Company's collection pattern is 30 percent in the month of sale, 48 percent in the month after sale, and 20 percent in the second month after the sale. Clevenger Company expects 2 percent of all credit sales to be uncollectible. Assume accounts receivable balances as of March 1 are $70,000 from February sales and $44,000 from January sales; no bad debts have been written off. Also assume expected March sales are $180,000. Based on this data, expected collections to be included in the cash budget are as follows:

From March sales (30% × $180,000). . . . . $ 54,000

From February sales $\left(\dfrac{\$70,000}{.70} \times 48\%\right)$ 48,000

From January sales $\left(\dfrac{\$44,000}{.22} \times 20\%\right)$ 40,000

$142,000

Note that the $70,000 accounts receivable remaining uncollected from February sales represent 70 percent of sales made in February (100% − 30% collected in February). Also, note that the $44,000 accounts receivable from January sales represents 22 percent of January sales [100% − (30% + 48%) = 22%].

Budgeted Statement of Income and Balance Sheet

After completing the sales budget and all expense budgets, we prepare a budgeted Statement of Income similar to that in Exhibit 11–7. We make no new estimates; instead, we take figures from budgets previously prepared as indicated. In practice, companies should prepare more detailed budgeted statements of income on a monthly basis. With monthly forecasted statements of income, management frequently can analyze actual performance and investigate causes for variances. In addition, most companies round these figures to hundreds of dollars or thousands of dollars. However, Exhibit 11–7 rounds figures to the nearest dollar to ease the carryover from one budget to another. The percentages shown represent vertical analysis.

Managers can study percentage changes by comparing the 19X2 budgeted statement of income to the 19X1 actual statement of income. For instance, even though Hart Company expects 19X2 sales to increase $600,100 from $3,200,000 to $3,800,100 or 18.8 percent ($600,100/$3,200,000), managers also expect the cost of goods sold as a percentage of sales to increase. This results in lower percentages for gross margin and net income after taxes.

Analysis of Gross Margin

A detailed analysis of the causes for the change in gross margin for Hart Company follows:

$960,000	Gross margin 19X1
916,067	Gross margin 19X2
$ 43,933	Decrease in gross margin

If the same conditions exist in 19X2 with no change in unit sales price:

Sales for 19X2	$3,800,100		
Cost of goods sold for 19X2		$2,884,033	
Cost based on 19X1 rate (70% x $3,800,100)		2,660,070	
Net increase in cost of goods sold			$223,963
Gross margin earned on increased sales			
(30% x $600,100)			180,030
Decrease in gross margin			$ 43,933

EXHIBIT 11-7   Income Statement Analysis

HART COMPANY
Budgeted and Actual Income Statement
For Year Ending December 31

	19X2 (Budgeted)		19X1 (Actual)	
	Amount	*Percent*	*Amount*	*Percent*
Sales (from Exhibit 10–6)	$3,800,100	100.0%	$3,200,000	100.0%
Cost of goods sold (from Exhibit 10–13)	2,884,033	75.9	2,240,000	70.0
Gross margin	$ 916,067	24.1	$ 960,000	30.0
Marketing and administrative				
expenses (from Exhibit 11–1)	494,013	13.0	320,000	10.0
Income before income taxes	$ 422,054	11.1	$ 640,000	20.0
Income taxes assumed	304,008	8.0	256,000	8.0
Net income after income taxes	$ 118,046	3.1%	$ 384,000	12.0%

Exhibit 11–8 illustrates a budgeted balance sheet representing all expected changes in assets, liabilities, and owners' equity. Companies can prepare similar budgets on a monthly basis. We could make a comparative analysis similar to that in Exhibit 11–7 for the balance sheet. Exhibit 11–8 shows how to calculate ending balances. We take most of these data from other budgets. As a result, we use a budgeted balance sheet to prove the accuracy of all other budgets. For example, the ending cash balance reported on Exhibit 11–6 also appears on the budgeted balance sheet along with all other changes in assets, liabilities, and owners' equity. We can apply ratio analysis to the budgeted balance sheet to discover expected unfavorable ratios in time to take corrective action. We also can prepare a return on investment ratio by relating expected net income to the capital employed. A lower return than desired by management may provide the stimulus to adjust management plans and budgets.

Government Budgeting

Budgeting differs depending on the profit status of the organization involved. For example, nonprofit budgets, such as government budgets, are appropriation budgets and differ from business budgets. An **appropriation budget** establishes fixed dollar amounts to achieve the objectives of the organizational unit for the period specified. Several factors in government cause the use of appropriation budgets. The stewardship function with its spending limits is very strong as the government unit is spending taxpayers' funds. The revenue sources of governments are limited and fixed for selected periods. Thus, we cannot base many expenditures on changing demands for services because revenues do not vary with demand. In addition, taxpayers' votes or legislative action earmark specific revenues, such as taxes, for certain activities. Available revenues limit expenditures on such activities.

Due to the appropriation budget concept, managers often focus more on spending resources than on obtaining results. At year-end, government managers are tempted to spend the appropriated amounts, even if not needed. Unfortunately, this budgeting concept encourages managers to think of incremental increases in budget amounts rather than to consider the services offered. A cost/benefit relationship is usually not the basis of performance evaluation. Further, failure to spend to the allowable limit implies managers do not need this large an amount, leading to reduced budgets for future periods.

A Step toward Improvement.   One modification in government budgeting results in more effective management control by relating costs to outputs or results. **Performance budgeting** achieves this by focusing on the government entity's results, such as the services performed and number of people served, rather than on dollars spent. In formulating a performance budget, managers make a precise definition of the work to be done and a careful estimate of what that work will cost. Work units and unit cost then become the basis for evaluating service levels. The functions and objectives of government agencies and departments become the basis for preparing performance budgets. An extreme form of **program budgeting**, performance budgeting involves attempts to describe program objectives and alternative methods of meeting them. Objectives are then matched with the costs of achieving them.

EXHIBIT 11-8 Budgeted Balance Sheet

HART COMPANY
Budgeted Balance Sheet
December 31, 19X2

Assets

Current Assets		*Amount*	*Percent*
Cash (from Exhibit 11–6)		$ 52,117	6.3%
Accounts receivable ($30,250 beginning balance			
+ $3,800,100 sales − $3,720,000 receipts)		110,350	13.2
Direct materials inventory (from Exhibit 10–9)		14,000	1.7
Work in process inventory (from Exhibit 10–13)		62,180	7.4
Finished goods inventory (from Exhibit 10–13)		$ 59,655	7.2
Total current assets		$298,302	35.8

Plant Assets

Land			$ 80,000	9.6
Buildings and Equipment ($2,080,603 beginning				
balance + $42,277 purchases)	$2,122,880			
Less: Accumulated depreciation ($600,000 beginning				
balance + $978,000 from Exhibit 10–12 + $90,000				
from Exhibit 11–1)	(1,668,000)		454,880	54.6
Total plant assets			$534,880	64.2
Total assets			$833,182	100.0%

Liabilities and Stockholders' Equity
Current Liabilities

Accounts payable (beginning balance + purchases of			
material, labor, overhead − disbursements of material,			
labor, overhead)		$ 40,933	4.9%
Income taxes payable (from Exhibit 11–7)		304,008	36.5
Total current liabilities		$344,941	41.4%

Stockholders' Equity

Common stock (from beginning balance sheet)		$ 200,500	24.1%
Retained earnings (from beginning balance sheet +			
$118,046 net income − $1,897 dividends from			
Exhibit 11–6)		287,741	34.5
Total stockholders' equity		$488,241	58.6
Total liabilities and stockholders' equity		$833,182	100.0%

Another budget modification, **zero-base budgeting** calls for a reevaluation of activities and their costs on a regular, rotating basis. For example, rather than review the entire organization every year, managers may apply zero-base budgeting to different departments on a three-year rotation. The focus in zero-base budgeting, similar to program budgeting, is on the objectives of the organization. When using the zero-base procedure, all programs are reviewed on a line item basis. This requires managers to justify their entire budgets, not just the changes proposed for the budget year. That is, managers assume that zero money will be spent on each activity until they can justify a greater expenditure—thus, the term *zero base*. The beginning point in the budgeting procedure is zero, rather than the amount already being spent as is often the approach used in incremental budgeting. Even though zero-base budgeting often generates much paperwork, companies can adapt certain of its aspects and acquire a valuable control process. A review of each department's purpose, costs, and methods of operation may reveal areas needing improvements.

Incremental Budgeting

Traditional budgeting directs attention to changes or differences between existing budget appropriations and proposed expenditures. Because such a budgeting procedure accepts the existing base and examines only the increments involved, it is called **incremental budgeting.** A decision maker focuses attention on a small number of the total relevant factors involved and analyzes only areas containing different alternatives. Incremental budgeting proponents argue that managers should move toward new projects slowly because of their limited ability to forecast the future. However, incremental budgeting has the weakness of encouraging companies to maintain functions and duties that have lost their usefulness. Often it is difficult to allocate resources away from outdated functions to new tasks. Companies need to periodically review all functions to obtain optimum utilization of resources.

Behavioral Aspects of Budgeting

A budgetary program needs the cooperation and participation of all members of management to yield its greatest benefits. Too often, a budgetary plan fails because top management lacks enthusiasm and pays only lip service to its execution. Some companies ignore the human factors and fail to educate personnel about the important benefits of the budgeting process. One cause of friction between budget and production personnel is the difference in their outlooks and backgrounds. Budgets emphasize past and future performance, while production personnel usually are more concerned with daily operations. In addition, management often fails to realize that, because the natural reaction to control and criticism is resistance and self-defense, they must sell the budget.

Budgets for Performance Evaluation

Top management may adopt a budget-constrained or a profit-conscious style for evaluating the performance of managers. A budget-constrained style evaluates performance on the ability to meet short-term budgets. A manager using a budget-constrained style of evaluation establishes well-defined work procedures and uses accounting data for evaluation because this information has the aura of clarity and objectivity. Efficiency of operations and strict role discernment—rather than individual employee needs—is this manager's concern. A manager using this style of evaluation is often insensitive to interpersonal relations and directs more attention to task and goal attainment.

Evaluation under a budget-constrained style encourages managers to avoid drastically reducing expenses for fear the company will cut next period's budgets. They also may attempt to have favorable variances by avoiding maintenance expenses and purchasing inferior material. Fear of failure keeps them from starting new projects that are expected to be profitable. Budget-constrained managers are likely to get the job accomplished without cost overruns, regardless of the human cost.

By way of contrast, a manager's ability to increase a unit's long-term effectiveness in relation to the organization's goals is the basis for evaluation under the profit-conscious style. This management style is much more concerned with cost measures within the profit center than with meeting budget considerations. Such managers are both efficient and people-conscious. Managers being evaluated under the profit-conscious style realize they will not be penalized for expenses in this period that would otherwise reduce later profits. They are more willing to take on new projects as long as such projects are expected to be profitable.

Fear of Failure

Unfortunately, budgets often become such inhibiting factors that management is afraid to take any risks for fear of not meeting the budget. Certainly, budgets are not a substitute for skilled management. They depict only a series of estimates that appear to represent good measurements at the time the budgets are established. When conditions change, managers should not believe that the budget is a straitjacket that they cannot revise.

Unrealistic Budgets

Despite increased recognition by managers that units should not be produced unless they can be sold, budgets often are a means of demanding higher productivity from employees. Even if managers do not overtly express this assumption to employees, it filters down to them in very subtle ways. An unrealistic budget that is almost impossible to meet does not motivate; it breeds resentment. Supervisors resent this practice for it places both them and their workers in situations in which they can never succeed. This practice also implies that a company does not believe the supervisor's own desire to do a good job is sufficient to meet a reasonable budget.

Often after meeting a budget, companies set a new higher goal in the next budget. Such constantly increasing pressure for greater production often leads to negative results in the long-run. People living under conditions of tension tend to become suspicious of every new move management makes to increase production. To combat such tensions, employees may establish informal groups antagonistic to management. These groups may be difficult to disband even after the tension dissipates.

Management needs to guard against demanding immediate increases in efficiency that hinder long-range growth in employee relations. Applying too much pressure to increase efficiency generates forces that decrease productivity in the long run. The better approach is to involve employees and thereby weaken the forces that tend to decrease efficiency.

Participative Budgeting and Continuous Improvement

Because a crucial problem in budget administration is for employees to accept budgets as a means of *continuous improvement,* a participative budgeting process may offer solutions. **Participative budgeting** is the practice of allowing individuals who are accountable for budgeted activities and performance to participate in establishing budgets. People directly involved in certain functions have more understanding of the resources each particular activity needs. Research in motivational theory has shown that it is in an organization's best interest to attempt to meet the esteem and self-actualization needs of participants. Making tasks more challenging and giving individuals a greater sense of responsibility can help meet these needs. Encouraging employees to participate in preparing budgets and comparing actual results often leads to increased performance and elimination of waste. Participation in the budgetary control system gets the participants' egos involved and committed to the budget; they are not just task involved.

Participative budgeting increases the probability that involved individuals will accept budget goals as their own and become personally committed to the control system. By participating, individuals accept budgeted objectives as their own aspiration levels or personal goals. When employees participate in the budget-setting process, they tend to believe that the budget is theirs and not just management's. Employees better understand how costs are assembled in a budget, as well as for which items they are responsible. Participative budget systems have a greater probability of achieving goal congruence than other models. Frequently, improved morale and greater initiative result from a high degree of participation.

Often management wants employees to believe that it is soliciting their suggestions when, in fact, it desires only false participation. Management may go through the motions of participative budgeting techniques without encouraging real participation. This may prove to be even more damaging because such insincere attitudes soon filter down the line to the employees. Employees strongly resent managers leading them to believe they are assisting in the budgetary process when they really are not. False participation is no better than imposing the budget—halfhearted acceptance is risky.

Limitations of Participation.   Participative budgeting does offer strong improvement over more traditional and authoritarian practices, however, employees may use their influence to arrive at goals that are less demanding or in conflict with companywide objectives. Managers can use participation to build organizational slack into their budgets by overestimating costs and underestimating revenues. **Slack** is the difference between the total resources available to the firm and the total resources necessary to maintain organizational activities. Repeatedly achieving easy goals or continually failing to attain goals that are too high can adversely influence aspiration levels and performance. Excessive slack is clearly detrimental to the best interests of an organization. In-depth reviews during budget development may detect slack.

Goal Congruence

A budgeting system should encourage **goal congruence** in which managers pursue objectives consistent with top-management's objectives. In addition, employees should participate in establishing performance goals and budgets that ensure attainment of company objectives. Managers must be certain that employees understand not only the reasons for budgets but also how budgets affect each of them. Participation in selecting measures of goal achievement increases employees' acceptance of a budgeting program.

Effective Communication

Expectancy theory suggests that individuals alter their behavior based on the expected outcome of an event. The utility derived from an expected outcome can be either intrinsic (such as praise or self-respect) or extrinsic (such as pay or promotion). Companies influence behavior and enhance performance by designing their budgeting systems to provide either intrinsic or extrinsic rewards in sufficient degrees.

A company's budgeting system provides the opportunity for much interaction between various management levels. Before beginning participative budgeting, top management should decide if they can be flexible and accept refined decisions jointly made by employees and low- and middle-level managers. Management should determine whether the personality and history of its work force are conducive to participation. Participative budgeting is not an all-or-nothing proposition. In practice, companies differ dramatically in both the amount and form of participation and influence they afford their operating managers in the budget- or target-setting process.

Basic Constraints.   By taking part in developing budgets, individuals become aware of the reasons for budget constraints. Budget staffs may increase line participation in developing budgets by giving employees a framework of basic constraints in advance. Budget staffs should explain management goals and future events expected to significantly affect operations. Managers should never discredit the intelligence and human dignity of employees at lower organizational levels. Employees who do not understand and accept their company's objectives are less willing to attempt to meet its goals.

Summary

Companies cannot operate or grow without adequate working capital or cash resources, making more timely, more detailed, and more reliable information about cash flows valuable. However, the true success of any budgetary system depends on its acceptance by all of the company members affected by the budget. Properly conducted participation should build acceptance of the budget by those responsible for meeting the budget. Accountants should not view their function as primarily one of criticizing the actions of others; instead, they should show they are willing to recommend needed budget revisions. Despite their advantages, budgets do have limitations because they can lead to faultfinding and pressure. The accountant should try to separate the budget from the person involved and look for the cause of, or reason for, unfavorable performance. Certainly the administration of the budget should not be rigid, since changed conditions may require budget revisions.

Important Terms and Concepts

Discretionary cost   330
Encumbered amount   330
Crashing   332
Program evaluation and review technique
  (PERT)   332
Yields   333
Liquidity   333
Security of principal   333
Appropriation budgeting   338

Performance budgeting   338
Program budgeting   338
Zero-base budgeting   339
Incremental budgeting   340
Participative budgeting   341
Slack   342
Goal congruence   342
Expectancy theory   342

Ethical Dilemma

**Ethics and Budgetary
Slack (CMA Adapted)**

Norton Company, a manufacturer of infant furniture and carriages, is in the initial stages of preparing the annual budget for 19X2. Scott Ford has recently joined Norton's accounting staff and wants to learn as much as possible about the company's budgeting process. During a recent lunch with Marge Atkins, sales manager, and Pete Granger, production manager, Ford said: "Since I'm new around here and am going to be involved with the preparation of the annual budget, I'd be interested to learn how the two of you estimate sales and production numbers."

Atkins: "We start out very methodically by looking at recent history, discussing what we know about current accounts, potential customers, and the general state of consumer spending. Then, we add that usual dose of intuition to come up with the best forecast we can."

Granger: "I usually take the sales projections as the basis for my budget projections. Of course, we have to make an estimate of what this year's closing inventories will be which is sometimes difficult."

Ford: "Why does that present a problem? There must have been an estimate of closing inventories in the budget for the current year."

Granger: "Those numbers aren't always reliable since Marge makes similar adjustments to the sales numbers before passing them on to me."

Ford: "What kind of adjustments?" Atkins: "Well, we don't want to fall short of the sales projections so we generally give ourselves a little breathing room by lowering the initial sales projection anywhere from 5 to 10 percent."

Granger: "So, you can see why this year's budget is not a very reliable starting point. We always have to adjust the projected production rates as the year progresses and, of course, this changes the ending inventory estimates. By the way, we make similar adjustments to expenses by adding at least 10 percent to the estimates. I think everyone around here does the same thing."

Required:

a. Marge Atkins and Pete Granger have described the use of budgetary slack.
   (1) Explain why Atkins and Granger behave in this manner and describe the benefits they expect to realize from the use of budgetary slack.
   (2) Explain how the use of budgetary slack can adversely affect Atkins and Granger.
b. As a management accountant, Scott Ford believes that the behavior described by Marge Atkins and Pete Granger may be unethical and that he may have an obligation not to support this behavior. Explain why the use of budgetary slack may be unethical considering such factors as competence, confidentiality, integrity, and objectivity.

Problem for Self-Study

Gross Margin Analysis

Comparative data for years 19X1 and 19X2 follow for Nolan Corporation:

	19X1	*19X2*	*Increase/Decrease*
Sales revenue	$5,000,000	$6,000,125	$1,000,125
Cost of sales	3,000,000	4,069,650	1,069,650
Gross margin	$2,000,000	$1,930,475	$ (69,525)
Number of units sold	10,000		

Required:

Prepare two quantitative analyses of the change in Gross Margin if the following exclusive conditions were to prevail:

a. Selling prices were 15 percent higher during 19X2.

b. In 19X2 the volume of sales was 10 percent higher. (Carry unit sales price and unit cost to four decimal places.)

Solution to Problem for Self-Study

NOLAN CORPORATION

---

a. $5,000,000 19X1 sales/10,000 units = $500 19X1 unit sales price

$500 × 115% = $575 19X2 unit sales price

$6,000,125 19X2 sales/$575 19X2 unit sales price = 10,435 units sold in 19X2

$4,069,650 19X2 cost of sales/10,435 19X2 units sold = $390 unit cost of sales in 19X2

Increase in amount of sales attributed to:

Quantity factor:				
Increase in number of units sold in 19X2	435			
Multiply by unit sales price in 19X1	× $500	$217,500		
Price factor:				
Increase in unit sales price in 19X2	$75			
Multiply by number of units sold in 19X2	× 10,435	782,625	$1,000,125	

Increase in amount of cost of goods sold attributed to:

Quantity factor:			
Increase in number of units sold in 19X2	435		
Multiply by unit cost price in 19X1	× $300	$130,500	
Price factor:			
Increase in unit cost price in 19X2	$ 90		
Multiply by number of units sold in 19X2	× 10,435	939,150	1,069,650
Decrease in gross profit on sales			$ 69,525

b. 10% × 10,000 = 1,000 units increase in sales for 19X2

$6,000,125 19X2 sales/11,000 units sold in 19X2 = $545.4659 unit sales price for 19X2

$4,069,650 19X2 cost of sales/11,000 19X2 units sold in 19X2 = $369.9682 unit cost of sales for 19X2

Increase in amount of sales attributed to:

Quantity factor:			
Increase in number of units sold in 19X2	1,000		
Multiply by unit sales price in 19X1	× $500	$500,000	
Price factor:			
Increase in unit sales price in 19X2	$45.4659		
Multiply by number of units sold in 19X2	× 11,000	500,125	
Net increase in amount of sales			$1,000,125

Increase in amount of cost of goods sold attributed to:

Quantity factor:			
Increase in number of units sold in 19X2	1,000		
Multiply by unit cost price in 19X1	× $300	$300,000	
Price factor:			
Increase in unit cost price in 19X2	$69.9682		
Multiply by number of units sold in 19X2	× 11,000	769,650	
Net increase in amount of cost of goods sold			1,069,650
Decrease in gross profit on sales			$ 69,525

Review Questions

1. Contrast budget-related behavior in organizations of different size, technology, and structure.

2. Why is it important that top management become involved in the budgeting process? How can budgets be viewed as a means of coordination and continuous improvement?

3. Discuss four different approaches to establishing an advertising budget.

4. Discuss how the design of the budgeting system influences managerial behavior and performance.

5. List several modifications of government budgeting that would allow more effective managerial control.

6. How could you use PERT in time budget analysis?

7. What advantages over zero-base budgeting do proponents of incremental budgeting stress?

8. Discuss the strengths as well as the weaknesses of participative budgeting.

9. Contrast budget-constrained style versus profit conscious style of using budgeted and accounting cost information in performance evaluation.

10. Define the expectancy theory of motivation and how it relates to budgets and cost accounting systems.

Exercises

E11–1 Cash Receipts from Credit Sales
You have been asked to forecast the cash receipts from credit sales for the month of May for the Reid Company. The company is engaged in seasonal production, and May credit sales are estimated to be only $144,000. Discount terms of 2/10, n/30 are offered customers as an incentive to pay their bills early. The collection pattern is assumed to be 20 percent during the discount period and month of sale; 7 percent after the discount period has expired, but within the month of sale; 43 percent in the first month after sale; 28.5 percent in the second month after sale. The accounts receivable balance as of April 30 is $164,250; one-third of the balance represents March sales and the remainder, April sales. All accounts receivable from months prior to March have been paid or written off.

Required:
Determine the May cash receipts from credit sales.

E11–2 Forecasting Cash Disbursements and Collections
Dorette Corporation management makes the following data available:

	Charge Sales	Purchases
February	$75,000	$50,000
March	85,000	58,000
April	50,000	31,000
May	60,000	45,000
June (budgeted)	80,000	62,000

The company takes full advantage of the 3 percent discount allowed on purchases paid for by the 10th of the following month. Dorette expects $13,560 June operating expenses, including $3,000 depreciation. The company's cash balance at June 1 is $8,500.

Collections from charge customers are normally 50 percent in the month of sale, 30 percent in the month following the sale, and 12 percent in the second month following the sale. The balance is expected to be uncollectible. June cash sales are expected to be $20,000.

Required:

a. Calculate the cash disbursement expected during June.
b. Compute the cash collections expected from charge customers during June.
c. Give the cash balance at June 30 which is forecasted.

E11–3 Cash Receipts by Month

Judging by management's experience with similar organizations, Chariott Company forecast their collection pattern for Accounts Receivable as follows:

Twenty percent of the credit sales are paid after the end of the month of sales but within the discount period.

An additional 70 percent of credit sales are paid in the month following the sale after the discount period has expired.

An additional 5 percent of credit sales are paid within the second month after the sale is made.

Operations began on January 1. Management has agreed to offer cash discounts for credit sales only on a term of 3/10 EOM, n/60. Cash and credit sales by month are forecast as follows:

	Cash Sales	Credit Sales
January	$6,000	$20,000
February	5,000	30,000
March	8,000	38,000

Required:

Prepare the cash receipts budget by month for the first quarter of the year.

E11–4 Cash Receipts from Accounts Receivable

Collections from Troy, Inc., customers conform to the following pattern:

20% in month of sale
50% in first month after sale
25% in the second month after sale

The $210,000 balance in Accounts Receivable on May 1 is made up of uncollected sales from the following months:

From January sales	$ 1,000
From February sales	5,000
From March sales	60,000
From April sales	144,000
	$210,000

May credit sales totaled $150,000 and the cash balance on May 1 was $32,000. Assume no bad debts have been written off.

Required:

Determine the cash collections for May from Accounts Receivable.

E11–5 Credit Sales Collections with Discounts

As an inducement to pay their bills early, Ingalls, Inc., offers a discount of 3/10, n/30 to its customers. Its credit sales for April are estimated to be $70,000. The collection pattern is assumed to be 25 percent within the discount period and month of sale; 30 percent after the discount period has expired, but within the month of sale; 20 percent in the first month after sale; 10 percent in the second month after sale, and 5 percent in the third month after sale. The remaining percent is considered uncollectible.

The accounts receivable account balance as of March 31 appears as follows:

Accounts Receivable

From January sales	5,000	
From February sales	18,000	
From March sales	27,000	

No bad debts were written off from February and March sales; however, Joe Brown's account balance of $1,000 resulting from a sale made in January was written off in March at the time Brown declared bankruptcy. The allowance method for recording the bad debts expense adjustment is used.

Required:

a. Determine the April cash receipts from credit sales.
b. If there is any difference between April cash receipts from March sales and the $27,000 balance in the Accounts Receivable account from March sales, explain the difference.

E11–6 Monthly Cash Budget

Salmon Corporation asks you to prepare its cash budget for November. Management expects $40,000 cash sales and $120,000 credit sales for November with a beginning cash balance of $80,000. Their collection pattern in the past, which you believe will continue in the future, has been 30 percent in the month of sale, 60 percent in the next month after sale, and 4 percent in the second month after sale.

The Accounts Receivable as of November 1 are $49,000 from October sales and $4,000 from September sales. No bad debts have been written off from the sales of these months.

The company has experienced a 20 percent gross profit on sales before considering the purchase discount. They have enough stock in inventory for lead time and safety stock and have been following the purchase pattern in the last three months of ordering only enough for current sales. Their payment pattern is 45 percent in the month in which the sale is made because their suppliers allow a cash discount then of 2 percent. The remaining 55 percent is paid in the month after the sale is made.

Payroll disbursements for November will be $55,700. Other disbursements will be as follows:

Rent	$ 1,000
Loan repayment and interest	15,000
Miscellaneous cash expenses	5,400

In addition, Salmon records $18,000 depreciation expense and $6,700 goodwill amortization in November.

Required:

Prepare a cash budget for November.

E11–7 Quarterly Cash Requirements

For the first quarter of 19X2, Bluefield Company prepared the following estimates of unit sales:

	Dolls	*Toy Drums*
January.	10,100	5,000
February	9,800	5,600
March	9,200	5,200
April	9,400	5,480

The company must have a beginning inventory of each type of product that is equal to 75 percent of the upcoming month's sales in units. During December 19X1, the company sold 9,900 dolls and 4,580 toy drums.

Bluefield's 19X1 cost was $15 per unit for dolls and $20 per unit for toy drums. The company pays for all purchases during the month following the purchase.

Required:

Determine the cash requirements for each of the first three months of 19X2 for merchandise purchases. Assume December budgeted sales were the same as actual sales.

E11–8 Detailed Monthly Cash Budget

The management of Doug, Inc., requests that you prepare a cash budget for January. The cash balance is $35,150 on January 1. Analysis of their collection pattern in the past shows that accounts receivable are paid as follows:

> 30 percent in the month of sale
> 40 percent in the first month after sale
> 15 percent in the second month after sale
> 5 percent in the third month after sale

On January 1, the accounts receivable is $255,000. Of this balance, $140,000 came from December sales, $45,000 from November sales, $60,000 from October sales, and $10,000 from September sales. No accounts receivable have been written off.

Management has been in negotiation with the National Bank and will receive a $60,000, 8 percent loan on January 1. Interest is to be paid at the end of each month.

Additional expenses for the month will be the following:

Salaries	$155,180
Materials and supplies	184,000
Depreciation	15,180
Rent	10,000
Amortization of goodwill	77,000

Total sales for January are forecasted to be $600,000.

Required:

Prepare a detailed cash budget for January.

Problems

P11–9 Behavioral Impact of Management Actions

What is the behavioral impact of:

a. The budgeting process being referred to in a budget orientation meeting as *meeting the budget.*

b. Using *concern with cost* as a means of evaluating a manager's performance more than his or her ability to meet the budget.

c. Providing supervisors with alternative sources of information allowing managers to continually test the validity of the accounting data rather than relying wholly on the budget.

P11–10 Monthly Detailed Cash Budget

The management of Bosco Company requests that you prepare a cash budget for December. The cash balance is $46,000 on December 1. Managers forecast December cash sales to be $30,000 and December credit sales to be $90,000. Analysis of their collection pattern in the past shows that accounts receivable are paid as follows: 50 percent during the month of sale, 35 percent in the first month after the sale, 10 percent in the second month after the sale, 2 percent in the third month after the sale.

On December 1, accounts receivable are $114,000. Of this balance, $80,000 came from November sales; $21,000 from October sales; $8,500 from September sales; and $4,500 from August sales. No accounts receivable have been written off.

A 6 percent $50,000 loan is due at the end of the month. Only interest has been paid at the end of each previous month. A final monthly interest payment is due at the end of December. Additional expenses for the month will be:

Payroll	$35,000
Materials and supplies	40,000
Depreciation	15,000
Insurance	4,000*

*This has not been prepaid in a previous month.

Required:

Prepare a detailed cash budget for December.

P11–11 Quarterly Cash Budget

Earl Douglass Wholesalers asks your advice in preparing cash and other budget information for October, November, and December 19X1. The September 30, 19X1, balance sheet showed the following balances:

Cash	$ 20,100
Accounts receivable	995,816
Accounts payable	289,915

Management supplies you with these assumptions to use in budget preparation: All sales are credit sales that are billed on the last day of the month; and customers are allowed a 3 percent discount if they pay within 10 days after the billing date. Receivables are recorded at gross. The estimated collection pattern is 60 percent within the discount period, an additional 25 percent in the month after billing that does not receive a discount, and 9 percent in the second month after billing.

Fifty-four percent of all material purchases and marketing and administrative expenses are expected to be paid for in the month purchased and the remainder in the following month. Each month's units of ending inventory are equal to 120 percent of the next month's units of sale. Each unit of inventory costs $50. Marketing and administrative expenses, of which $3,500 is monthly depreciation, are equal to 10 percent of the current month's sale. Actual and budgeted sales are as follows:

	Units	Dollars
August	10,000	$750,000
September	10,500	787,500
October	11,000	836,000
November	11,200	851,200
December	11,500	874,300
January 19X2	11,800	890,000

Equipment costing $200,000 is paid for in November. Dividends of $40,000 are paid in December.

Required:

a. Prepare a cash budget for the last quarter of 19X1, rounding to whole dollars.
b. Explain what you can logically conclude regarding accuracy and fluctuations in market demand, reliability of suppliers, and lead time in view of management's desired inventory level.

P11–12 Analysis of Gross Margin

Top management of O'Neill Company are concerned that gross margin has decreased from $183,000 in 19X1 to $146,700 in 19X2. They ask for your assistance in providing for an analysis of the causes of change. The company operates a plant in Dallas and one in Memphis. The plant in Memphis produces only one type of valve, while the Dallas plant manufactures several varieties. The following information concerns the plants:

	19X2	19X1
Dallas plant:		
Sales	$375,000	$450,000
Cost of sales	277,500	315,000
Gross margin	$ 97,500	$135,000

	19X2		19X1	
	Amount	Per Unit	Amount	Per Unit
Memphis plant:				
Sales	$125,000	$12.50	$120,000	$12.00
Cost of sales	75,800	7.58	72,000	7.20
Gross margin	$ 49,200	$ 4.92	$ 48,000	$ 4.80

Required:

Prepare a quantitative detailed analysis of the causes for the change in gross margin for each plant based on the preceding data. Explain your analysis indicating where management attention needs to be directed.

SPATS

P11–13 Additional Financing Necessary

Addemup, Inc., is a manufacturer of calculators. Actual credit sales for the last month of 19X2 and the first two months of 19X3 and projected credit sales for March and April are as follows:

December (actual)	$1,000,000
January (actual)	1,250,000
February (actual)	1,000,000
March (projected)	1,300,000
April (projected)	1,400,000

The average markup on cost for the company's merchandise is 50 percent. The company collects 50 percent of its sales during the month the sale is made; 30 percent is collected during the month following the sale; and 15 percent is collected in the second month following the sale. Managers predict March cash sales of $50,000.

Purchases of merchandise are paid for as follows: 20 percent paid during the month of purchase and 80 percent paid during the month following the purchase. Merchandise is purchased in the month preceding the sale. The company plans to maintain the current level of inventory.

To meet loan obligations, there must be a cash balance of $100,000 on hand at the end of the coming month of March. Other cash payments anticipated during the month of March are salaries and wages, $125,000; other expenses, $90,000, of which $12,000 is amortization of bond discount and $8,000 is depreciation; and equipment purchases, $200,000. The cash balance on March 1, 19X3, is $106,000.

Required:

a. Prepare a cash budget for March 19X3.
b. If additional financing is necessary to have the required ending cash balance, indicate the financing needed.

Cases

Writing

C11–14 Participative Management

President David Morgan of Waco Company was meeting with several other top executives when the subject of participative and autocratic management was introduced. Morgan began bragging about the success his company had when participative management was implemented. In supporting his convictions, he said, "Let me tell you about our latest adoption of a new budgeting technique called zero-based budgeting. Top management of our company left the decision whether to adopt this approach completely to the division controllers. After the approach was explained to the controllers, they voted on its adoption and have wholeheartedly supported it ever since."

However, the president's interpretation of participative management is somewhat biased. Division controllers received a letter from the vice president of finance inviting them to the headquarter's offices for a one-day seminar to learn about zero-based budgeting. The vice president indicated in the letter that he was extremely excited about this new approach, and he felt it offered the company many advantages.

Plans were made to bring in a nationally recognized consultant for a day to explain the theory of this new management tool. At noon the division controllers would vote on its adoption. If a positive vote was received, the consultant would spend the afternoon explaining the implementation of this budgeting technique.

The consultant was somewhat surprised by the questions he received during the morning session. He realized that if a positive vote was received, controllers would have the responsibility of selling the idea to the supervisors at their plants. A management by objective (MBO) system was in effect at all divisions in which each manager was given specific goals. However, the managers insisted that they were never given enough funds to fulfill these goals; as a result, they were reprimanded at year-end for having unfavorable variances. Repeatedly, managers asked the consultant if this new budgeting approach integrated objectives with funds. As one controller asked, "If you provide me with a certain sum of money on the condition that I promise to fulfill certain stated goals, will I be fussed at if I only achieve these goals and not those that are more stringent?" After the consultant convinced the controllers that zero-based budgeting required the preparation of various levels of effort and the proposed expenditures to meet each level, the controllers voted unanimously to adopt the new system.

Required:

Agree or disagree with the president's contention that participative management is in effect, discussing your reasons.

C11–15 Behavioral Role of Cost Accountants in Participation Processes

Management by objectives (MBO) is a participative process involving all management levels. This process measures and evaluates both segment and individual performance. MBO is a strategy of planning and obtaining results in the direction that management wishes to take while meeting the goals and needs of its participants. Upper and lower levels of management jointly identify the organization's goals. The relative areas of responsibility are defined and expressed in measurable terms. These terms are used to assess the performance of each manager.

The exact procedures employed in implementing MBO vary from organization to organization and from unit to unit; however, the basic elements of objective setting, participation of subordinates in objective setting, and feedback and evaluation are usually parts of any MBO program. The emphasis, for both the superior and the subordinate, is on participation, communication, and feedback.

Required:

a. Describe briefly the steps you think should be involved to have successful employee participation in setting goals.
b. Explain to what degree the process suffers if some of these steps are omitted.
c. Discuss what problems you can identify with a participative approach such as MBO.
d. Assume you are the chief cost accountant, what should be your role in a participative approach:
   (1) Within your own cost accounting department?
   (2) Within the entire organization?
e. Describe how the degree of goal congruence already achieved within an organization affects the successful implementation of a participative process.
f. Discuss why a participative system could stimulate interest in the products of the cost accounting system over a wider range of users.

C11–16 Top Management's Influence on Divisional Behavior

The six divisions of Beale, Inc., are in different regions of the United States, and all but one are situated a great distance from corporate headquarters. The Western Division is the exception; its offices as well as Beale's corporate headquarters are in San Diego. Two months ago, division managers received a notice from the president requesting their attendance at a meeting in San Diego to hear a presentation on a proposed budgeting system. Division managers were told to plan to be in attendance at the meeting for two days and to be certain that their assistant managers were in their division's office during their absence.

According to the agenda, the first morning of the meeting was to be spent in introducing the budgeting system. After lunch on the first day, the division managers were to vote concerning their acceptance of the system. Then, assuming the vote was positive to accept the system, the remainder of the two days would be spent in learning the system's details and how to implement it.

Under the present budgeting system, division managers submit budgeted revenue and expense figures to corporate headquarters. It is understood that since these were merely ball-park figures the corporate controller and president would refine them. However, before the expense and revenue projections are finalized, a conference call is made to each division to receive their input.

The morning of the first day of the division managers' meeting was spent in presenting the new budget system. Top management explained that they believed the divisions needed more autonomy and in turn, the division managers should have the opportunity to earn a bonus if they performed within the budget. The bonus would be calculated on divisional return on investment using an asset base composed of divisional plant assets employed. Corporate management would establish divisional budgets since they were more aware of the role of each division in achieving the overall company objectives. The previous year's data adjusted for economic and industry changes would be the basis for each division's budget. Since each division differs significantly in operating and marketing techniques used, corporate managers explained that they would consider these variations. In addition, after corporate management established divisional budgets, they cannot be modified by division managers under the new system because of the confusion it would create in developing the total companywide budget. As in the past, corporate managers would have the final decision regarding the commitment of funds to purchase machinery and other capital assets as well as to expand existing facilities. Division executives would continue to propose investment projects for their own segments for corporate review.

After the president outlined the proposed procedure, the Western Division manager explained the challenges each individual would have supporting the new system. Further, the opportunity to earn a bonus was presented as a significant advantage. The Western Division manager urged adoption of the system and used data from his segment to reveal what he expected his bonus to be next year if the plan was accepted.

Since he had more immediate access to the corporate managers and knew what was being planned for the meeting, he had previously taken the specifics of the proposal and applied them to his own situation in preparation for this presentation. To further his argument, he stressed how much more aware each division manager would be of the income/asset relationship. He concluded by stating that he was confident of their vote, and that if they had any questions, they could be answered in the implementation session which would begin after the vote was conducted.

As the division managers dismissed for lunch, several commented, "Where do we go from here?" The Northern Division manager remarked, "Now, you are smarter than that, do we have any choice? Besides if we render a negative vote, what do we do during the one and one-half days remaining?"

Required:

a. Identify the behavioral problems you expect the company to encounter as a result of the meeting.

b. Evaluate the proposed budgeting system, identifying the major disadvantages in implementation.

C11–17 Corporate and Individual Goals

The president of Ferony Company has spent several hours reviewing the previous year's financial statement. He is concerned that earnings declined last year. Ferony experienced steady growth in market share and excellent profit margins in its first eight years of operation, but in the last two years, its share of the market has remained level. In view of these developments, the president has called a meeting of the top management team, the firm's four vice presidents. After studying historical data and predicting future sales, members of the team presented their strategy for profit improvement.

The vice president of marketing suggested that the promotion mix be changed so that sales promotion is directed toward additional markets. He also recommended that additional funds be applied toward advertising so that a national television campaign can be included. He believes that this strategy can increase market share and earnings enough so that an increase in sales price is unnecessary.

The vice president of finance disagrees with the vice president of marketing's approach. She believes an increase in sales price is justified since competitors' prices are already higher than Ferony's prices. In addition, she is skeptical about increasing the advertising budget, because she is doubtful about the short-run benefit. The financial vice president's concern is that the company's cash flow and short-term investment position will be jeopardized.

The vice president of marketing insists that even though many of the additional sales generated by the national television campaign would be credit sales, 95 percent of them would be collected within 90 days.

The vice president of engineering and research agrees that additional markets should be sought, but that product improvement is the answer. He suggests that the company conduct extensive tests for the purpose of making innovations in the company's product line. He believes that with these additional features, the company will be recognized as an industry leader.

The vice president of production is concerned about rising labor rates and believes that unless Ferony increases its labor rates, many of the skilled labor workers will look for work elsewhere. She agrees with the vice president of engineering and research that the product could be improved by incorporating new features and possibly by using a higher grade of material. In addition, she believes that time and motion studies would result in an improvement in the work flow.

The president has listened intently to each suggestion and agrees with many of these ideas, as he recognizes the need for increasing labor rates. However, he believes that company management should become more involved in civic activities; in fact, he has just been approached by the campaign manager for the United Fund Drive about volunteers. He believes additional study is required before a specific management strategy is chosen.

Required:

State the implied corporate goals being expressed by each of the following and how these relate to their own personal goals:

a. Vice president of marketing.
b. Vice president of finance.
c. Vice president of engineering and research.
d. Vice president of production.
e. President.

C11–18 Budget Construction and Behavioral Implications of Management by Exception

Resorts Hotel is on the Mississippi gulf shores, a popular summer resort area. During the summer months, the population of the area doubles, and management relies on university students for much of its labor force. There is never a shortage of students to fill the positions. These university students are supervised by regular staff, many of whom have not completed a high-school education, but have learned their management skills through on-the-job training.

The hotel is organized by departments with each department head reporting to a recently hired central manager. She has instituted several new changes in the reporting system. One change she is trying to implement is to install standards in the routine area of operations. For instance, she has used time and motion studies to determine the average time it should take to clean a hotel room. Also, she has installed standards in the Linen Cleaning and Maintenance Department.

With the introduction of standards, she also began a new management-by-exception reporting system. The responsibility reports now show budget variances so that more attention can be given to costs that differ significantly from budget. The central manager explained this as an added advantage to the department heads. However, to be fair, she indicated that she would allow each department head a 3 percent cushion and not get exceedingly upset as long as the variance stayed within a 3 percent range either over or under budget.

In establishing the budget which is expressed on a quarterly basis, the central manager used last year's spring quarter as the basis with a 5 percent inflation factor added. The hotel operates on a calendar year basis. Motel rooms occupied is the primary activity level with additional activities pertinent to each department. For example, a copy of the Linen Cleaning and Maintenance Department's recently distributed report follows:

Resorts Hotel
Linen Cleaning and Maintenance
Third Quarter, 19X2

	Budget	Actual	Over (Under) Budget	Percent Over (Under) Budget
Rooms occupied	12,000	15,100		
Pounds of linens processed	60,000	74,800		
Expenses:				
Cleaning and				
maintenance labor	$160,000	$163,000	$ 3,000	1.9%
Electricity and water	36,000	37,000	1,000	2.8
Bleach and detergent	25,000	29,700	4,700	18.8
Other laundry supplies	15,000	18,500	3,500	23.3
Leasing of equipment	46,000	52,000	6,000	13.0
Marketing expenses—allocated ...	10,000	11,000	1,000	10.0
Administrative expenses—				
allocated	5,000	5,250	250	0.5

The central manager commented: "Department heads, please note that equipment leasing, marketing expenses, and administrative expenses exceeded budget by more than the 3 percent margin of error we agreed was acceptable. Also, attention must immediately be directed to bleach, detergent, and supplies expenses."

Required:

a. Enumerate any negative behavioral implications to management by exception as it is normally applied.

b. Describe the net effect of having a 3 percent cushion.

c. Evaluate the method used to construct the budget.

d. Decide if the information given to the department heads is sufficient for them to improve their performance. If not, what information should be communicated by budget variances?

e. Determine if the central manager can effectively appraise departmental performance with the system presently in effect.

f. List the advantages and disadvantages in employing university students during the peak season from a cost standpoint.

g. Assume a management viewpoint and describe the problems likely encountered with employing university students during the peak season on a part-time basis.

C11–19 Appropriation Budgets and Implications of Budgetary Systems

Five years ago Randy Mart, president of Leisure Products, announced plans to enter the computer market and began appointing senior executives to a microcomputer division. However, the company soon realized that competition was stiffer than anticipated and that they had failed to prepare adequate plans for this venture. As a result, the company suffered alarming financial reversals in this division, but Mart insisted that the fault was due to the executives' lack of expertise in this area as well as inadequate dedication to company goals. The president was correct in forecasting increased demand for company products other than microcomputers. Production activity was expanded in these divisions to meet the larger market.

Before leaving on a recent trip to visit plants in Japan that were developing unique software applications for microcomputers, Mart announced the reassignment of key senior executives. In his absence, four of the senior executives, who had formerly been in the microcomputer division, convinced the board of directors that Mart's reorganization was inappropriate and that he should be replaced. They were so successful that when Mart returned, he was handed a letter of resignation for his signature.

Guy Cunningham was brought in to assume presidency. Cunningham had worked his way up through factory operations and was an expert on matters dealing with production. However, his experience with administrative work was limited. He soon let it be known indirectly that he considered administrative departments as necessary evils because they represented expenses that had to be allocated to revenue producing departments.

Cunningham's former employment was as president of a manufacturing concern about the same size as Leisure Products, except that his former company manufactured few product lines in large lots and sold them to relatively few customers. Leisure Products, on the other hand, makes a wide variety of products in small lots and sells them in small orders to many customers. Cunningham was amazed at the size of the office force of Leisure Products and believed they were overstaffed.

Cunningham obtained past data showing the number of employees by administrative department. He was told by a number of the department heads that past top management had given them freedom to add to their staffs as they saw fit, except that new supervisors and assistants to department heads were to be cleared with the president. Budgets had been established for all factory departments, but no budgetary control procedures had been developed for the administrative departments. The administrative departments included Personnel, Purchasing, Credit and Collections, Order Filling, and Accounting. A monthly report of expenses was furnished to all department heads.

After studying the situation, Cunningham called a conference with the vice presidents and showed them his plan for adopting an appropriation budget for the administrative departments and for later expanding its adoption to all departments. Under this approach, fixed amounts were to be established for each department which could be applied to achieve the objectives of the organizational unit for the next period. The vice president of finance had previously worked in a governmental unit and did not believe this budgeting system would be appropriate for Leisure Products. He convinced Cunningham to postpone adoption of this budgeting plan.

Word leaked to the administrative department heads that the new president had been heard to remark, "I must turn this company around quickly; otherwise, I will also be asked to sign a letter of resignation. Therefore, I should be an autocratic boss and impose a budget even if it isn't an appropriation budget." These department heads began meeting informally to discuss possible future events. They knew that some of their departments had, in fact, overexpanded their staffs. Some of these department heads had been employed by Leisure for 15 years and commented, "I wish we could go back to the good ole days."

However, the Personnel and Purchasing department heads knew that their own departments could not handle additional work without more help and that, with announced plans for expansion, more work was expected. These two department heads realized that they would have to do their best to convince the new president that their departments should have increased budgets, reflecting the additional employees needed in the near future.

Required:

a. What behavioral impact would you expect the replacement of Randy Mart as president to have on implementing the budgetary system?

b. If Leisure Products should adopt an appropriation basis for its budgeting process
   (1) Describe the expected effect on the department head's behavior.
   (2) Explain why these department heads would likely behave in this manner.
c. Contrast the behavioral implications on the budgetary control system if Leisure Products employs a participative versus an imposed budgetary approach.
d. Suggest how Leisure's top management can effectively apply the expectancy theory of motivation in implementing their budgetary system.
e. Compare the administrative department heads' behavior before Cunningham assumed the presidency with their expected behavior after implementation of a new budget system by Cunningham. Explain the changes in behavior.
f. What accounting data could the purchasing and personnel department heads use to support their conviction that they are performing efficiently and need additional funding?
g. What role should the accounting department head play in light of the new management style, and how will the administrative department heads react to the accountant's monthly reports of departmental activity?

Writing

C11–20 Participative Budgeting

Realizing that in designing budgeting systems, cost accountants often are faced with the problem of deciding how much and what degrees of participation operating managers should be allowed in setting budgets, you are conducting a survey of various industries to gain an insight into budgeting procedures. After visiting four companies in the state of Maryland, you compile the following notes concerning their participative budgeting procedures:

In Company A, top management sets operating budgets using information generally available at the time. General managers of each operating division are usually not consulted when divisional earning targets are established because top management believes it has all the relevant data. Aggregate divisional sales forecasts are derived from the earnings targets. Division general managers and their marketing, finance, and production managers formulate their labor, material, and other production requirements and order forecasts from these estimates. These production budgets and forecasts are used to prepare each division's detailed operating plan. The president indicates that this procedure is best because fewer hours are spent in budgeting, and divisional managers are freed to spend their time in day-to-day operations.

In Company B, divisional general managers establish operating budgets for their divisions. However, before they set these budgets, the production manager for each division obtains detailed forecasts for usage of direct material, direct labor, and direct factory overhead by department from each department manager. Production managers review the forecasts submitted by department managers and adjust these where they deem appropriate. Adjusted forecasts are then submitted to the division's general manager for consideration and use in setting operation budgets for the division.

In Company C, a large manufacturing company, cost center managers work closely with department managers in preparing initial forecasts for their cost centers for the coming year. Then, department managers bring their cost center managers together for a series of group meetings to help set departmental goals. Each cost center manager presents an initial forecast for a joint evaluation by all of the cost center managers present and the department manager. Together, they make any necessary adjustments to meet overall company goals. Group target-setting meetings also are held at the various management levels. Finally, the budgets set in these meetings are compiled in an overall operating plan.

Management of Company D devotes much of its time in late October and November to preparing budget proposals. Weekends find many of the managers in group meetings trying to meet deadlines in the budgeting procedure. One division manager and his immediate subordinates refer to this season as "management's folly." Taking this as a cue, department managers in this division often refer to the efforts at forecasting dollar outlays in such terms as *playing with funny money.* Budgets in this department are often unrelated to actual expenditures and serve no control purpose. Funds are transferred from one account to another when it appears that certain budgeted expenses are far less than actual results. Also, at year-end, expenses are charged off to other expense classifications to prevent significant unfavorable variances in certain categories.

Required:

a. Define the term *participative budgeting.*
b. Discuss two advantages of participative budgeting.
c. Discuss the problems and limitations of participative budgeting.
d. Discuss the budgeting procedures used by each of the four companies.

CHAPTER 12

Target Costing, Kaizen Costing, and Standard Costing for Materials and Labor

Chapter Objectives

After studying this chapter, you should be able to:

1. Contrast the differences between target costing, kaizen costing, and standard costing.

2. Explain the benefits of a standard cost system and how traditional variance measures are changing.

3. Analyze and record material and labor variances in either a job order or process costing system.

4. Describe the role variances play in evaluating actual performance.

Introduction

Proper control of costs requires a comparison of actual cost results with some target or predetermined amount. Because historical data cannot satisfy the need for determining the acceptability of performance, accountants developed standard costing. **Standard costs** represent what costs should be under attainable, acceptable, but not perfect, performance. Standard costs are determined scientifically using such means as time studies and engineering estimates. When actual operations exceed standards, managers investigate the variances. Thus, companies use cost standards as a basis for measurement and comparison.

Most companies have traditionally used standard cost systems as their primary cost control vehicle. However, as they improve their cost management systems, they find deficiencies in their conventional standard costing system. For example, now managers recognize that standard cost variance analysis often ignores quality levels and disregards feedback concerning improvements. Further, companies often fail to use operating results to update standards frequently enough. Traditional standard cost systems measured labor efficiency crudely as a total output per person. Instead, the personnel whose performance is being evaluated should own the standards and play a significant role in continuous improvement. Additional deficiencies include standard costing efficiency and volume variances leading to dysfunctional behavior by encouraging more output than is needed so there would be more units over which to allocate fixed costs.

Target, Kaizen, and Standard Costing

With the advent of target costing and kaizen costing, managers are questioning if standard costing needs to be supplemented or modified to include these new approaches. This would give them a total cost management system with **target costing** supporting the cost reduction process in the developing and designing phases of new models and **kaizen costing** supporting the cost reduction process in the manufacturing phase of existing products. The Japanese word "kaizen" refers to continuous accumulations of small betterment activities rather than innovative improvement.

Target Costs Represent Market-Driven Standards

Target costing is the process of planning specific products that satisfy customers' needs and then establishing the target cost using this formula:

$$\text{Target sales price} - \text{Target profits} = \text{Target costs}$$

Using the formula, companies calculate backward from a product's sales price to arrive at a target cost the engineers' design cannot exceed. Serving as should costs, target costs become goals for designers and production personnel. **Target costs** are less than currently achievable costs that are based on standard processes and technologies. Standards serve as benchmarks that measure incremental progress toward meeting the target cost objectives.

- Target costs represent **market-driven standards:** competitive market price less desired mark-up = allowable cost.
- Standard costs represent **engineering-driven standards:** summation of engineering-driven standard cost + desired mark-up = desired market price.

Productivity

Current Cost Management Practice

Culp, Inc., a $260-million textile manufacturer for the home furnishings industry, has just completed the final stages of implementation of its newly designed costing system. They have undertaken a target costing program to help them build profit and decrease the cost of products at the design stage. Culp's approach was to combine the efforts of marketing, operations, and accounting; it presumes a relationship with and working knowledge of each to be successful. This relationship was achieved by no longer treating cost accountants as after-the-fact scorekeepers. Culp's No. 1 maxim of cost management is: unless cost management is treated as a viable part of the firm's strategic direction, ongoing cost management efforts are doomed to failure. Culp believed that cost accountants should not be treated as beancounters destined to crunch a lot of numbers without any input or explanation as to why the numbers are the way they are. Culp managers found that with target costing, the pricing decision became the focus point of their efforts, not the product's cost. Their second focus was on their profit plan because medium to long-term profit planning must be in place to incorporate target costing. They report that the largest change in their thinking has been to stop reporting what products should cost and instead to report what products will cost.

Gilda M. Agacer, Donald W. Baker, and Les Miles, "Beyond ABC: Target Costing," *Management Accounting,* November 1994, pp. 45–49.

Managers use value engineering to realize their target costs by further comparisons of target costs with achieved costs. The basic idea of **value engineering** is that products and services have functions to perform and the amount of their value is measured by the ratio of these functions to their costs. Target costing is applied in the developing and design stages unlike standard costing that is applied in the production stage. Value engineering differs from the control activities in traditional standard cost systems because it encourages finding creative ways to reduce cost standards. In contrast, standard cost systems emphasize establishing and meeting cost performance standards.

Further Differences.   Target costs and standard costs differ because target costing represents a cost planning method that emphasizes the control of design specifications and manufacturing techniques. As discussed in Chapter 5, target costs are market driven and come from external sources, such as customers, while standard costs are predetermined from an internal analysis of manufacturing processes.

Standard costs may not be as effective a cost management tool as target costs because they provide after-the-fact cost data while target costs provide before-the-fact information. Also, managers frequently change target costs during a product's life cycle as they continuously improve their activities. However, some companies are replacing engineered standards with rolling averages of historical actual costs, using the theoretical optimum as the long-range performance target. Although target costs represent costs they strongly want to achieve, top managers must recognize that the target cost must be attainable to motivate employees.

Kaizen Costing

Kaizen costing ensures continuous improvement by supporting the cost reduction process in the manufacturing phase. As discussed previously, target costing is effective in managing costs in the new product design and development stage. Used with target costing, kaizen costing helps reduce costs throughout the entire product design-development-manufacturing cycle. By relating target costing and kaizen costing, companies are better able to implement total cost management during the entire life of a product or service.

A kaizen costing system has specific cost-improvement activities for each department and each accounting period. Kaizen costing activities include cost reduction activities requiring changes in the way a company manufactures existing products. For example, a company will undertake kaizen costing activities if there is a large difference between actual and target costs after it has been producing a new product for several months. Companies implement other kaizen costing activities continuously to ensure constant improvement. The actual production cost of the previous year serves as the cost base of the current year. Projected reductions in manufacturing variable costs provide cost reduction targets. The ratio of the target reduction amount to the cost base is called the *target reduction rate.*

Kaizen Costing Compared with Standard Costing.   Kaizen costing operates outside a company's standard cost system and is not limited by the financial accounting focus of the standard costing system. It functions in a similar fashion as a budgetary control system. The strength of kaizen costing is its close link with a company's profit planning process. This link allows managers to monitor progress toward the company's long-term goals without focusing on meeting cost standards and studying variances in a traditional cost control system. Kaizen costing's aim is to reduce actual costs below the standard costs. This is in distinct contrast to a standard cost system's emphasis of meeting the cost standards in effect. Exhibit 12–1 contrasts standard costing concepts with kaizen costing concepts.

EXHIBIT 12–1 Standard versus Kaizen Costing

Standard Costing Concepts	*Kaizen Costing Concepts*
Cost control system concept.	Cost reduction system concept.
Assume current manufacturing conditions.	Assume continuous improvement in manufacturing.
Meet cost performance standards.	Achieve cost reduction targets.
Standard Costing Techniques	*Kaizen Costing Techniques*
Standards are set annually or semiannually.	Cost reduction targets are set and applied monthly.
	Continuous improvement (kaizen) is implemented during the year to attain target profit or to reduce the gap between target profit and estimated profit.
Cost variance analysis involves standard costs and actual costs.	Cost variance analysis involves target kaizen costs and actual cost reduction amounts.
Investigate and respond when standards are not met.	Investigate and respond when target kaizen amounts are not attained.

Source: Yasuhiro Monden and John Lee, "How a Japanese Auto Maker Reduces Cost," *Management Accounting,* August 1993, p. 26.

Standard Costing Systems

Establishing correct standards for a company's manufacturing expense is important because the accuracy of the standards usually determines the success of the standard cost system. Managers and employees responsible for meeting the standards should approve the bases for the standards. Also, those responsible for meeting standards should have the opportunity to participate in the standard setting process. They should believe that the standard is accurate and expressed in terms they understand. While accountants and industrial engineers provide technical information about the tightness of standards, the final decision should reflect input from the production line managers and their immediate supervisors. Standards should be set only after there has been face-to-face communication, bargaining, and interaction between the individuals involved. Finally, the basic plan should win the support of top management.

Standard Costs and Budgets

Standard costs become the unit building block for the company's budget. After establishing standards for each unit produced, accountants multiply standard costs by the total units they plan to produce to determine budgeted costs. When estimating costs for new products, managers do not completely rely on prevailing engineering standards. Instead, they establish target costs derived from estimates of a competitive market price.

Advantages of a Standard Cost System

A standard cost system makes managers and employees cost conscious because variances between standard costs and actual costs help pinpoint waste. By calling attention to cost variations, standards can serve as a compass guiding managers toward improvements. The process of setting standards also assists in management's planning for efficient and economical operations. Because managers should thoroughly study all factors affecting costs when setting standards, they often discover operations needing improvement.

Standard cost systems also integrate managerial, accounting, and engineering functions. Setting standards involves defining goals and reviewing with all concerned their roles in the attainment of those goals. For example, workers know what is expected of them when their standard is expressed as so many units per hour and they have helped establish this standard.

Levels of Activity and Efficiency

Managers should make certain decisions before setting standards: First, they must determine the number of units that a company plans to make and sell. Second, managers should decide how demanding they want their standards to be before estimating the hours of operation needed to provide for this production level. We use the theoretical, practical, normal, and expected actual capacity levels introduced in Chapter 4 for setting standards. Standards set on the basis of theoretical capacity are **ideal standards,** because they reflect maximum efficiency. Even though standards set on a theoretical or practical capacity are usually not attainable, they can be useful in motivating employees. Generally, accountants set standards on a less demanding level. **Normal** and **expected actual standards** make allowances for machine breakdowns, normal material loss, and expected lost time. However, normal standards make no allowances for abnormal loss or waste.

There are varying degrees of tightness in standards based on attainable performance. Many competent managers believe that to encourage high standards of performance, standards should provide a goal. However, this is often detrimental to employee morale. Tight standards may not only discourage those individuals whose efforts managers are measuring but also slow down their results. Cost figures derived from unrealistic standards can give management a false sense of security. Some managers may provide for contingencies in standards by making them fairly loose. However, standard costs based on comparatively low efficiency tend to hide and to perpetuate waste that should be highlighted. Loose standards provide unreliable data for measuring cost because they underwrite inefficiencies that need to be reviewed and corrected.

Rigid adherence to either extreme is usually unsound. Because inclusion of excessive contingencies and abnormal losses defeats the purpose of a standard cost system, accountants should not include budgetary slack in cost standards. Instead, they should set standards on a reasonable basis that considers all known normal factors and use of proper processing methods. Such standards involve expectation of more than a continuation of the past. Accountants usually set standards tightly enough so operating personnel consider achievement possible.

Incorporation in the Accounting System

Rather than enter standard costs in journals, managers sometimes use them only for statistical purposes with variances analyzed to determine corrective measures. Generally, managers take standard costs and variances more seriously and are more responsive to cost reduction if accountants enter standards in the ledger accounts. Incorporating cost standards in the accounting system provides an orderly and somewhat compulsory plan for cost analysis. However, the important factor is subjecting actual costs to proper measurement and control.

Setting Material Standards

Material standards consist of both price and usage standards. Industrial engineers develop specifications for the kinds and quantities of material used in producing the goods budgeted. Operation schedules list the materials and quantities required for the expected volume of production. The Purchasing Department receives the operation schedule and bills of material established jointly by the Engineering Department, the manufacturing supervisor, and the accountant. This information becomes the basis for the material price standard.

Material Quantity Standards

Managers can study results by placing a quantity of material in process under controlled conditions. There may, however, be a tendency for workers to produce with less scrap material under these test conditions. Accountants should watch for this artificial element because, if they fail to consider it, the material quantity standard could be understated.

Zero Defect's Influence on Material Quantity Standards. Traditionally, quantity standards contained an allowance for lost materials and inefficiencies in the production process. However, the popular zero defect philosophy does not include an allowance for waste. Including an allowance for defective items and scrap often prevents improvement because companies accept losses as normal and ignore product waste. Instead, the focus under zero defect is to avoid losses of material and to isolate them for study when they do occur. Companies charge resources lost due to waste directly to the supervisor whose group caused the error.

Also, more and more companies are not building in time for rework. As a result, their workers have become more careful in preventing errors because rework time comes out of regular production hours assigned to their job. However, accountants appropriately add a waste allowance when companies buy materials in bars or lengths and cut definite sizes of parts from sheet stocks of material.

Material Price Standards

Because purchasing agents are responsible for material price variances, they should help set the price standards. Price standards should reflect managers' study of market conditions, vendors' quoted prices, and the optimum size of a purchase order. The Just-in-Time (JIT) management philosophy minimizes inventories, keeping on hand only the amount needed in production until the next order arrives. The impact on material price standards of more frequent, smaller orders is a consideration.

Purchasing Responsible for Quality.   If a company holds its Purchasing Department accountable for only the price of purchased components, not their quality, Purchasing's motivation is to find inexpensive vendors. The department is less concerned about meeting the material quality specifications. Because cheaper materials often require substantial manufacturing rework time, unfavorable labor efficiency variances may result at the same time the purchasing department has a favorable material price variance. To prevent this from occurring, the purchasing department must meet the material quality specified.

Applied Rates for Material Handling.   When accountants apply material handling costs to the materials inventory accounts, as illustrated in Chapter 5, the price standard should also reflect this. Accountants can develop applied rates for freight in, purchasing, receiving, and other costs associated with the material handling function. An alternative to using applied rates for freight charges on raw material is to use only FOB destination prices in establishing the standards.

Setting Labor Standards

Like materials standards, labor standards also consist of price and usage (or efficiency) variances. However, the human factor makes it more difficult to set labor standard costs than material standard costs. There are many elements, such as the state of a person's health and fatigue, that can cause variances in productivity. A person's attitude toward a supervisor, along with other psychological factors, also affects productive efficiency. These factors, as well as skill and seniority, are important considerations in establishing labor standards.

Labor Efficiency Standards

Examination of past payroll and production records can reveal the worker-hours used on various jobs and can help determine standard performance. However, if the layout of the present plant differs from that of the past plant, a special investigation may be necessary to determine the probable effect of these changes. Also, historical records may include unnecessary operations. In industries where no data reflecting past performance are available, it may be necessary to obtain time reports from the workers for a limited period as a basis for the standards.

Time and Motion Study.   A time study develops time standards and piece rates that the average operator can meet daily without affecting his or her well-being; it is an appropriate basis for setting labor efficiency standards. A time study that breaks up the operating cycle into distinct elements can detect stalling attempts and irregularities earlier. Because the worker representative studied is important, plant supervisors should observe the employee's work habits before selection. The worker assigned should not be abnormally fast or slow but rather a seasoned worker who performs at a steady pace. There should be no evidence of an attempt to confuse the person making the time and motion study. The time-study analyst should exercise judgment in excluding those observations that reflect abnormal conditions. Advance estimates become the basis for setting labor standards if the operation has never been performed before or if the operation is of a special type not expected to be repeated.

Test Runs.   Test runs are another approach to establishing labor quantity standards. A weakness is that an average situation is difficult to find because plant conditions are never static and no two similar jobs take the same amount of manufacturing time. Past performance, on the other hand, gives an average, while time and motion study gives an objective result. Management should consider using a combination of these methods to obtain more accurate labor standards.

Labor Rate Standards

Referring only to the rates paid previously may result in inaccurate rate standards. Competitive markets in which supply and demand are active and constantly changing often determine labor rates. The labor rate standard should adhere closely to the actual labor rates paid in the next period.

A company may establish a standard rate for the job; regardless of who performs the job, the rate stays the same. Or, a company may establish a rate for an individual worker, and the worker receives this rate regardless of the work performed. The wage is relatively fixed and can be used as standard when labor contracts exist. If direct labor operations in each cost center are not uniform and require varying degrees of skill, each operation should have a separate standard hourly labor rate.

Group Piece Rates.   If managers have difficulty in applying a straight piecework plan, they can adapt a group piece rate plan. Departments performing multiple operations use this plan and pay for completed jobs, not for individual units. The total price of the completed job is the sum of the unit rates. This price includes an allowance for repairing defective work, supervision, and training new employees. Group rates also allow for time lost due to the handling of parts.

Incentive Wages.   If workers receive an opportunity to increase their earnings by producing more units than standard, time studies and job evaluations supply the hourly base rate for the standard. The hourly rate on the job evaluation sheet used for pricing the allowed time on the job also may be used. This base rate often becomes the guaranteed rate that a company pays its workers regardless of their output. Management may believe they should establish a guaranteed wage rate to be fair to new, inexperienced workers who cannot produce at a high level of output because of inadequate training and experience. In determining the guaranteed and incentive wage rates, management should make certain that the spread between the figure used as a base rate and possible earnings is great enough to encourage workers to greater productivity.

Current Cost Management Practice

Procter & Gamble is shifting to everyday low pricing—called value pricing—rather than maintaining high list prices punctured by frequent and irregular discounts. They also are tearing down and rebuilding nearly every activity that contributes to high costs. P&G is redesigning the way it develops, manufactures, distributes, prices, markets, and sells products to deliver better value at every point in the supply chain. Top managers believe this is the only way to rekindle the brand loyalty that earned P&G's profits in the first place. They recognize that consumers are not willing to subsidize costs that do not show up on the product so they are redefining consumer values by not charging customers for non-value-added costs. Managers realize that it is hard for the company to change its thinking—ironically, they are doing this by making a rule that it is okay to break an old rule.

Bill Saporito,"Behind the Tumult at P&G," *Fortune*, March 7, 1994, pp. 74–82.

Salaried Direct Labor Workers.   Because direct labor workers are performing a greater variety of tasks and working on multiple products, labor costs in an automated manufacturing system are largely fixed. When there is a temporary delay in production, companies do not stop paying their workers. The labor cost that remains in a flexible manufacturing system represents the cost of workers performing the initial machine and material loading, but only for a single shift of a three-shift operation. Accountants use an average salary figure that includes payroll taxes and such employee benefits as vacation pay, jury duty allowance, insurance, and pensions.

Material Variances Using Job Order Costing

After determining quantity and price standards, accountants prepare a **standard specification** for each product unit. Even though Chapter 13 discusses establishing overhead standards, the following standard specification for bread includes overhead to be complete. Note that overhead is applied on the basis of machine-hours. For instance, at the same time that 1.2 hours of labor occurs in making the bread, overhead is being applied. The standard does not specify 3.2 total hours to finish the product, but 1.2 hours of labor and 2 hours of machine time.

Flour material (3 pounds @ $4 per pound)	$12
Mixing and Baking labor (1.2 labor-hours @ $15 per hour)	18
Overhead (2 machine-hours @ $20 per hour)	40
Total standard cost per unit	$70

Material variances are as follows:

1. Material price variance: (Actual material price − Standard material price) × Actual material quantity. (Note the appropriate name of this variance; there is a price variance only if the actual price varies from the standard price.)

2. Material usage or quantity or efficiency variance: (Actual material quantity − Standard material quantity) × Standard material price.

The following data illustrate the calculation of material variances:

> Standard cost per unit as shown in the standard specification:
>   3 pounds of flour @ $4 per pound = $12
>   Actual pounds of flour purchased: 3,220 pounds @ $3.10 per pound
>   Actual pounds of flour used in production: 2,950
>   Loaves of bread finished: 900

Material Price Variances

Assume the company purchased 3,220 pounds of flour costing $3.10 per pound, but only used 2,950 pounds in production. We can compute the price variance either on the basis of material purchased or material used as follows:

Material purchase price variance

($3.10 Actual material price − $4.00 Standard material price) × 3,220 pounds purchased = $2,898 favorable **material purchase price variance**

Material usage price variance

($3.10 Actual material price − $4.00 Standard material price) × 2,950 pounds used = $2,655 favorable **material usage price variance**

Regardless of the approach used, the variance is favorable because flour was purchased at a savings of $0.90 per pound ($3.10 − $4). We assume that the company purchased the same grade of material specified and that the saving does not result from acquiring a lower and cheaper grade of material.

Material Quantity Variances

We apply standards to the actual production of finished units. Because there were 900 loaves produced, the **standard quantity allowed** must be 2,700 pounds (900 units × 3 pounds = 2,700). In computing the material usage variance, we compare 2,950 actual pounds used to produce the 900 loaves with the 2,700 standard pounds allowed. We multiply the difference in quantity used by the standard material price to arrive at the material usage variance.

Material usage (quantity or efficiency) variance

(2,950 Actual material quantity − 2,700 Standard material quantity) × $4 Standard material price = $1,000 unfavorable **material quantity variance**

The material usage variance is unfavorable since 250 more pounds were used to make the 900 units than was specified in the standard. Of course, one way to have favorable material quantity variances is to inject only a portion of the material required to make each finished unit. However, an imperfect product will result; quality control established in the factory should prevent this from occurring. We always assume that the units produced are perfect units that have passed inspection.

Diagram Approach.   Instead of using the equation approach of determining material price and usage variances, you may find the diagram approach easier. The diagram approach has a built-in proof when the quantity purchased exactly equals the quantity used. The built-in proof results because the two variances should equal the difference between actual and standard costs. When we are determining a material purchase price variance, we cannot determine the proof of a net variance because the quantity variance and the price variance are based on different amounts of input. We use the general terms *input* and *output* to make the approach applicable to all measures. Input, such as flour or labor efforts, is typically measured in gallons, pounds, machine-hours, or labor-hours. Output is the product manufactured, such as shirts or bread. Output may not be a finished product ready for use; instead, it is the product completed through the cost center's processing. Note that the variances are the same as we computed using equations.

Diagram Approach for Material Purchase Price Variance and Quantity Variance

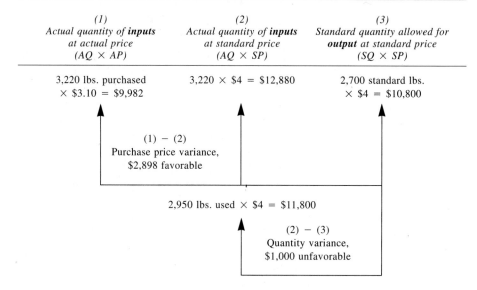

Diagram Approach for Material Usage Price Variance and Quantity Variance

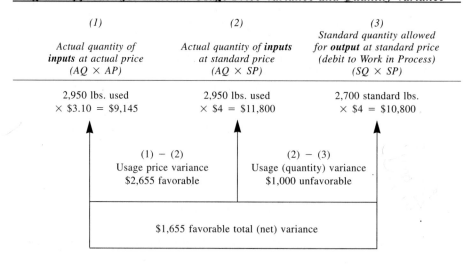

Avoid Rote Memory in Interpreting Variances.   We encourage you not to memorize the formulas for standard variances; instead, try to analyze the components of each variance. Also, think of comparing actual quantity and price with standard quantity and price. In turn, avoid seeing if their signs are negative or positive when labeling variances as favorable or unfavorable. Instead of using rote memory, think through the situation. If you were to use only 2,700 pounds of flour, but you used 2,950 pounds, logic tells you that the variance is unfavorable because you used 250 more pounds of flour than the standard said you should. Likewise, if you paid only $3.10 a pound for material and the standard price is $4, you have saved the company 90 cents a pound, resulting in a favorable variance. For this reason, we encourage you not to think of a negative or positive sign when comparing actual and standard.

Journal Entries for Material

As illustrated earlier, we can compute the material price variance on the basis of either pounds used or pounds purchased. The approach chosen depends on when we integrate the material standards in the accounting system. There are three different methods of reflecting material price and quantity variances.

1. Isolating the price variance at the time of purchase, and keeping the materials inventory at standard cost is one method. Recording material purchase price variances is the preferred method. This method saves a company clerical costs by not requiring an actual inventory costing method (such as FIFO, LIFO, or average cost). Also, this approach allows for more timely investigation of the variance.

2. Not recording the price variance until materials are issued from the storeroom into production is a second method. When recording material usage price variances, the Material Inventory ledger account must be kept on some actual costing basis which requires much clerical effort to account for inventories. An alternative treatment for recording the usage price variance is to wait until all unused materials are returned to the storeroom and total usage on the job is determined.

3. Recording the material purchase price variance when materials are received from a supplier and allowing the Direct Materials Inventory account to be kept at standard is a third method. Then the price variance on the material used is transferred from the Purchase Price Variance ledger account to the Material Usage Price Variance ledger account. The remaining balance in the purchase price variance is treated as a valuation account. This balance represents the price variance for the material remaining unused in inventory. It is deducted from (if a favorable or credit balance) or is added to (if an unfavorable or debit balance) the standard cost of material to arrive at an adjusted actual cost of material.

The last approach is a combination of the two previous methods; it determines both a material purchase price and a material usage price variance. If there is a large difference between the amount of material purchased and the amount of material used each accounting period, the additional effort required under this method is warranted. With recognition of JIT and inventory carrying costs, however, more companies are closely matching their material purchases with usage.

The following illustrates each of these methods using the data presented earlier for a job order costing system producing bread from a custom recipe:

> Standard cost per loaf: 3 pounds of flour @ $4 per pound = $12
> Pounds purchased: 3,220 pounds @ $3.10 per pound
> Pounds used in production: 2,950
> Loaves finished: 900
> No beginning inventory in the Direct Materials Inventory account

Note that because managers rarely know the eventual output at the time materials are issued, the practical procedure is to charge the entire quantity to work in process and determine any quantity variance after workers complete the job. Whenever lost or spoiled units are likely to result from the production process, or whenever managers do not know the eventual yield at the start of a job, they estimate how much material they need to complete the order and requisition accordingly.

Managers monitor progress and estimate costs at key points during production. Often there are inspection points where they can measure the ratio of bad units to good ones. Also, if the performance of certain machines or operators is typical of the entire process, these points can serve as reliable indicators of the job. These indicators serve as frequent performance appraisals without awaiting variance analyses. The journal entries are as follows under each of the three methods showing material variances:

Material price variance recognized at time of purchase (material inventory at standard)

Direct Materials Inventory (3,220 pounds × $4)	12,880	
Material Purchase Price Variance		
(3,220 pounds × $0.90 @ pound)		2,898
Accounts Payable (3,220 pounds × $3.10)		9,982
Work in Process Inventory (2,950 pounds × $4)	11,800	
Direct Materials Inventory (2,950 pounds × $4) .		11,800

We make the following entry after knowing the output of 900 loaves:

Material Quantity Variance (250 pounds × $4)	1,000	
Work in Process Inventory		1,000

Material price variance recognized at time of usage (material inventory at actual)

Direct Materials Inventory (3,220 pounds × $3.10) . . .	9,982	
Accounts Payable		9,982
Work in Process Inventory (2,950 pounds × $4)	11,800	
Direct Materials Inventory (2,950 pounds × $3.10)		9,145
Material Usage Price Variance		
(2,950 pounds × $0.90)		2,655

We make the following entry after knowing the output:

Material Quantity Variance (250 pounds × $4)	1,000	
Work in Process Inventory		1,000

Material purchase price and usage price variance

Direct Materials Inventory (3,220 pounds × $4)	12,880	
Material Purchase Price Variance		
(3,220 pounds × $0.90 @ pound)		2,898
Accounts Payable (3,220 pounds × $3.10)		9,982
Work in Process Inventory (2,950 pounds × $4)	11,800	
Direct Materials Inventory (2,950 pounds × $4) .		11,800
Material Purchase Price Variance	2,655	
Material Usage Price Variance		
(2,950 pounds × $0.90)		2,655
Material Quantity Variance (250 pounds × $4)	1,000	
Work in Process Inventory		1,000

This leaves a balance of $243 in the Material Purchase Price Variance account which reflects the $0.90 variance per pound for the 270 pounds of flour left in inventory.

Material Purchase Price Variance

2,950 pounds used × $0.90 variance	2,655	(3,220 pounds purchased × $0.90 variance)
		2,898
		(This equals 270 pounds in inventory ×
		$0.90 variance Balance 243

This method leaves a balance sheet like this:

Direct materials inventory (270 pounds × at $4 standard cost)	$1,080
Less material purchase price variance	243
Direct materials inventory (adjusted to actual)	$ 837

Other combinations of journal entries record the material price and quantity variances, depending on the sequence of events occurring. Remember that the net amount debited to Work in Process as the cost of the job should reflect standard quantity allowed × standard price. You do not have to determine the standard cost of a job to compute the material variances. However, when you enter standards in the journal, you compute the standard cost of the job. Thus, Finished Goods Inventory is always at standard cost.

JIT and Material Variance Analysis

The three materials variance analyses presented study only the efficiency of the production process and ignore the volume of inventory maintained, purchasing procedures, and consumer demand. In contrast, minimization of inventory holding costs is a central theme of JIT inventory procedures. Using JIT concepts, consumer demand pulls product through the production process.

We can modify the variance analysis presented by adding a Materials Inventory Variance as follows:[1]

(Actual quantity *purchased* − Actual quantity *used*) × Standard price

[1] For an in-depth discussion of this variance, see Horace W. Harrell, "Materials Variance Analysis and JIT: A New Approach," *Management Accounting,* May 1992, pp. 33–38.

Using the previous illustration in which the bakery purchased 3,220 pounds of flour and used 2,950 pounds, the following variance results:

(3,220 − 2,950) × \$4 = \$1,080 Unfavorable material inventory variance

An unfavorable material inventory variance results because purchases exceed usage. Conversely, a favorable variance results when inventory decreases, which is a movement in the direction of minimum inventory holding. This follows the JIT concept that manufacturers should not hold inventory waiting to be used in production, but instead materials should arrive as they are needed for production. Accountants also can compute a finished goods inventory variance to measure the waste of holding excessive finished goods.

Labor Variances Using Job Order Costing

We can compute labor variances identical to those illustrated for material after determining labor standards. The labor variances are

1. **Labor rate variance:** (Actual labor rate − Standard labor rate) × Actual labor-hours.
2. **Labor efficiency (quantity or time) variance:** (Actual labor-hours − Standard labor-hours) × Standard labor rate per hour.

Unlike materials, companies cannot purchase labor services in one period, store them, and then use these services in the next period. Thus, both labor variances relate to the same period. To illustrate the computation of these variances, assume the following for a job order company:

Standard cost per unit as shown in the standard specification:
1.2 hours @ \$15 per hour = \$18
Total direct wages paid: 1,280 hours @ \$15.20 per hour = \$19,456
Units: 900 units finished

Labor Rate Variance

(\$15.20 actual labor rate − \$15 standard labor rate) × 1,280 actual labor-hours = \$256 *unfavorable labor rate variance*

The labor rate variance is unfavorable because workers received \$0.20 more per actual hour worked than was indicated in the standard specifications.

Labor Efficiency Variance

The **standard hours allowed** for actual production amount to 1,080 (1.2 hours × 900 units produced). We compute standard hours in a similar manner as standard pounds. The labor efficiency variance is

Labor efficiency (quantity or time) variance

(1,280 actual labor-hours − 1,080 standard labor-hours) × \$15 standard labor rate per hour = \$3,000 unfavorable labor efficiency variance

The labor efficiency variance is unfavorable because workers used 200 more hours to manufacture the 900 loaves of bread than specified in the standard. We multiply the 200 excess hours by the standard labor rate to isolate the effects of quantity only. Alternatively, using the diagram approach, the variances are the same as follows:

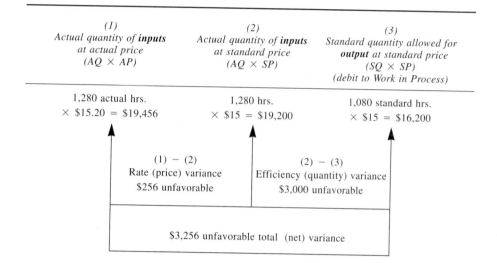

(1) Actual quantity of **inputs** at actual price (AQ × AP)	(2) Actual quantity of **inputs** at standard price (AQ × SP)	(3) Standard quantity allowed for **output** at standard price (SQ × SP) (debit to Work in Process)
1,280 actual hrs. × $15.20 = $19,456	1,280 hrs. × $15 = $19,200	1,080 standard hrs. × $15 = $16,200
(1) − (2) Rate (price) variance $256 unfavorable	(2) − (3) Efficiency (quantity) variance $3,000 unfavorable	
$3,256 unfavorable total (net) variance		

Labor Efficiency under JIT

Because productivity measures based on direct labor efficiency can be manipulated on the plant floor in dysfunctional ways, interpreting labor variances requires care. Standards for different products are not identical. Since products have different standards, managers may increase efficiency by running simple products and avoiding more complex, harder-to-run jobs. Also, managers can improve direct labor efficiency by increasing the lot size because setups and changeovers often are included in overhead rather than in direct labor. However, long production runs may not be profitable because there may be insufficient demand for the product manufactured.

Under traditional manufacturing systems, long runs lead to better use of direct labor for a given amount of indirect labor. Today, supervisors realize that keeping machines working to produce inventory not yet needed is contradictory to the JIT philosophy. Instead, they schedule short production runs coupled with frequent changeovers. Using a JIT system, if a worker's output during a day is lower than expected, bottlenecks either before or after the worker are the likely cause. Regardless of where bottlenecks occur, they force workers to stop producing through no fault of their own.

Also, when a company bases incentive pay on the total output produced, not the output that passes inspection, workers focus on the amount of goods produced, regardless of how much of the product is unusable. Therefore, companies should consider the quality of the products manufactured in measuring worker efficiency.

Because automated JIT production policies make the traditional evaluation of labor and machine time invalid, companies should change their evaluation measures to reflect this. Companies that maintain their previous efficiency measures after adopting the JIT production philosophy confuse both workers and managers. Using multiple performance measures—including the effect of a manager's operations on productivity and quality—is a better indicator than sole reliance on labor efficiency variances. Managers should ensure that labor efficiency does not reward production while demand is ignored. Otherwise, the Finished Goods storeroom may be overstocked with products no one wishes to buy.

Journal Entries for Labor

Several combinations of journal entries record the labor variances. The following one records only the rate variance while the job is in process. We do not know the amount nor the direction (whether favorable or unfavorable) until workers complete the job. We adjust Work in Process at that time, not while the job is in process.

Work in Process Inventory (1,280 hours × $15 per hour)	19,200	
Labor Rate Variance (0.20 × 1,280 hours)	256	
Wages Payable (1,280 hours × $15.20 per hour) .		19,456

After determining the output of 900 loaves, the Labor Efficiency Variance is recorded as follows:

Labor Efficiency Variance (200 hours × $15).......	3,000	
Work in Process Inventory		3,000

We do not transfer the job into Finished Goods Inventory until we have applied its factory overhead. Chapter 13 discusses the standards for factory overhead costs.

Combined Net Variances.   Rather than determine separate price and quantity variances for material and labor, some companies merely determine total variances for these factors. We do not recommend this approach, as it provides no way to identify factors that cause the variance. Instead of combining all contributing factors, an approach should pinpoint each.

Material and Labor Variances Using Process Costing

The previous examples illustrated standards in a job order costing system. Standards in process costing effectively eliminate the conflicts and complexities of the FIFO and weighted-average methods that Chapters 7 and 8 introduced. In a process costing system, as in a job order cost system, managers know in advance the standard cost specifications for all three cost components: material, labor, and overhead. However, they cannot determine the standard hours, gallons, pounds, or other measures allowed for process costing operations until the accounting period ends. Then they multiply the standard quantity per unit by the equivalent units for each cost element.

Assume another bakery employing a process costing system uses the same material standards illustrated for job order costing but processes bread from a standard recipe. There was no beginning inventory, and the following goods were transferred to or remain in ending inventory:

Units transferred .... 1,000 units
Ending Inventory (1/5 material, 3/4 labor) .... 100 units

The equivalent units (EU) for material and labor are

EU, material = 1,000 + 20 (100 units × 1/5) = 1,020
EU, labor = 1,000 + 75 (100 units × 3/4) = 1,075

Material Variances.   The standard pounds of flour allowed are 3,060 (1,020 EU × 3 pounds). If this process costing company used 3,000 pounds of flour, the material quantity variance would be favorable, as follows:

(3,000 actual material quantity − 3,060 standard material quantity) × $4 standard material price = $240 favorable material quantity variance

Assume further that this processing company purchased 3,150 pounds of flour costing $4.15 per pound. As in a job order costing system, we can compute the price variance in either of the following ways:

Material purchase price variance

($4.15 actual material price − $4.00 standard material price) × 3,150 pounds purchased = $472.50 unfavorable material purchase price variance

Material usage price variance

($4.15 actual material price − $4.00 standard material price) × 3,000 pounds used = $450 unfavorable material usage price variance

Labor variances.   Assuming the process costing company used 1,040 hours of labor this period at a $14.75 hourly rate, the labor variances are

Labor efficiency variance

Standard hours allowed: 1,290 hours (1,075 EU × 1.2)

(1,040 actual labor-hours − 1,290 standard labor-hours) × $15 standard labor rate per hour = $3,750 favorable labor efficiency variance

Labor rate variance

($14.75 actual labor rate − $15.00 standard labor rate) × 1,040 actual labor-hours = $260 favorable labor rate variance

Self-study problems at the end of Chapters 12 and 13 illustrate the use of standards in a process cost system.

Standard Costs in Factories of the Future

Companies are changing their traditional standard cost models to meet the needs of their flexible manufacturing systems. Managers perform many traditional performance evaluations using a standard cost system. However, conventional monthly variance analysis is becoming obsolete because the information arrives too late and at too aggregate a level to be helpful for operational control. Modern cost management systems compile standard cost variances quickly and frequently. Managers recognize effective control of materials, labor, and overhead occurs daily. If a problem arises in any of these areas, production managers strive to handle it immediately.

New cost accounting procedures are replacing the standard cost model to make standards current and relevant when: *(a)* short production runs are tailored for each customer, *(b)* product characteristics are changing, and *(c)* the production method changes for each batch depending on which machines are available when the order is processed. Because automation provides opportunities for more predictable yields, variances are being determined much more rapidly in time for corrections. The following summarize the impact of flexible manufacturing systems on standard costs:

1. Target costing and kaizen costing are modifying standard cost systems.

2. Standard cost models based on large-scale production of an item with unchanging specifications are less common.

3. Standard cost systems are less oriented toward standard direct labor-hours and direct material costs with more measurement of all significant resource costs. While an orientation directed to labor and material may be adequate for accounting purposes, it is insufficient for decision making and performance improvement/reporting purposes.

4. Emphasis solely on price variances is shifting to include the costs for rejected materials or late deliveries. By focusing on the lowest price, a system de-emphasizes material quality and delivery. This lack of attention creates downstream quality problems and forces the company to maintain inventory buffers to compensate for poor delivery performance.

5. Price fixation is shifting to consolidate vendors and to develop long-term partnership arrangements with them. Former systems measuring price variances forced buyers to judge vendors strictly on price. Thus, buyers showed no loyalty to suppliers and adversarial relationships with vendors resulted. Vendors were unwilling to raise quality, improve schedule performance, or work to solve supply problems because they knew the company bought strictly on price.

6. Costs of large orders are being traced to purchases and matched with their price variances. A system concentrating only on price variances encourages buyers to increase their order quantities for higher discounts. Large orders create the potential risk of excess inventory, tie up cash, and extend lead times. Also, large purchase quantities increase inventory buffers and require more warehousing space.

7. Material standard specifications do not include costs of rework and spoiled units. A company is more likely to accept a specified amount of defective items with no improvement if the standard includes spoiled unit costs. Instead, rework and spoiled unit costs are isolated so attention is directed to reducing these costs.

8. Timely variance analysis is replacing monthly aggregate material usage variances.

9. Less attention is given to direct labor efficiency because direct labor costs usually are such a small percent of product costs in machine-paced factories.

10. Incentive systems and traditional variance measures are changing because workers are performing a variety of tasks on multiple products.

11. By focusing less on direct labor variances, managers direct more attention to crucial manufacturing strategies.

12. Product costing is improved because standard cost models are less commonly based on the assumption that overhead cost is proportionate to the amount of direct labor consumed by the product.

Interactions among Factors of Input and Variances

Earlier in the chapter we assumed that when we purchased flour at a savings of $0.90 per pound we were buying the same grade of material specified. Instead, suppose a company buys a grade of material lower than standard because its price is lower. What is the likely impact on the resulting variances? The favorable material price variance may cause high material usage and poor labor efficiency. An unfavorable material quantity variance and unfavorable labor efficiency variance normally results. Under these circumstances, we cannot blame an unfavorable labor efficiency variance on the workers who require more time to handle lower grade materials. This illustrates that most variances are due to interactions among the factors of input. There is usually not a single, independent cause of each variance.

In deciding whether a company made a correct decision in purchasing the cheaper, lower-grade material, we compare the resulting variances. If the favorable material price variance more than offsets the unfavorable material usage and unfavorable labor efficiency variances, the trade-off was appropriate. Otherwise, the company should buy standard-grade materials. The following summary pinpoints possible causes of each variance including the impact of the interactions between factors of production.

Summary of Material and Labor Variances

Material Price Variances

(Actual material price − Standard material price) × Actual material quantity

Companies compute price variances at different times by recording a material *purchase* price and/or *usage* price variance. However, computing the price variance at the time of purchase provides better control. To compute a purchase price variance, we multiply the difference between actual and standard material price by the material quantity *purchased*. In computing a material *usage* price variance, we multiply this difference by the material quantity *used*. To delay the computation until the issuance of material usually destroys the usefulness of the information for control. Then corrective action is seldom possible. Since this treatment charges material inventory at standard, we simplify detailed record-keeping, for we keep records in quantities only. An objection to this procedure is that if buying is not closely allied to production and sales volume, variations in the volume of purchasing can cause a distortion in operating results.

Possible causes of unfavorable variances:

1. Fluctuations in material market prices.
2. Purchasing from distant suppliers, which results in additional transportation costs.
3. Failure to take cash discounts available.
4. Purchasing in nonstandard or uneconomical lots.
5. Purchasing from suppliers other than those offering the most favorable terms.

Material Usage (Quantity or Efficiency) Variances

Responsibility.   The Purchasing Department is usually responsible for material price variances. However, supervisory factory personnel are responsible when they specify certain brand-name materials or materials of certain grade or quality. If a price variance occurs because a request was made for a rush order, the Production Planning Department could be responsible, as this may be the result of poor scheduling.

$$\text{(Actual material quantity} - \text{Standard material quantity)} \times \text{Standard material price}$$

For control purposes, this variance should be isolated as quickly as possible; however, it may be impossible to calculate until the work is completed.

Possible causes of unfavorable variances:

1. Waste and loss of material in handling and processing.
2. Spoilage or production of excess scrap.
3. Changes in product specifications that have not been incorporated in standards.
4. Substitution of nonstandard materials.
5. Variation in yields from material.

Responsibility.   Line supervisors should be held responsible for material under their control.

Labor Rate Variances

$$\text{(Actual labor rate} - \text{Standard labor rate)} \times \text{Actual labor-hours}$$

Possible causes of unfavorable variances:

1. Change in labor rate that has not been incorporated in standard rate.
2. Use of an employee having a wage classification other than that assumed when the standard for a job was set.
3. Use of a greater number of higher paid employees in the group than anticipated. (This applies when the standard rate is an average.)

Responsibility.   If line supervisors have the authority to match workers and machines to tasks by using the proper grade of labor, line supervisors should be responsible. Line supervisors also should be responsible if they control the wage rate of their labor force. If they do not, the Personnel Department may be responsible.

Labor Time (Quantity or Efficiency) Variances

$$\text{(Actual labor-hours} - \text{Standard labor-hours)} \times \text{Standard labor rate per hour}$$

Possible causes of unfavorable variances:

1. Inefficient labor.
2. Poorly trained labor.
3. Rerouted work.
4. Inefficient equipment.
5. Machine breakdowns.
6. Nonstandard material being used.

Responsibility.   Line supervisors should be held responsible for labor under their control. The Production Planning Department or the Purchasing Department should be held responsible for any labor efficiency variance that results from the use of nonstandard material.

Summary

Standard cost systems are changing as companies direct more attention to quantifying resources that affect costs and vary proportionally with production volume. Companies also are finding they need a total cost management system that includes target costing to manage costs in the development stage and kaizen costing to manage costs in the manufacturing stage. However, analysis of variances between actual and standard costs remains a useful means of evaluating operations and finding areas that need correction. Since setting standards requires a review of the company's plant layout and workflow, managers obtain a better understanding of possible cost savings.

Important Terms and Concepts

Problem for Self-Study

Material and Labor Variances in a Process Costing System
Using an assembly line, Carson, Inc., processes cucumbers into pickles. The standard costs per batch are as follows:

	Total
Cucumbers—direct materials (4 gallons)	$28
Slicing and cooking labor—direct labor (5 hours)	$50

Workers completed 200 batches and transferred them to the next department this period; ending inventory consists of 400 batches, 25 percent complete for material and 10 percent complete for labor.

Beginning inventory contained 100 batches with the following costs:

60 gallons of material costing $448, 15% completion stage
520 hours of labor costing $5,219, 60% completion stage

Carson incurred the following costs in the current period:

Direct materials used	1,100 gallons costing $7,788
Direct labor used	980 hours costing $9,751

Required:

a. Prepare a variance analysis for material and labor using FIFO costing.
b. Prepare a variance analysis for material and labor using average costing.
c. Prove your variances using both costing methods.
d. Provide a possible explanation that is not due to worker efficiency or inefficiency for:
  (1) A favorable material usage variance and an unfavorable material price variance.
  (2) A favorable labor rate variance and an unfavorable labor efficiency variance.

Solution to Problem for Self-Study

Carson, Inc.

---

a. Using FIFO Costing

Material Usage (Quantity) Variance
  EU, Material $= 200 + 100 - 15 = 285$
  $\qquad\qquad\quad$ (25% $\times$ 400) (15% $\times$ 100)
  285×4 gallons $= 1,140$ standard gallons
  (1,100 actual gallons $-$ 1,140 standard gallons) $\times$ \$7 $=$ <u>\$280</u> favorable

Material Usage Price Variance
  $\dfrac{\$7,788}{1,100 \text{ actual gallons}} = \$7.08$ actual rate
  (\$7 standard rate $-$ \$7.08 actual rate) $\times$ 1,100 actual gallon $=$ <u>\$88</u> unfavorable

Labor Efficiency (Quantity) Variance
  EU, Labor $= 200 + 40 - 60 = 180$ batches
  180 batches $\times$ 5 hours $= 900$ standard hours
  (980 actual hours $-$ 900 standard hours) $\times$ \$10 $=$ <u>\$800</u> unfavorable

Labor Rate Variance
  $\dfrac{\$9,751}{980} = \$9.95$ actual rate
  (\$9.95 actual rate $-$ \$10.00 standard rate) $\times$ 980 actual hours $=$ <u>\$49</u> favorable

b. Using Average Costing

Material Usage (Quantity) Variance
  EU, Material $= 200 + 100 = 300$
  $\qquad\qquad\quad$ (25% $\times$ 400)
  300×4 gallons $= 1,200$ standard gallons
  $60 + 1,100$ gallons $= 1,160$ actual gallons
  (1,160 actual gallons $-$ 1,200 standard gallons) $\times$ \$7 $=$ <u>\$280</u> favorable

Material Usage Price Variance
  $\dfrac{\$448 + \$7,788}{1,160 \text{ actual gallons}} = \dfrac{\$8,236}{1,160} = \$7.10$ averaged actual rate
  (\$7.10 $-$ \$7.00) $\times$ 1,160 actual gallons $=$ <u>\$116.00</u> unfavorable

Labor Efficiency (Quantity) Variance
  EU, Labor $= 200 + 40 = 240$ batches
  $\quad$ 240 batches $\times$ 5 hours $= 1,200$ standard hours
  $980 + 520 = 1,500$ actual hours
  (1,500 actual hours $-$ 1,200 standard hours) $\times$ \$10 $=$ <u>\$3,000</u> unfavorable

Labor Rate Variance
  $\dfrac{\$9,751 + \$5,219}{1,500 \text{ actual hours}} = \$9.98$ averaged actual rate
  (\$9.98 actual rate $-$ \$10 standard rate) $\times$ 1,500 actual hours $=$ <u>\$30</u> favorable

c. Proof for FIFO Costing

Actual Material Cost	$ 7,788	
Standard Material Cost (1,140 standard gallons × $7)	7,980	
Total (net) Variance	$ 192	Favorable
Material Usage (Quantity) Variance	$ 280	Favorable
Material Usage Price Variance	88	Unfavorable
Net Variance	$ 192	Favorable
Actual Labor Cost	$ 9,751	
Standard Labor Cost (900 standard hours × $10)	9,000	
	$ 751	Unfavorable
Labor Efficiency (Quantity) Variance	$ 800	Unfavorable
Labor Rate Variance	49	Favorable
	$ 751	Unfavorable

Proof for Average Costing

Actual Material Cost ($7,788 + $448)	$ 8,236	
Standard Material Cost (1,200 standard gallons × $7)	8,400	
Total (net) Variance	$ 164	Favorable
Material Usage (Quantity) Variance	$ 280	Favorable
Material Usage Price Variance	116	Unfavorable
Total (net) Variance	$ 164	Favorable
Actual Labor Cost ($9,751 + $5,219)	$14,970	
Standard Labor Cost (1,200 standard hours × $10)	12,000	
Total (net) Variance	$ 2,970	Unfavorable
Labor Efficiency (Quantity) Variance	$ 3,000	Unfavorable
Labor Rate Variance	30	Favorable
Total (net) Variance	$ 2,970	Unfavorable

d. 1. A favorable material usage variance and an unfavorable material price variance as experienced by Carson, Inc., not due to worker efficiency could result from purchasing higher grade, more expensive materials resulting in less waste than anticipated under the standard in effect. This could cause a favorable material usage variance because less waste was experienced with the higher-grade materials.

2. A favorable labor rate variance and an unfavorable labor efficiency variance not due to worker inefficiency could result from employing less-skilled, lower-paid workers who were not able to complete the work in as short a time as the more skilled, higher paid workers used in establishing the standard. This set of labor variances could also result if on-the-job training is used and the newly hired, lower-paid workers required more time to complete the job since they are still in training

Review Questions

1. *a.* Contrast standard costing, target costing, and kaizen costing.
   b. How does value engineering play a role in these systems?
2. Discuss the similarities in and differences between budgets and standard costs.

3. *a.* Discuss why you agree or disagree that a primary focus on direct labor standards and variances leads to long production runs.
   b. Discuss whether long production runs are profitable.

4. Why is it incorrect in a labor efficiency variance to compare actual hours and budgeted hours?

5. Why is it imperative that a standard cost system have the support of top management before initiation of the system?

6. *a.* What factors should a company consider in deciding how tight standards should be?
   b. Why is the worker representative important to the success of time and motion studies?

7. Would you advise recognizing material quantity variances at the time the materials are charged to production? Why or why not?

8. Which departments should be held responsible for an
   a. Unfavorable material usage variance?
   b. Unfavorable material price variance?

9. When can the total standard quantity allowed be determined? How is it determined?

10. Why are yardsticks for performance measurement needed? What limitations are inherent in any approach in which actual current costs are compared with historical cost data?

Exercises

Writing

E12–1 Impact of Zero Defects and Quality on Standard Setting

The introduction of zero defect programs questions the traditional approach of including rework costs and waste in standards.

Required:

Write a memo to the vice president of production addressing these issues. Include in your memo answers to the following:

a. Should rework cost be built into the standard specifications for materials? If not, to what account should time lost due to rework be charged? Support your view.

b. Should an allowance for waste and shrinkage be made in material quantity standards? What factors should a company consider in making this decision?

E12–2 Journal Entries for Material and Labor

The Engineering Department of Federal, Inc., supplied the following standards per finished batch:

	Per batch
Material (10 pound @ $6 per pound)	$ 60
Labor (5 hours @ $20 per hour)	100

The Purchasing Department reported buying 200 pounds at a total cost of $1,160. The manager of the Production Department reported that 188 pounds were used to make 18 batches. Top management was quite upset as 20 batches were scheduled to be produced and the company's customers were anxious to have their orders filled. Actual labor cost was $1,900.80 for a total of 96 hours.

Required:

a. Prepare all journal entries for material transactions recording direct materials inventory at actual cost. Assume standards are incorporated within the accounting system.
b. Prepare all journal entries for the material transactions recording direct materials inventory at standard cost; record only one type of price variance.
c. Prepare all journal entries for labor transactions.

E12–3 Direct Labor Entries Using Standard Costs

The standard rate is $24 per direct labor-hour for Ace Company. In the current month, actual hours were 12,800 at an actual price of $23.50 per hour. For the output achieved, the standard direct labor-hours allowed were 12,000.

Required:

Prepare general journal entries isolating labor and efficiency variances under the following two systems assuming:

a. Work in Process Inventory is carried at standard hours allowed times standard prices.
b. Price variances are isolated when labor costs are originally journalized and efficiency variances are isolated when units are transferred to Finished Goods from Work in Process Inventory.

E12–4 Unit Standard and Actual Material Cost

Jeanne, Inc.'s records show the following data relating to direct materials cost for November:

Units of finished product manufactured	8,500
Standard direct materials per unit of production	8 lbs.
Quantity of direct materials used	68,750 lbs.
Direct materials quantity variance (unfavorable)	$ 2,850
Direct materials price variance (favorable)	$13,750

There is no work in process either at the beginning or the end of the month.

Required:

a. Calculate the standard direct material cost per unit of finished product.
b. Derive the actual direct material cost per unit of finished product.

E12–5 Material and Labor Variances

Dexter Company's management and production personnel analyzed factory conditions and determined the following material and labor standards:

	Per Finished Unit
Material (12 pounds @ $4)	$48
Labor (2 hours @ $5)	$10

Management had planned to produce 2,000 units, but due to machine breakdowns produced only 1,500 units. There were 15,000 pounds of material used at a cost of $75,000. There were 3,080 hours of labor employed at a cost of $13,860.

Required:

a. Calculate material and labor variances, indicating whether favorable or unfavorable.
b. Provide possible explanations for these variances.

E12–6 Material and Labor Variances in a Process Costing System

Mary Miller, Inc., produces batches of a petroleum product on an assembly line. The standard costs per batch are as follows:

	Total
Direct materials (80 gallons)	$ 40
Direct labor (60 hours)	216

Workers completed 480 batches this period; ending inventory consists of 69 batches, one-third complete. Assume all costs are incurred uniformly. There was no beginning inventory. The following costs were incurred:

Direct materials used (40,743 gallons)	$ 17,519.49
Direct labor (29,677 hours)	108,321.05

Required:

a. Prepare a variance analysis for material and labor.

b. Prove your material variances.

c. Prove your labor variances.

E12–7 Quantity Variances for Material and Labor

Cynthia Company uses standard costing as one of the controlling techniques to manage its manufacturing cost. For June, the following data apply to its two products, soup and tomato paste:

	Standard Material (tomatoes) per Unit	*Standard Labor per Unit*	*Units Produced in June*
Soup	5 lbs.	2 hrs.	500
Tomato paste	7	1.5	450

Actual usage in June was 5,750 pounds of tomatoes and 1,660 labor-hours.

Required:

a. Calculate the material usage variance in pounds and the labor efficiency variance in hours.

b. Restate the variances in monetary terms if the standard materials price is $20 per pound and the standard labor rate is $5.00 per hour.

E12–8 Impact of Planned and Sales Activity on Prime Cost Variances

Agatha Company produces two products, soup and chili, each of which uses tomatoes and beans as materials. The following unit standard costs apply:

	Tomatoes	*Beans*	*Direct Labor*
Soup	3 lbs. @ $5	2 lbs. @ $7	1 hour @ $8
Chili	2 lbs. @ $5	3 lbs. @ $7	2 hours @ $8

During May, 5,000 units of soup and 3,000 units of chili were produced. Also, 20,000 pounds of tomatoes were purchased and used at $4.95 per pound, and 20,000 pounds of beans were purchased and used at $6.90 per pound. All of these materials (but no other materials) were used for the month's production. This production required 10,000 direct labor-hours at $9.50 per hour.

Required:

a. Calculate the material price and usage variances for the month.
b. Calculate the labor rate and efficiency variances for the month.
c. How would your answers to Requirements *a* and *b* change if you had been told that May's sales were 4,500 units of soup and 2,500 units of chili?
d. How would your answers to Requirements *a* and *b* change if you had been told that May's planned production activity was 4,000 units of soup and 4,000 units of chili?

E12–9 Material Variances

Bowman Company's direct material costs for the manufacture of a product are as follows for a month:

Actual unit purchase price	$ 3.30
Standard quantity allowed tor actual production	5,100
Quantity purchased and used for actual production	5,500
Standard unit price	$ 3.00

Required:

a. Determine the material price variance.
b. Determine the material usage variance.
c. Prove your answers.

Problems

Writing

P12–10 Needed Changes in Reporting System

Ian, Inc., is a personal computer manufacturing company. It uses a standard cost system to record its production cost and the system allows for a small level of product defects. However, in its variance reports for last quarter, Ian's Assembly Department incurred large unfavorable labor efficiency and volume variances. The assembly supervisor claims that these variances were caused by the inefficiency of the Inspection Department. In the last three months, the quantity of parts approved by the Inspection Department have not been sufficient to meet the production schedule. As a result, the assembly workers have had to wait for parts. Therefore, the Assembly Department did not meet its production schedules. On the other hand, the supervisor of the Inspection Department argues that the unfavorable variances in the Assembly Department were not caused by his department. Instead, the main problem is caused by the major supplier. The inspection supervisor believes that the major supplier does not maintain a strict quality control standard. As a result, many computer parts are inferior and the Inspection Department has to increase its worker-hours to inspect the parts. Therefore, the Inspection Department also has unfavorable labor efficiency variances. Both supervisors claim that they should not be held accountable for their unfavorable variances.

Required:

Suggest ways that this matter should be settled. Make recommendations for any needed changes in the reporting system.

SPATS

P12–11 Standard Cost Using Weighted-Average and FIFO Costing

Lilly Company adopted a standard cost system several years ago to account for its single product, sausage. The company set the following standard:

Raw pork meat	3 pounds @ $6 per pound
Direct labor	4 hours @ $4.50 per hour

The following operating data were for June:

In process (beginning inventory): 200 units, 20 percent complete as to labor.
Material and labor cost incurred in May: 580 pounds of raw pork meat costing $4,496 and 200 hours of labor costing $667

In process (ending inventory): 600 units, 80 percent complete as to labor. Completed during the month: 6,400 units.

    In the current month, 20,900 pounds of pork meat were used in production for a total cost of $123,310. Pork meat is issued at the beginning of processing. Direct labor for June was $127,370, which was a rate of $4.70 per hour.

Required:

Prepare an analysis of variances for material and labor separating each into the factors that caused them using:
a. Weighted-average costing.
b. FIFO costing.

P12–12 Methods of Recording Materials Using a Standard Cost System

Murray, Inc., managers asked their CPA to provide them with three different approaches for recording material price variations. In their first month of operation, they decided to adopt a standard cost system and have purchased enough raw materials for several months of operations using the following data:

Standard cost per unit	4 gallons @ $3.00 per gallon
Gallons purchased	40,000 for $90,000
Gallons used in production	13,200
Units finished	3,000

Required:

a. Using the three different methods illustrated in this chapter for recording materials in a standard cost system, prepare the journal entries. Label your different methods.
b. Evaluate these methods using the data given.

Critical Thought

SPATS

P12–13 Analysis of Material and Labor

Evangeline Company employs just-in-time inventory in its operations. Its one product passes through two production operations. Under normal conditions, 200 pounds of direct material are required to make 100 units of product. The standard price of direct material is $2 per pound; all of the materials for a unit are issued to and used in Operation 1. In Operation 1, standard labor time is 12 units per direct labor-hour at a standard wage rate of $8. In Operation 2, standard output is six partially completed units per direct labor-hour, with a standard wage rate of $9 per hour. Normal volume is 364,000 units per month. In October, output was 364,200 units and 729,600 pounds of direct material were consumed. No spoilage occurred in Operation 2. There was no beginning or ending work in process inventory. October direct labor-hours and costs were as follows:

	Direct Labor	
	Hours	*Costs*
Operation 1	30,420	$241,839
Operation 2	60,600	554,490

Required:

a. Prepare an analysis of direct labor in October for Evangeline's two operations.

b. Compute the materials quantity variance.

c. Assume the labor usage standard in Operation 1 is still 12 units cut per direct-labor hour. In addition, suppose you learn that to cut 12 units, direct-labor employees process 10 pounds of direct material per hour. It has come to your attention that the unfavorable material quantity variance in October was caused by the purchasing agent's buying direct materials of an off-standard quality.

   (1) With this knowledge concerning the use of substandard materials, would you change your analysis of direct labor efficiency variance for October? How?

   (2) Who should be charged with the material quantity variance?

d. Can you determine if the purchasing agent made a wise decision in purchasing the off-standard direct material? Explain your answer.

P12–14 Material and Labor Variances

Standards for the only product manufactured by Overman Company were established as follows:

Direct Material A:	5 gallons @ $2 per gallon
Direct Material B:	2 gallons @ $1 per gallon
Direct labor:	4 hours @ $4 per hour
Factory overhead:	Applied at $3 per direct labor-hour

A summary of the first year's costs and related data for the manufacturing process follows:

1. Purchases of material were 2,500 gallons of Material A for a total of $5,125; 900 gallons of Material B for a total of $882. (Direct Materials Inventory is recorded at standard.)

2. Four hundred units were finished and 100 units were at the one-fifth stage of completion. This required 2,150 gallons of Material A, 820 gallons of Material B, and 1,750 hours of direct labor costing $7,140.

Required:

a. Indicate the total credits to the direct materials account for the issuance of Material A for the year.

b. Determine:

   (1) The material quantity variance for Materials A and B.

   (2) The material purchase price variance for Materials A and B.

   (3) The labor quantity variance.

   (4) The labor rate variance.

c. How would your answers to Requirement *b* change if management told you that the first year's sales were 380 units?

d. How would your answers to Requirement *b* change if management told you that they planned to make 500 units during their first year of operations?

P12–15 Recommendations for Changes in Reporting Variances

Osbert Company is a canned cat food manufacturer. The basic meat ingredients are fish, pork and beef, and all of these ingredients are supplied by an outside vendor. The production floor of Osbert Company is using a mass-production, assembly-line approach. This month,

Writing

the production supervisor discovered that more meat was required to produce the same amount of cat food than in past months. The supervisor suspects that the outside supplier tried to cut costs by not trimming meat fat out. In cooking the meats, an increased quantity of fat would result in less processed cat food. When the production supervisor and other top managers received this month's production report, the cost accountant indicated that the production supervisor is responsible for this month's unfavorable material price and quantity variances. The production supervisor objected to being held responsible for these unfavorable variances.

Required:

Who should be held responsible for these unfavorable variances? Make recommendations for any needed changes in the reporting system.

P12–16 Impact of Bonuses on Material Variances

Hill Corporation has installed a bonus system in which the purchasing agent receives 10 percent of any favorable purchase price variances. The production supervisor receives 10 percent of any favorable material usage variances.

The Engineering Department established the following standards per finished unit:

Material (5 pounds of Grade A @ $4 a pound) . . . . $ 20 per unit
Labor (8 hours @ $20 an hour) . . . . $160 per unit

The purchasing agent purchased 200 pounds of Grade C material at $3 per pound.

The production supervisor reported that even though 40 units were budgeted to be produced, only 30 units were finished. The supervisor used 180 pounds of material. Direct labor workers reported 260 hours of labor at a total pay of $7,800.

Required:

a. Make journal entries for all material transactions needed to record direct material inventory at actual cost assuming a standard cost system is used.
b. Make journal entries for all material transactions needed to record direct material inventory at standard cost; record only one price variance.
c. Make journal entries for all labor transactions.
d. Explain the oversight the company made in establishing the bonus.

SPATS

P12–17 Recording Material and Labor

Sharon Perfume Company had planned to produce each month 1,000 units of Vrago, a secret mixture. Sharon's budget included engineering standards of 6,000 pounds of direct material at a total cost of $12,000. The labor budget was for 4,000 hours at a total cost of $48,000.

At the end of the month, the accountant determined that 1,200 units of Vrago were produced and that 7,600 pounds of direct material were purchased at a cost of $18,000. The materials manager reported 600 pounds were not used and were still in the raw material inventory. The labor cost summary revealed 5,400 actual hours at a total cost of $70,200 were incurred.

Required:

a. Prepare all journal entries for material transactions in a system in which the only price variance used is a material purchase price variance.
b. Prepare all journal entries for material transactions in a system in which the only price variance used is a material usage price variance.
c. Make the labor journal entries needed to record price and quantity variances regardless of the system of recording material price variances used.

P12–18 Direct Material and Labor Variances

Scotty Chemical Co. produces chemicals to be used as base ingredients for a variety of products. The 19X1 budget for the two products was

	A	B	Total
Production output in gallons	855,400	902,400	1,757,800
Direct material	$2,011,100	$2,380,800	$4,391,900
Direct labor	$1,200,000	$1,215,352	$2,415,352
Total prime manufacturing cost	$3,211,100	$3,596,152	$6,807,252

Management assumes a direct-material yield of 94 percent and a direct-labor rate of $8 per hour in budgeting. The actual direct production cost for 19X1 was

	A	B	Total
Production output in gallons	790,500	894,240	1,684,740
Direct material	$1,564,000	$2,498,040	$4,062,040
Direct labor	$1,251,954	$1,274,955	$2,526,909
Total prime manufacturing cost	$2,815,954	$3,772,995	$6,588,949

The actual production yield was 93 percent for Product A and 92 percent for Product B. The direct-labor cost per hour for both products was $8.25.

Required:

a. Calculate for Product A:
   (1) The direct material price variance
   (2) The direct material quantity (yield) variance
b. Calculate for Product B:
   (1) The direct material price variance
   (2) The direct material quantity (yield) variance
c. Calculate for Product A:
   (1) The direct labor price variance
   (2) The direct labor efficiency variance
d. Calculate for Product B:
   (1) The direct labor price variance
   (2) The direct labor efficiency variance

Cases

C12–19 The Use of Standards as a Motivational Device

The management of Pinkerton Manufacturing Company has become alarmed over a consistent increase in production costs. Most of the increase is attributed to direct labor. Accountants advised the company that a standard cost system would help control labor as well as other costs.

Since detailed production records have not been maintained, the company has hired Comer Consulting Engineers to establish labor standards. On conclusion of a thorough study of the manufacturing process, Comer recommended a labor standard of one unit of production every 15 minutes, or 32 units per day per worker. As a part of their report to management, the engineers informed Pinkerton that their wage rates were below the industry average of $24.50 per hour.

The production manager was somewhat concerned about Comer's labor standard. She believed the employees could not attain this standard because it is too tight. Based on first-hand experience, she considered one unit of production every 20 minutes, or 24 units per day, more reasonable.

Management recognized that the standard should be at a high level to motivate workers, but not so high that it fails to provide adequate information for control and cost comparison purposes. After giving the matter much thought, management agreed on a dual standard. The engineers' labor standard of one unit every 15 minutes was adopted by the plant as a motivational device, but a labor standard of one unit every 20 minutes was adopted for reporting purposes. The workers were not to be informed of the different labor reporting standard.

The production manager held a meeting with the workers to inform them that a standard cost system was being implemented and to educate them about how the system works.

The new cost system was put into effect on March 1 along with a wage increase to $24.50 per hour. Six months later, the following data, based on the standards recommended by Comer, were reviewed by management:

	March	April	May	June	July	August
Production in units	10,000	9,800	9,200	9,000	8,600	8,800
Direct labor-hours	2,800	2,650	2,700	2,750	2,850	2,800
Variance from labor standard	$1,350(U)	$ 900(U)	$1,800(U)	$2,250(U)	$3,150(U)	$2,700(U)

U = Unfavorable.

Other factors of production had not changed materially during this six-month period.

Required:

a. Discuss the different standards and their influence on motivation. Include the effect on plant workers of Pinkerton's acceptance of the engineering firm's labor standard.
b. Discuss your reaction to the adoption of dual standards.

C12–20 Tight and Current Standards

BMD Corporation has recently installed a standard cost system. Management adopted fairly tight standards that can be achieved if the workers perform at an efficient level. The monthly labor budget established for 1,600 units called for 5,600 hours at a total cost of $79,800. The monthly direct material budget for 3,600 gallons was set at $10,800.

The vice president in charge of manufacturing believes that the quantity standards established are too tight and that an additional set of expected standards should be established. He believes that an extra hour of labor and three-fourths gallon of materials per unit should be added to the standards. He also believes, however, that the standard labor rate and the standard material prices correctly reflect current conditions. His reasoning is that top management is not going to get upset if the employees take an extra hour to complete the units or use more material because they recognize that the standards are tight.

The cost clerk determines that 1,550 units were completed during the month. The summary of labor time tickets reveals that 5,813 direct labor-hours were used at a cost of $81,382. There were 4,650 gallons used at an actual cost of $14,415.

··

Required:

a. Explain what you would advise the company to do in regard to establishing another set of standards.

b. Compute the direct material variances and labor variances using the tight standards. Label each variance indicating whether it is favorable or unfavorable.

c. Determine what the direct material variances and labor variances would be using the vice president's expected standards. Label each variance indicating whether it is favorable or unfavorable.

CHAPTER 13

Standard Costs and Factory Overhead Variances

Chapter Objectives

After studying this chapter, you should be able to:

1. Discuss the purpose of a standard cost system and explain how its value begins when the causes of variances are analyzed.

2. Prepare factory overhead variance analyses using a standard cost system.

3. Journalize and prorate overhead variances.

4. Explain why the overall objective of making money is achieved by reducing inventory and operating expenses, and by increasing throughput and product quality rather than by making certain a specific cost center has a favorable variance.

Introduction

Factory overhead cost standards provide a means of allocating factory overhead to cost inventories for pricing decisions and controlling expenses. However, cost accountants are recognizing that accounting measures such as standard cost variances require monitoring. Reporting variances for individual departments encourages cost center managers to focus only on improving their performance. When separate segments of an organization attempt to enhance their individual efficiencies with favorable standard cost variances without regard to subsequent effects, throughput decreases and the goal of making money is sacrificed.

Further, accountants recognize that it is a waste of their time to simply compute variances and place them neatly on a page for distribution to management. Computing variances is not as important as knowing what to do if a significant variance occurs. The benefit of a standard cost system comes from determining the cause of the variance and correcting the situation. Accountants do not investigate every variance. By studying only significant variances, they emphasize the management by exception principle.

Setting Overhead Standards

There is a close similarity between setting overhead standards and applying factory overhead in a **normal costing system** and in a standard cost system. An actual costing system uses actual overhead rates to apply indirect costs while a normal costing system uses budgeted rates to apply indirect costs based on actual hours or other cost drivers. A standard cost system uses budgeted rates based on standard hours or other cost drivers allowed for actual production. In a cost system not employing standards, there are no standard hours—actual hours or another cost driver is the only means available for applying overhead. A standard cost system has both actual and standard hours, but the system uses standard hours to apply overhead to Work in Process Inventory. Our definition of applied overhead in a standard cost system differs from applied overhead in a system not employing standards.

Selecting Budgeted Capacity

As discussed in Chapter 4, accountants select one of the four capacity levels—theoretical, practical, normal, and expected actual—as the volume basis or **denominator capacity. Theoretical capacity** is rarely chosen because it does not represent an attainable level of performance. Standards set on **practical capacity** are more likely to be attainable and are more realistic than theoretical standards. Either **normal capacity** or **expected actual capacity** is the basis for current standards. A disadvantage of using expected actual capacity is that frequent, costly revisions of the standards may be necessary.

After selecting the capacity level, accountants allocate costs on a volume-related or nonvolume-related base. Commonly used volume-related bases include machine-hours, direct labor-hours, direct labor costs, direct material costs, and units of production. The evaluation of these bases in Chapter 2 also applies to a standard cost system. An activity-based costing system also uses such nonvolume-related activities as number of scheduled production runs or inspections. After expressing volume based on machine-hours, the number of inspections, or another basis, managers estimate the factory overhead incurred at this level.

Current Cost Management Practice

Global

With Japan's growing backlog of idle production lines, Japanese companies are aggressively hawking used equipment. Among those on the prowl for buyers are such famous names as Mitsubishi Steel Manufacturing, Sumitomo Metal Industries, and Kawasaki Steel. This $206 billion excess Japanese production capacity has been accumulating for four years since Japan's bubble economy burst and put an end to its biggest-ever capital spending binge. Nippon Paper is shutting down 6 of its 60 mainstay paper machines this year and looking for buyers for them as well as for coating and spooling equipment. Sony Corp. shipped 12 machines for stamping parts onto circuit boards to a joint venture in Indonesia. As Japan undergoes a transformation from manufacturing to services, excess equipment keeps increasing. A slower-growing economy may spell the end of the frequent factory upgrades that have helped Japanese companies keep ahead of foreign rivals. Up until several years ago, Japanese executives considered it unpatriotic to sell used equipment overseas. Today the Japanese government is giving a hand in the sell-off. People holding the opinion that Japan is unique and won't suffer lags in the economy are disappearing.

Larry Holyoke with Keith L. Alexander and Teresa Albor, "Psst! Wanna Buy a Used Steel Plant?" *BusinessWeek,* August 22, 1994, pp. 48–49.

Plantwide or Departmental Rates

Some companies use a single plantwide rate for standard factory overhead while others set a standard overhead rate for each cost center or department. Each cost center should have its own rate if the amount of overhead varies significantly between departments. Departmental overhead rates also are appropriate if all products do not pass through the same departments.

We determine standard factory overhead rates to cost inventory for producing departments only. Chapter 4 illustrated a normal costing system of allocating budgeted indirect costs to production and service departments and then distributing the service department budgeted costs to production departments. Standard costing also uses this procedure. However, normal costing may give less attention to estimating factory overhead costs by referring only to historical cost.

Assume an automated factory selects a normal capacity level of 1,000 units or 2,000 machine-hours as its budgeted volume. The company uses machine-hours as its basis because it has found a causal relationship between machine-hours and the incurrence of factory depreciation, supplies, indirect labor, and other overhead costs. To determine the standard factory overhead rates, accountants then estimate the following standard variable and fixed factory overhead for this volume.

Normal capacity or budgeted volume (1,000 units x 2 hours each) .	2,000 machine-hours
Standard variable factory overhead	$ 8,000
Standard fixed factory overhead	32,000
Standard total factory overhead	$40,000

Standard variable factory overhead rate per machine-hour: $\dfrac{\$8{,}000}{2{,}000 \text{ machine-hours}} = \$4$

Standard (budgeted) fixed factory overhead rate per machine-hour: $\dfrac{\$32{,}000}{2{,}000 \text{ machine-hours}} = \$16$

Standard (budgeted) total factory overhead rate per machine-hour: $\dfrac{\$40,000}{2,000 \text{ machine-hours}} = \$20$

Because this $20 overhead rate is known throughout the accounting period, the company applies overhead to each job as it is finished. The firm also applies overhead to unfinished jobs remaining in work in process at the end of the period. A process costing system applies the standard overhead rate to the equivalent units calculated for overhead, as illustrated in the Problem for Self-Study at the end of the chapter.

Overhead Variance Methods

Accountants do not agree on which of the following three different sets of factory overhead variances is most appropriate. All sets analyze the **net overhead variance,** which is the difference between the actual overhead incurred and the overhead applied to the products using the total standard factory overhead rate. Note that the three- and four-variance methods are detailed variations of the two-variance method.

1. Two-variance method:
   a. Controllable variance.
   b. Production volume variance.

2. Three-variance method:
   a. Total overhead spending variance.
   b. Variable overhead efficiency variance.
   c. Production volume variance.

3. Four-variance method:
   a. Variable overhead spending variance.
   b. Fixed overhead spending variance.
   c. Variable overhead efficiency variance.
   d. Production volume variance.

All three methods compute the production volume variance in the same manner.

Data for Overhead Variance.   Exhibits 13–1, 13–3, and 13–4 present the three different methods of computing factory overhead variances based on the following data:

Standard variable overhead (2 machine-hours @ $4 per hour)	$8 per unit
Standard fixed overhead (2 machine-hours @ $16 per hour)	$32 per unit
Budgeted fixed factory overhead at standard	$32,000
Budgeted volume: 1,000 units × 2 hours = 2,000 machine-hours	
900 units of finished product were completed.	
Actual machine-hours	1,890 hours
Actual variable factory overhead	$ 9,000
Actual fixed factory overhead	31,000
Actual total factory overhead	$40,000

Three Volume Levels Used

Overhead variance analysis uses these three volume levels that become available at different times:

1. Known before operations begin: Budgeted, normal, denominator, predetermined capacity—2,000 machine-hours.

2. Known after operations end: Standard volume allowed—900 units × 2 hours = 1,800 machine-hours.

3. Known after operations end: Actual volume—1,890 machine-hours.

Accountants cannot correctly compute standard volume allowed when using units of production as the basis for standards. This explains why units of production are usually not an appropriate basis for a standard cost system.

EXHIBIT 13–1   Two-Variance Method Illustrated

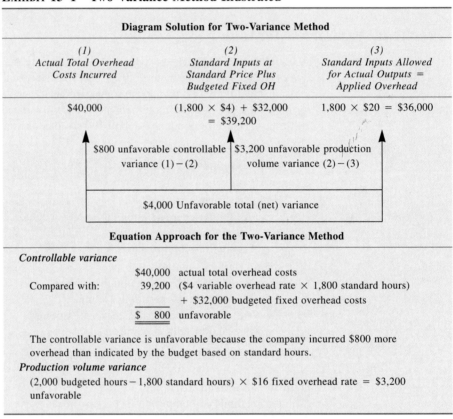

Diagram Solution for Two-Variance Method

(1) Actual Total Overhead Costs Incurred	*(2)* Standard Inputs at Standard Price Plus Budgeted Fixed OH	*(3)* Standard Inputs Allowed for Actual Outputs = Applied Overhead
$40,000	(1,800 × $4) + $32,000 = $39,200	1,800 × $20 = $36,000

$800 unfavorable controllable variance (1) − (2) | $3,200 unfavorable production volume variance (2) − (3)

$4,000 Unfavorable total (net) variance

Equation Approach for the Two-Variance Method

Controllable variance

Compared with:
	$40,000	actual total overhead costs
	39,200	($4 variable overhead rate × 1,800 standard hours)
		+ $32,000 budgeted fixed overhead costs
	$ 800	unfavorable

The controllable variance is unfavorable because the company incurred $800 more overhead than indicated by the budget based on standard hours.

Production volume variance

(2,000 budgeted hours − 1,800 standard hours) × $16 fixed overhead rate = $3,200 unfavorable

---

Two-Variance Method

These variances comprise the two-variance method for factory overhead:

1. **Controllable variance**
   Actual total factory overhead
   Compared with: Budget based on *standard* capacity used [(Standard variable factory overhead rate × Standard hours) + Total budgeted fixed factory overhead costs].

2. **Production volume variance** *(noncontrollable variance)*
   (Budgeted hours, such as normal capacity hours, used for determining standard overhead rates − Standard hours allowed for the output achieved) × Standard fixed factory overhead rate at budgeted capacity.

Exhibit 13–1 illustrates both the diagram and equation approaches for the two-variance method. You may select whichever approach you find easier. The diagram approach offers the advantage of containing a built-in proof.

EXHIBIT 13–2   Production Volume Variance

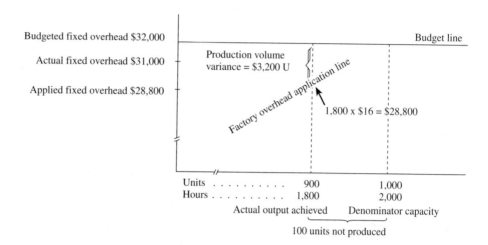

Units	900	1,000
Hours	1,800	2,000
	Actual output achieved	Denominator capacity

100 units not produced

Production Volume Variance.   A production volume variance arises whenever the volume level achieved for actual factory output differs from the denominator volume level used for determining the fixed overhead application rate. We refer to this as a production volume variance to distinguish it from the sales volume variance presented in Chapter 24. For simplicity, however, we often simply call it a volume variance. The production volume variance measures the costs or savings from not operating at the volume level planned. Exhibit 13–2 contains a graph illustrating the $3,200 production volume variance. If the volume variance is unfavorable, as shown in Exhibits 13–1 and 13–2, the company did not use its facilities to the extent planned. The company applied $28,800 (1,800 standard hours × $16) fixed overhead, but budgeted to have 2,000 hours on which to apply overhead. The volume variance is unfavorable because there were 200 idle hours to which the lump-sum budgeted fixed factory overhead could not be applied. Instead, if the company produced more than 1,000 units, the volume variance represents the advantage of a higher use of production facilities than expected.

Volume variances distinguish between resource spending and resource usage. **Resource spending** refers to acquiring the facilities to perform activities, such as manufacturing 1,000 units. The company has created a capacity of 1,000 units on which to spend money. **Resource usage** refers to actual performance (i.e., 900 units). Volume variances measure how many available resources are used and the cost of excess capacity or the savings from a better use of facilities than expected. As discussed later in this chapter, management must monitor production to ensure excess inventory is not manufactured merely to ensure a favorable production volume variance.

Three-Variance Method   In comparing the three-variance method with the two-variance method, note that further division occurs. The controllable variance for the two-variance method divides into the total overhead spending variance and the variable overhead efficiency variance for the three-variance method. The **total overhead spending variance** compares actual total factory overhead to a budget adjusted to actual capacity using the flexible budget formula presented in Chapter 10. These variances comprise the three-variance method:

Controllable variances

1. Total overhead spending variance:
   Actual total factory overhead
   Compared with: Flexible budget allowance adjusted to actual capacity used (Standard variable factory overhead rate × Actual hours) + Total budgeted fixed factory overhead costs.
   Note this is the same spending variance computed under a normal costing system using applied factory overhead rates introduced in Chapter 4.

2. Variable factory overhead efficiency variance:
   (Actual hours − Standard hours) × Standard variable factory overhead rate.

Noncontrollable variance

3. Production volume variance:
   (Budgeted hours − Standard hours) × Standard fixed factory overhead rate at budgeted capacity.

Using the same data as for the two-variance method, Exhibit 13–3 illustrates the three-variance method using the diagram and equation solution.

EXHIBIT 13–3   Three-Variance Method Illustrated

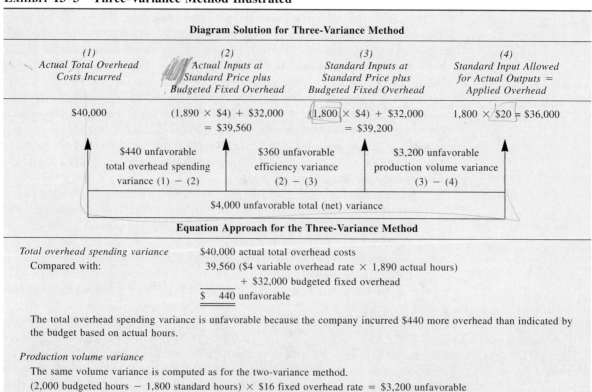

Diagram Solution for Three-Variance Method

(1) Actual Total Overhead Costs Incurred	*(2)* Actual Inputs at Standard Price plus Budgeted Fixed Overhead	*(3)* Standard Inputs at Standard Price plus Budgeted Fixed Overhead	*(4)* Standard Input Allowed for Actual Outputs = Applied Overhead
$40,000	(1,890 × $4) + $32,000 = $39,560	(1,800 × $4) + $32,000 = $39,200	1,800 × $20 = $36,000

$440 unfavorable total overhead spending variance (1) − (2)

$360 unfavorable efficiency variance (2) − (3)

$3,200 unfavorable production volume variance (3) − (4)

$4,000 unfavorable total (net) variance

Equation Approach for the Three-Variance Method

Total overhead spending variance
Compared with:
$40,000 actual total overhead costs
39,560 ($4 variable overhead rate × 1,890 actual hours)
+ $32,000 budgeted fixed overhead
$ 440 unfavorable

The total overhead spending variance is unfavorable because the company incurred $440 more overhead than indicated by the budget based on actual hours.

Production volume variance
The same volume variance is computed as for the two-variance method.
(2,000 budgeted hours − 1,800 standard hours) × $16 fixed overhead rate = $3,200 unfavorable

Variable Overhead Efficiency Variance.   The **variable overhead efficiency variance** reflects the efficient or inefficient use of the base on which a company applies variable overhead. Note the similarity between this variance and the labor efficiency variance computed in Chapter 12. We assume that inefficiencies in using the base (i.e., machine-hours or production runs scheduled) causes an increase in variable overhead. However, the assumption that variable overhead fluctuates in direct proportion to a specific production volume, such as machine-hours, is fairly weak. Whether this clear-cut relationship exists depends on the specific circumstances.

Machine-hours is the base used in Exhibit 13–3. Because actual machine-hours are greater than the standard allowed, the variance is unfavorable, reflecting an inefficient use of machine time. If, instead, a labor-intensive process uses direct labor-hours or direct labor costs, the variable overhead efficiency variance reflects the effect of labor efficiency on overhead. Managers responsible for the cost driver usually must account for variable overhead efficiency.

Four-Variance Method

The total overhead spending variance in the three-variance method divides into the variable overhead spending variance and the fixed overhead spending variance for the four-variance method. The variable factory overhead efficiency variance and the production volume variance are the same as for the three-variance method. These four variances make up this method.

Controllable variances

1. Variable overhead spending variance: Actual variable factory overhead
   Compared with: Budget allowance for variable costs adjusted to actual capacity used (Standard variable factory overhead rate $\times$ Actual hours). Alternatively, (Actual variable overhead rate $-$ Standard variable overhead rate) $\times$ Actual hours.
   (Note the similarity of this alternative computation and the material price and labor rate variances.)
2. Variable overhead efficiency variance: (Actual hours $-$ Standard hours) $\times$ Standard variable factory overhead rate.
3. Fixed overhead spending variance: Budgeted fixed factory overhead
   Compared with: Actual fixed factory overhead.

Noncontrollable variance

4. Production volume variance:
   (Budgeted hours $-$ Standard hours) $\times$ Standard fixed factory overhead rate at budgeted capacity.

Exhibit 13–4 illustrates the diagram and equation solution approach for the four-variance method.

Variable Overhead Spending Variance.   A **variable overhead spending variance** occurs because actual costs (such as utilities, supplies, and indirect labor) differ from those budgeted for the actual hours incurred. The spending variance in Exhibit 13–4 is unfavorable because the company incurred $1,440 more factory over-

EXHIBIT 13–4   Four-Variance Method Illustrated

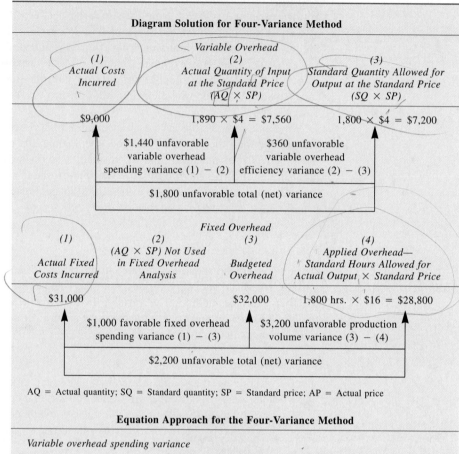

Diagram Solution for Four-Variance Method

Variable Overhead

(1) Actual Costs Incurred	(2) Actual Quantity of Input at the Standard Price (AQ × SP)	(3) Standard Quantity Allowed for Output at the Standard Price (SQ × SP)
$9,000	1,890 × $4 = $7,560	1,800 × $4 = $7,200

$1,440 unfavorable variable overhead spending variance (1) − (2) | $360 unfavorable variable overhead efficiency variance (2) − (3)

$1,800 unfavorable total (net) variance

Fixed Overhead

(1) Actual Fixed Costs Incurred	(2) (AQ × SP) Not Used in Fixed Overhead Analysis	(3) Budgeted Overhead	(4) Applied Overhead— Standard Hours Allowed for Actual Output × Standard Price
$31,000		$32,000	1,800 hrs. × $16 = $28,800

$1,000 favorable fixed overhead spending variance (1) − (3) | $3,200 unfavorable production volume variance (3) − (4)

$2,200 unfavorable total (net) variance

AQ = Actual quantity; SQ = Standard quantity; SP = Standard price; AP = Actual price

Equation Approach for the Four-Variance Method

Variable overhead spending variance

                 $9,000 actual variable overhead costs

Compared with :   7,560 budget allowance for variable overhead

                         ($4 variable overhead rate × 1,890 actual hours)

             $ 1,440 unfavorable

Alternatively: $9,000/1,890 actual hours = $4.762; ($4.762 − $4) × 1,890 = $1,440 unfavorable

Variable overhead efficiency variance

The variable factory overhead efficiency variance is as computed using the three-variance method.

(1,890 actual hours − 1,800 standard hours) × $4 variable overhead rate = $360 unfavorable

Fixed overhead spending variance

                 $31,000 actual fixed overhead

                 32,000 budgeted fixed overhead

              $ 1,000 favorable

Production volume variance

The volume variance is the same for the three methods presented:

(2,000 budgeted hours − 1,800 standard hours) × $16 fixed overhead rate = $3,200 unfavorable

head than indicated by the budget based on actual hours. Also, the spending variance could have occurred because the relationship between machine-hours and variable factory overhead is not perfect. The variable overhead spending variance compares the actual and standard price of overhead, hence it also is called a **variable overhead price variance.** For example, if supplies cost more than expected, the spending variance will be unfavorable.

The spending variance also contains some efficiency (usage) items. For example, employees may waste supplies, causing cost to be higher than expected. Some companies compute a separate spending variance for certain key components of variable overhead; for example, energy costs in an automated factory. This breakdown analyzes waste and efficiency by cost component. When a spending variance is computed for each cost center or department, the variance becomes the responsibility of the supervisor of the center involved.

Fixed Overhead Spending Variance.   The **fixed overhead spending or price variance** reflects the impact of the actual price level on fixed factory overhead. The variance measures changes in fixed overhead costs from the amounts budgeted. The fixed overhead spending variance in Exhibit 13–4 is favorable because actual fixed factory overhead is less than budgeted fixed factory overhead. However, if factory supervisors' salaries, machinery depreciation, or other fixed overhead costs are higher than expected, an unfavorable fixed overhead spending variance results. Even though lacking universal acceptance, we classify the fixed overhead spending variance as controllable. Although low-level and possibly middle managers may be unable to control fixed costs, top-level managers can. Despite being unable to control committed costs, line supervisors often can control discretionary fixed factory overhead.

Outline of Interrelationship.   Exhibit 13–5 contains an outline of the methods discussed showing their interrelationship. The four-variance method involves a more detailed breakdown of factors not directly related to volume than does the two-variance method. Thus, the four-variance method is more costly and time-consuming to prepare. Also, it is difficult often to separate actual overhead into fixed and variable components.

However, accountants usually prefer the four-variance method because it distinguishes between cost behavior better than the two- or three-variance methods. The additional variances computed give better insight into the reasons why actual overhead differed from that budgeted. Control and responsibility for fixed and variable overhead usually rests with different members of the management team. For example, it would be unfair to hold line supervisors responsible for the difference between actual fixed and budgeted fixed overhead because they usually lack the authority to select plant facilities or insurance policies to cover these facilities. As a result, top managers are accountable for fixed overhead variances.

Proof of Method Used.   Regardless of the method used, the variances computed represent a breakdown of the total difference between actual and standard costs. We use this difference, called the total or *net factory overhead variance,* to prove the variances computed regardless of the method used, as shown in Exhibit 13–5. Using the different methods, the total or net variance equals $4,000:

> $40,000 actual total overhead
> 36,000 (1,800 standard hours × $20 total standard overhead rate per hour)
> $ 4,000 unfavorable net factory overhead variance

EXHIBIT 13–5   Overhead Variance Analysis

Two-variance method

Controllable variance

Actual total overhead − [(standard variable overhead rate × standard hours) + total budgeted fixed overhead costs] =

$40,000 − [($4 × 1,800) + $32,000] =
$40,000 − ($7,200 + $32,000) =
$40,000 − $39,200   = $ 800(U)

Volume variance

(Budgeted hours − standard hours) × standard fixed overhead rate =

(2,000 − 1,800) × $16   =
200 × $16   =   3,200(U)

Total (net) variance $4,000(U)

Proof:

(Actual total overhead − applied overhead (standard direct labor-hours × standard overhead rate) =

$40,000 − (1,800 × $20)
$40,000 − $36,000
= $4,000(U)

Three-variance method

Total overhead spending variance

Actual total overhead − [(standard variable overhead rate × actual hours) + total budgeted fixed overhead costs] =

$40,000 − [($4 × 1,890) + $32,000] =
$40,000 − ($7,560 + $32,000) =
$40,000 − $39,560   = $ 440(U)

Variable overhead efficiency variance

(Actual hours − standard hours) × standard variable overhead rate =

(1,890 − 1,800) × $4
90 × $4   =   360(U)

Volume variance

(Same computation as for two-variance method)

=   3,200(U)
$4,000(U)

Four-variance method

Variable overhead spending variance

Actual variable overhead − (standard variable overhead rate × actual hours) =

$9,000 − ($4 × 1,890) =
$9,000 − $7,560   = $1,440(U)

Fixed overhead spending variance

Actual fixed overhead − total budgeted fixed overhead costs

$31,000 − $32,000   = 1,000(F)

Variable overhead efficiency variance

(Same computation as that for three-variance method)

360(U)

Volume variance

(Same computation as for two-variance method)

=   3,200(U)
$4,000(U)

U = unfavorable; F = favorable

Productivity

Current Cost Management Practice

A penny spent is a penny lost, figures Regal Cinemas' Chairman Mike Campbell, which explains why his is the most profitable movie house chain in the United States. Campbell won't reimburse traveling employees of the Knoxville, Tennessee-based theater chain more than $40 a night for a hotel room or more than $15 a day for meals. This kind of cost control pays off because Regal generates net profit margins of 8 percent, almost double the margin of the larger publicly held exhibitors such as AMC Entertainment, Cineplex Odeon, and Carmike Cinemas. As former grocers, Campbell and his partner haven't lost their grocer mentality of watching margins like hawks. Regal managers know exactly how much syrup should be in each softdrink serving, exactly how much popcorn should fill each container, and exactly how much popcorn oil goes into each batch. Computers at Regal's headquarters monitor concession yields on a regular basis. Campbell is convinced operations are still not at bare bones as he is looking to reduce general and administrative costs over the next two years to 3 percent, from a current 4.3 percent.

Matt Walsh, "Easy on the Popcorn," *Forbes,* September 26, 1994, pp. 126–27.

Journal Entries Illustrated

The following summary entry records actual fixed and variable factory overhead incurred:

Factory Overhead Control ($9,000 + $31,000)	40,000	
Various Credits		40,000

Accountants can use separate ledger accounts for fixed and variable overhead. Such accounts as supplies, inventory, payroll, accumulated depreciation, and prepaid insurance are credited during the accounting period to record actual factory overhead.

The following entry records the application of total overhead to the products included in the Work in Process Inventory based on the standard hours allowed. Note again that in a normal costing system not employing standards, we would use 1,890 actual hours to apply overhead of $37,800 ($20 × 1,890 actual hours).

Work in Process Inventory (1,800 standard hours × $20 total standard overhead rate)	36,000	
Factory Overhead Control		36,000

The Factory Overhead Control account now appears as follows:

Factory Overhead Control

Actual	40,000	Applied at standard	36,000
Balance 4,000			

The underapplied factory overhead balance of $4,000 reflects the four overhead variances computed. The Factory Overhead Control account is closed by recording these overhead variances under the four-variance method:

Variable Overhead Spending Variance	1,440	
Variable Overhead Efficiency Variance	360	
Volume Variance	3,200	
Fixed Overhead Spending Variance		1,000
Factory Overhead Control		4,000

We record the three unfavorable variances as debits, while the favorable fixed overhead spending variance is recorded as a credit. There is not always a special combination of unfavorable and favorable variances. Only the actual operating facts, in addition to the standards established, determine whether variances are favorable or not.

Disposition of Variances

To dispose of standard cost variances, we use two basic procedures: (1) close them entirely to Cost of Goods Sold or Income Summary; or (2) allocate them to inventories and Cost of Goods Sold. Chapter 4 introduces the disposition of over- or underapplied overhead as a period cost.

Variances Treated as Period Costs

If a company charges or credits its variances against the revenues of the period, it considers them as a cost of inefficiency rather than as a cost of the product. Variances either are closed entirely to Cost of Goods Sold or Income Summary. We use the $70 unit standard cost given in Chapter 12 and the related variances for material, labor, and overhead calculated in Chapters 12 and 13 for a job order system. The disposition of variances to Income Summary at the end of the period is

Material Purchase Price Variance	2,898	
Fixed Overhead Spending Variance.	1,000	
Income Summary	5,358	
Material Quantity Variance.		1,000
Labor Efficiency Variance		3,000
Labor Rate Variance		256
Variable Overhead Spending Variance		1,440
Variable Overhead Efficiency Variance		360
Volume Variance		3,200

If, instead, we consider the variances as the responsibility of production, we close them to Cost of Goods Sold. Later we close the balance in Cost of Goods Sold to Income Summary.

Assuming we close the variances to Income Summary, and the company sells 600 units at $160 each, Exhibit 13–6 illustrates a partial income statement stating Cost of Goods Sold at standard. We deduct favorable production cost variances from unfavorable production cost variances to yield a $5,358 deduction from the gross margin at standard. Since we closed these variances to Income Summary, they appear in the income statement. If, instead, we had closed the variances to the Cost of Goods Sold account, they would appear as adjustments to Cost of Goods Sold at standard.

Proration of Variances

The other procedure is to consider variances as a cost of the product and allocate them to Work in Process, Finished Goods, and Cost of Goods Sold. Significant material purchase price variances are allocated not only to these but also to Direct Materials Inventory and the Material Quantity Variance accounts. However, Direct Materials Inventory would not receive any of the material quantity variance or the labor and overhead variance allocation. Chapter 1 indicated the Cost Accounting Standards Board is an agency of the federal government; its regulations require significant standard cost variances to be included in inventories. Internal Revenue Service regula-

EXHIBIT 13–6   Gross Margin Adjusted for Variances

**Partial Income Statement
for Month Ended 19X1**

Sales (600 units @$160)			$96,000
Cost of goods sold at standard (600 units @$70)			42,000
Gross margin at standard			$54,000
Adjustments for standard cost variances:			
Material quantity variance	$1,000		
Labor efficiency variance	3,000		
Labor rate variance	256		
Variable overhead spending variance	1,440		
Variable overhead efficiency variance	360		
Volume variance	3,200		
Total unfavorable variances		$9,256	
Material purchase price variance	$2,898		
Fixed overhead spending variance	1,000		
Total favorable variances		3,898	5,358
Gross margin adjusted			$48,642

tions also require the inclusion of a portion of significant variances in inventories. However, if the variances are not significant, they need not be inventoried for tax purposes unless an allocation is made for financial reporting purposes. Internal Revenue Service regulations do require the consistent treatment for both favorable and unfavorable variances. However, the volume variance can be expensed irrespective of the treatment of other variances.

Exhibit 13–7 illustrates the allocation of variances. Assume that of the 900 units mentioned in earlier exhibits, the company sells 600 units, 200 units remain in finished goods, and 200 units were in process at a 50 percent stage of completion for all three cost elements. This yields 100 equivalent units in Work in Process Inventory. Exhibit 13–7 uses the unit standard cost of $12 for materials, $18 for labor, and $40 for overhead. As you recall from Chapter 12, of the 3,220 pounds of material purchased, production used 2,950 pounds. The 270 pounds remaining in

EXHIBIT 13–7   Variance Allocation

Accounts	Direct Materials (270 lbs. × $4)	Work in Process (100 EU × $70)	Finished Goods (200 units × $70)	Cost of Goods Sold (600 units × $70)	Total
Standard cost balances......	$1,080	$7,000	$14,000	$42,000	$64,080
Allocations:					
Material price	$ (243)	(270)	(540)	(1,620)	(2,673)*
Material quantity	–0–	86	172	517	775†
Labor	–0–	361	724	2,171	3,256
Overhead	–0–	444	888	2,668	4,000
Ending balances	$837	$7,621	$15,244	$45,736	$69,438

* $2,898 − $225 allocation to material quantity variance

† $1,000 material quantity variance − $225 material purchase price variance allocated

Direct Materials Inventory are valued at a standard price of $4 for a total of $1,080. (Note in advance that for simplicity we use very few digits to illustrate variance calculations. Do not be misled; prorating variances is not a waste of effort just because we allocate such small amounts in Exhibit 13–7.)

For distributing the material price variance, we use direct materials at standard prices within each of the inventories, cost of goods sold, and material quantity variance for a basis of $12,880 ($1,080 in Direct Material + $1,200 in Work in Process + $2,400 in Finished Goods + $7,200 in Cost of Goods Sold + $1,000 Material Quantity Variance = $12,880). For example, we credit Direct Materials Inventory for $243 ($1,080/$12,880 × $2,898 = $243) and Work in Process Inventory for $270 ($1,200/$12,880 × $2,898 = $270).

The journal entry is as follows:

Material Purchase Price Variance	2,898	
Direct Materials Inventory		243
Work in Process Inventory		270
Finished Goods Inventory		540
Cost of Goods Sold		1,620
Material Quantity Variance		225

If the material quantity variance is favorable, we divide the quantity used in production less the quantity in the material quantity variance by the equivalent units of production to arrive at the pounds per equivalent unit worked on. Then we apply the price variance per pound or gallon to each of the pounds or other measurement per equivalent unit worked on.

The materials quantity variance is now $775 ($1,000 − $225 prorated from materials price variance). We prorate the materials quantity variance to Work in Process, Finished Goods, and Cost of Goods Sold. We use the $10,800 original materials balance before prorating the material price variance as a basis ($1,200 in Work in Process + $2,400 in Finished Goods, and $7,200 in Cost of Goods Sold = $10,800). For example, we debit Work in Process Inventory for $86 ($1,200/$10,800 × $775 = $86). The same allocation results if we use the materials balances after the material price variance is prorated.

The journal entry to prorate the material quantity variance is

Work in Process Inventory	86	
Finished Goods Inventory	172	
Cost of Goods Sold	517	
Material Quantity Variance		775

We allocate the remaining labor and overhead variances to Work in Process, Finished Goods Inventory, and Cost of Goods Sold on the basis of their ending balance of standard labor and overhead costs. We allocate the $3,256 total labor variance on the basis of $16,200 ($1,800 Work in Process + $3,600 Finished Goods + $10,800 Cost of Goods Sold). For example, Cost of Goods Sold receives $10,800/$16,200 × $3,256 = $2,171 proration as shown in this journal entry:

Work in Process Inventory	361	
Finished Goods Inventory	724	
Cost of Goods Sold	2,171	
Labor Rate Variance		256
Labor Efficiency Variance		3,000

We allocate the overhead variances on the basis of $36,000 ($4,000 Work in Process + $8,000 Finished Goods + $24,000 Cost of Goods Sold). For example, Finished Goods receives $8,000/$36,000 × $4,000 = $888 proration as shown in this journal entry:

Work in Process Inventory.....................	444	
Finished Goods Inventory	888	
Cost of Goods Sold...........................	2,668	
Fixed Overhead Spending Variance...............	1,000	
Variable Overhead Spending Variance		1,440
Variable Overhead Efficiency Variance		360
Volume Variance		3,200

After posting this entry, the inventories and Cost of Goods Sold have the ending balances as indicated in Exhibit 13–7. We could have used equivalent units for the proration instead of costs and approximately the same amounts would have resulted, depending on what rounding of figures was used.

Most Appropriate Alternative.   The method chosen for allocating variances should depend on the significance of the amounts involved. If the variances are not material, we can close them to Cost of Goods Sold and Income Summary. However, when the variances arise because of some unforeseen condition, allocation is the more appropriate procedure.

Analysis of Material, Labor, and Overhead Variances

Netting out the separate variances aggregates the data so the need for corrective action is hard to detect. On the other hand, it is counterproductive to provide so many variances that managers ignore them. Just because a manual system calculated few variances, a computerized system does not have to calculate several variances. The first step in system redesign is to establish minimum information requirements for legal and management purposes within the context of the manufacturing process. Accountants should eliminate unnecessary detail and irrelevant information.

Role of Probabilities and Timing.   Chapter 17 discusses the use of probabilities in deciding when to investigate variances. Timing is very important in a standard cost system. The person responsible for a cost should know the standard in advance and receive variance information promptly. The more quickly a variance is isolated, the greater the chance that the cause of the variance is detected and corrected before the firm incurs excessive cost. One of operating management's most common problems is that cost information often arrives too late for effective decision making.

The effectiveness of the control is in direct proportion to the speed with which a change is recommended after discovering an unsatisfactory operating condition. The quality and price of materials are best controlled prior to or at the time of purchase. Overhead costs should be analyzed as the decisions creating such cost elements are made. Many times the accounting system fails by compiling lengthy reports that arrive long after the cost is incurred. Such reports are of little value for cost control.

As an initial step in interpreting variances, managers must identify who has primary responsibility for each of the variances. The individual who has authority to incur a cost should be held responsible for that cost. Thus, we must separate cost factors directly controllable by operating supervisors from those for which executive management is responsible.

Monitor Efficiency and Volume Variances to Prevent Excess Inventory

JIT production dictates that every process produces parts only when needed and only in the quantity needed. JIT recognizes profits when goods are sold, not when they are produced. Using a volume variance to measure segment performance encourages long production runs that may not meet market demand. Product life cycles are shorter today, and products change more frequently than in the past. A large inventory stored for future use may become obsolete before it can be sold. In addition, the expense of holding inventory increases.

Local Efficiencies.   Even though managers set standards to increase efficiency and encourage total utilization of the resource, the result may be decreased throughput of the organization as a whole. The local efficiency does increase but only at the expense of the entire entity. Use of **local efficiencies,** such as the incentive to incur a favorable efficiency or volume variance, may be in direct contradiction with the company's goal of making money. When an entire plant is not efficient, the productivity of any one department does not increase the profitability of the entire plant. The primary reason for this counterproductivity is evaluating managers on their efficiency and volume variances while ignoring market needs.

Computing labor efficiency and volume variances often encourages managers to keep workers busy in production activities without regard to market demand. Because of the influence of variance analysis, managers may act to achieve a high level of segment efficiency, while overall performance of the plant is declining. With uneven production capacity, accounting performance measures, such as standard cost variances that emphasize only local efficiencies, may place a company in a position of carrying excess inventory and increasing operating expenses while reducing throughput.

For example, assume a company has an older blending machine that performs operations equally well—but not as fast—as a blending machine purchased last year. The older machine produces a unit in 18 minutes while the newer machine takes only 13 minutes. The cost standard is set on the faster machine's operation. Even though ingredients blended with the older machine take 18 minutes, managers receive credit for only 13 minutes of earned standard minutes allowed based on output. All product managers strive to route their units through the faster machine rather than the older machine. Managers do not use the older machine unless absolutely necessary because they are motivated to run as many products as possible through the faster machine and have no incentive to run any products through the older machine. Thus, product managers are not willing to damage their performance by incurring unfavorable variances on all products processed through the older machine. Unless companywide performance affects their evaluations, it is doubtful that managers are concerned about the performance of the entire system.

As a result, managers delay throughput by waiting to use the newer machine to incur favorable variances. Frequently, the end result is that the newer blending machine becomes a temporary bottleneck. The company increases the time that its final product is shipped. Consequently, production costs increase instead of decrease because the new machine is the basis for the standard. Thus, the production standard appears to be disguising any benefits associated with using the older machine. Because the older machine cannot operate as quickly as the new one, any production on this machine appears inefficient. However, management has not considered the effect of the new machine's insufficient capacity on the system's throughput.

Cost accountants set the standard with a view to increasing efficiency. However, the result is excess inventory before the bottleneck resource that increases operating expenses (through increased inventory carrying cost) and decreases throughput. While segment managers maximize their own efficiencies, the organization as a whole suffers. The primary reason for this counterproductivity is basing the rating of managers on the faster machine.

Causes of and Responsibility for Variances

The following outline provides a basic understanding of possible causes of unfavorable controllable and noncontrollable variances. With this general knowledge, management gains insight into which operations they should investigate to determine more exact causes of the variances reported. In addition, the outline identifies the individual responsible for any deviation.

Possible causes of unfavorable controllable variances

1. Unfavorable terms in buying supplies and services.
2. Waste of indirect material.
3. Avoidable machine breakdowns.
4. Using wrong grade of indirect material or indirect labor.
5. Poor indirect labor scheduling.
6. Lack of operators or tools.

Responsibility for controllable (spending) variances

Supervisors of cost centers are responsible because they have some degree of control over these budget or expense factors.

Responsibility for variable factory overhead efficiency variances

Line supervisors are responsible because this variance reflects the effects of labor efficiency on factory overhead when labor dollars or labor-hours are the basis for applying factory overhead. This variance shows how much of the factory's capacity has been consumed or released by off-standard labor performance. If machine-hours are the basis for applying factory overhead, the variance measures the efficiency of machine usage.

Possible causes for unfavorable noncontrollable variances

1. Poor production scheduling.
2. Unusual machine breakdowns.
3. Storms or strikes.
4. Fluctuations over time.
5. Shortage of skilled workers.
6. Excess plant capacity.
7. Decrease in customer demand.

Responsibility for noncontrollable variances

Line supervisors can control fixed overhead when the costs are discretionary rather than committed.

Top sales executives may be held responsible if budgeted volume (i.e., theoretical, practice, or normal capacity) is matched with anticipated long-run sales.

Responsibility usually rests with top management, for the volume variance represents under- or overutilization of plant and equipment.

Revision of Standards

To be effective measures of performance, standards should be accurate. This requires that management continuously review standards and make any necessary revisions. However, managers should not adjust standards too frequently in an attempt to keep them in line with actual results. This destroys the control aspect of standards and adds clerical costs. Managers should adjust standards only when events such as labor rate changes, material price changes, changes in production flow, or technological advances warrant. If managers fail to revise standards when they automate plant operations, standard costs are based on the assumption that overhead cost is proportionate to the direct labor consumed by each product. The result is inaccurate product costs.

Summary

Recognizing that companies earn profits through selling, not by producing inventory for stock, affects variance analysis. Stressing lower production costs through long production runs no longer meets market needs. Performance measurements, such as efficiency and volume variances, may result in several types of conflict. In particular, segment managers may be torn between the performance that is most efficient for the overall company versus what appears efficient according to the accountant's performance measurements. While standard cost systems offer many advantages in quickly pointing out matters needing control, they require monitoring. This better ensures the discovery of opportunities for cost reduction and control and prevents misguided decisions on product pricing, product sourcing, product mix, and responses to rival products.

Important Terms and Concepts

Problem for Self-Study

Material, Labor, and Overhead Variances in a Process Costing System
Charlie Company manufactured yeast dinner rolls in batches of 12-dozen using a standard cost system. Management budgets 200 of these batches per period. Fixed factory overhead at this level is $15,000. The standard costs per batch are as follows:

	Total
Flour material (20 pounds)	$ 30
Mixing-Cooking direct labor (15 hours)	135
Total factory overhead (15 hours)	120
	$285

The following costs were incurred in finishing 225 batches of rolls during the period. In addition, 50 batches were one-half complete as to all cost elements in ending inventory; there was no beginning inventory.

Direct material used (5,220 pounds of flour)	$ 7,255.80
Mixing-Cooking labor (3,650 hours)	30,660.00
Actual variable factory overhead	11,050.00
Actual fixed factory overhead	15,500.00

Required:

Prepare a variance analysis and proof of variances for:
a. Material.
b. Labor.
c. Factory overhead: two-variance method.
d. Factory overhead: three-variance method.
e. Factory overhead: four-variance method.

Solution to Problem for Self-Study

Charlie Company

$$EU = 225 + 25 = 250 \text{ batches of rolls}$$
$$(50 \times 0.5)$$

a. Material quantity variance

$$250 \text{ batches} \times 20 \text{ pounds} = 5,000 \text{ standard pounds}$$
$$[(5,220 \text{ actual pounds} - 5,000 \text{ standard pounds}) \times \$1.50 \text{ standard rate}]$$
$$= \$ 330.00 \text{ unfavorable}$$

Material price variance

$$\frac{\$7,225.80 \text{ actual material cost}}{5,220 \text{ actual lbs.}} = \$1.39 \text{ actual rate}$$

$$[(\$1.39 \text{ actual rate} - \$1.50 \text{ standard rate}) \times 5,220 \text{ lbs.}] = \$574.20 \text{ favorable}$$

Proof:

Actual material cost	$7,255.80
Standard material cost (5,000 × $1.50)	7,500.00
Favorable	$ 244.20

Material price variance—favorable . . . . $ 574.20
Material quantity variance—unfavorable 330.00
Total (net) variance . . . : . . . . $ 244.20

b. *Labor quantity variance*

250 batches × 15 hours = 3,750 standard hours
[(3,650 actual hours − 3,750 standard hours) × $9.00 standard rate]
= $900.00 favorable

Labor rate variance

$$\frac{\$30,660.00}{3,650 \text{ hours}} = \$8.40 \text{ actual rate}$$

($8.40 actual rate − $9.00 standard rate) × 3.650 actual hours = $2,190 favorable

Proof:

Actual labor cost $30,660
Standard labor cost (3,750 × $9.00)   33,750
Favorable . . . . $ 3,090
Labor rate variance—favorable . . . . $ 2,190
Labor quantity variance—favorable   900
Total (net) variance . . . . $ 3,090

c.

200 batches × 15 hours = 3,000 budgeted hours
Total overhead rate $8.00 per hour ($120/15 hours)

Less: $$\frac{\$15,000 \text{ fixed overhead}}{3,000 \text{ budgeted hours}} = 5.00 \text{ fixed factory overhead rate}$$

Variable overhead rate $3.00

Two-variance method for factory overhead

1. *Controllable*

Actual overhead $26,550
Flexible budget
(3,750 standard hours × $3 variable overhead rate =
$11,250 variable + $15,000 budgeted fixed)   26,250
Unfavorable controllable variance . . . . $ 300

2. *Volume variance*

(3,000 budgeted hours − 3,750 standard hours) × $5
    fixed factory overhead . . . . $3,750 favorable

Proof:

Actual overhead $26,550
Standard overhead (3,750 standard hours × $8)   30,000
Favorable . . . . $ 3,450
Controllable variance—unfavorable . . . . $ 300
Volume variance—favorable   3,750
Total (net) variance . . . . $ 3,450

d. Three-variance method for factory overhead

Controllable

1. *Total overhead spending variance*

Total actual overhead costs	$26,550	
Flexible budget for actual hours		
$15,000 budgeted overhead + ($3 variable		
factory overhead × 3,650 actual hours)	25,950	
	$ 600 unfavorable	

2. *Variable overhead efficiency variance*

(3,650 actual hours − 3,750 standard hours) × $3 = $300 favorable

Noncontrollable

3. *Volume variance*

(3,000 budgeted hours − 3,750 standard hours) × $5 = $3,750 favorable

Proof:

Actual overhead		$26,550
Standard overhead		30,000
Favorable		$ 3,450
Total overhead spending variance—unfavorable		$ 600
Variable overhead efficiency variance—favorable	$ 300	
Volume variance—favorable	3,750	4,050
Total (net) variance		$ 3,450

e. Four-variance method for factory overhead

Controllable

1. *Variable overhead efficiency variance*

[(3,650 actual hours − 3,750 standard hours) × $3] = $300 favorable

2. *Variable overhead spending variance*

Actual variable overhead	$11,050	
Budget for actual hours (3,650 actual hours × $3)	10,950	
	$ 100 unfavorable	

3. *Fixed overhead spending variance*

Actual fixed overhead	$15,500	
Budgeted fixed overhead	15,000	
	$ 500 unfavorable	

Noncontrollable

4. *Volume variance*

(3,000 budgeted hours − 3,750 standard hours) × $5 = $3,750 favorable

Proof:

Actual overhead		$26,550
Standard overhead		30,000
Favorable		$ 3,450
Variable overhead spending variance—unfavorable	$ 100	
Fixed overhead spending variance—unfavorable	500	$ 600
Variable overhead efficiency variance—favorable	$ 300	
Volume variance—favorable	3,750	4,050
Total (net) variance		$ 3,450

Review Questions

1. How can the reporting of variances cause further breakdowns in the working relationship of employees and supervisors? Suggest a better approach for reporting variances.

2. Indicate which of the following data are known before operations begin or after operations end and how each is determined or computed.
   a. Actual hours.
   b. Standard variable overhead rate.
   c. Standard hours.
   d. Budgeted hours.
   e. Standard fixed overhead rate.
   f. Actual cost or actual rate.

3. Discuss the three different capacity levels that companies use in overhead variance analysis. Indicate the point in the operating cycle at which information used to determine these capacity levels becomes available.

4. What similarities are there between factory overhead application rates in an actual cost system and those in standard factory overhead rates? Discuss the difference between applying factory overhead in an actual cost system and applying it in a standard cost system.

5. What capacity level is normally chosen as a basis for establishing standard factory overhead rates? In what terms is the capacity level chosen as the basis for standard overhead most often expressed?

6. Why is a volume variance comparing budgeted hours with standard hours a better indication of the use of capacity than a volume variance comparing budgeted hours with actual hours?

7. What is the danger involved if a company automatically loosens a standard every time an unfavorable variance occurs? How often do you think standards should be reviewed for possible revisions? Why is there a danger in frequently revising standards?

8. *a.* Discuss two reasons that could cause factory overhead to be overapplied.
   b. How should an accountant dispose of an overapplied factory overhead balance if it is material?

9. Why is it necessary that managers using a standard cost system know the total standard factory overhead rate when operations begin? Why are the standard factory overhead rates used to cost inventory determined for production departments only?

10. Discuss some environmental conditions that have an effect on the standard cost system.

Exercises

Critical Thought

E13–1 Standard Cost Concepts
Before operations begin, management has analyzed the market and determined that 500 batches of their secret mixture TREX are budgeted to be produced. Time and motion studies show that 25 standard hours are needed per batch. In their planning for the next period, management budgets manufacturing overhead to be $437,500 of which $250,000 is fixed.

Required:

a. What capacity concept can you determine (i.e., budgeted, actual, or standard)?
b. How many hours is it?

c. In what variance do you use the capacity concept for Requirement *a* if the company uses the four-variance method? Use calculations to show how it is used.

d. In what variance do you use the $250,000 fixed overhead in total assuming the four-variance method is used?

e. What is the budgeted variable overhead and how do you use it?

f. What is the variable overhead rate per hour and in what variance do you use this rate?

E13–2 Theory and Computations of Overhead Variance

The following data are from the Tom Clevenger Company:

Budgeted fixed costs	$25,000
Standard fixed overhead rate	$ 25.00 per machine-hour
Standard variable overhead rate	2.25 per machine-hour
Standard machine-hours per unit	4
Actual machine-hours	1,460
Actual units produced	280
Actual total overhead	$28,940

Required:

a. Determine overhead variances using the three-variance method of analysis.

b. If you can perform a four-way variance analysis, do so. Explain why you can or cannot.

c. If you can perform a two-way variance analysis, do so. Explain why you can or cannot.

E13–3 Impact of Quality Control Program on Behavior

McSparrin Company is a manufacturer of costume jewelry and employs a standard cost system. The ingredients for the fake stones are combined in the Mixing Department. From there, the mixture is sent in 500-gallon batches to the Molding Department, where various sizes of stones are molded. After the stones are removed from the molds and cleaned, they are forwarded to the Assembly Department, where the stones are mounted in rings, bracelets, and necklaces. The frames for these are purchased from an outside vendor.

McSparrin operates a modified job order process system. For example, all operations use a mass-production, assembly-line approach; however, they do produce according to job order. A job order calling for 1,000 rings of a specified type may be received for inventory stock. After this order is completed, another job order is issued for the production of other types of jewelry. No jewelry is manufactured according to customer specification.

A standard cost system allows for some spoilage in the Assembly Department. However, the supervisor of the department has been complaining recently about the extra work her employees do when they cut stones to fit the bracelets they are assembling. If the stones are even 1/64 of an inch too large, the assembler must cut and polish the stone so that it can be inserted in the bracelet frame and clasped down.

The plant supervisor has had conferences with the Molding Department supervisor, and together they have inspected the quality control program. All stones are examined and measured before being forwarded to the Assembly Department. However, slight variations in size are difficult to detect. The Molding Department supervisor believes that the bracelet frames supplied by the outside vendor are at fault; he claims that many of these are not consistent in size.

The Assembly Department supervisor claims that she should not be held accountable for any unfavorable labor quantity variance. She admits that the quantity standard was explained to her before operations began and that an allowance for some stone cutting was made in the standard.

Required:

Suggest ways that this matter should be settled. Make recommendations for any needed changes in the reporting system.

E13–4 Labor and Overhead Variances

The following information is from the Daniel Company:

Standard labor hours allowed	1,170
Actual labor hours	1,220
Budgeted total overhead	$18,000
Actual labor cost	4,865
Actual variable cost	7,040
Actual fixed cost	12,500

Standard Specification per Finished Product

	Total
Direct labor (3 hours)	$12
Variable overhead	15
Fixed overhead	30

Required:

Compute labor and overhead variances. Show proof of your figures. Use the four-variance method for overhead.

Critical Thought

E13–5 Specific Standard Cost Data

On April 1, 19X1, Lake Company began the manufacture of a new device known as Whiz. The company installed a standard cost system in accounting for manufacturing costs. The standard costs for a unit of Whiz are as follows:

Direct materials (6 pounds at $1 per pound)	$ 6
Direct labor (1 hour at $4 per hour)	4
Overhead (75 percent of direct labor cost)	3
	$13

Lake's records included the following data for April:

Actual production of Whiz	2,000
Units sold of Whiz	1,250

	Debit	Credit
Sales		$25,000
Purchases	$13,650	
Material price variance	650	
Material quantity variance	500	
Direct labor rate variance	380	
Direct labor efficiency variance		400
Manufacturing overhead total variance	250	

The amount shown for the material price variance is applicable to direct material purchased during April.

Required:

Compute each of the following items for April:

a. Standard quantity of direct materials allowed (in pounds).

b. Actual quantity of direct materials allowed (in pounds).
c. Standard hours allowed.
d. Actual hours worked.
e. Actual direct labor rate.
f. Actual total overhead.

E13–6 Two-Variance Method for Overhead

The records revealed the following data for the Ajax Manufacturing Co.:

		Standard Cost per Unit
Direct material	10 lbs. at $2 per pound	$20.00
Direct labor	2 hours at $16 per hour	32.00
Factory overhead	4 machine-hours at $4 per hour	16.00
		$68.00

Factory overhead incurred during the month included indirect labor, $234,000; indirect materials, $220,000; depreciation, $54,000; and miscellaneous factory costs, $16,000. The fixed factory overhead incurred represented $60,500 of the total, while the variable factory overhead totaled $463,500.

Goods finished during the period totaled 32,000 units. Normal production capacity for the plant is 120,000 machine-hours with budgeted fixed costs of $60,000.

Required:

Compute the factory overhead controllable and volume variances, indicating if favorable or unfavorable.

E13–7 Material, Labor, and Two-Variance Overhead Method, Journalizing Variances

Zoe Company uses a standard cost system. Engineers have determined that the standard pounds of material in one of Zoe's finished products is 4 pounds per unit. The standard direct material cost is $5 per pound. Each unit requires one hour of direct labor time and one hour of machine time. Standard direct labor cost is $10 per hour. The overhead budget formula is $18,000 per month plus $4 per machine-hour for a normal volume of 3,600 units.

A total of 15,000 pounds of material costing $72,000 were purchased and received; 14,000 pounds of materials were used. Direct labor cost incurred (3,570 hours) was $42,840. Actual overhead of $32,000 was incurred in making 3,600 units.

Required:

a. Compute the:
   1. Material usage variance.
   2. Material purchase price variance.
   3. Material usage price variance.
b. Compute the labor efficiency and rate variances.
c. Calculate the absorption rate for overhead per machine-hour.
d. Compute the overhead variances using the two-variance method.
e. Prepare summary journal entries to record actual and applied factory overhead; also record overhead variances.

E13–8 Material, Labor, and Three-Way Overhead Variance

Shelly Company adopted a standard cost system several years ago for use in costing its single product. Standards per unit were set as follows:

Material	8 kilograms @ $0.10 per kilogram
Direct labor	6 hours @ $9 per hour
Factory overhead—variable	6 hours @ $2 per hour
Factory overhead—fixed	6 hours @ $3 per hour

The following operating data were for April:

In process, beginning inventory, none.

In process, ending inventory 800 units, which are 75 percent complete as to labor and overhead; material is issued at the beginning of processing.

Completed during month, 6,000 units.

Budgeted units were 7,000.

Issued to production were 54,100 kilograms of material @ $0.11 per kilogram.

Direct labor cost $354,000 which was a rate of $8.85 per hour.

Total actual factory overhead was $206,300.

Required:

An analysis of variances for:

a. Material.

b. Labor.

c. Factory overhead using a three-way analysis.

E13–9 Flexible Budget and Standard Costs

Writing

CD Company manufactured compact disc players. The company uses a standard cost system plus a flexible budget for overhead expense. The accountant determined the standard unit overhead cost by dividing budgeted costs at the normal volume by the number of compact disc players that volume level represented.

Certain cost information follows. When filling in the blank spaces, closely analyze the relationships among the figures given for allocated service and general overhead to determine normal volume.

	Actual Cost, June	Standard Charge per CD Player	Total Standard Cost, June	Flexible Overhead Budget, June	Overhead Budget Formula
Direct labor	$ 9,650	$ 10	$ ____	Not used	
Direct material	14,200	15	14,250	Not used	
Department direct overhead expense . . .	6,700	____	____	$ 6,900	$5,000 per month plus $2 per CD player
Allocated service and general overhead . . .	11,000	10	9,500	10,000	$10,000 per month
Total	$41,550	$	$	$16,900	

Required:

a. Determine how many disc players the company produced in June.

b. Calculate the normal volume of disc player output at which the standard unit overhead charge was determined.

c. Fill in the blanks.

d. Explain as much of the difference between total actual costs and total standard costs as you can on the basis of the information given by calculating all the variances you can for material, labor, and overhead.

Problems

SPATS

P13–10 Journal Entries for Variances

Goodwin Company has established two quarterly budgets, but there is some conflict as to which one they should use. The vice president believes that they should estimate their overhead rate using a long-range approach that would be an average of 1,500 machine-hours per quarter. The president does not agree as he believes that since they are a seasonal operation they should use the short-range approach and change their capacity estimate every quarter. The estimate for the first quarter is 1,800 machine-hours. Since the president believes he has supreme command, he decides to go with the short-range approach as their budgeted hours. The two proposed budgets are as follows:

Product Units	Machine-Hours	Total Budgeted Overhead
500	1,500	$8,805
600	1,800	9,468

Analysis of the actual factory overhead shows the following (none of these costs have been recorded):

Variable:	
Insurance expired	$ 811
Indirect labor	1,690
Indirect material	1,199
Total variable	$3,700
Fixed:	
Indirect labor	$1,180
Depreciation	4,230
Total fixed	$5,410

Analysis of the time sheets showed that actual machine-hours were 1,660 for the 548 units finished. The company uses the four-variance method of computing factory overhead variances.

Required:

Prepare all the necessary journal entries entering all variances into the accounting system. Close the variances into cost of goods sold. Subsidiary ledger accounts are not necessary.

P13–11 Labor and Four-Variance Method for Overhead

Jobb Manufacturing Company estimates that it will incur the following labor and overhead costs:

Estimated variable overhead	$ 72,000
Estimated fixed overhead	80,000
Total estimated overhead	$152,000
Estimated direct labor costs	$128,000

Estimates are that each unit will require 20 hours of labor. Management plans to produce 800 units next period.

At the end of that period, Jobb managers determined that workers used 14,250 actual direct labor-hours to produce 750 units. Actual costs for variable overhead was $62,275; for fixed overhead, $82,100; for direct labor costs, $117,562.50.

Required:

Prepare direct labor and factory overhead variances. Use the four-variance method of analyzing overhead. Prove your answers for labor and overhead.

P13–12 Material, Labor, and Overhead Variances Using Various Methods of Overhead Analysis

John Douglass, Inc., manufactures dried onion dip mix using a standard cost system. Each carton contains 400 packages. Management had planned to produce 50 cartons for the period. The following data were obtained from the Accounting and Production Departments for a recent operating period:

Standard cost per 400-package carton:

Onion and sour cream materials (2,000 gallons @ $1.20 per gallon)	$2,400
Direct labor (800 hours @ $7 per hour)	5,600
Variable factory overhead (800 hours @ $4 per hour)	3,200
Fixed factory overhead (800 hours @ $2 per hour)	1,600

	Total

Actual results for 44 cartons produced:

Onion and sour cream materials used (87,250 gallons)	$109,062.50
Direct labor (36,300 hours)	263,175.00
Variable factory overhead incurred	150,000.00
Fixed factory overhead incurred	83,000.00

Required:

Compute the following:

a. Material and labor variances.
b. Four-variance method for overhead.
c. Three-variance method for overhead.
d. Two-variance method for overhead.

P13–13 Journalizing Variances

Ross Manufacturing Company has established the following specifications for each unit:

	Total
Material (5 gallons @ $1.65 per gallon)	$ 8.25
Labor (4 hours @ $12.75 per hour)	51.00
Variable overhead (4 hours @ $2.00 per hour)	8.00
Fixed overhead (4 hours @ $3.00 per hour)	12.00
	$79.25

The company planned to produce 100 units per month. Workers completed 30 units on Job No. 1, completed 40 units on Job No. 2, and partially completed 20 units on Job No. 3. These 20 units were 100 percent complete for material and 80 percent complete for conversion costs. Actual variable overhead costs were $800, while actual fixed overhead costs were $1,259. The company paid $12.60 hourly labor rate. Total direct labor cost for Job No. 1 was $1,537.20; for Job No. 2, $2,268; and $982.80 for Job No. 3. Analysis of the material requisitions and purchase orders showed that 148 gallons were purchased and used on Job No. 1; 210 gallons on Job No. 2; and 87 gallons on Job No. 3. Total material costs amounted to $747.60. The company uses the four-variance method of analyzing factory overhead.

Required:

Journalize these transactions, entering all standard cost variances into the accounting system. Use job order subsidiary ledger accounts when recording the entries to Work in Process Inventory. All inventories are recorded at standard. Determine the material quantity and labor efficiency variances for each job. It is not necessary to close the variance accounts.

P13–14 Material, Labor, and Overhead Variances Using Different Bases for Standards

Regional Company assembles family-size dinners ready for the microwave. Standards for these frozen vegetable dinners are:

	Per Unit
Raw mixed vegetable materials (3 lbs. at $6 per lb.)	$18
Assembling labor (2 labor-hours at $8 per hr.)	16
Variable overhead (5 machine-hours at $2 per hr.)	10
Fixed overhead (5 machine-hours at $3 per hr.)	15

Management has budgeted to make 1,000 dinners monthly. Regional's records revealed the following monthly data:

Actual variable factory overhead	$ 8,670
Actual fixed factory overhead	$13,000
Actual dinners produced	850 units
Actual machine-hours	4,100 hours
Actual vegetables used	2,610 lbs. at a total cost of $15,399
Actual labor used	1,890 hours at a total cost of $19,013.40

Required:

Calculate these variances:
a. Material.
b. Labor.
c. Four-variance method for overhead.
d. Three-variance method for overhead.
e. Two-variance method for overhead.

P13–15 Variances for Material, Labor, and Overhead (Two-Way)

Brown Company has established the following standard costs per unit:

Material (6 pounds @ $0.50 per pound)	$ 3.00
Direct labor (1 hour @ $8 per hour)	8.00
Factory overhead (1 hour @ $5.50 per hour)	5.50
Total standard cost	$16.50

The $5.50 per direct labor-hour overhead rate is based on a normal capacity budgeted at 95 percent operating level. The following flexible budget information reveals:

	Operating Levels		
	85%	*95%*	*100%*
Units of production	4,250	4,250	5,000
Standard direct labor-hours	4,250	4,750	5,000
Variable factory overhead	8,500	9,500	10,000
Fixed factory overhead	16,625	16,625	16,625

During March, the company operated 85 percent of capacity, producing 4,250 units of product which they charged with the following standard costs:

Material (25,500 pounds @ $0.50 per pound)	$12,750
Direct labor (4,250 hours @ $8 per hour)	34,000
Factory overhead costs (4,250 hours @ $5.50 per hour)	23,375
Total standard cost	$70,125

Actual costs incurred during March were

Material (26,100 pounds)	$11,745
Direct labor (4,150 hours)	34,445
Fixed factory overhead costs	16,625
Variable factory overhead costs	7,650
Total actual costs	$70,465

Required:

Isolate the material and labor variances into price and quantity variances and isolate the overhead variance into the volume variance and controllable variance.

SPATS

P13–16 Interim Income Statements
Each subsidiary of the Beatle Corporation submits interim financial statements. The accountants combine these statements into companywide quarterly statements. One of its subsidiaries, the Dobbs Company, provides the following data regarding sales forecasts for the year:

Quarter	*Bug Killer Units*	*Percent*
First	100,000	10%
Second	400,000	40
Third	300,000	30
Fourth	200,000	20
	1,000,000	100%

Additional data are as follows:

1. The company has achieved first and second quarter sales as forecasted.
2. The president is considering raising the sales price of the bug killer spray from $80 to $100. Other managers are concerned, however, that this increase will reduce sales volume forecasts for the first and fourth quarters, which are already low.
3. Although manufacturing facilities can produce 1,400,000 units per year or 350,000 units per quarter during regular hours, the production schedule calls for only 1,000,000 units this year. This is the quarterly schedule for production:

Quarter	Units of Production Scheduled	Percent
First	375,000	37.5%
Second	400,000	40.0
Third	150,000	15.0
Fourth	75,000	7.5
	1,000,000	100.0%

4. The standard production cost, which does not incorporate any charges for overtime, was established at the beginning of the current year as follows:

Direct material	$35
Labor	10
Variable factory overhead	5
Fixed factory overhead	6
	$56

5. An unfavorable material price variance of $210,000 resulted in the second quarter because of a significant and permanent price increase.

6. An unfavorable direct labor variance also resulted in the second quarter in the amount of $277,500 partially due to overtime pay to meet the heavy production schedule. Whenever production requires work beyond regular hours, an overtime premium equal to 0.5 times the standard labor rate is paid. The remaining portion of the labor variance during the second quarter is due to expected inefficiencies.

7. In addition, a $40,000 unfavorable variable overhead variance resulted in the second quarter which was related to the excess direct labor costs.

8. A total of $6,000,000 fixed overhead expected to be incurred is budgeted for the year; $3,600,000 of fixed overhead has been absorbed into production through the first two quarters. Of this total, $2,400,000 was absorbed in the second quarter. For the first two quarters, a $600,000 total fixed overhead volume variance resulted due to the high manufacturing activity.

9. Marketing expenses are 10 percent of sales and are expected to total $8,000,000 annually.

10. The $6,000,000 annual administrative expenses are incurred uniformly throughout the period.

11. At the end of the second quarter, inventory balances are

Direct material—at actual cost	$ 750,000
Work in process—50% complete—at standard cost ..	168,000
Finished goods—at standard cost	1,680,000

12. The bug killer product line is expected to earn $10,000 before taxes this year with estimated state and federal income taxes at $4,200,000 for the year.

13. The accountant prorates any unplanned variances that are significant and permanent in nature to the applicable accounts during the quarter in which the variances were incurred.

Required:

a. Prepare the second quarter interim income statement for the Dobbs subsidiary of the Beatle Corporation.

b. Evaluate the production scheduling that Dobbs Company is proposing.

P13–17 Recording and Allocating Material, Labor and Overhead Variances

A total of 1,800 units are budgeted by Sly, Inc., for its first year of operations. Standards per unit have been established jointly by the cost accountants, management, and company engineers, as follows:

Direct material (8 pounds @ $3 per pound)	$ 24
Direct labor (5 hours @ $7 per hour)	35
Factory overhead:	
Variable (4 machine-hours @ $7.50 per hour)	30
Fixed (4 machine-hours @ $5 per hour)	20
	$109

A total of 12,825 pounds of direct material were used in production; 13,200 pounds were purchased at a cost of $2.85 per pound. A saving also resulted from employing lesser skilled workers at $0.20 per hour less than standard. Actual labor-hours totaled 8,375; actual machine-hours were 6,700. Actual variable overhead and fixed overhead totaled $46,000 and $38,400, respectively. A total of 1,340 units were finished and transferred out of production; 1,000 of these were sold. There were 1,500 units in ending Work in Process, one-fifth complete.

Even though much time was spent in establishing standards, significant variances did arise. Material variances are prorated at year-end on the basis of direct material balances in the appropriate accounts. Variances associated with direct labor and overhead are prorated based on the respective direct labor and overhead balances in the appropriate accounts.

Required:

a. Determine material, labor, and overhead variances using the four-variance method for analyzing overhead. Compute a purchase price variance for material.
b. Prepare summary journal entries to record the variances. For this problem, assume no entries involving standard costs have been made. Record Direct Materials Inventory at standard cost.
c. Prepare journal entries to allocate the variances.
d. Give the balances in Direct Materials Inventory, Work in Process, Finished Goods, and Cost of Goods Sold after all variances have been prorated.

P13–18 Standard Costs for a Process Operation (AICPA)

Webb & Company is engaged in the preparation of income tax returns for individuals. Webb uses the weighted-average method and actual costs for financial reporting purposes. However, for internal reporting, Webb uses a standard cost system. The standards, based on equivalent performance, have been established as follows:

Labor per return	5 hours @ $20 per hour
Overhead per return	5 hours @ $10 per hour

For March 19X7 performance, budgeted overhead is $49,000 for the standard labor-hours allowed. The following additional information pertains to the month of March 19X7:

Inventory Data

Returns in process, March 1 (25% complete)	200
Returns started in March	825
Returns in process, March 31 (80% complete)	125

Actual Cost Data

Returns in process March 1:

Labor	$ 6,000
Overhead	2,500
Labor, March 1 to 31,	
4,000 hours	89,000
Overhead, March 1 to 31	45,000

Required:

a. Using the weighted-average method, compute the following for each cost element:
   (1) Equivalent units of performance.
   (2) Actual cost per equivalent unit.
b. Compute the actual cost of returns in process at March 31.
c. Compute the standard cost per return.
d. Prepare a schedule for internal reporting analyzing March performance, using the following variances, and indicating whether these variances are favorable or unfavorable:
   (1) Total labor.
   (2) Labor rate.
   (3) Labor efficiency.
   (4) Total overhead.
   (5) Overhead volume.
   (6) Overhead controllable.

P13–19 Material, Labor and Overhead Variances (AICPA)

Tredoc Co. is in the business of seasonal tree-spraying and uses chemicals in its operations to prevent disease and bug infestation. Employees are guaranteed 165 hours of work per month at $8 per hour and receive a bonus equal to 75 percent of their net favorable direct labor efficiency variance. The efficiency variance represents the difference between actual time consumed in spraying a tree and the standard time allowed for the height of the tree (specified in feet), multiplied by the $8 standard hourly wage rate. For budgeting purposes, there is a standard allowance of one hour per customer for travel, setup, and clearup time. However, since several factors are uncontrollable by the employee, this one-hour budget allowance is excluded from the bonus calculation. Employees are responsible for keeping their own daily timecards.

Chemical usage should vary directly with the tree footage sprayed. Variable overhead includes costs that vary directly with the number of customers, as well as costs that vary according to tree-footage sprayed. Customers pay a service charge of $10 per visit and $1 per tree-foot sprayed.

The standard static budget and actual results for June are as follows:

	Static Budget		Actual Results
Service calls . . . .(200 customers)	$ 2,000	(210 customers)	$ 2,100
Footage sprayed . . . .(18,000 feet)	18,000	(21,000 feet)	21,000
Total revenues	$20,000		$23,100
Chemicals . . . .(1,800 gallons)	4,500	(2,400 gallons)	5,880
Direct labor:			
Travel, setup, and clearup .(200 hours) $1,600		(300 hours) $2,400	
Tree-spraying . . . .(900 hours) 7,200		(910 hours) 7,280	
Total direct labor	8,800		9,680

P13–19 Material, Labor and Overhead Variances (AICPA) *(continued)*

	Static Budget	*Actual Results*
Overhead:		
Variable based on number of customers . 1,200		
Variable based on tree-footage 1,800		
Fixed 2,000		
Total overhead	5,000	5,400
Total costs	$18,300	$20,960
Gross profit before bonus	$ 1,700	$ 2,140

July's demand is expected to be in excess of June's and may be met by either paying a 25 percent overtime premium to current employees or by hiring an additional employee. A new employee will cause fixed costs to increase by $100 per month. The potential increased demand may be estimated by considering the impact of increases of 20 and 30 customers, with probabilities of 70 percent and 30 percent, respectively.

Required:

a. Compute the following for June:
   (1) Direct materials price variance.
   (2) Direct materials usage (efficiency) variance.
   (3) Direct labor travel, setup, and clearup variance.
   (4) Direct labor bonus.
   (5) Overhead spending (flexible budget) variance.
   Indicate whether each variance is favorable or unfavorable.
b. Assume that Tredoc accepts all orders for services in July. Should Tredoc hire an additional employee? Provide supporting computations based on standard cost.

Cases

C13–20 Analysis of Standard Cost System and Variance Computation

Florida Company is a medium-size manufacturer located in a relatively small community to take advantage of a cheap labor force. Florida Company established standards four years ago based on a sequence of three job operations—A, B, and C—requiring a total elapsed time of four hours. Direct labor workers are paid $15 an hour. According to standard specifications, three pounds of Raw Material R at a cost of $6 per pound are mixed with two pounds of Material S costing $1 per pound. This results in a weighted average cost per pound of $4 that is used as the standard. Material R costs more because it is a durable, high-quality material needed to give strength and long life to the product the company's marketing department promotes. Material S is a filler that adds bulk to the product. Standard specifications per unit are as follows:

		Per Unit
Material: 5 pounds @ $4 per lb.		$ 20
Labor: 4 labor-hours @ $15 per hr.		60
Overhead—Variable: 8 machine-hours @ $3 per hour	$24	
Overhead—Fixed: 8 machine-hours @ $7 per hour	56	80
Total per unit		$160

Two years ago the company hired engineering consultants who evaluated the production work flow and revised the sequence of operations to B, C, A which reduced the required time to three hours. Because management believed that this was a production method change only, the cost accountant was not aware of this event.

The production manager has been experimenting with different combinations of Materials R and S and has found that with a slight altering of the raw material ingredient ratios, the product can still pass initial inspection.

The company budgeted a total of 120 units but actually produced only 100 units during the current period. According to company records, the following are actual results for the period:

Material R—100 lbs. for a total cost of	....	$ 800
Material S—400 lbs. for a total cost of	....	1,000
500 lbs.	....	$1,800
Labor—325 hours for a total cost of	....	$5,980
Overhead—860 machine-hours: Variable	....	$2,700
Fixed	....	6,900
Total overhead	....	$9,600

The following standard cost variances appeared on the cost production report for the period. The company uses the two-way variance analysis for overhead.

Material price variance

Standard cost (100 units × $20)	....	$2,000
Actual cost	....	1,800
Favorable price variance	....	$ 200

Material quantity variance

(100 units × 5 pounds each @ standard = 500 pounds used) ....   –0–

Labor variance

(100 units × $60 @ standard = $6,000 − $5,980 actual cost) = $20 favorable

Volume variance

(860 machine-hours—960 machine-hours) × $10 = $1,000 unfavorable

Controllable variance

Actual overhead	....	$9,600
Standard overhead (100 units x $80)	....	8,000
		$1,600 unfavorable

Required:

a. Evaluate the standard cost system employed by the company and list any weaknesses.
b. Suggest needed improvement; where appropriate, recalculate any variances you believe are incorrect.
c. List the objectives of a standard cost system.
d. Indicate specific ways that these objectives are not being met with Florida Company's present system.
e. Discuss briefly the critical information needs that an effective standard cost system can provide for the following:
   (1) Production manager.
   (2) Marketing manager.
   (3) President.

Writing

C13–21 Evaluating Standard Cost Systems Indicating Weaknesses

Standard cost data help managers keep cost centers under control and running efficiently according to predetermined plans. If appropriately applied, they can evaluate performance through variance analysis. While standard cost systems offer many opportunities for improving cost control, these systems often include features that destroy much of their usefulness. After studying the standard cost systems employed by the following companies, you may detect areas in which managers are being hindered in performing their functions. When this occurs, the company's profitability is endangered.

Company A management boasts of their performance by emphasizing that they have consistently had favorable variances for the last three reporting periods. Initially, standards were scientifically determined using time and motion studies and material sampling. However, management found over the years since, that these initial standards were not realistic because unfavorable variances were being reported. Thus, the standards were relaxed so that achievable standards were used. For example, after the Purchasing Department ordered materials costing $0.10 over standard one year, the price standard was raised $0.50 just to make certain that the extra $0.40 would be available to cover unforeseen possibilities. Likewise, industrial engineers estimated that the standard quantity per unit should be five pounds including normal waste, however, plant management convinced them to add another pound to the standard to give them some flexibility. Labor and overhead standards are handled in a similar manner. Standard markups for pricing are added to the full standard cost.

Company B is a relatively small manufacturer; in fact, they do not have an industrial engineering department. However, they did employ engineers as consultants when the standards were first set up four years ago. They have since revised standard unit prices for material and labor but the quantities for material or the time allotments for labor have remained fixed. Two years ago, Company B increased production capacity by more than 100 percent by adding a second labor shift. Existing standards are applied to this second shift. As a result, the company's income statement reported large unfavorable labor efficiency variances.

Company C prides itself on its strict schedule of events. For example, on the fifth working day after the end of a month, income statements are scheduled to be on the controller's desk for review. Managers also established official dates for revising standard cost cards that are the basis for preparing variance reports. Top management believes that this policy is most appropriate even though the company's cost accountant has some reservations. For example, at mid-year last year, the company changed its production techniques; the effect on standard costs was then incorporated six months later according to the official schedule for revising standards. The cost accountant recalls this also happening during the 1970s as a result of the Arab oil embargo when prices were accelerating.

Company D uses the following two-way analysis for factory overhead:

Controllable variance

Actual fixed overhead of $9,500 + $10,000 Budgeted fixed overhead $19,500
Compared with: [($4 fixed overhead rate + $3 variable overhead rate)
  × 2,000 standard hours] + $5,000 actual variable overhead   19,000
                                                                $ 500 unfavorable

Volume variance

   (2,500 budgeted hours − 2,300 actual hours) × $3 variable overhead rate = $600 favorable

Company E uses two sets of standards; they revise one set once a year and use it for interim financial statements. The other set is changed continually to keep price and quantity standards current for all three cost components.

Company F manufactures and sells a line of fabrics in three different manufacturing plants. There are significant differences among the various production lines; also some grades of fabric can be produced only on certain lines. Equipment capacities vary between plants so that the most efficient run size in each line differs. Production personnel constantly monitor sales orders with the equipment capacities to achieve the most economic production cost. They use a standard cost system in which standards are based on the one most efficient compatible production line with each order size.

Company G manufactures a plastic product in five strengths; to obtain the varying strengths, workers alter the ratios of the ingredients. However, the only standard product cost card represents an average of the strengths that are to be made. Accountants calculate mix variances based on this average standard. They compute the mix variance by comparing the standard formula to the standard cost of material or labor actually used. A mix variance results if the actual product strength does not match the strength on the cost card. Because management must take time in explaining these resulting mix variances, they are considering a proposal to base the standard on one of the five strengths.

Required:

a. Evaluate the standard cost systems employed by the seven companies: for each, indicate any impact on the company's financial statements and any behavioral effect of the system.
b. Suggest needed improvements, giving specific examples if appropriate. Set up your answers so that Requirements *a* and *b* follow each other for each company.

Capstone Case

Standard Variances, High-Low, and Cash Budget

L. Mosyer Company management is generally pleased with 19X1 operations in which net income of $72,000 is projected. The president is not satisfied, however, with the earnings per share projection and would like to increase this figure from a projected $3.60 for 19X1 to at least $4 for 19X2. She wants this projection to be included in the 19X2 budgets.

For 19X1, Mosyer expects to sell 50,000 units at $120 each and projects an annual increase of 10 percent in unit sales for 19X2 and 19X3. An increase of $8 per unit selling price will begin in 19X2, but the marketing staff is confident that demand is high enough that the sales price increase will not affect the expected increase in unit sales.

Mosyer uses two materials in production and has developed the following standard costs for all manufacturing costs reflecting 19X2 standard quantities and prices to produce one final unit:

Material A (3 pounds @ $2/pound) .... $ 6
Material B (4 gallons @ $3.75/gallon) 15
Direct labor (2 hours @ $15/hour) 30
Factory overhead (to be developed using the following budgets)

The following budgets have been developed for manufacturing overhead with the standard overhead rate based on a normal capacity of 100,000 direct labor-hours.

	Direct Labor-Hours		
	90,000	*100,000*	*115,000*
Indirect material and supplies	$ 630,000	$ 700,000	$ 805,000
Supervisory salaries	810,000	900,000	1,035,000
Plant maintenance	380,000	420,000	480,000
Plant rent	300,000	300,000	300,000
Depreciation on factory facilities	280,000	280,000	280,000
Total overhead	$2,400,000	$2,600,000	$2,900,000

   Mosyer management desires to have 20 percent of the expected annual unit sales for the coming year in ending finished goods inventory of the prior year. Finished goods inventory on December 31, 19X1, is forecasted to consist of 11,000 units at a total standard cost of $935,000. The company uses LIFO inventory costing.

   Marketing expenses are determined to be variable, while administrative expenses are all fixed. Budgeted marketing expense is expected to average 5 percent of sales revenue in 19X2; however, administrative expenses for 19X2 are expected to be 30 percent higher than the 19X1 estimated amount of $400,000. The price of Material B rose $0.25 a gallon to $4 per gallon near the end of 19X1; however, management believes this is temporary and did not revise its standard for this increase. Also the company has suffered a sharp increase in labor turnover recently; this has increased the production time per unit by 12 minutes. Managers expect that as the new workers become more skilled, they will meet the standard.

Required:

a. Prepare a budgeted income statement for 19X2 for the company incorporating management's specifications. Use the standards as developed but consider the most unfavorable situation for 19X2 with regard to Material B and direct labor. Identify production variances separately and add or subtract them from budgeted cost of goods sold. Assume Mosyer is subject to a 42 percent income tax rate.

b. Analyze the 19X2 budgeted income statement prepared to determine if the president's objective of $4 earnings per share is feasible.

c. Assume the company uses FIFO inventory costing and compute the budgeted cost of goods sold at standard cost.

PART IV

Cost Planning and Control

CHAPTER
14

Cost-Volume-Profit Analysis

Chapter Objectives

After studying this chapter, you should be able to:

1. Explain the cost-volume-profit relationships that exist in a company.
2. Compute and use breakeven analysis.
3. Explain why even though rigid assumptions underlie breakeven analysis, it can result in effective answers without costly analysis.
4. Use sensitivity analysis to examine the effect of changing an input value on profit and the breakeven point.

Introduction

Chapter 14 focuses on cost-volume-profit relationships and the impact of cost behavior patterns on decision making. An understanding of a company's cost behavior patterns is helpful in making management decisions on such matters as product pricing, accepting or rejecting sales orders, and promotion of more profitable product lines.

Cost-volume-profit analysis determines the target volume, which is the volume necessary to achieve target or desired operating income. One of the more popular forms of cost-volume-profit analysis is the computation of a company's breakeven point.

Computing Breakeven Point

The **breakeven point** is the volume of sales at which there is no profit or loss. Even though breakeven analysis is a static concept, its application to a dynamic situation aids management in planning and controlling operations. The focus of breakeven analysis is the impact of volume on costs and profits within a **relevant range,** as introduced in Chapter 3. Because operating at the breakeven point is not the goal of managers, they may question the benefit of breakeven analysis. However, breakeven analysis forces a study of a company's fixed and variable cost behavior. The actual breakeven point is of less importance than the effect of decisions on costs and sales. Cost-volume-profit analysis provides management with information about the impact on profit of changes in costs, revenues, volume, and product mix.

Impact of Automation on Breakeven

As machines replace laborers and factories become more automated, many formerly variable costs—such as payroll—become fixed. Plants with increased fixed costs resulting from automation have higher breakeven points and require higher levels of utilization to be profitable. Thus, understanding cost behavior becomes even more important in making management decisions on product pricing, accepting or rejecting sales orders, cost reduction analysis, and promotion of more profitable product lines. Cost accountants assign greater importance to the variable-fixed cost relationships in an automated environment.

Contribution Margin Approach

Accountants can use either an equation or a graph to determine a company's breakeven point. They express breakeven in units or in sales dollars. For example, assume a $10 unit sales price, $4 unit variable expenses, and fixed expenses of $36,000 for Sills Co. Its contribution margin is

$10 unit sales price − $4 variable expense = $6 unit contribution margin

Contribution margin is sales dollars less all production, marketing, and administration variable expenses. It represents the sales dollars that cover fixed costs and produce a profit. Contribution margin may be expressed as a total, as an amount per unit, or as a percentage. The following equation indicates sales equal expenses because there is no income at the breakeven point.

$$X = \text{Units to be sold at breakeven point}$$
$$S = \text{Variable expenses } + \text{ Fixed expenses}$$
$$\$10X = \$4X + \$36,000$$
$$\$6X = \$36,000$$
$$X = \frac{\$36,000 \text{ Fixed expense}}{\$6 \text{ Unit contribution margin}} = 6,000 \text{ Units to break even}$$

Strategic Planning

Current Cost Management Practice

Many economists believe productivity has dramatically improved compared with the prior two decades and improved productivity means the economy can grow more rapidly without triggering inflation. A pickup in manufacturing activity raises the specter of production bottlenecks, but American factories can shift excess order flows to factories overseas. While productivity has risen faster in the last three years than the rate assumed by the typical forecast, part of this reflects the typical productivity rebound following a recession. However, the heavy investment in business equipment is likely to cause the productivity surge to continue. The old rules about capacity utilization constraints and inflation flashpoints may no longer work because many U.S. companies have plenty of manufacturing capacity abroad. To its credit, U.S. industry has a highly flexible labor and entrepreneurial tradition. The biggest threat to faster growth comes from the troubling combination of zealous restraint by policy makers and the inflation jitters of the bond market investors. These two threaten to squander the economy's potential strength and all the jobs and wealth it would produce. Thus, the U.S. can do better, but not if it continues to fear growth.

Christopher Farrell, "Why Are We So Afraid of Growth?" *BusinessWeek,* May 16, 1994, pp. 62–72.

Remember that Chapter 3 defined **variable costs** as those costs varying directly with changes in the volume of output. For example, direct materials used is a variable cost. **Fixed costs,** on the other hand, remain the same in total for a given period and production level. Insurance and rent payments are examples of fixed costs. Note that we are substituting *expense* for *cost* as there is a widespread tendency to use these terms interchangeably. In this context, *costs* refer to costs expiring and thus become expenses in the period studied.

Breakeven Units.   The preceding equation indicates that if Sills Company sold in the range of 6,000 units, it would break even. We should not assume, however, that when Sills Company's volume is exactly 6,000 units, breakeven conditions automatically occur. Breakeven may not occur because actual costs may vary from those forecasted. For example, the actual unit variable expenses may not be $4, and actual total fixed expenses may vary from $36,000.

Breakeven Sales Dollars.   After arriving at the 6,000 units needed to sell to break even, Sills managers can determine breakeven sales. Breakeven sales result from multiplying breakeven units by the unit sales price to yield $60,000 (6,000 units × $10 sales price).

Variable Cost Ratio   Rather than multiplying breakeven units by unit sales price, we can use the variable cost ratio or the contribution margin ratio to determine breakeven sales dollars. The **variable cost ratio** results from dividing variable costs by sales. Using the previous illustration, the variable cost ratio is 40 percent ($4 unit variable cost/$10 unit sales price). We can also determine the variable cost ratio by subtracting the contribution margin ratio from 100 percent. The **contribution margin ratio** is the ratio

Service

Current Cost Management Practice

While touring a company-owned satellite plant, the CEO of Scientific-Atlanta realized the company needed communication between its divisions. To achieve better communications, they moved from a divisional to a group structure, with common manufacturing and a sharing of research and development, wherever possible. The objective was to remove the bottlenecks in the business. Increasing sales remains an important issue. Analysts believe for the past 10 years their biggest weakness has been that they have been an engineering-driven company rather than a customer-driven one. The CEO is starting to make these changes to remove this outdated mentality.

Russell Shaw, "Put Up or Shut Up," *Financial World*, May 24, 1994, pp. 32–33.

of contribution margin to sales price. With a 60 percent contribution margin ratio, the result is a 40 percent variable cost ratio. Dividing total fixed costs by the 60 percent contribution margin ratio, breakeven sales dollars are

$$100\% \text{ sales} = \$4/\$10 \text{ variable cost percentage} + \$36,000 \text{ fixed expenses}$$
$$100\% = 40\% + \$36,000$$
$$60\% = \$36,000$$

$$\frac{\$36,000 \text{ Fixed expense}}{60\% \text{ Contribution margin ratio}} = \$60,000 \text{ Breakeven sales}$$

Breakeven Chart

Breakeven charts graphically display the relationship of cost to volume and profits and show profit or loss at any sales volume within a relevant range. A breakeven chart may better indicate cost-volume-profit relationships to line managers and nonaccountants than a numerical exhibit. A breakeven chart vividly shows the impact of volume on costs and profits.

A breakeven chart expresses dollars of revenue, costs, and expenses on the vertical scale. Its horizontal scale indicates volume, that may represent units of sales, direct labor-hours, machine-hours, percent of capacity, or other suitable volume drivers. The relationships depicted in breakeven graphs are valid only within the relevant range that underlies the construction of the graph. We assume that 0 to $100,000 sales fall within Exhibit 14–1's relevant range, representing up to 75 percent capacity.

The three lines in Exhibit 14–1 represent fixed expenses, total expenses, and sales revenue. A horizontal line at $36,000 represents fixed expenses. Even if there are no sales, fixed expenses for this relative range remain at $36,000. Adding variable expenses to fixed expenses gives a total expense line. Variable expenses are zero if there are no sales because of the direct relationship between sales and variable expenses. As sales increase, the total expense line increases, reflecting the $4 per unit variable charge. The sales revenue line is drawn from the zero intersection of the horizontal and vertical scales to $100,000 maximum sales for this relevant range.

EXHIBIT 14–1   Breakeven Chart

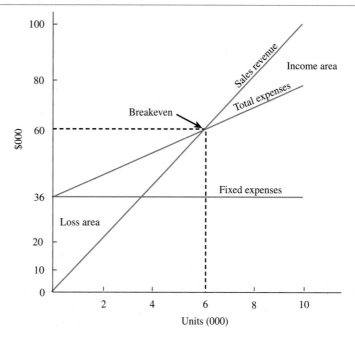

We can construct breakeven charts in an alternate manner that readily shows the contribution margin at any sales volume. Exhibit 14–2 illustrates capacity percentages, rather than units sold, on the horizontal axis using the facts given in the previous example.

EXHIBIT 14–2   Breakeven Chart Showing Contribution Margin

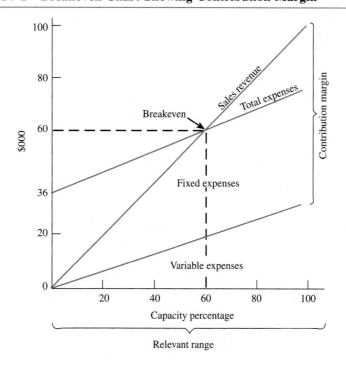

Because breakeven charts are best used as a simple means of illustrating various cost-volume-profit alternatives, the chapter does not include a complex breakeven chart. However, occasions may arise in which the probable effects of complex alternative proposals are best communicated through more elaborate breakeven charts. We can construct a curved sales line to indicate that the sales line does not have to be constant at all capacity levels. We also can divide fixed and variable expenses into production, administrative, and marketing expenses. And, we can draw fixed expenses in a step fashion to indicate the increase expected at various capacity levels. Even though all of the breakeven charts illustrated in this chapter depict a constant unit variable cost, we can alter the slope of the variable cost line at different capacity levels. Increases in variable costs and declines in sales are among other conditions shown on breakeven charts.

Extensions of Breakeven Analysis

Marginal Income

The term *contribution margin* is sometimes used interchangeably with **marginal income.** However, *marginal* often refers to only one product unit. Thus, when accountants refer to marginal income, they generally mean the contribution margin generated by the sale of one additional unit. The contribution margin ratio is known as the **profit-volume (P/V) ratio** or the **marginal income ratio.**

Margin of Safety

Margin of safety, another key concept of breakeven analysis, is the excess of actual or budgeted sales over the breakeven sales volume. This provides the buffer by which sales may decrease before a loss occurs. The margin of safety concept is a mechanical way of saying a company is (or is not) close to the breakeven point. With breakeven sales of $60,000 ($36,000 fixed cost ÷ 60 percent P/V ratio) and actual sales of $80,000, the margin of safety becomes:

Margin of safety = $80,000 actual sales − $60,000 breakeven sales = $20,000
Margin of safety ratio (M/S ratio) = $20,000/$80,000 actual sales = 25 percent.

Used with the contribution margin ratio (or P/V ratio), the margin of safety determines the percentage of sales that income represents. Using the 25 percent margin of safety ratio and the 60 percent contribution margin ratio from Exhibit 14–1, income is 15 percent (25 percent × 60 percent) of sales. When applied against $80,000 sales, this income percentage yields $12,000 (15 percent × $80,000) income before taxes.

Margin of safety draws management's attention to the importance of maintaining efficient operating conditions. Because not all administrators have financial backgrounds, the margin of safety concept may impress on them how close to breakeven the company's operations really are and how critical certain cost controls are. Examining its contribution margin and total fixed costs is an effective strategy when management finds its margin of safety is low. With high contribution margins and high fixed costs, management should concentrate on reducing the fixed costs or increasing sales. A low margin of safety accompanied by a low contribution margin ratio requires effort to increase the contribution margin ratio by either reducing variable costs or increasing sales price. While the preceding statements represent oversimplifications of uncertain real situations, management should act in those directions.

Operating Leverage   Closely related to the margin of safety is the **operating leverage** that measures the relationship between a company's variable and fixed expenses. Operating leverage is greatest in organizations that have high fixed expenses and low per unit variable expenses, such as universities, hospitals, and highly automated manufacturing companies. For these companies, income will be very sensitive to changes in sales because a small percentage increase in sales generates a significant increase in income. Companies having high operating leverage have high contribution margin ratios. Highly labor intensive companies, such as fast-food restaurants that have low fixed expenses and high per unit variable expenses, have low operating leverage.

The **degree of operating leverage** shows how a percentage change in sales volume affects income. The following formula measures the degree of operating leverage:

$$\text{Degree of operating leverage} = \frac{\text{Contribution margin}}{\text{Beforetax income}}$$

Exhibit 14–3 shows the degree of operating leverage is greatest at sales levels near the breakeven point of $60,000 previously computed. Exhibit 14–3 also shows that as sales increase from breakeven, margin of safety increases while the degree of operating leverage decreases. The following shows the relationship between the margin of safety and degree of operating leverage:

$$\text{Margin of safety \%} = 1 \div \text{Degree of operating leverage}$$
$$\text{Degree of operating leverage} = 1 \div \text{Margin of safety \%}$$

Cash Flow   In addition to calculating the breakeven point at which net taxable income equals
Breakeven Point   zero, Sills Company can determine the breakeven point at which cash flow equals zero. In calculating the breakeven point where sales equal expenses, Sills managers use the same expenses as they used for determining net income. For example, with $4 unit variable expenses and $36,000 fixed expenses, the contribution margin approach yields a breakeven point of $36,000 ÷ $6 = 6,000 units.

Assume Sills Company's fixed costs comprise the following:

Superintendent's salary	$17,000
Rent—building	11,000
Insurance	2,000
Depreciation—equipment	6,000
	$36,000

EXHIBIT 14-3

Sales	$65,000	$80,000	$95,000
Variable costs (40%)	26,000	32,000	38,000
Contribution margin	39,000	48,000	57,000
Fixed costs	36,000	36,000	36,000
Income before taxes	$ 3,000	$12,000	$21,000
Degree of operating leverage			
($39,000 CM ÷ $3,000 income)	13		
($48,000 CM ÷ $12,000 income)		4	
($57,000 CM ÷ $21,000 income)			2.7
Margin of safety %	8%	25%	37%

Because depreciation does not represent a cash outflow, **cash flow breakeven point** is

Cash flow fixed costs:

Superintendent's salary	$17,000
Rent	11,000
Insurance	2,000
	$30,000

$$\frac{\$30,000}{\$6} = 5,000 \text{ units for cash flow breakeven}$$

To simplify, the preceding cash flow breakeven ignores the tax shield that depreciation provides. Although most expenses involve cash payments, such charges as depreciation and amortization are noncash reductions in income. We deduct depreciation expense along with other expenses in arriving at net taxable income. Because depreciation does not require a cash expenditure, the tax rate multiplied by the depreciation charge yields a tax shield. We call it a **tax shield** because it protects that amount of income from taxation. Chapter 20 introduces this concept in capital expenditure analysis. Even though the company project or segment being examined has no income at breakeven point, companywide income may be taxed at the income tax rate. Because depreciation from this project may be a tax shield against any companywide income, the following improved cash flow breakeven point results. Note that Sills Company uses a 48 percent income tax rate and a $6 unit contribution margin and consider the tax effect.

Cash flow fixed costs:

Superintendent's salary	$17,000
Rent	11,000
Insurance	2,000
	$30,000
Less tax shield on noncash expense:	
Fixed costs of depreciation (48% × $6,000)	2,880
	$27,120

$$\frac{\$27,120}{\$6} = 4,520 \text{ units for cash flow breakeven}$$

Regardless whether the analysis considers the tax shield, the contribution margin used should represent *cash* variable expenses deducted from *cash* sales and all fixed costs used should represent cash flows out. Since few companies operate on a cash only basis, accruals of assets and liabilities and inventory changes affect the computation. Cash flow breakeven also ignores the different timing of cash flows; that is, cash outflows may occur faster than cash inflows. Despite its limitations and assumptions, cash flow breakeven gives management a different perspective because it reveals the volume needed for cash inflow to equal cash outflow.

Assumptions of Cost-Volume-Profit Analysis

Cost-volume-profit analysis is easy to use and inexpensive to apply; however, it has the following limiting assumptions:

1. The breakeven chart is fundamentally a static analysis; normally, changes can be shown only by drawing a new chart or a series of charts.

2. Relevant range is specified to define fixed and variable costs in relation to a specific period and designated range of production level. The relevant range is usually a range of activities in which the company has operated. This volume of activity is expressed in common terms for sales and expenses; direct labor or machine-hours, units produced, and sales value of production often are used. We must then redefine the amount of fixed and variable cost for any activity outside the relevant range.

3. All costs fall into either a fixed or variable cost classification or can be separated into fixed and variable components.

4. Unit variable costs remain the same and there is a direct relationship between costs and volume. For example, no quantity discounts on materials, increases in labor productivity, or other possible savings in cost are assumed.

5. Volume is assumed to be the only important factor affecting cost behavior. Other influencing factors such as unit prices, sales mix, labor strikes, and production method are ignored. A change in expected cost behavior causes a modification in the breakeven point.

6. Unit sales price and other market conditions are assumed to remain unchanged. No quantity discounts are assumed to be available.

7. Total fixed costs remain constant over the relevant range considered.

8. Inventory changes are so insignificant that they have no impact on the analysis.

9. No increase in efficiency occurs in the period of activity studied, and managerial policies and techniques have no effect on costs.

10. Product technology is assumed to remain unchanged.

11. If breakeven analysis covers more than one product line, there is a specific sales mix assumed that does not change. **Sales mix** is the combination of quantities of products that a company sells. For example, in a tennis sporting shop, it may be six cans of tennis balls to one tennis dress to one tennis racket. Some accountants argue that the constant sales mix assumption is not such a limiting assumption because the sales mix is relatively stable for most product lines. Many individual products have similar gross margins because companies price them to yield a targeted gross margin. Also, if there are many products, a change in the mix will not be significant.

Even though breakeven analysis assumes total fixed costs are constant over a relevant range, we know that fixed costs may change between periods. Management may decide, for example, to purchase machinery to replace direct labor workers, which, in turn, may lower unit variable costs but increase total fixed costs through increased depreciation costs. Increases in the sales force or advertising also alter fixed costs. When one of these events occurs, we construct a new breakeven point and a new breakeven chart.

Although the limitations of breakeven analysis do not invalidate the concept, the assumptions are so restrictive that a breakeven calculation should be interpreted cautiously. The value of breakeven analysis is the insight it gives into cost behavior patterns and the cost-volume-profit relationship. Effective managers recognize that breakeven analysis is not always a routine decision tool. There are other opportunity and relevant cost considerations. For example, maintaining good relations with current, large customers whose supplies are critical may override the decision that breakeven analysis suggests.

Sales Mix Effect on Breakeven

Breakeven analysis assumes sales of only one product or a specified sales mix for a company selling more than one product. We must assume a sales mix to compute average revenues and average costs. In the following example, using only two products to calculate a breakeven point for the overall company may not be realistic because many companies sell a number of product lines. However, to simplify, assume that a hammer sells for $16 and its unit variable cost is $12 while a saw sells for $20 with a unit variable cost of $12. This gives a $4 per unit or 25 percent ($4/$16 sales price) contribution margin for hammers and a $8 per unit or 40 percent ($8/$20) contribution margin for saws. Total fixed costs are $196,000. If the company only sells hammers, the breakeven point is

$$\frac{\$196,000}{\$4} = 49,000 \text{ hammers to break even}$$

If the company only sells saws, the breakeven point is

$$\frac{\$196,000}{\$8} = 24,500 \text{ saws to break even}$$

Assume management plans to sell a total of 5,000 units with a planned mix of 2 hammers (or 2,000) to 3 saws (or 3,000), resulting in this contribution margin for the combined products:

Hammers   Saws
$$2(\$4) + 3(\$8) = \$8 + \$24 = \$32/5 = \$6.40 \text{ weighted-average budgeted} \\ \text{contribution margin}$$

With a $6.40 weighted-average budgeted contribution margin, the breakeven point for the two products becomes:

$$\frac{\$196,000}{\$6.40} = 30,625 \text{ units resulting in 12,250 hammers and 18,375 saws}$$

This calculation indicates the company must sell 30,625 units to break even. When we apply the planned mix of 2:3 (2 hammers to 3 saws), there are 12,250 hammers (i.e., 2/5 × 30,625 = 12,250) and 18,375 (i.e., 3/5 × 30,625 = 18,375) saws at the planned breakeven point.

Market Bundle.   Rather than compute the average budgeted contribution margin, it may be easier to think of this combination as a **market bundle of goods** containing two hammers and three saws resulting in a total contribution margin for the bundle of $32. This results in a breakeven volume of 6,125 market bundles as follows:

$$\frac{\$196,000}{\$32} = 6,125 \text{ market bundles}$$

6,125 bundles × 2 hammers = 12,250 hammers
6,125 bundles × 3 saws = 18,375 saws

Change in Sales Mix.   Suppose, instead, that the company sells 4,000 units composed of 3,000 hammers and 1,000 saws, resulting in an actual sales mix of 3 hammers to 1 saw for a total of 4. Now the breakeven point for the two products is higher, as follows:

Hammers   Saws

$3(\$4) + 1(\$8) = \$12 + \$8 = \$20/4 = \$5$ average actual contribution margin

$$\frac{\$196,000}{\$5} = 39,200 \text{ units resulting in } 29,400^* \text{ hammers and } 9,800^\dagger \text{ saws}$$

$^*3/4 \times 39,200$ units $= 29,400$ hammers.
$^\dagger1/4 \times 39,200$ units $= 9,800$ saws.

Using the market bundle approach with a total contribution margin of $20, the computation is:

$$\frac{\$196,000}{\$20} = 9,800 \text{ market bundles}$$

$$9,800 \text{ bundles} \times 3 \text{ hammers} = 29,400 \text{ hammers}$$
$$9,800 \text{ bundles} \times 1 \text{ saw} = 9,800 \text{ saws}$$

The actual mix of 3:1 (three hammers to one saw) results in a higher breakeven point because the company sold fewer units of the higher contribution margin saws than planned. Breakeven analysis becomes less valid when involving more than one segment or division of a company because we must allocate companywide indirect fixed costs to each segment. Thus, we should determine the breakeven point for as small a segment as possible.

The company expressed its sales mix for hammers and saws in a ratio of units. Alternatively, sales mix can be stated in sales dollars. The following breakeven sales computation expresses sales mix as a percentage of sales dollars. Assume for 19X1 the following unit sales price and variable costs for three different products with $185,000 fixed costs. Assuming the sales mix in dollars is 30 percent dresses, 40 percent shirts, and 30 percent hats, the 19X2 breakeven sales dollars would be:

	Products		
	Dresses	*Shirts*	*Hats*
Sales price	$40	$30	$20
Variable costs	20	18	16
Contribution margin	$20	$12	$ 4
Contribution margin ratio	50%	40%	20%
Percentage of sales dollars	30%	40%	30%
Weighted contribution margin (Contribution margin ratio ×			
Percentage of sales dollars)	15% +	16%	+ 6% = 37%

$185,000/37% = $500,000 breakeven sales dollars resulting in $150,000* dress sales; $200,000† shirt sales; and $150,000* hat sales

$^*30\% \times \$500,000 = \$150,000.$
$^\dagger40\% \times \$500,000 = \$200,000.$

Now, assume the company expresses its sales mix in units as 30 percent dresses, 40 percent shirts, and 30 percent hats. This sales mix expression indicates that 30 percent of total units sold result from dress sales, 40 percent from shirt sales, and 30 percent from hat sales. Converting the percentages into ratios, the mix becomes 3:4:3 resulting in this contribution margin for the combined products:

$$3(\$20) + 4(\$12) + 3(\$4) = \$120/10 = \$12 \text{ average budgeted contribution margin}$$

With a $12 average budgeted contribution margin, the breakeven point for the three products becomes:

$$\frac{\$185,000}{\$12} = 15,417 \text{ units resulting in 4,625 dresses, 6,167 shirts and 4,625 hats}$$

Note that if the sales mix is stated in percentage of sales dollars, you determine the weighted contribution margin ratio and calculate the breakeven sales dollars. If the sales mix is expressed in units, then calculate the average budgeted contribution margin and determine the breakeven point in units.

Target Beforetax and Aftertax Income

We can adapt the breakeven equation to reveal useful information indicating the sales necessary to yield a specified target income. For example, assuming a $10 unit sales price, $4 unit variable cost, $36,000 fixed costs, Sills Co. must sell 7,000 units to earn a target income before taxes of $6,000.

Let X = Number of units to be sold to yield a target operating income
Sales = Variable expenses + Fixed expenses + Target income
$$\$10X = \$4X + \$36,000 + \$6,000$$
$$\$6X = \$42,000$$
$$X = 7,000 \text{ units}$$

Expressing the equation in a slightly different format, we determine the necessary sales dollars to earn an income expressed as a percent of sales. Assume that with a $10 unit sales price, $4 unit variable cost (or $4/$10 = 40% variable cost to sales), and $36,000 fixed costs, Sills management wishes to earn a 15 percent return on sales before taxes. Changing the equation, the sales level to earn this return is:

Sales − Variable expense − Fixed expense = Target beforetax income
$$100\%X - 40\%X - \$36,000 = 15\%X$$
$$45\%X = \$36,000$$
$$X = \$80,000 \text{ sales to earn 15 percent return on sales before tax.}$$

The following simplified statement of income proves that the sales figure determined is correct.

Statement of Income

Sales		$80,000
Expenses:		
Variable expenses (40% × $80,000)	$32,000	
Fixed expenses	36,000	68,000
Income before taxes (15% × $80,000)		$12,000

Aftertax Target Income. Sills' managers may desire a target return after taxes. Exhibit 14–4 indicates $88,300 target sales yields a 10 percent target aftertax return on sales assuming a 40 percent variable cost ratio, $36,000 fixed expenses, and a 48 percent tax rate. Alternatively, aftertax income can be converted to beforetax income using this equation:

$$\text{Aftertax income}/(1 - \text{tax rate}) = \text{Beforetax income}$$

Exhibit 14–4

Sales =	Variable Expense	+	Fixed Expense	+	Desired Aftertax Income
$100\%X =$	$40\%X$	+	$\$36,000$	+	$\dfrac{10\%X}{100\% - 48\%}$
$100\%X =$	$40\%X$	+	$\$36,000$	+	$19.23\%X$
$100\%X - 59.23\%X =$	$\$36,000$				
$40.77\%X =$	$\$36,000$				
$X =$	$\$88,300$		sales to earn 10 percent aftertax income		

With a 10 percent target aftertax return, the sales needed to fulfill this objective must not only support variable and fixed expenses but also cover income taxes before yielding an aftertax income. With a 48 percent income tax rate, the desired aftertax income represents 19.23 percent ($10\%X \div 52\%X$) of sales. The following statement of income proves this sales figure:

Income Statement for Sills Co.

Sales		$88,300
Expenses:		
Variable expenses (40% × $88,300)	$35,320	
Fixed expenses	36,000	71,320
Income before taxes		$16,980
Income taxes (48% × $16,980)		8,150
Net income after taxes (10% × $88,300)		$ 8,830

If Sills Co. is manufacturing a product with not only a declining market but also a decreasing volume, income, and profit margin, it may not be feasible to establish a $88,300 sales objective without additional sales promotion.

Maximum Expenditures to Achieve Objectives

Sills Co. may use cost-volume-profit analysis to estimate the maximum additional amount it can spend on advertising to earn a specific aftertax net income.

Assuming forecasted sales of $88,300, 40% variable costs, $36,000 fixed costs, and 48% tax rate, the following indicates $2,250 is the maximum additional advertising Sills can incur and earn $10,000 aftertax net income.

$$X = \text{maximum advertising}$$
$$\$10,000 = 1.00 - \text{tax rate (sales} - \text{variable cost} - \text{fixed cost} - \text{advertising)}$$
$$\$10,000 = .52 (\$88,300 - \$35,320 - \$36,000 - X)$$
$$\$10,000 = .52 (\$16,980 - X)$$
$$\$10,000 = \$8,830 - .52X$$
$$.52X = \$1,170$$
$$X = \$2,250$$

*Volume to Generate
Equal Income*

Assume Sills Co. is considering automating its factory which would reduce the variable cost percentage to 15 percent but raise fixed costs to $57,000. Managers question what sales volume would yield an identical income regardless whether Sills automates or continues with the same process. The following indicates estimated sales dollars of $84,000 generate the same income of $14,400 whether using present or automated facilities:

$$\textit{Costs Continuing with Same Process} = \textit{Costs with Automated Manufacturing}$$
$$X = \text{Sales volume}$$
$$0.40X + \$36,000 = 0.15X + \$57,000$$
$$0.25X = \$21,000$$
$$X = \$84,000$$

Proof:

Same process: 60% contribution margin × $84,000 = $50,400 − $36,000 fixed costs = $14,400 income
Automate: 85% contribution margin × $84,000 = $71,400 − $57,000 fixed costs = $14,400 income

Sensitivity Analysis

After using market research to determine which sales range is realistic, management may be forced to reassess its objectives or change the promotional expenditures planned. Sensitivity analysis is a helpful tool for making such decisions. **Sensitivity analysis** examines the effect on the outcome for changes in one or more input values and asks what if an input value changed. For example, when the unit variable cost, sales mix, sales price, total fixed cost, or other inputs for cost-volume-profit analysis change, the breakeven point changes, as well as the amount of profit or loss. Sensitivity analysis allows management to determine the impact on the breakeven point and profit if an input value changes.

To illustrate, assume Sills management believes that the $88,300 sales calculated in Exhibit 14–4 is unrealistic. However, it wishes to earn an aftertax income of $8,600. It investigates several alternatives, one of which involves the reduction of fixed costs by $6,000. They can use the following formula to determine the target sales dollars needed to earn an aftertax net income of $8,600 if this alternative is chosen assuming a 48 percent tax rate. They deduct variable costs of 40 percent and $30,000 fixed costs from sales. The resulting profit is subject to a 48 percent tax. They project this alternative to yield the target profit in the sales range of $77,564.

$$X = \text{Sales to earn } \$8,600 \text{ aftertax net income}$$
$$100\%X = \text{Sales to earn } \$8,600 \text{ aftertax net income}$$
$$\$8,600 = [(100\%X - 40\%X) - \$30,000] \times (1.00 - 0.48)$$
$$\$8,600 = 31.2\%X - \$15,600$$
$$31.2\%X = \$24,200$$
$$X = \$77,564$$

To prove this sales range, Sills managers could prepare the following income statement:

Sales		$77,564
Variable cost (40% × $77,564)	$31,026	
Fixed cost	30,000	61,026
Income before taxes		$16,538
Tax (48% × $16,538)		7,938
Aftertax income		$ 8,600

Effect of Volume Change

We also can use sensitivity analysis to estimate the effect on earnings if Sills Co. expands facilities, resulting in an increase in sales volume. In the example used earlier and displayed in Exhibit 14–1, Sills Co. must achieve 60 percent of its theoretical capacity to break even. If we estimate operations to reach 80 percent of capacity, sensitivity analysis estimates income to be: $80,000 − [$36,000 + (40% × $80,000)] = $12,000. Managers can use this information in estimating the most profitable alternative for expansion of plant facilities and product lines, as well as financing and dividend policies.

Assume that in the previous illustration, management has the opportunity to purchase an adjacent building and expand operations to a maximum sales volume of $125,000. However, this expansion would increase fixed costs to $42,000. With variable costs remaining at 40 percent of sales, we can make the following calculation:

	With Present Facilities	With Expanded Facilities
Sales at breakeven	$100\%X = 0.40X + \$36,000$ $= \$60,000$	$100\%X = 0.40X + \$42,000$ $= \$70,000$
Income at $80,000 sales	$\$80,000 - [(40\% \times \$80,000)$ $+ \$36,000]$ $= \$12,000$	$\$80,000 - [(40\% \times \$80,000)$ $+ \$42,000]$ $= \$6,000$
Sales necessary to earn $20,000 income before taxes	$X = \$36,000 + 0.40X$ $+ \$20,000$ $= \$93,333$	$X = \$42,000 + 0.40X$ $+ \$20,000$ $= \$103,333$
Income at 90% capacity	$\$90,000 - [(40\% \times \$90,000)$ $+ \$36,000]$ $= \$18,000$	$\$112,500 - [(40\% \times \$112,500)$ $+ \$42,000]$ $= \$25,500$

A breakeven chart, as shown in Exhibit 14–5, illustrates the effect of increasing fixed expense on the breakeven point. Broken dotted lines indicate the proposed total expense and fixed expense lines. On the chart, the proposed increase in fixed expenses has caused the breakeven point to be higher. Remember, however, assuming that cost behavior is linear over the relevant range may limit the reliability of breakeven analysis. Users of cost-volume-profit analysis must constantly reexamine the assumptions of breakeven analysis. Otherwise, they may mistakenly assume that volume is the only cost driver and that uncertainty does not exist.

In deciding whether the company should expand, management should determine potential sales possibilities. The plant expansion requires a higher sales volume to break even. In addition, a higher sales volume is necessary to earn $20,000 in income using the expanded facilities. However, if a significant market for the product

EXHIBIT 14–5   **Breakeven Chart with an Increase in Fixed Costs**

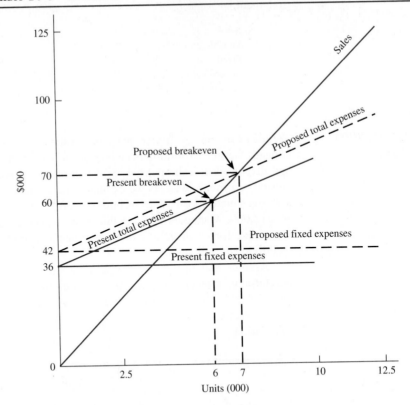

exists, the company has the chance of earning a higher level of income using expanded facilities operating at 90 percent capacity. (As previous chapters have emphasized, it is not realistic to assume a company can obtain maximum capacity.)

Price and Volume Alternatives

Cost-volume-profit analysis is helpful in predicting the change in income that occurs when altering sales price or sales volume. Using spreadsheet software and a personal computer, an accountant can generate an analysis similar to that in Exhibit 14–6. This analysis measures the effects of various sales prices and volumes. We expect no change in unit variable cost or total fixed costs. This analysis assumes that management's budget is based on selling 7,000 units at a $10 per unit sales price, yielding $6,000 net income before taxes, as shown in Column 1. Because of the influence of supply and demand, Column 2 assumes that an increase in sales price would result in a lower volume sold. Column 3 illustrates the results obtained if there is a decrease in sales price and an increase in volume. Marketing research should assist in arriving at such probable sales price and volume combinations. Column 4 indicates the effect on the breakeven point and income when a 5 percent increase in sales price occurs with no decrease in volume. Management may believe that demand for their product is high enough because of brand loyalty or product quality that a sales price increase would have no effect on volume.

Exhibit 14–6 shows projected income is highest when there is a 10 percent increase in sales price with a 5 percent decrease in volume. Breakeven sales with these conditions also are lower than at budgeted volume. The least favorable alter-

Current Cost Management Practice

Productivity

Geac/Collier-Jackson's software applications will put financial executives in control of their own destinies. With VisionShift, information never before available to them will be at their fingertips. With this brand new combination of accounting, human resources, and distribution client/server applications, they will be able to perform the usual accounting and finance functions with a click of a mouse. Financial executives will be able to do the job for which they have been trained—analyzing financial data or creating data to analyze and making strategic decisions almost instantly. What was once a mainframe host-based computer company that wrote programs is now a PC-based client/server company that builds applications to solve business problems from the desktop. Geac/Collier-Jackson believes their success results from understanding the business, the technology, and what people are doing.

Kathy Williams and James Hart, "Collier-Jackson Shifts Its Vision," *Management Accounting,* October 1994, pp. 22–26.

native is to lower the sales price 15 percent with a resulting 20 percent increase in volume. Not only is income lowest with this alternative but also breakeven sales are highest. A 5 percent increase in sales price, with no corresponding decrease in volume, causes a marked increase over budgeted income.

EXHIBIT 14–6   Effect of Sales Price and Volume Changes on Income and Breakeven

	(1) Budgeted 7,000 Units @ $10	*(2)* 10% Increase in Sales Price 5% Decrease in Volume	*(3)* 15% Decrease in Sales Price 20% Increase in Volume	*(4)* 5% Increase in Sales Price No Change in Volume
Sales:				
7,000 units @ $10	$70,000			
6,650 units @ $11		$73,150		
8,400 units @ $8.50			$71,400	
7,000 units @ $10.50				$73,500
Variable expense:				
7,000 units @ $4	28,000			
6,650 units @ $4		26,600		
8,400 units @ $4			33,600	
7,000 units @ $4				28,000
Contribution margin	$42,000	$46,550	$37,800	$45,500
Fixed costs	36,000	36,000	36,000	36,000
Income before taxes	$ 6,000	$10,550	$ 1,800	$ 9,500
Contribution margin ratio	60%	63.6%	52.9%	61.9%
Breakeven sales (fixed expenses ÷ P/V ratio)	$60,000	$56,604	$68,053	$58,158
Degree of operating leverage	7	4	21	5

P/V Charts

A **profit-volume graph,** also called a **P/V chart,** illustrates the impact of sale price and volume changes on income and breakeven. Even though the P/V chart appears quite different from the breakeven chart, it really is a reformatting of information already portrayed in the breakeven chart. The first graph in Exhibit 14–7 illustrates such a chart using data from Exhibit 14–1 in which fixed expenses are $36,000, unit variable expenses are $4, and unit sale price is $10. The vertical axis represents net income in dollars, while the horizontal axis is volume, expressed in units or sales dollars. If the company produces no units, the net loss will be $36,000, the amount of the fixed expense. The net income line intersects the volume axis at the breakeven point of 6,000 units, indicating zero net income at this breakeven volume. Net income at 10,000 units becomes $24,000.

EXHIBIT 14–7   P/V Chart

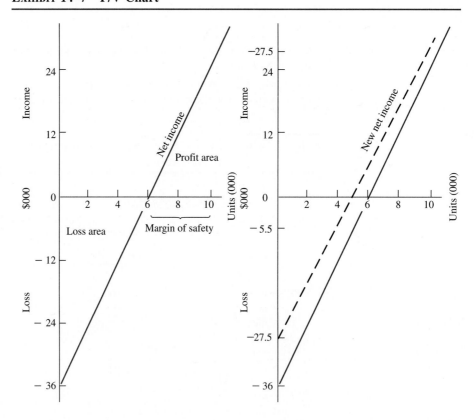

The second graph in Exhibit 14–7 shows the impact on net income and the breakeven point if the unit variable expense increases to $4.50 while total fixed expense decreases to $27,500. The breakeven point falls from 6,000 units to 5,000 units, as follows:

$$\frac{\$27,500}{\$5.50 \text{ unit contribution margin}} = 5,000 \text{ units}$$

The new net income, the dashed line in the second graph, is less steep, because the net income increases at a slower rate as volume increases. With a lower P/V ratio, profits climb slower because a larger portion of the sales dollar is being used to meet variable costs.

Data presented in any cost-volume-profit analysis such as those illustrated in Exhibits 14–6 and 14–7 are of great importance in analyzing which available alternative is most profitable. However, accountants usually have to spend time studying the information because cost-volume-profit analysis requires the segregation of fixed and variable costs. They cannot directly use data that appear on conventional absorption statements of income. Instead, they must break down semivariable expense into variable and fixed components. Accountants use the cost estimation methods presented in Chapter 3 and establish separate ledger accounts for fixed and variable costs. In addition, the data used in any cost-volume-profit analysis should reflect current conditions, since the behavior of variable and fixed costs tends to change over time.

Computer Spreadsheets and Cost-Volume-Profit Analysis

The widespread availability of personal computers encourages more managers to apply cost-volume-profit analysis. Even though this chapter gives the mathematical details of the manual process, the preprogrammed microcomputer applications written for this book introduce the ease of using sensitivity analysis. Computers can quickly make the computations for changes in the assumptions underlying proposed projects. For example, computer spreadsheets allow managers to determine the most profitable combination of selling price, variable and fixed costs, and volume. A manager enters into the computer various numbers for price and cost in an equation based on cost-volume-profit relationships to yield target income for each combination. Because of a computer's speed and accuracy in providing this information, the manager can select the most profitable actions.

Summary

Cost-volume-profit analysis provides useful information for making decisions about pricing, short-term bidding, and deleting or adding product lines. Management must know the contribution margin ratios for each product to promote high contribution margin products and reduce emphasis on less profitable products. Contribution margin analysis allows managers to decide whether to accept an extra order when capacity is less than normal.

While breakeven point analysis portrays only static cost-volume-profit relationships under limiting assumptions, it offers insight into the effect on profits when a change occurs in any of these components. A breakeven chart also may illustrate more vividly these relationships for line management than would detailed numerical statements. However, rigid limitations designed to simplify real-world situations underlie breakeven analysis. Nevertheless, rather than apply more complex decision-making tools requiring costly analysis, accountants often use computer spreadsheet programs to find cost-volume-profit answers quickly. Also, accountants make many decisions within the relevant volume range where the linearity assumption is more accurate.

Important Terms and Concepts

Problem for Self-Study

Breakeven Sales

Neville, Inc., manufactures three household appliances: dishwashers, refrigerators, and electric stoves. Market demand for each of these products varies; dishwashers are very seasonal and demand is extremely difficult to forecast more than four years in advance. Refrigerators are somewhat seasonal and fairly difficult to forecast more than four years in advance. Marketing personnel have less difficulty predicting electric stove demand as it is constant and easy to forecast four years in the future.

Management provides the following internal contribution income statement, based on standard costs:

	Dishwashers	Refrigerators	Electric Stoves	Total
Sales (1,000 dishwasher units)	$800,000	$560,000	$640,000	$2,000,000
Variable standard cost of goods sold	$510,000	(detail omitted)		
Variable marketing and administrative costs	130,000			
Total variable costs	$640,000			
Standard contribution margin	$160,000	$336,000	$480,000	$ 976,000
Fixed manufacturing overhead costs	$ 90,000	(detail omitted)		
Fixed marketing and administrative costs . .	30,000			
Total fixed costs	$120,000			
Standard operating income	$ 40,000	$132,000	$354,000	$ 526,000
Variances—Favorable–F/ Unfavorable–U				
Direct materials—Price–F	$ 6,000	(detail omitted)		
Usage–U	9,000			
Direct labor—Rate–U	1,000			
Efficiency–F	5,000			
Manufacturing overhead—total–U	3,000			
Marketing and administrative costs–F	1,500			
Operating income, net of variances	$ 39,500	$110,000	$310,500	$ 460,000

Required:

a. What is Neville's standard breakeven point in sales dollars for the overall company and for each product line for the actual sales mix achieved?

b. Because dishwashers are so seasonal, a salesperson is delighted to receive an offer to sell dishwashers to a segregated market during the off-season. Assume the standard cost pattern remains unchanged except that unit variable marketing and administrative costs will be twice the standard rate for this sale. Explain if Neville will break even if the sales price equals the variable cost of goods sold at the standard rate, plus twice the variable marketing and administrative costs at standard rate.

c. If Neville sells $20,000 more refrigerators than electric stoves, explain the effect on its breakeven point.

d. Management has these questions about cost classifications and standard variances:

    (1) Should the standard cost of repair supplies and maintenance materials be included in fixed manufacturing overhead?

    (2) Should normal spoilage costs be reported on an internal performance report as variable manufacturing overhead?

    (3) Was the total amount Neville paid for dishwasher direct materials put into process more than the standard cost allowed for the output completed?

    (4) What do the material variances suggest?

    (5) Did Neville pay above or below standard rate to its dishwasher direct labor employees?

    (6) Did dishwasher manufacturing employees take less time than standard in manufacturing?

    (7) Ignoring variances and assuming that Neville uses budgeted demand as the cost driver for allocating manufacturing overhead costs, which of its three products would likely have a substantial percentage of underapplied or overapplied manufacturing overhead on its quarterly statements?

    (8) How much of dishwasher's direct material and direct labor variances would you regard as wholly or partially the responsibility of direct labor employees.?

    (9) What is the dishwasher budgeted standard per unit cost for variable marketing and administrative costs if sales are 900 units?

    (10) What is the dishwasher budgeted standard fixed marketing and administrative costs if sales are 900 units?

Solution to Problem for Self-Study

Neville, Inc.

a. Total fixed costs = $976,000 total contribution margin − $526,000 standard operating income = $450,000

Dishwashers: $160,000/$800,000 = 20% CM ratio; $800,000/$2,000,000 = 40% sales mix;

   20% CM ratio × 40% sales mix = 8%.

Refrigerators: $336,000/$560,000 = 60% CM ratio; $560,000/$2,000,000 = 28% sales mix;

   60% CM ratio × 28% = 16.8%.

Electric Stoves: $480,000/$640,000 = 75% CM ratio; $640,000/$2,000,000 = 32% sales mix;

   75% CM ratio × 32% = 24%

8% Dishwashers + 16.8% Refrigerators + 24% Electric Stoves = 48.8%

$450,000/48.8% = $922,131 overall breakeven sales; broken down into product lines as follows:

$922,131 × 40% = $368,852 for dishwasher breakeven sales

$922,131 × 28% = $258,197 for refrigerator breakeven sales

$922,131 × 32% = $295,082 for electric stove breakeven sales

Dishwashers—$368,852; Refrigerators—$258,197; Electric Stoves—$295,082 for overall of $922,131 breakeven sales

b. Yes, Neville will break even on this order because sales price covers the differential costs of the order; fixed costs are covered by existing sales.

 c. Neville's breakeven point will increase because the 60 percent CM ratio of refrigerators is less than the 75 percent CM ratio of electric stoves.

 d. (1) No, the standard cost of repair supplies and maintenance materials are variable manufacturing overhead.

  (2) Yes, normal spoilage costs should be reported on an internal performance report as variable manufacturing overhead as this cost varies with production.

  (3) Yes, there was a $6,000 favorable direct materials price variance but a larger $9,000 unfavorable direct materials usage price variance.

  (4) It suggests that a cheaper grade of material was purchased, causing workers to use more of this material. The resulting variances indicate this was not a good decision.

  (5) Neville paid above standard since there is an unfavorable direct labor rate variance.

  (6) Yes, they took less time than standard since there is a favorable labor efficiency variance.

  (7) Dishwashers are most likely as they have the most seasonal demand and are most difficult to forecast.

  (8) $9,000 unfavorable direct materials usage − $5,000 favorable direct labor efficiency = $4,000 U

  (9) $130,000/1,000 dishwasher units = $130

  (10) $30,000 same as for selling 1,000 dishwasher units.

Review Questions

1. Why is breakeven analysis more accurate for one segment rather than for the overall company?

2. List five limitations of breakeven analysis in managerial decision making.

3. How does increased automation affect: (*a*) a company's breakeven point and (*b*) the importance of cost accountants fully understanding a company's cost behavior?

4. Discuss the relationship between contribution margin ratios and variable cost ratios.

5. (*a*) Assume the president of a company wishes to earn a 10 percent profit on sales. How can breakeven analysis be used to determine the unit sales to earn this desired profit percentage? (*b*) Discuss other uses management can make of the contribution margin and contribution margin ratio.

6. What is the relationship between a company's product mix and its breakeven point? Does a change in the assumed product mix affect the breakeven point previously determined?

7. What should management do when a low margin of safety is accompanied by (*a*) a high contribution margin and high fixed costs or (*b*) a low contribution margin ratio?

8. The budget formula for the Brown Company is $200,000 plus $0.75 per machine-hour. It takes four hours to manufacture a unit before it can be sold for $7. Based on the overhead budget formula, how many units must be sold for the company to generate $60,000 more than total budgeted overhead costs?

9. Assume the market saturation point for a product is almost met and management does not believe it can increase present sales volume; in fact, they would not be surprised if there is a decrease in volume. With these conditions, the company has the opportunity of replacing some of its equipment and machinery, which is being depreciated on a straight-line basis, with direct labor workers. Assume at present volume there is an equal exchange of total fixed costs for total variable costs. Ignoring other factors, what recommendations would you make?

10. A company sells its product for $45 per unit. Fixed costs amount to $600,000 per year. Variable expenses amount to $1,120,000 if 40,000 units are sold. Management anticipates that variable expenses will increase 15 percent per unit during the coming year, as a result of direct materials price increases and a new labor contract. How many units must the firm sell to make $40,000 in income before taxes?

Exercises

E14–1 Short-Run Bidding Decision

A Japanese computer manufacturing company has contacted Babbage Products with an offer to purchase 50,000 daisy wheels at a price of $4.25 each. Babbage's full cost of producing a daisy wheel is $4.50, of which $3.00 is variable. The regular selling price is $7.00. The computer manufacturer's offer is on an all-or-none basis. Annual sales to regular customers must be reduced by 15,000 daisy wheels to meet the terms of the Japanese order.

Required:

Determine if Babbage should accept the Japanese offer in the short run.

E14–2 Volume to Warrant Expansion

Michael Antonucci, Inc., owns a movie theater that has a seating capacity of 400. The price of one ticket is $3. The theater is open 52 weeks a year, and attendance averages 4,200 a week. Variable costs are $0.75 per person, and fixed annual costs are $131,040. Because consumer demand is far more than 400 seats for some movies, Antonucci is considering expanding the seating capacity to 600 for an additional annual fixed cost of $29,160. Variable costs per person will remain constant.

Required:

How much does average attendance have to increase to warrant the expansion if management wishes to maintain the same profit margin on sales? Show your calculations.

E14–3 Sales Price to Achieve Objectives

Gold Company has fixed expenses of $325,000, variable expenses of $5.60 per unit, and a selling price of $12 per unit. A 15 percent return on invested capital of $500,000 is desired.

Required:

a. Estimate the dollar sales required to obtain the desired return on capital.
b. Assume instead that the selling price per unit is unknown. Estimate the selling price per unit needed to earn a 15 percent return on the company's invested capital. Assume sales of 60,000 units.

Writing

E14–4 Breakeven Theory

Benjamin Company has determined the number of units of Product AA that it must sell to break even. However, Benjamin Company would like to attain a 15 percent profit on sales of Product AA.

Required:

a. Explain how to use breakeven analysis to determine the number of units of Product AA that Benjamin Company would have to sell to attain a 15 percent profit on sales.
b. Discuss how having the unit variable cost increase as a percentage of the sales price would affect the number of units of Product AA that Benjamin would have to sell to break even and explain why.
c. Identify the limitations of breakeven analysis in managerial decision making.

E14–5 High-Low and Breakeven Point

Each unit produced by Delman Company is sold for $8.40. Analysis of the cost records reveals the following costs at various capacity levels:

Months	Volume in Units	Costs
January	6,500	$35,100
February	9,000	40,500
March	8,000	37,080
April	7,000	36,200
May	4,000	30,000
June	6,000	34,800

Required:

Calculate the breakeven point in dollars.

E14–6 Breakeven Units and Units to Earn Target Profit Percentage

Covington Company has conducted cost studies and projected the following annual cost based on 50,000 units of production and sales:

	Total Annual Cost	Percent of Variable Portion of Total Annual Cost
Direct material	$150,000	100
Direct labor	90,000	65
Factory overhead	140,000	40
Marketing and administrative	250,000	40

Required:

a. Determine the number of units that must be sold for the company to break even if the unit sales price is $17.91.
b. Compute the company's unit sales price necessary to yield a return on sales of 15 percent before taxes if sales are 50,000 units.

E14–7 Determining the Breakeven Point and Breakeven Chart

Management of the Culver Company wants to earn a 20 percent return on sales. The sales price is $15 per unit, and the unit variable cost is $8. Fixed expenses amount to $12,000.

Required:

a. How many units must Culver sell to earn the income desired?
b. What is the breakeven point for the company? Express your answer in units.
c. Assuming a maximum capacity of 4,000 units, construct a breakeven chart.

E14–8 Calculating Aftertax Income, Operating Leverage

Armstrong Company produces quality wheels. The statement of income for the year ended December 31, 19X1, is as follows:

Sales (3,500 units)		$140,000
Less variable expenses:		
Direct material	$49,000	
Direct labor	42,000	
Variable overhead	10,500	
Total variable expenses		101,500
Contribution margin		$ 38,500
Fixed expenses		20,000
Income before taxes		$ 18,500

Company management believes that 4,000 units can be sold in 19X2. Assume a tax rate of 48 percent.

Required:

a. What is the forecasted aftertax income for 19X2, assuming the same cost behavior as in 19X1?
b. Compare the degree of operating leverage for 19X1 and 19X2. Explain why it changed.
c. Calculate the breakeven point for 19X2 in units.
d. What will the breakeven volume in dollars be if $16,000 additional fixed expenses are incurred?
e. How many sales dollars are required in 19X2 to maintain the aftertax net income in dollars for 19X2 (determined in Requirement *a*) if fixed marketing expenses of $5,000 are eliminated?

E14–9 Sales to Break Even
LAT Company is considering establishing a branch plant in Peru. Predicting sales of 50,000 units, they provide the following estimated expense:

	Total Annual Expenses	Percent of Total Annual Cost That Is Variable
Material	$ 30,000	70%
Labor	28,000	60
Factory overhead	36,000	55
Marketing and administrative	20,000	42
....	$114,000	

For each unit it sells, a marketing firm in Peru will receive a commission of 20 percent of the sales price. None of the home office expense will be allocated to the plant in Peru.

Required:

a. Compute the sales price per unit that would cover all total annual expenses for the plant in Peru.
b. Compute the breakeven point in sales dollars for the plant in Peru if the unit sales price is $3.

Problems

P14–10 Constructing Breakeven Charts under Varying Conditions

A product line of Adams Company produced the following results during 19X1:

Sales (8,000 units)	$304,000
Total fixed expenses	$154,000
Total variable expenses	$128,000

During 19X2, company management plans to slightly modify the product by increasing the direct labor cost per unit by $0.60. In addition, the sales price will be increased by $2.00 per unit. A part-time inspector will be hired, increasing total fixed expense by $6,000. Maximum capacity for the company is 15,000 units.

Required:

a. What is the breakeven point for the company in dollars and units before giving effect to the changes?

b. What is the margin of safety before giving effect to the changes?

c. What is the breakeven point for the company in dollars and units after giving effect to the changes?

d. Draw a breakeven chart using the original data—not giving effect to the expected changes.

e. On the breakeven graph that you prepared for Requirement *d,* draw in the following:
   (1) The 19X2 sales line, giving effect to the changes.
   (2) The 19X2 fixed expenses line.
   (3) The 19X2 total cost line.

SPATS

P14–11 Sales Mix Expressed in Units and in Dollars

Fixed costs of $299,300 are incurred by Jungle Company in its sales of products, R, S, and T. For 19X1 the unit sales price and variable costs of these products were

	Products		
	R	*S*	*T*
Sales	$20	$50	$10
Variable costs	14	25	6

Required:

a. Assuming the sales mix in dollars is 20 percent R, 30 percent S, and 50 percent T, compute the 19X2 companywide breakeven sales dollars broken down by sales dollars for each of the three products.

b. Instead assume the sales mix in units is 20 percent R, 30 percent S, and 50 percent T.
   1. What is the weighted-average contribution margin ratio? (Round to four decimal places.)
   2. What is the weighted-average unit contribution margin in dollars?
   3. What is the companywide breakeven broken down in dollars and units for each of the three products?

Writing

P14–12 Factors Affecting Profitability and Cost-Volume-Profit Analysis

Recently you agreed to act as a consultant to a company manufacturing high-tech audio equipment. The company produces remote control AM/FM stereo/CD players and receivers with 8 and 16-program memory modules, 5 and 10-band graphic equalizers, and various speaker systems. The company markets the audio equipment both as systems and component parts. Company headquarters are in Detroit, Michigan, with distribution centers scattered across the United States. The company employs 1,000 workers in production.

Required:

To assist in your consulting activities, provide probable answers to the following:
a. List the company's objectives.
b. Suggest ways the company can make a profit.
c. Determine which major external factors affect the audio company's profitability.
d. Determine which major internal factors affect the audio company's profitability.
e. Explain what impact each of the following would have on profitability:
  (1) Increase in labor rate.
  (2) Increase in prices of foreign audio equipment.
  (3) Increase in sales price of company products.
  (4) Increased quality control.
  (5) Increased automation.
  (6) Increased advertising.

P14–13 Choosing the Most Profitable Alternatives
Faber, Inc., produces fishing equipment. For one of its product lines, the 19X2 sales price will be $100 per unit with unit variable costs of $70; fixed costs are budgeted at $36,000. A tax rate of 40 percent is to be considered.

Required:

a. If management desires an aftertax income of $42,000, how many units must be sold?
b. What would breakeven units be for 19X2?
c. Late in 19X2, management finds that sales are not meeting expectations because of a recession. After selling 1,000 units at the established sales price with variable costs as planned, at midyear management realizes it will never meet the desired aftertax income of $42,000 unless action is taken. The following three alternatives are proposed. Indicate the remaining number of units that must be sold to achieve management's desired aftertax income.
  (1) Reduce sales price by $10 based on the Marketing Department's forecast that 3,000 units will be sold during the last six months of 19X2. Total fixed and unit variable costs will remain the same as budgeted.
  (2) Reduce variable cost per unit by $5 with a substitution of a cheaper grade of material. Sales price will be reduced by $2; sales of 2,400 units are expected for the remainder of the year.
  (3) Slash fixed costs by $8,000 and cut sales price by 3 percent. Variable costs per unit will remain the same. Sales of 2,400 units are forecast.

P14–14 Cash Flow Breakeven Point
Horrell Company provides you with the following budgeted income statement for one of its departments:

SPATS

Units sold	1,000	1,200
Sales	$20,000	$24,000
Less:		
Cost of material sold	$ 8,000	$ 9,600
Cost of direct labor sold	6,000	7,200
Repairs	1,000	1,200
Supervisor's salary	2,000	2,000
Rent	1,800	1,800
Depreciation	1,500	1,500
Amortization of patent	500	500
Total	$20,800	$23,800
Income before taxes	$ (800)	$ 200

Required:

a. Determine the breakeven point in number of units that must be sold.

b. Assuming a 48 percent tax rate, determine the cash flow breakeven point in the number of units that must be sold. Management expects other departments within the company to be profitable so that payment of income taxes will be required.

P14–15 Sensitivity Analysis

Flinn Corporation's accountant gathered the following data concerning the fixed and variable cost structure of the company:

Selling price per unit of product $325
Variable cost per unit of product 285
Fixed costs per unit of product (if the firm produces and sells 30,000 units) . . .   60

Required:

Compute the following, assuming each situation is a separate case:

a. Breakeven point in units and dollars.

b. Breakeven point in units if the variable costs per unit are expected to increase to $295.

c. Breakeven point in dollars, if the fixed costs are expected to increase by $80,000.

d. The number of units that must be sold if income before taxes is $132,000, and if the company variable expenses are to increase to $290 per unit.

e. The dollar sales necessary to produce an income before taxes of $150,000 if the selling price is reduced to $300 per unit.

f. The number of units that must be sold if income before taxes is $200,000 and fixed expenses are expected to increase by $60,000.

P14–16 Breakeven Operations Using Levels of Fixed Costs

Analysis of Daywitt Company's cost records reveals the following:

Production Volume in Units	Fixed Costs
0	$200,000
1–2,000	247,500
2,001–4,000	280,000

The unit sales price is $500; at full capacity of 4,000 units, the company's variable costs amount to $900,000.

Required:

a. Compute the company's breakeven point in:
   (1) Sales dollars.
   (2) Sales units.

b. Prove your answer to Requirement *a* using a simplified income statement.

c. Assume that the company is operating at 35 percent capacity when it decides to reduce the sales price to $300 in an attempt to increase sales. At what capacity is breakeven at the reduced sales price?

d. Explain why you would or would not advise such a drastic price cut.

e. Determine at which level of operations it would be more economical to close the factory than to operate it. Use the original sales price of $500.

f. Prove your answer to Requirement *e* using a simplified income statement.

g. Assume the company is presently operating close to the level of operations you determined in Requirement *e*. Indicate the factors management should consider in deciding whether to operate or close operations.

SPATS

P14–17 Sensitivity Analysis in an Automated Production Process

Towery Company presently has a highly automated production process. Management is concerned because annual budgeted fixed costs are $1.4 million for next year. The current sales price is $12 per unit, and unit variable cost is $5.

An outsider has approached the company about buying some machinery that Towery could sell at book value. Management has been considering replacing its machines with direct labor workers since the product could be produced as skillfully in this manner. This proposed change would lower fixed cost by $200,000, with a resulting increase of $2 per unit in variable costs.

Required:

a. Compute the budgeted breakeven point in units and sales dollars under present conditions.
b. Compute the breakeven point in units and sales dollars if the machines are replaced by direct labor workers.
c. Assume that market research indicates 300,000 units could be sold; prepare income statements and margin of safety ratios for each alternative using this sales volume. Indicate which alternative you recommend.
d. Prepare the same analysis as in Requirement c assuming that 420,000 units can be sold.
e. Prepare only income statements for the two alternatives assuming a depressed market in the future when 180,000 units will be sold. Indicate which alternative you recommend.
f. Based on your analyses in Requirements c through e, prepare a general recommendation statement.

Critical Thought

P14–18 Breakeven Analysis: Changing Costs

Operating results for the fiscal year just ended for Daniel Humphrey, Inc., follow:

Sales (3,500 units)		$70,000
Variable costs:		
Production	$31,500	
Marketing and administrative	10,500	
Total variable costs		42,000
Contribution margin		$28,000
Fixed costs:		
Production	$10,600	
Marketing and administrative	7,000	
Total fixed costs		17,600
Income before income taxes		$10,400
Income taxes (40%)		4,160
Net income after income taxes		$ 6,240

The manufacturing capacity of the company's facilities is 5,000 units.

Required:

Consider each of the following items independently of the other items:

a. Compute the breakeven volume in units.
b. Assume a potential foreign customer has offered to buy 1,700 units at $15 per unit. If all of Humphrey's costs and rates were to stay at last year's levels, what net income after taxes will Humphrey make if it takes this order and rejects some business from regular customers to prevent exceeding capacity?
c. Suppose the sales price is reduced by 20 percent and management expects to sell 4,100 units. What is the aftertax net income or loss that Humphrey can expect next year if costs and rates stay at the same levels?

d. Assume Humphrey is considering replacing a highly labor intensive process with an automatic machine; this should result in an annual increase of $16,000 in production fixed costs. However, variable production costs will decrease $4 per unit. Compute the:
   (1) New breakeven volume in units.
   (2) Sales volume in dollars that would be required to earn an aftertax net income of $8,340 next year if the automatic machine is purchased.

e. Suppose Humphrey has an opportunity to market the product in a new area. Using this strategy, an advertising and promotion program costing $8,400 annually must be undertaken for the next two or three years. A $2 per unit sales commission in addition to the current commission will be required for the sales force in the new territory. How many units will have to be sold in the new territory to maintain Humphrey's current aftertax income of $6,240? Show proof of your answer.

f. Assume management estimates that the per unit sales price should decline 15 percent next year. Production materials should increase $1 due to the scarcity of petroleum products, but fixed costs should not change. What sales volume in units will be required to earn an aftertax net income of $7,500 next year? Is this feasible?

P14–19 Using Cost-Volume-Profit Analysis to Select Alternatives (CMA)

Almo Company manufactures and sells adjustable canopies that attach to motor homes and trailers. The market covers both new unit purchasers as well as replacement canopies. Almo developed its 19X1 business plan based on the assumption that canopies would sell at a price of $400 each. The variable costs for each canopy were projected at $200, and the annual fixed costs were budgeted at $100,000. Almo's aftertax profit objective was $240,000; the company's effective tax rate is 40 percent.

While Almo's sales usually rise during the second quarter, the May financial statements reported that sales were not meeting expectations. For the first five months of the year, only 350 units had been sold at the established price, with variable costs as planned, and it was clear that the 19X1 aftertax profit projection would not be reached unless some actions were taken. Almo's president assigned a management committee to analyze the situation and develop several alternative courses of action. The following mutually exclusive alternatives were presented to the president:

- Reduce sales price by $40. The sales organization forecasts that with the significantly reduced sales price, 2,700 units can be sold during the remainder of the year. Total fixed and variable unit costs will stay as budgeted.

- Lower variable costs per unit by $25 through the use of less expensive raw materials and slightly modified manufacturing techniques. The sales price will also be reduced by $30, and sales of 2,200 units for the remainder of the year are forecast.

- Cut fixed costs by $10,000 and lower sales price by 5 percent. Variable costs per unit will be unchanged. Sales of 2,000 units are expected for the remainder of the year.

Required:

a. If no changes are made to the selling price or the cost structure, determine the number of units that Almo Company must sell (1) to break even; (2) to achieve its aftertax profit objective.

b. Determine which one of the alternatives Almo Company should select to achieve its annual aftertax profit objective. Be sure to support your selection with appropriate calculations.

c. The precision and reliability of cost-volume-profit analysis are limited by several underlying assumptions. Identify at least four of these assumptions.

Case

Critical Thought

C14–20 Analysis of Budgeted Revenue and Expense

To decentralize operations, Barnes Hospitals rents some of its facilities to for-profit entities for such specialized areas as psychiatry, pediatrics, and cardiac care. Barnes charges each separate entity for such common patient services as meals, laundry, and administrative services, including billings and collections. All uncollectible accounts are charged directly to each entity. Space and bed rentals are fixed for the year.

The Psychiatry Department's $70 average daily patient charge for 19X3 resulted in total revenue of $1,278,200. The Psychiatry Department had a capacity of 70 beds and operated 24 hours per day. Expenses charged by the hospital to the Psychiatry Department for the year ended June 30, 19X3, were as follows:

	Basis of Allocation	
	Patient Days	*Bed Capacity*
Dietary.	$ 63,255	
Laboratory, other than direct charges to patients.	29,785	
Repairs and maintenance	10,150	$ 8,280
Uncollectible accounts expense.	9,500	
Billings and collections	12,000	
Janitorial		16,420
Laundry	22,690	
Pharmacy	34,200	
General administrative services.		145,760
Rent.		261,470
Other	1,020	65,270
	$182,600	$497,200

The only personnel directly employed by the Psychiatry Department are supervising nurses, nurses, and aides. The hospital has minimum personnel requirements based on total annual patient days. Hospital requirements beginning at the minimum expected level of operation are

Annual Patient Days	*Aides*	*Nurses*	*Supervising Nurses*
10,000–14,000	10	8	5
14,001–17,000	11	10	5
17,001–23,725	11	11	5
23,726–25,550	12	12	5
25,551–27,375	13	12	6
27,376–29,200	14	13	7

These staffing levels represent full-time equivalents. Assume that the Psychiatry Department always employs only the minimum number of required full-time equivalent personnel.

Annual salaries for each class of employee follow: supervising nurses, $25,000; nurses, $21,000; and aides, $12,000. Salary expense for the year ended June 30,19X3, for supervising nurses, nurses, and aides was $125,000, $252,000, and $144,000, respectively.

The Psychiatry Department operated at 100 percent capacity during 111 days for the past year. It is estimated that during 90 of these capacity days, the demand averaged 15 patients more than capacity. The hospital has an additional 20 beds available for rent for the year ending June 30, 19X4.

Required:

a. Determine the minimum number of patient days required for the Psychiatry Department to break even for the year ending June 30, 19X4, if the additional 20 beds are not rented. Patient demand is unknown, but assume that revenue per patient day, cost per patient day, cost per bed, and employee salary rates will remain the same as for the year ended June 30, 19X3. Present calculations in good form.

b. Decide if the Psychiatry Department should rent the additional beds assuming that patient demand, revenue and cost per patient day, and employee salary rates remain the same for 19X4 as in 19X3. Show the annual gain or loss from the additional beds.

Chapter 15

Product Quality and Inventory Management in a JIT Environment

Chapter Objectives

After studying this chapter, you should be able to:

1. Explain the theories underlying the different methods of accounting for scrap material, spoilage, and defective units.
2. Apply selective controls to prevent inventory overages and shortages.
3. Compute economic order quantity and the optimum size of a production run using the EOQ model.
4. Discuss the impact of JIT on backflushing and on quality control.
5. Cost material inventory using FIFO, LIFO, or average costing methods.

Introduction

Traditionally, managers have found economic order quantity (EOQ) useful in establishing optimal inventory lot sizes that minimize the combined costs of production and inventory. Now, the just-in-time (JIT) concept that advocates zero or minimal, rather than optimal, lot sizes offers a major challenge to EOQ. The cost management view is that inventory is a waste. Properly implemented inventory management procedures can drastically reduce the associated costs of holding inventory and accounting for detailed cost tracking through inventory accounts. Using these procedures, manufacturing processes operate on a demand-pull basis. The demand of a subsequent work center activates each work center's activity. The emphasis is to avoid producing any unnecessary items.

Implementing Quality Assurance

Managers are increasingly considering quality as a key feature for reducing long-term manufacturing costs. On-the-spot correction is replacing the traditional produce-and-rework-if-defective routine. However, even with increased emphasis on improved quality, defects may occur and accountants must estimate and record their costs. Cost accountants assume leadership roles in product waste prevention and in the adoption of a zero defect program.

Zero Defect Approach

A **zero defect approach** reduces uncertainty in an organization by fostering closer coordination with its suppliers and customers. This approach evaluates management practices, rearranges plants to focus on products and procedures, and installs automated process controls and computers. In applying a zero defect program, organizations find if they permit suppliers a 2 percent defective rate, there may be 5 percent errors in parts received, but if they set the standard at zero, they come closer to obtaining perfect supplies. Thus, people and companies operate to the tolerance level of authority.

Waste control is an important element of inventory planning. Controlling scrap, spoilage, and defective units affects not only costs but also a company's reputation. Rather than risk selling imperfect goods, a company often decides that increased quality control techniques and additional inspection points affect long-run profitability. A company has several means for controlling excessive production costs. For example, some control is accomplished through more effective supervision of the manufacturing facilities. Also, using scrap and spoiled goods reports showing the dollars lost because of imperfect goods makes management more aware of the importance of avoiding unnecessary spoilage costs.

Scrap materials cannot be reused in the manufacturing process without additional refining. Scrap may or may not have a market value. Many companies pay to have unsalable scrap hauled away. Conversely, other scrap, such as silver and gold recovered from making jewelry, is very valuable. Still other types of scrap have limited dollar value. Even though each unit of scrap has limited dollar value, the total value of scrap for any period may amount to a significant amount of money. To earn profits, companies need to control their scrap so they can sell all that is marketable.

Current Cost Management Practice

Productivity

Founded in 1950, Southwire Company is America's largest wire maker, with an annual revenue of $1.3 billion. Like many large companies, Southwire has a quality process and has developed a corporate vision and philosophy as a basis for the quality process. Southwire sees itself in the future as a world-class organization in which teamwork continuously improves its people, profitability, and product and service quality. Southwire's quality process includes the following values: customer focus, integrity, dignity and respect, powerful people, continuous improvement, and prosperity. Southwire recognizes that to achieve excellence it must have leadership commitment; customer focus; continuous improvement; measurement; corrective action; and employee involvement, recognition, training, and education. Southwire identified three success factors for business excellence—people, product and service quality, and profits. To achieve business excellence, the company's people must be involved. Product and service quality means superior product performance, 100 percent on-time delivery, and low-cost production. To measure its performance in achieving business excellence, Southwire developed key indicators for business excellence. The company looks at turnover, safety, education, and error-cause removal in measuring its people. Customer retention, customer complaints, service level, scrap/recycle, and process improvement are used to measure product and service quality.

Gilda M. Agacer, Donald W. Baker, and Les Miles, "Implementing the Quality Process at Southwire Company," *Management Accounting,* November 1994, pp. 59–62.

Scrap Report

When scrap occurs, individual scrap tickets report the details. Periodically, companies prepare a summary of these scrap tickets in triplicate with the original given to the person responsible for maintaining the materials records, the second copy distributed to the accounting department for recording purposes, and the third copy retained in the department responsible for the scrap. Exhibit 15–1 illustrates a summary scrap report that shows not only the quantity of each item or part scrapped but also the cost and reason for the scrap. In addition, the scrap report can provide space for comparing the actual scrap against the scrap expected on that particular job. Often,

EXHIBIT 15-1

				Summary Scrap Report				
Job: 2509						*Supervisor: Kent Miller*		
Department: Fabricating						*Period: April 19X1*		
Material Part No.	*Description*	*Quantity Scrapped*	*Unit Cost*	*Total Cost*	*Expected Scrap*	*Variances*	*Sales Value*	*Causes of Actual Scrap*
20A	Supports	15	$12.50	$ 187.50	13	$ 25.00	$ 60	Defective material
39B	Copper pipe	5	48.00	240.00	1	192.00	None	Machine malfunction
39C	Plastic	11	87.00	957.00	5	522.00	$212	Defective molds
41E	Oak lumber	4	10.80	43.20	2	21.60	Not known	Operator inefficiency
41K	Tubing	12	6.00	72.00	8	24.00	$ 41	Inexperienced operator
		47		$1,499.70	29	$784.60		

companies include an allowance for scrap in the material issued. For example, the material cost may include a 1 percent factor for cutting waste. Because scrap is sometimes inherent in the production process, the concern is whether actual scrap loss is within the norms established. Exhibit 15–1 shows a fairly large unfavorable variance for Material Part 39C. After determining that the cause of the 39C scrap is defective molds, the company should direct attention to correcting the molds. When managers do not expect the cause of the scrap variance to occur again, they may decide not to spend much time and effort in trying to correct the problem. The company should return the defective material causing the scrap in Part 20A to the vendor for credit. Exhibit 15–1 includes a space for inserting the sales value of scrap if it is known in advance. Often companies do not know the value of scrap until a sale to the customer or scrap dealer.

Accounting for the Various Types of Material Waste

The methods used in accounting for scrap depend on whether or not the sales value is known when the scrapping of material occurs and whether scrap occurs on a regular basis.

Sales Value of Scrap Is Not Known

Time Scrap Occurs.   We make no journal entry, but itemize the quantity of scrap material on the material ledger card.

Time of Sale.   The accountant debits Cash or Accounts Receivable and may credit one of three possible accounts:

1. Credit the job or department in which the scrap occurs:

Cash or Accounts Receivable....................	XXX	
Work in Process Inventory..................		XXX

Accounting theory indicates that this is the most correct approach because it leaves the net cost in the job or department. Yet, it may present some practical problems. If the scrap is not significant for each job, it may not be feasible to associate scrap with a particular job. However, the company may agree to credit customers for any revenues from scrap on their jobs. This occurs more frequently on difficult manufacturing jobs in which significant scrap is expected.

2. Credit the factory overhead control:

Cash or Accounts Receivable....................	XXX	
Factory Overhead Control—Recovery of Scrap ..		XXX

We credit the subsidiary ledger account, Recovery of Scrap, for the sales price of the scrap. This method does not directly subtract the scrap sale from the cost of the job or department. Thus, it does not have as strong a theoretical justification as does the method crediting the sales value to Work in Process Inventory. Crediting Factory Overhead Control is easier but the scrap sales are not traced to individual jobs or departments. All products bear a portion of the scrap recovery under this practical approach. Using this approach requires that we estimate scrap revenue and deduct it from budgeted factory overhead costs when establishing factory overhead application rates. Deducting the value of scrap results in a lower factory overhead application rate.

3. Credit an Other Income account:

Cash or Accounts Receivable..................	XXX	
Income from the Sale of Scrap		XXX

While crediting other income lacks theoretical merit, accountants justify it when more accurate accounting is costly and burdensome, the scrap sales price is uncertain, or the scrap value is relatively small.

Sales Value of Scrap Can Be Reliably Estimated

Time scrap occurs.   If the market value of scrap can be estimated, both the quantity of scrap and the dollar value is recorded when the scrap is sent to the storeroom. An asset account titled Scrap Inventory records the market value with a credit to one of these three accounts:

1. Work in Process Inventory.
2. Factory Overhead Control—Recovery of Scrap.
3. Income from Sale of Scrap.

The same advantages and disadvantages apply as those mentioned earlier when one of these accounts is credited at the time of sale. However, Alternative 3 has some inherent problems because crediting the Income from Sale of Scrap account recognizes income when scrap occurs but before making a sale. However, as long as the income from scrap is not significant, we do not materially misstate the product or process cost by crediting income at the time scrap occurs.

Time of Scrap Sale.   Regardless of which of the accounts we credit, Scrap Inventory is credited at the time of sale as follows:

Cash or Accounts Receivable..................	XXX	
Scrap Inventory.........................		XXX

A company improperly records its assets by assigning no value to scrap inventory if the dollar value of scrap is material. This understatement of assets occurs even though the company does not know the exact sales price of the scrap at the time scrap occurs or expects a time lag before selling the scrap. Thus, the best approach is to estimate and assign the scrap's expected market value to Scrap Inventory.

Accounting for Scrap Illustrated

The following example describes the various methods used to account for scrap. Assume that in processing Job No. 42 managers determine that 10 parts have to be scrapped. We illustrate two different alternatives for scrap accounting.

First, assume that at the time the scrap occurs, managers cannot estimate the sales value of scrap. Later the scrap is sold for $3,000 cash.

Time Scrap Occurs

Ten parts scrapped on Job No. 42 (memo entry only).
(A material ledger card is set up showing quantity.)

Time of Sale

	1. Cash	3,000	
	Work in Process Inventory—Job No. 42		3,000
Or			
	2. Cash	3,000	
	Factory Overhead Control—Recovery of Scrap . .		3,000
Or			
	3. Cash	3,000	
	Income from Sale of Scrap.		3,000

A second possibility is that at the time the scrap occurs, managers reliably estimate they can sell the scrap for $3,000. Later the scrap is, in fact, sold for $3,000. Using the three methods available, the entry is as follows:

Time Scrap Occurs

	1. Scrap Inventory	3,000	
	Work in Process Inventory—Job No. 42		3,000
Or			
	2. Scrap Inventory	3,000	
	Factory Overhead Control—Recovery of Scrap . .	3,000	
Or			
	3. Scrap Inventory	3,000	
	Income from Sale of Scrap.		3,000

Time of Sale

	Cash	3,000	
	Scrap Inventory		3,000

Any difference between the amount recognized in the Scrap Inventory account and the sale price actually received is treated as a debit or credit adjustment. We adjust the Work in Process account, Factory Overhead Control account, or Scrap Income account, consistent with the account credited at the time scrap occurred.

Cause of Material Scrap.   When scrapping of parts with high unit costs occurs, management should account for the scrap and determine the cause so corrective action can occur. For example, in Exhibit 15–1 workers scrapped eleven 39C plastic parts having a total cost of $957. While the company expected some scrap, the actual quantity exceeds the norm. At this point, management should study the reasons for the scrap. Even though it may be possible to eliminate much scrap material, it may not always be economical to do so. Before establishing controls, managers should compare the value of the scrap lost to the cost of controlling this scrap. Cost-benefit analysis enables management to determine which corrective action is economical.

Defective Units

Another form of product waste is **defective units.** As opposed to scrap, defective units require extra work before they can be sold as first-quality products. Two methods are available to account for the added costs incurred to correct defective units:

1. If the defective units result from unusual job requirements, the additional rework costs should be treated as direct costs of that job order. For example, if a customer requests an order on a rush basis, the cost of defective units should be charged to the job when time pressure has caused the defective units.

2. If the defective units occur irregularly and are not the result of specific job requirements, the costs should be treated as departmental overhead costs. The rework costs are charged to Factory Overhead Control and to a subsidiary ledger account called Rework Costs. When determining the factory overhead application rate at the beginning of the year, accountants should include an estimate for rework costs as additional factory overhead costs.

Accounting for Rework Costs.   For example, assume that Job No. 50 accumulates $500 direct material costs, $120 direct labor costs, and $150 factory overhead costs. Then, we determine that four units are defective and require additional total direct material costing $65, direct labor of $40, and two machine-hours. Because we are applying factory overhead at $25 per machine hour, we apply an additional $50 factory overhead for reworking. The entries to record the cost of this job follow:

Original accumulation of costs

Work in Process Inventory—Job No. 50	770	
Direct Materials Inventory		500
Wages Payable		120
Factory Overhead Control—Overhead Applied. . .		150

Rework costs assigned to job
Accountants make the following entry when assigning rework cost to the job:

Work in Process Inventory—Job No. 50	155	
Direct Materials Inventory		65
Wages Payable		40
Factory Overhead Control—Overhead Applied. . .		50

Transferred to finished goods
The following entry transfers the job to the finished goods storeroom:

Finished Goods Inventory	925	
Work in Process Inventory—Job No. 50		925

The costs of all units in the job have increased because of the rework costs. Without the rework costs, the job would have cost $770. If the factory overhead application rate includes an estimate for rework costs, a minor overcharge of factory overhead results when rework costs are charged directly to the job. To remedy this overcharge, we can either use an independent factory overhead application rate or accumulate separate costs for this special job.

Rework Costs Assigned to Overhead.   If the defective units were not the result of the job specifications, the following approach charges rework costs to factory overhead:

Original accumulation of costs

Work in Process Inventory—Job No. 50	770	
Direct Materials Inventory		500
Wages Payable		120
Factory Overhead Control—Overhead Applied. . .		150

Rework costs assigned to factory overhead

Factory Overhead Control—Rework Costs	155	
Direct Materials Inventory		65
Wages Payable		40
Factory Overhead Control—Overhead Applied. . .		50

Transferred to finished goods

Finished Goods Inventory	770	
Work in Process Inventory—Job No. 50		770

Since all rework costs are transferred to Factory Overhead Control—Rework Costs, Job No. 50 does not directly bear any rework costs. However, because actual factory overhead is higher, accountants must apply more overhead costs to each job. Thus, all jobs worked on receive higher applied overhead.

Before reworking defective units, a company must determine that it is economical to perform such work. Sometimes, rather than spend many dollars to correct defective units so they can be sold as first quality, a company may find it more profitable to sell them in their current stage as seconds or spoiled goods. Operating procedures should prescribe when to rework defective units. Defective units should be reworked only after the production manager has authorized the rework or when company operating procedures indicate that it is economical.

Spoiled Goods   Although defective goods can be economically reworked so they can be sold as first-quality finished goods, it is usually not profitable to correct spoiled goods enough for sale as first quality. **Spoiled goods** are products containing such significant imperfections that even with additional expenditures for material, labor, and overhead, they cannot be made into perfect finished products. Effective spoilage control requires a distinction between spoilage due to factors in the overall production process versus spoilage that occurs because of the nature of the job being worked on. Some spoilage results from human error which is practically unavoidable. Workers become fatigued and cannot perform at peak efficiency during the entire workday. As a result, they may make errors in cutting fabric or wood or in mixing ingredients.

Treatment of Spoilage Costs.   Even though the preceding journal entries focus on job order costing, the procedures for process costing illustrated in Chapter 8 follow approximately the same treatment of spoilage costs. Basically we treat spoilage costs in one of two ways:

1. If spoilage is expected to occur regularly, the difference between the sales price of the spoiled goods and their total production costs should be accumulated in Factory Overhead Control.
2. If the spoilage is clearly traceable to a job because of its special requirements, the difference between the sales price of the spoilage and its costs is added to the cost of the good units only in that job.

We reduce the market value of spoiled goods for increased materials handling and storage costs. We may reduce the market value further by subtracting the cost of disrupting the production schedule when defective output is produced. These methods encourage the elimination of waste in the production process because the focus is on its cost.

The following example illustrates both methods of accounting for spoilage using a separate work in process account to accumulate each cost element. Assume a firm manufactures men's suits with the following cost per unit:

Materials $30
Labor 15
Factory overhead . . . . 20 (using the applied rate)

If Job No. 60 contains 100 suits, the entry to record the costs in production is as follows. (Note that the Work in Process subsidiary ledger details the cost components for illustration purposes.)

Work in Process—Job No. 60, Materials	3,000	
Work in Process—Job No. 60, Labor	1,500	
Work in Process—Job No. 60, Factory Overhead	2,000	
Direct Materials Inventory		3,000
Wages Payable		1,500
Factory Overhead Control		2,000

Assume spoilage resulting from many unpredictable factors causes 10 suits not to meet specifications; they will be sold as irregulars for $260. Spoilage cost of the suits is charged to Factory Overhead Control. This removes the entire cost of the spoiled units from the three Work in Process accounts. We transfer the 90 good units into finished goods inventory at a cost of $65 per unit (material, $30; labor, $15; and overhead, $20). The sales value of the spoiled goods enters a special inventory account labeled Spoiled Goods Inventory. Factory Overhead Control with its subsidiary ledger account, Loss on Spoiled Goods, absorbs the difference as illustrated next. Budgeted factory overhead costs should include an estimate for the loss on spoiled goods when factory overhead application rates are established.

Spoilage charge to total production

Spoiled Goods Inventory	260		
Factory Overhead Control—Loss of Spoiled Goods . . .	390		
Work in Process—Job No. 60, Materials		300	
Work in Process—Job No. 60, Labor		150	
Work in Process—Job No. 60, Factory Overhead .		200	
Finished Goods Inventory	5,850		
Work in Process—Job No. 60, Materials		2,700	
Work in Process—Job No. 60, Labor		1,350	
Work in Process—Job No. 60, Factory Overhead .		1,800	

Spoilage Charged to Job.   If the spoiled units result because the job requires a special fabric or difficult pattern details, the 90 good units should bear the cost of all 100 suits, including the 10 spoiled units. The entry to record the original costs under these circumstances is the same as shown earlier:

Work in Process—Job No. 60, Materials	3,000	
Work in Process—Job No. 60, Labor	1,500	
Work in Process—Job No. 60, Factory Overhead	2,000	
Direct Materials Inventory		3,000
Wages Payable		1,500
Factory Overhead Control		2,000

Instead of crediting the three work in process accounts for the full cost of the spoiled units, we remove only a portion of the cost. We determine the portion removed as follows:

$$\frac{\$260 \text{ sales recovery of 10 units}}{\$650 \text{ total cost of 10 units}} = 40 \text{ percent sales recovery}$$

40% × $300 material cost of 10 units	$120
40% × $150 labor cost of 10 units	60
40% × $200 overhead cost of 10 units	80
	$260

Spoiled Goods Inventory	260	
Work in process—Job No. 60, Material		120
Work in Process—Job No. 60, Labor		60
Work in Process—Job No. 60, Factory Overhead .		80

Similar computations can be determined using the following approach, which includes:

$$\frac{\$3,000 \text{ material cost of 100 units}}{\$6,500 \text{ total 100–unit job cost}} \times \$260 \text{ sales value } = \$120$$

$$\frac{\$1,500 \text{ labor cost of 100 units}}{\$6,500 \text{ total 100–unit job cost}} \times \$260 \text{ sales value } = \$60$$

$$\frac{\$2,000 \text{ overhead cost of 100 units}}{\$6,500 \text{ total 100–unit job cost}} \times \$260 \text{ sales value } = \$80$$

The cost of the remaining 90 good units has increased from $65 per unit to $69.33 ($6,500 total job cost − $260 sales recovery value of spoilage = $6,240 ÷ 90 good units = $69.33). We transfer the 90 good units to finished goods at the $69.33 unit cost as follows:

Finished Goods Inventory	6,240	
Work in Process—Job No. 60, Material		
($3,000 − $120)		2,880
Work in Process—Job No. 60, Labor		
($1,500 − $60)		1,440
Work in Process—Job No. 60, Overhead		
($2,000 − $80)		1,920

Defective and Spoilage Report.   A report similar to the one illustrated in Exhibit 15–1 for scrap can summarize defective units and spoilage. Alternatively, one summary report may combine all loss from scrap, defective units, and spoilage. These reports should include (1) the number of defective or spoiled units, (2) the cost involved, and (3) the cause of the spoilage. Often it is difficult to determine who is responsible for the mistake causing the scrap, defective units, or spoilage. The person responsible for the mistake is not likely to admit it; as a result, such losses go unreported. Requiring the supervisor to prepare such reports benefits the company when workers use the information to control scrap, defective units, and spoilage. Only if managers are willing to spend time in studying the causes of material waste can they have a quality program that keeps material costs under control.

Inventory Planning

Inventory planning and control involve much more than minimizing the loss from scrap, spoilage, and defective units. A company must schedule its purchasing; otherwise its inventory will be overstocked during some periods and out of stock during others. The goal of management is that its investment in inventory represent an optimum balance between the two extremes of having inadequate or excessive inventories. Between these two extremes is a desirable inventory level; the objective is to find this level. The controller wants to maintain the optimum inventory investment for the same reasons the financial manager wants to avoid idle cash on which no return is earned. The cost of carrying unnecessary inventory stock reduces the profitability of the firm.

Stockouts, Temporarily Out of Stock, and Back Orders

Stockouts, temporarily out of stock (TOS), and **back orders (B/O)** refer to a company running out of inventory. If raw material is not quickly available after the receipt of sales orders, there is a possibility that the production cycle must stop or slow down. Such delays cause lost sales. The type of product a company sells influences this risk; for example, when a stockout occurs for a convenience item, customers usually switch brands.

The degree of service reliability that a company wishes to offer its customers is a consideration when determining inventory size. The willingness of its customers to tolerate a delayed delivery also influences the size of inventory a company carries. In the past, managers using traditional inventory systems clearly recognized that the higher the degree of service reliability offered, the larger the investment in inventory. Fortunately, JIT, zero defect, flexible manufacturing, and other cost management concepts now make possible large reductions in inventory without sacrificing service reliability. JIT eliminates most safety stock; orders are smaller but more frequent. JIT depends on orders arriving regularly and on time to shorten production lead time.

Carrying a large inventory investment is not advisable for any materials, certainly not those used in the manufacture of products subject to short, intense sales periods, such as novelties or high-fashion products. The company involved in such sales should try to match its purchases with sales and maintain zero or minimum inventory. Often companies fail to meet this goal because their sales forecast is incorrect. Fortunately, carrying stocks of materials used in manufacturing products with longer sales lives and not subject to rapid market changes, technological obsolescence, or physical deterioration is less risky. However, companies should avoid inventory buildups because product life cycles are decreasing due to intense global competition. In addition, carrying costs increase with inventory buildups.

Costs of the Two Extremes.   In selecting an inventory level that minimizes costs in the long run, the company should weigh the costs of carrying too much inventory against the cost of not carrying enough. Many of these costs do not actually appear in accounting records because companies use them for planning purposes only. For example, accountants do not record the loss of customer goodwill or contribution margin on missed sales in formal accounting records. These costs are, of course, important in determining the **optimum inventory level.**

Under conventional manufacturing systems, there is a trade-off between carrying too much inventory and not carrying enough. As more companies adopt newer inventory management techniques, this trade-off may disappear.

The costs of not carrying enough inventory include:

Raw Material Inventory	*Finished Goods Inventory*
1. Additional costs due to interruptions of production.	1. Loss of customer goodwill.
2. Lost quantity discounts.	2. Contribution margin on lost sales.
3. Additional purchasing costs (due to rush).	3. Additional transportation costs.

Carrying both excessive raw material and excessive finished goods inventories causes:

1. Increased cost of storage space.
2. Increased insurance and property taxes.
3. Increased cost of handling and transferring inventory.
4. Increased risk of theft, technological obsolescence, and physical deterioration.
5. Increased clerical costs in maintaining records.
6. Loss of desired return on investments in inventory and storage space.
7. Cover up of costly problems in the production process.

To minimize costs in the long run, the company should decide which inventory items warrant the highest degree of control. Unless a company has unlimited funds to install all the control features the cost accountant wishes, managers must decide which controls are feasible for the type of inventories carried.

Materials Control Methods

Selective Control—
The ABC Plan

Selective control, also called **ABC analysis,** is a commonsense approach to deciding which inventories should receive tighter control. (Do not confuse this abbreviation with Activity-Based Costing discussed in Chapter 5.) This selective approach also is called 80/20 (i.e., 80 percent of the dollar cost of material used is in 20 percent of the inventory items). The method operates on the exception principle, because it is neither feasible nor possible to give the same amount of attention to all inventory stock. Those inventories that are important either because they are critical to production or have a large dollar value deserve frequent reviews and tight control. Managers can use a ranking of inventory, comparing the costs of running out of stock with carrying costs, to determine which inventories to closely control.

The inventory items in Exhibit 15–2 illustrate the **ABC inventory system.** In this system, managers first determine the future usage of each material item for a designated period. Then they estimate the unit price of each material to determine the total consumption cost.

Management chooses arbitrary criteria to reflect both the number and the break between classes. Class divisions depend on the storage facilities, personnel, and other resources available. Exhibit 15–2 shows that only 10 percent of the total units account

Exhibit 15-2 ABC Analysis of Inventory

Material Part Number	*Budgeted Unit Usage*	*Total Cost*
X1.................	3,300	$ 13,200
X2.................	11,900	6,426
X3.................	15,750	4,095
X4.................	3,600	47,340
X5.................	990	26,433
X6.................	9,980	8,982
	45,520	$106,476

After listing the material in descending order by total consumption cost, the items are divided into the following classes based on their total cost. In the three classes established, Class A contains Items X4 and X5; Class B, Items X1 and X6; and Class C, Items X2 and X3.

Class	Units Usage	Percent of Total Units	Total Cost	Percent of Total Cost
A—low safety stock, frequent reviews of order point, JIT, complete records, high number of orders per year .	4,590	10%	$ 73,773	69%
B—moderate safety stock, infrequent reviews of order point, simple records, moderate number of orders per year	13,280	29	22,182	21
C—high safety stock, use EOQ and order point, few records, small number of orders per year	27,650	61	10,521	10
....	45,520	100%	$106,476	100%

for 69 percent of the cost. As demonstrated here, management usually finds a relatively large percentage of its inventory costs tied up in a small percentage of the material items carried in stock.

Because Class A contains so much cost, managers should apply the greatest degree of control here. Class A is a good candidate for JIT purchasing techniques to minimize the funds tied up in inventory. Employees should frequently review the stock in Class A so the company can safely carry small inventory levels. Managers should apply less control to Class B items, and even less control for Class C items. The low-value items in Class C do not require elaborate controls.

Inexpensive Control Systems

For their low-value, noncritical items, some companies use a simple **two-bin system.** They use two bins, piles, or other measures, with the first bin containing enough material to meet manufacturing needs between the receipt of one order and the placement of another. The reserve bin contains enough stock to satisfy production requirements for the time between placing an order and receiving the goods. When the first bin is empty and the reserve bin tapped, personnel immediately prepare a purchase requisition for additional stock. If they fail to place a purchase order when units are first withdrawn from the reserve stock, the company may use all its inventory stock causing a stockout. A two-bin system does not require perpetual inventory records for material items because the expense of maintaining these records may outweigh the cost of the material being controlled. Because the two-bin system is an inexpensive means of material control, it is appropriate only for Class C, low-value material items.

Managers may use various other simple methods for indicating a reorder point. They may place a line or some other mark on the storage bins, indicating the point at which personnel should place a purchase order. This mark represents the minimum level the stock can reach before reordering. Because most companies have limited storage space and limited investments for inventory, they should establish quantity and dollar maximums for each inventory. There is less chance of overstocking if companies maintain only the maximum quantity of each inventory on hand.

Automatic Reorder System

Inventory systems can have an automatic reorder procedure built in that issues a purchase order whenever the balance on hand drops to a designated level. A computer can indicate the quantity to be ordered when it generates the purchase order. A company can use more elaborate inventory techniques depending on the capabilities of its electronic data processing equipment.

Impact of JIT on Inventory Accounting

Just-in-Time Concept

The **just-in-time (JIT)** concept is an inventory concept affecting not only accounting and production but also warehousing and marketing functions. Since the basic principle of just-in-time is receiving production parts as needed, long-term supplier relationships are important. Instead of stockpiling inventory, the just-in-time approach depends on orders arriving regularly and on time. It demands on-time deliveries from suppliers, rather than building in additional safety stocks to compensate for possible delays. Thus, JIT is based on short, rapidly changing production runs operating in a timely and efficient manner, rather than long, inflexible runs. This approach argues for no inventory stock, rather than a regular supply plus safety stock. It operates under the premise of zero defects in parts supplied by other companies as well as products manufactured internally.

Using the JIT approach, managers reduce inventory to a minimum level, keeping on hand only the amount needed in production until the next order arrives. JIT eliminates most safety stock, and orders are smaller but more frequent. Also, fewer goods on hand require less warehouse space and storage equipment with a resulting cost saving. While shipping and receiving cost may increase, the JIT concept eliminates the double handling of products by relocating storage to the work area. JIT shortens production lead time and virtually eliminates unnecessary work in process and finished goods inventories by having continuous delivery of items. Employees closely monitor purchases to ensure that the company receives the quantity ordered. Even though some companies may have difficulty adopting JIT in its entirety, often they can make changes in their operations to use some of its aspects to reduce costs.

Backflush Costing

As companies convert to JIT, they may modify their job order or process cost system by adopting **backflush costing** and avoid tracking input costs throughout the production process. Unlike both job order and process costing systems that record costs in subsidiary work in process accounts, a backflush costing system—also called **backflushing**—maintains no work in process or materials inventory accounts. Instead, a Raw and In Process Inventory general ledger account includes only the raw materials purchased. Accountants journalize direct labor and overhead into a Conversion Costs account and do not take costs out of this account until goods are completed or sold. At that time total costs incurred are allocated to cost of goods sold and to finished goods inventory using standard production costs. Backflushing speeds up the accounting process because no input usage journal entries are made as production occurs and no cost variances are journalized. Thus, backflush costing eliminates many nonvalue-added accounting activities in journalizing and recording.

Under a JIT system, accounting for the cost of products as they move through successive work cells is not necessary because employees monitor production and make corrections quickly. Also, fewer costs require allocation in a JIT system because more costs are directly traceable to their related output. Backflushing is a streamlined cost accounting method appropriate for a company that minimizes inventory balances, uses standard costs, and has minimal variance from standard. Exhibit 15–3 illustrates backflush costing assuming beginning inventory is zero.

Because management will not place all inventory on a JIT system, they will modify their inventory control to provide high-quality service to customers.

Materials Requirements Planning System

A **materials requirements planning (MRP) system** does not assume an even or constant demand throughout a production period. MRP is an actual demand-driven system rather than a system based on an average demand. Employees place purchase orders for materials only when a *master production schedule (MPS)* has materials actually scheduled for use in production. A MRP system examines the finished goods requirements before determining the demand for raw materials, compo-

---

EXHIBIT 15–3   Backflush Costing

Assume unit standard production costs are:

Direct material $12
Conversion costs 58
Total standard cost per unit $70

Purchased $130,000 direct materials in May at standard price under long-term purchase agreement so there is no price variance.

Raw and In Process Inventory	130,000	
Accounts Payable		130,000

Incurred $600,000 of conversion costs during May.

Conversion Costs	600,000	
Accumulated Depreciation, Wages Payable, Cash and various credits		600,000

Applied conversion costs to the 10,000 units completed.

Raw and In Process Inventory	580,000	
Conversion Costs		580,000

Transferred cost of 10,000 units completed.

Finished Goods	700,000	
Raw and In Process Inventory		700,000

Sold 9,900 units for cash at $100 each.

Cost of Goods Sold.	693,000	
Finished Goods		693,000
Cash	990,000	
Sales		990,000

This leaves a minimal inventory of: Raw and In Process $130,000 − $120,000 = $10,000
Finished Goods $700,000 − $693,000 = $7,000
Underapplied conversion costs: $600,000 − $580,000 = $20,000

There are modifications of the entries illustrated in this exhibit depending on the production time and how quickly goods are shipped to customers. Three alternatives are

Alternative one: Extreme use of JIT with record-keeping at a minimum:

Raw and In Process Inventory (recording material overpurchases)	10,000	
Cost of Goods Sold	693,000	
Finished Goods (recording small amount of overproduction)	7,000	
Accounts Payable		130,000
Conversion Costs.		580,000

Entry recording actual conversion costs and sales also would be made.

Alternative two: If goods are shipped immediately to customers, the entries to produce and sell are combined, as follows:

Cost of Goods Sold.	693,000	
Finished Goods (recording small amount of overproduction).	7,000	
Conversion Costs		580,000
Raw and In Process Inventory		120,000

Entries recording actual conversion costs and actual purchases also would be made.

EXHIBIT 15–3   **Backflush Costing** *(continued)*

Alternative three: If the production cycle is short, raw material purchases are not journalized until product completion as follows:

Raw and In Process Inventory		
(recording material overpurchases)	10,000	
Finished Goods	700,000	
Accounts Payable		130,000
Conversion Costs		580,000

Entries recording actual conversion costs, cost of goods sold, and sales also would be made.

nents, and subassemblies at each of the prior production stages. MRP's purpose is to maintain the lowest possible level of inventory while also making certain materials and parts are available.

Economic Order Quantity

Unlike MRP, the **economic order quantity (EOQ)** approach assumes a stable level of demand that is known with certainty. EOQ is the order size that minimizes the sum of the costs of ordering and the costs of carrying inventory in stock over time. The ordering costs include the costs of preparing and processing an order and receiving the materials. Carrying costs include costs that vary with the average number of units held in inventory, such as taxes and insurance on inventory and inventory spoilage costs, as well as the desired return on investment. In determining the desired return, the cost of capital is multiplied by the costs that vary with the number of units purchased, such as the purchase price, freight, and unloading costs. Firms often express carrying costs as a percent of the unit's purchase cost. Because costs such as depreciation and rent on plant facilities and supervisor's salary do not vary with the number of units held in inventory or the units purchased, these costs are usually irrelevant for this short-range decision even though they may be important for long-range decision making. We can calculate economic order quantity by table, graph, or formula. For this example, assume the following facts for a company:

Annual requirements	1,000 units
Ordering costs per purchase order (includes postage, telephone, clerical costs)	$15 per order
Carrying costs per unit for a year (taxes, insurance, and desired return on inventory investment)	$0.75 per unit

Tabular Determination of EOQ.   Exhibit 15–4 includes an approximate value for EOQ using a tabular analysis. Exhibit 15–4 uses varying order sizes to satisfy the annual requirement of 1,000 units. Because a zero inventory level is assumed at the receipt of each purchase order and the inventory level increases to the order size on the order's arrival, we compute the average inventory as one-half the order size.

EXHIBIT 15–4   Tabular Determination of EOQ

Order size (selected arbitrarily)	100	200	400	600	800	1,000
Average inventory (order size/2)	50	100	200	300	400	500
Number of orders:						
$\frac{\text{Annual requirements}}{\text{Order size}}$	10	5	2.5	1.6	1.25	1
Total order cost (no. of order @ $15)	$150	$ 75	$ 38	$ 24	$ 19	$ 15
Total order cost (average inventory @ $0.75)	38	75	150	225	300	375
Total costs of carrying and ordering inventory	$188	$150	$188	$249	$319	$390

Inventory stock decreases with the use of units so just before the receipt of another order, the stock is zero. As the order size increases, the number of orders necessary to meet annual total needs decreases. Conversely, total ordering costs decrease when employees make fewer orders, but the carrying costs increase because a company requires more space to hold the larger orders. Carrying costs and ordering costs move in opposite directions; at some point, an order size minimizes total costs. Because the total annual costs for carrying and ordering are lowest at 200 units, this order size reflects the EOQ, given the indicated order size.

Graphic Determination of EOQ.   Rather than calculating the EOQ using a tabular analysis, a company can prepare graphs. Exhibit 15–5 illustrates the graphic method of determining EOQ. The ordering costs curve shows that total ordering costs decrease as the order size increases. Carrying costs move in the opposite direction;

EXHIBIT 15–5   Graphic Determination of Economic Order Quantity

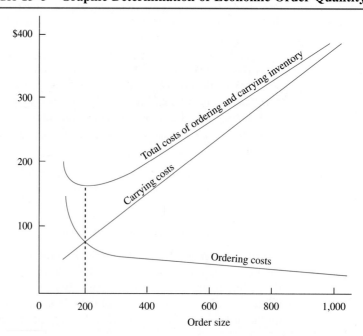

they increase as the order size increases because there is more inventory on hand. The curve representing the total costs of carrying and ordering begins to flatten between 200 and 400 units. After finding this range, we choose an order size in this area at the lowest point. In Exhibit 15–5, the low point is 200 units, which is the EOQ.

EOQ Formula.   A formula method of determining EOQ is even more accurate and timesaving than either the tabular or graphic approaches. We can express the widely used EOQ formula in several ways using a variety of symbols. One simple variation of the formula is as follows:

$$EOQ = \sqrt{\frac{2QO}{C}}$$

where

Q = Annual quantity required in units.
O = Cost of placing an order.
C = Annual cost of carrying a unit in stock.

Using the data presented earlier with Q = 1,000, O = \$15, and C = \$0.75, the EOQ is 200:

$$\sqrt{\frac{2(1,000)(\$15)}{\$0.75}} = 200$$

Not all calculations of EOQ result in such a round lot size as 200 units. Depending on annual requirements, ordering costs, and carrying costs, the answer could have been 218 or some other odd figure.

The EOQ determined by all three methods is the same only because we selected the order sizes in Exhibits 15–4 and 15–5 to correspond to the EOQ using the formula. If we used other data and the formula calculated an EOQ of 415, it would be very unlikely that an order size of 415 was arbitrarily chosen for the tabular analysis or the graphic approach. The tabular or graphic approaches are, after all, not as exact as the EOQ formula. This is why the answer obtained through the tabular or graphic approach is only an approximate value. Accountants usually prefer the formula method because of ease of application. However, even though we use the formula method, the graphical analysis provides a useful visual representation of the relationship between carrying and ordering costs and gives some appreciation of the consequences of ordering some amount greater or less than optimal. In addition, we can use the tabular presentation as a convenient form for communicating such relationships to some party not involved in the analysis.

Regardless of the method used to compute EOQ, we can determine the total cost of buying and carrying the units ordered through the following formula:

$$\frac{EOQ}{2} \text{ (Carrying cost per unit)} + \frac{\text{Annual requirements}}{EOQ} \text{ (Ordering cost per order)}$$

Using an EOQ of 200 units, \$0.75 carrying cost per unit, a 1,000-unit annual requirement, and a \$15 ordering cost per order, the buying and carrying costs become the following:

$$\frac{200}{2} (\$0.75) + \frac{1,000}{200} (\$15) = \$150$$

Ignoring Stockouts and Other Costs

In the past, accountants considered EOQ the most competent mechanism for maintaining an efficient level of materials inventories. With today's automated manufacturing environment, the EOQ model loses its practical usefulness. Use of the simple deterministic EOQ model encourages companies to carry inventory. Managers assume the setup cost of starting a new production run or switching from one model to another increases with each change in the production run. This generates a preference for production runs longer than needed to fill an immediate demand. Also, companies hold inventory as a buffer at work centers to prevent halting the entire assembly line when a breakdown or stoppage occurs at an individual work center. The excess inventory allows the production line to continue operating even when one or more work centers on the assembly line have halted production to rework defective output.

Although the answer determined using EOQ analysis is mathematically correct, a company may still buy a quantity other than the EOQ. Although economic order quantity does represent a trade-off between carrying and ordering costs that move in opposite directions, the EOQ model may not contain all relevant costs.

The prime objective using MRP and JIT is to minimize inventory levels while eliminating stockouts. However, EOQ balances carrying costs and ordering costs, usually ignoring stockout costs. Carrying costs and ordering costs may not cover all the costs associated with controlling and maintaining inventory. Not all manufacturing processes have a smooth or level production curve; for the majority, demand occurs at intermittent times. This means that they may maintain unneeded inventories or that costly stockouts occur. The EOQ formula in use by most companies today ignores this potentially costly problem. Also, having a few days of safety stock on hand to cover shipments that were not received on time usually does not solve this problem. In addition, safety stock sits in inventory, increasing costs even further.

The simplified EOQ models presented do not contain all the relevant costs affecting the order size decision. For example, a company may buy 50 or 100 units at a time rather than the 200 EOQ determined earlier in the illustrations because it cannot pay for the larger order even though it is more economical. In addition, a company may wish to maintain a larger stock of inventory than indicated by EOQ analysis, to provide a higher level of customer service. Also, because the basic EOQ formula ignores inventory's purchase price, the formula does not consider the reduction in material costs of taking quantity discounts. Therefore, we may have to formally consider additional costs in a more complicated model or informally through some judgmental process external to the model.

Effect of Quantity Discounts

The tabular approach to determining EOQ can include the effect of quantity discounts. Exhibit 15–6 employs the same data presented in Exhibits 15–4 and 15–5 except that the cost of forgoing the largest discount available is included for the smaller order sizes. Assuming that no safety stock is included, we calculate average inventory as one-half the order size. The data assumptions are as follows:

Annual quantity required	1,000 units
Costs of ordering per purchase order	$ 15.00
Carrying costs per unit	0.75 per unit
Material cost ($10 per unit at list price)	$10,000

The following discount is offered by the supplier:

Order Size in Units	Quantity Discount (Percent)	Price per Unit
0-99	0	$10.00
100-199	1 %	9.90
200-399	2	9.80
400-599	4	9.60
600-799	5	9.50
800-999	5	9.50
1,000 and over	5.5	9.45

EXHIBIT 15–6   Economic Order Table with Quantity Discount Effect

Order size (arbitrarily selected)	100	200	400	600	800	1,000
Average inventory	50	100	200	300	400	500
Number of orders:	10	5	2.5	1.6	1.25	1
Quantity discount	1%	2%	4%	5%	5%	5.5%
Total ordering costs	$150	$ 75	$ 38	$ 24	$ 19	$ 15
Total carrying costs	38	75	150	225	300	375
Additional expense of forgoing discount	450	350	150	50	50	—
Total	$638	$500	$338	$299	$369	$390

Each of the five smaller orders loses some quantity discount because these order sizes do not take advantage of the largest discount of 5.5 percent. For example, by ordering in lot sizes of 100, the material costs $9.90 rather than the $9.45 for units purchased in 1,000-unit orders. Thus, the forgone discount for 100-unit orders is $450 [1,000 units $\times$ ($9.90 − $9.45)]. The most economical order, as shown in Exhibit 15–6, is 600 units (increased from 200 units in Exhibit 15–4) because of the effect of quantity discounts. Depending on the size of the quantity discount, management may find it cheaper to buy in larger quantities and destroy units not needed. (Note that we determine a round lot size of 600 only because its cost is lower than any of the other five order sizes arbitrarily selected. Also, the company may not purchase 600 units because of an inadequate cash flow.)

Order Size Restrictions

We can use the EOQ formula in combination with the tabular approach when there are restrictions on the order size. Many companies accept only orders in round lot sizes because of packing and assembly-line requirements. The EOQ obtained through the formula may yield a size that is not an acceptable order quantity. In this case, it is necessary to determine the annual ordering and carrying costs through use of a tabular determination.

Assume a company can order only in lot sizes of 1,000 units. However, with costs to place each order of $128, a 360,000-unit annual demand, and $4 unit carrying cost, the EOQ formula yields the following:

$$\text{EOQ} = \sqrt{\frac{2\,(360,000)\,(\$128)}{\$4}} = \sqrt{\frac{\$92,160,000}{\$4}} = \sqrt{23,040,000} = 4,800 \text{ units}$$

Current Cost Management Practice

Total quality management (TQM) is finding acceptance in the government after becoming a proven management technique in the private sector. The Internal Revenue Service (IRS) introduced a quality improvement program in response to the millions of unnecessary taxpayer contacts made annually requiring countless hours of taxpayers' time. Also, even though the IRS collects and accounts for more than $1 trillion in revenue each year, another $100 billion of taxes owed each year are not collected. Three goals of the TQM program at the IRS were enhancing quality and productivity through its business processes, reducing the taxpayer burden, and improving voluntary compliance. While the IRS and its operations are unique, they can be broken down into processes similar to those in other private and public-sector organizations. The IRS also can use benchmarking by measuring and comparing the performance of its processes to the best performers in the private and public sector. This helps establish priorities and targets leading to process improvement.

Al Y. S. Chen and Roby B. Sawyers, "TQM at the IRS," *Journal of Accountancy,* July 1994, pp. 77–80.

Because the 4,800 units represent an unacceptable order quantity, Exhibit 15–7 shows the total annual costs of ordering and carrying the two acceptable quantities on either side of 4,800 (4,000 and 5,000 in this case).

The difference in the annual cost is relatively small ($304). Generally, when the EOQ determined through the formula is close to an acceptable order quantity, the EOQ formula is relatively insensitive to small changes in order quantity. In this example, the 4,800-unit order is close to the 5,000 acceptable order. However, when these differences are larger, cost changes may be significant and the tabular approach is justified.

Constraints from Storage.   Managers need additional analysis if the EOQ determined exceeds the storage available to receive the order. Assume that a company has facilities to store only 3,000 units. If the EOQ model indicates 4,800 units is optimum, the company should compare the cost of additional warehouse space with the cost savings obtained from ordering in a quantity larger than 3,000. In choosing the optimum solution, we must examine the differential costs of the alternative available, such as the extra warehousing cost. Chapters 9 and 17 further discuss differential costs.

Lead Time.   EOQ analysis determines the optimal order size; now the question is when to order. One of the factors affecting this decision is **lead time**—the time it takes

---

EXHIBIT 15–7   **Tabular Determination of Economic Order Quantity**

Order size	4,000	5,000
Average inventory (order size/2)	2,000	2,500
Number of orders:		
$\dfrac{\text{Annual requirements}}{\text{Order size}}$	90	72
Total ordering cost (no. of orders @ $128)	$11,520	$ 9,216
Total carrying cost (average inventory @ $4)	8,000	10,000
Total costs of carrying and ordering inventory	$19,520	$19,216

to receive an order after it is placed. If its supplier is reliable, a company can predict the time needed for delivery, or lead time, with a high degree of certainty. However, for most products, it is not possible to predict lead time because of uncertainties in delivery schedules. In addition, it may be difficult to estimate the amount of material that will be used during the lead time. If material usage is not steady, there is a danger of stockouts or of new customers' orders arriving before receipt of the stock ordered.

Calculating Safety Stock and Reorder Points

Because it is difficult to forecast lead time and inventory usage with a high degree of certainty, companies need an inventory buffer, or **safety stock,** to protect against stockouts. Often management is tempted to be conservative and maintain a large stock. However, this can be costly and may result in excessive inventory carrying cost. If a company maintains inadequate safety stock, interruptions and inconveniences can result and stockouts may become frequent. The ideal safety stock level minimizes the possibility of stockouts and the cost of carrying inventory. The intangible costs of stockouts are difficult to measure because a company cannot easily quantify the loss of a customer's goodwill and possible repeat sales.

Several means are available to estimate safety stock. According to one method, management arbitrarily decides to use a certain number of average days' usage as its safety stock. Another method allows for the fluctuations between maximum daily usage and average daily usage. To illustrate, the following data refer to one material item used by a company:

Maximum daily usage	40 units
Average daily usage	30 units
Minimum daily usage	15 units
Lead time	18 days

The safety stock is computed as follows:

10 units (40 maximum daily usage − 30 average daily usage)
$\times$ 18 days
180 units of safety stock

Another method is to calculate the probability of running out of stock at various levels of safety stock and to determine an annual expected stockout cost. The annual cost of carrying safety stock in inventory is added to this cost. Total annual carrying cost increases with the level of safety stock maintained, but stockout cost decreases as the level of stock increases. The goal is to determine which amount of safety stock results in the lowest annual cost. Assume the following options are available for a product:

Units of Safety Stock	Probability of Running Out of Safety Stock
20	50%
40	30
60	25
Stockout cost	$100 per occurrence
Carrying cost of safety stock	$4 per unit per year
Number of purchase orders	8 per year

Exhibit 15–8 contains an analysis of these costs. The lowest cost results with 40 units of safety stock.

Reorder Point.   After determining safety stock, it is possible to determine a **reorder point,** the inventory level to place an order. The reorder point is

$$
\begin{array}{l}
180 \text{ safety stock} \\
\underline{+540} \text{ (18 days lead time} \times 30 \text{ average daily usage)} \\
720 \text{ reorder point in units}
\end{array}
$$

We compute the reorder point by adding the safety stock to the average usage during the lead time. To build safety stock into the computation, we multiply the maximum daily usage by the lead time as follows:

$$
\begin{array}{l}
40 \text{ maximum daily usage} \\
\underline{\times 18} \text{ days lead time} \\
720 \text{ reorder points in units}
\end{array}
$$

We may need to expand this computation if lead time is long and/or the order quantity is small. Under these circumstances, there may be one or more orders placed but not received that must be included in the computation determining when to reorder. Using the preceding example, the company would reorder when units on hand plus **orders in transit** equal 720.

Reorder Point with Certainty.   We based the previous computation on realistic assumptions because we made an allowance for variations in lead time and in daily usage. Safety stock provides a cushion against stockouts and, in turn, this increases the reorder point. However, if usage is even throughout the year and lead time is always reliable, we can omit safety stock from the reorder point computation. The reorder point then becomes the average usage during the lead time or 540 (18 days' lead time $\times$ 30 average daily usage) for the preceding example.

EXHIBIT 15–8

	Safety stock costs			Stockout costs					
		Unit				*Probability*	*Annual*	*Expected Annual*	*Expected*
Units of Safety Stock	$\times$	*Carrying Cost per Year*	=	*Total Annual Carrying Cost*	*Cost per Stockout*	*of $\times$ Stockout*	*Purchase $\times$ Orders*	*Stockout = Cost*	*Total Cost*
20	$\times$	$ 4	=	$ 80	$100	$\times$ .50	$\times$ 8	= $400	$480
40	$\times$	4	=	160	100	$\times$ .30	$\times$ 8	= 240	400*
60	$\times$	4	=	240	100	$\times$ .25	$\times$ 8	= 200	440

*Lowest costs.

Economic Production Runs

If a company manufactures a product with constant demand that becomes inventory instantaneously, we can use the economic order quantity model to determine **economic production runs.** This model makes the implicit assumption that a company adds units to inventory while production is in process. That is, as a company produces units, it takes them to the storeroom and adds them to inventory stock. We substitute the setup cost for a new production run for the unit ordering cost in the EOQ model. The setup cost includes the labor and other costs involved in rearranging and adjusting machines for a run of a different production item. Setup costs include preparing facilities to perform the job and to dismantle them after the job is finished. The following example solves the problem of deciding when to start and stop production runs and the number of production runs needed per year. We can expand this simplified model to include other factors.

Assume management has determined the following costs are associated with one of its product lines:

$$Q = 60{,}000 \text{ units produced each year to meet demand.}$$
$$S = \$48 \text{ setup cost to change a production run.}$$
$$C = \$4 \text{ carrying cost per unit.}$$

A variation of the EOQ formula determines the following optimal production run:

$$\text{Optimal production run} = \sqrt{\frac{2 \times 60{,}000 \times \$48}{\$4}}$$

$$= \sqrt{\frac{\$5{,}760{,}000}{\$4}} = 1{,}200$$

$$\text{Annual runs} = \frac{60{,}000 \text{ annual demand}}{1{,}200 \text{ optimal run size}} = 50 \text{ runs}$$

The relatively low setup cost requires small production runs; as a result, using production runs of approximately 1,200 units minimizes overall cost. Based on this, the company needs 50 runs per year to meet demand.

Reducing Setup Cost

As illustrated in determining the optimal production run, the relatively high setup cost causes a preference for production runs longer than needed for immediate demand. A company that can reduce its setup costs to a minimum can match production closely with demand, eliminating the holding of inventory. Savings in holding excess inventory often occur when companies undertake investment projects to reduce setup costs or to schedule deliveries and production so there is less overall uncertainty in the production system.

Cost accountants may find that rather than use the EOQ formula to compute an optimal production run size that balances setup and holding costs, a better use of their time is to help find ways to reduce setup costs. Additionally, they may find that reducing the setup on different machines may involve the same expense, but if one machine is a bottleneck and the other is not, the effect of these actions is very different. Certainly if investigation shows setup costs are already at a minimum, the company can consider the market impact of offering less variety in the units they produce.

Summary

Some of the control tools introduced in this chapter, such as safety stock and EOQ, are approximations at best. However, they do allow management to find the range from which to choose the quantity ordered. The simplified EOQ model presented gives accurate answers if usage or demand is stable. Unfortunately, many companies experience erratic patterns. However, managers can gain insight into the relevant range of inventory levels by using the tabular, graphic, or formula methods of determining EOQ. If managers desire a more exact answer that considers variable usage rates and variable lead times as well as costs other than ordering and carrying costs, more complex models are available.

The ABC system of inventory control recognizes there is always a trade-off between the cost of the control tool used and the cost of the material controlled. By analyzing which inventory accounts for most of the company's cost, management can select its control sensibly. Efficient managers use frequent reviews and tight controls for material parts that are of high value or are critical to the manufacturing process.

Important Terms and Concepts

Zero defect approach   468
Scrap materials   468
Defective units   473
Spoiled goods   474
Stockouts, TOS, B/O   477
Optimum inventory level   478
Selective control (ABC analysis)   479
ABC inventory system   479
Two-bin inventory system   480
Just-in-time (JIT) concept   480

Backflush costing or backflushing   481
Materials requirements planning (MRP) system   481
Economic order quantity (EOQ)   483
Lead time   488
Safety stock   489
Reorder point   490
Orders in transit   490
Economic production runs   491

Appendix 15–A Inventory Costing Methods

Costing material differs somewhat from costing labor and overhead because the accountant must choose an inventory costing method. The primary goal is to achieve a proper matching of costs and revenues. The residual inventory values on the statement of financial position also receive some consideration. The following briefly describes several inventory costing methods.

FIFO Inventory Method

The first-in, first-out (FIFO) method assumes that the first costs incurred are the first costs issued, regardless of the physical flow. Accountants cost material issues at the unit cost of the oldest supply on hand. The ending inventory comprises the most recent costs of material or production of goods. Exhibit 15A–1 illustrates a material ledger card using FIFO under a **perpetual inventory system.** A perpetual system records each transaction to make available a book balance of the quantity of material on hand.

A disadvantage of using the FIFO inventory costing method is that a rise in material price matched by a corresponding increase in sales price tends to inflate income. Conversely, a decline in material price and sale price deflates income. This occurs because in periods of increasing costs and sales prices, the costs charged against revenue come from the older, lower-priced inventory on hand, while the newer, higher-priced stock makes up ending inventory. Cost of sales receives the lower cost and the new higher cost remains in inventory. Companies pay income taxes on the artificially inflated profits that result. The advantage of FIFO

EXHIBIT 15A–1

Material Ledger Card—FIFO—Perpetual Inventory

Item: Material A

Item Description

Reorder point 40   Reorder quantity 60

	Receipts				Issued					Balance		
Date	Quantity	Amount	Unit Cost	Date	Req. No.	Job No.	Quantity	Amount		Quantity	Amount	Unit Cost
Jan. 1	Balance									40	$88.00	$2.20
										40	$88.00	$2.20
Jan. 7	60	$150.00	$2.50							60	150.00	2.50
				Jan. 9	112	84	64	$148.00		36	90.00	2.50
										36	90.00	2.50
Jan. 18	60	152.40	2.54							60	152.40	2.54
				Jan. 22	113	86	75	189.06		21	53.34	2.54
										21	53.34	2.54
Jan. 24	60	156.00	2.60							60	156.00	2.60

January 9 issues:	January 22 issues:
40 units @ $2.20 = $ 88.00	36 units @ $2.50 = $ 90.00
24 units @ $2.50 = 60.00	39 units @ $2.54 = 99.06
$148.00	$189.06

EXHIBIT 15A–2

Material Ledger Card—LIFO—Perpetual Inventory

Item: Material A

Item Description

Reorder point 40   Reorder quantity 60

	Receipts				Issued					Balance		
Date	Quantity	Amount	Unit Cost	Date	Req. No.	Job No.	Quantity	Amount		Quantity	Amount	Unit Cost
Jan. 1	Balance									40	$88.00	$2.20
										40	$88.00	$2.20
Jan. 7	60	$150.00	$2.50							60	150.00	2.50
				Jan. 9	112	84	64	$158.80		36	79.20	2.20
										36	79.20	2.20
Jan. 18	60	152.40	2.54							60	152.40	2.54
				Jan. 22	113	86	75	185.40		21	46.20	2.20
										21	46.20	2.20
Jan. 24	60	156.00	2.60							60	156.00	2.60

January 9 issues:	January 22 issues:
60 units @ $2.50 = $150.00	60 units @ $2.54 = $152.40
4 units @ $2.20 = 8.80	15 units @ $2.20 = 33.00
$158.80	$185.40

is that it produces an ending inventory valuation that approximates current replacement costs. However, most companies currently rely on the income statement rather than the balance sheet for performance evaluation.

LIFO Inventory Method

Using the last-in, first-out (LIFO) method of inventory valuation, the price of the latest items purchased or produced is the first cost assigned to units issued or sold. The materials in ending inventory are costed at prices in existence at a much earlier date since they represent the cost of the oldest stock on hand. Exhibit 15A–2 illustrates the use of LIFO with a perpetual inventory method.

The LIFO inventory method has the advantage of matching current inventory costs with current revenues; this provides a more proper matching on the income statement. In a period of increasing prices, a tax savings results because the cost of goods used or sold is priced at the higher material costs of the latest inventory on hand. When prices are rising, the lower-priced, oldest inventory on hand comprises the ending inventory valuation; this does not reflect a current valuation. If a company experiences a decline in material prices, the reverse is true because accountants cost material used at the latest, lower-priced inventory. Ending inventory, on the other hand, is valued at the older, higher-priced inventory in a deflationary period.

Average Costing Methods

Instead of using FIFO or LIFO costing, variations of the average costing inventory method are available. Some of these are most appropriate for perpetual inventory systems, while others are used with a **periodic** inventory system. A periodic system updates the quantity of each material item only when a physical inventory occurs.

These methods assume that the cost of materials on hand at the end of an accounting period is the weighted average of the cost of the inventory on hand at the beginning of the period and the cost of the materials purchased during the period. Companies holding goods for a long time often use average methods that tend to even out the effects of net increases and decreases in costs. Average cost methods balance abnormally low and abnormally high material prices, giving stable cost figures. Although several methods are available, we only discuss the moving-average cost method with a perpetual inventory procedure.

Moving-Average Method. The moving-average method allows the issues to be costed out currently at the average unit cost of the goods on hand as of the withdrawal date. A new unit cost is calculated after each purchase. However, some companies follow the practice of making

EXHIBIT 15A–3

Material Ledger Card—Moving Average												
Item: Material A				Item Description						Reorder point 40	Reorder quantity 60	
Receipts				Issued						Balance		
Date	Quantity	Amount	Unit Cost	Date	Req. No.	Job No.	Quantity	Amount		Quantity	Amount	Unit Cost
Jan. 1	Balance									40	$88.00	$2.200
Jan. 7	60	$150.00	$2.50							100	238.00	2.380
				Jan. 9	112	84	64	$152.32		36	85.68	2.380
Jan. 18	60	152.40	2.54							96	238.08	2.480
				Jan. 22	113	86	75	186.00		21	52.08	2.480
Jan. 24	60	156.00	2.60							81	208.08	2.569

moving-average computations monthly. The established unit costs move upward or downward as new material purchases are made at higher or lower prices. Exhibit 15A–3 illustrates a material ledger card for Material A using the moving-average method. For example, adding the $152.40 cost of the January 18 purchase to the $85.68 balance on hand gives the following $2.480 unit cost:

$$\frac{\$152.40 + \$85.68}{96} = \frac{\$238.08}{96} = \$2.480$$

Problem for Self-Study

EOQ and Number of Orders

Cross Company's average demand for a special motor used in production is 12,000 per month. These motors cost Cross Company $20 each from the supplier and require only a one-day lead time from date of order to date of delivery. The ordering cost is $5 per order, and the carrying cost is 10 percent per annum.

Required:

a. Determine the economic order quantity.
b. Calculate the number of orders needed per year.
c. Calculate the total cost of buying and carrying motors for the year.
d. Assuming no safety stock is maintained and that the present inventory level of these motors is 400, when should the next order be placed?
e. Discuss the limitations in attempting to apply the EOQ formula to inventory problems.

Solution to Problem for Self-Study

CROSS COMPANY

a. The economic order quantity (EOQ) is

$$EOQ = \sqrt{\frac{2 \times 144,000 \times \$5}{10\% \times \$20}} = \sqrt{720,000} = 849 \text{ units per order}$$

b. The number of orders needed per year is

$$\frac{144,000 \text{ annual requirements}}{849 \text{ EOQ}} = 170 \text{ orders per year}$$

c. The total cost of buying and carrying motors for the year is

$$\frac{EOQ}{2} \times \text{carrying cost per unit} + \frac{\text{Annual requirements}}{EOQ} \times \text{ordering cost per order}$$

$$= \frac{849}{2} \times (\$20.00 \times 10\%) + \frac{144,000}{849} \times \$5.00 = \$1,697$$

d. The next order should be placed immediately. This conclusion is arrived at as follows:
   (1) Number of days' supply in each order:

$$\frac{360 \text{ days in year}}{170 \text{ orders per year}} = 2.12 \text{ days}$$

   (2) Number of days' supply left in inventory:

$$\frac{400 \text{ units in inventory}}{849 \text{ EOQ}} \times 2.12 \text{ days' supply in each order} = 1 \text{ day's supply left}$$

Or

$$\frac{144{,}000 \text{ annual requirements}}{360 \text{ days in business year}} = 400 \text{ average daily usage}$$

$$\frac{400 \text{ units in inventory}}{400 \text{ average daily usage.}} = 1 \text{ day's supply left in inventory}$$

(3) Days before next order should be placed: (Days' supply left) = (Delivery lead time)
= 1 day − 1 day = 0

e. Some of the limitations of applying the EOQ formula to inventory problems are
(1) Inventory is not always used at a constant rate, and the constant usage assumption is implicit in the EOQ formula.
(2) The EOQ formula requires estimates of (*a*) annual sales, (*b*) ordering costs, (*c*) purchase price per unit, and (*d*) cost of carrying inventories. These estimates may be extremely difficult to obtain.

Review Questions

1. What are the implications of an approach that does not attempt to minimize inventory ordering or carrying costs, but rather has as its goal to change the costs and parameters of a production process until it is no longer necessary to have any inventory?
2. At what point should cost information be accumulated under JIT manufacturing?
3. In what ways can scrap be recorded on the books? Discuss the theoretical basis and practical limitations of each.
4. (*a*) Discuss the lack of theoretical merit of crediting the sale of scrap to an other income account. When is this method justified? (*b*) To what account should the cost of reworking defective goods be charged if defective units are normal in the manufacturing of a product?
5. Discuss three ways of estimating safety stock.
6. Define and discuss the terms *safety stock, economic order quantity,* and *lead time.*
7. Indicate one way of determining the optimum size of production runs.
8. What are stockouts, TOS, and B/O? What risks does a company run when these conditions occur?
9. Contrast the three EOQ computational methods presented. What are the inherent limitations of each? Why is it important to recognize these weaknesses?
10. How can the effect of quantity discounts be added to the tabular approach of determining EOQ?
11. Discuss the impact of backflushing on the cost of inventory accounting.
12. Why is quality increasingly being considered by management as a key feature for reducing long-term manufacturing costs?

Exercises

Critical Thought

E15–1 Theory Concerning Accounting for Scrap
Susan Smith is confused about why the company she works for sets up scrap inventory as an asset. She believes the present system is strictly a waste of time and accounting effort because the value of scrap is not large. Smith's employer has a continuing agreement with a quilt-making specialty company that purchases all scrap fabrics.

Required:

a. Give as many reasons as you can for the company's policy.
b. Determine the result if the scrap inventory were ignored in this company.

E15–2 Calculating EOQ and Number of Orders

According to its production schedule, Jacksonville Company estimates that 12,000 yards of polyester at a cost of $45 per yard will be needed next year. The estimated carrying cost is 30 percent of purchase price for each yard, and the ordering cost per purchase order is $62.50. Use a 360-day business year.

Required:

a. Determine the most economical number of yards to order.
b. Calculate how many orders must be placed next year.
c. Decide how frequently the orders must be placed.

E15–3 Economical Production Runs

Management of James Machine Shop has been quite concerned as to the optimum production run. It produces special die castings for a customer who yearly orders 20,000 Type I castings and 25,000 Type II castings. Rather than manufacture these castings as the orders are received monthly from the customer, management believes that the customer will continue purchasing so James can manufacture in larger lots. The setup cost for Type I castings is $600 and $450 for Type II castings. Carrying costs are estimated to be 12 percent per year. The production cost per Type I casting is $8 and $10 for Type II casting.

Required:

Compute the most economical production run size for each type of casting. Also indicate the number of production runs per year for each type of casting.

E15–4 Safety Stock and EOQ

Jovan Corporation has developed a new type of industrial detergent. Sales are expected to be 78,000 gallons per year. The manager wishes to keep a safety stock of 2 weeks normal usage based on a 52-week year. Carrying costs are $4 per gallon; it costs $12 to place an order. Assume a five-day work week.

Required:

a. Determine the safety stock quantity the manager wishes to maintain.
b. Calculate the EOQ.
c. Identify the number of orders needed per year based on the EOQ you determined in Requirement *b*.
d. Using the EOQ you determined in Requirement *b*, calculate the annual ordering costs.

E15–5 Summary Scrap Report

On Job No. 3319 in the mixing department, John Brown, the supervisor for the Tracy Company, provides you with the following data concerning scrap for June 19X1:

Material Part No.	Description	Quantity Scrapped	Unit Cost	Expected Scrap
212B	Plastic wheels	28	$2.10	31
390E	Metal tops	16	8.80	10
118J	Electric motors	10	5.10	2
218C	Metal shells	3	1.10	1

The actual quantity of Part No. 212B scrapped has a sales value of $20, while the sales value of part No. 218C is unknown. The other scrap has no value. The cause of the scrap for Part No. 212B is defective molds; for 390E, operator inefficiency; for 118J, defective material; and for 218C, machine malfunction.

Required:

a. Prepare a summary scrap report indicating the variances from expected scrap.
b. Indicate the action you would advise management to take regarding this scrap loss.

E15–6 Determining EOQ and Number of Orders

The Carr Company uses two different types of motors. One motor costs $12 and the other costs $8. The ordering cost is $9 per order for the $12 motor and $7 per order for the $8 motor. The carrying cost per annum is 10 percent of the cost of the motor. Carr uses a total of 300,000 of each type of motor annually.

Required:

a. Determine the economic order quantity for each motor.
b. Identify the number of orders needed per year for each motor.
c. Indicate the annual carrying cost and ordering costs for each motor ignoring safety stock.

E15–7 Economic Production Run

Crain Company believes that it can save costs by determining the optimum production run for its chemical products. Annual demand for one of its products is forecasted to be 60,000 units. The setup cost is $5 per run and annual carrying costs are estimated to be 8 percent of gross material cost. The list price of material per finished unit is $40, subject to a 5 percent purchase discount.

Required:

a. Determine the most economic production run size.
b. Indicate the number of production runs per year.
c. Decide if Crain Company is using a traditional or flexible manufacturing system based on the financial data given.

E15–8 Alternative Approaches for Recording Scrap

Costley Company is processing Job No. 42 that is expected to yield some amount of scrap. On November 22, 19X1, Costley had to scrap 10 items.

Required:

Record entries for each situation:
a. (1) When the items were scrapped, their sales value could not be determined. Record any necessary entries.
    (2) On December 10, 19X1, the scrap was sold for $1,600. Record the sale using three alternative methods.
b. (1) When the items were scrapped, the sales value was estimated at $1,400. Make appropriate entries using three alternative approaches.
    (2) On December 10, 19X1, the scrap was sold for $1,600. Record the sale using three alternative methods.

Problems

Writing

P15–9 Viewing Zero Defect as Naive Management Tool

When Thoren Company adopted a zero defect program last year, workers greeted the program with skepticism. They believed a quality control and zero defects program was another new management fad—such as background music, suggestion boxes, and psychological counseling. Thoren employees remember trying suggestion boxes and abandoning them because workers feared retribution if they suggested something that management viewed negatively. Workers consider the zero defect concept as another naive attempt by management to increase productivity. Their skepticism toward the zero defect program is somewhat justified because they can cite many recent instances in which parts rejected for not meeting inspection standards were returned to the manufacturing department for correction. However, the manufacturing department did nothing to correct the parts and merely sent them back through inspection, only to find they passed quality control this time.

Required:

Evaluate Thoren Company's zero defect program.

P15–10 EOQ and Economic Production Run

Assume the following facts for Lambert Company:

Annual requirements for motors	10,000 units
Ordering cost per purchase order for motors (includes postage, telephone, clerical costs)	$40 per order
Carrying costs per motor for a year (taxes, insurance, and desired return on inventory investment)	$0.80 per unit
Wheels produced each year to meet demand	1,600,000 units
Setup cost to change a production run for wheels	$400
Carrying cost per wheel	$20

Required:

a. Determine the economic order quantity for motors.
b. Indicate the number of orders per year for motors.
c. Calculate the optimal production run for wheels.
d. Indicate the number of production runs per year for wheels.

Writing

P15–11 Control over Waste

Zelcer Company's president was quite concerned on reading the latest quality control report. He found the Finished Tire Department's percent of defects continues to remain high despite additional efforts to control waste. Recently Zelcer purchased new machines to replace the six-year-old ones thinking this would help reduce automobile tire waste. Fred Zelcer was especially concerned because their defective tires have so little recovery value; they have found it cost prohibitive to melt them down for reuse. In fact, employees bought defective tires at very reduced prices. Their children and grandchildren enjoyed using them as tire swings in their playgrounds. The president noted that the company incurred little expense in hauling off these tires so he assumed good use of the tires as playground equipment. However, he decided the hefty waste expense could no longer be ignored and began his own private investigation. On conclusion of this study, for which he had documentation, he walked into the Inspection Department unannounced and began slashing the so-called defective tires with a knife several times. He planned to continue this approach because he believed such drastic action was justified until Zelcer employees got the message.

Required:

Describe the findings President Fred Zelcer obtained that caused him to take these dramatic actions. Were these actions justified?

SPATS

P15–12 Economic Order Table with Quantity Discount Effect

Gaff, Inc., can order lubricating material for its fabricating operation in cartons weighing two pounds each. It projects annual usage to be 3,600 cartons and material list price to be $10 per carton. The cost of placing an order is estimated to be $15, while the annual carrying cost per carton is estimated at $25. Management does not believe it is feasible to order more than one month's usage at a time. The supplier offers the following discount:

Order Size (Cartons)	Quantity Discount (Percent)
0—60	3%
61—120	4
121—150	6
151—200	7
over 200	8

Required:

a. Prepare a tabular analysis for determining the most economical order quantity using selected order sizes of 40, 90, 100, 150, 180, 200, and 300 cartons.

b. Explain which size order you would advise based on your analysis in Requirement *a* as well as other factors.

SPATS

P15–13 ABC Analysis of Inventory Control

Pat's Manufacturing Company produces four different product lines. Each of the products requires varying amounts of the eight materials (M1 to M8) carried in stock.

The following table indicates the budgeted pounds required of each material. Materials M1 and M2 are subject to credit terms of 1/10, n/30; M4 and M5, 2/10, n/30; and M7 and M8, 3/10, n/30. Assume all discounts are taken.

	Material Part Numbers							
	M1	*M2*	*M3*	*M4*	*M5*	*M6*	*M7*	*M8*
Product A	1	—	—	30	6	5	1	2
Product B	2	4	3	2	8	3	—	7
Product C	3	2	2	6	4	—	5	1
Product D	—	6	—	4	3	—	10	—
Invoice price per pound	$11	$9	$5	$12	$5	$8	$4	$3

Management plans to produce the following units of each product line:

Product A	2,500 units
Product B	3,000 units
Product C	1,500 units
Product D	4,000 units

The storekeeper in a secured warehouse can only oversee the annual issuance of approximately 108,000 material parts.

Required:

Using the ABC analysis of inventory, divide the materials into three different classes for control purposes. Which inventory controls would you advise management to use for each of the three inventory classes? Explain your advice.

SPATS

P15–14 Matching Costs to Determine Optimal Activity

The unit costs which Shady Glen, Inc., incurs to produce fine porcelain figurines are as follows: direct material, $1; direct labor $0.50; variable overhead, $0.30; and $0.20 fixed overhead. At a sales price of $4.50, demand is so high that the company is unable to produce all that they could sell.

Figurines are baked in kilns in which bricks made of volcanic ash are used for heat. Flaws begin appearing as heat becomes less evenly distributed, causing color breaks in the figurines. At the beginning of each day, the kilns are fired and bricks can be added throughout the day to maintain the proper temperature at the supervisor's discretion. Past data reveals that of the 5,000 figurines produced each day, the number of rejects is equal to 108 divided by the number of bricks added. Each brick added during the day costs $6, but no figurines are lost during the time the brick is added. Any figurines rejected during inspection are worthless.

Required:

Determine the optimal number of bricks that should be added each day.

P15–15 Economic Purchase Lot Size

Tilley Company is trying to decide the most economical size purchase order for motors. The following estimates have been made for this analysis:

Purchase price: $5 per motor with quantity discounts of 1 percent on orders of 1,000 or more; 3 percent on orders of 10,000 or more.

Purchasing costs:
   Fixed costs: $8,000 per year
   Variable costs: 20 cents per motor plus $40 per order

Storage costs:
   Fixed costs: $15,000 per year
   Variable costs: 60 cents per year per motor in storage

Receiving Costs:
   Variable costs: 18 cents per motor received and issued

Annual requirements: 100,000 motors purchased in assorted sizes

Safety stock: 1,000 motors regardless of order size

The company can earn 10 percent interest on any funds not needed for operating purposes. For imputing interest, management considers only the variable purchasing costs and purchase price as funds invested in inventory. Assume the safety stock of 1,000 motors is already on hand. Ignore the opportunity cost of lost discounts.

Required:

a. Compare the relative advantages of buying in lots of 2,000 motors and 10,000 motors per year using the whole dollars. Show calculations to support your analysis.
b. Give two examples of the types of costs that should be included in the estimate for:
   (1) Fixed storage costs per year per motor in storage.
   (2) Variable purchasing costs per order.

P15–16 Alternative Treatment of Rework Costs with Defective Units

Wallace Company produces various types of lawn and garden tools. With one of its new product lines, lawn vacuum/shredders, it encountered some difficulty. The vacuums are produced in 500-unit lots with total costs per lot as follows:

Materials	$60,000
Labor	40,000
Factory overhead (applied on the basis of machine-hours)	30,000

Machine-hours average four hours per vacuum. When inspection was made at the end of the processing, it was discovered that 60 units were defective and had to be reworked. The total costs for reworking were as follows:

Materials	$7,500
Labor	2,200

The rework operations required two machine-hours per defective vacuum. The company uses a separate ledger account for each cost component of work in process inventory.

Required:

Assuming no entries have been made in connection with the order, record all journal entries to complete the order, to transfer it to the warehouse, and to sell 100 vacuums at $300 cash each when

a. The cost of the rework is to be charged to the production of the period.

b. The cost of the rework is to be charged to the job.

P15–17 Backflush Costing

With the adoption of JIT, Moser Inc. accountants believed they could reduce the time they spent in such nonvalued activities as detailed tracking of costs through production inventory accounts. Because they also were using standard costs, they decided to try backflush costing for a few of their products maintained under the JIT concept. The unit standard production cost for one of those products is

Direct material	$ 20
Conversion costs	80
Total standard cost per unit	$100

Monthly transactions summarized are

1. During the month Moser purchased $405,000 direct materials at the standard price. Since Moser has a long-term contract with its direct material supplier, there is no price variance because the standard price reflects this contract price.
2. Incurred $1,607,000 of conversion costs during May.
3. Applied conversion costs to the 20,100 units completed.
4. Transferred cost of 20,100 units completed.
5. Sold 20,000 units on account at $150 each.

Required:

a. What is the purpose of backflush costing?

b. Compare backflushing with the periodic and perpetual inventory methods.

c. Prepare all journal entries needed for the month assuming Moser places material purchases first in an in process inventory account and applies conversion costs to this account.

d. Indicate the balances in Raw and In Process Inventory and Finished Goods Inventory.

e. What are the over/underapplied conversion costs?

f. Make the entries if Moser uses a JIT system involving minimum record-keeping for back-flushing.

P15–18 Cost of Placing and Storing Order; EOQ and High Low Methods

Cook, Inc., is a manufacturer of electrical appliances; the company has decided to use the economic order quantity method to help determine the optimal quantities of motors to order from the different manufacturers. Annual demand for motors totals 66,000; the purchase price of each motor is $40. Values for the cost of placing an order and the annual cost of storage will be developed using cost data from last year. There were 4,100 purchase orders placed last year; during the highest activity month of April, 600 orders were placed, while only 300 orders were placed during the slack period of November.

The purchasing department places all orders. The accounts payable division of the accounting department processes the purchase orders for payment. Another division of the accounting department, accounts receivable, processes all amounts due from customers. The warehousing department handles both receiving and shipping. The receiving clerks inspect all incoming shipment and store items received. The shipping clerks process all sales orders to customers.

	Costs for April (600 orders)	Costs for November (300 orders)	Annual Costs
Purchasing department:			
Supervisor	$2,000	$ 2,000	$ 24,000
Agents	4,200	2,400	31,200
Supplies and other expenses	600	300	6,800
Accounting department:			
Accounts payable:			
Clerks	2,000	1,200	19,200
Supplies and other expenses	800	500	8,400
Accounts receivable:			
Clerks	2,000	1,000	18,000
Supplies and other expenses	600	400	6,100
Warehousing department:			
Supervisor	1,800	1,800	21,600
Receiving clerks	2,600	1,500	24,000
Other receiving expenses	650	450	7,200
Shipping clerks	2,500	1,580	27,600
Other shipping expenses	700	420	7,200
	$20,450	$13,550	$201,300

Space is leased in a public warehouse on a rental fee per square foot occupied. This charge totaled $55,000 last year. Motors are stored in boxes of approximately the same size; consequently, each motor occupies about the same amount of storage space in the warehouse. Fire and theft insurance and property taxes on the motors stored amounted to $3,000 and $6,104, respectively. The company pays 12 percent annual interest charge on a short-term seasonal bank loan. Long-term capital investment is expected to earn 15 percent after taxes. The effective tax rate is 42 percent. Inventory balances tend to fluctuate during the year, depending on the demand for motors. Selected data on inventory balances are

	Units	Cost
Beginning inventory	5,000	$200,000
Ending inventory	4,800	192,000
April inventory balance	7,000	280,000
November inventory balance	3,200	128,000
Average monthly inventory	5,500	220,000

Required:

a. Using last year's data determine estimated values for:
   (1) The cost of placing an order.
   (2) The annual cost of storing a unit.
b. Calculate the EOQ and the number of orders that will be made using the EOQ formula.
c. Explain why the company should or should not use the cost parameters developed solely from historical data in calculating EOQ.

Cases

C15–19 Implementing a Zero Defect Program

Boer Company's top management recently returned from a seminar emphasizing the importance of quality control and zero defects. Immediately, they began taking steps to implement such a program within their production ranks. However, to their disappointment, progress toward zero defects in the goods produced has been slow. For example, they investigated why Bill Smith, a parts manufacturing supervisor, is behind schedule. According to Smith, production control does not give him adequate parts on time and when he does get parts, they usually are not the correct size or of the specified material. Also, Smith believes that the Inspection Department has no sense of urgency and continually holds up his operations by not being reasonable about items. Smith supports this belief by showing a recent inspection report in which some of his parts were rejected for being a mere 1/16 of an inch off size. Smith's biggest complaint is the feeling that others in the organization ram the production schedule down his throat without fully understanding the constraints under which he has to work. He believes schedules are prepared by those who do not know what the production environment is really like.

When asked to describe the steps he has taken to inform others in the organization of these problems, Smith merely shook his head and replied, "What's the use?"

Required:

Discuss if these are merely excuses commonly given by a manufacturing person behind schedule or if these complaints merit further investigating.

Critical Thought

C15–20 Evaluating Departmental Reports

Michael Flint has reason to reflect on the past 10 years with pride, as his company has grown from a small operation to its present role as an industry leader. Much of the success is due to Flint's management. As majority owner, he became familiar with all facets of operation. The rapport he developed with factory supervisors encouraged a constant interchange of ideas for product improvement.

As the company grew, Flint devoted more and more of his time to planning and policy-making, so factory supervisors became responsible for operations. Flint regretted this situation because he believed it resulted in a breakdown in communications. In addition, factory supervisors are not bringing all problems in operations to Flint's attention. As a result, Flint has asked a cost consultant to prepare a system of monthly reports that would provide him with more information than he can obtain from his limited direct observation. After the cost consultant spent many hours of study and discussion with Flint and his supervisors, she prepared the following sample of a departmental report. The supervisor in charge of each department will receive a copy of this report, as will Flint.

FLINT COMPANY
July 19X2

Supervisor *Harold Douglass*   Department *Mixing*

	July 19X2	June 19X2	Average for Last Six Months	July 19X1
Direct material cost	$20,000	$18,800	$18,000	$15,000
Scrap as a percent of material cost	5%	5.5%	6%	5.8%
Direct labor cost	$24,000	$24,600	$23,000	$22,300
Sales value of production	82,000	80,000	76,000	72,000
Allocated administrative cost	6,000	5,800	5,400	5,000

Direct material cost represents a summary of the actual material used—obtained from material requisitions for each department.

Scrap as a percent of material cost represents the net cost of scrap (direct material cost less sales value of scrap recovered) expressed as a percentage of direct material cost.

Direct labor cost includes regular wages (regular hourly rate multiplied by actual hours worked) and overtime premiums. Individual supervisors are responsible for scheduling operations and top management expects them to keep overtime to a minimum.

Sales value of production represents the sales price of the production processed through the department. Actual sales price has increased an average of 10 percent each year due to the effect of inflation.

Allocated administrative cost represents the department's share of such costs as top management salaries, rent and utilities for the administrative offices, and administrative staff salaries. The basis for allocation is floor space occupied by each department.

Currently, managers compare monthly figures to the previous month's results, the average for the last six months, and results for the same month in the preceding year. In addition, the consultant suggested that Flint compare individual departmental reports with those from other departments.

Required:

a. List any weaknesses in the departmental report suggested by the cost consultant.
b. Give any suggestions for improving the report.

C15–21 Alternative Spoilage Treatment

In talking with a group of managers for Manchos, Inc., regarding the costly spoilage of 100 units on Job No. X20, you discover a variety of suggestions as to the proper accounting treatment for the spoilage.

The president believes that the original cost of the 100 units should be assigned to the Spoilage Inventory account with Work in Process Inventory—Job No. X20 credited. He acknowledges that the company will not recover their original full cost, but plans to record the loss at the time the 100 units are sold because the exact amount of the loss will be known then. That way, he claims, the accountant does not have to confuse the issue with estimates of a future sales price for the spoiled units.

The marketing manager disagrees because she stresses that the company's salespersons will be lucky if they find a buyer for the spoiled units. Even though she plays it safe by emphasizing that the salesperson must exert extra marketing effort in finding a buyer for the spoiled units, she has no real fear that they cannot find a buyer. Instead, she proposes the approach of recording only a memorandum entry at the time spoilage occurred indicating the number of units spoiled. At the time of sale, the cash proceeds are to be credited to an Other Income account.

The production manager, instead, argues that this spoilage is due to the nature of Job No. X20 and its related unique specifications. Thus, the approach he suggests is to record the 100 units at their expected market value in a Spoiled Goods Inventory account. The difference in the cost and the market value is assigned to Factory Overhead Control—Loss on Spoiled Goods using this approach.

The vice president of personnel agrees with the approach suggested by the production manager except that she prefers recording the difference between the market value of the spoilage and the original cost as an operating, nonmanufacturing expense rather than as a part of factory overhead.

Required:

a. Evaluate each of the approaches suggested by the four managers.
b. Indicate which of these four methods, if any, is the appropriate one to use in this case. If you do not agree with any of these methods, describe the method you would prefer.

C15–22 Cost-Plus Contracts

A company is so anxious for Karol, Inc., to make a special order of athletic uniforms that it is willing to let Karol's cost accountant decide the costing procedure to use in submitting a bid. The company agreed to pay Karol $19,750 for the 500 uniforms of special design, or to pay cost plus 15 percent. Even though the cost accountant intends to act ethically and according to good accounting principles, he is looking for the costing procedure most financially favorable to Karol, Inc. If a cost-plus contract is chosen, the cost accountant will be required to provide the supplier with source documents and other records in support of the cost figures.

In evaluating the alternatives, he determined:

Cost per Uniform

Material	$7	
Labor	2	hours @ $10 per hour
Factory overhead	$4	per direct labor-hour

Scrap from cutting out the uniforms will result; its exact sales value is not known at the time scrapping occurs. The production supervisor believes the scrap can be sold for $600, but the production manager doubts that the scrap will be worth anything. Both agree that it depends on the size of the scrap pieces, which cannot be determined at this time. Also, sale of this scrap is partially dependent on Karol's obtaining another order requiring material like that used in the uniforms. If both orders are received, Karol will have enough scrap to attract further scrap sales.

A quick examination of the details of the uniform requested by the potential customer indicates that rework is likely. To sew in the zipper, the sewers must be well trained; otherwise, units will be defective. Several of the workers now employed have completed other jobs requiring such detail, so they can be expected to create little rework. Workers who have less on-the-job training are expected to find the sewing more challenging. The production supervisor expects 25 of the uniforms to require reworking. A new zipper costing $0.20 each, including thread, will be required for each defective uniform. It will require one-half hour of a direct laborer's time to remove the old zipper and correct the uniform.

In addition to the 25 uniforms expected to be defective, the production supervisor expects the zippers in an additional 5 uniforms to be so badly sewn that it will be impossible to rework these and sell them as first-quality uniforms. Some of this error will be due to worker fatigue because careful attention must be paid to sewing in zippers. Management believes that it can remove the supplier's name from these five uniforms and sell them for $15 each. Inspection will occur only at the end of production, at which time spoiled and defective units will be identified.

Required:

a. Indicate which approach you would choose regarding the following if you were Karol's cost accountant:
   (1) Scrap.
   (2) Defective units.
   (3) Spoiled goods.
b. Determine the cost of the order using the approach chosen in Requirement *a*.
c. Indicate the price you would choose: $19,570 or a cost-plus contract.

Appendix Problem

P15–23A Using Various Inventory Costing Methods
Brown Company has 170 units, each costing $6 in its inventory on May 1. The company makes the following purchases:

Date	Units	Unit Cost
May 5	100	$6.80
16	80	7.10
22	65	7.05

Issues of material were recorded on these dates:

Date	Units
May 8	110
12	115
25	80

Required:

Compute the cost of material issued and the ending inventory under the following costing methods:
a. FIFO—perpetual
b. Moving average
c. LIFO—perpetual

CHAPTER

16 Payroll Accounting and Incentive Plans

Chapter Objectives

After studying this chapter, you should be able to:

1. Record labor distribution, employee withholdings, and payroll taxes.
2. Prepare adjusting and reversing labor entries.
3. Accrue vacation, holiday, and bonus pay.
4. Apply varieties of incentive wage plans and evaluate their impact on total product cost.
5. Evaluate the impact of JIT on incentive programs.
6. Calculate the learning rate and account for deferred learning curve costs.

Introduction

In many companies, labor is decreasing as a percentage of total production costs due to automation. Nevertheless, all companies need payroll accounting; this is time-consuming because of the many amounts deducted from employees' wages. These deductions include federal income taxes and Social Security taxes (FICA) and some voluntary withholdings, such as medical insurance premiums and charitable contributions. Each pay period employers withhold payroll deductions and remit them periodically to the appropriate parties. In addition to deductions from employees' wages, accountants must record the employer's payroll taxes. Because of the large volume of routine calculations, payroll accounting often is the first system that companies automate so they can prepare payroll checks and records in a timely, accurate manner.

Previous examples in this book have assumed that all employees' wages and salaries were payable directly to them. This chapter explains how to correctly account for payroll costs and liabilities. We also examine other aspects of employment such as legislation, fringe benefits, incentive compensation plans, and learning curve effect.

Withholdings from Employees' Wages

Voluntary Withholdings

Employees voluntarily agree to have various payments deducted from their pay. The employer remits these deductions to the appropriate party on the employee's behalf. Examples of voluntary withholdings include: (1) union dues, (2) pension funds, (3) medical and life insurance premiums, (4) withholding for the purchase of savings bonds or other savings deposits, and (5) charitable contributions.

For any such amount withheld, the company must establish a separate liability account that is reduced when the deduction is remitted to the appropriate party. For example, if the company has agreed to withhold union dues from employees' wages, accountants establish a liability account called Union Dues Collected at the time they make deductions. At specified intervals, they forward union dues to the union treasurer; then they debit the liability account and credit Cash. Often, companies share the costs of health and life insurance plans with employees. The amounts withheld from employees represent liabilities until payment to the insurer.

Another form of payroll deduction results from the payment of payroll advances. Due to the nature of their jobs and their travel requirements, salespersons and other employees often request payroll advances. Employees also may ask for advances for personal reasons. Prior authorization from the employee's supervisor, from a person in a higher management level, or from the treasurer's department is necessary because control over these advances is very important. After making such advances, accountants debit an asset account called Payroll Advances, Salespersons' Advances or Employee Advances, and credit Cash. At the time accountants make the advance, they record the repayment terms. When accountants deduct the advance from the employee's payroll check, they credit a Payroll Advance account. Before agreeing to handle optional payroll deductions, the company should recognize the additional accounting costs involved and establish a policy regarding the type of deductions made.

Global

Current Cost Management Practice

Responding to increased competition in the Asian power-generation market, General Electric plans to restructure its Industrial and Power Systems division and cut costs. The move will include elimination of 1,200 jobs or 13 percent of the work force at its facility which makes steam turbines and generators. In addition, the restructuring also will include significant streamlining of primary business processes, shifting some production among the unit's manufacturing facilities, and farming out production of some parts to outside suppliers. GE's focus has been on gas turbines where it has been a dominant player but the emerging competition is now forcing the company to pay greater attention to cost in the steam-turbine side of the business.

Amal Kumar Naj, "GE to Revamp Big Division, Cut 1,200 Jobs," *The Wall Street Journal*, August 31, 1994, pp. A2, A14.

Involuntary Withholdings

Various laws require that employers withhold from the pay of their employees certain taxes and remit these amounts periodically to the proper authorities. These tax withholdings are

1. *Income tax.* Federal, state, and city income tax authorities furnish tables indicating the amount to be withheld.
2. *Social Security taxes (FICA).* The FICA tax finances the Old Age Survivors and Disability Insurance (FICA:OASDI) and the FICA Medicare tax. Employers must pay a tax equal to the contributions of their employees. Because changes regularly occur and no single rate is likely to be correct for the years you use this text, we assume a total FICA tax rate of 8 percent.

Forms W–4 and W–2. Before starting work, employees must complete an **Employee's Withholding Exemption Certificate (Form W–4)** on which they indicate the income tax exemptions they claim. The federal income tax deduction from an employee's gross wages depends on the amount of the employee's earnings and the exemptions claimed on form W–4. Employers must furnish each employee with a **Wage and Tax Statement (Form W–2)** on or before January 31 of the year following the one in which wages were earned. If employment ends before December 31, employers must provide a W–2 form within 30 days of the last payday. Form W–2 indicates wages earned and taxes withheld.

Payroll Accounting Entries

Despite the variations found in practice, payroll accounting entries are of two basic types: One, recording salary and wage distribution, together with the liabilities from employee withholdings and net earnings. Two, recording the employer's payroll taxes. Understanding these two basic labor entries allows you to adjust to any payroll system found in practice.

1. Salary and Wage Distribution

The payroll distribution requires entries to record the direct labor costs to Work in Process Inventory, indirect labor costs to Factory Overhead Control, and marketing and administrative wages and salaries to their respective control accounts. In this process, accountants record the amount of employee withholdings from gross pay as liabilities and the net earnings in a liability account titled Payroll Payable, Accrued Salaries, or Salaries Payable. Voluntary and involuntary employee withholdings are not additional costs to the employer; an employer's cost is the employees' gross pay. However, accountants must make accounting entries to record these deductions from gross pay to arrive at net pay

The following general ledger entry records and pays a particular payroll of $3,910 in which direct labor workers earned $2,300; indirect labor workers, $710; marketing personnel, $400; and administrative personnel, $500.

Work in Process Inventory.....................	2,300.00	
Factory Overhead Control	710.00	
Marketing Expense Control	400.00	
Administrative Expense Control.................	500.00	
FICA Taxes Withheld or Payable		
(required liability)		312.80
Federal Income Tax Withheld (required liability) .		899.50
State Income Tax Withheld (required liability)...		203.00
Union Dues Collected (liability).............		125.00
Health Insurance Payable (liability)...........		180.00
Payroll Payable (liability).................		2,189.70
Payroll Payable...........................	2,189.70	
Cash....................................		2,189.70

The preceding entry shows the total effect on the general ledger accounts. However, it may not be possible to record the total effect at one time. At the time the company pays wages, the data may not be available to record the wage and salary distribution. In that case, accountants establish a temporary ledger account called Payroll for deferred recording purposes. The following entries use a deferred payroll distribution. At the end of each pay period, the financial accountant records:

Payroll.................................	3,910.00	
FICA Taxes Payable		312.80
Federal Income Tax Withheld...............		899.50
State Income Tax Withheld.................		203.00
Union Dues Collected		125.00
Health Insurance Payable..................		180.00
Payroll Payable.........................		2,189.70
Payroll Payable...........................	2,189.70	
Cash....................................		2,189.70

At the end of each month or some other period, the cost accountant analyzes the balance in the Payroll Summary account. Assume there were several additional pay periods in the month and the Payroll account has a balance of $6,010. The cost accountant determines that direct labor costs account for $2,810 (including $2,300 incurred in the first pay period); indirect labor of $1,270 (including $710 incurred in the first pay period); marketing salaries of $1,015 (including $400 incurred in the first pay period); and $915 of administrative wages and salaries (including $500 incurred in the first pay period). In this case, the labor distribution entry is

Work in Process Inventory....................	2,810.00	
Factory Overhead Control	1,270.00	
Marketing Expense Control	1,015.00	
Administrative Expense Control...............	915.00	
Payroll.......................................		6,010.00

2. Payroll Taxes

The second type of labor entry involves recording the taxes levied directly on the employer for the benefit of employees. The primary payroll taxes include Social Security (FICA), federal and state unemployment taxes, and state workers' compensation insurance. These are not withholdings from the individual employee's payroll check, but are additional labor costs to the employer.

FICA.   Unless they are in excluded classes of employment, all employers must withhold from employees and contribute an equal amount to the FICA taxes withheld from their employees.

Federal and State Unemployment Taxes.   Under the Federal Unemployment Tax Act, employers of one or more workers in covered employment must pay an unemployment insurance tax. The law specifies the annual earnings base on which to compute this tax. Employees do not contribute to federal unemployment tax. Various states require employers to contribute to a state unemployment compensation plan. Some states also tax employees, but not at the same rate as they tax employers. Employers with few employees collecting unemployment compensation receive certain credits.

State Workers' Compensation Insurance.   Workers' compensation insurance compensates workers or their survivors for losses caused by employment-related accidents or occupational diseases. Only employers pay this tax; the rate they pay varies according to the degree of occupational risk. This tax is determined by state law, with the benefits and premiums differing among states.

Recording Payroll Taxes.   Accountants can use two approaches to record an employer's payroll taxes on factory salaries and wages. One is to treat the taxes as a direct cost; the second is to treat them as an indirect cost. Treating payroll taxes as a direct cost means including them as an additional cost of direct labor and accumulating them in the Work in Process Inventory account. Even though accountants recognize the theoretical soundness of the direct cost approach, many do not believe the extra refinement is worth the effort. The practical approach to payroll taxes is to treat them as an indirect cost, which means including them in Factory Overhead Control.

The timing of the employer's liability for payroll taxes differs. Some companies record the payroll tax as a liability when employees earn the salaries and wages, while other employers wait until paying the salaries and wages because the legal liability is not incurred until then. However, payroll taxes are related to incurring salary and wage costs and not to their payment. Thus, the preferred treatment is to accrue payroll tax liability at the time salary and wage costs are recognized. The practice of waiting to recognize the liability at payroll payment is acceptable if the amounts are not material and if a company follows this practice consistently.

Data from the previous example illustrate the two approaches for recording the employer's payroll taxes. We use only three payroll taxes under the assumption that all wages are subject to these: 8 percent FICA tax, a 2.7 percent state unemployment tax, and 0.8 percent federal unemployment tax.

Employer's payroll tax treated as direct cost

Work in Process Inventory (11.5 percent total tax on $2,300 direct factory labor)	264.50	
Factory Overhead Control (11.5 percent total tax on $710 indirect factory labor)	81.65	
Marketing Expense Control (11.5 percent total tax on $400 marketing labor)	46.00	
Administrative Expense Control (11.5 percent total tax on $500 administrative labor)	57.50	
FICA Taxes Payable (8 percent × $3,910)		312.80
State Unemployment Taxes Payable (2.7 percent × $3,910).		105.57
Federal Unemployment Taxes Payable (0.8 percent × $3,910).		31.28

Employer's payroll tax treated as indirect cost

Factory Overhead Control (11.5 percent total tax on $2,300 direct and $710 indirect factory labor)	346.15	
Marketing Expense Control (tax on marketing labor as above)	46.00	
Administrative Expense Control (tax on administrative labor as above)	57.50	
FICA Taxes Payable		312.80
State Unemployment Taxes Payable		105.57
Federal Unemployment Taxes Payable.		31.28

Note that the entries for the employer's payroll taxes on marketing and administrative salaries and labor are identical regardless of the method used for factory salaries and wages.

The preceding illustration follows the typical practice of combining the employees' and employer's contributions to FICA into one account titled FICA Taxes Payable. However, accountants could use an account titled FICA Taxes Withheld to record the employees' deductions and another liability account titled FICA Taxes Payable to record the employer's tax. This entry records the payment of the $312.80 FICA tax withheld from the employees' gross wages and the $312.80 FICA tax reflecting the employer's contribution:

FICA Taxes Payable ($312.80 employees' withholdings + $312.80 employer's contribution).	625.60	
Cash		625.60

Productivity

Current Cost Management Practice

After Chairman Robert J. Eaton drove a prototype Cirrus sedan, the Chrysler Corp. chairman knew the car needed lots of improvement before it could roll into dealers' showrooms. The chairman quickly launched a major campaign to boost the quality of Chrysler cars. His first move was delaying production of Cirrus and its cousin, the Dodge Stratus, until fixes could be made. Chrysler workers scrambled to make last-minute changes because the lucrative market for family sedans is dominated by some of the world's highest-quality cars, such as the top-ranked Toyota Camry. The company's aim: to beat or at least match Japan's vaunted quality. The Cirrus is aimed at the heart of the family-sedan market which has been dominated by Japanese models even though these models cost $2,000 to $5,000 more. Many young affluent buyers remain extremely skeptical of Detroit's ability to build quality products and are willing to pay extra for Japanese models. Chrysler has hired a consulting firm to help it focus more on quality because they say, "We have talked about quality for 10 years, but this time we are actually doing it."

David Woodruff, "Bug Control at Chrysler," *BusinessWeek*, August 22, 1994, p. 26.

Employers must deposit the federal income tax and FICA withheld together with the employer's FICA tax to either an authorized commercial bank depository or a Federal Reserve Bank by a designated time. In addition, the employer must pay state and federal unemployment taxes. The following summary indicates the journal entry that a company makes when paying these taxes. In all cases, they debit a liability account and credit Cash.

Federal Income Tax Withheld.	XX	
State Income Tax Withheld	XX	
FICA Taxes Payable	XX	
State Unemployment Taxes Payable	XX	
Federal Unemployment Taxes Payable	XX	
Cash.		XX

Adjusting and Reversing Salary and Wage Entries

In addition to the two basic payroll accounting entries previously illustrated, the company may use adjusting and reversing labor entries. Adjusting entries record accrued payroll costs that properly match the period in which the employee earns compensation. If a company does not make adjusting entries to record accrued payroll costs, it misstates both its salary and wage costs and liabilities.

Assume that total earnings are $2,000 per day for direct labor workers, $1,000 for indirect labor, $500 for marketing personnel, and $750 for administrative personnel. Assume further that the company pays all employees working a five-day week every Friday for the previous week. If the company's accounting system is on a calendar year and December 31 is a Tuesday, the following adjusting journal entry should be dated as of December 31. (Note that the entry omits FICA tax and income tax liability on these wages.)

Work in Process Inventory ($2,000 × 2 days)	4,000	
Factory Overhead Control ($1,000 × 2 days)	2,000	
Marketing Expense Control ($500 × 2 days)	1,000	
Administrative Expense Control ($750 × 2 days)	1,500	
Payroll Payable		8,500

Most companies have a timing problem—they cannot pay payroll up to the day of earnings, so they often pay employees late. Some companies stagger payment throughout the week or month; for example, they pay Departments 1 to 20 on Monday, Departments 21 to 40 on Tuesday, and so forth. Under this plan, they make all payments 3 to 10 days after the end of the payroll period.

Reversing Labor Entry.   To reverse the adjusting entry that they made at the end of the preceding period, companies use reversing entries. They date reversing entries the first day of the next period. Reversing entries for salary and wage costs are optional, as companies can achieve the same result whether or not they use reversing entries.

A company can date a reversing entry as of the first working day of the next period, as it closes the balances in the three expense control accounts through a closing entry at year-end. A company can distribute the entire gross wages and payroll tax for the first pay period in the new year to the Work in Process Inventory and the three expense controls. The credits in the expense control accounts resulting from the reversing entry offset the gross wage and payroll tax expenses recorded for the first pay period. The net amount remaining in the expense control accounts represents the total wage costs incurred in the new accounting period. A company could date the following reversing entries on the first working day of the next accounting period.

Payroll Payable	8,500	
Work in Process Inventory		4,000
Factory Overhead Control		2,000
Marketing Expense Control		1,000
Administrative Expense Control		1,500

Government Legislation Affecting Employment

Government regulations cover various aspects of employment such as minimum and overtime wages, discrimination, and job hazards. Complying with these regulations normally falls within the scope of a Personnel Department, and this administration is a definite cost to the firm. For example, the Fair Labor Standards Act of 1938, called the Wages and Hours Law, established a minimum wage per hour with time-and-a-half pay for those working more than 40 hours in one week. However, certain types of workers and organizations are exempt from the act's provisions.

In 1964, Congress passed an amendment to the Civil Rights Act. Title VII specifically prohibits discrimination for reasons of race, creed, color, national origin, age, physical disability, political affiliation, and sex. Title VII established the Equal Employment Opportunity Commission (EEOC) to administer the law and to receive, investigate, and reconcile employment discrimination charges under Title VII. The commission's responsibility is to ensure that all Americans are considered for hiring and promotion on the basis of their ability and qualifications, without regard to race, color, religion, sex, or national origin.

Another government regulation that affects employment is the Occupational Safety and Health Act (OSHA). While protecting the worker and the environment, the act has had a costly impact on many companies. OSHA has required them to invest millions of dollars to change production methods to conform to OSHA regulations.

Indirect or Fringe Benefits

In addition to wages and salaries, employees receive other types of employment compensation that may not directly or immediately benefit them. Many of these require a year-end labor cost entry. Briefly, some of the major items include:

Holidays.   Each year, most firms pay employees for certain days that they do not work.

Vacations.   Most firms have a policy of granting vacations with pay to their employees; the length of vacation usually relates to tenure with the company. For example, a company may grant annual two-week vacations for employees with five years or less of service and annual three-week vacations for those with more than five years of service.

Bonus Pay.   Firms may reward employees—especially those in managerial positions—with bonuses based on the amount by which a company, division, or plant exceeds a specified income target. The agreement between employer and employee determines the amount; companies often calculate bonuses at year-end. For example, a company may give the manager of Plant A a bonus of 1 percent of all net income (after bonuses and taxes) that exceeds $2 million for the year. In all instances, companies must spell out the specifics so the bonus plan is an incentive to increase income. Otherwise, misunderstandings and hard feelings result. Because bonus payments based on income are not known until after the period ends, accountants estimate and accrue them throughout the accounting period.

Insurance.   Many firms pay all or part of their employees' premiums for medical, dental, or life insurance. This allows employees to obtain the insurance at cheaper group rates.

Pensions.   Pensions are an employee benefit that most firms provide; however, employees may not receive them until many years after earning them. The basic concept behind a pension is that employees earn this benefit each year they work, and they defer the receipt of cash payments until leaving the firm. It is not possible to generalize about pension plans; the agreement between the employees and management determines the actual specifics.

Stock and Thrift Plans.   Some companies have **thrift plans** that usually allow employees to borrow on a thrift fund or to purchase company stock. Another common compensation plan, primarily for salaried persons, is stock options; basically such plans grant employees options (rights) to purchase a certain number of shares of company stock at a specified price within a certain period. The employees' compensation is the difference between the option price and the price of the stock on the date they exercise the option.

Holidays, Vacations, and Bonus Pay

Even though companies calculate bonuses at specified points, and employees take holidays and vacations at irregular times throughout the year, employees earn these benefits throughout the year. They represent expenses of the entire year, rather than the period in which employees receive the benefits.

Therefore, Work in Process Inventory should accumulate vacation, holiday, and bonus payments earned by direct labor workers as additional labor cost. Companies rarely use this approach in practice, however, because it is difficult to apply. The more common procedure is to classify vacation and bonus payments to direct labor workers as indirect costs chargeable to the Factory Overhead Control account with the payments made to indirect labor workers. Companies should charge vacation, holiday, and bonus payments to the marketing and administrative staff for their respective control accounts.

Most companies do not attempt to classify vacations, holiday pay, and bonus pay as a direct labor cost; instead they use the simpler approach of accumulating these costs in the Factory Overhead Control. However, the problem still exists of charging the costs of these employee benefits to the accounting period in which the benefits are earned. Basically, companies should spread the cost of these employee benefits over the entire year by including an estimate for vacation, holiday, and bonus pay in the predetermined factory overhead rate. There are several ways to develop an estimate of the cost of holidays, vacations, and bonuses to charge to each accounting period. Accountants may estimate the total amount for each employee or for a homogeneous group of employees.

Accruing Vacations, Holiday Pay, and Bonus Pay. To illustrate the accrual of these benefits, assume that an employee earns $80 per day. The union contract, company policy, or employment agreement specifies the employee is to receive 10 working days of vacation and 5 working days of holidays. In addition, at fiscal year-end, the employee is to receive a bonus of 0.1 percent of company income. The company expects total net income to be $1 million. The accountant estimates benefit payments as follows:

Vacations (10 days × $80 per day)	$800	
Holidays (5 days × $80 per day)	400	$1,200
Bonus (0.1% of $1,000,000 expected net income)		1,000

The company spreads the cost of these employee benefits over the productive labor time of each employee. Assume the company pays employees weekly and spreads these employee benefit costs over 49 weeks [52 weeks − (2 weeks of vacation + 1 week of holidays)] as follows:

$$\frac{\$1,200}{49 \text{ weeks}} = \$24.49 \text{ per week for vacations and holiday pay}$$

$$\frac{\$1,000}{49 \text{ weeks}} = \$20.41 \text{ per week for bonus pay}$$

The following entries use a Payroll summary account rather than illustrate the withholding of taxes for five days of productive labor for an employee:

Work in Process (5 days × $80 per day)	400.00	
Factory Overhead Control ($24.49 + $20.41).	44.90	
Payroll.		400.00
Accrued Vacation and Holiday Pay		24.49
Accrued Bonus Pay		20.41

Payment for Holidays and Vacations.   The company records withholdings from the employees' gross pay when paying them for holidays and vacations. The following journal entry records vacation pay received by the employee in the previous example:

Accrued Vacation and Holiday Pay.	800.00	
Federal Income Tax Withheld.		160.00
State Income Tax Withheld.		48.00
FICA Taxes Payable (8% × $800)		64.00
Payroll Payable.		528.00
Payroll Payable.	528.00	
Cash.		528.00

A company makes an entry similar to the preceding one for bonus payments. Rather than calculate the cost of these employee benefits each pay period, a company may use a percentage of cost or time. For example, assume that the previous employee works 1,960 productive hours during the year. Because the company expects vacation and holidays to total 15 days or 120 hours (15 days × 8 hours assuming an 8-hour workday), it accrues a liability equal to 6.122 percent of wages every pay period.

$$\frac{120 \text{ nonproductive hours}}{1,960 \text{ productive hour}} = 6.122 \text{ percent}$$

Administrative and other personnel, who receive fixed salaries, regardless of the hours worked, receive holidays, vacations, and bonuses. A company can treat the cost of these employee benefits in the manner illustrated for direct labor workers to achieve proper matching of costs and benefits. However, some companies consider vacation pay and holiday pay as a cost of the period in which employees receive the benefit. Usually, a company does not temporarily employ other persons to assume the duties of administrators. While they are taking holidays or vacations, their workloads accumulate.

Overtime Premium Pay

Another added employee benefit is **overtime premium pay**. The Fair Labor Standards Act established a minimum wage for most nonfarm workers engaged in interstate commerce, prohibited child labor, and required time-and-a-half pay for those working more than 40 hours per week. For example, assume a company pays an individual $12 per hour. If the individual works 44 hours in a week, the payroll clerk computes the weekly earnings as follows:

Regular earnings (40 hours × $12)		$480
Overtime pay:		
At regular rate (4 hours × $12)	$48	
Overtime premium (4 hours × $6)	24	72
Total weekly gross earnings		$552

Accountants debit total hours at the regular pay for direct labor workers to Work in Process, as the following entry shows:

Work in Process Inventory (44 hours × $12)	528.00	
FICA Taxes Payable		42.24
Federal Income Taxes Withheld		105.35
Payroll Payable		380.41

In addition to federally mandated time-and-a-half pay, a union contract may specify additional premium pay. Examples include double pay for Sunday work and time-and-a-half pay for working more than eight hours per day. Companies should segregate such overtime earnings into the base pay component and the premium pay component for planning, control, and reporting purposes. A Work in Process Inventory account should accumulate the overtime premium pay as a cost of the job or department if the demands of the job or process cause the overtime hours. For example, assume a company accepts an order on Monday with a promised delivery date of Wednesday and requires its workers to work overtime to complete the order. Accountants should charge the premium pay to this job in addition to the regular direct labor charge for total hours computed at the regular rate. When employees work overtime because the workload is heavier than normal and the company cannot attribute the overtime to a specific job, the Work in Process Inventory account should accumulate only the total hours at the regular rate as a direct labor cost. Accountants should charge the overtime premium pay to the Factory Overhead Control account. In determining the overhead application rate, management should include an estimate for overtime premium pay when they expect overtime.

Shift Premium

Shift premium pay, similar to overtime pay, affects labor costs. Either a union contract agreement or company policy may require that evening- or night-shift employees receive a higher wage rate to compensate for the less desirable schedule. It is not logical to charge larger direct labor costs for a finished unit simply because it is manufactured on an evening or night shift. The preferred treatment is to accumulate the shift premium amount in the Factory Overhead Control account rather than to charge the entire wage (the regular pay and the shift premium) to Work in Process Inventory. In determining the factory overhead application rate, total indirect expenses should include an estimate of the shift premium. For example, assume that an employee on the night shift receives $12.40 per hour rather than the regular day-shift rate of $12 per hour. This entry distributes the weekly wage for this night-shift employee:

Work in Process Inventory (40 hours × $12)	480	
Factory Overhead Control—Shift Premium		
(40 hours × $0.40)	16	
Payroll		496

This approach facilitates the comparison of payroll costs for different work shifts.

Incentive Compensation Plans

In addition to meeting payroll deadlines and government requirements, management is concerned about maximizing the productivity of labor. One of the tools they use to achieve this goal is some form of **incentive compensation plan**. This provides additional compensation to employees whose performance exceeds a predetermined goal or standard. Companies adopt incentive plans for these reasons:

1. To give employees an opportunity to earn additional pay by performing at a more efficient level.
2. To reduce the cost per unit of finished products. Even though wages may increase with an incentive compensation plan, management does not expect factory overhead to increase significantly. They expect conversion cost per unit to decrease after spreading the increased direct labor cost and lower per unit factory overhead cost over additional finished units. For example, Exhibit 16–1 assumes workers produced 600 units before and 750 units after introduction of an incentive plan. Although direct labor cost increased from $180 to $240, we assume factory overhead did not change. The labor cost per unit has increased from $0.30 to $0.32, but the decrease in overhead costs per unit has been large enough to produce a lower total conversion cost per unit. The example in Exhibit 16–1 indicates that productivity, measured by units produced, has increased; however, incentive systems cannot guarantee higher production and greater efficiency.

Individual Incentive Plans

Several incentive plans are available, including the straight piecework plan, the 100 Percent Bonus Plan, and versions of Taylor Differential Piece Rate, Gantt Task, and the Emerson Efficiency System. As an example, a straight piecework plan computes the production standard in minutes per piece and then transforms it into money per piece. Assuming time studies showed that one unit required two minutes of time, the standard becomes 30 units per hour. If the worker's base rate is $9 per hour, the piece rate is $0.30. If the worker completes 260 units in an eight-hour day, the pay is $78 (260 units × $0.30). Workers often are guaranteed a base pay rate even if they do not meet the standard.

Some incentive plans express standards in units per hour rather than in money. For example, the following computations illustrate an incentive plan in which employees receive a guaranteed rate of $12 per hour and a premium of 70 percent of the

---

EXHIBIT 16–1   Effect on Unit Conversion Cost after Wage Incentive Plan Is Introduced

	Cost per Time Period			Cost per Unit		
	Units Produced	*Direct Labor*	*Overhead*	*Direct Labor*	*Overhead*	*Total Conversion*
Before initiating incentive plan	600	$180	$120	$0.30	$0.20	$0.50
After initiating incentive plan	750	240	120	0.32	0.16	0.48

time saved on production exceeding the standard of 50 units per hour. Assume an employee has produced 450 units on Monday and 525 units on Tuesday during the eight hours worked each day. The daily earnings would be:

Monday: $\dfrac{50 \text{ units}}{50}$ = 1 hr. saved $\times$ \$12 $\times$ 70% =   \$ 8.40 premium

                                                                96.00 (8 hours $\times$ \$12)

                                                                $\overline{\$104.40}$

Tuesday: $\dfrac{125 \text{ units}}{50}$ = 2.5 hours saved $\times$ \$12 = \$30 $\times$ 70% =   \$ 21.00 premium

                                                                96.00

                                                                $\overline{\$117.00}$

An incentive plan's effect on reducing the unit cost of finished products while providing the employees an opportunity to earn additional wages is important in evaluating a plan. As with all wage payment plans, managers should explain the mechanics of the system to production employees so they can compute their incentive payments. Unfortunately, in practice some incentive plans are so complex that this is not always possible.

Group Incentive Plans

Determining the individual production of each employee is impossible in some production processes because operations require the joint effort of a group of employees. When a process requires teamwork, one individual cannot increase output without increasing the productivity of the entire crew. Because individual incentive plans are impossible to implement under these conditions, companies use group incentive plans.

Exhibit 16–2 illustrates bonus computations under a group incentive plan. Each worker receives a guaranteed minimum hourly wage; in addition, each receives a bonus equal to 1 percent of the worker's hourly guaranteed minimum for each unit produced over standard. Standard production is 50 units per hour or 400 units per eight-hour day. Actual production for the group is 450 units.

Group incentive plans reduce the amount of clerical effort required to compute a bonus. Another advantage is employees have a stronger incentive to work together as a team and may be more cooperative because each employee's bonus depends on the group's output. Also, the group may apply pressure on slower workers because the bonus calculated depends on the group's efforts.

Group incentive plans have a danger of encouraging too much competition between individual departments and thereby threatening goal congruence. **Suboptimization** occurs when managers ignore what is best for the overall company while improving the profit performance of their own departments. Suboptimization occurs when individual managers disregard major company goals and inter-

---

EXHIBIT 16–2   Daily Earnings Summary—Eight-Hour Day*

	Guaranteed Hourly Minimum Wage	Regular Wage	Bonus	Total
Employee A	\$16.00	\$128	\$8 (50 $\times$ \$0.16)	\$136
Employee B	12.00	96	6 (50 $\times$ \$0.12)	102
Employee C	14.00	102	7 (50 $\times$ \$0.14)	109

*Standard production, 400 units; actual production, 450 units.

relationships and focus their attention solely on their own divisions' activities. Often, incentive plans force employees to look only at short-run benefits for themselves rather than at long-run benefits for both themselves and the company. In addition, incentive plans can lead to much quarreling within the team because individual members may believe they are doing more than a fair share of the group's tasks.

Impact of JIT on Incentive Plans

Just–in–time (JIT) production policies often make traditional incentive plans invalid. The objective of JIT is to keep inventory at a minimum and eliminate much of the warehousing and storage costs. Lot sizes are small, and the plant workload is uniform. Keeping employees working to produce inventory not yet needed is contradictory to the JIT philosophy. Whenever a company slows down or stops its machines or production line, workers can use their off time performing a variety of tasks. They will probably take more pride in their work and be more content performing these tasks:

1. Housekeeping to manage stock on hand, putting things in order, arranging the work site, discussing how to maintain work flow at the bottlenecks, and preparing notices and manuals.
2. Maintenance of machines, routine equipment, and tools.
3. Machine setups so workers can prepare for the next use of the same machine or another machine.
4. Educational or training activities help workers acquire skills for using other machines or different applications of the same machine.
5. Employee self-improvement seminars can help employees with any problems associated with drugs, alcohol, and so on.
6. Creativity experimentation programs encourage employees to develop better production techniques or different products.
7. Socialization gives workers an opportunity to meet employees who work with the product after they complete their tasks; this interchange may lead to suggestions for improvements.
8. Versatility programs train employees on other machines, to reduce the chance that absenteeism would antagonize an existing bottleneck.
9. Customer relations programs encourage employees to call customers and ask if they had any problems with products.
10. Team management allows workers to make internal work assignments, make production trade-off decisions, diagnose and solve production problems, and select personnel replacements for their team.

Avoid Creating Busy Work

Not only should managers avoid creating work to keep employees busy but they should also monitor a policy of allowing workers free time once they finish their workloads. This policy encourages workers to work as fast as possible to enjoy extra time if they do not have to keep working. In this case, there is a greater possibility of increased defects because of careless work. An effective quality control program should prevent this from occurring.

Current Cost Management Practice

Strategic Planning

The merger of Lockheed Corp. and Martin Marietta Corp. is causing shell-shocked managers and workers at every level to fret over job cuts and wonder about their fate. Such a combination accelerates the downsizing of the defense industry. This combination of the second-largest and third-largest arms makers makes many people think of the benefits of consolidation sooner rather than later. Despite years of industry and government emphasis on converting defense technologies to commercial use, this merger highlights the relatively limited success of those strategies so far. Lockheed has been on the leading edge of those touting the value of aggressive diversification moves. This combination sends the message to solidify core markets in the defense business while recognizing that defense conversion is a difficult and long-term proposition. While top management at both companies stress they hope to create jobs by expanding nondefense business, the sheer size of the new entity means the impact of such efforts will take longer to be felt.

Jeff Cole and Andy Pasztor, "Lockheed-Marietta Merger Sends Industry Scrambling," *The Wall Street Journal,* August 31, 1994, pp. A3–A4.

Also, if certain department workers continually finish early and have extra free time, managers should reexamine the workload of the employees' department in relation to bottlenecks. Managers need to reconsider the flow of production process to utilize the extra time of one department to prevent bottlenecks. Above all, managers must control machine down time with an adequate maintenance plan. The malfunctioning of certain equipment stops the whole production process. Therefore, managers must prepare a systematic maintenance schedule to minimize down time loss.

Under JIT if a worker's output during a day is lower than expected, bottlenecks either before or after the worker are the likely cause. Either situation compels workers to stop producing through no fault of their own. Thus, the adoption of the JIT production philosophy without a change in previous labor efficiency measures confuses both workers and managers. Also, a company must revise its incentive plans to reflect the impact of this change.

Learning Curve Theory

In estimating cost behavior, Chapter 3 made the assumption that the cost of securing each input is a linear function of the quantity acquired. However, the relationship between costs and independent variables is not always linear. When employees gain experience performing a specific task, managers often find a systematic, nonlinear relationship. The **learning curve theory,** also called the **improvement curve theory,** is based on the proposition that as workers gain experience in a task, they need less time to complete the job and productivity increases. The learning curve theory not only affects direct labor costs but also impacts direct labor-related costs, such as supervision. In addition, this learning affects direct material costs. As workers gain experience, they may have less waste and spoilage.

The time to perform many operations begins slowly and speeds up as employees become more skilled. Much fumbling is likely to occur at the start of a new process. Gradually the time needed to complete an operation becomes *progressively* smaller at a constant percentage as workers find rhythmic work patterns. Because this rate of improvement often has a regular pattern, we can draw **learning curves** to estimate the labor-hours required as workers become more familiar with the process. Learning curves also are called **progress functions** and **experience curves.**

The learning curve model is based on a constant percentage reduction in required inputs. We typically express these reductions in terms of the effect of doubling the output quantity. We state this pattern as follows: As cumulative quantities double, average time per unit falls by a certain percent of the previous time. For example, assuming this reduction is 20 percent and it took two hours to produce the first unit, the accumulated average rate to double the present output from one to two units is two hours × 0.80 = 1.6 hours. Because the cumulative hours are an average for the units completed, the total time to produce two units is 1.6 × 2 = 3.2 hours. To double production again from two to four units, the average per unit time decreases to 80 percent of the previous average, 1.6 hours × 0.80 = 1.3. This makes the total time to produce four units equal to 5.2 hours. We use this progression to obtain the values in the following table:

Cumulative Quantity	Cumulative Average Worker–Hours per Unit	Predicted Total Hours to Perform Task
1	2.0	2.0
2	1.6 (2.0 hours × 80%)	3.2 (2 × 1.6 hours)
4	1.3 (1.6 hours × 80%)	5.2 (4 × 1.3 hours)
8	1.0 (1.3 hours × 80%)	8.0 (8 × 1.0 hours)
16	0.8 (1.0 hours × 80%)	12.8 (16 × 0.8 hours)
32	0.6 (0.8 hours × 80%)	19.2 (32 × 0.6 hours)
64	0.5 (0.6 hours × 80%)	32.0 (64 × 0.5 hours)

The table shows the computations for an 80 percent learning curve, shown in Exhibit 16–3. In practice, managers plot these curves on log-log graph paper. The slope of the curve for operations that are complex and require much technical skill are steeper than that for routine, repetitive operations. We determine points on the graph by dividing the cumulative quantity at each point by the predicted total hours to perform the task. For example: 1 unit ÷ 2 hours = 0.50, 2 units ÷ 3.2 hours = 0.63, 4 units ÷ 5.2 hours = 0.76, 8 units ÷ 8 hours = 1.0, and so forth. The table shows that the reduction rate of 20 percent is constant at each doubling of the number of tasks performed. Eventually, workers learn the skill and further reductions in time become negligible. As shown in Exhibit 16–3, a constant productivity state is established.

Learning Rate   The reduction in time varies between 10 and 40 percent depending on the repetitiveness of labor operations, with 20 percent being a common reduction. In calculating the learning rate that applies to the specific situation, data on manufacturing the first two lots of a product can be used. We usually define the **learning rate** as:

$$\frac{\text{Average input quantity (cost) for the first } 2X \text{ units}}{\text{Average input quantity (cost) for the first } X \text{ units}}$$

EXHIBIT 16–3   Learning Curve

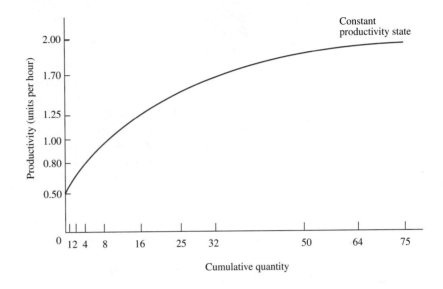

Assume that for another project the first lot of four units required a total of 4,000 direct labor-hours. The second lot of four more units requires an additional 2,800 direct labor-hours. We calculate the learning rate as follows for this operation:

$$\frac{(4,000\ +\ 2,800)/8}{4,000/4}\ =\ \frac{850\ \text{average direct labor-hours}}{1,000\ \text{average direct labor-hours}}\ =\ 85\%$$

Deferred Learning Curve Costs

Managers can use learning curves to estimate labor requirements and prepare cost estimates. In competitive bidding, we can estimate the effect of learning on costs if we expect repeat orders. For example, assume that a company has recently succeeded in winning a federal contract to build and assemble eight special TV sets. The prototype constructed to win the contract cost $2,000 in materials and $10,000 in labor. Materials are not subject to a learning effect. However, management estimates the labor costs are subject to a 90 percent learning rate. Using the doubling approach, average labor costs for the eight units are $7,290 as shown in the following table. (Note this analysis uses costs rather than hours.) Subtracting the $10,000 labor cost used on the first unit gives a total budgeted labor cost of $48,320 for the seven units needed later. Budgeted material costs for these seven units is $14,000 (7 × $2,000).

Total Units	Average Cost to Produce All Units to Date	Total Cost to Produce All Units to Date
1	$10,000	$10,000
2	9,000 ($10,000 × 90%)	18,000 (2 × $9,000)
4	8,100 ($9,000 × 90%)	32,400 (4 × $8,100)
8	7,290 ($8,100 × 90%)	58,320 (8 × $7,290)

For financial accounting purposes, we usually do not report an increasing trend of profits for each subsequent unit as the actual labor cost decreases. Instead, we charge units to cost of goods sold at the average cost expected to be incurred for all units in the production run. This is $7,290 average costs for the federal contract just described. The actual labor cost to produce the first unit is $10,000. However, we transfer the labor cost to finished goods as $7,290 resulting in a deferred cost of $2,710. We place the deferred cost of $2,710 in a suspense account titled **Deferred Learning Curve Costs.** Even though such costs have a possible relationship to future economic benefits, the disclosure of deferred learning curve costs on a company's balance sheet disagrees with generally accepted accounting principles.

In the early part of the production run, actual labor costs for the units manufactured exceed average production cost. The reverse occurs later in the run with the actual cost being less than average cost. Exhibit 16–4 illustrates the pattern of learning curve costs. By the time the learning effect becomes negligible and a constant productivity state sets in or the production run is complete, the balance in the Deferred Learning Curve Costs account is zero.

The following journal entry reflects *labor cost only* for the transfer of the first and eighth unit from work in process to finished goods inventory. An alternative treatment recognizes deferred learning curve costs at the time the finished product is sold and recorded as a cost of goods sold.

For Unit 1:

Deferred Learning Curve Costs	2,710	
Finished Goods Inventory	7,290	
Work in Process Inventory		10,000

For Unit 8:

Finished Goods Inventory	7,290	
Deferred Learning Curve Costs.		810
Work in Process Inventory		6,480

EXHIBIT 16–4   Pattern of Learning Curve Costs

Unit	Unit Actual Cost		Average Cost	Adjustment to the Deferred Learning Curve Cost Account	Balance in Deferred Learning Curve Cost Account
1	$10,000		$7,290	+ $2,710	$2,710
2	8,000	$18,000 − 10,000	7,290	+ 710	3,420
4	7,200	$32,400 − 18,000 $14,400/2 units	7,290	− 180 ($90 × 2)	3,240
8	$6,480	$58,320 − 32,400 $25,920/4 units	7,290	−3,240 ($810 × 4)	–0–

Even though the use of the Deferred Learning Curve Costs account causes a smoothing effect on reported company earnings, it does result in a deferred charge account which the company's balance sheet shows as an asset. The company recovers this asset in future cost of goods sold if it completes the production run.

However, if the company fails to produce and sell all the units in the production run for which the learning effect applies, accountants must write the deferred cost balance off as a loss. For example, assume that even though the initial contract was for a total of eight units, after delivering the first four sets (including the prototype), the buyer cancels the contract. Deferred learning curve costs must be written off at the time the buyer cancels the contract if the company valued the four units at the expected average cost for all eight units in the contract. Thus, with the manufacture of each unit, the labor cost portion of that unit for inventory valuation would have been $7,290, or a total for four units of $29,160 (4 × $7,290). This is lower than the actual unit cost for these early units. Actual labor cost for the first four units total $32,400. The difference is $3,240, calculated as follows:

$32,400 Total actual labor cost for four units
29,160 Total average cost for four units assuming eight units were made
$ 3,240 Deferred cost

A Deferred Learning Curve Costs account accumulates this $3,240 difference. Accountants must write the difference off as an additional cost of the job or as a loss at the time the buyer cancels the contract.

Advantages of Learning Curves

Since learning curve theory describes the phenomenon of improving efficiency as a function of time or increasing output, it provides an insight into the ability of workers to learn new skills. Managers use progress reports comparing actual results with estimated accomplishments as depicted by the learning curve to evaluate performance. Learning models bring the behavioral and the quantitative aspects of labor management together. This information assists management in establishing an incentive wage system. Companies should avoid giving bonus pay while workers are in a learning stage. After learning the skill, companies establish standards so employees may earn bonus pay for performing operations in less than standard time. Certainly if companies need standards before the constant productivity state becomes apparent, they should consider the learning curve effect.

Impact of Automation on Learning Curves

Learning curve theory has limited usefulness at the machine level in a flexible manufacturing system. These new technologies alter the whole concept of learning curve costs. After the system learns the operation method, it repeats the task identically each time. Also, direct labor comprises a small percent of total production costs in a machine-paced environment.

Summary

Companies often introduce incentive wage systems to lower the unit conversion cost while also giving workers an opportunity to earn additional wages. Companies use group incentive plans when the work flow requires a team effort and it is not possible to determine the number of units each employee produces. JIT has a significant impact on a company's incentive plans because keeping workers busy to produce inventory not yet needed is contradictory to the JIT concept.

In traditional manufacturing systems, direct labor is generally considered to be a variable cost. In practice, however, it is normally a semivariable cost because a temporary decrease in product demand normally does not result in extensive production worker layoffs. Instead, companies may provide employment to workers even though there is not enough work available to keep the full work force busy. After automating a production process, cost behavior changes significantly. Not only is there a sharp decrease in the proportion of product cost attributed to labor, but the remaining labor is also mostly a fixed cost.

Additionally, labor operations with much repetitiveness can experience a higher learning rate as workers become more familiar with the tasks and can complete it in less time. In the early stage of a production run, actual labor costs usually will exceed average costs resulting in deferred learning curve costs. However, by the time the learning effect becomes negligible and a constant productivity state sets in, the balance of the deferred costs is zero.

Important Terms and Concepts

Form W–4, Employee's Withholding
  Exemption Certificate   510
Form W–2, Wage and Tax Statement
  510
Thrift plans   516
Overtime premium pay   518
Shift premium pay   519
Incentive compensation plan   520

Suboptimization   521
Just-in-time (JIT)   522
Learning curve theory or improvement
  curve theory   523
Learning curves, progress functions,
  experience curves   524
Learning rate   524
Deferred learning curve costs   526

Ethical Dilemma

Recommendations for Ethical Situation

Victor, Inc., manufactures microcomputers with 60% of its sales made through personal sales calls. Salespersons receive a commission on each sale; however, successful sales often reflect many months of solicitation, entertaining, and promotional demonstrations. In this highly competitive market environment, salespersons also must travel extensively within the region searching for new clients.

Victor's most successful model, the Ap-IT, has been responsible for much of the company's growth within the last few years. However, two years ago, a major competitor introduced a more versatile microcomputer and Victor's sales have slowed down sharply. In fact, production management has begun manufacturing a more efficient model which they are introducing in the market. While Victor can use some of the Ap–IT model parts on the newer version, much of the material inventory is rapidly becoming obsolete. Unfortunately, Victor has a significant amount of this inventory in its parts warehouse.

Because of its dramatic impact on the entire company, you are surprised to hear the vice president's report to the officers of a local bank from whom a large note is outstanding. In this conversation, the vice president makes the assurance that Victor has no obsolete inventory. In your accounting records you have begun making provisions to write down the material and parts that are obsolete to their net realizable value. Just last week you had talked with the vice president, to whom you report directly, concerning the need for this write down and how detrimental it was going to be to the current period's financial statements. However, you recognize that this vice president's image and merit raise relates directly to the company's financial results.

In your position as controller, you also notice that travel and entertainment expenses have been increasing each month. In investigating the situation you find documents needed to support reimbursement are often missing. According to company tradition, superiors of the employee requesting reimbursement are responsible for reviewing expenditures and signing the request. Despite your earlier request to the president to establish tightly written travel and entertainment policies, you remember that the company took no action on this matter. The company requires salespersons, as well as all other management personnel, to submit receipts for any traveling, food, and lodging expenses incurred. However, in reviewing expenditures and talking with the travel clerks, you gain the distinct impression that the "line of least resistance" is the general rule. Underpayments are likely to provoke cries of outrage from the managers requesting travel reimbursement while they accept overpayments in courteous silence. Travel clerks often find it difficult to evaluate when client entertaining is cost justified; thus, their philosophy is "when in doubt, pay."

To further complicate the matter, evaluations from salespersons and other Marketing Department personnel are reviewed when the company considers travel clerks for raises and promotions. Naturally, those travel clerks that give the salespersons the least hassle in reimbursing their travel and entertainment claims receive higher evaluations.

As controller, you have also had difficulty in contacting travel clerks because of absences within the department. Victor, Inc., has a rule that should absences or lateness total five or more in any six-month period, employees must forfeit the entire 4 percent normal raise due at the next merit review. Victor counts a week's absence equally with a 10-minute lateness. Thus, workers in danger of accumulating a fifth absence within six months merely remain ill and away from work during their fourth absence until their first absence is more than six months old. There is a limit on how much younger workers can violate this rule because at some point their salary ceases and sickness benefits take over. This is usually sufficient to get the younger worker to return to work. Employees with 20 or more years of service, however, receive sickness benefits of 85 percent of normal salary.

These absences help explain why there is such a delay in recording travel expense. Several times within the last month, you have asked for an update on travel and entertainment expenses, only to find that the records are current through four weeks ago.

Required:

a. List the problems you are encountering as controller for the company.
b. Describe what you think is causing these problems.
c. Determine the ethical considerations you should recognize in this situation.
d. Recommend a course of action in this situation and give your reasons for selecting this action.

Problem for Self–Study

Daily Earnings and Effective Hourly Rate Using Proposed Incentive Plans
Standard production in the Emma Knight Company is 40 units per hour. For the first week in April, a worker's record shows the following:

Monday	330 units	8 hours
Tuesday	350 units	8 hours
Wednesday	310 units	8 hours
Thursday	320 units	8 hours
Friday	340 units	8 hours

Management is considering the adoption of one of two different incentive plans and wants to use this representative worker's record to study earnings using each proposed incentive plan.

With incentive Plan A, workers are guaranteed a rate of $12.40 per hour and a premium of 70 percent of the time saved on production in excess of standard.

With incentive Plan B, workers are paid $0.35 per unit when daily output is below standard, $0.45 per unit when daily output is at standard and up to 5 percent above standard, $0.50 per unit for all production when the daily output exceeds 5 percent above standard.

Required:

Compute daily earnings and the effective rate per hour for each day using each of the incentive plans proposed.

Solution to Problem for Self–Study

EMMA KNIGHT COMPANY

Plan A: $\dfrac{\$12.40}{40 \text{ units}}$ = $0.31 per unit × 70% = $0.217 per unit

$12.40 × 8 hours = $99.20 guaranteed daily wage

	Daily Earnings		Effective Rate per Hour
Monday	$101.37	[$99.20 + (10 units × $0.217)]	$12.67
Tuesday	105.71	[$99.20 + (30 units × $0.217)]	13.21
Wednesday	99.20		12.40
Thursday	99.20		12.40
Friday	103.54	[$99.20 + (20 units × $0.217)]	12.94
Weekly earnings	$509.02		

Plan B: Standard production = 320 units
105% standard production = 336 units

	Daily Earnings		Effective Rate per Hour
Monday	148.50	(330 × $0.45)	$18.56 $\left(\dfrac{\$148.50}{8 \text{ hours}}\right)$
Tuesday	175.00	(350 × $0.50)	21.88
Wednesday	108.50	(310 × $0.35)	13.56
Thursday	144.00	(320 × $0.45)	18.00
Friday	170.00	(340 × $0.50)	21.25
Weekly earnings	$746.00		

Review Questions

1. Give two examples frequently encountered in actual business organizations that suggest workers are compensating for each others' perceived errors.

2. What is the weakness in a system in which workers are continually compensating for others' perceived errors?

3. What impact do automated manufacturing systems have on the concept and applicability of learning curve theory?

4. Discuss the variety of labor-related costs that an employer can incur for each worker.

5. *a.* Discuss the advantages and the disadvantages of group incentive payroll plans.

   b. As a member of the management team, what factor would you consider most important when evaluating an incentive plan?

6. What is the impact of JIT and newer management philosophies on incentive plans?

7. Discuss the relation of a no-layoff policy and workers' acceptance of robots. What is a preferred approach when introducing automation?

8. As a manufacturing company's cost accountant, you recognize the importance of understanding the production process. Periodically, you walk through the plant to reorient yourself to any changes occurring. On a recent trip, you notice several Finishing Department employees standing around the last 1 1/2 hours each day waiting for the whistle to blow and end the work shift. Explain whether you think you should or should not report such actions to their supervisors.

9. Why might you advise companies to stagger payrolls throughout the week or month?

10. What is the basic assumption of the learning curve?

11. List some managerial applications of learning curves in the planning and controlling of business operations.

Exercises

E16–1 Learning Curve Application
Shell, Inc., manufactures complex units for submarines. Fabricating these units requires a high degree of technical skill. However, employees have an opportunity to learn how to produce the units more effectively. In estimating direct labor-hours, a 70 percent learning curve can be used. Completing one prototype unit required 1,200 direct labor-hours at a cost of $18,000.

Required:

a. Determine the cumulative average worker-hours per unit for a total of two units, four units, and eight units.

b. Estimate direct labor cost for an order of seven additional units, after completing one unit.

E16–2 Working Smarter, Not Harder

Writing

Management of Roget Company was surprised to learn that employees were complaining about posters that managers recently placed on departmental bulletin boards. The posters show an employee running to increase plant productivity. In selecting these posters, managers thought employees would interpret the message that the employee had a goal for which to work. Instead, the grapevine tells management that employees highly resent managers displaying these posters.

Required:

Explain why employees have such a negative attitude toward these posters.

E 16–3 Computing Daily Earnings under an Incentive Plan
Dobbs Company uses an incentive plan in which employees receive a guaranteed rate of $8 per hour and a premium of 60 percent of the time saved on production in excess of the standard of 80 units per hour. You have pulled the production records and find an employee has produced the following: Monday—700 units; Tuesday—720 units.

Required:

Compute the daily earnings.

E16–4 Vacation and Holiday Pay

Pauley, Inc., uses a payroll account to record its weekly payroll. The labor summary for March shows Pauley incurred $15,800 direct labor and $6,100 indirect labor. Vacation and holiday pay is charged to current production at a rate of 5 percent of total payroll and is treated as factory overhead. All wages are subject to an 8 percent FICA tax rate, 2.7 percent state unemployment tax rate, and 0.8 percent federal unemployment tax rate. Pauley treats payroll taxes as indirect costs.

Required:

Prepare the labor summary entry on March 30, distributing the payroll and recording payroll taxes and costs of vacations and holidays. Record subsidiary ledger accounts for factory overhead.

E16–5 Treatment of Overtime Premium Pay

An employee at the Russell Company is paid $4.60 per hour for a regular week of 40 hours. For the week ending July 19, the employee worked 43 hours on Job No. 502 and earned time and a half for overtime hours. A job order subsidiary ledger is used for work in process.

Required:

a. Prepare the entry to distribute the labor cost if the overtime premium is the result of a heavier than normal work load.
b. Prepare the entry to distribute the labor cost if the overtime premium is the result of a time deadline on No. 502.

Critical Thought

E16–6 Penalty and Incentive Pay

Jane Brown works for the Nashville Company. Jane's basic wage rate is $16.00 an hour. She receives 1 1/2 times her normal wage rate for hours in excess of 40 per week. Jane also receives $1.00 for each motor she produces. If Jane does not produce at least 14 motors on a given day, she has $18.00 deducted from her pay and does not receive the $1.00 per motor bonus. Given the following information, what is Jane's pay for the week?

Day	Hours	Motors Produced
Monday	6	10
Tuesday	12	20
Wednesday	7	12
Thursday	11	22
Friday	6	17

E16–7 Use of Learning Curve Theory in Bidding

Miller Manufacturers has just completed the production and sale of a complex electronic unit. Management believes an opportunity exists to apply a 70 percent learning curve. In determining the cost of the first unit manufactured, the following data were obtained:

Material (60 pounds @ $4 per pound)	$ 240
Direct labor (80 hours @ $10 per hour)	800
Factory overhead ($2 per direct labor-hour)	160
Total	$1,200

A potential customer approaches management wanting to buy three units for a total price of $2,500.

Required:

a. Provide supporting data indicating the estimated profit or loss if the bid is accepted. Assume no quantity discount exists for materials.
b. Explain how your approach would be different in determining whether the bid should be accepted if the potential customer brought specifications for the electronic unit; that is, Miller Manufacturers had never made a unit like the one requested.

E16–8 Incentive Wage Plan

The incentive wage system at Swindell Company provides for a guaranteed wage per hour plus a premium of 65 percent of the time saved on production in excess of the standard of 40 units per hour. The following actual production and the guaranteed wage for an eight-hour day are for two employees:

	Hourly Guaranteed Rate	Units Produced	
		Monday	*Tuesday*
Clyde	$13.40	315	400
Collins	$16.00	360	410

Required:

Calculate the daily wages for each employee.

E16–9 Treatment of Overtime Premium Pay

On Friday morning, a customer brings a rush order of 2,500 units of Product X210 at a unit sales price of $20. Searcy Company agrees to produce these units for the customer over the weekend for shipment on Monday. Fifty of the direct labor employees who earn $18 an hour work eight hours each on Saturday and Sunday to complete the order.

The union agreement specifies that the workers are to be paid time and one-half for weekend work.

Material costing $3 per unit was used on the order. The factory overhead application rate is $8 per direct labor-hour.

Required:

a. Determine the gross margin on the specific order.
b. Determine the gross margin on the order if, instead, the request was received earlier in the week but due to the heavy work load, the employees had to work overtime on Saturday and Sunday to complete the order.

E16–10 Reversing Entries for Labor Costs

Richard Company pays its employees every other Friday. Because the last pay period of 19X2 ended on December 24, the company made the following adjusting entry on December 31 so that its financial statements would be correctly stated:

Work in Process Inventory....................	2,000	
Factory Overhead Control	6,000	
Marketing Expense Control	1,500	
Administrative Expense Control.................	900	
Payroll Payable.........................		10,400

Gross regular earnings for the first payroll ending on January 7, 19X3, were direct labor, $4,000; indirect labor, $12,000; sales and distribution personnel, $3,000; administrative costs, $1,800. Because Job No. 49 had a time deadline, the company incurred overtime premium pay totaling $820. Authorizations from employees to withhold contributions to the United Neighbors charitable fund of $850 and union dues of $750 were received. Federal income taxes of $5,250 were withheld. The following taxes were imposed on 100 percent of wages at the rates indicated: FICA at 8 percent each for employer and employee; federal unemployment tax at 0.8 percent; and state unemployment tax at 2.7 percent.

Required

a. Record the reversing entry for wages on January 1.
b. Assuming a reversing entry was made, prepare the entries on January 7 to record the labor cost and its subsequent payment.
c. Prepare the entries on January 7 assuming no reversing entry was made.

Problems

P16–11 Impact of Incentive Plan on Conversion Costs

The management of Lucille Austin Company has recently adopted an incentive plan for its employees. Standards for each employee are expressed in time per unit of output. A performance efficiency ratio is computed for each employee by comparing actual output with standard output. This ratio then is applied against each employee's base rate. All employees are guaranteed $10.80 per hour if they do not meet standard production. The labor time sheets for the week ended June 15 are as follows:

Employee	Hours Worked	Hourly Rate for Standard Production	Actual Output	Standard Units per Hour
H. J. Adams	40	$13.00	690	15
A. R. Baker	40	12.25	944	20
L. T. Smith	35	11.90	425	13
B. J. Wallace	38	11.50	855	18

Required:

a. Compute the gross wages for each employee.
b. Prior to the enactment of the incentive plan, the weekly output of the four employees was 2,500 units for the same number of hours worked. Total weekly labor costs were $1,650. Total factory overhead averaged $550 per week prior to the incentive plan, but it was $551.29 after the plan was enacted. Calculate the conversion costs per unit prior to and after enactment of the incentive plan.

P16–12 Distributing Labor Costs and Alternative Treatment of Payroll Tax

Swift, Inc., is subject to the following tax rates: FICA, 8 percent, state unemployment, 2.7 percent, and federal unemployment, 0.8 percent. The company pays its employees biweekly and shows the following current pay period information for four employees:

1. Dodge, president, has earned $2,100, from which $580 federal income tax is withheld. None of her salary is subject to payroll tax.
2. Brown, marketing manager, has earned $1,800, from which $300 federal income tax is withheld. Of this salary, $800 is subject only to FICA tax.

3. Jones, production operator, has earned $600, from which $90 is withheld for federal income taxes. This salary is subject only to FICA tax.
4. Smith, maintenance worker, has earned $300, from which $30 is withheld for federal income taxes. This salary is subject to FICA and unemployment tax.

Required:

a. Record the distribution of labor cost for the current pay period and its subsequent payment.
b. Record the payroll taxes, treating them as indirect costs.

P16–13 Accounting for Vacation, Holiday, and Bonus Pay

A union agreement was recently entered into by the management of Greg Jones Company granting employees 10 working days of vacation and 5 working days of holidays. In addition, at fiscal year-end, each employee is to receive a bonus of 0.03 percent of net company income. Total net income is expected to be $500,000.

Required:

a. Prepare the journal entry to record the total weekly labor cost for one employee who earns $45 for one day of productive labor. Assume a payroll summary account has been used previously and you are to distribute only the labor cost.
b. Prepare the journal entry when the employee in Requirement *a* receives his entire vacation pay. Assume that amounts withheld are $90 federal income tax, $32 state income tax, and 8 percent FICA tax.
c. Compute the cost of holidays and vacations accruing to each pay period as a percentage of cost for this employee, assuming a 40-hour week.

Critical Thought

P16–14 Controls for Piecework

Paper Inc. has adopted an incentive plan. Employees earn 20 percent of their hourly minimum wage for each unit that they produce above standard. Because the nature of their jobs varies, a standard and hourly minimum is established for each job. Employees receive the guaranteed minimum wage if they do not meet the standard for a day. Employees work eight hours per day.

	Actual Output	Standard per Day	Minimum Hourly Wage
Employee Locke		50	$10.75
Monday	46		
Tuesday	58		
Wednesday	52		
Thursday	48		
Friday	52		
Employee Richards		60	11.50
Monday	50		
Tuesday	68		
Wednesday	48		
Thursday	76		
Friday	62		

Required:

a. Calculate each employee's daily wages.
b. Does a review of these employees' output lead you to believe that a control feature is needed? Explain your answer.

P16–15 Journal Entries for Payroll, Labor Distribution, and Payroll Tax

Taylor Motor Corporation has the following payroll for the pay period just ended:

	Gross Wages	Wages Subject to FICA
Direct labor	$7,000	$5,500
Indirect labor	4,500	1,500
Marketing salaries	2,500	2,000
Administrative salaries	4,000	3,500

Income tax withheld totals $3,050. Applicable tax rates are FICA, 8 percent; state unemployment, 2.7 percent, and federal unemployment, 0.8 percent. Of all wages, only $2,000 direct labor wages are subject to unemployment tax.

Required:

a. Using a temporary payroll account, prepare the payroll entry. Then prepare the labor distribution entry and the subsequent wage payment entry.

b. Record the payroll taxes using the direct cost method.

P16–16 Using Learning Curves in Standard Setting

Based on experience in similar production processes, James Hood, Inc., believes that learning curves can be used in setting the standard for production of a new product called LTT. This new product requires an extensive amount of labor in relation to materials.

Analysis of the first two lots of four units each of LTT is as follows:

> 4,800 total direct labor-hours for first lot of four units.
> 2,880 additional direct labor-hours for second lot of four units.

Management believes that the bugs and fumbling that occurred in the first two lots will soon be corrected so that there will be no significant improvement in production time after the first 16 units of LTT. Thus, the standard for direct labor-hours will be established based on the average hours per unit for Units 9–16.

Company policy requires that all bids submitted include a markup of 20 percent on total variable manufacturing cost. The direct labor workers employed on LTT production earn $18 per direct labor-hour; variable manufacturing overhead is assigned to products at 125 percent of direct labor costs. Each unit of LTT requires 20 square feet of direct material at a cost of $60 per square foot.

Required:

a. Calculate the learning rate that is applicable to LTT production based on the data for the first eight units.

b. Determine the standard for direct labor-hours that is appropriate for each unit of LTT.

c. Assume that after the first 16 units were manufactured, the company was asked to submit a bid for an additional 30 units. Using appropriate calculations, explain what price the company should bid on this order of 30 units.

SPATS

P16–17 Evaluating Alternative Incentive Plans

Blake Company, a management consulting firm, has designed two different incentive plans for a client. Plan A does not provide a guaranteed wage. Instead, workers are paid at a piece rate of $0.36 a unit. A bonus of 25 percent of the regular piece rate is paid for each unit over standard. The standard is 25 units per hour.

Plan B, a group incentive plan, includes an extra 4 percent on a guaranteed minimum wage for each 100 units over the group's weekly standard. The weekly standard for the group is 3,000 units. Data follow for all the employees in the group for a 40-hour week. The bonus will be calculated for every hour worked.

Employee	Units Produced	Guaranteed Hourly Minimum (for Plan B)
C. Xedus	900	$13.05
F. York	1,100	10.65
R. Zillis	1,200	10.95

Required:

a. Compute the gross earnings for each employee, first under Plan A and then under Plan B.
b. Evaluate the plans and indicate which is more appropriate in these circumstances.

P16–18 Estimating Learning Curves

The Jensen Company found it takes 600 hours to produce the first unit of a complex motor for a computer system at a labor cost of $7,200. Since much reference was made to the blueprint in making the first unit, management believes there is great opportunity to learn. In estimating direct labor-hours, an 80 percent learning curve can be used.

Required:

a. Determine the cumulative average work-hours per unit for a total 2 units, 4 units, 8 units, 16 units, 32 units, and 64 units. (Carry hours to two decimal places.)
b. Estimate the direct labor cost of an order for 63 additional units, after completing one unit.
c. Assuming an order for a total of 64 units was received, record the journal entry showing at what unit labor cost the second unit would be entered into finished goods inventory and what would be the deferred learning curve cost.
d. Assuming the firm had erroneously used an 80 percent learning curve when, in fact, the labor cost followed a 70 percent learning curve, by how much would the:
   (1) Budget over- or understate the hours? (Carry hours to two decimal places.)
   (2) Order cost for the 63 units have been over/under actual?

Critical Thought

SPATS

P16–19 Incentive Plan Evaluation

Williams Corporation is considering two different incentive plans for its production employees. Under Plan One, the worker receives a piece rate of $0.15 per unit. In addition, for each unit over the standard of 55 units per hour, the worker receives a bonus of 30 percent of the regular piece rate. There is no guaranteed wage.

Plan Two rewards group effort. For each full 250 units produced in excess of the weekly group standard of 6,500 units, each worker receives, in addition to his or her regular piece rate of $0.15 per unit, a bonus of 5 percent of a guaranteed hourly minimum. For the week ending October 30, 19X1, each employee worked 40 hours.

	Weekly Production in Units	Guaranteed Hourly Minimum (for Plan Two)
Gail Jackson	2,150	$4.50
Ann Watkins	2,690	4.25
Gerry James	2,245	5.00

Required:

a. Compute the gross earning for each employee under Plan One and then under Plan Two.

b. Evaluate the plans and indicate which you believe is most appropriate in these circumstances.

P16–20 Learning Rate and Deferred Costs

On the first unit produced by Arsenault, Inc., workers consulted a blueprint for almost all parts installed; the work required 2,500 direct labor-hours. On the second unit, workers were more familiar with the blueprint for the missile and could go rapidly to the part of the blueprint to review when installing the parts; this required an additional 1,700 direct labor-hours. This pattern is expected to continue until workers make 16 units, at which time they will remember how to install the parts without reference to the blueprint so that further learning is negligible. Workers are paid $10 an hour.

Required:

a. Calculate the learning rate for the company based on the data for the first 16 units.

b. Determine the average labor cost based on the learning pattern expected and the expected labor cost for units 3–16. Round to whole dollars.

c. Show in a schedule the pattern of learning curve cost with adjustments to the deferred learning curve cost account and the resulting balance in this account. Round to whole dollars.

d. Prepare the journal entry to transfer the labor cost for the 2nd unit and the 16th unit from work in process to finished goods.

e. Assume that even though the initial contract was for a total of 16 units, after the first 8 units were delivered (including the prototype), the contract was canceled. If the eight units had been valued at the expected average cost for all units in the contract, what is the amount that must be written off at the time the contract is canceled?

P16–21 Unit Conversion Cost under Two Proposed Incentive Plans

Two different incentive plans are presented to Nix Crawford, Inc., management for adoption. The standard per employee is 40 units per hour. Under Plan One, workers are paid 10 cents per unit when daily output is below standard; 12 cents per unit when daily output is at standard and up to and including 10 percent above standard; 15 cents per unit for all production when the daily output exceeds 10 percent above standard. With Plan Two, workers and the company will share in a ratio of 2:1 on the time saved on production in excess of standard. An hourly wage rate of $6 will be paid whether or not standard production is met.

In evaluating the plans, the following is a worker's eight-hour daily production record:

SPATS

Monday	310
Tuesday	350
Wednesday	315
Thursday	360
Friday	300

Total factory overhead averages $50 a day per worker.

Required:

a. Compute daily earnings and conversion cost per unit for each day using each of the proposed incentive plans. Carry unit cost to three decimal places.
b. Explain whether you see anything that arouses suspicion concerning the worker's performance.
c. Discuss whether this worker's performance would be a good basis for evaluating the plans.
d. Suppose, instead, Plan One is layered: workers receive 10 cents per unit for those units produced below standard, 12 cents per unit for those units produced at standard and up to and including 10 percent above standard, and 15 cents per unit for all extra units produced exceeding 10 percent above standard.
   (1) Using this layer effect, what is the daily wage for Tuesday and Thursday?
   (2) Why are earnings less under this revised Plan One than those calculated in Requirement *a*?

Cases

Critical Thought

C16–22 Internal Control over Payroll Procedures
Butler Company employs approximately 600 production workers and has the following payroll procedures. All hiring is performed by the factory supervisors, who make their decisions after interviewing applicants. After the interview, Butler either hires or rejects the applicant. If Butler hires the applicant, the new employee prepares a W–4 form indicating the number of exemptions claimed. This employee's Withholding Exemption Certificate serves as a notice to the payroll clerk that the employee has been hired; the hiring factory supervisor writes the hourly rate on the form and forwards it to the Payroll Department. The factory supervisors verbally inform the payroll clerks of any rate adjustments for employees under their supervision.

Near the entrance to the factory is a box containing blank time cards. At the beginning of the week, production workers remove blank cards and fill in their names in pencil. Workers record their arrival and departure times daily.

At the end of the pay period, payroll clerks replace the completed time cards with blank cards. If a worker does not have a time card, it is assumed that he or she is no longer employed, and his or her name is removed from the payroll. The chief payroll accountant manually signs payroll checks. Payroll checks for the majority of employees are distributed at the Payroll Department. During the days on which payroll is paid, employees go to the Payroll Department to pick up their checks. Unfortunately, some employees wait in line 45 minutes or more to receive them. This not only represents lost production time but also creates a traffic problem because space is limited outside the Payroll Department window.

Payroll checks for employees working in critical assembly lines are given to the factory supervisors for distribution. The supervisors arrange for the delivery of checks for workers who are absent.

The payroll bank account is reconciled by the chief payroll accountant, who also prepares state and federal payroll tax reports.

Required:

Make suggestions for improving control over hiring practices and payroll procedures.

Capstone Case

Behavioral Needs of Employees in a Changing Environment

Edmond Office Equipment Company began operations 30 years ago, specializing in the development of typewriters. Over the years, the company has earned average profits of $150,000 on sales of nearly $1.5 million annually. However, in recent years, sales have fallen to less than $300,000, and the company has become unprofitable.

Dan Edmond, the founder and president, is very conservative and views small businesses as risky. As a result, the company had no debt for 15 years; retained earnings financed all growth. Interest on bond investments played a larger role in helping to meet the obligations incurred by the sales and production aspects of the business.

Bob Edmond, a nephew of the founder of the organization, is frustrated that his efforts to improve the company have not been successful. While he agrees that he has obtained valuable experience first as director of marketing and now as vice president of finance, he questions whether he should leave the organization or attempt other tactics to turn the company around. He admits that he feels some responsibility to the company his uncle founded, especially since no other family member has made a definite commitment to the firm.

This is the same philosophy held by Dan Edmond. He views the company as a family trust because his two sisters each hold 20 percent of the stock. Actual voting has never occurred, since Dan owns 35 percent of the stock with Bob holding 5 percent. Bob believes that it is up to him to determine the company's future as his uncle wishes to retire and does not have any children.

When first organized, the founder ran the company very informally as a one-person operation. This philosophy is still prevalent as the president continues to exert a high degree of dominance over management. Personnel evaluation is extremely informal. The president believes he should tell employees what to do in performing the job and then let them be on their own. However, he did agree several years ago to establish three major product lines as separate profit centers with each manager having a significant amount of authority within their centers. These three profit centers are office furniture and fixtures, office supplies, and automatic typing. Each profit center consists of a sales department, production department, a service department, and an administrative department.

When word processing began using sophisticated input/output devices for text, the demand for office products changed. Because Edmond hesitated to invest funds in this new development, the company lagged behind its competitors and many grabbed a large share of Edmond's market. As a result, two firms became dominant and barriers to entry for most segments were significant. Edmond's marketing policy was not very aggressive as they allowed the two dominant competitors to do the missionary work for word processing equipment while they followed up with those potential customers who required less costly automatic typing equipment. Edmond distributes most of its typewriters through independent local dealers. Foreign sales account for about 2 percent of total current sales, down from 18 percent five years ago. Bob believes this decline resulted because German manufacturers have developed the technology to manufacture similar or better devices and can more favorably compete because of decreased shipping cost and import duties.

Because the greatest decline in sales has occurred in the automatic typing division, the president decided to establish a task force from the three different profit centers to identify this division's problems and make recommendations to correct them. He appointed the following people to the task force:

From Office Supplies Division: John Brown, personnel director; Mary Smith, budget supervisor.

From the Office Furniture and Fixture Division: Cindy Black, administrative department manager.

From the Automatic Typing Division: Bob Denton, profit center manager;

Jim Green, assistant profit center manager;

Ann Strong, salesperson; and

Louis Wells, service person.

Bob believes that his firm's product does have advantages over competitors' as Edmond's automated typewriter is more versatile and simpler to repair than the more advanced systems. However, the machine produced by Edmond does have one serious disadvantage—it is more difficult to learn to operate than competitors' products.

Employees' overall performance does not satisfy Bob. However, he places much of this blame on the lack of supervision and poor worker morale. He admits that it is hard to motivate employees when management also is disenchanted. Bob and his uncle have had several disagreements over the years about product development. Most of these stemmed from the uncle's unwillingness to fund a large capital commitment for new projects.

Bob worries that the professional scientists and engineers Edmond employed are not making sufficient progress in designing a new word processing system that will represent an improvement over those presently on the market. In talking with the automated typing profit center manager, he receives the following information:

1. There is widespread concern among these professionals that management may hire technical school graduates or individuals who have received only on-the-job training in this area from competing companies.

2. Engineers want more than competitive salaries and benefits.

3. Engineers wish to be treated as high-caliber professionals.

4. Several scientists also have expressed interest in gaining graduate education at a local university while employed.

5. These scientists want to be better qualified to publish some of their findings in technical journals.

6. Other professionals believe this graduate education will give them an opportunity for advancement in status and salary to higher management positions within the research division.

7. Others express interest in attending conventions of other professional scientists where they can discuss their work.

8. However, many of them have complaints about the resources and laboratory facilities.

9. All professionals believe they must have their ideas recognized and the opportunities to see these ideas put to use.

10. Another point in which there is agreement is that they want the freedom to solve problems and manage their own work within the constraints of the organization.

11. Others stress the importance of a local environment that offers good libraries, colleges, art museums, and other cultural opportunities.

Bob has been searching for ways that the company can diversify and has narrowed the alternatives down to five new products related to office products. An additional alternative for Bob developed recently when he saw an old college classmate who developed a different automatic typewriter. He is anxious for Bob to join him in forming a new company.

Required:

a. Enumerate the changes in the word processing industry that present threats and opportunities for the company.

b. Explain if the company could have changed its strategy within the last 20 years so it could have continued as a successful operation.

c. Describe the behavioral problems you see arising among the group members of the task force as a result of the composition of this group.

d. Discuss the contribution a person such as Mary Smith, the budget supervisor, could make in this task force.

e. Identify and discuss the specific needs expressed in the 11 issues by the scientists and engineers, using Maslow's and Herzberg's approaches.

Part V

Cost Accounting/Cost Management for Decision Making

Decision Models and Strategic Cost Analysis under Uncertainty

Chapter Objectives

After studying this chapter, you should be able to:

1. Discuss the factors affecting decision making and the constraints placed on the decision maker.

2. Employ different costs in various decision models used in uncertain situations.

3. Illustrate the various applications of differential costs in decision making, such as making or buying, accepting or rejecting sales orders, and eliminating segments.

4. Describe the advantages of calculating the payoff and expected values of the alternatives being considered as opposed to a subjective evaluation of opportunity cost.

5. Explain the role of probabilities in optimizing correction and inspection costs in deciding which variances to investigate.

Service

Current Cost Management Practice

Randy W. Kirk joined the virtual-corporation bandwagon when outsourcing seemed like a near perfect idea. At the time, he was an entrepreneur who considered any business with more than 10 employees to be midsize. When he and his partner raised start-up capital for AC International from nonactive, outside investors and opened the doors with no employees, they became a virtual-corporation. The owners created the company to manufacture a bicycle-tire liner that stops puncture flats. They outsourced the manufacturing to a job shop, the packaging and distribution to one owner's wholesale business, and the sales and billing to the other owner's company. Each owner billed for services rendered. The company grew by adding other products from domestic or foreign manufacturers. The company looked like a wholesaler but behaved like a manufacturer even though they owned no productive equipment. What initially seemed like a panacea began to spawn trouble because AC International customers were constantly complaining about late shipments and AC owners were always screaming at suppliers for not keeping promises. After numerous problems with suppliers, the owners began purchasing their own equipment, manufacturing on-site, and performing their own work. As their costs decreased, they gained better control of production timing and quality improvement. While there are business opportunities and situations in which virtual-corporations are effective, the vertical company that owns its own product sources remains an option for sources of products and services.

Randy W. Kirk, "It's About Control," *Inc.*, August 1994, pp. 25–26.

Introduction

When making decisions that affect the future, managers ask accountants to prepare special cost analyses. Because costs collected for inventory valuation often are inadequate for these analyses, accountants use other types of costs. Decision making requires costs such as opportunity costs and replacement costs that accountants do not enter in formal accounting records.

The environment of a firm affects the decision-making process by limiting the discretion of the decision maker and by presenting such resource constraints as governmental tariffs. The shorter the time planned for and the more time devoted to planning, the better the plans. However, managers should balance the benefit of the data accumulated and analyzed against the cost of obtaining information. Cost trade-offs occur in most decisions, and management may find that the first decision is too expensive.

Differential Cost Analysis

Differential costs are very useful in planning and decision making. **Differential costs,** or **incremental costs,** are the differences in the cost of two alternatives. Chapter 9 introduces differential costs as being useful when managers try to find the most profitable stage of production at which to sell a product. Differential cost analysis also involves such choices as accepting or rejecting orders, deciding to make or buy, and increasing or abandoning operations.

Differential and marginal costs are closely related because **marginal costs** refer to the change in total cost resulting from increasing the volume of activity by one unit per period. If fixed and semivariable costs do not increase due to the enlarged production, we measure marginal cost by the change in total variable cost.

Relevant-Irrelevant Costs

Accountants should emphasize only relevant costs in reports prepared for managerial decisions. **Relevant costs** are those that are pertinent and bear on the decision to be made. All others become **irrelevant costs** and do not apply to that particular selection process. The ability to distinguish between costs critical to the decision and costs having no significance is important in arriving at correct conclusions. Emphasizing the relevant costs avoids management's investment of time (also a scarce resource) in irrelevant details.

Out-of-pocket costs involve either an immediate or near-future cash outlay; they are usually relevant to decisions. Frequently, variable costs fall into this classification. For example, the direct materials needed to fill additional orders are relevant out-of-pocket costs while depreciation on the existing manufacturing facilities is not. Out-of-pocket costs are important in decision making because management should determine whether a proposed project would, at the minimum, return its initial cash outlay.

While not entered in the company's accounting records, replacement costs also represent relevant information for a decision maker. **Replacement cost** is what would be paid if an asset were acquired at present price levels. By valuing assets at current replacement cost, the accountant determines the cost that is currently required to purchase assets with the same service potential as those now used. Decision makers should use the lowest replacement cost based on prices in the current or anticipated future market.

In contrast to out-of-pocket and replacement costs, **sunk costs** are historical expenditures for equipment or other productive resources having no economic relevance to the present decision-making process. Managers decided in the past to incur these costs, and no present or future decision can change it. Thus, the costs are irrevocable in a given situation. Book value of plant assets are common examples of sunk costs. When exchanging an old asset for a new one, a company cannot change the old asset's undepreciated book value. The book value is irrelevant to the decision except in determining income tax liability. In deciding whether to continue or abandon operations, managers should ignore the book value of any equipment to be discarded at no salvage value. If operations are continued, depreciation of the equipment is a production cost. However, the book value of the equipment is irrelevant in deciding to abandon operations.

Cost Behavior for Volume and Transaction Changes

Understanding cost behavior is helpful for many short-term decisions such as accepting or rejecting special orders or bidding on small jobs to cover differential costs. The cost-volume-profit relationship presented in Chapter 14 uses variable direct costs, such as material, and variable indirect or overhead costs, such as utilities, in short-term decisions. These short-term costs should reflect the physical demands on a company's scarce or capacity resources made by the product or project under consideration. Even though a differential cost is more likely to be variable or semivariable, differential costs include fixed costs when management anticipates a change in capacity or production scheduling. For example, assume Fun Bike's present plant facilities can manufacture between 7,000 and 10,000 bicycles without adding plant space or machinery. Exhibit 17–1 shows that the differential cost between 7,000 and 8,500 bicycles is strictly variable costs. However, if Fun Bike increases

Exhibit 17–1   Differential Cost Analysis

	70%	Normal Capacity 85%	125%
Volume	70%	85%	125%
Number of bicycles	7,000	8,500	12,500
Variable costs: $29 per bicycle	$203,000	$246,500	$362,500
Fixed costs	85,000	85,000	100,000
Total costs	$288,000	$331,500	$462,500
Unit variable costs	$ 29.00	$ 29.00	$ 29.00
Unit fixed costs	12.14	10.00	8.00
Average unit costs	$ 41.14	$ 39.00	$ 37.00
Total differential costs		$ 43,500	$131,000
Unit differential costs ($43,500/1,500 bicycles = $29; $131,000/4,000 bicycles = $32.75)		$ 29.00	$ 32.75

production to 12,500 bicycles, it requires renting additional factory space, and equipment costing a total of $15,000. The variable costs of $29 per bicycle remains the same, yielding a total of $362,500 variable cost for manufacturing 12,500 bicycles. The differential costs for the extra 4,000 bicycles manufactured to yield a total production of 12,500 bicycles is $131,000 [$116,000 variable costs ($29 variable costs × 4,000 bicycles) + $15,000 additional fixed costs = $131,000].

As Exhibit 17–1 shows, Fun Bike can lower average bicycle cost from $41.14 ($288,000/7,000) to $39 ($331,500/8,500) by expanding production within the present facilities. The company reduces average unit costs by distributing the $85,000 total fixed cost over 1,500 more units. This results in a decrease in unit fixed costs from $12.14 to $10. Fixed costs do not increase because the company uses the idle capacity to produce the additional 1,500 units. Despite the increase in total fixed costs when renting additional plant facilities to produce 12,500 units, average unit costs have decreased from $39 to $37 due to the $2 decrease in unit fixed costs.

Transaction Changes.   Costs change with production volume in Exhibit 17–1. As discussed in Chapter 5, transactions such as engineering work orders, machine setups, and purchase orders also consume resources. A change in manufacturing volume is not the only activity that consumes overhead resources. Thus, differential cost analysis is also appropriate for analyzing cost changes based on managerial decisions using alternative transactions.

Accept-or-Reject Decisions

Exhibit 17–1 is useful for decision making and profit planning if a company faces an accept-or-reject sales offer. Managers should compare the differential costs of the additional 4,000 bicycles with the revenue they expect to receive in deciding whether manufacturing additional bicycles is profitable. For example, assume Fun Bike is producing 8,500 bicycles when an outside company makes a one-time offer to buy 4,000 bicycles at a unit sales price of $36. Exhibit 17–1 shows the average unit cost of $37 exceeds $36 sales price at the 125 percent capacity level. If, however, Fun Bike is producing at a 70 percent level, the fixed costs are irrelevant since they do not increase until the company reaches the 85 percent level.

Management may not take advantage of the sales offer if it relies on the unit average costs. Instead, managers should use differential costs in evaluating short-term projects when the objective is to make better use of existing facilities.

Fun Bike managers should compare the revenue received from this extra production with the differential cost as follows to determine whether the increased production is profitable:

Differential revenue (4,000 bicycles × $36) $144,000
Differential cost (4,000 × $32.75)   131,000
Differential income . . . . $ 13,000

If it accepts the sales offer, Fun Bike receives a $13,000 contribution to the recovery of fixed costs and, after full recovery, to income. Fun Bike should accept the sales price even though it is lower than average unit costs. Companies should accept new short-term business as long as they recover differential costs—differential costs represent the minimum sales price under these conditions. If a factory has excess capacity everywhere, it can produce additional products for essentially raw material costs in an automated environment, with direct labor and factory overhead displaying a fixed cost pattern. Likewise, for an existing plant to assign overhead rates on activity-based cost drivers at the product design stage provides appropriate signals only if the overhead rates represent differential costs.

Strategic Cost Analysis

Cost analysis can play a significant role in evaluating strategic opportunities when evaluating sales offers that affect current sales. While one-time orders often do not affect present sales, sales contracts covering several years often erode regular sales. Managers must then use strategic cost analysis to better assess the impact of selling to competitors. Companies usually find it unprofitable to be a significant supplier simultaneously in two price segments with a basically identical product. Cosmetics and price often are an insufficient differentiation competitive strategy.

Reducing Regular Sales Temporarily

For accept-or-reject decisions involving changes in present sales, companies must compare differential revenues to differential costs. Assume that when Fun Bike is operating at 85 percent capacity, it receives an offer of $250,000 for 5,000 bicycles that are slightly different from their regular products. Since this is a one-time order, management does not wish to rent plant facilities. After evaluating the requirements of the new order, Fun Bike managers find that they must temporarily cut regular production by one-third. Under these conditions, the company must calculate its net change in income, or **net differential income.** Assume simply that each of the 5,000 bicycles in the order requires $6 direct material, $8 direct labor, and $10 variable factory overhead. Fun Bike must purchase new tools costing $10,000 to make the 5,000 bicycles. These tools will have no use after they complete the order. Exhibit 17–2 illustrates the analysis needed to determine whether they should accept the order. We assume that the company can sell one-third of the regular production for $60 each or $169,980. As Exhibit 17–2 shows, the company will receive net differential income of $32,187 after comparing the $120,000 differential

Exhibit 17–2   Net Differential Income Analysis

Differential revenue from 5,000-bicycle order			$250,000
The differential cost of the 5,000-bicycle order:			
Costs incurred to fill the order:			
Direct materials (5,000 bicycles × $6)	$30,000		
Direct labor (5,000 bicycles × $8)	40,000		
Variable factory overhead (5,000 bicycles × $10) . .	50,000		
Tools	10,000		
Differential cost of 5,000-bicycle order		130,000	
Differential income from 5,000-bicycle order			$120,000
Less: Differential income from regular production:			
Regular production sales		$169,980	
Costs reduced for regular production:			
Variable costs (1/3 × $246,500)		82,167	87,813
Net differential income—advantage of accepting			
5,000-bicycle order			$ 32,187

income from the 5,000-bicycle order with the $87,813 income from regular production that the company will not earn. The company can prepare an analysis similar to that in Exhibit 17–2 comparing the $130,000 differential cost of the 5,000-bicycle order with the $82,167 differential cost of one-third regular production. Managers then compare this difference of $47,833, called **net differential cost,** to the $80,020 difference in revenue to yield a $32,187 advantage of accepting the order. Before accepting the order, they should consider many qualitative factors, such as *(1)* the impact on future earnings of temporarily cutting regular production by one-third, *(2)* the possibility of selling additional bicycles beyond the 5,000-unit initial order, and *(3)* the reliability of the cost estimates associated with the order.

Eroding Regular Sales

Differential analysis requires additional evaluation if the sales offer is repeated and long term, rather than one term. Rather than Fun Bike receiving a one-time order, assume an outside company, Outbike Inc., approaches Fun Bike to produce bicycles. Since Fun Bike is not operating at 100 percent capacity and facing declining sales, the added volume appears attractive. Outbike would sign a three-year contract agreeing to buy 1,500 bicycles a year at $45 each. Outbike wants the bikes to look different from Fun Bike's other bicycles even though the frame and some parts could be the same.

For simplicity, assume that the variable costs of producing an Outbike bicycle are $8 direct material + $15 direct labor + $6 variable overhead = $29, the same as for regular production. Also, Fun Bike's purchasing and inventorying costs would increase from producing 1,500 more bicycles. Since fixed costs are already being covered by the regular business, there is no need for the Outbike line to cover these costs. Assume Fun Bike requires no additional plant assets, but that the 1,500-order requires approximately the following differential working capital investment:

Direct materials—Two month's stock:

1,500 annual sales/12 = 125 bikes × 2 × $8	$ 2,000
Less 30 days trade credit from suppliers: 125 bikes × $8	1,000
	$ 1,000

Work in process—20 average bikes, having 100% material and

$1/4$ labor and overhead [$8 material + $1/4$ ($15 labor + $6 overhead) =	
$8 + $5 = $13; 20 bikes × $13]	260
Finished goods: One month's stock: 125 bikes × $29	3,625
Accounts receivable: (30 days sales): 125 bikes × $45 sales price	5,625
Net approximate extra investment	$10,510

Cannibalization Charge

With assumed aftertax carrying costs of 15 percent, the approximate annual cost estimate is $10,510 × 15 percent = $1,577 or $1.05 per Outbike over the 1,500 bikes. Assuming a 50 percent tax rate, this price is less than the $8 aftertax contribution margin [($45 − $29) × 50 percent]. However, before accepting the Outbike order, managers should determine if they should include an erosion or cannibalization charge for the regular Fun Bike sales lost because of Outbike's entry into the market. If managers include an erosion charge, it is the lost contribution margin from lost sales. For example, if Fun Bike loses 2,000 units of sales, the impact on profits is $60 sales − $29 variable costs = $31; $31 × 2,000 = $62,000. Partially offsetting this, the 2,000-unit Fun Bike sales decline would cause the differential working capital investment to somewhat decline.

Whether the erosion charge is relevant is debatable. This profit is relevant to Fun Bike assuming sales do decline. However, if Fun Bike rejects the offer, Outbike will find some other company to make its bicycles, and Fun Bike's sales will decline regardless of Fun Bike's action. Thus, new products may erode the sales of regular products even if Fun Bike does not accept the offer. In this case, the erosion charge is not an additional charge to accepting Outbike's offer.

Strategic Repositioning

Before accepting the outside offer, Fun Bike management should answer such questions as:

1. If Fun Bike makes the Outbike line, will it alienate Fun Bike's current suppliers?
2. Is Fun Bike creating another direct competitor for its regular customers and also offering that competitor a lower price than Fun Bike's regular customers?
3. Is it profitable in the long run, as well as ethical, to differentiate its bikes only in cosmetics and price?
4. Will this strategy backfire on Fun Bike?
5. In the long run will current Fun Bike dealers drop the Fun Bike line and concentrate instead on other brands?
6. If this happens, will Fun Bike be driven to change its sales mix and reduce its price?
7. Can Fun Bike compete as a supplier of another price range of bikes after eroding its present image?

Answering these questions may force Fun Bike to strategically reposition itself in the market. Selling this product to Outbike may result in a strategic repositioning with major, long-run implications. Engaging in this cost analysis may open new channels of distribution in a growth market or move it to a different price market segment. Managers may discover Fun Bike's strategic niche is eroding, slowly but definitely. Strategic cost analysis encourages managers to outline Fun Bike's alternatives and the risks and advantages of each. Strategic cost analysis includes marketing and competitive strategy to help evaluate the relative attractiveness of Fun Bike's options.

Additional Applications of Differential Analysis

Differential cost analysis is also appropriate for short-run make-or-buy decisions involving the construction of plant assets or component parts of a finished product on the company premises rather than acquiring them outside. As in accept-or-decline decisions, the company's objective is to profitably use the various levels of productive capacity available with the existing facilities. Differential cost analysis is especially valid if the company can use idle capacity and personnel to realize a cost saving.

Make-or-Buy Decisions

For example, suppose a company has determined these standard costs for two component parts it uses in processing:

	Part X2	Part Y4
Variable materials, labor, and overhead	$ 6	$ 7
Fixed factory overhead	3	4
Total	$ 9	$11
Machine-hours per part	7	5

Assume the company has been producing the 10,000 units of X2 and the 9,000 units of Y4 needed annually. However, a recent fire destroyed part of the building where manufacturing of the parts occurred. As a result, the company can devote only 87,000 hours of otherwise idle machine-hours to the production of these two parts. An outside company has offered to supply comparable quality parts at $9.50 for X2 and $12.50 for Y4. Management wants to schedule the 87,000 available machine-hours to maximize potential cost savings. Since machine-hours is the constraint, management wishes to maximize the contribution relative to this constraint. Exhibit 17–3 illustrates the allocation of machine time based on potential cost savings per machine-hour. Note that only variable production costs are relevant in this make-or-buy decision. The company should include any additional overhead incurred in the buying process, such as purchasing agents' salaries, as a differential cost.

EXHIBIT 17–3   Make-or-Buy Analysis

	Part X2	Part Y4
Outside purchase price	$ 9.50	$12.50
Relevant unit production cost	6.00	7.00
Potential cost savings per unit	$ 3.50	$ 5.50
Machine-hours per unit	÷ 7	÷ 5
Potential cost savings per machine-hour	$ 0.50	$ 1.10

Because the potential cost saving is greater for Y4, the company should give priority to using as much capacity as possible to produce Y4. After using the remaining capacity to manufacture part X2, the company would make the following purchases from the outside supplier:

Available machine-hours	87,000
Part Y4 annual usage (9,000 $\times$ 5 hours)	45,000
Remaining machine-hours	42,000
Part X2 annual usage in units	10,000
Units to be manufactured:	
$\left(\dfrac{42,000 \text{ remaining machine-hours}}{7 \text{ machine-hours per unit}} \right)$	6,000
Part X2 units to be purchased from outside suppliers	4,000

It is difficult to make clear-cut rules for make-or-buy decisions because each individual circumstance warrants additional considerations. On-site construction may be necessary because the company cannot purchase the asset from an outside supplier due to required specifications or the allotted time period. The company also may base the decision to make the parts or plant assets on their desire to control quality. In comparing the cost to make with the purchase price, management should use identical quantities and product quality levels, and consider quantity discounts. The price quoted by an outside supplier to make the products should be competitive. The first quoted price may be high, so bargaining may be necessary.

The make-or-buy decision is often complex, involving not only present costs but also projections of future costs resulting from such factors as capacity, trade secrets, technological innovation, product quality, seasonal sales, and production fluctuations. For example, many alternatives may be available in designing the product, including various types of material. Top management should, therefore, provide basic policies identifying the factors to be taken into account in make-or-buy decisions. They also should specify the division of responsibility among the management team. Make-or-buy decisions are not the exclusive problem of top management. In making these decisions, management must keep prevailing market forces in mind. The Purchasing Department and the Production and Industrial Engineering Departments often have more responsibility in such cost studies than does the Cost Accounting Department. Before undertaking make-or-buy cost studies, management should analyze the capacity available. It may not be feasible to operate the number of shifts required to manufacture both normal production and the asset in question.

The technical ability of the labor force making the product is an important factor in make-or-buy decisions. Managers should evaluate workers' ability against any special training or skills required. A company needs assurance that workers' knowledge is adequate to manufacture a product of the quality desired. Likewise, a company may need to acquire specialized plant facilities and equipment to manufacture the new asset. In addition, the firm may require new material sources.

It is difficult to find a comparative cost figure for making an asset rather than buying it from an outside supplier. Likewise, accountants encounter special cost measurement problems when companies contemplate buying a component part or service that they have been producing. While the experience of the past may prove helpful, historical cost data have serious limitations for planning and decision making because conditions may have changed. Companies should use the current and prospective level of costs, rather than historical costs in the estimation process. By using the costs the company incurs by continuing to perform the work rather than employing an outside supplier, management makes a more valid decision.

Escapable Costs

Costs that a company eliminates by discontinuing an activity are **escapable costs**. **Nonescapable costs** are costs that a company does not eliminate by discontinuing the activity. Instead, accountants reassign nonescapable costs to other segments. When management is considering dropping a product line or customer group, the only relevant costs are those that a company would avoid by dropping the product or customer. For example, if the company stops manufacturing component parts and purchases parts instead, the material costs for making the parts is an escapable cost. On the other hand, factory rent and insurance may remain unchanged. The remaining product lines must absorb these nonescapable costs, as shown in the following example. Suppose a company furnishes the following recent operating statement for its three product lines, televisions, computers, and radios:

	Televisions	Computers	Radios	Total
Sales	$200,000	$180,000	$150,000	$530,000
Variable expenses	$140,000	$108,000	$120,000	$368,000
Fixed expenses:				
Salaries of product line supervisors	15,000	16,000	20,000	51,000
Marketing costs allocated to product lines on basis of sales	4,000	3,600	3,000	10,600
Administrative costs allocated equally	11,000	11,000	11,000	33,000
Total expenses	$170,000	$138,600	$154,000	$462,600
Operating income (loss)	$ 30,000	$ 41,400	$ (4,000)	$ 67,400

Managers are considering discontinuing radio production and expect television sales to increase 10 percent as a result. They expect computer sales to increase 15 percent if this happens. They project no increase in fixed costs as a result of the increased television sales. However, the salaries of computer supervisors would increase 10 percent due to the increased sales. Managers expect no increase in total assets required. The company can sell assets used in radio operations at book value and lay off the radio supervisor with no termination pay.

Exhibit 17–4 illustrates the projected operating statement assuming the company discontinues radio operations. Notice that variable expenses for televisions and computers remain the same percentage of sales, and the radio operation's variable expenses are escapable. However, fixed marketing and administrative expenses are nonescapable, and television and computer sales must now cover radio's share. As shown in Exhibit 17–4, net income increases slightly from $67,400 to $72,600 with no increase in total assets required. However, management should consider other factors such as future radio sales and whether the increased sales of televisions and computers will continue or would occur without eliminating radio manufacturing.

Management also considers escapable and nonescapable costs in make-or-buy decisions, as shown in Exhibit 17–5. Assume a company that has the costs indicated in Exhibit 17–5 receives an offer from an outside company to supply the parts at $7 per unit. On first observation, this offer appears lower than the manufacturing

EXHIBIT 17–4   Projected Income Statement If Radio Manufacturing Is Discontinued

	Product Lines		
	Televisions	*Computers*	*Total*
Sales	$220,000	$207,000	$427,000
Variable costs and expenses	$154,000 (70%)	$124,200 (60%)	$278,200
Fixed expenses:			
Salaries of product line supervisors ..	15,000	17,600 (110%)	32,600
Marketing costs $\left(\dfrac{\$10,600}{\$427,000} = 2.4824\% \text{ of sales} \right)$	5,461	5,139	10,600
Administrative costs	16,500	16,500	33,000
Total expenses	$190,961	$163,439	$354,400
Operating income (loss) before taxes ..	$ 29,039	$ 43,561	$ 72,600

cost of $9 per unit. However, accountants must determine which costs are relevant in the future. If the company can avoid all $3,000 direct fixed costs in the future by buying units, these costs are escapable costs and relevant. However, if the $4,000 indirect fixed cost continues regardless of the decision, it is a nonescapable cost and irrelevant.

Assume for the data given in Exhibit 17–5 that by buying the units, the company avoids $3,000 direct fixed overhead, but $4,000 indirect fixed overhead is nonescapable. Thus, the escapable costs total $2,000 + $3,000 = $5,000 or $5 per unit, which is lower than the outside price of $7 per unit. This indicates that the company should continue manufacturing the unit. Exhibit 17–3 illustrates a make-or-buy decision in which variable costs are the only relevant costs. However, as we see in Exhibit 17–5, fixed costs also may be relevant.

EXHIBIT 17–5   Make-or-Buy Decisions

	Per Unit	*Per 1,000 Units*
Full cost:		
Direct material, direct labor, variable overhead	$2	$2,000
Fixed overhead, direct	3	3,000
Fixed overhead, indirect but allocated	4	4,000
	$9	$9,000
Escapable costs:		
Direct material, direct labor, variable overhead	$2	
Fixed overhead, direct	3	
	$5	
Outside purchase price	$7 which is higher	

Opportunity Cost Analysis

When a company is considering eliminating one activity and using plant facilities advantageously in another activity, opportunity costs are relevant. **Opportunity costs** are the profits lost by the diversion of an input factor from one use to another. Usually, formal accounting systems do not record opportunity costs because such costs do not involve cash receipts or outlays. Accountants usually record only data concerning the alternative selected rather than alternatives rejected. However, these rejected alternatives do have significance in decision making. The merits of any particular course of action are relative merits because they involve the difference between this action and some alternative.

Even though most managers are continually weighing alternatives, they may not actually use opportunity cost to their advantage. Some managers may resort to rough, subjective evaluations of opportunity cost. These rough evaluations are risky because opportunity costs are significant for many decisions. For example, a single proprietor or partner has forgone the opportunity to earn a salary elsewhere by owning a company. In deciding to own a business, the proprietor weighs the salary that would have been earned if he or she worked elsewhere. Likewise, the opportunity cost of using a machine or laborer to manufacture a product is the sacrifice of the earnings from using that machine or laborer to make other products. In deciding which product to manufacture, the earnings received from other products should be a major influencing factor. Wholly owned company assets also involve opportunity costs, because the company could invest the funds used to purchase company assets elsewhere and earn a return.

Opportunity costs are called **alternative costs**. When a firm uses resources in the manufacture of a product, society must forego certain quantities of other products that those resources aid in producing. This is true because the economy has limited supplies of economic resources in relation to human wants.

In Exhibit 17–5 illustrating escapable and nonescapable costs, the $5,000 escapable cost is lower than the outside offer to supply parts for $7,000. In addition, there is the opportunity cost of continuing to make the part; this is the earnings the company could have made if it had applied the capacity to some alternative use. Suppose forecasts show that another company wants to rent the plant capacity for $500. Because this opportunity cost becomes relevant to the decision, we should consider the following factors:

	Make	Buy
Cost of obtaining parts	$5,000	$7,000
Opportunity cost, rental income lost	500	
	$5,500	$7,000

Even with opportunity cost included, the company should continue to manufacture the parts.

Payoffs of Alternative Actions

The preceding examples illustrate that even though the statement of income does not include them, opportunity costs are important factors in decision making. For example, when a company has a large sum of money to invest, management should identify

EXHIBIT 17–6   Payoffs of Alternative Actions

Alternative Actions	Payoffs under Various Environmental Conditions		
	Excellent	*Average*	*Poor*
Physical improvements to present golf clubs currently produced	$200,000	$ 80,000	$ –15,000
Advertising campaign for present golf clubs . . .	100,000	75,000	–10,000
Manufacture new exercise bikes	500,000	100,000	–100,000
Manufacture new weight-lifting equipment	300,000	200,000	–80,000

the alternative actions and determine the respective payoffs of each. A payoff table displays the results expected for each alternative under consideration using possible states of the environment. The net benefit expressed in cash flow or income is the **payoff.** The first step in preparing a payoff table is to identify the alternative actions management is analyzing. As seen in Exhibit 17–6, management has established payoffs for four alternatives considered feasible in view of the company's funds and objectives. Two of these alternatives involve the introduction of new products, while the other two involve strategy changes for golf clubs the company presently manufactures. Exhibit 17–6 lists only four of many alternatives. For instance, the company could invest its funds in stocks or bonds of other companies. Exhibit 17-6 omits other alternatives for simplification. Speed in gathering data is important, for management could delay action by taking too much time in analyzing alternatives.

The second step in preparing a payoff table involves adding the environmental conditions influencing the payoff. The payoff table lists these environmental conditions across the top. Each cell on the payoff table contains a unique combination of an alternative action and an environmental condition. The third step involves estimating the payoff for each alternative and environmental condition since conditions prevailing in the future affect the income generated. Each cell indicates the estimated payoff for the alternative actions studied if the environmental condition at the head of the column prevails. For example, management forecasts that physical improvements to golf clubs would result in $200,000 in income in an excellent environment, $80,000 in income in an average environment, and a $15,000 loss if a poor market exists. Exhibit 17–6 indicates that manufacturing exercise bikes is most profitable in an excellent market, while producing weight-lifting equipment is the most profitable alternative in an average market. However, the strategy of an advertising campaign for golf clubs involves less loss in a poor environment.

If managers base their decisions solely on the information in Exhibit 17–6, they assume one environmental condition to exist. An improvement to this analysis considers the likelihood of the various environmental conditions. A decision problem exists because the payoff table in Exhibit 17–6 does not contain a clearly dominant alternative.

Quantified Regrets Table

A conservative way of choosing the most desirable alternative is to select the alternative whose maximum opportunity cost is the smallest. The **quantified regrets table** in Exhibit 17–7 shows that the maximum opportunity costs for physical improvements are $300,000 to golf clubs, $400,000 for an advertising campaign for golf clubs, $100,000 to manufacture exercise bikes, and $200,000 to manufacture weight-

EXHIBIT 17–7　Opportunity Costs of Alternative Actions

Alternative Actions	Opportunity Costs under Various Environmental Condition		
	Excellent	Average	Poor
Physical improvements to present golf clubs	$300,000	$120,000	$ 5,000
Advertising campaign for present golf clubs	400,000	125,000	—
Manufacture new exercise bikes	—	100,000	90,000
Manufacture new weight-lifting equipment	200,000	—	70,000

lifting equipment. Management should manufacture exercise bikes since the $100,000 maximum opportunity cost associated with their manufacture is lowest. As with the payoff table in Exhibit 17–6, this analysis fails to consider the probabilities of the various environmental conditions.

Decision Making Under Uncertainty

Management may know enough about the likelihood of each environment to attach probabilities of occurrence to each alternative. If so, management certainly wants to select the alternative that appears to produce the largest income, as long as that alternative does not expose the company to a high probability of a large loss. We can reduce the payoffs using each alternative to one figure. One way to do this is to weigh the possible payoffs according to the relative probabilities that the various conditions will occur.

Assigning Probabilities

Because decision makers normally deal with uncertainty, rather than certainty, they must estimate the probability of various outcomes. It is useful to assign probabilities that represent the likelihood of various events occurring. A **probability distribution** describes the chance or likelihood of each of the collectively exhaustive and mutually exclusive set of events. Decision makers have much information to guide the assignment of probabilities in some cases. Managers can base the probability distribution on past data if they believe that the same forces will continue to operate in the future. For instance, if certain machines have turned out 1 percent defective units for the last several operating periods, management could reasonably expect this same defective percentage to continue. In other cases, such as the introduction of a new product line or service, decision makers have little information on which to base the probability assignments. In these circumstances, they assign probabilities appropriate to the possible states of nature. The probabilities for the states of nature (market conditions) usually vary among the alternatives according to management's evaluation of market forecasts. The state of the economy also causes the probabilities to vary. When possible, the decision maker should use relevant and reliable evidence to improve the assignment of probabilities.

Assume the probabilities assigned are 30 percent each for an excellent or average environment and 40 percent for a poor environment. We find the resultant weighted payoff, called the **expected monetary value** (or simply **expected value**), by multiplying each possible payoff by its probability and adding the products, as shown in Exhibit 17–8. The higher the expected value, the more favorable the investment. The difference between the highest expected value and that of other alternatives represents an **opportunity gain** from investing in the most desirable alternative rather than the other alternatives. Given the estimated probabilities, the expected values indicate manufacturing exercise bikes maximizes profits. If managers chose this approach, $118,000 is lost from the manufacture of weight-lifting equipment; $78,000 from the physical improvements to golf clubs; and $48,500 from the advertising campaign.

Like all models, the expected monetary value criterion is logically oversimplified even though it is mathematically distinctive. Since the payoffs and the probabilities of success for various strategies are forecasts, they can be inaccurate. The probabilities of success are subject to management's bias and preference for one alternative over another. In addition, the expected value criterion does not consider risk. The model omits other important considerations or assumptions. For example, the model excludes psychological factors that may require an adjustment such as aversion to risky alternatives. The degree of risk that a company is willing to assume influences the alternative chosen. Management's preference for or aversion to risky alternatives may depend on how much it subjectively values the dollar amounts in Exhibit 17–8. For example, if a $100,000 loss in manufacturing exercise bikes would throw the company into bankruptcy or, less seriously, cut working capital considerably, management should be cautious and weigh the possible loss by a factor much larger than its relative probability. Under these circumstances, management may want to use a criterion other than expected value.

On the other hand, if the company needs income of at least $300,000 to satisfy a certain goal such as paying off a pressing debt, the decision maker may consider the production of only exercise bikes and weight-lifting equipment with the hope of operating in excellent environmental conditions. In this way, factors that affect the subjective worth of income or loss do influence the decision process.

Expected Value of Perfect Information

Even though the $140,000 expected value of manufacturing exercise bikes is highest in Exhibit 17–4, management and/or owners may resist exposure to the percentages involved in making a decision under risk. The probabilities of which environmental conditions will actually occur (for instance, a 30 percent probability of an excellent

---

EXHIBIT 17–8   Probability of the Payoffs of Alternative Actions

Alternatives	Excellent Environmental Conditions (Probability × Payoff)	Average Environmental Conditions (Probability × Payoff)	Poor Environmental Conditions (Probability × Payoff)	Expected Value
Physical improvements to golf clubs				
	.3 × $200,000 = $ 60,000	.3 × $ 80,000 = $24,000	.4 × −$ 15,000 = −$ 6,000	$78,000
Advertising campaign for golf clubs				
	.3 × $100,000 = $ 30,000	.3 × $ 75,000 = $22,500	.4 × −$ 10,000 = −$ 4,000	$48,500
Manufacture exercise bikes				
	.3 × $500,000 = $150,000	.3 × $100,000 = $30,000	.4 × −$100,000 = −$40,000	$140,000
Manufacture weight-lifting equipment				
	.3 × $300,000 = $ 90,000	.3 × $200,000 = $60,000	.4 × −$ 80,000 = −$32,000	$118,000

environment) are based on existing information. The company may hire a marketing consultant to obtain additional information on the environmental situation. The **expected value of perfect information** is the amount that the company is willing to pay for the marketing research team's errorless advice. If we assume the research team could indicate with certainty which condition would occur, the managers would decide with complete certainty. For example, if the research team tells management that an excellent environment will prevail, the company would manufacture exercise bikes and obtain a $500,000 payoff.

Of course, perfect information isn't perfect in the sense of absolute predictions. Thus, we identify the probabilities of each event or environmental condition. Assume that as before these probabilities are 30 percent each for an excellent or average environment and 40 percent for a poor environment. This allows the computation of the expected value with perfect information using the highest payoff for each given environment. The expected value of the decision with perfect information is the sum of the optimum outcome for each event multiplied by its probability as follows:

$$(.3 \times \$500,000) + (.3 \times \$200,000) + (.4 \times -\$10,000) = \$206,000$$

We then compare the expected values with perfect information and existing information to arrive at the following expected value of perfect information:

Expected value with perfect information	$206,000
Expected value with existing information	140,000
Expected value of perfect information	$ 66,000

In this example, $66,000 represents the upper limit that a decision maker would be willing to spend to reduce uncertainty. This amount is the maximum amount to spend for perfect information because in a real world, perfect forecasters are difficult to find.

Probabilities in Investigating Variances

Other types of decision making use probabilities. For example, Chapter 15 introduces the role of probability in determining the optimum level of safety stock. Managers can estimate the probability of running out of safety stock for various inventory levels and use this information to arrive at the expected stockout cost. As the units of safety stock and the resulting carrying cost increase, stockout cost decreases to a level at which total cost is at its lowest point.

Managers can use probabilities in deciding when to investigate variances from standards and budgets. As Chapter 13 emphasizes, accountants use the management-by-exception principle and investigate both significant favorable and unfavorable variances. The size of the variance may be a crucial factor in assessing the probabilities of deciding whether to investigate.

Expected Value of Investigation

When we use the payoff table format introduced earlier with the two possible conditions or states—being in control or being out of control—we have two alternatives available, investigating or not investigating. Assume management believes there is a 20 percent probability of a process being out of control; thus, there is an 80 percent chance of that process being in control. Managers estimate a $4,000 cost of investigation and an additional $5,000 cost of correction if, in fact, the process is out of control. However, if the process is out of control but the company takes no action, managers assume $18,000 is the present value of the extra costs over the relevant planning period. This planning period may be the time

EXHIBIT 17–9   Probability of the Payoffs of Alternative Actions of Investigating Variances

Alternatives	In Control	Out of Control	Expected Cost
Investigate variances	.8 × $4,000	.2 × $ 9,000	$5,000
Do not investigate variances	–0–	.2 × $18,000	3,600

EXHIBIT 17–10   Effect of Probabilities Assigned to Investigation

Alternatives	In Control	Out of Control	Expected Cost
Investigate variances	.6 × $4,000	.4 × $ 9,000	$6,000
Do not investigate variances	–0–	.4 × $18,000	7,200

until the company schedules a routine periodic inspection or the time until managers expect the process to go out of control again. This present value depends on expected future action.

As shown in Exhibit 17–9, the costs of investigation and correction are $9,000 ($4,000 inspection cost + $5,000 correction cost) if managers investigate the variance and find the process out of control. Thus, the company should not undertake the investigation because the expected value or costs of investigating are $1,400 more than not investigating the variances.

Changing Probabilities.   When the probability of the process being out of control is higher, the expected costs and benefits are affected, possibly resulting in a different optimal action. Assume, for instance, that the probability of being out of control is 40 percent as shown in Exhibit 17–10. At this higher probability of being out control of 40 percent, the expected cost of investigating is less than the cost of not investigating.

Point of Indifference.   Exhibits 17–9 and 17–10 show the optimal action depends on the probability of an out-of-control occurrence and the costs and benefits related to each alternative. Using the following formula, a **point of indifference** can be determined at which the expected cost of each alternative is the same.

Let:

p = Level of probability where alternatives are the same
I = Inspection cost
C = Correction cost
E = Extra cost of later actions

$$I(1 - p) + (I + C)p = Ep$$
$$I - Ip + Ip + Cp = Ep$$
$$I + Cp = Ep$$
$$I = Ep - Cp$$
$$p = \frac{I}{E - C}$$

Current Cost Management Practice

Five months after taking over as Eastman Kodak Co.'s CEO, George Fisher stunned outsiders by announcing that Kodak would auction off three big units, including the Sterling Drug Inc. operations. In a single stroke, Fisher repudiated the failed diversification strategy of his predecessors, shored up a debt-laden balance sheet, and underscored his commitment to Kodak's imaging business. Fisher's turnaround strategy is simple: Concentrate on wringing improved earnings from Kodak's core photography business. Further, the strategy includes building a future with digital technologies such as all-electronic cameras, thermal printers, and image-storage devices such as photo CDs. Also, any peripheral businesses, such as pharmaceuticals, should be sold. Fisher admits the strategy is not novel and agrees that "The difficulty is not knowing what to do, it's doing it." A key target has been employee moral, shattered by years of ineffectual restructurings and uncertainty. Fisher frequents the company cafeteria and sends hand-written notes to congratulate staffers for solid work.

Mark Maremont, "The New Flash at Kodak," *BusinessWeek*, May 16, 1994, p. 32.

Using the cost data from Exhibits 17–9 and 17–10 and substituting $I = \$4,000$, $C = \$5,000$, and $E = \$18,000$:

$$p = \frac{I}{E - C} = \frac{\$4,000}{\$18,000 - \$5,000} = .307$$

Thus, investigation is desirable only if the probability of being out of control exceeds 30 percent.

Summary

Accounting records and financial statements do not provide all of the costs that decision makers need. This is true because accounting records normally show only costs that have or will require an outlay of cash or its equivalent at a future date. Some decision-making costs, such as opportunity costs, do not involve cash outlays. Costs prepared for financial statement purposes thus may be of limited use when management is choosing between alternative courses of action. To be effective, accountants tailor costs to fit the specific problem and consider only relevant costs.

Relevant costs are generally those that respond to managerial decision making, but they vary with individual projects and the length of the project planning period. Differential costs should form the base for defensive decision making, with the objective of better utilizing existing facilities to increase profits or reduce loss. A cost study prepared for a make-or-buy decision merely indicates the direction of a decision. Other factors such as trade secrets, seasonal sales, production fluctuations, and the quality and design of the product are considerations.

Certainly, most managers are continually weighing alternatives. Managers must make decisions not only when problems exist but also when opportunities arise. In decision making, many managers try to incorporate a subjective evaluation of opportunity cost into the final decision. Many, however, fail to fully understand its significance and do not focus enough attention on the sacrifice of the profit that might have been made if an alternative decision were chosen.

The opportunity cost approach is primarily an economic concept that should be included only in internal cost analysis. Managers can apply opportunity cost when evaluating the relative economies of different methods of production, make-or-buy decisions, or proposals for investment of assets. As a rule, managers should not accept a potential investment unless the rate of return at least equals what they can earn from other investment alternatives in the same risk category. Assembling the outcomes of each alternative on a payoff table directs attention to the profit lost from rejected alternatives.

Important Terms and Concepts

Problem for Self-Study

Accept-Decline Bid

Lee Corporation faces the alternative of bringing in a construction crew to construct a storage building for the corporation on Lee's plant site or having it built by an outside contractor. The employees performing construction will be hired for this purpose only. Lee's bookkeeper obtained the following construction costs:

Building material and supplies		$25,000
Wages of employees performing construction		6,000
One-fourth of the plant superintendent wages (he estimates spending one-fourth of his time supervising building construction)		7,000
Depreciation on production machinery that was previously used in manufacturing:		
Straight-line basis	$10,000	
Machine-hour basis	15,000	25,000
General and administration—allocated share		2,000
Total construction cost		$65,000

Since the bookkeeper compared this $65,000 to the outside bid of $50,000, he advises the company to accept the bid.

Required:

Before making the final decision, management asks you to evaluate the situation and recommend what Lee Corporation should do.

Solution to Problem
for Self-Study

Lee Corporation		
Depreciation	$15,000	
Material	25,000	
Direct labor	6,000	
Total cost of building within organization		$46,000
Outside cost		50,000
Savings from building inside		$ 4,000

Note: There is support for excluding the machine-hour basis depreciation since it does not require a cash flow out. However, it is a differential cost.

Lee Corporation should construct the building itself and reap the savings of $4,000.

Review Questions

1. *a.* Comment on this statement: "All accounting information is relevant for some purpose."

   b. What are relevant costs, and why is the ability to determine relevant costs necessary in decision making?

2. In what type of business decision making would differential cost be more appropriate to use than full cost? What is an appropriate use of full cost?

3. Discuss the types of cost analysis that are important in internal decision making. Should you use the same cost for all decisions?

4. What is the objective in evaluating short-term projects?

5. Discuss the constraints on decision making and how their impact may alter the course of action taken. What is the relationship between time and planning?

6. Support your agreement or disagreement with the following statement: "If a plant has excess capacity everywhere, it can produce additional products for essentially raw material costs."

7. Explain if differential costs are composed only of variable costs.

8. Why may differential cost analysis not be appropriate for determining the asset value of the component parts manufactured rather than purchased?

9. What is the danger in using historical cost when a shift from making to buying is contemplated? What costs should be used instead?

10. Distinguish between escapable and nonescapable costs.

11. List four criticisms of using the expected monetary value criterion in decision making.

Exercises

Writing

E17–1 Costs for Decision Making
Decision makers often need a new set of cost data that is not provided by financial accounting:

Required:

a. Discuss the following terms as they relate to decision making:

   (1) Relevant cost

(2) Sunk cost

(3) Incremental cost or differential cost

(4) Marginal cost

(5) Escapable cost

(6) Opportunity cost

(7) Imputed cost

(8) Out-of-pocket cost

b. Suggest at least one type of decision in which the terms used in (2) through (8) would be appropriate.

E17–2 Make or Buy

Wickers, Inc., has been purchasing a part for $30 per unit. The cost of producing this part based on absorption costing is $34 computed as follows:

Direct material	$ 4
Direct labor	15
Factory overhead (100% of direct labor cost)	15
	$34

Since Wickers is presently operating with excess capacity, there is enough capacity to provide facilities to make the part with no increase in the total amount of fixed factory overhead costs. Variable overhead costs are estimated at 80 percent of direct labor costs.

Required:

Determine whether the part should be manufactured, indicating the unit cost savings from choosing the alternative you select.

E17–3 Determining Unit and Differential Cost of Various Capacity Levels

Paternal, Inc., owns a manufacturing plant that processes textiles. The variable costs including direct material and direct labor amount to $4 per yard. Fixed costs of operating the present facilities whose normal capacity is 30,000 yards amount to $120,000. Management is considering renting an additional building for $5,000 per period; it could process 2,500 yards per period. Other fixed costs associated with the rented building total $1,750.

Required:

Determine unit variable costs, unit fixed costs, average unit cost, total differential cost, and unit differential cost at these three capacity levels: 25,000 yards, 30,000 yards, and 32,500 yards. (Compare with preceding lower volume.)

E17–4 Accept-Reject Order

Siegel Company is considering manufacturing an order of 3,000 units for another company. Without the special order, the company had planned to produce 42,000 units of the product for a total cost of $168,000. If the special order is accepted, the unit cost of all units produced will decrease from $4.00 to $3.75.

The 42,000 units of regular production will be sold for $5 each; however, the other company is willing to pay only $3 per unit for the 3,000 units.

Required:

Prepare an analysis indicating the advantage or disadvantage if the company accepts the special order.

E17–5 Make-or-Buy Decision

Waters Company manufactures Part A for use in its production cycle. The costs per unit for 1,000 units of Part A are as follows:

Direct materials	$ 2
Direct labor	10
Variable overhead	3
Fixed overhead	6
	$21

Another company has offered to sell Waters 1,000 units of Part A. If Waters accepts this offer, the released facilities could be used to save $4,000 in relevant costs in the manufacture of Part B. In addition, $2 per unit of the fixed overhead applied to Part A would be totally eliminated.

Required:

Using the following three different purchase prices, determine if the company should manufacture Part A or buy the part and indicate by what amount the alternative is more desirable:

a. $16.
b. $20.
c. $23.

E17–6 Determining Capacity Level to Operate Using Unit and Differential Cost Analysis

The variable costs of Gretts Company including direct material and direct labor amount to $15 per hour with each unit requiring two hours of processing. Fixed costs of operating the present facilities whose normal capacity is 25,000 units amount to $500,000. Management is considering renting an additional building for $180,000 per period; it could process 5,000 units per period more than the normal capacity. Other fixed costs associated only with the rented building total $70,000.

Required:

a. Determine unit variable costs per hour, unit fixed costs per hour, average cost per hour, total differential cost, and differential cost per hour at these four capacity levels: 30,000 hours, 40,000 hours, 50,000 hours, and 60,000 hours. (Compare with preceding lower level.)
b. Which alternative would you advise? Explain the factors involved in your decision.

E17–7 Evaluating Alternative Investments

Irma McHood, manager of an office building, is considering putting certain concessions in the main lobby. An accounting study produces the following estimates, on an average annual basis.

Sales of merchandise	$55,000
Salaries	8,000
Licenses and payroll taxes	300
Beginning inventory	2,100
Purchases of merchandise	40,800
Ending inventory of merchandise	5,000
Share of heat, light, etc.	600
Pro rata building depreciation	1,200
Concession advertising	100
Share of company administrative expense	350

The investment in equipment, which would last 10 years, would be $30,000. As an alternative, a catering company has offered to lease the space at $3,050 per year for 10 years and to put in and operate the same concessions at no cost to the company. Heat and light are to be furnished by the office building at no additional charge. Assume the current market rate for interest is 8 percent.

Required:

What is your advice to the company? Support your calculations.

E17–8 Calculating Unit and Total Differential Costs

Case Manufacturing Company establishes the following standard specification based on a normal capacity of 10,000 units:

	Standard Specification per Unit
Direct material (variable)	$ 3.50
Direct labor (variable)	2.60
Variable factory overhead	1.50
Fixed factory overhead	3.00
	$10.60

Management believes the present manufacturing facilities are adequate to produce a maximum of 11,000 units. If they produce additional units, they must acquire additional plant space and equipment at an annual cost of $6,000 and employ additional supervisors at a cost of $5,000.

If its volume is larger than 10,000 units, the company can take a 5 percent quantity discount on direct materials because of the increased purchases. Management hesitates to produce more than 10,000 units in the present factory because the additional direct labor workers required would be eligible for a 5 percent night-shift differential pay. Management plans to employ only one day shift in the new factory producing 1,000 units.

Required:

a. Prepare flexible budgets for volume levels of 9,000, 10,000, 11,000, and 12,000 units.
b. Calculate average unit cost, broken down into unit variable and unit fixed costs. (Carry to three decimal places.)
c. Calculate total differential cost, comparing with the preceding lower volume.
d. Calculate unit differential cost.
e. Advise management about which alternative to choose.

E17–9 Deciding When to Investigate Variances

As manager of Dufour, Inc., you receive a report indicating a $20,000 unfavorable labor efficiency variance for the past week's operations. You estimate the probability of the process being out of control at .40 and the cost to investigate at $1,000. If the process is out of control, the cost to correct the error is estimated to be $2,000 in addition to the $1,000 cost of investigating. Further, if you do not investigate and the process is out of control, the present value of future unfavorable variances that would be saved by making the necessary changes if the process is operating improperly is $7,600.

Required:

a. Use the expected cost of investigation and no investigation as the basis for your decision. Should the process be investigated?
b. Determine the level of probability that the process is out of control where the expected costs of each action would be the same.
c. Explain why the present value of the cost savings over the planning period ($7,600 in this case) is not equal to the unfavorable variance ($20,000 in this case).

E17–10 Accepting a Single Order

Schmidt Production Company signs a five-year lease on a building in which to manufacture large decorated flowerpots. At the beginning of the lease, management purchases a machine costing $9,000 that mixes the clay and other ingredients. The machine has a life of 10 years and can be economically removed from the building. Schmidt expects the salvage value to be $1,000 at the end of 10 years and uses double-declining-balance depreciation.

Schmidt also purchased a molding machine costing $37,500. Engineers estimate that the machine can mold 7,500 pots per year for eight years. The molding machine cannot be removed from the manufacturing facilities without incurring more expense than the machine is worth. The productive-output method of depreciation is used.

During the first year of operations, Schmidt produced 5,000 pots and sold 4,800 pots for a total sales revenue of $24,000. Costs per flowerpot exclusive of depreciation were as follows:

Direct material	$1.40
Direct labor	0.80
Variable factory overhead	0.15
Fixed factory overhead	0.24

Required:

a. Calculate the total cost per flowerpot for the first year of operations.
b. Assume that early in the second year of operations, a European buyer approaches the company wanting to buy a single order of 2,000 flowerpots for a unit sales price of $3.85. The company estimates that it will cost $0.10 per flowerpot to ship the order. The company believes that the annual domestic market for flowerpots will become saturated above a 5,000-unit level. Management does not believe accepting this order will affect the domestic sales price, nor will the company face difficulty in securing the material and labor necessary to fill the foreign order. What would you advise management to do?

Problems

P17–11 Unit and Total Differential Cost

The president of the King Company has asked you, the company's accountant, to advise him concerning several alternatives. King Company presently rents a building to house its processing plant. The landlord does not plan to raise rent from $1,000 per month. These facilities are presently being used with one work shift to manufacture 5,000 units monthly. The following sales price and unit cost have been determined based on a 5,000-unit normal capacity:

	Per unit
Sales price	$35.00
Direct material	$10.00
Direct labor	8.00
Variable factory overhead	5.00
Fixed factory overhead (including rent)	4.20
	$27.20

The president is considering the following alternatives and wants you to provide cost studies for each:

1. Renew the lease on the present building but increase to two work shifts. Management would produce 5,000 units on the day shift and 3,000 units on the night shift. Night-shift workers would get a shift differential causing a $0.10 per unit cost increase for units produced on the night shift. Because a larger quantity of raw material would be purchased, the company can take an 8 percent quantity discount. However, to sell this larger volume, the sales price must be lowered to $33. No additional machinery would be required.

2. A smaller building nearby is available for a monthly rent of $850. However, King Company must purchase additional machinery costing $960 that would be depreciated over four years with no salvage value. Other fixed factory overhead would amount to $17,000 monthly. Unit variable factory overhead would be $5.20. Two shifts would produce 4,000 units each. The night-shift differential presented in Alternative 1 would be used. The material quantity discount also would be available; a $33 sales price would be in effect.

Required:

Determine the following on a monthly basis for present conditions and for each of the two alternatives presented:
a. Income before taxes.
b. Average unit cost, broken down into variable and fixed components.
c. Total differential cost compared to present operations.
d. Unit differential cost compared to present operations.

P17–12 Eliminating a Product Line

Wallace Company furnished the following recent operating statement for its three product lines, A, B, and C:

	A	B	C	Total
Sales	$300,000	$260,000	$190,000	$750,000
Variable costs and expenses	$180,000	$160,000	$133,000	$473,000
Fixed expenses				
Salaries of product line supervisor	25,000	80,000	20,000	125,000
Marketing costs allocated to product				
lines on basis of sales	9,000	8,000	3,000	20,000
Administrative costs allocated equally .	20,000	20,000	20,000	60,000
Total costs and expenses	$234,000	$268,000	$176,000	$678,000
Operating income (loss)	$ 66,000	$(8,000)	$ 14,000	$ 72,000

Management is considering discontinuing Product B operations. If they discontinue Product B operations, managers expect Product A sales to increase 20 percent and Product C sales to increase 25 percent. No increase in fixed costs is projected as a result of the increased sales of Product A. However, the salaries of Product C's product line supervisors will increase 10 percent due to the increased sales. No increase in total assets required is expected. Assets used in Product B operations can be sold at book value. Product B supervisors will be laid off with no termination pay.

Required:

a. Prepare a projected operating statement based on the assumption that Product B operations are discontinued.
b. List other factors to consider before making the decision to eliminate Product B.

SPATS

P17–13 Evaluating Alternatives

The Freeman Company produces three different products, U–1, U–2, and U–3. All fixed costs are allocated as follows: fixed cost of units sold according to various allocation bases, such as square footage for factory rent and machine-hours for repairs; fixed general and administrative expenses based on a percentage of revenues.

These pro forma income statements by product line are for next year:

	U-1	U-2	U-3	Total
Sales (units)	20,000	400,000	200,000	620,000
Revenue	$1,000,000	$800,000	$650,000	$2,450,000
Variable cost of units sold	$ 200,000	$250,000	$175,000	$ 625,000
Fixed cost of units sold	350,000	325,000	200,000	875,000
Gross margin	$ 450,000	$225,000	$275,000	$ 950,000
Variable general and administrative expenses	175,000	200,000	52,500	427,500
Fixed general and administrative expenses	120,000	96,000	78,000	294,000
Income (loss) before taxes	$ 155,000	$(71,000)	$144,500	$ 228,500

Because management is concerned about the loss for U–2, it has taken under advisement two alternative courses of action, either of which should remedy the situation:

First alternative—discontinue producing U–2. This will have several effects. Some of the machinery used in the production of U–2 can be sold at scrap value. The proceeds will just cover the removal costs. Without this machinery, however, fixed costs allocated to U–2 will be reduced by $55,000 a year. The remaining fixed costs allocated to U–2 include $130,000 annual rent expense. The space used for production of U–2 can be rented to another firm for $135,000 annually. The selling price of U–1 and U–3 will remain constant. U–3 production and revenues should increase by 30 percent.

Second alternative—purchase some new machinery for the production of U-2. This will require an initial cash outlay of $500,000. The new machinery will reduce total variable costs (cost of units sold and general and administrative expenses) for U–2 to 50 percent of revenues. Total fixed costs allocated to U–2 will increase to $450,000. No additional fixed costs will be allocated to U–1 and U–3.

Required:

Analyze the effects of each alternative on total projected income before taxes.

P17–14 Relevant Costs for Make-or-Buy Decision

Cash Enterprises established the following standard cost for two component parts it uses in processing:

	A	B
Direct material	$ 4.00	$ 3.70
Direct labor	3.50	3.00
Factory overhead:		
Variable	2.00	1.80
Fixed	2.70	3.90
Total	$12.20	$12.40

The company has been producing the 5,000 units of A and 9,000 units of B needed annually. However, a recent flood destroyed part of the building in which workers manufactured parts. As a result, Cash Enterprises can devote only 41,000 hours of otherwise idle machine-hours to the production of these two parts. An outside company offers to supply a comparable quality of parts at $15 for A and $13 for B. Management wants to schedule the 41,000 available machine-hours so the company realizes maximum potential cost savings. Each unit of A requires six machine-hours, while B requires five and one-half machine-hours.

Required:

a. Determine the costs relevant to the make-or-buy decision on a unit cost basis.
b. To meet the company's current needs, determine the number of units of A and B that Cash must produce, assuming they base the allocation of machine time on potential cost savings per machine-hour.

Critical Thought

P17–15 Accept-Reject Bid

Management of the Maybe Company was quite upset when receiving the following income statement for the first six months of the year:

MAYBE COMPANY
Income Statement
For the Six-Month Period Ended June 30, 19X1

Sales (15,000 units @ $70)		$1,050,000
Cost of sales:		
Material (15,000 units @ $25.10)	$376,500	
Labor (15,000 units @ $10.15)	152,250	
Factory overhead—variable (15,000 units @ $16)	240,000	
Factory overhead ($600,000 × ½)	300,000	
Marketing expense—fixed (at $12,000 per month)	72,000	1,140,750
Loss		$ (90,750)

The production cost for the company's single product, which normally sells for $70, is as follows:

Direct material	$25.10 per unit
Direct labor	10.15 per unit
Factory overhead—variable	16.00 per unit
Factory overhead—fixed ($600,000 for the year applied to production on the basis of 50,000 units of production for the year)	12.00 per unit
	$63.25 per unit

Managers are not optimistic that sales for the last half of the year will improve; in fact, they expect sales to be significantly below the initial forecast of 50,000 units which the production plant can handle.

In July the president received a letter from a governmental agency inviting the company to bid on a contract for 10,000 units of Material 1R–15, which is similar to the product Maybe now produces. The agency will entertain a bid not to exceed $53 per unit to be completed within six months. The letter assures the company that the submission of such a bid in no way obligates or binds the company in bidding for similar government contracts in the future.

In studying the requirements of Material 1R–15, the engineering department believes that $4,000 of outside designing and drafting time will be required. However, since the same type of material and labor will be needed as for the present product, no additional machinery need be purchased. Material 1R–15 is expected to take slightly less material than the present product; on the other hand, it will require a higher quality material, which will result in more spoilage than experienced on the present product. These factors will offset each other. They expect no change in the amount of labor required for the present product. Because of the existing idle capacity, management expects to complete the contract without overtime work.

Required:

a. Prepare an analysis management can use to decide if the bid should be entered.

b. Assuming sales stay at the same level for the remainder of the year, prepare statements of income for the entire year comparing the results if the government contract is not processed with those if it is processed.

SPATS

P17–16 Payoff Table and Expected Value of Perfect Information

At year-end, the Bradshaw Company is pleased to find that it has $1 million cash not needed for operations. After investigating available strategies, management has determined that the following alternatives are practical:

1. Purchase machinery and equipment to manufacture Product A, whose operations are expected to yield $100,000 income if excellent environmental conditions exist, $60,000 income in average conditions, and a $40,000 loss in poor conditions.

2. Purchase different machinery that can manufacture Product B, whose operations will result in a $300,000 income if excellent environmental conditions exist, $100,000 income in average conditions, and a $30,000 loss in poor conditions.

3. Purchase machinery to manufacture Product C, whose operations are expected to yield $120,000 income in excellent market conditions, $75,000 income in average conditions, and a $10,000 loss in poor conditions.

The current assessment of the probabilities for each environmental condition are excellent, 30 percent; average, 20 percent; and poor, 50 percent.

Required:

a. Prepare a payoff table for the alternative actions.

b. Calculate the opportunity cost of alternative actions for each environmental condition.

c. Determine the expected value for each alternative action.

d. Calculate how much the company should be willing to pay for perfect advance information as a consultant can be hired to study the situation.

P17–17 Differential and Opportunity Costs of Taking an Additional Order

Jean Company builds regular and deluxe truck oil filters. A customer has asked whether the company could produce 2,000 super filters. Because managers believe that this may be a one-time order, they do not wish to expand plant facilities. Instead, they have evaluated the requirements of the super filter and find that if they cut regular filter production by one-fourth and deluxe filters by one-third, the super filter order can be completed in one year.

The customer has agreed to pay $12 for each super filter at the end of the year when the entire order is completed. The engineering staff of Jean estimates that the direct material cost will be $5 per unit and the direct labor cost will be $3 per unit. In addition to using the machines presently located in the regular and deluxe facilities, super filter production will require a special machine costing $5,000. Management expects to be able to sell the machine after one year for $2,400. Cash will be required initially for the purchase. Jean management expects to sell an investment currently earning 10 percent interest to provide these funds. The special machine purchased for super filter production will require $515 annual power expense in addition to the power required for the regular and deluxe filter machines that will be devoted to super filter production.

Rent and other utilities, heating and lighting, are allocated on the basis of floor space. The accountant furnishes you with this portion of last year's financial statements:

	Regular	Deluxe
Sales	$8,000	$6,000
Direct material	$2,400	$1,500
Direct labor	1,600	900
Factory overhead:		
Indirect labor	300	150
Depreciation	500	450
Power	400	600
Rent	200	60
Other utilities	552	90
Total expenses	$5,952	$3,750
Operating income	$2,048	$2,250

Required:

a. Calculate the net differential cost of the order for 2,000 super filters.
b. Determine the opportunity cost of taking the order.
c. Compute the full cost of the super filter order.
d. Decide if Jean Company should accept the order. Support your decision with quantitative as well as qualitative findings.

P17-18 Make-or-Buy Decision

The Marketing Research Department of the Chester Company has developed a unique idea that will appeal to children. They are presently packaging their chewing gum in a simple paper wrapper in a stick form. They are considering processing the gum in individual balls and placing them in a decorated plastic bank. A child desiring a gum ball must deposit a nickel in the bank.

The company could make the plastic banks in the present facilities by converting a machine to process the banks. The machine cost $100,000 and is being depreciated on a straight-line basis over a five-year period. The only other fixed costs to be allocated to the production of chewing gum and banks will be $10,000, which represents a portion of the company's present fixed costs.

The cost accounting department estimates the company can sell 100,000 banks if they are placed on the market before the Christmas season begins. Accountants developed estimates of the costs, including chewing gum and the banks, as follows:

Direct material	$1.25
Direct labor	0.80
Total overhead*	$0.90
	$2.95

*The overhead does include the machine's depreciation and allocated fixed costs.

A plastic specialties company has approached the Chester Company and offered to supply the banks for $0.40 per unit. Based on their study, Chester believes that if it buys the banks and merely puts gum balls in them, the firm can cut its direct material cost by 6 percent, variable overhead by 15 percent, and direct labor by 25 percent.

Required:

a. Determine if Chester Company should purchase the plastic banks or manufacture them in their own facilities. Support your answer with cost data.

b. Assume that after the marketing department conducts more extensive tests, they believe that since they will be able to sell the banks through a variety of distribution channels, 150,000 banks can be sold. The company's present facilities will not be able to exceed the production of 100,000 banks. The company must rent a nearby empty building for $20,000 and equipment for $6,300 to handle the extra production. How would you advise management to obtain the plastic banks under these conditions?

c. List the qualitative factors you would advise the company to consider before making a decision.

Critical Thought

SPATS

P17–19 Capacity Issues; Acceptance of Order

Elizah Corporation manufactures only one product; its budget for the following year is

ELIZAH CORPORATION
Budgeted Income Statement
For the Year Ended December 31, 19X1

Sales (270,000 units of LX7 @ $67 per unit)		$18,090,000
Variable costs and expenses:		
Direct material (LX material, 6 pounds per unit		
@ $1.25 per pound)	$2,025,000	
Direct labor (8 hours per unit @ $4.45 per hour)	9,612,000	
Manufacturing overhead (30% of direct labor cost)	2,883,600	
Marketing and administrative expense ($1.22 per unit)	329,400	14,850,000
Contribution margin		$ 3,240,000
Fixed expenses		1,049,000
Income before tax		$ 2,191,000

Required:

Consider each part independent of the others.

a. Compute the income if actual sales in 19X1 are 10 percent less than the budgeted figure.

b. Calculate the income if actual sales in 19X1 are 15 percent more than the budgeted figure.

c. Assume that the existing capacity is sufficient to handle the transaction. What cost per unit would the company incur if it made additional sales beyond the budgeted figure?

d. Assume the beginning inventory of LX7 is 45,000 units; the company wants to have an ending inventory of 50,000 units. How many LX7 units must be produced this year according to the budget? Based on this production level, how many pounds of LX material must be acquired, assuming management wants to have 15,000 pounds in ending inventory and beginning inventory of LX material is 12,000 pounds?

e. Assume Elizah Corporation is operating at capacity when it sells 270,000 units of LX7. The company receives an additional order for 25,000 units of LX7 at a sales price of $59 per unit. If the firm accepts the order, it will incur an additional $91,000 of fixed expense. If the only criterion in this decision is the impact on income, should the order be accepted? Support your conclusion by showing the change in income.

P17–20 Differential Cost and Cash Flow Analysis in Make-or-Buy Decision

Jeffrey, Inc., a manufacturer of mopeds, is trying to decide whether to continue manufacturing its own engine units or to purchase them from an outside supplier. Bids have been taken, and a unit that meets all specifications costs $35 each. Jeffrey needs 12,000 units a year.

The Fabricating Department makes all of the engine parts. The unit is completed by direct labor in the Finishing Department and then is installed in the moped by the Assembly Department.

The Fabricating Department is used 25 percent for the production of the engine parts; however, phasing out this segment will reduce the labor, utilities, and supplies allocated to the engine units. Last year's records show the following information for the Fabricating Department for 12,000 units:

	Total Costs	Allocation to Engine Units
Direct materials	$1,200,000	$125,000
Direct labor	700,000	160,000
Indirect labor	90,000	30,000
Utilities	24,000	6,000
Depreciation	25,000	6,250
Property taxes and insurance	32,000	8,000
Miscellaneous supplies	18,000	2,000

The Finishing Department incurred $60,000 of direct labor costs on the engine units. The basis for overhead allocation in the Finishing Department is 25 percent of direct labor cost. If the engine units are not manufactured, the direct labor cost in the Finishing Department will be eliminated.

Machinery can be sold at its book value of $50,000 and the proceeds invested to yield 10 percent. The machinery has a remaining useful life of eight years with no estimated salvage value. Sale of the machinery will reduce property taxes and insurance by $2,000 a year. Purchasing the units will result in shipping costs of $2 a unit, and receiving, handling, and inspection costs of $6,000 annually.

Required:

a. Compare the total annual differential cost of engine units, if they are manufactured, to their annual cost if purchased. Ignore income taxes.
b. Assume that the annual cost of engine units if manufactured or purchased was $425,000 each, without regard to your answer in Requirement *a*. Compute the annual net cash flow (ignoring income taxes) if:
   (1) Engine units are manufactured.
   (2) Engine units are purchased.
c. Explain the working capital requirements that should be considered in deciding whether to make or buy.

P17–21 Escapable/Nonescapable Cost

Ledbetter Company maintains its home office in Chicago and leases a plant and office facilities in each of its three territories. All plants manufacture the company's single product; however, there is some variation in the production process at each plant. Management supplies you with the following data concerning last year's operations:

	Western Territory	Northern Territory	Eastern Territory
Sales ($20 per unit)	$400,000	$360,000	$200,000
Variable costs:			
Material	$120,000	$126,000	$ 70,000
Labor	40,000	36,000	30,000
Factory overhead	10,000	10,800	60,000
Direct fixed costs:			
Factory overhead	60,000	80,000	20,000
Marketing	70,000	37,000	10,000
Administrative	40,000	30,000	12,000
Allocated home office expense	20,000	18,000	10,000
Total	$360,000	$337,800	$212,000
Income from operations	$ 40,000	$ 22,200	$ (12,000)

Home office expense is allocated on the basis of sales dollars. The company is undecided over whether certain territory operations should be expanded or reduced. Because of the unprofitable operations in the Eastern Territory, management is considering closing the plant facilities there. There are two alternatives available to continue serving the Eastern Territory customers. One is to enter into a contract with an outside plant that will pay Ledbetter Company a commission of 8 percent of sales price. The outside plant plans to increase the sales price to $22 even though their marketing research department believes that the higher price will cause them to sell 20 percent fewer units. The other alternative is that the western plant can be expanded to absorb the units presently produced by the eastern facilities. An additional production supervisor earning $22,000 and a marketing manager earning $25,000 will be required. There will be additional shipping and selling costs of $4 per unit on the increased production.

Required:

a. Prepare a schedule showing the company's total income:
   (1) If they enter into the commission agreement.
   (2) If the western plant is expanded.
b. Discuss briefly some other factors Ledbetter should investigate before entering either agreement.

Case

Writing

C17–22 Differential Margin under Various Volumes in a Nonprofit Organization

Harry Moss, administrator of Las Vegas General Hospital, requests your assistance in preparing a cost analysis for a proposed addition to the telemetry unit. The hospital presently has 10 telemetry units in operation on a 40-bed floor. A telemetry unit monitors patients who had heart attacks or have cardiac problems. This unit allows a patient to move about freely in that particular hospital wing without being confined to a hospital bed. A radio-controlled device attached to the patient monitors the cardiac system. The present 10-unit telemetry monitoring system is located in the nursing station that can accommodate the proposed 8 additional units without renovation.

Telemetry units represent a step down in the level of care from cardiac intensive care rooms. Telemetry units not only offer patients more freedom but also offer a considerable cost saving. Cardiac care rooms average $300 per day, while the telemetry unit charge is the regular room charge of $120 plus an additional $80 to $120 daily.

Expected revenue. Hospital management is undecided whether to charge a $80 or $120 differential a day for the proposed unit. Also, there is lack of consensus among the managers regarding the rate of utilization. The expected range is from 40 to 60 percent. A 10 percent allowance for bad debts and insurance discount is estimated.

Expected cost. Space for the unit will be obtained by converting a wing of the hospital presently being used for medical-surgical patients; the regular room rate is charged for this wing. The equipment's total cost is expected to be $44,570; the life is estimated to be only five years due to technological changes. Straight-line depreciation will be used.

The administrator indicates that you are to determine total cost for the five-year period for each cost element and then divide by five years to obtain an average for the five-year period.

Service contract costs for routine maintenance and service call costs for overtime, labor, and parts are expected to be $3,060 and $2,400 respectively in Year 2, with an increase of 10 percent per year thereafter for inflation; no such costs are expected for Year 1 since the equipment will be under warranty during this time. Costs of supplies will be $2,800 for the first year, with a 12 percent annual increase thereafter due to inflation and aging of the equipment. One registered nurse earning $25,000 annually, and two licensed practical nurses, each earning $17,000 annually, will staff the eight-bed unit. Personnel cost in the hospital industry has increased 8 percent annually in the last few years. For simplicity, assume the service contract, service call, supplies, and personnel costs are fixed, unaffected by changes in volume.

Required:

a. Determine differential margin that will be received and the annual percentage return on equipment using a:
   (1) $ 80 charge per day and a 40 percent use rate.
   (2) $ 80 charge per day and a 50 percent use rate.
   (3) $ 80 charge per day and a 60 percent use rate.
   (4) $120 charge per day and a 40 percent use rate.
   (5) $120 charge per day and a 60 percent use rate.
b. Advise management as to the alternative to choose.
c. List other factors that should be considered before installation of the unit.

CHAPTER

18

Performance Evaluation and Segment Analysis

Chapter Objectives

After studying this chapter, you should be able to:

1. Explain the conceptual framework for measuring and evaluating segment performance.

2. Discuss the advantages and disadvantages of the various degrees of decentralization.

3. Analyze segment performance using contribution margin, segment margin, ROI, and residual income.

4. Explain how short-term performance measures have many weaknesses, such as rewarding undesirable behavior.

5. Discuss the advantage of using multiple performance measures that include nonfinancial evaluations.

Productivity

Current Cost Management Practice

S.C. Johnson & Son has long profited by sticking to the have-a-nice-niche school of marketing, using strong research and development, and heavy advertising. Since consumers continue to buy such Johnson Wax products as Pledge furniture polish, Glade air freshener, and Raid bug spray, these products are not highly sensitive to price competition. Their products command fat premiums while still repelling private-label incursion. After buying Drackett Co. from Bristol-Myers Squibb, Johnson Wax found itself competing against such heavyweights as Procter & Gamble Company and Clorox Company. But Johnson has been training for the big leagues for years by overhauling factories, consolidating international operations, and recasting itself more clearly as a provider of products that clean, shine, and debug the home. They are more focused, using their resources where they have a better chance of success. Self-directed work teams are replacing check-your-brains-at-the-door assembly lines. In the past employees were not involved in decisions, now they are finding it is amazing how many different ways people try to save money.

Ronald Henkoff, "When to Take on the Giants," *Forbes,* May 30, 1994, pp. 111–14.

Introduction

Many companies recently have expanded their activities into different markets, foreign countries, and various industries. The resulting size and complexity of these companies make it urgent that their operations be decentralized. This creation of various company segments, in turn, requires that accountants provide some measure of each segment's level of efficiency. Accountants recognize they should design manufacturing cost and control systems for the needs of production and line management. Cost accountants are developing new performance measures causing executives to emphasize long-range rather than short-range results. Further, these measures recognize that profits are earned when the sale of goods occurs, not when they are produced.

Accountants expect their measurements to change in the future due to extensive automation that has created the need for measurement and control points. New performance measures will focus on optimizing an organization's performance globally, not locally. As labor cost and productivity become less relevant, firms will implement measurement systems that help product line managers monitor raw materials. Managers need these systems because raw material will be one of the major variable costs in the factory of the future. Future accounting measures will also motivate managers to look beyond segmental interest to organizational cost reduction and profit improvement.

Responsibility Accounting

Responsibility accounting involves using accounting to evaluate performance. Variance analysis and budgeting, as discussed in Chapters 10 through 13, comprise part of the responsibility accounting process. These systems accumulate costs by **responsibility centers** to evaluate their effectiveness.

Responsibility
Centers

Cost centers are the smallest areas of responsibility for which accountants accumulate costs. A cost center is a segment responsible only for costs; it may be a department or a grouping within a department. At a somewhat higher level, the branch or territory manager's cost center is the entire segment for which he or she is responsible. The chief operating executive's cost center is the entire company, because he or she performs certain duties of the overall company. Thus, every operating cost is traceable to a responsibility center, whether that center makes a product or not.

The classification of costs by cost centers should follow a company's responsibility accounting system. Costs should be accumulated following lines of responsibility and authority within an organization. Thus, accountants consider the organization chart and chart of accounts as the basic framework of the responsibility accounting system. The organization chart defines functional responsibility for each manager. Accountants should design a chart of accounts around cost centers to establish proper accountability for costs. After assigning costs to cost centers, managers set the budget for each output level.

Some companies find it more profitable to establish profit centers which allows managers to control or influence revenues as well as costs. Changing from a cost center to a profit center may make managers more concerned with finding ways to increase the center's revenue by expanding production or improving distribution methods. A **profit center** is accountable for both revenues and costs. Accountants should base the performance measure for a profit center on controllable revenues and expenses that are matched to determine the segment's income. A profit center, however, must have the authority to earn revenue and incur costs.

Some companies go one step further and establish **investment centers.** Investment center managers are responsible for the expenses, profits, and assets of their center. In evaluating performance, accountants relate investment center income to the invested capital in each segment to determine the return on investment.

Principal-Agent
Relationships

Many companies fail to distinguish between controllable and noncontrollable costs in performance evaluation. They base managers' bonuses and other rewards on income figures that contain some uncontrollable elements. According to **agency theory, principal-agent relationships** are found when authority is decentralized. A principal delegates duties to a subordinate, called an *agent.* Corporate managers represent principals; segment managers represent agents. Principals use accounting information to evaluate agents' performances and as a basis for employee bonuses and commissions. As discussed in the next chapter, agents sometimes act only in their own best interests, to the detriment of their companies.

Degree of Decentralization

As companies grow larger and more diverse, they generally divide into several segments or divisions. Each segment becomes a separately identifiable center of operating activity and managerial responsibility. The degree of autonomy enjoyed by these segments varies because some companies establish tightly defined policies for segment managers. Other companies give their segment managers flexibility and hold them responsible only for the broad task of operating efficiently and profitably. This degree of autonomy reflects the extent of a company's decentralization. The more autonomous each segment, the more decentralized the company is as a whole.

A company's human relations philosophy also influences its degree of decentralization. When a company adopts a behavioral science approach, it is likely to decentralize operations.

At one extreme is **total decentralization**, in which managers operate under minimum constraints and have maximum freedom because there is a lack of central authority. At the other extreme is **total centralization**, in which division managers have limited authority because top management maintains tight constraints. Few companies use either of these extremes. Absolute centralization is rarely effective because large volumes of decisions are difficult to administer at the top management level. On the other hand, absolute decentralization is rarely practical because each division may focus only on its own operations, disregarding companywide goals.

Not All Profit Centers Are Decentralized.   Accounting and management literature often spreads the misconception that the profit center concept is synonymous with a decentralized subunit. However, not all profit centers have the freedom to make most of their decisions. A highly centralized organization could have many segments called profit centers, but the segment managers may have little autonomy in decision making. These segment managers may need corporate approval before buying or selling to outsiders or purchasing capital assets over a set amount, say, $5,000. Corporate staff closely monitor segment managers in highly centralized organizations. Conversely, in other companies, managers of cost centers have more latitude in making decisions affecting their divisions. Thus, the terms *profit center* and *cost center* may provide no accurate gauge about the degree of decentralization.

Advantages of Decentralization

Because decentralization has various degrees, management should determine which arrangement best meets their needs. Decentralization offers the following advantages:

1. Frees top management from daily operating problems so they can direct their attention to strategic planning.
2. Allows decision making as near as possible to the scene of action. This encourages teamwork among all executives, each skilled in his or her own area.
3. Results in more accurate, timely decisions because segment managers are more familiar than top management with local conditions.
4. Provides training in decision making for segment managers so they are better prepared to advance in the organizational hierarchy.
5. Offers stimulus for more efficient performance because decentralization gives managers authority to match their responsibility.
6. Eliminates unprofitable activities more rapidly since, for example, decentralization may give managers authority to purchase direct materials from outside parties rather than force them to buy from one of the company's segments.
7. Encourages each segment manager to look for outside markets for the division's products.

Disadvantages of Decentralization

Although the preceding advantages should lead to profits greater than those in a more heavily centralized organization, we cannot ignore the costs associated with decentralization. One of decentralization's greatest threats comes from the barriers it presents to goal congruence. The goals of the individual segments of a decentralized company may not be in harmony with overall company goals. Decentralization encourages segment managers to focus attention on local operating conditions. Decentralization fails to fully emphasize the contribution that each segment should make to the profitability of the overall company. In addition, because decision making is decentralized, there may be little communication among segment managers. As a result, decentralization may require a more elaborate and effective information system, which can be expensive.

Traditional Methods for Evaluating Segment Performance

Regardless of the degree of decentralization, top management needs a dependable method of measuring segment performance. We define the term **segment** in various ways. Generally, a segment refers to any logical subcomponent of a company, identified with the responsibility of supplying a product or service. Some companies formally designate distinct organization subcomponents, such as divisions, as their segments. An example is the Truck and Coach Division of General Motors Corporation. Other companies designate territories, departments, service centers, or branch offices as segments.

In analyzing marketing operations, we also find other types of segments, such as product lines, classes of customer, or channels of distribution. Although segments are not separate organizational entities, an important characteristic is that their operating performance is separately identifiable and measurable. Products or services may be related based on similar characteristics such as rates of profitability, degrees of risk, or opportunities for growth. Or products may be related based on similar production processes, labor skills, or marketing methods.

Contribution Reporting

Determining cost behavior patterns provides a helpful starting point in evaluating segment performance. Exhibit 18–1 uses **contribution reporting** to present a condensed profitability analysis of two territories. (In practice, companies detail the expenses thoroughly.) Exhibit 18–1 illustrates two kinds of segments: territories and salespersons; each territory has two salespersons. As you read across Exhibit 18–1, the focus becomes narrower, going from the overall company, to the East and West Territories, and then to the salespersons in each territory.

Contribution Margin.   Deducting only segment variable costs from segment revenue yields a **contribution margin** that companies use to evaluate segments. We can usually determine each segment's revenue and variable costs directly because they are identifiable with a specific segment. (This chapter assumes no intersegment sales; Chapter 19 discusses pricing of intersegment sales.) Contribution margin is useful in understanding the impact on income of short-run volume changes. We calculate changes in income by multiplying any sales increase by the contribution margin ratio. For example, the increase in pretax income resulting from a $10,000 increase in Mr. A's sales volume is 46% × $10,000, or $4,600. If Ms. D also earns a similar $10,000 sales volume increase, pretax income increases 48.5% × $10,000, or $4,850. These calculations of contribution margin assume no change in sales price, operating efficiency, or fixed costs.

Segment Margin

The best contribution reporting method for evaluating segments is segment margin. **Segment margin** reflects each segment's contribution to indirect expenses and to the income of the company as a whole. Segment margin represents what remains after subtracting both the direct, or traceable, variable and fixed costs from each segment's revenue. Traceable expenses include both fixed and variable expenses, with the larger part composed of variable expenses. Examples of traceable variable costs include salaries earned by those employees who devote their efforts strictly to the segment and material and supplies used for the segment. If a company discontinues a segment, it would eliminate these traceable, or direct, expenses. Nonvariable costs traceable to the segment include depreciation, rent, and insurance on plant assets used by the individual territories and salespeople. For performance measurement, accountants do not allocate **nontraceable costs** that benefit more than one segment.

As shown in Exhibit 18–1, the East Territory has a much more favorable operating performance, because of its larger segment margin. The segment margins generated by Mr. A and Ms. D also are greater than the performances of the other two salespersons.

EXHIBIT 18-1

DOUGLASS COMPANY
Contribution Analysis for Territories and Salespeople
For Period Ending 19X1
($ thousands)

	Company Totals	East	West	Mr. A	Ms. B	Mr. C	Ms. D
		Territory		East Territory		West Territory	
Sales	$500	$300	$200	$175.0	$125.0	$70	$130
Less: Variable production expense	200	140	60	80.0	60.0	25	35
Variable marketing and administrative expenses	80	25	55	14.5	10.5	23	32
Total variable expenses	280	165	115	94.5	70.5	48	67
Contribution margin	$220	$135	$ 85	$ 80.5	$ 54.5	$22	$ 63
Contribution margin as a percent of sales	44%	45%	42.5%	46%	43.6%	31.4%	48.5%
Less: Fixed costs traceable to segments	130	69	61	33.5	35.5	18	43
Segment margin	$ 90	$ 66	$ 24	$ 47	$ 19.0	$ 4	$ 20
Segment margin as a percent of sales	18%	22%	12%	26.9%	15.2%	5.7%	15.4%
Nontraceable costs	20						
Income before taxes	$ 70						
Beforetax income as a percent of sales	14%						

Adding Segments.   Segment margin is useful when making decisions about long-run capacity and the allocation of resources to each segment. For example, suppose Douglass Company is considering adding another salesperson to the West Territory. Estimates reveal that the fifth salesperson would generate the following revenue and costs:

Sales		$ 90,000
Less: Variable production expense	$40,000	
Variable marketing and administrative expenses	10,000	50,000
Contribution margin		$ 40,000
Less: Fixed costs traceable to fifth salesperson		45,000
Segment margin		$ (5,000)

The fifth salesperson incurs $45,000 fixed costs because the company must rent additional office space and equipment that results in a negative segment margin. Even though this segment projects a $40,000 contribution margin, segment margin should form the basis for the decision because long-run capacity is involved. Contribution margin is most useful for short-run decisions such as the pricing of special orders; however, segment margin is the best gauge of the long-run profitability of a segment.

Nontraceable Costs.   Arbitrary allocations of indirect or nontraceable costs distort the costs over which a segment manager has control. Typical indirect or nontraceable costs include rent, building depreciation, and corporate expenses such as salaries. As a result, internal performance appraisal does not include nontraceable costs. Arbitrary allocations of nontraceable costs may imply that a specific segment is unprofitable when, in fact, there is a positive segment margin. This segment margin is contributing to overall indirect costs and any income. Generally, a company should retain a segment as long as its segment margin is positive, unless a more profitable investment alternative is available.

Breakeven Analysis   Another means of evaluating segments is to apply the breakeven analysis presented in Chapter 14. The breakeven point is the level of sales at which the segment recovers all expenses and shows neither income nor loss. However, breakeven analysis has limitations when applied to segments, because we must consider fixed costs in determining the breakeven point. Allocating fixed costs may be difficult and involve some arbitrary allocations. Chapter 14 discusses additional limitations of breakeven analysis.

Return on Investment   The relationship of profit margin to invested capital or assets is a better measure of profitability than income or sales dollars alone, particularly if the amount of resources committed to segments differs. The following formula outlines this relationship called **return on investment (ROI)**:

$$\text{Segment ROI} = \underbrace{\frac{\text{Segment revenues}}{\text{Investment center assets}}}_{\textbf{Asset Turnover}} \times \underbrace{\frac{\text{Operating profits}}{\text{Revenues}}}_{\substack{\textbf{Profit Margin} \\ \textbf{Percentage on Revenue}}} = \frac{\text{Operating profits}}{\text{Investment center assets}}$$

Asset turnover ratio measures the investment center's ability to generate revenue for each dollar of assets invested in the segment. **Profit margin** measures the investment center's ability to control costs for a specific level of revenue. The lower the cost required to generate a dollar of revenue, the higher the profit margin.

ROI focuses attention on the optimum asset investment. ROI enables management to determine whether the activity is profitable enough to support the amount of resources devoted to it. In addition, ROI analyses can identify segments needing top management's attention. For example, if a segment's ROI is lower than planned or than that earned by other segments, corrective action may be taken to improve performance. On the other hand, management also may be able to capitalize on a situation in which the ROI is higher than expected. ROI analysis emphasizes that long-run profits will be maximized if the optimum level of investment in each asset is achieved.

Companies use return on investment (ROI), **rate of return, return on assets (ROA), and return on assets committed (ROAC)** to refer to the same performance measurement. Even though ROAC and ROA are more descriptive because they emphasize that the return is calculated on the assets committed, ROI is more popularly used.

Segment Assets.   The important factor is that only those assets used exclusively by the segment should be included. Assets that the overall company controls and uses for the general benefit of all segments should not be included. Some companies calculate a return on the assets employed by excluding standby equipment and other assets available but not used. This has the obvious result of increasing the rate of return because we assume idle assets generate no income. However, it fails to measure how efficiently assets are used. The presence of idle assets suggests inefficient utilization of resources, and the rate of return should reflect this.

Determining the appropriate measurement of a segment's assets to compute the ROI is difficult. Although the most readily available measure is usually the book value of the assets, as reported in the company's accounts, this measure may be least useful. When a significant portion of a segment's assets are depreciable, using the book value of assets committed causes the rate of return to increase as the assets become older and increasingly depreciated. The rate of return rises as long as the segment's margin does not decline as rapidly as the book value of the assets identifiable with the segment. Using the gross value of depreciable assets without a deduction for depreciation eliminates such a meaningless increase in the rate of return. However, this basis still does not reflect the current economic value of the assets. Use of the current replacement costs of the assets committed is generally a more appropriate basis on which to measure the segment's performance. Even though ledger accounts do not reflect replacement cost, it can be obtained fairly readily. Quoted market prices can be used for inventories and equipment for which an actual market exists, and appraisals can be made of building, land, and other assets. Reliable replacement costs for intangible assets and special equipment are more difficult to obtain. However, if no other current value estimate is possible, the original cost of the asset can be adjusted for a change in the general price level.

Measuring segment profit also poses many difficulties. Just as companies use different terms in referring to the rate of return calculated, they also use various profit figures. For example, if assets are based on replacement cost, depreciation expense should be calculated on this basis in determining segment margin. To calculate ROI for an entire company, accountants use operating profit after income taxes but they prefer segment margin for computing a segment's ROI.

Computing Segment ROI.   Since capital investments are scarce resources, relating profits to capital investment provides an intuitively appealing performance measure. For example, Exhibit 18–1 indicates that the East Territory is more profitable than the West Territory and that Mr. A is the most profitable salesperson. However, a danger exists in the use of segment margin expressed as a percentage of sales. The East Territory and Mr. A are not the most profitable if they require more resources. If a large difference in the resources committed to each segment exists, firms should express segment margin as a return on the assets employed.

Assets employed can include working capital and the current value of long-term assets or, less desirably, their gross value. For example, assume the assets of the West Territory are as follows, resulting in a 15 percent ROI:

Assets Employed by West Territory
For Period Ending 19X1

Working capital	$ 40,000
Current replacement cost of long-term assets	120,000
Net assets	$160,000
Segment margin (from Exhibit 18–1)	$ 24,000
Return on assets committed ($24,000/$160,000)	15%

Certainly, if the assets employed vary as significantly as they do in Exhibit 18–2, ROI evaluation is necessary. The segment margin for each division as calculated in Exhibit 18–1 is divided by the assets employed to determine how profitably the resources are being used. In Exhibit 18–2, the return generated by Mr. C is highest although his segment contribution margin is lowest. A similar situation arises when product lines are being evaluated if the hours to complete a unit vary considerably. In this case, segment margin per hour required to complete the product is a better means of evaluating the segments than the total segment contribution. As you can see, ROI analysis provides different results from segment margin analysis.

By evaluating the segments through ROI, managers focus attention on the factors that increase ROI by either increasing sales or reducing invested capital or expenses. Likewise, an improvement in capital turnover or the gross margin percentage without a change in the other factors increases ROI.

EXHIBIT 18–2

DOUGLASS COMPANY
Segment Margin as a Percentage of Assets Employed
For Period Ending 19X1

	Territory		East Territory		West Territory	
	East	West	Mr. A	Ms. B	Mr. C	Ms. D
Segment margin	$66,000	$24,000	$47,000	$19,000	$4,000	$20,000
Assets employed	660,000	160,000	335,714	324,286	20,000	140,000
Return on investment	10.0%	15.0%	14.0%	5.9%	20.0%	14.3%

Residual Income

Instead of using ROI or segment margin to evaluate a segment, a company may use residual income. **Residual income** is the segment margin of the investment center after deducting the imputed interest on the assets used by the center. Residual income eliminates some of the problems associated with expressing a rate of return because it is not expressed as a ratio. Accountants normally use a company's average cost of capital, which Chapter 20 discusses, to compute imputed interest.

Rather than compute imputed interest on the segment's *invested capital* or assets, analysts may consider only interest on the segment's *controllable investment* (assets). This approach recognizes that segment managers cannot currently control much of the segment's plant and equipment because plant assets remain unchanged for long periods. Instead, firms evaluate their segment managers on the investment in working capital, especially receivables and inventories. Segment managers can control the receivable investment through their credit and collection policies. Likewise, the reordering levels chosen affect inventory investment. Usually, accountants subtract a segment's accounts payable and accrual balances from its receivables and inventories to arrive at the controllable investment.

To calculate residual income, assume a segment earns a $50,000 segment margin while employing $200,000 of assets, with a 12 percent cost of capital:

Segment margin	$50,000
Less imputed interest on investment center assets (12% × $200,000)	24,000
Residual income	$26,000

ROI and Residual Income Compared.   To compare the effect of using ROI or residual income on manager motivation, assume the preceding segment manager can purchase a new asset for $50,000. This purchase would generate a segment margin of $10,000, even though the rate on the asset is not as high as the 25 percent ($50,000/$200,000) ROI currently earned. Assume the overall company's cost of capital is 12 percent and it has excess cash of $50,000 that the company may otherwise invest in marketable securities yielding 10 percent. The new asset earns only a 20 percent ($10,000/$50,000) ROI, which is higher than the cost of capital, with an increased residual income as follows:

Segment margin	$60,000
Less imputed interest on investment center assets (12% × $250,000)	30,000
Residual income	$30,000

If the company evaluates the segment manager strictly on the basis of the rate of return rather than also giving some attention to the dollar amount of segment margin generated, the segment manager may not make the purchase. If evaluated on ROI, the segment manager may be tempted to dispose of any asset that is not earning a 25 percent ROI. For example, if the manager holds an asset valued at $100,000 that can be disposed of with a resulting reduction in segment margin of less than $25,000, the manager's ROI increases in the short run when he or she disposes of the asset. However, this decision may weaken the company in the long run.

Also, by using controllable assets rather than invested assets, the evaluation does not hold the segment manager responsible for plant and equipment decisions that top managers usually make. By using residual income as a performance measure, a company encourages segment managers to concentrate on maximizing dollars of residual income rather than maximizing a percentage return. Thus, the residual income concept overcomes one of the dysfunctional aspects of the ROI measure in which managers can increase their reported ROI by rejecting investments that yield returns greater than their company's or segment's cost of capital, but that are less than their current average ROI. However, since no external reporting authority requires an explicit charge for the use of invested capital, companies lack an incentive to use residual income in their profit center income analysis.

Budget-Performance Reports and Ratios

Companies often use budget-performance reports to evaluate cost centers. Accountants measure the performance of a cost center by comparing actual controllable costs with budgeted controllable costs for a specified period. Controllable costs result from decisions made by the manager of the cost center. Accountants also can compute a limitless number of ratios for each segment operation. These ratios range from the current ratio, which compares current assets to current liabilities, to ratios of various expenses to sales. Many trade associations collect and make available to their members information in ratio form for comparative purposes. However, because of the wide variation in classifying items such as marketing and distribution expenses, these comparisons may have little meaning. Thus, the value of this analysis depends on the analysts' ability to interpret differences between a given company and the industry average.

Full Costing

Even though full costing is necessary for external segment reporting, it has limited usefulness in segment evaluation. As we discuss in Chapter 17, accountants should not use **full costing** to test alternatives because the alternative does not affect some of the costs allocated. For example, if a territory reports a net loss, the company cannot avoid the entire loss reported by eliminating the territory because the indirect costs allocated to the territory are nonescapable.

Instead of using contribution reporting, if the accountant applied full costing to the data in Exhibit 18–1, the performance picture would be quite different. In arriving at a full-costing income, the accountants would allocate $20,000 nontraceable cost to the territories and salespersons. Using full-cost reporting is likely to cause the performance of Mr. C in the West Territory to reflect a net loss.

An evaluation of profitability is especially important when managers must decide whether to eliminate a segment. A segment is considered profitable if its revenue exceeds its traceable costs, regardless of whether it covers what someone has determined is its fair share of the nontraceable costs. A company should retain a segment as long as it yields a positive contribution and management cannot put the segment resources to better use.

Controllable and Noncontrollable Costs

Regardless whether analysts use full costing or contribution reporting, controllable costs should be separated from noncontrollable costs. Advocates of contribution reporting argue that noncontrollable costs should not be shown in segment reports at all. Instead, full-costing proponents believe that segment managers should be aware of the costs of the services they receive from other parts of the company so they are supportive of cost control. However, the company should assure its segment managers that even though their controllable costs are small in relation to noncontrollable costs, it is urgent that they direct full attention to those areas over which they have authority and responsibility.

Because it is unfair to hold segment managers responsible for costs over which they have no control, segment reporting may use the full-costing approach, but *segment evaluation* should not. However, this does not imply that a company should not expect each segment to contribute toward these indirect costs. Only the overall company can earn income; all that each segment can do is to contribute to that income.

Limitations of Traditional Methods for Evaluating Segment Performance

As companies decentralize their operations, accountants use quantifiable short-term financial measurements, such as ROI and segment margin, for evaluating profit center performance. However, these evaluation methods give too much weight to short-term benefits and costs. Further, they assign no cost to lost opportunities and no benefit to potential strategic advantages. In most companies, bonuses for short-term performance are larger than payments from long-term incentive programs. Thus, managers are motivated to pursue their own interests and ignore the long-term financial advantages of effective manufacturing performance.

ROI in Automated Manufacturing Environments

Although quality and inventory control are of increasing importance today, most segment evaluation methods, including ROI, neglect them. ROI is inadequate for estimating the advantages of robots and automated equipment (which are added in as segment assets), particularly where the company narrowly defined the analysis as a comparison of the return on the investment in one segment with the return on the investment in another. Also, the development of customer loyalty, recruiting costs, and research expenditures have a value beyond the current accounting period. Accountants do not usually capitalize such costs as assets. Accountants also rarely estimate the earnings effect of intangible assets such as employee talent and morale, an efficient distribution network, and knowledge of high-quality, flexible manufacturing processes.

Often analysts make monthly estimates for income and expense adjustments, such as depreciation, interest, and amortization. They then wait until year-end to determine more exact figures. Because ROI uses both revenues and profit, they may determine an inaccurate ratio by using estimated monthly revenues and expenses. On the other hand, waiting until year-end to calculate ROI is limiting as management needs current information concerning operations.

In addition, historical cost and current economic value may have no direct relationship because some assets depreciate in value while others appreciate. Historical cost is the result of decisions made several years ago. Its current economic usefulness depends on the current market, technology, and other facts. Both the numerator and the denominator in ROI are the result of and/or subject to wide ranges of arbitrary decisions that make them somewhat unreliable.

Therefore, ROI is a useful index of performance only if reasonable criteria for comparison are available. Such criteria include the ROI for the same segment in previous periods, the ratio in other segments, the rate in another company, or some desired rate of return. However, considerable danger exists in comparing the ROI of one company with that earned by another company, even if they are approximately the same size and are in the same industry. This is because a segment can rely on overall company management for many services that a separate company must provide for itself. In addition, analysts consider a segment to be more profitable per sales dollar volume than a separate company. Otherwise, there would be little advantage to having a large company with many operating segments. ROI can most effectively evaluate segment operations that are somewhat independent of each other and produce output that can be objectively valued.

Local versus Overall Performance Measurements

A performance measure is fundamentally wrong when the actions that benefit a company hurt the segment manager and vice versa. For example, emphasizing only local or segment performance fails to encourage the use of standard parts. Using stand-

Strategic Planning

Current Cost Management Practice

The videogame powerhouse Sega Enterprises Ltd. is blasting beyond games and racing to build a high-tech entertainment empire. A bloody price war with Nintendo Co. may cause profits to plunge. Rather than hold down expenses and cut prices like Nintendo, Sega is pursuing a two-pronged campaign to rebuild earnings. To broaden the market for videogames, it is completing a compact-disk machine that will play more realistic games than the ones on current CDs or cartridges. Sega wants to challenge Walt Disney Co. with virtual reality theme parks. To get to this level, Sega is relying on its twin strengths of computer prowess and a deep bond with children as Sega knows what kids find cool. Sega's strategy includes diversifying into two new businesses, toys and indoor amusement parks; forming alliances; riding the information superhighway; and keeping today's players happy.

Richard Brandt, Neil Gross, and Peter Coy, "SEGA!" *BusinessWeek,* February 21, 1994, pp. 66–74.

ard parts lowers material costs because of aggressive volume buying for the whole company. Segment managers may not recognize these economies on a product-by-product basis. For example, assume a company produces several different products. The products all use one or two parts bought in approximately equal amounts. Part X costs $15 per unit and Y, $8. Because Part X can be used in place of Part Y, a supplier has offered to sell Part X at $10 per unit, if the company doubles its present purchase volume. For products that incorporate both parts, substituting X for Y makes sense to qualify for the discount because the total parts cost is $23 using X and Y, but only $20 using Xs only. Part X should become a standard part for the factory. Segments building products that only require Part Y, however, would hesitate to substitute the higher-priced Part X. Even discounted, the cost of X exceeds that of Y.

Additional conflicts in local versus overall performance measurements result because many companies suffer from the end-of-reporting period "hockey-stick phenomenon." These plants issue shipments at a steady rate for a period, then shipments rise sharply near the end of the period and later drop even more rapidly to the original rate. As the end of the reporting period approaches, corporate management focuses on the overall performance of the company, instead of segment performance. Corporate managers want to know how much product will be shipped and how much money the company will make. Top management pushes shipments aggressively, emphasizing productivity over efficiency by using small runs to finish orders. As a result, companies ship most of the month's production in the last week of the month, disrupting any semblance of uniform flow. Manufacturing departments push to make their numbers, regardless of cost. Shops schedule overtime, expedite vendors, and cherry pick orders. Segment managers engage in such inefficient practices as running jobs on less-efficient machines, authorizing additional overtime, and splitting and overlapping batches to get the shipments out.

Such a system appears to work as each company ships more product and makes more money than it would have by following efficient practices. This phenomenon creates a management mindset that focuses on shipping targets and not cost control. To meet its targets, management believes it must ship a certain number of units. After the reporting period ends, however, managers reinstitute the old measurement systems. Thus, the conflict between local and overall performance measurements continues.

Performance Measures for World-Class Companies

As previously discussed, traditional performance measures focus on achieving short-run financial success and encourage **suboptimization;** this occurs when each segment benefits to the detriment of the overall company. Segment managers attempt to make their own segments look good in the short run. This especially occurs in companies with bonus systems from which they can personally gain by profitable performance. Managers learn how to manipulate ROI targets, not by selling more products or services, but by reducing discretionary expenditures, exploiting accounting conventions, and other nonproductive procedures. With only a short-term view, managers fail to perceive the need for automation and improved technology because the company gears its measurement and reward systems to achieving short-term results. To overcome this, companies are using additional performance measures that focus on longer-term objectives and plans.

Segregate Discretionary Expenses

Exhibit 18–3 illustrates the sacrificing of a company's long-term financial health by postponing discretionary costs, such as advertising, research, and repairs. **Discretionary costs** arise from periodic appropriation decisions and include expenditures for advertising, research, repairs, customer relations, human resources, and quality improvements. All of these criteria are vital to a company's long-term competitive position. Discretionary costs reflect management judgment in deciding the amount to incur each accounting period.

EXHIBIT 18–3   Highlighting Discretionary Expenses

DOUGLASS COMPANY
Segment Analysis
For the Year Ending May 31, 19X1
($ thousands)

	Companywide	East Territory	West Territory
Revenue	$500,000	$300,000	$200,000
Less: Variable production expense	200,000	140,000	60,000
Manufacturing contribution margin	$300,000	$160,000	$140,000
Less traceable variable expenses:			
Discretionary variable marketing expenses	$ 30,000	—	$ 30,000
Other variable marketing expenses	12,000	10,000	2,000
Discretionary variable administrative expenses	20,000	—	20,000
Other variable administrative expenses	18,000	15,000	3,000
Total traceable variable expenses	$ 80,000	$ 25,000	$ 55,000
Net contribution margin	$220,000	$135,000	$ 85,000
Less traceable fixed expenses:			
Discretionary fixed marketing expenses	$ 19,000	—	$19,000
Other fixed marketing expenses	32,000	$ 30,000	2,000
Discretionary fixed administrative expenses	10,000	—	10,000
Other fixed administrative expenses	69,000	39,000	30,000
Total traceable fixed expenses	$130,000	$ 69,000	$ 61,000
Segment margin	$ 90,000	$ 66,000	$ 24,000

The segment income statement in Exhibit 18–3 segregates discretionary expenses to clarify which segments are achieving their profit goals by risking their future competitive positions. Variable production expenses include factory repairs and maintenance. Advertising and public relations are variable marketing expenses. It appears that the East Territory manager is reducing or deferring such discretionary expenditures as preventive maintenance, advertising, and research solely to increase short-run segment margin. A format such as Exhibit 18–3 encourages this detection. Otherwise, the evaluation would unduly penalize the West Territory manager in the short run.

The allocation base selected for discretionary expenses often leads to dysfunctional consequences. For example, accountants often allocate repair and maintenance departmental cost on the basis of usage. As a result, accountants assign a larger share of the repair cost to the department that is properly maintaining its equipment than to the department neglecting its equipment. Segment managers rationalize that incurring regular maintenance and servicing, engaging in research, or purchasing depreciable safety equipment unfavorably affects their profits (and, in turn, their bonuses). Such evaluation encourages segment managers to postpone regular repairs, sell off equipment, and stifle research to develop short-term advantages. It takes several months before costly breakdowns and repairs occur to offset the apparent savings from deferring such maintenance. Obviously, such behavior may be dysfunctional in the long run. An organization must rapidly replace the equipment in a segment that incurs less short-run repair expense because it is not under a preventive maintenance program.

Historical cost accounting procedures and generally accepted accounting principles provide opportunities to time revenues and expenses to achieve a targeted ROI. Such one-shot opportunities as changing from accelerated to straight-line depreciation, lengthening depreciable lives, and amortizing pension costs over a longer period are examples. Selling assets whose market values exceed their book values also create one-shot profits. A segment that needs these assets can lease them back. Leasing and pension costs offer opportunities for clever financial accounting maneuvers, too. Creative rearrangement of ownership claims through mergers and acquisitions, divestitures and spin-offs, and leveraged buy-outs create earnings. Because of the opportunity for misapplication of financial accounting, companies need performance measures highlighting such tactics.

Productivity Measurements.   Local performance measurements, such as efficiencies, variances, and direct and indirect labor ratios, are attempts to measure the effective use of current capacity. These productivity measures generally increase when output expands because the firm's capital resources receive greater use. This productivity gain is due to external market forces, however, not to improved efficiency within the factory. Productivity measurements estimate the effects of substitution among labor, capital, materials, energy, and other key inputs.

Nonfinancial Evaluations

Some useful measures of performance do not involve financial data. For example, companies emphasizing quality could measure such internal failure indicators as scrap, rework, and unscheduled machine downtime. The quality measure includes external failure indicators, such as customer complaints, warranty expenses, and service calls. Companies wishing to become lower-cost producers develop productivity measures to show trends in their ability to produce more with less. When the focus is on just-in-time production and delivery systems, average setup times, throughput times, and lead times would support this objective. Companies wanting to improve their design and process flexibility can measure the total parts per product, the percentage common versus unique parts in products, and the number of subassembly levels.

Analysts also evaluate a segment on the basis of employee attitudes, delivery schedules, customer relations, and plant asset maintenance. While corporate management may hope for employee effort in the area of interpersonal relations, creativity, and team building, often these are not formally rewarded. Companies may not reward this behavior simply because it is hard to observe. However, use of nonfinancial indicators such as safety programs, decreased absenteeism, improved morale, reduced turnover, recruiting success, and improved promotability rates convince employees that management is giving more than mere lip service to these measures. Although all these factors affect the financial performance of a segment, the direct measurement itself involves nonfinancial data.

Multiple Performance Measures

Performance evaluations with a short-range time frame often reward behavior the company is trying to discourage while desired behavior goes unrewarded. Measures of performance covering three to five years more appropriately evaluate managers. Multiple criteria, rather than a single performance measure, provide flexible evaluations because they study short-range as well as long-range objectives. Additionally, companies are more likely to achieve goal congruence by evaluating segment managers on their contribution to the overall organizations, rather than their segments' performance only.

Application of Segment Analysis.   The approach to profitability analysis suggested in this chapter has a wide range of applicability regardless of whether the company is profit oriented. For example, in hospitals the segments could be patient floors, therapy services, X-ray, and pharmacy. In a university, the segments could be various graduate and undergraduate programs in the different colleges. A continuing education division can consider each course offering as a separate segment, such as CPA Review, CMA Review, or Art Appreciation. Managers can compare the tuition generated by each course with the instructor's salary and other traceable costs to determine whether the course can pay for itself. Both of these institutions, however, have other objectives that may assume priority over profitability.

Summary

Multiple performance measures, which include a variety of short-range and long-range financial and nonfinancial indicators, provide better targets and predictors for the firm's long-term profitability goals. Recognizing that any single financial measure is inadequate is important. Each company should select the measures most appropriate for its individual circumstances.

A danger exists in managers maximizing the segment's short-run performance to the detriment of the overall company. Companies should not reject projects profitable to the overall company but not as favorable to a specific segment as alternative projects. To be meaningful, an understanding of the consequences of the costs being incurred must accompany short-term market evaluations. Also, measurement needs change as companies become more automated.

Important Terms and Concepts

Problem for Self-Study

Profitability of Product Lines

Dulcie Douglass, Inc., makes three different products and wishes to evaluate the profitability of each product line. The following data are for the year ended September 30, 19X2:

Sales—Product A (2,000 units)	$200,000
Sales—Product B (4,000 units)	500,000
Sales—Product C (6,000 units)	100,000
Direct cost—Product A	80,000
Direct cost—Product B	360,000
Direct cost—Product C	90,000
Indirect costs—allocated on per unit basis	240,000

Each unit of Product A requires six hours to produce; Product B, four hours; and Product C, five hours.

Required:

Evaluate the profitability of each product line.

Solution to Problem for Self-Study

DULCIE DOUGLASS, INC.
Segmental Contribution Analysis
For Year Ended September 30, 19X2

	Company Totals	Products A	B	C
Sales	$880,000	$200,000	$500,000	$180,000
Direct costs	530,000	80,000	360,000	90,000
Segment margin	$350,000	$120,000	$140,000	$ 90,000
Indirect costs	240,000			
Income	$110,000			
Hours to complete		12,000	16,000	30,000
		(6 × 2,000)	(4 × 4,000)	(5 × 6,000)
Segment margin per hour		$10	$8.75	$3

Review Questions

1. Describe a situation often encountered in business when a company's overall profitability will be maximized if one segment will take a loss that will be more than made up in another segment.
2. Give some advantages and disadvantages of decentralization.
3. Discuss three dysfunctional consequences of accounting measurements. Be specific in your examples.
4. Define a segment and explain what factors should be studied in grouping segments.
5. Define residual income and discuss its use as a performance measurement.
6. *a.* What misleading inferences can be made if segment margin is expressed as a percentage of sales?
   b. When should segment margin be expressed as a percentage of asset employed or on a per hour basis?
7. Discuss ways the typical corporate manager is guilty of rewarding undesirable behavior.
8. *a.* Do you believe that idle assets should be included in the asset base when calculating ROI? Why or why not?
   b. How could the use of ROI encourage unprofitable behavior?
9. Do you believe that full costing has limited usefulness in evaluations of segments? Support your answer.
10. Discuss your views of the trend toward more extensive use of nonfinancial indicators. Include in your discussion some examples of nonfinancial measures.
11. Explain why you agree or disagree that short-term profits are no index of the ability of top management. Regardless whether you agree or disagree with this statement, indicate other indicators of productivity or profitability which reflect good management.

Exercises

E18–1 Segment Performance Measures

Management of Nan Mischke Company wishes to earn a 25 percent return on assets employed by all segments. Assets employed by the Northern Territory amount to $500,000, while fixed costs directly attributable to this product line amount to $86,000. The accountant for this territory informs you that the variable cost per unit is $5.50.

Required:

a. Calculate how many units must be sold if the sales price is $8 per unit to earn the desired rate of return.
b. Determine breakeven sales in units for this division.
c. Compute the rate of return earned if 60,000 units were sold at a $7.50 sales price.
d. Calculate the segment's residual income assuming an interest rate of 12 percent if 75,000 units are sold at an $8 unit sales price.

Writing

E18–2 Disclosure of Segment Information

Luther, Inc.'s controller advocates segment reporting and argues the merits of management identifying and reporting significant aspects of the organization's operations. Other members of the management team are not convinced that the effort involved is worth it.

Required:

a. Present arguments against the disclosure of segment information.
b. Present arguments for the disclosure of segment information.

E18–3 Residual Income
Data for the Ellen Company's records are as follows:

	Products			
	A	B	C	D
Units sold	8,000	6,000	6,200	5,800
Unit sales price	$ 30	$ 55	$ 40	$ 44
Unit cost of goods sold:				
Direct material	$6	$ 14	$ 13	$ 12
Direct labor	4	6	9	8
Variable factory overhead	8	3	4	6
Fixed factory overhead	3	2	5	4
Unit variable marketing and				
administrative expense	2	2	6	3
Other traceable fixed costs	8,000	17,500	2,080	6,010

Various types of machinery are required to manufacture each product, depending on the features involved. In addition, the plant facilities housing each production process differ. As a result, the invested capital for each product line is as follows: A, $200,000; B, $800,000; C, $100,000; D, $350,000. A recent study indicates the company's cost of capital is 12 percent.

Required:

Prepare a profit report for use in appraising product line performance. Use the residual income approach.

E18–4 Contribution Margin, Segment Margin, Residual Income
Management of Roan, Inc., is concerned about the profitability of its plant food line and requests your help in preparing segment analysis. Roan supplies the following data:

Units sold	25,000
Unit sales price	$ 8
Unit variable production expense	5
Unit variable marketing and administrative expense .	2
Traceable fixed costs	5,000

Roan invested $500,000 of capital in this product line.

Required:

Prepare contribution margin, segment margin, and residual income for this product line assuming a 14 percent cost of capital.

E18–5 Divisional Breakeven and Rate of Return
Management of Herbert, Inc., set an objective of a 20 percent return on assets employed by all segments. The XRX product line employed assets totaling $800,000, while $75,000 fixed costs relate directly to this product line. Variable costs amount to $4 per unit.

Required:

a. Determine breakeven sales in units for this division if the sales price is $9 per unit.

b. Compute how many units must be sold at the $9 sales price to earn the desired rate of return.
c. Calculate the segment's residual income assuming an interest rate of 12 percent if 50,000 units are sold at a $10 unit sales price.
d. Compute the rate of return earned if 20,000 units were sold at a $12 sales price.

E18–6 Segment Margin and ROI

Erwin Company manufactures Products A and B and employs Ms. X and Mr. Y to sell Product A and Mr. R and Ms. S to sell Product B. For the year ended December 31, 19X1, Erwin presents the following data:

	Product A		Product B	
	Ms. X	*Mr. Y*	*Mr. R*	*Ms. S*
Revenue	$240,000	$170,000	$290,000	$215,000
Variable production expense	40%	45%	60%	50%
Variable marketing and administrative expense	10%	8%	6%	12%
Traceable fixed costs	$ 70,000	$ 38,600	$ 30,500	$ 21,500

Nontraceable costs totaled $23,750.

Required:

a. Prepare segment analysis for each product line and for each of the salespersons by determining contribution margin and segment margin. Express each of these and income for the overall company as a percentage of sales.
b. Prepare any additional analysis you believe is necessary if the assets employed are as follows: Product A—Ms. X, $271,250; Product A—Mr. Y, $170,000; Product B—Mr. R, $758,750; and Product B—Ms. S, $440,000.

E18–7 Residual Income in Appraising Performance

Data for the Savell Company is extracted from their records as follows:

	Products			
	A	*B*	*C*	*D*
Units sold	6,000	8,000	7,500	5,500
Unit sales price	$ 21	$ 26	$ 32	$ 45
Unit cost of goods sold:				
Direct material	4	12	10	12
Direct labor	3	5	8	10
Variable factory overhead	6	3	2	5
Fixed factory overhead	2	1	2	2
Unit variable marketing and administrative expense	2			
Other traceable fixed costs	5,000			

Various types of machinery manufacture each product depen⌐ addition, the plant facilities housing each production process⌐ capital for each product line is as follows: A, $180,000; B, $350,000. A recent study indicates the company's cost of ca⌐

Required:

Prepare a profit report for use in appraising product line performance. Use the residual income approach.

E18–8 Territorial Contribution Margin and Segment Margin

K. Jones Company analyzes its Eastern and Western Territories by product line as well as by total territory performance. The Eastern Territory manufactures and sells Products A and B, while the Western Territory manufactures and sells Products C and D. For the quarter ending March 31, 19X1, you extract the following data from the records:

	Products			
	A	B	C	D
Units sold	1,500	2,600	3,000	3,800
Unit sales price	$ 5	$ 8	$ 10	$ 6
Unit variable production expense . . .	2	4	7	3
Unit variable marketing and				
administrative expense	1	2	1	2
Traceable fixed costs	1,000	1,800	4,200	1,200

Costs that could not be traced to a segment totaled $5,400.

Required:

a. Prepare a contribution margin and segment margin for the two territories and the four product lines. Express both of these measures and income for the overall company as a percent of sales.
b. Prepare additional analysis for the territories and product lines if the hours to complete each unit are Product A, two hours; Product B, one hour: Product C, one-half hour; and Product D, one and one-half hours.

E18–9 Profitability of Product Lines

Top management of the Park Company is concerned about the profitability of its three product lines, A, B, and C. The following data are from its financial statements:

Sales (2,500 units of A, 1,200 units of B, and 3,000 units of C)	$216,200
Cost of goods sold	156,600
Salespeople's commissions	8,772
Direct selling	25,000
Sales manager's salary	9,000
Administrative salaries and other expenses	36,000

Each unit of A sells for $20; of B, $26; and of C, $45. The cost per unit is composed of 25 percent direct material, 30 percent direct labor, and 5 percent variable factory overhead. The full cost per unit is $12 for A, $18 for B, and $35 for C.

Salespeople receive commissions equal to 3 percent of sales of A, 6 percent of sales of B, and 4 percent of sales of C. The provision for bad debt is estimated to be 0.5 percent of sales. The marketing manager informs you that 20 percent of direct selling is devoted to Product A, 25 percent to B, and the remainder to C.

Required:

a. Prepare a segment analysis of the profitability of each product.
b. Evaluate Park Company's present sales commission arrangement. Use cost analysis to support or refute the appropriateness of their present plan.

Chapter 18   Performance Evaluation and Segment Analysis   **599**

Problems

SPATS

P18–10 Product Line Evaluation

Buell Edmonds Company manufactures a special design of children's shirts and pants. During 19X1 the company's costs, revenues, and capital employed in the production of these two items were as follows:

	Shirts	Pants
Sales in units	500,000	800,000
Sales dollars	$1,250,000	$3,720,000
Material costs	250,000	800,000
Labor	300,000	600,000
Variable factory overhead	150,000	1,160,000
Variable marketing expense	125,000	640,000
Fixed factory overhead	300,000	305,000
Fixed marketing and administrative expense	100,000	150,000
Variable capital committed	8% of sales	10% of sales
Fixed capital committed	$ 100,000	$ 180,000

Nontraceable costs of the company amount to $60,000.

Because management is not pleased with the return generated by the divisions, it is considering a number of alternatives to improve this return. Market research indicates that sales of shirts can be expanded by 50 percent if the company engages in an advertising campaign costing $80,000. To produce these extra shirts, the company would need sewing machines and other equipment now being used by the pants division. A transfer of $20,000 fixed factory overhead and $15,000 of fixed capital would be made for this equipment.

The transfer of this equipment would mean limiting the production of pants to 600,000. These pants could either be sold at a sales price increase of $0.15 with an increase of $10,000 in fixed advertising expense or be sold at the same sales price with a $60,000 reduction in fixed advertising expense.

Required:

a. Calculate the segmental margin and ROI for each product line for 19X1.
b. Calculate the segmental margin and ROI for each product line and income for the company using each alternative presented.

Writing

P18–11 Segment Analysis for Product Lines

The following Ostendorf Company data are available for segment analysis:

	Northern Territory		Southern Territory	
	Product A	Product B	Product A	Product C
Sales	$ 40,000	$ 12,000	$ 80,000	$100,000
Contribution margin	30%	60%	30%	40%
Traceable fixed expenses	$ 4,000	$ 1,000	$ 9,000	$ 15,000

Nondirect fixed costs total $12,000 for the company.

Required:

a. Prepare segment analyses by product line and determine income before taxes for the overall company.

b. Assume the company's Research and Development Department has found ways that improvements can be made in Products B and C. However, company funds are limited so that only $5,000 can be spent to complete the improvements to either Product B or Product C. These improvements would increase the sale of Product B by 40 percent and Product C by 25 percent. On which product line should the company spend the funds?

c. Assume a proposed advertising campaign for Product A costing $6,000 in the Northern Territory is expected to increase sales by $27,500. Would you advise management to conduct the campaign?

d. Assume that after you present your segment statements computed in Requirement *a* to the president, she asked you to explain why segment statements prepared by another accountant on a territorial basis showed traceable costs of $7,000 for the Northern Territory and $28,000 for the Southern Territory. What would you tell her?

Critical Thought

SPATS

P18–12 Divisional Profitability

The California and Arizona Divisions of a company produce and sell equipment designed for oil drilling in Arctic conditions. California's manager prefers to use machines for labor-intensive tasks, while Arizona's manager prefers to maintain a large work force and avoid the expenditure of capital funds for expensive equipment. These are the respective costs of the two companies.

	Cost per Equipment	
	California	*Arizona*
Materials	$2.50	$7.00
Labor	1.60	2.00
Variable factory overhead	1.90	4.00
Fixed factory overhead	4.00	2.00

Fixed costs for California are $400,000 per year and for Arizona, $200,000 per year.

A total of 100,000 units will continue to be used as the normal volume for each division's sales and production. Each unit of drilling equipment is expected to sell for $18.

Required:

a. Calculate the manufacturing volume level at which both divisions would have the same operating results.

b. Prove your answer to Requirement *a*.

c. Compute the expected operating results for both divisions at the normal level of output.

d. Explain why one division outperformed the other in your answer to Requirement *c*.

e. (1) Assume that the sales outlook for next year is bleak and each division will produce and sell only 80,000 units. Compute their respective profits or losses.

(2) Explain why one division would outperform the other.

f. Discuss which division manager would most likely be willing to reduce the sales price to obtain a larger volume of sales. Why?

P18–13 Divisional ROI as Performance Measure

Thompson Corporation has divided its organization into autonomous divisions. Each division is an investment center since it has responsibility and authority for purchases of assets as well as marketing, product development, and manufacturing. Senior corporate managers evaluate the performance of division managers on divisional return on investment (ROI) solely.

This policy is justified by top management because quantitative data from both the divisions' income statements and balance sheets are used. In addition, both divisions produce and sell the same type of product. For example, data for Division A and Division B follow:

	(In millions)	
	Division A	*Division B*
Sales	$80	$50
Less: Variable cost of goods sold	60	20
Fixed cost of goods sold	4	15
Gross margin	$16	$15
Operating expenses:		
Repairs	–0–	$ 8
Allocated corporate expense	$ 4	6
Total operating expense	$ 4	$14
Net income	$12	$ 1
÷ Invested capital	$30	$50
ROI	40%	2%

Division A's manager is evaluated much more favorably than Division B's manager because of the higher ROI. However, Division B's manager argues that this is unfair since Division B occupies a large, old plant space and corporate expense is allocated on the basis of square footage. Division B's manager contends that the difference in the bonus received is not justified.

Required:

a. Evaluate Division B's manager's complaint that using ROI as the sole criterion to evaluate division managers is unfair.

b. Discuss which other criteria would be appropriate for use in evaluating division managers.

c. Describe the advantages in using multiple criteria for this evaluation rather than one single criterion.

d. List any problems you anticipate in implementing multiple criteria in this performance evaluation.

SPATS

P18–14 Income Statements for Territories
Management of the Carlton Company believes that it should be analyzing its marketing costs in more detail. The company has learned that its competitors are classifying their marketing costs into variable and fixed order-getting and order-filling categories. The company serves three territories: Mississippi, Kentucky, and Tennessee.

Costs incurred by the home office are as follows:

Regional warehousing	$11,000
Regional advertising	30,000
Regional administrative	27,000

Regional warehousing is allocated to the three territories on the basis of pounds shipped; regional advertising, on the basis of sales; and regional administration equally to all territories.

The salespeople receive a base salary plus 3 percent of all items sold within their territories.

Each territory has responsibility for its own advertising in addition to the fixed yearly retainer fee contracted by the entire organization for regional advertising. Each territory manager has signed a contract with an advertising agency in which they pay a fee equal to 0.5 percent of sales.

Travel expense is incurred by the salesperson calling on the customer. Territorial salespeople each have a budget for customer entertainment. Freight-out averages $0.30 per pound shipped for each territory warehouse. Warehouse supplies average $0.05 per pound shipped. Warehouse salaries are considered fixed costs.

Standards are set for the manufacturing process; the standard specification per unit is

Direct material	$3.00
Direct labor	2.83
Variable factory overhead	1.27
Fixed factory overhead	0.78
	$7.88

Partial results of operations for the year ended April 30, 19X1, are as follows:

	Mississippi	Kentucky	Tennessee	Total
Sales	$200,000	$600,000	$400,000	$ 1,200,000
Territory office expense	6,100	6,900	5,810	18,810
Territory manager salary	24,000	27,000	23,600	74,600
Salespersons' salaries (excluding commissions)	20,000	24,000	21,000	65,000
Advertising retainer fee	25,000	15,000	20,000	60,000
Travel	4,000	4,800	3,900	12,700
Warehouse salaries	10,050	11,800	9,900	31,750
Warehouse insurance	960	1,170	2,310	4,440
Warehouse depreciation	1,810	1,990	1,508	5,308
Pounds shipped	18,000	19,500	17,500	55,000
Units sold	5,100	18,000	9,700	32,800

Required:

a. Prepare an income statement for each territory in which costs are separated into their variable and fixed components in the following categories: cost of sales; marketing—order-getting; marketing—order-filling; and administrative.

b. Prepare a statement in another format if you believe it is more appropriate for evaluating each territory.

P18–15 Awarding Bonus on ROI

Sadhwani Company is the leading food distributor in the nation. The company is organized by geographical regions: North, East, South, and West, and each region has its own sales department. At the beginning of each year, corporate officers of Sadhwani Company determine the desired minimum return on investment (ROI) of the regional branches. Bonuses are awarded to the sales personnel in the region with the highest return on investment, provided that return exceeds the established goal. The current year company goal is 10 percent ROI, and the regional results follow:

	North	East	South	West	Total
Estimated market	$ 250,000	$ 350,000	$500,000	$400,000	$1,500,000
Regional sales	$ 175,000	$ 210,000	$150,000	$120,000	$ 655,000
Variable costs	$ 52,500	$ 63,000	$ 45,000	$ 36,000	$ 196,500
Discretionary costs* . . .	22,500	32,000	$ 55,000	44,000	153,500
Common fixed costs† . .	13,500	16,000	11,500	9,000	50,000
Total costs	$ 88,500	$ 111,000	$111,500	$ 89,000	$ 400,000
Net income	$ 86,500	$ 99,000	$ 38,500	$ 31,000	$ 255,000
Assets committed	$1,000,000	$1,500,000	$800,000	$1,250,000	$4,550,000
Liabilities	135,000	600,000	433,000	850,000	2,018,000
Net investment	$ 865,000	$ 900,000	$367,000	$ 400,000	$2,532,000

* Discretionary costs include costs for research, advertising, and other avoidable activities.
† The allocation of the common fixed cost is based on the percentage of each region's sales to the total sales.

The South region recently purchased several personal computers, the cost was treated as an office expense.

Although the company policy requires each regional branch to purchase a company car for every salesperson, the North region decided not to follow the policy. Instead, the North region reimburses sales personnel for gasoline only.

Required:

a. Decide which region deserves the bonuses based on the preceding information. Show all supporting calculations.
b. Discuss the effect on their ROI if the South region debited the capital asset account for the personal computers and North region purchased company cars for its sales personnel.
c. Explain which factor makes the company's established minimum return on investment criterion inappropriate for measuring the performance of each region.
d. Recommend which methods Sadhwani corporate officers should use to evaluate the performance of each region.

P18–16 Contributions Margins by Markets and Products

R. Reynolds, Inc., manufactures two types of computer chips, RAM and ROM. Both chips are sold in a local market and an overseas market. The following is the latest quarterly income statement:

	Local	Overseas	Total
Sales	$150,000	$200,000	$350,000
Cost of goods sold	50,000	165,000	215,000
Gross margin	$100,000	$ 35,000	$135,000
Marketing expenses	$ 20,000	$ 15,000	$ 35,000
Administrative expenses	10,000	10,000	20,000
Total expenses	$ 30,000	$ 25,000	$ 55,000
Operating income	$ 70,000	$ 10,000	$ 80,000

The management is very concerned with its overseas market because of the low return on sales. Many computer chip manufacturers are retreating from their overseas markets and the demand for computer chips does not seem like it will increase in the near future. Thus, management desires a final analysis of its overseas market so it can decide whether to leave this market. The cost structure is as follows for the individual products:

	RAM	*ROM*
Sales	$200,000	$150,000
Variable production cost as a percentage of its sales	24%	28%
Variable marketing expense as a percentage of its sales	4%	8%
Sales by markets		
Local	$100,000	$50,000
Overseas	$100,000	$100,000

All fixed production expenses and all administrative expenses are indirect to the two products and the two markets and are fixed for the period. The remaining marketing expenses are fixed for the period and traceable to the markets. Reynold's management bases fixed expenses on a prorated yearly amount.

Required:

a. Prepare the quarterly income statement showing contribution margin and segment margin by markets.
b. Assume R. Reynolds, Inc., decides to abandon its overseas market under the assumption there are no alternative uses for the capacity. Prepare the new income statement based on the preceding information. Should R. Reynolds, Inc., keep the overseas market?
c. Prepare the quarterly income statement showing contribution margin by products.
d. Assume that according to its production department, R. Reynolds, Inc., can begin producing a new version of the ROM chip next year. Then, the company will no longer produce the current ROM chip. However, to manufacture the new version, R. Reynolds, Inc., needs to buy a new machine that costs $200,000, has $0 salvage value, and has a useful life of 10 years. Reynolds uses straight-line depreciation. Besides the purchase of the new machine, Reynolds will not incur any additional cost if the new ROM is produced. What must be the minimum contribution margin per quarter for the new product to make the changeover financially feasible?

P18–17 CVP Analysis of Segments

Beckett Company's condensed statements for last year, prepared on an absorption costing basis by product line, follow:

BECKETT COMPANY
Income Statement
For the Year Ended January 31, 19X5

	A	*B*	*C*	*Total*
Sales	$780,000	$590,000	$900,000	$2,270,000
Cost of sales:				
Direct material and labor	$300,000	$240,000	$360,000	$ 900,000
Factory overhead *a*	300,000	180,000	120,000	600,000
Total cost of sales	$600,000	$420,000	$480,000	$1,500,000
Gross margin	$180,000	$170,000	$420,000	$ 770,000

BECKETT COMPANY (*continued*)

	A	B	C	Total
Marketing and administrative expenses:				
Packaging [b]	$ 7,800	$ 5,900	$ 27,000	$ 40,700
Salaries [c]	100,000	30,000	25,000	155,000
Advertising [d]	40,000	28,000	42,000	110,000
Rent [e]	35,000	9,000	16,000	60,000
Total marketing and administrative expense	$182,800	$72,900	$110,000	$365,700
Operating income before taxes	$ (2,800)	$97,100	$310,000	$404,300

Notes to income statement:

[a] Factory overhead is applied on the basis of $6 per machine-hour based on 100,000 machine-hour normal capacity. In processing Product Line A, 50,000 machine-hours were incurred; 30,000 hours in Product B; and 20,000 hours in Product C. Analysis of factory overhead reveals the following. (At year-end there was no overapplied or underapplied overhead.)

Rent and insurance	$ 90,000
Depreciation—per unit basis	120,000
Supervisor's salaries	160,000
Variable indirect labor and benefits	80,000
Variable indirect materials	150,000
	$600,000

[b] Packaging costs amount to 1 percent of sales for Products A and B and 3 percent on Product C.

[c] Marketing and administrative personnel devote effort to all product lines; allocation of their salaries is based on management's estimates of time spent on each product line.

[d] Each product has its own advertising campaign.

[e] Rent is allocated on the basis of square footage occupied by each division.

Required:

a. As Beckett's new accountant you suggest that the company use cost/volume/profit (CVP) analysis for a better evaluation of its product lines. Prepare a statement utilizing CVP analysis that shows the profit contribution of each product line and the net income before taxes for the company as a whole.

b. Discuss three dangers and difficulties management could experience in using CVP analysis.

c. Discuss three advantages to management if CVP analysis were used.

Cases

C18–18 Increasing the Divisional Manager's Bonus

As a management accountant employed by Sanks, Inc., you were involved with the decentralization plan of organization. Three years ago top management made each division a profit center and began giving bonuses to each division head based on the gross margin percentage. This plan of organization has worked rather smoothly.

Recently, the company has suffered sharp financial setbacks and lost a major customer. This change of events has caused a freeze on all salaries. However, marketing management has convinced top management that sales promotion should not be curtailed since the objective is to generate additional sales. Also, the company is planning the introduction of a new product line, and the salespersons strongly argued for extensive advertising campaigns to support this new product line.

Yesterday, Joe Brown, the production manager, called for a confidential appointment. When he arrived at your office, he closed the door and asked for your help in one of his difficult management problems. He stated that Sara Jones, a division manager, has felt the financial crunch from not receiving a salary raise. She had just begun construction on a new family residence when the freeze was announced. In addition, since that time, she has had to help her elderly parents pay some medical bills. Jones is threatening to leave the company unless some help can be found for her.

Brown explains that since he is not an accountant, he wants your advice on what kinds of entries can be made to increase the gross margin percentage for Jones' division. This would increase Jones' bonus based in part on gross margin. Brown reemphasizes that Jones is a key person and if she does not receive a monetary increase, he is certain that she will leave.

Before you can interrupt Brown, he pulls out his clipboard and begins asking if the division ignores the costing of some of their sales, would this have a favorable impact on gross margin? He continues by asking what could be done with ending inventory to effect the desired result—should ending inventory be overstated or understated? He further states that he believes one of the best policies to achieve a higher gross margin for Jones' division is to charge Advertising Expense and credit Purchases Discount for various amounts throughout the period. His logic is that since top management has not frozen sales promotion, this practice is less likely to be detected.

Your telephone rings and since it is a long distance call, Brown leaves saying, "I will be in touch."

Required:

a. Discuss what you, as Sanks' management accountant, would do with Brown's request to manipulate the gross margin percentage. List the alternatives available and the reasons for choosing one of these.
b. Describe what role, if any, you should assume in suggesting alternative evaluation techniques or changes in the salary freeze policy.
c. Discuss the impact on gross margin of:
   (1) Ignoring the recording of Jones' division sales.
   (2) Understating ending inventory.
   (3) Overstating ending inventory.
   (4) Charging Advertising Expense with fictitious purchase discounts.
d. Evaluate the behavioral impact Brown's actions or encouragement could have on future actions of subordinates like Jones.

Writing

C18–19 Merits of Decentralization and Centralization

Potts Processing Company is a manufacturer of a wide variety of industrial cleaning products. The company has total sales of $200 million and eight processing divisions located in six northern states. Top management has always believed that division managers should have authority to run their plants as they feel is best. The degree of decentralization enjoyed has been rather extreme as it allows each division manager to set prices and decide on the optimal product mix.

Purchasing of raw materials is performed by each division. Division managers are able to approve capital expenditures. In addition, each division establishes its own objectives and budgets. Top management at the home office performs a cursory review of these objectives and budgets.

Top management receives quarterly performance reports for each division showing income before taxes for each segment. Recently the New York division has been reporting a loss; however, the manager of the New York division believes that the loss results from unfair allocation of home office fixed expenses. This issue is coupled with a proposal from Kimberly Wells, a former management consultant with the company's auditor, and presently assistant controller for Potts Company, concerning the purchase of larger computer facilities and greater centralization of decision-making responsibility. Ms. Wells strongly believes that management should be receiving more current performance reports in a different format. In addition, she thinks that the increased capabilities of the new computer will provide enough relevant information to enable corporate management to effectively make major decisions for each division. In fact, she argues that to justify the cost of such a large computer, all accounting functions including billing, budgeting, performance reporting, cost accounting, purchasing of raw materials and credit extension should be performed at the home office rather than at each divisional level.

A strong supporter of centralization, Wells further argues that many of the functions presently performed by the division managers should be centralized including recruitment of personnel, production scheduling, and pricing. She supports her proposal by emphasizing the lack of coordination between the divisions as evidenced by a recent case where the Boston division and the Albany division were marketing competing products. She claims that much of the poor performance of the New York division is due to lack of strong top-management leadership.

Top management is undecided if the policy of decentralization should be abandoned. However, managers all agree that this issue should be decided before acquiring a larger computer.

Required:
a. Give some additional advantages and disadvantages of decentralization.
b. Explain which of the functions cited by Wells could be more effectively performed if centralized.
c. Explain which functions should remain decentralized.
d. Describe the information now available to division managers that would not probably be available to top management through a formal centralized information system.
e. Suggest any improvements to the present division performance reports received by top management.
f. Decide which action the company should take in regard to Wells's proposal. State your reasons for this action.

C18–20 Behavioral Impact of Short/Long Trade-Offs

Three years ago, Klammer, Inc., suffered a recession along with other firms in the industry. As a result of the poor economic condition, administrative staff was reduced by 30 percent. Top management issued a policy stating that it was trying to create an atmosphere that stimulated creative thinking and some risk taking. This staff reduction eliminated three layers of management leaving division managers responsible for implementing corporate strategic goals. Decisions regarding capital outlays, personnel, product mix and promotion, which formerly were jointly decided by division managers and top management are now under the authority of division managers. Along with this change which leaves division managers responsible for the success or failure of their operations, the company instituted a bonus for each division manager determined on the basis of these three items:

1. Division net income.
2. Return on investment for each division.
3. Achievement of budgeted profit.

Klammer, Inc., uses a fixed or static budgeting system assembled during the prior year; for the budget to be printed and distributed, it is prepared five months before the operating year begins. Because there are now few top managers and their time is valuable, the budget for each division is not changed after its preparation. As a result of the recent financial downturn, division managers are encouraged to think optimistically when submitting raw financial budget data that are translated into the final budget by top management. Rather than express future division performance in realistic terms, many division managers overstate revenues or understate expenses in the hope that conditions will improve. In fact, word has leaked out that the division managers who failed to follow this optimistic approach were called into corporate offices to explain why they thought conditions would be so unfavorable for their divisions.

Evaluation is made quarterly for each division for all revenue and expense items used to arrive at divisional net income. Since the budget is not adjusted for competitors' actions or the state of the economy, division managers that failed to live within their budgets received unfavorable performance evaluations. Several division managers have been heard to remark that there is no way to win with this system because they are criticized for presenting realistic data, but if they fail to meet the optimistic budget, they receive no bonus.

Required:

a. Describe the expected behavior of division managers as a result of the present system of performance evaluation regarding:
   (1) Operating expenses.
   (2) Product mix.
   (3) Capital outlays.
b. Evaluate whether these behavioral patterns are normal for division managers under the current evaluation system. Why or why not?
c. Discuss some disastrous long-term effects resulting from performance evaluation plans such as that used by Klammer, Inc.
d. Outline five features of a evaluation system that would overcome some of the problems inherent in the present one used by Klammer.

Critical Thought

C18–21 Criteria for Performance Measures (CMA)

The Star Paper Division of Royal Industries is located outside of Los Angeles. A major expansion of the division's only plant was completed in April of 19X0. The expansion consisted of an addition to the existing building, additions to the production-line machinery, and the replacement of obsolete and fully depreciated equipment that was no longer efficient or cost effective.

On May 1,19X0, George Harris became manager of Star. Harris had a meeting with Marie Fortner, vice president of operations for Royal, who explained to Harris that the company measured the performance of divisions and division managers on the basis of return on gross assets (ROA). When Harris asked if other methods were used in conjunction with ROA, Fortner replied "Royal's top management prefers to use a single performance measure. There is no conflict when there is only one measure. Star should do well this year now that it has expanded and replaced all of that old equipment. You should have no problem exceeding the division's historical rate. I'll check with you at the end of each quarter to see how you are doing."

Fortner called Harris after the first quarter results were completed because Star's ROA was considerably below the historical rate for the division. Harris told Fortner that he did not believe that ROA was a valid performance measure for Star. Fortner indicated that she would discuss this with others at headquarters and get back to Harris. However, there was no further discussion of the use of ROA, only reports on divisional performance at the end of the second and third quarters. Now that the fiscal year has ended, Harris has received the memorandum shown here.

To:	George Harris, Star Paper Division
From:	Marie Fortner, Royal Industries
Subject:	Divisional Performance

The operating results for fourth quarter and for our fiscal year ended on April 30 are now complete. Your fourth quarter return on gross assets was only 9 percent, resulting in a return for the year of slightly under 11 percent. I recall discussing your low return after your first quarter and reminding you after the second and third quarters that this level of return is not considered adequate for the Star Paper Division.

The return on gross assets at Star has ranged from 15 to 18 percent for the past five years. An 11 percent return might be acceptable at some of Royal's other divisions, but not at a proven winner like Star, especially in the light of your recently improved facility. Please arrange to meet with me in the near future to discuss ways to restore Star's return on gross assets to its former level.

Harris is looking forward to meeting with Fortner as he plans to pursue the discussion about the appropriateness of ROA as a performance measure for Star. While the ROA for Star is less than historical levels, the division's profits for the year are higher than at any previous time. Harris is going to recommend that ROA be replaced with multiple criteria for evaluating performance, namely, dollar profit, receivable turnover, and inventory turnover.

Required:

a. Identify general criteria that should be used in selecting performance measures to evaluate operating managers.
b. Describe the probable cause of the decline in Star Paper Division's return on gross assets during the fiscal year ended on April 30, 19X1.
c. On the basis of the relationship between Marie Fortner and George Harris, as well as the memorandum from Fortner, discuss apparent weaknesses in the performance evaluation process at Royal Industries.
d. Discuss whether the multiple performance evaluation criteria suggested by George Harris would be appropriate for the evaluation of the Star Paper Division.

C18–22 Decentralized versus Centralized Organization Structure

In the 1940s, John Lewis, an energetic and talented engineer, invented an item that revolutionized the assembly of motors. He formed a closely held company to manufacture and market this product. As the company grew, more stock was issued, but only to family members. Lewis also maintained a majority interest in the company, which has now been given to his only daughter, Jean.

At his encouragement Jean attended engineering school and also received a masters in business administration. Now that John has retired, Jean is the president, overseeing each of the four territories. Jean travels to each of the divisions regularly. She says, "I just do not have time for tennis and bridge, because I have to fly weekly from one territory to another to put out fires. My boys in the four territories just do not have the historical background to understand the overall company as I do. Why, Daddy let me work in his office beginning when I was a teenager." She continues, "But, I want my territory managers to be able to express themselves and to have the freedom to experiment with various ideas and styles of management. They do not have to get my approval first. Now that I am approaching middle age, I want to relieve myself of some duties. That is what a decentralized organization with managers who have complete autonomy is supposed to be about.

Each of the four territories is headed by a division manager who reports to Lewis. In recruiting and hiring these division managers, extensive procedures were used in an attempt to secure the best person. Since the territories are established as profit centers, performance evaluation is based on segment margin. In addition to using segment margin as the basis for bonus calculation, Lewis then adds her own evaluation based upon the difficulty of the tasks involved. Two of the territories are producing intricate items requiring much supervision.

Lewis believes that the company recently has experienced more tension than ever before. The Eastern Territory has expanded its facilities to a maximum due to what is considered a temporary demand for its products. The territory manager, Bill Oury, wanted to buy a new building, but Lewis would not agree to review his proposal. Instead she made the decision to remain in the present building and operate three labor shifts. This has placed an increased burden on Oury since there is a lack of trained supervisors willing to work at night. The result has been an increase in waste and defective products.

When Oury called to ask for four days off work, Lewis reminded him of the trouble he was having at his plant. Oury insisted that he really needed to have these days off and counted on his accumulated vacation days even though he could understand the possible inconvenience to the plant. Finally, Oury informed Lewis that he was interviewing elsewhere because he needed more opportunity to test his abilities. To this, Ms. Lewis exploded, "You have all the responsibility and opportunity that you can adequately handle now."

Lewis is somewhat surprised at her outburst but attributes this loss of composure to several other management problems that have arisen lately. Don Brown, a sales supervisor in the Western Territory, has requested a demotion to a sales position; his request was accompanied by a letter from his physician. Brown indicates that he cannot handle the pressure of work and fears that he will have a heart attack if he continues under the present conditions. Lewis did not expect to receive such a request because four months ago Brown was assigned an experienced assistant to relieve him of some marketing, clerical, and management duties. The purpose was to allow Brown to concentrate his efforts on creative ventures in promotion. The Southern Territory is also experiencing a high turnover of middle management personnel. She has felt that this could be explained by the opening of increased job opportunities for all workers as more companies make a move to more favorable geographical and economic surroundings. However, Lewis admits that she is surprised at what is happening to "Daddy's Company," and she wonders what needs to be corrected.

Required:

a. Choose examples and descriptions of company activities that characterize centralized and those that characterize decentralized management.
b. Evaluate Ms. Lewis's recommendation not to expand facilities in the Eastern Territory.
c. Explain how recent events at Lewis Company could have been expected.

C18–23 Segment Performance Evaluation
Vanderbilt, Inc., produces many products in the metal works industry. Because the company is separated geographically, a decentralized management structure is used. Each territory manager receives a bonus whenever actual residual income exceeds budgeted residual income. Residual income for this company is computed by determining each segment's contribution to company profits before taxes less an investment charge of 20 percent on each segment's investment base. The investment base used is the total of the segment's year-end balances of accounts receivable, inventories, and the book value of plant assets for each segment. Top management has informed each manager that each segment's investment in receivables and inventories is to be minimized because of its unfavorable impact on cash flow.

Each segment manager is responsible for production and marketing of company products in the geographical area surrounding the territory served. Also, requests for each territory's plant asset purchases are initiated by the segment manager. They are then evaluated based upon need for the asset, feasibility studies, and available company funds.

Bob Weatherly, manager of the Northern Territory, is very proud of his segment's performance for the current year. In fact, he is so confident that he will receive a significant bonus that he has already purchased airline tickets for his family to spend Christmas in Hawaii. The current year's income statement in comparison with the annual budget is as follows for the Northern Territory with $000 omitted:

	Annual budget	Annual Actual
Sales	$2,300	$2,500
Territory costs and expenses:		
Direct materials	460	540
Direct labor	115	140
Repairs and maintenance	120	70
Depreciation on production facilities	40	30
Other traceable costs	100	100
Segment margin.	$1,465	$1,620
Allocated company fixed costs	250	200
Segment contribution to company profits	$1,215	$1,420
Imputed interest on segment investment (20%)	300	276
Residual income for segment	$ 915	$1,144

	Budgeted End-of-Year Account Balance	Actual End-of-Year Account Balances
Segment investment:		
Accounts receivable	$ 150	$ 200
Inventories	350	380
Plant and equipment (net)	1,000	800
Total	$1,500	$1,380
Imputed interest (20%)	$ 300	$ 276

Beginning of the year territorial assets were: accounts receivable—$120,000; inventories—$280,000; and plant and equipment—$800,000.

Required:

a. Evaluate Weatherly's performance and decide if he should receive a bonus. Support your decision with relevant facts from the data given.

b. Identify any weaknesses in the company's performance evaluation, and indicate how they should be corrected.

C18–24 Decentralization Issues

Within a company, decentralization exists in various degrees, often reflecting the scope of the decision-making authority given to a particular segment manager. Under this classification scheme, the decentralized units are often referred to as investment centers, profit centers, or cost centers.

Required:

a. Describe the characteristics that distinguish an investment center, a profit center, and a cost center from each other.

b. Discuss how the performance of a manager of each type of center should be evaluated.

c. Define return on investment and residual income and discuss whether or not these measures are appropriate for measuring the performance of managers responsible for each type of center.

    d. Explain the ramifications of using residual income as compared to the more traditional return on investment approach for internal decisions for those centers where appropriate.

    e. Discuss if residual income, or a variation of it, could be usable in the future for financial reports for external users.

    f. Discuss the limitations of return on investment and residual income as performance measures and indicate some additional measures that could be used for performance evaluation. For each measure you list, give reasons why it would be appropriate for evaluating performance.

Chapter
19

Transfer Pricing in Multidivisional Companies

Chapter Objectives

After studying this chapter, you should be able to:

1. Explain the relationship between the degrees of interdependence and the need for establishing transfer prices.

2. Apply appropriate criteria for choosing transfer prices.

3. Use variations of the two transfer pricing methods that impact a segment's profitability.

4. Discuss how transfer prices should reflect the factors surrounding each specified situation.

5. Explain the behavioral implications inherent in decentralized segments and the potential for suboptimization and other dysfunctional behavior.

Current Cost Management Practice

After General Motors Corp. bought Hughes Aircraft, it kept it growing. Often when giant companies take over smaller ones, the smaller ones suffer. As military spending decreases, Hughes has more than made up the difference by selling more commercial satellites. To help the transition, GM supplied capital and credit enabling Hughes to invest more than $2 billion in telecommunications and space since 1987. Other than providing cash and credit, GM has pretty much left Hughes on its own. GM plans to continue making heavy investments in Hughes. Hughes' fastest growing division is its commercial satellite and telecommunications group. However, Michael Armstrong, Hughes' chief executive, an IBM veteran, knows the danger of overconfidence and corporate bloat. Armstrong has cut costs at Hughes arguing that doing things that work and cost less gains market advantage. This formula for success is hard to achieve, but immensely effective.

Howard Banks, "GM's Hidden Treasure," *Forbes*, August 1, 1994, pp. 36–37.

Introduction

When all companies were small and management was centralized, accountants transferred goods and services from one cost center to another at the cost of production. Today, many companies are giant conglomerates having multiple divisions. Simply transferring goods and services at cost no longer serves the needs of these decentralized organizations.

Transfer pricing becomes complex because of the need to evaluate an organization's segments. To the department selling goods and services, the transfer price is its revenue. To the department buying the goods and services, the transfer price is its cost. Therefore, transfer prices have a direct bearing on segment margin. Corporate managers should set transfer pricing policies ensuring that divisions do not purchase outside when high-fixed-cost internal facilities can *provide* the product. Allowing these facilities to be idle is detrimental to overall company profitability.

Transfer Pricing Bases

Transfer pricing refers to the unit price assigned to goods or services that one segment transfers to another segment within the same company. Accountants use transfer prices for purposes other than inventory costing. Regardless of the transfer price in effect, consolidated financial statements still show the unit production cost computed according to generally accepted accounting principles. On consolidated financial statements, accountants eliminate transactions between segments to reduce inventories on hand to cost. Usually, the greater the degree of interdependence among segments, the greater the transfer pricing problem. For instance, large volumes of intracompany transfers occur in a vertically integrated firm such as a paper supply company that owns timberland and manufactures paper cut to customer specification.

The transfer price that accountants derive internally replaces the independent market transaction for directing the allocation of economic resources. The appropriate price used for transferring goods and services from one organizational segment to another is important because it affects the reported income of both the selling segment and the buying segment. A particular transfer pricing basis also may be an excellent management tool for motivating division managers, for establishing and maintaining cost control systems, and for measuring internal performance.

There are two basic methods for establishing transfer prices. The first involves some form of cost derived from the company accounting records or from financial analysis. Included are differential or variable cost, opportunity cost, marginal cost, full cost, and full cost plus a markup for a reasonable profit. The second method includes market price, negotiated price, or some variation of the two. The chapter discusses the merits of each method; however, any solution is situation specific and depends on the individual circumstances of the divisions involved.

Transfer Pricing Illustrated

To illustrate the application of several transfer prices, assume the Transistor Division of Entertainment, Inc., supplies transistors to outside customers at a price of $3.50 each. Entertainment, Inc., has just acquired a radio assembly company. Entertainment's president believes this newly acquired Radio Division should purchase transistors from the company's own Transistor Division because this division has excess capacity. Until the acquisition, the radio assembly company had purchased transistors for $3.50 less a 10 percent discount.

Assume no additional machines or supervisors will be acquired for the internal transfers and the Transistor Division's unit cost is

Direct material	$1.00
Direct labor	1.15
Variable overhead	0.50
Fixed overhead (based on full capacity of 100,000 units)	0.30
Total cost	$2.95

General Formula for Transfer Prices

The following general formula provides a beginning point for computing a minimum transfer price:

Differential costs per unit $+$ lost contribution margin on outside sales

The formula indicates that the minimum transfer price should equal the unit differential cost of the product being transferred, plus the contribution margin per unit that the selling division loses as a result of giving up outside sales. If the selling division is not operating at full capacity, it does not lose contribution margin unless it has to give up some of its present outside customers. **Differential cost** is the increase in total company cost if a company adds the contemplated alternative to its present volume of activities. For transfer pricing purposes, the **opportunity cost of internal transfers** is the maximum lost contribution margin on outside sales; this results from a company not selling the goods outside, but transferring them internally. Although the accounting records show differential costs, they do not show opportunity costs.

If the intermediate product has a perfectly competitive market in which the maximum available output may be sold at unchanging prices, the opportunity cost to the selling segment is the market price less the differential costs incurred for the product. The reason is that in refusing to accept outside business and, instead, making an internal transfer, the selling segment has forgone income that it could have earned on this business. If there is no intermediate market, the opportunity costs are zero, and the most appropriate transfer price is the differential cost. The buying segment's opportunity cost is the lower of either its net marginal revenue or the price at which it could obtain the intermediate product in the open market.

Differential/Variable/Prime Cost Transfer Prices

Entertainment, Inc., could add the transistor direct material and direct labor to give a **prime cost** of $2.15 as the transfer price. However, this price would not be appropriate because it does not cover all the differential costs of the Transistor Division since variable overhead is not included.

Instead, Entertainment may use all variable or differential costs as a transfer price. Variable costs approximate differential costs in many situations. However, when fixed costs increase because of a transfer of goods between segments, they are differential costs and accountants should include these fixed costs in the transfer price. Variable-cost transfer pricing has the advantage of ensuring, in the short run, the best use of total corporate facilities. Because total fixed costs do not change in the short run, variable cost pricing focuses attention on the contribution margin a transfer generates and on how it increases short-run profitability.

The transistor differential cost of $2.65 is an appropriate transfer price for guiding top management in deciding whether there should be transfers between the two divisions as long as the total differential costs are less than the outside purchase price of the buying division. Since Entertainment's radio assembly company had purchased transistors for $3.50 less a 10 percent discount or $3.15, the transistor differential cost of $2.65 is less. This transfer price would be appropriate only when the selling division has excess capacity as it does in this example. A differential-cost transfer price also would be appropriate in situations where there is no outside market.

One limitation of variable-cost transfer pricing is that a company must cover all costs before earning a profit. A company cannot ignore fixed costs. As a result, a variable-cost transfer price may be profitable in the short run, but not in the long run. Another weakness of a variable- or differential-cost transfer price is that it allows one segment manager to make a profit at the expense of another segment manager, because the buying segment receives all the profit.

In addition, if a segment must forgo outside sales to make products for other internal segments, the use of variable- or differential-cost transfer prices can lead to dysfunctional decisions. For example, assume the Transistor Division presently sells 70,000 transistors at $3.50 to outside customers, but the Radio Division wants to buy at $2.65 all 100,000 transistors they could make. A dysfunctional decision might result if only the Radio Division's position is considered by comparing their $3.15 outside purchase price with a $2.65 differential cost transfer price that gives the Radio Division a $50,000 savings in purchasing.

The following shows it would be unfair to penalize Transistor Division profits by requiring transfers at $2.65 when $3.50 reflects its opportunity costs. All benefits with this transfer price accrue to the Radio Division. The Transistor Division and the overall company have lost the $59,500 contribution margin even though there is a $50,000 savings in the Radio Division by not buying outside at $3.50.

	Sales to Radio Division	Sales to Outsiders
Sales	$265,000 (100,000 × $2.65)	$245,000 (70,000 × $3.50)
Variable expense	265,000 (100,000 × $2.65)	185,500 (70,000 × $2.65)
Contribution margin.	$ 0	$ 59,500

Also, transfer prices based on differential costs diminish the decision-making autonomy of the profit center. If differential cost increases with volume, the segment is dependent on the total demands of the buying division and the supplying division's external customers. This means that neither segment can make its output decisions independently.

Full-Cost Transfer Prices

Using full cost as a transfer price is probably the oldest transfer pricing method. **Full cost** includes actual manufacturing cost plus portions of marketing and administrative costs. Full cost is firmly established in centralized companies, because almost all companies use full cost to value inventory for external reporting. The full-cost transfer price of $2.95 would be appropriate if Entertainment treats both divisions as cost centers rather than as independent, autonomous profit centers. Transistor Division profits are reflected in the profits of the Radio Division when using a full-cost transfer price.

Companies primarily use full cost because it is convenient to apply. Probably the greatest single advantage of any cost-based pricing method is its simplicity. Full-costing data are already available and can be obtained at very low expense and at tremendous time saving. Another important advantage of the full-cost transfer price is that it leaves no intracompany profits in inventory to eliminate when preparing consolidated statements. When accountants record intracompany transfers below cost, they must increase inventories to cost before consolidating the inventory accounts. When accountants record intracompany transfers at prices above cost, they must eliminate all profits in ending inventories before consolidating inventory accounts. Managers may compare transferred costs with budgeted costs to measure production efficiency. This method allows simple and adequate end-product costing for profit analysis by product lines.

Despite these advantages, full cost is not suitable for companies with decentralized structures that measure the profitability of autonomous units. Full-cost transfer pricing has little worth for evaluating performance because it shows no income on interdivisional sales. A criticism of full cost as well as all cost pricing methods is that they do not create incentives for segment managers to control or reduce costs. All cost-based transfer prices reflect the accumulated efficiency level of the supplying division. As a result, accumulated inefficiencies from divisions that previously handled the product affect the reported income of the division in question.

Full cost does not provide management with a divisional profit figure for the selling division. Therefore, decentralized companies that must measure the profitability of autonomous units do not find cost-based transfer prices appropriate. In addition, segments tend to become complacent and less concerned about controlling costs when they know their costs are merely passed along to the next segment.

Another justifiable criticism of the full-cost method is that it departs from goal congruence. The use of full-cost transfer prices can lead to decisions that are not goal congruent when the supplying division is not operating at capacity. For example, a division may decide to purchase outside the company at an apparent savings. However, a reduction of the full-cost transfer price to the market price would recover all variable costs and a portion of fixed costs. The company fails to cover these fixed costs because of the decision to purchase outside. To avoid such suboptimization, top management must order the lowering of transfer prices or require internal purchasing. Yet, both of these solutions dilute the authority of individual divisions.

Standard Full Cost. The use of standard full cost rather than historical average cost eliminates the negative effect of fluctuations in production efficiency in one division on the reported income of another division. Standard full cost also permits division managers to know in advance what price they will receive or what price they will pay for transferred goods. This eliminates one source of delay in processing transfers.

Using either actual or standard full cost weakens the income statement as a performance measure because the firm's long-range profitability is not emphasized. The local unit lacks the incentive to control or reduce cost when cost recovery is assured. A full-cost transfer price also does not provide an accurate guide for decision making because it offers no sound basis on which management can delegate decision-making authority to segment managers. For this reason, companies should restrict full-cost transfer prices to situations where segment managers lack decision-making authority.

Full Cost Plus Markup. A $3.50 transfer price represents full costs plus a markup but it is not appropriate because it exceeds the price that the Radio Division pays an outside supplier. In addition, the Transistor Division has excess capacity, and its opportunity costs are zero because it loses no contribution margin if the internal transfer occurs. However, if the Transistor Division receives more outside orders than it can fill and has no excess capacity, $0.85 represents the Transistor Division's opportunity cost ($3.50 − $2.65 = $.85). Using the general formula of adding opportunity cost to differential costs results in a $3.50 transfer price as follows: $2.65 differential costs per unit + $0.85 lost contribution margin on outside sales = $3.50.

Market-Based Transfer Prices

Using **market price** as a transfer price is essentially an opportunity cost approach. Company segments and outside customers pay the same price. However, a division might transfer products at a price lower than market price to reflect trade discounts and economies obtained by intracompany transfers. The market price of $3.15 ($3.50 − $.35 discount) represents the price that the Radio Division pays an independent, outside supplier and is appropriate if the company treats both divisions as independent units.

The principal argument for use of market price is that it represents the opportunity cost of the intermediate product. The price the buying unit is paying is the same as if it bought from an outside source. The use of the market price creates a fair and equal chance for both the buying and selling departments to make the most profit they can. Market-based pricing also places segment operations on a competitive basis. Market-based pricing results in charging all internal and external customers the same price and reflects product profitability at various stages of production.

Also, if a segment cannot improve on the product sufficiently to recover both the acquisition cost of the product on the open market and the production cost of the department, the segment should not be in operation. For example, if a segment cannot afford to pay market prices, the company should not allow it to buy internally at less than market. Conversely, if a segment can sell outside at market, the company should not require it to sell internally for less. In the short run, however, a lower transfer price may allow a segment to become profitable by acquiring a larger share of the market.

The use of market prices as transfer prices is especially appropriate when evaluating the performance of segments. We determine segment income by how well the division functions in a competitive market because intermediate products are transferred from one segment to another at market price. The income determined in this way also shows how effectively the segment can perform in an outside independent market. In appraising efficiency, this income measurement has stronger appeal than the arbitrary income that results when using variable cost or full-cost transfer pricing.

A serious disadvantage to market-based transfer pricing, however, is that it requires the existence of a well-developed outside competitive market. Transfers based on market prices work well in a decentralized organization if there is a perfectly competitive intermediate market and the supply and demand of segments are practically independent of one another. However, the product may not be actively traded on the open market and have no market price. This is most likely to occur when all companies in the industry are fully integrated and each division produces only for internal consumption. For example, a department may produce a unit that is not sold to outsiders, as when parts are secretly designed. Also, if the transfer is nonrepetitive, there may not be a large enough market for the product to give a valid market price.

Negotiated Transfer Prices

To overcome the difficulties of market-based transfer prices, very often we use a compromise transfer price that takes into consideration the competition and a fair return to the supplying division. The supplying and receiving departments can negotiate a price, with top management serving as arbitrator to avoid time-consuming, inflammatory negotiations.

A **negotiated price** is an attempt to simulate an arm's-length transaction between supplying and buying segments. A negotiated price of $2.90 would be appropriate if Entertainment treats both divisions as profit centers and both divisions share in the benefits. The firm could take the $0.50 ($3.15 − $2.65) difference between the Transistor Division's differential cost and the net outside purchase price and divide it between the two divisions, thus yielding $2.65 + $0.25 = $2.90.

Generally, we use a negotiated price if there is no competitive outside market price. In theory, we can make a strong case for market-based negotiated prices because all market prices are based on negotiation between buyer and seller. It follows then that if companies give segment managers autonomous authority to buy and sell as they think necessary and if they bargain in good faith, the result of this bargaining is the equivalent of a market price.

An additional advantage of pricing through negotiation is that usually sales of intracompany products are in such large volume that the use of any market price is meaningless because the quoted market price is based on smaller, normal order sizes. For example, assume that the selling division has excess capacity and the buying division can use more of the product. A negotiated price somewhere between the market price and the seller's differential cost increases the profits of both segments and is advantageous to the company as a whole.

However, negotiation may be very time-consuming and require frequent reexamination and revision of prices. Also, the process may reflect the negotiating skill of the managers rather than the actual economic circumstances. For this method to work, the company must allow subunits to go to the outside markets if negotiation fails. In addition, negotiated prices eliminate the objectivity necessary to ensure maximization of companywide profits. As a result, the negotiated price may distort segment financial statements and mislead top management in its attempts to evaluate performance and make decisions.

A primary problem with negotiated transfer pricing arises when there is no established market price and the segment managers cannot reach agreement. Top management must then intervene to establish an arbitrary transfer price. This central control should exist to prevent suboptimization of company profits by division managers when the purchasing division can buy more cheaply outside than it can within the company. If the segment managers cannot agree on the transfer price and the purchasing manager has the option of purchasing in the outside market without the approval of top management, overall profit may be reduced.

When arbitration between subunits becomes necessary, divisional authority is breached and the purpose of decentralization and profit centers is subverted. In fact, frequent arbitration completely nullifies the purpose of decentralization. Certainly, such arbitrary pricing severely hampers the profit incentive of segment managers. However, executives cannot carry decentralization to the point where they ignore all profits to allow local managers full control of purchasing when the product is available within the company.

Transfer Prices for Services

Divisions of many large organizations sell products and perform services for customers and for each other internally. One department's transfer of services to a second department is part of its sales yielding income. That same transfer is the second department's purchase of services. Companies typically bill administrative services, such as accounting, computer processing, personnel, and payroll, to the divisions they support. In each of the cases, they must establish equitable transfer prices to appraise division performance for its own return on invested capital. We can adopt many of the principles applied to the transfer of products for the transfer of services.

A first step in setting transfer pricing for services is to identify the different departments contributing various services and to estimate the corresponding skill and experience of personnel involved in delivering services. The second step is estimating each department's contribution to the value of the service generated. Because services are intangible, the service unit is often difficult to define.

Impact of Product/Service Life Cycles on Transfer Prices

Managers should recognize the stage in the life cycle of the product or service function and incorporate it in transfer pricing issues. A different set of environmental and technological factors characterizes each stage in the life cycle. The transfer pricing mechanism should vary according to these stages. Chapter 1 discusses life-cycle costing and includes planning and product design in addition to the generally accepted four stages of the product life cycle: introduction, growth, maturity, and decline. Because planning and product design do not need transfer prices, the following list excludes these two stages when describing the characteristics of the stages and the appropriate transfer prices.

1. *Introduction*   Low sales volume and high introduction costs result in a loss situation; near monopoly exists for service or product; intensive marketing activity generates awareness of product or service. Because the division has a monopoly for the product/service and there are no close substitutes available in the market, a market price is ambiguous. Thus, a company should use a transfer price based on the outlay cost plus a fixed fee or the outlay cost plus a profit share depending on whether the buying or selling division should bear the risk.

2. *Growth*   Unit cost is the lowest as a result of large sales increases and production and distribution economies; profits reach their highest level. The degree and extent of competition in the market, strength of the marketing department in the entity, and the speed of improvements in the service function affect the transfer price. Generally, the most appropriate

transfer price is market price less any savings in transaction costs because of the internal transfer. The more unique the product or service, the less the competition, and the more difficult it is to determine a market reference price.

3. *Maturity*   Costs increase as a result of product/service modifications, increased marketing mix expenditures and other efforts to maintain market position; profits decline causing weak firms to withdraw from the market; price competition intensifies as the factors responsible for the monopoly disappear. Gradually, identical products or services become available from many sources; marketing conditions become highly competitive, and rate of sales growth declines. At the maturity stage, the degree of elasticity of buyers switching to other suppliers, the extent and degree of standardization, degree of differentiation and price competition, relative intensity of price competition, and the relative strength of the marketing department should affect the transfer price chosen.

4. *Decline*   The market for the product or service decreases causing sales and profits to decline; divisions usually leave the market. The extent of cost control possible by the transferor, the degree of sophistication among customers, the relative degree of a firm's overcapacity vis-a-vis industry's capacity, and the extent of product differentiation influence the transfer price.

Recording Internal Transfers

Regardless of the basis used for transfer prices, the accounting system should provide a means of adjusting internal company data to a cost basis for external financial reporting. If the transfer price is less than inventory cost as when using variable costing as a basis, accountants should apply a portion of the fixed cost to goods remaining in inventory. Conversely, if the transfer price is more than inventory cost as with market or negotiated prices, accountants must subtract the excess from inventory and profit accounts in consolidation.

Consolidated income statements eliminate intradivisional sales including transfers made at standard full cost. Managers must distinguish between external and internal purchases to consolidate financial data and to provide information about the relative importance of intracompany transactions.

With this approach, an accountant uses the following entries to record a shipment from one segment to another at a 20 percent markup on sales.

On the supplying division's books:

Accounts Receivable—Purchasing Division.........	1,000	
Intracompany Sales		1,000
Cost of Goods Sold—Intracompany	800	
Inventory		800

On the purchasing division's books:

Inventory—from Supplying Division	1,000	
Accounts Payable—Supplying Division........		1,000

Assume the Purchasing Division sells one-fourth of these goods to an external customer for $500. The entries on the Purchasing Division's books are as follows:

Productivity

Current Cost Management Practice

Chicago's Tribune Co. is entering multimedia in a big way by pushing into on-line services and CD-ROM. At the thoroughly modern Tribune, editors are electronically converting newspaper articles to be distributed on Chicago Online, a data network owned by Tribune and affiliated with America Online, Inc. Reporters use a remote-controlled TV camera to tape sound bites for a local TV cable channel owned by Tribune. While Tribune was formerly a classic publishing and broadcasting company, it is becoming one of America's most aggressive multimedia players. Once reliant on papers and TV stations, it now wants to distribute its products—everything from news and country and western TV shows to children's books—via CD-ROM, on-line computer services, and interactive cable.

Richard A. Melcher with Ronald Grover, "Not Just Ink-Stained Wretches," *BusinessWeek,* March 28, 1994, pp. 56–59.

Accounts Receivable—External Customer	500	
Sales		500
Cost of Goods Sold—External Customer (1/4 × $1,000)	250	
Inventory—from Supplying Division		250

Assuming intracompany sales are handled in this manner, the accountant makes the following adjusting entry at the end of the period:

Intracompany Sales	1,000	
Cost of Goods Sold—Intracompany		800
Cost of Goods Sold—External		
Customer (20% × $250)		50
Inventory Adjustment Allowance (20% × $750) . .		150

The **Inventory Adjustment Allowance** account credited in the preceding journal entry is a contra account to inventory for external financial reporting. This allows for the elimination of intracompany inventory sales at prices above cost from both the overall company balance sheet and the income statement. Segment income is computed from the segment books, unadjusted.

Multinational Transfer Pricing

Many companies transfer goods and services between segments located in different countries. The transfer prices for these goods and services should reflect that countries have different tax rates and tax regulations. Because of these varying tax rates, a corporate group has an incentive to transfer most of its income to the subsidiary that has a tax advantage over other members of the corporate group. In addition, some countries restrict the payment of income or dividends to parties outside their national borders. Under these circumstances, the company often increases the transfer price so they pay more funds out of these countries while appearing to follow regulations. Transfers from foreign countries, where the wage level and/or tax rate is low, also may be made at a domestic market price rather than on a cost basis because foreign economic conditions are so different from domestic conditions. Foreign currency exchange rates, tariffs, and custom duties are additional factors influencing the multinational transfer price chosen.

Dual Transfer Pricing

In discussing transfer pricing, this chapter has emphasized the advantage of each base and the effect of specific circumstances. Having only one transfer-pricing method may not be appropriate for a company because it is unlikely that any one method fulfills all management's needs. **Dual pricing** allows each segment to use the transfer price that provides the optimum decision for the segment and still meet the goals of the overall company. Accountants apply dual pricing primarily to evaluate performance, while still allowing goal congruence and autonomy. Dual pricing does not fit into the neat balancing act of accounting. Company profit does not equal the sum of division profits. Therefore, accountants must eliminate some of the segment profits.

For example, suppose that Segment A can sell its product in the market for $20 but its differential cost is only $14, and Segment B can further refine this product. However, the Segment B manager is unwilling to pay the same price as an outsider, especially because top management is forcing a purchase from Segment A. If management wishes to evaluate the performance of Segment A, it should consider using the market price as the transfer price. There is no reason for Segment A to transfer its product at a lower price. This gives Segment A credit for the opportunity it loses in the market by making the sale to another segment of the company. If this market price is, in turn, imposed on the buying division that does not have the complete authority to choose whether to buy from Segment A or not, a conflict can arise. Segment B manager probably resents Segment A's making a profit at Segment B's expense when the manager does not have the authority to buy elsewhere. The better procedure in this circumstance is to charge the buying division with differential cost. This recognizes the interdependence of the subunits. This solution does not allow one segment manager to make a profit at the expense of another segment manager.

Missing Incentive to Control Cost

In practice, companies have not adopted dual pricing widely because of a major inherent weakness—all segment managers may win, but the overall company may lose. This results because the buying segment purchases at a low price while the supplying segment sells at a high price. As a result, the incentive to control cost is missing and inefficiencies may develop.

Do not assume, however, that dual pricing always uses market price as the selling segment's transfer price and a cost-based transfer price for the buying division. For example, suppose the full cost or differential cost of a product from Segment X is $10 and Segment Y further refines this product. Also, assume that Segment Y could purchase this elsewhere for $9. The solution using dual pricing should involve Segment X's selling the product to the home office for $10 and, in turn, Segment Y's buying it for $9 from the home office. In this case, the home office has created a fictitious loss that is eliminated when determining the overall company profit.

If a company fails to take this approach, the manager of Segment Y will try to buy from the outside resulting in a $1 savings. However, this lower external price could be the result of temporary excess capacity in a competitor's plant. If management fails to investigate the situation and eliminates Segment X because it believes it can buy all the products it needs on the outside for $9, the company may be hurt financially when the outside party sells its excess supply and raises prices above $10. A company should guard against such suboptimization.

Behavioral Implications of Transfer Pricing

As we have just discussed, when decentralization leads to **suboptimization**, the goals of the whole organization become secondary. Transfer prices do, however, offer a behavioral advantage by providing for units to operate autonomously in a decentralized organization even when there is no externally determined market price for the products and services exchanged internally. When managers determine transfer prices logically, segments can maintain their autonomy while also making decisions that benefit the entire organization. Because segment managers are closer to the marketplace, they provide more relevant information concerning the price of inputs and outputs.

Suboptimization

The use of opportunity cost and differential cost gives an immediate indication of the proper decision about selling the product inside or outside the company if a perfectly competitive market for the intermediate product exists. However, where there is imperfect competition in the intermediate market, the manager of either the buying or selling division can decrease the overall income of the company by attempting to maximize his or her own income. This might result in improved performance for the segment, but it does not result in goal congruence because the income of the company as a whole is less than optimum.

For example, suppose the selling division is operating at capacity and can sell all of its products at $5 each. However, the buying division must operate at 70 percent capacity because it cannot secure enough products. Should management force the selling division to transfer products at $4 if the selling division's unit differential cost is $3? For the selling segment to maximize income, it should continue to sell outside the company, yet this strategy hurts overall company income. Assume the buying division's cost of the finished product is as follows:

Part (being manufactured by selling division)	$ 4
Other variable cost	6
Allocated expenses	7
	$17

Assuming the allocated expenses represent expenses that the company incurs regardless, the company gains $6 ($7 allocated expenses minus $1 difference in outside sales price and inside transfer price) to contribute to unavoidable fixed expenses by transferring internally rather than selling outside. This assumes the buying division sells its product for at least $17. In the short run, there is an advantage to the internal transfer even though this action is counter to the purposes of decentralized decision making. This results because it requires top management to overrule the selling management's decision. If this action occurs on a regular basis, this situation would not be viable in a divisional organizational structure.

Suboptimization also often occurs when the total full cost at the transfer point is greater than the outside purchase price available to the purchasing division. To maximize division income, a manager will buy from the outside source. Assuming the supplying division has excess capacity, the outside purchase decreases the total profit of the company. This decrease occurs if the difference between the full-cost transfer price and the outside purchase price is less than the difference between the differential cost in the selling division and the full-cost transfer price. Stated differently, suboptimization can arise if the outside purchase price is greater than the differential cost in the supplying division, but less than the full cost of the supplying division.

The following example illustrates suboptimization; assume Selling Division A is not operating at full capacity:

	Unit Cost
Material	$ 20
Labor	30
Overhead, 40% fixed	100
Full-cost transfer price of product in Division A	$150
Outside purchase price available to Division B for product identical in quality, delivered	$130

Given these conditions, the Division B manager has an incentive to purchase the product outside, which results in a $20 savings to the division. Yet, Division A's managers may argue for coverage of its full cost. The differential costs in this division amount to $110 (material, $20; labor, $30; and variable overhead, $60). If Division B accepts the competitor's bid, the loss in company total income is $20 per unit, as shown here:

Addition to total company cost to purchase externally	$130
Addition to total company cost if produced by Division A . . .	110
Decrease in total company income	$ 20

The company should not adhere to completely decentralized decision making in this situation. Management also should be cautious in establishing policies requiring that divisions always purchase internally.

Divisional Performance Evaluation

The ideal transfer pricing system should motivate segment managers to most effectively fulfill overall company objectives. Often, this is difficult because of the division performance evaluation used by many companies. Such companies evaluate division managers on the basis of the profit the segment earns; but if one segment charges another segment too much, overall company performance decreases. When setting transfer prices, accountants must consider the interests of both the buyer and the seller. The problem becomes even more crucial if the company gives each segment manager a bonus based on the segment's performance. This may cause managers to try all the harder to get maximum beneficial prices from the other segments. Under these circumstances, segment managers have good reason to argue for a high transfer price for the goods they sell to other segments. In turn, they argue for a low price for goods bought from other segments. The transfer price thus chosen is likely to lead to a lack of goal congruence for the overall company.

A bonus system actually encourages segment managers to make decisions that may be good for their segments but detrimental to the entire company. For instance, using the previous example illustrating suboptimization, if segment managers receive bonuses based on their divisions' income, the Division B manager will be more eager to accept the outside offer resulting in a $20 savings per unit. Buying outside increases the segment's income which, in turn, increases the manager's bonus.

The company can solve this problem with complete goal congruence by reducing the transfer price to $130 at which both the individual segments and the overall company benefit because the selling division has excess capacity. Another solution is a transfer price that divides the difference between Division A's differential cost and the outside purchase price. For example, the $20 ($130 − $110) difference can be divided equally, resulting in a transfer price of $120 [$110 differential cost + $10 difference ($20/2)]. Even though transfer pricing should be a tool for motivating segment managers, it also should lead to segment actions benefiting the entire company.

Reward Team Players. A company's reward system should encourage segment managers to be team players. Companies should carefully establish transfer prices so segments do not purchase outside when there are high-fixed-cost internal facilities that would remain idle. Often, as in the case when idle facilities exist, the company must make decisions for its overall benefit.

Internal Competition

Internal competition between segments of a company often is very healthy. Division managers may feel assured of a market for their production if the company does not allow buying segments the freedom to purchase externally. A supply division with a captive source of sales is less likely to be aggressive in developing more efficient methods that lower costs than if it must meet competition on each sale. **Internal competition** is, therefore, one means of preventing division managers from becoming complacent and failing to incorporate current technological developments.

In addition, companies should compare division performance to that of outside companies. A company may overlook how outdated and unprofitable a division really is by failing to compare its performance with like companies outside the organization. In determining transfer prices, a company should focus attention on uneconomical activities that otherwise might go undetected. Further, the firm should force managers to check outside markets and supplies carefully.

External Procurement

Management should establish a policy concerning outside purchases of products and services. When the company's own product is superior to or equal in quality and performance to that from outside sources, segments should buy the product internally. This assumes meeting an acceptable delivery schedule. If the internal source of supply is not competitive, however, management may agree to outside procurement as long as the receiving division can justify its action. It is reasonable to allow division managers the freedom to purchase externally if the external price is lower and the quality comparable. In justifying outside purchasing, the division should supply evidence of a reasonable effort to bring the internal supplier's terms into competition with those of the outside source.

Some companies have a policy of splitting purchases between external and internal supplying divisions. This policy is appropriate only when management considers it important to have alternative sources available or when internal facilities are not adequate.

Not imposing the strict requirement that segments can purchase only from other segments allows segment managers some flexibility in purchasing from outsiders. This arrangement may motivate segment managers to determine whether to sell intermediate products in their present form or process them further. Learning that a competitor's price is cheaper stimulates segment managers to find the reasons. Flexible purchasing encourages them to seek each other's advice about the best plant layout and work flow. This approach emphasizes each segment manager's contribution to the overall company.

Although some conflict of interest is usually unavoidable no matter how well developed the transfer-pricing system, management can design a workable system that resolves much of this conflict by monitoring certain issues. Management should avoid holding division managers responsible for their segments' performance, while restricting their purchasing function. If managers have income responsibility, they need the authority to purchase material that best meets their requirements. It is, therefore, important that the system provides objective measures of division income as free from administrative bias as possible. The objective should be to prevent the transfer price from becoming an alibi for poor income performance.

Summary

The shift from centralized to decentralized organizations has increased the role of transfer pricing as portions of the revenue from one income center become portions of the costs of another. Transfer pricing and divisional income measurement serve several purposes: to guide division managers in decision making; to help evaluate divisional performance; and to aid top management in allocating resources and in long-range planning. A supplying division that is always assured of a market for its products may lapse into inefficiencies that are difficult and expensive to discover and correct. There is no single best pricing method from an absolute point of view, but there may be a best method for a particular set of circumstances. Product type, degree of decentralization, stage in the life cycle, and managerial skills are considerations in selecting a transfer price. In establishing transfer prices, management should encourage segment managers not only to communicate with each other but also to study and eliminate uneconomical activities within their divisions.

Companies guard against suboptimization, that can arise if the outside purchase price is greater than the supplying division's differential cost but less than its full cost. Companies should establish transfer pricing policies so divisions do not purchase outside when there are high-fixed-cost internal facilities that remain idle, thus hurting the overall company. Extreme decentralization granting complete freedom to decide in the best interests of the segment alone, and not of the overall company, is not advisable. To prevent such dysfunctional behavior, a company's reward system should encourage segment managers to become team players.

Important Terms and Concepts

Transfer pricing	614	Negotiated price	619
Differential cost	615	Inventory Adjustment Allowance	
Opportunity cost	615	account	622
Prime cost	616	Dual pricing	623
Full cost	617	Suboptimization	624
Market price	618	Internal competition	626

Problem for Self-Study

Recommendations Regarding Transfer Prices
Newberg Division's budget for next year for producing 60,000 storage containers is as follows:

Direct material	$162,000
Direct labor	156,000
Factory overhead—variable	66,000
Factory overhead—fixed	170,000
Marketing expense	42,000
Administrative expense	49,000
	$645,000

Of the fixed factory overhead, $50,000 represents allocated joint costs. Management's analysis shows that shipping and handling expense, which is included in the marketing expense, amounts to $0.50 per unit; the remainder is divisional fixed expense. The division manager's salary of $30,000 is included in administrative expenses. This represents the only administrative expense that could be eliminated because the other components are allocated home office expense.

Required:

a. Give the segment cost per unit.

b. Assume Newberg Division has no market for its containers except for inside sales to other divisions and is not operating at normal capacity. What should the transfer price be?

c. Assume buying divisions within the company are able to purchase containers at a price of $14, less 8 percent discount from outside suppliers. What should the transfer price be?

d. Assume that Newberg Division can sell all its production to outsiders for $15. Which transfer price would you recommend?

Solution to Problem for Self-Study

NEWBERG DIVISION

a. Segment cost

Direct material	$2.70 ($162,000/60,000 units)
Direct labor	2.60 ($156,000/60,000 units)
Factory overhead—variable	1.10 ($66,000/60,000 units)
Factory overhead—fixed	2.00 [($170,000 − $50,000)/60,000 units]
Marketing expense	.70 ($42,000/60,000 units)
Administrative expense	.50 ($30,000/60,000 units)
Unit segment cost	$9.60

---

b. The minimum transfer price should be $6.90 differential cost ($2.70 + $2.60 + $1.10 + $.50 shipping and handling) as long as this does not exceed the outside purchase price of containers available to internal buying divisions. Some price between $6.90 and $9.60 is likely. However, since Newberg sells exclusively to inside divisions, fixed segment (traceable) costs must be covered and $9.60 appears most appropriate with the possibility of covering some of the allocated cost.

c. A price of $12.88 [$14.00 − (8% × $14.00)] is recommended since this is the price now being paid externally by purchasing divisions. Newberg Division should be willing to meet this price because it covers full unit cost of $10.75 ($645,000/60,000 units). An argument can be made for a transfer price less than $12.88, but not less than $9.60 because Newberg Division has excess capacity. If the buying divisions pay $12.88, all benefits accrue to Newberg Division. If the difference between $10.75 and $12.88 is split between Newberg and the internal buying division, both segments benefit from the intracompany transaction.

 d. With these conditions, Newberg has no excess capacity, and a transfer price of $15 should be used. However, unless Newberg containers have superior qualities worth the cost differential, no transfers will take place since the internal buyers can secure containers for $12.88.

Review Questions

 1. Define *transfer pricing* and indicate when it is necessary to establish transfer prices.

 2. Discuss three transfer pricing methods, indicating under what conditions each would be appropriate. State any variations of these methods.

 3. Indicate the relationship between the degree of interdependence and diversification among company segments and the significance of the transfer pricing problem.

 4. What effect does the use of transfer pricing information have on the pricing basis chosen?

 5. With regard to both the segment and the overall company, how should the transfer pricing system motivate segment managers?

 6. What is the impact of product life cycles on transfer prices?

 7. Discuss some advantages and limitations of using full cost as the transfer price.

 8. How can opportunity cost be used as the basis on which transfer prices are established?

 9. Discuss several arguments supporting the use of market transfer pricing.

 10. What important requirement is necessary for market transfer pricing to be successfully applied?

 11. Discuss how a service company uses transfer prices.

Exercises

Writing

E19–1 Transfer Pricing Issues
In a company in which income responsibility is centralized, managers are evaluated on their ability to control cost. However, as businesses grow and become decentralized, evaluating managerial performance becomes more complex. Part of this complexity arises because divisions transfer goods and services to other divisions of the same company. Since the transfer from the supplying division represents their sales, a price is assigned to these goods or services. That same transfer is the receiving department's purchase of service or cost of materials. There is inherent conflict because division managers are interested in receiving the best price for their segments. The best price for the buying segment is a low price while it becomes a high price for the selling segment. Thus, the growth of enterprises and trend toward decentralization of management within these companies creates challenges. The improper setting of transfer prices could lead subunit managers to purposely pursue a course of action not benefiting the organization as a whole. Thus, transfer pricing is a complicated issue that can cause many problems in a diverse corporate setting.

Required:

a. Transfers between departments within the same company create the problem of determining the best procedure(s) for calculating the proper transfer prices of products being sent for further production before ultimate consumption. Briefly list several possible situations complicating the transfer pricing issue.

b. Describe the two basic methods of establishing transfer prices. Give one advantage and one disadvantage of each method.

c. Discuss some behavioral problems associated with using transfer prices.

d. Describe how service industries use transfer prices.

E19–2 Conditions Conducive to Transfers

The Motor Division of French Company produces components that the Fabricating Division incorporates into a final product. Components from the Motor Division also can be sold to outsiders. Each division is a separate profit center. Data gathered from records of both segments reveal the following:

Market price—final product	$600
Market price—components	300
Motor Division—variable cost	170
Fabricating Division—variable completion cost	375

Required:

a. Describe the conditions under which transfers should be made to the Fabricating Division. Support your answer with a quantitative analysis.

b. Assume the conditions that you suggested in Requirement *a* exist. At which price should transfers be made?

Critical Thought

E19–3 Behavioral Problems Associated with Segmentation and Transfer Prices

Multidivisional corporations benefit by establishing independent and autonomous profit centers. Each division manager's nearness to the marketplace provides relevant information regarding the price of inputs and outputs. Also, more effective coordination of production factors is possible at the divisional level. However, dividing an organization into independent segments has strong behavioral implications.

Required:

Discuss the behavioral problems often encountered in establishing segments and the related transfer pricing situations that normally arise.

E19–4 Short-Run Economic Advantage of Interdivisional Sales

Eastern Division of Platt Company requests that the Western Division supply it with No. A854 valves. Western Division presently operates at capacity and sells valves to outside customers at $2.50 each. The variable costs of these valves produced by the Western Company is $1.40.

Eastern Division, operating at 60 percent capacity because it cannot secure enough valves, is willing to pay $2 for each valve. The cost of the finished product built by the Eastern Division based on normal capacity is as follows:

Valve (the type now being manufactured by Western Division)	$ 2.00
Other purchased parts	13.00
Other variable costs	8.20
Fixed factory overhead, marketing, and administrative expense	9.00
Total	$32.20

Platt Company uses dollar net income return on investment in measuring division managers' performance.

Required:

a. Ignoring income tax, should the Eastern Division be supplied valves by the Western Division?

b. Ignoring income tax, discuss the short-run economic advantage per unit to the Platt Company if the Western Division supplies valves at $2 each to the Eastern Division.

c. In view of the present organizational structure and long-run economic profits, what recommendation would you make to Platt top management regarding the transfer?

E19–5 Transfer Price to Meet Target Return

The cost accountant for the Mischke Company provides you with the following data for the Tire Division:

Division assets	
Cash	$ 100,000
Inventories	250,000
Plant assets, net	1,150,000
	$1,500,000

	Per Unit
Variable costs	$10
Fixed costs (based on normal volume of 40,000 tires)	5

She also informs you that 5,000 of the 40,000 tires usually are sold to the Motorcycle Division of the company. Currently, the two division managers cannot agree on the price to transfer these tires. The Motorcycle Division manager has offered to pay $14, claiming he can purchase these tires from another company at that price. The Tire Division manager believes that the Motorcycle Division should pay the same $18 price as other customers.

Analysis shows that the Tire Division can eliminate $5,000 of inventories, $10,000 in plant assets, and $20,000 in cash fixed costs if the Tire Division manager does not sell to the Motorcycle Division. The assets can be converted into cash.

Required:

a. Should the Tire Division sell to the Motorcycle Division at a transfer price of $14?

b. Assume that top management decides that the tires will be sold to the Motorcycle Division at a $14 transfer price. At which price must the 35,000 tires be sold to outsiders to achieve a 15 percent desired return on assets employed?

E19–6 Conditions for Profitable Transfer

The Assembly Division of Waltz Company produces components that the Finishing Division incorporates into a final product. Components from the Assembly Division also can be sold to outsiders. Each division has been established as a separate profit center. Data gathered from both divisions' records reveal the following:

Market price—final product	$350
Market price—Assembly Division components	200
Assembly Division—variable cost	150
Finishing Division—variable completion cost	175

Required:

a. Under what conditions should transfers be made to the Finishing Division? Support your answer with a quantitative analysis.

b. Assuming the conditions exist that you suggested in Requirement *a*, at what price do you think transfers should be made?

E19–7 Transfer Pricing to Provide Normal Return

Division A of the Diamond Company manufactures motors used by other divisions of the company and sold to outside customers. Division B of Diamond Company has requested that Division A supply a certain style of motor, and Division A has computed a proposed transfer price on this motor, as follows:

	Per 800 Motors
Variable cost	$35
Fixed cost	25
	$60
Markup on full cost to provide a normal return	6
Transfer price	$66

Management of Division B believes this transfer price is too high because it knows that this style of motor is sold to outside customers for $62 per 800 motors. Management of Division A indicates that it is forced to lower the price below $66 to meet competition. Even though it cannot earn a normal return from outside customers, it believes that Division B should pay for this return.

Required:

Explain what the transfer price should be.

E19–8 Impact of Outside Sales Offer

The Supply Division of Hilton Company has the following budgets when it receives an order for an additional 20,000 units from an outside customer for a bid price of $2.20 per unit. At present, all 80,000 units being produced are sold at $2.40 to the company's Buying Division.

	80,000 Units	*100,000 Units*
Direct material	$ 32,000	$ 40,000
Direct labor	40,000	50,000
Variable overhead	60,000	75,000
Supervision	15,000	17,000
Rent	6,000	10,000
Depreciation	20,000	20,000
	$173,000	$212,000

Required:

a. Should the order from the outside customer be accepted?
b. In view of the outside order, the Buying Division asks that the Supply Division cut their price to match the bid price. Prepare an analysis showing your recommendations to the Supply Division.

E 19–9 Rejection of Outside Order

At practical capacity, the Fabricating Division of Crossville Company has facilities to produce 8,000 units per month. Each unit requires five direct labor-hours. The Assembly Division of the company has forwarded a requisition for 8,000 units to the Fabricating Division. Since Crossville Company uses a market-based transfer pricing system, contribution margin using a $50 market price would be $168,000. The receipt of this requisition from the Assembly Division upset the Fabricating Division manager as he had just been approached by an outside buyer with a rush order for 5,000 units at a $56 unit sale price. Top management's initial reaction to the conflict is that the outside order should be rejected so that the Assembly Division's order can be filled.

Required:

a. Determine how the income of the Fabricating Division and Crossville Company would be affected if the outside order is rejected.
b. List four additional factors that should be known before a final decision is made.

P19–10 Differential Cost Per Unit and Desired ROI

A division of Neale Equipment Company manufactures motors exclusively for the Assembly Division. Annual sales and production volume is 5,000 units, which represents normal capacity. All unit fixed costs are based on normal capacity. Analysis of the records revealed the following unit cost:

	Per Motor
Direct material	$ 10
Direct labor	5
Variable overhead	7
Traceable fixed overhead	12
Allocated fixed overhead	4
Variable marketing expense	6
	$ 44
Assets committed	$300,000

If the Motor Division were discontinued, $10,000 of the annual traceable fixed costs could be eliminated.

Required:

a. Determine the differential cost per motor.
b. Assuming that 2,000 motors are transferred to the Assembly Division at a transfer price based on the differential cost determined in Requirement *a,* at what price must the other 3,000 motors be sold to outsiders to earn a 10 percent desired return on assets employed?

Problems

P19–11 Decentralization in a CPA Firm

The firm of Myrtle Douglass, CPA, has prepared the following budgets for its three groups. The firm recently organized into three independent groups; each group provides services to outside clients as well as to other groups within the firm. The fees budgeted are representative of those of other CPA firms in the geographical area.

	Tax Group	Auditing Group	Management Services Group
Budgeted consulting hours	10,000	16,000	12,000
Fees	$450,000	$960,000	$780,000
Variable cost	280,000	720,000	456,000
Fixed cost	50,000	96,000	60,000

The firm asks your advice in evaluating each group as if it were an autonomous company.

Required:

a. Assume that the auditing group has need for tax consulting services. The tax accountants are busy preparing tax returns to meet approaching deadlines. What transfer price should the tax group charge the auditing group?

b. Use the conditions given in Requirement *a* but assume that the services are needed during the summer months when the tax accountants are less rushed and have fewer deadlines to meet. If the tax accountants did not perform this work, they would be spending time catching up on their professional reading. What transfer price should now be charged to the auditing group?

c. Assume that a former employee of the firm started her own tax practice and, to acquire clients, charges $35 per hour. The auditing group needs some tax analysis that would become part of the audit. Since the company's own tax group has adequate opportunity to use its time with outside clients, would you advise the auditing group to go outside the firm? What nonfinancial factors must be considered?

d. Discuss if, in view of the characteristics of this firm and its employees, you think the three groups should be established as autonomous companies.

P19–12 Capacity Impact on Transfer Price

SPATS

Edmonds Company is a producer of various kinds of batteries. After recently acquiring a lawn mower assembly company, management questions if they should establish two autonomous divisions. Presently the lawn mower company is purchasing 500 batteries a month for $20 each from Miller Company, which then gives them a 4 percent quantity discount.

The Battery Division supplies you with the following costs per battery:

Direct materials	$ 9
Direct labor	3
Variable factory overhead	1
Fixed factory overhead, based on 1,850	
batteries (normal capacity) per month	3
	$16

The Battery Division presently sells 1,850 batteries of this line with a 25 percent markup on sales price. No quantity discount is given by the Battery Division.

Required:

a. Would you advise the Battery Division to sell to the Lawn Mower Division? If so, at what transfer price?

b. Assume instead that the Battery Division presently sells 1,300 to outsiders. With these conditions should the Battery Division sell to the Lawn Mower Division? If so, at what transfer price?

c. Disregard your answer to Requirement *b,* and assume that presently the Battery Division sells 1,300 batteries to outsiders and the Lawn Mower Division manager offers to purchase 500 batteries a month for $14.50 each. What decision would you advise them to make? Why?

P19–13 Economic Advantage of Interdivisional Sales

Richards, Inc., management has recently incorporated a companywide policy for their 20 divisions; it states that a selling division always must sell to a buying division at current market price. The Seattle Division was asked to submit bids to the Boston Division on 2,500 standard parts representing 15 percent of its normal capacity for the year. Seattle Division quoted a price of $40, but was forced by company policy to fill the order at $32, the price an outside supplier quoted. At a price of $40, Seattle Division could have earned a contribution margin of $36,000.

Required.

a. Calculate how much the total contribution margin of Seattle Division decreased when it sold at the price of $32.
b. Describe the impact on the total income of Richards, Inc., of requiring Boston Division to buy internally.
c. Assume further that by selling to Boston Division, Seattle Division must forgo an order to an outside company for 2,200 units of special design. These specially designed parts could be sold for $45 each; the variable cost per unit is $28. Seattle is unable to process both Boston's standard parts and the outside order because of volume limitations. By requiring Boston to buy inside, how will the income of Seattle Division and overall income be affected? What would you suggest as a solution?

P19–14 Evaluating Various Transfer Prices

The Battery Division of the Herndon Company supplies batteries to outside customers at a price of $100 per 100 batteries. The company has just acquired a flashlight company and the president believes the newly acquired Flashlight Division should purchase batteries from the company's own Battery Division, even though the latter now has all the outside orders it can process.

Until the acquisition, the flashlight company had purchased batteries for $95 per 100 batteries.

The Battery Division's cost per lot of 100 batteries as follows:

Direct material	$30
Direct labor	18
Variable overhead	17
Fixed overhead (now operating at a 1 million battery lot level)	10
Total cost	$75

Herndon Company management is undecided as to the transfer price for sales between the two divisions.

Required:

a. Explain why each of the following transfer prices would or would not be appropriate to charge the Flashlight Division on the intracompany sales:
   (1) $60   (4) $80
   (2) $65   (5) $95
   (3) $75   (6) $100
b. Assume instead that the Battery Division has excess capacity. In view of this changed condition, explain why each of the transfer prices in Requirement *a* would or would not be appropriate to charge the Flashlight Division.

P19–15 Sales to Company Division

Schnell Company is a producer of various kinds of gaskets. After recently acquiring a washing machine assembly company, management wonders if they should establish two autonomous divisions. Presently the washing machine company is purchasing 2,000 gaskets monthly at $60 each from an outside supplier, which gives them a 10 percent quantity discount from the $60. The Gasket Division supplies you with the following costs per gasket:

Direct material	$20
Direct labor	12
Variable factory overhead	3
Fixed factory overhead, based on 4,000 gaskets (normal capacity) per month	8
	$43

The Gasket Division presently sells 2,000 gaskets of this line with a 30 percent markup on cost. No quantity discount is given by the Gasket Division.

Required:

a. Advise the Gasket Division whether to sell to the Washing Machine Division. If so, at what transfer price?

b. Assume instead that the Gasket Division presently sells 4,000 gaskets to external customers. With these conditions should the Gasket Division sell to the Appliance Division? If so, at what transfer price?

c. Disregard your previous answers and assume that presently the Gasket Division sells 3,100 gaskets to outsiders and the Washing Machine Division manager offers to purchase 2,000 gaskets a month for $40 each. Provide quantitative data to support whether the Gasket Division manager would favor this alternative.

d. Assume that presently the Gasket Division sells 3,100 gaskets to outsiders and that a partial internal transfer of the 2,000 needed can be made. Provide quantitative data to support whether the overall company profits would increase if top management forces a transfer between the divisions. Calculate the cost to Schnell for three alternative sale and purchase arrangements between the Gasket Division and the Washing Machine Division.

e. Advise top management about what decision to make. Why?

SPATS

P19–16 Comparison of Gross Margin Using Different Transfer Prices

The Cathode Ray Tube Division of Emmett Company sells various styles of tubes to outsiders. Recently, an engineer for Emmett Company's newly acquired toy company has developed a unique idea for a television game employing a cathode ray tube.

The Tube Division presently produces and sells 120,000 tubes of this style for $140. The plant has an annual capacity of 150,000 tubes with a variable cost of $80. Fixed costs related to this style amount to $3.6 million per year.

The Toy Division plans to sell the television game for $350 and has received offers from outside companies to supply the tubes needed for $125. Total variable costs per game amount to $155 including the outside purchase price of the tubes. Fixed costs for 30,000 games assembled per year amount to $3 million.

The Tube Division offers to supply the Toy Division with the style of tubes needed for $140; however, the Toy Division manager wants to refuse the offer. Top management believes that full costs should be the transfer price, but they ask for your recommendation.

Required:

a. Compare the gross margin for both divisions and the total company if tubes are purchased outside with internal purchases made using a transfer pricing system based on full cost, assuming a production level of 150,000 tubes.

b. Explain which cost factors are relevant to the decision whether the Tube Division should sell to the Toy Division.

c. Discuss if the Tube Division's unit full cost is relevant to this decision.

P19–17 Profitable Volume for Decentralized Organization

Emma's Deodorant Company organized several years ago to manufacture both men's and women's deodorant. When first organized, the company sold the deodorant as a paste in a plain jar. Then, one of the supervisors developed a roll-on bottle and sales skyrocketed. It was so successful that Emma's management decided to set up a Manufacturing Division and a Bottle Division. Competition between the two divisions has become quite intense because each division manager receives a bonus based on the center's contribution margin.

The president is quite concerned that the transfer price used is not fair and has called you in as a consultant to evaluate the circumstances. Your first project is to determine the costs of each division; then your second project is to discover the prices charged by competitive bottle companies. Your findings are as follows:

Cases	Bottle Division's Cost per Case	Average Competitor's Sales Price per Case
1,000,000	$10.00	$12.00
4,000,000	9.50	11.00
8,000,000	9.10	10.50

The Manufacturing Division's costs of ingredients and sales prices are as follows:

Cases	Cost per Case	Sales Price per Case for Packaged Product
1,000,000	$25.00	$45.00
4,000,000	23.40	43.60
8,000,000	22.60	41.80

Required:

a. Evaluate the success of decentralizing the divisions.

b. Assume the market price is used as the transfer price and calculate the income for each division and for the overall organization using a volume of 1 million cases, 4 million cases, and 8 million cases.

c. Recommend the most profitable volume for each of the divisions and for the overall company.

SPATS

P19–18 Segment Margin for Divisions

Gray Cosmetics Company manufactures pressed powder in compacts. The manufacturing process is a series of mixing operations with various coloring ingredients added to obtain specified shades. Workers then press the powder into company-produced compacts and pack them in cases containing 24 compacts. Gray Cosmetics management believes that the sale of its product is heavily influenced by the highly decorated compact. Much advertising has stressed the uniqueness of the compact's decorative style.

The company has organized its process into the Powder Division and the Compact Division. Each division is supervised by a plant superintendent; supervisors of the various cost centers report to the plant superintendent. All compact production has been used by the Powder Division. Little interchange of management ideas or personnel takes place between the two divisions; unfortunately, this has caused intense rivalry to develop between the divisions. Top management believes that their decision several years ago to establish each division as a profit center also may have contributed to the rivalry. Each plant superintendent receives a commission based on the net income generated by the division.

You are to determine a proper transfer price for the Compact Division to use in charging the powder profit center. The compact plant superintendent informs you that cost studies have determined variable costs are $11 per case, while total annual fixed costs are $1 million. An outside compact production company has contacted the company president and supplied the following price quotations:

Cases	Price per Case
250,000	$18
500,000	16
750,000	13

Top management has reviewed the reliability of the outside supplier and is confident that a compact identical in quality to that of the Compact Division can be supplied.

In addition to the compact costs, the Powder Division has the following costs. The sales price for the finished product reflects the price-demand relationship.

Cases	Powder Cost per Case	Sales Price per Case
250,000	$19	$60
500,000	18	54
750,000	16	48

The current market value is presently used as the transfer price.

Required:

a. Determine the segment margin for each division and income for the overall company at a volume of 500,000 cases.
b. Determine the volume that would be most profitable for each division and the overall company.
c. Explain the conditions that should exist for a division to be established as a profit center.
d. Discuss if the Compact and Powder Divisions should be organized as profit centers.
e. Indicate two other transfer pricing methods Gray could use and show the prices at various volume levels.

Cases

Writing

C19–19 Interference by Top Management in Transfer Pricing
Ten years ago, Subbett Company, a midsize subsidiary of Paulett Corporation began research on developing a chemical, similar in nature to CHEMX, for mixture in a commercial detergent. Within Paulett Corporation, CHEMX is presently being purchased by Stoney Company, another subsidiary. Stoney began purchasing CHEMX eight years ago from Outter Company.

While Stoney has been pleased with the quality of CHEMX, its relationships with Outter have been somewhat disagreeable at times. For instance, Stoney recognizes that even though it is not the only Outter buyer, its demand is significant in relation to Outter's capacity. Further, in making suggestions to Outter for product improvement, Stoney realizes that its competitors buying from Outter also are going to reap the benefit from these suggestions. However, of even more concern is the fear of monopolistic pricing practices as Stoney does not have a second source for CHEMX.

Five years ago Subbett was successful in developing a chemical substitute for CHEMX. Subbett required $40 million of capital equipment to enter the market. One of Subbett's objectives is to supply chemicals that support Paulett Corporation's worldwide consumer markets. However, Paulett has a policy of decentralized operations. Given these policies, only Subbett resources funded the project. Subbett knew that Stoney Company was free to select the chemical it thought best met its needs.

When Subbett entered the market, Outter Company immediately lowered its CHEMX price to Stoney. Outter explained this move by stating that after several years of manufacturing, it has been able to maximize production efficiencies and could achieve lower costs. Subbett realized that it was at a cost disadvantage and might meet resistance if it tried to price on a full cost basis with an additional percent return on invested capital. Subbett also recognized that it must beat Outter's prices and minimize production costs. Otherwise, it would never be more than Stoney's second source of supply even though Subbett had the capacity to produce all the chemicals required by Stoney.

Subbett's president requested a meeting with Paulett's chief executive officer in hopes of getting the CEO to force Stoney to buy internally at full cost plus a return on invested capital. However, a letter received by both Stoney and Subbett's presidents from Paulett's CEO indicated that this matter should first be presented to the executive committee of the parent company. After meeting with the executive committee, there was no consensus as to the transfer price. Then the presidents of Stoney and Subbett brought the problem to the CEO.

In a short meeting, the CEO made it clear that this was the two subsidiary presidents' problem. Based on their extensive prior experience, if they could not work out a solution, new presidents could. Thus, the division presidents were sent back to their companies.

In reflecting on his action, the CEO questioned if he had done the right thing. In his earlier days as the new top manager, subordinates were constantly asking for his suggestions. Finally, when asked for a solution, he began asking subordinates, "What do you recommend?" Subordinates thus realized that they would be asked for suggestions and began thinking through their problems before approaching him. Often times, subordinates found they could arrive at the solution themselves and did not need the CEO's advice. However, the CEO found that because he keeps space between those he manages and himself, he is sometimes lonely; he misses workers dropping in and taking up his time just chatting. He questions whether he adopted the correct management style after all.

Required:

a. Explain the problem from each of the following points of view.
    (1) Subbett Company, the selling division
    (2) Stoney Company, the buying division
    (3) Paulett, the parent company.
b. Forecast the result if Subbett establishes a full cost plus markup price for its product.
c. Suggest a more appropriate price rather than a full cost plus markup price for their product.
d. Evaluate if Paulett's CEO took the correct stance from:
    (1) An accounting-financial (income statement) regard.
    (2) A behavioral view.
e. Discuss if there are good reasons for the cliché about it being lonely at the top.

C19–20 The Impact of Product Life Cycle Stages on Transfer Pricing
Product life cycle has been classified into four different stages; each of the stages has its own distinct characteristics. It is because of their unique characteristics, the following four different product life cycle stages have varying effects on transfer pricing.

1. *Introduction*—low sales volume and high product introduction costs resulting in a loss situation; firm frequently has a near monopoly; intensive marketing activity to generate awareness of product is used.

2. *Growth*—sales increase, costs per unit decline and profits result; costs per unit are the lowest as a result of large sales increases and production and distribution economies; profits reach their highest level during the growth stage.

3. *Maturity*—costs increase as a result of product modifications, increased marketing mix expenditures and other efforts to maintain market position; profits are declining which causes weak firms to withdraw from the market; price competition will intensify as the factors responsible for the monopoly disappear. Gradually, identical products will become available from many sources; marketing conditions become highly competitive and the rate of sales growth declines.

4. *Decline*—market for the product contracts causing sales and profits to decline; firms usually leave the market.

As previously described, each stage in the product life cycle is characterized by a different set of environmental and technological factors. The choice of a specific transfer pricing policy is, therefore, a function of the relative variation in the nature and the intensity of these contextual variables. The overall factor affecting the choice is of course the management philosophy on the treatment given to individual parties at stake—the transferor and transferee. The treatment accorded to a specific responsibility center as a cost center or profit center affects the way transfer price will be set in any given situation. Broadly speaking, the transferor has a general preference for market-based transfers, and the transferee has a general preference for full cost transfer, assuming that full cost is less than market price. Such behavior, though, maximizes individual utility, each preference is usually opposite to each other at a given point of time which gives rise to interdivision conflict. Any attempt by a transferor to maximize its utility will prevent the transferee from maximizing its own utility. Hence, a trade-off is sought to be achieved in practice which is subject to the interacting forces of the underlying environmental and technological factors.

Required:

a. Assume there has been limited attention given to the relationship between transfer price and product life cycle. What influence, if any, should the product life-cycle stage have on the transfer price used?

b. Discuss the factors in choosing the most appropriate transfer price at the various stages of a product's life cycle.

c. Describe what role, if any, the transfer pricing mechanism used has in a company adopting product life-cycle costing?

C19–21 Negotiating a Transfer Price

Formerly independently owned, Abbott and Bennett Companies merged to form AB, Inc., several years ago. Since each of the two companies had spent large sums of money in promotions recently, they each retained their own names, but insiders simply refer to them as Division A and Division B. Each division also maintained its own production and marketing staff and facilities. Division management is responsible for acquiring and financing current and plant divisional assets, revenue, and cost of operations. They evaluate division managers on return on investment generated. Corporate management has no restrictions regarding where each division must purchase parts and supplies as long as corporate profits are not adversely affected.

Division B recently received a contract for a product that uses a component Division A manufactures and sells to outsiders for $5. In submitting its bid, Division B used a cost figure of $2.70 for the component Division A produces. Division A would still incur variable marketing expenses on sales to Division B. Division B management had obtained an outside purchase price for the component of $5.10 but reasoned that it should only be charged $2.70

by Division A which represented the total variable cost of the part to Division A. Before preparing the bid, Division B secured the following unit cost data for the component from Division A.

Standard variable production cost $2.20
Standard variable marketing expenses 0.50
Standard fixed production cost 0.80
Selling price to outsiders 5.00

Division A's salespeople are actively securing new customers but do not believe the demand will be so great that they would lose any regular customers if Division A produced the component for Division B.

Since this transfer pricing issue has never arisen before in the company, there is no policy regarding the price. Division A and B management have been meeting trying to decide on a fair price while still protecting their own segments because whatever price is chosen will affect their performance evaluation.

Required:

a. Assume management believes that controversy between its divisions can lead to disharmony affecting long-range profits. It proposes to settle the transfer pricing issue by choosing a price. Explain why you do or do not advise such a procedure.

b. Assume Division A and B managers agree that they should be allowed to work out a satisfactory solution to this transfer pricing issue.
   (1) Would you advise such a procedure?
   (2) List three surrounding circumstances needed for a negotiated transfer pricing method to work satisfactorily.

c. Discuss the impact of the following proposed transfer prices and indicate if they should be accepted:
   (1) Standard variable production cost.
   (2) Standard variable production cost plus 10 percent of that cost.
   (3) Standard variable production plus variable marketing expenses.
   (4) Division A's sales price to outsiders.
   (5) Standard full production cost.

d. Assume the division managers cannot agree on a transfer price and Division B begins making arrangements to buy externally for $5.10. Explain why Division B should or should not be allowed to do this.

e. Determine the upper and lower limits within which a fair transfer price should fall in this situation.

Critical Thought

C19–22 Conflict in Pricing Quotes

Robert Bingham, Inc., manufactures force pumps for water wells and fire engines. Force pumps resemble lift pumps, the simplest type of reciprocating pump used to pump water from wells. However, force pumps discharge water at high pressure instead of merely lifting the water out. Force pumps generally are run by mechanical power rather than by hand power.

Bingham has three divisions, each specializing in various components of the pump. Sales of these components also are made to outsiders. The Southern Division produces the piston and valve; the Northern Division, the pump handles that attach to the piston, and the Western Division, the cylinder and outside container.

Bingham, Inc., is highly decentralized, with each division being judged independently as a profit center. Management uses profit and return on investment to evaluate each division manager. Top management believes that in the past five years, while this decentralized policy has been in force, profits have improved. Each division manager is normally free to buy from whichever supplier he or she desires. For sales within the company, divisions are expected to meet the current market price.

Juan Weston, the Western Division manager, has completed the design of a special water well for leisure home owners. Such wells are smaller than those for residential homes and less expensive. After requesting bids for 1,000 completed pistons and valves, the following bids per completed unit were received: Southern Division—$500; Outboard Company—$400; Exxel Company—$425. The Southern Division had received an agreement from the Northern Division to supply pump handles at the present market price of $112.50 per unit. The Northern Division presently is operating at full capacity and does not have excess inventory; however, the Northern Division has agreed to sell the needed handles to Southern by adding more workers to avoid losing any sales to outside customers. The differential cost of pump handles is $65.

Scarlett Smith, the division manager of the Southern Division, indicates that she cannot quote a unit price lower than $500 because she must cover full cost as well as give her division some profit for their efforts. She provides further support for her position by arguing that her salespeople have been told they must cover full costs in all price quotes. An analysis of the accounting records reveals that the differential cost of each completed piston and valve is $375. Of this amount, 30 percent represents the cost of the pump handles to Southern.

In the Exxel Company bid, there was an agreement to buy certain unassembled parts from both the Southern and Northern Divisions. The price agreed to with Southern for a portion of the valve is $50 for each part. Exxel agreed to purchase 1,000 handles from the Northern Division for $70 each. The unit differential cost of Southern's valve is $20, and it is $30 for Northern's handles.

Weston is quite annoyed that Southern's price quote is so much higher than the competitors' quotes. He calls the controller at corporate headquarters for advice. Weston indicates that unless told otherwise, he plans to accept the lowest bid.

The controller is concerned that Smith has submitted such a high bid in view of the recent slack in work experienced by her division. However, the controller also knows that intervention by top management must be carefully handled because a precedent may be established that could raise similar problems later.

Required:

You may find it useful to diagram the alternatives with the respective prices and differential costs.

a. Provide support indicating the most profitable action for:
   (1) The Western Division.
   (2) Bingham, Inc.
b. Decide if the controller should instruct Western to buy from Southern. If so, at what price?
c. Assume the controller intervenes in this situation. What will the effect be on:
   (1) The division profit measurement system?
   (2) Outside firms?
d. Determine if the controller should ask Northern to lower its bid of $112.50 to Southern. Why or why not?
e. Assume Southern had idle capacity for several months. How would your answer be affected?
f. Discuss the impact on the situation if division managers receive a bonus based on division profits.

C19–23 Transfer Pricing for Auto Dealers

The New York Automobile Dealership serves as a leader in its field because it has undertaken innovative techniques that have received the recognition of its peers. Sales are expected to exceed 1,500 units or $10 million next year.

The dealership maintains separate Parts and Service Departments in addition to the Sales Department. The Sales Department is treated as a customer of both Service and Parts Departments.

Management of New York Automobile Dealership is basically uninformed about the merits of transfer pricing theory. Transfer prices are arbitrarily set to ensure profitability of all company segments. The dealer-owner set the following prices in conjunction with the service manager and parts manager. The implied intention is to give both the Service and Parts Departments a share of the Sales Department's profit. The following prices are not retail or wholesale prices; they simply are arbitrary transfer prices. This is the practice that the dealer-owner has found commonly used by the company's competitors also.

All the items purchased by Sales from Parts and Services are products the Sales Department can readily obtain as there is an excess in the market of these products.

Products, Services	Invoice Price to Parts Department	Cost to Service Department	Hours to Install*	Cost to Sales Department
Vinyl seatcovers	$150	NA	1	$200.00
Material for paint protection	10	$ 10	1.3	86.40
AM-FM stereocassette	200	210	1.2	302.40
Air conditioning	400	450	5.0	800.00

*The cost to install averages $20 per hour .

The sales manager believed that he was being charged excessive prices for these four products and services and began soliciting bids from outsiders. The sales manager was especially frustrated because all three department managers are paid a bonus on their departments' net income. After a short time, he found a subcontractor willing to supply comparable products at considerable savings. The outside price for seatcovers was $190; for stereocassettes installed, $282.40; and for air conditioners, $660 installed.

This practice continued for three years; during this period the sales manager was excited about his increased bonuses, while the parts and service managers were upset over their departments' declining profits and idle capacity. The Sales Department sold and had installed 400 seatcovers, 300 stereocassettes, and 800 air conditioners. Of these, 150 seatcovers, 100 stereocassettes, and 200 air conditioners were purchased internally.

Finally, in the third year, the dealer-owner called in all three department managers to analyze and solve the problems that were developing. After agreeing that a problem did exist and that long-run survival of the company should be the chief concern, the three department managers and the dealer-owner reluctantly agreed on the following transfer prices:

Products and Services	
Vinyl seatcovers	$170
Material for paint protection	40
AM-FM stereocassette	220
Air conditioning	690

The dealer-owner, however, decided to call in a management accountant to analyze departmental costs and operations before any changes were implemented. The accountant was also asked to investigate the revised transfer prices that the four individuals agreed on and determine if further revisions were needed. The management accountant began her investigation by calling together the three managers in a conference to discuss the problem. All managers argued their respective points to support their position and practice. The sales manager was unwilling to pay more for a product than the outside competitors' prices. The sales manager further argued that he and his family had become accustomed to a higher standard of living because of the bonus and he did not believe it was fair for the company to ask him to take a cut in pay just because he had to assume some of the costs of the Parts and Service Departments' inefficiencies. The parts and service managers argued that they could not afford to sell their products and services to the Sales Department without earning a reasonable profit; they also wanted to provide a higher standard of living for their families.

After several days of negotiation, the three department managers agreed to leave the responsibility for establishing the transfer prices with the management accountant. These three individuals recognized that an outsider would not be biased and would use cost accounting theory in arriving at a decision. Further, they all admitted that close interaction and harmony was essential for long-run survival and that one individual should not be allowed to benefit at the expense of the other two managers.

Required:

a. Use the present transfer prices and determine the markup on cost for each of the four products or services sold to the Sales Department.

b. Compute how much the Sales Department saved on air conditioners, stereocassette radios, and seatcovers by purchasing externally.

c. Calculate how much the company as a whole lost by the Sales Department making the outside purchases.

d. Identify the person who should bear the blame for the amount the company as a whole lost from the Sales Department buying externally.

e. Calculate the opportunity cost of the four products and services being transferred between departments.

f. Determine if the transfer prices suggested by the four individuals within the company were fair and acceptable. Provide support for your answer.

g. Indicate what transfer prices you would suggest as the management accountant given responsibility for solving the problem.

CHAPTER
20

Capital Budgeting

Chapter Objectives

After studying this chapter, you should be able to:

1. Discuss the issues encountered in estimating the hurdle rate or cost of capital.
2. Explain the present value concept and how it applies to capital expenditure analysis.
3. Demonstrate discounted cash flow methods of evaluating capital assets.
4. Use payback and other alternatives to discounted cash flow methods.

Introduction

Because capital expenditures involve significant resources that companies commit for a long time in the future, much time and effort should go into the evaluation of proposed capital investments. The length of time for which companies commit resources makes capital expenditures more risky than short-term investments. Capital expenditure analysis is also crucial because after making a commitment for a capital investment, management may have difficulty in recovering the cost other than through using the capital asset. Thus, high initial equipment costs hinder a company's ability to change products and processes to respond to shorter product life cycles and changing consumer demands.

Most companies do not have all the funds necessary to finance all proposed capital expenditure projects. Thus, they can put their available funds to different uses. As a result, before beginning a capital expenditure program involving a large outlay of funds that a company would tie up for several years, management should seek assurance that the company will receive an acceptable return on the investment. When managers evaluate projects on quantitative criteria, they compare predicted cash flows with the investment required. Management then determines whether the return generated by these projects exceeds the minimum acceptable return. Determining which rate is acceptable is a difficult problem involving more financial than accounting concepts. This chapter discusses the discounted cash flow methods and alternative methods for evaluating capital expenditures. The next chapter addresses the impact of automation on capital budgeting techniques, sensitivity analysis, and other related topics.

Top Management Involvement.   Top management should evaluate large capital expenditure proposals because individual projects must be consistent with overall company objectives. However, top managers must delegate some authority to middle managers who have the required competence for properly evaluating capital expenditure proposals. Companies vary in decentralization of authority for capital expenditure approval. For example, some companies allow division managers much discretion in selecting the plant and equipment to use in operating their divisions. Other companies specify a small dollar amount as the limit for approval by division managers; only top management can approve capital expenditure proposals greater than this limit.

Managers should establish policies reflecting their goals in advance so the firm's capital expenditure evaluation can be objective and consistent. Detailed capital expenditures guidelines are especially necessary at lower management levels. Policy manuals usually detail the procedures and document flow for administering capital expenditure proposals. Managers should design these manuals to encourage employees to search for profitable investments within their own technical specialties. Although a thorough review is important, management must guard against having such detailed, time-consuming procedures that employees hesitate to introduce new projects, thus impeding rapid project development. Employees also are more likely to search for capital improvements when they believe that their proposals will be given a fair review.

Sunk Cost in Replacement Decisions.   Managers facing replacement of plant assets should consider only future cost savings and revenue changes. This type of analysis is difficult to prepare because managers must estimate the economic life

Productivity

Current Cost Management Practice

Charles Knight is chairman and chief executive of the St. Louis-based manufacturer, Emerson Electric Co. Emerson has an unbroken string of 36 years of increased earnings. Emerson makes refrigerator compressors, pressure gauges, and In-Sink-Erator garbage disposals. Because its markets are so competitive, it has operated without significant price increases since the mid-1980s. Rather than complain about unfair foreign competition, Knight has a focused strategy. Emerson's best cost producing strategy was achieving the lowest cost consistent with quality. The objective was to reduce expenses to a point where the company could compete effectively with imports. Knight worries that the pressure of the last 10 years has been so great that managers have neglected growth. Emerson's exceptionally detailed planning seeks to identify problems before they emerge and block them. As part of Knight's concern for worker morale, employees complete surveys evaluating supervisors every two years. Forecasts were beginning to show that further gains from cost cutting would be marginal. Now risk taking is encouraged, and making mistakes is more accepted. Knight has set a target of pushing revenue growth to as high as 10 percent per year while keeping profit margins and return on equity steady. While Knight sets tremendously aggressive expectations for his managers, he also creates a belief that they can do just about anything they set their minds to.

Seth Lubove, "It Ain't Broke, but Fix It Anyway," *Forbes,* August 1, 1994, pp. 56–60.

of the new asset in addition to the prospective purchase price less any salvage value they expect. Book value is the original cost less the accumulated depreciation; book value on the equipment being replaced is a **sunk cost.** Because a company cannot change the cost by any future decision, sunk cost is irrelevant to the decision regarding the replacement of the equipment. However, book values do affect the income tax liability related to plant asset transactions because of Internal Revenue Service regulations regarding the recognition of gains and losses on exchanges of plant assets.

Tax Impact on Capital Decisions

Income tax laws that apply to capital budgeting situations often are complex. Because the main objective of this book is not to explain current tax law and tax provisions change frequently, we use only a few pertinent provisions in our illustrations. Even though the illustrations and problems represent an attempt to follow the current tax rulings regarding depreciation and other aspects of capital budgeting, the coverage does not necessarily reflect current tax treatment.

Income Tax Deduction for Depreciation

An allocated share of the purchase cost of capital assets is deductible as yearly depreciation. Sometimes the amount allowable for depreciation is equal to the purchase cost of the asset. In other cases, it is less than or more than the cost of the asset acquired. In those countries where companies have the option of claiming investment tax credits, they may reduce the amount allowable for depreciation to less than the cost of the asset acquired. An **investment tax credit** is a direct reduction of income taxes arising from acquiring depreciable assets. Governments use the investment tax credit option to stimulate capital investment in specific industries and in certain assets. Tax authorities allow these three main methods of depreciation:

1. *Straight-line depreciation.*   Each year companies claim an equal amount of depreciation.

2. *Accelerated depreciation.*   Companies write off depreciable assets more quickly than by using straight-line depreciation.

3. *Allowable percentage write-offs.*   Tax legislation specifies a table of percentages for depreciation. These tables usually allow companies to recover the cost of plant assets for tax purposes over a shorter period than the assets' physical lives. Capital projects are more attractive because this tax incentive makes projects' cost recovery larger in the early years.

Tax Shield

Although depreciation does not involve a cash outflow, it is deductible from taxable income. Thus, depreciation reduces the amount of cash outflow for income taxes. Because depreciation expense protects an equal amount of income from taxation, it creates a tax shield or tax savings. Multiplying the tax rate by the amount of depreciation gives the **tax shield** or savings. The formula is

$$\text{Depreciation deduction} \times \text{Tax rate} = \text{Tax shield}$$

To illustrate the impact of this tax shield, assume a company is considering the purchase of a new machine costing $120,000. Managers expect the life of the machine to be eight years with no salvage value. They expect the machine to produce cash inflow of $95,000 and cash outflows of $60,000 per year. Assuming a straight-line depreciation deduction of $15,000 per year for tax purposes and a 40 percent tax rate, the amount of the tax shield is $6,000 (40 percent $\times$ $15,000 depreciation). Considering taxes and depreciation, Exhibit 20–1 gives the annual net cash inflow generated from the $120,000 machine investment.

If no tax shield resulted from the depreciation expense, the income tax would have been $14,000 ($35,000 $\times$ 40%), and the net aftertax cash inflow from the investment would have been $21,000 [$35,000 − $14,000 or $35,000 $\times$ (1 − 40%) = $21,000]. In the same way that additional income causes income taxes to increase, depreciation expense causes income taxes to decrease. The tax shield reduces income

EXHIBIT 20–1   Aftertax Net Cash Inflow

	Change in Net Income	*Change in Cash Flow*
Cash inflows generated	$95,000	$95,000
Cash outflows	60,000	60,000
Beforetax net cash inflow	$35,000	$35,000
Depreciation	15,000	
Beforetax net income	$20,000	
Tax at 40%	8,000	8,000
Aftertax net income	$12,000	
Aftertax net cash inflow		$27,000

tax by $6,000 ($15,000 × 40%) and increases the investment's aftertax net cash inflow by $6,000. Thus, the following formula also can determine the aftertax net cash inflow from an investment:

$$\begin{matrix} \text{Aftertax net} \\ \text{cash inflow} \end{matrix} = \left[\begin{matrix} \text{Beforetax} \\ \text{net cash inflow} \end{matrix} \times (1 - \text{Tax rate}) \right] + \overbrace{\left[\begin{matrix} \text{Depreciation} \\ \text{deduction} \end{matrix} \times \begin{matrix} \text{Tax} \\ \text{rate} \end{matrix} \right]}^{\substack{\text{Tax shield attributable} \\ \text{to depreciation}}}$$

Present Value

After arriving at the aftertax net cash inflow, we must express these cash flows in dollars at the same time for a useful comparison. This requires discounting future dollars or bringing them back to the present using present value concepts. The value of money today is its **present value.** The present value concept is important because capital budgeting involves long-term projects. Most capital-budgeting decisions involve a comparison of cash flows in and out of the company.

The **time value of money** concept explains why a dollar today is preferred over receiving a dollar at some future date. For example, the present value of one dollar is $1, while the present value of $1 available at some time in the future is less than $1, assuming no deflation. This preference results because (1) there is risk that the company will never receive the future dollar, and (2) the company can invest the dollar on hand at present, resulting in an increase in total dollars possessed at that future date.

Present Value of a Dollar

In present value terms, the rights to future cash receipts are owned now. For example, assume a company expects a machine it is considering buying to generate $10,000 in cash receipts one year from now. The present value is less than $10,000 because the company will not have access to the receipts for one year.

We use a process called **discounting** to convert the cash inflows for each period to their present value by multiplying each period's cash inflow by the appropriate factor from a present value table. The appendix at the end of the book includes present value tables to facilitate applying the discounted cash flow methods. Table A on page 868 gives the present value for a single amount to be received n periods from now. By multiplying the appropriate present value factor from the table by an expected future cash flow, you can determine the present value of the cash flow.

Present Value of an Annuity

An **annuity** is a series of equal cash flows equally spaced in time. We can use Table B on page 869 to find the present value of a stream of equal cash inflows received annually for any given number of periods. Tables A and B are both based on the assumption that cash inflows are received only once annually on the last day of the year.

Present Value of Depreciation Tax Shield

Tax policymakers use the tax allowance for depreciation to stimulate long-term capital investments. The faster we depreciate an asset's cost for tax purposes, the sooner the tax reductions are realized. Thus, the greater the net present value of the tax shield.

EXHIBIT 20–2   Present Value of Depreciation Tax Shield

	(1) Depreciation Deduction on the Tax Return	(2) Tax Shield (35% × Depreciation Deduction)	(3) Present Value Factor at 10% Discount	(4) (2) × (3) = Present Value
Year				
1	$ 350,000	$122,500	.909	$111,353
2	260,000	91,000	.826	75,166
3	170,000	59,500	.751	44,685
4	110,000	38,500	.683	26,296
5	110,000	38,500	.621	23,909
	$1,000,000	$350,000		$281,409

(35 percent tax rate, $1 million depreciation basis)

Assume a company depreciates an asset having a $1 million depreciation tax basis over five years. Exhibit 20–2 computes the annual depreciation tax shield and the present value of the tax shield, using a 35 percent tax rate and a 10 percent discount rate. We assume no salvage value.

Depreciation deducted for tax purposes is shown in Column 1. The tax shield shown in Column 2 is the tax savings from deducting the depreciation that protects an equal amount of income from taxation. We determine the tax shield by multiplying the tax rate by the depreciation deduction. Column 3 indicates the present value factors using Table A, Present Value of $1, in the appendix. Column 4 shows the present value of each year's tax shield. Note that even though Years 4 and 5 reported the same $110,000 depreciation deduction, the present value of the expense deduction for Year 4 is $26,296. For Year 5, it is only $23,909, illustrating the present value concept.

When applying present value to a capital investment, the future return is in the form of cash inflows generated by the asset acquired. Because a company must make an outflow of cash in the present to purchase the asset, management questions whether the cash inflow generated by this asset warrants making the investment.

Evaluation Techniques for Capital Expenditures

Management uses several techniques for evaluating capital expenditure proposals. These range from simple methods such as cash payback to more sophisticated methods using the time value of money in computing an estimated return on investment. We discuss three capital budgeting quantitative methods and their advantages and weaknesses: (1) discounted cash flow, (2) payback or payout, and (3) unadjusted return on investment. Two variations of the discounted cash flow method are net present value (also called excess present value) and internal rate of return (often called time-adjusted rate of return). In evaluating proposals involving large sums of money, the use of more than one approach may be advantageous. However, when comparing several proposals, we should use the same evaluation techniques consistently for each project across all segments of the company. Because the details and costs of applying each evaluation technique vary, the dollar amount of the prospective investment becomes the criteria in justifying the evaluation technique used.

EXHIBIT 20–3   Aftertax Cash Flow for Krebs Company Robot

Year	(1) Pretax Increase in Cash Inflow	(2) Income Tax Deduction for Depreciation	(3) (1 − 2) Cash Inflow Subject to Tax	(4) Column 3 × Rate for Federal and State Income Tax*	(5) (1 − 4) Net Increase in Aftertax Cash Flow
1	$52,000	$32,000	$20,000	$ 6,000	$ 46,000
2	46,000	17,600	28,400	14,000	32,000
3	50,000	14,000	36,000	15,000	35,000
4	58,000	10,400	47,600	20,000	38,000
5	40,000	6,000	34,000	16,000	24,000
		$80,000			$175,000

* Percentage varies each year

Net Cash Inflow

In capital budgeting, the net increase in aftertax cash flow (or simply net cash inflow) is the net cash benefit expected from a project in a period. The **net cash inflow** is the difference between the periodic cash inflows and the periodic cash outflows of a proposed project.

To illustrate the calculation of net cash inflow, assume Krebs Company considers expanding its production facilities by purchasing a robot costing $80,000, having a five-year life. Exhibit 20–3 shows the cash flows associated with the proposal. We use these cash flows to illustrate the application of the four evaluation techniques discussed. (Note that this is a slightly different format for computing aftertax cash flow than presented earlier using data in Exhibit 20–1.)

For ease of computation, Exhibit 20–3 expresses the net increase in aftertax cash flow in even thousands of dollars. However, to reach these figures, we use a varying federal and state income tax rate. The pretax cash inflow is the difference between cash revenue and expenditures. For example, assume in Year 1 that the cash revenue generated from use of the capital asset is $92,000 while cash costs were $40,000, yielding $52,000 pretax cash flow increase. The depreciation percentages are 40 percent, 22 percent, 17.5 percent, 13 percent and 7.5 percent for Years 1 through 5, respectively. The effect of subtracting federal and state income tax from the pretax increase in cash flow is to add depreciation back in to measure the full amount of cash that flows into the business. One of the most difficult and important stages in the capital budgeting process involves defining and estimating cash flows.

Cost of Capital

The interest rate used in discounted cash flow methods is the minimum rate that must be earned to prevent dilution of shareholders' interests. This rate is called the **cost of capital, required rate of return, hurdle rate, discount rate,** or **cutoff rate;** this is the rate at which we discount cash inflows to the present.[1] The cost of capital is a composite of the cost of various sources of funds from the debt and equity that make up a firm's capital structure. To find this weighted average, we determine the costs of the individual types of capital and multiply the cost of each by its proportion in the firm's total capital structure. For example, assume a company uses three

[1] For additional exploration of this subject, see Statement on Management Accounting No. 4A, "Cost of Capital" (Montvale, NJ: National Association of Accountants, 1984).

EXHIBIT 20–4   **Weighted Cost of Capital**

	Aftertax Costs	Percent of Capital Structure	Weighted Cost
Debt	5%	20%	1.0%
Preferred stock	16	35	5.6
Common equity	12	45	5.4
		100%	12.0%

types of financing: debt, preferred stock, and common equity (retained earnings and common stock), with aftertax costs of 5 percent, 16 percent, and 12 percent, respectively. Exhibit 20–4 shows a 12 percent cost of capital if debt comprises 20 percent of the capital structure, preferred stock is 35 percent, and common equity is 45 percent. We multiply the cost of capital by the prospective cost of the various capital components, rather than by a company's historical costs.

In computing the cost of each of the various components of the capital structure, we should consider the amortization of premiums or discounts as part of the debt cost. Because the firm deducts interest payments when determining taxable income, the effective cost of debt is lower than the interest rate stated. To equate the tax treatment of debt and equity, we use the interest rate net of the applicable tax rate in determining the weighted cost of capital. In computing the cost of preferred stock, we divide the preferred dividend by the actual proceeds (cost) of the stock or the current price per share. The cost of equity capital is the most difficult component to calculate, and there are several methods available for use in the estimation process.

The historical rate of return, earnings/price ratio, dividend growth model, capital asset pricing model, and bond yield plus risk premium are five methods we use to estimate the cost of equity capital.

- Using the historical rate of return method, we calculate and use the rate of return earned by an investor, who is assumed to have purchased the stock in the past, held it until the present, and sold it at current market prices.
- Dividing earnings per share by the average price per share yields an earnings/price ratio.
- Reflecting a market value approach to determining the cost of equity capital is the dividend growth model. This method assumes the market price of a stock equals the cash flow from such expected future incomes as dividends and market price appreciation, discounted to their present value.
- Using the capital asset pricing model assumes the required rate of return on any security equals the riskless rate of interest plus a premium for risk.
- Using the bond yield plus risk premium method results in adding a risk premium to the interest rate on the firm's long-term debt to arrive at an estimated cost of equity. The risk premium is judgmental and varies depending on market conditions and other factors.

After estimating the costs of its capital structure components, a company must weight the components before calculating its cost of capital. Preferably, a company bases the weight on the proportions that it should maintain in its target capital structure

Global

Current Cost Management Practice

Years ago when oil companies did not know what to do with all their money, many blundered into the copper business and lost their shirts. Richard Osborne, chief executive of Asarco, Inc.—the one time American Smelting and Refining Co.—realized he was in the wrong business because Asarco owned much copper production in Peru. However, Peru left-wing governments soaked Asarco with taxes and fees, making profitable operations impossible. So Asarco earned its profits in the United States by processing copper mined by others, but it was leaving the biggest profit to others. Osborne realized that if his company mined, everything between the cost and the market price would belong to the firm. As disillusioned oil companies dumped the mines they had so expensively acquired, Asarco began buying them and increased its copper ore reserves almost tenfold. In 1991 Osborne cut a deal with Peru's more reasonable Fujimori government. In return for $300 million invested in new projects there, Peru ended the discriminatory taxes, ore pricing, and exchange rates. Despite these changes, Asarco is still a high-cost producer with its costs per pound in the mid-to-high-70s while its main competitors have costs per pound in the 60-to-70-cent range. That is Asarco's next goal—to cut costs eventually to 60 cents per pound.

James R. Norman, "The Ordeal of Richard Osborne," *Forbes,* September 26, 1994, pp. 45–46.

to provide an optimum balance of risk and return. However, a company can use the existing proportions of the capital components on its balance sheet or the current proportions of the market values of the firm's outstanding securities. The advantage of using the balance sheet book value weight is that consistency is preserved since it corresponds to the amounts shown on the financial statement. However, the market value of the firm's securities may differ from their book value. Using the market value weight is consistent with using market values to determine the cost of the individual components of capital. Finally, we multiply the cost of each source of capital by its proportion in the capital structure to obtain a weighted cost for each element. The sum of these weighted costs is the weighted cost of capital.

Discounted Cash Flow Methods

The net present value method and the internal rate of return are variations of the **discounted cash flow method** that consider the time value of money. We represent cash inflows and outflows of a capital investment at a common point for better comparison. The discounted cash flow models focus on cash flows, rather than on net income. Because of this focus and of the weight given to the time value of money, the discounted cash flow model is generally the preferred model for long-range decisions.

Net Present Value Method

The **net present value method** also is called the *excess present value method.* Just as we arrive at a future value by adding interest earned to an investment made today, we can determine present value if we know the future value as well as the interest earned over the respective time period. The present value method assumes some minimum desired rate of return or hurdle rate to discount cash inflows to the present.

Exhibit 20–5   Net Present Value Method

Year	Aftertax Cash (Outflow) or Inflow	Present Value of $1 at 12%	Net Present Value of Flow
0	$(80,000)	1.000	$ (80,000)
1	46,000	0.893	41,078
2	32,000	0.797	25,504
3	35,000	0.712	24,920
4	38,000	0.636	24,168
5	24,000	0.567	13,608
Net present value			$ 49,278

Managers consider a capital investment proposal acceptable if the present value of its future expected net cash inflows equals or exceeds the amount of the initial investment. When considering more than one investment, managers compare the net present value of each alternative with that of the others to choose the investment with the highest net present value.

Tables A and B indicate the higher the required rate of return, the lower the present value of the cash inflows. As a result, if managers use a higher required rate of return, fewer capital expenditure proposals have cash inflows that exceed the initial outflow of the investment cost. This means that a company may have to adjust its desired rate of return if it rejects too many proposals. Conversely, if the company finds that more proposals are acceptable than management believes are warranted, the firm should consider raising the rate of return.

The rate used is usually greater than the general level of interest rates at which banks and other institutions are lending money because there is greater risk with a capital investment than with a bank loan. We use this approach for investment proposals considered to involve average risk. For projects considered higher risks, we raise the required rate of return for this uncertainty. Also, the discount rate may be raised for future inflation.

After managers estimate a company's required rate of return (cost of capital), they apply the present value method. Exhibit 20–5 illustrates the net present value concept using the data from Exhibit 20–3 with a 12 percent estimated cost of capital. The starting point for capital expenditures is assumed to be time 0. Thus, we do not discount cash outlays at the beginning of the project. We enter these cash outlays at their full amount.

Since the project in Exhibit 20–5 has a positive net present value, the effective rate of return earned is greater than the 12 percent cost of capital used. When the annual cash flows vary as they do in this illustration, we must use Table A showing the present value of $1 for each period. However, if the cash flows are uniform, we use Table B, the present value of $1 received annually for *n* years. We multiply the cumulative factor by the cash flow of one period. For example, if the $175,000 annual net increase in aftertax cash flows in Exhibit 20–3 had been earned uniformly, giving a $35,000 annual cash flow ($175,000/5 years), we could make the following computation using a cumulative factor of 3.605 from Table B for the annual cash flow:

Present value of annual cash flows	$126,175	($35,000 × 3.605)
Less initial investment	80,000	
Net present value	$ 46,175	

Weighted Net Present Value or Expected Value

Managers can make an allowance for risk and uncertainty by determining the present value of the net cash flows for each alternative investment according to various assumptions about future conditions. For example, managers should determine the present value of the net cash flows for normal conditions, for pessimistic conditions, and for optimistic conditions. Management determines the probability of each of these conditions occurring and then applies them to the net cash flows so they can calculate the **weighted net present value,** or **expected value.** The net present value calculated in Exhibit 20–5 is rounded to $49,000. Managers assume this represents the normal condition most likely to occur. Managers make similar computations to arrive at a $66,000 net present value for the optimistic conditions and $30,000 for the pessimistic conditions. Exhibit 20–6 shows the weighted net present value, or expected present value, for this investment.

In Exhibit 20–6 we determined the net present values given for the optimistic conditions and pessimistic conditions using the present value method; however, the calculations are not shown. Managers employ this method to estimate the most likely amount of future cash receipts.

Profitability Index

The net present value method does not provide a valid means by which to rank projects' contribution to income or desirability when companies compare investment projects costing different amounts. However, we can relate a proposal's present value of cash inflows to initial outlay to obtain a profitability index. As the following formula shows, the **profitability index** method is simply a further refinement of the net present value method; this is why it is called the **present value index.**

$$\text{Profitability Index} = \frac{\text{Present value of aftertax net cash benefits}}{\text{Initial outlay (or present value of cash outlays if future outlays are required)}}$$

Use of the formula allows managers to evaluate all possible proposals and rank them according to their desirability. Only those proposals with a profitability index greater than or equal to 1.00 are eligible for further consideration. Those with a profitability index of less than 1.00 would not yield the minimum rate of return because the present value of the expected cash inflows is less than the initial cash outlay. The higher the profitability index, the more profitable the project per dollar of investment.

EXHIBIT 20–6   Weighted Net Present Value

	Net Present Value	×	*Probability Weights*	=	*Weighted Net Present Value*
Normal conditions	$49,000		0.60		$29,400
Optimistic conditions	66,000		0.25		16,500
Pessimistic conditions	30,000		0.15		4,500
Weighted net present value or expected present value					$50,400

EXHIBIT 20–7   Internal Rate of Return

Year	Cash (Outflow) or Inflow	Present Value of $1 (35 Percent)	Net Present Value of Flow	Present Value of $1 (40 Percent)	Net Present Value of Flow
0	$(80,000)	1.000	$(80,000)	1.000	$(80,000)
1	46,000	0.741	34,086	0.714	32,844
2	32,000	0.549	17,568	0.510	16,320
3	35,000	0.406	14,210	0.364	12,740
4	38,000	0.301	11,438	0.260	9,880
5	24,000	0.223	5,352	0.186	4,464
			$ 2,654		$ (3,752)

The following formula illustrates the profitability index using the data for the equipment in Exhibit 20–5. Note that in calculating the profitability index we are not using the net present value of $49,278, which is the present value of cash inflows less initial outlays, as shown in Exhibit 20–5.

$$\text{For Krebs Co. Robot: } \frac{\$129,278 \text{ present value of cash inflows}}{\$80,000 \text{ initial outlay}} = 1.62$$

Internal Rate of Return

A second variation of the discounted cash flow method is the **internal rate of return,** often called the **time-adjusted rate of return.** Similar to the present value method, the internal rate of return approach measures project profitability. However, it differs from the net present value method in that no discount rate is known in advance with this approach. We determine the computation in Exhibit 20–7 by trial and error before finding a discounted rate that yields a zero net present value. To obtain a starting point, we compute an approximate payback period by dividing the average annual cash flow into the plant asset cost. For example, $80,000/$35,000 average cash flow (determined by dividing $175,000 by five years) yields 2.286. Then we look for a factor of 2.286 on the horizontal row of an annuity for five years in Table B in the appendix. This asset is not yielding a 35 percent return so interpolation is necessary. If the factor had exactly matched the factor of one of the percent returns, the asset would have yielded that exact return.

The discounted rate is greater than 35 percent because a positive net present value results, but it is less than 40 percent because we determine a negative present value at this level. If we do not use the payback period clue to the starting point, the trial-and-error search should continue until we find adjacent rates in the table such that a positive net present value is achieved with the lower rate and a negative net present value with the higher rate. If using present value tables no more detailed than Tables A and B, we can obtain an approximation of the percentage by interpolation, as follows:

$$35\% + \left(5\% \times \frac{\$2,654}{\$6,406^*} \right) = 35\% + (5\% \times 0.414)$$
$$= 35\% + 2.07\% = 37.07\%$$
$$= 37\%$$

*$2,654 + $3,752.

Using the internal rate of return, management can choose the proposal with the highest rate of return. This return should be higher than the company's cost of capital. Using either present value or internal rate of return does not normally affect the indicated desirability of investment proposals. However, the rankings of mutually exclusive investments determined using the internal rate of return often are different from those determined using the net present value method. This can occur when the mutually exclusive proposals have unequal lives or when the size of the investment differs even though the lives are identical. The differences in these two variations of discounted cash flow result from the assumptions made regarding the reinvestment rate of return. With the internal rate of return, earnings are assumed to be reinvested at the same rate earned by the shorter-lived project. However, many people argue it is more reasonable to adopt the net present value method assumption that earnings are reinvested at the rate of discount, which is the company's minimum rate of return.

Exhibit 20–8 indicates the different rankings for mutually exclusive capital investment proposals obtained using the net present value and internal rate of return methods. With identical annual aftertax net cash inflows, but with varying investments and years of life, the rankings differ. (Because Exhibit 20–8 omits the computations, check your understanding of the methods by making the calculations using the present value tables.) There is a difference in results because the internal rate of return method assumes that Proposal A's amount at the end of the fourth year will be reinvested to earn a 22 percent rate of return. However, the net present value method assumes the Proposal A's amount at the end of the fourth year will be reinvested to earn only a 12 percent return, which is presumed to be the minimum desired rate of return.

Thus, as long as the minimum desired rate of return is lower than the internal rate of return, projects with shorter lives will show a higher rank with the internal rate of return. A company that expects reinvestment at the minimum desired rate of return should use the net present value approach because it better reflects the opportunity rate of return.

Opinions differ concerning comparison of the profitability of projects with different lives or significantly different cash inflow patterns. The rate of return earned on the reinvestment of funds recovered by the project with the shorter life span is thus an important factor. One way to reflect different asset lives is to consider the shorter-lived investment's period only and include an estimate of the recoverable value of the longer-lived investment at the end of the shorter period. The analysis would cover only the shorter period, with the recoverable value of the longer-lived investment treated as a cash inflow at the end of the period.

EXHIBIT 20–8   Comparison of Rankings for Mutually Exclusive Proposals

Capital Investment Proposal	Investment	Life (Years)	Annual Aftertax Net Cash Inflow	Net Present Value Method Using 12 Percent Discount		Internal Rate of Return	
				Net Present Value	Rank	Rate of return	Rank
A	$2,500	4	$1,000	$ 537	3	22%	1
B	5,000	12	1,000	1,194	2	17	2
C	6,000	18	1,000	1,250	1	15	3

Alternatives to Discounted Cash Flow Methods

Other capital expenditure evaluation techniques do not consider the time value of money. Such evaluation may satisfy an immediate pressing need because time or data does not permit a more sophisticated analysis. Although these techniques may be intuitively appealing because they are easy (present value concepts are not used) or quick to apply, they have many limitations. The time value of money is such an important concept to capital budgeting that accountants prefer discounted cash flow methods. Computer programs can ease the complexities of discounted cash flow methods. However, all methods share the weakness of assuming that future cash flows are certain.

Payback or Payout Method

The **payback** or **payout method** is a simple approach measuring the length of time required to recover the initial outlay for a project. Despite this model's lack of sophistication, it represents an improvement over merely basing the decision on management's intuition. A company can appropriately use the payback method if managers must screen proposals rapidly and if decisions involve extremely risky proposals. The payback formula is

$$\text{Payback period} = \frac{\text{Investment (cash outflow)}}{\text{Annual aftertax cash inflow}}$$

If the net increase in aftertax cash flow in Exhibit 20–3 were an even $35,000 ($175,000/5 years) each year, we could divide the $80,000 purchase price of the asset by the cash flow to give the payback of 2.29 ($80,000/$35,000). However, because the annual net increase in cash flow is not uniform, a different calculation is required, as shown in Exhibit 20–9. We accumulate each year's net cash inflows until we recover the initial investment. With the net annual cash inflows as a given, we recover the amount of the investment in 2.06 years.

Payback Reciprocal.   When the annual cash inflows are equal and the useful life of the project is at least twice the payback period, we may use the **payback reciprocal** to estimate the investment's rate of return. The payback reciprocal for the robot illustrated in Exhibit 20–9 is

$$\text{Payback reciprocal} = \frac{1}{\text{Payback time}} = \frac{1}{2.06} = .49 \text{ or } 49\%$$

Even though the payback reciprocal approximates the internal rate of return reasonably well, it is better to calculate the internal rate of return rather than depend on an approximation of it.

EXHIBIT 20–9   Traditional Payback for Krebs Company Robot

	Aftertax Cash Flow	Payback Years	
Year 1	$46,000	1.00	
Year 2	32,000	1.00	
Year 3	2,000	0.06	$\left(\dfrac{\$2,000}{\$35,000} \right)$
Investment	$80,000	2.06	

Companies often hesitate to apply methods more sophisticated than the payback method because many investment decisions are automatic if the company wishes to maintain operations. In these cases, management relies on professional judgment coupled with the payback method. In other cases, management may find the proposals unacceptable when presented and use the payback method to screen them. The payback method emphasizes liquidity, is easy to understand and apply, and gives a quick evaluation that offers some improvement over strictly intuitive judgment. Serious inherent weaknesses of the payback method are that it ignores the time value of money and the salvage value of the investment. It also ignores cash flows generated beyond the payback period. Nor does the payback method measure profitability. Despite these disadvantages, companies use the payback method as an initial screening for capital expenditure proposals.

Bailout Payback Method.   The **bailout payback method** is a variation of the payback method focusing on measuring the risk involved in a capital expenditure. The traditional payback approach attempts to answer the question, "How soon will I recover my investment if operations proceed as planned?" The bailout payback method asks, "If conditions go wrong, which alternative offers the best bailout protection?" For example, if the capital item is of a special type, and its disposal value is less than that of standard equipment, the bailout payback reflects these disposal values. Suppose we are comparing the robot under consideration in Exhibits 20–3 and 20–9 with a bottling machine costing $60,000 that we expect to produce uniform annual cash savings of $15,000. We expect the robot's disposal value to be $20,000 at the end of Year 1 and to decline to $1,000 at the end of Year 2 due to the special nature of its technology. We expect the bottling machine's disposal value to be $45,000 at the end of Year 1 and decline only $5,000 annually because of its general adaptability. Both are five-year property items. The bailout payback period is reached when the cumulative net increase in aftertax cash flow plus the disposal value equals the original cost. As seen in Exhibit 20–10, there is less risk with purchasing the bottling machine because it reaches its bailout period at the end of Year 1. However, as Exhibit 20–10 shows, its traditional payback period is four years, which is longer than the robot's traditional payback period of 2.06 years. Exhibit 20–10 also indicates that different analyses of the payback method can yield different results.

EXHIBIT 20–10   Bailout Payback

	At End of Year	*Cumulative Cash*	*Disposal Value*	*Cumulative Total*
Robot	1	$ 46,000	$20,000	$ 66,000
	2	78,000	1,000	79,000
	3	113,000	–0–	113,000
Bailout payback is between Years 2 and 3, depending on assumptions made regarding cash flow.				
Bottling machine .	1	$15,000	$45,000	$60,000
Bailout payback is at the end of Year 1.				
Traditional payback of bottling machine: $60,000/$15,000 = 4 years				

EXHIBIT 20–11   **Present Value Payback**

Year	Net Present Value of Cash Flow	Payback Years	
1	$41,078	1.00	
2	25,504	1.00	
3	13,418	0.54	$\left(\dfrac{\$13,418}{\$24,920}\right)$
	$80,000	2.54	

Present Value Payback. With the **present value payback method,** management knows the minimum necessary life over which a project will recover its initial investment and still earn the desired rate of return. Exhibit 20–11 shows the present value payback years required using the net present value of the flow from Exhibit 20–5. Based on the calculations in Exhibit 20–11, 2.54 years are required to recover the $80,000 initial investment and earn the desired 12 percent rate of return on the annual unrecovered investment balance.

Unadjusted Return on Investment

The **unadjusted return on investment** also is called the book value rate of return, the **accounting rate of return**, the financial statement method, or the approximate rate of return. We use the following equation to determine the unadjusted return on investment:

$$\frac{\text{Average annual net aftertax income}}{\text{Initial investment}}$$

Using the data from Exhibit 20–3, we deduct depreciation of $80,000 from the $175,000 net increase in aftertax cash and divide the remainder by five years to give a $19,000

$$\frac{\$175,000 - \$80,000}{5 \text{ years}} = \$19,000$$

average annual income after taxes. We then divide the average annual income by the $80,000 initial investment to give a 23.75 percent return as follows:

$$\frac{\$19,000 \text{ average annual net aftertax income}}{\$80,000 \text{ initial investment}} = 23.75 \text{ percent}$$

Instead of computing the return on initial investment, we can determine a return on average investment. Because this illustration does not use straight-line depreciation, the original book value and the book values at the end of each year must be averaged to determine average investment as follows:

Year	Book Value (End of Year)
1	$ 48,000
2	30,400
3	16,400
4	6,000
5	–0–
Original investment	80,000
	$180,800

$180,800/6 = \$30,133$ average investment

Using these data, the return on average investment becomes:

$$\frac{\$19,000 \text{ average annual net aftertax income}}{\$30,133 \text{ average investment}} = 63 \text{ percent}$$

If, instead, we use straight-line depreciation, we divide the original investment by 2 to arrive at the average investment since this $80,000 asset had no salvage value. When an asset has a scrap value at the end of its economic life, we would add the scrap value to determine average investment, regardless of the depreciation method used. Scrap value represents the investment at the end of its economic life.

The unadjusted return on investment does improve on the weaknesses of the payback method by taking into account profitability. However, it fails to consider the time value of money and it does not emphasize cash flows. Also, the unadjusted rate of return compares savings to be received in the future to an investment that requires a current outlay of funds. Thus, we misstate the true return of projects. However, the unadjusted return on investment is familiar because it is based on the accrual method of preparing financial statements and is easy to apply. It facilitates follow-up of expenditures because the data are available in the accounting records. It also ties in with performance evaluation. Despite its advantages, the unadjusted return on investment is not appropriate if a company makes additional capital expenditures after the project has started.

Summary

Capital budgeting decisions are among the most difficult that management must make, primarily because they usually involve large commitments. Also, the returns on these commitments are complex to forecast. This chapter presented three techniques for evaluating capital expenditures: (1) discounted cash flow, (2) payback or payout, and (3) unadjusted return on investment. Chapter illustrations include two variations of the discounted cash flow method—net present value (also called excess present value) and internal rate of return (often called time-adjusted rate of return).

Accountants prefer the present value and internal rate of return methods because they consider the time value of money. We determine the present value of expected future cash inflows by applying appropriate present value factors for the rate of return required. We can base the required rate of return on the cost of capital employed, or it can be a rate greater than the general level of interest rates at which institutions are lending money. The internal rate of return differs from the present value method because no discount rate is known in advance. We find a discounted rate that yields a zero net present value.

The payback method determines the length of time a project requires to recover the initial outlay. However, we ignore the time value of money and the salvage value of the investment. Profitability is considered in the unadjusted return on investment method by determining the relationship of average annual net aftertax income to the initial or average investment. While the adjusted return on investment method is familiar because it is based on the accrual method of financial statement preparation, it fails to take into consideration the time value of money.

Important Terms and Concepts

Sunk cost 647	Net present value method 653
Investment tax credit 647	Weighted net present value or expected
Tax shield 648	value 655
Present value 649	Profitability index (present value index)
Time value of money 649	655
Discounting 649	Internal rate of return or time-adjusted rate
Annuity 649	of return 656
Net cash inflow 651	Payback or payout method 658
Cost of capital 651	Payback reciprocal 658
Required rate of return 651	Bailout payback method 659
Hurdle rate 651	Present value payback method 660
Discount rate 651	Unadjusted return on investment
Cutoff rate 651	(accounting rate of return) 660
Discounted cash flow method 653	

Problem for Self-Study

Net Present Value and Internal Rate of Return

Krebs Company is considering the purchase of Machine A or B. Machine A costs $35,000 and has a life of 12 years, while Machine B costs $60,000 and has a life of 18 years. The cost of removing either machine at the end of its life is expected to equal any salvage value. Annual aftertax cash inflow for Machine A is expected to be $5,000 and $7,000 for Machine B.

Required:

For both machines, prepare the following analysis:
a. Internal rate of return.
b. Net present value at 6 percent.
c. Which machine would you recommend that the company buy?

Solution to Problem for Self-Study

KREBS COMPANY

a. Internal rate of return

For Machine A

Cash Inflow	PV at 8%		PV at 10%	
$(35,000) × 1.000	$(35,000)		$(35,000)	
$5,000 for 12 years	37,680	($5,000 × 7.536)	34,070	($5,000 × 6.814)
Net present value	$ 2,680		$ −930	

$$8\% + \left(2\% \times \frac{\$2,680}{\$3,610}\right) = 8\% + 2\% \ (0.74238) = 9.485\% \text{ rate of return}$$

For Machine B

Cash Inflow	PV at 8%		PV at 10%	
$(60,000) × 1.000	$(60,000)		$(60,000)	
$7,000 for 18 years	65,604	($7,000 × 9.372)	57,407	($7,000 × 8.201)
Net present value	$ 5,604		$ −2,593	

$$8\% + \left(2\% \times \frac{\$5,604}{\$8,197}\right) = 8\% + 2\% \ (0.68366) = 9.367\% \text{ rate of return}$$

b. Net present value at 6%

	Machine A			Machine B	
	$(35,000) × 1.000 =	$(35,000)		$(60,000) × 1.000 =	$(60,000)
	$5,000 × 8.384 =	41,920		$7,000 × 10.828 =	75,796
	Net present value	$ 6,920		Net present value	$ 15,796

c. Machine B appears to be more acceptable because it not only has a larger net present value at 6% but also is expected to have a cash inflow for 18 years. Machine A's life is expected to be only 12 years. Even though the internal rate of return for both machines is approximately the same, Machine B is recommended.

Review Questions

1. What one weakness do all the capital budgeting methods discussed in the chapter share?
2. How does depreciation affect capital asset decisions?
3. Define sunk cost and indicate the role this cost plays in replacement decisions.
4. As the cost accountant of a company requesting a loan for the purchase of expensive robots, what is your reaction when the banker says, "I will not lend money for new equipment unless your company can demonstrate by statistical evidence that you are using your present equipment to reasonably full capacity"?
5. How can the probability of occurrence be given consideration in the net present value approach to evaluating plant asset proposals?
6. How does use of the profitability index overcome a weakness of the net present value method in ranking projects in order of contribution to income or desirability when comparing investment projects costing different amounts?
7. *a.* Which capital budgeting method assumes that funds are reinvested at the company's cost of capital?
   b. Which capital budgeting methods require use of present value tables?
8. What methods are used to arrive at the required rate of return in the present value method of evaluation?
9. Discuss the strengths and weaknesses of these capital budgeting methods:

    a. Net present value method.

    b. Internal rate of return.

    c. Unadjusted return on investment.

    d. Payback.

10. Assume proposed Project A has a profitability index greater than 1.00 while proposed Project B has a profitability index of less than 1.00. What does this mean and how do these indexes affect their selection of capital assets?

11. How is the tax shield computed and how is it used in capital expenditure analysis?

12. Discuss the concept underlying the present value method. What strengths does this evaluation method have over the payback method or the unadjusted rate of return?

Exercises

E20–1 Maximum Interest Rate to Be Paid

Ryan, Inc., purchased equipment at a cost of $67,000. The equipment is estimated to yield $12,000 for each of its eight years of life. Use the following data in answering the requirements:

Interest Rate	Present Value of $1 Received Annually for 8 Years
8%	5.747
10%	5.335
12%	4.968

Required:

Determine the maximum interest rate that could be paid for the capital employed over the equipment's life without incurring a loss on the project.

E20–2 Weighted Cost of Capital

Bellview Company uses three types of financing: debt, preferred stock, and common equity (the sum of retained earnings and common stock), with aftertax costs of 6 percent, 12 percent, and 16 percent, respectively. Debt comprises 30 percent of the capital structure, the preferred stock 45 percent, and the common equity 25 percent.

Required:

What is Bellview's weighted cost of capital with the preceding capital structure?

E20–3 Present Value of Net Cash Flow

An investment of $100,000 is planned by Tanglewood, Inc., for a three-year project. Cash flow, net of income taxes, will be $37,756, having a present value of $34,320, for the first year and $40,000, having a present value of $33,040, for the second year.

Required:

Assuming the rate of return is exactly 10 percent, what will the cash flow, net of income taxes, be for the third year?

E20–4 Net Present Value Analysis in Purchasing

Beal, Inc., a large construction firm is interested in replacing a mainframe computer with a new model. The cost of the new equipment is $1,000,000 and has an expected useful life of 10 years. The company elects to take straight-line depreciation over a five-year period for tax purposes. The equipment will have a disposal value of $100,000 at the end of its useful life. However, salvage value is ignored in computing depreciation for tax purposes. Due to increased efficiency, the company expects to save 9,000 hours per year in machine operator labor costs with the new machine. A machine operator earns $18 per hour including fringe benefits.

Presently the old mainframe computer is being carried on the books at $500,000 less $350,000 accumulated depreciation. Currently, Beal can sell it for $50,000; however, it will have no disposal value at the end of its useful life. The minimum aftertax rate on its investments management will consider is 12 percent. The company's income tax rate is 35 percent.

Required:

Determine whether Beal should purchase the equipment using net present value analysis.

E20–5 Aftertax Benefits, Present Value, Payback Period

Hodges Company is planning to purchase a machine costing $117,000 to use in their Mixing Department. Management determined that this machine has a 10-year life with an estimated salvage value of $5,000. Depreciation for tax purposes is $9,360 for Year 1. The estimated annual cash savings from using this machine is $22,000. The company's cost of capital is 14 percent and its income tax rate, including state income tax, is 45 percent.

Required:

a. Calculate the annual aftertax net cash benefits of this machine for Year 1.
b. Calculate the net present value of this investment if the annual aftertax cash benefits of this machine were $20,000 each year for the machine's life.
c. Calculate the payback period assuming that the annual aftertax cash benefits of this machine were $20,000 each year for the machine's life.

E20–6 Top Management Behavior

Clifton Key, president, remarked casually to the data processing manager, Robert Knight, that it would be helpful if he had the printouts concerning the proposed capital expenditures by Friday. Key wanted to study them over the weekend before meeting with the equipment salespersons and the board of directors the following week.

Knight immediately called a halt to all programs being run so his staff could concentrate on having these reports for the president. This meant delaying the monthly income statement with its detailed cost of production reports comparing actual costs to standard costs for several days.

Knight and his staff worked overtime and were pleased to be able to produce the reports for the president by Friday. However, on the following Tuesday, the fifth working day after the end of the month, when they normally delivered the income statement and budget comparisons to the president, the statements were incomplete. The data processing manager thought the president would understand the delay. He became upset after receiving an angry phone call asking for an explanation of the missing reports.

Required:

Explain what caused the problem. Could anything have prevented this situation from occurring?

E20–7 Net Present Value and Expected Value

Wallis, Inc., is considering the purchase of a machine to use in manufacturing a new product developed by the firm's engineering department. The cost of the machine is $150,000, and the machine dealer requires a cash payment on delivery. Life of the machine is expected to be six years; salvage value at the end of the machine's life is forecasted to be $20,000.

Estimates for the success of this new product are difficult to determine; however, based on various market tests, management believes that the availability of personal disposable income will be a critical factor. The following estimates of aftertax cash flow from operations are based on three different market conditions. The probability of a poor market is 30 percent; of a normal market, 55 percent; and the probability of an excellent market, 15 percent.

Year	Poor Market	Normal Market	Excellent Market
1	$10,000	$20,000	$30,000
2	21,000	30,000	45,000
3	35,000	40,000	50,000
4	40,000	45,000	57,000
5	32,000	38,000	45,000
6	18,000	25,000	30,000

Required:

a. Using an interest rate of 8 percent, determine the net present value of the cash flow for each of the three market conditions assumed.
b. Using the information determined in Requirement a, calculate the weighted net present value or expected value of the investment.

Problems

P20–8 Capital Budgeting Techniques

Whitehead Company is considering purchasing a blending machine costing $75,000. The firm is using straight-line depreciation, with no estimated salvage value at the end of the machine's useful life of five years. Net annual aftertax cash flow is forecasted to be $18,000 for each of the five years.

Required:

Determine the following:

a. Payback period.
b. Unadjusted rate of return on initial investment.
c. Unadjusted rate of return on average investment.
d. Net present value at 12 percent.
e. Internal rate of return.

P20–9 Net Present Value and Expected Value

Crawford Company managers are considering the purchase of a machine to use in their processing plant. Its cost is $75,000, and the machine salesperson requires a cash payment on delivery. Life of the machine is expected to be five years; there is no value at the end of the equipment's life.

The following estimates of aftertax cash flow are based on three different market conditions: The probability of a poor market is 30 percent, of a normal market, 50 percent; and of an excellent market, 20 percent.

Year	Poor Market	Normal Market	Excellent Market
1	$18,000	$20,000	$28,000
2	10,000	15,000	16,000
3	11,000	18,000	19,000
4	18,000	20,000	22,000
5	20,000	25,000	28,000

Required:

a. Using an interest rate of 12 percent, determine the net present value of the cash flow for each of the three market conditions assumed.

b. Assuming the net present value was ($15,000) for the poor market, ($3,000) for the normal market, and $8,000 for the excellent market, calculate the weighted net present value or expected value of the investment.

SPATS

P20–10 Capital Budgeting Techniques

Salespersons have approached Camp Company management with promotional material introducing a machine with innovative technological devices. The machine whose initial cost is $50,000 has an estimated life of six years. The expected salvage value is $2,000 with straight-line depreciation being used; a $14,000 aftertax cash inflow for six years is forecasted.

Required:

Calculate the following:

a. Payback period.

b. Unadjusted rate of return on initial investment.

c. Unadjusted rate of return on average investment.

d. Net present value at 8 percent and present value payback period.

e. Internal rate of return.

Writing

P20–11 Present Value Analysis

The Raymond Dairy Company manually wraps its sticks of butter for sale. One part-time employee, who is paid minimum wage, performs this operation involving no machines. Direct costs of operations are

Salaries and payroll taxes	$7,608
Paper wrappers and other supplies	2,000

A company has offered to sell Raymond an automatic machine to use in the butter wrapping operations. The machine will cost $30,000 with $2,000 disposal value at the end of a seven-year life. Sales terms are cash on delivery. The machine is expected to become jammed periodically, resulting in the waste of 10 percent more paper wrappers and supplies. Even though the machine is automatic, it will require some supervision. However, management plans to have an employee presently working in the processing plant perform these duties in addition to those duties he now has. He is expected to devote an average of one-tenth of his time to loading and supervising the machine; his annual salary including payroll taxes is $20,000.

Annually the machine will cost a total of $500 for electricity and utilities. All machine repairs are guaranteed by the manufacturer. The new machine will occupy the space presently being used by the manual operations.

Required: (Ignore income tax effect.)

a. Assume a 14 percent cost of capital and use present value analysis to show whether the new equipment should be purchased.

b. Determine which additional factors Raymond should consider before making a decision regarding the purchase.

P20–12 Capital Budgeting Techniques

Johns Company is considering a machine whose initial outlay is $50,000. Straight-line depreciation is to be used, with $2,000 estimated salvage value. Net annual aftertax cash inflow excluding salvage value is forecasted to be $6,000 for six years.

Required: ·

a. Payback period.
b. Unadjusted rate of return on initial investment.
c. Unadjusted rate of return on average investment.
d. Net present value at 8 percent.
e. When would a company invest in a machine yielding the preceding results?

P20–13 Net Present Value, Profitability Index, Internal Rate of Return, and Bailout Payback

Fentress Company management is evaluating the purchase of either a machine built by the Pullen Company or a longer-life machine built by the Adler Company. The Pullen machine costs $60,000 and has a useful life of 12 years, while the Adler machine costs $65,000 with a useful life of 18 years. Managers expect neither machine to have any salvage value at the end of its life. They expect the annual aftertax net cash inflow for both machines to be $15,000. Managers expect the Pullen machine's disposal value to be $35,000 at the end of the first year and decline at the rate of $5,000 annually. They expect the Adler machine's disposal value to be $25,000 at the end of the first year and decline $8,000 annually.

Required:

a. Prepare the following analyses for both machines:
  (1) Net present value at 8 percent.
  (2) Profitability index using present value at 8 percent.
  (3) Internal rate of return.
  (4) Bailout payback.
b. Discuss which machine you would advise purchasing and explain why.

SPATS

P20–14 Numerous Capital Budgeting Techniques

Management of Frank Barton Company is considering expanding its operations through the purchase of a blending machine costing $165,000. The tax and economic life of the asset is five years. The estimated salvage value at the end of its life is $45,000. Depreciation is deducted for tax purposes as follows: Year 1, $60,000; Year 2, $42,000; Year 3, $25,000; Year 4, $20,000; and Year 5, $18,000. Based on engineering and accounting studies, management believes the pretax increase in cash inflow will be as follows: Year 1, $65,000; Year 2, $73,000; Year 3, $85,000; Year 4, $98,000; and Year 5, $96,000. Federal and state income taxes have averaged 52 percent in the past, and no change is expected in this rate.

Required:

Determine the following:
a. Payback period.
b. Unadjusted rate of return on investment based on initial investment and on average investment (ignore salvage).
c. Net present value of the machine assuming the cost of capital is 14 percent.
d. Present value payback.
e. Internal rate of return approach to determine the discount rate.
f. Payback period assuming that the aftertax cash flow was even over the five years.
g. Profitability index using present value of 14 percent.

P20–15 Aftertax Cash Flow Net Present Value

Springfield Company is considering replacing its present manufacturing equipment with robots costing $200,000 and having an estimated five-year life. The robotics supplier promises that if the equipment is purchased at the beginning of the project year, the robots will be in operation by the end of the second quarter of the project year. This will result in 50 percent of the estimated annual savings being realized in the project's first year. The estimated savings in direct labor from the use of robots is $100,000 annually. Management expects no change in capacity from the use of the robots.

Springfield will incur a $20,000 one-time expense to transfer manufacturing activities from its present equipment to the automated equipment. Because operations are well arranged, no loss in sales is expected in the transfer to robots.

The current equipment is carried in the accounts at zero book value since it is fully depreciated. However, Springfield engineers believe the equipment can be used an additional five years based on their recent examination. Springfield Company would receive $10,000 net of removal costs if it elected to buy the new equipment and dispose of its current equipment at this time.

Springfield currently leases its manufacturing plant. The annual lease payments are $50,000. The lease, which will have five years remaining when the equipment installation begins, is not renewable. Springfield Company would be required to remove any equipment in the plant at the end of the lease. The cost of equipment removal is expected to equal the salvage value of either the old or new equipment at the time of removal. The company is subject to a 30 percent income tax rate and requires an aftertax return of at least 10 percent on any investment.

Required:

a. Calculate the annual incremental aftertax cash flows for Springfield Company's proposal to acquire the new manufacturing equipment. For ease of calculation, use straight-line depreciation for tax purposes. Take a full year's depreciation in the first year the asset is put into use.

b. Calculate the net present value of Springfield Company's proposal to acquire the new manufacturing equipment using the cash flows calculated in Requirement *a* and indicate what action Springfield's management should take. For ease in calculation, assume all recurring flows take place at the end of the year.

P20–16 Capital Budgeting Techniques

Keat Company is considering the purchase of a machine with an initial outlay of $43,000. Accountants will use a straight-line depreciation with no salvage value at the end of the machine's useful life of 10 years. Net annual *aftertax* cash inflow is forecasted to be $9,000 for 10 years.

Required:

Determine the following:
a. Payback period.
b. Unadjusted rate of return on initial investment.
c. Unadjusted rate of return on average investment.
d. Net present value at 10 percent and present value payback period.
e. Internal rate of return.

P20–17 Capital Budgeting Techniques

McNeely Company is considering the purchase of a large cutting machine costing $300,000. The estimated cash benefit is as follows:

SPATS

Year	Beforetax Cash Benefit
1	$ 80,000
2	90,000
3	95,000
4	100,000
5	90,000
6	85,000
7	70,000
8	60,000

The machine is to be depreciated over eight years on a straight-line basis. No salvage value is expected. Assume a 48 percent tax rate and a 12 percent cost of capital.

Required:

Calculate the following:
a. Payback period.
b. Unadjusted rate of return on initial investment.
c. Unadjusted rate of return on average investment.
d. Net present value and present value payback period.
e. Profitability index using present value at 12 percent.
f. Internal rate of return method.

P20–18 Capital Budgeting Techniques
Logo Company is considering replacing an obsolete machine with new equipment costing $15,000 and having an estimated useful life of five years. The old machine is fully depreciated, and no salvage value can be realized on its disposal. The new machine would provide annual cash savings of $5,000 before income taxes. No salvage value would be used for depreciation purposes because the equipment is expected to have no value at the end of five years.

Logo uses the straight-line depreciation method on all equipment for both book and tax purposes. The company is subject to a 30 percent tax rate. Logo has an aftertax cost of capital of 12 percent.

Required:
a. Use each of the following methods to evaluate Logo Company's proposed investment. Assume all operating revenues and expenses occur at the end of the year.
   (1) Net present value.
   (2) Profitability index using present value at 12 percent.
   (3) Internal rate of return.
   (4) Payback period.
   (5) Accounting rate of return on initial investment.
   (6) Accounting rate of return on average investment.
b. Assume you are a cost accounting consultant employed by Logo Company. Identify and discuss the issues management should consider in choosing one of the five capital budgeting techniques to compare and evaluate alternative capital investment projects.

P20–19 Evaluating Discounted Cash Flow Techniques
The Mann Company designs and sews a nationally known brand of men's shirts. On January 2, 19X1, Mann purchased a special fabric cutting machine; this machine has been utilized for three years. A sales representative has been talking with Mann's production manager

concerning the purchase of a newer, more efficient machine. If purchased, the new machine would be acquired on January 2, 19X4. Mann expects to sell 50,000 shirts in each of the next four years. The unit selling price of the shirts is expected to average $10.

Mann Company has two options: (1) continue to operate the old machine, or (2) sell the old machine and purchase the new machine. No trade-in was offered by the seller of the new machine. The following information has been assembled to help decide which option is more desirable:

	Old Machine	New Machine
Original cost of machine at acquisition	$90,000	$200,000
Salvage value at the end of useful life for depreciation purposes	$20,000	$ 40,000
Useful life from date of acquisition	7 years	4 years
Estimated cash value of machines:		
January 2, 19X4	$50,000	$200,000
December 31, 19X7	10,000	40,000
Expected annual cash operating expenses:		
Variable cost per shirt	$ 4	$ 3
Total fixed costs	20,000	19,500

Mann Company is subject to an overall income tax rate of 30 percent. Assume that all operating revenues and expenses occur at the end of the year. Assume that any gain or loss on the sale of machinery is treated as an ordinary tax item and will affect the taxes paid by Mann Company at the end of the year in which it occurred. Assume for simplicity that straight-line depreciation will be used for tax purposes on both machines.

Required:

a. Identify and discuss the advantages and disadvantages of using discounted cash flow techniques (such as the net present value method and the internal rate of return) for capital investment decisions.

b. Use an aftertax return of 14 percent and determine whether Mann Company should purchase the new machine based on the net present value method.

c. Assume Mann's cost accountant believes that the information assembled to help decide which option is more desirable fails to consider all factors. For example, the cash operating expenses include only product costs such as labor, materials, and overhead. There is no consideration given to the savings in manufacturing cost that result because the new machine will have a lower incidence of defects. Additionally, the higher quality of the product that can be produced from the new machine is ignored. Do you think such factors should be included to obtain a more realistic and accurate analysis? If so, how would you arrive at the savings a company would have if its defect rate was reduced?

d. List some other important nonquantitative factors that Mann Company should consider in addition to the quantitative analysis using a capital budgeting technique.

P20–20 Capital Budgeting for CAD/CAM Project (AICPA)
Spara Corporation is considering the various benefits of shortening its product cycle by changing from the company's present manual system to a computer-aided design/computer-aided manufacturing (CAD/CAM) system. The proposed system can provide productive time equivalency close to the 20,000 hours currently available with the manual system. The incremental annual out-of-pocket costs of maintaining the manual system are $20 per hour.

The incremental annual out-of-pocket costs of maintaining the CAD/CAM system are estimated to be $200,000, with an initial investment of $480,000 in the proposed system. The estimated useful life of this system is six years. For tax purposes, assume a level accelerated cost recovery with a full year allowable in each year. The tax rate is expected to remain constant at 30 percent over the life of the project. Spara requires a minimum aftertax return of 20 percent on projects of this type. Full capacity will be utilized.

Required:

a. Compute the relevant annual aftertax cash flows related to the CAD/CAM project.
b. Based on the computation in Requirement *a*, compute the following on an aftertax basis:
   (1) Payback period for recovery of investment.
   (2) Internal rate of return.
   (3) Net present value.
   (4) Excess present value index (profitability index).

Capital Budgeting— Additional Topics

Chapter Objectives

After studying this chapter, you should be able to:

1. Apply sensitivity analysis to capital budgeting decisions.
2. Prepare aftertax analyses for equipment replacement using the total-cost and differential-cost approaches.
3. Incorporate inflation into capital budgeting analysis.
4. Identify and quantify the subjective benefits of new automated plant assets that should be incorporated into conventional capital expenditure analysis.
5. Compare the costs of constructing assets for a company's own use versus leasing or purchasing.

Introduction

Traditional **differential cost studies** and capital budgeting techniques often fail when managers propose purchasing automated equipment. Accountants find it difficult to quantify many of the important advantages of automation, such as increased flexibility, improved quality and customer service; and increased opportunities for responding to changes in material availability, product design, or product-mix demand. If companies ignore these gains from improved manufacturing performance, their conventional single-purpose, high-volume machines prevent them from changing products and operations. A narrow interpretation of the discounted cash flow procedures may inhibit desirable investment projects.

Chapter 20 presented several evaluation techniques for capital expenditures. This chapter demonstrates the use of sensitivity analysis and the effect of changing prices on capital budgeting. Changes in purchasing power cause future cash flows to have a different real value than dollars received today.

Capital expenditure proposals involve not only additions of new plant assets but also expansion and improvement of existing investments and the replacement of capital assets. The basis of analyzing the improvement and replacement of capital assets involves comparing the costs of existing facilities with future cost savings.

Sensitivity Analysis for Capital Budgeting Decisions under Uncertainty

All of the capital budgeting methods presented in Chapter 20 share the weakness of assuming future cash flows are certain. Companies can use **sensitivity analysis** to offset this certainty weakness by measuring the effect on the estimate if the critical data inputs change. Computer spreadsheets are particularly helpful in performing sensitivity analysis. Sensitivity analysis attempts to determine the effect on the internal rate of return, net present value, or other calculations if the various predictions, such as cash flow or economic life, change or are in error.

For example, accountants use sensitivity analysis to determine how much net cash inflow can decrease before net present value equals zero or before the internal rate of return equals the required rate of return. Also, we can calculate the net present value and the internal rate of return using pessimistic and optimistic cash flow estimates. Sensitivity analysis also determines how short a proposed capital asset's useful life would have to be before net present value equals zero or before the internal rate of return equals the required rate of return. In addition, sensitivity analysis measures the potential increases in net present value and in the rate of return if cash inflow is larger or if the economic life is longer than expected. We can determine the cost of errors in estimating an asset's cash flow or life assuming there are or are not acceptable alternatives. The financial cost of possible errors as measured by sensitivity analysis helps management focus attention on more crucial and reactive decisions.

Cash Flow Changes and Present Value

We can use sensitivity analysis to determine how much annual cash savings can decrease before a company breaks even on an investment. Sensitivity analysis also measures the impact on net present value or internal rate of return if actual cash flows differ from estimated cash inflows. For example, assume a company's cost of

Service

Current Cost Management Practice

The food-processing section of the Seaboard Corp. runs a major chicken processor in the United States, is building one of the biggest hog processing plants, owns flour mills in Nigeria, and has stakes in mills in Guyana, Zaire, and Sierra Leone. It owns shrimp operations in Honduras and Ecuador, fruit and vegetable farms in Guatemala and Costa Rica, and the largest bakery in Puerto Rico. Seaboard also owns the largest shipping fleet operating out of Miami. Current revenues totaled $1.1 billion. Seaboard's headquarters are in Shawnee Mission, Kansas, but it is run out of an office in suburban Boston by Harry Breskey, who with his family, owns 78 percent of the company and is worth some $200 million. Harry Breskey's father, Otto Breskey, started the company as a flour broker. Otto Breskey expanded abroad in places such as Ecuador and Nigeria while General Mills and Pillsbury Company integrated vertically into value-added goods like cereal and bakery products. To deliver grist to his far-flung mills, Otto Breskey built a shipping business. He delivered wheat to West Africa for processing, then refilled his ships with shrimp and other goods for the return voyage. Keeping the ships as full as possible on all legs of their voyages was a lesson Otto taught Harry early and well.

Marcia Berss, "Papa Knew Best," *Forbes*, September 26, 1994, pp. 80–82.

capital is 12 percent and management estimates $35,000 annual cash inflow for equipment having a cost of $80,000 and a five-year life. Managers wish to know how much these cash savings can decrease before reaching the point of indifference about the investment. Using a cumulative factor of 3.605 from Table B in the Appendix, letting X = annual cash inflows and net present value = 0, then

$$3.605(X) - \$80,000 \text{ initial investment} = 0$$
$$3.605(X) = \$80,000$$
$$X = \$80,000 \div 3.605 = \$22,191$$

Sensitivity analysis indicates that the annual cash savings can decrease $12,809 ($35,000 − $22,191) before the net project value equals zero.

Should managers fear the actual cash inflow may be only $20,000 rather than the optimistic estimate of $35,000, the following sensitivity analysis measures the impact on net present value of using the pessimistic cash flow estimate:

Present value of $20,000 × 3.605	$72,100
Less initial investment	80,000
Net present value	$ (7,900)

The original net present value was $46,175, determined by subtracting $80,000 from $126,175 ($35,000 × 3.605). The net present value using the revised cash inflow is $(7,900). This indicates the impact of a $15,000 annual difference in cash flow is a $54,075 difference in net present value (i.e., $7,900 + $46,175 = $54,075).

Cost of Estimation Errors in Cash Flows and Present Value

Before management purchases the $80,000 worth of equipment, accountants should calculate the **cost of estimation error** or the **cost of prediction error.** This is the cost to a company of incorrectly estimating the value of one or more parameters used in evaluating the project. Such costs occur in two situations: (1) a company has no other acceptable projects to choose if managers reject the project under study, and (2) a company has other acceptable projects from which to choose if managers reject the project in question.

No Acceptable Alternatives.   When a company has no other projects that are acceptable, the cost of estimation error analysis involves comparing the cost of selecting the project with the cost of not selecting the project. If the cash flow from the project is only $20,000, sensitivity analysis reveals that the best decision is to reject the project because if the company purchases $80,000 worth of equipment, a $7,900 cost of estimation error occurs as follows:

Net present value of optimal decision of not investing	$ -0–
Less net present value if project gives $20,000 cash flow	(7,900)
Cost of estimation error	$ 7,900

If instead of a $15,000 error in annual cash savings, the error is only $5,000 (i.e., cash flows are $30,000 annually instead of the $35,000 originally expected), the net present value is positive as follows:

Present value of cash inflows ($30,000 x 3.605)	$108,150
Less initial investment	80,000
Net present value	$ 28,150

Because the net present value of the equipment is positive with either a $30,000 or $35,000 annual cash flow, the decision in both cases is to invest in the project. Remember that net present value represents the difference between the discounted cash inflow and outflow. Whether the difference is positive or negative only indicates that the actual return on the capital asset is larger or smaller than the cost of capital.

Acceptable Alternatives.   If a company has more acceptable projects than it can engage in, management accepts the project that best meets its goals. When a company accepts one project and turns down another project, the cost of estimation error is a comparison of the net present value of the accepted investment with the net present value of the best project rejected. Using the original net present value of $46,175 calculated on page 655 and assuming the company does not accept a comparable project with a $32,000 net present value, the $32,000 is an opportunity cost representing the best investment forgone. However, if the $35,000 annual cash flow estimated is overly optimistic and $30,000 cash flow results each year, the cost of estimation error in this analysis is:

Net present value of best alternative forgone	$32,000
Net present value of project accepted with actual cash flow of $30,000	28,150
Cost of estimation error	$ 3,850

Cash Flow Changes and Internal Rate of Return

Sensitivity analysis indicates the following impact on internal rate of return if actual cash flow is $20,000 instead of the $35,000 estimate:

Interest rate of return with expected cash flow	
$80,000/$35,000 = 2.286; from Exhibit 20–7 by interpolation	37.07 percent
Internal rate of return with actual cash flow	
$80,000/$20,000 = 4; by interpolation	7.94 percent
Difference in internal rate of return	29.13 percent

If the cash flow is not as favorable as originally expected, selecting this project would result in approximately 29.13 percent less return than anticipated.

Cost of Estimation Errors in Cash Flows and Internal Rate of Return

No Acceptable Alternatives.   The cost of estimating the incorrect internal rate of return when there are no acceptable alternative projects is the difference between the expected and actual annual return. With an expected internal rate of return of 37.07 percent and an actual return of 7.94 percent, if the cash flow is $20,000 rather than $35,000, the cost of estimation error is

Expected annual return ($80,000 × 37.07%)	$29,656
Actual annual return ($80,000 × 7.94%)	6,352
Cost of estimation error	$23,304

A shorter calculation is to multiply the project's cost by the difference between expected and actual internal rate of return as follows: $80,000 × 29.13% = $23,304 yielding the same cost of estimation error.

Acceptable Alternatives.   If the internal rate of return of the best alternative forgone is 10 percent and that for the actual annual return is 7.94 percent, the cost of estimation error is

$$\$80,000 \times 2.06\%^* = \$1,648$$

*10.00% − 7.94% = 2.06%

Economic Life Changes and Present Value

Companies also use sensitivity analysis to measure the uncertainty attached to a capital asset's useful life. For example, if the proposed project's life is three years rather than five years, the net present value is $4,070 as shown next, instead of $46,175 as computed on page 655:

Present value using revised life ($35,000 × 2.402, cumulative factor for 3 years, 12% from Table B)	$84,070
Less initial investment	80,000
Net present value	$ 4,070

Even though the net present value still exceeds the original investment cost, this analysis does not tell management how much the estimation error costs the company.

Cost of Estimation Errors in Economic Lives

As just illustrated, errors in estimation also may occur in the useful life of a project. If instead of a five-year life, the project's actual life is only two years, its net present value is

Present value of revised life ($35,000 × 1.609 cumulative factor for two years, 12% from Table B)	$ 56,315
Less initial investment	80,000
Net present value	$(23,685)

Because the net present value is negative, the optimal decision is not to invest in the project. If the investment is made based on the original five-year estimate and there are no alternative investments, the cost of the estimation error or cost of prediction error is

Net present value of optimal decision of not investing	$ –0–
Net present value if equipment's life is two years	(23,685)
Cost of prediction error	$23,685

If, however, an alternative with a positive net present value of $5,000 exists, the cost of estimation error is $28,685.

Computer Studies.   Various computer models simulating possibilities and probabilities offer management additional means of evaluation that are not feasibly done manually. For example, a computer simulation can combine probabilistic estimates of cash flows into a probabilistic distribution of the internal rate of return. Computer studies yield more reliable information than manual evaluation techniques.

Managers should carefully examine projects with forecasted results very near the cutoff point because there is little room for error. For example, if they expect an investment proposal to yield an 11 percent return when the required rate of return is 10 percent, there is a smaller zone for error than for an investment forecasted to yield a 20 percent return. Companies need more sophisticated evaluation to better determine the profitability of the proposal. This additional cost is warranted if two alternative proposals yield approximately the same acceptable results, or if the evaluation indicates results that are near the rejection point.

Choice of a Method.   Managers often hesitate to apply present value or internal rate of return and rely on nondiscounting criteria, such as professional judgment, the payback method, or the unadjusted rate of return. These managers do not use discounting techniques because they believe that cash flows and economic life represent such rough estimates that many times they cannot justify the cost of applying such refined methods. Granted, it is difficult to determine the cost of capital used to discount the cash flows. Also, the cash flows used are point estimates rather than more realistic estimates of ranges. Therefore, it is difficult to relate this variability or risk to an appropriate discount factor. However, discounted cash flow techniques consider the time value of money and the cash flows over the entire life of the project. Discounted cash flow techniques have the advantage of using cash flows rather than accounting income. Using the payback method or the unadjusted return is understandable if a company has no choice but to purchase the asset. For example, the Environmental Protection Agency may require a particular pollution device. Similarly, profitability is not the prime consideration when incurring some capital expenditures, such as luxurious offices, because they are status symbols.

Even though management should apply one or more evaluation techniques in making capital investment decisions, they cannot ignore such factors as legal requirements and social responsibilities. The capital investment program also must allow for emergencies. For example, a machine that managers expect to operate efficiently for several more years may break down. If this machine is crucial to production, management may have no choice but to incur major expenditures in repairing or replacing it. Managers must make provisions to handle proposals of this nature more rapidly than less critical projects.

Aftertax Analysis of Equipment Replacement

Computing net cash flow is more complex for a replacement decision than for an acquisition decision because we are considering cash inflows and outflows for the asset being replaced and the new asset. Exhibits 21–1 and 21–2 provide a step-by-step analysis illustrating the expansion of net present value to include the total-cost and differential-cost approaches when considering income taxes.

Global

Current Cost Management Practice

Chairman and Chief Executive Richard M. Rosenberg intends to make BankAmerica Corp. live up to its ambitious name. Already the dominant force in western-state banking, BankAmerica is pushing east with its plans to buy Chicago-based Continental Bank Corp., one deal in a string of acquisitions that has boosted BankAmerica's already huge asset base. The deal put BankAmerica among the nation's biggest corporate lenders. This latest acquisition provides a rich market for BankAmerica's loans and fee-based services. With its better credit rating and huge retail network, BankAmerica should make Continental stronger. In addition, the extra capital and the international reach will provide an incentive for investors to deal with them. However, these benefits depend on the CE's ability to refrain from growth for growth's sake.

Russell Mitchell, "Dick Rosenberg's Manifest Destiny," *BusinessWeek*, February 14, 1994, p. 31.

Assume Maddox Theater management is considering replacing its floor cameras with new cameras having a purchase price of $150,000. Annual operating costs for the old floor cameras total $62,000. However, Maddox will realize savings with the new cameras since total annual operating costs would decrease to $50,000. After five years' use, Maddox can sell the new cameras for $18,000, but we ignore this salvage value in computing annual depreciation charges. If Maddox makes the purchase, management cannot sell the old cameras for their book value of $60,000 because the expected present salvage value is only $25,000.

If Maddox does not replace the old cameras, the theater can use them for five more years and then scrap them for $3,000 salvage. (For simplicity, assume we originally estimated no salvage value in calculating annual depreciation on the old cameras.) However, in two more years Maddox must make major repair expenses costing $36,000 on the old cameras. Maddox would depreciate the new cameras for tax purposes as indicated and use straight-line depreciation for the old cameras. The theater's tax rate is 45 percent, and its aftertax cost of capital is 12 percent. Note that we ignore the cash inflow from revenue generated from the cameras because we assume it to be the same whether the old cameras are replaced or not.

In deciding whether to keep the old cameras or replace them, Maddox may use either the total-cost or differential-cost approach. When there are only two alternatives (i.e., keep or replace a capital asset), the differential-cost approach is appropriate. However, when a company is considering more than two alternatives, the total-cost approach reflects additional computations.

Exhibits 21–1 and 21–2 contain a complete solution for Maddox Theater. They sketch out of the relevant cash flows by years, which may be helpful. For simplicity, we assume all cash outflows or inflows occur at the beginning or end of a year. Also, we separate cash operating costs from the income tax savings generated by depreciation deductions even though we could have combined them if preferred. The separation of these helps compare alternative depreciation effects and allows the use of annuity tables when either depreciation or cash operating costs are equal each year. We are assuming that any cash receipts or disbursements and their related tax effects occur in the same period. We can refine the analysis to reflect possible lags in tax payments and related pretax operating cash flows. Assume that gains and losses on capital asset disposal are taxed as ordinary gains and losses. However, note that rules on tax rates and other impacts on taxes vary considerably depending on the type of asset and period involved.

Total-Cost
Approach

In deciding whether to replace the old cameras, the analysis in Exhibit 21–1 using the **total-cost approach** indicates a net present value advantage in keeping the old cameras. Notice that depreciation charges, which do not require a cash outflow, do provide a tax shield equal to the deduction multiplied by the 45 percent tax rate for Maddox Theater.

Differential-Cost
Approach

If, instead, we use the **differential-cost approach** for deciding whether to keep the cameras, we include only differences in cash operating costs, depreciation tax shield, and salvage value as shown in Exhibit 21–2. We obtain the $31,932 net present value advantage to keeping the old cameras as computed in Exhibit 21–1.

Inflation in the Capital Budgeting Process

An important aspect of capital budgeting is the impact of inflation on budgeting techniques, particularly incorporating price-level changes into the model. In a taxless economy, inflation would affect cash flows and the applicable discount rate in a comparable manner. Therefore, the effect on present value calculations would be irrelevant. However, we do not live in such an economy, and we must consider the impact of taxes in almost all business decisions. In addition, assuming a constant price level is erroneous because the general price level changes over the life of the project. An increase in the general price-level index increases future revenues, wages, materials, and other project costs.

Inflation's Effect.   To illustrate the **impact of inflation on capital budgeting,** assume that in the current year, 19X0, a company is considering the purchase of equipment with an expected life of five years. The controller indicates that the company's cost of capital unadjusted for inflation is 8 percent. Economic advisors determine that the general price level index should rise by 6 percent a year for the next five years. The company anticipates operations from the equipment to yield $55,000 in cash revenues and require $20,000 cash expenses, all in 19X0 prices. The requested 8 percent rate for the cost of capital (the discount rate) is adjusted for inflation and rounded to 15 percent as follows:

$$1.08 \times 1.06 = 1.145 - 1.000 = 15\%$$

Adding the cost of capital to the inflation rate is not appropriate; instead, these values should be multiplied to incorporate the compounding effect of inflation.

Exhibit 21–3 illustrates an adjustment for inflation for both the discount rate and the predicted cash inflows. Each year is adjusted for an inflation increase of 6 percent for the next five years; for example, in Year 2, 106 percent × 106 percent = 112.4 percent. Alternatively, we could have used the estimated specific year-end index value for each of the next five years in Exhibit 21–3. The present value factors obtained from Table A in the Appendix reflect the discount rate adjusted for inflation (15 percent in Exhibit 21–3). Note that inflation does not affect depreciation

Exhibit 21–1   Capital Budgeting Using Total-Cost Approach

Items and Computations	Year(s) Having Cash Flows	Amount of Cash Flows	12% Factor	Present Value of Cash Flows	Year 1	Year 2	Year 3	Year 4	Year 5
Buy the new cameras:									
Initial investment	Now	$(150,000)	1.000	$(150,000)	($150,000)				
Annual cash operating expenses $50,000									
Multiply by 1 – 45% . . . × 55%									
Aftertax expenses $27,500	1–5	(27,500)	3.605	(99,138)	($27,500)	($27,500)	($27,500)	($27,500)	($27,500)
Depreciation (see below) . . . 1	1	27,000	0.893	24,111	27,000				
. . . . 2	2	14,850	0.797	11,836		14,850			
. . . . 3	3	10,125	0.712	7,209			10,125		
. . . . 4	4	8,325	0.636	5,295				8,325	
. . . . 5	5	7,200	0.567	4,082					7,200
Cash from disposal of the old cameras:									
Cash received from sale . . .	Now	25,000	1.000	25,000	25,000				
Tax shield from loss:									
Book value now $60,000									
Less sale price 25,000									
Loss from disposal . . . 35,000									
Income tax savings at 45% × 45%									
Income tax savings . . . $15,750	Now	15,750	1.000	15,750	15,750				
Salvage value of the new cameras $18,000									
Multiply by 1 – 45% . . . × 55%									
Net cash inflow . . . . . $ 9,900	5	9,900	0.567	5,613					9,900
Present value of cash flows of buying new cameras				$(150,242)					

(continued)

Exhibit 21–1   Capital Budgeting Using Total-Cost Approach *(concluded)*

Depreciation:

Year	Cameras, Cost	Income Tax Depreciation Deduction	Tax Shield: Income Tax Savings at 45%
1	$150,000	$60,000	$27,000
2	150,000	33,000	14,850
3	150,000	22,500	10,125
4	150,000	18,500	8,325
5	150,000	16,000	7,200

Items and Computations		Year(s) Having Cash Flows	Amount of Cash Flows	12% Factor	Present Value of Cash Flows
Keep the old cameras:					
Annual cash operating costs	$62,000				
Multiply by 1 − 45%	× 55%				
Aftertax cost	$34,100	1–5	$(34,100)	3.605	$(122,931)
Repairs needed	$36,000				
Multiply by 1 − 45%	× 55%				
Aftertax cost	$19,800	2	(19,800)	0.797	(15,781)
Depreciation deduction	$12,000*				
Multiply by 45%	× 45%				
Income tax savings	$ 5,400	1–5	5,400	3.605	19,467
Salvage value	$ 3,000				
Multiply by 1 − 45%	× 55%				
Net cash inflow	$ 1,650	5	1,650	0.567	935
Present value of cash flows of keeping old cameras					$(118,310)
Net present value in favor of keeping the old cameras					$ (31,932)

*$60,000/5 years = $12,000

	Now	1	2	3	4	5
Years Having Cash Flows		($34,100)	($34,100)	($34,100)	($34,100)	($34,100)
			(19,800)			
		5,400	5,400	5,400	5,400	5,400
						1,650

EXHIBIT 21–2   Capital Budgeting Using Differential-Cost Approach

Items and Computations	Year(s) Having Cash Flows	Amount of Cash Flows	12% Factor	Present Value of Cash Flows	Now	1	2	3	4	5
Initial investment	Now	$(150,000)	1.000	$(150,000)	($150,000)					
Savings in cash operating expenses $12,000										
Multiply by 1 − 45% . . . × 55%										
Net cash inflow . . . . $ 6,600	1–5	6,600	3.605	23,793		$6,600	$6,600	$6,600	$6,600	$6,600
Difference in depreciation: (see below)	1	21,600	0.893	19,289		21,600				
	2	9,450	0.797	7,532			9,450			
	3	4,725	0.712	3,364				4,725		
	4	2,925	0.636	1,860					2,925	
	5	1,800	0.567	1,021						1,800
Cash from disposal of the old cameras:										
Cash received from sale. .	Now	25,000	1.000	25,000	25,000					
Income tax savings from loss (see Exhibit 21–1)	Now	15,750	1.000	15,750	15,750					
Repairs avoided $36,000										
Multiply by 1 − 45% . . . × 55%										
Net cash inflow $19,800	2	19,800	0.797	15,781			19,800			
Difference in salvage value in 5 years $15,000										
Multiply by 1 − 45% . . . × 55%										
Net cash inflow . . . . $ 8,250	5	8,250	0.567	4,678						8,250
Net present value in favor of keeping old cameras				$ (31,932)						

Depreciation on Cameras

Year	New	Old	Difference in Depreciation	Income Tax Savings @ 45%
1	$60,000	$12,000	$48,000	$21,600
2	33,000	12,000	21,000	9,450
3	22,500	12,000	10,500	4,725
4	18,500	12,000	6,500	2,925
5	16,000	12,000	4,000	1,800

EXHIBIT 21-3   The Effects of Inflation on Capital Budgeting Procedures

Revenue	19X1	19X2	19X3	19X4	19X5	Total
Revenue	$55,000	$55,000	$55,000	$55,000	$55,000	
Less: Cash expenses	20,000	20,000	20,000	20,000	20,000	
Pretax cash flow unadjusted for inflation	$35,000	$35,000	$35,000	$35,000	$35,000	
Inflation index	1.06	1.124	1.191	1.262	1.338	
Inflation adjusted pretax cash flow	$37,100	$39,340	$41,685	$44,170	$46,830	
Less: Depreciation	35,000	27,000	18,000	12,000	8,000	
Inflation adjusted taxable income	$ 2,100	$12,340	$23,685	$32,170	$38,830	
Less: Income tax (45%)	945	5,553	10,658	14,477	17,474	
Inflation adjusted aftertax income	$ 1,155	$ 6,787	$13,027	$17,693	$21,356	
Add: Noncash depreciation expense	35,000	27,000	18,000	12,000	8,000	
Net aftertax cash flow adjusted for inflation	$36,155	$33,787	$31,027	$29,693	$29,356	
Present value factor	0.870	0.756	0.658	0.572	0.497	
Present value	$31,455	$25,543	$20,416	$16,984	$14,590	$108,988
Less: Investment in equipment						100,000
(1.00 × $100,000)						
Net present value						$ 8,988

and its tax shield because we must base the income tax deduction on the original cost of the asset in 19X0 dollars. Assume we deduct a 45 percent tax rate and the depreciation shown in Exhibit 21–3 for tax purposes.

The project appears acceptable because the real cash inflows from the equipment purchase are adequate. To prevent the erroneous acceptance of capital investment projects and provide optimum resource allocation during times of changing prices, the capital budgeting process should incorporate the effects of inflation.

Capital Budgeting in the Automated Environment

The difficulty of justifying the large investment required in computerization is a big obstacle to purchasing an automated manufacturing system. Traditional capital expenditure analysis focuses on future cash inflows that come mainly from savings in labor costs. Traditional models often do not provide managers with enough incentive for changing to flexible manufacturing systems because of inadequate means for quantifying the benefits from increased manufacturing flexibility, reduced inventory levels, and the capacity for increased product innovations. As a result, companies may ignore these benefits and delay automation.

Replacement-
Trigger Thinking

In studying proposed capital expenditures in the past, most managers used **replacement-trigger thinking** that assumes they replace only worn-out or unworkable equipment. Important advantages of automated factory equipment include increased flexibility and opportunities for responding to changes in material availability, product design, or product-mix demand. Replacement-trigger thinking destroys the advantages of automated equipment. Usually, managers cannot legitimately evaluate advanced automated equipment on a machine-for-machine-basis. Even though the advantages derived from replacing a single machine have merit, that is not the final goal. Instead, greater benefits flow from such systematic, overall changes as reductions in design time and errors, and an increase in product quality.

Advantages of Automating

Acquiring equipment capable of manufacturing varieties of quality products leads to increased revenues. This equipment allows companies to better meet changing consumer needs. Computers and robots are consistent because they perform the same tasks. Unfortunately, human beings do not operate in the same manner for every task because they make random errors. Robots and automation make **deterministic errors.** If a computer is programmed that one plus one is three, it produces a three every time it encounters one plus one. Deterministic errors are much easier to correct; this is the reason automation produces higher-quality products.

Robots perform many functions more accurately and at lower cost than human workers. Robots are useful for dirty jobs such as automobile spot welding where welding errors can cause large losses. Robots also are effective for intricate, repetitive jobs such as assembling computer components. However, highly automated equipment may not be cost-effective for operations involving nonrepetitive short production runs.

The management of some companies view flexible, automated machines as offering additional capabilities, and in turn, profitable challenges. Robots are investments in overcapacity that keeps pressure on the company to grow, to develop new products and services, and to market these products and services effectively and aggressively. Automated equipment forces managers to search for new markets or to increase their market share in present markets. Their incentive is to profitably use the automated machine's competence and volume capabilities.

Automation also provides a capability that never existed before. Continuous tracking of parts occurs as parts flow through factories with automated reading devices. Managers find it valuable knowing where inventories are, what operations are in process, and how long inventories remain at any given operation.

Flexible manufacturing systems facilitate **repetitive manufacturing** that involves assembling components into a product rather than fabricating a product. The characteristics of repetitive manufacturing are small lot sizes, fast setup times, pull material systems, total quality control, significantly reduced inventories and floor space, rate scheduling, fixed routings, short cycle times, and a flexible work force. Repetitive manufacturing implies the elimination of job order production in which costs are assigned to each order or unit of production manufactured according to customers' specifications. Repetitive manufacturing also eliminates cost collection by work orders.

Failure of Traditional Capital Budgeting Techniques

Managers began to recognize the need for change in capital asset evaluation while studying proposed acquisitions of capital investments in computer-integrated manufacturing (CIM) technology. Investment evaluation and decision criteria must be broader when considering automated equipment because these purchases involve more company segments and activities. Additionally, the criteria include more qualitative than quantitative factors. Thus, traditional capital budgeting models fail to truly evaluate automated manufacturing systems for several reasons.

Benefits of Quality Improvement

Traditional capital budgeting models often overlook various indirect and intangible benefits. Discounted cash flow models focus on future net cash savings in reduced labor costs and energy costs that the proposed equipment generates. The danger is relying solely on the easily quantified savings in labor, energy, and materials from new capital investments and ignoring those subjective gains more difficult to quantify.

When robots and other new equipment cause increases in product quality, capital budgeting analysis should reflect these benefits. Anticipated savings from fewer customer complaints and reduced warranty costs from achieving a lower incidence of defects represent additional benefits of proposed capital assets. Also, the proposed capital expenditure may permit faster, more flexible, or more reliable production scheduling that reduces inventory levels. The purchase decision should include the decrease in total inventory carrying costs from releasing factory space. With increased flexibility available to accommodate product changes, inventory buffers are no longer needed and turnaround time can drop dramatically. Shorter lead times allow companies to respond quickly to customer demands. An increase in the quality of the products also may lead to an increase in demand.

Quantifying the benefits from increased manufacturing flexibility, reduced inventory levels, and the capacity for increased product innovation is subjective. However, this does not justify ignoring such benefits. If ignored, managers assume the value of these benefits is zero. Instead, improving the measurement of these factors should promote more congruence and improved profitability. No longer should managers reject proposed equipment on the basis of its insufficient labor or energy savings without considering the equipment's impact on product or service quality.

Profitable Quality.   However, justifying capital expenditures solely on the basis of quality is inadvisable. Even though quality is important, the main objective of a company is to make money in the present and in the future. For public relations purposes, companies advertise that their objectives are to provide customers with better quality products; however, profitability also should be their goal. For example, companies manufacturing personal computers should not install expensive keyboards with speed capabilities that exceed the typing ability of users. For improved quality to have real merit, higher revenues and/or lower expenses should result.

Hurdle Rate Set Too High

Managers may use a high discount, hurdle, and payback rate because they believe automation increases operating leverage which increases risk. However, the rate should not be higher than what a company could earn on its common stock or other investments. A company can justify a lower hurdle rate if the new investment involves the installation of flexible manufacturing systems. New technologies enable companies to manufacture products of better quality with fewer rejects and recalls, thereby reducing the risk in the product output and the capital expenditure.

Projects Rather Than Strategies Justified

Traditional capital budgeting techniques also attempt to justify projects rather than strategies. Management often overlooks a long-run opportunity because of its orientation toward short-term returns. Standard evaluation criteria like net present value, payback, and return on investment typically assume that change involves replacement of individual machines. This assumption reinforces the short-term focus because it permits consideration of only differential benefits. Also, publicly traded companies are required to issue quarterly financial reports emphasizing a short-term orientation.

*Effects of Not
Automating Not
Evaluated*

Traditional capital budgeting techniques that consider the time value of money assume money in hand is worth more than money promised in the future. By implication, a cost deferred is preferable to a cost incurred. Although this is often true—and sometimes useful—managers extend this concept to a point where they view present activities as bearing little or no risk and see new activities as risky. Thus, conventional capital budgeting analysis fails to quantify the difference between making and not making the investment.

Companies find that they need to not only carefully analyze the impact of purchasing automated equipment but also closely evaluate the impact of not acquiring new equipment. Companies that spend millions of dollars on single-purpose, high-volume equipment are likely to lock themselves into unchanging products and processes. Because of high machinery cost and the difficulty of replacing equipment, companies are often slow to respond to changing tastes and demands, with serious consequences for market share and cost positions. However, greater flexibility allows companies to use automated equipment for successive generations of products, providing a longer useful life than conventional equipment.

After the purchase, it is very difficult to measure whether an investment in a robot or a numerically controlled machine tool accomplished what managers expected. Much of the investment in new manufacturing technology provides increased quality, reduced lead time, and maximum flexibility for product and volume change. After purchasing and using automated equipment, now managers are evaluating the dollar impact of their greater flexibility. Even after quantifying indirect benefits, the investment may not meet the heightened expectations of production managers.

*All Trade-Offs Not
Considered*

Managers give the substitution of machines for production labor as a justification for factory automation. Many times robots can perform more consistently, accurately, and at lower cost than human workers. However, significant trade-offs are involved in substituting machinery for factory labor. In justifying the investment in robots, numerically controlled machine tools, and other techniques of automation, discounted cash flow or ROI calculations make certain assumptions about future operating costs. Management believes costs will decrease while quality increases with automation. Yet, automation affects other indirect costs, such as programming, material handling, setup, inventory levels, and relationships with suppliers. Automated factories require higher-skilled personnel, and a company may find such qualified personnel unavailable. Reductions in direct labor may have already been optimized, so that total out-of-pocket costs may actually increase with automation.

Assets Constructed for Own Use

Measurement problems arise in determining the asset cost that companies should capitalize when they construct assets for their own use. The material, labor, and factory overhead costs that accountants can identify directly with the assets present little difficulty. However, determining the normal factory overhead to capitalize is more complex.

In determining the amount of factory overhead to assign, the capacity level at which the plant operates is an influencing factor. For example, if the plant is operating at planned capacity at the time a company constructs the asset, management must postpone manufacturing some products so plant space, machinery, and personnel are available to build the asset. Under these conditions, managers should allocate a fair share of general factory overhead to the asset on the same basis as that applied to goods manufactured for sale.

If the plant is operating with idle capacity, managers may use part of this capacity to manufacture the asset rather than purchasing from an outsider. Then, the question arises whether managers should assign any of the general factory overhead normally allocated to the units produced to the constructed asset. No doubt exists about the capitalization of direct material, direct labor, and additional factory overhead caused by the construction. However, accountants have differing views concerning general factory overhead.

Capitalizing General Factory Overhead

Some accountants believe the full cost of constructed assets should include general factory overhead; otherwise, they overstate the cost of idle capacity. They argue for not penalizing normal manufacturing operations by having it bear all general factory overhead when other assets are using some of the facilities. They also argue that future periods will reap the benefit of constructed assets. Further, these accountants believe the costs should be deferred since special status should not be given to these assets.

Other accountants believe they should assign no general factory overhead to constructed assets when utilizing idle plant capacity. They argue that the company did not consider this cost in the differential cost analysis used in deciding to make the asset. They believe that the cost of this idle capacity would occur regardless of whether they undertook construction or not. Thus, they assign no general factory overhead to keep from affecting the cost of producing units. Admittedly, both positions have merit. However, this author argues for assigning a fair portion of general factory overhead to determine the cost of assets constructed for a company's own use. This approach conforms more closely to the cost principle that an allocation is necessary to determine appropriate costs for both the units produced and the asset constructed. This position does not penalize either asset involved.

Excess Construction Cost

If the constructed asset cost materially exceeds its fair market value, accountants should treat the excess cost as a period cost. Under these conditions, full construction cost does not represent a valid charge against future operations through capitalization. The company may have been less efficient than an outside producer, and they should recognize this in the current period.

After approving a project, accountants must apply control techniques to ensure that the company is following planned objectives. Periodically, accountants should compare actual costs incurred on the project with budgeted costs and note variances. If actual costs begin exceeding the original estimate, managers must either approve additional appropriations of funds or revise plans. After the capital expenditure is operating, managers should compare its actual performance with expected performance to determine whether overly optimistic claims were made about its efficiency. Even though the investment now represents a sunk cost, this comparison is helpful for future decisions and evaluation of managers involved in the process. If individuals realize that the company makes postmortem examinations of all capital expenditures, this discourages them from making overly optimistic estimates. They are more likely to support their claims with as much data as is feasible.

Summary

Labor or energy savings are not the only justification for new capital investments. Qualitative factors, such as improvements in product quality, market share, customer service, and competitive posture, are relevant. Managers should include such factory floor benefits as reduced raw materials and work in process inventory and the resulting increases in inventory turnover. The hidden benefits of CIM result from the close integration, improved speed and flexibility, higher quality, and greater product variation these systems can support.

It is no longer a question of whether to replace older technologies. Instead, the question is whether survival is possible if companies fail to acquire new technologies. The price of delay may be disastrous. Strict reliance on traditional capital budgeting techniques without quantifying the additional benefits automation brings is inadvisable. Although the benefits of automation may be difficult to quantify, they are significant.

Important Terms and Concepts

Differential cost studies   674
Sensitivity analysis   674
Cost of estimation error (cost of prediction error)   675
Total-cost approach   680
Differential-cost approach   680

Inflation impact on capital budgeting   680
Replacement-trigger thinking   684
Deterministic errors   685
Repetitive manufacturing   685

Problem for Self-Study

Comparing Methods of Accounting for Inflation
In evaluating the purchase of finishing equipment, June Allen, Inc., estimates that two positions could be eliminated if the equipment was purchased. However, additional inspection would be required for optimal operations. In current 19X0 annual prices, the wages and benefits of the two positions eliminated total $50,000 while the inspection amounts to $8,000 annually.

The equipment can be purchased and installed at a cost of $75,000. The economic and tax life is three years. Depreciation is deducted for tax purposes as follows: Year 1, $28,500; Year 2, $27,750; and Year 3, $18,750.

Management insists that a 5.4 percent rate for cost of capital be used. This rate does not include an allowance for inflation, which is expected to occur at an average annual rate of 10 percent over the next three years. The company adjusts for inflation in capital expenditure analyses by adding the anticipated inflation rate to the cost of capital and then using the inflation-adjusted cost of capital to discount the projected cash flows. The company pays an average income tax rate of 46 percent. Assume all operating revenues and expenditures occur at the end of the year and would be subject to the effects of inflation.

Required:

a. Analyze the expenditure under consideration using the company's method.
b. Assume a consulting firm proposes a different adjustment for inflation in capital expenditure analyses, adjusting the cash flows by an estimated price level index. The adjusted aftertax cash flows are then discounted using the appropriate discount rate. The discount rate used is the cost of capital multiplied by the inflation rate. The estimated year-end index values for the next four years are as follows:

Year	Year-End Price Index
19X0 (current year)	1.00
19X1	1.10
19X2	1.16
19X3	1.20

Prepare a schedule, using the price index values provided, showing the aftertax annual cash flows adjusted for inflation for the equipment under consideration.

c. Determine the net present value for the equipment using the method proposed by the consulting firm.

d. Discuss the advice you would give management regarding the purchase.

e. Compare the consulting firm's approach to the one presently used to compensate for inflation.

Solution to Problem for Self-Study

JUNE ALLEN, INC.

	Year 1	Year 2	Year 3	Total
a. Wages and benefits saved	$50,000	$50,000	$50,000	
Less: Additional inspection	−8,000	−8,000	−8,000	
Net cost savings	$42,000	$42,000	$42,000	
Less: Increase in depreciation expense	−28,500	−27,750	−18,750	
Increase in taxable income	$13,500	$14,250	$23,250	
Increase in income taxes (46 percent)	−6,210	−6,555	−10,695	
Increase in aftertax income	$ 7,290	$ 7,695	$12,555	
Add back: Noncash depreciation expense ...	28,500	27,750	18,750	
Net aftertax annual cash inflow unadjusted for inflation	$35,790	$35,445	$31,305	
Present value factor*	0.870	0.756	0.658	
Present value	$31,137	$26,796	$20,599	$78,532
Investment required				75,000
Net present value				$ 3,532

*Present value of $1 at 15 percent, which is 5.4 percent cost of capital plus 10 percent inflation rate.

	19X1	19X2	19X3
b. Wages and benefits saved..................	$50,000	$50,000	$50,000
Less: Additional inspection	8,000	8,000	8,000
Net cost savings	$42,000	$42,000	$42,000
Inflation index	1.10	1.16	1.20
Inflation adjusted cost savings	$46,200	$48,720	$50,400
Less: Depreciation.......................	−28,500	−27,750	−18,750
Inflation adjusted taxable income	$17,700	$20,970	$31,650
Income tax (46 percent)....................	−8,142	−9,646	−14,559
Inflation adjusted aftertax income............	$ 9,558	$11,324	$17,091
Add: Noncash depreciation.................	28,500	27,750	18,750
Net aftertax cash flow adjusted for inflation....	$38,058	$39,074	$35,841

An alternative approach is to subtract income tax from inflation adjusted cost savings; for example, in 19X1, $46,200 − $8,142 = $38,058.

c. Cost of capital adjusted for inflation = 1.054 × 1.10 = 1.159 = 16%

Year	Net Aftertax Cash Flow Adjusted for Inflation	Discount Rate = 16%*	Present Value
19X0 (current)	($75,000)	1.000	$(75,000)
19X1	38,058	0.862	32,806
19X2	39,074	0.743	29,032
19X3	35,841	0.641	22,974
Net present value			$ 9,812

*Using present value of $1 Table.

d. Greater weight should be placed on the consulting firm's method; therefore, the purchase should probably be made because the consulting firm's method yields a positive present value. At least an additional investigation of the equipment's potential should be made.

e. The consulting firm's method is sound and should be adopted. Using the company's present approach, aftertax cash flows are not adjusted for the effect of the expected rate of inflation. The cost of capital and the inflation rate should be multiplied, not added, to incorporate the compounding effect of inflation.

Review Questions

1. Contrast the hard automation used traditionally with flexible automation; include a definition of flexible manufacturing systems.
2. Discuss the impact of inflation on capital budgeting.
3. When comparing plant asset proposals, suggest guidelines to follow about the use of the various evaluation techniques.
4. How can two projects with different lives be compared in a plant asset expenditure program?
5. How can sensitivity analysis be used in capital budgeting?
6. Discuss why some accountants believe conventional capital budgeting uses too high a hurdle rate.
7. Why is the required rate of return used in the present value method usually above the general level of interest rates at which banks and lending institutions are loaning money?
8. Discuss the ideal conditions under which to introduce automation.
9. Name some benefits of automated equipment that are difficult to quantify.
10. In justifying the purchase of new capital equipment, explain why reliance on labor or energy savings may not be adequate for management's evaluation process.
11. Discuss the reasons why a manager might make the following comment: "My company needs to evaluate very carefully not only the impact of purchasing a robot but also the impact of not acquiring the latest automated equipment."

Exercises

Critical Thought

E21–1 Limiting Cost of Capital Rate
PDB Company has purchased a new machine for $71,830. It has an estimated life of six years. Annual aftertax cash benefits are estimated to be $20,000.

Required:

Determine the maximum interest rate that could be paid for the capital over the life of this asset without a loss on the project.

E21–2 Determining Cost of Capital Asset
Management of Winters Company is planning to purchase a new tooling machine with a payback period estimated to be eight years. Straight-line depreciation of $2,500 will be expensed each year of the payback period. Cash flow from operations, net of income taxes, for years 1 to 3 will be $4,000 and will then decrease by $500 from the previous year for each of the remaining years.

Required:

Determine the cost of the tooling machine.

Writing

E21–3 Maintenance Costs Replacing Repair Costs
With the automation of factories, cost accountants and production managers are changing their views regarding repair costs. As a result of this change in approach, more organizations are using the term *Maintenance Costs* in their accounting ledgers rather than Repair Costs.

Required:

a. Cite reasons for this change in account titles.
b. Discuss the behavioral implications of this change.

E21–4 Profit Difference in Machine Acquisition
Gonld Company is considering the purchase of a new machine, whose initial outlay would be $110,000. Its expected useful life is estimated to be five years, with no salvage value. Variable operating costs are forecasted to be $90,000 per year. The current machine has a book value of $45,000, with a remaining useful life of five years. Its disposable value now is $8,000 but would be zero at the end of five years. Variable operating costs are $115,000 per year.

Required:

Considering the five years in total, what would be the difference in profit between acquiring the new machine and retaining the old one? Ignore present value and income tax considerations.

E21–5 Aftertax Cash Benefit, Payback Period, and Cost of Estimation Error in Economic Lives
Short Company is planning to purchase equipment costing $70,000 to use in their Cooking Department. Management estimates that the life of the machine will be 10 years, and depreciation for tax purposes for Year 1 is $5,600. The company estimates the first year's cash savings from using this machine will be $20,000. The company's income tax rate is 48 percent.

Required:

a. Calculate the annual aftertax net cash benefits of this machine for Year 1.
b. Suppose the annual aftertax cash benefits of this machine were $13,500 for each of the years of its life, what would the net present value of this investment be, assuming the company's cost of capital is 12 percent?

c. Assuming the annual aftertax cash benefits of this machine were $13,500, what would the payback period be?

d. Suppose the useful life should be seven years and annual aftertax net cash benefits are $13,500. What is the cost of estimation error if there are no alternative investments and the machine is purchased based on the original 10-year estimate?

E21–6 Equipment Costs to Capitalize

Brodnax, Inc., received bids from several companies for a machine needed in production. Bids range from $100,000 to $125,000. Management decided to construct the machine using its own facilities. Costs incurred are as follows:

Materials	$40,000 (2/10, n/30 discount not taken because of a cash shortage)
Direct labor	30,000
Variable overhead	34,000
Fixed overhead	10,000 (allocated on basis of direct labor cost)
Installation	1,000
Operational test time and test material	600

Brodnax would bear the installation and the testing costs if they purchase the machine.

Required:

Ignore interest capitalization.

a. Determine what costs management should consider in arriving at the decision to make or buy the machine. Indicate the dollar amount.

b. Decide which costs should be entered in the accounting records. Provide support for your answer.

c. Determine if management was correct in deciding to construct the machine rather than to buy it.

Problems

P21–7 Make or Buy Machine

Clark Manufacturing Company secured bids from several outside companies for a machine needed in production. The bids ranged from a high of $60,000 to a low of $53,000.

Management decided to construct the machine using its own facilities by adding a third work shift to perform the construction. Workers used materials with a list price of $20,000 subject to 2/10, n/30 terms. A shortage of cash prevented the company from paying the invoice within the discount period and the discount was lost. Clark's costs included direct labor of $15,000 and variable overhead of $17,000. Fixed overhead allocated on the basis of direct labor-hours amounted to $6,600.

Installation of the new machine cost $700. The machine required 40 hours of an operator's time, costing $200, in testing its performance; materials of $180 were wasted in this testing process. Clark must bear the same installation and testing costs if they purchase the machine.

Required:

a. Indicate the costs management should consider in arriving at the decision to make or buy the machine.

b. Determine what advice you would give management in arriving at a decision.

c. Compute the new machine's cost that should be entered in the accounting records.

P21–8 Net Present Value, Sensitivity Analysis
A new machine costing $480,000 was purchased by Brown, Inc., on January 1, 19X1. Engineers expect the machine to have a useful life of eight years with no salvage value. The straight-line depreciation method will be used; the net increase in annual aftertax cash flow is forecasted to be $110,000. The present value of $1 for eight years,14 percent is 0.351; the present value of $1 received annually for eight years, 14 percent is 4.639.

Required:

a. Suppose Brown uses a time-adjusted rate of return of 14 percent, what is the net present value?
b. Calculate how much the aftertax cash flow can drop before the point of indifference regarding the investment is reached.
c. Assume management is concerned that actual cash flow may only be $60,000. What is the impact on net present value using the less favorable cash flow?
d. Using the less favorable cash flow, what is the cost of estimation error:
   (1) If there are no acceptable alternatives?
   (2) If the net present value of the best alternative forgone is $20,000?

P21–9 Sensitivity Analysis in Cash Flow Estimates, Payback Period, and Tax Shield
Bibb Corporation is planning to sell a new mineral that it can extract in addition to its normal product line. New equipment costing $1,500,000 with a useful life of 10 years (salvage value is zero) will be required. Depreciation is computed on a straight-line basis. The new equipment will be in an existing building that is fully depreciated and has been idle for several years. Sales of the new mineral are estimated at $1,800,000 per year for the duration of the life of the equipment. Annual cash flow costs are cost of sales, $1,280,000 and marketing expenses, $35,000. Assume a 40 percent income tax rate.

Required:

a. Ignoring the half-year convention for depreciation, determine the:
   (1) Internal rate of return to find the discount rate.
   (2) Payback period.
   (3) Tax shield from depreciation expense in dollars.
b. If management's estimates were overly optimistic and actual annual aftertax cash should be $223,545, what is the difference in the internal rate of return from that predicted in Requirement *a*?
c If the company had no other projects that are acceptable, what is the cost of estimating the incorrect rate of internal return?

P21–10 Present Value and Cash Inflow Related to Purchasing
After careful study, top management of Jan Humphreys, Inc., has agreed on a model of equipment for use in manufacturing. However, management is undecided whether a purchase or leasing arrangement should be made. The equipment may be acquired by an outright cash purchase of $50,000 or by a leasing alternative of $13,000 per year for the life of the machine plus $0.25 per hour operated. Salvage value is estimated to be $2,000 with a six-year life; straight-line depreciation will be used. If the equipment is purchased, the annual cost of its maintenance contract will be $650. In addition, the electricity cost per hour operated is expected to cost $5. The lease would cover plant maintenance and all other normal operating costs except the electricity used.

   If the equipment is purchased, the full purchase price could be borrowed from the bank at 8 percent annual interest and repaid in one payment at the end of the fifth year. No funds will be borrowed if the leasing arrangement is chosen. For purpose of this analysis, assume all expenditures including the lease rental will be made at the end of the year.

Assume a 48 percent income tax rate and an 8 percent minimum desired rate of return on investment. Management expects to operate the machine 1,800 hours the first year with an additional 200 hours each additional year.

Required:

a. Determine the present value of the purchase price of the equipment and the present value of the estimated salvage value under the purchase alternative.
b. Assume the purchase alternative is chosen and determine the annual cash inflow (tax reduction) related to depreciation.
c. Determine the annual aftertax cash outflow for interest and maintenance if the purchase alternative is chosen.
d. Advise the company if it should lease or buy. Support your answer with cost data.

P21–11 Payback Period and Internal Rate of Return

Cave Corporation is planning to sell a new mineral that it can extract in addition to its normal product line. This requires new equipment costing $400,000 with a useful life of 10 years (salvage value is zero). Depreciation is computed on a straight-line basis.

Cave plans to install the new equipment in an existing building which is fully depreciated and has been idle for several years. Sales of the new mineral are estimated at $1 million per year for the duration of the life of the equipment.

Annual cash flow costs are $770,000 cost of sales and $40,000 marketing expenses. The income tax rate is 45 percent.

Required:

a. Determine the:
    (1) Payback period.
    (2) Internal rate of return to find the discount rate.
b. Assuming the actual annual aftertax cash flow should instead be $95,420, what is the difference in the internal rate of return?
c. Decide what is the cost of estimation error using $95,420 cash flow if
    (1) The best alternative forgone is 22 percent.
    (2) There are no acceptable alternative projects.

P21–12 Differential Costs and Cash Flows

Management of Freeman Company is considering the purchase of manufacturing facilities needed to process a new product. The new equipment will cost $200,000, with a useful life of five years with no salvage value. Straight-line depreciation will be used. The processing facilities will occupy space in the existing plant that is now being used by the office staff. Actual depreciation on this office space is $15,000 based on a 15-year life. When the new product occupies the office space, Freeman Company will rent an adjacent building for an annual cost of $18,500. These are estimates of differential revenue and expense on an average annual basis:

Sales	$800,000
Cost of products sold (excluding depreciation)	600,000
Administrative and marketing expense (excluding rent)	30,000

Freeman Company requires an accounting rate of return of 12 percent after income taxes on average investment proposals. The effective income tax rate is 48 percent. Ignore the time value of money.

Required:

a. Determine the average annual differential costs for the first five years (including income taxes) that must be considered in evaluating this decision.
b. Calculate the minimum annual net income needed to meet the company's requirement for this investment.

c. Estimate the differential cash flow during the second year.

d. Estimate the annual operating income after allowing for income taxes and the return on investment in the new equipment resulting from introducing the new product.

P21–13 Automatic versus Manual Operation

McBride Corporation has been manually placing the label on its designer bottles containing perfume. Part-time employees earning minimum wages place the labels on these perfume bottles. Direct costs of performing this task have been:

Wages and payroll taxes	$10,500
Labels, glue, and other supplies	3,000

The company presently uses a machine to seal labels for its other cosmetic products since these containers are of standard design.

A salesperson for an equipment dealer has recently approached management with an automatic machine that seals labels on unique containers. The machine costs $40,000 and has a $2,000 salvage value at the end of an eight-year life. Straight-line depreciation will be used. Sales terms are cash on delivery. Since the machine is expected to become jammed periodically, 15 percent more labels and supplies will be used than were used with manual operations. In addition to the labor required to place labels in the machine, some supervision will be required while the machine is in operation. Management proposes to use an employee presently working in the manufacturing plant; she also will perform her present duties. This employee will devote one-fifth of her time to the supervision of the new machine; the annual salary of this employee is $25,000, including payroll taxes.

Utilities are expected to increase $1,200 annually due to the operations of the proposed machine; however, all machinery repairs costing more than $800 per year will be covered by the equipment company. The machine will occupy space presently being used for the manual operations.

The company presently has taxable income on its other operations and pays an average 42 percent income tax rate.

Required:

a. Assume an 18 percent cost of capital and use present value analysis to determine whether the new equipment should be purchased.

b. Determine the payback period.

c. Decide which additional factors McBride should consider before making a decision regarding the purchase.

P21–14 Discounted Cash Flow Analysis

Kent Company manufactures several lines of industrial products. The specialized machinery that Kent uses to make rotary wheels needs to be replaced. These machines were designed especially for this product. Management has decided that the only alternative to replacing these machines is to acquire the rotary wheels from an outside source. A sales price of $25 per rotary wheel has been quoted by a supplier if at least 75,000 units are ordered annually.

Over the past three years, Kent's average usage of rotary wheels has been 80,000 units a year. This volume is expected to remain constant over the next five years. According to Kent's cost records, unit manufacturing costs for the last several years have been as follows:

Direct material.	$ 5.80
Direct labor	4.20
Variable overhead	1.80
Fixed overhead*	6.00
Total unit cost	$17.80

*Cash expenditures for factory cost account for one-third of the fixed overhead; the balance is depreciation.

If purchased, the specialized machines will cost $2.8 million and have a disposal value of $200,000 after their expected economic life of five years. Depreciation for tax and book purposes will be as follows: Year 1, $1,200,000; Year 2, $900,000; and Year 3, $700,000. The company has 45 percent marginal tax rate, and management requires a 12 percent after-tax return on investment.

In its sales promotion, the machine manufacturer provided evidence that direct labor and variable overhead would be reduced by $1.50 per unit through use of the new machinery. Kent's production managers contracted a customer of the machine manufacturer using identical facilities and confirmed these findings except that this customer had annual production exceeding Kent's of 20,000 to 30,000 units. Also, the customer indicates that it experienced an increase in direct material cost due to the higher quality of material that had to be used with the new machinery. The customer indicated that its costs have been as follows:

Direct material	$ 6.50
Direct labor	3.70
Variable overhead	0.80
Fixed overhead	6.50
Total unit cost	$17.50

Required:

a. Present a discounted cash flow analysis covering the economic life of the new specialized machinery to determine whether Kent Company should replace the old machines or purchase the rotary wheels from an outside supplier. Give consideration to all typical tax implications. (Round to the nearest dollar.)

b. List additional factors Kent Company should consider before deciding to replace the machines or purchase the rotary wheels from an outside supplier.

c. Using only the data given in this problem and no other sources, could you prepare an internal rate of return analysis?

SPATS

P21–15 Total-Cost and Differential-Cost Approach

Management of Celery Manufacturers, Inc., is considering replacing its electric fans at a purchase price of $200,000. Annual operating costs for the old fans total $92,000; however, savings would be realized with the new fans since total annual operating costs would decrease to $60,000. After five years' use, the new fans could be sold for $55,000 but this disposal value is to be ignored in computing annual depreciation charges. If the purchase is made, the old fans cannot be sold for their book value of $75,000 because only $64,500 is the expected present disposal value. If, instead, the old fans are not replaced, they can be used for five more years at which time they will be scrapped for $10,000 salvage. (For simplicity, ignore this $10,000 salvage value in computing annual depreciation on the old fans.) However, in Year 4, major repair expenses costing $16,000 would be required on the old fans. The old fans are being depreciated on the straight-line basis. The new fans are five-year property class. Depreciation on the new fans is deducted for tax purposes as follows: Year 1, $80,000; Year 2, $44,000; Year 3, $34,000; Year 4, $26,000; and Year 5, $16,000. The company's tax rate is 40 percent and its aftertax cost of capital is 10 percent.

Required:

(A sketch of the relevant cash flows by years is not required, but you may find it helpful in preparing your solution. Round to whole dollars.)

a. Prepare an analysis using the total-cost approach incorporating the effects of income tax and present value.

b. Use the differential-cost approach incorporating the effects of income tax and present value to prepare an analysis.

P21–16 Discounting Differential Cost in a Make-or-Buy Decision

Because Lamb Company's old equipment for making motor parts is no longer operable, the company principals are faced with the following alternatives:

1. Replace the old equipment with new equipment.
2. Buy motor parts from an outside supplier who quoted a unit price of $2 per part on an eight-year contract for a minimum of 70,000 units per year.

For the past three years, production has averaged 80,000 units in each year, and forecasts are that this level will remain unchanged for the next eight years. Records for the past three years reveal the following costs of manufacturing the motor parts on the old equipment:

Direct material	$0.38
Direct labor	0.37
Variable factory overhead	0.17
Fixed factory overhead (including $0.30 depreciation and $0.15 for supervision and other direct departmental fixed overhead)	0.45
	$1.37

The new equipment would cost $250,000 and have a disposal value of $10,000 at the end of its eight-year life. Straight-line depreciation is to be used on the new equipment. Assume a tax rate of 40 percent.

The sales representative for the new equipment provides the following information regarding operations. The new machine will allow direct labor and variable overhead to be reduced by $0.16 per unit. Based on cost data supplied by a competitor using identical equipment and similar operating conditions, except that production generally averages 60,000 units per year, the unit costs are:

Direct material	$0.45
Direct labor	0.30
Variable factory overhead	0.08
Fixed factory overhead including $0.30 depreciation	0.50
	$1.33

Required:

a. Determine which alternative is more attractive, assuming the company desires a 12 percent return on investment. Support your decision with calculations.
b. List additional factors to consider before a decision is made.

SPATS

P21–17 Comparing Methods of Compensating for Inflation

In analyzing the purchase of finishing equipment, Fonda, Inc., estimates that the annual cash cost savings expected from the machine will be $42,000 in current 19X0 annual prices. The equipment can be purchased and installed at a cost of $90,000. The economic and tax life is three years. Depreciation is deducted for tax purposes as follows: Year 1, $34,200; Year 2, $33,300; and Year 3, $22,500.

Management insists on using a 10 percent rate for cost of capital. This rate does not include an allowance for inflation that is expected to occur at an average annual rate of 5.2 percent over the next three years. The company adjusts for inflation in capital expenditure analyses by adding the anticipated inflation rate to the cost of capital and then using the inflation-adjusted cost of capital to discount the projected cash flows. The company pays an average income tax rate of 38 percent. Assume all operating revenues and expenditures occur at the end of the year and would be subject to the effects of inflation.

Required:

(Round to the nearest percentage to determine the cost of capital.)
a. Analyze the expenditure under consideration using the company's method.

b. Assume a consulting firm proposes a different adjustment for inflation in capital expenditure analyses by adjusting the cash flows by an estimated price level index. The adjusted aftertax cash flows are then discounted using the appropriate discount rate. The estimated year-end index values for each of the next four years are as follows:

Year	Year-End Price Index
19X0 (current year)	1.00
19X1	1.04
19X2	1.09
19X3	1.15

Prepare a schedule, using the price index values provided, showing the aftertax annual cash flows adjusted for the equipment under consideration.

c. Determine the net present value for the equipment using the method proposed by the consulting firm, assuming the discount rate used is the cost of capital multiplied by a 5.2 percent inflation rate.

d. Advise management regarding the purchase.

e. Compare the consulting firm's approach to the one presently used to compensate for inflation.

P21–18 Comparison of Return on Investment and Discounted Cash Flow

Two years ago when Perishing Corporation purchased new equipment costing $200,000, an internal rate of return analysis showed that the equipment would save $69,832 in operating expenses per year over a five-year period, or a 22 percent return on capital before taxes per year.

Management has generally been pleased with the new equipment's performance and is surprised to read the accountant's report showing only a 16.6 percent return on investment (ROI) for the first year. To support the calculation, the accountant provides the following analysis:

Reduced operating expenses due to new equipment . .	$ 69,832
Less: Depreciation—20% of cost	40,000
Beforetax contribution	$ 29,832
Investment—beginning of Year 1	$200,000
Investment—ending of Year 1	$160,000
Average investment for Year 1	$180,000

$$\text{ROI} = \left(\frac{\$29,832}{\$180,000} \right) = 16.6\%$$

The accountant used the internal rate of return method for capital expenditure analysis, while ROI is used for performance evaluation.

Required:

a. Give some reasons why the 16.6 percent return on investment for the new equipment as calculated by the accountant is not identical to the 22 percent internal rate of return calculated at the time the machine was approved for purchase.

b. Explain how the ROI calculation performed by Pershing's accountant differs from the unadjusted return on investment as illustrated in the chapter.

c. (1) Name the one factor that accounts for the major difference between the accountant's ROI calculation and internal rate of return analysis.

(2) Discuss if the internal rate of return analysis can be restructured to make it consistent with ROI as calculated by Pershing's accountant.

P21–19 Capital Budgeting Techniques

Stafford Company is considering a machine whose initial outlay is $80,000. Straight-line depreciation is to be used, with no salvage value at the end of its useful life of five years. Net annual aftertax cash receipts are forecasted to be $22,000 for each of the five years.

Required:

Determine the:
a. Payback period.
b. Unadjusted rate of return on initial investment.
c. Unadjusted rate of return on average investment.
d. Net present value at 12 percent.
e. Internal rate of return approach.

P21–20 Sensitivity Analysis (continuation of P21–19)

Using the data given in P21–19 for Stafford Company, and assuming a 12 percent cost of capital, provide management with the following sensitivity analysis:

Required:

a. Calculate how much net annual aftertax cash receipts would have to increase before the net project value equals zero.
b. Determine the net present value if the cash flow is $30,361. How much does the $8,361 increase in cash flow affect net present value?
c. Compute the internal rate of return if the cash flow is $30,361. How much does the $8,361 increase in cash flow affect the internal rate of return?
d. Calculate the net present value if the life of the proposed project should be eight years instead of the originally estimated life of five years? (Use $22,000 annual cash flow in your analysis.)
e. Assume the annual aftertax cash flow is $22,000 and the company has no other projects which are acceptable, what is the cost of the estimation error, and what is the best decision for the company to make?
f. Give the cost of the estimation error if the company rejected a project estimated to have a $5,000 net present value to invest in this project yielding a $22,000 annual aftertax cash flow?
g. Refer to Requirement *f*: What factors could cause a company to wisely invest in the $80,000 machine when it has an alternative project estimated to have a $5,000 net present value?

SPATS

P21–21 Total-Cost and Differential-Cost Approaches

Management of Barton Feeds, Inc., is considering replacing its floor motors at a purchase price of $180,000. Annual operating costs for the old motors total $85,000; however, savings would be realized with the new motors since total annual operating costs would decrease to $70,000. After five years' use, the new motors could be sold for $6,000 but this salvage value was not originally expected in computing annual depreciation charges. If the purchase is made, the old motors cannot be sold for their book value of $42,000 because only $32,000 is the expected present disposal value. If, instead, the old motors are not replaced, they can be used for five more years at which time they will be scrapped for $8,000 salvage. However, in two more years major repair expenses costing $42,000 would be required on the old motors. The old motors are being depreciated on the straight-line basis. The new motors are expected to have a life of five years. Depreciation on the new motors is deducted for tax purposes as follows: Year 1, $70,000; Year 2, $39,600; Year 3, $37,800; Year 4, $19,600; and Year 5, $13,000. The company's tax rate is 42 percent and its aftertax cost of capital is 8 percent.

Required:

(A sketch of the relevant cash flows by years is not required, but you may find it helpful in preparing your solution. Round to whole dollars, and for simplicity, ignore salvage value in calculating annual depreciation for the old and new motors.)

a. Prepare analysis using the total-cost approach incorporating the effects of income tax and present value.

b. Use the differential-cost approach to prepare an analysis incorporating the effects of income tax and present value.

CHAPTER

22

Activity-Based Management for Marketing and Pricing Decisions

---

Chapter Objectives

After studying this chapter, you should be able to:

1. Use activity-based management to establish standards based on cost drivers for marketing activities.
2. Perform segment profitability analyses.
3. Compute variances using marketing standards and understand the care needed to interpret them.
4. Explain the role of cost in the final pricing decision.
5. Evaluate the various cost-based methods on which prices can be established, such as variable costs, differential costs, full costs, and conversion costs.

Introduction

Changes in marketing strategy require the rapid introduction of new and modified products. An overriding concern is to accomplish all these changes at reduced cost. Increasingly, cost accountants are assisting production and engineering personnel to ensure that companies' products and services meet global standards for quality, cost, product design, and competitive production technology. Activity-based management offers opportunities to better understand how companies generate profits at the customer level by using standards for marketing cost activities.

It is difficult to separate price determination from other market mix elements, such as advertising, product quality, and delivery terms. While a product's sales price is only one of many elements that determine its success or failure, price determination certainly warrants much of the manager's time and consideration. This chapter discusses ways of establishing the sales price according to various cost concepts and explains when each approach is most appropriate. For example, differential cost pricing may be appropriate for short-run, specialized situations, but it could be risky to use in the long run.

Objectives of Marketing Cost Accounting

Marketing costs arise from exchanges between companies and consumers. These costs include sales promotion and advertising, as well as physical distribution, market research, and product development. Accountants sometimes use the terms **distribution costs** and **selling costs** interchangeably with *marketing costs*. Using the **marketing management concept**, a marketing manager assumes an important role in production/marketing decisions and helps develop a companywide plan that involves all aspects of the operating cycle.

Cost Control and Cost Analysis

Cost control and cost analysis use different approaches involving divergent techniques. Efficient utilization of company assets is a concern of **cost control**. Marketing cost control employs budgets, standards, and such operation research techniques as transportation and assignment models. **Cost** or **activity analysis** searches for better ways to perform tasks. Accountants collect marketing costs in such meaningful classifications as advertising, warehousing, and transportation so they can compare costs with alternative expenditures and with related sales volumes and gross margins.

Marketing cost accounting tries to ensure the most effective use of marketing expenditures to increase profits. This approach differs from production cost accounting whose objective usually is cost reduction. Production cost accounting emphasizes full utilization of manufacturing capacity so that additional units absorb fixed costs. The result is that unit production cost decreases as manufacturing volume increases. The effect on marketing of increased production volume is that companies must exert more effort to find additional customers and to open new territories. Hence, unit marketing cost normally increases when the company attempts to expand sales volume, especially during periods of strong competition.

Current Cost Management Practice

Global

Dr Pepper/Seven-Up Companies' domestic sales have grown by 38 percent since 1989, twice the rate of the soft drink industry. Coca-Cola Company and PepsiCo still retain 42 percent and 31 percent of the domestic market respectively. However, Dr Pepper's sales growth does not strike terror at the Coca-Cola or PepsiCo executive offices. John Albers, the chief executive of Dr Pepper/Seven-Up does make competitors notice with lavish spending on promotion, generous allowances to bottlers, and a feisty management style. As a percentage of revenue, Dr Pepper's marketing spending of 51 percent of revenues outclasses the largest companies. Refinancing and reducing average interest costs from 13.9 percent to 7.2 percent enabled Dr Pepper to go public. Albers cannot relax because Dr Pepper/Seven-Up lacks the money and muscle that Coca-Cola has. Also, the growing popularity of flavored teas, sports drinks, and juice water threaten Dr Pepper. Despite this competition, Albers is optimistic and admits if the company received a bona fide purchase offer, he would have a fiduciary responsibility to shareholders to seriously consider it. Albers believes he has done his job by building the brands to where they are worth a lot more money.

Howard Rudnitsky, "Lots of Fizz," *Forbes*, August 1, 1994, p. 44.

*Government
Regulations*

Generally, there are two purposes of marketing cost accounting. First, companies need more effective means of controlling and analyzing marketing costs. Second, companies must be able to justify courses of action to regulatory bodies concerned with marketing policies. With the passage of the **Robinson-Patman Amendment**, knowledge of marketing costs became a prerequisite for intelligent price determination. The amendment concerns price differentials caused by charging different prices to different customers in a single market. Because companies can avoid discriminatory price setting if complete cost information is available, the amendment continues to be a motivator for improving marketing cost accounting methods. ABC techniques for marketing costs represent one such improvement.

ABC System for Marketing Costs

Activity-based costing (ABC) concepts not only improve resource utilization in manufacturing but also readily apply to marketing functions. Marketing activities consume resources; customer groupings, territories, and other segments require activities. ABC more appropriately costs the marketing activities needed to service each customer or order size. The extensive variability in marketing costs across customer types and distribution channels merits attention in the costing system. ABC helps manage the customer mix by encouraging the elimination of low-volume customers for whom prices cannot be raised. Alternatively, ABC provides costing to support the addition of a surcharge on small orders.

As discussed in Chapter 5, an activity-based accounting system is a two-stage allocation process that fully allocates costs to customers, products, or other ultimate cost objects. In the first stage of an ABC system, accountants separate costs into detailed activities or other cost pools. In the second stage, they allocate cost pools to customers, products, or other segments based on activity measures or cost drivers unique to each cost pool.

Steps for Implementing ABC for Marketing Activities

We use the following steps to measure the profitability of marketing costs:

1. Select the segments on which to base profitability analyses. Territories, customer groupings, and product lines are examples.
2. Establish detailed marketing activities for these broad functions: Warehousing and handling, transportation, credit and collection, general marketing activities, personal selling, and advertising and sales promotion.
3. Accumulate the direct costs for each activity and separate them into variable and fixed cost categories.
4. Determine cost drivers for each activity; this chapter lists a representative sample.
5. Compute unit costs for each activity by dividing the budgeted activity cost by the cost driver selected. Use the unit cost to establish standards and flexible budgets.
6. Allocate costs to segments to analyze segment profitability.
7. Compare budgeted/standard costs with actual costs for each marketing activity and compute the price and efficiency variances.
8. Determine the cause of resulting variances.

Natural Expense Classification.   Most companies initially record costs by the nature or object of the expenditure—for example, material, wages, and rent. This **natural expense classification** identifies the kind of service the company secures for its expense. Accountants then determine how to accumulate the costs. Territories, products, salespersons, or customer groupings are typical cost pools or segments that they use. After determining the production, marketing, or administrative costs, accountants distribute individual natural expense items to products and activities within each segment.

Segmentation

The cost of marketing and delivering a product varies dramatically by distribution channel. For example, in a direct channel, customers simply call and place their orders. Sales in other channels that require frequent customer calls by specially trained salespersons incur higher marketing costs. **Segmentation** is the difficult task of tracing marketing costs to individual segments such as product lines or salespersons. Accurately attributing marketing costs to segments involves interviewing marketing and salespeople to learn how they allocate their time and effort across buyer segments and distribution channels.

Marketing Activities

After choosing the segments, accountants determine which activities to cost, such as transportation, warehousing, or personal selling. For instance, marketing activities are the separate and distinct marketing functions a company undertakes. Then accountants accumulate costs by these functions. They consider cost responsibility and control because assignment of responsibility to individuals within a company is generally by activity. For example, one individual is responsible for warehousing and handling while another employee is in charge of advertising. Marketing executives and accountants should jointly determine the activities to be costed. The selection depends on the degree of cost control and cost responsibility desired. The size of the company and its method of operation also help determine the number of activities chosen. Representative marketing activities are difficult to establish because companies engage in many marketing procedures and practices. To illustrate the procedures involved, this chapter uses the following broad marketing activities: warehousing and handling, transportation, credit and collection, personal selling, advertising and sales promotion, and general marketing.

Detailed Activities.   Expenses included in each of these marketing activities should be not only closely related but also vary according to the same activity or cost driver. We divide major activities into small classifications of responsibility to ensure that the work performed is homogeneous. For example, advertising and sales promotion may be further broken down into such detail as radio, television, and direct mail. The extent of homogeneity within marketing activities varies. For example, pricing and tagging finished products for storage and shipment is so different from soliciting sales orders by telephone that these two marketing activities need different cost drivers.

Cost Assignment to Marketing Activities.   Direct marketing costs require no allocation. However, accountants must distribute indirect costs on some basis. This requires the same process used in allocating indirect manufacturing overhead costs to producing and service departments. Accountants allocate wages and salaries on the basis of the duties performed by the individuals involved. They allocate depreciation of assets used solely by marketing personnel to their respective activities. Where possible, accountants designate the ledger accounts so as many costs as possible are charged to the activity directly rather than through allocation.

Marketing Standards Based on ABC Drivers

Accountants use standards to help control and interpret marketing costs; however, the methods of establishing these standards differ somewhat from the approach suggested for production costs. In setting standards for marketing costs, accountants identify the **ABC driver, unit of variability,** or **work unit** that causes the marketing costs to vary.

Because accountants base standards on the ABC driver, they should exercise great care in selecting cost drivers. A company should be practical so its cost drivers are measurable and produce reasonably accurate results that are economical in application. It may not be feasible, for instance, for a small company to detail all its activities. Instead, it can establish a standard for the entire marketing activity using the most appropriate ABC driver.

The same marketing standards may not be applicable in different geographical areas. The distance of the territory from the manufacturing plant, for example, is an important factor. Obviously, markets farther from the manufacturing plant have greater transportation expense per unit than markets in the same territory as the plant.

Companies also use different advertising media in selected territories because they find dissimilar consumers in various geographical areas. For example, an industrial goods manufacturer likely has only a few practical media alternatives, such as advertising in the one trade publication or direct mail. A consumer products manufacturer has more potential customers and several media from which to choose. A salesperson working in a highly populated area also has a lower standard cost per customer than does a salesperson traveling in a sparsely settled area. The nature of the coverage also affects the time and cost required to serve a territory. Salespersons in some locales may visit customers weekly while their counterparts in other territories must see their customers less frequently. The nature of the competition in the different regions also affects the standard costs for advertising and personal selling.

Order-Getting and Order-Filling Costs

Marketing cost can be broken down into two categories: order-getting and order-filling. Personal selling, advertising, and sales promotion activities incur **order-getting costs. Order-filling** activities relate to the other marketing costs necessary to complete a sale. For example, marketing costs to perform warehousing and handling, transportation, and credit and collection functions are necessary to complete a sale even after a customer has made a commitment to buy the product. These are order-filling costs. Standards are easier to establish for order-filling costs because many of these activities are repetitive, such as the physical handling of goods and clerical operations. In contrast, order-getting activities are generally nonrepetitive. The ABC driver for order-getting activities usually measures efforts expended rather than results obtained. For example, we may base the standard for personal selling cost on a unit cost per customer or sales call, while the standard for advertising may be cost per item mailed or per newspaper inch.

Even though most order-filling costs vary with sales volume, the individual cost units respond to different sales activities. For example, managers expect warehousing costs to increase as the number of shipments made increases. However, the receiving function varies with the number of items received, and the cost of handling returns relates more to the number of returns handled. Managers should establish this relationship between the cost component and an appropriate activity measure or cost driver. Companies that sell products on consignment, for example, incur the costs of transporting the product to the consignee in one month, while sales of the product may not occur until several months later.

Warehousing and Handling

Warehousing and handling involve receiving finished goods from the manufacturing process or from another business concern and storing them until they are delivered to customers. Because the nature of such operations is largely repetitive, accountants can apply standardization and cost control like that applied for manufacturing operations. If each territory or other segment has its own warehousing and handling facilities and clerical employees for handling the orders, these costs are direct segment costs requiring no allocation. However, when the segments use central facilities, accountants allocate cost to the segments. To facilitate this allocation, the employees involved may record the time spent for each segment's orders.

JIT Inventory Management Systems.   A just-in-time (JIT) inventory management system affects not only accounting and production but also warehousing, purchasing, transportation, and other marketing activities. A JIT system purchases products and manufactures products only when needed and only in the quantity needed. JIT directs attention to work in process inventory and turnover performance. Managers monitor what they have in their inventory, from raw materials to finished goods, virtually on a real-time basis.

Transportation

The transportation activity consists of the shipping and delivery operations in getting products to customers. To set standard costs for this activity, a company establishes economic traffic routings for the required distribution pattern. Because most transportation activities involve physical operations, time and motion studies and other techniques applied to manufacturing operations are appropriate to develop transportation standards. However, rather than conduct time and motion studies for each procedure, as for production operations, time studies for marketing functions represent longer periods involving several operations.

Credit and Collection

The costs of extending credit to customers for the purchase of goods and later processing collections vary considerably among companies. Accountants apply industrial engineering methods to study repetitive office operations such as preparing invoices, posting charges and credits to accounts receivable, and preparing customers' statements.

General Marketing Activities

Additional marketing costs, such as clerical, office, and accounting costs, vary in importance in different companies. In some companies, these activities are not significant enough to be treated as a separate activity. A company generally needs past experience and knowledge of the segment's activities before successfully establishing standards for general marketing activities. Analysis of invoices and charges, for example, provides information for establishing an ABC driver for such factors as supplies, telephone, and stationery. Typically, costs of general marketing activities are indirect costs of the segment and require allocations.

Personal Selling

As opposed to advertising, personal selling involves securing orders through personal contact. Repetitive personal selling activities are easier to standardize than nonrepetitive activities. Despite individual differences among salespersons and sales situations, certain sales techniques—such as product presentation—are standardized enough that managers can determine an allotted time for each sales call. Industry's widespread use of sales training programs is evidence of this trend toward uniformity.

To determine sales call standards, a time-study observer can accompany salespersons on calls to examine how they spend their working time. This approach, however, has some inherent weaknesses because the presence of the observer may embarrass both the salesperson and the customer and cause atypical salesperson behavior. A more practical approach may be to obtain data from the salesperson's daily reports showing the time spent with each customer and the number of sales made. This information yields a standard list of activities that salespersons perform so accountants can develop standards for the number of accounts per salesperson and calls per day. The type of assistance salespersons render each customer and the number of individual products they sell are considerations in establishing standards for sales calls per day. The standard number of calls increases if the salesperson conducts calls by telephone rather than through personal contact.

An analysis of sales salaries provides the basis for setting standard salary rates for each class of employee in each segment. In addition, accountants study each segment before preparing the standards for salespersons' traveling expenses. The estimated customer calls required to meet the sales quota becomes the basis for determining the expected sales calls per day. Since segment conditions significantly influence personal selling expenses, each segment requires different standards. For example, the variety of products sold and the channel of distribution among company segments cause differences in the cost drivers selected. For expediency, companies express personal selling standards as a percentage of gross margin or gross or net sales. However, other cost drivers achieve better control.

Advertising and Sales Promotion

The advertising and sales promotion function creates a demand for the company's products and services while building and maintaining goodwill toward the organization. Some companies handle all their own advertising and produce their own advertising campaigns and sales promotion material. Other companies contract all their advertising to an outside firm. The cost measure for specific-product advertising should differ from the driver for institutional promotional expenditures whose objective is to develop favorable consumer attitudes toward the company. For example, since the objective of institutional advertising extends beyond increasing sales in the short run, standard costs should not be expressed as a percentage of sales.

ABC Drivers for Marketing Activities

Accountants should chose the most appropriate of the following cost drivers to determine standard and actual unit costs. The degree to which they break down each marketing activity into detailed activities varies.

Detailed Activity	ABC Drivers
Warehousing and Handling— Receiving, pricing, tagging, and marking, assembling stock for shipment, and packing	Dollars of merchandise purchased, shipments, weight or number of shipping units, or purchase invoice lines
Transportation—Loading and unloading, handling claims, gasoline, repairs, and planning and supervision	Deliveries or shipments, truck-miles, truck-hours of operation, units of products shipped, or dollars of shipments
Credit and collection—Preparing invoices, making street or window collections, credit correspondence, records, and files, and credit investigation and approval	Accounts sold, credit sales transactions, invoices, collections, sales orders, accounts sold, or letters
General marketing activities—Sales analyses and statistics, letters, vouchering, cashiering, and mail handling	Orders, invoice lines, customers' orders, units filed, transactions, sales slips, time spent, or vouchers
Personal selling—telephone solicitation, salesperson subsistence, and customer entertainment	Customers served, sales transactions, sales orders, units of product sold, days, or customers
Advertising and sales promotion— Newspaper advertising, outdoor billboards and sign advertising, radio and television advertising, and product demonstrations	Newspaper inches, sign units, cost-per-thousand consumers reached, prospects secured, sales transactions, or product units sold

Marketing Profitability Analysis Illustrated

Exhibits 22–1 through 22–5 provide information about marketing profitability using standard costs based on ABC cost drivers. Exhibit 22–1 shows sales prices, unit production costs, units sold, and cost drivers. Exhibit 22–2 shows total variable and fixed costs for each marketing activity and develops standard rates. To simplify, warehousing and handling is the only broad marketing activity broken down into detailed activities. In practice, we would detail all marketing activities.

EXHIBIT 22–1   Monthly Budgeted Data for Product Line and Territory Analyses

	Product A	Product B	Northern Territory	Southern Territory	Total
Unit sales price	$40	$60			
Unit production cost	$ 8	$12			
Shipments	300	200	100	400	500
Units handled	300	400	500	200	700
Customers' orders	100	60	50	110	160
Returns	20	80	30	70	100
Warehouse units	1,500	500	400	1,600	2,000
Units sold	400	600	50 A	350 A	
			200 B	400 B	
Accounts sold	20	80	70	30	100
Sales calls	60	140	150	50	200
Clerical items	500	400	150	750	900
Newspaper advertising inches	300	200	100	400	500

EXHIBIT 22–2   Budgeted Unit Costs for ABC Drivers

		Variable		Fixed	
Marketing Activity	*Total ABC Drivers*	*Total*	*Unit*	*Total*	*Unit*
Warehousing and handling					
Variable costs:					
Receiving	500 shipments	$10,500	$21.00		
Pricing, tagging, and marking	700 units handled	4,200	6.00		
Sorting	160 customers' orders	800	5.00		
Handling returns	100 returns	1,000	10.00		
Taking physical inventory	2,000 warehouse units	1,000	0.50		
Clerical handling of shipping					
orders	900 clerical items	1,800	2.00		
Fixed costs:					
Rent	$600 per month per territory				
Depreciation	450 per month per territory				
Transportation	500 shipments	$2,000	$ 4	$ 500	$1
Credit and collection	100 accounts sold	900	9	300	3
General marketing activities	160 customers' orders	320	2	800	5
Personal selling	200 sales calls	2,000	10	800	4
Advertising and sales					
promotion	500 newspaper inches	1,500	3	1,000	2

The profitability analysis by territories in Exhibit 22–3 shows that the Southern Territory is more profitable than the Northern Territory. Exhibit 22–3 assumes for simplicity that actual unit sales prices, unit production costs, and units sold were the same as budgeted. For example, the Southern Territory's sales revenue is (350 Product A units × $40 = $14,000) + (400 Product B units × $60 = $24,000) for a total of $38,000.

However, both territories had several actual cost drivers that differed from those budgeted. Also, Southern Territory's actual rent and depreciation varied from budgeted. We allocate marketing costs in the profitability analysis on these actual cost drivers:

	Northern	Southern
Shipments	80	420
Units handled	477	223
Customers' orders	52	108
Returns	29	71
Warehouse units	370	1,630
Clerical items	120	780
Accounts sold	70	30
Sales calls	150	50
Newspaper advertising inches.............	100	400

The profitability statement by product line in Exhibit 22–4 indicates an operating loss of $3,605 for Product line A. Although the overall company is profitable, one of its product lines requires further analysis. Accountants can prepare additional exhibits using data by product line for each separate territory to further isolate the operating loss of Product A.

EXHIBIT 22–3   Territory Profitability Analysis

	Northern	Southern	Total
Sales revenue	$14,000	$38,000	$52,000
Less cost of sales	2,800	7,600	10,400
Gross margin	$11,200	$30,400	$41,600
Less: Expenses:			
Warehousing and handling:			
Receiving	$ 1,680 (80 × $21)	$ 8,820 (420 × $21)	$10,500
Pricing, tagging, and marking	2,862 (477 × $6)	1,338 (223 × $6)	4,200
Sorting	260 (52 × $5)	540 (108 × $5)	800
Handling returns	290 (29 × $10)	710 (71 × $10)	1,000
Taking physical inventory ...	185 (370 × $0.50)	815 (1,630 × $0.50)	1,000
Clerical handling of shipping			
orders	240 (120 × $2)	1,560 (780 × $2)	1,800
Rent	600	650	1,250
Depreciation	450	445	895
Transportation	400 (80 × $5)	2,100 (420 × $5)	2,500
Credit and collection	840 (70 × $12)	360 (30 × $12)	1,200
General marketing activities ...	350 (50 × $7)	770 (110 × $7)	1,120
Personal selling	2,100 (150 × $14)	700 (50 × $14)	2,800
Advertising and sales promotion	500 (100 × $5)	2,000 (400 × $5)	2,500
Total expense	$10,757	$20,808	$31,565
Operating income	$ 443	$ 9,592	$10,035

EXHIBIT 22–4   Product Line Profitability Analysis

	A	B	Allocation Basis
Sales revenue	$16,000	$36,000	
Less cost of sales	3,200	7,200	
Gross margin	$12,800	$28,800	
Less: Expenses:			
Warehousing and handling			
Receiving	$ 6,300	$ 4,200	$21 per shipment
Pricing, tagging, and marking	1,800	2,400	$6 per unit handled
Sorting	500	300	$5 per order
Handling returns	200	800	$10 per return
Taking physical inventory	750	250	$0.50 per warehouse unit
Clerical handling of shipping orders	1,000	800	$2 per unit sold
Rent	625	625	
Depreciation	450	445	
Transportation	1,500	1,000	$5 per shipment
Credit and collection	240	960	$12 per account
General marketing activities	700	420	$7 per customers' order
Personal selling	840	1,960	$14 per sales call
Advertising and sales promotion	1,500	1,000	$5 per newspaper inch
Total expense	$16,405	$15,160	
Operating income (loss)	$ (3,605)	$13,640	

Flexible Budgets

After establishing standards for marketing costs, we prepare a flexible (variable) budget using the approaches suggested in Chapter 10. Levels of marketing activity appropriate to the levels of production output are most practical. We estimate the marketing requirements needed to achieve the sales goals by applying the standards previously established.

Variance Analysis

As with production costing, analysis of marketing cost variances is the basic step toward identifying the factors that caused any difference between standard and actual costs and eliminating any inefficiencies. Each company selects its own specific variance analyses. Often companies compute only a net variance for marketing costs and do not attempt to break the variance down into causal factors. We do not encourage this practice, however, since it tends to hide inefficiencies. Instead, to be meaningful, we compute price and efficiency variances. This is the computation for each of these variances:

Price variance
(Standard price − Actual price) × Actual cost drivers

Quantity or efficiency variance
(Budgeted or standard cost drivers − Actual cost drivers) × Standard price

*Expense Variance
Report*

Exhibit 22–5 illustrates a detailed variance report for the warehousing and handling activity analyzed for the Southern Territory. The standards and actual costs for the warehousing and handling activities repeated from Exhibit 22–2 are

	Total Standard for Direct and Indirect Costs (in Dollars)	Actual Cost
Variable costs:		
Receiving	$ 21.00 per shipment	$6,400
Pricing, tagging, and marking	6.00 per unit handled	1,115
Sorting	5.00 per order	565
Handling returns	10.00 per return	680
Taking physical inventory	0.50 per warehouse unit	880
Clerical handling of shipping orders . . .	2.00 per clerical unit	500
Fixed costs:		
Rent	$600.00 per month per territory	650
Depreciation	450.00 per month per territory	445

The company allocates the following actual indirect costs to its Southern and Northern Territories:

Receiving (allocated on actual shipments:
  Southern, 420; Northern, 80) $2,500
Clerical handling of shipping orders (allocated on actual clerical unit:
  Southern, 780; Northern, 120) $1,223

Repeating, Southern Territory's budgeted and actual ABC drivers for January relating to warehousing and handling are

	Budgeted	Actual
Shipments	400	420
Units handled	200	223
Customers' orders	110	108
Returns	70	71
Warehouse units	1,600	1,630
Clerical items	750	780

Efficiency Variance

Shipments received is the cost driver chosen for the receiving activity. The firm received a total of 420 shipments, while they budgeted for only 400 shipments. This results in an unfavorable efficiency variance because actual shipments exceeded those budgeted. The efficiency variance in this case is unfavorable because they received 20 more shipments than planned. Hence, the company should encourage orders of larger quantities to save costs in receiving, but only if they need the parts received for production. Large-size shipments are not cost justified if the increase in inventory carrying costs exceeds the savings in receiving cost.

EXHIBIT 22–5

HILL COMPANY—SOUTHERN TERRITORY
Expense Variance Report—Warehousing and Handling
January 19X1

	ABC Drivers	(1) Actual Cost (Actual Drivers @ Actual Price)	(2) Actual Drivers @ Standard Price	(3) Budgeted Costs (Budgeted Drivers @ Standard Price)	(2–1) Price Variance	(3–2) Efficiency Variance	(3–1) Net Variance
Detailed Activity:							
Receiving:							
Direct costs	Shipment	$6,400					
Indirect costs	$\left(\dfrac{420}{500} \times \$2,500\right)$	2,100					
Total		$ 8,500	$8,820 (420 × $21)	$ 8,400 (400 × $21)	320F	$420U	$100U
Pricing, tagging, and marking:	Unit handled						
Direct costs		1,115	1,338 (223 × $6)	$1,200 (200 × $6)	223F	138U	85F
Sorting: Direct costs	Order	565	540 (108 × $5)	550 (110 × $5)	25U	10F	15U
Handling returns:							
Direct costs	Return	680	710 (71 × $10)	700 (70 × $10)	30F	10U	20F
Taking physical inventory	Warehouse Unit	880	815 (1,630 × $0.50)	800 (1,600 × $0.50)	65U	15U	80U
Clerical handling of shipping orders:	Clerical item	$ 500					
Direct costs							
Indirect costs	$\left(\dfrac{780}{900} \times \$1,223\right)$	1,060					
Total		1,560	1,560 (780 × $2)	1,500 (750 × $2)	–0–	60U	60U
Total variable expense		$13,300		$13,150	$483F	$633U	$150U
Fixed expense:							
Rent		650		600			50U
Depreciation		445		450			5F
Total warehousing and handling		$14,395		$14,200			$195U

F = favorable; U = unfavorable

However, if actual sales exceeded budgeted sales by more than 5 percent (20 extra shipments over budgeted shipments/400 budgeted shipments) it would not be appropriate to classify the receiving efficiency variance as unfavorable. It is reasonable to assume that a larger than budgeted sales volume requires additional receiving activity. Managers should exercise care in analyzing marketing cost variances because it is easy to misinterpret the results associated with marketing costs. Initially, they should consider each marketing cost variance as favorable or unfavorable in reference to that individual detailed activity, not for its effect on the overall company. Later they can interpret marketing cost variances in view of other factors, such as sales volume achieved.

Some situations use standard cost drivers rather than budgeted cost drivers in variance analysis for marketing functions, following a treatment similar to that for production activities. If some measure of marketing output, such as sample kits, is available, accountants can set standards for the components of this output. It is more appropriate to compute the standard allowed for this level of marketing activity using a treatment identical to direct material and direct labor efficiency or quantity variances. We then compare the standard cost drivers allowed with actual cost drivers in the efficiency variance.

Price Variance

Exhibit 22–5 shows a favorable receiving price variance because the $21 standard price exceeds $20.238 actual cost per shipment ($8,500 total actual receiving cost divided by 420 actual units). We multiply this difference in price by the actual shipments to give a total favorable variance of $320. We do not have to compute the actual cost per unit using the format illustrated in Exhibit 22–5. We can determine the price variance by comparing total actual cost to the actual cost driver at the standard price shown in Column (2).

We compute efficiency and price variances for variable costs only. Exhibit 22–5 shows only net variances for the two fixed expenses. Net variances measure the difference between budgeted costs (budgeted drivers at standard price) and actual costs (actual drivers at actual price).

Cost–Plus Pricing Methods

While the relationship between cost and price exists, how close this relationship actually is in practice varies. The measurement of cost is especially important when the buyer has agreed to pay a price based on cost, such as government contracts that reimburse providers for their cost plus an allowance for profits. In other cases, managers consider costs as simply a floor below which price cannot fall. The product's cost forces a company to resist lowering the selling price, both in the short run and the long run. Certainly, regardless of the cost concept used, companies strive to keep cost to a minimum by adopting the most efficient methods of production and marketing.

Variable Cost Pricing

Variable cost pricing emphasizes the contribution margin by delineating the behavior of variable and fixed cost. One form of variable cost pricing involves adding a markup on variable costs to full costs. Proponents of variable costing argue that this method allows management to determine prices for either the short run or the long run because it relates the effect of different prices to total

Global

Current Cost Management Practice

Kellogg, the largest ready-to-eat cereal producer in the world with $5.5 billion in cereal sales and 51 percent of the foreign market, wants to become the first Western cereal producer to apply its trade in mainland China, India, and the republics of the former Soviet Union. Kellogg managers recognize that staying put is not the answer. With a rise in marketing costs and a shrinking North American market share, they believe they must invest heavily to develop the China, Russia, and India market. Despite differences in culture regarding cereal eating, Kellogg does not plan to alter their products to suit regional tastes. That leaves many questions about the growth potential.

John Kimelman, "Beijing Bound," *Financial World,* April 26, 1994, pp. 34–35.

fixed costs. However, there is a danger in focusing all attention on variable costs and contribution margin. Suppose a company has two products, lotion and soap, for which monthly operating statements show the following:

	Lotion	*Soap*
Sales (1,000 units each)	$23,000	$16,000
Less variable expense	15,000	8,000
Contribution margin	$ 8,000	$ 8,000

Because lotion and soap have identical contribution margins, there may be a temptation to treat them as equals in pricing. However, such an analysis of only the contribution margin may lead to erroneous conclusions. If these products require different effort and costs of marketing, executive analysis, and research and engineering, management should arrive at the cost by including these expenses. For example, assume that fixed manufacturing costs are $2,000 for each product; fixed marketing costs for the period are $3,000; engineering costs, $1,000; and executive analysis, $2,000. The marketing staff estimates that it spends 60 percent of its time on the lotion product and 40 percent on the soap line because of the unstable market demand for lotion. In addition, workers package lotion in glass containers. The engineering staff estimates that over the last several years it has spent 70 percent of its time in redesigning the lotion container. Despite these attempts to improve the container, there have been several lawsuits from customers for damages. Because managers normally spend many hours in consultation with the company's attorneys and in court trials, they believe they spend 75 percent of their time with lotion. As a result of this information, they developed the following analysis:

	Lotion	*Soap*
Contribution margin	$8,000	$8,000
Fixed expenses:		
Manufacturing	$2,000	$2,000
Marketing	1,800 (60%)	1,200 (40%)
Engineering	700 (70%)	300 (30%)
Executive analysis	1,500 (75%)	500 (25%)
	$6,000	$4,000
Operating income	$2,000	$4,000
Cost per unit	$ 6	$ 4
Income per unit	2	4

This analysis shows why managers should not treat the products as equals. Even though the allocations may not be precise, they give management a better insight into the costs to use for pricing than does a contribution approach. Note, however, the allocations may change next period depending on the attention given to either of the products.

Contribution margin analysis also labels fixed costs as irrelevant and omits them from consideration in pricing. Assume that the company has determined the span of control for a supervisor is five direct labor workers employed. The company has received several bids of $2,000 each for processing 100 additional units per month. Because the present work force cannot handle any increase in workload, each 100-unit order requires one additional direct labor worker earning $900 monthly. Variable material and overhead amount to $8 per unit; supervisors earn $1,200 monthly.

EXHIBIT 22–6

Worker Number	**Contribution Margin Approach**			
	Revenue	*Cost*	*Contribution*	*Decision*
51	$2,000	$1,700	$300	Accept
52	2,000	1,700	300	Accept
53	2,000	1,700	300	Accept
54	2,000	1,700	300	Accept
55	2,000	2,900	(900)	Reject

Worker Number	**Alternative Approach**			
	Revenue	*Cost**	*Contribution*	*Decision*
51	$2,000	$1,940	$60	Accept
52	2,000	1,940	60	Accept
53	2,000	1,940	60	Accept
54	2,000	1,940	60	Accept
55	2,000	1,940	60	Accept

*$900 per direct labor worker + $800 variable materials and overhead + ($1,200/5 supervisors' costs).

As Exhibit 22–6 shows, contribution margin analysis generally does not include a charge for the supervisor until the company employs the 55th worker and adds the supervisor. However, we could argue that the supervisor's cost is really due to adding the 51st, 52nd . . . 55th worker as well and the 56th and 57th worker in the future. Contribution marginal analysis could cause a company to reject profitable opportunities, as illustrated in Exhibit 22–6.

Differential Cost Pricing

Differential cost pricing (also called **marginal cost pricing**) focuses attention on the contribution to fixed costs and profit that an additional order generates. This method involves adding a markup on differential cost. The differential cost of an order is the increase in total costs resulting from the production of additional units. Differential cost pricing differs from variable cost pricing that adds a markup only on variable costs. Differential cost pricing includes both variable and fixed costs as differential costs on which a markup is determined. Differential cost pricing is appropriate for some specific situations, especially those of a short-run nature.

To illustrate differential cost pricing, assume the following product costs from accounting records:

	Belts	Hats
Direct material	$ 5	$ 5
Direct labor	6	2
Factory overhead:		
Variable	4	1
Differential fixed	3	2
Allocated fixed	3	2
Total production cost	$21	$12

The differential cost of material, labor, and factory overhead for belts is $18 and $10 for hats. With a 25 percent markup on differential cost, the sales price becomes:

	Belts	Hats
Markup on differential costs	$ 4.50 (25% × $18)	$ 2.50 (25% × $10)
Full cost	21.00	12.00
Sales price	$25.50	$14.50

Companies can appropriately use differential cost and variable cost pricing theories when they face difficult times and must improve profits by receiving any revenue that exceeds variable or differential costs rather than no revenue at all. Such revenue makes some contribution to the fixed costs for which the company has already made a commitment. Admittedly, contribution margin is helpful in short-run pricing and profit planning because companies can compare the increase in cost resulting from a sale with the revenue increment to determine whether to accept the order.

With some even rarer short-run projects, it may be more profitable in the long run for the company to sell below variable costs. Generally, variable cost is the floor below which the sales price cannot fall. However, we can challenge this statement in some situations. For example, if a company has a skilled labor force that is difficult to replace, management might accept an order in which sales price is less than variable costs to receive some revenue to apply to existing wages and other costs. This approach might be more profitable in the long run than laying off the workers and running the risk of not being able to replace them.

Full-Cost Pricing

While we can set sales prices by adding a markup on differential cost or variable cost, full-cost pricing predominates. This **full-cost pricing** involves not only determining the product's direct costs but also allocating the company's indirect costs that cannot be traced to one product line. If management establishes a sales price of $28 for belts and $16 for hats, the gross margin is 25 percent of the selling price. The $7 gross margin for belts and the $4 gross margin for hats is a 33 1/3 percent mark-on ($7/$21 of belt's full cost and $4/$12 of hat's full cost) to the production cost.

Conversion Cost Pricing

The use of **conversion cost pricing** does not consider the material used in the product; instead, the emphasis is on the labor and factory overhead required, known as conversion cost. Companies mainly use conversion cost pricing when the customers furnish the material. The rationale behind this pricing theory is that companies can realize greater profits if they direct efforts to the products requiring less labor and overhead because they can produce and sell more units. Companies can use this pricing theory effectively if they have limited factory capacity when the capacity constraint is labor and overhead cost.

In the full-cost pricing example, hats require the same amount of material as belts, but only $7 of direct labor and factory overhead, while belts require $16 direct labor and overhead. When using a 25 percent markup on conversion cost, the sales price for each product becomes the following:

	Belts	*Hats*
Full cost	$21.00	$12.00
Markup on conversion cost..	4.00 (25% × $16)	1.75 (25% × $7)
Sales price	$25.00	$13.75

Using this pricing strategy, each product generates the same profit per unit of scarce resource.

Standard Costs.   A company can base its pricing decision on standard costs regardless of whether managers adopt the full-cost or variable cost approach. Standard costs represent the costs of efficient production methods at a normal capacity. However, before using standard costs as a basis for the pricing decision, managers should be certain that the standards established reflect current conditions. An advantage of this approach is that standard costs usually are broken down into fixed and variable components, and this is critical in many pricing decisions.

Direct Cost Pricing

When using the **direct cost pricing** theory, companies establish selling prices at a certain percentage above the direct, or traceable, costs incurred in manufacturing the product. This resembles the use of uniform gross profit percentages by merchandising companies. This pricing procedure has validity when the amount of indirect costs that should be equitably borne by each product line is essentially the same percentage of direct costs and when the assets employed by product lines are similar. Some managers believe that this method is more valid to apply in practice because it does not require that companies base prices on indirect costs. They believe that accountants cannot allocate indirect costs with a high degree of accuracy and that the pricing decision should not use indirect costs.

The following illustrates direct cost pricing for shirts. With indirect costs of approximately 18 percent of direct costs and management wishing to earn a profit equal to 25 percent of total cost, the following calculation compares the direct cost pricing method with the full-cost pricing method.

	Shirts	
	Direct Cost Pricing	*Full-Cost Pricing*
Direct costs	$17	$17
Indirect costs		3
Total costs		$20
Mark-on [18% + 25% + (25% × 18%) = 47%]	8 ($17 × 47%)	5 ($20 × 25%)
Selling price	$25	$25

We multiply total costs of $20 under the full-cost method by the desired profit percentage to arrive at a markup of $5 and a resulting sales price of $25. If, instead, we use the direct cost pricing method, the mark-on percentage must cover indirect costs plus the desired 25 percent profit. A 47 percent mark-on is as follows [18% + 25% + (25% × 18%)] = 47 percent. After applying this 47 percent mark-on to direct costs, we determine a $25 selling price, which is identical to that computed using the full-cost pricing method.

As stated earlier, direct cost pricing has validity if the cost characteristics of the various product lines are similar. Some managers might argue that even if their product lines do have different margins, the difference is offset because one product line's losses counterbalance gains on other product lines. However, this reasoning is faulty, for these differences only counterbalance each other if the sales quantities of each product line are in the proportion originally assumed when the sales prices were set. For example, if a company sells a larger proportion of the high-cost products and a smaller proportion of the low-cost products, overall company profits would be less than planned. In addition, the company may be unable to justify the sales price of each product line, because they sell some products for a price lower than their costs require, while other products have a higher price than required by cost. In the latter case, the company runs the risk of losing sales to competitors.

Evaluation of All Cost-Based Pricing Methods.   There is little agreement about which costing theory is most appropriate for use in pricing, and we can criticize each method. The volume level at which companies calculate unit fixed costs significantly affects full costs, as emphasized in previous illustrations. There is also a danger in using only differential costs or variable costs in pricing, because a company must cover all fixed or variable expenses to earn a profit. The marketing staff might be misled or tempted to cut prices to the point where they cover only variable costs; this results in underpricing and ultimate disaster for the company.

Pricing includes much more than totaling the specific costs involved and adding a mark-on to these costs. Cost information only provides an estimate of the sales price. In fact, many companies merely accept the existing market price without any involved pricing decision. They realize that customers will not pay more than this price and there is no justification for charging less. While each of the costing theories presented is appropriate for specific pricing decisions, pricing strategy involves many considerations. Basing prices solely on one costing approach is risky; managers must consider other factors.

Even after conducting cost studies to arrive at the optimum price for a product or service, effective managers monitor the profitability of price revisions. This phase of pricing is almost a continual process; management should be constantly studying the changing market environment in which the product or service is offered for sale. For example, effective managers study the effect of price changes in sales of substitute and complementary products. More specifically, although golf balls and golf clubs are complementary products, they are substitute goods for tennis balls and rackets. A company may find it profitable to decrease its price of golf clubs to improve the market for golf balls. However, if the sporting goods dealer is not careful, this price reduction can cause some sporting enthusiasts to switch from playing tennis to golf. Management thus should not assume that the optimum price will be static.

Summary

Global competition has increased the importance of efficient marketing activities. Because repetitive marketing operations are fully as measurable as manufacturing activities, accountants can adapt the techniques used in setting production standards. ABC offers an opportunity for continuous improvement by establishing standards based on cost drivers for each detailed marketing activity. This allows management to examine marketing activities more thoroughly than it could by comparing actual cost only to historical data.

The numerous factors in a pricing decision, many of which are difficult to measure and quantify, add complexity. Companies need sophisticated analysis of full cost, differential cost, and elasticity of supply and demand—not just a slight consideration of the additional revenue and cost generated by a price change. While costs have a major influence on pricing decisions, companies cannot disregard their competitors and customers. Managers must consider the impact of a pricing decision on these influences, as well as on the profitability and survival of the company.

Important Terms and Concepts

Marketing costs   703
Distribution costs   703
Selling costs   703
Marketing management concept   704
Cost control   704
Cost or activity analysis   704
Robinson-Patman Amendment   704
Natural expense classification   705
Segmentation   705

ABC driver unit of variability, or work
  unit   706
Order-getting costs   707
Order-filling costs   707
Variable cost pricing   715
Differential cost pricing (marginal cost
  pricing)   718
Full-cost pricing   719
Conversion cost pricing   719
Direct cost pricing   720

Problem for Self-Study

Determining Sales Price to Achieve Objectives

Sills Company produces valves and motors for industrial use. The company expects to sell 5,000 valves and 7,000 motors next year. Unit costs have been estimated as follows:

	Cost per Unit	
	Valves	*Motors*
Cost of goods sold	$ 8	$18
Direct marketing and administrative costs	2	10
Total direct costs	$10	$28
Indirect costs	4	6
Total costs	$14	$34

Management estimates that $500,000 of assets are employed annually in the production of valves, while $560,000 in assets are employed annually in the production of motors. The president believes the company can earn a 10 percent return on assets employed. Disregard income taxes.

Required:

a. Using the sales estimates given, how much total profit per product line and profit per motor and valve must the company earn to yield a 10 percent return on assets employed?

b. Decide at what uniform percentage above total costs for both products the selling prices should be established to earn the total profit required.

c. Assume management establishes a sales price that earns a 10 percent return on the assets employed on each product. What should the sales prices be?

d. Assume management establishes the sales price based on direct cost. What uniform percentage above direct cost should be used? What should the sales price be?

e. Assume total sales were 12,000 units as estimated, but the sales mix was 4,000 valves and 8,000 motors. Calculate the return on assets employed using the sales prices computed in Requirements b through d.

f. Compare the traditional procedures used in Requirements a through d with sales price determination using target costing. Assume market research data indicates customers are willing to pay $15 each for valves and $40 each for motors on a long-range basis. Sill managers normally expect to earn $4 per unit in profit on valves and $8 per unit on motors. What are the sales prices using target costing? Discuss possible considerations.

Solution to Problem for Self-Study

SILLS COMPANY

a.	$500,000 assets employed with valves × 10% =	$ 50,000
	$560,000 assets employed with motors × 10% =	56,000
	Total profit required	$106,000

$$\frac{\$50,000}{5,000 \text{ valves}} = \$10.00 \text{ profit per valve}$$

$$\frac{\$56,000}{7,000 \text{ motors}} = \$8.00 \text{ profit per motor}$$

b.

Total costs ($14 × 5,000) + ($34 × 7,000)		$308,000
Desired profit (from Requirement a)		106,000
Total sales revenue		$414,000

Sales price must be 134.42% ($414,000/$308,000) of total costs. The unit sales price of valves would be $18.82 ($14 × 134.42%) and $45.70 ($34 × 134.42%) for motors.

		Valve	*Motor*
c.	Profit per product (from Requirement *a*) ...	$10.00	$ 8.00
	Cost per product	14.00	34.00
		$24.00	$42.00

d.   Direct costs ($10 × 5,000 valves) + ($28 × 7,000 motors) = $246,000

Sales price must be 168.29% ($414,000 revenue from Requirement *b*/$246,000) of direct costs.

The sales price of valves would be $16.83 (168.29% × $10) and $47.12 (168.29% × $28) for motors.

e.

	Sales Price Based on Total Cost	Sales Price on Assets Employed	Sales Price Based on Direct Cost
Sales			
Valve	$ 75,280 ($18.82 × 4,000)	$ 96,000 ($24.00 × 4,000)	$ 67,320 ($16.83 × 4,000)
Motors	365,600 ($45.70 × 8,000)	336,000 ($42.00 × 8,000)	376,960 ($47.12 × 8,000)
Total sales	$440,880	$432,000	$444,280
Less costs:			
Valves	$ 56,000 ($14 × 4,000)	$ 56,000	$ 56,000
Motors	272,000 ($34 × 8,000)	272,000	272,000
Total cost	$328,000	$328,000	$328,000
Income before taxes	$112,880	$104,000	$116,280
Return on assets	10.65% $\dfrac{\$\ 112,880}{\$1,060,000}$	9.81% $\dfrac{\$\ 104,000}{\$1,060,000}$	10.97% $\dfrac{\$\ 116,280}{\$1,060,000}$

f. As Chapter 5 discusses, managers using target costing go to the end of the valve chain—the customers—to find the acceptable price and then work back through all the stages of a product by subtracting profit margins. Thus, the unit sales prices would be:

Valves: $15 target price − $4 target profit = $11 target cost
Motors: $40 target price − $8 target profit = $32 target cost

Since these target costs exceed the full cost of valves and motors, Sill managers will try to reduce the overall cost of these products over the entire life cycle by controlling design specifications and production techniques. Sill may also try to expand its market to increase capacity utilization so indirect costs per unit will decrease. Over the life of the products, they will cut target cost to encourage a process of continuous reduction in actual costs. This improvement allows Sill Company to keep its profit margin relatively stable as valve and motor prices are reduced over the products' life cycles.

Review Questions

1. Why are marketing costs presented on a per production unit basis not as meaningful as production costs presented on the same basis?
2. *a.* Why is the selection of the ABC cost drivers for marketing costs so important?

    b. What basic criteria should be considered in choosing an appropriate unit of variability?
3. Discuss the various segments that can be used to analyze marketing costs.
4. Should direct selling standards be expressed as a percentage of gross margin or as a percentage of gross sales?
5. Why are cost standards most difficult to develop for advertising and sales promotion?
6. What type of variance analyses can be used for variable and fixed marketing costs?
7. Discuss the factors that can cause future costs to be different from historical costs.
8. *a.* Discuss the role of cost in pricing decisions.

    b. When would a company establish a sales price less than variable cost?
9. Describe several cost-plus pricing methods.
10. Explain why you agree or disagree with the following: Managers should ask themselves, "Do I really know what my products cost?"

Exercises

E22–1 Direct and Full-Cost Pricing

Indirect costs of a product manufactured by Worth Company amount to 75 percent of direct costs. Direct costs of the product are $45. Management wishes to add a 20 percent markup on the cost basis used to arrive at the sales price.

Required:

a. Determine the sales price if:
   (1) Direct cost pricing is used.
   (2) Full-cost pricing is used.
b. Evaluate the direct cost pricing policy.

E22–2 Volume to Justify Advertising

Sales of a diet drink have not been as high as expected. To combat this, the marketing manager of Opaque, Inc., is planning an extensive advertising campaign costing $60,000. The president is concerned that the market is saturated with other diet drinks and colas to the point that the demand is not sufficient to absorb the extra volume that must be sold to achieve management's budgeted aftertax net income.

Based on a budgeted sales volume of 75,000 cases, the fixed expenses per case are $30 while unit variable expenses are $20 per case. The budgeted aftertax income at this level is $350,000.

Required:

a. Calculate how many total units must be sold to achieve the budgeted aftertax income of $350,000 if the advertising campaign is undertaken and cost behavior and the unit sales price remain the same. Assume the company is in a 30 percent tax bracket. Round all figures to the nearest dollar.

b. Prove your answer to Requirement *a.*

E22–3 Minimum Order Size

Louis Wells, salesperson for Ann Martin Manufacturing, was upset about the amount of time he thought he was wasting with customers that ordered only small amounts. He discussed his complaint with Harold Douglass, the sales manager. Douglass informed him that other salespersons had raised the same question.

   Together, they approached the controller to prepare a sales order analysis so that top management would be better able to set guidelines for the salespeople. A cost clerk prepared the following average processing cost per order, based on 2,000 orders per period:

Receiving	$0.40
Warehousing and handling	0.50
Preparing invoices	0.25
Posting charges and credits to Accounts Receivable	0.35
Credit investigation	0.30
Total cost per order	$1.80

A markup of 25 percent over production cost is planned.

Required:

a. Compute the minimum order size in dollars that the company should accept using the $1.80 unit processing cost per order.

b. Evaluate any weaknesses in this approach for deciding on minimum order sizes.

E22–4 Standards for Sample Distribution Costs Similarly Established as in Manufacturing

MUS, Inc., has been fortunate in controlling its costs through standards for its manufacturing activities. However, management believes there is enough similarity in some of its repetitive marketing operations that it plans to apply the same techniques to some of them. The company distributes trial sizes of shampoo along with educational material describing the herbal ingredients of the shampoo. Cents-off coupons also are enclosed in the sample kit not only for future purchases of shampoo but also for MUS's other cosmetic products. MUS's budgeted data follows:

	Budgeted Operations
Sample kits distributed	1,000
Shampoo:	
Quantity	2 tubes per kit
Total budgeted cost	$4,000
Advertising pieces:	
Quantity	3 pieces per kit
Total budgeted cost	$300

For the 920 sample kits distributed, 1,940 tubes of shampoo were used or destroyed in handling. These tubes cost $4,074. Also for these 920 kits, 3,100 advertising pieces were used at a total cost of $260.40.

Required:

a. Using the approach for production, compute price and efficiency variances from standard cost and prove your variances for: (Use the most appropriate method for computing efficiency variances.)
   (1) Shampoo.
   (2) Advertising pieces.

b. Evaluate the situation using only 2,100 advertising pieces for the 920 kits.

E22–5 Analyzing Financial Trends in Inventory

John Schmidt is owner of Big John's, a barbecue restaurant with a separate carryout-counter. Schmidt's accountant usually prepares adjustments, financial statements, and tax returns at year-end only. This year, Schmidt has noticed that sales receipts seem to be lower, although business seems to be as good as usual. Schmidt has decided to have his accountant prepare condensed statements for each month, to find out what the problem is before the whole year passes by. Schmidt expects a gross margin of 38 percent. A physical inventory taken by Schmidt and his accountant for each of the four months follows:

	May		June	
	Restaurant	Carryout-Counter	Restaurant	Carryout-Counter
Sales	$37,200	$54,600	$39,500	$43,200
Cost of goods sold	24,100	32,400	24,850	30,950
Gross margin	$13,100	$22,200	$14,650	$12,250

	July		August	
	Restaurant	Carryout-Counter	Restaurant	Carryout-Counter
Sales	$38,750	$39,450	$41,550	$35,700
Cost of goods sold	23,050	30,800	25,600	31,200
Gross margin	$15,700	$ 8,650	$15,950	$ 4,500

Required:

Analyze these financial reports and indicate any suspicions you have. To correct this condition, which sales control techniques does Schmidt need?

E22–6 Evaluating Pricing Policy

Dill Corporation was formed as a method of benefiting key employees of a national corporation. The employees invested in this company with the assurance that they would receive a high yield on their funds. For the first few years of its existence, the corporation showed a small but consistent growth with profitable operations. Various business ventures were continually suggested to Dill Corporation for consideration. After a venture was considered as being a good risk, having good growth possibilities, and being compatible with current operations, Dill would either buy an established company or set up a new company operating the new business as a division.

In the past few years, Dill Corporation has begun to show large losses despite tremendously increasing sales volume. At this time the corporation has four operating divisions: a service company, a brokerage and speciality division, a printing company, and a retail sales division. Each division was established as an independent company with a part-time bookkeeper.

After analysis, Dill management discovered that the retail sales operation appeared to be the cause of much of the loss. At this time a new manager was hired for the retail sales division, and an experienced accountant was hired to be the controller for the entire corporation. A primary job of the new accountant was to determine and correct the problems with the retail sales division because as sales in the division continued to increase, losses also became larger.

After much analysis, the controller discovered that salespersons were allowed to determine the discounts they would give their customers and to whom credit would be issued. In addition, the retail sales division kept a warehouse full of inventory although almost any product needed could be supplied by one of their local wholesalers usually on the same day. There were many cases of items being purchased that were in stock in the warehouse. Top management has informed the controller that the gross margin on the products sold by the retail division was supposed to average 40 percent on sales price; however, in studying a typical sale, the controller found the following:

$100	Cost
40	40 percent markup
$140	Sales price

The manager of the retail sales division is hesitant to make any changes as he fears salespersons will quit if discounts are cut back and sales prices increased.

Required:

Suggest how to improve the profitability of the retail sales division.

E22–7 Are Marketing Cost Standards Based on ABC Drivers Customer Driven?

Critical Thought

As controller of a large organization, you receive the following proposal from your marketing manager and cost accountant. They argue that some marketing activities do not relate to the number of units sold. Thus, using only volume-based (unit-based) allocations distorts the cost they use in product line sales analysis. They believe that applying marketing costs on the number of units sold incorrectly implies that a reduction in units sold results in corresponding reductions in the cost of sales analysis and statistics. Also, they state that nonunit-level activities, such as institutional advertising campaigns and generating vendor/customer relationships, are also unrelated to the number of units available for sale. They provide company statistics showing that for the last five years increasing the quantity of each product line carried in stock did not increase the company's advertising or entertaining activities.

The marketing manager and cost accountant believe activity-based costing (ABC) would provide them with better costing data due to the difference in volume and complexity of their product lines. They provide the following data for four product lines and ask you to compare conventional costing and ABC.

	Product A	*Product B*
Units sold	100	100
Marketing executive hours spent per product line	30	70
Budgeted marketing personnel cost—$43,500		

	Product C	*Product D*
Units sold	1,000	100
Outdoor advertising signs	5	5
Total budgeted outdoor advertising sign cost—$8,800		

Required:

a. 1. How much marketing personnel cost would you allocate to each Product A and B line if you use a traditional cost allocation system?
    2. What is the cost per unit for Product A and B?
    3. Evaluate the allocations.
b. 1. If instead, you use ABC, how much marketing personnel cost would you allocate to each Product A and B line?
    2. What is the cost per unit for Product A and B?
c. 1. How much outdoor advertising sign cost would you allocate to each Product C and D line if you use a traditional cost allocation system?
    2. What is the cost per unit for Product C and D?
    3. Evaluate the allocations.
d. 1. If instead, you use activity-based costing, how much outdoor advertising sign cost would you allocate to each Product C and D line?
    2. What is the cost per unit for Product C and D?
e. Requirements *a* through *d* illustrate product and volume diversity. You should have found ABC allocated more marketing personnel cost to each unit of Product B than Product A and more advertising cost to each unit of Product D than Product C. This resulted in a higher unit advertising cost for each Product D unit sold. While you may agree that this results in improved costing, discuss what actions could result from using ABC costing that hurt long-run relationships with consumers.

E22–8 Discontinuing a Product Line

The management of Grove Electronics is holding a meeting in five days to discuss whether to discontinue its handheld calculator product line. Each person attending the meeting is expected to express an opinion and to substantiate that opinion with a quantitative analysis. Management has furnished the following product statement for the year just ended:

Revenue	$ 900,000
Cost of goods sold	850,000
Gross margin	$ 50,000
Marketing and administrative expenses	70,000
Net loss	$ (20,000)

Cost of goods sold is 35 percent factory overhead, of which 15 percent is fixed.

Required:

a. Discuss what opinion and supporting data you would present if you were to attend this meeting.
b. Compute the breakeven sales dollar for the product.

Problems

P22–9 Revising Sales Price on Order Size Cost

Milam, Inc., requests that you allocate its marketing costs on order size as a way of determining if its sales price per unit reflects any variation in the nonmanufacturing cost per volume-unit. Their order sizes fall into these three categories: small (1 to 4 items), medium (5 to 26 items), and large (over 26 items). The actual marketing costs incurred last year and the basis for allocation are:

Marketing Cost	Amount	Basis for Distribution
Transportation	$ 7,920	Units shipped
Sales promotion	8,000	Circulation pieces distributed
Credit and collection	5,000	Number of orders
Marketing salaries	36,000	Direct charge

An analysis of their records produced the following statistics:

| | Order Sizes | | | |
	Small	Medium	Large	Total
Units shipped	500	1,800	2,100	4,400
Circulation pieces distributed	50,000	75,000	125,000	250,000
Number of orders	150	70	30	250
Marketing salaries	$2,400	$16,900	$16,700	$36,000

Required:

a. Prepare a detailed schedule showing the marketing cost per order size and per unit within each order size. Carry cost per unit to three decimal places.

b. Assume that presently the company charge a constant price per unit. Management desires an analysis showing the revised sales price per unit based on marketing costs. However, managers believe marketing cost per unit decreases with an increase in the size of the order. Prepare a schedule showing the unit sales price revised upward or downward for each order size while also maintaining total sales of $500,000.

P22–10 Variance Analysis for Customer Groups

The controller for the Brown Company has helped establish the following standards for each detailed area of the advertising activity broken down by customer group:

| | Retailers | | Wholesalers | |
	Unit Cost	Estimated ABC Drivers	Unit Cost	Estimated ABC Drivers
Demonstrations (per demonstration)	$50.00	150	$45.00	130
Dealers' aids (per customer)	40.00	800	50.00	750
Store and window display (per day of window trimming)	100.00	50	125.00	60
Letters, circulars (per item distributed)	1.00	1,000	1.15	900
Catalogs (per standard space unit)	20.00	600	22.00	500

The following actual ABC drivers and actual costs were incurred for each customer grouping:

| | Retailers | | Wholesalers | |
	Cost per Unit of Variability	Actual ABC Drivers	Cost per Unit of Variability	Actual ABC Drivers
Demonstrations	$52.00	155	$47.00	125
Dealers' aids	42.50	750	46.40	785
Store and window display	105.00	54	132.00	65
Letters, circulars	1.30	980	1.35	960
Catalogs	24.15	615	24.16	438

Required:

Prepare a variance analysis for each customer group; a formal statement is not required. Assume budgeted sales were achieved.

Writing

P22–11 Trade-Off of Excess Inventory Cost versus Improved Customer Service

As a management consultant specializing in cost accounting systems, you are in consultation with Dawn Smith, production manager of Smith Producers, when she receives an important telephone call. Smith insists that you remain in her office when she takes the call. It is a call from one of the company's major customers, and you hear her say, "Why, Bill, you know this request is really going to interrupt our regular production schedule, but since you are such a valuable customer, I will try to honor your order. We are really pushed on an order now, but we will try to work something out with you. I will get back with you shortly."

Smith Producers manufactures custom-designed motors with technology so complex that only three other companies in the country have the machinery to produce these motors. Smith Producers has built an excellent reputation for the quality of its motors because it has been willing to engage in extensive research to improve them.

Two years ago Smith Producers began a new policy designed to expand its customer service. This policy included manufacturing a larger volume of motors than a customer needed and keeping the motors in inventory so that later if the customer had an emergency need for motors, Smith Producers could fill the request within hours. Smith's customers are unaware of this policy and are highly impressed that their business is so valued that the Smith production department stops all manufacturing in process to honor emergency requests. Smith management believes that this policy, along with the excellent engineering quality of its motors, has created a group of loyal customers even though a specific customer will rarely, if ever, use this service. Word about this service, however, has spread among Smith's customers despite its infrequent use.

Unfortunately, Smith is running out of storage space for the extra motors produced that remain unsold awaiting a customer's emergency. The fact that each order received differs even in some small aspects prevents Smith from easily adapting extra motors produced on one order to fill another customer's order. Smith Producers has followed the practice of expensing the extra cost of production overruns as a component of the cost of the motors sold. However, it is uncertain as to what policy to follow and what price to charge its customers when it sells any of the motors produced as part of the production overruns. In addition, some members of the management team question the profitability of these overruns.

Required:

Write a technical memo to Smith Producers's top management outlining factors to study before abandoning or continuing the production overrun policy.

Critical Thought

SPATS

P22–12 Using Expected Monetary Value in Transportation Decisions

The Supply Company, supplier of raw manufacturing materials, agrees to furnish materials to the Buying Company. Because these materials are essential to the Buying Company's process, it is agreed that the Supply Company will pay a penalty of $1,500 for any shipment that does not reach the Buying Company on the day it is needed.

The Supply Company makes other materials, and often when it receives orders from the Buying Company, it cannot interrupt its other production process to manufacture these raw materials. However, the Buying Company recognizes this and agrees to forward orders two weeks in advance. The Supply Company can produce the materials in five days of operation after initiating processing. This arrangement requires timing in delivery because sometimes the Supply Company may finish production only one or two days before the raw materials are needed by the Buying Company. Fortunately, the contract between the two companies allows the Supply Company to choose its mode of transportation and also specifies the day the Buying Company's manufacturing division requires the materials.

The following table shows the degree of reliability and costs of the three modes of transportation available for the Supply Company. (For example, using water transportation there is a 60 percent probability that the materials will not reach the Buying Company in four days.)

| | | **Probability That the Shipment** | | | | | |
| | | | | *Will Take _____ days* | | | |
Transportation Mode	*Cost per Shipment*	*1*	*2*	*3*	*4*	*5*	*6*
Water	$200	*	*	.10	.30	.40	.20
Rail	300	*	.30	.50	.20	†	†
Air	500	.80	.20	†	†	†	†

*Cannot reach Buying Company in this length of time.
†100 percent probability will have reached Buying Company by this time.

Required:

Using the expected monetary value decision criteria, prepare a decision table that the Supply Company transportation clerk can use in deciding which mode of transportation to use.

P22–13 Cost per Order Size

Although Outland Company managers realize that they need additional marketing cost studies, they lack the personnel and funds at present to establish marketing cost standards. They suspect that Outland may be accepting orders that are too small. As a result, they analyzed the orders received last year and broke them down into categories: small (1 to 20 items), medium (21 to 100 items), and large (over 100 items). The actual marketing costs incurred last year were as follows:

Marketing Cost	*Amount*	*Basis for Distribution*
Marketing personnel salaries	$27,000	Number of personnel
Marketing manager's salary	20,000	Time spent
Salespeople's commissions	3,000	Sales dollars
Advertising and direct selling	37,500	Sales dollars
Packing and shipping	26,250	Weight shipped
Delivery	19,000	Weight shipped
Credit and collection	15,000	Number of orders

An analysis of their records produced the following statistics:

| | **Order Sizes** | | | |
	Small	*Medium*	*Large*	*Total*
Number of personnel	5	3	1	9
Time spent by marketing manager	60%	10%	30%	100%
Amount of sales	$250,000	$300,000	$200,000	$750,000
Weight	6,090	2,940	1,470	10,500
Number of orders	612	170	68	850

Required:

a. Prepare a detailed schedule showing the marketing cost per order size and marketing cost as a percentage of total sales for each order size.
b. Make recommendations to management about the size of order Outland should accept.

P22–14 Overhead Rate and Pricing

Bulloch, Inc., presents the factory overhead incurred by the company during two recent years. The data have been adjusted for the effect of price level.

	19X1	*19X2*
Direct labor-hours worked	1,380,000	1,130,000
Manufacturing overhead costs incurred (adjusted for changes in current prices and wage rates):		
Indirect material	$10,801,200	$10,416,200
Indirect labor	4,498,800	3,683,800
Utilities	2,980,000	1,600,000
Inspection and maintenance supplies	4,600,000	3,130,000
Rent	10,000,000	10,000,000
Supervisory salaries	2,100,000	2,100,000
Total overhead costs	$34,980,000	$30,930,000

Required:

a. Assume the company expects to operate at a 1,200,000 direct labor-hour level of activity next year. Using the data from two recent years, calculate the rate that should be used to assign total factory overhead to the products manufactured.
b. Indicate the cost behavior of supervisory salaries and indirect labor.
c. Use the overhead application rates from Requirement *a* and assume each product requires $20 direct material and five hours of direct labor at a wage per hour of $10. Determine the sales price per unit using the following approaches in which the markup is added to full cost to give the sales price:
(1) 20 percent markup on variable cost.
(2) 5 percent markup on full cost.
(3) 10 percent markup on conversion cost.

P22–15 Product Line Profitability Analysis

The management of the Scenic Toy Company plans to establish marketing standards in the near future. Now all they do in analyzing marketing costs is to allocate actual costs at the end of the period to three major product lines: bicycles, tricycles, and wagons. Scenic Toy incurred the following direct and indirect actual marketing costs last year:

Marketing Costs	*Amount*	*Basis for Distribution*
Sales salaries	$90,000	Direct charge
Warehousing and handling	7,500	Item handled
Transportation	6,000	Shipments
Credit and collection	10,500	Amount of sales orders
Direct selling	18,000	Customers served
Advertising and sales promotion	7,500	Amount of sales orders
General accounting	5,400	Customers served

Statistics extracted from the records of the company are as follows:

	Bicycle	Tricycle	Wagon
Sales salaries	$ 32,000	$ 40,000	$ 18,000
Items handled	40,000	25,600	14,400
Shipments	800	500	700
Sales orders	$300,000	$504,000	$396,000
Customers served	50	30	20

Required:

Distribute these actual marketing costs to the three product lines and then compare marketing costs as a percentage of sales for each product line.

P22–16 Analyzing Marketing Cost Variances

The following data concern the personal selling function of the Dale Company for the period ending December 31, 19X1.

	Northern Territory		Southern Territory	
	Cost per Driver	*Estimated Cost Drivers*	*Cost per Driver*	*Estimated Cost Drivers*
Budgeted data:				
Salespersons' salaries (per call)	$25.00	280	$35.00	200
Entertainment (per customer)	15.00	100	20.00	80
Salespersons' traveling expense (per day traveled)	30.00	15	35.00	12
Telephone solicitation (per telephone call)	0.40	1,000	0.20	900
Actual results:				
Salespersons' salaries	28.00	260	31.00	215
Entertainment	12.00	110	26.00	70
Salespersons' traveling expense	32.00	17	34.00	16
Telephone solicitation	0.35	1,040	0.30	930

Required:

a. Analyze each detailed function by computing two variances for each function assuming budgeted sales were achieved.

b. Indicate what interpretation you would place on the quantity variances if the salespeople exceed their sales quota by 25 percent.

P22–17 Use of Contribution Margin in Pricing Decisions

As a consultant strongly supportive of the contribution reporting concept, you are surprised to find that contribution reporting is not employed to a great extent at Spritt, Inc. Instead, you find that marketing, engineering, and administrative expenses are allocated in detail. When you ask Ann Brown, director of financial planning at Spritt, why contribution reporting is not employed more extensively, she indicates that while the concept is employed to some degree, management also believes that the profit after allocating marketing, administrative, and engineering expenses is very important. Management believes an analysis of only contribution margin may lead to false conclusions, especially in pricing decisions.

When you press Brown for an explanation, she gives you the following monthly data for two of the firm's products:

	Totals
Sales—Product A (500 units)	$100,000
Sales—Product B (700 units)	210,000
Variable manufacturing cost—Product A	35,000
Variable manufacturing cost—Product B	87,500
Variable marketing and administrative—Product A	15,000
Variable marketing and administrative—Product B	52,500
Fixed manufacturing cost	40,000
Marketing (fixed)	20,000
Executive analysis (fixed)	42,000
Research and patent (fixed)	10,000

All four products processed use approximately the same amounts of floor space and supervision. However, of the hours spent in promoting these two products, the marketing staff estimates that 45 percent of their time is spent on Product A, 20 percent on Product B, and the remainder equally on the other two company products. A customer claims physical damage from using Product A. Consequently, management has spent many hours in consultation with their lawyers. In estimating the time spent on each product, management believes an allocation of 30 percent to Product A and 20 percent to Product B is appropriate. Because the customer claims Product A's glass container is defective, management is concerned there may be additional lawsuits unless changes are made. The engineering staff has been working on a new design for the container that management hopes to patent soon. However, the explosive nature of Product A will always present additional hazards, and it is doubtful that a container can be designed that is completely free of potential problems. Time sheets for the research department show 70 percent of their hours were spent in analyzing and testing Product A, while the remainder of the time was divided equally among the other three products.

Brown further believes that while marginal analysis is a very useful tool, its benefits are overemphasized. One reason for this, she says, is that too many costs are omitted because they are labeled as fixed and irrelevant. She describes the following situation that occurred recently in the Fabricating Department. When the Fabricating Department was employing two supervisors and 16 direct labor workers, several orders were received for processing 100 additional units per month. The revenue from each 100 unit order would amount to $1,000 monthly. Since the work force could not handle any increase in workload, one additional direct labor worker was required to handle each 100-unit increase. The supervisor will be added when the 24th worker is employed. Direct labor workers and supervisors earn $700 and $1,248 per month, respectively. Variable materials and overhead amount to $1 per finished unit.

Brown claims that the use of marginal analysis in this situation would have been a costly mistake. Instead, a total cost approach was used, further supporting her contention that fixed costs and allocated costs are indispensable in the operation of a business and that they should not be omitted from the accountant's analysis in pricing decisions.

Required:

a. Agree or disagree with Brown's contention that contribution reporting can lead to false conclusions. Support your position with financial analyses of Products A and B.
b. Prepare marginal and total cost analyses for use in deciding whether to accept any one of eight additional 100-unit orders.

P22–18 Determining Minimum Bid

Because of idle capacity, management of MacDuck Company wants to submit a bid to Adrienne Camera Company to produce a camera under Adrienne's name. The president of MacDuck wants you to suggest a bid for the company. All of the relevant data for the bid are as follows:

1. Because Adrienne's camera is less sophisticated than MacDuck's, it requires MacDuck to spend $1,000 to set up the machinery.
2. The job for Adrienne is to produce 1,000 cameras. Costs of each camera are:

Direct labor	10 hours
Direct material	
Plastic	2 pounds
Lens	1 unit
Electronic component	5 units

After you have checked the inventory, you find the following information:

Direct Material	Inventory on Hand	Acquisition Cost	Current Replacement Cost
Plastic	3,000 pounds	$4 per pound	$5 per pound
Lens	800 units	50 per unit	52 per unit
Electronic component	4,500 units	10 per unit	12 per unit
XR	500 pounds	2 per pound	2.10 per pound

Material XR may be substituted for the plastic material on a pound for pound basis. MacDuck made Material XR under their own patent; Material XR has a current salvage value of $300.

MacDuck pays its workers $5 per hour. MacDuck Camera Company has 8,000 hours idle time and after the company reaches its full capacity, it pays workers $7.50/hour for every overtime hour.

3. Based on your regression analysis, you identify the fixed overhead cost is $10,000 and variable overhead cost is $2 per unit.
4. Additional sales to Adrienne are not expected.

Required:

a. Determine the minimum bid that would neither increase nor decrease total profits for MacDuck.
b. Assume the president believes that the chief competitor of MacDuck, Ursula Camera Company also will submit a bid to Adrienne. Based on information MacDuck obtained, Ursula has the same production cost behavior as MacDuck does. However, Ursula does not have any inventory to produce Adrienne cameras, and only has 2,000 hours idle time, but Ursula has no setup cost for its machinery. What is the minimum bid (i.e., the bid that would neither increase nor decrease total profits) Ursula might submit?
c. Explain how you would use the information obtained from Requirements *a* and *b* in actually submitting a bid.

P22–19 Variance Report—Warehousing and Handling

Standard costs are applied to marketing costs for the Capp Company. Management supplies you with the following budgeted unit cost and estimated ABC drivers for the warehousing and handling activity:

SPATS

Activity	Budgeted Unit Cost	Estimated ABC Drivers	
Receiving	$ 0.10	2,000	purchase invoice lines
Sorting	15.00	500	orders
Handling returns	2.00	50	returns
Packing and shipping	18.00	450	shipments
Clerical handling of shipping orders	5.00	500	orders

By the end of the period, Capp incurred the following actual unit cost and actual ABC drivers:

	Actual Unit Cost	Actual ABC Drivers	
Receiving	$ 0.12	1,890	purchase invoice lines
Sorting	14.75	480	orders
Handling returns	2.10	55	returns
Packing and shipping	20.00	460	shipments
Clerical handling of shipping orders	5.25	480	orders

Capp budgeted a fixed cost of $1,000 for depreciation and $1,500 for supervision. Actual costs were depreciation, $1,100 and supervision, $1,450.

Required:

Prepare an expense variance report showing price, quantity, and net variances for the detailed functions. Indicate the ABC driver on the report. Assume Capp achieved budgeted sales.

P22–20 Determining Sales Price to Achieve Objectives

Kimberly Wells plans to establish a drapery company specializing in the manufacture of custom-made draperies and bedspreads, as well as hardware parts, exclusively for the residential market of Butler County. The company will have manufacturing, display, and office space in a light industrial area occupied by similar businesses. Management expects very little walk-in trade; thus, location is important only from a general geographic standpoint. After extensive research, Wells estimated the following sales and costs for the first year:

Total Market—United States (millions)	
Drapery hardware	$ 334
Draperies	935
Bedspreads	534
Curtains	334
Total expected sales	$2,137
U. S. population	203,300,000
Butler county population	722,017

Management is confident that their company can capture 10 percent of the Butler County custom market, recognizing that custom drapes represent 20 percent of all drapery sales. From previous experience in this field, management expects that 10 percent of total hardware sales are for custom drapes. In addition, it expects 1 percent of all bedspread sales to be for the custom market. No curtains are custom made.

Drapery shops typically base the quoted price of their product on the estimated material and labor used to manufacture the product. Butler Drapery Shop has taken the following typical product and estimated its material and labor cost. Material and labor for custom bedspreads bear the same relationship to sales price as do drapery costs.

*Manufactured Items (Typical Product 48" × 84"
Lined Drapery Made of Satin)*

Direct material cost	$13.52
Labor cost	9.36
	$22.88
Markup	29.12
Sales price	$52.00

Less markup is realized on drapery hardware parts that are purchased since the material cost constitutes 50 percent of the sales price, while direct labor on such parts remains at 18 percent of sales price.

Management expects all other costs to total $19,100 for the year.

Required:

a. Develop a market forecast providing (1) the expected Butler County expenditures for drapery and curtain hardware, draperies, bedspreads, and curtains; (2) the portion of these expenditures that represents the custom-made market; and (3) Butler Drapery Shop's projected sales and expenses for the year.

b. Calculate the percentage the sale price must increase if management wishes to earn a 25 percent return on the $125,000 in assets employed in the company.

SPATS

P22–21 Use of High-Low with Marketing Costs

Patricia Lyerly, cost accountant for the Dyersburg Manufacturing Company provides you with data for selected marketing costs determined on the basis of sales. She informs you that management has decided that the relevant range for the company is 70,000 to 100,000 units of sales per period. Budgeted sales are set at 85,000 units. The company set the following standards for these two volumes:

Units of sale	70,000	100,000
Sales (@ $10 per unit)	$700,000	$1,000,000
Marketing expenses:		
Transportation	$ 17,000	$ 23,000
Credit and collection	21,300	28,800
General marketing activities	36,000	48,000
Direct selling	28,500	39,000
Advertising and sales promotion . .	40,500	57,000

During the period, the cost accountant reported these sales and marketing expenses:

Sales (@ $10 per unit) . . . .   82,000 units

	Variable	Fixed
Marketing expenses:		
Transportation	$16,900	$2,600
Credit and collection	21,000	4,000
General marketing activities	33,100	8,100
Direct selling	28,900	3,700
Advertising and sales promotion	44,800	1,850

Required:

a. Prepare an expense variance report, breaking marketing costs down into their fixed and variable components. Compute two variances for individual marketing expenses where appropriate: otherwise, only one variance for each expense item.

b. Explain if, based on the report you prepared in Requirement *a*, you see any disadvantages of using units of sales as the factor of variability on which to establish the standards.

P22–22 Using Costs in Bid Prices (CMA)

Marcus Fibers Inc. specializes in the manufacture of synthetic fibers that the company uses in many products such as blankets, coats, and uniforms for police and firefighters. Marcus has been in business since 1975 and has been profitable each year since 1983. The company uses a standard cost system and applies overhead on the basis of direct labor-hours.

Marcus has recently received a request to bid on the manufacture of 800,000 blankets scheduled for delivery to several military bases. The bid must be stated at full cost per unit plus a return on full cost of no more than 9 percent after income taxes. Full cost has been defined as including all variable costs of manufacturing the product, a reasonable amount of fixed overhead, and reasonable incremental administrative costs associated with the manufacture and sale of the product. The contractor has indicated that bids in excess of $25.00 per blanket are not likely to be considered.

To prepare the bid for the 800,000 blankets, Andrea Lightner, cost accountant, has gathered the following information about the costs associated with the production of the blankets:

Raw material	$1.50 per pound of fibers
Direct labor	$7.00 per hour
Direct machine costs*	$10.00 per blanket
Variable overhead	$3.00 per direct labor-hour
Fixed overhead	$8.00 per direct labor-hour
Incremental administrative costs	$2,500 per 1,000 blankets
Special fee†	$.50 per blanket
Material usage	6 pounds per blanket
Production rate	4 blankets per direct labor-hour
Effective tax rate	40 percent

*Direct machine costs consist of items such as special lubricants, replacement of needles used in stitching, and maintenance costs. These costs are not included in the normal overhead rates.

†Marcus recently developed a new blanket fiber at a cost of $750,000. In an effort to recover this cost, Marcus has instituted a policy of adding a $0.50 fee to the cost of each blanket using the new fiber. To date, the company has recovered $125,000. Lightner knows that this fee does not fit within the definition of full cost as it is not a cost of manufacturing the product.

Required:

a. Calculate the minimum price per blanket that Marcus Fibers Inc. could bid without reducing the company's net income.

b. Using the full cost criteria and the maximum allowable return specified, calculate Marcus Fibers Inc.'s bid price per blanket.

c. Assume that—without prejudice to your answer to Requirement *b*—the price per blanket that Marcus Fibers Inc. calculated using the cost-plus criteria specified is greater than the maximum bid of $25.00 per blanket allowed. Discuss the factors that Marcus Fibers Inc. should consider before deciding whether or not to submit a bid at the maximum acceptable price of $25.00 per blanket.

Capstone Case

Profit Centers in the Evaluation System

According to Jay Doran, president of Baltimore Company, one reason morale is so high among employees is that the company adopted a stock option plan several years ago. Thus, key people can see the immediate impact of their personal efforts on company sales and earnings as well as on the stock price. He admits, however, that as the company has grown from 100 employees to 500, stock options have become less motivational.

Now the company relies more on the profit center concept as a motivational tool and pays a percentage of division profits to all employees from supervisors upward. With corporate objectives losing their importance as a motivational force, individual personal objectives are clearly becoming dominant. For instance, Doran explains, learning that the profits of a particular division exceeded the overall profitability of the total company is of more personal interest to its supervisor than is learning that the overall company profits were X percent during the previous quarter. In addition, Doran informs you that the profit center concept allows individuals to combat the feeling that as the company grows, they become smaller and smaller fish in a bigger and bigger pond. Doran further contends that employees favorably identify with profit centers psychologically—what the company calls their center does make a difference to the division managers.

The philosophy of Baltimore management is that profit centers are primarily educational devices to get lower-level management to think of corporate-level objectives. This method of training exposes supervisors to various environmental constraints, which they soon realize vary with management level. To illustrate his point, Doran presented the following partial organization chart:

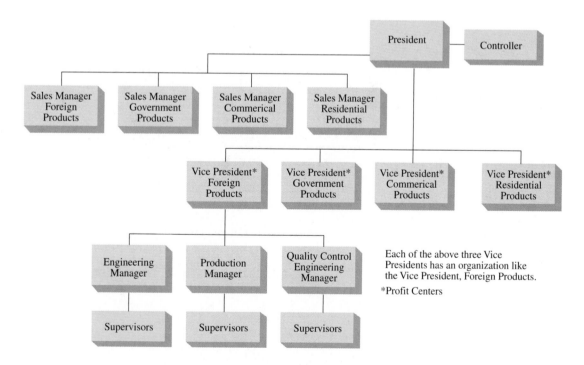

To reinforce this treatment of each product line serving as a profit center, Baltimore establishes prices for transfers of semifinished components between product lines. Where available, they use competitive outside market prices as the bases; otherwise, the sales managers impose a transfer price. When questioned as to how successful transfer pricing has been at Baltimore, Doran acknowledged that he has heard some grumbling from managers and vice presidents.

Even though Doran is the first to admit that he lacks accounting expertise, he believes that Baltimore has not made enough changes in the accounting system as the company has grown. For example, supervisors often have to wait a month after the quarter ends before receiving profit reports. Also, many of them do not understand how accountants allocate marketing and administrative costs to their departments or why in some quarters they have exceeded budget merely because the marketing and administrative expense allocations were larger than budgeted.

Annually, the president and the sales managers review the product lines and make sales projections and consider price levels. These individuals work closely with the controller in arriving at logical bases for allocating marketing and administrative expenses. From this analysis, the team forecasts profits for the product lines.

Required:

a. Discuss any existing factors that could lead to problems in the company's evaluation system. Give possible solutions to these problems.
b. Suggest improvements in the design of the accounting information system.

Analysis of Costs and Profits

Variable Costing

Chapter Objectives

After studying this chapter, you should be able to:

1. Contrast the application of variable and absorption costing in product costing and income determination.

2. Convert variable costing income to absorption costing income.

3. Show that changes in inventory affect absorption costing income.

4. Evaluate the impact of automation and changes in the manufacturing environment on variable costing.

5. Discuss the advantages variable costing offers in decision making, as well as its dangers.

Introduction

Previous chapters discussed only absorption costing that treats variable and fixed costs as product costs. **Absorption costing** (also called **conventional costing** or **full costing**) is required for external reporting. This chapter discusses a different approach to product costing known as *variable* or *direct costing* that is used only for internal reporting and analysis. Variable and absorption costing are not mutually exclusive. Accountants find that variable costing more effectively meets internal requirements because it provides better insight into cost relationships while the absorption costing method meets external reporting requirements.

Variable Costing (Direct Costing)

The **variable** or **direct costing** concept considers only those production costs varying directly with volume as **product costs**. This leaves all other manufacturing costs to be treated as **period costs**. Since direct material and direct labor are usually variable in a labor intensive environment, variable costing treats these costs and variable factory overhead as product costs. Accountants therefore charge off all other costs as expenses in the period incurred. In an automated factory, however, direct labor is usually fixed and a smaller component of product costs. Thus, in a machine-driven environment, direct material and variable factory overhead may be the only product costs using variable costing. Variable costing considers all other costs as the costs of providing for a level of capacity and charges the entire costs against the revenue of the period.

Cost Flows under Variable Costing

Exhibit 23–1 graphically shows the cost flows under variable costing. Accountants assign all variable manufacturing costs to production, and they become part of the unit costs of the products manufactured. Accountants do not assign fixed costs to inventory; they consider them as expenses for the year and charge them to Income Summary.

When referring to variable costing, this book prefers not to use the often-heard term *direct costing*. *Variable costing* is the more accurate term because it treats those costs that vary with production volume (generally direct material, direct labor, and variable overhead) as product costs. Variable costing treats all fixed costs as period costs. On the other hand, recall that direct costs are traceable to a cost center. Because indirect costs are not traceable, they must be allocated to the cost center. Direct and indirect costs may be either product or period costs. Variable costing treats variable overhead costs (indirect costs), as well as other variable manufacturing costs, as product costs. Using the term *direct costing* implies that the method treats only traceable costs as product costs. Traceability is not the emphasis, however, as both variable and fixed costs can be direct costs. For example, in a department that makes only one product, direct product costs are all costs that accountants can trace to the department, including supervision, depreciation, and other fixed costs as well as variable costs.

Variable costing differs from **prime costing** that inventories only direct material and direct labor. The prime cost method is based on a weak theoretical concept and is not acceptable for external reporting either.

Current Cost Management Practice

Global

Since becoming chief executive of Mattel, Inc., in 1987, John Amerman has extended the Barbie name and image. There are 90 different dolls in the Barbie line, Barbie doll-houses, Barbie sports cars, Barbie on a cruise ship, Kidsize Barbies that come in wear-able wedding dresses, and adult collector Barbies. This Barbie brand extension has turned Mattel into a money machine. However, with a goal of doubling revenues in five years, Amerman knows Mattel needs more than the Barbie line. Last year Mattel paid $1 billion in stock for Fisher-Price, Inc., the leading maker of preschool and infant toys. In early 1994, they paid $260 million in cash for Kransco, which makes Frisbees and Hula Hoops. Mattel has high hopes for its new Fisher-Price unit's overseas sales as they believe there is plenty of room for growth there. Mattel is weak in electronics, but their electronic disaster in the mid-1980s makes them cautious. They are using talking Barbies to test the electronic market.

Seth Lubove, "Barbie Does Silicon Valley," *Forbes,* September 26, 1994, pp. 84–85.

Absorption Costing

Absorption costing, as discussed previously, distinguishes between production and nonproduction costs in determining which costs to capitalize as assets. Absorption costing only inventories production costs and expenses marketing and administrative costs in the period incurred. Absorption costing defers both fixed and variable manufacturing cost until the sale of the product. At that time, the cost is matched

EXHIBIT 23–1   Cost Flows under Variable Costing

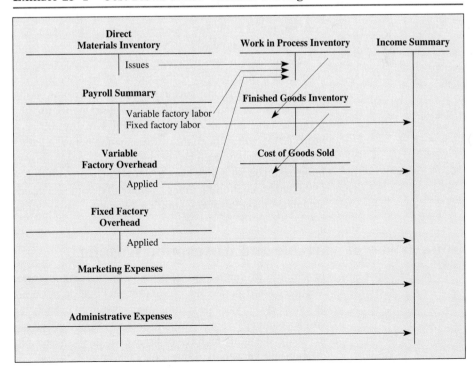

with revenue. Variable costing distinguishes between fixed and variable costs in addition to making the same distinction as absorption costing among production, marketing, and administrative costs.

Both absorption and variable costing exclude marketing and administrative costs from inventory; thus, these two methods differ only in this: Variable costing excludes fixed production costs from the costs of goods manufactured, while absorption costing does not. This treatment of fixed factory costs—whether it is charged off against income when the cost is incurred, or against income when the goods are sold—is the primary difference between variable and absorption costing.

Impact of Automated Manufacturing Environment

Variable costing was appropriate when variable costs were a high proportion of total production costs. Also, variable costing was appropriate when product diversity was small and there was not a wide variation of product demands made on the firm's production and marketing resources. Changes in the factory environment have decreased the percentage of variable costs in total manufacturing cost. With automation on the increase in industry, fixed costs become an ever larger element. Depreciation and related costs of automated equipment cause a large portion of overhead to be fixed, not variable. The spread of guaranteed annual wage contracts also causes more of the labor costs to be fixed.

Thus, fixed costs are becoming a larger share of total manufacturing costs. The competitive environment is forcing companies to produce an increasing variety of products that make different demands on equipment and support departments. Some accountants argue that in this cost accounting environment, absorption costing becomes the only meaningful costing method. Other accountants believe that as automation increases, variable costing becomes more important for decision making, and that absorption costing is dysfunctional for management accounting decisions. Their view is rooted in the idea that all product costs are based on assumptions, estimates, allocations, and averages. This is especially prevalent for assigning factory overhead cost and other indirect product costs. Variable costing overcomes the dysfunctionality of absorption costing, but it excludes fixed cost elements that many accountants believe they should assign to products.

Such shifts in the cost characteristics of a company emphasize the importance of management understanding the impact of fixed cost. The company has less flexibility in altering decisions, because it has invested more dollars in machinery and plant. However, merely grouping fixed overhead items together to charge to the period under variable costing may be insufficient to control a company's rising fixed overhead costs. On the other hand, differentiating between fixed and variable costs as plants become more automated can be a first step in controlling costs. Managers need better information because they have to deliberate more carefully over the expansion of labor force and production facilities. Admittedly, with increased fixed costs experienced in automated manufacturing, omitting fixed costs from products may have less merit.

Comparison of Variable and Absorption Costing

In addition to long-range statements to evaluate factors affecting income, companies need short-period income statements that do not consider the entire production and sales cycle. Variable costing meets this need even in small businesses with limited cost accounting systems. Variable costing is an overhead costing approach that consolidates the desirable features of breakeven analysis and profit planning involving the relationship between volume, costs, and profits.

Production and Sales Variations Cause Income Distortion

With an increase in fixed costs, seasonal variations in production and sales cause a distortion in income reported on the income statement. Absorption costing assumes that existing facilities and management were set up to make and sell an average volume of goods over a period of years. Absorption costing supplies a base for cost determination and eliminates great fluctuations in inventory values, but it still distorts income as Exhibit 23–2 illustrates. To simplify, Exhibit 23–2 assumes no partially completed units are in inventory. The top part of the exhibit provides production and sales statistics. Exhibit 23–2 assumes a $10 unit sales price, $6 unit variable production costs (direct material, $2; direct labor, $3; and variable overhead, $1), and $250,000 total production fixed costs at a budgeted capacity of 125,000 units each year. Fixed marketing and administrative expenses total $30,000. Both absorption and variable costing treat marketing and administrative expenses as period costs. However, the variable costing concept separates fixed and variable marketing and administrative expenses to determine the net **contribution margin.**

With absorption costing, when production volume exceeds sales in the first year, fixed costs are built up in inventory and are not charged off until the inventory is sold. Thus, even though there is a lag in sales, absorption costing shows higher profits than does variable costing during this period of heavy production. The opposite is true during the reverse cycle, as can be seen for the second year in Exhibit 23–2. Even though the sales volume has increased from 80,000 to 140,000 units, absorption costing income does not reflect this increase as dramatically as does variable costing. Management could become confused as income often seems to have no direct relationship to sales volume in absorption costing.

Because production was only 100,000 units in the first year, $50,000 of under-applied fixed production expenses resulted. Under the variable cost approach, units of production receive no application of fixed expenses. Instead, variable costing charges off the entire $250,000 fixed production expense each year.

In studying Exhibit 23–2, which compares absorption and variable costing, observe the following:

1. Absorption costing income statements presented in the traditional or functional format make no distinction between fixed and variable costs. As a result, absorption costing income statements do not show cost-volume-profit relationships as clearly as variable costing income statements.

2. Inventory values are smaller with variable costing because it capitalizes only $6 variable cost as assets. Inventory values using absorption costing have an additional $2 fixed factory overhead per unit.

3. Variable costing income in the first year is lower than that for absorption costing because production exceeds sales. Variable costing charges total fixed cost incurred against sales revenue, while absorption costing applies part of it to inventory and defers the cost until sale of the product. If there is an increase in inventories, variable costing income will be less than absorption costing income, as seen in the first year.

4. In the second year, variable costing income is higher than absorption costing income because units sold exceed units produced. Variable costing income always moves in the same direction as sales volume. The cost of goods sold using variable costing includes only a $6 per unit variable cost. The unit cost of goods sold is $8 with absorption costing.

EXHIBIT 23–2

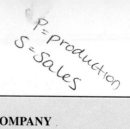
P = Production
S = Sales

HICKS COMPANY
Comparison of Absorption and Variable Costing Income Statements
For Years Indicated

	First Year	Second Year	Two Years Combined
Production and sales statistics	*P>S*	*P<S*	*P>S*
Finished goods inventory:			
Units in beginning inventory	–0–	20,000	
P Units produced	100,000	130,000	230,000
S Units sold	80,000	140,000	220,000
Units in ending inventory	20,000	10,000	10,000
Absorption costing:			
Sales @ $10	$800,000	$1,400,000	$2,200,000
Less: Cost of goods sold:			
Cost of goods manufactured	$800,000	$1,040,000	$1,840,000
Add: Beginning inventory @ $8		160,000	
Available for sale	$800,000	$1,200,000	$1,840,000
Less: Ending inventory @ $8	160,000	80,000	80,000
Cost of goods sold	$640,000	$1,120,000	$1,760,000
Volume variance*	(50,000)	10,000	40,000
Adjusted cost of goods sold	$690,000	$1,110,000	$1,800,000
Gross margin	$110,000	$ 290,000	$ 400,000
Marketing and administrative expense	60,000	80,000	140,000
Absorption costing income before taxes	$ 50,000	$ 210,000	$ 260,000
Variable costing:			
Sales @ $10	$800,000	$1,400,000	$2,200,000
Less Cost of goods sold:			
Total variable manufacturing cost	$600,000	$ 780,000	$1,380,000
Add: Beginning inventory @ $6		120,000	
Available for sale	$600,000	$ 900,000	$1,380,000
Less: Ending inventory @ $6	120,000	60,000	60,000
Cost of goods sold	$480,000	$ 840,000	$1,320,000
Manufacturing contribution margin	$320,000	$ 560,000	$ 880,000
Less: Variable marketing and administrative expense	30,000	50,000	80,000
Net contribution margin	$290,000	$ 510,000	$ 800,000
Less: Fixed factory overhead	250,000	250,000	500,000
Fixed marketing and administrative expense	30,000	30,000	60,000
Variable costing income before taxes	$ 10,000	$ 230,000	$ 240,000

*Volume variance based on normal capacity of 125,000 units.

$$\frac{\$250,000 \text{ fixed overhead}}{125,000 \text{ units}} = \$2$$

First year: $50,000 underapplied (125,000 − 100,000) × $2
Second year: $10,000 underapplied (125,000 − 130,000) × $2
overapplied

5. Conventional absorption costing determines an intermediate income figure called **gross margin** that reflects the difference between sales and the fixed and variable costs of sales. This figure normally varies significantly from the **manufacturing contribution margin** determined with variable costing, because we subtract only the variable expenses of the goods sold from sales revenue in determining manufacturing contribution margin. We subtract all production, marketing, and administrative variable expenses from sales to determine **net contribution margin**.

6. The income for the two years combined using the two concepts, differs by $20,000 ($260,000 absorption costing income; $240,000 variable costing income). This $20,000 difference in income results from the 10,000 units remaining in ending inventory; they have $2 fixed overhead assigned to each under absorption costing. However, over a complete cycle of inventory buildup and liquidation, total income is identical. Note that we cannot add the costs available for sale horizontally in Exhibit 23–2 because of the inclusion of inventory values more than once. (Exhibit 23–3 illustrates the difference in income for each year.)

7. As discussed in Chapters 4 and 13, we should prorate the volume variance computed for absorption costing if it is a significant amount. However, to simplify the illustration, Exhibit 23–2 treats the volume variance as a period cost.

Later in this chapter, Exhibits 23–6 and 23–7 illustrate that changes in inventory do not affect variable costing profits as they do absorption costing profits.

Volume Variance

Absorption costing determines both fixed and variable factory overhead application rates. In Exhibit 23–2, the variable factory overhead rate is $1 and the fixed overhead rate is $2. However, variable costing does not inventory fixed costs. As a result, variable costing does not determine an application rate for fixed factory overhead. With the absorption costing concept, a favorable or unfavorable **volume variance** results when actual production differs from budgeted production used to compute the fixed overhead rate. The bottom of Exhibit 23–2 shows a volume variance for the absorption costing method. For example, in the first year, the company budgeted to produce 125,000 units but produced only 100,000 units. This results in a $50,000 [(125,000 units − 100,000 units) × $2] underapplication of overhead. Variable costing computes no volume variance, since it closes total fixed factory overhead directly to the temporary account, Income Summary.

Standard Costs for Absorption and Variable Costing

Variable costing can use either strictly actual costs or standard costs. If accountants combine a variable costing system with standard costs, they establish estimates for only variable production costs (i.e., direct material, direct labor in a labor-intensive operation, and variable factory overhead). They set no standard for fixed factory costs in a variable costing system.

Both variable and absorption costing determine variable cost variances. If a company uses a three- or four-variance method of analysis for overhead, the spending and efficiency variances reflect differences between actual and standard variable costs. If, instead, a company uses a two-variance method of overhead analysis, it determines a controllable variance for both variable and absorption costing since the controllable variance reflects variable cost efficiency. When using a four-variance method, a company computes a fixed overhead spending variance only for absorption costing since this variance reflects the difference between budgeted and actual fixed costs.

Adjustments to Include Fixed Costs

Overhead Application Rate Unchanged.   Because external reporting does not allow variable costing, companies must adjust to an absorption costing basis. Exhibit 23–3 shows this adjustment for periods in which the application rate remains unchanged. We determine the adjustment by multiplying the change in the quantity of all inventory by the $2 fixed factory cost per unit. For example, in the first year, there was an increase of 20,000 units in finished goods inventory (from a zero beginning inventory to 20,000 units). We multiply this change of 20,000 units by the $2 fixed factory overhead rate to arrive at an adjustment of $40,000. We add this adjustment to the variable costing income from Exhibit 23–2 to determine absorption costing income. In the second year, there is a 10,000-unit decrease in inventory. We multiply this decrease by a $2 fixed factory overhead cost per unit to arrive at the $20,000 adjustment. We then deduct the adjustment from the variable costing income in calculating absorption costing income. In a period like the second year in which the units sold exceed the units produced, we deduct the fixed factory overhead adjustment for the change in inventory from variable costing income to determine absorption costing income.

Overhead Application Rate Changed.   Admittedly, Exhibit 23–3 represents an oversimplification of the reconciliation of absorption and variable costing. Exhibit 23–3 assumes that the $2 fixed overhead application rate did not change over the two-year period. If beginning and ending inventories carry different fixed overhead rates, the reconciliation of absorption costing and variable costing income becomes more complex. Assuming first-in, first-out inventory costing, Exhibit 23–4 uses the data given in Exhibit 23–2, but the fixed overhead application rate increases to $2.20. This increase causes the second-year ending inventory under absorption costing to be valued at $8.20 × 10,000 units = $82,000.

Rather than use the formula multiplying the change in inventory by the fixed overhead rate, we use the analysis in Exhibit 23–5. This analysis is appropriate for periods in which a rate change occurs as well as for periods in which the rate remains unchanged.

EXHIBIT 23–3   Adjustment of Variable Costing Income to Absorption Costing Basis with Overhead Application Rate Unchanged

	First Year	Second Year	Two Years Combined
Variable costing income per Exhibit 23–2	$10,000	$230,000	$240,000
Variation for fixed cost influence of inventory (Units produced − Units sold) × Fixed factory overhead per unit at normal capacity	40,000	(20,000)	20,000
Absorption costing income per Exhibit 23–2	$50,000	$210,000	$260,000

EXHIBIT 23–4

HICKS COMPANY
Comparison of Absorption and Variable Costing Income Statements
With Change in Application Rate
For Years Indicated

	First Year	Second Year
Production and sales statistics		
Finished goods inventory		
Units in beginning inventory	–0–	20,000
Units produced	100,000	130,000
Units sold	80,000	140,000
Units in ending inventory	20,000	10,000
Absorption costing:		
Sales @ $10	$800,000	$1,400,000
Less: Cost of goods sold:		
Cost of goods manufactured	$800,000	$1,066,000
Add: Beginning inventory @ $8		160,000
Available for sale	$800,000	$1,226,000
Less: Ending inventory @ $8, @ $8.20	160,000	82,000
Cost of goods sold	$640,000	$1,144,000
Volume variance*	$ (50,000)	11,000
Adjusted cost of goods sold	$690,000	$1,133,000
Gross margin	$110,000	$ 267,000
Marketing and administrative expense	60,000	80,000
Absorption costing income before taxes	$ 50,000	$ 187,000
Variable costing:		
Sales @ $10	$800,000	$1,400,000
Less Cost of goods sold:		
Total variable manufacturing cost	$600,000	$ 780,000
Add: Beginning inventory @ $6		120,000
Available for sale	$600,000	$ 900,000
Less: Ending inventory @ $6	120,000	60,000
Costs of goods sold	$480,000	$ 840,000
Manufacturing contribution margin	$320,000	$ 560,000
Less: Variable marketing and administrative expense	30,000	50,000
Net contribution margin	$290,000	$ 510,000
Less: Fixed factory overhead	250,000	275,000
Fixed marketing and administrative expense	30,000	30,000
Variable costing income before taxes	$ 10,000	$ 205,000

*Volume variance based on normal capacity of 125,000 units.

First Year	Second Year
$\dfrac{\$250{,}000 \text{ fixed overhead}}{125{,}000 \text{ units}} = \$2$	$\dfrac{\$275{,}000 \text{ fixed overhead}}{125{,}000 \text{ units}} = \$2.20$

First year: $50,000 underapplied (125,000 − 100,000) × $2.
Second year: $11,000 overapplied (125,000 − 130,000) × $2.20.

Exhibit 23–5   Adjustment of Variable Costing Income to Absorption Costing Basis with Overhead Application Rate Changed

	First Year		Second Year	
Variable costing income before taxes	$10,000		$205,000	
Add: Fixed costs of period deferred in ending inventory	40,000	($160,000 − $120,000)	22,000	($82,000 − $60,000)
	$50,000		$227,000	
Less: Fixed costs of prior year absorbed in period through beginning inventory	–0–		40,000	($160,000 − $120,000)
Absorption costing income before taxes ...	$50,000		$187,000	

Advantages of Variable Costing

Once you realize the inadequacies of absorption costing, you can more easily understand the advantages of variable costing. The greatest of these is that management can easily comprehend variable costing data. Accountants want to provide information that is accurate, complete, and timely; but none of this matters if the information cannot be understood. When managers find company reports are too complex, they have no faith in the figures and do not realize their importance. Variable costing overcomes this problem.

Inventory Changes Do Not Affect Profit

Managers can better understand variable costing statements because profits more rapidly move in the same direction as sales. Sales and changes in inventory affect absorption costing profits. For example, if sales exceed production, inventory decreases and absorption costing profits are lower than variable costing profits. This difference results when sales exceed production because we take the cost for the excess of the number of units sold over the number of units produced out of inventory and add it to cost of goods sold. In both variable costing and absorption costing, we take the variable costs of these excess units out of inventory. However, in absorption costing, we take one additional cost, fixed manufacturing overhead, out of inventory and add it to cost of goods sold. Recall that in variable costing, we do not add fixed manufacturing overhead to inventory. Rather, we treat it as a period cost along with all other fixed costs. This additional cost in cost of goods sold using absorption costing causes net income to be lower than the net income using variable costing.

If production exceeds sales, inventory increases and profits using absorption costing are higher than profits using variable costing. Both variable and absorption costing add the variable costs of the excess units produced to inventory. However, absorption costing also adds fixed manufacturing overhead to inventory. Because absorption costing treats fixed manufacturing overhead as a product cost, absorption costing profits are higher than when using variable costing where fixed manufacturing overhead is treated as a period cost along with all other fixed costs. If production and sales are equal, profits are the same under both absorption and variable costing.

EXHIBIT 23–6   Income Statement under Absorption Costing

TRAUGH COMPANY
Absorption Costing Income Statement
For the Years Ending May 31
(in thousands)

	19X1		19X2	
Sales (4,000,000 units)		$28,000		$28,000
Cost of goods sold:				
Beginning inventory (1,000,000 units)	$ 6,500		$ 6,500	
Cost of goods manufactured ($4 unit variable				
+ $10,000,000 fixed overhead)	26,000		30,000	
Goods available for sale	$32,500		$36,500	
Less: Ending inventory	6,500		12,000	
Cost of goods sold		26,000		24,500
Gross margin		$ 2,000		$ 3,500
Fixed marketing and administrative expenses . .		3,000		3,000
Absorption costing income (loss) before taxes .		$ (1,000)		$ 500

For example, assume that Traugh Company operations for 19X1 resulted in a loss as shown in Exhibit 23–6. An individual agreeing to accept compensation equal to only 50 percent of profits generated replaced the president. Within the next year the president had the production facilities operating at full capacity of 5,000,000 units, up from 19X1's production of 4,000,000 units. Despite no growth in sales, the next period's income statement showed a profit with no change in total fixed costs or unit variable costs. The new president was delighted with his compensation, but is it deserved?

In 19X1, absorption costing applied fixed manufacturing overhead costs at $2.50 per unit produced ($10,000,000/4,000,000 units). In 19X2, Traugh Company applied fixed manufacturing overhead costs at $2.00 per unit produced ($10,000,000/5,000,000 units). Therefore, the full cost per unit of inventory in 19X1 is $6.50, the total of the direct materials, direct labor, and variable and fixed manufacturing overhead. Using absorption costing, product cost in 19X2 is $6 resulting in an ending inventory of $12,000,000 ($6 × 2,000,000 units).

If, instead, Traugh Company uses variable costing in 19X2, the income statement would show a loss as Exhibit 23–7 illustrates, and the president would not receive a bonus. Variable costing inventories $4 variable costs of production as product costs. Variable costing considers all $10,000,000 fixed manufacturing overhead costs as period costs, charged to expense in 19X2.

Note that sales volume is constant and variable costing shows a loss of $1,000,000 for 19X2 that equals the loss reported for 19X1. A change in inventory does not affect variable costing profits or losses. The new president does not deserve a bonus because true profits are not generated by merely increasing production with no increase in sales.

Phantom Profits Are Ignored

The president's action resulted in larger inventory, which increases absorption costing income on the financial statement, although the company sold no additional goods. Absorption costing uses this dysfunctional concept—the larger the volume

EXHIBIT 23–7   Income Statement under Variable Costing

TRAUGH COMPANY
Variable Costing Income Statement
For the Period Ending May 31, 19X2
(in thousands)

Sales (4,000,000 units)			$28,000
Cost of goods sold:			
Beginning inventory (1,000,000 units)		$ 4,000	
Cost of goods manufactured			
($4 unit variable × 5,000,000 units)		20,000	
Goods available for sale		$24,000	
Less: Ending inventory (2,000,000 units)		8,000	
Cost of goods sold			16,000
Manufacturing contribution margin			$12,000
Fixed manufacturing overhead		$10,000	
Fixed marketing and administrative expenses		3,000	13,000
Variable costing loss before taxes			$ (1,000)

of operations, the more inventory to absorb overhead, the lower the unit cost, and the more profit generated. Increasing production without a corresponding rise in sales assumes converting raw materials to work in process increases profits. Usually raw materials have a higher resale value than work in process and are easier to sell. Absorption costing profits reflect absorbed labor and overhead costs as assets and ignore expenses associated with carrying additional inventory. These inventory profits or **phantom profits** are a contradiction in terms generated by manufacturing more products, not selling more.

Further, absorption costing ignores expenses associated with carrying additional inventory. Holding inventory is expensive because of increased costs for insurance, property taxes, storage space, inventory handling and transfer, and record maintenance. In addition, increased risk of theft, technical obsolescence, and physical deterioration occur. Further, a company does not receive any return on investments in inventory and storage space.

Cost-Volume-Profit Relationships

Another advantage of variable costing is that it facilitates the analysis of cost-volume-profit relationships by separating fixed and variable costs on the income statement. Management is able to identify the cost-volume-profit ratio therefore without working with two and sometimes several sets of data. In addition, variable costing emphasizes the contribution margin discussed in Chapter 14. This emphasis aids management in selecting product lines, in determining the optimal sales mix for pricing purposes, and in solving other problems involving choices. The data are especially important to companies that face make-or-buy decisions because variable costing facilitates comparing company costs with the costs of buying from outsiders. In addition, the cost-volume-profit relationship provides a valuable tool for other short-run planning activities.

Marginal Products

Variable costing also is of use in appraising **marginal products** or **marginal volume,** because variable costs correspond closely with current out-of-pocket expenditures for a product. The problem of product line simplification is not always easy. Yet, an important aspect of the appraisal becomes apparent using variable costing because it provides a sharper focus on the profitability of products, customers, and territories. Multiplying the volume of an item by its unit contribution margin discloses the relative importance of a product's contribution. Management then can study the contribution the product has made to fixed overhead and more easily identify the unprofitable items to eliminate. This is true because the allocation of fixed costs does not obscure the data.

Because accountants can present variable costing data in an uncomplicated manner, managers without strong accounting backgrounds can understand and use the information for profit planning. Often, the application of fixed overhead may be difficult for a nonaccountant to understand because budgeted costs and budgeted capacity must be estimated. The nonaccountant can better grasp the relationship of variable costs and profit planning. Forecasting costs and profits is easier if fixed factory overhead applications are not included.

Impact of Fixed Costs

Some managers argue that they can make decisions more easily if fixed expenses are separated and not buried in inventory or cost of sales. Showing the total fixed expense for the period in the variable costing income statement emphasizes the impact of fixed expenses on profits. Variable costing proponents contend that fixed costs represent **committed costs** arising from a basic organization of providing property, plant, equipment, and other facilities to produce. This justifies treating fixed costs as period costs because, they argue, product costs should reflect only those costs that expire when they sell the asset.

Variable costing advocates believe that variable costs are the crucial costs for decision making. Thus, they claim that one of the important purposes of variable costing is helping management control operating costs. They contend that separating fixed and variable costs automatically focuses a manager's attention on cost reduction. Variable costing advocates also believe that the concept is an accurate means of measuring responsibility for departmental supervisors. Responsibility accounting is easier with variable costing than it is with conventional absorption costing. Variable costing does not allocate fixed costs to products; it simplifies tracing costs by lines of managerial responsibility.

This fixed-variable manufacturing cost breakdown aids in the preparation of budgets. Each account is broken down into variable and fixed costs. Multiplying the unit variable cost by actual monthly sales and adding the fixed costs yields expected costs. Managers then can easily compare monthly budgeted costs and actual costs.

Pricing Policies

Variable costing advocates also believe variable costing provides more relevant information concerning pricing policies than does absorption costing. Managers often assume they should not keep a product line for an extended time unless its price is higher than average full cost. However, pricing to cover average full costs may not be advantageous for a company in specialized situations because pricing decisions must consider the effect of prices on volume and the effects of volume on cost. With variable costing, management has the data to determine when it is advisable to accept orders if other than normal conditions exist. In this way, management can take advantage of sales that may contribute only partly to fixed expenses. A knowledge of the contribution margin provides guidelines for the most profitable pricing policies.

EXHIBIT 23-8   **Use of Variable Costing in Pricing**

	10,000	12,000
Volume in units		
Variable costs:		
Direct materials @ $2	$ 20,000	$ 24,000
Direct labor @ $5	50,000	60,000
Factory overhead @ $12	120,000	144,000
Fixed factory overhead	180,000	180,000
Total cost	$370,000	$408,000
Absorption cost per unit	$ 37	$ 34

For example, assume Yunker Company is producing and selling 10,000 units at a $40 unit sales price when it receives an offer from a foreign distributor to buy 2,000 units at a unit sales price of $30. The absorption cost per unit as shown in Exhibit 23–8 indicates that this $30 sales price is less than the $34 average unit full cost to make 12,000 units. Management may not take advantage of the sales offer if it relies on the absorption cost per unit to make the decision. Instead, managers should use variable costs along with any extra costs of the foreign sale in evaluating this sales offer.

With $19 unit variable costs, $40 unit sales price, and $180,000 annual fixed costs, current net income before taxes is $30,000, computed as follows:

Sales (10,000 units at $40)		$400,000
Costs:		
Variable (10,000 units at $19)	$190,000	
Fixed	180,000	370,000
Net income before taxes		$ 30,000

If the order is accepted and can be produced without any plant expansion, net income will be $52,000, computed as follows:

Sales (10,000 units at $40, 2,000 units at $30)		$460,000
Costs		
Variable (12,000 units at $19)	$228,000	
Fixed	180,000	408,000
Net income before taxes		$ 52,000

Yunker Company should accept the $30 sales price even though it is lower than average unit cost because a unit contribution margin of $11 on the new units results. By accepting the sales offer, the company makes a $22,000 contribution to the recovery of fixed costs and, after full recovery, to income. Net income of only $30,000 results from continuing to produce 10,000 units. Because the export of the product at a sharply reduced price is unlikely to affect the regular market, the company should accept the order, assuming it does not violate international trade agreements.

Finally, variable costing highlights the serious results that often accompany price cutting. Cutting prices by a certain percentage and trying to increase volume by the same percentage under the assumption that the volume increase will compensate for the price reduction is a common error. To gain market share from a competitor, however, one should understand just how far a cut in price can go before it becomes unprofitable. Managers who understand how price cutting to gain market share seriously affects profits, should be more cautious about cutting prices to undersell a competitor; they may be cutting themselves out of business.

Dangers of Variable Costing

The simplicity of variable costing allows management to easily understand the resulting figures. However, managers may misapply the principle of variable costing. Many accountants contend that variable costing does not provide all the answers or the best answers in certain business situations.

Many nonaccountants outside and inside companies use accounting figures. These people have become accustomed to the normal relationship of sales to total costs and to using gross margin and net income data. A change to another accounting method that gives a completely different picture under similar labels may confuse them. Although the purpose of the change in costing methods is to bring about better understanding, it may cause more confusion instead.

Another danger is that managers may assign variable costing income a broader significance than it deserves. When sales substantially exceed current production, for instance, variable costing profits are higher than those under absorption costing, and management may take improper action based on these increased profits. These profits may mislead marketing executives to ask for lower prices. Managers also may demand higher employee benefits or sales bonuses when, in fact, there is no justification for such actions. At the other extreme, variable costing results may mislead management during a business recession because, when sales lag behind production during early recession stages, the variable costing profit will be minimized and the variable costing loss maximized. Management may miss future profit opportunities by thus misreading the severity of the recession.

When management decides to expand or eliminate activities connected with specific product lines or other specific business units, it may need to adjust income figures determined using variable costing. For example, most businesses produce or sell several products differing in ratios of variable costs to sales revenue and contribution rates. They can improve the total profit picture by eliminating the products contributing the smallest amount and by continuing to carry the products making large contributions to profits. On the other hand, this approach, too, can be misleading. If companies drop the items contributing small amounts of profits, the fixed unit cost that other products must cover will increase. As a result, profits will likely decrease if the company fails to add other products to its line. A company also must consider intangible factors because a product with a low contribution margin ratio may be necessary for the convenience of customers. The loss in customer goodwill that might result from dropping this item could easily offset any gain from products with higher contribution margin ratios.

Long-Range Pricing Policies

Since variable costing income is higher than absorption costing income when sales substantially exceed current production, opponents of variable costing argue that managers who receive only variable cost data are tempted to cut prices to the degree that company profits suffer. Yet, an adequate pricing system avoids this because companies allocate fixed overhead on some volume base for long-range pricing policies. Admittedly, allocations are somewhat arbitrary; however, more companies are improving their cost allocation techniques as they gain access to computer facilities. Thus, variable costing generates product figures providing little basis for long-range pricing policies.

In addition, opponents of variable costing argue that all costs are variable in the long run. Further, companies should avoid too great an emphasis on the arbitrary classification of costs into variable and fixed categories. Strictly separating costs into two categories is impossible, as many costs have both fixed and variable components. It is not enough merely to define fixed and variable costs according to the rate of output. Classifying a cost as fixed or variable depends on how managers measure output, the period allowed for adjustments, the degree of flexibility, and the extent to which managers calculate certain costs in advance. Even strict fixed costs have some variable characteristics. The behavior of certain costs, especially overhead, is exceedingly complex. Thus, managers occasionally separate costs into fixed and variable categories on the basis of practicality or expediency rather than strict adherence to an established accounting principle. There may be a strong temptation to include as product costs only those obviously variable costs such as direct material and direct labor in a labor-intensive process. In extreme cases, companies use the *prime cost method* that eliminates variable overhead from product cost. This produces misleading profit contribution data. Variable costing advocates, however, argue that although this separation of fixed and variable costs sometimes is arbitrary, accountants can usually arrive at figures that are accurate enough. They believe cost behavior is usually not so erratic that managers cannot reasonably predict it.

Because variable costing considers fixed expenses as period costs, it minimizes over- or underapplied factory overhead. An additional weakness is variable costing's failure to express the volume variance in monetary terms.

Fixed Costs Must Be Covered.   Elimination of fixed overhead costs from inventories is questionable in view of the increased fixed costs automation brings. It is possible to foresee a time when direct material constitutes the only variable manufacturing cost. Thus, the company with the largest fixed expenses would have the smallest unit inventory costs. This appears contrary to management's objective of having expenses covered by sales—regardless of how they value inventory. With automation, higher ratios of fixed costs to variable costs limit the ability of companies to respond to changes in the economy. While labor-intensive industries can cut costs during a recession by laying off workers, companies with robots lack this flexibility. This is a serious threat to the usefulness of variable costing and its acceptability for inventory valuation. This is one reason the FASB and the Internal Revenue Service have not recognized variable costing as an acceptable method of inventory costing.

Variable Costing for External Reporting

FASB Position.   Even though most accountants agree that variable costing provides valid information for internal decision making, there is no agreement concerning its appropriateness for external reporting. The FASB has not recognized variable costing as a generally accepted inventory valuation method because of its belief that fixed production costs are as much a part of manufacturing the product as are variable costs. In addition, variable costing violates the cost attaching and matching principle.

IRS Regulations.   Likewise, the IRS does not recognize variable costing as an acceptable inventory valuation method. The Tax Reform Act (TRA) of 1986 changed inventory accounting for income tax purposes by requiring the capitalization of additional costs to inventory. Product costing under pre-TRA regulations followed the

Strategic Planning

Current Cost Management Practice

Disillusioned shoppers, nervous shareholders, and discouraged employees are wondering if Liz Claiborne, who flew high in the 1980s, can remake itself for the 1990s. While baby-boomer women climbing the career ladder in the 1980s favored the Claiborne's clothing, the company has done little to instill loyalty to the brand among these women. Sales have fallen, but Claiborne executives are conducting a reimaging campaign to lure shoppers back by sprucing up Claiborne boutiques and advertising differently. Also, the company has brought in consultants to help cut its production cycle time from 40 weeks to 30 weeks. The company knows it has to raise its profile in shoppers' minds.

Laura Zinn, "A Sagging Bottom Line at Liz Claiborne," *BusinessWeek,* May 16, 1994, pp. 56–57.

absorption costing concepts specified by generally accepted accounting principles. TRA requires capitalizing additional indirect product costs, making product costing more complicated.

Variable Costing Need Not Replace Absorption Costing

While reporting for external purposes must conform to generally accepted accounting principles, financial data prepared for internal uses need not. The unacceptability of variable costing for external reporting does not affect its importance and special usefulness as an analysis tool. The basic objective of costing should be to meet internal requirements. Variable costing can contribute to this objective because it overcomes many of the weaknesses in reporting with conventional absorption costing. Many companies have converted to variable costing to obtain certain advantages and have found many others not thought of initially. Variable costing need not replace absorption costing. A well-informed management needs both contribution margin analysis and full cost data in budgeting and decision making.

Combined Approach.   This chapter suggests arranging the income statement to show both an income under variable costing and the net income required for external reporting. To variable costing income, we can add or deduct an increment measuring the effect of the change in the fixed cost components of inventory variation to arrive at conventional profits. We can distinguish income resulting only from sales from that resulting from inventory changes. One advantage of this approach is the income statement separates variable costs from fixed costs.

Having both sets of profit figures enables the executive to form judgments with much greater facility than if only one profit figure were available; it also facilitates responsibility accounting by making it possible to have information by organizational level. This dual approach provides the additional information that management needs for making decisions and still follows generally accepted accounting principles. A system combining variable costing and absorption costing with standard costs and flexible budgets provides more effective cost control.

Summary

With full absorption costing, fixed production costs are product costs that become period costs when the product is sold. Full absorption costing is consistent with external inventory valuation rules. External reports cannot use variable costing because it treats fixed production costs as period costs. However, it is difficult to state with full assurance which costing concept presents the best measure of unit cost. Thus, we recommend a combined approach that adjusts inventories to include fixed costs on all external reports. We can prepare a variable costing income statement by first subtracting variable costs from sales to give a net contribution to fixed costs and income. Then, we subtract fixed costs to give income before taxes.

Rather than reject variable costing because companies cannot use the concept for external reporting, accountants should be aware of its advantages. For example, in evaluating the effectiveness of individual and departmental performance, variable costing is useful. It readily offers solutions to such problems as determination of the effect on overall profits of a new product. Also, in preparing cost control reports, there is little need to include such cost items as insurance and depreciation if the manager lacks the authority to incur the expense. A departmental income statement prepared on the variable costing basis is more useful.

There is danger in the exclusive use of variable costing because a company must cover both fixed and variable costs in the long run to be profitable. Variable costing can jeopardize a company whose managers only add a profit allowance to a product's variable cost to determine the sales price, thus ignoring fixed costs. Although variable costing may be superior to absorption costing in giving the short-range view of profits, its merit is questionable in long-range profit planning. Usually companies commit period costs for relatively long periods; such costs are important in long-term, not day-to-day, decisions. Average full cost is a better measure of the resources required for other than short-run decisions. Yet, when accountants use variable costing with an awareness of its limitations and weaknesses, it is one of their most useful tools in aiding management.

Important Terms and Concepts

Absorption (conventional or full)
  costing   744
Variable (direct) costing   744
Product costs   744
Period costs   744
Prime costing   744
Contribution margin   747
Gross margin   749

Manufacturing contribution margin   749
Net contribution margin   749
Volume variance   749
Phantom profits   754
Marginal products or marginal volume   754
Committed costs   755

Problem for Self-Study

Absorption Costing and Variable Costing Income
The following information pertains to BBC Company's first year of operation when it produced 25,000 units:

Sales ($50 per unit)	$850,000
Total fixed production cost	200,000
Total variable production cost	250,000
Total variable marketing and administrative costs	150,000
Total fixed marketing and administration costs	82,000

Required:

a. Determine income without preparing a formal income statement using:

   (1) Absorption costing.

   (2) Variable costing.

b. Explain the differences in absorption costing income and variable costing income.

Solution to Problem for Self-Study

BBC COMPANY

a. (1) Sales		$850,000
Less: Variable production cost		
($250,000/25,000 = $10 × 17,000)	$170,000	
Fixed production cost		
($200,000 /25,000 = $8 × 17,000)	136,000	306,000
Gross margin		$544,000
Less: Variable marketing and administration costs	150,000	
Fixed marketing and administration costs	82,000	232,000
Absorption costing income		$312,000
(2) Sales		$850,000
Less: Variable production costs	$170,000	
Variable marketing and administration costs	150,000	320,000
Contribution margin		$530,000
Fixed production costs	$200,000	
Fixed marketing and administration costs	82,000	282,000
Variable costing income		$248,000

b.   25,000 units produced

   −17,000 units sold ($850,000/$50 = 17,000 units)

   8,000 units × $8 fixed production cost = $64,000

Review Questions

1. How does a variable costing structure facilitate the calculation of breakeven point and contribution margin analysis?

2. Can variable costing be used in a strictly actual cost system as well as in a standard cost system? How can it be implemented?

3. Discuss the development of variable costing and why there was a need for this concept.

4. A company produced 1,000 units having costs as follows: direct materials—$32,000; direct labor—$45,000; variable overhead—$62,000; and fixed overhead—$70,000. What is the product unit cost under

   a. Variable costing?

   b. Absorption costing?

5. Contrast and explain the difference in income using absorption and variable costing if:

   a. Production volume exceeds sales volume.

   b. Sales volume exceeds production volume.

    c. Sales volume equals production volume.

    d. Sales volume remains constant, while production volume fluctuates.

6. Why is the unit cost assigned to inventory using variable costing generally considered to be uniform?

7. What is the future of variable costing with the current emphasis on robots and automated manufacturing?

8. Why may an income statement prepared using absorption costing continue to show a profit even if sales decline?

9. What factor related to manufacturing costs causes the difference in net income computed using absorption costing and using variable costing?

10. Which features associated with variable costing income measurement should marketing managers find attractive?

11. Why are inventory valuations smaller with variable costing than with absorption costing?

Exercises

E23–1 Determining Costing Method Used

Oury Company has established the following unit standards:

Direct material (2 pounds @ $ 3)	$ 6
Direct labor (3 hours @ $5)	15
Factory overhead—variable (3 hours @ $ 1)	3
Factory overhead—fixed (3 hours @ $ 2)	6
	$30

The Finished Goods Inventory account contains 2,000 units for a total of $42,000. No significant standard cost variances exist.

Required:

a. Indicate the inventory costing method used by the company.

b. Decide if an adjustment must be made to the balance before reporting the account on the balance sheet; determine the amount of the adjustment.

E23–2 Variable Costing Impact on Inventory

Baddour, Inc., manufactures a product whose unit variable and fixed production costs are $5 and $3, respectively. There was no beginning inventory of this product, but 80 units remained unsold at the end of the year.

Required:

Assume the variable (direct) costing method is used instead of the absorption costing method. What would be the change in the dollar amount of ending inventory?

E23–3 Effect of Variable Costing

Jumbo Jet Company manufactures a product that employs expensive automated machinery in its processing. Jumbo Jet uses straight-line depreciation for this automated machinery. Because of a lag in the economy, Jumbo Jet has a large stock of Finished Goods Inventory, this constitutes a material item on the balance sheet at year-end. A departmental cost accounting system assigns production costs to the units processed each period.

The controller of the company informs you that management is considering adopting variable costing as a method of accounting for plant operations and inventory valuation for internal decision making. They understand that conventional or absorption costing must continue to be used for external purposes.

Required:

Explain the effect, if any, such a change would have on:

a. Year-end financial statements.

b. Net income for the year.

E23–4 Absorption Costing and Variable Costing Income

The following information is for the Rue Company's first year of operation when it produced 20,000 units:

Sales ($40 per unit)	$720,000
Total fixed production cost	80,000
Total variable production cost	400,000
Total variable marketing and administrative costs ..	120,000
Total fixed marketing and administration costs	60,000

Required:

a. Determine income without preparing a formal income statement, using:
   (1) Absorption costing.
   (2) Variable costing.

b. Explain the differences in absorption costing income and variable costing income.

E23–5 Calculation of Variable Costing from Absorption Income Data

Normal capacity of the Benn Company is 80,000 units per quarter, or 320,000 units per year. Standard variable cost per unit is materials, $4; labor, $2.50; and overhead, $0.90; or a total of $7.40 per unit. Standard fixed manufacturing expenses are $224,000 per year. In the following data there is no variance except the volume variance. This was closed to income each quarter as the absorption costing income statements were prepared. Thus, all inventories are stated at standard cost.

	1st Quarter	2nd Quarter	3rd Quarter	4th Quarter
Units produced	80,000	86,000	75,000	79,000
Units sold	80,000	78,000	83,000	77,000
Absorption costing income	$128,000	$129,000	$129,300	$122,500

Required:

Using the given data, compute the variable costing income for each quarter.

E23–6 Determining Cost of Goods Sold and Inventory Valuation

Accounting records for the Douglas Company reveal the following production cost for the year ending December 31, 19X1:

Direct material	$480,000
Direct labor	260,000
Factory overhead—variable	44,000
Factory overhead—fixed	36,800

Douglas purchased 40,000 units and sold 35,000 units. The company is considering adopting variable costing for internal purposes and asks that you determine what effect this adoption would have on inventory valuation.

Required:

a. Determine the cost of the 5,000 units in inventory and the total cost expensed using variable costing.
b. Determine the cost of the 35,000 units sold and the 5,000 units in inventory using absorption costing.

E23–7 Specific Information Using Variable and Absorption Costing

The following information is available for Bragg Company's new product line:

Variable production cost per unit	$ 6
Total annual fixed production cost (15,000 units budgeted capacity)	30,000
Total annual fixed marketing and administrative costs	18,000
Variable marketing and administrative cost per unit of sales	3
Selling price per unit	15

There was no inventory at the beginning of the year. During the year 15,000 units were produced and 13,500 units were sold.

Required:

a. Determine the ending inventory assuming Bragg uses absorption costing.
b. Determine the ending inventory assuming Bragg uses variable costing.
c. Determine the total variable costs charged to expense for the year assuming Bragg uses variable costing.
d. Determine the total fixed costs charged against the current year's operations assuming Bragg uses absorption costing
e. Determine income using variable costing without preparing a formal income statement.
f. Determine income using absorption costing without preparing a formal income statement.
g. Account for the difference in income between the two concepts.

E23–8 Variable and Absorption Costing Comparison for Income and Inventory

At the end of last year, management of Tiller, Inc., planned to produce 1,000 units for the current year. Fixed factory overhead was budgeted for $5,000 and variable factory overhead for $3,000. Based on the standards established, direct material was expected to be $6 per unit and direct labor $2 per unit. There were 300 units in inventory at the beginning of the current year.

Of the 900 units produced during the current year, 700 units sold at a $25 unit sales price. Variable marketing and administration expenses totaled $2,000, and fixed marketing and administration expenses totaled $1,000. There were no price or efficiency variances for factory costs.

Required:

a. Using both variable costing and absorption costing
   (1) Determine the cost of goods sold.
   (2) Determine the value of ending inventory.
   (3) Compute the volume variance.
   (4) Calculate income before taxes.
b. Account for the difference in income using the two methods.

E23–9 High-Low, Comparison of Income

Hicks Company provides you with the following condensed budgets for standard costs and expenses:

	14,000 Units	16,000 Units
Direct material	$ 32,200	$ 36,800
Direct labor	117,600	134,400
Factory overhead	82,100	87,400
Total	$231,900	$258,600

Marketing and administrative expense budgets were as follows:

Marketing expense:
    Variable . . . . $1.50 per unit sold
    Fixed $25,000

Administrative expense:
    Variable . . . . $2.40 per unit sold
    Fixed $42,000

Hicks applies overhead on the basis of a standard capacity of 15,000 units.

Required:

a. Using the high-low method of separating cost components, determine the standard cost per unit under absorption costing.
b. Assume that 14,500 units are manufactured and 13,800 are sold at a price of $38. Determine the income using:
 (1) Absorption costing.
 (2) Variable costing.
c. Account for the difference in absorption costing income and variable costing income.

Problems

P23–10 Adjustment from Variable Costing Income to Absorption Costing Income

Mason Company uses variable costing for internal purposes with income adjustments to an absorption costing basis made at year-end. FIFO inventory costing is used. Analysis over the first three years of operation shows the following data:

	First Year	Second Year	Third Year
Units sold	690,000	555,000	580,000
Units produced	700,000	560,000	600,000
Variable costing income	$ 34,500	$ 28,000	$ 30,000
Budgeted capacity in units	500,000	600,000	600,000
Budgeted fixed overhead	$1,500,000	$1,650,000	$1,680,000

Required:

Indicate the absorption costing income for each year by determining the adjustment necessary each year to convert the variable costing income to an absorption costing income.

P23–11 Reconciling Differences between Absorption Costing and Variable Costing
The September 1, 19X1, balance sheet for Watkins Company contained an inventory amounting to $300,000, which included fixed overhead costs of $50,000. The September 30, 19X1, balance sheet revealed an inventory amounting to $130,000: this included fixed overhead amounting to $19,000. Operations for the month of September 19X1 resulted in the following:

Variable costs:	
Direct materials used in production	$620,000
Direct labor used in production	418,000
Factory overhead	300,000
Marketing expenses	30,000
Administrative expenses	85,000
Fixed costs:	
Factory overhead	$ 16,570
Marketing expenses	70,000
Administration expenses	90,000

Net sales for September 19X1 were $2,000,000.

Required:

a. Prepare an income statement for the month using variable costing.
b. Prepare an income statement for the month using absorption costing.
c. Reconcile the difference in the income figures reported using each of these costing methods.

P23–12 Standard Absorption Costing Recast to Variable Costing
Terry Company uses a standard absorption costing system. The engineering department has determined that the variable production cost is $18 per unit, while standard fixed factory overhead is $180,000 ÷ 60,000 units of normal activity = $3 per unit. Variable marketing and administrative costs are $4 per unit sold, while fixed marketing and administrative costs are $75,000. Variances from standard variable production costs during the year totaled $35,000 favorable. Sales during 19X1 were 55,000 units at $40 unit sales price. Beginning inventory was 5,000 units; ending inventory was 3,000 units.

Required:

a. Prepare an absorption costing income statement for 19X1 assuming all variances are written off directly as an adjustment to cost of goods sold at year-end.
b. Recast the income statement as it would appear using variable costing.
c. Explain the difference in income as calculated in Requirements *a* and *b*.

P23–13 Absorption Costing and Variable Costing Income Statements
L. Tatikonda, president of Tatikonda Enterprises, projects the following data for November 19X1:

	Units
Beginning inventory	5,000
Production	18,000
Available for sale	23,000
Sales	21,800
Ending inventory	1,200

Tatikonda has established the following standard cost per unit for the product her company manufactures:

	Standard Cost per Unit
Direct material (all variable)	$45.00
Direct labor (all variable)	16.00
Factory overhead:	
Variable cost	2.00
Fixed costs (based on 20,000 units per month)	7.50
Marketing and administration:	
Variable cost (based on units sold)	1.25
Fixed costs (based on 20,000 units per month)	2.70

The sales price per unit is projected to be $90 per unit. The fixed costs remain static within the relevant range of 15,000 to 25,000 units of production.

Required:

a. Prepare projected income statements for November 19X1 for management purposes using each of the following product-costing methods:
   (1) Absorption costing with all variances charged to cost of goods sold each month.
   (2) Variable (direct) costing.
b. Reconcile the difference in the income reported with the two methods.

P23–14 Absorption and Variable Costing's Influence on Bonus
Management of the Sharon Russell Company is concerned because last year's operations resulted in the worst loss in the history of the company, as shown here:

Sales (50,000 units)		$ 500,000
Cost of goods sold:		
Beginning inventory (10,000 units)	$ 75,000	
Cost of goods manufactured (50,000 units)	375,000*	
Goods available for sale	$450,000	
Less: Ending inventory (10,000 units)	75,000	
Cost of goods sold		375,000
Gross margin		$125,000
Marketing and administrative expense		140,000
Loss		$ (15,000)

*Includes $125,000 fixed factory overhead, remaining costs are $5 variable per unit.

The board of directors replaced the president with an individual who agreed to assume the position if he would receive a bonus of 60 percent of profits generated. The new president agreed to reimburse the company for any losses incurred. Within a short period, the new president had the production facilities operating at full capacity of 75,000 units.

Despite no growth in sales, the next period's income statement showed a profit with no change in the cost behavior patterns or normal volume. Immediately after the income statement was prepared, the new president accepted his bonus and resigned with no explanation. The board of directors cannot understand the president's actions.

Kaylee

Required:

a. Explain why you know that the company's income statement for last year was prepared on a variable costing or an absorption costing basis.

b. Determine normal volume used for overhead application.

c. Prepare an income statement for the next year based on absorption costing assuming there was no change in sales, cost behavior patterns, or normal volume.

d. Using an alternative reporting procedure, prepare an income statement which would have contradicted the new president's stance.

e. Explain why the new president deserved, or did not deserve, the bonus.

P23–15 Absorption Costing and Variable Costing Income Statements

Cayson Corporation projects the following data for the month of September 19X1:

	Units
Beginning inventory	7,000
Production	23,000
Available for sale	30,000
Sales	26,000
Ending inventory	4,000

Management has established the following standard cost per unit for the one product the company manufactures:

	Standard Cost per Unit
Direct material (all variable)	$21.00
Direct labor (all variable)	17.00
Factory overhead:	
Variable cost	5.00
Fixed costs (based on 24,000 units per month)	3.00
Marketing and administrative:	
Variable cost (per unit sold)	2.00
Fixed costs (based on 24,000 units per month)	1.50

The sales price per unit is projected to be $60 per unit. The fixed costs remain static within the relevant range of 20,000 to 30,000 units of production.

Required:

a. Prepare projected income statements for September 19X1 using each of the following product costing methods:
  (1) Absorption costing with all variances charged to cost of goods sold each month.
  (2) Variable (direct) costing.

b. Reconcile the difference in the income reported with the two methods.

SPATS

P23–16 Variable Costing Where All Costs Are Fixed

Several years ago, the city of Oxford approached the management of Mississippi Fertilizer Company concerning the possibility of using garbage obtained from the city's residents in manufacturing fertilizer. After conducting many engineering studies, the company built a completely automated processing plant with its own source of utilities. Under the agreement with the city, garbage is delivered to the plant daily at no cost to the company. Because of the factory's unique features, volume can be easily adjusted. All operating costs are fixed, and employees are paid a fixed salary. Fertilizer is sold in bulk at $2 per pound to farmers who drive their trucks to the factory for filling. The following data relate to the first three years of operation:

	19X1	19X2	19X3
Pounds processed	10,000	6,000	12,000
Pounds sold	6,000	10,000	11,000
Fixed production costs	$15,000	$15,000	$15,000
Fixed marketing and administrative expense	$ 2,000	$ 2,000	$ 2,000

Required:

a. Using 10,000 pounds as normal capacity, prepare income statements using variable costing and absorption costing.
b. Indicate the inventory value shown on the balance sheet at year-end for each of the three years using each method.
c. Assume that if the company changes its manufacturing facilities, purchases utilities from the city, and pays its employees on an hourly basis, fixed costs will be reduced to $10,000 per year and variable cost per pound will become $0.60. Using the same data except for the change in cost behavior, prepare income statements using variable costing and absorption costing.
d. Account for the difference in income for 19X2 using conditions in which all costs are fixed as compared to having both fixed and variable costs.

P23–17 Variable Costing and Absorption Costing Income Statements

The executives of Evans Company have been pleased that their accounting staff is using variable costing for internal management purposes because they have obtained valuable information through its use. At year-end, the variable costing data is converted to absorption costing for external reporting.

Forecasts prepared at the end of 19X1 indicated that sales would increase 20 percent the following year. To meet this predicted sales increase, production was increased from 10,000 units to 12,000 units. However, there was no sales increase in 19X2. The following data pertain to 19X1 and 19X2:

	19X1	19X2
Selling price per unit	$ 15	$ 15
Sales (units)	10,000	10,000
Beginning inventory (units)	1,000	1,000
Production (units)	10,000	12,000
Ending inventory (units)	1,000	3,000
Unfavorable labor, materials, and variable		
overhead variances (total)	$ 2,500	$ 2,000

Standard variable costs per unit for 19X1 and 19X2 were

Labor	$3.75
Materials	2.25
Variable overhead	1.50
	$7.50

Budgeted and annual fixed costs for 19X1 and 19X2 are as follows:

Production	$30,000
Marketing and administrative	35,000
	$65,000

There was no variance between actual and budgeted fixed costs. The overhead rate under absorption costing is based on practical plant capacity, which is 15,000 units per year. All variances and under- or overabsorbed overhead are charged to cost of goods sold.

Required: (Ignore all taxes.)

a. Present the income statement based on variable costing for 19X2.
b. Present the income statement based on absorption costing for 19X2.
c. Explain the difference, if any, between the net income figures. Give the entries needed to adjust the book figures, if any are necessary.
d. Discuss the advantages and disadvantages attributed to variable costing for internal purposes.

P23–18 Adjusting from Variable Costing to Absorption Costing Basis
Campbell Company records reveal the following:

	Per Unit:
Sales price	$10
Direct material	2
Direct labor	3
Variable overhead	1
Fixed overhead	2
Total variable marketing and administrative expense	$ 48,000
Total fixed marketing and administrative expense	$ 50,000
Budgeted production	125,000 units
Units in beginning inventory	10,000
Units produced	140,000
Units sold	145,000

Required:

a. Prepare absorption costing income statement.
b. Prepare variable costing income statement.
c. Calculate the amount needed to adjust the variable costing income to an absorption costing basis.

P23–19 Increased Sales with Corresponding Income Decline

Coffee Company management is concerned about the firm's decline in income despite a sales increase of $10,000. The company requests your expertise in determining where management should focus attention. Management realizes that a shortage in its raw material caused a delay in manufacturing; workers produced only 45,000 units instead of the 50,000 units as planned. However, there was no change in sales price or sales mix.

COFFEE COMPANY
Operating Forecast

	Budgeted Forecast as of 1/1/19X1	Adjusted Forecast as of 12/31/19X1
Sales	$180,000	$190,000
Cost of sales at standard	126,000	139,500 *
Gross margin	$ 54,000	$ 50,500
Marketing expense ($8,000 is fixed cost) ..	14,000	17,000
Administrative expense (all fixed cost)	12,000	14,000
Total operating expenses	$ 26,000	$ 31,000
Income before taxes	$ 28,000	$ 19,500

* Standard cost of sales includes over- or underabsorbed fixed overhead.

Additional cost data:

1. Budgeted fixed manufacturing cost was $65,000.
2. Actual variable cost of sales remained the same as budgeted.
3. Finished Goods Inventory was large enough to fill all sales orders received.

Required:

a. Explain in report form why there is a $8,500 decrease in income before taxes at the same time that sales have increased $10,000.
b. Suggest ways management can improve its performance as reflected in the company's operating statements.
c. Recast the two operating forecasts to a variable costing basis. Briefly explain why variable costing better reflects the company's financial picture.
d. Account for any difference in the income generated using variable costing and the $19,500 income before taxes as of 12/31/19X1.

P23–20 Variable Costing Income Statement (CMA)

Portland Optics, Inc., specializes in manufacturing lenses for large telescopes and cameras used in space exploration. As the specifications for the lenses are determined by the customer and vary considerably, the company uses a job order cost system. Factory overhead is applied to jobs on the basis of direct labor-hours, utilizing the absorption (full) costing method. Portland based its predetermined overhead rates for 19X2 and 19X3 on the following estimates:

	19X2	19X3
Direct labor-hours	32,500	44,000
Direct labor cost	$325,000	$462,000
Fixed factory overhead	130,000	176,000
Variable factory overhead	162,500	198,000

Jim Bradford, Portland's controller, would like to use variable (direct) costing for internal reporting purposes as he believes statements prepared using variable costing are more appropriate for making product decisions. To explain the benefits of variable costing to the other members of Portland's management team, Bradford plans to convert the company's income statement from absorption costing to variable costing and has gathered the following information for this purpose, along with a copy of Portland's 19X2–19X3 comparative income statement.

PORTLAND OPTICS, INC.
Comparative Income Statement
For the Years 19X2–X3

	19X2	*19X3*
Net sales	$1,140,000	$1,520,000
Cost of goods sold		
Finished goods at January 1	16,000	25,000
Cost of goods manufactured	720,000	976,000
Total available	736,000	1,001,000
Finished goods at December 31	25,000	14,000
Cost of goods sold:		
Before overhead adjustment	711,000	987,000
Overhead adjustment	12,000	7,000
Cost of goods sold	723,000	994,000
Gross profit	417,000	526,000
Selling expense	150,000	190,000
Administrative expense	160,000	187,000
Operating income	$ 107,000	$ 149,000

Portland's actual manufacturing data for the two years are

	19X2	*19X3*
Direct labor-hours	30,000	42,000
Direct labor cost	$300,000	$435,000
Raw materials used	140,000	210,000
Fixed factory overhead	132,000	175,000

The company's actual inventory balances on December 31 were

	19X1	*19X2*	*19X3*
Raw material	$32,000	$36,000	$18,000
Work in process			
Costs	$44,000	$34,000	$60,000
Direct labor-hours	1,800	1,400	2,500
Finished goods			
Costs	$16,000	$25,000	$14,000
Direct labor-hours	700	1,080	550

For both years, all administrative costs were fixed, while a portion of the selling expense resulting from an 8 percent commission on net sales was variable. Portland reports any over- or underapplied overhead as an adjustment to the cost of goods sold.

Required:

a. Prepare the revised income statement for the year ended December 31, 19X3, for Portland Optics, Inc., utilizing the variable costing method. Be sure to include the contribution margin on the revised income statement.

b. Describe two advantages of using variable costing rather than absorption costing.

Revenue Variances, Material Mix and Yield Variances, and Labor Mix and Yield Variances

Chapter Objectives

After studying this chapter, you should be able to:

1. Explain how different levels of detail in variance analysis are appropriate and cost justified depending on the individual circumstance.
2. Prepare sales price, sales mix, and sales quantity variances for each product sold.
3. Calculate market size and market share variances that detail the sales quantity variance.
4. Determine material and labor mix and yield variances and interpret their meaning.
5. Describe the constraints involved with assumed substitution.

Introduction

One of cost accountants' prime responsibilities is assisting management in evaluating performance by determining variances between actual operations and planned operations. Chapters 12 and 13 describe how standard costing enables the computation and interpretation of variances for direct materials, direct labor, and factory overhead in a single product company and for a single ingredient product. This chapter applies standard cost, variance analysis, and budgeting principles presented in earlier chapters to a multiproduct company and a multi-ingredient product.

In addition, we discuss the computation and analysis of a revenue variance comprised of the sales price variance and the sales volume variance for a multiproduct company. The chapter also presents the direct materials and direct labor mix and yield variances for a multi-ingredient product; these are simply a further breakdown of the material and labor quantity variances studied in Chapters 12 and 13.

Revenue Variances for Multiproduct Companies

For planning purposes, a company that sells several products may assume that sales of its products occur in constant proportions. For example, a grocery may assume it sells two gallons of milk for every pound of steak. Management may intentionally use a low markup on one product (milk) to attract customers and increase sales of other products (such as steak) with higher contribution margins. Not only is the quantity of products sold important for management but also the relative mix of products.

A multiproduct company concentrates on a product-by-product analysis of sales price and sales volume. Companies often use sales price and sales volume variances to evaluate marketing performance. We determine the **sales price variance** by multiplying the difference between actual sales price and budgeted sales price times the actual quantity sold. The **sales volume variance** (also called **sales activity variance**) compares budgeted and actual quantity and mix.

To illustrate the revenue variances, assume Clevenger Company provides the estimated and actual results for its two product lines for the first quarter of the year as shown in Exhibit 24–1.

Based on the sales forecast, managers expect industrywide sales to total 12,500 units for gloves and 10,000 units for belts. Managers expect Clevenger Company to sell 2,000 units of gloves and 3,000 units of belts. This is equivalent to a 16 percent share of the glove market and a 30 percent share of the belt market. However, actual industry sales were only 6,000 units of gloves and 5,000 units of belts. Clevenger sold 3,000 units of gloves and 1,000 units of belts, yielding an actual market share of 50 percent (3,000/6,000 units) for gloves and 20 percent (1,000/5,000 units) for belts.

Sales Price Variance

The sales price variance is computed as:

$$(\text{Actual sales price} - \text{Budgeted sales price}) \times \text{Actual quantity sold}$$

For gloves of Clevenger Company:

$$(\$17 - \$16) \times 3,000 = \$3,000 \text{ Favorable price variance}$$

For belts of Clevenger Company:

$$(\$18 - \$20) \times 1,000 = \$2,000 \text{ Unfavorable price variance}$$

EXHIBIT 24–1

| | CLEVENGER COMPANY | | |
	Gloves	Belts	Total
Budgeted unit sales price	$16	$20	—
Actual unit sales price	17	18	—
Standard variable cost per unit	12	12	—
Budgeted unit contribution margin	4	8	—
Budgeted sales volume	2,000 units	3,000 units	5,000 units
Budgeted sales mix percentage	40%	60%	100%
Actual sales volume	3,000 units	1,000 units	4,000 units
Actual sales mix percentage	75%	25%	100%
Total budgeted market for industry	12,500	10,000	
Budgeted market share	16%	30%	
Actual industry sales	6,000	5,000	
Actual market share	50%	20%	

The sales price variance is favorable for gloves because of the $1 increase in sales price. Conversely, the sales price variance is unfavorable for belts because there is a $2 per unit decrease in sales price. The sales price variance can be broken down by such causal factors as changes in quantity discount, early payment discount, and list price.

Sales Volume Variance

We use contribution margin to calculate sales volume variances. Therefore, we can call this variance a **contribution margin variance**. We need a knowledge of cost behavior to determine contribution margin, which is revenue less variable costs. If a company cannot break costs down easily into their variable and fixed components, we compute a **gross margin variance**. We calculate the gross margin variance the same as the contribution margin variance except that we substitute gross margin for contribution margin in the formulas.

Weighted-Average Budgeted Contribution Margin.   Before computing the sales volume variance, we must calculate the weighted-average budgeted contribution margin per unit. Using the information from Exhibit 24–1, the planned mix of 2 units of gloves (or 2,000) to 3 units of belts (or 3,000) results in the following unit contribution margin for the product mix:

Gloves Belts
2($4) + 3($8) = $8 + $24 = $32/5 = $6.40 average budgeted contribution margin

The sales volume variance is

Budgeted contribution margin: (5,000 units × $6.40) $32,000
Actual contribution margin:
       Gloves   Belts
(3,000 units × $4) + (1,000 units × $8)   20,000
Sales volume variance—unfavorable $12,000

The sales volume variance is broken down into sales mix and sales quantity variances. We can subdivide the sales quantity variance into a market size variance and a market share variance. Alternatively, we can break down the sales mix variance by geographic region or customer class. The following illustrates the interrelationship between these variances:

Strategic Planning

Current Cost Management Practice

Southwest Airlines Co. CEO H. D. Kelleher does not appear to be bracing for the war declared by United Airlines. Southwest still boasts the lowest costs among the industry's major carriers and commands a 50 percent share of the lucrative intra-California air-travel market. But Kelleher takes the showdown seriously because it is United's first attempt at proving that concessions won as part of an employee buyout will make the carrier competitive with any rival. For scrappy Southwest, it is a fight to keep United and other Southwest wannabes out of its short-haul niche. To beef up its fight, Southwest has oral agreements to lease two additional planes this year and is looking for two more. Despite their size difference—Southwest revenue accounts for only 16 percent of United's—most observers give Southwest the edge in this battle. United argues that people will want to fly with them because they can consolidate their frequent flyer miles. However, to succeed, United must drop its fare. For now, Southwest's more frequent flights and lower costs will beat United's perks. After the dust settles, both airlines may be able to coexist if other carriers drop off those routes. Most observers give Southwest the edge in this battle.

Wendy Zellner, "Dogfight over California," *BusinessWeek,* August 15, 1994, p. 32.

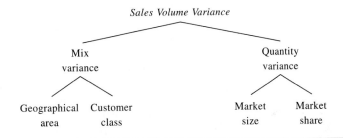

Sales Mix Variance   The **sales mix variance** adjusts for the change in contribution margin because the company did not sell the products in the proportions anticipated in the master budget. Using the information from Exhibit 24–1, the sales mix variance is

$$\text{Sales mix variance} =$$

$$\left[\left(\begin{array}{c}\text{Actual}\\\text{sales mix}\\\text{percentage}\end{array} - \begin{array}{c}\text{Budgeted}\\\text{sales mix}\\\text{percentage}\end{array}\right) \times \begin{array}{c}\text{Actual total sales}\\\text{volume of all}\\\text{products in units}\end{array}\right]$$
$$\times (\text{Budgeted individual unit contribution margin}$$
$$- \text{Budgeted average unit contribution margin})$$

For gloves:

$$= [(75\% - 40\%) \times 4{,}000] \times (\$4 - \$6.40)$$
$$= (35\% \times 4{,}000) \times -\$2.40 = \qquad \$3{,}360 \text{ unfavorable}$$

For belts:

$$= [(25\% - 60\%) \times 4{,}000] \times (\$8 - \$6.40) =$$
$$= (-35\% \times 4{,}000) \times \$1.60 = \qquad \underline{2{,}240} \text{ unfavorable}$$
$$\underline{\$5{,}600} \text{ unfavorable}$$

The sales mix variance measures the effect of changes from the budgeted average unit contribution margin combined with a change in the quantity of specific product lines. A sales mix variance provides useful information when a company sells multiple products because it captures the effect on income arising from a change in the mix of products sold. The overall sales mix variance just computed was unfavorable for two reasons: First, the company sold more gloves than budgeted, and the $4 unit contribution margin for gloves is lower than the $6.40 average. Second, the company sold fewer belts than planned, and the $8 unit contribution margin for belts is higher than the $6.40 average.

Sales Quantity Variance

We calculate the **sales quantity variance** by multiplying the difference between the actual units sold and the master fixed budget units by the weighted-average budgeted contribution margin per unit as follows:

Sales quantity variance = (Actual sales volume in units − Fixed budget volume in units) × Budgeted average unit contribution margin

For gloves in Exhibit 24–1:

$$\begin{array}{ll}
(3{,}000 \text{ units} - 2{,}000 \text{ units}) \times \$6.40 & \\
\text{budgeted contribution margin} = & \$\ 6{,}400 \quad \text{favorable}
\end{array}$$

For belts in Exhibit 24–1:

$$\begin{array}{ll}
(1{,}000 \text{ units} - 3{,}000 \text{ units}) \times \$6.40 & \\
\quad \text{budgeted contribution margin} = & \underline{12{,}800} \text{ unfavorable} \\
\text{Sales quantity variance, total} & \underline{\$\ 6{,}400} \text{ unfavorable}
\end{array}$$

The sales quantity variance weights all units at the budgeted average contribution margin, showing the impact on profits of a change in physical volume.

Note that the sales quantity variance formula uses a fixed budget volume that we do not adjust to the actual volume achieved. (Chapter 10 discusses fixed and flexible budgeting concepts.) Because the physical volume used in flexible budgeting equals actual physical volume (except, possibly, where the flexible budget is prepared for standard capacity), we could express the sales quantity variance formula as:

(Flexible budget volume in units − Fixed budget volume in units) × Budgeted average unit contribution margin = Sales quantity variance

Thus, the actual sales volume in units is sometimes called the *flexible budget unit sales*.

Proof of Variances.   We can prove the sales mix and the sales quantity variances by totaling them as follows to produce the sales volume variance:

Sales mix variance, total	$ 5,600 unfavorable
Sales quantity variance, total	6,400 unfavorable
Sales volume variance	$12,000 unfavorable

Market Size and Market Share Variances

We can further break down each product's sales quantity variance into market size and market share variances. We use budgeted average contribution margin for these two products; however, if we were analyzing only one product, we would use that individual product's contribution margin.

Market size variance = Budgeted market share percentage ×
(Actual industry sales volume in units − Budgeted
industry sales volume in units) × Budgeted average
contribution margin per unit

For gloves:

= .16 × (6,000 − 12,500) × \$6.40
= .16 × 6,500 × \$6.40
= \$6,656 unfavorable

For belts:

= .30 × (5,000 − 10,000) × \$6.40
= \$9,600 unfavorable

Market share variance = (Actual market share percentage − Budgeted market
share percentage) ×
(Actual industry sales volume in units × Budgeted
average contribution margin per unit)

For gloves:

= (.50 − .16) × (6,000 × \$6.40)
= .34 × \$38,400
= \$13,056 favorable

For belts:

= (.20 − .30) × (5,000 × \$6.40)
= \$3,200 unfavorable

	Gloves	Belts
Market size variance	\$ 6,656 unfavorable	\$ 9,600 unfavorable
Market share variance	13,056 favorable	3,200 unfavorable
Sales quantity variance	\$ 6,400 favorable	\$12,800 unfavorable

Gloves' total market size sharply decreased, but the company increased its share
of gloves' market from 16 to 50 percent. However, belts lost when its actual
share of the total market was 20 percent and not the 30 percent budgeted. Belts'
industry sales also suffered with a drop in sales from 10,000 budgeted to 5,000
actual sales.

Material and Labor Mix and Yield Variances for Multi-Ingredient Products

We can apply sales mix and quantity variances to production inputs. Many production procedures, especially process costing operations, use a recipe or formula to
indicate the specifications for each class of material or labor ingredient. Management may vary the mix in an attempt to improve the yield. Or, the price of an ingredient or labor class may increase, and management may respond by reducing the

quantity of this specific ingredient or labor grade. In some cases, varying the mix does not affect the quantity of the resulting product; in other cases, it does. Although a product's specifications may allow changes in the various material and labor classes when a substitute becomes less costly, managers usually establish tolerance limits beyond which they cannot change the specifications.

Separation of Quantity Variance.   Breaking the quantity variance for material and labor down into mix and yield variances can lead to better management control. We calculate price or rate variances for each type of material or each category of labor in the usual manner described in Chapter 13. The total material price variance is the sum of the price variances for all material types. On the other hand, the total labor rate variance is the sum of the rate variances for all labor classes.

Production Mix and Yield Variances

When a company uses several inputs to process its products and the inputs are partially substitutable for each other (for example, substituting beans for peas in vegetable soup), we can calculate mix and yield variances that identify the costs or savings of substituting one material for another. We compute a *mix variance* by comparing the standard formula to the standard cost of material or labor actually used. The resulting variance arises from mixing raw material or classes of labor in a ratio that differs from standard specifications. For example, the textile or chemical industry can mix different combinations of raw material and still yield a perfect product.

A *yield variance* results because the yield obtained differs from the one expected on the basis of material or labor input. A yield variance reflects the extra costs or savings incurred because we used more inputs than the original specifications or recipe called for. To make fudge, for example, we cook sugar, corn syrup, cocoa, and milk. We expect a certain quantity of these raw materials to yield a specified number of pounds of fudge. A yield variance results if the actual output of fudge differs from that expected. Often an advantage created by a mix or yield variance cancels the disadvantage of the other variance. For example, the new mix may result in a favorable mix variance, but an unfavorable yield variance offsets it. Likewise, the advantages gained from a favorable yield variance may result in an unfavorable mix variance. Accountants usually consider a *labor yield* variance as the result of the quantity and/or the quality of the material handled.

Material Mix and Yield Variances

We can calculate production mix and yield variances in total for the batch of material or for each grade of material. Our calculations use the following data.

Standard ingredient mix
    The standard ingredient mix for a certain type of sausage is

	Standard Pounds	*Standard Price*	*Standard Cost*
Meat A	250	$0.40	$100
Meat B	600	0.25	150
Meat C	50	0.88	44
Meal	200	0.18	36
Input	1,100		$330
Output	1,000		

Standard cost per pound of material input ($330/1,100 pounds) $0.30
Cost per pound of output ($330/1,000 pounds) $0.33

At the end of the month, the company determined that they used the following actual pounds of meat and meal to produce 40,000 pounds of sausage:

	Actual Quantity	*Actual Cost per Pound*	*Actual Quantity at Standard Price*
Meat A	9,900	$0.44	$ 3,960 (9,900 × $0.40)
Meat B	24,600	0.22	6,150 (24,600 × $0.25)
Meat C	2,400	0.93	2,112 (2,400 × $0.88)
Meal	8,100	0.17	1,458 (8,100 × $0.18)
	45,000		$13,680

In contemplating the mix variance, one realizes that the actual quantities used did not conform to the standard formula. For example, workers finished 40,000 pounds of sausage; if they had used the standard formula they would have used 10,000 pounds (250 pounds × 40 batches) of Meat A instead of the 9,900 pounds actually used.

To determine the mix variance, we calculate the budgeted mix quantity by determining the amount of each ingredient to use at budgeted mix. For example, Meat A includes 22.73 percent of the total material ingredients (250/1,100 pounds = 22.73%). If workers had applied this percentage to the total actual quantity, they should have used 22.73% × 45,000 = 10,229 pounds of Meat A. Exhibit 24–2 illustrates mix and yield variances in detail for each class of material using the diagram approach. Even though we are calculating individual mix and yield variances, we recognize that each input is related to each other. Part of the reason for developing these variances is to determine the effect of altering the mix on the total product output made up of all the ingredients. Exhibit 24–2 also illustrates the material price variances.

Total Material Mix and Yield Variances.   Rather than compute individual mix and yield variances for each ingredient as shown in Exhibit 24–2, managers may find **total material mix and yield variances** better meet their needs. In the following mix variance, we multiply the actual quantities used by the standard price per pound and then compare it to the actual quantities multiplied by the standard cost per pound of material input.

Total material mix variance
    Actual quantity at standard price:

Meat A (9,900 pounds @ $0.40)	$3,960	
Meat B (24,600 pounds @ $0.25)	6,150	
Meat C (2,400 pounds @ $0.88)	2,112	
Meal (8,100 pounds @ $0.18)	1,458	$13,680
Actual quantity at standard input cost (45,000 pounds × $0.30)		13,500
Unfavorable material mix variance		$ 180

Total material yield variance
    The total yield variance is

Actual input quantity at standard input cost (45,000 pounds × $0.30)	$13,500
Actual output quantity at standard output cost (40,000 pounds × $0.33)	13,200
Unfavorable material yield variance	$ 300

An alternative approach to computing material yield variances is to compare the expected loss from processing with the actual loss as follows:

Expected loss from processing . . . . .100/1,100 = 9.09%
Expected yield percent . . . . .100.00% − 9.09% = 90.91%
5,000 Actual loss . . . .(45,000 − 40,000 pounds)
4,091 Expected loss . . . .(9.09% × 45,000 pounds put into process)
  909 (909 × $0.33 cost per pound of output = $300 unfavorable yield variance)

Stated another way, the yield is unfavorable because we put 45,000 pounds into processing and expected to receive 40,909 (45,000 × 90.91%) of output. We only received 40,000 pounds, giving us an unplanned loss of 909 pounds.

Not separating the quantity variance into mix and yield variances would result in the following $480 unfavorable material quantity variance. This does not give managers adequate information for a multi-ingredient product.

$480 U materials quantity variance

Materials mix	Materials yield
variance	variance
$180 U	$300 U

Materials quantity variance

	Standard pounds		Actual pounds				
(10,000*	—	9,900)	×	$.40	=	$ 40 F
(24,000	—	24,600)	×	$.25	=	150 U
(2,000	—	2,400)	×	$.88	=	352 U
(8,000	—	8,100)	×	$.18	=	18 U
		Total materials quantity variance				$480 U

*250 pounds per batch × 40 batches.

Journalizing Material Mix and Yield Variances. If a company keeps its direct materials inventory at standard costs, accountants record a material price variance for each of the four materials at the time the company purchases the material, using the analysis presented in Chapter 12. Company accountants would make the following journal entry to record the material mix and yield variances:

Work in Process Inventory (40,000 pounds × $0.33) 13,200
Material Mix Variance 180
Material Yield Variance 300
   Direct Materials Inventory (kept at standard) 13,680

If, instead, a company keeps its Direct Materials Inventory at actual cost, the credit to Direct Materials Inventory is actual quantity used multiplied by the actual cost. Accountants would record a Material Price Variance at the time of purchase with this system.

EXHIBIT 24–2   Material Price, Mix and Yield Variances

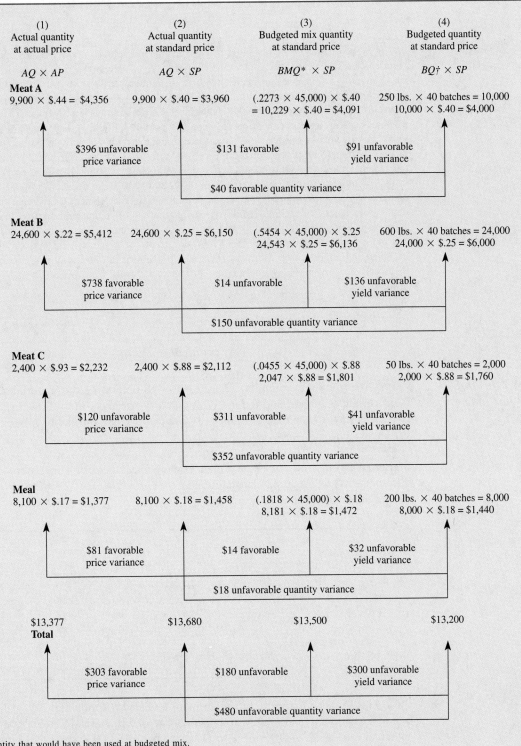

	(1) Actual quantity at actual price	(2) Actual quantity at standard price	(3) Budgeted mix quantity at standard price	(4) Budgeted quantity at standard price
	$AQ \times AP$	$AQ \times SP$	$BMQ^* \times SP$	$BQ\dagger \times SP$

Meat A
9,900 × $.44 = $4,356   9,900 × $.40 = $3,960   (.2273 × 45,000) × $.40   250 lbs. × 40 batches = 10,000
                                                                = 10,229 × $.40 = $4,091   10,000 × $.40 = $4,000

$396 unfavorable price variance $131 favorable $91 unfavorable yield variance

$40 favorable quantity variance

Meat B
24,600 × $.22 = $5,412   24,600 × $.25 = $6,150   (.5454 × 45,000) × $.25   600 lbs. × 40 batches = 24,000
                                                                24,543 × $.25 = $6,136   24,000 × $.25 = $6,000

$738 favorable price variance $14 unfavorable $136 unfavorable yield variance

$150 unfavorable quantity variance

Meat C
2,400 × $.93 = $2,232   2,400 × $.88 = $2,112   (.0455 × 45,000) × $.88   50 lbs. × 40 batches = 2,000
                                                              2,047 × $.88 = $1,801   2,000 × $.88 = $1,760

$120 unfavorable price variance $311 unfavorable $41 unfavorable yield variance

$352 unfavorable quantity variance

Meal
8,100 × $.17 = $1,377   8,100 × $.18 = $1,458   (.1818 × 45,000) × $.18   200 lbs. × 40 batches = 8,000
                                                              8,181 × $.18 = $1,472   8,000 × $.18 = $1,440

$81 favorable price variance $14 favorable $32 unfavorable yield variance

$18 unfavorable quantity variance

$13,377 $13,680 $13,500 $13,200
Total

$303 favorable price variance $180 unfavorable $300 unfavorable yield variance

$480 unfavorable quantity variance

*Quantity that would have been used at budgeted mix.
†Budgeted quantity using standard formula.

Global

Current Cost Management Practice

Wattie Frozen Foods (WFF) Limited of New Zealand developed a work center management system that illustrates Tom Johnson's philosophy as expressed in his book *Relevance Regained.* Some of the specific features of the company's system that embody the regaining of relevance are (1) the organizational culture is changed from top-down control to bottom-up empowerment; (2) the focus is on continuous improvement, (3) physical measures are used for daily process control (costing without dollars), and (4) dollar signs are attached to the physical measures to create a dynamic activity-based costing system. Earlier, WFF had adopted the principle of work center management by dividing the organization into a set of semiautonomous work centers. Supervisors and employees in each work center were empowered with the authority to make decisions critical to the manufacture of a quality product in a timely fashion. The work center management system requires managers to be empowered, responsible, and highly competent because they are fully responsible for their outputs and the use of inputs and resources including labor, equipment, services, and inventories. Staff should be proactive and systems should be designed and implemented with performance improvement in mind—not just control. To be effective, there must be a deliberate shift in focus away from the result and to the process.

William D. J. Cotton, "Relevance Regained Downunder," *Management Accounting,* May 1994, pp. 38–42.

Labor Mix and Yield Variances

Just as the previous example illustrates how to determine the material mix and yield variances comprising the material quantity variance, the following example illustrates how to separate the labor efficiency variance into labor mix and yield variances.

Standard Crew Mix.   Assume a crew of employees performs operations in three different pay grades. A standard crew mix consists of 20 worker-hours distributed among the pay grades as follows:

Pay Grade	Hours	Standard Rate	Standard Cost
A2	6	$20	$120
C4	5	16	80
D5	9	24	216
	20		$416

Output: 400 gallons
Standard cost per crew ($416/20 hours) = $20.80

During the month, charges to the department included 570 hours of A2 at an actual rate of $20.40, 420 hours of C4 at an actual rate of $16.20, and 700 hours of D5 at an actual rate of $23.72, giving a total labor cost of $35,036 for 1,690 hours. For 32,000 gallons of the product finished during the month, we compute the **labor mix** and **labor yield variances** as shown in Exhibit 24–3 using the diagram approach.

EXHIBIT 24–3   Labor Rate and Mix and Yield Variance

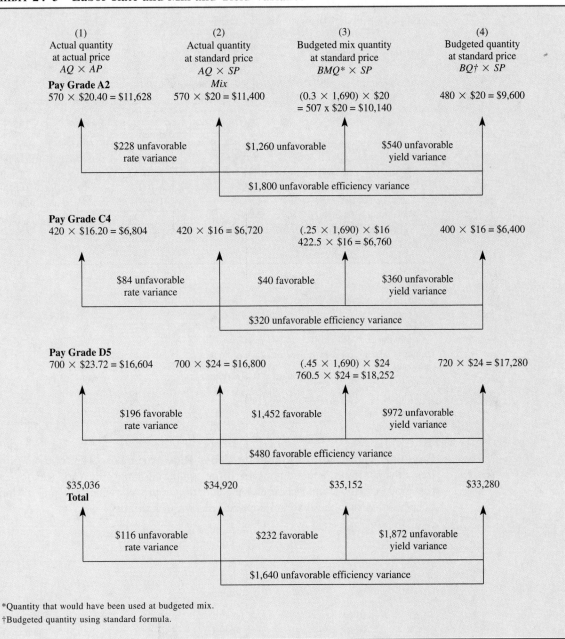

(1) Actual quantity at actual price $AQ \times AP$	(2) Actual quantity at standard price $AQ \times SP$ *Mix*	(3) Budgeted mix quantity at standard price $BMQ^* \times SP$	(4) Budgeted quantity at standard price $BQ† \times SP$

Pay Grade A2
$570 \times \$20.40 = \$11,628$ $570 \times \$20 = \$11,400$ $(0.3 \times 1,690) \times \$20$ $= 507 \times \$20 = \$10,140$ $480 \times \$20 = \$9,600$

$228 unfavorable rate variance $1,260 unfavorable $540 unfavorable yield variance

$1,800 unfavorable efficiency variance

Pay Grade C4
$420 \times \$16.20 = \$6,804$ $420 \times \$16 = \$6,720$ $(.25 \times 1,690) \times \$16$ $422.5 \times \$16 = \$6,760$ $400 \times \$16 = \$6,400$

$84 unfavorable rate variance $40 favorable $360 unfavorable yield variance

$320 unfavorable efficiency variance

Pay Grade D5
$700 \times \$23.72 = \$16,604$ $700 \times \$24 = \$16,800$ $(.45 \times 1,690) \times \$24$ $760.5 \times \$24 = \$18,252$ $720 \times \$24 = \$17,280$

$196 favorable rate variance $1,452 favorable $972 unfavorable yield variance

$480 favorable efficiency variance

$35,036 **Total** $34,920 $35,152 $33,280

$116 unfavorable rate variance $232 favorable $1,872 unfavorable yield variance

$1,640 unfavorable efficiency variance

*Quantity that would have been used at budgeted mix.
†Budgeted quantity using standard formula.

We compute the labor mix variance similarly to the material mix variance. For example, of the 1,690 actual hours used, 30 percent (6/20 hours) should have been Pay Grade A2 hours or a total of 507 hours. Instead, the company employed 570 Grade A2 hours; they used a higher proportion of this more expensive pay grade than indicated by the crew formula. If they had followed the standard formula exactly for the 80 batches completed (32,000 gallons of output/400 gallons per batch = 80 batches), Pay Grade A2 hours should have totaled 80 × 6 hours = 480 hours. Using more A2 hours results in an unfavorable yield variance for Pay Grade A2 of $540.

We calculate mix and yield variances similarly for the other pay grades. If we use total, rather than individual, mix and yield variances as shown in Exhibit 24–3, the computation is as follows:

Total labor mix variance

Actual Hours at Standard Rate

	Actual Hours	Standard Rate	Total Standard Cost for Actual Hours
A2	570	$20	$11,400
C4	420	16	6,720
D5	700	24	16,800
....	1,690		$34,920
Actual hours at weighted standard cost:			
(1,690 actual hours × $20.80 standard hourly rate)			35,152
Favorable labor mix variance			$ 232

Total labor yield variance

Actual hours at standard cost
  (1,690 hours × $20.80) $35,152
Output at standard cost expressed in standard hours:

$$\frac{32,000}{400} = 80 \text{ batches} \times 20 \text{ hours} = 1,600 \text{ hours}$$

1,600 hours × $20.80 standard hourly rate 33,280
Unfavorable labor yield variance .... $ 1,872

Equation Approach to Computing Labor Rate Variance.   The following illustrates the short-cut, equation approach for computing labor rate variances for each pay grade of labor. You may prefer the equation approach, which Chapter 12 introduced, rather than the diagram approach shown in Exhibit 24–3.

Labor rate variance

Pay Grade	Actual Rate	Standard Rate	Rate Variance		Total Rate Variance
A2	$20.40	$20	$0.40 U*	$228 U*	($0.40 × 570 hours)
C4	16.20	16	0.20 U	84 U	($0.20 × 420 hours)
D5	23.72	24	0.28 F	196 F	($0.28 × 700 hours)
				$116 U	

*U = Unfavorable; F = Favorable.

Journalizing Labor Rate, Mix and Yield Variances.   The following journal entry records the labor mix, labor yield, and labor price variances:

Work in Process Inventory...............	33,280	
Labor Yield Variance....................	1,872	
Labor Rate Variance	116	
Labor Mix Variance.................		232
Payroll		35,036

Assumed Substitutability of Material and Labor in Products

We assume that a company can substitute inputs in its products as well as finished products in its sales mix. For example, we assume a company can substitute Meat C for Meat A or swap a sale of Product B for Product A. However we know there is a limit to this exchange. While Meat C may replace Meat A in limited amounts without changing the taste of sausage, there is an even greater limit to the amount of cheap meal that can be used instead of meat in sausage.

Assume instead we pay all classes of labor the same, all material inputs cost the same per pound, or all products sold have the same contribution margin. Under any of these conditions, there would be no mix variance for that ingredient or product. For example, if the engineer and the janitor on a crew of workers earned the same wage per hour, the substitution of laborers would have no effect on the total cost of a job. We do know that other constraints prevent us from complete substitutability, however. The engineer can sweep the floor, but the janitor lacks the skills needed to perform an engineering task. Managers must remember these general concepts when interpreting mix and yield variances.

A question arises: Should we routinely calculate mix and yield variances? The answer depends on the opportunity management has for substitution between material ingredients and various skills of labor. If trade-off alternatives are available, cost/benefit analysis usually indicates that calculations are worthwhile because they provide insight that managers could not obtain through the quantity variance.

Summary

Chapter 12 introduces material and labor price and quantity variances, and Chapter 13 discusses factory overhead variances. Management may use additional revenue and cost variances to further pinpoint responsibility for other major sources of deviations from plans. Companies selling multiple products or using multiple material and labor inputs in their manufacturing process especially have supplementary sources of variances available.

Because products have different unit contribution margins, the mix of their sales affect net income. Companies may not sell products in the proportions anticipated by management. The sales mix variances capture the effect of these changes on net income. Likewise, the production mix variance reflects the extra cost or savings from substituting material and labor inputs. Yield variances measure the impact on costs and profits of a change in physical volume.

However, merely calculating the variance does not complete the cost accountant's full responsibility. More importantly, managers must understand the specific impact of the various factors measured before they can take appropriate corrective actions.

Important Terms And Concepts

Problem for Self-Study

Material Price, Mix and Yield Variances, and Journal Entries

Nancy Sills Manufacturers processes and cans tomato catsup in 24-ounce jars. The standard input for a batch of materials is as follows:

	Pounds	Standard Price per Pound
Tomatoes	340	$.60
Corn syrup	75	.10
Vinegar	25	.40
Salt	10	.20
Onion powder, spice, and flavoring	50	.53
Input	500	
Output	400	

The recipe used not only is secret but also allows for some variation in ingredients in obtaining the special flavor. The following materials were purchased during the month. Direct materials inventory is kept at standard.

	Pounds	Actual Cost
Tomatoes	23,000	$14,950
Corn syrup	5,000	250
Vinegar	3,000	1,320
Salt	800	176
Onion powder, spice, and flavoring	2,500	1,200

During the month, 18,000 jars were filled with the following materials put in process:

	Pounds
Tomatoes	22,100
Corn syrup	3,900
Vinegar	1,900
Salt	500
Onion powder, spice and flavoring	1,950
	30,350

Required:

a. Compute a material purchase price variance for each of the materials and a material total mix and total yield variance for the month. Indicate if the variance is favorable or unfavorable.

b. Prepare journal entries to record the issuance of material, the variances, and the disposition of variances.

Solution to Problem for Self-Study

NANCY SILLS MANUFACTURERS

a.

	Pounds	Standard Cost
Tomatoes	340	$204.00
Corn syrup	75	7.50
Vinegar	25	10.00
Salt	10	2.00
Onion powder, spices, and flavorings	50	26.50
Input	500	$250.00
Output	400	
Standard cost per pound of input ($250/500)	$.50	
Standard cost per pound of output ($250/400)	$.625	

Material purchase price variance

	Actual Pounds	Standard Price	Actual Price	Price Variance per Pound	Total Purchase Price Variance
Tomatoes	23,000	$.60	$.65	$ .05 U	$1,150 U
Corn syrup	5,000	.10	.05	.05 F	250 F
Vinegar	3,000	.40	.44	.04 U	120 U
Salt	800	.20	.22	.02 U	16 U
Onion powder, spices, and flavoring	2,500	.53	.43	.05 F	125 F
					$ 911 U

Material mix variance

	Actual Quantity	Standard Price	Amounts
Tomatoes	22,100	$.60	$13,260.00
Corn syrup	3,900	.10	390.00
Vinegar	1,900	.40	760.00
Salt	500	.20	100.00
Onion powder, spices and flavoring	1,950	.53	1,033.50
	30,350		$15,543.50
Actual quantity at standard input cost (30,350 pounds × $.50)			15,175.00
Unfavorable material mix variance			$ 368.50

Material yield variance

Actual quantity at standard input cost	$15,175.00
Actual output at standard output cost (27,000* × $.625)	16,875.00
Favorable material yield variance	$ 1,700.00

*18,000 jars × 24 ounces = 432,000 ounces ÷ 16 ounces = 27,000 pounds

Alternative way of computing yield variance

100/500 = 20% Expected loss from processing

6,070	Expected loss (20% × 30,350 materials put into process)
3,350	Actual loss (30,350 − 27,000)
2,720	× $.625 = $1,700 Favorable

b.

Direct Materials Inventory	16,985.00	
Material Purchase Price Variance	911.00	
Accounts Payable		17,896.00
Work in Process Inventory	16,875.00	
Material Mix Variance	368.50	
Material Yield Variance		1,700.00
Direct Materials Inventory		15,543.50
Material Yield Variance	1,700.00	
Material Mix Variance		368.50
Material Purchase Price Variance		911.00
Cost of Goods Sold		420.50

Review Questions

1. Should material mix and yield variances be routinely calculated for all companies?

2. What does the sales mix variance capture and how does this information assist management?

3. (*a*) At a low level of analysis for sales variances, what variances would you compute? (*b*) What types of variances would these low detailed variances be decomposed into at higher levels of analysis?

4. What would you review in a company to determine the cause of a (*a*) mix variance and (*b*) yield variance?

5. Discuss any constraints you see in the substitutability that we assume when calculating sales mix and production mix variances.

6. Assume you are making a product that has two ingredients, oil and vinegar, which are substitutable. The recipe for one batch of 10 gallons is oil—5 gallons @ $6 a gallon and vinegar—5 gallons @ $10 a gallon. At the end of the month, you find the company made 500 gallons of finished products using 210 gallons of oil costing $5.90 a gallon and 300 gallons of vinegar costing $11 a gallon. What is the mix variance for each of the two ingredients?

7. Using the data in Question 6, determine the price and yield variances for each of the ingredients.

8. Assume a company makes a special vegetarian diet soup and all beans, carrots, celery, and onions cost the same per pound. Also, the company prides itself on having an across-the-board pay scale so all workers are paid the same per hour. How would this situation affect the company's production mix variances?

9. Assume a company has a planned mix of 5 units of Product X to 2 units of Product Y. The individual unit contribution margin for X is $6 and $13 for Y. What is the weighted-average budgeted contribution margin? How do you use the weighted-average budgeted contribution margin in variance analysis?

10. For what types of operations would material mix and labor yield variances be appropriate?

11. Describe circumstances in which the overall sales mix variance would be unfavorable.

Exercises

E24–1 Sales Quantity and Sales Mix Variances

The First Company sells Products A and B whose sales prices are $6 and $12, respectively. The variable cost for Product A is $4 and $7 for Product B. Total fixed costs for the company are estimated at $30,000. Assume management plans to sell a total of 9,000 units with a planned mix of 1 unit of Product A to 2 units of Product B. Suppose, instead, that 8,000 units composed of 1,600 units of Product A and 6,400 units of Product B are actually sold.

Required:

Compute for each product the sales quantity and sales mix variances. Prove your answer.

E24–2 Market Size and Market Shares Sales Variances

Midnight Co. is a leading manufacturer of designer dresses. The average selling price is $500 and the average variable production cost of each dress is $300. In preparing its 19X3 sales budget, managers expect their dress sales to reach 400,000 units. This is equivalent to a 40 percent share of the designer dress market. Based on an industry sales forecast, there will be 1,000,000 dresses sold in 19X3. At the end of 19X3, the actual sales figure indicates that Midnight Co. sold 432,000 units and actual industry sales were 1,200,000 units.

Required:

Compute the market size and market share sales variances for Midnight Co.

E24–3 Sales Quantity, Sales Mix, and Sales Price Variances

Wash Company produces three types of children's dancing shoes: ballet, tap, and acrobatic. Its budget for the next period is based on the following:

		Product Lines	
	Ballet Shoes	*Tap Shoes*	*Acrobatic Shoes*
Sales price	$8.00	$12.00	$10.00
Variable expenses	4.00	9.00	4.00
Budgeted volume	3,000	7,500	4,500
Total fixed expenses $26,650			

Required:

At the end of the period, you determine that Wash sold 12,000 units consisting of 2,000 ballet shoes, 4,000 of tap shoes, and 6,000 of acrobatic shoes.

a. Determine the sales quantity and sales mix variance for each product line.

b. Prove your answer to Requirement a.

c. Compute sales price variances for each of the products assuming actual sales revenue was $12,000 for ballet shoes, $64,000 for tap shoes, and $78,000 for acrobatic shoes.

E24–4 Unit Material Yield, Mix, and Price Variances

Vance Company has determined that after allowing for normal processing losses, the standard mix of material used in producing a finished product is as follows:

Material A (3 gallons @ $2.00)	$ 6.00
Material B (8 gallons @ $0.75)	6.00
Material C (9 gallons @ $1.00)	9.00
	$21.00

During a given period, the actual cost per fully inspected unit was as follows:

Material A (4 gallons @ $2.05)	$ 8.20
Material B (7 gallons @ $0.70)	4.90
Material C (8 gallons @ $0.90)	7.20
	$20.30

Required:

a. Determine the material yield variance per finished unit.

b. Determine the material mix variance per finished unit.

c. Determine the material price variance per finished unit.

d. Prepare a journal entry to record the issuance of material and the material variances. The direct materials inventory is kept at actual cost.

E24–5 Sales Quantity and Sales Mix Variances

This year's budget for Pattie, Inc., a multiproduct firm, is as follows:

	Products Lines			
	Dishes	*Cookware*	*Utensils*	*Total*
Sales	$1,060,000	$800,000	$880,000	$2,740,000
Less: Variable costs	580,000	600,000	740,000	1,920,000
Fixed costs allocated				
on square footage	140,000	150,000	91,300	381,300
Income before taxes	$ 340,000	$ 50,000	$ 48,700	$ 438,700
Units	160,000	100,000	140,000	400,000

At year-end, you determine that sales price, total fixed costs, and unit variable costs were exactly as budgeted, but the following units per product line were sold:

Product Line	*Units*
Dishes	175,000
Cookware	175,000
Utensils	150,000
Total	500,000

Required:

a. Compute sales quantity variances and sales mix variances for each product line.

b. Prove your answer to Requirement *a.*

E24–6 Journal Entries to Record Unit Material Yield, Mix and Price Variances

Dean Company uses standard costing in its manufacturing process. The following is the standard mix of one unit of copper steel:

	Pounds	*Standard Rate*	*Standard Cost*
Copper	3	$2.00	$ 6.00
Iron	5	1.50	7.50
Carbon	2	1.00	2.00
	10		$15.50

In the month of June, Dean Company produced 1,000 units of copper steel and the material cost of each unit is as follows:

	Pounds	*Total Cost*
Copper	2.5	$ 7.50
Iron	6.0	7.50
Carbon	1.0	2.00
	9.5	$17.00

Required:

a. Determine the material yield, the material mix, and the material price variance per finished unit. Compute a total mix and total yield variance for the unit, but individual price variances for each material.

b. Prepare a journal entry to record the issuance of material and the material variances. The materials inventory is kept at actual cost.

E24–7 Sales Quantity and Sales Mix Variances

This year's budget for Well Company, a multiproduct firm is as follows:

	Product Lines			
	A	*B*	*C*	*Total*
Sales	$1,500,000	$1,100,000	$800,000	$3,400,000
Less: Variable costs	906,000	489,500	503,000	1,898,500
Fixed costs allocated on direct labor dollars	300,000	300,000	200,000	800,000
Income before taxes	$ 294,000	$ 310,500	$ 97,000	$ 701,500
Units	297,000	203,500	49,500	550,000

At year-end, you determine that sales price, total fixed costs, and unit variable costs were exactly as budgeted, but the following units per product line were sold:

Product Line	*Units*
A	280,000
B	224,000
C	56,000
Total	560,000

Required:

a. Compute sales quantity variances and sales mix variances for each product line.

b. Prove your answer to Requirement *a.*

Problems

P24–8 Material Price, Mix, and Yield Variances

Edsel Company is the leading sausage producer in the nation. In its beef sausage, Edsel uses three grades of beef. The standard amount of each grade of beef in each 10-pound batch of sausage is as follows:

	Pounds	*Standard Price per Pound*	*Standard Cost*
Grade A	5	$4	$20
Grade B	3	2	6
Grade C	2	1	2
	10		$28

During March, Edsel produced 1,100 pounds of beef sausage; the actual amount of beef consumption and cost is as follows:

	Pounds	*Total Cost*
Grade A	450	$2,025
Grade B	320	800
Grade C	380	304
	1,150	$3,129

Required:

a. Compute a material price variance, a material mix, and a yield variance for each grade of beef for the month. Indicate if each is favorable or unfavorable.

b. Prepare the journal entry to record these variances for March. Assume direct materials are kept at actual cost.

P24–9 Sales Quantity, Sales Mix, and Sales Price Variances

Chris, Inc.'s budget reveals the following for the three products lines they manufacture:

		Product Lines	
Per Unit	*A*	*B*	*C*
Sales price	$100	$80	$60
Variable expenses	$ 40	$30	$20
Budgeted volume	8,000	16,000	16,000
Total fixed expenses: $1,200,000			

Required:

a. Determine sales quantity variances and sales mix variances for each product line assuming that actual variable costs were the same as budgeted and there was a sales mix of 6,000 units of Product A for a total sales revenue of $588,000; 12,000 units of Product B for a total sales revenue of $84,000; and 18,000 units of Product C for a total sales revenue of $1,188,000.

b. Prove your answer to Requirement *a.*

c. Compute sales price variances for each product.

P24–10 Labor Rate and Mix and Yield Variances

Walther Industrial Company's standard direct labor costs for the manufacture of a product are as follows for a month:

Labor rate per hour:		
3 skilled workers @ $20	$	60
5 semiskilled workers @ $12		60
Total cost of standard combination of labor	$	120
Average price per hour, $120 ÷ 8 = ...	$	15
Standard labor price per unit of output at 5 units per hour, $15 ÷ 5 = ...	$	3
Standard labor cost of 40,000 units of output, 40,000 × $3, or 8,000 × $15	$120,000	
Actual inputs: 8,640 hours		
2,500 hours of skilled workers @ $21	$ 52,500	
6,140 hours of semiskilled workers @ $12.50	76,750	
	$129,250	

Skilled workers were paid a higher average wage rate than standard because of a temporary shortage of this skill. Walther's management used more semiskilled workers per skilled workers than usual in an attempt to save costs.

Required:

a. Compute a labor rate, labor mix, and a labor yield variance for each class of worker skill.

b. Prepare the journal entry to record these variances.

c. Determine what the actual cost probably would have been if the standard labor mix had been maintained even though the actual labor prices were incurred.

P24–11 Unit Material Yield, Mix, and Price Variances

The standard mix of material used in producing a finished product is as follows for the Postman Company; an allowance is made for normal processing loss:

Material A (12 gallons @ $8)	$ 96	
Material B (8 gallons @ $1.50)	12	
Material C (10 gallons @ $7.20)	72	
	$180	

During a given period, the actual cost per unit was as follows:

Material A (14 gallons @ $8.10)	$ 113.40	
Material B (7 gallons @ $1.40)	9.80	
Material C (8 gallons @ $7.05)	56.40	
	$179.60	

Required:

a. Determine the following:

  (1) Material price variance per finished unit.

(2) Material yield variance per finished unit.

(3) Material mix variance per finished unit.

b. Prepare a journal entry to record the issuance of material and the material variances. The material inventory is kept at actual cost.

P24–12 Sales Quantity and Sales Mix Variances

This year's budget for Bodnar Company, a multiproduct firm follows:

	Products Lines			
	X	Y	Z	Total
Sales	$1,200,000	$1,500,000	$900,000	$3,600,000
Less: Variable costs	795,000	600,000	450,000	1,845,000
Fixed costs allocated on square footage occupied	200,000	300,000	300,000	800,000
Income before taxes	$ 205,000	$ 600,000	$150,000	$ 955,000
Units	300,000	562,500	75,000	937,500

At year-end, you determine that sales price, total fixed costs, and unit variable costs were exactly as budgeted, but the following units per product line were sold:

Product Line	Units
X	282,600
Y	612,300
Z	47,100
Total	942,000

Required: (Use three decimal places for dollar unit calculations.)

a. Compute sales quantity variances and sales mix variances for each product line.

b. Prove your answer to Requirement a.

P24–13 Labor Rate, Mix, and Yield Variances

SPATS

Felix Industries is the leading cordless telephone manufacturer in the Southwest. Its manufacturing process is performed by a crew of employees in different pay grades. A standard crew hour consists of 20 direct labor-hours distributed as follows:

Pay Grade	Hours	Standard Rate	Standard Cost
G7	4	$12	$48
G8	8	8	64
G9	8	6	48
	20		$160
Output: 5 cordless telephones			

In April, Felix produced 500 cordless telephones; the actual hours and labor cost were

Pay Grade	Hours	Total Costs
G7	350	$ 4,900
G8	775	6,975
G9	950	6,650
	2,075	$18,525

Required:

a. Compute a labor rate, a labor mix, and a labor yield variance for each pay grade.

b. Prepare the journal entry to record these variances for April.

SPATS

P24–14 Material Price, Mix and Yield Variances, and Journal Entries

Anderson Company sells a chemical to industrial companies for cleaning purposes. Inspection of the chemical content is made at frequent intervals because some of the material is subject to evaporation. The standard product mix for a 50-gallon batch is

> 20 gallons of Chemical A @ $0.40 per gallon
> 5 gallons of Chemical B @ $0.80 per gallon
> 30 gallons of Chemical C @ $0.30 per gallon
> 5 gallons of Chemical D @ $0.60 per gallon

The company records the material price variance at the time of purchase. Materials purchased were as follows:

> 2,500 gallons of Chemical A @ $0.44 per gallon = $1,100.00
> 650 gallons of Chemical B @ $0.85 per gallon =   552.50
> 3,650 gallons of Chemical C @ $0.32 per gallon = 1,168.00
> 550 gallons of Chemical D @ $0.57 per gallon =   313.50

In producing the 120 batches during the month, the following actual material quantities were put into production:

> 2,450 gallons of Chemical A
> 540 gallons of Chemical B
> 3,620 gallons of Chemical C
> 475 gallons of Chemical D

Required:

a. Determine individual material purchase price variances, a total material mix variance, and a total yield variance.

b. Prepare journal entries to record the variances determined in Requirement *a* and the disposition of variances assuming all completed units are sold. Assume all variances are treated as period costs.

SPATS

P24–15 Labor Crew Rate, Mix and Yield Variances

LC Company's production process is performed by a crew of employees in different pay grades. A standard crew hour consists of 50 worker-hours distributed as follows:

Pay Grade	Hours	Standard Rate	Standard Cost
K10	20	$ 6	$120
J4	23	8	184
H2	5	16	80
L5	2	30	60
	50		$444
Output	100 tons		

During the month, charges to the department included 1,300 hours of K10 at a total cost of $9,100; 1,250 hours of J4 at a total cost of $9,750; 310 hours of H2 at a total cost of $5,053; and 125 hours of L5 at a total cost of $3,625. There were 6,000 tons of finished goods produced during the month.

Required:

a. Compute a labor rate, a labor mix, and a labor yield variance for each pay grade.

b. Prepare the journal entry to record these variances.

P24–16 Labor Rate, Mix, and Yield Variances

Dunston Company's production process is performed by a crew of employees in different pay grades. A standard crew hour consists of 60 labor-hours distributed as follows:

Pay Grade	Hours	Standard Rate	Standard Cost
A	25	$ 8	$200
B	12	12	144
C	18	10	180
D	5	20	100
	60		$624
Output	100 tons		

During the month, charges to the department included 1,260 hours of Pay Grade A at a total cost of $10,332; 610 hours of B at a total cost of $7,076; 925 hours of C at a total cost of $9,620; and 265 hours of D at a total cost of $5,830. There were 5,000 tons of finished goods produced during the month.

Required: (Round budgeted mix quantity percents to two decimal places.)

a. Compute a labor rate, a labor mix, and a labor yield variance for each pay grade.

b. Prepare the journal entry to record these variances and the direct labor cost.

P24–17 Market Share and Size Variances

Forecasts indicated industry sales of 7,500 units of Product C and 25,000 units of Product D. Wright, Inc., managers expected sales to be: 3,000 units (40% market share) of Product C and 5,000 units of Product D (20% market share). Actual industry sales were 17,000 units of Product C and 22,000 units of Product D. This yields an actual market share of 20 percent (3,400/17,000 units) for Product C and 30 percent (6,600/22,000 units) for Product D. Wright's managers summarized data for Products C and D as follows:

	Product C	Product D	Total
Budgeted unit sales price	$25	$50	—
Actual unit sales price	22	56	—
Standard variable cost per unit	10	30	—
Budgeted unit contribution margin	15	20	—
Budgeted sales volume	3,000 units	5,000 units	8,000 units
Budgeted sales mix percentage	37.5%	62.5%	100%
Actual sales volume	3,400 units	6,600 units	10,000 units
Actual sales mix percentage	34%	66%	100%
Total budgeted market for industry	7,500	25,000	
Budgeted market share	40%	20%	
Actual industry sales	17,000	22,000	
Actual market share	20%	30%	

Required:

a. Calculate sales price variances for each product.

b. Determine the sales volume variance.

c. Calculate sales mix variances for each product.

d. Determine sales quantity variances for each product.

e. Prove your sales mix and sales quantity variances.

f. Calculate market size variances for each product.

g. Calculate market share variances for each product.

h. Prove your sales size and sales share variances.

i. Explain Wright, Inc.'s market size and market share variances.

P24–18 Labor Rate, Mix and Yield Variances, Performance Evaluation

Good Time Company manufactures tires in two plants, one in Dayton, Ohio, and the other in Oklahoma City. Because the plants are not automated, labor costs comprise a large component of the production costs. Thus, management watches labor costs carefully. The standard underlying the May budget for each batch of 1,000 tires is

Direct Labor Category	Dayton Plant	Oklahoma City Plant
Semiskilled	36 hours at $20 an hour	30 hours at $10 an hour
Skilled	32 hours at $25 an hour	18 hours at $15 an hour
Specialist	12 hours at $32 an hour	12 hours at $20 an hour

On the third working day of June, actual results from May were released. Dayton's plant output was 430 batches and Oklahoma City's output was 660 batches. Actual direct labor costs were

Direct Labor Category	Dayton Plant	Oklahoma City Plant
Semiskilled	15,000 at $20 an hour = $300,000	20,050 at $ 8 an hour = $160,400
Skilled	11,900 at $20 an hour = 238,000	8,000 at $18 an hour = 144,000
Specialist	5,000 at $30 an hour = 150,000	7,550 at $18 an hour = 135,900
	$688,000	$440,300

Required:

a. Compute a labor rate, a labor mix, and a labor yield variance for each skill level for the Dayton plant.
b. Compute a labor rate, a labor mix, and a labor yield variance for each skill level for the Oklahoma City plant.
c. Evaluate the performance of the Dayton and Oklahoma City plant managers regarding direct labor costs.

P24–19 Sales, Material, Labor, Overhead, and Contribution Margin Variances (CMA)
Allglow Company is a cosmetics manufacturer specializing in stage makeup. The company's best selling product is SkinKlear, a cream used under the stage makeup to protect the skin from frequent use of makeup. SkinKlear is packaged in three sizes—8 ounces, 1 pound, and 3 pounds—and regularly sells for $21 per pound. The standard cost per pound of Skin-Klear, based on Allglow's normal monthly production of 8,000 pounds, is as follows:

Cost Item	Quantity	Standard Cost	Total Cost
Direct materials			
Cream base	9.0 oz.	$0.05/oz.	$0.45
Moisturizer	6.5 oz.	0.10/oz.	0.65
Fragrance	0.5 oz.	1.00/oz.	0.50
			$ 1.60
Direct labor*			
Mixing	0.5 hr.	$4.00/hr.	$2.00
Compounding	1.0 hr.	5.00/hr.	5.00
			7.00
Variable overhead†	1.5 hr.	$2.10/hr.	3.15
Total standard cost per pound			$11.75

*Direct labor dollars include employee benefits.
†Applied on the basis of direct labor-hours.

Based on these standard costs, Allglow prepares monthly budgets. The budgeted performance and the actual performance for May 19X1, when the company produced and sold 9,000 pounds of SkinKlear, follow:

Contribution Report for SkinKlear
For May 19X1

	Budget	Actual	Variance	
Units	8,000	9,000	1,000	F
Revenue	$168,000	$180,000	$12,000	F
Direct material	12,800	16,200	3,400	U
Direct labor	56,000	62,500	6,500	U
Variable overhead	25,200	30,900	5,700	U
Total variable costs	$ 94,000	$109,600	$15,600	U
Contribution margin	$ 74,000	$ 70,400	$ 3,600	U

Barbara Simmons, Allglow's president, was not pleased with these results; despite a sizable increase in the sales of SkinKlear, there was a decrease in the product's contribution to the overall profitability of the firm. Simmons has asked Allglow's cost accountant, Brian Jackson, to prepare a report that identifies the reasons why the contribution margin for SkinKlear has decreased. Jackson has gathered the following information to help in the preparation of the report:

Cost Item	Quantity	Actual Cost
Direct materials		
Cream base	84,000 oz.	$4,200
Moisturizer	60,000 oz.	7,200
Fragrance	4,800 oz.	4,800
Direct labor		
Mixing	4,500 hr.	18,000
Compounding—Manual	5,300 hr.	26,500
Compounding—Mechanized	2,700 hr.	13,500
Compounding—Idle	900 hr.	4,500
Variable overhead		30,900
Total standard cost per pound		$109,600

While doing his research, Jackson discovered that the manufacturing department had mechanized one of the manual operations in the compounding process on an experimental basis. The mechanized operation replaced manual operations that represented 40 percent of the compounding process.

The workers' inexperience with the mechanized operation caused increased usage of both the cream base and the moisturizer; however, Jackson believed these inefficiencies would be negligible if mechanization became a permanent part of the process and the workers' skills improved. The idle time in compounding was traceable to the fact that fewer workers were required for the mechanized process. During this experimental period, the idle time was charged to direct labor rather than overhead. The excess workers could either be reassigned or laid off in the future. Jackson also determined that all of the variable manufacturing overhead costs over standard could be traced directly to the mechanization process.

Required:

a. Prepare an explanation of the $3,600 unfavorable variance between the budgeted and actual contribution margin for SkinKlear during May 19X1 by calculating the following variances:
   (1) Sales price variance.
   (2) Material price variance.
   (3) Material quantity variance.
   (4) Labor efficiency variance.
   (5) Variable overhead efficiency variance.
   (6) Variable overhead spending variance.
   (7) Contribution margin volume variance.
b. Assume Allglow Company must decide whether the compounding operation in the SkinKlear manufacturing process that was mechanized on an experimental basis should continue to be mechanized. Calculate the variable cost saving that can be expected to rise in the future from the mechanization. Explain your answer.

Gantt Charts, PERT, and Decision Tree Analysis

Chapter Objectives

After studying this chapter, you should be able to:

1. Prepare graphs and networks for use in planning and controlling processes where there are time flows.
2. Compare actual and budgeted time and cost for each activity so the resulting variance reflects the impact one activity's delay has on the overall project.
3. Provide, through decision tree analysis, a systematic framework for analyzing a sequence of interrelated decisions.
4. Apply the time value of future earnings by discounting the expected value of future decisions.

Introduction

Increasingly, cost accountants are devoting more attention to furnishing management and other interested parties with data they can use in cost control and planning rather than emphasizing cost accumulation and determination. Cost accounting now considers the predictive ability of data rather than solely emphasizing the past. Accountants are integrating control models within the cost accounting system for monitoring actual results against plans to provide feedback for corrective action. This involvement in managerial planning and control has led to the use of Gantt charts, Program Evaluation and Review Technique (PERT), and decision tree analysis.

Gantt Charts

One aid to planning that is simple to prepare is a **Gantt chart**, a bar chart with time shown on the horizontal axis and the duration of the task represented as a bar running from the starting date to the ending date. Industry uses Gantt charts as a method of recording progress toward goals. On a given date, a Gantt chart easily shows how expected performance of a specific task compares with actual performance, which tasks should be in progress on a specific date, and how close to completion a task should be on a given date.

Control Device

Gantt charts are a control technique because they readily allow the comparison of actual production with scheduled production to identify variations and initiate corrective action. As shown in Exhibit 25–1, a Gantt chart involves (1) identifying and showing the sequence of activities and (2) scheduling the work by periods. The *Y*-axis of a Gantt chart represents the tasks or activities workers must perform, while the *X*-axis represents the time available for work. The horizontal broken line represents work scheduled by periods within the departments. The short vertical broken

---

Strategic Planning

Current Cost Management Practice

Chrysler Corporation took extraordinary precautions to camouflage the new design of its minivan. If it seems unnecessary to protect a vehicle that however designers jazz it up will always essentially remain a box on wheels, you have underestimated one of the most profitable consumer products ever built. By all accounts, the minivan's market is growing; all major auto companies plan to launch minivans. Chrysler has virtually owned the market for five-to-seven-passenger, $15,000 to $29,000 vehicles.

Chrysler's introduction of the minivan reflects creativity and innovation in a large organization. Because of its flexibility of management, absence of institutional barriers, strong leadership, and urgency of mission, Chrysler had crucial advantages over its competition during the early 1980s. Chrysler's minivan success is a tribute to superior market research and to the extraordinary consumer instinct of Lee Iacocca. The appeal of the minivan that Iacocca built is based almost entirely on utility, not on style or marketing.

Alex Taylor III, "Iacocca's Minivan," *Fortune*, May 30, 1994, pp. 57–66.

EXHIBIT 25–1   Gantt Chart—Each Block Represents One Workweek Beginning on Monday and Ending on Friday

Tasks

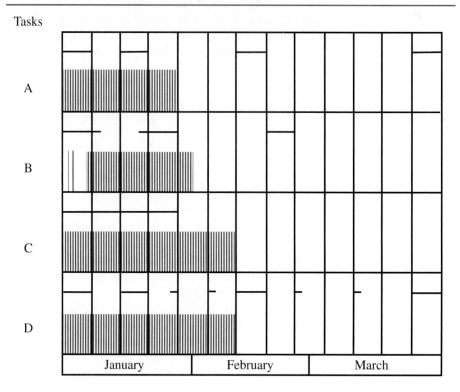

lines represent work unfinished or carried over from previous periods. The large shaded bar line is a summation of the individual horizontal broken lines and represents cumulative work to be performed.

Exhibit 25–1 divides time into weeks for each month. Management schedules Task A for the first and third weeks of January, the middle of February, and the last week of March. The four horizontal lines show this scheduled work for Task A. When added, these lines represent four weeks of cumulative work; the heavy horizontal line indicates this work. On examination, the chart shows that management could schedule additional jobs during the second and fourth weeks of January. Note that the workers have no backlog of work to complete on Task A because it has no short vertical lines as Task B does.

Advantages of Gantt Charts

Gantt charts provide a visual display of planned utilization of facilities so managers can make appropriate revisions to obtain better use of resources. After managers study the horizontal broken lines illustrating when work is scheduled, they can plan additional tasks for the time periods represented by breaks in the horizontal lines. The heavy bold line representing cumulative work assists managers in computing total work-hours required for each task as well as in scheduling repairs and maintenance. Gantt charts also alert managers to areas in which large variations in planned and actual performance exist so they can reallocate resources.

Network Models

Even though Gantt charts are simple systematic tools for planning, they fail to indicate which tasks workers must complete before beginning others. This failure results because all activities are arranged vertically on a Gantt chart. Network models provide for this aspect of planning. Program Evaluation Review Technique (PERT) is one of the more sophisticated planning and control devices.

Program Evaluation Review Technique

Program Evaluation Review Technique (PERT) is a systematic procedure for using network analysis to plan and measure actual progress toward scheduled events. The United States military developed PERT for the Polaris program to aid in controlling this large-scale project. Generally, organizations use PERT for exceptional projects whose managers have limited experience. The **critical path method (CPM)** developed by industry closely relates to PERT.

As illustrated in Exhibit 25–2, PERT diagrams are free-form, network diagrams showing each activity as an arrow between events. A network for **PERT-Time analysis** contains a sequence of arrows showing interrelationships among activities with time being the basic element in these activities. A circle represents an **event,** indicating the beginning or completion of a task. Events are discrete points, numbered for identification, that consume no resources. Arrows represent **activities** or tasks to be accomplished to go from one event to the next. An activity consumes resources and has a duration over time starting at one event and ending with the occurrence of the next event. We show activities from left to right in the necessary order of their accomplishment. Workers must complete all the activities leading to an event before an event occurs. This explains why an event at the head of the arrow should have a higher number, if possible, than an event at the end of the arrow.

EXHIBIT 25–2   Network for PERT-Time

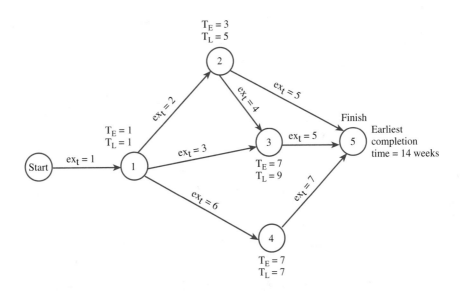

Expected Activity Time.   After developing the network diagram, managers make an estimate of the time needed to complete each activity. We base the **expected activity time** on the 1–4–1 three-estimate method, a weighted average of the shortest time, the average time, and the longest time. We weight the shortest and the longest times, one; and the average time, four. The formula for time estimations is

$$ex_t = 1/6 \text{ (optimistic time } + 4 \text{ most likely time } + \text{ pessimistic time).}$$

Exhibit 25–2 shows only the expected time (ex_t); to illustrate, the expected time of the activity beginning at 1 and ending at 4 is computed as: optimistic estimate = 3 weeks; most likely estimate = 6 weeks; pessimistic estimate = 9 weeks

$$\frac{3 + 4(6) + 9}{6} = 6 \text{ weeks } ex_t$$

We compute the expected times for the other activities similarly and write them on the upper sides of the arrows in Exhibit 25–2. Rather than expressing time in weeks, daily units can express the time estimates.

Critical Path.   We can determine the longest duration for completion of the entire project using a PERT network. The **critical path** is this longest path. Managers can reduce the total time of the project only by shortening the critical path. The reason this path is critical is that if any activity on the path takes longer than expected, a delay in the entire project occurs. Every network has at least one critical path. To find the critical path, we compute the cumulative expected activity time along each of the paths. In Exhibit 25–2, the cumulative paths are

Paths	Cumulative Expected Activity Time (in weeks)
0–1–2–5	1 + 2 + 5 = 8
0–1–2–3–5	1 + 2 + 4 + 5 = 12
0–1–3–5	1 + 3 + 3* + 5 = 12
0–1–4–5	1 + 6 + 7 = 14†

*Time lag of three weeks waiting until completion of activity 2–3.
†Critical path with cumulative activity time of 14 weeks.

Slack.   Paths that are not critical have **slack time;** however, activities along the critical path do not. The slack associated with an event is the amount of time a company can delay the event without affecting the completion of the project. The larger the amount of slack, the less critical the activity, and vice versa. Slack is the difference between the latest allowable time that a worker may complete an event and the earliest expected time. Exhibit 25–2 also indicates the earliest completion time. The **earliest completion time (T_E)** is the cumulative time of the event. In Exhibit 25–2, the T_E of event 2 is three weeks (1 + 2), the duration of activity 0–1 and 1–2. The T_E for event 3 is more complex because it has two cumulative paths, one along path 0–1–2–3 (seven weeks) and the other along the path 0–1–3 (four weeks). When an event has more than one cumulative path, the longest completion time of any path is the T_E for that event. This means the earliest completion time for event 3 is seven weeks. Note that this causes a time lag for path 0–1–3–5 as production cannot leave event 3 until week seven. Exhibit 25–2 indicates the T_E for all other events.

After computing the earliest completion time for all events, we determine the **latest completion time (T_L).** The T_L on the critical path equals the T_E because there is no slack on this path. We compute the other events' latest completion times by working backwards through the network. For instance, the T_L for event 3 is nine weeks, the latest completion time for event 5, the event that follows it, and the five weeks of activity 3–5 ($14 - 5 = 9$ weeks). If an event has several activities flowing from it, there may be several latest completion times. However, the minimum of these times is the T_L for that event. Slack now can be computed using the following formula:

$$S = T_L - T_E$$

The slack at event 2 is two weeks ($S = 5 - 3 = 2$ weeks). This allows management to delay event 2 up to two weeks without delaying the overall project's expected completion time of 14 weeks. However, if a noncritical activity uses more than its expected time, we must recompute the slack time for subsequent events. For example, if activity 1–2 takes three weeks instead of the estimated two weeks, event 2's slack time has been reduced one week, for a total slack of one week.

Flexibility with Slack.   Slack introduces flexibility into the network because it serves as a buffer for events not located on the critical path. When time lags appear on the critical path, managers can transfer materials, labor, and equipment to the problem areas. However, managers must be alert to the effect of these transfers on other paths because they have made little or no progress if transfers in turn create problems on other paths.

Crashing.   Not only does information about slack time allow management to continually monitor a project's status but these data also may serve as a guide in rescheduling tasks to shorten the overall project's completion time. In Exhibit 25–2, event 3 has two weeks of slack. If these weeks represent idle resources, it may be possible to use these resources in critical events and cut the 14-week completion time of the project. Of course, there are limits to transferring idle resources, depending on the task's specifications. Activity time also may be reduced by hiring more labor, overtime, or acquiring more equipment. **Crashing** is what we call these efforts designed to complete the project ahead of schedule. However, when managers use crashing, the project's variable costs increase. Crashing the network means finding the minimum cost for completing the project in minimum time to achieve an optimum trade-off between time and cost. Determining the appropriate trade-off is referred to as *PERT-Cost analysis.*

PERT-Cost Analysis   **PERT-Cost analysis** of the trade-off between time and cost is essential to determine the cost effectiveness of crashing. We use the same type of network illustrated in Exhibit 25–2 for PERT-Time as employed in PERT-Cost. However, we include two estimated times, a crash time and a normal expected time, for each activity. Exhibit 25–3 indicates the expected time *(ex_t)* from Exhibit 25–2 along with the crash time *(cr_t)* for each activity. If the activity is as shown in 1–3 and 3–5 in Exhibit 25–3 and managers cannot crash it, there is no difference in these times and we can omit the crash time.

EXHIBIT 25–3   Network for PERT-Cost

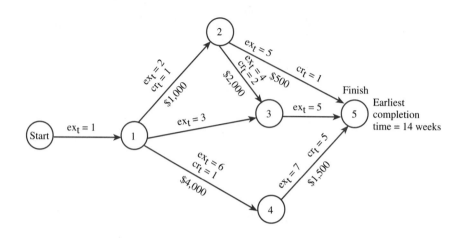

We estimate the costs of completing the activity under normal expected conditions and under crash conditions. A comparison of these two cost projections results in the determination of the *differential, or incremental, crash cost* for each activity that managers can crash. For example, assume the expected cost of activity 2–5 is $18,000 requiring five weeks. If instead, workers complete the activity in one week and management projects the cost at $20,000, the result is $500 differential cost per week [($20,000 − $18,000 ÷ (5 − 1 week)]. In Exhibit 25–3, differential crash cost per week is written below the arrow for each activity. Note that activity 1–3 and 3–5 have no differential crash cost because managers cannot crash either of these activities.

In PERT-Cost analysis of the trade-off between time and cost, managers study the status of the project. Assume that the project illustrated in Exhibits 25–2 and 25–3 has a normal cost of $100,000, shown as follows, if no crashing occurs:

No activities crashed

Paths	Cumulative Expected Weeks
0–1–2–5	8
0–1–2–3–5	12
0–1–3*–5	12
0–1–4–5	14†

*Time lag as cannot leave event 3 until week 7.
†Critical path—14 weeks for project completion.
$100,000—project cost.

In studying trade-offs, the company should crash first the critical activity with the lowest differential cost on the critical path. Even though activity 2–5 has the lowest differential cost ($500) in the network, it is not on the critical path. Crashing activity 2–5 will not shorten the overall project's completion time until managers first crash another activity. Crashing activity 2–5 would only increase slack time from 6 to 10 weeks on this path. Instead, activity 4–5, with a differential cost of $1,500, is the one to crash because its differential cost is the lowest of those activities on the critical path. However, managers can shorten it only two weeks before paths 0–1–2–3–5 and 0–1–3–5 also become critical. This results in the following status analysis showing crashing reduced project time by two weeks but increased cost $3,000 (2 weeks $\times$ $1,500). Now we have three critical paths and we can shorten the schedule only by reducing the lengths of all of them.

First Iteration

Activity 4–5 Crashed Two Weeks

Paths	Cumulative Expected Weeks
0–1–2–5	8
0–1–2–3–5	12*
0–1–3–5	12 (still cannot leave event 3 until week 7)
0–1–4–5	12*

*Critical paths —12 weeks for project completion.
$100,000 + 2 ($1,500) = $103,000 project cost.

Second Iteration.   A next iteration is to shorten activity 1–2 by one week because this activity has the lowest differential cost on path 0–1–2–3–5.

This also reduces the time on path 0–1–3–5 since now the project can leave event 3 at the sixth week of operation. However, this does not shorten overall project completion time until further crashing of activities occurs.

Thus, there is no overall time savings unless additional crashing occurs on path 0–1–4–5. You might have started in a different order or used a different combination than that illustrated in this second and third iteration. The important factor is to arrive at the final overall project time of nine weeks.

Activity 1–2 Crashed One Week

Paths	Cumulative Expected Weeks
0–1–2–5	7
0–1–2–3–5	11
0–1–3–5	11 (now can leave event 3 at week 6)
0–1–4–5	12*

* Critical path—12 weeks for project completion.
$103,000 + $1,000 = $104,000 project cost.

Third Iteration.   A next iteration involves shortening activity 2–3 by two weeks and activity 1–4 by three weeks. By crashing activity 2–3 there is no longer a time lag at event 3 for path 0–1–3–5 since the project can leave event 3 at the fourth week now. By crashing these two activities, overall project cost has increased with extra weeks saved, as the following illustrates:

Current Cost Management Practice

When Thomas C. Graham was president of U.S. Steel back in the mid-1980s, he spent most of his time ripping out excess mills. He blamed most of the U.S. steel industry's woes on the overvalued dollar. Today Graham heads AK Steel Corp., based in Middletown, Ohio, and his fellow top steel executives are the ones who are laughing. Thanks to the dirty work done in the 1980s, the U.S. steel industry is lean, efficient, and primed to cash in on a newly exuberant market. Also, Americans can jack up prices without worrying much about a flood of imports. With economic recovery moving ahead in Europe and Japan, steel prices are rising fast. Because steel is no longer at the heart of the U.S. economy, no crackdown on price is expected from the White House as experienced from Presidents Harry Truman and John Kennedy. The key players in the U.S. economy today are goliaths such as health care and software.

Stephen Baker and Keith L. Alexander with James B. Treece and Douglas Harbrecht, "Fat City for Big Steel," *BusinessWeek*, August 22, 1994, pp. 24–25.

**Activity 2–3 Crashed Two Weeks
and Activity 1–4 Crashed Three Weeks**

Paths	Cumulative Expected Weeks
0–1–2–5	7
0–1–2–3–5	9*
0–1–3–5	9* (now can leave event 3 at week 4)
0–1–4–5	9*

*Critical paths—9 weeks for project completion.

$104,000 + 2 ($2,000) + 3 ($4,000) = $120,000 project cost.

Even though we can further crash paths 0–1–4–5 and 0–1–2–5, we cannot reduce overall project time because there is no further reduction in paths 0–1–3–5 and 0–1–2–3–5. We cannot crash the remaining activities along these paths. This results in a final trade-off of crashing four activities and finishing the project in nine weeks, or five weeks earlier, at a minimum crash cost of $20,000, or total project cost of $120,000.

Deciding When to Crash

In deciding whether the company should proceed at the normal pace or attempt a crash program, we should compare the total differential cost of the crash program ($20,000 in our example) with the cost savings or benefits of the crash program. If we expect the contribution margin earned to be $6,000 a week, we should undertake the crash program because the $30,000 ($6,000 × 5 weeks) exceeds the $20,000 differential cost. If, however, the additional contribution profit the company expects to receive by completing the project early does not exceed $20,000, the company should follow the normal schedule.

Construction contracts may include penalties for failing to complete the project by a specified time. We can compare these penalties to differential cost in determining if crashing is profitable. For example, assume these penalties were in effect for the preceding case presented in Exhibit 25–3: no penalty if completed within 9 weeks, $5,000 penalty for a 12-week completion, and $15,000 for a 14-week completion. We should undertake crashing to reduce the project from 14 weeks to 12 weeks because the differential cost is $3,000 ($103,000 cost for 12 weeks − $100,000 normal cost for 14 weeks), which is less than the $10,000 penalty increase from $5,000 to $15,000. However, we cannot financially justify avoiding completely a penalty because it costs us $17,000 ($120,000 − $103,000) to reduce completion time from 12 weeks to 9 weeks. This $17,000 differential cost exceeds the $5,000 penalty we would save.

Variance Analysis and PERT-Cost

The PERT-Cost network may display expected and actual time and cost so managers can direct immediate attention to time slippage of the activities on the critical path. Comparison of actual time and costs with budgeted figures can reveal variances for each activity so management may direct corrective action. Penalties are also a factor in analyzing variances for each activity.

We illustrate variance analysis using the previous example in which we plan to crash activity 4–5 by 2 weeks to avoid the $15,000 penalty with total planned completion time of 12 weeks and a $5,000 penalty incurred. We assume project costs occur evenly over time.

Assume activity 2–5, which is not on the critical path, requires seven weeks instead of the expected five weeks at a total actual cost of $5,500. Although this does not affect overall project completion time because this path had available slack, it does increase activity costs such as rental of plant facilities and labor costs. Assume management budgeted in advance that the differential cost of extending completion per week on activity 2–5 was $100. Assume further that the normal cost to complete activity 2–5 in five weeks was $5,000. The variances for activity 2–5 are

Actual cost	$5,500
Normal cost	5,000
Net unfavorable variance	$ 500

This net unfavorable variance can be broken down into a **spending variance** and **activity time variance** reflecting the cost of extending completion. The spending variance reflects price and quantity variances for direct material, direct labor, and overhead. We compute the spending variance similarly to using variable (flexible) budgeting. While the flexible budgeting approach, first presented in Chapter 10, adjusts for actual units produced or hours worked, the PERT-Cost budget adjusts for the time required to complete the activity. Activity 2–5's variances are

Unfavorable activity time variance (2 weeks × $100 cost of extending completion per week)	$200
Unfavorable spending variance ($5,500 actual cost − $5,200 which is $5,000 normal cost for five weeks + $200 additional cost for the extra two weeks)	300
Total unfavorable variance	$500

Assume instead that activity 4–5, in which management planned to crash two weeks down to five weeks, required seven weeks at an actual cost of $21,000. These 2 weeks could not be made up elsewhere on the critical path so the overall project required 14 weeks which resulted in a $15,000 penalty. Assume that the normal cost for activity 4–5 was $20,000 with the differential cost of extending completion per week on this activity of $1,000. The following variances result:

Actual cost ($21,000 + $10,000 penalty increase)	$31,000
Normal cost adjusted for planned crashing [$20,000 + (2 × $1,500 weekly differential cost of crashing)]	23,000
Net unfavorable variance	$ 8,000

Three variances comprise the net unfavorable variance. By computing a **project time variance,** the activity manager is not only less likely to focus attention on activity 4–5 but also to recognize the impact of the delay on the overall project. Recognizing a project time variance discourages the tendency to suboptimize, which is choosing actions that are in one activity's best interest but not for the benefit of the overall project. The $8,000 net variance comprises the following:

Unfavorable project time variance which is the penalty increase	$10,000	
Unfavorable spending variance ($21,000 − $20,000 normal cost)	1,000	$11,000
Favorable activity time variance which is the differential cost to shorten two weeks that were saved (2 weeks × $1,500)		3,000
Net unfavorable variance		$ 8,000

The computation of a project time variance also may motivate activity managers to search for ways to speed up completion time especially if time has slipped on other activities. Assume instead that even though activity 4–5 required seven weeks instead of the crash time of five weeks, workers could make up the two weeks on activity 1–4. The normal cost of activity 1–4 for six weeks was $10,000 with the weekly differential cost of extending this activity, $2,000. Workers complete activity 1–4 in four weeks at a cost of $15,000. The variances for activity 4–5 are identical to those in the previous example; variances for activity 1–4 are

Normal cost		$10,000
Actual cost ($15,000 − $10,000 penalty increase saved)		5,000
Net favorable variance		$ 5,000
Favorable project time variance (the penalty increase)	$10,000	
Favorable spending variance [$15,000 actual cost − $18,000 normal cost adjusted for shortening two weeks which is $10,000 + (2 × $4,000 weekly differential cost to crash)]	3,000	$13,000
Unfavorable activity time variance (the differential cost to crash two weeks: 2 × $4,000)		8,000
Net favorable variance		$ 5,000

This analysis shows that it cost $8,000 to shorten the activity 1–4 completion time, but the company saved the $10,000 penalty increase. This indicates we made a correct decision because the increased cost was more than offset by the penalty saved.

If there had been a time slippage on activities on separate critical paths and the overall project time had extended to 14 weeks, a $15,000 penalty would have been in effect. Under these conditions, we would allocate the $10,000 penalty increase between the activities failing to meet their budgeted time. While the accountant must use professional judgment in making the allocation, a general guideline is that the allocation should result in both an unfavorable project time and activity time variance for the activities having a time slippage.

Decision Tree Analysis

Another method with potential as a decision-making tool is **decision tree analysis.** Decision trees provide a systematic framework for analyzing a sequence of inter-related decisions the manager may make over time. This technique expresses decision making in a sequence of acts, events, and consequences under the assumption that the projects management considers today often have strong implications for future profitability. In turn, the relationship between the investment decision that managers must make at present and the results of that decision in the future is complex. Stemming from the present investment decisions are alternative scenarios that depend on the occurrence of future events and the consequences of those events. Decision tree analysis encourages the study and understanding of these scenarios. Also, if a decision tree is on a computer spreadsheet, sensitivity analysis can show the impact on the decision of varying the cash flow estimates and the discount rate.

Advantages of Decision Tree Analysis

The decision tree can clarify for management the choices, risks, monetary gains, objectives, and information needs involved in an investment problem. In comparison with other analytical tools, a decision tree may be a more effective means of presenting the relevant information. Regardless of its size, a decision tree always combines action choices with different possible events or results of action that chance or other uncontrollable circumstances partially affect.

Managers should make today's decisions by considering not only the anticipated effect of these decisions but also the outcome uncertain events can have on future decisions and goals. Today's decisions affect tomorrow's decisions both directly and indirectly, and decision tree analysis allows management to focus on this relationship. Managers can use analytical techniques, such as discounted cash flow and present value methods, to obtain a better picture of the impact of future events and decision alternatives. Use of a decision tree permits management to consider various alternatives with greater ease and clarity. The interactions among present decision alternatives and uncertain events and their possible payoffs become clearer. Because decision trees present no new financial data, they do not show anything that management does not already know. The advantage is this concept presents data in a manner that enables systematic analysis and better decisions.

Weaknesses of Decision Tree Analysis

A decision tree does not give management the answer to an investment problem. Instead, it helps management determine which alternative yields the greatest expected monetary gain at any particular choice point, given the information and the alternatives important to the decision. A decision tree does not identify all possible events nor does it list all the decisions that must be made on a subject under analysis. The business environment does not restrict the number of possible choices to two or three. However, it is impossible to analyze all the implications of every act into the indefinite future and take them formally into account in selecting a decision strategy. We include only those decisions and events or results that are important to management and have consequences they wish to compare. With more than a small number of choices, decision tree analysis by hand becomes tedious and complicated. The use of computers is especially suitable when studying the effect of variations in figures and/or when the events involved continue for some time. The interactions of such decisions with the objectives of other parts of the business organization would be too complicated to compute manually.

Decision tree analysis treats uncertain alternatives as if they were discrete, well-defined possibilities. For example, we often assume uncertain situations depend basically on a single variable, such as the level of demand or the success or failure of a development project. While cash flow may depend solely on demand in some situations, it also may depend on several independent or partially related variables subject to such chance influences as cost, demand, yield, and economic climate.

Requirements for Decision Tree Preparation

Making a decision tree requires the following steps, which this chapter illustrates later:

1. Identification of the points of decision and the alternatives available at each point.

2. Determination of the points of uncertainty and the type or range of alternative outcomes at each point.

3. Estimates of the probabilities of different events or results of actions.

4. Estimates of the costs and gains of various events and actions.

5. Analysis of the alternative values in choosing a course of action.

Investment problems like those of Tucker Industries are appropriate for the application of the decision tree. The management of Tucker Industries must decide whether to build a small plant or a large one to manufacture a new product with a market life of 12 years. The company's managers are uncertain about the size of the market for their product. The company grew rapidly between 1983 and 1993; however, the last few years have seen only small market gains.

If the market for this new product turns out to be large, present management will be able to push the company into a new period of profitable growth. Consequently, the Research and Development Department—particularly the development project engineer—argues that building a large plant will enable the company to exploit the first major product development the department has produced in several years. However, if it builds a big plant, the company must incur increased fixed costs whatever the market demand. If demand is low in the first years, the fixed costs of operating a large plant will result in unprofitable operations. A large plant costs $4.8 million, while a small plant costs $3.2 million with expansion costing an additional $2.4 million later.

The marketing manager supports the large plant because she fears that competitors will enter the market with equivalent products if Tucker is unable to fill the demand for the new product. Further, the marketing manager is confident that the company's sales personnel will be aggressive enough to promote the product sufficiently. Ideas for an exhaustive advertising campaign are already on the drawing board.

The controller is wary of large, unneeded plant capacity. This officer favors building a small plant and expanding it in two years if demand is high during the introductory period. However, the controller recognizes that later expansion to meet high-volume demand involves a total plant cost greater than the cost of a large plant built initially. In addition, a large plant is more efficient to operate than an expanded plant.

After consultation, top management arrives at the following marketing estimates:

		Initially	*Long Term*
Initially low demand and long-term high	20%		
Initially high demand and continued high	40%		60%
Initially low demand and continued low	10%		
Initially high demand and long-term low	30%		40%

Management estimates an initial high demand of 70 percent (40 + 30); if it is high initially, there is a 57 percent (40/70) conditional probability that demand will continue at a high level. Comparing 57 percent with 40 percent, a high initial sales level increases the estimated chance of high sales in later periods. On the other hand, there is a 30 percent (20 + 10) chance that sales will be low initially; the chances are 33 percent (10/30) that initial low sales will lead to low sales in the later period, and a 67 percent (20/30) chance that initial low sales will lead to high demand after the first two years. However, if Tucker experiences an initial low demand with a small plant, management has agreed there will be no expansion. Based on these projections, management estimates a 60 percent chance of a large market in the long run and a 40 percent chance of a low demand in the long run.

The accounting staff arrives at the following estimated cash flows:

1. Small plant:
   a. With expansion after two years and continuous high demand, annual $600,000 cash flow for the first two years and annual cash flows of $1 million thereafter would result.
   b. With expansion after two years and high demand not sustained, estimated annual cash flows of $280,000 from year three onward would result.
   c. With initially high and sustained demand and no expansion, $600,000 annual cash flows would be the yield for the first two years. Competition would cause this to drop to $480,000 in the long run when other companies are attracted by the high demand.
   d. With initially high demand and low long-term demand and no expansion, $600,000 annual cash flows for the first two years and $350,000 a year thereafter.
   e. With initially low demand and high long-term demand and no expansion, $350,000 annual cash flows for the first two years increasing to $480,000 per year thereafter.
   f. With a continuous low demand, annual net cash flows of $350,000 would be the yield.
2. Large plant:
   a. With an initially low demand and long-term high demand, $200,000 cash flows each for the first two years and $1.2 million annually thereafter since this large plant is more costly to operate than the small plant for the first 2 years, but more efficient to operate for the last 10 years than would be a small, expanded plant.
   b. With continuous high demand, $1.2 million annual cash flows would be the yield.
   c. With continuous low demand, only $200,000 annual cash flows because of high fixed costs and inefficiencies.

EXHIBIT 25–4   Decision Tree with Financial Data

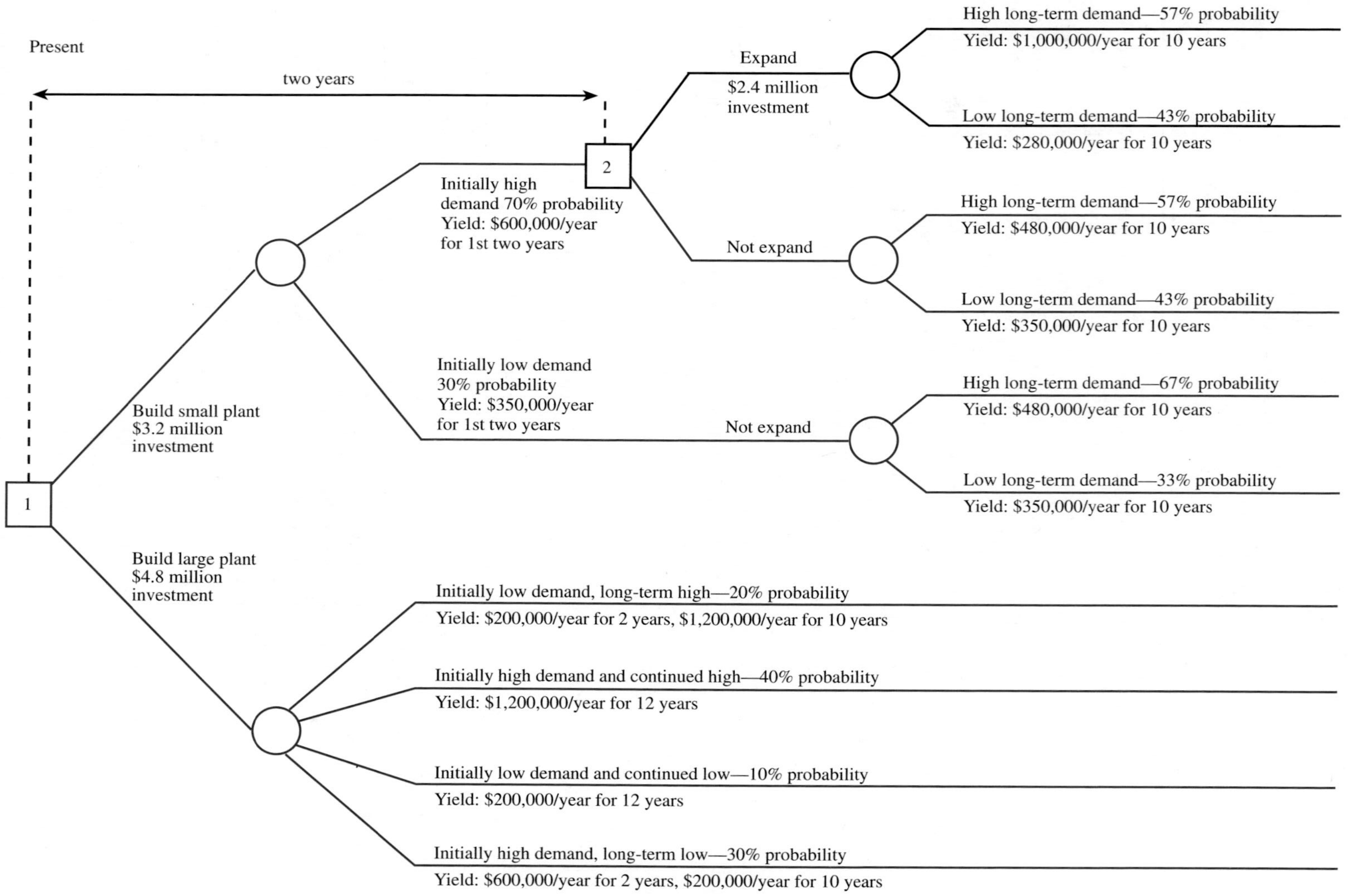

Present

two years

Build small plant
$3.2 million
investment

Build large plant
$4.8 million
investment

1

Initially high
demand 70% probability
Yield: $600,000/year
for 1st two years

Initially low demand
30% probability
Yield: $350,000/year
for 1st two years

2

Expand
$2.4 million
investment

Not expand

Not expand

High long-term demand—57% probability
Yield: $1,000,000/year for 10 years

Low long-term demand—43% probability
Yield: $280,000/year for 10 years

High long-term demand—57% probability
Yield: $480,000/year for 10 years

Low long-term demand—43% probability
Yield: $350,000/year for 10 years

High long-term demand—67% probability
Yield: $480,000/year for 10 years

Low long-term demand—33% probability
Yield: $350,000/year for 10 years

Initially low demand, long-term high—20% probability
Yield: $200,000/year for 2 years, $1,200,000/year for 10 years

Initially high demand and continued high—40% probability
Yield: $1,200,000/year for 12 years

Initially low demand and continued low—10% probability
Yield: $200,000/year for 12 years

Initially high demand, long-term low—30% probability
Yield: $600,000/year for 2 years, $200,000/year for 10 years

d. With initially high but long-term low demand, $600,000 cash flow for each of the first two years and $200,000 for each of the next years.

The decision tree in Exhibit 25–4 incorporates the preceding data. This decision tree indicates the **action** or **decision points (forks)** by square nodes and the **chance event forks** by round ones. There is no single way to diagram a decision problem: rather than using squares and circles, we could place the terms *act* and *event* above or below the appropriate fork. However, all variations of the shape of the tree rarely change the order of the acts and events from left to right. While Tucker management knew all the information in Exhibit 25–4 before preparing the decision tree, its use leads to better decisions by encouraging executives to engage in a more systematic analysis. The decision tree shows management which decision today will contribute most to its long-term goals.

Roll-Back Concept

The next step in the analysis uses the **roll-back concept**. Briefly, the roll-back method involves: (1) proceeding from right to left on each terminal point, (2) finding the total expected value at every chance event, and (3) choosing that course of action with the highest expected value. At the time of deciding whether to build a large or small plant (Decision 1), management does not involve itself with Decision 2. Also, it may not even have to make a second decision, as in initially building a large plant. Exhibit 25–5 illustrates this analysis. Using the maximum expected total cash flow as the criterion, and rolling back to Decision 2, we see that the company would expand the plant if it had the option. The total expected value of the expansion alternative is $263,000 ($4,504,000 − $4,241,000) more than the no-expansion alternative over the 10-year life remaining. (We ignore discounting future profits now and introduce them later.)

EXHIBIT 25–5   Expected Value of Decision 2

Choice	Chance Event	(1) Probability	(2) Total Yield (10 years)		(1) × (2) Expected Value
Expand	High long-term demand	.57	$10,000,000		$5,700,000
	Low long-term demand	.43	2,800,000		1,204,000
				Total	$6,904,000
				Less expansion cost	2,400,000
				Net	$4,504,000
Not expand ...	High long-term demand	.57	$4,800,000		$2,736,000
	Low long-term demand	.43	3,500,000		1,505,000
				Total	$4,241,000
				No expansion cost	–0–
				Net	$4,241,000

Even though the present issue is how to make Decision 1, we start at Decision 2 using the roll-back concept. By putting a monetary value on Decision 2, management can compare the gain from building a small plant (the upper branch) to initially building a large plant (the lower branch). The $4,504,000 net expected value from expansion with Decision 2 is its **position value.** Thus, if you repeated Decision 2 again and again, you would expect annually to get a $1 million yield 57 percent of the time and a $280,000 yield 43 percent of the time. It is worth $4,504,000 for Tucker management to get to the position where it can make Decision 2. Given this value, management can ask, what is the best action at Decision 1?

Exhibit 25–6 compiles the cash flows for Decision 1. In the top half are the yields for a small plant, including the Decision 2 position value of $4,504,000 plus a $1.2 million yield for the two years before Decision 2. In the lower half are the yields for 12 years for various events if Tucker builds a large plant. These yields are the annual cash flow from Exhibit 25–4 multiplied by the appropriate number of years. We obtain the following comparison when we reduce these yields by their probabilities:

Build small plant: ($5,704,000 × .70) + ($5,500,000 × .20) + ($4,200,000 × .10) − $3,200,000 = $2,312,800

Build large plant: ($12,400,000 × .20) + ($14,400,000 × .40) + ($2,400,000 × .10) + ($3,200,000 × .30) − $4,800,000 = $4,640,000

The choice that maximizes expected total cash yield at Decision 1 is to build the large plant initially.

Discounted Expected Value of Decisions

Because the time between successive decision stages on a decision tree may be long, we must consider the time value of future earnings. We must weight the differences in immediate cost or revenue against differences in value at the next stage. We can place the two alternatives on a Decision 2 basis if the value assigned to the next stage is discounted by an appropriate percentage. This is similar to the use of a discount rate in the present value or discounted cash flow techniques and makes allowance for the cost of capital. We discount both cash flows and position value.

Accounting for Time

Using a 12 percent discount rate applied to the cash flows from Exhibit 25–4, we can obtain Exhibit 25–7 data. When considering the time value of money, we first prepare the decision tree as in Exhibit 25–4; Exhibit 25–7 is the second step. (There is no need to prepare the analysis illustrated earlier in Exhibits 25–5 and 25–6.) We discount the cash flow for all 10 years, including the first year's cash flow. The figures in the present value column represent the present value at the time of making Decision 2, not at the time of making Decision 1. (Remember that if a large plant is built initially, there is no Decision 2.)

Exhibit 25–8 uses the same approach as previously illustrated in Exhibit 25–5; however, we now use discounted yield figures to arrive at a **discounted expected value.** Since the discounted expected value of the no-expansion alternative is higher, the $2,396,165 becomes the position value of Decision 2.

We repeat the same analytical procedure used previously for Decision 1 in Exhibit 25–9; however, now we incorporate discounting. We treat the Decision 2 position value of $2,396,165 at the time of Decision 1 as if it were a lump sum received at the end

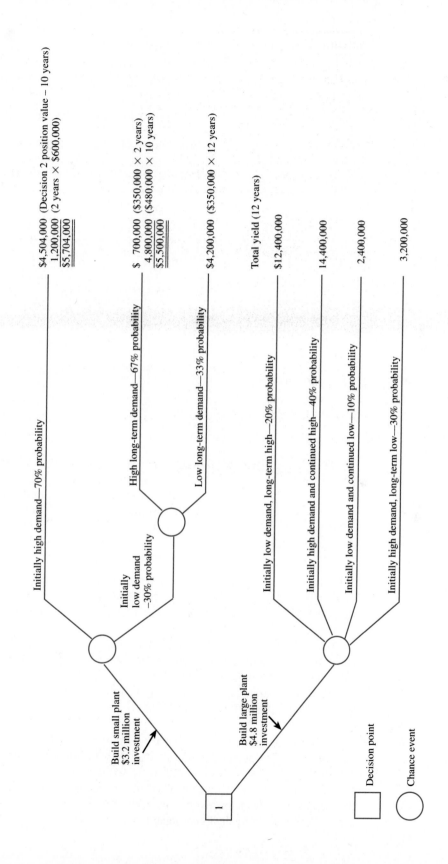

EXHIBIT 25–6   Cash Flows for Decision 1

Initially high demand—70% probability

$4,504,000 (Decision 2 position value – 10 years)
1,200,000 (2 years × $600,000)
$5,704,000

High long-term demand—67% probability

$ 700,000 ($350,000 × 2 years)
4,800,000 ($480,000 × 10 years)
$5,500,000

Low long-term demand—33% probability

$4,200,000 ($350,000 × 12 years)

Initially low demand –30% probability

Build small plant $3.2 million investment

Initially low demand, long-term high—20% probability

Total yield (12 years)

$12,400,000

Initially high demand and continued high—40% probability

14,400,000

Initially low demand and continued low—10% probability

2,400,000

Initially high demand, long-term low—30% probability

3,200,000

Build large plant $4.8 million investment

☐ Decision point

◯ Chance event

819

Exhibit 25–7   Decision 2 with Discounting

	Yield	Present Value
Expand—High demand ...	$1,000,000/year for 10 years	$5,650,000 ($1,000,000 × 5.65)
Expand—Low demand ...	280,000/year for 10 years	1,582,000 ($280,000 × 5.65)
Not expand— High demand	480,000/year for 10 years	2,712,000 ($480,000 × 5.65)
Not expand— Low demand	350,000/year for 10 years	1,977,500 ($350,000 × 5.65)

Exhibit 25–8   Discounted Expected Value of Decision 2

Choice	Chance Event	(1) Probability	(2) Present Value Yield		(1) × (2) Discounted Expected Value
Expand	High long-term demand	.57	$5,650,000		$3,220,500
	Low long-term demand	.43	1,582,000		680,260
				Total	$3,900,760
				Less expansion cost	2,400,000
				Net	$1,500,760
Not expand ...	High long-term demand	.57	$2,712,000		$1,545,840
	Low long-term demand	.43	1,977,500		850,325
				Total	$2,396,165
				No expansion cost	–0–
				Net	$2,396,165

of the two years. Note that the discount factor of .797 comes from Table A, present value of $1 for two years, at a 12 percent rate, in the Appendix to this book. Again, we assume a 12 percent discount rate with the cash flow for all years discounted, including the first year's cash flow. Using Table B in the Appendix, we discount cash flows for Years 3 through 12 to the present by a factor derived by subtracting 1.690, the factor for 12 percent, 2 years, from 6.194, the factor for 12 percent, 12 years. The large-plant alternative is again the preferred decision based on the discounted expected cash flow. The margin of difference of $405,905 ($20,000 + $385,905) is smaller than the $2,327,200 ($4,640,000 − $2,312,800) obtained without discounting.

Other Factors to Consider

We must consider the expected monetary gains along with the risks. Because managers have different viewpoints toward risk, they draw different conclusions about the various alternatives. The controller will likely see the uncertainty surrounding the decision in a much different light than will the marketing manager or the development project engineer. A major investment might also pose risk to an individual's job and career. While one individual may stand to gain much from a project's success and lose

EXHIBIT 25–9 Decision 1 Analysis

Choice	Chance Event	(1) Probability	Yield	(2) Discounted Value of Yield	(1) × (2) Discounted Expected Yield
Build small plant	Initially high demand	.70	$600,000/year, 2 years	$1,014,000 (600,000 × 1.690)	$2,046,621
			Decision 2 value: $2,396,165 at end of 2 years	1,909,744 ($2,396,165 × .797)	
				$2,923,744	
	Initially low demand high long-term	.20	$350,000/year, 2 years	$ 591,500 ($350,000 × 1.690)	550,684
			$480,000/year, 10 years	2,161,920 [$480,000 × (6.194 − 1.690)]	
				$2,753,420	
	Continuous low demand	.10	$350,000/year, 12 years	$2,167,900 ($350,000 × 6.194)	216,790
				Total	$2,814,095
				Less investment	3,200,000
				Net	$ (385,905)
Build large plant	Initially low demand high long-term	.20	$200,000/year, 2 years	$ 338,000 ($200,000 × 1.690)	$1,148,560
			$1,200,000/year, 10 years	5,404,800 [$1,200,000 × (6.194 − 1.690)]	
				$5,742,800	
	Continuous high demand	.40	$1,200,000/year 12 years	$7,432,800 ($1,200,000 × 6.194)	2,973,120
	Continuous low demand	.10	$200,000/year, 12 years	$1,238,800 ($200,000 × 6.194)	123,880
	Initially high demand, low long-term	.30	$600,000/year, 2 years	$1,014,000 ($600,000 ×1.690)	574,440
			$200,000/year, 10 years	900,800 [($200,000 × (6.194 − 1.690)]	
				$1,914,800	
				Total	$4,820,000
				Less investment	4,800,000
				Net	$ 20,000

little from its failure, others in the company may be risking much if a project fails. The types of risks and how individuals regard them from a personal viewpoint affect not only the assumptions they make but also the strategy they follow in handling risks.

Top management should jointly consider the political environment when selecting plant size. They should ask what risks and prospects are at stake. Is it a possible bankruptcy or an opportunity for large profit increases and job stability? Is it a major career opportunity? The individuals who bear the risks—whether employees, stockholders, managers, or the community—and the numbers affected, assume significance. In addition, the character of the risk that each person bears merits evaluation. How disastrous would a failure be to individuals as well as to the company and the community's economy? Whether the risk is once in a lifetime, insurable, or unique is important. The decision tree does not eliminate these risks; however, it shows management which decision makes the largest contribution to long-term goals.

Summary

Chapter 25 presents several techniques and analyses that prove helpful in planning complex projects and in investment analysis. A Gantt chart is a simple control technique that compares scheduled and actual production. However, Gantt charts are inadequate for sophisticated projects requiring an understanding of what tasks to complete before beginning others. Network models, such as PERT, show interrelationships among activities. Use of a PERT network determines a project's critical path so managers can prevent delaying overall completion time. Paths that are not critical have slack and thus provide some flexibility for managers. Slack time also serves as a guide in rescheduling tasks to shorten the project's overall completion time. Managers use PERT-Cost analysis in deciding whether crashing the project is economically feasible.

Decision tree analysis clarifies choices and risks and the related profits of long-term investment alternatives. Because decision trees present financial data in a systematic manner, the relationships and consequences of present decision alternatives and uncertain events and their possible payoffs become clearer. Certainly, decision tree analysis does not provide the single, accurate solution to an investment decision. Instead, the objective is to assist managers in assessing which alternative at any particular choice point yields the greatest expected monetary gain given the information available and alternatives to the decision. In using decision tree analysis, we recognize that we must consider the expected monetary gains along with the risks. Further, we realize that members of the management team view these risks differently. Unless we recognize these differences initially, those who must assist in making the decision by supplying data and analyses, and those who are operating the plant and promoting the product will view the decision in conflicting ways. The criteria for success may be vastly different.

Important Terms and Concepts

Gantt charts   803
PERT (Program Evaluation Review
  Technique)   805
Critical path method (CPM)   805
PERT-Time analysis   805
Event   805
Activities   805
Expected activity time *(ex_t)*   806
Critical path   806
Slack time   806
Earliest completion time *(T_E)*   806
Latest completion time *(T_L)*   807

Crashing   807
PERT-Cost analysis   807
Spending variance   811
Activity time variance   811
Project time variance   812
Decision tree analysis   813
Action or decision points   817
Chance event forks   817
Roll-back concept   817
Position value   818
Discounted expected value   818

Problem for Self-Study

PERT Network and Critical Path

In building a PERT-Time network, management of Medlock, Inc., listed the events necessary to finish a project. They next arrived at the following activities leading to these events:

Activity	Time Estimates in Weeks		
	Optimistic	*Most Likely*	*Pessimistic*
0–1	2.0	2.5	3.0
1–2	1.0	2.0	3.0
1–3	1.5	2.0	2.5
1–4	0.6	2.0	4.0
2–5	0.6	3.5	7.0
3–6	2.0	2.8	6.0
4–7	0.8	1.9	2.4
5–7	1.0	4.5	5.0
6–7	0.6	0.9	1.8

Required:

a. Construct the PERT network.
b. Determine the expected completion times for all activities and place on network.
c. Determine the critical path.

Solution to Problem for Self-Study

a. *MEDLOCK, INC.*

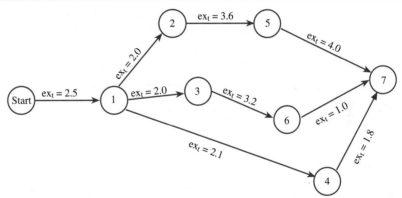

Activity	Optimistic	Most Likely	Pessimistic	Expected Time
0–1	2.0	2.5	3.0	2.5
1–2	1.0	2.0	3.0	2.0
1–3	1.5	2.0	2.5	2.0
1–4	0.6	2.0	4.0	2.1
2–5	0.6	3.5	7.0	3.6
3–6	2.0	2.8	6.0	3.2
4–7	0.8	1.9	2.4	1.8
5–7	1.0	4.5	5.0	4.0
6–7	0.6	0.9	1.8	1.0

Paths	Cumulative Expected Time in Weeks
0 – 1 – 2 – 5 – 7	2.5 + 2.0 + 3.6 + 4.0 = 12.1*
0 – 1 – 3 – 6 – 7	2.5 + 2.0 + 3.2 + 1.0 = 8.7
0 – 1 – 4 – 7	2.5 + 2.1 + 1.8 = 6.4

c.

*Critical Path

Review Questions

1. Outline the characteristics of (*a*) Gantt chart techniques and (*b*) PERT.
2. Give the requirements for making a decision tree.
3. *a.* Why should the time value of future earnings be considered in decisions?
   b. How can the time value of future earnings be used in decision tree analysis?
4. What is meant by crashing the network and what is the differential crash cost of an activity?
5. What is the advantage of holding an activity manager responsible for a project time variance?
6. What is slack and how can management utilize it?
7. If an activity has a favorable spending variance, what does this indicate?
8. Define the roll-back concept; discuss how it is used in decision tree analysis.
9. Should management analyze time slippage on all activities?
10. Define the term *critical path* and explain why it is considered critical.
11. What is the expected activity time for each of the following, given these estimates?

	Optimistic	Most Likely	Pessimistic
Activity 1–2	9	1	19
Activity 2–3	6	9	12

Exercises

E25–1 Analyzing Progress on PERT-Cost Network
Van, Inc.'s engineering and accounting staff has prepared the following PERT-Cost network with expected time (ex_t) noted for all activities. Also indicated on the network is the actual time (ac_t) for the three activities already completed. The budgeted (Bud) cost for each activity and the actual (Act) cost incurred is indicated for the completed activities. Actual time and cost incurred also are shown for activities 2–6 and 3–5 that are partially completed.

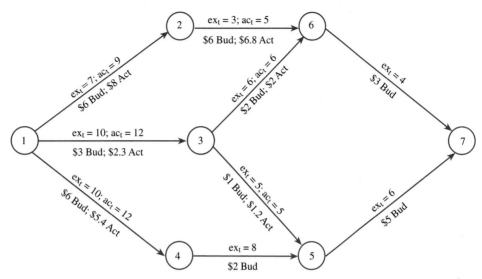

Time expressed in weeks, and dollars in millions.

Required:

a. Determine the critical path before operations began; indicate the time for all paths.
b. Compute the budgeted cost of completing the project.
c. Indicate which activities need management's immediate attention and why this attention is needed.
d. Determine the amount of any overall cost overrun.

E25–2 Computing Expected Time for Activities on a PERT Network

Milan, Inc., management estimated the following days required for various activities while constructing a large building:

Activities	Optimistic	Most Likely	Pessimistic
0–1	9	11	19
1–2	6	9	12
1–3	2	3	4
3–4	3	7	11
2–5	1	2	9
5–6	3	4	11
4–6	1	5	15

Required:

a. Determine the expected time for each activity.
b. Draw a PERT-Time network for the listed activities showing the earliest time (T_E) and the latest time (T_L) for each event.
c. Identify the paths indicating the critical one(s).

E25–3 PERT-Time Chart and Critical Path

Burns Company management regularly employs the Program Evaluation and Review Technique (PERT) in planning and coordinating its construction projects. The firm developed the following schedule of separable activities and their expected completion times for a ship it plans to construct.

Activity Description	Expected Activity Completion Time in Weeks
1–2	4
1–6	17
1–3	12
1–7	13
2–5	15
2–3	3
3–4	4
4–9	2
5–9	8
7–8	6
8–9	5
6–9	9

Required:

a. Draw a PERT-Time chart.
b. Identify the critical path for this project and determine the expected project completion time in weeks.
c. Discuss briefly how the expected activity completion times are derived in the PERT method and what the derived value for the expected activity completion times means in the PERT method.

E25–4 Critical Path and Slack

Washington Company has contracted with a local business group to construct a large addition to a building. To help the managers organize and control this project, the accountant developed the following PERT-Time network. The expected time of each activity (ex_t) is expressed in weeks.

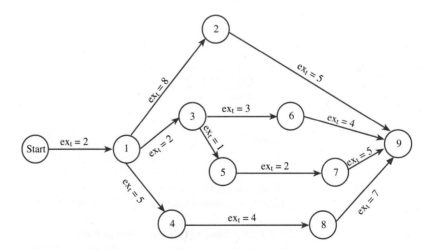

Required:

a. Determine the critical path.
b. Discuss the slack at each event.

E25–5 Developing PERT Network with T_E and T_L

Cabincraft, Inc., management is making plans for a complex missile and has estimated the activities needed. The expected completion time for each activity follows:

Activity	Estimated Completion Time in Weeks
0–1	2
1–2	4
1–3	3
1–4	7
2–5	6
3–5	8
4–6	2
5–6	3
6–7	4
6–8	5
7–8	5

Required:

a. Develop a PERT network for these activities indicating the earliest completion time and the latest completion time.
b. Identify the critical path(s).

E25–6 Critical path, T_E and T_L

The accountants for Trent, Inc., along with the assistance of production management, have prepared the following PERT-Time network system. Time is expressed in weeks.

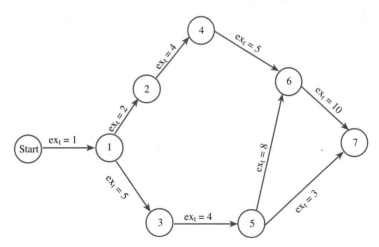

Required:

a. List the various paths in the PERT network.
b. Identify which path is the critical path.
c. Determine the earliest time (T_E) and the latest time (T_L) for each event.
d. Determine the difference between the T_E and T_L for the entire project and indicate what it represents.
e. Indicate if any of the paths have a lag before an event.

E25–7 Crashing from a Prepared PERT-Cost Network

McMickle, Inc. hired engineers to work closely with its management accountants in preparing PERT-Cost analyses. From their experience, they determined the following activities should be displayed on the PERT network for construction of a machine. Along with each activity is its estimated normal time (ex_t), the crash time for each activity (cr_t), and the related additional cost required to meet the crash time expressed per week. The normal cost is $10,000.

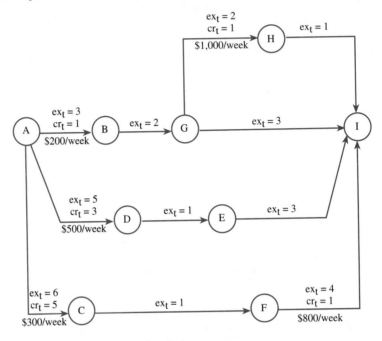

Required:

a. Identify all paths and the time involved on each path; determine the critical path.

b. Determine the minimum time in which the machine could be installed, and the costs incurred to achieve this earlier installation.

E25–8 Gantt Charts and Flexible Manufacturing

Steam Boat, Inc., just received four separate orders to produce electric motors. Each motor must go through Department 1 and Department 2 in sequence. Due to different specifications, the production floor of Steam Boat, Inc., needs one day to adjust its machines in both departments before a new order can be started. Supervisors of the company estimate the time required for each order as the following:

	Order			
	1	*2*	*3*	*4*
Department 1 (days)	7	6	9	4
Department 2 (days)	4	5	7	6

There is no backlog in the departments and a new order can be started immediately. To finish the job as soon as possible, the supervisors decide to start the order with the least production time in Department 1. Then, they start with the order having the second least time and so on. However, they schedule the last order with the least amount of time in Department 2.

Required:

a. Develop a Gantt chart for the four orders.

b. Determine how long it will take to complete work on all four orders.

c. Discuss why the supervisors decide to start the order with the least production time in Department 1.

d. Describe the support you have for arguing that Steam Boat does or does not have a flexible manufacturing system.

E25–9 Critical Path and Slack Time

Rim Company's management provides the following activities and their related expected completion times in building a complex missile:

Activity	Expected Completion Time in Months
0–1	2
1–2	3
1–3	4
1–4	4
2–3	2
3–5	3
4–6	9
5–6	1

Required:

a. Develop a PERT network for the listed activities.

b. Identify the critical path.

c. Indicate on the PERT network the earliest completion time and the latest completion time.

d. Determine how many days Rim can delay Event 4 and Event 5 without extending the time of the overall project.

Problems

P25–10 Network Preparation and Crash Time

Recently MTT, Inc. received an order to produce a piece of computerized electronic equipment. Anxious to acquire the equipment early, the buyer promised $1,200 a day for delivery sooner than the normal time. The cost accountant suggested applying network analysis to the construction and prepared the following schedule for use in this analysis:

Activity	Expected Normal Time in Days	Crash Time in Days	Total Cost for Normal Conditions	Total Cost for Crash Conditions
0–1	3	NC	$1,000	NC
1–2	6	3	3,000	$4,500
1–3	5	2	4,000	5,800
2–4	4	2	7,000	9,000
3–4	3	NC	2,000	NC

NC = No change in time or cost is possible.

Required:

a. Prepare a network for PERT-Cost, showing the expected time and the crash time.
b. Calculate the normal costs to be incurred in constructing the equipment.
c. Determine the critical path under normal conditions.
d. Compute the minimum time in which the equipment could be constructed and the costs to achieve this earlier delivery.
e. Indicate the number of days you advise MTT Inc. to crash; support your advice with financial data.

P25–11 PERT Network and Completion Time

The management of Cannon, Inc., gives the following time estimates for activities required in the construction of a major project:

Activities	Expected Completion Time in Days
0–1	12
1–2	18
1–3	28
1–6	26
2–5	10
3–4	7
4–7	15
5–8	14
6–7	9
7–8	3

Required:

a. Develop a PERT network for the listed activities.
b. Identify the critical path.
c. Indicate on the PERT network the earliest completion time and the latest completion time.

P25–12 PERT-Cost Analysis (continuation of P25–11)

Management of Cannon, Inc., estimates that the project mentioned in P25–11 has a normal cost of $200,000, but some activities can be crashed. Following are the crash times in days and the related total differential cost to achieve the crash program:

Activities	Crash Time	Total Differential Cost
0–1	NC	—
1–2	12	$16,200
1–3	15	11,700
1–6	20	9,000
2–5	8	6,000
3–4	NC	—
4–7	14	1,400
5–8	11	1,800
6–7	5	7,200
7–8	NC	—

NC = No change in time or cost is possible.

Required:

a. Prepare a PERT network (or insert in the network prepared in P25–11) showing the expected and crash times and the differential cost per day.

b. Indicate the minimum time in which the project could be completed and the costs incurred to achieve this earlier opening.

c. Compute the minimum additional contribution to profits needed to justify completing the project early.

P25–13 PERT—Cost with Variance Analysis

Whitney Corporation is about to undertake an important new project. Managers have identified the relevant activities and the expected time associated with each. They also have estimated the cost if an activity exceeds its normal time as well as the feasibility of crashing an activity. Results of this analysis show:

Activity	Expected Time in Weeks	Crash Time in Weeks	Normal Cost	Differential Cost to Shorten Each Week	Additional Cost of Extending Completion by One Week
1–2	6	0	$700	—	$150
1–3	10	6	425	$250	140
1–4	12	9	600	250	200
2–6	4	2	375	100	50
3–6	2	0	300	—	—
4–5	4	2	350	400	240
4–7	16	13	800	90	—
5–6	2	0	100	—	90
6–7	6	0	450	—	125

A $5,000 penalty is levied on Whitney by the buyer if workers complete the project in 30 weeks; a $3,000 penalty if within 28 weeks; a $2,600 penalty if within 25 weeks; a $2,000 penalty within 22 weeks; and no penalty if completion is within 20 weeks. Project costs are assumed to occur evenly over time.

Required:

a. Prepare a PERT network analysis showing the expected and crash times and the differential cost per week.

b. Determine the critical path.

c. Show calculations to support your decision about how much time the project should be crashed to save all or part of the penalty.

d. Assume management planned to crash Activity 4–7 three weeks but during construction found this could not be accomplished, and the time slippage could not be made up on other activities on this path. If completion of Activity 4–7 occurs in 16 weeks at a cost of $900, what are its variances?

e. Assume Activity 1–2 is completed in nine weeks at a cost of $900. What are its variances?

P25–14 Decision Tree Using Discounted Expected Yield

After two years of study, Kingsberry Company's engineering staff presented a proposal for an expanded installation of their computer-based control system. The present system has been in operation for four years and cash savings are being achieved. The expected cost of the new system is $1.2 million. A reduction in labor costs and less material waste are the claimed advantages. The equipment needed for the expansion can be purchased and installed quickly because the supplier is anxious to further test the system in an actual application. The supplier's bid of $1.2 million represents a reduced price for this on-site testing; the price will be $1.4 million in one year. Possible technical malfunctions, as well as uncertain product demand, have convinced several Kingsberry vice presidents that additional engineering studies should be conducted. The vice president of production suggests that action be postponed until the Tire Industry Association completes both its one-year study of the technical capacities of the system and a forecast of market demand; cost of this survey to Kingsberry will be $25,000. The marketing vice president argues that more reliance could be placed on analysis conducted by an independent research team than on that from industry studies; the cost of an independent research team's analysis will be $40,000. However, all vice presidents agree that cost studies and probabilities of various events should be carefully estimated since the investment is substantial. They also agree that one of the three alternatives must be chosen. After many hours of study, they produced the following data:

	Probability
Postpone expansion and use industry studies:	
Weak initial market, negative technical studies	30%
Strong initial market, positive technical studies . . . . . , ...	70
Postpone expansion and hire independent research team:	
Weak initial market, negative technical studies	35%
Strong initial market, positive technical studies	65

If the expansion is made in year 1, there is a 55 percent chance of an initial weak market and many technical problems and a 45 percent chance of an initial strong market and limited technical malfunctions. Using either the industry study or the independent research study, it will be one year before the results can be examined and the machine installed. The system's impact is expected to extend eight years from the present, regardless of the date of installation. Probabilities for long-term market demand for the three different alternatives follow:

Market Based on Industry Study or for Immediate Expansion	*Percent*
Weak long term after a weak initial	70%
Strong long term after a weak initial	30
Weak long term after strong initial	20
Strong long term after strong initial	80
Market Based on Independent Study	
Weak long term after a weak initial	60%
Strong long term after weak initial	40
Weak long term after strong initial	25
Strong long term after strong initial	75

The annual cash savings for the weak and strong markets by years is as follows:

| Market | Year 1 | | Years 2–8 | |
	Without Expansion	With Expansion	Without Expansion	With Expansion
Weak	$40,000	$200,000	$ 50,000	$240,000
Strong	75,000	450,000	100,000	580,000

Required:

a. Using a 10 percent discount rate for the cash flow, prepare a decision tree; discount the cash flow for all years.
b. Indicate the course of action you would advise.

P25–15 PERT-Cost with Variance Analysis and Crashing Limitations

In planning for the construction of a project, Houston, Inc., estimates the cost if an activity exceeds its normal time as well as the feasibility of crashing an activity. The following results of this study indicate that some activities cannot be crashed while other activities must be crashed in their entirety rather than partially.

Activity	Expected Time in Weeks	Crash Time in Weeks	Normal Cost	Differential Cost to Shorten Each Week	Additional Cost of Extending Completion by One Week
A–B	7	2*	$4,000	$500	$400
A–C	6	1	900	100	150
A–D	3	1	1,800	400	100
B–E	8	—	1,000	?	200
C–E	4	3*	750	800	100
D–G	4	1	600	200	300
E–F	2	—	400	—	500
F–H	6	—	500	—	300
G–H	4	3	200	50	80

*Cannot be partially crashed.

Management agrees to pay the buyer a $4,000 penalty if the project is completed in 23 weeks; a $2,000 penalty if within 20 weeks; and no penalty if completion occurs within 16 weeks. Project costs are assumed to occur evenly over time.

Required:

a. Prepare a PERT network analysis showing the expected and crash times and the differential cost per week.
b. Determine the critical path.
c. Show calculations to support your decision about how much time the project should be crashed to save all or part of the penalty.
d. Assume that Activity A–D requires six weeks at a cost of $2,600. Determine the variances.

P25–16 Short-Run Decision Tree Analysis

Last week, Kent Miller, president of Miller Chemicals, Inc., signed a contract with Everett Manufacturing Company to produce 200,000 gallons of HHX, an industrial lubricant, at a fixed price of $10. Delivery of the first 20,000 gallons is scheduled for 90 days with the remainder to be delivered in 15,000-gallon batches each month thereafter.

Although Miller believes that his company can meet the product specifications, he is concerned about available production capacity. Construction of a research laboratory has just been completed, and it is possible that HHX could be processed in this facility. Miller knows that the research director is anxious to experiment with a new mixing process, and this would give her that opportunity. The research director's initial tests show that the new mixing process can cut costs by 10 to 15 percent, to $5.50 per gallon; however, she has tried neither to process such a large quantity nor to process it under the time constraints of the Everett contract. If numerous failures occur, the cost would increase to as much as $8.80 per gallon. Management estimates the following: a 20 percent probability that the mixing process will require no rework, resulting in a cost of $5.50 per gallon; a 40 percent probability of limited rework, resulting in a $7.10 cost per gallon; a 30 percent probability of additional rework, resulting in an $8 per gallon cost; and finally, a 10 percent probability of many failures resulting in an $8.80 cost per gallon.

With proper planning, 200,000 gallons of HHX could be produced in the company's regular production operations. This would require additional labor shifts, but no undue problems are anticipated. The regular process cost is estimated to be $7 per gallon, but the company's labor union is negotiating for a wage increase that would result in a $0.25 increase in cost per gallon. There is a 30 percent chance that the labor union will receive its requested raise. However, if regular production facilities are used, it may delay production on some existing orders. Also, the company had planned to introduce a new product line with additional labor shifts using existing facilities. If, instead, HHX is produced with these facilities, the introduction of the new product will be delayed. The impact that this delay will have on demand has not been determined.

With these thoughts in mind, Miller contacted a local real estate agency concerning leasing a building next door. Machinery to process HHX also could be leased. Preliminary cost studies reveal that the cost will be $8.60 with a probability of 60 percent, $8.50 with a probability of 30 percent, and $8.30 with a probability of 10 percent.

Chemical companies were contacted to determine the availability of manufacturing capacity; only one of these companies was interested. Douglass Company indicated that they were presently experimenting with a new process with a success rate, under testing conditions, of 40 percent. If success were achieved, their bid would be $5.80 per gallon. However, if they are not able to use this new process in the production of HHX, they must resort to a more elaborate process involving less automated techniques. If the new process fails and a more elaborate process is used, management is willing to submit only maximum and minimum prices of $7.40 and $5.90 per gallon, respectively, with equal chances that this will be the bid. Douglass Company has a good reputation, so quality is not an issue.

In talking with Carr Chemicals' management last week, Miller learned from Carr's president that they had experienced an unforeseen drop in customers' orders but were anxious to keep their present labor force employed by securing short-term orders until they could shift production from lubricants to other chemicals. In view of his pressing capacity problem, Miller asked whether they were willing to engage in subcontracting work. After much discussion, Carr management proposed purchasing the Everett Manufacturing Company contract from Miller for $600,000 and assuming all liabilities. Miller is not concerned about Carr's quality; however, he does have some reservations concerning the impact that a transfer would have on future business with Everett.

Required:

a. Discuss the advantages of a decision tree.

b. List the requirements for making a decision tree.

c. Draw a decision tree incorporating the financial data given.

d. Describe the course of action you would advise management to take. Support your answer.

P25–17 Adjusting Cash Flow for Time Value of Money

Spece, Inc., presently sells a line of hand tools. Production has been fairly even over the last several years with competition increasing. Many of Spece's competitors have expanded their line of tools, but Spece has continued with its present style and variety.

However, management is worrying that it may need to upgrade its product line, either now or in three years. At the end of three years, if no upgrading is performed presently, management must again face this decision. The cost of upgrading the product line is forecasted to be $15,000 regardless of when it occurs.

A team of marketing experts analyzed short-run and long-run market conditions and worked with the accountants to arrive at expected cash yields for the next eight years. After much study, the team initially believed there were two alternatives:

1. Do not upgrade the product line now: There is a 20 percent probability for an initial successful market environment for the next three years; the annual cash flow for the next three years under these circumstances would be $4,000. If, however, conditions are not favorable, an unsuccessful market will yield an annual cash flow for the next eight years of $2,000, since if the initial market environment is unsuccessful, they will not upgrade their product line.

   If the initial market is successful, management can either:
   a. Upgrade the product line. There is a 40 percent probability of a successful market with cash flows of $10,000 annually for five years. If the market is unsuccessful, they expect annual cash flows to be $2,000 for the five years.
   b. Not upgrade the product line: There is a 30 percent probability of a successful market with cash flows of $6,000 annually for five years. If instead, an unsuccessful market exists, annual cash flow is predicted to be $1,000 for the five years.

2. Upgrade the product line now: If the market is successful, both in the short run and long run (a 40 percent probability), a $14,000 annual cash flow for the eight years under study is expected. With an unsuccessful market, $3,000 is the forecasted annual cash flow for the eight years.

Required:

a. Draw a decision tree; adjust the cash flows for the time value of money using a discount rate of 10 percent.
b. Indicate the course of action you would advise.

P25–18 Weaknesses of Decision Tree: Adjusting Cash Flow for Time Value of Money

As a consultant for Yale Company, you are assisting it to decide the optimal size of plant facilities expansion. In talking with you, members of top management, who are all in their 50s and 60s, are quick to emphasize that they want some conventional decision tools used to answer this investment problem rather than some cutesy, way-out approach, such as decision tree analysis. Later, in talking with younger management personnel on lower levels, you begin to understand the significance of top management's remark regarding decision tree analysis. These younger managers had recently used it as a scientific tool to support their main argument for another problem, only to be strongly rebuffed by top management.

Yale has recently developed a new product with an expected life of 10 years. Present manufacturing facilities are inadequate to produce the product, so Yale must decide how much to expand the present plant. Market research believes it has reliable tests indicating that the domestic market alone is sufficient to require a 20,000-square-foot expansion. Data concerning an export market are less accurate; however, marketing personnel believe that if demand is high in the export market, a 40,000-square-foot expansion is warranted. Management is faced with the immediate decision of whether to expand by 20,000 square feet now with a possible later 20,000-square-foot expansion, or to expand 40,000 square feet initially. Management is in agreement that there is not enough space available in the present site to exceed a total 40,000-square-foot expansion.

Bids from local contractors have averaged $75 per square foot; however, if a second expansion of 20,000 square feet is undertaken, the price is expected to be $120 per square foot for this additional space. This price is estimated to reflect inflation as well as additional costs due to remodeling the first expansion. If the smaller expansion is undertaken, it will be four years before a second expansion is made, if at all.

Market research studies indicate there is a 60 percent chance that the initial demand will be high. Management agrees that if the initial demand is low, there is complete assurance that the long-term demand will also be low, and they will not expand. It believes there is a 50 percent chance that if initial demand is high it will continue, while only a 10 percent chance that a low long-term demand will follow a high-demand initial market. The projections of net annual cash flow follow.

You are convinced that decision tree analysis is appropriate and believe that you can demonstrate this to top management.

Years 1–4	Demand Level	Annual Cash Flow
1. Small expansion	High	$300,000
2. Small expansion	Low	200,000
3. Large expansion	High	700,000
4. Large expansion	Low	100,000
Years 5–10		
1. Small expansion with later additional expansion	High	600,000
2. Small expansion with later additional expansion	Low	200,000
3. Small expansion, no further expansion	High	400,000
4. Small expansion, no further expansion	Low	250,000
5. Large initial expansion	High	700,000
6. Large initial expansion	Low	100,000

Required:

a. Discuss potential reasons for top management's resistance to decision tree analysis.
b. Give the weaknesses or limitations of decision tree analysis.
c. Draw a decision tree; adjust the cash flow for the time value of money using a discount rate of 14 percent. Discount the cash flow for all years.
d. Indicate the course of action you would advise.
e. Discuss other factors that could affect your decision.

P25–19 Payoff Table and Decision Tree Analysis (CMA)

Steven Company has been producing component parts and assemblies for use in the manufacture of microcomputers and microcomputer peripheral equipment for 10 years. The company plans to introduce a magnetic tape cartridge back-up unit for IBM-compatible microcomputers in the near future.

Steven's Research and Development (R&D) and Market Research Departments have been working on this project for an extended period and the combined development costs incurred to date amount to $1.5 million. R&D designed several alternative back-up units. Three of the designs were approved for development into prototypes; from these only one will be manufactured and sold. Market Research has determined that the appropriate selling price would be $400 per unit, regardless of the model selected.

The estimated demand schedule for three different market situations follows. These three demand levels are the only ones the company considers feasible, and other demand levels are not expected to occur. Steven can meet all demand levels because its plant currently is below full capacity.

	Unit Sales	Probability of Occurrence
Light demand	20,000	25%
Moderate demand	80,000	60
Heavy demand	120,000	15

Steven's accounting and engineering staffs have worked together to develop manufacturing cost estimates for each of the three model designs. Costs for the three models follow. Manufacturing overhead, 40 percent of which is variable, is applied to Steven's products using a plantwide application rate of 250 percent of direct labor-dollars.

	Model A	Model B	Model C
Unit costs:			
Direct materials	$150	$100	$114
Direct labor	40	50	48
Manufacturing overhead	100	125	120
Total unit costs	$290	$275	$282
Other costs:			
Tooling and advertising	$3,000,000	$4,500,000	$4,100,000
Incurred development costs	1,500,000	1,500,000	1,500,000

Steven has decided to employ an expected value model in its analysis to reach a decision as to which of the three prototypes it will manufacture and sell.

Required:

a. Develop a payoff table to determine the expected monetary value for each of the three models Steven Company could manufacture. Based on your analysis, identify the prototype model Steven should manufacture and sell.

b. Assume Steven Company's costs for a back-up unit design that was not developed into a prototype were estimated as follows:

Unit costs:	
Direct materials	$130
Direct labor	46
Manufacturing overhead	115
Total unit costs	$291
Other costs:	
Tooling and advertising	$4,000,000
Incurred development costs	1,500,000

If this design had been developed by Steven into a viable model, it would have sold for $400 and had the same expected demand as the other models. Steven's management eliminated this model from consideration because it was considered an inadmissible act (i.e., the calculation of its payoff would have been irrelevant). Explain why the model design was considered an inadmissible act, thus making the calculation of its payoff irrelevant.

c. Explain how Steven Company could have employed a decision tree model in this situation. (No calculations are required.)

Case

C25–20 Behavioral Impact of PERT Diagrams

Chicago, Inc., has recently been awarded a bid for a complex machine. Prior to submitting the bid, the vice president of research and the vice president of engineering prepared a PERT chart showing the network of activities required to complete the tasks. They also estimated the crash time and costs involved with each activity. The construction is quite detailed involving the coordination of three different production departments. In addition, Chicago, Inc., has never manufactured a machine similar to this so that the two vice presidents had to use their best judgment in arriving at the times required for each task.

In accepting the bid the buyer indicated that the machine must be completed within the crash time. In fact, in talking with the company president, the buyer offered to pay $1,000 a day for any days that the machine was completed in advance of the crash time. The company president promised the buyer that he would check into this matter.

After formal receipt of the bid, the three production managers whose departments will be involved in the construction were called together for a meeting. The two vice presidents responsible for preparing the PERT chart and bids presented the data. The Machining Department manager began asking specific questions as to the type of molds and materials that will be needed. The research vice president tried unsuccessfully to convey to her the specific grade of material included in the bid. The Finishing Department manager was equally concerned about the time allotted for the molds and paint to dry. In the midst of this confusion, the Pattern Department manager realized that only two weeks were estimated for the design of the machine. He was especially worried that the skill level of personnel presently employed will be inadequate for this duty. Finally after trying to communicate his concern to the vice presidents he remarked, "I wish I had known about this machine construction three weeks ago because I would have given Karen Jones the raise she wanted; then I would have had a better chance of retaining her. She has since resigned to work as a draft person for a competitor."

The two vice presidents become perplexed as well as annoyed with all the questions and worries expressed. In concluding the meeting, the vice presidents warn the department managers that they must "live with the PERT-Cost chart" and that all their necks are on the line. They further informed the Production Department managers that the president was expected to put pressure on all of them to finish before the crash time because of the $1,000-a-day offer for early completion.

Required:

a. Identify what has caused the confusion and concern expressed by the department managers.
b. Explain why you do or do not expect the machine to be completed by the crash time.

CHAPTER 26

Linear Programming and the Cost Accountant

Chapter Objectives

After studying this chapter, you should be able to:

1. Apply linear programming techniques to cost accounting issues either through computer usage or manually.
2. Interpret linear programming solutions.
3. Use linear programming to maximize profits with specific constraints.
4. Explain model formulation in linear programming to minimize cost.

Introduction

As the problems of management become more complex, it becomes urgent to have more accurate information. For accountants to satisfy this need, they must have expertise in the use of quantitative tools. One of the major benefits of using such tools is the low expense involved in calculating the impact of change on a proposed course of action. One of the best-known operations research models used in the business environment is linear programming.

Linear Programming Defined

Linear programming is a mathematical approach to maximizing profits or minimizing costs by finding a feasible combination of available resources that accomplishes either objective. Linear programming recognizes that resources not only are limited but also have alternative uses. Linear programming is a powerful planning tool, but it is complex and usually requires a computer to derive solutions.

We can apply linear programming to the following business-related problems:

1. Allocating resources (e.g., assigning jobs to machines) to maximize profits.
2. Selecting product ingredients (e.g., blending chemical products) to minimize costs.
3. Assigning personnel, machines, and other business components (e.g., scheduling flight crews).
4. Scheduling output to balance demand, production, and inventory levels.
5. Determining transportation routes to minimize distribution cost.

Accountants should possess basic knowledge of linear programming; that is, they should recognize problems they can analyze using linear programming. The ideal situation is for the accountant to understand the mathematics involved and be able to communicate with operations researchers and mathematicians. In this chapter, however, we take the position that the accountant should focus on drafting and formulating the models and then analyzing the solution obtained. This approach leaves the technical details to the operations researchers. If you desire a solid understanding of linear programming, consult books on quantitative models.

Effects of Constraints

The focus in linear programming is on scarce resources. Managers face few challenges in decision making if there are unlimited resources; selecting a course of action to achieve a specific objective in this situation is relatively easy. Unfortunately, most managers make few decisions involving unlimited resources because production and marketing constraints affect their choice of action.

Constraints Absent   Assume, for example, that a company has unlimited resources and its aim is to maximize profits. Its manufacturing facilities can produce either of two products, A or B. Assume further that the entire output of either product can be sold, and the contribution margin per machine-hour is as follows:

	Product	
	A	*B*
Unit sales price	$10.00	$ 4.50
Unit variable cost	8.00	3.00
Unit contribution margin	$ 2.00	$ 1.50
Machine-hours required per unit	1	4
Contribution margin per machine-hour	$ 2.00	$0.375

Since the company can sell all it manufactures, the obvious decision is to use all available capacity in manufacturing Product A, because it has the higher contribution per hour of capacity.

Constraints Present   Unfortunately, most business problems are not this simple. Assume, instead, that the manufacturer has a total of 1,000 machine-hours available per period (a production constraint) and that it can sell only 600 units of Product A and 500 units of Product B (a marketing constraint). In this simple situation with few constraints, the decision is to produce as many units of the more profitable Product A as the company can sell. The company uses the remaining machine time to produce Product B. The maximum contribution to fixed costs and income is $1,350 by producing 600 units of Product A and 100 units of Product B to fully utilize the 1,000 machine-hours.

Product A—600 units @ $2 contribution margin per unit	$1,200
Product B—100 units @ $1.50 contribution margin per unit	150
Maximum contribution margin	$1,350

Since we assume fixed costs to be the same whether we manufacture Product A or B, fixed costs are irrelevant and ignored in the calculation. In addition, even though Product A's $2 unit contribution margin is higher than Product B's $1.50 contribution margin, the contribution margin per hour is important. This results because the limit of 1,000 machine-hours is a scarce resource.

Linear Programming Terms

The previous example introduced production and marketing constraints. However, this simple data does not require linear programming analysis. In many situations, we cannot obtain the solution so readily and need linear programming to find the optimal combination of resources that maximizes profits or minimizes costs. The purpose of linear programming is to find a mix of the products that yields the **objective function,** or the factor to maximize or minimize. In this example, the objective function is to maximize the total contribution margin that, in turn, maximizes profit. In other uses of linear programming, the objective function might be to minimize costs. The **constraints** determine limitations on the feasible solution. Constraints are the conditions that restrict the optimal value of the objective function. In this example, the following three constraints are present: a 600-unit maximum sales demand for Product A, a 500-unit maximum sales demand for Product B, and a total of 1,000 available machine-hours. The optimal feasible solution represents all the possible combinations of Product A and Product B that the company can manufacture and sell. We use the following mathematical symbols in linear programming equations:

$$\geq \text{ equal to or greater than}$$
$$\leq \text{ equal to or less than}$$
$$= \text{ equal to}$$

Linear Programming Requirements

In summary, the following requirements must be present in a decision situation to employ linear programming:

1. Express the objective function and the limitations as mathematical equations or inequalities because we base the decision on a determinate solution.
2. Specify the objective function; it is either a profit-maximizing or cost-minimizing function.
3. Specify and quantify the constraints because resources are limited. Constraints also must be consistent and define a feasible region for a solution. The constraints cannot be specified so there is no solution for every value of the objective function.
4. The objective function and the constraints must be linear and continuous.
5. Both the objective function and the constraints must be independent and known with certainty.
6. The objective function and all constraints must be a function of a prespecified set of quantitative variables, and these variables must be interrelated. They generally represent resources that must be combined to produce one or more products.

Solution Methods

The following solution methods are available for linear programming problems:

1. *Graphic method*: The easiest technique, but limited to simple problems. The basic rule is that the optimum solution lies at the extreme point of feasible combinations of products without going beyond the constraints.

Productivity

Current Cost Management Practice

When Larry Clark, the vice president and controller of Chaparral Steel Co. in Midlothian, Texas, realized his company was awash in paper, he suggested they move toward a paperless office. The goal was to convert all new paper documents and some of the old ones into electronic images and eventually close a warehouse clogged with old documents. However, managers did not want to lose access to the information these documents contained. With a computerized system, the company's past and future documents could be stored in a fraction of the space needed for paper files; in addition, staff could gain access to the images of the documents almost instantly. Clark met employee resistance by involving his staff in the planning and providing comprehensive training in the uses of the technology. An important initial decision was how to organize the filing system and the indexing scheme—the database that would locate and retrieve all the documents. Generally, images and documents are stored on optical drives because, while slower, they can store more data. The index database from which all retrievals are triggered and for which speed is a priority is usually on a hard drive. Chaparral Steel Co. found the best approach was to move in small steps, making corrections before moving on.

James E. Hunton, "Setting up a Paperless Office," *Journal of Accountancy,* November 1994, pp 77–85.

2. *Simplex method:* Managers more commonly use this technique because it is very effective. The simplex method is a stepwise process that approaches an optimum solution. It is an algorithm to move from a possible solution to another solution at least as good. We reach the optimum solution when we cannot find a better solution. Many computer facilities have linear programming packages available that use the simplex algorithm to find the optimal solution.

Graphic Method

When a linear programming problem involves only two variables, we can use a two-dimensional graph to determine the optimal solution.

Maximizing Profits. Exhibit 26–1 illustrates the **graphic method** where the x-axis represents the number of Product A units and the y-axis represents the number of Product B units. The combination of Product A and B that results in the largest contribution margin attainable within the limits set by the constraints will maximize profits. In the example presented in Exhibit 26–1, this can be stated algebraically:

$$CM = \$2.00A + \$1.50B$$

Three Constraints Plotted. The constraints also can be expressed algebraically as follows:

Sales demand for Product A: A $\leq$ 600
Sales demand for Product B: B $\leq$ 500
Machine-hours available: 1A + 4B $\leq$ 1,000

In addition, we need the following obvious statements so we do not mathematically determine negative quantities of products:

A $\geq$ 0 B $\geq$ 0

We first plot the constraints. If we devote all 1,000 machine-hours to the production of A, we can produce 1,000 units of A, but we do not manufacture any Product B. If, instead, we devote all the hours to manufacturing Product B, we can produce 250 B units (1,000 hours/4 hours per Product B), but no Product A. We determine the maximum limits of production possibilities by connecting these points. All combinations of Products A and B that we can manufacture, fully utilizing the machine-hours limitation of 1,000 hours, lie along this line. We next plot the marketing constraints, a 600-unit sales demand for Product A and 500 units for Product B. However, in Exhibit 26–1, the marketing constraint that sales demand for Product B will not exceed 500 units is redundant since the production constraint indicates that we can manufacture only 250 units of Product B with the 1,000 machine-hours available. We do not connect lines for Product A's and Product B's marketing constraint because they each involve only one product.

We establish the boundaries of the feasible area of combination after plotting all constraints. In Exhibit 26–1, this area is a polygon with four corners labeled *a, b, c,* and *d*. Within this feasible area, many combinations of Products A and B exist that we can manufacture and sell. For example, the following are a few of these combinations available:

Units of A	Units of B
0	250
200	200
400	150
600	100

Even though many combinations of Products A and B satisfy the production and marketing constraints, one combination maximizes the contribution margin. According to mathematical laws, the best feasible solution is at one of the four corner points. (As discussed later, the optimal solution may be at more than one corner point; in this case, any point on the line joining these two points is also optimal.) As a result, we test all corner point variables to find the combination that maximizes profits.

	Combination		
Corner Point	*Units of A*	*Units of B*	*Contribution Margin =* *$2.00 A + $1.50 B*
a	0	0	($2 × 0) + ($1.50 × 0) = $0
b	0	250	($2 × 0) + ($1.50 × 250) = $375
c	600	100	($2 × 600) + ($1.50 × 100) = $1,350*
d	600	0	($2 × 600) + ($1.50 × 0) = $1,200

*Optimum.

The company maximizes profits at corner *c* representing 600 units of A and 100 units of B, giving a total contribution margin of $1,350.

EXHIBIT 26–1   Graphic Solution Depicting Profit Maximization, Three Constraints Plotted, Products A and B

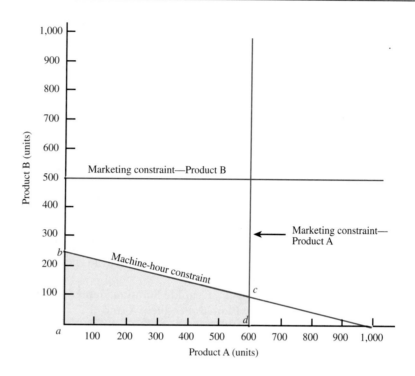

Objective Functions Plotted.   Instead of the trial and error method of working with the coordinates of the corners of the polygon, we can plot **objective function lines** as Exhibit 26–2 illustrates. We can determine the slope of the objective function line from the two products' contributions as follows using the total contribution margin equation:

$$CM = \$2.00 \text{ A} + \$1.50 \text{ B}$$

To find the slope reflecting the rate of change of B for one additional A, divide by the coefficient of B and then transfer B to the left side of the equation:

$$\frac{CM}{\$1.50} = \frac{\$2.00}{\$1.50} \text{ A} + \text{B}$$

$$\text{B} = \frac{CM}{\$1.50} = \frac{\$2.00}{\$1.50} \text{ A}$$

Thus, the slope of the objective function is a negative $2.00/$1.50 or $-4/3$. In our example, Product A contributes $2 per unit and Product B contributes $1.50 per unit. Therefore, one unit of A equals one and one-third units of Product B. If we connect any of two quantities of Products A and B in the ratio of A, 1 and B, $4/3$ (or A, $3/4$; B, 1), we can calculate many product combinations, each having the same marginal contribution. Exhibit 26–2 shows the following four lines drawn.

Line	Units of Product A ($2.00 CM/Unit)	Units of Product B ($1.50 CM/Unit)
1	100	133
2	300	400
3	675	900
4	800	1,066

Along Line 1, any combination of Products A and B yields a total contribution margin of $200; along Line 2, the total contribution is $600; along Line 3, a $1,350 contribution margin; and along Line 4, a $1,600 contribution margin. These lines illustrate that as the objective function lines move out from the point of origin, the total contribution margin increases. We realize the optimum profit when we can draw no further lines without going beyond the constraints. The optimum profit occurs in Exhibit 26–2 at corner c. If the objective function is optimized at two corner points, any point on the line joining these two points is also optimal. Even though along line 4 the $1,600 contribution margin is greater than at corner c, the combinations of Products A and B along this line are outside the constraints.

EXHIBIT 26–2   Graphic Solution Depicting Profit Maximization, Objective Functions Plotted, Products A and B

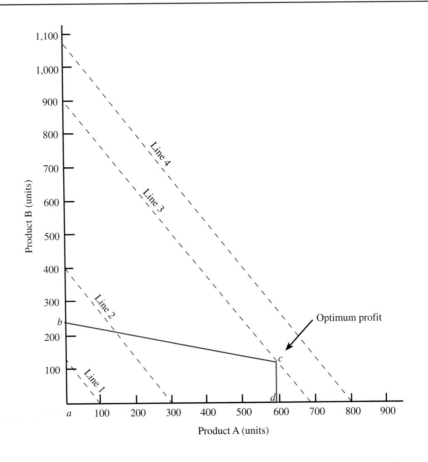

Four Constraints Plotted.   The previous example involving Products A and B is less complex than many business problems because we limited the constraints. For example, if a company's labor-hours per period are divided into two departments and each product requires varying amounts of time in each department, the solution is not as obvious. A linear programming model can determine how many units of each product should be produced each period to obtain the maximum profit.

Consider a company that manufactures regular and super products in its Mixing and Finishing Departments. There are 400 hours of mixing capacity and 240 hours of finishing capacity each day. Regular products require 2 hours of mixing and 0.8 hour of finishing per unit. If the company devotes all production facilities to manufacturing regular products, the maximum daily output is 200 units (400/2 hours per regular product) in the Mixing Department and 300 units (240/0.8 hours per regular product) in the Finishing Department. Super products, however, require $1 \frac{1}{4}$ hours of mixing and one hour of finishing per unit. If, instead, they devote all facilities to processing the super products, maximum daily output of super products in the Mixing Department is 320 units ($400/1.25 hours per super product) and 240 units (240/1 hour per super product) in the Finishing Department. In addition to these constraints, there is such a critical shortage of material used in processing super products that the company must limit production to a maximum of 180 units per day. Management worries that this shortage exists because market demand is sufficient for the company to sell all it produces. (In effect, there is no marketing constraint for super products.) However, sales forecasts indicate the company can sell a maximum of 150 units of regular products daily. The following summarizes these constraints and the contribution margin per unit:

	Regular Products	*Super Products*
Mixing—Maximum daily output	200 units	320 units
Finishing—Maximum daily output	300 units	240 units
Material shortage constraint	—	180 units
Marketing constraint	150 units	—
Unit contribution margin	$5	$3

The objective is to find the combination of regular and super products that maximizes the following profit function:

Let R = number of units of regular product.
Let S = number of units of super product.
$$CM = \$5R + \$3S$$

Exhibit 26–3 plots these constraints:

Production hour constraint: Mixing: $2R + 1.25S \leq 400$
                                                      Finishing: $0.8R + 1S \leq 240$
Material shortage constraint: $S \leq 180$
Marketing constraint: $R \geq 150$
Additionally: $R \geq 0$
                                                      $S \geq 0$

**EXHIBIT 26–3   Graphic Solution Depicting Profit Maximization, Four
Constraints Plotted, Regular and Super Products**

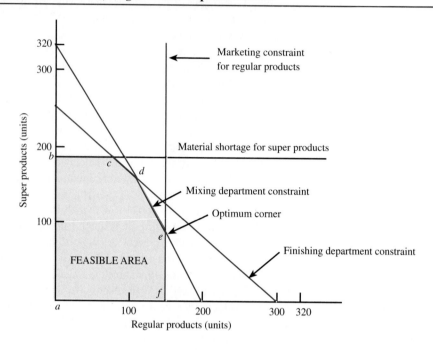

As shown in Exhibit 26–3, the area of feasible production combinations is a polygon with six corners denoted by *a, b, c, d, e,* and *f.* Contributions at each of these corners are as follows:

Corner Point	Regular Units	Super Units	CM = $5R + $3S
a	–0–	–0–	$0
b	–0–	180	$540
c	80	180	$940
d	100	160	$980
e	150	80	$990*
f	150	–0–	$750

*Optimum.

If, instead, we plot objective function lines, the slope is $-5/3$ indicating that 1 unit of regular product equals 1 2/3 units of super product. Exhibit 26–4 plots the objective function lines for the regular and the super products. Along Line 1, the contribution margin is $500; along Line 2, $752; and along Line 3, $990, which is the largest margin that the company can earn within production constraints. Note how close Line 3 comes to corner *d* since the contribution margin at corner *d* is $980, which is $10 less than at corner *e*. We could argue that either corner *d* or *e* is the optimum combination.

EXHIBIT 26–4   Graphic Solution Depicting Profit Maximization, Objective Functions Plotted, Regular and Super Products

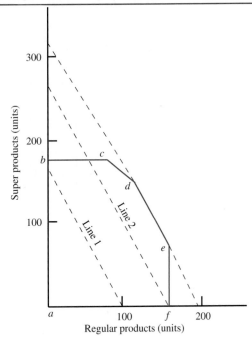

Minimizing Costs.   We also can use linear programming to select product ingredients that minimize costs. For example, assume that to produce a more beautiful green for its golf course, a country club plans to spread at least 4,800 pounds of fertilizer and 5,600 pounds of special chemicals on the soil. However, club management is able to buy only fertilizer and chemicals in a mixture, not in a pure form.

A dealer has offered to sell management 100-pound bags of Mixture A at $2 each; this mix contains the equivalent of 30 pounds of fertilizer and 70 pounds of chemicals. Mixture B is also available in 100-pound bags at $4 each; it contains the equivalent of 80 pounds of fertilizer and 20 pounds of chemicals.

The objective is to find the combination of Mixtures A and B that satisfies the chemical and fertilizer requirements and also minimizes cost.

$$Let\ A = \text{Bags of Mixture A}$$
$$Let\ B = \text{Bags of Mixture B}$$

The following summarizes these constraints and the cost per bag of mixture:

$$\text{Minimize: } \$2A + \$4B$$

Subject to: Fertilizer requirements: $30A + 80B \geq 4{,}800$
Chemical requirements: $70A + 20B \geq 5{,}600$
Additionally: $A \geq 0$
$B \geq 0$

After plotting these constraints in Exhibit 26–5, the feasible area has three corners denoted as *a, b,* and *c*. Note that this solution differs from the linear programming exhibits shown earlier in the chapter because cost minimization is the objective. Its feasible area lies beyond the constraints rather than within the constraints as shown in previous exhibits. Cost at each of these corners is as follows:

**EXHIBIT 26–5   Graphic Solution Depicting Cost Minimization, Two
Constraints Plotted, Mixtures A and B**

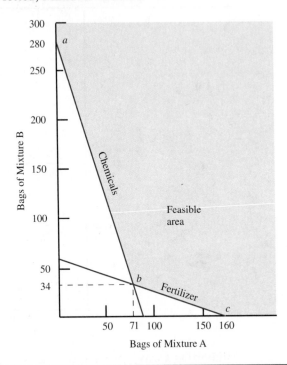

Corner Point	Bags of Mixture A	Bags of Mixture B	Cost = $2A + $4B
a	0	280	$1,120
b	71	34	$142 + $136 = $278*
c	160	0	$320

*Optimum.

As shown in Exhibit 26–5, the club minimizes cost by purchasing 71 bags of Mixture
A and 34 bags of Mixture B.

Simplex Method

The graphic approach works best when there are only two products involved, therefore requiring only a two-dimensional treatment. We use the **simplex method** to
solve more complex problems involving many cost centers and products.

Maximizing Profits.   We use matrix algebra in the simplex method to reach an
optimum solution. We arrange the equations that form the constraints in a matrix of
coefficients and manipulate them as a group with matrix algebra. Even though it is
too detailed to describe extensively in this book, the simplex method basically involves
solving sets of simultaneous equations where the number of unknowns in each set
is equal to the number of constraints.

   We must take the following steps before applying the method. (Note that the
first two steps are identical to those used with the graphic method.)

1. Establish the relationships for the constraints or inequalities. The set of constraints for the super and regular product is

Mixing:	$2R + 1.25S \leq 400$
Finishing:	$0.8R + 1S \leq 240$
Material shortage:	$S \leq 180$
Marketing:	$R \leq 150$

Both R and S must be zero or positive values:

$$R \geq 0;\ S \geq 0$$

2. Establish the objective function. The company expects a contribution of $5 and $3 for each unit of regular product and super product respectively, thus:

$$CM = \$5R + \$3S$$

3. Change the set of inequalities into a set of equations by introducing slack variables. By adding an arbitrary variable to one side of the inequality, an equality results. This arbitrary variable is called a **slack variable** because it takes up the slack in the inequality. The resulting equalities from the four inequalities introduced earlier are

$$2R + 1.25S + s_1 = 400$$
$$0.8R + 1S + s_2 = 240$$
$$S + s_3 = 180$$
$$R + s_4 = 150$$

Maximize: $CM = \$5R + \$3S + 0s_1 + 0s_2$

Slack variable s_1 represents unused mixing hours; s_2, unused finishing hours; s_3, unused material; and s_4, unused marketing demand. Because the slack variables do not contribute to profits, we do not add them to the profit equation. In tabular format this is

		s_1	s_2	s_3	s_4	R	S
Solution Variable	*Solution Values*	0	0	0	0	5	3
	400	1	0	0	0	2	1.25
	240	0	1	0	0	0.8	1
	180	0	0	1	0	0	1
	150	0	0	0	1	1	0

z
$C_j - z_j$

The tableau results from rewriting the equations of the problem. Row 1 results from the first constraint written as:

$$400 = 2R + 1.25S + 1s_1 + 0s_2$$

Row 2 results from the second constraint written as:

$$240 = 0.8R + 1S + 0s_1 + 1s_2$$

After the tableau is manipulated using the simplex algorithm, the final solution tableau is generated by a computer program:

			s_1	s_2	s_3	s_4	R	S	
Cj	Solution Variable	Solution Values	Cj0	0	0	0	5	3	
0	s_2	40	− 0.8	1	0	0.8	0	0	
0	s_3	100	− 0.8	0	1	1.6	0	0	
3	S	80	0.8	0	0	− 1.6	0	1	
5	R	150	0	0	0	1	1	0	Profit
		Zj	2.4	0	0	0.2	5	3	990
		Cj − Zj	− 2.4	0	0	− 0.2	0	0	

Reading the solution value, the optimal solution is 80 units of super product and 150 units of regular products with an optimal value of $Z = 990$, from:

$$Z = 5R + 3S + 0s_1 + 0s_2$$

$$Z = 5(150) + 3(80) = 990$$

Sensitivity Analysis.   This final tableau is the key to sensitivity analysis because we use its data to calculate how much the contribution margin can vary, if at all, without changing the optimal solution. The term sensitivity analysis describes how sensitive the linear programming optimal solution is to a change in any one number. **Sensitivity analysis** answers what-if questions about the effect of changes in prices or variable costs; changes in value; addition or deletion of constraints, such as available machine-hours; and changes in industrial coefficients, such as the labor-hours required in manufacturing a specific unit. An exhaustive treatment of sensitivity analysis is beyond the scope or intent of this chapter; however, a discussion of shadow prices is appropriate.

Shadow Price.   The preceding output produced with the linear programming computer package provides additional information of economic significance. In the last row of the table $(Cj - Zj)$ is the amount of profit the company will add if they add one unit of the variable j to the solution. This measure of the contribution forgone by failing to have one more unit of scarce capacity in a specific incident is a **shadow price.** Earlier, slack variables s_1 and s_2 were added to convert the constraints into equalities as follows:

Mixing: $2R + 1.25S + s_1 = 400$

Finishing: $0.8R + 1S + s_2 = 240$

The tableau indicates that increasing slack variables s_1 by 1 unit will make Z increase by $2.40 from $990 to $992.40. If we increase the right side of the constraint from 400 to 401, this is the same as adding a negative one unit of s_1 and will increase Z by $+$2.40. This number, -2.4, is the shadow price or dual price of s_1, the slack variable in the first constraint. This represents the maximum amount we should pay for an additional unit of the resource described in the first constraint. Thus, shadow prices facilitate the calculation of the potential variation in contribution margin from expanding capacity and alleviating the constraint.

The value in the s_2 column, $C_j - Z_j$ row, is -0 representing the shadow price of s_2, and the opposite of the amount Z increases with every additional unit of Finishing Department resource. Since in the solution, we already have enough finishing capacity to make 40 additional units, no gain would occur if we added more finishing resources.

We need caution in interpreting shadow prices because these variations in the right side of the constraints produce the shadow price change in the objective function only within a certain range of their optimal values. Shadow prices are effective quantifications of opportunity cost only if the products and idle capacity do not change. In our example, if all regular products or all super products become the optimal solution, the shadow prices would change.

Summary

As the emphasis in cost accounting shifts even more from providing costs for inventory valuation to determining relevant costs for decision making and internal planning, accountants use such quantitative tools as linear programming. However, cost accountants seldom have full responsibility for the development and use of linear programming models. Instead, the primary concern of cost accountants is in determining objective function coefficients. In addition, the cost accountant's focus should be on recognizing situations in which linear programming may be applicable and then obtaining any needed operations research assistance in solving the problem. Certainly, linear programming is a powerful management tool, but it is complex and usually requires the use of a computer.

Important Terms and Concepts

Problem for Self-Study

Linear Programming and Minimum Cost

To produce more attractive grounds and surrounding flower beds in his front and back yards, Max Rico wanted to spread at least 240 pounds but no more than 360 pounds of fertilizer and at least 300 pounds of topsoil. However, Rico will save a lot of money if he buys the topsoil and fertilizer mixture instead of the pure forms.

Rico can buy 20-pound bags of Mixture A at $5 each; it contains the equivalent of 8 pounds of fertilizer and 12 pounds of topsoil. Mixture B is also available in 20-pound bags at $8 each, it contains the equivalent of 15 pounds of fertilizer and 5 pounds of topsoil.

Required:

Express the relationships as inequalities. How many bags of Mixture A and Mixture B should Rico buy to obtain the required nutrients and fertilizer at minimum cost? Solve graphically.

Solution to Problem for Self-Study

	Max Rico

Let A = Mixture A
     B = Mixture B
Minimize $5A$ + $8B$
Subject to: Fertilizer requirements: $8A + 15B \geq 240$
                                        $8A + 15B \leq 360$
            Topsoil requirements: $12A + 5B \geq 300$
            $A \geq 0$
            $B \geq 0$

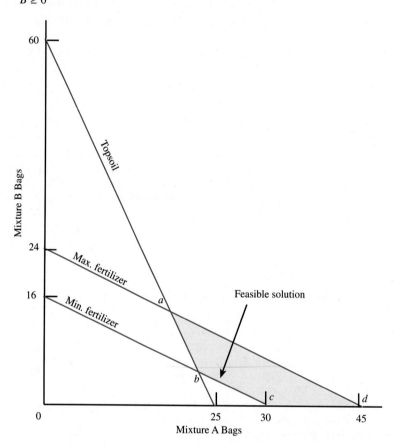

There are four possible answers.

Answer	Bags of Mixture A @ $5	Bags of Mixture B @ $8	Cost
a	20	14	$212
b	24.37	3	146*
c	30	0	150
d	45	0	225

*Optimal.

Review Questions

1. Define linear programming. How are resources regarded in a linear programming model?
2. To use linear programming, what requirements must be satisfied?
3. Give three applications of linear programming.
4. Define the term *objective function* and give an example.
5. What are constraints in linear programming, and how do they affect the decision?
6. Give three examples of constraints encountered in business problems.
7. Contrast the two solution methods used with linear programming.
8. How is the area of feasible combinations determined? Where is the optimal solution located?
9. How is the slope of objective function lines determined and how is the optimum profit determined with their use?
10. Discuss the relationship between sensitivity analysis and shadow prices.
11. What is the major benefit of using models to represent real-world situations?

Exercises

E26–1 Algebraic Expressions

Gleim Company manufactures Products A and B; each requires two processes, mixing and grinding. The contribution margin is $5 for Product A and $8 for Product B. One unit of A requires two hours of mixing and three hours of grinding time. One unit of B requires three hours of mixing and two hours of grinding time. There are 60 hours of mixing available daily and 48 hours of grinding available. The following graph shows the maximum number of units of each product that may be processed in the two departments.

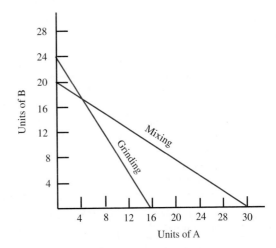

Required:

a. Give the objective function expressed algebraically.
b. Give the production constraint expressed algebraically.
c. Consider the constraints (restrictions) on processing and determine which combination of Products A and B maximizes the total contribution margin.

E26–2 Machine-Time Constraints

Wyatt Company processes two products, A and B, using two mixing machines. Product A requires 3 hours of processing time on Machine 1 and 5 hours time on Machine 2. Machine 2 is not employed in manufacturing Product B, but two hours time on Machine 1 is required for Product B. Machine 1 has 12 hours available time and Machine 2 has 10 hours for processing. Product A yields a contribution margin of $3 per unit; Product B, $2 per unit. These products must be sold in proportions such that the quantity of A will be equal to or less than the quantity of B.

Required:

Determine which product combination will maximize profits based on an analysis using graphic techniques. Use mathematical formulas to express the relationships.

E26–3 Linear Programming and Minimum Cost

To produce a more durable, beautiful green for its golf course, Civic Country Club is advised to spread at least 9,600 pounds of special chemicals and 10,000 pounds of fertilizer. However, club management is only able to buy the fertilizer and chemicals in a mixture, not in a pure form.

A dealer has offered 100-pound bags of Mixture X at $6 each; it contains the equivalent of 20 pounds of fertilizer and 16 pounds of chemicals. Mixture Y is also available in 100-pound bags, at $9 each; it contains the equivalent of 50 pounds of fertilizer and 50 pounds of chemicals.

Required:

Express the relationships as inequalities. How many bags of Mixture X and Mixture Y should the club buy to obtain the required fertilizer and chemicals at minimum cost? Solve graphically with Mixture X on the vertical axis.

E26–4 Expressing Objective Function and Constraints

Griffin, Inc., produces three items. Estimates of next year's sales prices and costs are as follows:

	Products		
	A	*B*	*C*
Annual market demand	4,000 Units	2,000 Units	1,000 Units
		Per Unit	
Sales price	$450	$250	$300
Direct material	300 pounds at $1 per pound	50 pounds at $2 per pound	100 pounds at $2 per pound
Direct labor	2 hours at $10 per hour	4 hours at $12 per hour	5 hours at $10 per hour
Variable overhead	$50	$20	$10
Fixed overhead	$40	$60	$30

Capacity available within the company:
  Direct material handling facilities—900,000 pounds per year
  Direct labor* ($10 per hour labor)—7,500 hours per year
  Direct labor* ($12 per hour labor)—10,000 hours per year

*$12 labor can be substituted for $10 labor, but not vice versa.

Required:

a. Express the objective function algebraically.

b. Express all the constraints involved for the three products algebraically.

E26–5 Profit-Maximizing Schedule

The following graph for White, Inc., presents the constraint functions for a machine manufacturing company whose production problem can be solved by linear programming. The company earns $50 for each calculator sold and $20 for each typewriter sold.

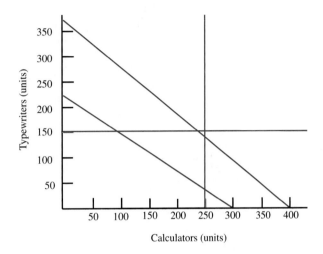

Required.

Determine the profit-maximizing production schedule. Provide support for your answer.

E26–6 Formulating Objective Function

Johnson Company has assigned a unit sales price of $200 for Product A and $160 for Product B. Johnson requires ten pounds of material to manufacture Product A while 8 pounds are needed for Product B. The cost of direct material is $10 per pound. Direct material is the only variable manufacturing cost; all other costs are fixed and total $5,000 per period.

The material used in manufacturing is of a specialized nature and no other material can be substituted. This is especially critical for management since the maximum number of pounds available for next period is 500 pounds.

Marketing studies reveal that 40 units of Product A and 50 units of Product B are the maximum number of units expected to be sold next period.

Required:

Set up the constraints and objective function to help Johnson Company decide how many units of Products A and B to produce next period to maximize its profits. Solve using the graphic method.

E26–7 Maximizing a Production Schedule

The Shell Corporation manufactures and sells two grades, A and B, of a single wood product. Each grade must be processed through three phases—mixing, fitting, and finishing—before it is sold. Shell provides the following unit information:

| | Grades | |
	A	B
Selling price	$18.00	$12.00
Direct materials	0.85	2.00
Direct labor	7.30	5.60
Variable overhead	1.15	1.80
Fixed overhead	0.60	0.30
Materials requirements in pounds	5	4
Labor requirements in hours:		
Mixing	2	5
Fitting	4	3
Finishing	1	6

Only 3,000 pounds per week can be obtained. The Mixing Department has 1,000 hours of labor available each week; the Fitting Department, 800 hours; and the Finishing Department, 980 hours. No overtime is allowed.

Contract commitments require the company to make 220 units of A per week. In addition, company policy is to produce at least 60 additional units of A and 40 units of B each week to actively remain in each of the three markets. Because of competition, only 150 units of B can be sold each week.

Required:

Formulate and label the linear objective function and the constraint functions necessary to maximize the contribution margin.

E26–8 Expressing Objective Function

The Cannon Company produces and sells Products X, Y, and Z. The company has such limited production capacity that only 2,500 direct labor-hours and 24,000 pounds of direct materials are available each month. All three products use the same type of direct material which costs $2 per pound. Direct labor is paid at the rate of $6 per hour.

A consultant suggests that the company consider using linear programming for determining optimum product mix. Based on prior years' operations, the accountants gather the following data concerning each product; it includes expected sales prices and labor and material costs by product line. Costs for variable overhead and fixed overhead are assumed to be the same for each product line since approximately the same quantity of each product was produced and sold last year.

| | Price and Cost Information (per Unit) | | |
	X	Y	Z
Selling price	$25.00	$30.00	$40.00
Direct labor	9.00	12.00	15.00
Direct materials	8.00	6.00	10.00
Variable overhead	5.00	5.00	5.00
Fixed overhead	1.00	1.00	1.00

Required:

Formulate and label the linear objective function and the constraint functions necessary to maximize the contribution margin. Use X, Y, and Z to represent units of the three products.

E26–9 Graphic Solution

Evans, Inc., can produce Parts A and B on either of two machines. When using Machine 1, workers need eight minutes to make Part A, and six minutes for Part B. The comparable times on Machine 2 are 10 minutes for Part A and 4 minutes for Part B. During each working day, 72 minutes are available on Machine 1 and 80 minutes on Machine 2. Daily marketing demands are not expected to exceed 12 units of Part A and 7 units of Part B.

Required:

a. Formulate and label the linear objective function and the constraint functions necessary to maximize the contribution margin, assuming the contribution margin for Part A is $9 and $12 for Part B.

b. Use the graphic solution to find the product mix that optimizes contribution margin.

Problems

P26–10 Graphic Linear Programming

Johns Corporation manufactures Products A and B. The daily production requirements are

| Product | Contribution Margin Per Unit | Hours Required per Unit per Department | | |
		Machining	Plating	Finishing
A	$ 8	5	3	2.5
B	12	2	6	2.0
Total hours per day in department		10,000	12,000	8,000

Maximum daily demand is expected to be 1,500 units for A and 3,000 units for B.

Required:

a. Indicate the objective function in determining daily production of each unit.

b. Set linear equations for the constraints.

c. Determine the optimal solution using the graphic method.

P26–11 Production Constraints and Optimum Combination

Disk Company manufactures two products Regular and Super. Each product must pass through two processing operations. All materials are introduced in the Mixing Department. There are no work in process inventories. Either one product exclusively or various combinations of both products may be produced subject to the following constraints:

	Mixing Dept.	Spinning Dept.	Contribution Margin per Unit
Hours required to produce one unit			
Regular	6.25 hours	2 hours	$5.00
Super	8 hours	1.5 hours	$4.00
Total capacity, hours per day	2,500	600	

A shortage of technical labor has limited Super production to 250 units per day. There are no constraints on the production of Regular products other than the hour constraints in the previous schedule. Assume that all relationships between capacity and production are linear, and that all data and relationships are deterministic rather than probabilistic.

Required:

a. Identify the production constraints for the Mixing Department and the Spinning Department, given the objective to maximize total contribution margin.
b. Identify the labor constraint for production of Super products, given the objective to maximize total contribution margin.
c. Indicate the objective function of the data presented.
d. Determine graphically the optimum combination to maximize contribution analysis.

P26–12 Linear Programming and Minimum Cost

To produce more attractive grounds and surrounding flower beds that might attract a more mature market, the Dallas Amusement Park wants to spread at least 3,000 pounds of special nutrients and 6,000 pounds of fertilizer on its soil. However, management is able to buy the nutrients and fertilizer only in a mixture, not in a pure form.

Management can buy 50-pound bags of Mixture A at $2 each; it contains the equivalent of 20 pounds of nutrients and 30 pounds of fertilizer. Mixture B is also available in 50-pound bags at $4 each; it contains the equivalent of 10 pounds of nutrients and 40 pounds of fertilizer.

Required:

Express the relationships as inequalities. How many bags of Mixture A and Mixture B should the amusement park buy to obtain the required nutrients and fertilizer at minimum cost? Solve graphically.

P26–13 Maximum and Minimum Production Constraints

Smith Company manufactures Products A and B through two processing operations. The company may produce either Product B exclusively or various combinations of both products except that Product B must equal or exceed 50 units per day. A shortage of material has limited production of Product A to 100 units per day. Assume all relationships between capacity and production are linear, and that all the data and relationships are deterministic rather than probabilistic. The following constraints are given:

	Hours Required to Produce One Unit		Unit Contribution Margin
	Process 1	*Process 2*	
Product A	4	5	$3
Product B	2	3	$5
Total capacity, hours per day .	800	750	

Required.

Using graphic techniques, determine how many units of each product the company should produce to maximize profits. Express the relationships in mathematical form and indicate the total contribution margin. (Graph Product A on the *x*-axis for consistency.)

P26–14 Graphic Solution

Management of Herch, Inc., is analyzing the requirements for producing chemicals on idle machines during January and February. Based on past results, the production of each gallon of Calciux requires two hours of labor in January and two hours of labor, $70 in cash, and

2 $1/2$ hours of machine time in February. To produce a gallon of Potasiux, four hours of labor are required in January; 10 hours of labor, $50 in cash, and five hours of machine time are required in February. Available for the production of these chemicals are 20,000 labor-hours in January; 16,000 labor-hours, $210,000 cash, and 10,000 machine-hours in February. The contribution margin is $1.50 per gallon of Calcium and $2.50 per gallon of Potasiux.

Required:

Using graphic techniques, determine how the company should divide its production between Calciux and Potasiux for the two-month period to maximize profits. Express the relationships in mathematical form and indicate the total contribution margin.

P26–15 Linear Programming Techniques

Ray Company furnished the following information about its two products, tables and chairs:

	Maximum Daily Capacities in Units			
	Shaping Department	*Sanding Department*	*Sales Price per Unit*	*Variable Cost per Unit*
Tables	300	250	$75	$45
Chairs	225	150	20	14

Ray can produce any combination of tables and chairs as long as the maximum capacity of the department is not exceeded because the daily capacities of each department represent the maximum production for either product assuming each department devoted full time to that product. For example, the company can shape 300 tables and no chairs or shape 225 chairs and no tables or some combination of the two products. Shortages of skilled labor prohibit the production of more than 200 tables per day. The company used the preceding production information to develop the following graph:

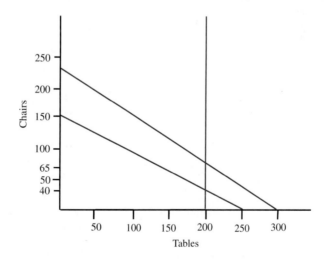

Required:

a. Comparing the information in the table with the graph, identify and list the graphic location (coordinates) of the:
  (1) Shaping department's capacity.
  (2) Production limitation for tables because of the labor shortage.
  (3) Area of feasible production combinations.

b. Determine the total contribution margin at each of the points of intersections of lines bounding the feasible production area, identifying the best production alternative.

P26–16 Graphic Solution of Linear Programming—Two Constraints

Bartlett, Inc., manufactures two products, A and B. Their cost data are

	Product A	Product B
Selling price per unit	$80	$50
Variable costs per unit	70	32

Machine-hours needed to produce one unit:

On machine X	3 hours	5 hours
On machine Y	10 hours	8 hours

Total machine hours available

> Machine X (4 machines @ 1,500 hours each)
> Machine Y (5 machines @ 2,760 hours each)

The company has no problem in selling Product A but research indicates 1,000 units of Product B is the most the company can sell during a period. The president argues for producing as many units of Product A as possible because of the higher sales price while the vice president of marketing argues that Product B is more profitable.

Required:

a. Indicate the objective function.
b. Set linear equations for the constraints.
c. Determine the optimal solution using the graphic method. (Plot Product A on the X axis.)

P26–17 Optimal Mixture to Minimum Cost

Naynes School Supplier is planning to assemble a kit for preschoolers containing a mixture of pencils and/or crayons. Management wants to find the optimal mixture for this product. The pencils and crayons will be in a colorful plastic box with removable sections that affect the space of the box. These plastic boxes can range from 50 to 70 square inches depending on the spacing and location of the removable sections. Data concerning the box, pencils, and crayons are as follows:

	Plastic Box	Pencils	Crayons
Number of units	40 or greater		
Weight per unit	25 or more ounces	1.0 ounce	0.5 ounce
Space per unit	50 to 70 square inches	2 square inches	1.0 square inch
Cost per unit	$7.00 maximum	$0.20	$0.10

Required:

a. Using the graphic technique, find the optimal mixture that minimizes cost.
b. Use the same data as in Requirement *a* except that at least five pencils must be in the plastic box. Find the optimal mixture that minimizes cost.

P26–18 Graphic Solution with Varying Conditions

Wind, Inc., manufactures two products, Regular and Super. Each product must be processed in each of three departments: Machining, Assembling, and Finishing. The hours needed to produce one unit per department, and the maximum possible hours per department follow:

| | **Production Hours per Unit** | | |
	Regular	*Super*	*Maximum Capacity Hours*
Machining	4	6	1,200
Assembling	5	7.5	2,000
Finishing	10	6.25	2,500
Minimum restrictions follow:			
Regular: ≥ 100			
Super: ≥ 20			

The objective is to maximize profits where the unit contribution margin is $5—Regular and $10—Super.

Required:

a. Calculate the most profitable number of units of Regular product and units of Super product to manufacture given the objective and constraints. Determine your answer by utilizing the graphic solution method.
b. Indicate your answer to Requirement *a* if there were no minimum restrictions on the products, and the sales price for Regular products decreased from $12 to $9.

P26–19 Linear Programming and Minimum Cost

Commerce Co. is the leading appliance manufacturing company. A component of one of its dishwashers is made of a special alloy. Every unit of alloy contains 12 ounces of Metal XXR and 7.5 ounces of steel. To meet its production schedule, Commerce Co. needs to buy at least 8,000 units but no more than 12,000 units of the alloy. Because the alloy is not currently available in the market, Commerce Co. decides to purchase the closest substitute from its two suppliers and reproduce the alloy in house.

Supplier W can supply an alloy that has 4.5 ounces of Metal XXR and 5 ounces of steel and sells at $60 per unit. The alloy from Supplier Y has 5 ounces of Metal XXR and 2 ounces of steel and the price is $45 per unit.

Required:

Calculate the maximum and minimum requirement for Metal XXR and steel in ounces. Express the relationship as inequalities. How many units of alloy should Commerce Co. purchase from the suppliers at minimum cost? Solve graphically. (For consistency, graph Supplier Y on the vertical axis.)

Capstone Case

Differential Contribution with Hospital Capacity: Payoff Table

Last year, administrators of Chicago General Hospital converted an unused wing of the hospital to a 12-bed ambulatory surgery unit (ASU). Patients whose conditions require minor surgery use an ASU; these patients enter the hospital early on the day of surgery and usually are discharged late that afternoon. It was hoped that this arrangement would relieve the delay for elective surgery experienced by some patients, caused by the high occupancy of the medical-surgical floors. The creation of the ASU also was intended to result in a higher turnover of the surgery suites or operating rooms. Hospital administrators believed there were sufficient surgery suites to handle an increased volume per day, but that a problem resulted from too few rooms for patients.

Administrators hoped for not only higher utilization of the operating room facilities, but also additional benefits to the patients. Patient costs should be reduced by the elimination of unnecessary days of hospitalization, even though there would be no reduction in the quality of care delivered in the ASU as compared to that delivered to other patients. This elimination of unnecessary hospitalization could be partially accomplished by preadmission testing. In addition, there would be a psychological benefit to the patient who was able to spend the pre- and postoperative period at home with minimal disruption of schedule and habits. Physicians would also save time because they would spend fewer hours on pre- and postoperative rounds.

Management's objective was to reduce the bed shortage through better utilization of hospital beds. Reducing the stay of ambulatory patients would free beds for the more acutely ill patients.

The ASU was opened for 5 1/2 days per week, excluding holidays, resulting in 281 possible days of usage. Cost to the patient was reduced by an average 1 1/2 days of hospital stay, with the majority of the other charges remaining the same. Management was satisfied that the quality of care rendered to ambulatory surgery patients was the same as that given to other patients. However, even though 1,360 patients using this facility resulted in 1 1/2 days saved, or a total of 2,040 days (1,360 × 1 1/2 days), better utilization of the hospital beds was not achieved because of the low occupancy rate of the ASU. In addition, the objective of increasing utilization of the operating room facilities was only partially attained because of this low occupancy rate. Consequently, hospital administration is considering alternative courses of action for the wing. After much discussion, the following alternatives were deemed worthy of further analysis:

1. Retain the present 12-bed ASU as private rooms with the hope that utilization will increase as physicians become more accustomed to this facility. Management is uncertain that the excess space could be utilized in other ways.

2. Convert the wing to a combination of (*a*) a 16-bed medical-surgical floor consisting of 12 private rooms and one 4-bed ward and (*b*) one 4-bed ward used as an ASU.

3. Convert the wing completely to a medical-surgical floor with 12 private rooms and two 4-bed wards.

4. Convert the wing to a psychiatric floor or a combination psychiatric and medical-surgical floor.

After the initial study, management determined that converting the wing to a psychiatric floor would not be feasible because of the potential increase in problems associated with another psychiatric floor and the restrictive admission laws. If the wing were converted to a combined psychiatric and medical-surgical floor, it would be difficult to admit medical-surgical or other categories of patients to the floor, considering the nature of the nursing personnel and routine on the floor.

Management asks that you ignore indirect expenses in your analysis, since they are convinced that inclusion of these expenses would not materially affect the results. Instead, they prefer the use of differential analysis. Your review of the records and interviews with hospital personnel yields the following for each alternative:

Retain ASU.   Gross revenue from the ASU would be $111,276 at 100 percent occupancy; however, management does not believe it is realistic to prepare an analysis based on this level. Instead, they can foresee occupancy ranging from 30 to 80 percent of full capacity. Discussion with numerous hospital employees convinces you that the probability of 80 percent occupancy is 5 percent; of 70 percent occupancy, 10 percent; 60 percent occupancy, 20 percent; 50 percent and 40 percent occupancy, 30 percent each; and 30 percent occupancy, 5 percent. Gross revenue is expected to have a direct relationship to occupancy.

Bad debts and courtesy discounts are expected to average 4 percent of gross revenue. Total salaries for 80 percent occupancy are forecasted to be $41,787; for 60 and 70 percent occupancy, $38,037 each; for less than 60 percent occupancy, $34,287. FICA and pensions average 11.054 percent of total salaries. Since supplies and other expenses contain an element of fixed and semivariable expenses, they cannot be expressed as a percentage of gross revenue. After much analysis, you determine supplies and other expenses to be: 80 percent occupancy—$3,483; 70 percent occupancy—$3,209; 60 percent occupancy—$2,959; 50 percent occupancy—$2,709; 40 percent occupancy—$2,459; and 30 percent occupancy—$2,259.

Medical-Surgical and ASU Wing.   For simplicity, management indicates that you are to assume a constant 75 percent occupancy of the 4-bed ASU ward, open 281 days a year, resulting in gross revenues of $27,819 regardless of the utilization rate of the medical-surgical beds. At 100 percent occupancy, assuming seven days a week utilization, managers estimate gross revenue on the medical-surgical unit to be $346,020; a direct relationship between medical-surgical occupancy and revenue is assumed. The probability of 90 percent occupancy is 20 percent; of 85 percent occupancy, 50 percent; of 80 percent occupancy, 20 percent; and of 75 percent occupancy, 10 percent.

The bad debt and courtesy discount rate is higher on the medical-surgical floor than the 4 percent rate for the ASU unit because the hospital admits emergency patients who may not have insurance and may not be able to pay. ASU patients tend to undergo an elective form of surgical procedure, so the hospital's insurance department has more time to verify insurance coverage and establish realistic payment schedules for patients whose insurance is inadequate. Past records indicate that the hospital can expect a 15 percent bad debt and discount rate for the medical-surgical unit.

Managers expect total salaries for alternative 2 at 100 percent capacity are expected to be $137,660; $100,000 of these salaries are fixed. FICA and pension average 10 percent of total salaries; this is slightly lower than for the ASU in alternative 1 because of the differences in salary ranges. For simplicity, assume supplies and other expenses will average 3 percent of gross revenue.

Medical-Surgical Wing.   If conversion to a medical-surgical floor is made, $423,400 in gross revenue is expected if the hospital achieves 100 percent occupancy. However, managers do not anticipate such a high utilization rate. In fact, they estimate the probability of a 90 percent occupancy is 20 percent; 85 percent occupancy, 60 percent; and 80 percent occupancy and 75 percent occupancy, 10 percent each. Gross revenue is expected to have a direct relationship to occupancy.

Bad debts and courtesy discounts are expected to be 17 percent of gross revenue. Managers expect total salaries at 100 percent capacity to be $150,000; $100,000 of these salaries are fixed. FICA and pensions average 10 percent of total salaries. Assume managers expect supplies and other expenses to average 3 percent of gross revenue.

Required: (Round to whole dollars.)

a. Prepare an estimated differential contribution if the hospital retained the ASU; use occupancy ranges of 80, 70, 60, 50, 40, and 30 percent.

b. Prepare a payoff table using the capacity utilization probabilities given for retaining the ASU.

c. Prepare an estimated differential contribution if conversion is made to a medical surgery unit and four-bed ASU; use an occupancy rate of 75 percent for the ASU ward and ranges of 90, 85, 80, and 75 percent for the medical-surgical unit.

d. Prepare a payoff table for the alternative analyzed in Requirement *c.*

e. Prepare an estimated differential contribution if conversion is made to a medical-surgical floor; use occupancy ranges of 90, 85, 80, and 75 percent.

f. Prepare a payoff table for the alternative analyzed in Requirement *e.*

g. Indicate which alternative you would advise management to choose.

h. Give some limitations of your analysis.

Present Value Tables

Appendix: Present Value Tables

TABLE A: **Present Value of $1**

Period Hence	1%	2%	4%	6%	8%	10%	12%	14%	15%	16%	18%	20%	22%	24%	25%	26%	28%	30%	35%	40%	45%	50%
1	0.990	0.980	0.962	0.943	0.926	0.909	0.893	0.877	0.870	0.862	0.847	0.833	0.820	0.806	0.800	0.794	0.781	0.769	0.741	0.714	0.690	0.667
2	0.980	0.961	0.925	0.890	0.857	0.826	0.797	0.769	0.756	0.743	0.718	0.694	0.672	0.650	0.640	0.630	0.610	0.592	0.549	0.510	0.476	0.444
3	0.971	0.942	0.889	0.840	0.794	0.751	0.712	0.675	0.658	0.641	0.609	0.579	0.551	0.524	0.512	0.500	0.477	0.455	0.406	0.364	0.328	0.296
4	0.961	0.924	0.855	0.792	0.735	0.683	0.636	0.592	0.572	0.552	0.516	0.482	0.451	0.423	0.410	0.397	0.373	0.350	0.301	0.260	0.226	0.198
5	0.951	0.906	0.822	0.747	0.681	0.621	0.567	0.519	0.497	0.476	0.437	0.402	0.370	0.341	0.328	0.315	0.291	0.269	0.223	0.186	0.156	0.132
6	0.942	0.888	0.790	0.705	0.630	0.564	0.507	0.456	0.432	0.410	0.370	0.335	0.303	0.275	0.262	0.250	0.227	0.207	0.165	0.133	0.108	0.088
7	0.933	0.871	0.760	0.665	0.583	0.513	0.452	0.400	0.376	0.354	0.314	0.279	0.249	0.222	0.210	0.198	0.178	0.159	0.122	0.095	0.074	0.059
8	0.923	0.853	0.731	0.627	0.540	0.467	0.404	0.351	0.327	0.305	0.266	0.233	0.204	0.179	0.168	0.157	0.139	0.123	0.091	0.068	0.051	0.039
9	0.914	0.837	0.703	0.592	0.500	0.424	0.361	0.308	0.284	0.263	0.225	0.194	0.167	0.144	0.134	0.125	0.108	0.094	0.067	0.048	0.035	0.026
10	0.905	0.820	0.676	0.558	0.463	0.386	0.322	0.270	0.247	0.227	0.191	0.162	0.137	0.116	0.107	0.099	0.085	0.073	0.050	0.035	0.024	0.017
11	0.896	0.804	0.650	0.527	0.429	0.350	0.287	0.237	0.215	0.195	0.162	0.135	0.112	0.094	0.086	0.079	0.066	0.056	0.037	0.025	0.017	0.012
12	0.887	0.788	0.625	0.497	0.397	0.319	0.257	0.208	0.187	0.168	0.137	0.112	0.092	0.076	0.069	0.062	0.052	0.043	0.027	0.018	0.012	0.008
13	0.879	0.773	0.601	0.469	0.368	0.290	0.229	0.182	0.163	0.145	0.116	0.093	0.075	0.061	0.055	0.050	0.040	0.033	0.020	0.013	0.008	0.005
14	0.870	0.758	0.577	0.442	0.340	0.263	0.205	0.160	0.141	0.125	0.099	0.078	0.062	0.049	0.044	0.039	0.032	0.025	0.015	0.009	0.006	0.003
15	0.861	0.743	0.555	0.417	0.315	0.239	0.183	0.140	0.123	0.108	0.084	0.065	0.051	0.040	0.035	0.031	0.025	0.020	0.011	0.006	0.004	0.002
16	0.853	0.728	0.534	0.394	0.292	0.218	0.163	0.123	0.107	0.093	0.071	0.054	0.042	0.032	0.028	0.025	0.019	0.015	0.008	0.005	0.003	0.002
17	0.844	0.714	0.513	0.371	0.270	0.198	0.146	0.108	0.093	0.080	0.060	0.045	0.034	0.026	0.023	0.020	0.015	0.012	0.006	0.003	0.002	0.001
18	0.836	0.700	0.494	0.350	0.250	0.180	0.130	0.095	0.081	0.069	0.051	0.038	0.028	0.021	0.018	0.016	0.012	0.009	0.005	0.002	0.001	0.001
19	0.828	0.686	0.475	0.331	0.232	0.164	0.116	0.083	0.070	0.060	0.043	0.031	0.023	0.017	0.014	0.012	0.009	0.007	0.003	0.002	0.001	
20	0.820	0.673	0.456	0.312	0.215	0.149	0.104	0.073	0.061	0.051	0.037	0.026	0.019	0.014	0.012	0.010	0.007	0.005	0.002	0.001	0.001	
21	0.811	0.660	0.439	0.294	0.199	0.135	0.093	0.064	0.053	0.044	0.031	0.022	0.015	0.011	0.009	0.008	0.006	0.004	0.002	0.001		
22	0.803	0.647	0.422	0.278	0.184	0.123	0.083	0.056	0.046	0.038	0.026	0.018	0.013	0.009	0.007	0.006	0.004	0.003	0.001	0.001		
23	0.795	0.634	0.406	0.262	0.170	0.112	0.074	0.049	0.040	0.033	0.022	0.015	0.010	0.007	0.006	0.005	0.003	0.002	0.001			
24	0.788	0.622	0.390	0.247	0.158	0.102	0.066	0.043	0.035	0.028	0.019	0.013	0.008	0.006	0.005	0.004	0.003	0.002	0.001			
25	0.780	0.610	0.375	0.233	0.146	0.092	0.059	0.038	0.030	0.024	0.016	0.010	0.007	0.005	0.004	0.003	0.002	0.001	0.001			
26	0.772	0.598	0.361	0.220	0.135	0.084	0.053	0.033	0.026	0.021	0.014	0.009	0.006	0.004	0.003	0.002	0.002	0.001				
27	0.764	0.586	0.347	0.207	0.125	0.076	0.047	0.029	0.023	0.018	0.011	0.007	0.005	0.003	0.002	0.002	0.001	0.001				
28	0.757	0.574	0.333	0.196	0.116	0.069	0.042	0.026	0.020	0.016	0.010	0.006	0.004	0.002	0.002	0.002	0.001	0.001				
29	0.749	0.563	0.321	0.185	0.107	0.063	0.037	0.022	0.017	0.014	0.008	0.005	0.003	0.002	0.002	0.001	0.001	0.001				
30	0.742	0.552	0.308	0.174	0.099	0.057	0.033	0.020	0.015	0.012	0.007	0.004	0.003	0.002	0.001	0.001	0.001	0.001				
40	0.672	0.453	0.208	0.097	0.046	0.022	0.011	0.005	0.004	0.003	0.001	0.001										
50	0.608	0.372	0.141	0.054	0.021	0.009	0.003	0.001	0.001	0.001												

TABLE B: Present Value of $1 Received Annually for *N* Years

Period (N)	1%	2%	4%	6%	8%	10%	12%	14%	15%	16%	18%	20%	22%	24%	25%	26%	28%	30%	35%	40%	45%	50%
1	0.990	0.980	0.962	0.943	0.926	0.909	0.893	0.877	0.870	0.862	0.847	0.833	0.820	0.806	0.800	0.794	0.781	0.769	0.741	0.714	0.690	0.667
2	1.970	1.942	1.886	1.833	1.783	1.736	1.690	1.647	1.626	1.605	1.566	1.528	1.492	1.457	1.440	1.424	1.392	1.361	1.289	1.224	1.165	1.111
3	2.941	2.884	2.775	2.673	2.577	2.487	2.402	2.322	2.283	2.246	2.174	2.106	2.042	1.981	1.952	1.923	1.868	1.816	1.696	1.589	1.493	1.407
4	3.902	3.808	3.630	3.465	3.312	3.170	3.037	2.914	2.855	2.798	2.690	2.589	2.494	2.404	2.362	2.320	2.241	2.166	1.997	1.849	1.720	1.605
5	4.853	4.713	4.452	4.212	3.993	3.791	3.605	3.433	3.352	3.274	3.127	2.991	2.864	2.745	2.689	2.635	2.532	2.436	2.220	2.035	1.876	1.737
6	5.795	5.601	5.242	4.917	4.623	4.355	4.111	3.889	3.784	3.685	3.498	3.326	3.167	3.020	2.951	2.885	2.759	2.643	2.385	2.168	1.983	1.824
7	6.728	6.472	6.002	5.582	5.206	4.868	4.564	4.288	4.160	4.039	3.812	3.605	3.416	3.242	3.161	3.083	2.937	2.802	2.508	2.263	2.057	1.883
8	7.652	7.325	6.733	6.210	5.747	5.335	4.968	4.639	4.487	4.344	4.078	3.837	3.619	3.421	3.329	3.241	3.076	2.925	2.598	2.331	2.108	1.922
9	8.566	8.162	7.435	6.802	6.247	5.759	5.328	4.946	4.772	4.607	4.303	4.031	3.786	3.566	3.463	3.366	3.184	3.019	2.665	2.379	2.144	1.948
10	9.471	8.983	8.111	7.360	6.710	6.145	5.650	5.216	5.019	4.833	4.494	4.192	3.923	3.682	3.571	3.465	3.269	3.092	2.715	2.414	2.168	1.965
11	10.368	9.787	8.760	7.887	7.139	6.495	5.937	5.453	5.234	5.029	4.656	4.327	4.035	3.776	3.656	3.544	3.335	3.147	2.757	2.438	2.185	1.977
12	11.255	10.575	9.385	8.384	7.536	6.814	6.194	5.660	5.421	5.197	4.793	4.439	4.127	3.851	3.725	3.606	3.387	3.190	2.779	2.456	2.196	1.985
13	12.134	11.343	9.986	8.853	7.904	7.103	6.424	5.842	5.583	5.342	4.910	4.533	4.203	3.912	3.780	3.656	3.427	3.223	2.799	2.468	2.204	1.990
14	13.004	12.106	10.563	9.295	8.244	7.367	6.628	6.002	5.724	5.468	5.008	4.611	4.265	3.962	3.824	3.695	3.459	3.249	2.814	2.477	2.210	1.993
15	13.865	12.849	11.118	9.712	8.559	7.606	6.811	6.142	5.847	5.575	5.092	4.675	4.315	4.001	3.859	3.726	3.483	3.268	2.825	2.484	2.214	1.995
16	14.718	13.578	11.652	10.106	8.851	7.824	6.974	6.265	5.954	5.669	5.162	4.730	4.357	4.033	3.887	3.751	3.503	3.283	2.834	2.489	2.216	1.997
17	15.562	14.292	12.166	10.477	9.122	8.022	7.120	6.373	6.047	5.749	5.222	4.775	4.391	4.059	3.910	3.771	3.518	3.295	2.840	2.492	2.218	1.998
18	16.398	14.992	12.659	10.828	9.372	8.201	7.250	6.467	6.128	5.818	5.273	4.812	4.419	4.080	3.928	3.786	3.529	3.304	2.844	2.494	2.219	1.999
19	17.226	15.678	13.134	11.158	9.604	8.365	7.366	6.550	6.198	5.877	5.316	4.844	4.442	4.097	3.942	3.799	3.539	3.311	2.848	2.496	2.220	1.999
20	18.046	16.351	13.590	11.470	9.818	8.514	7.469	6.623	6.259	5.929	5.353	4.870	4.460	4.110	3.954	3.808	3.546	3.316	2.850	2.497	2.221	1.999
21	18.857	17.011	14.029	11.764	10.017	8.649	7.562	6.687	6.312	5.973	5.384	4.891	4.476	4.121	3.963	3.816	3.551	3.320	2.852	2.498	2.221	2.000
22	19.660	17.658	14.451	12.042	10.201	8.772	7.645	6.743	6.359	6.011	5.410	4.909	4.488	4.130	3.970	3.822	3.556	3.323	2.853	2.498	2.222	2.000
23	20.456	18.292	14.857	12.303	10.371	8.883	7.718	6.792	6.399	6.044	5.432	4.925	4.499	4.137	3.976	3.827	3.559	3.325	2.854	2.499	2.222	2.000
24	21.243	18.914	15.247	12.550	10.529	8.985	7.784	6.835	6.434	6.073	5.451	4.937	4.507	4.143	3.981	3.831	3.562	3.327	2.855	2.499	2.222	2.000
25	22.023	19.523	15.622	12.783	10.675	9.077	7.843	6.873	6.464	6.097	5.467	4.948	4.514	4.147	3.985	3.834	3.564	3.329	2.856	2.499	2.222	2.000
26	22.795	20.121	15.983	13.003	10.810	9.161	7.896	6.906	6.491	6.118	5.480	4.956	4.520	4.151	3.988	3.837	3.566	3.330	2.856	2.500	2.222	2.000
27	23.560	20.707	16.330	13.211	10.935	9.237	7.943	6.935	6.514	6.136	5.492	4.964	4.524	4.154	3.990	3.839	3.567	3.331	2.856	2.500	2.222	2.000
28	24.316	21.281	16.663	13.406	11.051	9.307	7.984	6.961	6.534	6.152	5.502	4.970	4.528	4.157	3.992	3.840	3.568	3.331	2.857	2.500	2.222	2.000
29	25.066	21.844	16.984	13.591	11.158	9.370	8.022	6.983	6.551	6.166	5.510	4.975	4.531	4.159	3.994	3.841	3.569	3.332	2.857	2.500	2.222	2.000
30	25.808	22.396	17.292	13.765	11.258	9.427	8.055	7.003	6.566	6.177	5.517	4.979	4.534	4.160	3.995	3.842	3.569	3.332	2.857	2.500	2.222	2.000
40	32.835	27.355	19.793	15.046	11.925	9.779	8.244	7.105	6.642	6.234	5.548	4.997	4.544	4.166	3.999	3.846	3.571	3.333	2.857	2.500	2.222	2.000
50	39.196	32.424	21.482	15.762	12.234	9.915	8.304	7.133	6.661	6.246	5.554	4.999	4.545	4.167	4.000	3.846	3.571	3.333	2.857	2.500	2.222	2.000

Index